Tax Formula for Corporate Taxpayers

Income (*from whatever source*)	$xxx,xxx
Less: Exclusions from gross income	− xx,xxx
Gross Income..................................	$xxx,xxx
Less: Deductions	− xx,xxx
Taxable Income	$xxx,xxx
Applicable tax rates.........................	× xx%
Gross Tax	$ xx,xxx
Less: Tax credits and prepayments	− x,xxx
Tax Due (*or refund*)...........................	$ xx,xxx

Study Guide Available

For more practice problems that help you to expand your understanding of Corporations, Partnerships, Estates, and Trusts, we recommend the Study Guide that accompanies West's Federal Taxation: Corporations, Partnerships, Estates, and Trusts. The Study Guide uses a workbook approach and includes chapter outlines and summaries highlighting major points in the text, self-evaluation tests, problems, and drills using furnished tax forms.

If you cannot locate copies of the Study Guide in your bookstore, ask your bookstore manager to order a copy for you.

1993 ANNUAL EDITION

WEST'S FEDERAL TAXATION:

CORPORATIONS, PARTNERSHIPS, ESTATES, AND TRUSTS

West's Federal Taxation:

Corporations, Partnerships, Estates, and Trusts

General Editors

William H. Hoffman, Jr., J.D., Ph.D., C.P.A.   **William A. Raabe,** Ph.D., C.P.A.

James E. Smith, Ph.D., C.P.A.

Contributing Authors

James H. Boyd,
Ph.D., C.P.A.
Arizona State University

D. Larry Crumbley,
Ph.D., C.P.A.
Texas A & M University

Steven C. Dilley,
J.D., Ph.D., C.P.A.
Michigan State University

Patrica C. Elliott,
D.B.A., C.P.A.
University of New Mexico

Mary Sue Gately,
Ph.D., C.P.A.
Texas Tech University

William H. Hoffman, Jr.,
J.D., Ph.D., C.P.A.
University of Houston

Jerome S. Horvitz,
J.D., LL.M. in Taxation
University of Houston

David M. Maloney,
Ph.D., C.P.A.
University of Virginia

Marilyn Phelan,
J.D., Ph.D., C.P.A.
Texas Tech University

William A. Raabe,
Ph.D., C.P.A.
University of Wisconsin-Milwaukee

Boyd C. Randall,
J.D., Ph.D.
Brigham Young University

W. Eugene Seago,
J.D., Ph.D., C.P.A.
Virginia Polytechnic Institute and State University

James E. Smith,
Ph.D., C.P.A.
College of William and Mary

Eugene Willis,
Ph.D., C.P.A.
University of Illinois at Urbana

West Publishing Company

St. Paul   New York   Los Angeles   San Francisco

Copyediting: Patricia Lewis
Composition: Carlisle Communications, Ltd.
Index: E. Virginia Hobbs
Cover and
Interior Design: John Rokusek

West's Commitment to the Environment

In 1906, West Publishing Company began recycling materials left over from the production of books. This began a tradition of efficient and responsible use of resources. Today, up to 95 percent of our legal books and 70 percent of our college texts are printed on recycled, acid-free stock. West also recycles nearly 22 million pounds of scrap paper annually—the equivalent of 181,717 trees. Since the 1960s, West has devised ways to capture and recycle waste inks, solvents, oils, and vapors created in the printing process. We also recycle plastics of all kinds, wood, glass, corrugated cardboard, and batteries, and have eliminated the use of styrofoam book packaging. We at West are proud of the longevity and the scope of our commitment to our environment.

Production, Prepress, Printing and Binding by West Publishing Company.

TurboTax is a registered trademark of ChipSoft, Inc.

Copyright © 1992
Copyright © 1978, 1979, 1980, 1981, 1982,
1983, 1984, 1985, 1986, 1987, 1988, 1989, 1990, 1991
By **West Publishing Company**
610 Opperman Drive
P.O. Box 64526
St. Paul, MN 55164−0526

**Library of Congress
Cataloging in Publication Data**

Main entry under title:
  West's Federal Taxation.
  Includes index.
  1. Income tax—United States—Law
I. Hoffman, William H.   III.   Willis, Eugene

ISBN 0−314−00821−7
KF6335.H63   343′.73′04   76−54355

ISSN 0270−5265
1993 ANNUAL EDITION

PREFACE

This work was inspired by and designed to relieve the absence of suitable textual material for a second course in Federal taxation—the follow-up to a course outlining the Federal income taxation of individuals. It is especially valuable (a) for a second course offered at either the undergraduate or graduate level, (b) in the context of continuing professional education as a means to broaden one's professional capabilities, (c) as a reference for practitioners needing a refresher or review of seldom-encountered tax provisions, and (d) as a tool for self-study.

Throughout the text, the authors stress the practical application of the materials through a liberal use of examples, most of which have been classroom tested and found to be effective learning devices. At the same time, the evolution of specific statutory provisions through the interaction of case law, political compromise, and economic considerations is discussed to offer the student a broad base for understanding and applying the tax law. Our text does not purport to be a treatise on historical and fiscal policy considerations; its primary concern is tax practice. For this reason, such discussions of the law's development were minimized. In our opinion, this minimization does not compromise the subject matter's presentation.

Special Features

- At the center of the practical application of tax law is tax planning—the legal minimization of the tax burden. The authors are sensitive to this facet of tax law education; therefore, all chapters conclude with a special section—*Tax Planning Considerations.*
- Most chapters contain one or more *Concept Summaries* that synthesize important concepts in chart or tabular form.
- Any advanced Federal tax course should offer the student the opportunity to learn and utilize the methodology of tax research; therefore, Chapter 1 is devoted in part to this topic, and each chapter contains several research projects. The effectiveness of the text does not, however, depend upon the use of these research materials. They may be omitted without diminishing the presentation of all other topics.
- The text is divided into parts to facilitate a compartmentalization of the subjects covered. Thus, Part II, which includes Chapters 2 through 9,

largely deals with C corporations. Part III, which is designated Flow-through Entities, contains the material on partnerships (Chapters 10 and 11) and S corporations (Chapter 12). Further groupings are made to improve the organization of the text.

■ The material on C corporations is arranged to flow logically. Because of changes in the tax law and the expiration of phase-out rules, stock redemptions are treated similarly to liquidations. For this reason, redemptions and liquidations are discussed in the same chapter. The increased importance of the alternative minimum tax (AMT) warrants emphasis. As a result, the AMT is the highlight of Chapter 6, and the chapter title prominently reflects its presence.

■ Part IV (Advanced Tax Practice Considerations) contains three chapters that treat four subjects. Chapter 13 presents a detailed analysis of the various considerations that enter into the decision-making process in choosing the form of doing business. As such, the material is the capstone of what has been previously discussed and furnishes the foundation for choosing the appropriate business form. Chapter 14 deals with tax-exempt organizations, a controversial area that is receiving considerable media attention and Congressional inquiry, and one that plays an important role in the CPA exam.

■ Chapter 9 covers international transactions in a comprehensive manner. Increased foreign investment in U.S. enterprises, erosion of the dollar against major foreign currencies, and continuing trade deficits have increased interest in the tax aspects of this area. Chapter 15 explores the problems encountered when business is (or could be) conducted in more than one state. Many of the multistate taxation issues are of vital interest in today's climate of competitive economic development, and are increasingly important to tax practitioners.

■ The purpose of Part IV is to illustrate *some* of the specialized areas that tax practice involves. Furthermore, the subjects are arranged so as to maximize selectivity. For example, the user may wish to omit tax-exempt organizations (Chapter 14) and emphasize the material on multi-state taxation (Chapter 15). Since these modules are not interdependent, selective omission does not detract from the effectiveness of what the user chooses to cover.

■ There is a great deal of useful material contained in the appendixes to the text. In addition to the usual Subject Index, the following items are included: Tax Rates and Tables (Appendix A); Tax Forms (Appendix B); Glossary of Tax Terms (Appendix C); Table of Code Sections Cited (Appendix D–1); Table of Regulations Cited (Appendix D–2); Table of Revenue Procedures and Revenue Rulings Cited (Appendix D–3); and Table of Cases Cited (Appendix E).

The 1993 Edition of our text contains some innovative changes. In addition to improved readability, some of these changes are summarized below:

■ Increased coverage of corporations (Part II).

■ A new Chapter 8 devoted entirely to consolidated returns. For users who do not desire this extensive coverage, a short summation is still included at the end of Chapter 2.

■ Significant reorganization of the material on partnerships (Chapters 10 and 11).

■ Division of some of the material into separate chapters (Chapters 3 and 4 and Chapters 13 and 14). This improves the user's ability to select which subjects to cover and which to omit. It also reduces the length of some of the chapters.

For the Instructor

Accompanying the text is a comprehensive package of instructional aids.

- INSTRUCTOR'S GUIDE with Lecture Notes that contains the following materials:

  - Instructor's Summaries that can be used as lecture outlines and provide the instructor with teaching aids and information not contained in the text.
  - Incorporated as part of the Instructor's Summaries are selected queries that facilitate the use of WESTLAW, a computerized compilation of legal sources (judicial, legislative, and administrative) pertinent to the area of taxation. WESTLAW, a service available from West Publishing Co., provides a sophisticated short cut for carrying out in-depth analysis of various tax issues. Limited free use of WESTLAW is available to qualified adopters.
  - The solutions to the Research Problems contained in the text.
  - The solutions to the Comprehensive Tax Return Problems contained in the text.

- A separate SOLUTIONS MANUAL contains the answers to the Discussion Questions and Problems. These solutions are referenced to pages in the text.
- A separate TEST BANK contains examination questions and their solutions, page-referenced to the text. The questions are arranged in accordance with the sequence of the material in the chapter. To assist the professor in selecting questions for an examination, all questions are labeled by topical coverage in a matrix which also includes which questions are new, modified, or unchanged in the new edition.
- WESTEST, a microcomputer test generation program for IBM PC's and compatibles and the Macintosh family of computers.
  WEST'S FEDERAL TAXATION NEWSLETTER is mailed to adopters twice a year. It focuses on new tax legislation and updated information.
- WEST'S CD-ROM FEDERAL TAX LIBRARY (Compact Disk with Read-Only Memory) provides a complete tax research library on a desktop. The Federal Tax Library is a set of compact disks with a software package that reads the disks through a PC. Each of these disks has a remarkable storage capacity—roughly 1,000 times more than a single-sided floppy disk. A brief list of the library contents includes: complete Code and Regulations, 1986 Tax Reform Act with Amendments and Legislative History, Federal Court Cases on tax topics, Tax Court Cases, Revenue Rulings, and Revenue Procedures. This vital resource is available to qualified adopters.

For the Student

- A STUDENT STUDY GUIDE, prepared by Paul R. O'Brien, Governors State University, includes key concepts, self-evaluation tests, return problems and flowcharts of various sections of the Internal Revenue Code.
- WEST'S INTERNAL REVENUE CODE OF 1986 AND TREASURY REGULATIONS: ANNOTATED AND SELECTED: 1992 EDITION by James E. Smith, College of William and Mary.

We are delighted to have the opportunity, as editors, to coordinate the efforts of our authors in this, the 1993 Annual Edition of *West's Federal Taxation: Corporations, Partnerships, Estates and Trusts.* The fifteen years that have elapsed since our text was first made available to the academic and professional communities have more than justified the hope that it would fulfill a real need.

Acknowledgements

We are extremely grateful to the users of our text who were kind enough to provide us with constructive comments concerning its effectiveness both as a teaching and as a learning device. In particular, we express our gratitude to all those who have called or written with suggestions for improving the book and those who did comprehensive reviews for us this past year, including:

William T. Appleyard	Salem State College
John W. Baker, Jr.	Northwest Missouri State University
Susan Bates	Boise State University
John F. Bussman	University of South Florida
Alan D. Campbell	Arkansas State
Edmund D. Fenton, Jr.	Gonzaga University
Brian R. Greenstein	Drexel University
Larry Maples	Tennessee Technical University
Susan L. Megaard	Eastern Washington University
Lee J. Ness	University of North Dakota
Joseph F. Schirger	University of Wisconsin, Oshkosh
Robert Tabor	Emporia State University
James P. Trebby	Marquette University

We also thank those people who have painstakingly worked through all the problems and test questions and generally acted as problem checkers to insure accuracy of the book and ancillary package. They are Karen J. Boucher, University of Wisconsin-Milwaukee; Mary Sue Gately, Texas Tech University; Mark Persellin, St. Mary's University; Debra L. Sanders, Washington State University; and Raymond Wacker, Southern Illinois University at Carbondale.

Lastly, we appreciate the invaluable assistance provided to us by Bonnie S. Hoffman, M.S.A., C.P.A., Jill D. Robertson, M.S.T., and Thomas M. Hoffman, M.P.A.

William H. Hoffman, Jr.
William A. Raabe
James E. Smith

April 1992

CONTENTS IN BRIEF

◆ **Part V** Family Tax Planning

TABLE OF CONTENTS

PART II CORPORATIONS

PART III FLOW-THROUGH ENTITIES

PART IV   ADVANCED TAX PRACTICE CONSIDERATIONS

WEST'S FEDERAL TAXATION:

CORPORATIONS, PARTNERSHIPS, ESTATES, AND TRUSTS

PART

INTRODUCTION

The Federal tax law is an unbelievably complex set of rules. In working with these rules, however, it is helpful to understand *why* they came about. Also necessary is the ability to locate the sources of these rules. Part I, therefore, is devoted to the "whys" of the tax law and the applications of the tax research process.

CHAPTER

1

Understanding and Working with the Federal Tax Law

CHAPTER

UNDERSTANDING AND WORKING WITH THE FEDERAL TAX LAW

OBJECTIVES

Explain how economic, social, equity, and political considerations have influenced the evolution of the Federal tax law.

Describe how the IRS (as the protector of the revenue) and the courts (as the interpreter of congressional intent) have influenced the Federal tax law.

Aid the reader in dealing with the complexity of the Federal income tax as it currently exists.

Familiarize the reader with tax law sources (statutory, administrative, and judicial).

Explain how to locate and cite appropriate tax law sources.

Assess the weight of tax law sources.

Identify and resolve tax problems.

Explain the importance of particular tax planning measures.

Introduce computer-assisted tax research concepts.

OUTLINE

The Whys of the Tax Law

◆

The Federal tax law is a mixture of statutory provisions, administrative pronouncements, and court decisions. Anyone who has attempted to work with this body of knowledge is familiar with its complexity. Commenting on his 48-page tax return, the author James Michener said, "it is unimaginable in that I graduated from one of America's better colleges, yet I am totally incapable of understanding tax returns." For the person who has to wade through rule upon rule to find the solution to a tax problem, it may be of some consolation to know that the law's complexity can be explained. There is a reason for the formulation of every rule. Knowing these reasons, therefore, is a considerable step toward understanding the Federal tax law.

The major objective of the Federal tax law is the raising of revenue. Despite the importance of the fiscal needs of the government, however, other considerations explain certain portions of the law. In particular, economic, social, equity, and political factors play a significant role. Added to these factors is the marked impact the Internal Revenue Service (IRS) and the courts have had and will continue to have on the evolution of Federal tax law. These matters are treated in the first part of this chapter. Wherever appropriate, the discussion is related to subjects covered later in the text.

Revenue Needs

The foundation of any tax system has to be the raising of revenue to absorb the cost of government operations. Ideally, annual outlays should not exceed anticipated revenues. This leads to a balanced budget with no deficit. Many states have achieved this objective by passing laws or constitutional amendments precluding deficit spending. Unfortunately, the Federal government has no such prohibition, and mounting annual deficits have become an increasing concern for many. This concern has had a definite impact on the Federal tax system as evidenced by recent legislation enacted by Congress. The Deficit Reduction Act of 1984, for example, made modest inroads on the deficit by modifying certain income exclusions and deductions and by strengthening penalties for taxpayer noncompliance.

When finalizing the Tax Reform Act (TRA) of 1986, a deficit-conscious Congress was guided by the concept of revenue neutrality. This means that the changes made neither increase nor decrease the net revenues raised under the prior rules. Revenue neutrality does not mean that any one taxpayer's tax liability will remain the same, since this result would depend upon the circumstances involved. Thus, one taxpayer's increased tax liability could be another's tax saving. Revenue neutral tax reform does not reduce deficits, but at least it does not aggravate the problem.

One can expect budget deficit considerations to play an ever-increasing role in shaping tax policy. The most recent legislation, the Revenue Reconciliation Act of 1990, is intended to generate considerable revenue. Although it contains certain revenue loss provisions, these are more than made up by new taxes and increases in tax rates.

Economic Considerations

Using the tax system in an effort to accomplish economic objectives has become increasingly popular in recent years. Generally, this involves amending the Internal Revenue Code[1] through tax legislation and emphasizes measures designed to help control the economy or encourage certain activities and businesses.

---

1. The Internal Revenue Code is a compilation of Federal tax legislation.

Control of the Economy. Congress has made use of depreciation write-offs as a means of controlling the economy. Theoretically, shorter asset lives and accelerated methods should encourage additional investment in depreciable property acquired for business use. Conversely, longer class lives and the required use of the straight-line method of depreciation dampen the tax incentive for capital outlays.

Compared to past law, TRA of 1986 generally retrenched on faster write-offs for property acquired after 1986. Particularly hard hit was most depreciable real estate where class lives were extended from 19 years to as long as 31½ years and the straight-line method was made mandatory. These changes were made in the interest of revenue neutrality and in the belief that the current economy is stable.

A change in the tax rate structure has a more immediate impact on the economy. When tax rates are lowered, taxpayers are able to obtain additional spendable funds. Generally, TRA of 1986 lowered tax rates for most taxpayers. But since it also reduced or eliminated many deductions and credits, lower rates may not lead to lower tax liabilities.

Encouragement of Certain Activities. Without passing judgment on the wisdom of any such choices, it is quite clear that the tax law does encourage certain types of economic activity or segments of the economy. For example, the desire to foster technological progress helps explain the favorable treatment accorded to research and development expenditures. Under the tax law, such expenditures can be deducted in the year incurred or, alternatively, capitalized and amortized over a period of 60 months or more. In terms of timing the tax saving, such options usually are preferable to a capitalization of the cost with a write-off over the estimated useful life of the asset created.[2]

The encouragement of technological progress can also explain why the tax law places the inventor in a special position. Not only can patents qualify as capital assets, but under certain conditions their disposition automatically carries long-term capital gain treatment.[3]

Are ecological considerations a desirable objective? If they are, it explains why the tax law permits a 60-month amortization period for costs incurred in the installation of pollution control facilities.

Does stimulating the development and rehabilitation of low-income rental housing benefit the economy? The tax law definitely favors these activities since taxpayers incurring such costs are allowed generous tax credits.

Is saving desirable for the economy? Saving leads to capital formation and thus makes funds available to finance home construction and industrial expansion. The tax law provides incentives to encourage saving by giving private retirement plans preferential treatment. Not only are contributions to Keogh (H.R. 10) plans and certain Individual Retirement Accounts (IRAs) deductible, but income from such contributions accumulates on a tax-free basis. As noted in a following section, the encouragement of private-sector pension plans can be justified under social considerations as well.

Is it wise to stimulate U.S. exports of goods and services? Considering the pressing and continuing problem of a deficit in the U.S. balance of payments, the answer should be clear. Along this line, Congress has created Foreign Sales Corporations (FSCs), a unique type of organization designed to encourage exports. A portion of the export income from eligible FSCs is exempt from

---

2. If the asset developed has no estimated useful life, no write-off would be available without the two options allowed by the tax law.

3. At this point, a long-term capital gain has a slight favorable tax advantage.

Federal income taxes. Further, a domestic corporation is allowed a 100 percent dividends received deduction for distributions from an FSC out of earnings attributable to certain foreign trade income. Congress has also deemed it advisable to establish incentives for U.S. citizens who accept employment overseas. Such persons receive generous tax breaks through special treatment of their foreign-source income and certain housing costs.

Encouragement of Certain Industries. Who can question the proposition that a sound agricultural base is necessary for a well-balanced national economy? Undoubtedly, this belief can explain why farmers are accorded special treatment under the Federal tax system. Among the benefits are the election to expense rather than capitalize certain soil and water conservation expenditures and fertilizers and the election to defer the recognition of gain on the receipt of crop insurance proceeds.

The tax law also favors the development of natural resources by permitting the use of percentage depletion on the extraction and sale of oil and gas and specified mineral deposits and a write-off (rather than a capitalization) of certain exploration costs. The railroad and banking industries also receive special tax treatment. All of these provisions can be explained, in whole or in part, by economic considerations.

Encouragement of Small Business. At least in the United States, a consensus exists that what is good for small business is good for the economy as a whole. This assumption has led to a definite bias in the tax law favoring small business.

In the corporate tax area, several provisions can be explained by the desire to benefit small business. One provision enables a shareholder in a small business corporation to obtain an ordinary deduction for any loss recognized on a stock investment. Normally, such a loss would receive the less attractive capital loss treatment. The point of this favoritism is to encourage additional equity investments in small business corporations.[4] Another provision permits the shareholders of a small business corporation to make a special election that generally will avoid the imposition of the corporate income tax.[5] Furthermore, such an election enables the corporation to pass through to its shareholders any of its operating losses.[6]

The tax rates applicable to corporations tend to favor small business in that size is relative to the amount of taxable income generated in any one year. Since the full corporate tax rate of 34 percent applies only to taxable income in excess of $75,000, corporations that stay within this limit are subject to lower average tax rates.

EXAMPLE 1

For calendar year 1992, X Corporation has taxable income of $75,000, and Y Corporation has taxable income of $100,000. Based on this information, the corporate income tax is $13,750 for X Corporation and $22,250 for Y Corporation (see Chapter 2). X Corporation is subject to an average tax rate of 18.33% ($13,750/$75,000), while Y Corporation is subject to an average rate of 22.25% ($22,250/$100,000). ◆

If a corporation has taxable income in excess of $100,000, the benefits of the lower brackets are phased out until all income is taxed at the maximum rate of 34 percent.

---

4. Known as Section 1244 stock, this subject is covered in Chapter 3.

5. Known as the S corporation election, the subject is discussed extensively in Chapter 12.

6. In general, an operating loss can benefit only the corporation incurring the loss through a carryback or carryover to profitable years. Consequently, the shareholders of the corporation usually cannot take advantage of any such loss.

One of the justifications for the enactment of the tax law governing corporate reorganizations (see Chapter 7) was the economic benefit it would provide for small businesses. By allowing corporations to combine without adverse tax consequences, small corporations would be in a position to compete more effectively with larger concerns.

Social Considerations

Some of the tax laws, especially those related to the Federal income tax of individuals, can be explained by social considerations. The following are some notable examples:

- The nontaxability of certain benefits provided to employees through accident and health plans financed by employers. It is socially desirable to encourage such plans, since they provide medical benefits in the event of an employee's illness or injury.
- The nontaxability to the employee of some of the premiums paid by an employer for group term insurance covering the life of the employee. These arrangements can be justified in that they provide funds to help the family unit adjust to the loss of wages caused by the employee's death.
- The tax treatment to the employee of contributions made by an employer to qualified pension or profit sharing plans. The contribution and any income it earns will not be taxed to the employee until the funds are distributed. Private retirement plans are encouraged because they supplement the subsistence income level the employee would otherwise have under the Social Security system.[7]
- The deduction allowed for contributions to qualified charitable organizations. The deduction attempts to shift some of the financial and administrative burden of socially desirable programs from the public (the government) to the private (the citizens) sector.
- The credit allowed for amounts spent to furnish care for certain minor or disabled dependents to enable the taxpayer to seek or maintain gainful employment. Who could deny the social desirability of encouraging taxpayers to provide care for their children while they work?
- The disallowance of a tax deduction for certain expenditures that are deemed to be contrary to public policy. This disallowance extends to such items as fines, penalties, illegal kickbacks, and bribes to government officials. Public policy considerations also have been used to disallow gambling losses in excess of gambling gains and political campaign expenditures in excess of campaign contributions. Social considerations dictate that the tax law should not encourage these activities by permitting a deduction.
- The imposition of the Federal estate tax on large estates. From one viewpoint, permitting large accumulations of wealth to pass by death from generation to generation without being subject to some type of transfer tax would be socially undesirable.[8]

Many other examples could be included, but the conclusion would be unchanged: Social considerations do explain a significant part of the Federal tax law.

---

7. The same rationale explains the availability of similar arrangements for self-employed persons (the H.R. 10, or Keogh, plan).

8. Portions of Chapter 18 are devoted to procedures that permit taxpayers to pass wealth from one generation to another with minimal tax consequences.

Equity Considerations

The concept of equity is relative. Reasonable persons can, and often do, disagree about what is fair or unfair. In the tax area, moreover, equity is generally tied to a particular taxpayer's personal situation. To illustrate, it may be difficult for Ms. Jones to understand why none of the rent she pays on her apartment is deductible. However, her brother, Mr. Jones, is able to deduct a large portion of the monthly payments he makes on his personal residence in the form of interest and taxes.[9]

In the same vein, compare the tax treatment of a corporation with that of a partnership. Two businesses may be of equal size, similarly situated, and competitors in the production of goods or services, but they are not comparably treated under the tax law. The corporation is subject to a separate Federal income tax; the partnership is not. Whether the differences in tax treatment can be logically justified in terms of equity is beside the point. The tax law can and does make a distinction between these business forms.

Equity, then, is not what appears fair or unfair to any one taxpayer or group of taxpayers. It is, instead, what the tax law recognizes. Some recognition of equity does exist, however, and explains part of the law. The concept of equity appears in tax provisions that alleviate the effect of multiple taxation and postpone the recognition of gain when the taxpayer lacks the ability or wherewithal to pay the tax. Equity also helps mitigate the effect of the application of the annual accounting period concept and helps taxpayers cope with the eroding result of inflation.

Alleviating the Effect of Multiple Taxation. The same income earned by a taxpayer may be subject to taxes imposed by different taxing authorities. If, for example, the taxpayer is a resident of New York City, income might generate Federal, State of New York, and City of New York income taxes. To compensate for this inequity, the Federal tax law allows a taxpayer to claim a deduction for state and local income taxes. The deduction, however, does not neutralize the effect of multiple taxation since the benefit derived depends on the taxpayer's Federal income tax rate.[10]

Equity considerations can explain the Federal tax treatment of certain income from foreign sources. Since double taxation results when the same income is subject to both foreign and U.S. income taxes, the tax law permits the taxpayer to choose either a credit or a deduction for the foreign taxes paid.

The imposition of a separate income tax on corporations leads to multiple taxation of the same income.

EXAMPLE 2

During the current year, M Corporation has net income of $100,000, of which $5,000 was received as dividends from stock it owns in Xerox Corporation. Assume M Corporation distributes the after-tax income to its shareholders (all individuals). At a minimum, the distribution received by the shareholders will be subject to two income taxes: the corporate income tax when the income is earned by M Corporation and the individual income tax when the balance is distributed to the shareholders as a dividend. The $5,000 M Corporation receives from Xerox Corporation fares even worse. Because it is paid from income earned by Xerox Corporation, it has been

---

9. The encouragement of home ownership can be justified on both economic and social grounds. In this regard, it is interesting to note that some state income tax laws allow a form of relief (e.g., tax credit) to the taxpayer who rents his or her personal residence.

10. A tax credit, rather than a deduction, would eliminate the effects of multiple taxation on the same income.

subjected to a third income tax (the corporate income tax imposed on Xerox Corporation).[11] ◆

For corporate shareholders, for whom triple taxation is possible, the law provides a deduction for dividends received from certain domestic corporations. The deduction, usually 70 percent of the dividends, would be allowed to M Corporation for the $5,000 it received from Xerox Corporation. (See the discussion in Chapter 2.)

In the area of the Federal estate tax, several provisions reflect attempts to mitigate the effect of multiple taxation. Some degree of equity is achieved, for example, by allowing a limited credit against the estate tax for foreign death taxes imposed on the same transfer. Other estate tax credits are available and can be explained on the same grounds.[12]

The Wherewithal to Pay Concept.   The wherewithal to pay concept recognizes the inequity of taxing a transaction when the taxpayer lacks the means with which to pay the tax. It is particularly suited to situations when the taxpayer's economic position has not changed significantly as a result of a transaction.

———————————————— EXAMPLE 3 ————————————————

T Corporation holds unimproved land held as an investment. The land has a basis to T Corporation of $60,000 and a fair market value of $100,000. The land is exchanged for a building (worth $100,000) that the corporation will use in its business.[13] ◆

———————————————— EXAMPLE 4 ————————————————

T Corporation owns a warehouse that it uses in its business. At a time when the warehouse has an adjusted basis of $60,000, it is destroyed by fire. T Corporation collects the insurance proceeds of $100,000 and, within two years of the end of the year in which the fire occurred, uses all of the proceeds to purchase a new warehouse.[14] ◆

———————————————— EXAMPLE 5 ————————————————

T, a sole proprietor, decides to incorporate his business. In exchange for the business's assets (adjusted basis of $60,000 and a fair market value of $100,000), T receives all of the stock of X Corporation, a newly created corporation.[15] The X Corporation stock is worth $100,000. ◆

———————————————— EXAMPLE 6 ————————————————

R, S, and T want to develop unimproved land owned by T. The land has a basis to T of $60,000 and a fair market value of $100,000. The RST Partnership is formed with the following investment: land worth $100,000 transferred by T, $100,000 cash by R, and $100,000 cash by S. Each party receives a one-third interest in the RST Partnership.[16] ◆

———————————————— EXAMPLE 7 ————————————————

A Corporation and B Corporation decide to consolidate to form C Corporation.[17] Pursuant to the plan of reorganization, T exchanges her stock in A Corporation (basis

---

11. The result materializes because under the tax law a corporation is not allowed a deduction for the dividend distributions it makes.

12. See Chapter 17.

13. The nontaxability of like-kind exchanges applies to the exchange of property held for investment or used in a trade or business for property to be similarly held or used.

14. The nontaxability of gains realized from involuntary conversions applies when the proceeds received by the

taxpayer are reinvested within a prescribed period of time in property similar or related in service or use to that converted. Involuntary conversions take place as a result of casualty losses, theft losses, and condemnations by a public authority.

15. Transfers of property to controlled corporations are discussed in Chapter 3.

16. The formation of a partnership is discussed in Chapter 10.

17. Corporate reorganizations are discussed in Chapter 7.

of $60,000 and fair market value of $100,000) for stock in C Corporation worth $100,000. ◆

In all of the preceding examples, either T Corporation or T had a realized gain of $40,000 [$100,000 (fair market value of the property received) – $60,000 (basis of the property given up)].[18] It seems inequitable to force the taxpayer to recognize any of this gain for two reasons. First, without disposing of the property or interest acquired, the taxpayer would be hard-pressed to pay the tax.[19] Second, the taxpayer's economic situation has not changed significantly. To illustrate by referring to Example 5, can it be said that T's position as sole shareholder of X Corporation is much different from his prior status as owner of a sole proprietorship?

Several warnings are in order concerning the application of the wherewithal to pay concept. Recognized gain is merely postponed and not necessarily avoided. Because of the basis carryover to the new property or interest acquired in these nontaxable transactions, the gain element is still present and might be recognized upon a subsequent taxable disposition. Referring to Example 5, suppose T later sold the stock in X Corporation for $100,000. T's basis in the stock is $60,000 (the same basis as in the assets transferred), and the sale results in a recognized gain of $40,000. Also, many of the provisions previously illustrated prevent the recognition of realized losses. Since such provisions are automatic in application (not elective with the taxpayer), they could operate to the detriment of a taxpayer who wishes to obtain a deduction for a loss. The notable exception involves involuntary conversions (Example 4). Here, nonrecognition treatment is elective with the taxpayer and will not apply to a realized loss if it is otherwise deductible.

The wherewithal to pay concept has definitely served as a guideline in shaping part of the tax law. Nevertheless, it is not a hard and fast principle that is followed in every case. Only when the tax law specifically provides for no tax consequences will this result materialize.

EXAMPLE 8

T exchanges stock in A Corporation (basis of $60,000 and fair market value of $100,000) for stock in B Corporation (fair market value of $100,000). The exchange is not pursuant to a reorganization. Under these circumstances, T's realized gain of $40,000 is recognized for Federal income tax purposes.[20] ◆

The result reached in Example 8 seems harsh in that the exchange does not place T in a position to pay the tax on the $40,000 gain. How can this result be reconciled with that reached in Example 7 when the exchange was nontaxable? In other words, why does the tax law apply the wherewithal to pay concept to the exchange of stock pursuant to a corporate reorganization (Example 7) but not to certain other stock exchanges (Example 8)?

Recall that the wherewithal to pay concept is particularly suited to situations in which the taxpayer's economic position has not changed significantly as a result of a transaction. In Example 7, T's stock investment in A Corporation really continues in the form of the C Corporation stock since C was formed

---

18. Realized gain can be likened to economic gain. However, the Federal income tax is imposed only on that portion of realized gain considered to be recognized under the law. Generally, recognized (or taxable) gain can never exceed realized gain.

19. If the taxpayer ends up with other property (boot) as part of the transfer, gain may be recognized to this extent. The presence of boot, however, helps solve the wherewithal to pay problem, since it provides property (other than the property or interest central to the transaction) with which to pay the tax.

20. The exchange of stock does not qualify for nontaxable treatment as a like-kind exchange (refer to Example 3).

through a consolidation of A and B Corporations.[21] However, continuation of investment is not the case in Example 8. Here T's ownership in A Corporation has ceased, and an investment in an entirely different corporation has been substituted.

Mitigating the Effect of the Annual Accounting Period Concept. For purposes of effective administration of the tax law, all taxpayers must report to and settle with the Federal government at periodic intervals. Otherwise, taxpayers would remain uncertain as to their tax liabilities, and the government would have difficulty judging revenues and budgeting expenditures. The period selected for final settlement of most tax liabilities is one year. At the close of each year, a taxpayer's position becomes complete for that particular year. Referred to as the annual accounting period concept, the effect is to divide each taxpayer's life into equal annual intervals for tax purposes.

The finality of the annual accounting period concept can lead to dissimilarity in tax treatment for taxpayers who are, from a long-range standpoint, in the same economic position.

─────────────────── EXAMPLE 9 ───────────────────

R and S are two sole proprietors and have experienced the following results during the past four years:

| | **Profit (or Loss)** | |
Year	R	S
1989	$50,000	$150,000
1990	60,000	60,000
1991	70,000	70,000
1992	50,000	(50,000)

Although R and S have the same profit of $230,000 over the period 1989–1992, the finality of the annual accounting period concept places S at a definite disadvantage for tax purposes. The net operating loss procedure offers S some relief by allowing him to apply some or all of his 1992 loss to the earliest profitable years (in this case 1989). Thus, S, with a net operating loss carryback, would be in a position to obtain a refund for some of the taxes he paid on the $150,000 profit reported for 1989. ◆

The same reasoning used to support the deduction of net operating losses can be applied to explain the special treatment excess capital losses and excess charitable contributions receive. Carryback and carryover procedures help mitigate the effect of limiting a loss or a deduction to the accounting period in which it is realized. With such procedures, a taxpayer may be able to salvage a loss or a deduction that might otherwise be wasted.

The installment method of recognizing gain on the sale of property allows a taxpayer to spread tax consequences over the payout period.[22] The harsh effect of taxing all the gain in the year of sale is avoided. The installment method can also be explained by the wherewithal to pay concept since recognition of gain is tied to the collection of the installment notes received from the sale of the property. Tax consequences tend to correspond to the seller's ability to pay the tax.

---

21. This continuation is known as the continuity of interest concept. It forms the foundation for all nontaxable corporate reorganizations. The concept is discussed at length in Chapter 7.

22. Under the installment method, each payment received by the seller represents a return of basis (the nontaxable portion) and profit from the sale (the taxable portion).

—————————————— EXAMPLE 10 ——————————————

In 1990, T sold unimproved real estate (cost of $40,000) for $100,000. Under the terms of the sale, T receives two notes from the purchaser, each for $50,000 (plus interest). One note is payable in 1991 and the other note in 1992. Without the installment method, T would have to recognize and pay a tax on the gain of $60,000 for the year of the sale (1990). This is a harsh result, since none of the sale proceeds will be received until 1991 and 1992. With the installment method, and presuming the notes are paid when each comes due, T recognizes half of the gain ($30,000) in 1991 and the remaining half in 1992. ◆

The annual accounting period concept has been modified to apply to situations in which taxpayers may have difficulty accurately assessing their tax positions by year-end. In many such cases, the law permits taxpayers to treat transactions taking place in the next year as having occurred in the prior year.

—————————————— EXAMPLE 11 ——————————————

T, a calendar year individual taxpayer, is a participant in an H.R. 10 (Keogh) retirement plan. (See Appendix C for a definition of a Keogh plan.) Under the plan, T contributes 20% of her net self-employment income, such amount being deductible for Federal income tax purposes. On April 10, 1992, T determines that her net self-employment income for calendar year 1991 was $80,000. Consequently, she contributes $16,000 (20% × $80,000) to the plan. Even though the $16,000 contribution was made in 1992, the law permits T to claim it as a deduction for tax year 1991. Requiring T to make the contribution by December 31, 1991, in order to obtain the deduction for that year would force her to arrive at an accurate determination of net self-employment income long before her income tax return must be prepared and filed. ◆

Similar exceptions to the annual accounting period concept cover certain charitable contributions by accrual basis corporations (Chapter 2), dividend distributions by S corporations (Chapter 12), and the dividend deduction allowed in applying the tax on unreasonable accumulation of corporate earnings and the tax on personal holding companies (Chapter 6).

Coping with Inflation.   During periods of inflation, bracket creep has plagued the working person. Because of the progressive nature of the income tax, any wage adjustment to compensate for inflation can increase the income tax bracket of the recipient. The overall impact is an erosion of purchasing power. Congress recognized this problem and began to adjust various income tax components (the indexation procedure) in 1985, based upon the rise in the consumer price index over the prior year. For example, due to the inflation factor, the amount of a personal and dependency exemption has been increased over the years. Indexation also applies to dollar amounts of the tax brackets and the standard deduction.

Political Considerations

A large segment of the Federal tax law is made up of statutory provisions. Since these statutes are enacted by Congress, is it any surprise that political considerations influence tax law? For purposes of discussion, the effect of political considerations on the tax law is divided into the following topics: special interest legislation, political expediency, and state and local influences.

Special Interest Legislation.   Unquestionably, certain provisions of the tax law can be explained largely by looking to the political influence some pressure groups have exerted on Congress. For example, is there any other reason why prepaid subscription and dues income are not taxed until earned while prepaid rents are taxed to the landlord in the year received? The reason these exceptions came about is because certain organizations (e.g., the American Automobile Association) convinced Congress that special tax treatment was needed to cover income received from multiyear dues and subscriptions.

Special interest legislation is not necessarily to be condemned if it can be justified on economic or social grounds. At any rate, it is an inevitable product of our political system.

Political Expediency. Various tax reform proposals rise and fall in favor, depending upon the shifting moods of the American public. That Congress is sensitive to popular feeling is an accepted fact. Therefore, certain provisions of the tax law can be explained on the basis of the political climate at the time of enactment. Once the general public became aware that certain large and profitable corporations were able to avoid the corporate income tax, Congress responded in TRA of 1986 with a new alternative minimum tax. Since a portion of a corporation's adjusted current earnings has been made a tax preference item, many corporations no longer will escape taxation (see Chapter 6).

Measures that deter more affluent taxpayers from obtaining so-called preferential tax treatment have always had popular appeal and, consequently, the support of Congress. Provisions such as the alternative minimum tax, the imputed interest rules, and the limitation on the deductibility of interest on investment indebtedness can be explained on this basis. In the same vein are the provisions imposing penalty taxes on corporations that unreasonably accumulate earnings or are classified as personal holding companies (see Chapter 6).

Other changes partially founded on the basis of political expediency include lowering individual income tax rates, increasing the amount of the dependency exemption, and increasing the earned income credit.

State and Local Influences. Political considerations have played a major role in the exclusion from gross income of interest received on state and local obligations. In view of the furor that has been raised by state and local political figures every time repeal of this tax provision has been proposed, one might well regard it as sacred.

Somewhat less apparent has been the influence state law has had in shaping our present Federal tax law. Of prime importance in this regard has been the effect of the community property system employed in nine states.[23] At one time, the tax position of the residents of these states was so advantageous that many common law states actually adopted community property systems.[24] The political pressure placed on Congress to correct the disparity in tax treatment was considerable. To a large extent, this was accomplished in the Revenue Act of 1948, which extended many of the community property tax advantages to residents of common law jurisdictions.[25] Thus, common law states avoided the

---

23. The states with community property systems are Louisiana, Texas, New Mexico, Arizona, California, Washington, Idaho, Nevada, and Wisconsin. The rest of the states are classified as common law jurisdictions. The difference between common law and community property systems centers around the property rights possessed by married persons. In a common law system, each spouse owns whatever he or she earns. Under a community property system, one-half of the earnings of each spouse is considered owned by the other spouse. Assume, for example, H and W are husband and wife and their only income is the $40,000 annual salary H receives. If they live in New York (a common law state), the $40,000 salary belongs to H. If, however, they live in

Texas (a community property state), the $40,000 salary is divided equally, in terms of ownership, between H and W.

24. Such states included Michigan, Oklahoma, and Pennsylvania.

25. The major advantage extended was the provision allowing married taxpayers to file joint returns and compute the tax liability as if the income had been earned one-half by each spouse. This result is automatic in a community property state since half of the income earned by one spouse belongs to the other spouse. The income-splitting benefits of a joint return are now incorporated as part of the tax rates applicable to married taxpayers.

trauma of discarding the time-honored legal system familiar to everyone. The impact of community property law on the Federal estate and gift taxes is further explored in Chapters 17 and 18.

Influence of the Internal Revenue Service

The IRS has been influential in many areas beyond its role in issuing administrative pronouncements. In its capacity as the protector of the national revenue, the IRS has been instrumental in securing the passage of much legislation designed to curtail the most flagrant tax avoidance practices (closing tax loopholes). In its capacity as the administrator of the tax laws, the IRS has sought and obtained legislation to make its job easier (administrative feasibility).

The IRS as Protector of the Revenue. Innumerable examples can be given of provisions in the tax law that have stemmed from the direct efforts of the IRS to prevent taxpayers from exploiting a loophole. Working within the letter of existing law, ingenious taxpayers and their advisers devise techniques that accomplish indirectly what cannot be accomplished directly. As a consequence, legislation is enacted to close the loophole that taxpayers have located and exploited. The following examples can be explained in this fashion and are discussed in more detail in the chapters to follow:

- The use of a fiscal year by personal service corporations, partnerships, S corporations, and trusts to defer income recognition to the owners (see Chapters 2, 10, 12, and 19).
- The use of the cash basis method of accounting by certain large corporations (see Chapter 2).
- The deduction of passive investment losses and expenses against other income (see Chapter 11).
- The shifting of income to lower-bracket taxpayers through the use of reversionary trusts (see Chapter 19).

In addition, the IRS has secured from Congress legislation of a more general nature that enables it to make adjustments based upon the substance, rather than the formal construction, of what a taxpayer has done. One provision, for example, authorizes the IRS to establish guidelines on the thin capitalization issue. This question involves when corporate debt will be recognized as debt for tax purposes and when it will be reclassified as equity or stock (see the discussion of thin capitalization in Chapter 3). Another provision permits the IRS to make adjustments to a taxpayer's method of accounting when the method used by the taxpayer does not clearly reflect income. The IRS also has been granted the authority to allocate income and deductions among businesses owned or controlled by the same interests when the allocation is necessary to prevent the evasion of taxes or to reflect clearly the income of each business.

EXAMPLE 12

X Corporation and Y Corporation are brother-sister corporations (the stock of each is owned by the same shareholders), and both use the calendar year for tax purposes. For the current tax year, each has taxable income as follows: $335,000 for X Corporation and $50,000 for Y Corporation. Not included in X Corporation's taxable income, however, is $10,000 of rent income usually charged Y Corporation for the use of some property owned by X Corporation. Since the parties have not clearly reflected the taxable income of each business, the IRS can allocate $10,000 of rent income to X

Corporation. After the allocation, X Corporation has taxable income of $345,000, and Y Corporation has taxable income of $40,000.[26] ◆

Also of a general nature is the authority Congress has given the IRS to prevent taxpayers from acquiring corporations to obtain a tax advantage when the principal purpose of such acquisition is the evasion or avoidance of the Federal income tax. The provision of the tax law that provides this authority is discussed briefly in Chapter 7.

Administrative Feasibility.   Some of the tax law is justified on the grounds that it simplifies the task of the IRS in collecting the revenue and administering the law. With regard to collecting the revenue, the IRS long ago realized the importance of placing taxpayers on a pay-as-you-go basis. Elaborate withholding procedures apply to wages, while the tax on other types of income may have to be paid at periodic intervals throughout the year. The IRS has been instrumental in convincing the courts that accrual basis taxpayers should pay taxes on prepaid income in the year received and not when earned. This approach may be contrary to generally accepted accounting principles, but it is consistent with the wherewithal to pay concept.

Of considerable aid to the IRS in collecting revenue are the numerous provisions that impose interest and penalties on taxpayers for noncompliance with the tax law. These provisions include penalties for failure to pay a tax or to file a return that is due and the negligence penalty for intentional disregard of rules and regulations. Various penalties for civil and criminal fraud also serve as deterrents to taxpayer noncompliance. This aspect of the tax law is discussed in Chapter 16.

One of the keys to the effective administration of our tax system is the audit process conducted by the IRS. To carry out this function, the IRS is aided by provisions that reduce the chance of taxpayer error or manipulation and therefore simplify the audit effort that is necessary. An increase in the amount of the standard deduction, reduces the number of individual taxpayers who will be in a position to claim itemized deductions. With fewer deductions to check, the audit function is simplified.[27] The same objective can be used to explain the $192,800 unified estate and gift tax credit and the $10,000 annual gift tax exclusion (see Chapter 17). These provisions decrease the number of tax returns that must be filed (as well as reduce the taxes paid) and thereby save audit effort.[28]

The audit function of the IRS has also been simplified by provisions of the tax law dealing with the burden of proof. Suppose, for example, the IRS audits a taxpayer and questions a particular deduction. Who has the burden of proving the propriety of the deduction? Except in the case of fraud (see Chapter 16), the burden is always on the taxpayer.

Influence of the Courts

In addition to interpreting statutory provisions and the administrative pronouncements issued by the IRS, the Federal courts have influenced tax law in

---

26. By shifting $10,000 of income to X Corporation (which is in the 34% bracket), the IRS gains $3,400 in taxes. Allowing the $10,000 deduction to Y Corporation (which is in the 15% bracket) costs the IRS only $1,500. See Chapter 2 for a further discussion of the income tax rates applicable to corporations.

27. The same justification was given by the IRS when it proposed to Congress the $100 per event limitation on personal casualty and theft losses. Imposition of the limitation eliminated many casualty and theft loss

deductions and, as a consequence, saved the IRS considerable audit time. Also, an additional limitation equal to 10% of adjusted gross income applies to the total of nonbusiness losses after reduction by the floor of $100 for each loss.

28. Particularly in the case of nominal gifts among family members, taxpayer compliance in reporting and paying a tax on such transfers would be questionable. The absence of the $10,000 gift tax exclusion would create a serious enforcement problem for the IRS.

two other respects.[29] First, the courts have formulated certain judicial concepts that serve as guides in the application of various tax provisions. Second, certain key decisions have led to changes in the Internal Revenue Code. Understanding this influence helps explain some of our tax law.

Judicial Concepts Relating to Tax Law.   It is difficult to rank the tax concepts developed by the courts in order of importance. If this ranking were attempted, however, the concept of substance over form would be near the top of the list. Variously described as the "telescoping" or "collapsing" process or the "step transaction approach," it involves determining the true substance of what occurred. In a transaction involving many steps, any one step may be collapsed (or disregarded) to arrive directly at the result reached.

EXAMPLE 13

In the current year, Mrs. G, a widow, wants to give $20,000 to S without incurring any gift tax liability.[30] She knows that the law permits her to give up to $10,000 each year per person without any tax consequences (the annual exclusion). With this in mind, the following steps are taken: a gift by Mrs. G to S of $10,000 (nontaxable because of the $10,000 annual exclusion), a gift by Mrs. G to B of $10,000 (also nontaxable), and a gift by B to S of $10,000 (nontaxable because of B's annual exclusion). Considering only the form of what Mrs. G and B have done, all appears well from a tax standpoint. In substance, however, what has happened? By collapsing the steps involving B, it is apparent that Mrs. G has made a gift of $20,000 to S and therefore has not avoided the Federal gift tax. ◆

The substance over form concept plays an important role in transactions involving corporations.

Another leading tax concept developed by the courts deals with the interpretation of statutory tax provisions that operate to benefit taxpayers. The courts have established the rule that these relief provisions are to be narrowly construed against taxpayers if there is any doubt about their application. Suppose, for example, X Corporation wants to be treated as an S corporation (see Chapter 12) but has not literally satisfied the statutory requirements for making the required election. Because S corporation status is a relief provision favoring taxpayers, chances are the courts will deny X Corporation this treatment.

Important in the area of corporate-shareholder dealings (see the discussion of constructive dividends in Chapter 4) and in the resolution of valuation problems for estate and gift tax purposes (see Chapters 17 and 18) is the arm's length concept. Particularly in dealings between related parties, transactions can be tested by questioning whether the taxpayers acted in an "arm's length" manner. The question to be asked is: Would unrelated parties have handled the transaction in the same way?

EXAMPLE 14

The sole shareholder of a corporation leases property to the corporation for a monthly rental of $50,000. To test whether the corporation should be allowed a rent deduction for this amount, the IRS and the courts will apply the arm's length concept. Would the corporation have paid $50,000 a month in rent if the same property had been leased from an unrelated party (rather than from the sole shareholder)? ◆

---

29. A great deal of case law is devoted to ascertaining congressional intent. The courts, in effect, ask: What did Congress have in mind when it enacted a particular tax provision?

30. The example assumes that Mrs. G has exhausted her unified tax credit. See Chapter 17.

The continuity of interest concept originated with the courts but has, in many situations, been incorporated into statutory provisions of the tax law. Primarily concerned with business readjustments, the concept permits tax-free treatment only if the taxpayer retains a substantial continuing interest in the property transferred to the new business. Due to the continuing interest retained, the transfer should not have tax consequences because the position of the taxpayer has not changed. This concept applies to transfers to controlled corporations (Chapter 3), corporate reorganizations (Chapter 7), and transfers to partnerships (Chapter 10). The continuity of interest concept helps explain the results reached in Examples 5 through 7 of this chapter. This concept is further discussed in Chapter 7.

Also developed by the courts, the business purpose concept principally applies to transactions involving corporations. Under this concept, some sound business reason that motivates the transaction must be present in order for the prescribed tax treatment to result. The avoidance of taxation is not considered to be a sound business purpose.

EXAMPLE 15

B and C are equal shareholders in X Corporation. They have recently disagreed about the company's operations and are at an impasse about the future of X Corporation. This shareholder disagreement on corporate policy constitutes a sound business purpose and would justify a division of X Corporation that will permit B and C to go their separate ways. Whether the division of X Corporation would be nontaxable to the parties depends on their compliance with the statutory provisions dealing with corporate reorganizations. The point is, however, that compliance with statutory provisions would not be enough to ensure nontaxability without a business purpose for the transaction. ◆

The business purpose concept is discussed further in Chapter 7.

Judicial Influence on Statutory Provisions. Some court decisions have been of such consequence that Congress has incorporated them into statutory tax law. An illustration of this influence appears in Example 16.

EXAMPLE 16

In 1982, T claimed a capital loss of $100,000 for Z Corporation stock that had become worthless during the year. In the absence of any offsetting gains, the capital loss deduction produced no income tax savings for T either in 1982 or in future years. In 1984, T institutes a lawsuit against the former officers of Z Corporation for their misconduct that resulted in the corporation's failure and thereby led to T's $100,000 loss. In settlement of the suit, the officers pay $50,000 to T. The IRS argued that the full $50,000 should be taxed as gain to T. The stock in Z Corporation was written off in 1982 and had a zero basis for tax purposes. The $50,000 recovery received by T on the stock was, therefore, all gain. The position of the IRS was logical, but not equitable. The court stated that T should not be taxed on the recovery of an amount previously deducted unless the deduction produced a tax savings. Since the $100,000 capital loss deduction in 1982 produced no tax benefit, none of the $50,000 received in 1984 results in gain. ◆

The decision reached by the courts in Example 16, known as the tax benefit rule, is part of the statutory tax law. The tax benefit rule is discussed later in connection with transfers to controlled corporations (Chapter 3).

Court decisions sometimes produce uncertainty in the tax law. Such decisions may reach the right result but do not produce the guidelines necessary to enable taxpayers to comply. In many situations, Congress may be compelled to add certainty to the law by enacting statutory provisions specifying when a particular tax consequence will or will not materialize. The following are examples of this type of judicial "cause" and the statutory "effect":

- When a stock redemption will be treated as an exchange or as a dividend (see Chapter 5).
- What basis a parent corporation will have in the assets received from a subsidiary that is liquidated shortly after its acquisition (see Chapter 5).

Some of the statutory provisions can be explained by a negative reaction by Congress to a particular court decision. One decision, for example, held that the transfer of a liability to a controlled corporation should be treated as boot received by the transferor (see Chapter 3). Congress apparently disagreed with this treatment and promptly enacted legislation to change the result.

Summary

In addition to its revenue-raising objective, the Federal tax law has developed in response to several other factors:

- *Economic considerations.* Here, the emphasis is on tax provisions that help regulate the economy and encourage certain activities and types of businesses.
- *Social considerations.* Some tax provisions are designed to encourage or discourage certain socially desirable or undesirable practices.
- *Equity considerations.* Of principal concern in this area are tax provisions that alleviate the effect of multiple taxation, recognize the wherewithal to pay concept, mitigate the effect of the annual accounting period concept, and recognize the eroding effect of inflation.
- *Political considerations.* Of significance in this regard are tax provisions that represent special interest legislation, reflect political expediency, and illustrate the effect of state law.
- *Influence of the IRS.* Many tax provisions are intended to aid the IRS in the collection of the revenue and the administration of the tax law.
- *Influence of the courts.* Court decisions have established a body of judicial concepts relating to tax law and have, on occasion, led Congress to enact statutory provisions that either clarify or negate their effect.

These factors explain various tax provisions and thereby help in understanding why the tax law developed to its present state. The next step involves learning to work with the tax law.

WORKING WITH THE TAX LAW—TAX SOURCES

◆

Understanding taxation requires a mastery of the sources of tax law. These sources include not only the legislative provisions in the Internal Revenue Code, but also Congressional Committee Reports, Regulations, Treasury Department pronouncements, and court decisions. Thus, the primary sources of tax information are the pronouncements of the three branches of government: legislative, executive, and judicial.

The law is of little significance, however, until it is applied to a set of facts and circumstances. A tax researcher must not only be able to read and interpret the sources of the law but must also understand the relative weight of authority within the rules of law. Learning to work with the tax law involves the following three basic steps:

1. Familiarity with the sources of the law.
2. Application of research techniques.
3. Effective use of planning procedures.

The remainder of this chapter introduces the sources of tax law and explains how the law is applied to problems and conditions of individual and business transactions. Statutory, administrative, and judicial sources of the tax law are considered first.

Statutory Sources of the Tax Law

Origin of the Internal Revenue Code. Before 1939, the statutory provisions relating to taxation were contained in the individual revenue acts enacted by Congress. The inconvenience and confusion that resulted from dealing with many separate acts led Congress to codify all of the Federal tax laws. Known as the Internal Revenue Code of 1939, the codification arranged all Federal tax provisions in a logical sequence and placed them in a separate part of the Federal statutes. A further rearrangement took place in 1954 and resulted in the Internal Revenue Code of 1954.

Perhaps to emphasize the magnitude of the changes made by TRA of 1986, Congress redesignated the Internal Revenue Code of 1954 as the Internal Revenue Code of 1986. This change is somewhat deceiving since a recodification of the tax law, as occurred in 1954, did not take place in 1986. TRA of 1986 merely amended, deleted, or added provisions to the Internal Revenue Code of 1954. For example, before TRA of 1986, § 336 provided the general rule that no gain or loss would be recognized by a corporation when it distributed assets in kind to its shareholders in complete liquidation (see Chapter 5). After the effective date of TRA of 1986, § 336 provides that gain or loss will be recognized upon the same distributions.

The following observations will help clarify the significance of the three Codes:

■ Neither the 1939, the 1954, nor the 1986 Code changed all of the tax law existing on the date of enactment. Much of the 1939 Code, for example, was incorporated into the 1954 Code. The same can be said for the transition from the 1954 to the 1986 Code. This point is important in assessing judicial and administrative decisions interpreting provisions under prior Codes. For example, a decision interpreting § 121 of the Internal Revenue Code of 1954 will have continuing validity since this provision carried over unchanged to the Internal Revenue Code of 1986.

■ Statutory amendments to the tax law are integrated into the existing Code. Thus, the Revenue Reconciliation Act of 1990 became part of the Internal Revenue Code of 1986.

The Legislative Process. Federal tax legislation generally originates in the House of Representatives, where it is first considered by the House Ways and Means Committee. Tax bills originate in the Senate when they are attached as riders to other legislative proposals.[31] If acceptable to the House Ways and Means Committee, the proposed bill is referred to the entire House of Representatives

---

31. The Tax Equity and Fiscal Responsibility Act of 1982 originated in the Senate; its constitutionality was unsuccessfully challenged in the courts. The Senate version of the Deficit Reduction Act of 1984 was attached as an amendment to the Federal Boat Safety Act.

for approval or disapproval. Approved bills are sent to the Senate, where they are referred to the Senate Finance Committee for further consideration.

The next step in the legislative process involves referral from the Senate Finance Committee to the whole Senate. Assuming no disagreement between the House and the Senate, passage by the Senate means referral to the President for approval or veto. If the bill is approved or if the President's veto is overridden, the bill becomes law and part of the Internal Revenue Code.

When the Senate version of the bill differs from that passed by the House, the Joint Conference Committee is called upon to resolve these differences. The Joint Conference Committee includes members of the House Ways and Means Committee and the Senate Finance Committee.

Referrals from the House Ways and Means Committee, the Senate Finance Committee, and the Joint Conference Committee are usually accompanied by Committee Reports. These Committee Reports often explain the provisions of the proposed legislation and are therefore a valuable source in ascertaining the intent of Congress. What Congress has in mind when it considers and enacts tax legislation is, of course, the key to interpreting such legislation. Since Regulations normally are not issued immediately after a statute is enacted, taxpayers often look to legislative history materials to ascertain congressional intent.

The typical legislative process dealing with tax bills can be summarized as follows:

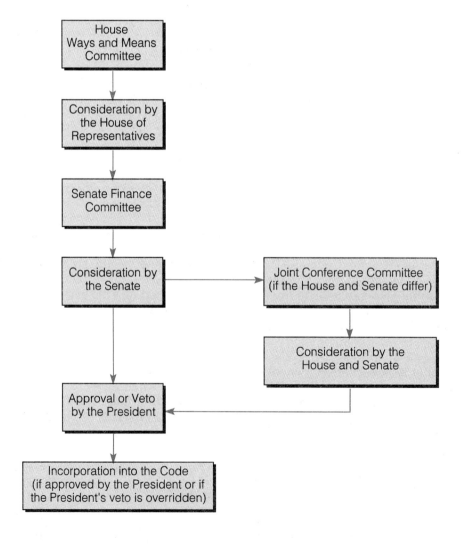

The role of the Joint Conference Committee indicates the importance of compromise in the legislative process. The practical effect of the compromise process can be illustrated by reviewing what happened in TRA of 1986 (H.R. 3838) with respect to the maximum income tax rates applicable to corporations beginning in 1988.

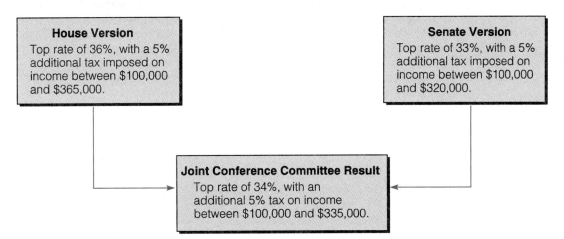

Some tax provisions are commonly referred to by the number the bill received in the House when first proposed or by the name of the member of Congress sponsoring the legislation. For example, the Self-Employed Individuals Tax Retirement Act of 1962 is popularly known as H.R. 10 (the House of Representatives Bill No. 10) or as the Keogh Act (Keogh being one of the members of Congress sponsoring the bill).

Arrangement of the Code.　In working with the Code, it helps to understand the format. Note the following partial table of contents:

> Subtitle A. Income Taxes
>
> 　Chapter 1. Normal Taxes and Surtaxes
>
> 　　Subchapter A. Determination of Tax Liability
>
> 　　Part I. Tax on Individuals
>
> 　　　Sections 1–5
>
> 　　Part II. Tax on Corporations
>
> 　　　Sections 11–12
>
> 　　　　　*　*　*

In referring to a provision of the Code, the key is usually the Section number. In citing Section 2(a) (dealing with the status of a surviving spouse), for example, it is unnecessary to include Subtitle A, Chapter 1, Subchapter A, Part I. Merely mentioning Section 2(a) will suffice since the Section numbers run consecutively and do not begin again with each new Subtitle, Chapter, Subchapter, or Part. Not all Code Section numbers are used, however. Note that Part I ends with Section 5 and Part II starts with Section 11 (at present there are no Sections 6, 7, 8, 9, and 10).[32]

---

32. When the 1954 Code was drafted, Section numbers were intentionally omitted. This omission provided flexibility to incorporate later changes into the Code without disrupting its organization. When Congress does not leave enough space, subsequent Code Sections are given A, B, C, etc., designations. A good example is the treatment of §§ 280A through 280H.

Tax practitioners commonly refer to a specific area of income taxation by Subchapter designation. Some of the more common Subchapter designations include Subchapter C (Corporate Distributions and Adjustments), Subchapter K (Partners and Partnerships), and Subchapter S (Tax Treatment of S Corporations and Their Shareholders). Particularly in the last situation, it is much more convenient to describe the subject of the applicable Code provisions (Sections 1361 through 1379) as S corporation status rather than as the "Tax Treatment of S Corporations and Their Shareholders."

Citing the Code. Code Sections often are broken down into subparts.[33] Section 2(a)(1)(A) serves as an example.

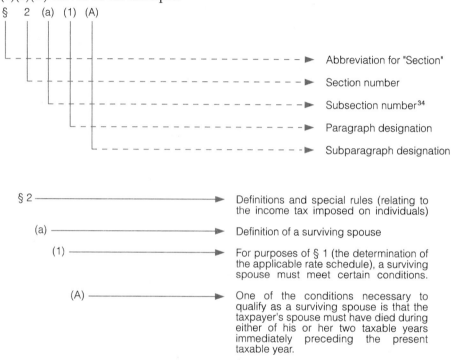

§ 2 ─────────────────────▶ Definitions and special rules (relating to the income tax imposed on individuals)

(a) ─────────────────────▶ Definition of a surviving spouse

(1) ─────────────────────▶ For purposes of § 1 (the determination of the applicable rate schedule), a surviving spouse must meet certain conditions.

(A) ─────────────────────▶ One of the conditions necessary to qualify as a surviving spouse is that the taxpayer's spouse must have died during either of his or her two taxable years immediately preceding the present taxable year.

Throughout the remainder of the text, references to Code Sections are in the form just given. The symbols "§" and "§§" are used in place of "Section" and "Sections." Unless otherwise stated, all Code references are to the Internal Revenue Code of 1986. The format followed in the remainder of the text is summarized as follows:

Complete Reference	Text Reference
Section 2(a)(1)(A) of the Internal Revenue Code of 1986	§ 2(a)(1)(A)
Sections 1 and 2 of the Internal Revenue Code of 1986	§§ 1 and 2
Section 2 of the Internal Revenue Code of 1954	§ 2 of the Internal Revenue Code of 1954
Section 12(d) of the Internal Revenue Code of 1939[35]	§ 12(d) of the Internal Revenue Code of 1939

---

33. Some Code Sections do not have subparts. See, for example, § 482.

34. Some Code Sections omit the subsection designation and use, instead, the paragraph designation as the first subpart.

See, for example, §§ 212(1) and 1221(1).

35. Section 12(d) of the Internal Revenue Code of 1939 is the predecessor to § 2 of the Internal Revenue Code of 1954. Keep in mind that the 1954 Code superseded the 1939 Code.

Administrative Sources of the Tax Law

The administrative sources of the Federal tax law can be grouped as follows: Treasury Department Regulations, Revenue Rulings and Procedures, and other administrative pronouncements. All are issued either by the U.S. Treasury Department or by one of its instrumentalities (e.g., the IRS or a District Director). The role played by the IRS in this process is considered in greater depth in Chapter 16.

Treasury Department Regulations. Regulations are issued by the U.S. Treasury Department under authority granted by Congress. Interpretative by nature, they provide taxpayers with considerable guidance on the meaning and application of the Code. Although not issued by Congress, Regulations do carry considerable weight. They are an important factor to consider in complying with the tax law.

Since Regulations interpret the Code, they are arranged in the same sequence. Regulations are, however, prefixed by a number that indicates the type of tax or administrative, procedural, or definitional matter to which they relate. For example, the prefix 1 designates the Regulations under the income tax law. Thus, the Regulations under Code § 2 would be cited as Reg. § 1.2, with subparts added for further identification. The numbering of these subparts often has no correlation with the Code subsections. The prefix 20 designates estate tax Regulations; 25 covers gift tax Regulations; 31 relates to employment taxes; and 301 refers to Regulations dealing with procedure and administration. This listing is not all-inclusive.

New Regulations and changes in existing Regulations usually are issued in proposed form before they are finalized. The time interval between the proposal of a Regulation and its finalization permits taxpayers and other interested parties to comment on the propriety of the proposal. Proposed Regulations under Code § 2, for example, would be cited as Prop.Reg. § 1.2.

Sometimes temporary Regulations relating to elections and other matters where speed is critical are issued by the Treasury Department. Temporary Regulations often are needed for recent legislation that takes effect immediately. Temporary Regulations have the same authoritative value as final Regulations and may be cited as precedent for three years. Temporary Regulations also are issued as Proposed Regulations and automatically expire within three years after the date of issuance. Temporary Regulations and the simultaneously issued Proposed Regulations carry more weight than traditional Proposed Regulations.

Proposed, final, and Temporary Regulations are published in the *Federal Register* and are reproduced in major tax services. Final Regulations are issued as Treasury Decisions (TDs).

Revenue Rulings and Revenue Procedures. Revenue Rulings are official pronouncements of the National Office of the IRS. Like Regulations, they are designed to provide interpretation of the tax law. However, they do not carry the same legal force and effect of Regulations and usually deal with more restricted problems. Both Revenue Rulings and Revenue Procedures serve an important function in that they provide guidance to both IRS personnel and taxpayers in handling routine tax matters.

A Revenue Ruling often results from a specific taxpayer's request for a letter ruling. If the IRS believes that a taxpayer's request for a letter ruling deserves official publication due to its widespread impact, the holding will be converted into a Revenue Ruling. In making this conversion, names, identifying facts, and money amounts will be changed to disguise the identity of the requesting taxpayer. The IRS then will issue what would have been a letter ruling as a Revenue Ruling.

Revenue Procedures are issued in the same manner as Revenue Rulings, but deal with the internal management practices and procedures of the IRS. Familiarity with these procedures increases taxpayer compliance and helps make the administration of the tax laws more efficient.

Both Revenue Rulings and Revenue Procedures are published weekly by the U.S. Government in the *Internal Revenue Bulletin* (I.R.B.). Semiannually, the bulletins for a six-month period are gathered together, reorganized by Code Section classification, and published in a bound volume called the *Cumulative Bulletin* (C.B.).[36] The proper form for citing Rulings and Procedures depends on whether the item has been published in the *Cumulative Bulletin* or is available in I.R.B. form. Consider, for example, the following transition:

Temporary Citation { Rev.Rul. 90–109, I.R.B. No. 52, 17.
Explanation: Revenue Ruling Number 109, appearing on page 17 of the 52nd weekly issue of the *Internal Revenue Bulletin* for 1990.

Permanent Citation { Rev.Rul. 90–109, 1990–2 C.B. 191.
Explanation: Revenue Ruling Number 109, appearing on page 191 of volume 2 of the *Cumulative Bulletin* for 1990.

Since the second volume of the 1990 *Cumulative Bulletin* was not published until August of 1991, the I.R.B. citation had to be used until that time. After the publication of the *Cumulative Bulletin*, the C.B. citation became proper. The basic portion of both citations (Rev.Rul. 90–109) indicates that this was the 109th Revenue Ruling issued by the IRS during 1990.

Revenue Procedures are cited in the same manner, except that "Rev.Proc." is substituted for "Rev.Rul." Procedures, like Rulings, are published in the *Internal Revenue Bulletin* (the temporary source) and later transferred to the *Cumulative Bulletin* (the permanent source).

Other Administrative Pronouncements. Treasury Decisions (TDs) are issued by the Treasury Department to promulgate new Regulations, to amend or otherwise change existing Regulations, or to announce the position of the Government on selected court decisions. Like Revenue Rulings and Revenue Procedures, TDs are published in the *Internal Revenue Bulletin* and subsequently transferred to the *Cumulative Bulletin*.

Technical Information Releases (TIRs) are usually issued to announce the publication of various IRS pronouncements (e.g., Revenue Rulings, Revenue Procedures).

Letter rulings are issued upon a taxpayer's request and describe how the IRS will treat a proposed transaction for tax purposes. In general, they apply only to the taxpayer who asks for and obtains the ruling, but post-1984 rulings may be substantial authority for purposes of avoiding the accuracy-related penalties.[37] This procedure may sound like the only real way to carry out effective tax planning. However, the IRS limits the issuance of letter rulings to restricted, preannounced areas of taxation. Thus, it is not possible to obtain a ruling on many of the problems that are particularly troublesome for taxpayers.[38] For

36. Usually, only two volumes of the *Cumulative Bulletin* are published each year. However, when major tax legislation has been enacted by Congress, other volumes may be published containing the Congressional Committee Reports supporting the Revenue Act. See, for example, the two extra volumes for 1984 dealing with the Deficit Reduction Act of 1984. The 1984–3 *Cumulative Bulletin*, Volume 1, contains the text of the law itself; 1984–3, Volume 2, contains the

Committee Reports. This makes a total of four volumes of the *Cumulative Bulletin* for 1984: 1984–1; 1984–2; 1984–3, Volume 1; and 1984–3, Volume 2.

37. Notice 90–20, 1990–1 C.B. 328, part V (A).

38. Rev.Proc. 92–3, I.R.B. No. 1, 55, contains a listing of areas in which the IRS will not issue advance rulings. From time to time, subsequent Revenue Procedures are issued that modify or amplify Rev.Proc. 92–3.

example, the IRS will not issue a ruling as to whether compensation paid to shareholder-employees is reasonable (see Chapter 4) or whether § 269 applies (the acquisition of a corporation to evade or avoid income tax [see Chapter 7]). The main reason the IRS will not rule on such matters is that these areas involve fact-oriented situations.

The IRS must make letter rulings available for public inspection after identifying details are deleted. Published digests of private letter rulings can be found in *Private Letter Rulings* (published by Prentice-Hall), *BNA Daily Tax Reports*, and Tax Analysts & Advocates *TAX NOTES*. *IRS Letter Rulings Reports* (published by Commerce Clearing House) contains both digests and full texts of all letter rulings. *Letter Ruling Review* (Tax Analysts), a monthly publication, selects and discusses the more important of the more than 300 letter rulings per month.

The National Office of the IRS releases Technical Advice Memoranda (TAMs) weekly. TAMs resemble letter rulings in that they give the IRS's determination of an issue. Letter rulings, however, are responses to requests by taxpayers, whereas TAMs are issued by the National Office of the IRS in response to questions raised by IRS field personnel during audits. TAMs deal with completed rather than proposed transactions and are often requested for questions relating to exempt organizations and employee plans. Although TAMs are not officially published and may not be cited or used as precedent, post-1984 TAMs may be substantial authority for purposes of the accuracy-related penalties. See Chapter 16 for a discussion of these penalties.

Both letter rulings and TAMs are issued with multidigit file numbers. Consider, for example, the following ruling dealing with disability benefits: Ltr.Rul. 9111027. Broken down by digits, the file number reveals the following information:

Like letter rulings, determination letters are issued at the request of taxpayers and provide guidance concerning the application of the tax law. They differ from individual rulings in that the issuing source is the District Director rather than the National Office of the IRS. Also, determination letters usually involve completed (as opposed to proposed) transactions. Determination letters are not published but are made known only to the party making the request.

The following examples illustrate the distinction between individual rulings and determination letters:

─────────────── EXAMPLE 17 ───────────────

The shareholders of X Corporation and Y Corporation want assurance that the consolidation of the corporations into Z Corporation will be a nontaxable reorganization (see Chapter 7). The proper approach would be to request from the National Office of the IRS an individual ruling concerning the income tax effect of the proposed transaction. ◆

─────────────── EXAMPLE 18 ───────────────

T operates a barber shop in which he employs eight barbers. To comply with the rules governing income tax and payroll tax withholdings, T wants to know whether the barbers working for him are employees or independent contractors. The proper procedure would be to request from the appropriate District Director a determination letter on the status of such persons. ◆

Judicial Sources of the Tax Law

The Judicial Process in General.   After a taxpayer has exhausted some or all of the remedies available within the IRS (no satisfactory settlement has been reached at the agent or at the conference level discussed in Chapter 16), the dispute can be taken to the Federal courts. The dispute is first considered by a court of original jurisdiction (known as a trial court) with any appeal (either by the taxpayer or the IRS) taken to the appropriate appellate court. In most situations, the taxpayer has a choice of any of four trial courts: a Federal District Court, the U.S. Claims Court, the Tax Court, or the Small Claims Division of the Tax Court. The trial and appellate court system for Federal tax litigation is illustrated in Figure 1–1.

The broken line between the Tax Court and the Small Claims Division indicates that there is no appeal from the Small Claims Division. Currently, the jurisdiction of the Small Claims Division of the Tax Court is limited to $10,000 or less. The proceedings of the Small Claims Division are informal, and its decisions are not precedents for any other court decision and are not reviewable by any higher court. Proceedings can be more timely and less expensive in the Small Claims Division.

American law, following English law, is frequently "made" by judicial decisions. Under the doctrine of *stare decisis*, each case (except in the Small Claims Division) has precedential value for future cases with the same controlling set of facts. Most Federal and state appellate court decisions and some decisions of trial courts are published. Almost three and a half million judicial opinions have been published in the United States; over 30,000 cases are published each year.[39] Published court decisions are organized by jurisdiction (Federal or state) and level of court (appellate or trial).

Trial Courts.   The differences between the various trial courts (courts of original jurisdiction) can be summarized as follows:

▪ There is only one Claims Court and only one Tax Court, but there are many Federal District Courts. The taxpayer does not select the District

FIGURE 1–1
Federal Judicial Tax Process

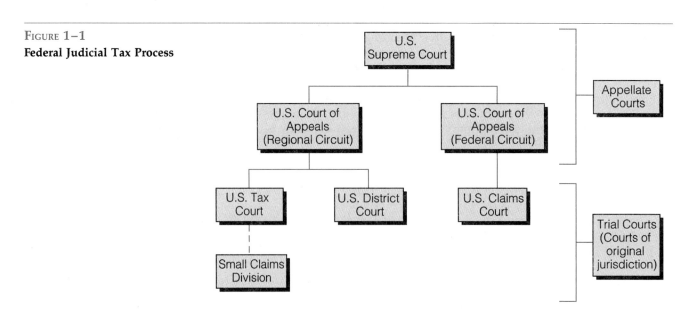

---

39. Jacobstein and Mersky, *Fundamentals of Legal Research,* 5th edition (Mineola, N.Y.: The Foundation Press, 1990).

Court that will hear the dispute but must sue in the one that has jurisdiction.

■ The U.S. Claims Court has jurisdiction over any claim against the United States that is based on the Constitution, any Act of Congress, or any regulation of an executive department.

■ Each District Court has only one judge, the Claims Court has 16 judges, and the Tax Court has 19. In the case of the Tax Court, the whole court will decide a case (the court sits *en banc*) only when more important or novel tax issues are involved. Most cases will be heard and decided by one of the 19 judges.

■ The Claims Court meets most often in Washington, D.C., while a District Court meets at a prescribed seat for the particular district. Since each state has at least one District Court and many of the populous states have more, the inconvenience and expense of traveling for the taxpayer and counsel (present with many suits in the Claims Court) are largely eliminated. The Tax Court is officially based in Washington, D.C., but the various judges travel to different parts of the country and hear cases at predetermined locations and dates. This procedure eases the distance problem for the taxpayer, but it can mean a delay before the case comes to trial and is decided.

■ The Tax Court hears only tax cases; the Claims Court and District Courts hear nontax litigation as well. This difference, as well as the fact that many Tax Court justices have been appointed from IRS or Treasury Department positions, has led some to conclude that the Tax Court has more expertise in tax matters.

■ The only court in which a taxpayer can obtain a jury trial is a District Court. Juries can decide only questions of fact and not questions of law, however. Therefore taxpayers who choose the District Court route often do not request a jury trial. In this event, the judge will decide all issues. Note that a District Court decision is controlling only in the district in which the court has jurisdiction.

■ Before the Claims Court or a District Court can have jurisdiction, the taxpayer must pay the tax deficiency assessed by the IRS and then sue for a refund. If the taxpayer wins (assuming no successful appeal by the Government), the tax paid plus appropriate interest will be recovered. Jurisdiction in the Tax Court, however, is usually obtained without first paying the assessed tax deficiency. In the event the taxpayer loses in the Tax Court (and no appeal is taken or any appeal is unsuccessful), the deficiency must be paid with accrued interest.

■ Appeals from a District Court or a Tax Court decision are to the appropriate U.S. Court of Appeals. Appeals from the Claims Court go to the Court of Appeals for the Federal Circuit.

Some of the characteristics of the judicial system described above are summarized in Concept Summary 1–1.

Appellate Courts. An appeal from a trial court goes to the Court of Appeals of appropriate jurisdiction, as shown in the list on the next page. Two of these Courts of Appeals are of recent vintage and may cause some confusion. The Eleventh Court of Appeals came into being in late 1981 and comprises states (Alabama, Florida, and Georgia) that formerly were within the jurisdiction of the Fifth Court of Appeals. The reason for the division was the increase in population in some of the Sun Belt states and the enormous geographical area previously covered by the Fifth Court of Appeals.

The Court of Appeals for the Federal Circuit was created in late 1982 and was given jurisdiction over all appeals from the U.S. Claims Court. Previously, such appeals went directly to the U.S. Supreme Court, bypassing the Court of Appeals level. As a matter of identification, the same legislation that established the Court of Appeals for the Federal Circuit changed the name of what used to be the U.S. Court of Claims to the U.S. Claims Court.

JURISDICTION OF THE COURTS OF APPEALS

First
Maine
Massachusetts
New Hampshire
Rhode Island
Puerto Rico

Second
Connecticut
New York
Vermont

Third
Delaware
New Jersey
Pennsylvania
Virgin Islands

District of Columbia
Washington, D.C.

Fourth
Maryland
North Carolina
South Carolina
Virginia
West Virginia

Fifth
Canal Zone
Louisiana
Mississippi
Texas

Sixth
Kentucky
Michigan
Ohio
Tennessee

Seventh
Illinois
Indiana
Wisconsin

Eighth
Arkansas
Iowa
Minnesota
Missouri
Nebraska
North Dakota
South Dakota

Ninth
Alaska

Arizona
California
Hawaii
Idaho
Montana
Nevada
Oregon
Washington
Guam

Tenth
Colorado
Kansas
New Mexico
Oklahoma
Utah
Wyoming

Eleventh
Alabama
Florida
Georgia

Federal Circuit
All of the jurisdictions
(where the case originates
in the Claims Court)

CONCEPT SUMMARY 1–1
FEDERAL JUDICIAL SYSTEM

Issue	U.S. Tax Court	U.S. District Court	U.S. Claims Court
Number of judges per court	19	1	16
Payment of deficiency before trial	No	Yes	Yes
Jury trial available	No	Yes	No
Types of disputes	Tax cases only	Most criminal/civil decisions	Claims against the United States
Jurisdiction	Nationwide	Location of taxpayer	Nationwide
IRS acquiescence policy	Yes	No	No
Appeal route	U.S. Court of Appeals	U.S. Court of Appeals	U.S. Court of Appeals for the Federal Circuit

If the Government loses at the trial court level (District Court, Tax Court, or Claims Court), it need not (and frequently does not) appeal. The fact that an appeal is not made, however, does not indicate that the IRS agrees with the result and will not litigate similar issues in the future.

The IRS may decide not to appeal for a number of reasons. First, the current litigation load may be heavy. As a consequence, the IRS may decide that available personnel should be assigned to other, more important, cases. Second, the IRS may determine that this is not a good case to appeal. For example, the taxpayer may be in a sympathetic position, or the facts may be particularly strong in his or her favor. In such event, the IRS may wait to test the legal issues involved with a taxpayer who has a much weaker case. Third, if the appeal is from a District Court or the Tax Court, the Court of Appeals of jurisdiction could have some bearing on whether the IRS decides to pursue an appeal. Based on past experience and precedent, the IRS may conclude that the chance for success on a particular issue might be more promising in another Court of Appeals. The IRS will wait for a similar case to arise in a different jurisdiction.

District Courts, the Tax Court, and the Claims Court must abide by the precedents set by the Court of Appeals of jurisdiction. A particular Court of Appeals need not follow the decisions of another Court of Appeals. All courts, however, must follow the decisions of the U.S. Supreme Court.

The Tax Court is a national court, meaning that it hears and decides cases from all parts of the country. For many years, the Tax Court followed a policy of deciding cases based on what it thought the result should be, even when its decision might be appealed to a Court of Appeals that had previously decided a similar case differently.

Some years ago, this policy was changed. Now the Tax Court will still decide a case as it feels the law should be applied *only* if the Court of Appeals of appropriate jurisdiction has not yet passed on the issue or has previously decided a similar case in accordance with the Tax Court's decision. If the Court of Appeals of appropriate jurisdiction has previously held otherwise, the Tax Court will conform even though it disagrees with the holding.[40] This policy is known as the *Golsen* rule.

EXAMPLE 19

Taxpayer T lives in Texas and sues in the Tax Court on Issue A. The Fifth Court of Appeals, the appellate court of appropriate jurisdiction, has already decided, based on similar facts and involving a different taxpayer, that Issue A should be resolved against the Government. Although the Tax Court feels that the Fifth Court of Appeals is wrong, under the *Golsen* rule, it will render judgment for T. Shortly thereafter, Taxpayer U, a resident of New York, in a comparable case, sues in the Tax Court on Issue A. Assume that the Second Court of Appeals, the appellate court of appropriate jurisdiction, has never expressed itself on Issue A. Presuming the Tax Court has not reconsidered its position on Issue A, it will decide against Taxpayer U. Thus, it is entirely possible for two taxpayers suing in the same court to end up with opposite results merely because they live in different parts of the country. ◆

Appeal to the U.S. Supreme Court is by Writ of Certiorari. If the Court accepts jurisdiction, it will grant the Writ (*Cert. Granted*). Most often, it will deny jurisdiction (*Cert. Denied*). For whatever reason or reasons, the Supreme Court rarely hears tax cases. The Court usually grants certiorari to resolve a conflict among the Courts of Appeals (e.g., two or more appellate courts have assumed opposing positions on a particular issue). The granting of a Writ of Certiorari

---

40. *Jack E. Golsen,* 54 T.C. 742 (1970).

indicates that at least four members of the Supreme Court believe that the issue is of sufficient importance to be heard by the full Court.

The role of appellate courts is limited to a review of the record of trial compiled by the trial courts. Thus, the appellate process usually involves a determination of whether or not the trial court applied the proper law in arriving at its decision. Usually, an appellate court will not dispute a lower court's fact-finding determination.

The result of an appeal can be any of a number of possibilities. The appellate court may approve (affirm) or disapprove (reverse) the lower court's finding, and it may also send the case back for further consideration (remand). When many issues are involved, it is not unusual to encounter a mixed result. Thus, the lower court may be affirmed (*aff'd.*) on Issue A and reversed (*rev'd.*) on Issue B, while Issue C is remanded (*rem'd.*) for additional fact finding.

When more than one judge is involved in the decision-making process, disagreement is not uncommon. In addition to the majority view, one or more judges may concur (agree with the result reached but not with some or all of the reasoning) or dissent (disagree with the result). In any one case, the majority view controls. But concurring and dissenting views can have influence on other courts or, at some subsequent date when the composition of the court has changed, even on the same court.

Judicial Citations—General. Having briefly described the judicial process, it is appropriate to consider the more practical problem of the relationship of case law to tax research. As previously noted, court decisions are an important source of tax law. The ability to cite a case and to locate it is therefore a must in working with the tax law. The usual pattern for a judicial citation is as follows: case name, volume number, reporter series, page or paragraph number, and court (where necessary).

Judicial Citations—The U.S. Tax Court. A good starting point is the U.S. Tax Court. The Court issues two types of decisions: Regular and Memorandum. The distinction between the two involves both substance and form. In terms of substance, Memorandum decisions deal with situations necessitating only the application of already established principles of law. Regular decisions involve novel issues not previously resolved by the Court. In actual practice, this distinction is not always preserved. Not infrequently, Memorandum decisions will be encountered that appear to warrant Regular status and vice versa. At any rate, do not conclude that Memorandum decisions possess no value as precedents. Both represent the position of the Tax Court and, as such, can be relied upon.

The Regular and Memorandum decisions issued by the Tax Court also differ in form. The Memorandum decisions are published officially in mimeograph form only, but Regular decisions are published by the U.S. Government in a series called *Tax Court of the United States Reports.* Each volume of these reports covers a six-month period (January 1 through June 30 and July 1 through December 31) and is given a succeeding volume number. But, as was true of the *Cumulative Bulletin,* there is usually a time lag between the date a decision is rendered and the date it appears in bound form. A temporary citation may be necessary to help the researcher locate a recent Regular decision. Consider, for example, the temporary and permanent citations for *James A. Barrett,* a decision filed on May 20, 1991:

| Temporary Citation | { | *James A. Barrett,* 96 T.C. __, No. 31 (1991). |
| | | *Explanation:* Page number left blank because not yet known. |

| Permanent Citation | { | *James A. Barrett,* 96 T.C. 713 (1991). |
| | | *Explanation:* Page number now available. |

Both citations tell us that the case ultimately will appear in Volume 96 of the *Tax Court of the United States Reports*. But until this volume is bound and made available to the general public, the page number must be left blank. Instead, the temporary citation identifies the case as being the 31st Regular decision issued by the Tax Court since Volume 95 ended. With this information, the decision can be easily located in either of the special Tax Court services published by Commerce Clearing House and by Research Institute of America (formerly by Prentice-Hall). Once Volume 96 is released, the permanent citation can be substituted and the number of the case dropped.

Before 1943, the Tax Court was called the Board of Tax Appeals, and its decisions were published as the *United States Board of Tax Appeals Reports* (B.T.A.). These 47 volumes cover the period from 1924 to 1942. For example, the citation *Karl Pauli*, 11 B.T.A. 784 (1928) refers to the 11th volume of the *Board of Tax Appeals Reports*, page 784, issued in 1928.

One further distinction between Regular and Memorandum decisions of the Tax Court involves the IRS procedure of acquiescence ("A" or "Acq.") or nonacquiescence ("NA" or "Nonacq."). If the IRS loses in a Regular decision, it usually indicates whether it agrees or disagrees with the result reached by the Court. The acquiescence or nonacquiescence is published in the *Internal Revenue Bulletin* and the *Cumulative Bulletin*. The procedure is not followed for Memorandum decisions or for the decisions of other courts. The IRS can retroactively revoke an acquiescence. The IRS sometimes issues an announcement that it will *or* will not follow a decision of another Federal court on similar facts.

Although Memorandum decisions are not published by the U.S. Government, they are published by Commerce Clearing House (CCH) and by Research Institute of America (RIA) [formerly by Prentice-Hall (P-H)]. Consider, for example, the three different ways that *Walter H. Johnson* can be cited:

Walter H. Johnson, T.C.Memo. 1975–245
The 245th Memorandum decision issued by the Tax Court in 1975.

Walter H. Johnson, 34 TCM 1056
Page 1056 of Vol. 34 of the *CCH Tax Court Memorandum Decisions*.

Walter H. Johnson, P-H T.C.Mem.Dec. ¶75,245
Paragraph 75,245 of the *P-H T.C. Memorandum Decisions*.

Note that the third citation contains the same information as the first. Thus, ¶75,245 indicates the following information about the case: year 1975, 245th T.C.Memo. decision.[41]

Judicial Citations—The U.S. District Courts, Claims Court, and Courts of Appeals. District Court, Claims Court, Court of Appeals, and Supreme Court decisions dealing with Federal tax matters are reported in both the CCH *U.S. Tax Cases* (USTC) and the P-H (now RIA) *American Federal Tax Reports* (AFTR) series.

Federal District Court decisions, dealing with *both* tax and nontax issues, are also published by West Publishing Company in its Federal Supplement Series. The following examples illustrate how a District Court case can be cited in three different forms:

---

41. In this text, the Prentice-Hall citation for Memorandum decisions of the U.S. Tax Court is omitted. Thus, *Walter H. Johnson* would be cited as: 34 TCM 1056, T.C.Memo. 1975–245. Prentice-Hall Information Services has been acquired by Thomson Professional Publishing. While this edition continues to use the Prentice-Hall name in most instances, subsequent editions will reflect any name changes made to the former Prentice-Hall products by the Research Institute of America, a Thomson publisher.

Simons-Eastern Co. v. U.S., 73–1 USTC ¶9279 (D.Ct.Ga., 1972). *Explanation:* Reported in the first volume of the *U.S. Tax Cases* (USTC) published by Commerce Clearing House for calendar year 1973 (73–1) and located at paragraph 9279 (¶9279).

Simons-Eastern Co. v. U.S., 31 AFTR2d 73–640 (D.Ct.Ga., 1972). *Explanation:* Reported in the 31st volume of the second series of the *American Federal Tax Reports* (AFTR2d) published by Prentice-Hall and beginning on page 640. The "73" preceding the page number indicates the year the case was published but is a designation used only in recent decisions.

Simons-Eastern Co. v. U.S., 354 F.Supp. 1003 (D.Ct.Ga., 1972). *Explanation:* Reported in the 354th volume of the *Federal Supplement Series* (F.Supp.) published by West Publishing Company and beginning on page 1003.

In all of the preceding citations, note that the name of the case is the same (Simons-Eastern Co. being the taxpayer), as is the reference to the Federal District Court of Georgia (D.Ct.Ga.,) and the year the decision was rendered (1972).[42]

Beginning in October of 1982, decisions of the new Claims Court are reported by West Publishing Company in a series designated *Claims Court Reporter*. Thus, the Claims Court decision in *Recchie v. U.S.* appears as follows:

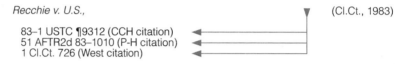

Recchie v. U.S.,   (Cl.Ct., 1983)

83–1 USTC ¶9312 (CCH citation)
51 AFTR2d 83–1010 (P-H citation)
1 Cl.Ct. 726 (West citation)

Decisions of the Claims Court (previously called the Court of Claims) and the Courts of Appeals are published in the USTCs, AFTRs, and a West Publishing Company reporter designated as the Federal Second Series (F.2d). Illustrations of the different forms follow:

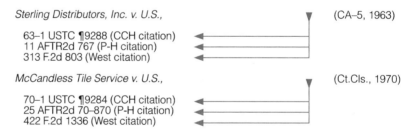

Sterling Distributors, Inc. v. U.S.,   (CA–5, 1963)

63–1 USTC ¶9288 (CCH citation)
11 AFTR2d 767 (P-H citation)
313 F.2d 803 (West citation)

McCandless Tile Service v. U.S.,   (Ct.Cls., 1970)

70–1 USTC ¶9284 (CCH citation)
25 AFTR2d 70–870 (P-H citation)
422 F.2d 1336 (West citation)

Note that *Sterling Distributors, Inc.* is a decision rendered by the Fifth Court of Appeals in 1963 (CA–5, 1963) while *McCandless Tile Service* was rendered in 1970 by the Court of Claims (Ct.Cls., 1970), the predecessor of the Claims Court.

Judicial Citations—The U.S. Supreme Court. Like all other Federal tax cases (except those rendered by the U.S. Tax Court), Supreme Court decisions are published by Commerce Clearing House in the USTCs and by Prentice-Hall in the AFTRs. The U.S. Government Printing Office also publishes these decisions in the *United States Supreme Court Reports* (U.S.) as does West Publishing Company in its *Supreme Court Reporter* (S.Ct.) and the Lawyer's Co-operative Publishing Company in its *United States Reports, Lawyer's Edition* (L.Ed.). The following illustrates the different ways the same decision can be cited:

---

42. In this text, the case will be cited in the following form: 73–640, 354 F.Supp. 1003 (D.Ct.Ga., 1972).
Simons-Eastern Co. v. U.S., 73–1 USTC ¶9279, 31 AFTR2d

U.S. v. The Donruss Co.,   (USSC, 1969)

69–1 USTC ¶9167 (CCH citation)
23 AFTR2d 69–418 (P-H citation)
89 S.Ct. 501 (West citation)
393 U.S. 297 (U.S. Government Printing Office citation)
21 L.Ed.2d 495 (Lawyer's Co-operative Publishing Co. citation)

The parenthetical reference (USSC, 1969) identifies the decision as having been rendered by the U.S. Supreme Court in 1969. The citations given in this text for Supreme Court decisions will be limited to the CCH (USTC), P-H (AFTR), and the West (S.Ct.) versions.

WORKING WITH THE TAX LAW—TAX RESEARCH
◆

Tax research is the method used to determine the best available solution to a situation that possesses tax consequences. In other words, it is the process of finding a competent and professional conclusion to a tax problem. The problem may originate from either completed or proposed transactions. In the case of a completed transaction, the objective of the research is to determine the tax result of what has already taken place. For example, is the expenditure incurred by the taxpayer deductible or not deductible for tax purposes? When dealing with proposed transactions, the tax research process is concerned with the determination of possible tax consequences. To the extent that tax research leads to a choice of alternatives or otherwise influences the future actions of the taxpayer, it becomes the key to effective tax planning.

Tax research involves the following procedures:

- Identifying and refining the problem.
- Locating the appropriate tax law sources.
- Assessing the validity of the tax law sources.
- Arriving at the solution or at alternative solutions while giving due consideration to nontax factors.
- Effectively communicating the solution to the taxpayer or the taxpayer's representative.
- Following up on the solution (where appropriate) in light of new developments.

This process is depicted schematically in Figure 1–2. The broken lines indicate steps of particular interest when tax research is directed toward proposed, rather than completed, transactions.

Identifying the Problem

Problem identification starts with a compilation of the relevant facts involved. In this regard, *all* of the facts that might have a bearing on the problem must be gathered as any omission could modify the solution reached. To illustrate, consider what appears to be a very simple problem.

───────────── EXAMPLE 20 ─────────────

A widowed mother advances $52,000 to her son in 1985 to enable him to attend a private college. Seven years later, the mother claims a bad debt deduction for $42,000 that the son has not repaid. The problem: Is the mother entitled to a bad debt deduction? ◆

Refining the Problem.   Before a bad debt deduction can arise, it must be established that a debt really existed. In a related-party setting (e.g., mother and son), the IRS may contend that the original advance was not a loan but, in reality, a gift. Of key significance in this regard would be whether the lender (the mother) had an honest and real expectation of payment by the borrower (the son).[43] Indicative of this repayment expectation is whether the parties preserved the formalities of a loan, including the following:

- The borrower issued a written instrument evidencing the obligation.
- Interest was provided for as part of the loan arrangement.
- The note specified a set due date.
- Collateral was available to the lender in the event of default by the borrower.[44]

The presence of some or all of these formalities does not, however, guarantee that a bona fide loan will be found. By the same token, the absence of some or all of the formalities does not make the advance a gift. Applying the formalities criteria to Example 20 is not possible since key facts (e.g., the presence or absence of a written note) are not given. Nevertheless, several inferences might be made that lead to a loan interpretation:

- It appears that the son has repaid at least $10,000 of the $52,000 that he borrowed. If the parties intended a gift of the full amount of the loan, why was partial repayment made?
- Although one would not expect a son on his way to college to have assets to serve as collateral for a loan, the fact that he was obtaining additional education could reinforce any expectation of repayment. In most

FIGURE 1–2

Tax Research Process

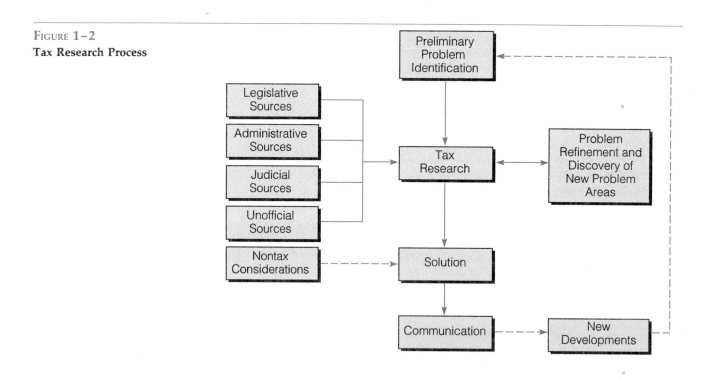

43. *William F. Mercil*, 24 T.C. 1150 (1955), and *Evans Clark*, 18 T.C. 780 (1952), *aff'd*. 53–2 USTC ¶9452, 44 AFTR 70, 205 F.2d 353 (CA–2, 1953).

44. *Arthur T. Davidson*, 37 TCM 725, T.C.Memo. 1978–167.

situations, a person with a college education will possess a higher earning potential than one without such education. This education would improve the son's financial ability to repay the loan.

Further Refinement of the Problem. It may be impossible to determine whether the advance constitutes a loan or a gift with any degree of certainty. In either event, however, the tax consequences of each possibility must be ascertained.

If the advance is determined to be a gift, it is subject to the Federal gift tax.[45] Whether or not a gift tax results depends upon how much of the unified tax credit the mother has available to absorb the gift tax on $42,000 [$52,000 (total gift) − $10,000 (annual exclusion)].[46] Whether the transfer results in a gift tax or not, it must be reported on Form 709 (United States Gift Tax Return) since the amount of the gift exceeds the annual exclusion.

Even if it is assumed that the mother made a gift to the son in 1985, does not the intervention of seven years preclude the IRS from assessing any gift tax that might be due as a result of the transfer?[47] Further research indicates that the statute of limitations on assessments does not begin to run when a tax return is not filed.[48]

To complete the picture, what are the tax consequences if the advance is treated as a loan? Aside from the bad debt deduction aspects (covered later in the chapter), the tax law provides more immediate tax ramifications: [49]

- If interest is not provided for, it is imputed with the following effect:

  a. The lender (the mother) must recognize interest income as to the imputed value.
  b. Since the lender has not received the interest, a gift of such interest is deemed to have taken place from the lender to the borrower.
  c. The borrower (son) is entitled to deduct (as an itemized expense) in some tax years a portion of the amount of interest deemed paid to the lender (mother).

- If interest is provided for but the rate is lower than market (as determined by the yield on certain U.S. government securities), the differential is treated as noted above.
- For gift loans of $100,000 or less, the imputed element cannot exceed the net investment income of the borrower.

Locating the Appropriate Tax Law Sources

Once the problem is clearly defined, what is the next step? Although this is a matter of individual judgment, most tax research begins with the index volume of the tax service. If the problem is not complex, the researcher may bypass the tax service and turn directly to the Internal Revenue Code and the Treasury Regulations. For the beginner, this latter procedure saves time and will solve

---

45. The transfer does not come within the unlimited gift tax exclusion of § 2503(e)(2)(A) since the mother did not pay the amount directly to an educational institution. Besides, the exclusion covers only tuition payments and not other costs attendant on going to college (e.g., room and board).

46. The tax, in turn, depends upon the amount of taxable gifts the mother has made in the past. For a discussion of the mechanics of the Federal gift tax, see Chapter 17.

47. Throughout the discussion of Example 20, the assumption has been made that if a gift occurred, it took place in 1985. That need not be the case. Depending upon the mother's intent, she could have decided to make a gift of the unpaid balance anytime after the loan was made (e.g., 1986, 1987, etc.).

48. See § 6501(c)(3) and the discussion of the statute of limitations in Chapter 16.

49. § 7872.

many of the more basic problems. If the researcher does not have a personal copy of the Code or Regulations, resorting to the appropriate volume(s) of a tax service is necessary. Several of the major tax services publish paperback editions of the Code and Treasury Regulations and can be purchased at modest prices. These editions are usually revised twice each year. The following major services are available:

Standard Federal Tax Reporter, Commerce Clearing House.

Federal Taxes, Prentice-Hall (before acquisition mentioned in Footnote 41).

United States Tax Reporter, Research Institute of America (entitled *Federal Taxes* prior to July, 1992).

Mertens Law of Federal Income Taxation, Callaghan and Co.

Tax Coordinator, Research Institute of America.

Tax Management Portfolios, Bureau of National Affairs.

Rabkin and Johnson, *Federal Income, Gift and Estate Taxation*, Matthew Bender, Inc.

Bender's Federal Tax Service, Matthew Bender, Inc.

Working with the Tax Services. In this text, it is not feasible to teach the use of any particular tax service; this can be learned only by practice. The representatives of the various tax services provide users with printed booklets and individual instruction on the use of the services. However, several important observations cannot be overemphasized about the use of tax services. First, never forget to check for current developments. The main text of any service is revised too infrequently to permit reliance on that portion as the *latest* word on any subject. Where such current developments can be found depends on which service is being used. Both the Commerce Clearing House and Prentice-Hall (now RIA) services contain a special volume devoted to current matters. Second, when dealing with a tax service synopsis of a Treasury Department pronouncement or a judicial decision, remember there is no substitute for the original source.

To illustrate, do not base a conclusion solely on a tax service's commentary on *Simons-Eastern Co. v. U.S.*[50] If the case is vital to the research, look it up. It is possible that the facts of the case are distinguishable from those in the problem being researched. This is not to say that the case synopsis contained in the tax service is wrong; it might just be misleading or incomplete.

Tax Periodicals. Additional sources of tax information are the various tax periodicals. The easiest way to locate a journal article on a particular tax problem is through Commerce Clearing House's *Federal Tax Articles*. This three-volume service includes a subject index, a Code Section number index, and an author's index. In addition, the P-H (now RIA) tax service has a topical "Index to Tax Articles" section that is organized using that service's paragraph index system.

The following are some of the more useful tax periodicals:

The Journal of Taxation Warren, Gorham and Lamont 210 South Street Boston, MA 02111	*Taxation for Accountants* Warren, Gorham and Lamont 210 South Street Boston, MA 02111
Tax Law Review Warren, Gorham and Lamont 210 South Street Boston, MA 02111	*The Tax Executive* 1300 North 17th Street Arlington, VA 22209

---

50. Cited in Footnote 42.

TAXES—The Tax Magazine
Commerce Clearing House, Inc.
4025 West Peterson Avenue
Chicago, IL 60646

National Tax Journal
21 East State Street
Columbus, OH 43215

The Tax Adviser
1211 Avenue of the Americas
New York, NY 10036

The Practical Accountant
1 Penn Plaza
New York, NY 10119

Journal of Corporate Taxation
Warren, Gorham and Lamont
210 South Street
Boston, MA 02111

Trusts and Estates
Communication Channels, Inc.
6255 Barfield Road
Atlanta, GA 30328

Estate Planning
Warren, Gorham and Lamont
210 South Street
Boston, MA 02111

Journal of Partnership Taxation
Warren, Gorham and Lamont
210 South Street
Boston, MA 02111

Oil and Gas Tax Quarterly
Matthew Bender & Co.
235 East 45th Street
New York, NY 10017

The International Tax Journal
Panel Publishers
14 Plaza Road
Greenvale, NY 11548

The Tax Lawyer
American Bar Association
1800 M Street, N.W.
Washington, DC 20036

Journal of the American Taxation
    Association
American Accounting Association
5717 Bessie Drive
Sarasota, FL 33583

Tax Notes
6830 Fairfax Drive
Arlington, VA 22213

Assessing the Validity of Tax Law Sources

After a source has been located, the next step is to assess the source in light of the problem at hand. Proper assessment involves careful interpretation of the tax law and consideration of the law's relevance and validity.

Interpreting the Internal Revenue Code.   The language of the Code can be extremely difficult to comprehend. For example, a subsection [§ 341(e)] relating to collapsible corporations contains *one* sentence of more than 450 words (twice as many as in the Gettysburg Address). Within this same subsection is another sentence of 300 words. One author has noted 10 common pitfalls in interpreting the Code:[51]

1. Determine the limitations and exceptions to a provision. Do not permit the language of the Code Section to carry greater or lesser weight than was intended.
2. Just because a Section fails to mention an item does not necessarily mean that the item is excluded.
3. Read definitional clauses carefully. Note, for example, that § 7701(a)(3) defines a corporation as including "associations." This inclusion (further developed in Chapter 2) becomes essential in determining how professional associations are to be treated for Federal income tax purposes.

---

51. H. G. Wong, "Ten Common Pitfalls in Reading the Internal Revenue Code," *The Practical Accountant* (July–August 1972), pp. 30–33.

4. Do not overlook small words such as "and" and "or." There is a world of difference between these two words.
5. Read the Code Section completely; do not jump to conclusions.
6. Watch out for cross-referenced and related provisions since many Sections of the Code are interrelated.
7. At times Congress is not careful when reconciling new Code provisions with existing Sections. Conflicts among Sections, therefore, do arise.
8. Be alert for hidden definitions; terms in a particular Code Section may be defined in the same Section *or in a separate Section.*
9. Some answers may not be found in the Code. Therefore, it may be necessary to consult the Regulations and/or judicial decisions.
10. Take careful note of measuring words such as "less than 50 percent," "exceeds 35 percent," "at least 80 percent," and "more than 80 percent."

Assessing the Validity of a Treasury Regulation. Treasury Regulations are often said to have the force and effect of law. This statement is certainly true for most Regulations, but some judicial decisions have held a Regulation or a portion thereof invalid. Usually, this is done on the grounds that the Regulation is contrary to the intent of Congress.

Keep the following observations in mind when assessing the validity of a Regulation:

■ In a challenge, the burden of proof is on the taxpayer to show that the Regulation is wrong. However, a court may invalidate a Regulation that varies from the language of the statute and has no support in the Committee Reports.
■ If the taxpayer loses the challenge, the negligence penalty may be imposed. This accuracy-related provision deals with the "intentional disregard of rules and regulations" on the part of the taxpayer and is further explained in Chapter 16.
■ Some Regulations merely reprint or rephrase what Congress has stated in its Committee Reports issued in connection with the enactment of tax legislation. Such Regulations are "hard and solid" and almost impossible to overturn, because they clearly reflect the intent of Congress.
■ In some Code Sections, Congress has given to the "Secretary or his delegate" the authority to prescribe Regulations to carry out the details of administration or to otherwise complete the operating rules. Under such circumstances, it could almost be said that Congress is delegating its legislative powers to the Treasury Department. Regulations issued pursuant to this type of authority truly possess the force and effect of law and are often called "legislative" Regulations. They are to be distinguished from "interpretative" Regulations, which purport to explain the meaning of a particular Code Section. Examples of legislative Regulations are those dealing with consolidated returns issued under §§ 1501 through 1505. As a further example, note the authority granted to the Treasury Department by § 385 to issue Regulations setting forth guidelines on when corporate debt can be reclassified as equity (see Chapter 3).

Assessing the Validity of Other Administrative Sources of the Tax Law. Revenue Rulings issued by the IRS carry less weight than Treasury Department Regulations. Rulings are important, however, in that they reflect the position of the IRS on tax matters. In any dispute with the IRS on the interpretation of tax law, taxpayers should expect agents to follow the results reached in any applicable Rulings.

Revenue Rulings further tell the taxpayer the IRS's reaction to certain court decisions. Recall that the IRS follows a practice of either acquiescing (agreeing) or nonacquiescing (not agreeing) with the *Regular* decisions of the U.S. Tax Court. This practice does not mean that a particular decision of the Tax Court has no value if the IRS has nonacquiesced in the result. It does, however, indicate that the IRS will continue to litigate the issue involved.

The validity of individual letter rulings issued by the IRS is discussed in Chapter 16.

Assessing the Validity of Judicial Sources of the Tax Law. The judicial process as it relates to the formulation of tax law has been described. How much reliance can be placed on a particular decision depends upon the following variables:

- The level of the court. A decision rendered by a trial court (e.g., a Federal District Court) carries less weight than one issued by an appellate court (e.g., the Fifth Court of Appeals). Unless Congress changes the Code, decisions by the U.S. Supreme Court represent the last word on any tax issue.
- The legal residence of the taxpayer. If, for example, a taxpayer lives in Texas, a decision of the Fifth Court of Appeals means more than one rendered by the Second Court of Appeals. This is the case because any appeal from a U.S. District Court or the U.S. Tax Court would be to the Fifth Court of Appeals and not to the Second Court of Appeals.
- Whether the decision represents the weight of authority on the issue. In other words, is it supported by the results reached by other courts?
- The outcome or status of the decision on appeal. For example, was the decision appealed and, if so, with what result?

In connection with the last two variables, the use of a manual citator or a computer search is invaluable to tax research.[52] The use of a manual citator is described in the last section of this chapter.

Assessing the Validity of Other Sources. Primary sources of tax law include the Constitution, legislative history materials, statutes, treaties, Treasury Regulations, IRS pronouncements, and judicial decisions. The IRS regards only primary sources as substantial authority. However, reference to secondary materials such as legal periodicals, treatises, legal opinions, general counsel memoranda, technical memoranda, and written determinations can be useful. In general, secondary sources are not authority.

Although the statement that the IRS regards only primary sources as substantial authority is generally true, there is one exception. In Notice 90–20,[53] the IRS expanded the list of substantial authority for purposes of the accuracy-related penalty in § 6662 to include:

> . . . applicable provisions of the Internal Revenue Code and other statutory provisions; temporary and final regulations construing such statutes; court cases; administrative pronouncements (including revenue rulings and revenue procedures); tax treaties and regulations thereunder, and Treasury Department and other official explanations of such treaties; and congressional intent as reflected in committee reports, joint explanatory statements of managers included in conference committee reports, and floor statements made prior to enactment by one of the bill's managers.

52. The major manual citators are published by Commerce Clearing House, Prentice-Hall, and Shepard's Citations, Inc.

53. 1990–1 C.B. 328, part V (A).

[T]he Service also will treat as authority General Explanations of tax legislation prepared by the Joint Committee on Taxation (the "Blue Book"), proposed regulations, information or press releases, notices, announcements and any other similar documents published by the Service in the Internal Revenue Bulletin. In addition, . . . the Service will treat as authority private letter rulings, technical advice memoranda, actions on decisions, and general counsel memoranda after they have been released to the public and provided they are dated after December 31, 1984 (the date that is five years prior to the general effective date of the penalty provisions of the Act).

As under former § 6661, "authority" does not include conclusions reached in treatises, legal periodicals, and opinions rendered by tax professionals.

Arriving at the Solution or at Alternative Solutions

Returning to Example 20, assume it is decided that the loan approach can be justified from the factual situation involved. Does this lead to a bad debt deduction for the mother? Before this question can be resolved, the loan needs to be classified as either a business or a nonbusiness debt. One of the reasons the classification is important is that a nonbusiness bad debt cannot be deducted until it becomes entirely worthless. Unlike a business debt, no deduction for partial worthlessness is allowed.[54]

It is very likely that the loan the mother made in 1985 falls into the nonbusiness category. Unless exceptional circumstances exist (e.g., the lender was in the trade or business of lending money), loans in a related-party setting are treated as nonbusiness. The probability is high that the mother would be relegated to nonbusiness bad debt status.

The mother has the burden of proving that the remaining unpaid balance of $42,000 is *entirely* worthless.[55] In this connection, what collection effort, if any, has the mother made? But would any such collection effort be fruitless? Perhaps the son is insolvent, ill, unemployed, or has disappeared for parts unknown.

Even if the debt is entirely worthless, one further issue remains to be resolved. In what year did the worthlessness occur? It could be, for example, that worthlessness took place in a year before it was claimed.[56]

A clear-cut answer may not be possible as to a bad debt deduction for the mother in year 1992 (seven years after the advance was made). This does not detract from the value of the research. Often a guarded judgment is the best possible solution to a tax problem.

Communicating Tax Research

Once the problem has been researched adequately, a memo setting forth the result may need to be prepared. The form such a memo takes could depend on a number of considerations. For example, is any particular procedure or format recommended for tax research memos by either an employer or an instructor? Is the memo to be given directly to the client, or will it first pass to the preparer's employer? Whatever form it takes, a good research memo should contain the following elements:

- A clear statement of the issue.
- In more complex situations, a short review of the factual pattern that raises the issue.

---

54. See § 166 and the discussion on "Investor Losses" in Chapter 3.

55. Compare *John K. Sexton*, 48 TCM 512, T.C.Memo. 1984–360, with *Stewart T. Oatman*, 45 TCM 214, T.C.Memo. 1982–684.

56. *Ruth Wertheim Smith*, 34 TCM 1474, T.C.Memo. 1975–339.

- A review of the tax law sources (e.g., Code, Regulations, Rulings, judicial authority).
- Any assumptions made in arriving at the solution.
- The solution recommended and the logic or reasoning in its support.
- The references consulted in the research process.

In short, a good tax memo should tell the reader what was researched, the results of that research, and the justification for the recommendation made.

WORKING WITH THE TAX LAW—TAX PLANNING
◆

Tax research and tax planning are inseparable. The primary purpose of effective tax planning is to reduce the taxpayer's total tax bill. The reduction does not mean that the course of action selected must produce the lowest possible tax under the circumstances. The minimization of tax payments must be considered in the context of the legitimate business goals of the taxpayer.

A secondary objective of effective tax planning is to reduce, defer, or eliminate the tax. Specifically, this objective aims to accomplish one or more results. Some possibilities are eradicating the tax entirely, eliminating the tax in the current year, deferring the receipt of income and, proliferating taxpayers (i.e., forming partnerships and corporations or making lifetime gifts to family members). Further examples include eluding double taxation, avoiding ordinary income, or creating, increasing, or accelerating deductions. However, this second objective should be pursued with considerable reservation. Although the maxim "A bird in the hand is worth two in the bush" has general validity, the rule frequently breaks down. For example, a tax election in one year may accomplish a current reduction in taxes, but it could saddle future years with a disadvantageous tax position.

Nontax Considerations

There is a danger that tax motivations may take on a significance that does not conform to the true values involved. In other words, tax considerations can operate to impair the exercise of sound business judgment. Thus, the tax planning process can lead to ends that are socially and economically objectionable. Unfortunately, a tendency exists for planning to move toward the opposing extremes of either not enough or too much emphasis on tax considerations. The happy medium is a balance that recognizes the significance of taxes, but not beyond the point at which planning detracts from the exercise of good business judgment.

The remark is often made that a good rule to follow is to refrain from pursuing any course of action that would not be followed were it not for certain tax considerations. This statement is not entirely correct, but it does illustrate the desirability of preventing business logic from being "sacrificed at the altar of tax planning." In this connection, the following comment is significant:

> The lure of a quick tax dollar is often the only justification for a transaction that might have been accomplished with much sounder economic results and equivalent tax savings if more careful and deliberate consideration had been given to the problem. Certainly in this atmosphere of the tax-controlled economy a very heavy obligation is cast upon the tax adviser to give serious consideration as to whether a proposed action achieves a desirable economic result apart from tax savings or whether the immediate tax advantages may be more than offset by later economic or personal disadvantage. We cannot afford to develop successful cures that are killing our patients.[57]

---

57. Norris Darrell, "Some Responsibilities of the Tax Adviser in Regard to Tax Minimization Devices," *Proceedings of the New* *York University Eighth Annual Institute on Federal Taxation* (Albany, N.Y.: Matthew Bender & Co., 1950), pp. 988–989.

Tax Avoidance and Tax Evasion

A fine line exists between legal tax planning and illegal tax planning—tax avoidance versus tax evasion. Tax avoidance is merely tax minimization through legal techniques. In this sense, tax avoidance becomes the proper objective of all tax planning. Though eliminating or reducing taxes is also a goal of tax evasion, the term implies the use of subterfuge and fraud as a means to this end. Perhaps because common goals are involved, popular usage has blurred the distinction between the two concepts. Consequently, the association of tax avoidance with tax evasion has kept some taxpayers from properly taking advantage of planning possibilities. The now-classic words of Judge Learned Hand in *Commissioner v. Newman* reflect the true values a taxpayer should have:

> Over and over again courts have said that there is nothing sinister in so arranging one's affairs as to keep taxes as low as possible. Everybody does so, rich or poor; and all do right, for nobody owes any public duty to pay more than the law demands: taxes are enforced extractions, not voluntary contributions. To demand more in the name of morals is mere cant.[58]

Follow-up Procedures

Tax planning usually involves a proposed (as opposed to a completed) transaction and is based upon the continuing validity of the advice resulting from tax research. A change in the tax law (either legislative, administrative, or judicial) could alter the original conclusion. Additional research may be necessary to test the solution in light of current developments.

Under what circumstances does a tax practitioner have an obligation to inform a client as to changes in the tax law? The legal and ethical aspects of this question are discussed in Chapter 16.

Tax Planning—A Practical Application

Returning to the facts in Example 20, what should be done to help protect the mother's bad debt deduction?

- All formalities of a loan should be present (e.g., written instrument, definite and realistic due date).
- Upon default, the lender (mother) should make a reasonable effort to collect from the borrower (son). If not, the mother should be in a position to explain why any such effort would be to no avail.
- If interest is provided for, it should be paid.
- Any interest paid (or imputed under § 7872) should be recognized as income by the mother.
- Because of the annual exclusion of $10,000, it appears doubtful that actual (or imputed) interest would necessitate the filing of a Federal gift tax return by the mother. But should one be due, it should be filed.
- If § 7872 applies (not enough or no interest is provided for), the son should keep track of his net investment income. This is advisable since the income the mother must recognize may be limited by such amount.

Throughout this text, each chapter concludes with observations on Tax Planning Considerations. Such observations are not all-inclusive but are intended to illustrate some of the ways in which the material in the chapter can be effectively used to minimize taxes.

---

58. 47–1 USTC ¶9175, 35 AFTR 857, 159 F.2d 848 (CA–2, 1947).

Computer-Assisted Tax Research

The computer is being used more frequently in the day-to-day practice of tax professionals, students, and educators. Many software vendors offer tax return software programs for individual, corporate, partnership, and fiduciary returns. The use of computers, however, is not limited to batch-processed tax returns. Computer timesharing for quantitative tax and problem-solving planning and calculations has added a new dimension to tax research.

The microcomputer has become the revolutionary tool of the present—much as the electronic calculator did in the 1970s. Electronic spreadsheets are replacing the 14-column worksheet. The electronic spreadsheet approach can be used anytime projections and calculations are needed. Examples include retirement planning, Form 1040 projections, real estate projections, partnership allocations, consolidated tax return problems, and compensation planning. Internally prepared tax-related programs are used by many public accounting firms. Microcomputer software is available for estate planning calculations.

LEXIS, a computerized legal data bank, has been available since 1973 as a complement to the conventional manual research approach. WESTLAW, a competitive system from West Publishing Company, has been operational since 1975. Research Institute of America has a national computer network, called RIATAX (formerly P-H's PHINet), which makes its loose-leaf service accessible by computer. WESTLAW, LEXIS and RIATAX are in actuality document retrieval systems and cannot interpret the law.

Users have access to these computerized data banks through special terminals and long-distance telephone lines. A user selects key words, phrases, or numbers and types the search request on the terminal keyboard. A display screen shows the full text or portions of the various documents containing the words, phrases, or numbers in the search request. A printer can be used to obtain hard copy of any documents or portions of a document. For example, a researcher can obtain the decisions of a particular judge or court over a specified time period. It is also possible to access judicial opinions containing specific words or phrases of statutory language. These computer-assisted tax systems can be used as a citator by collecting all judicial decisions that have cited a particular decision or statute as well as all decisions that have a specific combination of two or more earlier decisions or statutes.

Computer-assisted tax research is useful in searching for facts since human indexing evolves around legal theories rather than fact patterns. Computer searching also is useful in finding new court decisions not yet in the printed indexes. Computer searching probably does not find as many relevant cases as does manual searching. Consequently, a combination of manual and computer searching is preferred.[59]

Illustration of the Use of the P-H Citator

USE OF THE CITATOR
◆

Background. The *Federal Tax Citator* is a separate multivolume service with monthly supplements. Cases that are reported by the *Citator* are divided into the various issues involved. Since the researcher may be interested in only one or two issues, only cases involving the particular issue need to be checked.

The volumes of the *Federal Tax Citator* and the period of time covered by each are as follows:

---

59. For more detail, see W. A. Raabe, G. E. Whittenburg, and J. C. Bost, *West's Federal Tax Research*, 2d edition (St. Paul: West Publishing Co., 1990), Chapter 13.

- Volume 1 (1863–1941)
- Volume 2 (1942–1948)
- Volume 3 (1948–1954)
- Volume 1, Second Series (1954–1977)
- Volume 2, Second Series (1978–1989).
- Annual and monthly cumulative paperback supplements.

Through the use of symbols, the *Citator* indicates whether a decision is followed, explained, criticized, questioned, or overruled by a later court decision. These symbols are reproduced in Figure 1–3.

─────────────────────── EXAMPLE 21 ───────────────────────

Determine the background and validity of *Adda v. Comm.*, 49 USTC ¶ 9109, 37 AFTR 654, 171 F.2d 457 (CA–4, 1948). ◆

FIGURE 1–3
Prentice-Hall Citator Symbols

Citator Symbols*
COURT DECISIONS
Judicial History of the Case

a	affirmed (by decision of a higher court)
d	dismissed (appeal to a higher court dismissed)
m	modified (decision modified by a higher court, or on rehearing)
r	reversed (by a decision of a higher court)
s	same case (e.g., on rehearing)
rc	related case (companion cases and other cases arising out of the same subject matter are so designated)
x	certiorari denied (by the Supreme Court of the United States)
(C or G)	The Commissioner or Solicitor General has made the appeal
(T)	Taxpayer has made the appeal
(A)	Tax Court's decision acquiesced in by Commissioner
(NA)	Tax Court's decision nonacquiesced in by Commissioner
sa	same case affirmed (by the cited case)
sd	same case dismissed (by the cited case)
sm	same case modified (by the cited case)
sr	same case reversed (by the cited case)
sx	same case–certiorari denied

Syllabus of the Cited Case

iv	four (on all fours with the cited case)
f	followed (the cited case followed)
e	explained (comment generally favorable, but not to a degree that indicates the cited case is followed)
k	reconciled (the cited case reconciled)
n	dissenting opinion (cited in a dissenting opinion)
g	distinguished (the cited case distinguished either in law or on the facts)
l	limited (the cited case limited to its facts. Used when an appellate court so limits a prior decision, or a lower court states that in its opinion the cited case should be so limited)
c	criticized (adverse comment on the cited case)
q	questioned (the cited case not only criticized, but its correctness questioned)
o	overruled

*Reproduced from the *Federal Taxes 2nd Citator* with the permission of the publisher, Research Institute of America, Englewood Cliffs, N.J. 07632.

Turning directly to the case itself (reproduced as Figure 1–4), note the two issues involved ("1." and "2."). For purposes of emphasis, these issues have been bracketed and identified by a marginal notation added to Figure 1–4. The reason for the division of the issues becomes apparent when the case is traced through the *Citator*.

ADDA v. COMMISSIONER OF INTERNAL REVENUE   457   FIGURE 1–4

Cite as 171 F.2d 457   **Actual Court Case**

ADDA v. COMMISSIONER OF INTERNAL REVENUE.

No. 5796.

United States Court of Appeals
Fourth Circuit.

Dec. 3, 1948.

ISSUE 1

1. Internal revenue ☞792

Where nonresident alien's brother residing in United States traded for alien's benefit on commodity exchanges in United States at authorization of alien, who vested full discretion in brother with regard thereto, and many transactions were effected through different brokers, several accounts were maintained, and substantial gains and losses realized, transactions constituted a "trade or business," profits of which were "capital gains" taxable as income to the alien. 26 U.S.C.A. § 211(b).

See Words and Phrases, Permanent Edition, for other judicial constructions and definitions of "Capital Gains" and "Trade or Business".

ISSUE 2

2. Internal revenue ☞792

The exemption of a nonresident alien's commodity transactions in the United States provided for by the Internal Revenue Code does not apply where alien has agent in United States using his own discretion in effecting transactions for alien's account. 26 U.S.C.A. § 211(b).

On Petition to Review the Decision of The Tax Court of the United States.

Petition by Fernand C. A. Adda to review a decision of the Tax Court redetermining a deficiency in income tax imposed by the Commissioner of Internal Revenue.

Decision affirmed.

Rollin Browne and Mitchell B. Carroll, both of New York City, for petitioner.

Irving I. Axelrad, Sp. Asst. to Atty. Gen. (Theron Lamar Caudle, Asst. Atty. Gen., and Ellis N. Slack and A. F. Prescott, Sp. Assts. to Atty. Gen., on the brief), for respondent.

Before PARKER, Chief Judge, and SOPER and DOBIE, Circuit Judges.

PER CURIAM.

[1, 2] This is a petition by a non-resident alien to review a decision of the Tax Court. Petitioner is a national of Egypt, who in the year 1941 was residing in France. He had a brother who at that time was residing in the United States and who traded for petitioner's benefit on commodity exchanges in the United States in cotton, wool, grains, silk, hides and copper. This trading was authorized by petitioner who vested full discretion in his brother with regard thereto, and it resulted in profits in the sum of $193,857.14. The Tax Court said: "While the number of transactions or the total amount of money involved in them has not been stated, it is apparent that many transactions were effected through different brokers, several accounts were maintained, and gains and losses in substantial amounts were realized. This evidence shows that the trading was extensive enough to amount to a trade or business, and the petitioner does not contend, nor has he shown, that the transactions were so infrequent or inconsequential as not to amount to a trade or business." We agree with the Tax Court that, for reasons adequately set forth in its opinion, this income was subject to taxation, and that the exemption of a non-resident alien's commodity transactions in the United States, provided by section 211(b) of the Internal Revenue Code, 26 U.S.C.A. § 211(b), does not apply to a case where the alien has an agent in the United States using his own discretion in effecting the transactions for the alien's account. As said by the Tax Court, "Through such transactions the alien is engaging in trade or business within the United States, and the profits on these transactions are capital gains taxable to him." Nothing need be added to the reasoning of the Tax Court in this connection, and the decision will be affirmed on its opinion.

Affirmed.

Refer to Volume 3 for the AFTR Series (covering the period from October 7, 1948, through July 29, 1954) of the *Federal Tax Citator*. Reference to the case is located on page 5505 (reproduced in Figure 1–5).

FIGURE 1–5
From Volume 3

» Adamson — Adler «   5505

ADAMSON, JAMES H. & MARION C. v
U. S., — F Supp —, 36 AFTR 1529, 1946
P.-H. ¶ 72,418 (DC Calif) (See Adamson
v U. S.)

ADAMSON, R. R., MRS., — BTA —, 1934 (P.-
H.) BTA Memo. Dec. ¶ 34,370

ADAMSON v U. S., 26 AFTR 1188 (DC Calif,
Sept 8, 1939)
iv—Coggan, Linus C., 1939 (P.-H.) BTA
Memo. Dec. page 39—806

ADAMSON; U. S. v, 161 F(2d) 942, 35 AFTR
1404 (CCA 9)
1—Lazier v U. S., 170 F(2d) 524, 37 AFTR
545, 1948 P.-H. page 73,174 (CCA 8)
1—Grace Bros., Inc. v Comm., 173 F(2d)
178, 37 AFTR 1014, 1949 P.-H. page 72,433
(CCA 9)
1—Briggs; Hofferbert v, 178 F(2d) 744, 38
AFTR 1219, 1950 P.-H. page 72,267 (CCA
4)
1—Rogers v Comm., 180 F(2d) 722, 39 AFTR
115, 1950 P.-H. page 72,531 (CCA 3)
1—Lamar v Granger, 99 F Supp 41, 40
AFTR 270, 1951 P.-H. page 72,945 (DC Pa)
1—Herbert v Riddell, 103 F Supp 383, 41
AFTR 975, 1952 P.-H. page 72,383 (DC
Calif)
1—Hudson, Galvin, 20 TC 737, 20-1953
P.-H. TC 418

ADAMSON v U. S., — F Supp —, 36 AFTR
1529, 1946 P.-H. ¶ 72,418 (DC Calif, Jan
28, 1946)

ADAMS-ROTH BAKING CO., 8 BTA 458
1—Gunderson Bros. Engineering Corp., 16
TC 129, 16-1951 P.-H. TC 72

ADAMSTON FLAT GLASS CO. v COMM.,
162 F(2d) 875, 35 AFTR 1579 (CCA 6)
4—Forrest Hotel Corp. v. Fly, 112 F Supp
789, 43 AFTR 1080, 1953 P.-H. page 72,856
(DC Miss)

ADDA v COMM., 171 F(2d) 457, 37 AFTR 654,
1948 P.-H. ¶ 72,655 (CCA 4, Dec 3, 1948)
Cert. filed, March 1, 1949 (T)
No cert. (G) 1949 P-H ¶ 71,050
x—Adda v Comm., 336 US 952, 69 S Ct 883,
93 L Ed 1107, April 18, 1949 (T)
sa—Adda, Fernand C., 10 TC 273 (No.
33), ¶ 10.33 P.-H. TC 1948
iv—Milner Hotels, Inc., N. Y., 173 F (2d)
567, 37 AFTR 1170, 1949 P.-H. page 72,528
(CCA 6)
1—Nubar; Comm. v, 185 F(2d) 588, 39 AFTR
1315, 1950 P.-H. page 73,423 (CCA 4)
g-1—Scottish Amer. Invest. Co., Ltd.,
The, 12 TC 59, 12-1949 P.-H. TC 32
g-1—Nubar, Zareh, 13 TC 579, 13-1949
P.-H. TC 318

ADDA, FERNAND C. A., 10 TC 273 (No.
33), ¶ 10.33 P.-H. TC 1948 (A) 1918-2 CB 1
a—Adda v Comm., 171 F(2d) 457, 37 AFTR
654, 1948 P.-H. ¶ 72,655 (CCA 4)
1—Nubar; Comm. v, 185 F(2d) 588, 39 AFTR
1315, 1950 P.-H. page 73,423 (CCA 4)
g-1—Scottish Amer. Invest. Co., Ltd.,
The, 12 TC 59, 12-1949 P.-H. TC 32
g-1—Nubar, Zareh, 13 TC 579, 13-1949
P.-H. TC 318

ADDA, FERNAND C. A., 10 TC 1291 (No.
168), ¶ 10.168 P.-H. TC 1948 (A) 1953-1
CB 3, 1953 P.-H. ¶ 76,453 (NA) 1948-2
CB 5, 1948 P.-H. ¶ 76,434 withdrawn
1—Scottish Amer. Invest. Co., Ltd., The,
12 TC 59, 12-1949 P.-H. TC 32

ADDA INC., 9 TC 199 (A) 1949-1 CB 1, 1949
P.-H. ¶ 76,260 (NA) 1947-2 CB 6 withdrawn
a—Adda, Inc.; Comm. v, 171 F(2d) 367, 37
AFTR 641, 1948 P.-H. ¶ 72,654 (CCA 2)
a—Adda, Inc.; Comm. v, 171 F(2d) 367, 37
AFTR 641, 1949 P.-H. ¶ 72,303 (CCA 2)
e-1—G.C.M. 26069, 1949-2 CB 38, 1949 P.-H.
page 76,226
3—Koshland, Execx.; U.S. v, 208 F(2d)
640, — AFTR —, 1953 P.-H. page 73,597
(CCA 9)
4—Kent, Otis Beall, 1954 (P. H.) TC
Memo. Dec. page 54—47

ADDA, INC.; COMM. v, 171 F(2d) 367, 37
AFTR 641, 1948 P.-H. ¶ 72,654 (CCA 2, Dec
6, 1948)
sa—Adda, Inc., 9 TC 199
s—Adda, Inc.; Comm. v, 171 F(2d) 367, 37
AFTR 641, 1949 P.-H. ¶ 72,303 (CCA 2) reh.
den.
e-1—G.C.M. 26069, 1949-2 CB 39, 1949 P.-H.
page 76,227
e-2—G.C.M. 26069, 1949-2 CB 39, 1949 P.-H.
page 76,227

ADDA, INC.; COMM. v, 171 F(2d) 367, 37
AFTR 641, 1949 P.-H. ¶ 72,303 (CCA 2, Dec
6, 1948) reh. den.
sa—Adda, Inc., 9 TC 199
s—Adda, Inc.; Comm. v, 171 F(2d) 367, 37
AFTR 641, 1918 P.-H. ¶ 72,654 (CCA 2)

ADDISON-CHEVROLET SALES, INC. v
CHAMBERLAIN, L. A. & NAT. BANK
OF WASH., THE, — F Supp —, — AFTR
—, 1954 P.-H. ¶ 72,550 (DC DC) (See
Campbell v Chamberlain)

ADDISON v COMM., 177 F(2d) 521, 38 AFTR
821, 1949 P.-H. ¶ 72,637 (CCA 8, Nov 3,
1949)
sa—Addison, Irene D., — TC —, 1948
(P.-H.) TC Memo. Dec. ¶ 48,177
1—Roberts, Supt. v U. S., 115 Ct Cl 439,
87 F Supp 937, 38 AFTR 1314, 1950 P.-H.
page 72,292
1—Cold Metal Process Co., The, 17 TC
934, 17-1951 P.-H. TC 512
1—Berger, Samuel & Lillian, 1954 (P.-H.)
TC Memo. Dec. page 54—232
2—Urquhart, George Gordon & Mary F.,
20 TC 948, 20-1953 P.-H. TC 536

ADDISON, IRENE D., — TC —, 1948 (P.-
H.) TC Memo. Dec. ¶ 48,177
App (T) Jan 14, 1949 (CCA 8)
a—Addison v Comm., 177 F(2d) 521, 38
AFTR 821, 1949 P.-H. ¶ 72,637 (CCA 8)
1—Urquhart, George Gordon & Mary F.,
20 TC 948, 20-1953 P.-H. TC 536

ADDITON, HARRY L. & ANNIE S., 3
TC 427
1—Lum, Ralph E., 12 TC 379, 12-1949 P.-H.
TC 204
1—Christie, John A. & Elizabeth H., —
TC —, 1949 (P.-H.) TC Memo. Dec.
page 49—795

ADDRESSOGRAPH - MULTIGRAPH
CORP., 1945 (P.-H.) TC Memo. Dec.
¶ 45,058
f-10—Rev. Rul. 54-71, 1954 P.-H. page
76.453

ADDRESSOGRAPH-MULTIGRAPH CORP.
v U. S., 112 Ct Cl 201, 78 F Supp 111, 37
AFTR 53, 1948 P.-H. ¶ 72,504 (June 1, 1948)
No cert (G) 1949 P.-H. ¶ 71,041
1—New Oakmont Corp., The v U. S., 114
Ct Cl 686, 86 F Supp 901, 38 AFTR 924, 1949
P.-H. page 73,181

ADELAIDE PARK LAND, 25 BTA 211
g—Amer. Security & Fidelity Corp., — BTA
—, 1940 (P.-H.) BTA Memo. Dec. page
40—571

ADELPHI PAINT & COLOR WORKS,
INC., 18 BTA 436
1—Neracher, William A., — BTA —, 1939
(P.-H.) BTA Memo. Dec. page 39—69
1—Lyman-Hawkins Lumber Co., — BTA —,
1939 (P.-H.) BTA Memo. Dec. page 39—350

ADEMAN v U. S., 174 F(2d) 283, 37 AFTR
1406 (CCA 9, April 25, 1949)

ADICONIS, NOELLA L. (PATNAUDE),
1953 (P.-H.) TC Memo. Dec. ¶ 53,305

ADJUSTMENT BUREAU OF ST. LOUIS
ASSN., OF CREDIT MEN, 21 BTA 232
1—Cook County Loss Adjustment Bureau,
— BTA —, 1940 (P.-H.) BTA Memo. Dec.
page 40—331

ADKINS, CHARLES I., — BTA —, 1933
(P.-H.) BTA Memo. Dec. ¶ 33,457

ADLER v COMM., 77 F(2d) 733, 16 AFTR 162
(CCA 5)
g-2—McEuen v Comm., 196 F(2d) 130, 41
AFTR 1172, 1952 P.-H. page 72,604 (CCA 5)

Correlating the symbols in Figure 1–3 with the shaded portion of Figure 1–5 reveals the following information about *Adda v. Comm.*:

- Application for certiorari (appeal to the U.S. Supreme Court) filed by the taxpayer (T) on March 1, 1949.
- Certiorari was denied (x) by the U.S. Supreme Court on April 18, 1949.
- The trial court decision is reported in 10 T.C. 273 and was affirmed on appeal (sa) to the Fourth Court of Appeals.
- During the time frame of Volume 3 of the *Citator* (October 7, 1948, through July 29, 1954), one decision (*Milner Hotels, Inc.*) has agreed "on all fours with the cited case" (iv). One decision (*Comm. v. Nubar*) has limited the cited case to its facts (l), and two decisions (*The Scottish American Investment Co., Ltd.* and *Zareh Nubar*) have distinguished the cited case on issue 1 (g–1).

Reference to Volume 1 of the *Citator* Second Series (covering the period from 1954 through 1977) shows the *Adda v. Comm.* case on page 25. This page is reproduced in Figure 1–6.

Correlating the symbols in Figure 1–3 with the shaded portion of Figure 1–6 reveals the following additional information about *Adda v. Comm.*:

- The case was cited without comment in two rulings and two cases: Rev.Rul. 56–145 and Rev.Rul. 56–392, *Balanovski* and *Liang.*
- It was followed in *Asthmanefrin Co.* (f–1).
- It was distinguished in *de Vegvar* and *Purvis* (g–1).
- It was reconciled in *deKrause* (k–1).

Reference to the "Court Decisions" section of Volume 2, Second Series of the *Citator* covering the period from 1978 through 1989 shows that *Adda v. Comm.* was cited in *Robert E. Cleveland* and *Judith C. Connelly,* each case limited to its facts (l).

The *Citator* includes a cumulative supplement (i.e., 1990–1991), and each month there is a cumulative paperback supplement. Be sure to refer to these monthly supplements, or very recent citations might be overlooked.

Except as otherwise noted, it would appear that *Adda v. Comm.* has withstood the test of time.

PROBLEM MATERIALS

DISCUSSION QUESTIONS

1. What is meant by revenue neutral tax reform?
2. In what manner does the tax law encourage technological progress?
3. Does the tax law provide any stimulus for the development of international trade? Explain.
4. What purpose is served by provisions in the tax law that encourage private-sector pension plans?
5. TRA of 1986 eliminated many low-income persons from being subject to the Federal income tax. On what grounds can this be justified?
6. State the manner in which the following tax provisions encourage small business:

FIGURE 1–6

ADASKAVICH—ADELSON
25

From Volume 1, Second Series

ADASKAVICH, STEPHEN A. v U.S., 39 AFTR2d
77-517, 422 F Supp 276 (DC Mont) (See Wiegand,
Charles J., Jr v U.S.)
AD. AURIEMA, INC., 1943 P-H TC Memo ¶ 43,422
e-1—Miller v U.S., 13 AFTR2d 1515, 166 Ct Cl 257, 331
F2d 859
ADAY v SUPERIOR CT. OF ALAMEDA COUNTY, 8
AFTR2d 5367, 13 Cal Reptr 415, 362 P2d 47 (Calif,
5-11-61)
ADCO SERVICE, INC., ASSIGNEE v CYBERMATICS,
INC., 36 AFTR2d 75-6342 (NJ) (See Adco Service,
Inc., Assignee v Graphic Color Plate)
ADCO SERVICE, INC., ASSIGNEE v GRAPHIC
COLOR PLATE, 36 AFTR2d 75-6342 (NJ, Supr Ct,
11-10-75)
ADCO SERVICE, INC., ASSIGNEE v GRAPHIC
COLOR PLATE, INC., 36 AFTR2d 75-6342 (NJ) (See
Adco Service, Inc., Assignee v Graphic Color Plate)
ADDA v COMM., 171 F2d 457, 37 AFTR 654 (USCA 4)
Rev. Rul. 56-145, 1956-1 CB 613
1—Balanovski: U.S. v. 236 F2d 304, 49 AFTR 2013
(USCA 2)
1—Liang. Chang Hsiao. 23 TC 1045, 23-1955 P-H TC
624
f-1—Asthmanefrin Co., Inc., 25 TC 1141, 25-1956 P-H
TC 639
g-1—de Vegvar, Edward A. Neuman. 28 TC 1061.
28-1957 P-H TC 599
g-1—Purvis, Ralph E. & Patricia Lee, 1974 P-H TC
Memo 74-669
k-1—deKrause. Piedad Alvarado, 1974 P-H TC Memo
74-1291
1—Rev. Rul. 56-392, 1956-2 CB 971
ADDA, FERNAND C.A., 10 TC 273, ¶ 10,133 P-H TC
1948
1—Balanovski: U.S. v. 236 F2d 303, 49 AFTR 2012
(USCA 2)
1—Liang. Chang Hsiao. 23 TC 1045, 23-1955 P-H TC
624
g-1—de Vegvar, Edward A. Neuman. 28 TC 1061.
28-1957 P-H TC 599
g-1—Purvis, Ralph E. & Patricia Lee, 1974 P-H TC
Memo 74-669
k-1—deKrause. Piedad Alvarado, 1974 P-H TC Memo
74-1291
ADDA, INC., 9 TC 199
Pardee, Marvin L., Est. of, 49 TC 152, 49 P-H TC 107
[See 9 TC 206-208]
f-1—Asthmanefrin Co., Inc., 25 TC 1141, 25-1956 P-H
TC 639
1—Keil Properties, Inc. (Dela). 24 TC 1117, 24-1955 P-H
TC 615
1—Saffan, Samuel, 1957 P-H TC Memo 57—701
1—Rev. Rul. 56-145, 1956-1 CB 613
1—Rev. Rul. 56-392, 1956-2 CB 971
4—Midler Court Realty, Inc., 61 TC 597, 61 P-H TC
368
ADDA, INC.; COMM. v, 171 F2d 367, 37 AFTR 641
(USCA 2)
1—Pardee, Marvin L., Est. of, 49 TC 152, 49 P-H TC
107
1—Saffan, Samuel, 1957 P-H TC Memo 57-701
2—Midler Court Realty, Inc., 61 TC 597, 61 P-H TC
368
ADDELSTON, ALBERT A. & SARAH M., 1965 P-H TC
Memo ¶ 65,215
ADDISON v COMM., 177 F2d 521, 38 AFTR 821 (USCA
8)
g-1—Industrial Aggregate Co. v U.S., 6 AFTR2d 5963,
284 F2d 645 (USCA 8)
1—Sturgeon v McMahon. 155 F Supp 630, 52 AFTR
789 (DC NY)
1—Gilmore v U.S., 16 AFTR2d 5211, 5213, 245 F Supp
384, 386 (DC Calif)
1—Waldheim & Co., Inc., 25 TC 599, 25-1955 P-H TC
332
g-1—Galewitz. Samuel & Marian, 50 TC 113, 50 P-H TC
79
1—Buder, G. A., Est. of, 1963 P-H TC Memo 63-345
e-1—Rhodes, Lynn E. & Martha E., 1963 P-H TC
Memo 63-1374
2—Shipp v Comm., 217 F2d 402, 46 AFTR 1170 (USCA
9)

ADDISON—Contd.
g-2—Industrial Aggregate Co. v U.S., 6 AFTR2d 5964,
284 F2d 645 (USCA 8)
e-2—Buder, Est. of v Comm., 13 AFTR2d 1238, 330
F2d 443 (USCA 8)
2—Iowa Southern Utilities Co. v Comm., 14 AFTR2d
5063, 333 F2d 385 (USCA 8)
2—Kelly, Daniel, S.W., 23 TC 687, 23-1955 P-H TC 422
f-2—Morgan, Joseph P., Est. of, 37 TC 36, 37, 37-1961
P-H TC 26, 27
n-2—Woodward, Fred W. & Elsie M., 49 TC 385, 49
P-H TC 270
ADDISON, IRENE D., 1948 P-H TC Memo ¶ 48,177
1—Waldheim & Co., Inc., 25 TC 599, 25-1955 P-H TC
332
f-1—Morgan, Joseph P., Est. of, 37 TC 36, 37, 37-1961
P-H TC 26, 27
1—Buder, G. A., Est. of, 1963 P-H TC Memo 63-345
e-1—Rhodes, Lynn E. & Martha E., 1963 P-H TC
Memo 63-1374
ADDISON, JOHN MILTON, BKPT; U.S. v, 20 AFTR2d
5630, 384 F2d 748 (USCA 5) (See Rochelle Jr., Trtee;
U.S. v)
ADDRESSOGRAPH - MULTIGRAPH CORP., 1945
P-H TC Memo ¶ 45,058
Conn. L. & P. Co., The v U.S., 9 AFTR2d 679, 156 Ct
Cl 312, 314, 299 F2d 264
Copperhead Coal Co., Inc. 1958 P-H TC Memo 58-33
1—Seas Shipping Co., Inc. v Comm., 19 AFTR2d 596,
371 F2d 529 (USCA 2)
e-1—Hitchcock, E. R., Co., The v U.S., 35 AFTR2d
75-1207, 514 F2d 487 (USCA 2)
f-2—Vulcan Materials Co. v U.S., 25 AFTR2d 70-446,
308 F Supp 57 (DC Ala)
f-3—Marlo Coil Co. v U.S., 1969 P-H 58.133 (Ct Cl
Comr Rep)
4—United Gas Improvement Co. v Comm., 240 F2d 318,
50 AFTR 1354 (USCA 3)
10—St. Louis Co. (Del) (in Dissolution) v U.S., 237 F2d
156, 50 AFTR 257 (USCA 3)
ADDRESSOGRAPH - MULTIGRAPH CORP. v U.S.,
112 Ct Cl 201, 78 F Supp 111, 37 AFTR 53
f-1—St. Joseph Lead Co. v U.S., 9 AFTR2d 712, 299
F2d 350 (USCA 2)
e-1—Central & South West Corp. v U.S., 1968 P-H
58,175 (Ct Cl Comr Rep)
1—Smale & Robinson, Inc. v U.S., 123 F Supp 469, 46
AFTR 375 (DC Calif)
1—St. Joseph Lead Co. v U.S., 7 AFTR2d 401, 190 F
Supp 640 (DC NY)
1—Eisenstadt Mfg. Co., 28 TC 230, 28-1957 P-H TC 132
f-2—St. Joseph Lead Co. v U.S., 9 AFTR2d 712, 299
F2d 350 (USCA 2)
f-3—Consol, Coppermines Corp. v U.S., 8 AFTR2d
5873, 155 Ct Cl 736, 296 F2d 745
ADELAIDE PARK LAND, 25 BTA 211
g—Custom Component Switches, Inc. v U.S., 19
AFTR2d 560 (DC Calif) [See 25 BTA 215])
O'Connor, John C., 1957 P-H TC Memo 57-190
ADELBERG, MARVIN & HELEN, 1971 P-H TC Memo
¶ 71,015
ADELMAN v U.S., 27 AFTR2d 71-1464, 440 F2d 991
(USCA 9, 5-3-71)
sa—Adelman v U.S., 24 AFTR2d 69-5769, 304 F Supp
599 (DC Calif)
ADELMAN v U.S., 24 AFTR2d 69-5769, 304 F Supp 599
(DC Calif, 9-30-69)
a—Adelman v U.S., 27 AFTR2d 71-1464, 440 F2d 991
(USCA 9)
ADELSON, SAMUEL; U.S. v, 52 AFTR 1798 (DC RI)
(See Sullivan Co., Inc.: U.S. v)
ADELSON v U.S., 15 AFTR2d 246, 342 F2d 332 (USCA
9, 1-13-65)
sa—Adelson v U.S., 12 AFTR2d 5010, 221 F Supp 31
(DC Calif)
g-1—Greenlee, L. C. & Gladys M., 1966 P-H TC Memo
66-985
f-1—Cochran, Carol J., 1973 P-H TC Memo 73-459
f-1—Marchionni, Siro L., 1976 P-H TC Memo 76-1321
f-2—Krist, Edwin F. v Comm., 32 AFTR2d 73-5663, 483
F2d 1351 (USCA 2)
f-2—Fugate v U.S., 18 AFTR2d 5607, 259 F Supp 401
(DC Tex) [See 15 AFTR2d 249, 342 F2d 335]

    a. The nature of a shareholder's loss on a stock investment.
    b. The tax rates applicable to corporations.
    c. Nontaxable corporate reorganizations.

7. Although death taxes imposed on large estates can be justified on the grounds of social desirability, can such taxes carry economic implications? Explain.

8. What purpose is served by the credit allowed for certain child or disabled dependent care expenses?

9. Why should the deductibility of excess political campaign expenditures be contrary to public policy?

10. In the past, Congress has considered proposals that would allow a taxpayer to claim a tax credit for tuition paid to send a dependent to a private school. Is there any justification for such a proposal?

11. What purpose is served by allowing a deduction for home mortgage interest and property taxes?

12. Some states that impose a state income tax allow the taxpayer a deduction for any Federal income taxes paid. What is the justification for such an approach?

13. A provision of the Code allows a taxpayer a deduction for Federal income tax purposes for state and local income taxes paid. Does this provision eliminate the effect of multiple taxation of the same income? Why or why not? In this connection, consider the following:

    a. Taxpayer, an individual, has itemized deductions less than the standard deduction.
    b. Taxpayer is in the 15% tax bracket for Federal income tax purposes. The 31% tax bracket.

14. T operates a profitable sole proprietorship. Because the business is expanding, she would like to transfer it to a newly created corporation. T is concerned, however, over the possible tax consequences that would result from incorporating. Please comment.

15. Assume the same facts as in Question 14. T is also worried that once she incorporates, the business will be subject to the Federal corporate income tax. Any suggestions?

16. In situations in which the tax law recognizes the wherewithal to pay concept, discuss the effect of the following:

    a. The basis to the transferor of property received in an exchange.
    b. The recognition by the transferor of any realized loss on the transfer.
    c. The receipt of boot or other property by the transferor.

17. Can it be said that the application of the wherewithal to pay concept permanently avoids the recognition of any gain or loss by a transferor? Explain.

18. T, an individual, exchanges 100 shares of X Corporation stock for 100 shares of Y Corporation stock. The exchange is not pursuant to a nontaxable reorganization. Does the wherewithal to pay concept shield T from the recognition of gain or loss? Why?

19. U, a calendar year cash basis taxpayer, is a participant in an H.R. 10 (Keogh) retirement plan for self-employed persons. To get the deduction for 1992, U makes his contribution on December 30, 1992.

    a. Why was there an element of urgency in U's action?
    b. Was U misinformed about the tax law? Explain.

20. What purpose is served by the indexation procedure? To what items is indexation applicable?

21. Give an example of how the community property system has affected the Federal tax law.

22. W operates a service business as a sole proprietor. For tax purposes, she recognizes income using the cash method but deducts expenses as they accrue.

a. What is W trying to accomplish?
b. Is this procedure proper?
c. Does the IRS have any recourse?

23. In what way does the wherewithal to pay concept aid the IRS in the collection of tax revenue?

24. Describe how the IRS achieves administrative feasibility through each of the following tax provisions:

a. The standard deduction allowed to individual taxpayers.
b. The $192,800 unified tax credit allowed for estate tax purposes.
c. The $10,000 annual exclusion allowed for gift tax purposes.
d. The burden of proof in the audit of a taxpayer.

25. What is meant by the concept of substance over form? Why is it variously described as the "telescoping," "collapsing," or "step transaction" approach?

26. What is meant by the concept that statutory relief provisions of the tax law are to be narrowly construed? Where did the concept originate?

27. When does the tax benefit rule apply? With what effect?

28. W Corporation loans $10,000 to Z Corporation with no provision for interest. W Corporation and Z Corporation are owned by the same shareholders. In what manner might the IRS restructure this transaction with adverse tax consequences to W Corporation?

29. Under what circumstances can court decisions lead to changes in the Code?

30. Judicial decisions interpreting a provision of the Internal Revenue Code of 1954 are no longer of any value in view of the enactment of the Internal Revenue Code of 1986. Assess the validity of this statement.

31. Where do the primary sources of tax information originate?

32. What is the function of the Joint Conference Committee of the House Ways and Means Committee and the Senate Finance Committee?

33. Why are Committee Reports of Congress important as a source of tax law?

34. How much reliance may be placed upon temporary Regulations?

35. Distinguish between Treasury Regulations and Revenue Rulings, between Revenue Rulings and Revenue Procedures, and between Revenue Rulings and letter rulings.

36. What is the difference, if any, between the *Internal Revenue Bulletin* (I.R.B.) and the *Cumulative Bulletin* (C.B.)?

37. Explain the fact-finding determination of a Federal Court of Appeals.

38. Taxpayer lives in Michigan. In a controversy with the IRS, taxpayer loses at the trial court level. Describe the appeal procedure under the following different assumptions:

a. The trial court was the Small Claims Division of the U.S. Tax Court.
b. The trial court was the U.S. Tax Court.
c. The trial court was a U.S. District Court.
d. The trial court was the U.S. Claims Court.

39. Suppose the U.S. Government loses a tax case in the U.S. District Court of Idaho but does not appeal the result. What does the failure to appeal signify?

40. What is the *Golsen* rule?

41. Explain the following abbreviations:

a. CA–2
b. Cls.Ct.
c. *aff'd.*
d. *rev'd.*
e. *rem'd.*
f. *Cert. denied*
g. *acq.*
h. B.T.A.
i. USTC
j. AFTR
k. F.2d
l. F.Supp.
m. USSC
n. S.Ct.
o. D.Ct.

42. What is the difference between a Regular and a Memorandum decision of the U.S. Tax Court?

43. In assessing the validity of a court decision, discuss the significance of the following:

  a. The decision was rendered by the U.S. District Court of Wyoming. Taxpayer lives in Wyoming.
  b. The decision was rendered by the U.S. Claims Court. Taxpayer lives in Wyoming.
  c. The decision was rendered by the Second Court of Appeals. Taxpayer lives in California.
  d. The decision was rendered by the U.S. Supreme Court.
  e. The decision was rendered by the U.S. Tax Court. The IRS has acquiesced in the result.
  f. Same as (e) except that the IRS has issued a nonacquiescence as to the result.

44. Interpret each of the following citations:

  a. Rev.Rul. 80–28, 1980–1 C.B. 304.
  b. *Jack E. Golsen,* 54 T.C. 742 (1970).
  c. Ltr.Rul. 9046036.

45. Is tax avoidance illegal? Explain.

PROBLEMS

46. T owns some real estate (basis of $100,000 and fair market value of $60,000) that she would like to sell to her son, S, for $60,000. T is aware, however, that losses on sales between certain related parties are disallowed for Federal income tax purposes [§ 267(a)(1)]. T therefore sells the property to P (an unrelated party) for $60,000. On the same day, P sells the same property to S for the same amount. Is T's realized loss of $40,000 deductible? Explain.

47. P exchanges some real estate (basis of $80,000 and fair market value of $100,000) for other real estate owned by R (basis of $120,000 and fair market value of $90,000) and $10,000 in cash. The real estate involved is unimproved and is held by P and R, before and after the exchange, as investment property.

  a. What is P's realized gain on the exchange? Recognized gain?
  b. What is R's realized loss? Recognized loss?
  c. Support your results to (a) and (b) under the wherewithal to pay concept as applied to like-kind exchanges (§ 1031).

48. Using the legend provided, classify the overall objective of the particular tax provision:

Legend

CE	=	Control of the economy
EA	=	Encouragement of certain activities
EI	=	Encouragement of certain industries
SC	=	Social considerations
W	=	Wherewithal to pay concept
AF	=	Administrative feasibility
ESB	=	Encouragement of small business

  a. Involuntary conversion of a business building.
  b. A decrease in the individual tax rate.
  c. The S corporation election.
  d. Write-off of research and development expenditures.
  e. Percentage depletion.
  f. Unified estate tax credit.
  g. Charitable contribution deduction.

49. M exchanges common stock in X Corporation (adjusted basis of $43,000 and fair market value of $91,000) for common stock in Y Corporation (fair market value of $91,000). The exchange is not pursuant to any reorganization. Calculate the realized gain and any recognized gain to M.

50. T sells property (basis of $20,000) to V Corporation for $30,000. Based on the following conditions, how could the IRS challenge this transaction?

   a. T is the sole shareholder of V Corporation.
   b. T is the son of the sole shareholder of V Corporation.
   c. T is neither a shareholder in V Corporation nor related to any of V's shareholders.

51. Using the legend provided, classify each of the following statements (Note: more than one answer per statement may be appropriate):

Legend

D =	Applies to the U.S. District Court
T =	Applies to the U.S. Tax Court
C =	Applies to the U.S. Claims Court
A =	Applies to the U.S. Court of Appeals
U =	Applies to the U.S. Supreme Court
N =	Applies to none of the above

   a. Decides only Federal tax matters.
   b. Decisions are reported in the F.2d Series.
   c. Decisions are reported in the USTCs.
   d. Decisions are reported in the AFTRs.
   e. Appeal is by Writ of Certiorari.
   f. Court meets generally in Washington, D.C.
   g. A jury trial is available.
   h. Trial court.
   i. Appellate court.
   j. Appeal is to the U.S. Court of Appeals for the Federal Circuit.
   k. Has a Small Claims Division.
   l. The only trial court where the taxpayer does not have to pay the tax assessed by the IRS first.

52. Identify the governmental unit that produces the following tax sources:

   a. Proposed Regulations.
   b. Revenue Procedures.
   c. Letter rulings.
   d. Determination letters.
   e. Technical Advice Memoranda.

53. Locate the following Internal Revenue Code citations and give a brief description of each:

   a. § 461(b).
   b. § 542(a)(1).
   c. § 721(a).

54. Locate the following Regulation citations and give a brief description of each:

   a. Reg. § 1.408(a)(1).
   b. Reg. § 1.532–1(b).
   c. Reg. § 1.761–1(b).

55. What is the subject matter of Revenue Ruling 325 that begins on page 124 of the 1978–2 *Cumulative Bulletin*?

56. Determine the acquiescence/nonacquiescence position of the IRS with respect to the following:

    a. *Sidney Merians*, 60 T.C. 187 (1973).
    b. *Charles Crowther*, 28 T.C. 1293 (1957).
    c. *Ray Durden*, 3 T.C. 1 (1944).
    d. *John P. White*, 48 T.C. 430 (1967).

57. Locate the following tax services in your library and indicate the name of the publisher and whether the service is organized by topic or by Code Section:

    a. *Federal Taxes* or *United States Tax Reporter.*
    b. *Standard Federal Tax Reporter.*
    c. *Tax Coordinator 2d.*
    d. *Mertens Law of Federal Income Taxation.*
    e. *Tax Management Portfolios.*
    f. Rabkin & Johnson, *Federal Income, Gift and Estate Taxation.*
    g. Bender's, *Federal Tax Service.*

RESEARCH PROBLEMS

RESEARCH PROBLEM 1 Locate the following court decision and describe the proposition that this case created (i.e., the *Sutter* rule): *Richard A. Sutter*, 21 T.C. 170 (1953). Using a citator, determine if subsequent courts have accepted this rule.

RESEARCH PROBLEM 2 Locate and summarize Ltr.Rul. 9046036.

RESEARCH PROBLEM 3 Determine the disposition of the following decisions at the appellate level:

    a. *Anderson, Clayton & Co. v. U.S.*, 562 F.2d 972 (CA–5, 1977).
    b. *American Medical Assn. v. U.S.*, 688 F.Supp. 358 (D.Ct.Ill., 1988).
    c. *Redhouse v. Comm.*, 728 F.2d 1249 (CA–9, 1984).
    d. *Jack O. Chertkof*, 72 T.C. 1113 (1979).
    e. *Estate of Grace E. Lang*, 64 T.C. 404 (1975).

RESEARCH PROBLEM 4 Did the IRS agree or disagree with the following court decisions?

    a. *Stuart Bart*, 21 T. C. 880 (1954).
    b. *Phillip G. Larson*, 66 T.C. 159 (1978).
    c. *Intervest Enterprises, Inc.*, 59 T.C. 91 (1972).

RESEARCH PROBLEM 5 O Corporation has declared Chapter 11 bankruptcy during 1991. Can the taxpayer designate tax payments first to trust fund liabilities and next to non-trust fund liabilities? Be sure to indicate why a taxpayer may take such a position. Why might the IRS disagree with the taxpayer?

RESEARCH PROBLEM 6 In December of last year, T, a cash basis and calendar year taxpayer, embezzles $200,000 from a bank where he is employed as an assistant cashier. T disappears for parts unknown and goes on a three-month spending spree. In the current year, T is apprehended by law enforcement authorities and forced to make restitution of the $150,000 still unspent. Comment on T's income tax position, with special reference to the mitigation of the annual accounting period concept.

Partial list of research aids:

Code §§ 61, 172, and 1341.
Bernard A. Yerkie, 67 T.C. 388 (1976).

RESEARCH PROBLEM 7 Complete the following citations to the extent the research materials are available to you:

    a. *Edith G. McKinney*, _____ TCM 1272 (1981).
    b. *Horace B. Rickey, Jr. v. U.S.*, 592 F.2d 1251 (CA– _____ , _____).
    c. *U.S. v. Cumberland Public Service Co.*, 38 AFTR _____ (USSC, _____).
    d. Rev.Proc. 77–28, 1977–2 C.B. _____ .

e. *Harriet C. Flower v. U.S.*, 57–1 USTC ¶_____ (D.C.Pa., _____).
f. _____ _____ , 9 T.C. 1097 (1947).
g. *L. Weiner*, 10 B.T.A. _____ (_____).
h. Rev.Rul. 63–144, 1963– _____ C.B. 129.

RESEARCH PROBLEM 8   By using the research materials available to you, answer the following questions:

a. Has Prop.Reg. § 1.79–1(d)(7) been finalized?
b. What happened to *Barry D. Pevsner*, 38 TCM 1210, T.C.Memo. 1979–311, on appeal?
c. Does Rev.Rul. 60–97 still represent the position of the IRS on the issue involved?
d. What is the underlying Code Section for Reg. § 1.9101–1? Summarize this Regulation.

PART

CORPORATIONS

Corporations are separate entities for Federal income tax purposes. Subchapter C of the Code is devoted to the tax treatment of regular corporations. Part II deals mainly with the operating rules contained in Subchapter C that apply to regular corporations and with the effects of various capital transactions on the C corporation and its shareholders.

CHAPTER

2

CORPORATIONS: INTRODUCTION, OPERATING RULES, AND RELATED CORPORATIONS

OBJECTIVES

Summarize the income tax treatment of various forms of conducting a business.

Determine when an entity will be treated as a corporation for Federal income tax purposes.

Review the general income tax provisions applicable to individuals.

Establish the tax rules peculiar to corporations.

Illustrate the computation of the corporate income tax.

Describe the procedural aspects of filing and reporting for corporate taxpayers.

Describe the tax rules unique to multiple corporations that are controlled by the same shareholders.

Introduce some fundamental concepts relating to consolidated returns.

Evaluate the corporate form as a means of conducting a trade or business.

OUTLINE

Business operations can be conducted in a number of different forms. Among the various possibilities are the following:

- Sole proprietorships.
- Partnerships.
- Trusts and estates.
- S corporations (also known as Subchapter S corporations).
- Regular corporations (also called Subchapter C or C corporations).

For Federal income tax purposes, the distinctions between these forms of business organization are very important. The following discussion of the tax treatment of sole proprietorships, partnerships, and regular corporations highlights these distinctions. Trusts and estates are covered in Chapter 19,[1] and S corporations are discussed in Chapter 12.

Sole Proprietorships

A sole proprietorship is not a taxable entity separate from the individual who owns the proprietorship. The owner of a sole proprietorship reports all business transactions of the proprietorship on Schedule C of Form 1040. The net profit or loss from the proprietorship is then transferred from Schedule C to Form 1040, which is used by the taxpayer to report taxable income. The proprietor reports all of the net profit from the business, regardless of the amount actually withdrawn during the year.

Income and expenses of the proprietorship retain their character when reported by the proprietor. For example, ordinary income of the proprietorship is treated as ordinary income when reported by the proprietor, and capital gain is treated as capital gain.

--------------------------------------- EXAMPLE 1 ---------------------------------------

T is the sole proprietor of T's Record Shop. Gross income of the business in 1993 is $200,000, and operating expenses are $110,000. During 1993, T withdraws $60,000 from the business for living expenses. T reports the income and expenses of the business on Schedule C, resulting in net profit of $90,000. Even though he withdrew only $60,000, T reports the $90,000 net profit from the business on Form 1040, where he computes taxable income for the year. ◆

Partnerships

Partnerships are not subject to the income tax. However, a partnership is required to file Form 1065, which reports the results of the partnership's business activities. Most income and expense items are aggregated in computing the net profit of the partnership on Form 1065. Any income and expense items that are not aggregated in computing the partnership's net income are reported separately to the partners. Some examples of separately reported income items are interest income, dividend income, and long-term capital gain. Examples of separately reported expenses include charitable contributions and expenses related to interest and dividend income. Partnership reporting is discussed in detail in Chapter 10.

The partnership net profit and the separately reported items are allocated to each partner according to the partnership's profit sharing agreement, and the

---

1. The tax treatment of Real Estate Investment Trusts (REITs) presents peculiar problems and is not covered in this text. See §§ 856–859.

partners receive separate K–1 schedules from the partnership. Schedule K–1 reports each partner's share of the partnership net profit and separately reported income and expense items. Each partner reports these items on his or her own tax return.

────────────────── EXAMPLE 2 ──────────────────

X and Y are equal partners in XY Enterprises, a calendar year partnership. During 1993, XY Enterprises had $500,000 gross income and $350,000 operating expenses. In addition, the partnership sold land that had been held for investment purposes for a long-term capital gain of $60,000. During the year, X withdrew $40,000 from the partnership, and Y withdrew $45,000. The partnership's Form 1065 reports net profit of $150,000 ($500,000 income − $350,000 expenses). The partnership also reports the $60,000 long-term capital gain as a separately stated item on Form 1065. X and Y both receive a Schedule K–1 reporting net profit of $75,000 and separately stated long-term capital gain of $30,000. Each partner reports net profit of $75,000 and long-term capital gain of $30,000 on his own return. ◆

Regular Corporations

Regular corporations are governed by Subchapter C of the Internal Revenue Code. Thus, they are frequently referred to as C corporations. Unlike proprietorships and partnerships, C corporations are taxpaying entities. This results in what is known as a double tax effect. A C corporation reports its income and expenses on Form 1120 (or Form 1120–A, the corporate short form). The corporation computes tax on the net income reported on the corporate tax return using the rate schedule applicable to corporations (refer to the rate schedule inside the front cover of this text). When a corporation distributes its income, the corporation's shareholders report dividend income on their own tax returns. Thus, income that has already been taxed at the corporate level is also taxed at the shareholder level.

────────────────── EXAMPLE 3 ──────────────────

X Corporation files Form 1120, which reports net profit of $100,000. The corporation pays tax of $22,250. This leaves $77,750, all of which is distributed as a dividend to T, the sole shareholder of the corporation. T, who is in the 31% tax bracket, pays income tax of $24,103. The combined tax on the corporation's net profit is $46,353. ◆

if Bonus of 100,000 is pd then No corp tax now the 100,00 is taxed at 31% personal tax saving 15353.

────────────────── EXAMPLE 4 ──────────────────

Assume the same facts as in Example 3, except that the business is organized as a sole proprietorship. T reports the $100,000 net profit from the business on her tax return and pays tax of $31,000 ($100,000 net profit × 31% marginal rate). Therefore, operating the business as a sole proprietorship results in a tax saving of $15,353 ($46,353 tax from Example 3 − $31,000). ◆

Comparison of Corporations and Other Forms of Doing Business.   Comparison of the tax results in Examples 3 and 4 might lead to the conclusion that incorporation is not a wise tax strategy. In some cases that would be a correct conclusion, but in others it would not. While corporate taxes are generally higher than individual taxes, in many situations tax and nontax factors combine to make the corporate form of doing business the only reasonable choice.

Chapter 13 presents a detailed comparison of sole proprietorships, partnerships, S corporations, and C corporations as forms of doing business. However, it is appropriate at this point to consider some of the tax and nontax factors that favor corporations over proprietorships.

Consideration of tax factors requires an examination of the corporate rate structure. The income tax rate schedule applicable to corporations is reproduced below.

Taxable Income	Tax Rate
■ $50,000 or less	15%
■ Over $50,000 but not over $75,000	25%
■ Over $75,000	34%
■ Additional tax on $100,000 to $335,000	5%

As this schedule shows, corporate rates on taxable income up to $75,000 are lower than individual rates for persons in the 28 and 31 percent brackets. Therefore, corporate tax will be lower than individual tax. When dividends are paid, however, the double taxation problem occurs. This leads to an important question: Will incorporation ever result in Federal income tax savings? The following example illustrates a situation where this occurs.

EXAMPLE 5

T, an individual in the 31% tax bracket, owns a business that produces net profit of $50,000 each year. T has significant income from other sources, so he does not withdraw any of the profit from the business. If the business is operated as a proprietorship, T's Federal income tax on the net profit of the business is $15,500 ($50,000 × 31%). However, if the business is operated as a corporation and pays no dividends, the tax will be $7,500 ($50,000 × 15%). Operating as a corporation saves $8,000 of Federal income tax each year. If T invests his $8,000 tax saving each year for several years, it is possible that a positive cash flow will result, despite the fact that T will be required to pay tax on dividends distributed by the corporation some time in the future. ◆

The preceding example deals with a specific set of facts. The conclusions reached in this situation cannot be extended to all decisions about a form of business organization. Each specific set of facts and circumstances requires a thorough analysis of the tax factors.

Another tax consideration involves the nature of dividend income. All income and expense items of a proprietorship retain their character when reported on the proprietor's tax return. In the case of a partnership, several separately reported items (e.g., charitable contributions and long-term capital gains) retain their character when passed through to the partners. However, the tax attributes of income and expense items of a corporation are lost as they pass through the corporate entity to the shareholders.

EXAMPLE 6

During the current year, X Company receives tax-exempt interest, which is distributed to its owners. If X Company is a regular corporation, the distribution to the shareholders constitutes a dividend. The fact that it originated from tax-exempt interest is of no consequence.[2] On the other hand, if X Company is a partnership or an S corporation, the tax-exempt interest retains its identity and passes through to the individual partners. ◆

---

2. As noted in Chapter 4, such items will, however, affect the distributing corporation's earnings and profits.

Losses of a C corporation are treated differently than losses of a proprietorship, partnership, or S corporation. A loss incurred by a proprietorship may be deductible by the owner, because all income and expense items are reported by the proprietor. Partnership losses are passed through the partnership entity and may be deductible by the partners, and S corporation losses are passed through to the shareholders. C corporation losses, however, have no effect on the taxable income of the shareholders. Income from a C corporation is reported when the shareholders receive dividends. C corporation losses are not reported by the shareholders.

Nontax Considerations. Nontax considerations will sometimes override tax considerations and lead to a conclusion that a business should be operated as a corporation. The following are some of the more important nontax considerations:

- Sole proprietors and general partners in partnerships face the danger of unlimited liability. That is, creditors of the business may file claims not only against the assets of the business but also against the personal assets of proprietors or general partners. Shareholders are protected against claims against their personal assets by state corporate law.
- The corporate form of business organization can provide a vehicle for raising large amounts of capital. Most major businesses in the United States are operated as corporations.
- Shares of stock in a corporation are freely transferable, whereas a partner's sale of his or her partnership interest is subject to approval by the other partners.
- Shareholders may come and go, but a corporation can continue to exist. This *continuity of life* is a distinct advantage of the corporate form of doing business.

A more in-depth discussion of the different forms of business organizations is presented in Chapter 13. See especially the Concept Summary in Chapter 13 that contains a detailed comparison of the tax attributes of the sole proprietorship, the partnership, the S corporation, and the regular C corporation.

The tax consequences of operating a business in the regular corporate form fall within Subchapter C of the Code and are the subject of this chapter and Chapters 3 through 5 and Chapter 7.[3] Corporations that either unreasonably accumulate earnings or meet the definition of a personal holding company may be subject to further taxation. These so-called penalty taxes are imposed in addition to the corporate income tax and are discussed in Chapter 6.

Clearly, the form of organization chosen to carry on a trade or business has significant Federal income tax consequences. Though tax considerations may not control the choice, it could be unfortunate if they are not taken into account.

The first step in any discussion of the Federal income tax treatment of corporations must be definitional. Specifically, what is a corporation? At first glance, the answer to this question appears to be quite simple. Merely look to the appropriate state law to determine whether the entity has satisfied the requirements for corporate status. Have articles of incorporation been drawn up

WHAT IS A CORPORATION?

---

3. Special rules apply to cooperative organizations (§ 521 and Subchapter T), banking institutions (Subchapter H), insurance companies (Subchapter L), and regulated investment companies (Subchapter M). In the interest of space and because of limited applicability, these rules are not discussed in this text. Tax-exempt organizations (§ 501) are discussed in Chapter 14.

and filed with the state regulatory agency? Has a charter been granted? Has stock been issued to shareholders? These are all points to consider.

Compliance with state law, although important, may not tell the full story as to whether an entity will be recognized as a corporation for tax purposes. On the one hand, a corporation qualifying under state law may be disregarded as a taxable entity if it is a mere sham. On the other hand, an organization not qualifying as a regular corporation under state law may be taxed as a corporation under the association approach. These two possibilities are discussed in the following sections.

Disregard of Corporate Entity

In most cases, the IRS and the courts will recognize a corporation legally constituted under state law. In exceptional situations, however, the corporate entity may be disregarded because it lacks substance.[4] The key to such treatment is the degree of business activity conducted at the corporate level. The more the corporation does in connection with its trade or business, the less likely it will be treated as a sham and disregarded as a separate entity.

EXAMPLE 7

C and D are joint owners of a tract of unimproved real estate that they wish to protect from future creditors. Consequently, C and D form R Corporation, to which they transfer the land in return for all of the latter's stock. The corporation merely holds title to the land and conducts no other activities. In all respects, R Corporation meets the requirements of a corporation under applicable state law. ◆

EXAMPLE 8

Assume the same facts as in Example 7. In addition to holding title to the land, R Corporation leases the property, collects rents, and pays the property taxes. ◆

R Corporation probably would not be recognized as a separate entity under the facts set forth in Example 7. In Example 8, however, the opposite should prove true. It appears that enough activity has taken place at the corporate level to warrant the conclusion that R Corporation should be treated as a real corporation for Federal income tax purposes.[5]

Depending on the circumstances, either the IRS or the taxpayers may attempt to disregard the corporate entity. More often than not, the IRS may try to disregard (or "collapse") a corporation to make the corporation's income taxable directly to the shareholders. In other situations, a corporation may try to avoid the corporate income tax or permit its shareholders to take advantage of excess corporate deductions and losses.[6]

Theoretically speaking, the disregard-of-corporate-entity approach should be equally available to both the IRS and the taxpayers. From a practical standpoint, however, taxpayers have enjoyed considerably less success than has the IRS. Courts generally conclude that since the taxpayers created the corporation in the first place, they should not be permitted to disregard it later in order to avoid taxes.

---

4. The reader should bear in mind that the textual discussion relates to the classification of an entity for *Federal* income tax purposes. State corporate income taxes or other corporate taxes (e.g., franchise taxes) may still be imposed. An entity may possibly be treated as a corporation for state tax purposes and not for Federal and vice versa. This will become even more apparent when dealing with S corporations (Chapter 12) because some states do not recognize this status.

5. A classic case in this area is *Paymer v. Comm.*, 45–2 USTC ¶9353, 33 AFTR 1536, 150 F.2d 334 (CA–2, 1945). Here, two corporations were involved. The Court chose to disregard one corporate entity but to recognize the other.

6. An election under Subchapter S would generally accomplish this if the parties qualify and the election is made on a timely basis. See Chapter 12.

Associations Taxed as Corporations

The definition of a corporation in § 7701(a)(3) includes "associations, joint stock companies, and insurance companies." What Congress intended by including associations in the definition has never been entirely clear. Judicial decisions have clarified the status of associations and the relationship between associations and corporations.

The designation given to the entity under state law is not controlling. In one case, an entity that was a business trust under state law was deemed to be an association (and therefore taxable as a corporation) for Federal income tax purposes.[7] In another case, a partnership of physicians was held to be an association even though state law applicable to the tax year in question prohibited the practice of medicine in the corporate form.[8] As an association, the partnership was taxed as a corporation.

Whether an entity will be considered an association for Federal income tax purposes depends upon the number of corporate characteristics it possesses. According to court decisions and Regulation § 301.7701–2(a), corporate characteristics include the following:

1. Associates.
2. An objective to carry on a business and divide the gains.
3. Continuity of life.
4. Centralized management.
5. Limited liability.
6. Free transferability of interests.

The Regulations state that an unincorporated organization shall not be classified as an association unless it possesses more corporate than noncorporate characteristics. In making the determination, the characteristics common to both corporate and noncorporate business organizations are disregarded.

Both corporations and partnerships generally have associates (shareholders and partners) and an objective to carry on a business and divide the gains. In testing whether a particular partnership is an association, these criteria would be disregarded.

It then becomes a matter of determining whether the partnership possesses a majority of the remaining corporate characteristics (items 3 through 6). Does the partnership terminate upon the withdrawal or death of a partner (no continuity of life)? Is the management of the partnership centralized, or do all partners participate? Are all partners individually liable for the debts of the partnership, or is the liability of some limited to their actual investment in the partnership (limited partnership)? May a partner freely transfer his or her interest without the consent of the other partners?

Courts have ruled that any partnership lacking two or more of these characteristics will not be classified as an association. Conversely, any partnership having three or more of these characteristics will be classified as an association.[9]

For trusts, the first two characteristics are considered in testing for association status. The conventional type of trust often does not have associates and usually restricts its activities to investing rather than carrying on a trade or business. These characteristics, however, are common to corporations. Consequently, whether a trust qualifies as an association depends upon the satisfaction of the first two corporate characteristics.

---

7. *Morrissey v. Comm.*, 36–1 USTC ¶9020, 16 AFTR 1274, 56 S.Ct. 289 (USSC, 1935).

8. *U.S. v. Kintner*, 54–2 USTC ¶9626, 46 AFTR 995, 216 F.2d 418 (CA–9, 1954).

9. See *Zuckman v. U.S.*, 75–2 USTC ¶9778, 36 AFTR2d 6193, 524 F.2d 729 (Ct.Cls., 1975), and *P. G. Larson*, 66 T.C. 159 (1976).

From a taxpayer's standpoint, the desirability of association status turns on the tax implications involved. In some cases, the parties may find it advantageous to have the entity taxed as a corporation while in others they may not. These possibilities are explored at length under Tax Planning Considerations in this chapter.

An Introduction to the Income Taxation of Corporations
◆

An Overview of Corporate versus Individual Income Tax Treatment

In a discussion of how corporations are treated under the Federal income tax, a useful approach is to compare their treatment with that applicable to individual taxpayers.

Similarities. Gross income of a corporation is determined in much the same manner as it is for individuals. Thus, gross income includes compensation for services rendered, income derived from a business, gains from dealings in property, interest, rents, royalties, dividends—to name only a few items [§ 61(a)]. Both individuals and corporations are entitled to exclusions from gross income. However, corporate taxpayers are allowed fewer exclusions. Interest on municipal bonds is excluded from gross income whether the bondholder is an individual or a corporate taxpayer.

Gains and losses from property transactions are handled similarly. For example, whether a gain or loss is capital or ordinary depends upon the nature of the asset in the hands of the taxpayer making the taxable disposition. Code § 1221, in defining what is not a capital asset, makes no distinction between corporate and noncorporate taxpayers.

In the area of nontaxable exchanges, corporations are like individuals in that they do not recognize gain or loss on a like-kind exchange (§ 1031) and may defer recognized gain on an involuntary conversion of property (§ 1033).[10] The nonrecognition of gain provisions dealing with the sale of a personal residence (§§ 121 and 1034) do not apply to corporations. Both corporations and individuals are vulnerable to the disallowance of losses on sales of property to related parties [§ 267(a)(1)] or on wash sales of securities (§ 1091). The wash sales rules do not apply to individuals who are traders or dealers in securities or to corporations that are dealers if the securities are sold in the ordinary course of the corporation's business.

Upon the sale or other taxable disposition of depreciable property, the recapture rules (i.e., §§ 1245 and 1250) generally make no distinction between corporate and noncorporate taxpayers. However, § 291(a) does cause a corporation to have more recapture on § 1250 property. This difference is discussed later in the chapter.

The business deductions of corporations also parallel those available to individuals. Deductions are allowed for all ordinary and necessary expenses paid or incurred in carrying on a trade or business under the general rule of § 162(a). Specific provision is made for the deductibility of interest, certain taxes, losses, bad debts, accelerated cost recovery, charitable contributions, net operating losses, research and experimental expenditures, and other less common deductions. No deduction is permitted for interest paid or incurred on amounts

---

10. For definitions of terms such as "like-kind exchange" and "involuntary conversion," see the Glossary of Tax Terms in Appendix C.

borrowed to purchase or carry tax-exempt securities. The same holds true for expenses contrary to public policy and certain unpaid expenses and interest between related parties.

Some of the tax credits available to individuals can also be claimed by corporations. This is the case with the foreign tax credit. Not available to corporations are certain credits that are personal in nature, such as the child care credit, the credit for the elderly, and the earned income credit.

Dissimilarities. The income taxation of corporations and individuals also differs significantly. As noted earlier, different tax rates apply to corporations (§ 11) and to individuals (§ 1). Corporate tax rates are discussed in more detail later in the chapter (see Examples 29 and 30).

All allowable corporate deductions are treated as business deductions. Thus, the determination of adjusted gross income (AGI), so essential for individual taxpayers, has no relevance to corporations. Taxable income is computed simply by subtracting from gross income all allowable deductions and losses. Corporations need not be concerned with itemized deductions or the standard deduction. The deduction for personal and dependency exemptions is not available to corporations.

Because corporations can have only business deductions and losses, the $100 floor on the deductible portion of personal casualty and theft losses does not apply. Also inapplicable is the provision limiting the deductibility of nonbusiness casualty losses to the amount by which the losses exceed 10 percent of AGI.

─────────────── EXAMPLE 9 ───────────────

During 1992, X, a calendar year taxpayer with AGI of $10,000, suffers a casualty loss of $4,000. If X is an individual, only $2,900 ($4,000 – $100 – $1,000) of the casualty loss can be deducted (assuming the loss is personal and there has been no actual insurance recovery and none is reasonably anticipated). Chances are the casualty loss can be claimed only as an itemized deduction and will not be available if X chooses not to itemize. On the other hand, if X is a corporation, the item is deductible in full as a business expense under § 162. ◆

Specific Provisions Compared

In comparing the tax treatment of individuals and corporations, the following areas warrant special discussion:

- Accounting periods and methods.
- Capital gains and losses.
- Recapture of depreciation.
- Passive losses.
- Charitable contributions.
- Net operating losses.
- Special deductions available only to corporations.

Accounting Periods and Methods

Accounting Periods. Corporations generally have the same choices of accounting periods as do individual taxpayers. Like an individual, a corporation may choose a calendar year or a fiscal year for reporting purposes. Corporations, however, enjoy greater flexibility in the selection of a tax year. For example, corporations usually can have different tax years from those of their shareholders. Also, newly formed corporations (as new taxpayers) usually have a choice of any approved accounting period without having to obtain the consent of the IRS.

Personal service corporations (PSCs) and S corporations are subject to severe restrictions in the use of a fiscal year. The rules applicable to S corporations are discussed in Chapter 12. A PSC, often an association treated as a corporation (refer to the earlier discussion in the chapter), has as its principal activity the performance of personal services. Such services are substantially performed by owner-employees. The performance of services must be in the fields of health, law, engineering, architecture, accounting, actuarial science, performing arts, or consulting.[11]

Because a significant deferral of income can occur by placing a PSC on a fiscal year and retaining a calendar year for the employee-owner, a PSC must generally use a calendar year.[12] However, a PSC can *elect* a fiscal year under any of the following conditions:

- A business purpose for the year can be demonstrated.
- The PSC year results in a deferral of not more than three months' income. The corporation must pay the shareholder-employee's salary during the portion of the calendar year after the close of the fiscal year. Furthermore, the salary for that period must be at least proportionate to the employee's salary received for the fiscal year.[13]
- The PSC retains the same year that was used for its fiscal year ending 1987, provided the latter two requirements applicable to the preceding option are satisfied.

EXAMPLE 10

R & T is a professional association of public accountants. Because it receives over 40% of its gross receipts in March and April of each year from the preparation of tax returns, R & T has a May 1 to April 30 fiscal year. Under these circumstances, the IRS might permit R & T to continue to use the fiscal year chosen since it reflects a natural business cycle (the end of the tax season). R & T has a business purpose in using a fiscal year. ◆

EXAMPLE 11

A's corporation paid A $120,000 in salary during its fiscal year ending September 30, 1992. The corporation cannot satisfy the business purpose test for a fiscal year. However, the corporation can continue to use its fiscal year without any negative tax effects, provided A receives at least $30,000 (3 months/12 months × $120,000) as salary during the period October 1 through December 31, 1992. ◆

Accounting Methods. As a general rule, the cash method of accounting is unavailable to regular corporations.[14] Exceptions apply in the following situations:

- S corporations.
- Corporations engaged in the trade or business of farming and timber.
- Qualified personal service corporations.
- Corporations with average annual gross receipts of $5 million or less. (In applying the $5 million or less test, the corporation uses the average of the three prior taxable years.)

---

11. § 448(d)(2)(A).
12. § 441(i).

13. §§ 444 and 280H.
14. § 448.

Both individuals and corporations that maintain inventory for sale to customers are required to use the accrual method of accounting for determining sales and cost of goods sold.

Capital Gains and Losses

Capital gains and losses result from the taxable sales or exchanges of capital assets. Whether these gains and losses are long term or short term depends upon the holding period of the assets sold or exchanged. Each year, a taxpayer's long-term capital gains and losses are combined, and the result is either a *net* long-term capital gain or a *net* long-term capital loss. A similar aggregation is made with short-term capital gains and losses, the result being a *net* short-term capital gain or a *net* short-term capital loss. The following combinations and results are possible:

1. A net long-term capital gain and a net short-term capital loss. These are combined, and the result is either a net capital gain or a net capital loss.
2. A net long-term capital gain and a net short-term capital gain. No further combination is made.
3. A net long-term capital loss and a net short-term capital gain. These are combined, and the result is either capital gain net income or a net capital loss.
4. A net long-term capital loss and a net short-term capital loss. No further combination is made.

Capital Gains. Before TRA of 1986, long-term capital gains (combination 2 and, possibly, combination 1) enjoyed favorable tax treatment. Individuals were allowed a 60 percent deduction, which meant that only 40 percent of net capital gains were subject to the income tax. For corporations, the gains were subject to the lower of the applicable corporate rate or an alternative rate of 28 percent.

Although the capital gain and loss classification has been retained, the capital gain deduction for individuals has been eliminated. For tax years beginning after 1990, the tax rate on net capital gain is limited to a maximum of 28 percent for all taxpayers except corporations.

Capital Losses. Net capital losses (refer to combinations 3 and 4 and, possibly, to combination 1) of corporate and noncorporate taxpayers receive different income tax treatment. Generally, noncorporate taxpayers can deduct up to $3,000 of such net losses against other income.[15] Any remaining capital losses can be carried forward to future years until absorbed by capital gains or by the $3,000 deduction.[16] Carryovers do not lose their identity but remain either long term or short term.

───────────────── EXAMPLE 12 ─────────────────

T, an individual, incurs a net long-term capital loss of $7,500 for calendar year 1992. Assuming adequate taxable income, T may deduct $3,000 of this loss on his 1992 return. The remaining $4,500 ($7,500 – $3,000) of the loss is carried to 1993 and years thereafter until completely deducted. The $4,500 will be carried forward as a long-term capital loss. ◆

---

15. The limitations on capital losses for both corporate and noncorporate taxpayers are contained in § 1211.

16. Carryback and carryover rules for both corporate and noncorporate taxpayers can be found in § 1212.

Unlike individuals, corporate taxpayers are not permitted to claim any net capital losses as a deduction against ordinary income. Capital losses, therefore, can be used only as an offset against capital gains. Corporations may, however, carry back net capital losses to three preceding years, applying them first to the earliest year in point of time. Carryforwards are allowed for a period of five years from the year of the loss. When carried back or forward, a long-term capital loss is treated as a short-term capital loss.

EXAMPLE 13

Assume the same facts as in Example 12, except that T is a corporation. None of the $7,500 long-term capital loss incurred in 1992 can be deducted in that year. T Corporation may, however, carry back the loss to years 1989, 1990, and 1991 (in this order) and offset it against any capital gains recognized in these years. If the carryback does not exhaust the loss, it may be carried forward to calendar years 1993, 1994, 1995, 1996, and 1997 (in this order). Either a carryback or a carryforward of the long-term capital loss converts the loss to a short-term capital loss. ◆

Recapture of Depreciation

Depreciation recapture for § 1245 property is computed in the same manner for individuals and for corporations. However, corporations have more recapture of depreciation under § 1250 than do individuals. Corporations that sell depreciable real estate that is § 1250 property are subject to additional recapture of depreciation under § 291(a)(1). This provision requires recapture of 20 percent of the excess of any amount that would be treated as ordinary income under § 1245 over the amount treated as ordinary income under § 1250. The amount of ordinary income under § 291 is computed as shown in Figure 2–1.

EXAMPLE 14

A corporation purchased an office building on January 3, 1984, for $300,000. Accelerated depreciation was taken in the amount of $193,500 before the building was sold on January 5, 1992, for $250,000. Straight-line depreciation would have been $161,667 (using a 15-year recovery period under ACRS). The corporation's depreciation recapture and § 1231 gain are computed as follows.

Determine realized gain:	
Sales price	$250,000
Less: Adjusted basis [$300,000 (cost of building) – $193,500 (ACRS depreciation)]	106,500
Realized gain	$143,500

Because the building is 15-year real estate, it is § 1245 recovery property. The gain of $143,500 is recaptured to the extent of all depreciation taken. Thus, all gain is ordinary income under § 1245 and there is no § 1231 gain. ◆

FIGURE 2–1

Computation of Depreciation Recapture under § 291

Ordinary income under § 1245	$xx,xxx
Less: Ordinary income under § 1250	(x,xxx)
Equals: Excess ordinary income under § 1245 as compared to ordinary income under § 1250	$ x,xxx
Apply § 291 percentage	×20%
Equals: Amount of ordinary income under § 291	$ xxx

(handwritten top margin: always 1245 / always 100% recapture)

————————— EXAMPLE 15 —————————

Assume the building in Example 14 is residential rental property, making it § 1250 property. Gain recaptured under § 1250 would be $31,833 [$193,500 (depreciation taken) − $161,667 (straight-line depreciation)]. However, for a corporate taxpayer, § 291(a) causes additional § 1250 ordinary income of $22,333, computed as follows:

Ordinary income under § 1245	$143,500
Less: Ordinary income under § 1250	31,833
Excess ordinary income under § 1245	$111,667
Apply § 291 percentage	20%
Additional § 1250 income (ordinary income under § 291)	$ 22,333

(handwritten right margin: 1245 all recapture / 1250 only to extent to straight line)

Thus, of the total gain of $143,500, $54,166 [$31,833 (§ 1250 recapture) + $22,333 (§ 291 recapture)] would be ordinary income, and $89,334 would be § 1231 gain. ◆

(handwritten left margin: don't worry)

————————— EXAMPLE 16 —————————

Assume the building in Example 15 is commercial property and straight-line depreciation was used. An individual would report all gain as § 1231 gain. However, a corporate taxpayer would recapture as ordinary income (under § 291) 20% of the depreciation that would be ordinary income if the property were § 1245 property.

First, determine realized gain:	
Sales price	$250,000
Less: Adjusted basis [$300,000 (cost of building) − $161,667 (straight-line depreciation)]	138,333
Realized gain	$111,667
Second, determine § 291 gain:	
Ordinary income if property were § 1245 property	$111,667
Less: Ordinary income under § 1250	–0–
Excess ordinary income under § 1245	$111,667
Apply § 291 percentage	20%
Ordinary income under § 291	$ 22,333

(handwritten right margin: only corp. not personal)

For a corporate taxpayer, $22,333 of the $111,667 gain would be ordinary, and $89,334 would be § 1231 gain. ◆

Passive Losses

The passive loss rules apply to noncorporate taxpayers and to closely held C corporations and personal service corporations (PSCs).[17] For S corporations and partnerships, passive income or loss flows through to the owners, and the passive loss rules are applied at the owner level. The passive loss rules are applied to closely held corporations and to PSCs to prevent taxpayers from incorporating to avoid the passive loss limitation.

A corporation is closely held if, at any time during the taxable year, more than 50 percent of the value of the corporation's outstanding stock is owned, directly or indirectly, by or for not more than five individuals. A corporation is classified as a PSC for purposes of § 469 (passive loss provision) if it meets the following requirements:[18]

17. § 469(a).

18. § 469(j)(2).

- The principal activity of the corporation is the performance of personal services.
- Such services are substantially performed by owner-employees.
- More than 10 percent of the stock (in value) is held by owner-employees. *Any* stock held by an employee on *any* one day causes the employee to be an owner-employee.

The general passive activity loss rules apply to PSCs. Passive activity losses cannot be offset against either active income or portfolio income. The application of the passive activity rules is less harsh for closely held corporations. They may offset passive losses against active income, but not against portfolio income.

───────────────── EXAMPLE 17 ─────────────────

T Corporation, a closely held corporation, has $300,000 of passive losses from a rental activity, $200,000 of active business income, and $100,000 of portfolio income. The corporation may offset $200,000 of the $300,000 passive loss against the $200,000 active business income, but may not offset the remainder against the $100,000 of portfolio income. ◆

Individual taxpayers are not allowed to offset passive losses against *either* active or portfolio income.

Charitable Contributions

Both corporate and noncorporate taxpayers may deduct charitable contributions if the recipient is a qualified charitable organization. Generally, a deduction will be allowed only for the year in which the payment is made. However, an important exception is made for *accrual basis corporations*. They may claim the deduction in the year preceding payment if two requirements are met. First, the contribution must be authorized by the board of directors by the end of that year. Second, it must be paid on or before the fifteenth day of the third month of the next year.[19]

─────────────────── EXAMPLE 18 ───────────────────

On December 28, 1992, XYZ Company, a calendar year accrual basis taxpayer, authorizes a $5,000 donation to the Atlanta Symphony Association (a qualified charitable organization). The donation is made on March 14, 1993. If XYZ Company is a partnership, the contribution can be deducted only in 1993.[20] ◆

─────────────────── EXAMPLE 19 ───────────────────

Assume the same facts as in Example 18, except that XYZ Company is a corporation. Presuming the December 28, 1992, authorization was made by its board of directors, XYZ Company may claim the $5,000 donation as a deduction for calendar year 1992. If it was not, the deduction may still be claimed for calendar year 1993. ◆

Property Contributions. The amount that can be deducted for a noncash charitable contribution depends on the type of property contributed. Property must be identified as long-term capital gain property or ordinary income property. Long-term capital gain property is property that, if sold, would result in long-term capital gain for the taxpayer. Such property generally must be a capital asset and must be held for the long-term holding period (more than one year). Ordinary income property is property that, if sold, would result in ordinary income for the taxpayer.

19. § 170(a)(2).
20. Each partner will pick up his or her allocable portion of the charitable contribution deduction as of December 31, 1993 (the end of the partnership's tax year). See Chapter 10.

The deduction for a charitable contribution of long-term capital gain property is generally measured by fair market value.

─────────────── EXAMPLE 20 ───────────────

In 1992, XYZ Corporation donated a parcel of land (a capital asset) to Oakland Community College. XYZ acquired the land in 1987 for $60,000, and the fair market value on the date of the contribution was $100,000. The corporation's charitable contribution deduction (subject to a percentage limitation discussed later) is measured by the asset's fair market value of $100,000, even though the $40,000 appreciation on the land has never been included in income. ◆

In two situations, a charitable contribution of long-term capital gain property is measured by the basis of the property, rather than fair market value. If the corporation contributes *tangible personal property* and the charitable organization puts the property to an unrelated use, the appreciation on the property is not deductible. Unrelated use is defined as use that is not related to the purpose or function that qualifies the organization for exempt status under § 501.

─────────────── EXAMPLE 21 ───────────────

X Corporation donates a painting worth $200,000 to Western States Art Museum (a qualified organization), which exhibits the painting. X Corporation had acquired the painting in 1980 for $90,000. Because the museum put the painting to a related use, X Corporation is allowed to deduct $200,000, the fair market value of the painting. ◆

─────────────── EXAMPLE 22 ───────────────

Assume the same facts as in the previous example, except that X Corporation donated the painting to the American Cancer Society, which sells the painting and deposits the $200,000 proceeds in the organization's general fund. X Corporation's deduction is limited to the $90,000 basis because it contributed tangible personal property that was put to an unrelated use by the charitable organization. ◆

The deduction for charitable contributions of long-term capital gain property to certain private nonoperating foundations [as defined in § 509(a)] is also limited to the basis of the property.

Ordinary income property is property that, if sold, would result in ordinary income. Examples of ordinary income property include inventory and capital assets that have not been held long term. In addition, § 1231 property (depreciable property used in a trade or business) is treated as ordinary income property to the extent of any ordinary income recaptured under § 1245 or § 1250. As a general rule, the deduction for a contribution of ordinary income property is limited to the basis of the property. However, corporations enjoy two special exceptions where 50 percent of the appreciation (but not to exceed twice the basis) on property is allowed on certain contributions. The first exception concerns inventory if the property is used in a manner related to the exempt purpose of the charity. Also, the charity must use the property solely for the care of the ill, the needy, or infants.

─────────────── EXAMPLE 23 ───────────────

Z Corporation, a grocery chain, donated canned goods to the Salvation Army to be used to feed the needy. Z's basis in the canned goods was $2,000, and the fair market value was $3,000. Z's deduction is $2,500 [$2,000 basis + 50% of ($3,000 − $2,000)]. ◆

The second exception involves gifts of scientific property to colleges and certain scientific research organizations for use in research, provided certain conditions are met.[21] As was true of the inventory exception, 50 percent of the appreciation on such property is allowed as an additional deduction.

Limitations Imposed on Charitable Contribution Deductions. Like individuals, corporations are not permitted an unlimited charitable contribution deduction.[22] For any one year, a corporate taxpayer's contribution deduction is limited to 10 percent of taxable income. For this purpose, taxable income is computed without regard to the charitable contribution deduction, any net operating loss carryback or capital loss carryback, and the dividends received deduction. Any contributions in excess of the 10 percent limitation may be carried forward to the five succeeding tax years. Any carryforward must be added to subsequent contributions and will be subject to the 10 percent limitation. In applying this limitation, the current year's contributions must be deducted first, with excess deductions from previous years deducted in order of time.[23]

―――――――――――――――――――― EXAMPLE 24 ――――――――――――――――――――

During 1992, T Corporation (a calendar year taxpayer) had the following income and expenses:

Income from operations	$140,000
Expenses from operations	110,000
Dividends received	10,000
Charitable contributions made in May 1992	5,000

For purposes of the 10% limitation *only*, T Corporation's taxable income is $40,000 ($140,000 – $110,000 + $10,000). Consequently, the allowable charitable deduction for 1992 is $4,000 (10% × $40,000). The $1,000 unused portion of the contribution can be carried forward to 1993, 1994, 1995, 1996, and 1997 (in that order) until exhausted. ◆

―――――――――――――――――――― EXAMPLE 25 ――――――――――――――――――――

Assume the same facts as in Example 24. In 1993, T Corporation has taxable income (for purposes of the 10% limitation) of $50,000 and makes a charitable contribution of $4,500. The maximum deduction allowed for 1993 would be $5,000 (10% × $50,000). The first $4,500 of the allowed deduction must be allocated to the contribution made in 1993, and $500 of the balance is carried over from 1992. The remaining $500 of the 1992 contribution may be carried over to 1994, etc. ◆

Net Operating Losses *Know*

Like the net operating loss (NOL) of an individual, the NOL of a corporation may be carried back 3 years and forward 15 to offset taxable income for those years. A corporation does not adjust its tax loss for the year for capital losses as do individual taxpayers, because a corporation is not permitted a deduction for net capital losses. Nor does a corporation make adjustments for nonbusiness deductions as do individual taxpayers. Further, a corporation is allowed to include the dividends received deduction (discussed below) in computing its NOL.[24]

---

21. These conditions are set forth in § 170(e)(4). For the inventory exception, see § 170(e)(3).

22. The percentage limitations applicable to individuals and corporations are set forth in § 170(b).

23. The carryover rules relating to all taxpayers are in § 170(d).

24. The modifications required to arrive at the amount of net operating loss that can be carried back or forward are in § 172(d).

EXAMPLE 26

In 1992, X Corporation has gross income (including dividends) of $200,000 and deductions of $300,000 excluding the dividends received deduction. X Corporation had received taxable dividends of $100,000 from Exxon stock. X Corporation has an NOL computed as follows:

Gross income (including dividends)		$200,000
Less:		
Business deductions	$300,000	
Dividends received deduction		
(70% of $100,000)	70,000	370,000
Taxable income (or loss)		($170,000)

The NOL is carried back three years to 1989. (X Corporation may forgo the carryback option and elect instead to carry forward the loss.) Assume X Corporation had taxable income of $40,000 in 1989. The carryover to 1990 is computed as follows:

Taxable income for 1989	$ 40,000
Less NOL carryback	170,000
Taxable income for 1989 after NOL carryback (carryover to 1990)	($130,000)

◆

Deductions Available Only to Corporations

Dividends Received Deduction. The purpose of the dividends received deduction is to prevent triple taxation. Without the deduction, income paid to a corporation in the form of a dividend would be subject to taxation for a second time (once to the distributing corporation) with no corresponding deduction to the distributing corporation. Later, when the recipient corporation paid the income to its individual shareholders, the income would again be subject to taxation with no corresponding deduction to the corporation. The dividends received deduction alleviates this inequity by causing only some or none of the dividend income to be subject to taxation at the corporate level.

As the following table illustrates, the amount of the dividends received deduction depends upon the percentage of ownership the recipient corporate shareholder holds in a domestic corporation making the dividend distribution.[25]

Percentage of Ownership by Corporate Shareholder	Deduction Percentage
Less than 20%	70%
20% or more (but less than 80%)	80%
80% or more*	100%

*The payor corporation must be a member of an affiliated group with the recipient corporation.

The dividends received deduction is limited to a percentage of the taxable income of a corporation. For this purpose, taxable income is computed without regard to the NOL, the dividends received deduction, and any capital loss

25. § 243(a).

carryback to the current tax year. The percentage of taxable income limitation corresponds to the deduction percentage. Thus, if a corporate shareholder owns less than 20 percent of the stock in the distributing corporation, the dividends received deduction is limited to 70 percent of taxable income. However, the taxable income limitation does not apply if the corporation has an NOL for the current taxable year.[26]

In working with this myriad of rules, the following steps must be taken:

1. Multiply the dividends received by the deduction percentage.
2. Multiply the taxable income by the deduction percentage.
3. The deduction is limited to the lesser of Step 1 or Step 2, unless subtracting the amount derived in Step 1 from 100 percent of taxable income *generates* an NOL. If so, the amount derived in Step 1 should be used. This is referred to as the NOL rule.

--- EXAMPLE 27 ---

P, R, and T Corporations, three unrelated calendar year corporations, have the following transactions for 1992:

	P Corporation	R Corporation	T Corporation
Gross income from operations	$ 400,000	$ 320,000	$ 260,000
Expenses from operations	(340,000)	(340,000)	(340,000)
Dividends received from domestic corporations (less than 20% ownership)	200,000	200,000	200,000
Taxable income before the dividends received deduction	$ 260,000	$ 180,000	$ 120,000

In determining the dividends received deduction, use the three-step procedure described above:

Step 1 (70% × $200,000)	$140,000	$140,000	$140,000
Step 2			
70% × $260,000 (taxable income)	$182,000		
70% × $180,000 (taxable income)		$126,000	
70% × $120,000 (taxable income)			$ 84,000
Step 3			
Lesser of Step 1 or Step 2	$140,000	$126,000	
Deduction generates an NOL			$140,000

◆

R Corporation is subject to the 70 percent of taxable income limitation. It does not qualify for NOL rule treatment since subtracting $140,000 (Step 1) from $180,000 (100 percent of taxable income) does not yield a negative figure. T Corporation does qualify for NOL rule treatment because subtracting $140,000 (Step 1) from $120,000 (100 percent of taxable income) yields a negative figure. In summary, each corporation has a dividends received deduction for 1992 as follows: $140,000 for P Corporation, $126,000 for R Corporation, and $140,000 for T Corporation.

Deduction of Organizational Expenditures. Expenses incurred in connection with the organization of a corporation normally are chargeable to a capital account. That they benefit the corporation during its existence seems clear. But

---

26. § 246(b).

how can they be amortized when most corporations possess unlimited life? The lack of a determinable and limited estimated useful life would therefore preclude any tax write-off. Code § 248 was enacted to solve this problem.

Under § 248, a corporation may elect to amortize organizational expenditures over a period of 60 months or more. The period begins with the month in which the corporation begins business.[27] Organizational expenditures *subject to the election* include the following:

- Legal services incident to organization (e.g., drafting the corporate charter, bylaws, minutes of organizational meetings, terms of original stock certificates).
- Necessary accounting services.
- Expenses of temporary directors and of organizational meetings of directors or shareholders.
- Fees paid to the state of incorporation.

Expenditures that *do not qualify* include those connected with issuing or selling shares of stock or other securities (e.g., commissions, professional fees, and printing costs) or with the transfer of assets to a corporation. Such expenditures reduce the amount of capital raised and are not deductible at all.

To qualify for the election, the expenditure must be *incurred* before the end of the taxable year in which the corporation begins business. In this regard, the corporation's method of accounting is of no consequence. Thus, an expense incurred by a cash basis corporation in its first tax year qualifies even though not paid until a subsequent year.

The election is made in a statement attached to the corporation's return for its first taxable year. The return and statement must be filed no later than the due date of the return (including any extensions). The statement must set forth the description and amount of the expenditure involved. Also, it should include the date the expenditures were incurred, the month in which the corporation began business, and the number of months (not less than 60) over which the expenditures are to be deducted ratably.

If the election is not made on a timely basis, organizational expenditures cannot be deducted until the corporation ceases to do business and liquidates. These expenditures will be deductible if the corporate charter limits the life of the corporation.

─────────────────── EXAMPLE 28 ───────────────────

T Corporation, an accrual basis taxpayer, was formed and began operations on May 1, 1992. The following expenses were incurred during its first year of operations (May 1– December 31, 1992):

Expenses of temporary directors and of organizational meetings	$500
Fee paid to the state of incorporation	100
Accounting services incident to organization	200
Legal services for drafting the corporate charter and bylaws	400
Expenses incident to the printing and sale of stock certificates	300

Assume T Corporation makes a timely election under § 248 to amortize qualifying organizational expenses over a period of 60 months. The monthly amortization is $20 [($500 + $100 + $200 + $400) ÷ 60 months], and $160 ($20 × 8 months) is deductible

─────────────────────────────

27. The month in which a corporation begins business may not be immediately apparent. See Reg. § 1.248–1(a)(3). For a similar problem in the Subchapter S area, see Chapter 12.

for tax year 1992. Note that the $300 of expenses incident to the printing and sale of stock certificates does not qualify for the election. These expenses cannot be deducted at all but reduce the amount of the capital realized from the sale of stock. ◆

Organizational expenditures are to be distinguished from start-up expenditures covered by § 195. Start-up expenditures refer to various investigation expenses involved in entering a new business, whether incurred by a corporate or a noncorporate taxpayer. At the election of the taxpayer, such expenditures (e.g., travel, market surveys, financial audits, legal fees) can be amortized over a period of 60 months or longer rather than capitalized as part of the cost of the business acquired.

DETERMINING THE CORPORATE INCOME TAX LIABILITY
◆

Corporate Income Tax Rates

Although corporate income tax rates have fluctuated widely over past years, the general trend has been a reduction in rates. Refer to the inside front cover of the text for a schedule of current corporate income tax rates.

——————— EXAMPLE 29 ———————

X Corporation, a calendar year taxpayer, has taxable income of $90,000 for 1992. Its income tax liability is $18,850, determined as follows: $7,500 (15% × $50,000) + $6,250 (25% × $25,000) + $5,100 (34% × $15,000). ◆

For a corporation that has taxable income in excess of $100,000 for any taxable year, the amount of the tax is increased by the lesser of (1) 5 percent of the excess or (2) $11,750. In effect, the additional tax means a 39 percent rate for every dollar of taxable income from $100,000 to $335,000.[28]

——————— EXAMPLE 30 ———————

Y Corporation, a calendar year taxpayer, has taxable income of $335,000 for 1992. Its income tax liability is $113,900, determined as follows: $7,500 (15% × $50,000) + $6,250 (25% × $25,000) + $88,400 (34% × $260,000) + $11,750 (5% × $235,000). Note that the tax liability of $113,900 is 34% of $335,000. Thus, due to the 5% additional tax on taxable income between $100,000 and $335,000, the benefit of the lower rates on the first $75,000 of taxable income completely phases out at $335,000. ◆

Qualified PSCs are taxed at a flat 34 percent rate on all taxable income. Thus, PSCs do not enjoy the tax savings of being in the 15 percent (on the first $50,000) and 25 percent (on the next $25,000) brackets applicable to other corporations. For this purpose, a qualified PSC is one that is substantially employee owned. Also, it must engage in one of the following activities: health, law, engineering, architecture, accounting, actuarial science, performing arts, or consulting.

Alternative Minimum Tax

Corporations are subject to an alternative minimum tax (AMT) that is similar to the AMT applicable to individuals. The AMT for corporations, as for individuals, involves a more expansive tax base than does the regular tax. Like individuals, the corporation is required to apply a minimum tax rate to the expanded base and pay the difference between the AMT tax liability and the regular tax. Many of the adjustments and tax preference items necessary to arrive at alternative minimum taxable income (AMTI) are the same for individuals and corporations.

28. § 11(b).

Although the objective of the AMT is the same for individual and corporate taxpayers, the rate and exemptions are different. Computation of the AMT for corporations is discussed in Chapter 6.

Tax Liability of Related Corporations

Related corporations are subject to special rules for computing the income tax, the accumulated earnings credit, the AMT exemption, and the environmental tax exemption.[29] If these restrictions did not exist, the shareholders of a corporation could gain significant tax advantages by splitting a single corporation into *multiple* corporations. The next two examples illustrate the potential *income tax* advantage of multiple corporations.

─────────────── EXAMPLE 31 ───────────────

X Corporation annually yields taxable income of $300,000. The corporate tax on $300,000 is $100,250, computed as follows:

15% of $50,000	$ 7,500
25% of $25,000	6,250
34% of $225,000	76,500
5% of $200,000	10,000
Tax liability	$100,250

◆

─────────────── EXAMPLE 32 ───────────────

Assume the business in the previous example is divided equally among four corporations. Each corporation would have taxable income of $75,000, and the tax for each would be computed as follows:

15% of $50,000	$ 7,500
25% of $25,000	6,250
Tax liability	$13,750

The total liability for the four corporations would be $55,000 ($13,750 × 4). The savings would be $45,250 ($100,250 − $55,000). ◆

To preclude the advantages that could be gained by using multiple corporations, the tax law requires special treatment for *controlled groups* of corporations. A comparison of Examples 31 and 32 reveals that the income tax savings that could be achieved by using multiple corporations results from having more of the total income taxed at lower rates. To close this potential loophole, the law provides that controlled groups are limited to taxable income in the first two tax brackets (the 15 percent and 25 percent brackets) as though they were one corporation. Thus, in Example 32, under the controlled corporation rules, only $12,500 (one-fourth of the first $50,000 of taxable income) for each of the four related corporations would be taxed at the 15 percent rate. The 25 percent rate would apply to the next $6,250 (one-fourth of the next $25,000) of taxable income of each corporation. This equal allocation of the $50,000 and $25,000 amounts is required unless all members of the controlled group consent to an apportionment plan providing for an unequal allocation.

Similar limitations apply to the $250,000 accumulated earnings credit for controlled groups and to the $40,000 exemption amount for purposes of computing the AMT. Both the accumulated earnings tax and the AMT are discussed in Chapter 6.

───────────────

29. § 1561(a).

Know

Controlled Groups

A controlled group of corporations includes parent-subsidiary groups, brother-sister groups, combined groups, and certain insurance companies. Groups of the first three types are discussed in the following sections. Insurance groups are not discussed in this text.

Parent-Subsidiary Controlled Group. A parent-subsidiary controlled group consists of one or more *chains* of corporations connected through stock ownership with a common parent corporation. The ownership connection can be established through either a *voting power test* or a *value test.* The voting power test requires ownership of stock possessing at least 80 percent of the total voting power of all classes of stock entitled to vote.[30]

EXAMPLE 33

P Corporation owns 80% of S Corporation. P and S Corporations are members of a parent-subsidiary controlled group. P is the parent corporation, and S Corporation is the subsidiary. ◆

The parent-subsidiary relationship illustrated in Example 33 is easy to see because P Corporation is the direct owner of S Corporation. Real-world business organizations are often much more complex, sometimes including numerous corporations with chains of ownership connecting them. In these complex corporate structures, determining whether the controlled group classification is appropriate becomes more difficult. The ownership requirements can be met through direct ownership (refer to Example 33) or through indirect ownership, as illustrated in the two following examples.

EXAMPLE 34

X Corporation owns 80% of the voting stock of Y Corporation, and Y Corporation owns 80% of the voting stock of Z Corporation. X, Y, and Z Corporations constitute a controlled group in which X is the common parent and Y and Z are subsidiaries. The same result would occur if X Corporation, rather than Y Corporation, owned the Z Corporation stock. This parent-subsidiary relationship is diagrammed in Figure 2–2. ◆

FIGURE 2–2
Controlled Groups—Parent-Subsidiary Corporations

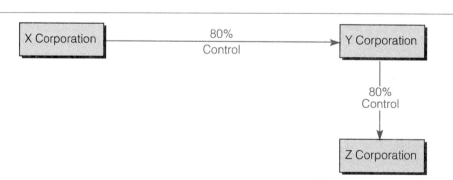

X is the common parent of a parent-subsidiary
controlled group consisting of X, Y, and Z Corporations.

---

30. § 1563(a)(1).

EXAMPLE 35

X Corporation owns 80% of the stock of Y Corporation, which owns 30% of Z Corporation. X also owns 80% of A Corporation, which owns 50% of Z Corporation. X, Y, Z and A Corporations constitute a parent-subsidiary controlled group in which X is the common parent and Y, Z and A are subsidiaries. This parent-subsidiary relationship is diagrammed in Figure 2–3. ◆

The value test requires ownership of at least 80 percent of the total value of all shares of all classes of stock of each of the corporations, except the parent corporation, by one or more of the other corporations.

Brother-Sister Corporations. A brother-sister controlled group *may* exist if two or more corporations are owned by five or fewer *persons* (individuals, estates, or trusts). Brother-sister status will apply if such a shareholder group meets an 80 percent total ownership test *and* a 50 percent common ownership test.[31]

- The *total* ownership test is met if the shareholder group possesses stock representing at least 80 percent of the total combined voting power of all classes of stock entitled to vote, *or* at least 80 percent of the total value of shares of all classes of stock of each corporation.
- The *common* ownership test is met if the shareholder group owns more than 50 percent of the total combined voting power of all classes of stock entitled to vote, *or* more than 50 percent of the total value of shares of all classes of stock of each corporation.

In applying the common ownership test, the stock held by each person is considered only to the extent that the stock ownership is *identical* for each corporation. That is, if a shareholder owns 30 percent of X Corporation and 20 percent of Y Corporation, such shareholder has identical ownership of 20 percent of each corporation.

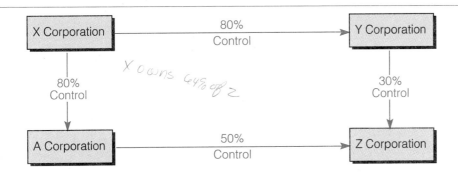

X is the common parent of a parent-subsidiary
controlled group consisting of X,Y,Z, and A Corporations.*
*Reg. § 1.1563–1(a)(2).

FIGURE 2–3
Controlled Groups—Parent-Subsidiary Corporations

---

31. § 1563(a)(2).

———————— EXAMPLE 36 ————————

The outstanding stock of Corporations W, X, Y, and Z, each of which has only one class of stock outstanding, is owned by the following unrelated individuals:

Individuals	Corporations W	X	Y	Z	Identical Ownership
A	40%	30%	60%	60%	30%
B	50%	20%	30%	20%	20%
C	10%	30%	10%	10%	10%
D		20%		10%	
Total	100%	100%	100%	100%	60%

Five or fewer individuals (A, B, and C) with more than a 50% common ownership own at least 80% of all classes of stock in W, X, Y, and Z. They own 100% of W, 80% of X, 100% of Y, and 90% of Z. Consequently, W, X, Y, and Z are regarded as members of a brother-sister controlled group. ◆

———————— EXAMPLE 37 ————————

Changing the facts in Example 36, assume the ownership is as follows:

Individuals	Corporations W	X	Y	Z	Identical Ownership
A	20%	10%	5%	60%	5%
B	10%	20%	60%	5%	5%
C	10%	70%	35%	25%	10%
D	60%			10%	
Total	100%	100%	100%	100%	20% *Not 50%*

In this instance, the identical ownership is only 20%. Consequently, the four corporations are not members of a brother-sister controlled group. X and Y would be brother-sister corporations because both the total ownership and the common ownership tests are met. A, B, and C own 100% of each corporation, and common ownership exceeds 50% (5% by A, 20% by B, and 35% by C). ◆

———————— EXAMPLE 38 ————————

The outstanding stock of Corporations X and Y, each of which has only one class of stock outstanding, is owned as follows:

Individuals	Corporations X	Y	Identical Ownership
A	55%	100%	55%
B	45%		
Total	100%	100%	55%

Although the 50% common ownership test is met, the 80% test is not since there is no common ownership in Y Corporation. Are X and Y brother-sister corporations? No, according to the U.S. Supreme Court.[32] ◆

———

32. *U.S. v. Vogel Fertilizer Co.*, 82–1 USTC ¶9134, 49 AFTR2d 82–491, 102 S.Ct. 821 (USSC, 1982). See also Reg. § 1.1563–1(a)(3), which was amended to comply with the conclusions reached in *Vogel*.

Combined Groups.   A combined controlled group exists if all of the following conditions are met:

- Each corporation is a member of either a parent-subsidiary controlled group or a brother-sister controlled group.
- At least one of the corporations is a parent of a parent-subsidiary controlled group.
- The parent corporation is also a member of a brother-sister controlled group.

─────────── EXAMPLE 39 ───────────

A, an individual, owns 80% of all classes of stock of X and Z Corporations. X Corporation, in turn, owns 80% of all classes of stock of Y Corporation. Z owns all the stock of W Corporation. X, Y, Z, and W are members of the same combined group. As a result, X, Y, Z, and W are limited to taxable income in the first two tax brackets and the $250,000 accumulated earnings credit as though they were one corporation. This is also the case for the election to expense certain depreciable business assets under § 179 and the $40,000 exemption for purposes of computing the AMT. ◆

Application of § 482.   Congress has recognized that a parent corporation has the power to shift income among its subsidiaries. Likewise, shareholders who control brother-sister groups can shift income and deductions among the related corporations.

When the true taxable income of a subsidiary or other related corporation has been understated or overstated, the IRS can reallocate the income and deductions of the related corporations under § 482. Section 482 permits the IRS to allocate gross income, deductions, and credits between any two or more organizations, trades, or businesses that are owned or controlled by the same interests. This is appropriate when the allocation is necessary to prevent evasion of taxes or to reflect income correctly. Controlled groups of corporations are particularly vulnerable to § 482.

Filing Requirements for Corporations

A corporation must file a Federal income tax return whether or not it has taxable income.[33] A corporation that was not in existence throughout an entire annual accounting period is required to file a return for the fraction of the year during which it was in existence. In addition, a corporation must file a return even though it has ceased to do business if it has valuable claims for which it will bring suit. A corporation is relieved of filing income tax returns only when it ceases to do business and retains no assets.

The corporate return is filed on Form 1120 unless the corporation is a small corporation entitled to file the shorter Form 1120–A. Corporations may file Form 1120–A if *all* the following requirements are met:

- Gross receipts or sales do not exceed $500,000.
- Total income (gross profit plus other income including gains on sales of property) does not exceed $500,000.
- Total assets do not exceed $500,000.
- The corporation is not involved in a dissolution or liquidation.

───────────

33. § 6012(a)(2).

- The corporation is not a member of a controlled group under §§ 1561 and 1563.
- The corporation does not file a consolidated return.
- The corporation does not have ownership in a foreign corporation.
- The corporation does not have foreign shareholders who directly or indirectly own 50 percent or more of its stock.

Corporations electing under Subchapter S (see Chapter 12) file on Form 1120S. Forms 1120, 1120–A, and 1120S are reproduced in Appendix B.

The return must be filed on or before the fifteenth day of the third month following the close of a corporation's tax year. As noted previously, a regular corporation can use either a calendar or a fiscal year to report its taxable income. The tax year of the shareholders has no effect on the corporation's tax year.

Corporations can receive an automatic extension of six months for filing the corporate return by filing Form 7004 by the due date for the return.[34] However, the IRS may terminate the extension by mailing a 10-day notice to the taxpayer corporation. A Form 7004 must be accompanied by the corporation's estimated tax liability.

Estimated Tax Payments

A corporation must make payments of estimated tax unless its tax liability can reasonably be expected to be less than $500. For tax years beginning in 1992, the required annual payment (which includes any estimated AMT liability) is the lesser of (1) 93 percent of the corporation's final tax or (2) 100 percent of the tax for the preceding year (if that was a 12-month tax year and the return filed showed a tax liability).[35] Estimated payments can be made in four installments due on or before the fifteenth day of the fourth month, the sixth month, the ninth month, and the twelfth month of the corporate taxable year. The full amount of the unpaid tax is due on the due date of the return. For a calendar year corporation, the payment dates are as follows:

April 15

June 15

September 15

December 15

A corporation failing to pay 93 percent of its final tax liability as estimated tax payments will be subjected to a nondeductible penalty on the amount by which the installments are less than 93 percent of the tax due. However, the underpayment penalty will not be imposed if the estimated payments are timely and are either equal to the tax liability of the corporation for the prior year or equal to 93 percent of the tax due computed on an annualized basis. If the annualized method is used for one installment and the corporation does not use this method for a subsequent installment, any shortfall from using the annualized method for a prior payment(s) must be made up in the subsequent installment payment. The penalty is imposed on each installment; that is, a corporation must pay one-fourth of its required annual payment by the due date of each installment.

---

34. § 6081.

35. §§ 6655(d) and (e) as amended by the Tax Extension Act of 1991.

A *large* corporation cannot base its installment payments on its previous year's tax liability except for its first installment payment. A large corporation is one with taxable income in excess of $1 million in any of its three preceding years.

Reconciliation of Taxable Income and Financial Net Income

Schedule M–1 on the last page of Form 1120 is used to reconcile net income as computed for financial accounting purposes with taxable income reported on the corporation's income tax return. The starting point on Schedule M–1 is net income per books (financial accounting net income). Additions and subtractions are entered for items that affect net income per books and taxable income differently. The following items are entered as additions (see lines 2 through 5 of Schedule M–1):

- Federal income tax liability (deducted in computing net income per books but not deductible in computing taxable income).
- The excess of capital losses over capital gains (deducted for financial accounting purposes but not deductible by corporations for income tax purposes).
- Income that is reported in the current year for tax purposes that is not reported in computing net income per books (e.g., prepaid income).
- Various expenses that are deducted in computing net income per books but not allowed in computing taxable income (e.g., charitable contributions in excess of the 10 percent ceiling applicable to corporations).

The following subtractions are entered on lines 7 and 8 of Schedule M–1:

- Income reported for financial accounting purposes but not included in taxable income (e.g., tax-exempt interest).
- Expenses deducted on the tax return but not deducted in computing net income per books (e.g., a charitable contributions carryover deducted in a prior year for financial accounting purposes but deductible in the current year for tax purposes).

The result is taxable income (before the NOL deduction and the dividends received deduction).

─────────────────── **EXAMPLE 40** ───────────────────

During the current year, T Corporation had the following transactions:

Net income per books (after tax)	$92,400
Taxable income	50,000
Federal income tax liability (15% × $50,000)	7,500
Interest income from tax-exempt bonds	(5,000)
Interest paid on loan, the proceeds of which were used to purchase the tax-exempt bonds	500
Life insurance proceeds received as a result of the death of a key employee	(50,000)
Premiums paid on key employee life insurance policy	2,600
Excess of capital losses over capital gains	2,000

For book and tax purposes, T Corporation determines depreciation under the straight-line method. T Corporation's Schedule M–1 for the current year is as follows:

Schedule M-1	Reconciliation of Income per Books With Income per Return *(This schedule does not have to be completed if the total assets on line 15, column (d), of Schedule L are less than $25,000.)*				
1	Net income per books	92,400	7	Income recorded on books this year not included on this return (itemize):	
2	Federal income tax	7,500			
3	Excess of capital losses over capital gains	2,000	a	Tax-exempt interest $ ...$5,000..Life insurance proceeds on key employee $50,000	55,000
4	Income subject to tax not recorded on books this year (itemize):				
	....		8	Deductions on this return not charged against book income this year (itemize):	
5	Expenses recorded on books this year not deducted on this return (itemize):		a	Depreciation . . . . $	
a	Depreciation . . . . $		b	Contributions carryover $	
b	Contributions carryover $			....	
c	Travel and entertainment $ ...Int..on... tax-exempt bonds $500 Prem. on key employee ins. $2,600	3,100	9	Add lines 7 and 8	55,000
6	Add lines 1 through 5	105,000	10	Income (line 28, page 1)—line 6 less line 9	50,000

Schedule M–2 reconciles unappropriated retained earnings at the beginning of the year with unappropriated retained earnings at year-end. Beginning balance plus net income per books, as entered on line 1 of Schedule M–1, less dividend distributions during the year equals ending retained earnings. Other sources of increases or decreases in retained earnings are also listed on Schedule M–2.

——————————— EXAMPLE 41 ———————————

Assume the same facts as in Example 40. T Corporation's beginning balance in unappropriated retained earnings is $125,000. During the year, T Corporation distributed a cash dividend of $30,000 to its shareholders. Based on these further assumptions, T Corporation's Schedule M–2 for the current year is as follows:

Schedule M-2	Analysis of Unappropriated Retained Earnings per Books (Line 25, Schedule L) *(This schedule does not have to be completed if the total assets on line 15, column (d), of Schedule L are less than $25,000.)*				
1	Balance at beginning of year	125,000	5	Distributions: a Cash	30,000
2	Net income per books	92,400		b Stock	
3	Other increases (itemize):			c Property	
	....		6	Other decreases (itemize):	
	....				
			7	Add lines 5 and 6	30,000
4	Add lines 1, 2, and 3	217,400	8	Balance at end of year (line 4 less line 7)	187,400

◆

Form 1120 Illustrated

Swift Corporation was formed on January 10, 1985, by James Brown and Martha Swift to sell men's clothing. Pertinent information regarding Swift is summarized as follows:

- The business address is 6210 Norman Street, Buffalo, TX 79330.
- The employer identification number is 75–3284680; the principal business activity code is 5600.
- James Brown and Martha Swift each own one-half of the outstanding common stock; no other class of stock is authorized. James Brown is president of the company, and Martha Swift is secretary-treasurer. Both are full-time employees of the corporation, and each has a salary of $70,000. James's Social Security number is 299–50–2593; Martha's Social Security number is 400–40–6680.

■ The corporation uses the accrual method of accounting and reports on a calendar basis. The specific chargeoff method is used in handling bad debt losses, and inventories are determined using the lower of cost or market method. For book and tax purposes, the straight-line method of depreciation is used.

■ During 1991, the corporation distributed a cash dividend of $35,000. Selected portions of Swift's profit and loss statement reflect the following debits and credits:

Account	Debit	Credit
Gross sales		$1,040,000
Sales returns and allowances	$ 50,000	
Purchases	506,000	
Dividends received from stock investments in less than 20% owned U.S. corporations		60,000
Interest income		
State bonds	$ 9,000	
Certificates of deposit	11,000	20,000
Premiums on term life insurance policies on the lives of James Brown and Martha Swift; Swift Corporation is the designated beneficiary	8,000	
Salaries—officers	140,000	
Salaries—clerical and sales	100,000	
Taxes (state, local, and payroll)	35,000	
Repairs	20,000	
Interest expense		
Loan to purchase state bonds	$ 4,000	
Other business loans	10,000	14,000
Advertising	8,000	
Rental expense	24,000	
Depreciation	16,000	
Other deductions	21,000	

A comparative balance sheet for Swift Corporation reveals the following information:

Assets	January 1, 1991	December 31, 1991
Cash	$ 240,000	$ 165,550
Trade notes and accounts receivable	404,200	542,300
Inventories	300,000	356,000
Federal and state bonds	150,000	150,000
Buildings and other depreciable assets	120,000	120,000
Accumulated depreciation	(44,400)	(60,400)
Land	10,000	10,000
Other assets	1,800	1,000
Total assets	$1,181,600	$1,284,450

Liabilities and Equity	January 1, 1991	December 31, 1991
Accounts payable	$ 150,000	$ 125,000
Other current liabilities	40,150	33,300
Mortgages	105,000	100,000
Capital stock	250,000	250,000
Retained earnings	636,450	776,150
Total liabilities and equity	$1,181,600	$1,284,450

Net income per books (before any income tax accrual) is $234,000. During 1991, Swift Corporation made estimated tax payments to the IRS of $56,000. Swift Corporation's Form 1120 for 1991 is reproduced on the following pages.

Although most of the entries on Form 1120 for Swift Corporation are self-explanatory, the following comments may be helpful:

- In order to arrive at the cost of goods sold amount (line 2 on page 1), Schedule A (page 2) must be completed.
- Reporting of dividends requires the completion of Schedule C (page 2). Gross dividends are shown on line 4 (page 1), and the dividends received deduction appears on line 29b (page 1). Separating the dividend from the deduction facilitates the application of the 80 percent and 70 percent of taxable income exception (which did not apply in Swift's case).
- Income tax liability is $59,300, computed as follows:

15% of $50,000	$ 7,500
25% of $25,000	6,250
34% of $120,000 (taxable income in excess of $75,000)	40,800
5% of $95,000 (taxable income in excess of $100,000)	4,750
	$59,300

The result is transferred to line 3 of Schedule J and ultimately is listed on line 31 (page 1). Because the estimated tax payment of $56,000 is less than the tax liability of $59,300, Swift has a tax liability of $3,300.

- In completing Schedule M–1 (page 4), the net income per books (line 1) is net of the Federal income tax ($234,000 − $59,300). The left-hand side of Schedule M–1 (lines 2–5) represent positive adjustments to net income per books. After the negative adjustments are made (line 9), the result is taxable income before net operating losses and special deductions (line 28, page 1).
- In completing Schedule M–2 (page 4) the beginning retained earnings figure of $636,450 is added to the net income per books as entered on Schedule M–1 (line 1). The dividends distributed in the amount of $35,000 are entered on line 5 and subtracted to arrive at the ending balance in unappropriated retained earnings of $776,150.
- Because this example lacks certain details, supporting schedules that would be attached to Form 1120 have not been included. For example, a Form 4562 would be included to verify the depreciation deduction (line 20, page 1), and other deductions (line 26, page 1) would be supported by a schedule.

pg 1 of 1120

CHAPTER 2
CORPORATIONS: INTRODUCTION,
OPERATING RULES, AND RELATED
CORPORATIONS

◆

2–31

Form 1120
Department of the Treasury
Internal Revenue Service

U.S. Corporation Income Tax Return

For calendar year 1991 or tax year beginning ...., 1991, ending ...., 19 ...
▶ Instructions are separate. See page 1 for Paperwork Reduction Act Notice.

OMB No. 1545-0123

1991

A Check if a—	Use IRS label. Other-wise, please print or type.	Name	B Employer identification number
(1) Consolidated return (attach Form 851) ☐		Swift Corporation	75-3284680
(2) Personal holding co. (attach Sch. PH) ☐		Number, street, and room or suite no. (If a P.O. box, see page 6 of instructions.)	C Date incorporated
(3) Personal service corp. (as defined in Temp. Regs. sec. 1.441-4T— see instructions) ☐		6210 Norman Street	1-10-85
		City or town, state, and ZIP code	D Total assets (see Specific Instructions)
		Buffalo, TX 79330	$ 1,284,450 00

E Check applicable boxes: (1) ☐ Initial return (2) ☐ Final return (3) ☐ Change in address

Income Statement
RE

Income

1a	Gross receipts or sales ▶	1,040,000 00	b Less returns and allowances	50,000 00	c Bal ▶ 1c	990,000 00
2	Cost of goods sold (Schedule A, line 7)				2	450,000 00
3	Gross profit. Subtract line 2 from line 1c				3	540,000 00
4	Dividends (Schedule C, line 19)				4	60,000 00
5	Interest				5	11,000 00
6	Gross rents				6	
7	Gross royalties				7	
8	Capital gain net income (attach Schedule D (Form 1120))				8	
9	Net gain or (loss) from Form 4797, Part II, line 18 (attach Form 4797)				9	
10	Other income (see instructions—attach schedule)				10	
11	**Total income.** Add lines 3 through 10 ▶				11	611,000 00

Deductions (See instructions for limitations on deductions.)

12	Compensation of officers (Schedule E, line 4)				12	140,000 00
13a	Salaries and wages	100,000 00	b Less jobs credit		c Balance ▶ 13c	100,000 00
14	Repairs				14	20,000 00
15	Bad debts				15	
16	Rents				16	24,000 00
17	Taxes				17	35,000 00
18	Interest				18	10,000 00
19	Contributions (**see instructions for 10% limitation**)				19	
20	Depreciation (attach Form 4562)		20	16,000 00		
21	Less depreciation claimed on Schedule A and elsewhere on return	21a		21b	16,000 00
22	Depletion				22	
23	Advertising				23	8,000 00
24	Pension, profit-sharing, etc., plans				24	
25	Employee benefit programs				25	
26	Other deductions (attach schedule)				26	21,000 00
27	**Total deductions.** Add lines 12 through 26 ▶				27	374,000 00
28	Taxable income before net operating loss deduction and special deductions. Subtract line 27 from line 11				28	237,000 00
29	Less: a Net operating loss deduction (see instructions)		29a			
	b Special deductions (Schedule C, line 20)		29b	42,000 00	29c	42,000 00

Tax and Payments

30	**Taxable income.** Subtract line 29c from line 28				30	195,000 00
31	**Total tax** (Schedule J, line 10)				31	59,300 00
32	Payments: a 1990 overpayment credited to 1991	32a				
b	1991 estimated tax payments	32b	56,000 00			
c	Less 1991 refund applied for on Form 4466	32c (	) d Bal ▶	32d	56,000 00	
e	Tax deposited with Form 7004		32e			
f	Credit from regulated investment companies (attach Form 2439)		32f			
g	Credit for Federal tax on fuels (attach Form 4136). See instructions		32g		32h	56,000 00
33	Estimated tax penalty (see page 4 of instructions). Check if Form 2220 is attached ▶ ☐				33	
34	**Tax due.** If the total of lines 31 and 33 is larger than line 32h, enter amount owed				34	3,300 00
35	**Overpayment.** If line 32h is larger than the total of lines 31 and 33, enter amount overpaid				35	
36	Enter amount of line 35 you want: **Credited to 1992 estimated tax** ▶ Refunded ▶				36	

Please Sign Here

Under penalties of perjury, I declare that I have examined this return, including accompanying schedules and statements, and to the best of my knowledge and belief, it is true, correct, and complete. Declaration of preparer (other than taxpayer) is based on all information of which preparer has any knowledge.

▶ Signature of officer	Date	▶ Title

Paid Preparer's Use Only

Preparer's signature ▶	Date	Check if self-employed ☐	Preparer's social security number
Firm's name (or yours if self-employed) and address ▶		E.I. No. ▶	
		ZIP code ▶	

Cat. No. 11450Q

look at

Consolidated Returns

Requirements.   Corporations that are members of a parent-subsidiary affiliated group, as defined in § 1504(a) of the Code, may file a consolidated income tax return for a taxable year. An affiliated group for this purpose is one or more chains of includible corporations connected through stock ownership with a common parent but only if the following requirements are met.

Pg 2 of 1120

Schedule A   Cost of Goods Sold (See instructions.)

1	Inventory at beginning of year	1	300,000	00
2	Purchases	2	506,000	00
3	Cost of labor	3		
4a	Additional section 263A costs (see instructions—attach schedule)	4a		
b	Other costs (attach schedule)	4b		
5	**Total.** Add lines 1 through 4b	5	806,000	00
6	Inventory at end of year	6	356,000	00
7	**Cost of goods sold.** Subtract line 6 from line 5. Enter here and on line 2, page 1	7	450,000	00

8a Check all methods used for valuing closing inventory:

    (i) ☐ Cost   (ii) ☒ Lower of cost or market as described in Regulations section 1.471-4 (see instructions)

    (iii) ☐ Writedown of "subnormal" goods as described in Regulations section 1.471-2(c) (see instructions)

    (iv) ☐ Other (Specify method used and attach explanation.) ▶ ....

  b Check if the LIFO inventory method was adopted this tax year for any goods (if checked, attach Form 970) . . . . . ▶ ☐

  c If the LIFO inventory method was used for this tax year, enter percentage (or amounts) of closing inventory computed under LIFO | 8c | |

  d Do the rules of section 263A (for property produced or acquired for resale) apply to the corporation? . . . . . ☐ Yes ☐ No

  e Was there any change in determining quantities, cost, or valuations between opening and closing inventory? If "Yes," attach explanation . . . . . ☐ Yes ☐ No

Schedule C   Dividends and Special Deductions (See instructions.)

		(a) Dividends received	(b) %	(c) Special deductions: (a) × (b)
1	Dividends from less-than-20%-owned domestic corporations that are subject to the 70% deduction (other than debt-financed stock)	60,000	70	42,000
2	Dividends from 20%-or-more-owned domestic corporations that are subject to the 80% deduction (other than debt-financed stock)		80	
3	Dividends on debt-financed stock of domestic and foreign corporations (section 246A)		see instructions	
4	Dividends on certain preferred stock of less-than-20%-owned public utilities		41.176	
5	Dividends on certain preferred stock of 20%-or-more-owned public utilities		47.059	
6	Dividends from less-than-20%-owned foreign corporations and certain FSCs that are subject to the 70% deduction		70	
7	Dividends from 20%-or-more-owned foreign corporations and certain FSCs that are subject to the 80% deduction		80	
8	Dividends from wholly owned foreign subsidiaries subject to the 100% deduction (section 245(b))		100	
9	**Total.** Add lines 1 through 8. See instructions for limitation			42,000
10	Dividends from domestic corporations received by a small business investment company operating under the Small Business Investment Act of 1958		100	
11	Dividends from certain FSCs that are subject to the 100% deduction (section 245(c)(1))		100	
12	Dividends from affiliated group members subject to the 100% deduction (section 243(a)(3))		100	
13	Other dividends from foreign corporations not included on lines 3, 6, 7, 8, or 11			
14	Income from controlled foreign corporations under subpart F (attach Forms 5471)			
15	Foreign dividend gross-up (section 78)			
16	IC-DISC and former DISC dividends not included on lines 1, 2, or 3 (section 246(d))			
17	Other dividends			
18	Deduction for dividends paid on certain preferred stock of public utilities (see instructions)			
19	**Total dividends.** Add lines 1 through 17. Enter here and on line 4, page 1 . . ▶	60,000		
20	**Total deductions.** Add lines 9, 10, 11, 12, and 18. Enter here and on line 29b, page 1 . . . . . ▶			42,000

Schedule E   Compensation of Officers (See instructions for line 12, page 1.)

Complete Schedule E only if total receipts (line 1a plus lines 4 through 10 of page 1, Form 1120) are $500,000 or more.

Compensat

	(a) Name of officer	(b) Social security number	(c) Percent of time devoted to business	(d) Common	(e) Preferred	(f) Amount of compensation
1	James Brown	299-50-2593	100 %	50 %	%	70,000
	Martha Swift	400-40-6680	100 %	50 %	%	70,000
			%	%	%	
			%	%	%	
			%	%	%	

2	Total compensation of officers		140,000
3	**Less:** Compensation of officers claimed on Schedule A and elsewhere on return	(	)
4	Compensation of officers deducted on line 12, page 1		140,000

1. the common parent owns stock that represents at least 80 percent of the total voting power *and* 80 percent of the total value of stock of at least one of the includible corporations and

2. stock representing at least 80 percent of the total voting power *and* 80 percent of the total value of stock in each of the includible corporations (except the common parent) is owned directly by one or more of the includible corporations.

Each corporation that has been a member of the group during any part of the taxable year for which the consolidated return is to be filed must consent by

Pg 3

CHAPTER 2
CORPORATIONS: INTRODUCTION,
OPERATING RULES, AND RELATED
CORPORATIONS
◆
2–33

Form 1120 (1991)   Page **3**

Schedule J   Tax Computation

1	Check if you are a member of a controlled group (see sections 1561 and 1563) . . . . . . ▶ ☐			
2	If the box on line 1 is checked:			
a	Enter your share of the $50,000 and $25,000 taxable income bracket amounts (in that order):			
	(i) | $ | | | (ii) | $ | | |			
b	Enter your share of the additional 5% tax (not to exceed $11,750) . . . . ▶ | $ | | |			
3	Income tax (see instructions to figure the tax). Check this box if the corporation is a qualified personal service corporation (see instructions on page 13) . . . . ▶ ☐	**3**	59,300	00
4a	Foreign tax credit (attach Form 1118)	4a		
b	Possessions tax credit (attach Form 5735)	4b		
c	Orphan drug credit (attach Form 6765)	4c		
d	Credit for fuel produced from a nonconventional source (see instructions) . . .	4d		
e	General business credit. Enter here and check which forms are attached: ☐ Form 3800 ☐ Form 3468 ☐ Form 5884 ☐ Form 6478 ☐ Form 6765 ☐ Form 8586 ☐ Form 8830 ☐ Form 8826	4e		
f	Credit for prior year minimum tax (attach Form 8827)	4f		
5	**Total.** Add lines 4a through 4f	**5**		
6	Subtract line 5 from line 3	**6**	59,300	00
7	Personal holding company tax (attach Schedule PH (Form 1120))	**7**		
8	Recapture taxes. Check if from: ☐ Form 4255 ☐ Form 8611	**8**		
9a	Alternative minimum tax (attach Form 4626). See instructions . . .	**9a**		
b	Environmental tax (attach Form 4626)	**9b**		
10	**Total tax.** Add lines 6 through 9b. Enter here and on line 31, page 1	**10**	59,300	00

Schedule K   Other Information (See page 15 of the instructions.)

		Yes	No
1	Check method of accounting:		
a	☐ Cash		
b	☒ Accrual		
c	☐ Other (specify) ▶		
2	Refer to the list in the instructions and state the principal:		
a	Business activity code no. ▶ 5600		
b	Business activity ▶ Sales		
c	Product or service ▶ Men's Clothing		
3	Did the corporation at the end of the tax year own, directly or indirectly, 50% or more of the voting stock of a domestic corporation? (For rules of attribution, see section 267(c).)		X
	If "Yes," attach a schedule showing: (a) name, address, and identifying number; (b) percentage owned; and (c) taxable income or (loss) before NOL and special deductions of such corporation for the tax year ending with or within your tax year.		
4	Did any individual, partnership, corporation, estate, or trust at the end of the tax year own, directly or indirectly, 50% or more of the corporation's voting stock? (For rules of attribution, see section 267(c).) If "Yes," complete a and b		X
a	Attach a schedule showing name, address, and identifying number.		
b	Enter percentage owned ▶		
5	Did one foreign person (see instructions for definition) at any time during the tax year own at least 25% of:		
a	The total voting power of all classes of stock of the corporation entitled to vote, or		
b	The total value of all classes of stock of the corporation?		X
	If "Yes," the corporation may have to file Form 5472.		
	If "Yes," enter owner's country(ies) ▶ .... Enter number of Forms 5472 attached ▶		

		Yes	No
6	Was the corporation a U.S. shareholder of any controlled foreign corporation? (See sections 951 and 957.)		X
	If "Yes," attach Form 5471 for each such corporation. Enter number of Forms 5471 attached ▶		
7	At any time during the tax year, did the corporation have an interest in or a signature or other authority over a financial account in a foreign country (such as a bank account, securities account, or other financial account)? (See page 15 of the instructions for more information, including filing requirements for Form TD F 90-22.1.)		X
	If "Yes," enter name of foreign country ▶		
8	Was the corporation the grantor of, or transferor to, a foreign trust that existed during the current tax year, whether or not the corporation has any beneficial interest in it?		X
	If "Yes," the corporation may have to file Forms 3520, 3520-A, or 926.		
9	During this tax year, did the corporation pay dividends (other than stock dividends and distributions in exchange for stock) in excess of the corporation's current and accumulated earnings and profits? (See sections 301 and 316.)		X
	If "Yes," file Form 5452. If this is a consolidated return, answer here for parent corporation and on **Form 851,** Affiliations Schedule, for each subsidiary.		
10	Check this box if the corporation issued publicly offered debt instruments with original issue discount . . ▶ ☐		
	If so, the corporation may have to file Form 8281.		
11	Enter the amount of tax-exempt interest received or accrued during the tax year ▶ | $ 9,000 | 00 |		
12	If there were 35 or fewer shareholders at the end of the tax year, enter the number ▶ 2		

filing Form 1122.[36] It may also consent by the actual filing of a consolidated return on Form 1120 with an affiliations schedule on Form 851 that includes all the member corporations. Once a consolidated return is filed, the controlled group must continue to file consolidated returns unless it secures permission from the IRS to discontinue the filing of such returns.[37] Applications to discontinue should be made to the IRS by the ninetieth day preceding the return's due date. A corporation that

---

36. § 1501 and Reg. §§ 1.1502–75(a) and (b).   **37.** Reg. § 1.1502–75(c).

Form 1120 (1991)
Page **4**

Schedule L — Balance Sheets

		Beginning of tax year		End of tax year	
	Assets	(a)	(b)	(c)	(d)
1	Cash		240,000		165,550
2a	Trade notes and accounts receivable		404,200		542,300
b	Less allowance for bad debts	( )		( )	
3	Inventories		300,000		356,000
4	U.S. government obligations		150,000		150,000
5	Tax-exempt securities (see instructions)				
6	Other current assets (attach schedule)				
7	Loans to stockholders				
8	Mortgage and real estate loans				
9	Other investments (attach schedule)				
10a	Buildings and other depreciable assets	120,000		120,000	
b	Less accumulated depreciation	44,400 ( )	75,600	60,400 ( )	59,600
11a	Depletable assets				
b	Less accumulated depletion	( )		( )	
12	Land (net of any amortization)		10,000		10,000
13a	Intangible assets (amortizable only)				
b	Less accumulated amortization	( )		( )	
14	Other assets (attach schedule)		1,800		1,000
15	Total assets		1,181,600		1,284,450
	Liabilities and Stockholders' Equity				
16	Accounts payable		150,000		125,000
17	Mortgages, notes, bonds payable in less than 1 year				
18	Other current liabilities (attach schedule)		40,150		33,300
19	Loans from stockholders				
20	Mortgages, notes, bonds payable in 1 year or more		105,000		100,000
21	Other liabilities (attach schedule)				
22	Capital stock: a Preferred stock				
	b Common stock	250,000	250,000	250,000	250,000
23	Paid-in or capital surplus				
24	Retained earnings—Appropriated (attach schedule)		636,450		776,150
25	Retained earnings—Unappropriated				
26	Less cost of treasury stock		( )		( )
27	Total liabilities and stockholders' equity		1,181,600		1,284,450

Schedule M-1 — Reconciliation of Income per Books With Income per Return (This schedule does not have to be completed if the total assets on line 15, column (d), of Schedule L are less than $25,000.)

1	Net income per books	174,700	7	Income recorded on books this year not included on this return (itemize):	
2	Federal income tax	59,300			
3	Excess of capital losses over capital gains		a	Tax-exempt interest $ 9,000	
4	Income subject to tax not recorded on books this year (itemize):				9,000
5	Expenses recorded on books this year not deducted on this return (itemize):		8	Deductions on this return not charged against book income this year (itemize):	
a	Depreciation . . . . $		a	Depreciation . . . . $	
b	Contributions carryover $		b	Contributions carryover $	
c	Travel and entertainment $				
	Prem.--life ins. . $8,000				
	Int.--state bonds, $4,000	12,000	9	Add lines 7 and 8	9,000
6	Add lines 1 through 5	246,000	10	Income (line 28, page 1)—line 6 less line 9	237,000

Schedule M-2 — Analysis of Unappropriated Retained Earnings per Books (Line 25, Schedule L) (This schedule does not have to be completed if the total assets on line 15, column (d), of Schedule L are less than $25,000.)

1	Balance at beginning of year	636,450	5	Distributions: a Cash	35,000
2	Net income per books	174,700		b Stock	
3	Other increases (itemize):			c Property	
			6	Other decreases (itemize):	
			7	Add lines 5 and 6	35,000
4	Add lines 1, 2, and 3	811,150	8	Balance at end of year (line 4 less line 7)	776,150

ceases to be a member of a consolidated group must generally wait five years before it can again file on a consolidated basis.

The privilege of filing a consolidated return is based on the concept that the affiliated group constitutes a single taxable entity despite the existence of technically separate businesses. By filing a consolidated return, the corporations can eliminate intercompany profits and losses on the principle that tax liability should be based on transactions with outsiders rather than on intragroup affairs.

The filing of consolidated returns is available only to parent-subsidiary affiliated groups; it is not available to brother-sister corporations.

Advantages and Disadvantages of Filing a Consolidated Return. Filing a consolidated return offers distinct advantages. Income of a profitable company is offset by losses of another. Capital losses of one corporation can offset capital gains of another. Without this possibility, net capital losses cannot be deducted in the year incurred as noted previously. Further, there is no § 482 problem. Section 482 permits the IRS to reallocate income and deductions among related organizations, trades, or businesses. The allocation is permitted when it is necessary to prevent evasion of taxes or to reflect income correctly.

Filing a consolidated return also has certain disadvantages. Losses on intercompany transactions must be deferred. Accounting for consolidated taxable income and deferral of intercompany transactions can be perplexing. Another problem is that the consolidated returns filed for tax purposes and the consolidated financial statements may not include the same corporations. For example, most foreign corporations cannot be consolidated for Federal income tax purposes but should be consolidated when preparing financial statements. This variance will cause some compliance problems in computing the taxable income and the AMT of the group.

Sections 1501–1504 and 1552 and the related Regulations, prescribing the manner of computing consolidated income, are quite complex. The rules for determining consolidated taxable income are discussed in Chapter 8.

CONCEPT SUMMARY 2–1
INCOME TAXES OF INDIVIDUALS AND CORPORATIONS COMPARED

	Individuals	Corporations
Computation of gross income	§ 61.	§ 61.
Computation of taxable income	§§ 62, 63(b) through (h).	§ 63(a). Concept of AGI has no relevance.
Deductions	Trade or business (§ 162); nonbusiness (§ 212); some personal and employee expenses (generally deductible as itemized deductions).	Trade or business (§ 162).
Charitable contributions	Limited in any tax year to 50% of AGI; 30% for long-term capital gain property unless election is made to reduce fair market value of gift.	Limited in any tax year to 10% of taxable income computed without regard to the charitable contribution deduction, net operating loss, and dividends received deduction.
	Excess charitable contributions carried over for five years.	Same as for individuals.
	Amount of contribution is the fair market value of long-term capital gain property; ordinary income property will be limited to adjusted basis; capital gain property will be treated as ordinary income property if certain tangible personalty is donated to a nonuse charity or a private nonoperating foundation is the donee.	Same as individuals, but exceptions allowed for certain inventory and for scientific property where one-half of the appreciation will be allowed as a deduction.
	Time of deduction—year in which payment is made.	Time of deduction—year in which payment is made unless accrual basis taxpayer. Accrual basis corporation can take deduction in year preceding payment if contribution was authorized by board of directors by end of year and contribution is paid by fifteenth day of third month of following year.
Casualty losses	$100 floor on personal casualty and theft losses; personal casualty losses deductible only to extent losses exceed 10% of AGI.	Deductible in full

	Individuals	Corporations
Depreciation recapture under § 1250	Recaptured to extent accelerated depreciation exceeds straight-line.	20% of excess of amount that would be recaptured under § 1245 over amount recaptured under § 1250 is additional ordinary income.
Net operating loss	Adjusted for several items, including nonbusiness deductions over nonbusiness income and personal exemptions.	Generally no adjustments.
	Carryback period is 3 years while carryforward period is 15 years.	Same as for individuals.
Dividends received deduction	None	70%, 80%, or 100% of dividends received depending on percentage of ownership by corporate shareholder.
Net capital gains	Taxed in full. Tax rate cannot exceed 28% for tax years beginning after 1990.	Taxed in full.
Capital losses	Only $3,000 of capital loss per year can offset ordinary income; loss is carried forward indefinitely to offset capital gains or ordinary income up to $3,000; carryovers retain their character as long term or short term.	Can offset only capital gains; carried back three years and forward five; carryovers and carrybacks are short-term losses.
Passive losses	Passive activity losses cannot be offset against either active income or portfolio income.	Passive loss rules apply to closely held C corporations and personal service corporations.
		For personal service corporations, the rule is the same as for individuals.
		For closely held corporations, passive losses may offset active income but not portfolio income.
Tax rates	Mildly progressive with three rates (15%, 28%, and 31%).	Mildly progressive with three rates (15%, 25%, and 34%); lower brackets phased out between $100,000 and $335,000 of taxable income.
Alternative minimum tax (see Chapter 6)	Applied at a 24% rate to AMTI; exemption allowed depending on filing status (e.g., $40,000 for married filing jointly); exemption phase-out begins when AMTI reaches a certain amount (e.g., $150,000 for married filing jointly).	Applied at a 20% rate on AMTI; $40,000 exemption allowed but phase-out begins when AMTI reaches $150,000; adjustments and tax preference items are similar to those applicable to individuals but also include 75% adjusted current earnings over AMTI.

TAX PLANNING CONSIDERATIONS

Corporate versus Noncorporate Forms of Business Organization

The decision to use the corporate form in conducting a trade or business must be weighed carefully. Besides the nontax considerations attendant to the corporate form (limited liability, continuity of life, free transferability of interest, and centralized management), tax ramifications will play an important role in any such decision. Close attention should be paid to the following:

1. Operating as a regular corporate entity (C corporation) results in the imposition of the corporate income tax. Corporate taxable income will be taxed twice—once as earned by the corporation and again when distributed to the shareholders. Since dividends are not deductible, a closely held corporation has a strong incentive to structure corporate distributions in a deductible form. Thus, profits can be bailed out by the shareholders in the form of salaries, interest, or rents. Such procedures

lead to a multitude of problems, one of which, the reclassification of debt as equity, is discussed in Chapter 3. The problems of unreasonable salaries and rents are covered in Chapter 4 in the discussion of constructive dividends.

2. Assuming the current tax rates remain in effect, the top rates favor the noncorporate taxpayer over the corporate taxpayer. For example, the top rate for individuals is 31 percent. For corporations, the top rate is 34 percent. The differential is not so pronounced, however, if a shareholder has a top rate of 31 percent and a corporation limits its taxable income to $100,000 to avoid the phase-out of the 15 percent and 25 percent lower brackets. Here, the time value of the taxes saved (by not distributing dividends and postponing the effect of the double tax that otherwise results) could make operating a business in the corporate form advantageous (refer to Example 5).

3. Corporate-source income loses its identity as it passes through the corporation to the shareholders. Thus, items possessing preferential tax treatment (e.g., interest on municipal bonds) are not taxed as such to the shareholders.

4. As noted in Chapter 4, it may be difficult for shareholders to recover some or all of their investment in the corporation without an ordinary income result. Most corporate distributions are treated as dividends to the extent of the corporation's earnings and profits.

5. Corporate losses cannot be passed through to the shareholders.[38]

6. The liquidation of a corporation will normally generate tax consequences to both the corporation and its shareholders (see Chapter 5).

7. The corporate form provides the shareholders with the opportunity to be treated as employees for tax purposes if the shareholders render services to the corporation. Such status makes a number of attractive tax-sheltered fringe benefits available. They include, but are not limited to, group term life insurance (§ 79), the $5,000 death benefit [§ 101(b)(1)], and excludible meals and lodging (§ 119). These benefits are not available to partners and sole proprietors.

The Association Route

Consideration 7 in the preceding section led to the popularity of the professional association. The major tax incentive involved was to cover the shareholder-employees under a qualified pension plan. Professionals, particularly physicians, who were not permitted to form regular corporations either because of prohibitions under state law or professional ethics restrictions, created organizations with sufficient corporate attributes to be classified as associations. The position of the IRS on the status of these professional associations (whether or not they should be treated as corporations for tax purposes) vacillated over a period of years. After a series of judicial losses, however, the IRS has accepted their association status, assuming certain conditions are satisfied.[39]

Over recent years, the popularity of the association approach has diminished significantly. Changes in the tax law have curtailed the deferral opportunities of qualified pension and profit sharing plans available to employees. At the same time, rules for H.R. 10 (Keogh) plans available to self-employed taxpayers have

---

38. Points 1, 2, and 5 could be resolved through a Subchapter S election (see Chapter 12), assuming the corporation qualifies for such an election. In part, the same can be said for point 3.

39. See, for example, *U.S. v. Empey*, 69–1 USTC ¶9158, 23 AFTR2d 69–425, 406 F.2d 157 (CA-10, 1969).

been liberalized. Since the two types of plans have been placed on a parity with each other, one of the major incentives to achieving employee status through association status no longer exists.

Operating the Corporation

Tax planning to reduce corporate income taxes should occur before the end of the tax year. Effective planning can cause income to be shifted to the next tax year and can produce large deductions by incurring expenses before year-end. Particular attention should be focused on the following.

Charitable Contributions. Recall that accrual basis corporations may claim a deduction for charitable contributions in the year preceding payment. The contribution must be authorized by the board of directors by the end of the tax year and paid on or before the fifteenth day of the third month of the following year. Even though the contribution may not ultimately be made, it might well be authorized. A deduction cannot be thrown back to the previous year (even if paid within the two and one-half months) if it has not been authorized.

Timing of Capital Gains and Losses. A corporation should consider offsetting profits on the sale of capital assets by selling some of the depreciated securities in the corporate portfolio. In addition, any already realized capital losses should be carefully monitored. Recall that corporate taxpayers are not permitted to claim any net capital losses as deductions against ordinary income. Capital losses can be used only as an offset against capital gains. Further, net capital losses can only be carried back three years and forward five. Gains from the sales of capital assets should be timed to offset any capital losses. The expiration of the carryover period for any net capital losses should be watched carefully so that sales of appreciated capital assets occur before that date.

Net Operating Losses. In some situations, electing to forgo an NOL carryback and utilizing the carryforward option may generate greater tax savings.

--- EXAMPLE 42 ---

XYZ Corporation incurred a $50,000 NOL in 1992. XYZ, which was in the 15% bracket from 1989 through 1991, has developed a new product that management predicts will push the corporation into the 34% bracket in 1993. If XYZ carries the NOL back, the tax savings will be $7,500 ($50,000 × 15%). However, if XYZ elects to carry the NOL forward, assuming management's prediction is accurate, the tax savings will be $17,000 ($50,000 × 34%). ◆

When deciding whether to forgo the carryback option, take into account three considerations. First, the time value of the tax refund that is lost by not using the carryback procedure should be calculated. Second, the election to forgo a net operating loss carryback is irrevocable. Thus, one cannot later choose to change if the predicted high profits do not materialize. Third, consider the future increases (or decreases) in corporate income tax rates that can reasonably be anticipated. This last consideration is the most difficult to work with. Although corporate tax rates have remained relatively stable in past years, projected budget deficits do little to assure taxpayers that future rates will remain constant.

Dividends Received Deduction. The dividends received deduction normally is limited to the lesser of 70 percent of the qualifying dividends or 70 percent of taxable income. An exception is made when the full deduction yields an NOL.

In close situations, therefore, the proper timing of income or deductions to generate an NOL may yield a larger dividends received deduction.

Organizational Expenditures.   To qualify for the 60-month amortization procedure of § 248, only organizational expenditures incurred in the first taxable year of the corporation can be considered. This rule could prove to be an unfortunate trap for corporations formed late in the year.

─────────────────── EXAMPLE 43 ───────────────────

T Corporation is formed in December 1992. Qualified organizational expenditures are incurred as follows: $2,000 in December 1992 and $3,000 in January 1993. If T Corporation uses the calendar year for tax purposes, only $2,000 of the organizational expenditures can be written off over a period of 60 months. ◆

The solution to the problem posed by Example 43 is for T Corporation to adopt a fiscal year that ends beyond January 31. All organizational expenditures will then have been incurred before the close of the first taxable year.

Shareholder-Employee Payment of Corporate Expenses.   In a closely held corporate setting, shareholder-employees often pay corporate expenses (e.g., travel and entertainment) for which they are not reimbursed by the corporation. The IRS often disallows the deduction of these expenses by the shareholder-employee, since the payments are voluntary on his or her part. If the deduction is more beneficial at the shareholder-employee level, a corporate policy against reimbursement of such expenses should be established. Proper planning in this regard would be to decide before the beginning of each tax year where the deduction would do the most good. Corporate policy regarding reimbursement of such expenses could be modified on a year-to-year basis depending upon the circumstances.

In deciding whether corporate expenses should be kept at the corporate level or shifted to the shareholder-employee, the treatment of unreimbursed employee expenses must be considered. First, since employee expenses are itemized deductions, they will be of no benefit to the taxpayer who chooses the standard deduction option. Second, these expenses will be subject to the 2 percent of AGI floor. No such limitation will be imposed if the corporation claims the expenses.

Related Corporations

Controlled Groups.   Recall that § 1561 was designed to prevent shareholders from operating a business as multiple corporations to obtain lower tax brackets and multiple accumulated earnings tax credits or AMT exemptions. Corporations in which substantially all the stock is held by five or fewer persons are subject to the provisions of § 1561. Dividing ownership so that control of each corporation does not lie with individuals having common control of all corporations avoids the prohibitions of § 1561.

─────────────────── EXAMPLE 44 ───────────────────

A, B, and C, individuals, have voting stock in Corporations X, Y, and Z as follows:

Shareholder	X	Y	Z	Common Ownership
A	40%	30%	30%	30%
B	40%	20%	30%	20%
C	20%	50%	40%	20%
Total	100%	100%	100%	70%

Because the total combined ownership is more than 50% and the three individuals own at least 80% of the combined voting power, X, Y, and Z are treated as a controlled group and are subject to § 1561. Thus, Corporations X, Y, and Z are limited to taxable income in the first two tax brackets and to the $250,000 accumulated earnings tax credit as though they were one corporation. ◆

Assume, however, that the voting stock is divided differently so that each of the individuals—A, B, and C—controls one of the corporations rather than having common control of all the corporations.

───────────────── EXAMPLE 45 ─────────────────

A, B, and C hold voting stock in Corporations X, Y, and Z in the following percentages:

Shareholder	X	Y	Z	Common Ownership
A	80%	10%	10%	10%
B	10%	80%	10%	10%
C	10%	10%	80%	10%
Total	100%	100%	100%	30%

Now the total combined ownership is less than 50%. Consequently, the corporations are not treated as a controlled group, since the prohibitions of § 1561 are not applicable. ◆

The differences in ownership in the corporations can be alleviated somewhat by issuing nonvoting preferred stock to the shareholders with the 10 percent ownership. (Nonvoting stock is not considered to be stock for purposes of § 1563.)

PROBLEM MATERIALS

DISCUSSION QUESTIONS

1. Briefly discuss the income tax consequences of the various forms of business organization in relation to the following:

   a. The tax treatment of sole proprietorships.
   b. Partnerships as reporting entities.
   c. The similarities and dissimilarities between the tax treatment of individuals and regular corporations. *pg. 2-2, 2-3 & Concept Summary 2-1 on pg 2-35 & 36*

2. Evaluate the disadvantages of using the corporate form in carrying on a trade or business in light of the following:

   a. No deduction is permitted for dividend distributions. *2-3*
   b. Corporate losses are not passed through to shareholders. *2-5*

3. What effect does state law have in determining whether an entity is to be treated as a corporation for Federal income tax purposes? *2-6*

4. Under what circumstances may a corporation legally constituted under state law be disregarded for Federal income tax purposes? *Examples 7 & 8*

5. Individuals X and Y own a building and a lot situated in a favorable location in a large city. X and Y want to sell the property but do not want the potential purchaser to know their identities. Therefore, X and Y transfer the building and lot to a newly

organized corporation, T Corporation, in exchange for all the stock of T Corporation. T Corporation sells the building and lot, collects the proceeds from the sale, distributes the proceeds to X and Y, and liquidates. T Corporation conducts no other activities. In all respects, T Corporation meets the requirements of a corporation under applicable state law. Would T Corporation be recognized as a separate entity for tax purposes? Why or why not? *Examples 7&8*

6. Why might the IRS attempt to disregard a legally constituted corporate entity? Why might the shareholders attempt to disregard such an entity? *Pg 2-6*

7. What is an association? How is it taxed for Federal income tax purposes? *2-7*

8. Under what circumstances might the owners of a business wish to have the business classified as an association? Not so classified? *Pg 2-7, 8, 37 & 38*

9. In testing for association status, what criteria are considered for partnerships? For trusts? *2 - 7*

10. Compare the income tax treatment of corporations and individuals in the following respects:

    a. Applicable tax rates. *Concept Summary 2-1 on Pg 2-36*
    b. Adjusted gross income determination. *2-9*
    c. The deduction for casualty losses. *Example 9*
    d. Allowable tax credits. *2-9*
    e. Recapture of depreciation. *Examples 14 to 16*
    f. Dividends received from domestic corporations *pg 2-17&18*
    g. Net operating losses. *2-16 &17*
    h. The alternative minimum tax. *2-20 & 21*

11. C corporations have greater flexibility in the selection of a tax year than personal service corporations and S corporations. Why is this the case, and what are the requirements that must be met for a PSC to elect a fiscal year? *2-10*

12. Under what conditions are corporations allowed to use the cash method of accounting? *2-10 & 11*

13. Compare the tax treatment of corporate and noncorporate taxpayers' capital gains and losses with respect to the following:

    a. Net capital gains. *2-11*
    b. A net long-term capital loss. *Examples 12 & 12*
    c. A net short-term capital loss. *Pg 2-12 Example 13*
    d. Capital loss carrybacks. *Examples 12 & 13*
    e. Capital loss carryovers. *pg 2-11 & 2*

14. What is the justification for the dividends received deduction? *2-17*

15. The amount of the dividends received deduction depends on the percentage of ownership held by the corporate shareholder. Explain. *2-17 & 2-18*

16. A taxpayer sells a warehouse for a gain of $50,000. The warehouse has been depreciated as 15-year property under ACRS. Depreciation recapture will be higher if the taxpayer is a corporation than if the taxpayer is an individual. Explain. *Example 14*

17. The passive loss rules apply differently to personal service corporations than to closely held corporations. Explain. *Pg 2-13 & 14*

18. Compare the tax treatment of corporate and noncorporate taxpayers' charitable contributions with respect to the following:

    a. The year of the deduction for an accrual basis taxpayer. *Examples 18 & 19*
    b. The percentage limitations on the maximum deduction allowed for any one year. *Pg 2-14 & 15 Summary 2-1 Pg 2-35*
    c. The amount of the deduction allowed for the donation of certain inventory. *Examples 21, 22 & 23*

19. In connection with organizational expenditures, comment on the following:

    a. Those that qualify for amortization. *Pg 2-18 to 2-20*
    b. Those that do not qualify for amortization. *Pg 2-18 to 2-20*
    c. The period over which amortization can take place. *Pg 2-19 Example 28*
    d. Expenses incurred but not paid by a cash basis corporation. *pg 2-19*

e. Expenses incurred by a corporation in its second year of operation. *Example 43*

f. The alternative if no election to amortize is made. *2-19*

g. The timing of the election to amortize. *2-19*

20. The corporate income tax can be expressed by the following formula: $13,750 + 34% of taxable income in excess of $75,000.

a. Do you agree? Explain. *2-20 Ex. 29*

b. When would the formula work? *Ex. 29 & 30*

21. Qualified personal service corporations need not be concerned about keeping taxable income at $100,000 or less. Please comment. *Pg 2-20*

22. How does treatment as a controlled group of corporations work to the disadvantage of the corporate group? *Ex 31 & 32*

23. What is the difference between a brother-sister controlled group and a parent-subsidiary controlled group? *2-22 & 23*

24. Assume an individual, A, owns 80% of all classes of stock of two corporations, X and Y. X Corporation, in turn, owns all the stock of Z Corporation, and Y Corporation owns 80% of the stock of W Corporation. Would X, Y, Z, and W Corporations be members of a combined group? Explain. *Ex: 39*

25. What are the conditions for filing a Form 1120–A? *2-25 & 26*

26. Taxable income and financial accounting income for a corporation are seldom the same amount. Discuss some common reasons for differences and how these differences affect the reconciliation of taxable income and financial accounting income on Schedule M–1 of Form 1120. *2-27*

27. What groups of corporations may file consolidated returns? *2-31 to 2-34*

28. What are the advantages and disadvantages of filing a consolidated return? *2-35*

PROBLEMS

29. X Corporation and A and B, individuals, form a limited partnership on January 1 to construct office buildings. X Corporation is the general partner, and A and B are both limited partners. The partnership agreement provides that X Corporation will have sole management of the business. A's and B's liabilities for debts of the partnership will be limited to their investments. The partnership agreement provides that the partnership will not end upon the death of any of the partners. The agreement also provides that either A or B may sell their interests without the consent of the other parties. A and B each invest $50,000 in the partnership. X Corporation, which has a net worth of only $20,000, invests $10,000. The partnership secures a loan from the bank to help finance the initial cost of construction. How will the partnership be classified for tax purposes? Explain. *2-7*

30. In the current year, T, a calendar year taxpayer, suffers a casualty loss of $9,000. How much of the casualty loss will be a tax deduction to T under the following circumstances?

a. T is an individual and has AGI of $20,000. The casualty loss was a personal loss. T recovered insurance of $3,000.

b. T is a corporation. T recovered insurance of $3,000. *2-9 Ex: 19*

31. R Corporation is a professional association. It paid its only shareholder T, a medical doctor, a salary of $240,000 during its fiscal year ending September 30, 1992. How much salary must R Corporation pay T during the period October 1 through December 31, 1992, to permit R Corporation to continue to use its fiscal year without negative tax effects? *Example 11*

32. In 1992, a business sells a capital asset, which it had held for two years, at a loss of $15,000. How much of the capital loss may be deducted in 1992 and how much is carried back or forward under the following circumstances?

a. The business was a sole proprietorship owned by A, an individual. A had a short-term capital gain in 1992 of $3,000 and a long-term capital gain of $2,000. A had ordinary net income from the proprietorship of $60,000.

b. The business is incorporated. The corporation had a short-term capital gain of $3,000 and a long-term capital gain of $2,000. Its ordinary net income from the business was $60,000. *Examples 12 & 13*

33. XYZ Corporation realized net short-term capital gains of $30,000 and net long-term capital losses of $80,000 during 1992. Taxable income from other sources was $400,000. Prior years' transactions included the following:

1988	Net long-term capital gains	$80,000
1989	Net short-term capital gains	20,000
1990	Net long-term capital gains	10,000
1991	Net long-term capital gains	10,000

   a. How are the capital gains and losses treated on the 1992 tax return?
   b. Compute the capital loss carryback to the carryback years.
   c. Compute the amount of capital loss carryover, if any, and designate the years to which the loss may be carried. *2-11   2-12*

34. X Corporation acquired residential rental property on January 3, 1984, for $100,000. The property was depreciated using the accelerated method and a 15-year recovery period under ACRS. Depreciation in the amount of $64,500 was claimed. Straight-line depreciation for the period would have been $53,888. X Corporation sold the property on January 1, 1992, for $110,000. What is the gain on the sale, and how is it taxed? *Ex. 15 & Figure 2-1*

35. Assume the property in Problem 34 was a commercial building and X Corporation used the straight-line method of depreciation with a 15-year recovery period under ACRS. What would be the gain on the sale, and how would it be taxed? *Ex. 14 & Fig 2-1*

36. In 1992, X Corporation has passive losses of $200,000 from a rental activity. It has active business income of $100,000 and $50,000 of portfolio income. What is X Corporation's taxable income for 1992 under the following circumstances?

   a. X Corporation is a closely held corporation.
   b. X Corporation is a personal service corporation. *2-14   Ex. 7*

37. T, a calendar year taxpayer engaged in the catering business, makes the following donations to qualified charitable organizations during the current year:

	Adjusted Basis	Fair Market Value
Used delivery van to half-way house, which sold it immediately	$3,200	$2,900
IBM stock held two years as an investment to Goodwill, which sold it immediately	3,000	9,500
Canned groceries to Catholic Meals for the Poor	4,000	4,100

What is the amount of the charitable contribution deduction if T is an individual? A corporation? *Example 23*

38. During the current year, T Corporation (a calendar year taxpayer) had the following income and expenses:

Income from operations	$225,000
Expenses from operations	165,000
Qualifying dividends from domestic corporations	15,000
NOL carryover from prior year	4,500

On June 3, T Corporation made a contribution to a qualified charitable organization of $10,500 in cash (not included in any of the above items).

   a. Determine T Corporation's charitable contribution deduction for the current year.
   b. What happens to any excess charitable contribution deduction not allowable for the current year? *Ex. 24 & 25*

39. Pursuant to a resolution adopted by its board of directors, X Corporation, a calendar year accrual basis taxpayer, authorizes a $50,000 donation to City University (a qualified charitable organization) on December 20, 1991. The donation is made on March 10, 1992. Is the corporation correct in claiming a deduction (subject to statutory limitations) in 1991? What if the donation were made on April 10, 1992?

40. During 1992, a corporation has $100,000 of gross income and $125,000 in allowable business deductions. Included in gross income is $30,000 in qualifying dividends from less than 20% owned domestic corporations.

   a. Determine the corporation's net operating loss for 1992.
   b. What happens to the loss if the corporation was newly created in 1992? In 1989?

41. In each of the following independent situations, determine the dividends received deduction. Assume that none of the corporate shareholders owns 20% or more of the stock in the corporations paying the dividends.

	E Corporation	F Corporation	G Corporation
Income from operations	$ 700,000	$ 800,000	$ 700,000
Expenses from operations	(600,000)	(900,000)	(740,000)
Qualifying dividends	100,000	200,000	200,000

42. P Corporation was formed on December 1, 1992. Qualifying organizational expenses were incurred and paid as follows:

Incurred and paid in December 1992	$10,000
Incurred in December 1992 but paid in January 1993	5,000
Incurred and paid in February 1993	3,000

Assume P Corporation makes a timely election under § 248 to amortize organizational expenditures over a period of 60 months. What amount may be amortized in the corporation's first tax year under each of the following assumptions?

   a. P Corporation adopts a calendar year and the cash basis of accounting for tax purposes.
   b. Same as (a), except that P Corporation chooses a fiscal year of December 1– November 30.
   c. P Corporation adopts a calendar year and the accrual basis of accounting for tax purposes.
   d. Same as (c), except that P Corporation chooses a fiscal year of December 1– November 30.

43. T Corporation, an accrual basis taxpayer, was formed and began operations on July 1, 1992. The following expenses were incurred during the first tax year (July 1 to December 31, 1992) of operations:

Expenses of temporary directors and of organizational meetings	$2,500
Fee paid to the state of incorporation	300
Accounting services incident to organization	600
Legal services for drafting the corporate charter and bylaws	1,400
Expenses incident to the printing and sale of stock certificates	500
	$5,300

Assume T Corporation makes an appropriate and timely election under § 248(c) and the related Regulations.

   a. What is the maximum organizational expense T may write off for tax year 1992?
   b. What would be the result if a proper election had not been made?

44. In each of the following independent situations, determine the corporation's income tax liability. Assume that all corporations use a calendar year for tax purposes and that the tax year involved is 1992.

	Taxable Income
J Corporation	$ 40,000
K Corporation	120,000
L Corporation	380,000
M Corporation	70,000

Examples 29 & 30

45. A regular corporation did not distribute any dividends in tax year 1992. It had no capital gains or losses. What is its 1992 income tax liability under the following independent situations?

a. Its taxable income was $30,000.
b. Its taxable income was $70,000.
c. Its taxable income was $130,000.
d. Its taxable income was $2 million.
e. Same as (a) except that the corporation distributed $20,000 in dividends to its sole shareholder.
f. Same as (a) except that the corporation had a $20,000 capital loss. *2-12*

46. X Corporation owns 80% of the total combined voting power of all classes of stock entitled to vote in Y Corporation. Y Corporation owns 20% of the stock in Z Corporation. X Corporation owns 90% of W Corporation, while the latter owns 60% of Z Corporation. Which corporations are part of a controlled group? *2-22* *figures 2-2 & 23*

47. The outstanding stock of X, Y, Z, W, and U Corporations is owned by the following *2-22 & 2-23* unrelated individual and corporate shareholders:

can claim consolidated return *Z is the only one on its own for filing its return* *can claim consolidated*

Shareholders	**Corporations**				
	X	Y	Z	W	U
A	20%		5%	10%	5%
B	30%		40%	50%	30%
C	20%		15%	10%	10%
D	10%		20%	10%	10%
X Corporation		90%			
W Corporation					85%

55% Pg 2-25 EX: 39

80% 90% 80% 80% 85%

Which, if any, of the above corporations are members of a controlled group? *all are members of controlled group*

48. The outstanding stock in X and Y Corporations, each of which has only one class of stock, is owned by the following unrelated individuals:

Shareholders	**Corporations**	
	X	Y
A	20	16
B	5	54
C	75	30
Total	100	100

16 5 30 51 a. yes they are brother-sister controlled group

a. Determine if a brother-sister controlled group exists. *EX: 36*
b. Assume that B owns no stock in X Corporation and C owns 80 shares. Would a brother-sister controlled group exist? Why or why not? *EX: 37* *NO the 50% rule doesn't apply*

49. The outstanding stock in corporations R, S, T, U, and W, which have only one class of stock outstanding, is owned by the following unrelated individuals:

Individuals	Corporations				
	R	S	T	U	W
A	55%	51%	55%	55%	55%
B	45%	49%	–0–	–0–	–0–
C	–0–	–0–	45%	–0–	–0–
D	–0–	–0–	–0–	45%	–0–
E	–0–	–0–	–0–	–0–	45%
Total	100%	100%	100%	100%	100%

Determine if a brother-sister controlled group exists.

50. Indicate in each of the following independent situations whether the corporation may file Form 1120–A:

	A Corporation	B Corporation	C Corporation
Sales of merchandise	$600,000	$400,000	$300,000
Total assets	200,000	360,000	400,000
Total income (gross profit plus other income, including gains)	480,000	490,000	380,000
Member of controlled group	no	yes	no
Ownership in foreign corporation	no	no	no
Entitled to file Form 1120–A (Circle Y for yes or N for no)	Y N	Y N	Y N

51. For 1992, T Corporation, an accrual basis calendar year taxpayer, had net income per books of $172,750 and the following special transactions:

Life insurance proceeds received through the death of the corporation president	$100,000
Premiums paid on the life insurance policy on the president	10,000
Prepaid rent received and properly taxed in 1991 but credited as rent income in 1992	15,000
Rent income received in 1992 ($10,000 is prepaid and relates to 1993)	25,000
Interest income on tax-exempt bonds	5,000
Interest on loan to carry tax-exempt bonds	3,000
ACRS depreciation in excess of straight-line (straight-line was used for book purposes)	4,000
Capital loss in excess of capital gains	6,000
Federal income tax liability for 1992	22,250

Using Schedule M–1 of Form 1120 (the most recent version available), compute T Corporation's taxable income for 1992.

52. Using the legend provided, classify each of the following statements:

Legend

I Applies only to individual taxpayers
C Applies only to corporate taxpayers
B Applies to both individual and corporate taxpayers
N Applies to neither individual nor corporate taxpayers

a. A net capital loss can be carried back.
b. Net long-term capital losses are carried forward as short-term capital losses.

c. A $4,000 net short-term capital loss in the current year can be deducted against ordinary income only to the extent of $3,000.   Εx 12 I

d. The carryforward period for net capital losses is five years. 2-12 C

e. The alternative minimum tax does not apply. 2-20 N

f. Net operating losses are not allowed to be carried back. 2-16 N

g. The credit for the elderly applies. 2-9 I

h. The carryback period for excess charitable contributions is three years. 2-14 N

i. Excess charitable contributions can be carried forward indefinitely. 2-14

j. On the disposition of certain depreciable real estate, more ordinary income may result. C   Ex 14-16

k. Percentage limitations may restrict the amount of charitable deductions that can be claimed in any one tax year. 2-16 B

l. Casualty losses are deductible in full. Ex 9 I

m. More adjustments are necessary to arrive at a net operating loss deduction. 2-14 c/S 2-1   I

COMPREHENSIVE TAX RETURN PROBLEM

Novelco Corporation was formed on October 1, 1976, by Jim and Anne Adams to manufacture and assemble novelty items (mainly key chains, ballpoint pens, and compaign buttons). These items usually are customized with the client's name (and/or logo) for distribution as promotional material. Pertinent information regarding Novelco is summarized as follows:

- The business address is 5210 Union Street, Leesville, IL 60930.
- The employer identification number is 71–0395674; the principal business activity code is 3998.
- Jim and Anne Adams, brother and sister, each own one-half of the outstanding common stock, and no other class of stock is authorized. Every three years, they rotate the positions of president and vice president. Currently, Anne is the president and Jim the vice president. Both are full-time employees, and the corporation has no other officers. Each receives a salary of $60,000. Jim's Social Security number is 581–00–0836; Anne's is 581–00–2604.
- The corporation uses the accrual method of accounting and reports on a calendar year basis. The specific chargeoff method is used in handling bad debt losses, and inventories are determined under the lower of cost or market method with full absorption of cost. For book and tax purposes, the straight-line method of depreciation is used.
- During 1991, the corporation distributed a cash dividend of $50,000. Because a customer was injured on the business premises and has threatened legal action for personal damages, a reserve for contingencies is to be established in the amount of $40,000.
- In November 1991, the corporation received a refund of $24,000 from the IRS due to overpayment on its 1990 estimated income tax liability.

Selected portions of Novelco's profit and loss statement reflect the following debits and credits:

Account	Debit	Credit
Gross sales		$2,500,000
Sales returns and allowances	$ 20,000	
Cost of goods sold	1,450,000	
Dividends received from stock investments in less than 20% owned U.S. corporations		30,000
Interest income		
Certificates of deposit	$12,000	
State bonds	14,000	26,000
Premiums on term life insurance (the policies are owned by the corporation and cover Jim and Anne Adams; the corporation is the designated beneficiary)	14,000	

Account	Debit	Credit
Compensation of officers	120,000	
Salaries and wages—indirect	70,000	
Repairs	4,000	
Bad debts	5,000	
Rental expense	12,000	
Taxes (state, local, payroll—indirect)	23,000	
Interest expense		
Loan to purchase state bonds	$ 2,000	
Other business loans and mortgages	27,000 29,000	
Charitable contributions	31,000	
Depreciation—indirect	5,000	
Advertising in trade journals	10,000	
Other expenses (e.g., office expenses, sales commissions, legal and accounting fees)	60,000	
Long-term loss from the sale of stock held as an investment—no carryback was available	4,000	

Information regarding the cost of goods sold:

Beginning inventory (1–1–91)	$120,000
Ending inventory (12–31–91)	160,000
Purchases (including subcontracted parts and raw materials)	900,000
Cost of labor—direct	450,000
Other costs (e.g., utilities, small tools, depreciation—direct [$14,000])	140,000

Net income per books (before any income tax accrual) is $699,000.

A comparative balance sheet for Novelco reveals the following information:

Assets	January 1, 1991	December 31, 1991
Cash	$ 28,682	$ 53,122
Trade notes and accounts receivable	125,000	140,000
Inventories	120,000	160,000
Federal and state government bonds	140,000	140,000
Other current assets	18,000	24,000
Other investments	108,000	240,000
Buildings and other depreciable assets	304,000	304,000
Accumulated depreciation	(105,000)	(124,000)
Land	115,000	165,000
Other assets	17,000	24,000
Total assets	$ 870,682	$1,126,122

Liabilities and Equity		
Accounts payable	$ 24,000	$ 12,000
Other current liabilities	11,000	6,000
Mortgages	168,000	—
Capital stock	200,000	200,000
Retained earnings (appropriated and unappropriated)	467,682	908,122
Total liabilities and equity	$ 870,682	$1,126,122

During 1991, Novelco made estimated tax payments to the IRS of $240,000. Prepare a Form 1120 for Novelco for tax year 1991.

RESEARCH PROBLEMS

RESEARCH PROBLEM 1   In 1985, several unrelated individuals created Joya Trust with a transfer of undeveloped real estate located near a large metropolitan area. In return for the transfer, the grantors received beneficial interests in Joya that were of a stated value and freely transferable. Under the trust instrument, the trust was to last 25 years or until dissolution by the trustees, whichever occurred sooner. The trust was not to terminate upon the death of a trustee, and the trustees were empowered to appoint their own successors. The trustees were authorized to call annual meetings of the beneficiaries, but the votes of the beneficiaries were advisory only. Under applicable state law, the liability of the beneficiaries was limited to their investment in the trust. Pursuant to authority granted by the trust instrument, Joya Trust arranged for the development of the real estate into recreational facilities (e.g., golf courses, tennis courts) and luxury housing units. When developed, the real estate was either sold or leased to the general public. Joya continued to manage the unsold and leased units as well as the recreational facilities until it was dissolved by action of its trustees in 1991. During its existence, how should Joya Trust be treated for Federal income tax purposes? Why?

RESEARCH PROBLEM 2   U and V are brothers and equal shareholders in X Corporation, a calendar year taxpayer. In 1990, they incurred certain travel and entertainment expenditures, as employees, on behalf of X Corporation. Because X Corporation was in a precarious financial condition, U and V decided not to seek reimbursement for these expenditures. Instead, each brother deducted what he spent on his own individual return (Form 1040). Upon audit of the returns filed by U and V for 1990, the IRS disallowed these expenditures. Do you agree? Why or why not?

RESEARCH PROBLEM 3   A, an individual, owns all the stock of X Corporation and 90% of the stock of Y Corporation. Y Corporation has had profitable years whereas X Corporation has suffered losses for several years. Y Corporation loaned X Corporation $90,000 in 1990 and did not charge X Corporation any interest on the loan. Upon audit of its 1990 return, the IRS determined that Y Corporation had interest income for 1990 in the amount of $9,900, causing Y Corporation to have a tax deficiency of $3,366 for 1990. Y Corporation is challenging the tax deficiency. It contends that X Corporation produced no taxable income from the use of the $90,000. Is the IRS correct in increasing the taxable income of Y Corporation?

Partial list of research aids:

Reg. §§ 1.482–2(a)(1) and 1.482–1(d)(4).

CHAPTER

CORPORATIONS: ORGANIZATION AND CAPITAL STRUCTURE

OBJECTIVES

Describe the tax consequences of incorporating a new or an existing business.

Explain how to deal with subsequent property transfers to a controlled corporation.

Describe the capital structure of a corporation and explain what it means for tax purposes.

Discuss the advantages and disadvantages of preferring debt over an equity investment.

Describe the nature and treatment of shareholder debt and stock losses.

OUTLINE

Chapter 2 dealt with three principal areas fundamental to working with corporations: (1) the recognition of an entity as a corporation for Federal income tax purposes, (2) the tax rules applicable to the day-to-day operation of a corporation, and (3) the filing and reporting procedures governing corporations.

Chapter 3 addresses more sophisticated problems in dealing with corporations:

- The tax consequences to the shareholders and the corporation upon the organization of the corporation.
- Once the corporation has been formed, the tax result that ensues when shareholders make later transfers of property.
- The capital structure of a corporation, including the treatment of capital contributions by nonshareholders and shareholders and the handling of investor losses suffered by shareholders. *debt vs capital*

ORGANIZATION OF AND TRANSFERS TO CONTROLLED CORPORATIONS
◆

In General

Unless special provisions in the Code apply, a transfer of property to a corporation in exchange for stock is a sale or exchange of property and constitutes a taxable transaction. Gain or loss is measured by the difference between the tax basis of the property transferred and the value of the stock received. Section 351 provides for the nonrecognition of gain or loss upon the transfer of property to a corporation solely in exchange for stock if the persons transferring the property are in control of the corporation immediately after the transfer.

The nonrecognition of gain or loss under § 351 reflects the principle of continuity of the taxpayer's investment. The taxpayer's economic status has not really changed. The investment in certain properties carries over to the investment in corporate stock. Since the taxpayer has received only stock in the new corporation, he or she is hardly in a position to pay a tax on any realized gain. As noted later, when the taxpayer receives property other than stock (i.e., boot) from the corporation, realized gain may be recognized.

The same principle governs the nonrecognition of gain or loss on like-kind exchanges under § 1031. The nonrecognition concept causes gain to be postponed until a substantive change in the taxpayer's investment occurs (a sale to or a taxable exchange with outsiders). This approach is justified under the wherewithal to pay concept discussed in Chapter 1.

─────────────── EXAMPLE 1 ───────────────

R is considering incorporating his donut shop. He is concerned about his potential liability for the shop's obligations in case he encounters financial difficulties in the future. R realizes that if he incorporates his shop, he will be liable only for the debts of the business that he has personally guaranteed. If R incorporates, he will transfer the following assets to the corporation:

	Tax Basis	Fair Market Value
Cash	$10,000	$ 10,000
Furniture and fixtures	20,000	60,000
Building	40,000	100,000
	$70,000	$170,000

R will receive stock in the newly formed corporation worth $170,000 in exchange for the assets. Without the nonrecognition provisions of § 351, R would recognize a taxable gain of $100,000 on the transfer. Under § 351, however, R does not recognize any gain because his economic status has not really changed. R's investment in the assets of his unincorporated donut shop carries over to his investment in the incorporated donut shop. Thus, § 351 provides for tax neutrality on the initial incorporation of R's donut shop. ◆

If property or money other than stock is received by the transferor shareholders, § 351(b) provides that gain is recognized to the extent of the lesser of the gain realized or the boot received (the amount of money and the fair market value of other property received). The gain is characterized according to the type of asset transferred.[1] Loss is never recognized. The nonrecognition of gain or loss is accompanied by a carryover of basis.[2]

boot is money received [handwritten note]

EXAMPLE 2

A and B, individuals, form X Corporation. A transfers property with an adjusted basis of $30,000, fair market value of $60,000, for 50% of the stock. B transfers property with an adjusted basis of $70,000, fair market value of $60,000, for the remaining 50% of the stock. The transfer qualifies under § 351. A has an unrecognized gain of $30,000, and B has an unrecognized loss of $10,000. Both have a carryover basis in the stock in X Corporation. A has a basis of $30,000 in her stock in X Corporation, and B has a basis of $70,000 in his stock in X Corporation. ◆

No Boot was received [handwritten note]

Section 351 is mandatory. If a transaction falls within its provisions, neither gain nor loss is recognized on the transfer (except that realized gain is recognized to the extent of boot received), and there is a carryover of basis.

There are three requirements for nonrecognition of gain or loss: (1) property is transferred for (2) stock and (3) the transferors must be in control of the transferee corporation.

Transfer of Property

Questions concerning what constitutes property for purposes of § 351 have arisen. Services rendered are specifically excluded by the Code from the definition of property. With this exception, the definition of property is comprehensive. Unrealized receivables for a cash basis taxpayer and installment obligations are considered property, for example.[3] The transfer of an installment obligation in a transaction qualifying under § 351 is not a disposition of the installment obligation. Thus, gain is not recognized to the transferor. Secret processes and formulas, as well as secret information in the general nature of a patentable inventory, also qualify as property under § 351.[4]

Services are not considered to be property under § 351 for a critical reason. A taxpayer must report as income the fair market value of property received as compensation for services rendered.[5] Thus, if a taxpayer receives stock in a corporation as consideration for rendering services to the corporation, the taxpayer has taxable income. The amount of income is the fair market value of the stock received. The taxpayer's basis in the stock then is the fair market value of the stock.

---

1. Rev.Rul. 68–55, 1968–1 C.B. 140.

2. §§ 358(a) and 362(a). See the discussion preceding Example 20.

3. *Hempt Brothers, Inc. v. U.S.*, 74–1 USTC ¶9188, 33 AFTR2d

74–570, 490 F.2d 1172 (CA–3, 1974), and Reg. § 1.453–9(c)(2).

4. Rev.Rul. 64–56, 1964–1 C.B. 133.

5. §§ 61 and 83.

———————————————— EXAMPLE 3 ————————————————

A and B form X Corporation and transfer the following property to it:

	Property Transferred		
	Basis to Transferor	Fair Market Value	Number of Shares Issued
From A:			
Personal services rendered to X Corporation	$ –0–	$20,000	200
From B:			
Installment obligation	5,000	40,000	
Inventory	10,000	30,000	800
Secret process	–0–	10,000	

The value of each share in X Corporation is $100. A has income of $20,000 on the transfer because services do not qualify as "property." A has a basis of $20,000 in the 200 shares of stock in X. B has no gain on the transfer because all the property he transferred to X qualifies as "property" under § 351. B has a basis of $15,000 in his stock in X. ◆

Stock

If property is transferred to a corporation in exchange for any property other than stock, the property constitutes boot. The boot is taxable to the transferor shareholder to the extent of any realized gain. The Regulations state that the term "stock" does not include stock rights and stock warrants.[6] Generally, however, the term "stock" needs no clarification. It includes both common stock and preferred stock.

Currently, securities (i.e., long-term debt) constitute boot under § 351.[7] Thus, the receipt of securities in exchange for the transfer of appreciated property to a controlled corporation causes recognition of gain.

Control of the Transferee Corporation

To qualify as a nontaxable transaction under § 351, the transferor must be in control of the transferee corporation immediately after the exchange. Control means that the person or persons transferring the property must have an 80 percent stock ownership in the transferee corporation. The transferor shareholders must own stock possessing at least 80 percent of the total combined voting power of all classes of stock entitled to vote and at least 80 percent of the total *number* of shares of all other classes of stock.[8]

Control Immediately after the Transfer. Control can apply to a single person or to several individuals if they are all parties to an integrated transaction. Section 351 requires control "immediately after the exchange." The Regulations provide that when more than one person is involved, the exchange does not necessarily require simultaneous exchanges by two or more persons. The Regulations do, however, require that the rights of the parties (e.g., those transferring property to the corporation) be previously set out and determined.

---

6. Reg. § 1.351–1(a)(1)(ii).

7. Prior to October 3, 1989, transfers of property for stock *or* securities in a controlled corporation were subject to the provisions of § 351. The Revenue Reconciliation Act of 1989

amended § 351 by deleting "or securities." As a result, securities are treated as boot for transfers after October 2, 1989.

8. § 368(c).

Also, the agreement to transfer property should be executed "... with an expedition consistent with orderly procedure."[9]

If two or more persons transfer property to a corporation for stock, the transfers should occur close together in time and should be made in accordance with an agreement among the parties.

─────────────── EXAMPLE 4 ───────────────

A exchanges property, basis of $60,000 and fair market value of $100,000, for 70% of the stock of X Corporation. The other 30% is owned by B, who acquired it several years ago. The fair market value of A's stock is $100,000. A recognizes a taxable gain of $40,000 on the transfer. ◆

─────────────── EXAMPLE 5 ───────────────

A, B, and C incorporate their respective businesses and form X Corporation. A exchanges her property for 300 shares in X on January 5, 1992. B exchanges his property for 400 shares of X Corporation stock on January 10, 1992, and C exchanges her property for 300 shares in X on March 5, 1992. The three exchanges are part of a prearranged plan. The nonrecognition provisions of § 351 apply to all the exchanges. ◆

Stock need not be issued to the transferring parties in proportion to the interest each held in the transferred property. However, when stock received is not proportionate to the value of the property transferred, the transaction could be treated as a gift from one transferor to the other.

─────────────── EXAMPLE 6 ───────────────

C and D organize a corporation with 500 shares of stock. C transfers property worth $10,000 for 100 shares, and D transfers property worth $5,000 for 400 shares. The transaction qualifies under § 351; however, if C did in fact make a gift to D, the transfer might be subject to a gift tax (see Chapter 17). ◆

Control is not lost if stock received by shareholders in a § 351 exchange is sold or given to persons who are not parties to the exchange shortly after the transaction. A different result might materialize if a plan for the ultimate sale or gift of the stock existed before the exchange.[10]

─────────────── EXAMPLE 7 ───────────────

A and B form X Corporation. They transfer appreciated property to the corporation with each receiving 50 shares of the stock. Shortly after the formation, A gives 25 shares to his son. Because A was not committed to make the gift, A is considered to own his original shares of the X Corporation stock "immediately after the exchange." The requirements of § 351 are met, and neither A nor B is taxed on the exchange. ◆

Transfers for Property and Services.   Section 351 treatment is lost if stock is transferred to persons who did not contribute property, causing those who did to lack control immediately after the exchange.

─────────────── EXAMPLE 8 ───────────────

A transfers property with a value of $60,000 and a basis of $5,000 for 600 shares of stock in newly formed X Corporation. B receives 400 shares in X Corporation for services rendered to the corporation. Each share of stock is worth $100. Both A and B have taxable gain on the transaction. B is not part of the control group because he did

───────────────

9. Reg. § 1.351–1.
10. *Wilgard Realty Co. v. Comm.*, 42–1 USTC ¶9452, 29 AFTR

325, 127 F.2d 514 (CA–2, 1942).

not transfer "property" for stock. B has taxable income of $40,000 (400 shares × $100). A has a taxable gain of $55,000 [$60,000 (fair market value of the stock in X Corporation) − $5,000 (basis in the transferred property)]. A is taxed on the exchange because she received only 60% of the stock in X Corporation. ◆

NOT 80%

A person who performs services for the corporation in exchange for stock and also transfers some property is treated as a member of the transferring group. That person is taxed on the value of the stock issued for services. In this case, all the stock received by the person transferring both property and services is counted in determining whether the transferors acquired control of the corporation.[11]

--- EXAMPLE 9 ---

Assume the same facts as in Example 8 except that B transfers property worth $30,000 (basis of $3,000) in addition to the services rendered to the corporation (valued at $10,000). Now B becomes a part of the control group. A and B together received 100% of the stock in X Corporation. Consequently, § 351 is applicable to the exchanges. A has no recognized gain. B does not recognize gain on the transfer of the property but has taxable income to the extent of the value of the shares issued for services rendered. Thus, B has income of $10,000. ◆

Transfers for Services and Nominal Property. To be a member of the group and aid in qualifying all transferors under the 80 percent test, the person contributing services must transfer property having more than a relatively small value compared to the services performed. Stock issued for property whose value is relatively small compared to the value of the stock already owned (or to be received for services rendered) will not be treated as issued in return for property. This will be the result when the primary purpose of the transfer is to qualify the transaction under § 351 for concurrent transferors.[12]

--- EXAMPLE 10 ---

A and B, individuals, transfer property to X Corporation, each in exchange for one-third of the stock. C, an individual, receives the other one-third of the stock for services rendered. The transaction will not qualify under § 351 because C is not a member of the group transferring property and A and B together received only 66⅔% of the stock. The post-transfer control requirement is not met.

Assume instead that C also transfers property. Then he is a member of the group, and the transaction qualifies under § 351. C is taxed on the value of the stock issued for services, but the remainder of the transaction is tax-free. However, if the property transferred by C is of a relatively small value in comparison to the stock he receives for his services, and the primary purpose for including the property is to cause the transaction to be tax-free for A and B, the exchange does not qualify under § 351. Gain or loss is recognized by all parties. ◆

The IRS generally requires that before a transferor who receives stock for both property and services can be included in the control group, the value of the property transferred must be at least 10 percent of the value of the services provided.[13] If the value of the property transferred is less than this amount, the IRS will not issue an advance ruling that the exchange meets the requirements of § 351.

Skip

---

11. Reg. § 1.351–1(a)(2), Ex. 3.
12. Reg. § 1.351–1(a)(1)(ii).

13. Rev.Proc. 77–37, 1977–2 C.B. 568, § 3.07.

─────────────── EXAMPLE 11 ───────────────

A and B form X Corporation. A transfers land (worth $100,000, basis of $20,000) for 50% of the stock in X. B transfers equipment (worth $50,000, adjusted basis of $10,000) and provides services worth $50,000 for 50% of the stock. B's stock in X Corporation is counted in determining control for purposes of § 351; thus, the transferors own 100% of the stock in X. All of B's stock, not just the shares received for the equipment, is counted in determining control because property he transferred has more than a nominal value in comparison to the value of the services rendered. A does not recognize gain on the transfer of the land. She will have a basis of $20,000 in the X Corporation stock. B, however, must recognize income of $50,000 on the transfer. Even though the transfer of the equipment qualifies under § 351, his transfer of services for stock does not. ◆

─────────────── EXAMPLE 12 ───────────────

Assume the same facts as in Example 11 except that the equipment was worth only $1,000 (basis of $400) and the services B provided were worth $99,000. The transfers do not qualify under § 351. A does not have the requisite 80% control. Thus, she has a taxable gain of $80,000 [$100,000 (value of the land) − $20,000 (basis in the land)]. B has income of $99,000 for services rendered plus gain of $600 on the transfer of the equipment. ◆

Transfers to Existing Corporations.   Once a corporation is in operation, § 351 also applies to any later transfers of property for stock by either new or former shareholders.

─────────────── EXAMPLE 13 ───────────────

A and B formed T Corporation three years ago. Both A and B transferred appreciated property to T in exchange for 50 shares each in the corporation. The original transfers qualified under § 351, and neither A nor B was taxed on the exchange. In the current year, A transfers property (worth $90,000, adjusted basis of $5,000) for 50 additional shares in T Corporation. A has a taxable gain of $85,000 on the transfer. The exchange does not qualify under § 351 because A does not have 80% control of T Corporation. (A will have 100 shares of the 150 shares outstanding, or a 66⅔% ownership.) ◆

Due to the 80 percent control rule, it is difficult for a transfer by a new shareholder to qualify for nonrecognition of gain under § 351.

Assumption of Liabilities—§ 357

Without § 357 of the Code, the transfer of mortgaged property to a controlled corporation could trigger gain to the extent of the mortgage whether the corporation assumed the mortgage or took property subject to it. This is the rule in nontaxable like-kind exchanges under § 1031. Liabilities assumed by the other party are considered the equivalent of cash and treated as boot. Section 357(a) provides, however, that when the acquiring corporation assumes a liability or takes property subject to a liability in a § 351 transaction, the transfer does not result in boot to the transferor shareholder. Nevertheless, liabilities assumed by the transferee corporation are treated as boot in determining the basis of the stock received. The basis of the stock received is reduced by the amount of the liabilities assumed by the corporation.

─────────────── EXAMPLE 14 ───────────────

C transfers property with an adjusted basis of $60,000, fair market value of $100,000, to X Corporation for 100% of the stock in X. The property is subject to a liability of $25,000 that X Corporation assumes. The exchange is tax-free under §§ 351 and 357.

However, the basis to C of the stock in X Corporation is $35,000 [$60,000 (basis of property transferred) − $25,000 (amount of mortgage)]. ◆

The rule of § 357(a) has two exceptions. Section 357(b) provides that if the principal purpose of the assumption of the liabilities is to avoid tax *or* if there is no bona fide business purpose behind the exchange, the liabilities are treated as boot. Further, § 357(c) provides that if the sum of the liabilities exceeds the adjusted basis of the properties transferred, the excess is taxable gain.

Tax Avoidance or No Bona Fide Business Purpose Exception. Unless liabilities are incurred shortly before incorporation, § 357(b) generally poses few problems. A tax avoidance purpose for transferring liabilities to a controlled corporation seems unlikely in view of the basis adjustment as noted above. Since the liabilities transferred reduce the basis of the stock received, any realized gain is deferred and not avoided. The gain materializes when and if the stock is disposed of in a taxable sale or exchange.

Satisfying the bona fide business purpose is not difficult if the liabilities were incurred in connection with the transferor's normal course of conducting a trade or business. But the bona fide business purpose requirement can cause difficulty if the liability is taken out shortly before the property is transferred and the proceeds are utilized for personal purposes.[14] This type of situation is analogous to a cash distribution by the corporation, which is taxed as boot.

EXAMPLE 15

D transfers real estate (basis of $40,000 and fair market value of $90,000) to a controlled corporation in return for stock in the corporation. Shortly before the transfer, D mortgages the real estate and uses the $20,000 proceeds to meet personal obligations. Along with the real estate, the mortgage is transferred to the corporation. In this case, it appears that the assumption of the mortgage lacks a bona fide business purpose. The amount of the liability is boot, and D has a taxable gain on the transfer of $20,000.[15] ◆

The effect of the application of § 357(b) is to taint *all* liabilities transferred even though some are supported by a bona fide business purpose.

EXAMPLE 16

T, an accrual basis taxpayer, incorporates his sole proprietorship. Among the liabilities transferred to the new corporation are trade accounts payable of $100,000 and a MasterCard bill of $5,000. T had used the MasterCard to purchase a wedding anniversary gift for his wife. Under these circumstances, all of the $105,000 liabilities are boot. ◆

Liabilities in Excess of Basis Exception. Unlike § 357(b), § 357(c) has posed numerous problems in § 351 transfers. Much litigation has centered around this provision in recent years, particularly with respect to cash basis taxpayers who incorporate their businesses. Section 357(c) states that if the sum of liabilities assumed and the liabilities to which transferred property is subject exceeds the total of the adjusted bases of the properties transferred, the excess is taxable gain. Without this provision, if liabilities exceed basis in property exchanged, a taxpayer would have a negative basis in the stock received in the controlled

---

14. See, for example, *Campbell, Jr. v. Wheeler,* 65–1 USTC ¶9294, 15 AFTR2d 578, 342 F.2d 837 (CA–5, 1965).

15. § 351(b).

corporation.[16] Section 357(c) precludes the negative basis possibility by treating the excess over basis as gain to the transferor.

────────────────────── EXAMPLE 17 ──────────────────────

A, an individual, transfers assets with an adjusted tax basis of $40,000 to a newly formed corporation in exchange for 100% of the stock. The corporation assumes liabilities on the transferred properties in the amount of $50,000. Without § 357(c), A's basis in the stock of the new corporation would be a negative $10,000 [$40,000 (basis of property transferred) + $0 (gain recognized) − $0 (boot received) − $50,000 (liabilities assumed)]. Section 357(c) causes A to recognize a gain of $10,000. As a result, the stock will have a zero basis in A's hands, determined as follows:

Basis in the property transferred	$40,000
Add: Gain recognized	10,000
Less: Boot received	–0–
Less: Liabilities assumed	50,000
Basis in the stock received	$ –0–

Thus, no negative basis results. ◆

Accounts payable of a cash basis taxpayer that give rise to a deduction and amounts payable under § 736(a) (payments to a retiring partner or payments in liquidation of a deceased partner's interest) are not considered to be liabilities for purposes of § 357(c).

────────────────────── EXAMPLE 18 ──────────────────────

T, a cash basis individual, incorporates her sole proprietorship. In return for all of the stock of the new corporation, she transfers the following items:

	Adjusted Basis	Fair Market Value
Cash	$10,000	$10,000
Unrealized accounts receivable (amounts due to T but not yet paid to her)	–0–	40,000
Trade accounts payable	–0–	30,000
Note payable	5,000	5,000

Unrealized accounts receivable and trade accounts payable have a zero basis. Under the cash method of accounting, no income is recognized until the receivables are collected, and no deduction materializes until the payables are satisfied. The note payable has a basis because it was issued for consideration received.

The accounts receivable and the trade accounts payable are disregarded. Thus, T has only transferred cash ($10,000) and a note payable ($5,000) and does not have a problem of liabilities in excess of basis. ◆

The definition of liabilities under § 357(c) excludes obligations that would have been deductible to the transferor had he or she paid those obligations before the transfer. Consequently, T, in Example 18, has no gain.

If §§ 357(b) and (c) both apply to the same transfer, § 357(b) predominates.[17] This could be significant because § 357(b) does not create gain on the transfer, as

───────────────

16. *Easson v. Comm.*, 33 T.C. 963 (1960), *rev'd.* in 61–2 USTC ¶9654, 8 AFTR2d 5448, 294 F.2d 653 (CA–9, 1961).

17. § 357(c)(2)(A).

does § 357(c), but merely converts the liability to boot. Thus, the realized gain limitation continues to apply to § 357(b) transactions.

EXAMPLE 19

A forms X Corporation by transferring land with a basis of $100,000, fair market value of $1,000,000. The land is subject to a mortgage of $300,000. One month prior to incorporating X, A borrows $200,000 for personal purposes and gives the lender a second mortgage on the land. X Corporation issues stock worth $500,000 to A and assumes the mortgages on the land. Section 357(c) applies to the transfer. The mortgages on the property ($500,000) exceed the basis of the property ($100,000). Thus, A has a gain of $400,000 under § 357(c). Section 357(b) also applies to the transfer. A borrowed $200,000 just prior to the transfer and used the $200,000 for personal purposes. Under § 357(b), A has boot of $500,000 in the amount of the liabilities (all of which are treated as boot). A has realized gain of $900,000 [$1,000,000 (fair market value of the land) − $100,000 (basis in the land)]. Gain is recognized to the extent of the boot of $500,000. Note that § 357(b) predominates over § 357(c). ◆

Basis Determination

Recall that § 351(a) postpones gain until the taxpayer's investment changes substantially. Postponement of the realized gain is accomplished through a carryover of basis under §§ 358(a) and 362(a).

Section 358(a). For a taxpayer transferring property to a corporation in a § 351 transaction, the basis of stock received in the transfer is the same as the basis the taxpayer had in the property transferred, increased by any gain recognized on the exchange and decreased by boot received. For basis purposes, boot received includes any liabilities transferred by the shareholder to the corporation.

Section 362(a). The basis of properties received by the corporation is determined under § 362(a). The basis to the corporation is the basis in the hands of the transferor increased by the amount of any gain recognized to the transferor shareholder.

The basis rules are summarized in Figures 3–1 and 3–2 and illustrated in Examples 20 and 21.

FIGURE 3–1

Shareholder's Basis in Stock Received

Adjusted basis of property transferred	$xx,xxx
Plus: Gain recognized	x,xxx
Minus: Boot received (including any liabilities transferred)	(x,xxx)
Equals: Basis of stock received	$xx,xxx

FIGURE 3–2

Corporation's Basis in Properties Received

Adjusted basis of property transferred	$xx,xxx
Plus: Gain recognized by transferor shareholder	xxx
Equals: Basis of property to corporation	$xx,xxx

EXAMPLE 20

M and N form Y Corporation. M transfers land (basis of $30,000 and fair market value of $70,000); N invests cash ($60,000). They each receive 50 shares in Y Corporation, worth $1,200 per share, but M also receives $10,000 cash from Y. The transfers of property, the realized and recognized gain on the transfers, and the basis of the stock in Y Corporation to M and N are as follows:

	A	B	C	D	E	F
	Basis of Property Transferred	FMV of Stock Received	Boot Received	Realized Gain (B + C − A)	Recognized Gain (Lesser of C or D)	Basis of Stock in Y (A − C + E)
From M: Land	$30,000	$60,000	$10,000	$40,000	$10,000	$30,000
From N: Cash	60,000	60,000	−0−	−0−	−0−	60,000

Y Corporation has a basis of $40,000 in the land. The basis to Y is M's basis of $30,000 plus M's recognized gain of $10,000. ◆

EXAMPLE 21

Assume the same facts as in Example 20 except that M's basis in the land is $68,000 (instead of $30,000). Because recognized gain cannot exceed realized gain, the transfer generates only $2,000 of gain to M. The realized and recognized gain and the basis of the stock in Y Corporation to M are as follows:

	A	B	C	D	E	F
	Basis of Property Transferred	FMV of Stock Received	Boot Received	Realized Gain (B + C − A)	Recognized Gain (Lesser of C or D)	Basis of Stock in Y (A − C + E)
Land	$68,000	$60,000	$10,000	$2,000	$2,000	$60,000

◆

Stock Issued for Services Rendered. Section 1032 provides that a corporation's disposition of stock for property is not a taxable exchange. A transfer of shares for services is also not a taxable transaction to a corporation.[18] Can a corporation deduct the fair market value of the stock it issues in consideration of services as a business expense? Yes, unless the services are such that the payment is characterized as a capital expenditure.[19]

EXAMPLE 22

C and D form Y Corporation. C transfers cash of $500,000 for 100 shares of Y Corporation stock. D transfers property worth $480,000 (basis of $90,000) and agrees to serve as manager of the corporation for one year; in return, D receives 100 shares of stock in Y. The value of D's services to Y Corporation is $20,000. The transfers qualify under § 351. D is not taxed on the transfer of the appreciated property. However, D has income of $20,000, the value of the services he will render to Y Corporation. Y Corporation has a basis of $90,000 in the property it acquired from D. It has a business deduction under § 162 of $20,000 for the value of services D will render. ◆

---

18. Reg. § 1.1032–1(a).
19. Rev.Rul. 62–217, 1962–2 C.B. 59, modified by Rev.Rul.

74–503, 1974–2 C.B. 117.

EXAMPLE 23

Assume, in Example 22, that D receives the 100 shares of Y Corporation stock in consideration for the appreciated property and for providing legal services in organizing the corporation. The value of D's legal services is $20,000. D has no gain on the transfer of the property but has income of $20,000 for the value of the services rendered. Y Corporation has a basis of $90,000 in the property it acquired from D and must capitalize the $20,000 as organizational expenses. ◆

Holding Period for Shareholder and Transferee Corporation. The shareholder's holding period for stock received for a capital asset or for § 1231 property includes the holding period of the property transferred to the corporation. The holding period of the property is "tacked on" to the holding period of the stock.[20] The holding period for stock received for any other property (e.g., inventory or property held primarily for sale) begins on the day after the exchange.[21] The transferee corporation's holding period for property acquired in a § 351 transfer is the holding period of the transferor shareholder regardless of the character of the property to the transferor.

Recapture Considerations

Recapture of Accelerated Cost Recovery (Depreciation). In a pure § 351(a) nontaxable transfer (no boot involved) to a controlled corporation, the recapture of accelerated cost recovery rules do not apply.[22] Moreover, any recapture potential of the property carries over to the corporation as it steps into the shoes of the transferor-shareholder for purposes of basis determination.

EXAMPLE 24

T transfers equipment (basis of $30,000 and fair market value of $100,000) to a controlled corporation in return for additional stock. If T had sold the equipment, it would have yielded a gain of $70,000, all of which would be recaptured as ordinary income under § 1245. If the transfer comes within § 351(a), T has no recognized gain and no accelerated cost recovery to recapture. If the corporation later disposes of the equipment in a taxable transaction, it will have to take into account the § 1245 recapture potential originating with T. ◆

Tax Benefit Rule. A taxpayer may have to take into income the recovery of an item previously expensed. Such income, however, is limited to the amount of the deduction that actually produced a tax saving. The relevance of the tax benefit rule to transfers to controlled corporations under § 351 was first raised in connection with accounts receivable and the reserve for bad debts.

EXAMPLE 25

T, an accrual basis individual, incorporates her sole proprietorship. In return for all of the stock of the corporation, T transfers, among other assets, accounts receivable with a face amount of $100,000 and a reserve for bad debts of $10,000 (book value of $90,000). T had previously deducted the addition to the reserve. The $10,000 deduction resulted in a tax benefit to T. ◆

The IRS took the position that § 351 did not insulate the transfer from the tax benefit rule.[23] Since T had previously deducted the reserve for bad debts and the reserve was no longer necessary, she should take the full $10,000 into income. In

---

20. § 1223(1).
21. § 1223(2).

22. §§ 1245(b)(3) and 1250(d)(3).
23. Rev.Rul. 62–128, 1962–2 C.B. 139.

Nash v. U.S.,[24] the Supreme Court disagreed. Operating on the assumption that the stock T received must be worth only $90,000 (the book value of the receivables), the Court compared the situation to a sale. No gain would have resulted if T had sold the receivables for $90,000. Why should it matter that they were transferred to a controlled corporation under § 351?

The Supreme Court decision in *Nash* does not imply that the tax benefit rule is inapplicable to transfers to controlled corporations when no gain is recognized. Returning to the facts in Example 25, suppose T was one of several transferors and the value of the stock she received exceeded the book value of the receivables ($90,000). Could the excess be subject to income recognition by virtue of the application of the tax benefit rule? The courts have not specifically addressed this question.

CAPITAL STRUCTURE OF A CORPORATION

Capital Contributions

The receipt of money or property in exchange for capital stock (including treasury stock) produces neither gain nor loss to the recipient corporation. Nor does a corporation's gross income include shareholders' contributions of money or property to the capital of the corporation. Additional funds received from shareholders through voluntary pro rata payments are not income to the corporation. This is the case even though there is no increase in the outstanding shares of stock of the corporation. The payments represent an additional price paid for the shares held by the shareholders and are treated as additions to the operating capital of the corporation.[25]

Contributions by nonshareholders, such as land contributed to a corporation by a civic group or a governmental group to induce the corporation to locate in a particular community, are also excluded from the gross income of a corporation.[26] Property that is transferred to a corporation by a nonshareholder for services rendered or for merchandise is taxable income to the corporation.[27]

EXAMPLE 26

A television company charges its customers an initial fee to hook up to a new television system installed in the area. These payments are used to finance the total cost of constructing the television facilities. The customers will make monthly payments for the television service. The initial payments are used for capital expenditures, but they represent payments for services to be rendered by the television company. As such, they are taxable income and not contributions to capital by nonshareholders. ◆

The basis of property received by a corporation from a shareholder as a contribution to capital is the basis of the property in the hands of the shareholder increased by any gain recognized to the shareholder. The basis of property transferred to a corporation by a nonshareholder as a contribution to capital is zero.

If a corporation receives money as a contribution to capital from a nonshareholder, a special rule applies. The basis of any property acquired with the money during a 12-month period beginning on the day the contribution was received is reduced by the amount of the contribution. The excess of money received over

24. 70–1 USTC ¶9405, 25 AFTR2d 1177, 90 S.Ct.1550 (USSC, 1970).

25. § 118 and Reg. § 1.118–1.

26. See *Edwards v. Cuba Railroad Co.*, 1 USTC ¶139, 5 AFTR 5398, 45 S.Ct. 614 (USSC, 1925).

27. Reg. § 1.118–1. See also *Teleservice Co. of Wyoming Valley v. Comm.*, 27 T.C. 722 (1957), *aff'd*. in 58–1 USTC ¶9383, 1 AFTR2d 1249, 254 F.2d 105 (CA–3, 1958), *cert. den*. 78 S.Ct. 1360 (USSC, 1958).

the cost of new property is used to reduce the basis of other property held by the corporation. The excess is applied to reduce the basis of property in the following order:

- Depreciable property.
- Property subject to amortization.
- Property subject to depletion.
- All other remaining properties.

The basis of property within each category is reduced in proportion to the relative bases of the properties.[28]

─────────────── EXAMPLE 27 ───────────────

A city donates land to X Corporation as an inducement for X to locate in the city. The receipt of the land does not produce taxable income. However, the land's basis to the corporation is zero. Assume the city also pays the corporation $10,000 in cash. The money is not taxable income to the corporation. However, if the corporation purchases property with the $10,000 within the next 12 months, the basis of the property is reduced by $10,000. ◆

Debt in the Capital Structure

Advantages of Debt. Shareholders must be aware of the difference between debt and equity in the capital structure. The advantages of receiving long-term debt are numerous. Interest on debt is deductible by the corporation, while dividend payments are not. Further, the shareholders are not taxed on loan repayments unless the repayments exceed basis. As long as a corporation has earnings and profits (see Chapter 4), an investment in stock cannot be withdrawn tax-free. Withdrawals will be deemed to be taxable dividends to the extent of earnings and profits of the distributing corporation.

─────────────── EXAMPLE 28 ───────────────

A, an individual, transfers cash of $100,000 to a newly formed corporation for 100% of the stock. In the first year of operations, the corporation has net income of $40,000. The income is credited to the earnings and profits account of the corporation. If the corporation distributes $9,500 to A, the distribution is a taxable dividend with no corresponding deduction to the corporation. Assume A transfers cash of $50,000 for stock. In addition, A loans the corporation $50,000, transferring cash of $50,000 to the corporation for a note in the amount of $50,000. The note is payable in equal annual installments of $5,000 and bears interest at the rate of 9%. At the end of the year, the corporation pays A $4,500 interest, which is tax deductible. The $5,000 principal repayment on the loan is not taxed to A. ◆

Reclassification of Debt as Equity ("Thin Capitalization" Problem). In certain instances, the IRS contends that debt is really an equity interest and denies the shareholders the tax advantages of debt financing. If the debt instrument has too many features of stock, it may be treated as a form of stock. In that case, the principal and interest payments are considered dividends. Under § 385, the IRS has the authority to characterize corporate debt wholly as equity or as part debt and part equity.

Section 385 lists several factors that *may* be used to determine whether a debtor-creditor relationship or a shareholder-corporation relationship exists. The thrust of § 385 is to authorize the Treasury to prescribe Regulations that

─────────────────────────

28. § 362 and Reg. § 1.362–2(b).

provide more definite guidelines for determining when debt should be reclassified as equity. To date, the Treasury has not drafted acceptable Regulations.[29] Consequently, taxpayers must rely on judicial decisions to determine whether a true debtor-creditor relationship exists.

Together, § 385 and the courts have identified the following factors to be considered in resolving the thin capitalization problem:

- Whether the debt instrument is in proper form. An open account advance is more easily characterized as a contribution to capital than a loan evidenced by a properly written note executed by the shareholder.[30]
- Whether the debt instrument bears a reasonable rate of interest and has a definite maturity date. When a shareholder advance does not provide for interest, the return expected is that inherent in an equity interest (e.g., a share of the profits or an increase in the value of the shares).[31] Likewise, a lender unrelated to the corporation will usually be unwilling to commit funds to the corporation for an indefinite period of time (i.e., no definite due date).
- Whether the debt is paid on a timely basis. A lender's failure to insist upon timely repayment (or satisfactory renegotiation) indicates that the return sought does not depend upon interest income and the repayment of principal.
- Whether payment is contingent upon earnings. A lender ordinarily will not advance funds that are likely to be repaid only if the venture is successful.
- Whether the debt is subordinated to other liabilities. Subordination tends to eliminate a significant characteristic of the creditor-debtor relationship. Creditors should have the right to share with other general creditors in the event of the corporation's dissolution or liquidation. Subordination also destroys another basic attribute of creditor status—the power to demand payment at a fixed maturity date.[32]
- Whether holdings of debt and stock are proportionate. When debt and equity obligations are held in the same proportion, shareholders are, apart from tax considerations, indifferent as to whether corporate distributions are in the form of interest or dividends.
- Whether funds loaned to the corporation are used to finance initial operations or capital asset acquisitions. Funds used to finance initial operations or to acquire capital assets the corporation needs to operate are generally obtained through equity investments.
- Whether the corporation has a high ratio of shareholder debt to shareholder equity. Thin capitalization occurs when shareholder debt is high relative to shareholder equity. This indicates the corporation lacks reserves to pay interest and principal on debt when corporate income is insufficient to meet current needs.[33] In determining a corporation's debt-equity ratio, courts have looked at the relation of the debt both to the book value of the corporation's assets and to their actual fair market value.[34]

29. Neither the proposed Regulations that were scheduled to be completed in 1980 nor the proposed revisions, as published in January 1982, fully reflected the position of either the IRS or the Treasury on debt/equity matters. Consequently, the final Regulations and the proposed revisions were withdrawn.

30. *Estate of Mixon v. U.S.,* 72–2 USTC ¶9537, 30 AFTR2d 72–5094, 464 F.2d 394 (CA–5, 1972).

31. *Slappey Drive Industrial Park v. U.S.,* 77–2 USTC ¶9696, 40 AFTR2d 77–5940, 561 F.2d 572 (CA–5, 1977).

32. *Fin Hay Realty Co. v. U.S.,* 68–2 USTC ¶9438, 22 AFTR2d 5004, 398 F.2d 694 (CA–3, 1968).

33. A court held that a debt-equity ratio of approximately 4:1 was not excessive. See *Tomlinson v. 1661 Corp.,* 67–1 USTC ¶9438, 19 AFTR2d 1413, 377 F.2d 291 (CA–5, 1967).

34. In *Bauer v. Comm.,* 84–2 USTC ¶9996, 55 AFTR2d 84–433, 748 F.2d 1365 (CA–9, 1984), a debt-equity ratio of 92:1 resulted when book value was used. But the ratio ranged from 2:1 to 8:1 when equity included both paid-in capital and accumulated earnings.

For the most part, the principles used to classify debt as equity developed in connection with closely held corporations. Here, the holders of the debt are also shareholders. The rules have often proved inadequate for dealing with such problems in large, publicly traded corporations.

In 1989, Congress amended § 385 to authorize the Treasury to issue Regulations classifying an instrument either as *wholly* debt or equity or as *part* debt and *part* equity. This flexible approach is important because some instruments cannot readily be classified either wholly as stock or wholly as debt. It may also provide an avenue for the IRS to address problems in publicly traded corporations.

The authority of the Treasury to reclassify *some* debt as equity may be appropriate in circumstances where a debt instrument provides for payments that are dependent on corporate performance. This objective may be accomplished through provisions allowing contingent interest, significant deferral of payment, or subordination of debt. It enables the IRS to reclassify debt instruments as part equity where the interest rate is sufficiently high to suggest a significant risk of default.[35]

Investor Losses

The choice between debt and equity financing leads to a consideration of the tax treatment of worthless stock and securities versus the treatment of bad debts.

Stock and Security Losses.   If stocks and bonds are capital assets in the hands of the holder, losses from their worthlessness are governed by § 165(g)(1). Under this provision, a capital loss materializes as of the last day of the taxable year in which the stocks or bonds become worthless. No deduction is allowed for a mere decline in value. The burden of proving complete worthlessness is on the taxpayer claiming the loss. One way to recognize partial worthlessness is to dispose of the stocks or bonds in a taxable sale or exchange.[36] But even then, the loss is disallowed under § 267(a)(1) if the sale or exchange is to a related party.

When the stocks or bonds are not capital assets, worthlessness yields an ordinary loss under § 165(a).[37] For example, if the stocks or bonds are held by a broker for resale to customers in the normal course of business, they are not capital assets. Usually, however, stocks and bonds are held as investments and are capital assets.

Under certain circumstances involving stocks and bonds of affiliated corporations, an ordinary loss is allowed upon worthlessness. These conditions are set forth in § 165(g)(3). A corporation is an affiliate of another corporation if the corporate shareholder owns at least 80 percent of the voting power of all classes of stock entitled to vote and 80 percent of each class of nonvoting stock. An ordinary loss is allowed upon worthlessness of the stock if the affiliated corporation derived 90 percent of its aggregate gross receipts for all taxable years from sources other than passive income. Passive income includes such items as rents, royalties, dividends, and interest.

The possibility of an ordinary loss on the stock of small business corporations (§ 1244) is discussed later in the chapter.

Business versus Nonbusiness Bad Debts.   In addition to the possible worthlessness of stocks and bonds, the financial end of a corporation can lead to bad debt deductions. These deductions can be either business bad debts or nonbusi-

---

35. H.Rep. No. 101–247, 101st Cong., 1st Sess. 1235–1236 (1989).

36. Reg. § 1.165–4(a).

37. Reg. § 1.165–5(b).

ness bad debts. The distinction between the two types of deductions is important for tax purposes in the following respects:

- Business bad debts are deducted as ordinary losses while nonbusiness bad debts are treated as short-term capital losses.[38] A business bad debt can generate a net operating loss while a nonbusiness bad debt cannot.[39]
- A deduction is allowed for the partial worthlessness of a business debt. Nonbusiness debts can be written off only when they become entirely worthless.[40]
- Nonbusiness bad debt treatment is limited to noncorporate taxpayers. All of the bad debts of a corporation qualify as business bad debts.[41]

When is a debt business or nonbusiness? Unfortunately, since the Code sheds little light on the matter, the distinction has been left to the courts.[42] In a leading decision, the Supreme Court somewhat clarified the picture when it held that being an investor does not, by itself, constitute a trade or business.[43] According to the Supreme Court, if individual shareholders loan money to a corporation in their capacity as investors, any resulting bad debt is classified as nonbusiness. Nevertheless, the Court did not preclude the possibility of a shareholder-creditor's incurring a business bad debt.

If a loan is made in some capacity that qualifies as a trade or business, nonbusiness bad debt treatment is avoided. For example, has the loan been made to protect the shareholder's employment with the corporation? Employee status is a trade or business, and a loss on a loan made for this purpose qualifies for business bad debt treatment.[44] Shareholders also receive business bad debt treatment if they are in the trade or business of loaning money or of buying, promoting, and selling corporations.

Suppose the shareholder has multiple motives for making the loan. Again the Supreme Court was called upon to resolve the problem.[45] According to the Court, the "dominant" or "primary" motive for making the loan controls the classification of the loss.

--- EXAMPLE 29 ---

T owns 48% of the stock of X Corporation, acquired several years ago at a cost of $100,000. T is also employed by the corporation at an annual salary of $40,000. At a time when X Corporation is experiencing financial problems, T loans it $50,000. Subsequently, the corporation becomes bankrupt, and both T's stock investment and his loans become worthless. ◆

Granted that T's stock investment is treated as a long-term capital loss (assuming § 1244 does not apply, as discussed below), how is the bad debt classified? If T can prove that his dominant or primary reason for making the loan was to protect his salary, a business bad debt deduction results. If not, it is assumed that T was trying to protect his stock investment, and nonbusiness bad debt treatment results. Factors to be considered in resolving this matter include the following:

---

38. Compare § 166(a) with § 166(d)(1)(B).

39. Note the adjustments necessitated by § 172(d)(2).

40. Compare § 166(a)(2) with § 166(d)(1)(A).

41. § 166(d)(1).

42. For definitional purposes, § 166(d)(2) is almost as worthless as the debt it purports to describe.

43. *Whipple v. Comm.*, 63–1 USTC ¶9466, 11 AFTR2d 1454, 83 S.Ct. 1168 (USSC, 1963).

44. *Trent v. Comm.*, 61–2 USTC ¶9506, 7 AFTR2d 1599, 291 F.2d 669 (CA–2, 1961).

45. *U.S. v. Generes*, 72–1 USTC ¶9259, 29 AFTR2d 72–609, 92 S.Ct. 827 (USSC, 1972).

- A comparison of the amount of the stock investment with the trade or business benefit derived. In Example 29, the stock investment of $100,000 is compared with the annual salary of $40,000. In this regard, the salary should be considered as a recurring item and not viewed in isolation. A salary of $40,000 each year means a great deal to a person who has no other means of support and who may have difficulty obtaining similar employment elsewhere.
- A comparison of the amount of the loan with the stock investment and the trade or business benefit derived.
- The percentage of ownership held by the shareholder. A minority shareholder, for example, is under more compulsion to loan the corporation money to protect his or her job than one who is in control of corporate policy.

In summary, it is impossible to conclude whether the taxpayer in Example 29 suffered a business or nonbusiness bad debt without additional facts. Even with such facts, the guidelines are vague. Recall that a taxpayer's intent or motivation is at issue. For this reason, the problem is the subject of frequent litigation.[46]

Section 1244 Stock. Section 1244 permits ordinary loss treatment for losses on the sale or worthlessness of stock of so-called small business corporations. By placing shareholders on a more nearly equal basis with proprietors and partners in terms of the tax treatment of losses, the provision encourages investment of capital in small corporations. Gain on the sale of § 1244 stock remains capital. Consequently, the shareholder has nothing to lose and everything to gain by complying with § 1244.

Only a small business corporation can issue qualifying § 1244 stock. The total amount of stock that can be offered under the plan to issue § 1244 stock cannot exceed $1,000,000. For these purposes, property received in exchange for stock is valued at its adjusted basis, reduced by any liabilities assumed by the corporation or to which the property is subject. The fair market value of the property is not considered. The $1,000,000 limitation is determined by property and money received for the stock as a contribution to capital and as paid-in capital on the date the stock is issued. Consequently, even though a corporation fails to meet these requirements when the stock later is sold, the stock can still qualify as §1244 stock if the requirements were met on the date the stock was issued.

The corporation must derive more than 50 percent of its aggregate gross receipts from sources other than royalties, rents, dividends, interest, annuities, and sales and exchanges of stock or securities (only the gains are considered). The test applies for the corporation's most recent five tax years. The gross receipts requirement applies only if the corporation's receipts equal or exceed its deductions other than a net operating loss deduction or the dividends received deduction.

The amount of ordinary loss deductible in any one year on § 1244 stock is limited to $50,000 (or $100,000 for husband and wife filing a joint return). If the amount of the loss sustained in the taxable year exceeds these amounts, the remainder is considered a capital loss.

--- EXAMPLE 30 ---

A taxpayer acquires § 1244 stock at a cost of $100,000. He sells the stock for $10,000 in one tax year. He has an ordinary loss of $50,000 and a capital loss of $40,000. On a joint return, the entire $90,000 loss is ordinary. ◆

---

46. See, for example, *Kelson v. U.S.*, 74–2 USTC ¶9714, 34 AFTR2d 74–6007, 503 F.2d 1291 (CA–10, 1974).

Only the original holder of § 1244 stock, whether an individual or a partnership, qualifies for ordinary loss treatment. If the stock is sold or donated, it loses its § 1244 status.

If a partnership is involved, the individual must have been a partner at the time the partnership acquired the stock. In addition, the partnership must not distribute the stock to the partners. Each partner's share of partnership tax attributes includes the share of the loss the partnership sustains on the stock.

EXAMPLE 31

A and B are partners in the AB Partnership. AB Partnership acquires 100 shares of § 1244 stock in X Corporation at a cost of $100,000. A few months later AB Partnership distributes 25 shares to A and 25 shares to B. X Corporation suffers financial difficulties and files for bankruptcy two years later. The X Corporation stock is worthless. AB Partnership can claim an ordinary loss of $50,000 (the cost of the remaining 50 shares in X Corporation), which is then passed to A and B as ordinary loss. However, A and B have a capital loss of $25,000 each on the shares distributed to them by AB Partnership. The 50 shares AB Partnership distributed to A and B lose their § 1244 status. A and B were not the original holders of the stock.[47] If AB Partnership had not distributed the stock to A and B, it would have claimed an ordinary loss of $100,000, which would have passed to A and B as ordinary loss. Thus, A and B could each have claimed ordinary loss of $50,000 on their individual returns. ◆

Recall the advantages of issuing some debt to shareholders in exchange for cash contributions to a corporation. A disadvantage of issuing debt is that it does not qualify under § 1244. Should the debt become worthless, the taxpayer generally has a short-term capital loss rather than the ordinary loss for § 1244 stock.

The basis of § 1244 stock issued by a corporation in exchange for property that has an adjusted basis above its fair market value immediately before the exchange is reduced to the fair market value of the property on the date of the exchange. The basis is reduced for the purpose of determining ordinary loss upon a subsequent sale.

EXAMPLE 32

A taxpayer transfers property with a basis of $10,000 and a fair market value of $5,000 to a corporation in exchange for shares of § 1244 stock. Assuming the transfer qualifies under § 351, the basis of the stock is $10,000, the same as the taxpayer's basis in the property. For purposes of § 1244, the basis is only $5,000. If the stock is later sold for $3,000, the total loss sustained is $7,000 ($10,000 − $3,000); however, only $2,000 is ordinary loss ($5,000 − $3,000). The remaining portion, $5,000, is capital loss. ◆

If a shareholder contributes additional property or money to a corporation after acquiring § 1244 stock, the amount of ordinary loss upon a sale of the § 1244 stock is limited to his or her original contribution.

Working with § 351

TAX PLANNING CONSIDERATIONS

Effective tax planning with transfers of property to corporations involves a clear understanding of § 351 and its related Code provisions. The most important question in planning is simply: Does compliance with the requirements of § 351 yield the desired tax result?

---

47. Reg. § 1.1244(a)–1(b)(2). *Jerome Prizant*, 30 TCM 817, T.C.Memo. 1971–196.

Utilizing § 351.   In using § 351(a), ensure that all parties transferring property (which includes cash) receive control of the corporation. Simultaneous transfers are not necessary, but a long period of time between transfers is vulnerable if the transfers are not properly documented as part of a single plan. To do this, the parties should document and preserve evidence of their intentions. Also, it is helpful to have some reasonable explanation for any delay in the transfers.

To meet the requirements of § 351, mere momentary control on the part of the transferor may not suffice if loss of control is compelled by a prearranged agreement.[48]

EXAMPLE 33

For many years, T operated a business as a sole proprietor employing R as manager. To dissuade R from quitting and going out on her own, T promised her a 30% interest in the business. To fulfill this promise, T transfers the business to newly formed X Corporation in return for all its stock. Immediately thereafter, T transfers 30% of the stock to R. Section 351 probably would not apply to the transfer by T to X Corporation. It appears that T was under an obligation to relinquish control. If this is not the case and the loss of control was voluntary on T's part, momentary control would suffice.[49] ◆

Be sure that later transfers of property to an existing corporation satisfy the control requirement if recognition of gain is to be avoided. In this connection, a transferor's interest cannot be counted if the value of stock received is relatively small compared with the value of stock already owned. Further, the primary purpose of the transfer may not be to qualify other transferors for § 351 treatment.[50]

To keep the matter in perspective, be in a position to recognize when § 351 is not relevant.

EXAMPLE 34

The stock in Q Corporation is held equally by F and D (father and daughter). F transfers real estate (basis of $40,000 and fair market value of $100,000) to Q Corporation. F receives no additional stock in Q as a result of the transfer. F has made a capital contribution, and § 351 is of no consequence. The transfer causes no gain to F, but other tax consequences can result.[51] F should increase his basis in his Q Corporation stock. ◆

Avoiding § 351.   Section 351(a) provides for the nonrecognition of gain on transfers to controlled corporations. As such, it is often regarded as a relief provision favoring taxpayers. In some situations, however, avoiding § 351(a) may produce a more advantageous tax result. The transferors might prefer to recognize gain on the transfer of property if they cannot be particularly harmed by the gain. For example, they may be in low tax brackets, or the gain may be a capital gain from which substantial capital losses can be offset. The corporation will then have a stepped-up basis in the transferred property.

Another reason a particular transferor might wish to avoid § 351 concerns possible loss recognition. Recall that § 351 refers to the nonrecognition of both gains and losses. Section 351(b)(2) specifically states: "No loss to such recipient shall be recognized." A transferor who wishes to recognize loss has several alternatives:

48. Rev.Rul. 54–96, 1954–1 C.B. 111.

49. Compare *Fahs v. Florida Machine and Foundry Co.*, 48–2 USTC ¶9329, 36 AFTR 1151, 168 F.2d 957 (CA–5, 1948), with *John C. O'Connor*, 16 TCM 213, T.C.Memo. 1957–50, *aff'd.* in 58–2 USTC ¶9913, 2 AFTR2d 6011, 260 F.2d 358 (CA–6, 1958).

50. Reg. § 1.351–1(a)(1)(ii). Refer to Example 10 of this chapter. The stock attribution rules of § 318 (see Chapter 5) do not

apply to § 351 transfers.

51. The daughter has benefited from F's capital contribution (her shares are, as a result, worth more). Therefore, a gift has taken place, and F's capital contribution could lead to the imposition of a gift tax liability. In this connection, see Chapter 17.

- Sell the property to the corporation for its stock. The IRS could attempt to collapse the "sale," however, by taking the approach that the transfer really falls under § 351(a).[52] If the sale is disregarded, the transferor ends up with a realized, but unrecognized, loss.
- Sell the property to the corporation for other property or boot. Because the transferor receives no stock, § 351 is inapplicable.
- Transfer the property to the corporation in return for securities. Recall that § 351 does not apply to a transferor who receives securities. In both this and the previous alternatives, watch for the possible disallowance of the loss under § 267.

Suppose the loss property is to be transferred to the corporation and no loss is recognized by the transferor due to § 351(a). This could present an interesting problem in terms of assessing the economic realities involved.

─────────────── EXAMPLE 35 ───────────────

E and F form X Corporation with the following investment: property by E (basis of $40,000 and fair market value of $50,000) and property by F (basis of $60,000 and fair market value of $50,000). Each receives 50% of the X Corporation stock. Has F acted wisely in settling for only 50% of the stock? At first, it would appear so, since E and F each invested property of the same value ($50,000). But what about tax considerations? Due to basis carryover, the corporation now has a basis of $40,000 in E's property and $60,000 in F's property. In essence, E has shifted a possible $10,000 gain to the corporation while F has transferred a $10,000 potential loss. With this in mind, an equitable allocation of the X Corporation stock would call for F to receive a greater percentage interest than E. ◆

Other Considerations in Incorporating a Business

When a business is incorporated, the organizers must determine which assets and liabilities should be transferred to the corporation. A transfer of assets that produce passive income (rents, royalties, dividends, and interest) can cause the corporation to be a personal holding company in a tax year when operating income is low. Thus, the corporation could be subject to the personal holding company penalty tax (see the discussion in Chapter 6).

A transfer of the accounts payable of a cash basis taxpayer prevents the taxpayer from taking a tax deduction when the accounts are paid. These payables should generally be retained.

Leasing some property to the corporation may be a more attractive alternative than transferring ownership. Leasing provides the taxpayer with the opportunity of withdrawing money from the corporation without the payment being characterized as a dividend. If the property is donated to a family member in a lower tax bracket, the lease income can be shifted as well. If the depreciation and other deductions available in connection with the property are larger than the lease income, the taxpayer would retain the property until the income exceeds the deductions.

Shareholder debt in a corporation can be given to family members in a lower tax bracket. This technique also causes income to be shifted without a loss of control of the corporation.

─────────────

52. *U.S. v. Hertwig,* 68–2 USTC ¶9495, 22 AFTR2d 5249, 398 F.2d 452 (CA–5, 1968).

Debt in the Capital Structure

The advantages of debt as opposed to equity have previously been emphasized. The main hurdle to overstressing debt is the thin capitalization problem. In avoiding the problem, consider the following observations:

- Preserve the formalities of the debt. This includes providing for written instruments, realistic interest rates, and specified due dates.
- If possible, have the corporation repay the debt when it becomes due. If this is not possible, have the parties renegotiate the arrangement. Try to proceed as a third-party (i.e., nonshareholder) creditor would. It is not unusual, for example, for bondholders of publicly held corporations to extend due dates when default occurs. The alternative is to foreclose and perhaps seriously impair the amount the creditors will recover.
- Avoid provisions in the debt instrument that make the debt convertible to equity in the event of default. These provisions are standard practice when nonshareholder creditors are involved. They make no sense if the shareholders are also the creditors.

EXAMPLE 36

C, D, and E are equal shareholders in Z Corporation. Each transfers cash of $100,000 to Z in return for its bonds. The bond agreement provides that the holders will receive additional voting rights in the event Z Corporation defaults on its bonds. The voting rights provision is worthless and merely raises the issue of thin capitalization. C, D, and E already control Z Corporation, so what purpose is served by increasing their voting rights? The parties probably used a "boiler plate" bond agreement that was designed for third-party lenders (e.g., banks and financial institutions). ◆

- Pro rata holding of debt is difficult to avoid. For example, if each of the shareholders owns one-third of the stock, then each will want one-third of the debt. Nevertheless, some variation is possible.

EXAMPLE 37

Assume the same facts as Example 36 except that only C and D acquire the bonds. E leases property to Z Corporation at an annual rent that approximates the yield on the bonds. Presuming the rent passes the arm's length test (i.e., what unrelated parties would charge), all parties reach the desired result. C and D withdraw corporate profits in the form of interest income, and E is provided for with rent income. Z Corporation can deduct both the interest and rent payments. ◆

- Try to keep the debt-equity ratio within reasonable proportions. A frequent pitfall arises when the parties first form the corporation. Often the amount invested in capital stock is the minimum required by state law. For example, if the state of incorporation permits a minimum of $1,000, limiting the investment to this amount does not provide much safety for later debt financing by the shareholders.
- Stressing the fair market value of the assets rather than their tax basis to the corporation can be helpful in preparing to defend debt-equity ratios.

EXAMPLE 38

F, G, and H form W Corporation with the following capital investments: cash of $200,000 from F; land worth $200,000 (basis of $20,000) from G; and a patent worth $200,000 (basis of $0) from H. Saying the equity of W Corporation is $220,000 (the tax basis to the corporation) does not reflect reality. The equity account is more properly stated at $600,000 ($200,000 + $200,000 + $200,000). ◆

- The nature of the business can have an effect on what is an acceptable debt-equity ratio. Capital-intensive industries (e.g., manufacturing, transportation) characteristically rely heavily on debt financing. Consequently, larger debt should be tolerated.

Investor Losses

In connection with § 1244, be aware that there is a danger of losing § 1244 attributes. Recall that only the original holder of § 1244 stock is entitled to ordinary loss treatment. If a corporation is formed to shift income within the family group by transferring shares of stock to family members, the benefits of § 1244 are lost.

─────────────── EXAMPLE 39 ───────────────

F incorporates his business by transferring property worth $100,000 for 100 shares of stock. The stock qualifies as § 1244 stock. F later gives 50 shares each to his children, S and D. Eventually, the business fails, and the corporation becomes bankrupt. The shares of stock become worthless. If F had retained the stock, he would have had an ordinary loss deduction of $100,000 (assuming he filed a joint return). S and D, however, have a capital loss of $50,000 each because the § 1244 attributes were lost. ◆

PROBLEM MATERIALS

DISCUSSION QUESTIONS

1. In terms of justification and effect, § 351 (transfer to corporation controlled by transferor) and § 1031 (like-kind exchanges) are much alike. Explain. 3-2

2. In terms of the wherewithal to pay concept, why does it matter whether a transfer is wholly or partially nontaxable under § 351? 3-2 Ex: 1

3. F and S (father and son) form a corporation with a transfer of property valued at $200,000 and $100,000, respectively. In return for this property, F and S each receive 50% of the corporation's stock. Explain the tax consequences of these transfers to F and to S. Ex: 2 44

4. What does the term "property" include for purposes of § 351? 3-3

5. How does a corporation account for stock issued for services? Ex. 3

6. Is the transfer of an installment obligation in a § 351 transaction a disposition of the installment obligation that triggers gain on the transfer? Explain. 3-3

7. If gain is recognized in a § 351 transfer because boot is received, how is the gain characterized? 3-3

8. In arriving at the basis of stock received by a shareholder in a § 351 transfer, describe the effect of the following:

   a. The receipt of other property (boot) in addition to stock by the shareholder. Ex 20 & 21
   b. Transfer of a liability to the corporation, along with the property, by the shareholder. 3-7 to 3-10
   c. The shareholder's basis in the property transferred to the corporation. 3-10 & 11

9. How does a corporation determine its basis in property received pursuant to a § 351 transfer? 3-10 & 3-11

10. What is the control requirement of § 351? Describe the effect of the following in satisfying this requirement: 3-4 to 3-9

    a. A shareholder renders services to the corporation for stock. Ex. 8
    b. A shareholder both renders services and transfers property to the corporation for stock. 3-6
    c. A shareholder has only momentary control after the transfer. Ex. 33

d. A long period of time elapses between the transfers of property by different shareholders. ℰⲕ: 5

11. Assuming a § 351(a) nontaxable transfer, explain the tax effect, if any, of the following transactions:

a. The transfer of depreciable property with recapture potential under § 1245 or § 1250. ℰⲕ:24

b. The later sale of such property by the corporation.

12. At a point when X Corporation has been in existence for six years, shareholder T transfers real estate (adjusted basis of $20,000 and fair market value of $100,000) to the corporation for additional stock. At the same time, P, the other shareholder, purchases one share of stock for cash. After the two transfers, the percentage of stock ownership is as follows: 79% by T and 21% by P.

a. What were the parties trying to accomplish?
b. Will it work? Explain. pg 3-6-37
c. Would the result change if T and P are father and son? footnote 58

13. Assume the same facts as in Question 12, except that T receives nothing from X Corporation for the transfer of the real estate to the corporation. Does this change the tax result as to T? Ex 34

14. Before incorporating her apartment rental business, B takes out second mortgages on several of the units. B uses the mortgage funds to make capital improvements to her personal residence. Along with all of the rental units, B transfers the mortgages to the newly formed corporation in return for all of its stock. Discuss the tax consequences to B of these procedures. Ex 15

15. K's sole proprietorship includes assets that, if sold, would yield a gain of $100,000. It also includes assets that would yield a loss of $30,000. K incorporates his business using only the gain assets. Two days later, K sells the loss assets to the newly formed corporation.

a. What was K trying to accomplish? pg 3-20&21
b. Will it work? Explain.

16. What is the holding period to the shareholder of stock received from a controlled corporation? 3-12

17. In structuring the capitalization of a corporation, what are the advantages of utilizing debt rather than equity? 3-14&15

18. In determining whether the debt of a corporation should be reclassified as stock, comment on the relevance of the following:

a. The loan is an open account.
b. The loan is a demand loan.
c. Although the loan has a definite maturity date, the corporation has not made payments on a timely basis.
d. Payments on the loan are contingent upon corporate earnings.
e. The corporation's shareholders loaned funds to the corporation in the same proportion as their shareholdings, and the debt was used to purchase a new building.
f. The corporation has a debt-equity ratio of 5:1.

19. Assuming § 1244 does not apply, what is the tax treatment of stock that has become worthless? 3-16&17

20. Under what circumstances, if any, may a shareholder deduct a business bad debt on a loan he or she has made to the corporation? 3-16&17

21. T, an unmarried individual taxpayer, had invested $75,000 in the stock of X Corporation, which recently declared bankruptcy. Although T is distressed over the loss of her investment, she is somewhat consoled by the fact that the $75,000 will be an ordinary (rather than a capital) loss. Is T fully apprised of the tax result? Why or why not?

22. Several years ago, M purchased stock in Y Corporation for $40,000. The stock has a current value of $5,000. Consider the following alternatives:

a. Without selling the stock, M deducts $35,000 for partial worthlessness of the Y Corporation investment.

(handwritten top-left: 3-16 to 3-19)

b.   M sells the stock to his son for $5,000 and deducts a $35,000 long-term capital loss.
c.   M sells the stock to a third party and deducts a $35,000 long-term capital loss.
d.   M sells the stock to a third party and deducts a $35,000 ordinary loss.

23. T incorporates her sole proprietorship, but does not transfer the building the business uses to the corporation. Subsequently, the building is leased to the corporation for an annual rental. What tax reasons might T have for not transferring the building to the corporation when the business was incorporated? *3-21*

PROBLEMS

24. G and H form Z Corporation with the following investment:

| | **Property Transferred** | | **Number of** |
	Basis to Transferor	**Fair Market Value**	**Shares Issued**
From G—			
Cash *(considered property)*	$20,000	$ 20,000	
Installment obligation *3-5*	70,000	180,000	40
From H—			
Cash	70,000	70,000	
Machinery	60,000	90,000	60
Equipment	95,000	140,000	

(handwritten: 225)

The installment obligation has a face amount of $180,000 and was acquired last year from the sale of land held for investment purposes (adjusted basis of $70,000).

a.   How much gain, if any, must G recognize? *3-3*
b.   What will be G's basis in the Z Corporation stock? *Fig 3-1*
c.   What will be Z Corporation's basis in the installment obligation? *Fig 3-2*
d.   How much gain, if any, must H recognize? *3-3*
e.   What will be H's basis in the Z Corporation stock? *Fig 3-1*
f.   What will be Z Corporation's basis in the machinery and equipment? *3-2*
g.   How would your answer change if G received common stock and H received preferred stock? *3-4*
h.   How would your answer change if H were a partnership? *Pg 3-3, 3-10 & 3-11*

25. A, B, C, and D (all individuals) form W Corporation with the following investment:

| | **Property Transferred** | | **Number of** |
	Basis to Transferor	**Fair Market Value**	**Shares Issued**
From A— *depends on what the service is*			
Personal services rendered to W Corporation	$ –0–	$ 10,000	10 *10,000*
From B— *Realized Loss 15,000*			
Equipment *115-100=15*	115,000	100,000	90* *+10,000 90,000 +10000 cash*
From C—			
Cash	20,000	20,000	50 *50,000*
Unrealized accounts receivable	–0–	30,000	
From D—			
Land & building	70,000	150,000	50 *50,000*
Mortgage on land & building	100,000	100,000	

(handwritten left margin: 115000 Boot 10,000 / 105,000 / 351 - NO LOSS)

*B receives $10,000 in cash in addition to the 90 shares.

The mortgage transferred by D is assumed by W Corporation. The value of each share of W Corporation stock is $1,000.

a. What, if any, is A's recognized gain or loss?
b. What basis will A have in the W Corporation stock?
c. How much gain or loss must B recognize? 3-3
d. What basis will B have in the W Corporation stock?
e. What basis will W Corporation have in the equipment?
f. What, if any, is C's recognized gain or loss?
g. What basis will C have in the W Corporation stock?
h. What basis will W Corporation have in the unrealized accounts receivable?
i. How much gain or loss must D recognize?
j. What basis will D have in the W Corporation stock?
k. What basis will W Corporation have in the land and building?

26. J, K, L, and M form V Corporation with the following investment:

	Property Transferred		
	Basis to Transferor	Fair Market Value	Number of Shares Issued
From J—			
Inventory	$10,000	$32,000	30*
From K—			
Equipment ($10,000 of depreciation taken by K in prior years)	15,000	33,000	30**
From L—			
Secret process	5,000	30,000	30
From M—			
Cash	10,000	10,000	10

*J receives $2,000 in cash in addition to the 30 shares.
**K receives $3,000 in cash in addition to the 30 shares.

Assume the value of each share of V Corporation stock is $1,000.

a. What, if any, is J's recognized gain or loss? How is any such gain or loss treated? 3-3
b. What basis will J have in the V Corporation stock? 3-10 & 11
c. What basis will V Corporation have in the inventory? 3-10 & 11
d. How much gain or loss must K recognize? How is the gain or loss treated? 3-3
e. What basis will K have in the V Corporation stock? 3-10 & 3-11
f. What basis will V Corporation have in the equipment? 3-10 & 11
g. What, if any, is L's recognized gain or loss? 3-3
h. What basis will L have in the V Corporation stock? 3-10 11
i. What basis will V Corporation have in the secret process? 3-10 & 11
j. How much income, if any, must M recognize? 3-3
k. What basis will M have in the V Corporation stock? 3-10 & 3-11

27. A and B organize X Corporation by transferring the following property:

	Property Transferred		
	Basis to Transferor	Fair Market Value	Number of Shares Issued
From A—			
Unimproved land	$10,000	$100,000	
Mortgage on land	50,000	50,000	50
From B—			
Receivables	60,000	50,000	50

Assume the value of each share of X Corporation stock is $1,000.

a. What, if any, is A's recognized gain or loss? 3-9
b. What basis will A have in the X Corporation stock?
c. What basis will X Corporation have in the land?
d. What, if any, is B's recognized gain or loss?

e. What basis will B have in the X Corporation stock?

f. What basis will X Corporation have in the receivables?

28. A organized Y Corporation 10 years ago by contributing property worth $500,000, basis of $100,000, for 2,000 shares of stock in Y, representing 100% of the stock in Y Corporation. A later gave each of his children, B and C, 500 shares of stock in Y Corporation. In the current year, A transfers property worth $160,000, basis of $50,000, to Y Corporation for 500 shares in Y Corporation. What gain, if any, will A recognize on this transfer?

29. C and D form T Corporation. C transfers property worth $140,000 (basis of $50,000) for 70 shares in T Corporation. D receives 30 shares for property worth $55,000 (basis of $10,000) and for legal services in organizing the corporation; the services are worth $5,000.

a. What gain, if any, will the parties recognize on the transfer?

b. What basis will C and D have in the stock in T Corporation?

c. What basis will T Corporation have in the property and services it received from C and D?

30. Assume in Problem 29 that the property D transfers to T Corporation is worth $5,000 (basis of $1,000) and his services in organizing the corporation are worth $55,000. What are the tax consequences to C, D, and T Corporation?

31. A and B formed X Corporation on January 2, 1990. Each transferred property to X Corporation and received 50 shares in X in return. On July 1, 1992, C transfers property worth $200,000 (basis of $30,000) for 50 shares, or a one-third interest, in X Corporation. What are the tax consequences to C and to X Corporation on the transfer of property for stock?

32. T is an employee of X Corporation. In 1992, T receives a salary of $30,000 and is also given 10 shares of X stock for services she renders to the corporation. The shares in X Corporation are worth $1,000 each. How will the transfer of the 10 shares to T be handled for tax purposes by T and by X Corporation?

33. R, a sole proprietor, was engaged in a service business and reported her income on a cash basis. On February 1, 1992, she incorporated her business and transferred the assets of the business to the corporation in return for all the stock in the corporation plus the corporation's assumption of the liabilities of her proprietorship. All the receivables and the unpaid trade payables were transferred to the newly formed corporation. The balance sheet of the corporation immediately following the incorporation was as follows:

**R CORPORATION
BALANCE SHEET
February 1, 1992**

Assets

	Basis to R	Fair Market Value
Cash	$ 20,000	$ 20,000
Accounts receivable	–0–	60,000
Equipment (cost $90,000; depreciation $60,000)	30,000	80,000
Building (straight-line depreciation)	40,000	100,000
Land	10,000	40,000
	$100,000	$300,000

Liabilities and Stockholders' Equity

Liabilities:		
Accounts payable—trade	$ 30,000	
Notes payable—bank	90,000	
Stockholders' equity:		
Common stock	180,000	
	$300,000	

a. Will R recognize any taxable gain as a result of the incorporation of her business? Explain. 3–7

b. What basis will R have in the stock in R Corporation? 3 70 7:8 3–1

c. What basis will R Corporation have in the assets transferred to it by R? 3-10 Fig 3-2

34. A forms T Corporation transferring land with a basis of $50,000, fair market value of $300,000. The land is subject to a mortgage of $150,000. Two weeks prior to incorporating T, A borrows $50,000 for personal purposes and gives the lender a second mortgage on the land. T Corporation issues stock worth $100,000 to A and assumes the mortgages on the land.

a. What are the tax consequences to A and to T Corporation? 3-7 to3-10

b. Assume that A does not borrow the $50,000 prior to incorporating T. A transfers the land to T Corporation for all the stock in T. T Corporation then borrows $50,000 and gives the lender a mortgage on the land. T Corporation distributes the $50,000 to A. What are the tax consequences to A and to T Corporation?

35. T organized X Corporation and transferred land with a basis of $200,000, fair market value of $600,000, and subject to a mortgage of $150,000. A month before incorporation, T borrowed $100,000 for personal purposes and gave the bank a lien on the land. X Corporation issued stock worth $350,000 to T and assumed the loans in the amount of $150,000 and $100,000. What are the tax consequences of the incorporation to T and to X Corporation? 3-7 to 3-10

36. A transfers land to X Corporation for 85% of the stock in X Corporation plus a note payable to A in the amount of $50,000 and the assumption by X Corporation of a mortgage on the land in the amount of $90,000. The land, which had a tax basis to A of $60,000, was worth $150,000.

a. What gain, if any, would A recognize on the transfer? 3-3,4 & 7

b. What basis would A have in the stock in X Corporation? 3-10 &7:8 3-1

c. What basis would X Corporation have in the land? 3-10

37. Indicate whether the following statements are true or false:

a. If both § 357(b) and § 357(c) apply, the latter will control. 3-7

b. For § 357(b) to apply, the transfer of the liability must be for the purpose of tax avoidance *and* must lack a bona fide business purpose. 3-8

c. Section 357(c) will not apply if there is no realized gain on the transfer.

d. T transfers depreciable property to a controlled corporation. The property possesses a recapture potential under § 1245. A later sale of the property by the corporation could trigger recapture of depreciation to T. 3-8 & 7

e. T transfers supplies (tax basis of zero, fair market value of $10,000) for stock in a controlled corporation worth $10,000. Under these circumstances, the tax benefit rule will not cause any recognition of gain to T. 3-12 ex 25

38. A city donates land to X Corporation as an inducement for X to locate there. The land is worth $100,000. The city also donates $50,000 in cash to X.

a. What income, if any, must X recognize as a result of the transfer of land and cash to it by the city?

b. What basis will X have in the land?

c. If X purchases property six months later with the $50,000 cash, what basis will it have in the property?

39. T, an individual, transfers cash of $400,000 to a newly formed corporation for 100% of the stock. In the first year of operations, the corporation has net taxable income of $90,000. If the corporation distributes $68,000 to T, how will the distribution be treated for tax purposes to T? To the corporation?

40. Assume in Problem 39 that T transferred the cash for stock in the amount of $200,000 and debt in the amount of $200,000, payable in equal annual installments of $50,000 plus interest at the rate of 9%. Assume again that the corporation has net taxable income of $90,000. If the corporation distributes $68,000 to T as payment on the debt, how will the distribution be treated for tax purposes to T? To the corporation?

41. T forms X Corporation with an investment of $200,000 cash, for which he receives $20,000 in stock and $180,000 in 8% interest-bearing bonds maturing in nine years. Several years later, T loans the corporation an additional $50,000 on open account. X Corporation subsequently becomes insolvent and is adjudged bankrupt. During the corporation's existence, T was paid an annual salary of $40,000. How might T's losses be treated for tax purposes? 3-16 to 3-19 EX 29

42. Stock in X Corporation is held equally by A, B, and C. X seeks additional capital to construct a building in the amount of $900,000. A, B, and C each propose to loan X Corporation $300,000, taking from X Corporation a $300,000 four-year note with interest payable annually at two points below the prime rate. X Corporation has current taxable income of $2,000,000. How might the payments on the notes be treated for tax purposes? 3-15

43. T, a single taxpayer, acquired stock in a corporation that qualified as a small business corporation under § 1244, at a cost of $100,000 three years ago. He sells the stock for $10,000 in the current tax year. How will the loss be treated for tax purposes? EX. 30

44. Assume that T in Problem 43 gave the stock to his brother a few months after he acquired it. The stock was worth $100,000 on the date of the gift. T's brother sells the stock for $10,000 in the current tax year. How will the loss be treated for tax purposes? 3-19

45. T, an individual, transfers property with a basis of $40,000 and a fair market value of $20,000 to X Corporation in exchange for shares of § 1244 stock. (Assume the transfer qualifies under § 351.)

   a. What is the basis of the stock to T?
   b. What is the basis of the stock for purposes of § 1244 to T?
   c. If T sells the stock for $10,000 two years later, how will the loss be treated for tax purposes? EX. 32

RESEARCH PROBLEMS

RESEARCH PROBLEM 1 A cash basis partnership is incorporated. The newly formed corporation elects the cash method of accounting. The partnership transfers $30,000 of accounts receivable along with equipment, land, and cash. The corporation also agrees to pay accounts payable of the partnership in the amount of $40,000. The corporation files its return for its first year of operation and does not report the $30,000 received on accounts receivable of the partnership as income. It does deduct the $40,000 it paid on the partnership's accounts payable. The IRS disallows the deductions totaling $40,000 and increases the corporation's taxable income by $30,000, which represents the collection of partnership accounts receivable. What is the result?

RESEARCH PROBLEM 2 Individuals A, B, C, and D organize T Corporation with 100 shares of common stock. Each individual receives 25 shares in T Corporation in exchange for $60,000 worth of stock in different corporations. All of the stock transferred to T Corporation is listed on the New York Stock Exchange and is readily marketable. A transferred stock in X Corporation; B transferred stock in Y Corporation; C transferred stock in Z Corporation; and D transferred stock in several corporations. The stock will be held by T Corporation for investment purposes. A, B, C, and D all have a low basis in the stock they transferred to T Corporation. Will they recognize gain on the transfer? Assume A, B, C, and D form a partnership rather than T Corporation and transfer their readily marketable stock to the partnership. The partnership will hold the stock for investment purposes. Will gain be recognized on the transfer?

RESEARCH PROBLEM 3 A and B, two doctors, form W, a professional association, to engage in the practice of medicine. W purchases X-ray equipment to be used in the business. A and B later form Y, an S corporation, to perform X-ray services for W. All the stock in Y is transferred by A and B to their children. W transferred the X-ray equipment to Y, with Y executing a note payable to W for the equipment. Y then hires an X-ray technician to perform the X-ray services for W. The X-ray equipment and the X-ray technician's office are located in the building owned by W. W does all the billing for X-ray services and then remits a percentage of its collections to Y. Y then pays the technician for his services, pays rent to W for use of the building, and pays W on the note it executed for payment of the X-ray equipment. During the tax year, Y had a profit that the children of A and B reported on their individual income tax returns. Upon audit, the IRS assessed a deficiency against W, asserting that all income and expenses of Y must be attributed to W because Y was a sham corporation. The IRS also assessed a deficiency against A and B, stating that all distributions from Y to A's and B's children are constructive dividends to A and B from W Corporation. What are the results?

Partial list of research aids:

§§ 61 and 482.
Edwin D. Davis, 64 T.C. 1034 (1975).
Engineering Sales, Inc. v. U.S., 75–1 USTC ¶9347, 35 AFTR2d 75–1122, 510 F.2d 565 (CA–5, 1975).

RESEARCH PROBLEM 4   T purchased 100 shares of stock in X Corporation at a cost of $20,000, relying on a magazine advertisement regarding X Corporation and on information furnished by his friend F, who owned some stock in X Corporation. T then purchased another 200 shares in X Corporation from F at a cost of $40,000. During the tax year, X Corporation became bankrupt, and T lost his entire investment. T deducted the $60,000 in full as a theft loss rather than reporting it as a capital loss, contending that the president of X Corporation and his friend F had defrauded him and other investors because they knew the claims they made about X Corporation were erroneous. T thus claimed that the money was stolen from him. Is T correct in reporting the loss as a theft loss?

Partial list of research aids:

Perry A. Nichols, 43 T.C. 842 (1965).

RESEARCH PROBLEM 5   T Corporation, a qualified small business corporation under § 1244, was incorporated in 1985. C, an individual, acquired 50 shares of T Corporation common stock in 1985. The stock had a tax basis to C of $50,000. In 1989, T Corporation redeemed C's 50 shares of common stock by issuing 10 shares of its preferred stock to her. In 1990, T experienced financial difficulties. It arranged for financing with a local bank, but the bank required adequate collateral. C agreed to transfer her shares in GM Corporation, a large publicly traded corporation, to T with the understanding that the GM shares would be used as collateral for the loan. T Corporation then issued 20 shares of its common stock to C. C had a tax basis of $40,000 in the GM stock. In 1991, T Corporation went bankrupt. Its shares, both preferred and common, were worthless. On her 1991 tax return (filed jointly with her husband), C claimed an ordinary loss of $90,000, her tax basis in her preferred and common stock in T Corporation. Upon audit of C's 1991 return, the IRS denied the $90,000 loss on the ground that neither the preferred stock nor the common stock qualified as § 1244 stock. According to the IRS, C has a capital loss of $90,000 and can deduct only $3,000 of that loss on her 1991 return. C contends that the 20 shares of common stock were issued to her in consideration of the cancellation of T Corporation's indebtedness to her. She argues that T Corporation owed her a debt when she contributed the GM stock to the corporation. The debt was then canceled when T Corporation issued its common stock to her.

Is C correct in contending that both her preferred stock and her common stock in T Corporation qualify as § 1244 stock? Explain.

CHAPTER

CORPORATIONS: EARNINGS & PROFITS AND DIVIDEND DISTRIBUTIONS

OBJECTIVES

Explain the concept of earnings and profits and its importance in measuring dividend income.

Discuss the tax consequences of a property dividend to the recipient shareholder and to the corporation making the distribution.

Describe the nature and treatment of constructive dividends.

Differentiate between taxable and nontaxable stock dividends and stock rights.

OUTLINE

Retained earnings — numerous Dividends are not out (handwritten margin note)

After a corporation begins operations, one of the most important tax considerations is the tax treatment of corporate distributions to the shareholders. The form of distributions can have varying tax results to the shareholders and to the corporation. Dividends are taxed as ordinary income to the recipient shareholder unless stock dividends are distributed. In that case, the distribution may or may not be taxed to the shareholder. Distributions that qualify as stock redemptions, or that are made in partial or complete liquidation of the shareholder's interest in the corporation, are treated as a return of the shareholder's capital. They are tax-free to the extent of the shareholder's investment in the corporation, with any excess being a capital gain.

For tax purposes, corporate distributions are classified as follows:

1. Regular distributions of a corporation's earnings. These are taxed as dividend income to the extent of the earnings and profits of the corporation.
2. Distributions of stock and stock rights.
3. Distributions to a shareholder in exchange for the shareholder's stock that qualify as stock redemptions for tax purposes.
4. Distributions in partial or complete liquidation of the corporation. A distribution in partial liquidation is treated as a stock redemption for tax purposes.
5. Distributions of stock of a subsidiary of the parent corporation. If these distributions qualify under § 355, they do not represent a taxable event.

Regular distributions of a corporation's earnings and distributions of stock and stock rights are covered in this chapter. The other types of corporate distributions are discussed in Chapter 5.

TAXABLE DIVIDENDS— IN GENERAL

◆

*order of Taxability
After E&P look at what
basis is in stock, then
after basis is 0, then
becomes capital gain* (handwritten margin note)

Distributions by a corporation to its shareholders are presumed to be dividends unless the parties can prove otherwise. Section 316 makes such distributions ordinary dividend income to a shareholder. Dividend income results to the extent of the distribution's pro rata share of earnings and profits (E & P) of the distributing corporation accumulated since February 28, 1913, or to the extent of corporate E & P for the current year.

───────────────── EXAMPLE 1 ─────────────────

X Corporation had accumulated E & P of $40,000 at the beginning of the tax year. During the current year, X Corporation has net earnings of $50,000 (current E & P). At the end of the tax year, X distributes $70,000 cash to its sole shareholder, A (an individual). A will have ordinary dividend income of $70,000. Although X's current E & P was only $50,000, the remaining $20,000 of the $70,000 distribution is also a taxable dividend. X Corporation had accumulated E & P at the beginning of the year in excess of that amount. ◆

Under § 301(c), the portion of a corporate distribution that is not taxed as a dividend (because of insufficient E & P) is nontaxable to the extent of the shareholder's basis in the stock. This reduces the stock basis accordingly. The excess of the distribution over the shareholder's basis is treated as a capital gain if the stock is a capital asset.

───────────────── EXAMPLE 2 ─────────────────

At the beginning of the year, X Corporation (a calendar year taxpayer) has accumulated E & P of $30,000. The corporation has no current E & P. During the year, the corporation distributes $40,000 to its *equal* shareholders, C and D. Only $30,000 of the $40,000 distribution is a taxable dividend. Suppose C's basis in his stock is $8,000, while D's basis is $4,000. Under these conditions, C must recognize a taxable dividend of $15,000 and reduce the basis of the stock from $8,000 to $3,000. The $20,000 D receives from X Corporation is accounted for as follows: a taxable dividend of $15,000, a reduction in stock basis from $4,000 to zero, and a capital gain of $1,000. ◆

Since E & P is the key to dividend treatment of corporate distributions, its significance cannot be emphasized enough. Beginning in 1990, E & P assumed added importance. A concept based on adjusted E & P replaced pretax book income in the determination of adjusted current earnings for purposes of the alternative minimum tax (refer to the discussion in Chapter 6).

EARNINGS AND PROFITS (E & P)—§ 312
◆

The Code does not define the term *earnings and profits*. Although § 312 lists certain transactions that affect E & P, it stops short of a complete definition. E & P does possess similarities to the accounting concept of retained earnings (earnings retained in the business). However, E & P and retained earnings are often not the same. For example, for financial accounting purposes, a stock dividend is treated as a capitalization of retained earnings (it is debited to the retained earnings account and credited to a capital stock account), but it does not decrease E & P. Similarly, the elimination of a deficit in a quasi reorganization increases retained earnings but does not increase E & P.

Several observations are helpful in understanding the concept of E & P. First, E & P might well be described as the factor that fixes the upper limit on the amount of dividend income shareholders would have to recognize as a result of a distribution by the corporation. In this sense, E & P represents the corporation's economic ability to pay a dividend without impairing its capital. The effect of a specific transaction on the E & P account can be determined simply by considering whether or not the transaction increases or decreases the corporation's capacity to pay a dividend.

Computation of E & P

Barring certain important exceptions, E & P is increased by earnings for the taxable year computed in the same manner as taxable income is determined. If the corporation uses the cash method of accounting in computing taxable income, it must also use this method to determine the changes in E & P.[1]

E & P is increased for all items of income. Interest on municipal bonds, for example, though not taxed to the corporation, increases the corporation's E & P. The dividends received deduction under § 243 is added back to compute E & P. Gains and losses from property transactions generally affect the determination of E & P only to the extent they are recognized for tax purposes. Thus, a gain on an involuntary conversion not recognized by the corporation because the insurance proceeds are suitably reinvested does not affect E & P. But the E & P account can be affected by both deductible and nondeductible items. Consequently, excess capital losses, expenses incurred to produce tax-exempt income, and Federal income taxes all reduce E & P. Such items do not enter into the calculation of taxable income.

The E & P account can be reduced only by cost depletion, even though the corporation may be using percentage (statutory) depletion for income tax

---

1. Regulations relating to E & P begin at Reg. § 1.312–6.

purposes. E & P cannot be reduced by accelerated depreciation.[2] However, if a depreciation method such as units-of-production or machine hours is used, the adjustment to E & P is determined on this basis.[3]

The alternative depreciation system must be used for purposes of computing E & P.[4] If cost recovery is figured under MACRS, E & P must be computed using the straight-line recovery method over a recovery period equal to the asset's Asset Depreciation Range (ADR) midpoint life.[5] Later, when the asset is sold, the increase or decrease in E & P is determined by using the adjusted basis of the asset for E & P purposes.[6]

A corporation's E & P for the year in which it sells property on the installment basis is increased by the amount of any deferred gain. This is accomplished by treating all principal payments as having been received in the year of sale.[7]

Intangible drilling costs and mine exploration and development costs are required to be capitalized for purposes of computing E & P. Once capitalized, these expenditures can be charged to E & P over a specified period: 60 months for intangible drilling costs and 120 months for mine exploration and development costs.[8]

EXAMPLE 3

A corporation sells property (basis of $10,000) to its sole shareholder for $8,000. Because of § 267 (disallowance of losses on sales between related parties), the $2,000 loss cannot be deducted in arriving at the corporation's taxable income. But since the overall economic effect of the transaction is a decrease in the corporation's assets by $2,000, the loss reduces the current E & P for the year of sale. ◆

EXAMPLE 4

A corporation pays a $10,000 premium on a key employee life insurance policy (the corporation is the owner and beneficiary of the policy) covering the life of its president. As a result of the payment, the cash surrender value of the policy is increased by $7,000. Although none of the $10,000 premium is deductible for tax purposes, current E & P is reduced by $3,000. ◆

EXAMPLE 5

A corporation collects $100,000 on a key employee life insurance policy. At the time the policy matured on the death of the insured employee, it possessed a cash surrender value of $30,000. None of the $100,000 is included in the corporation's taxable income, but $70,000 is added to the current E & P account. ◆

EXAMPLE 6

During 1992, a corporation makes charitable contributions, $12,000 of which cannot be deducted in arriving at the taxable income for the year because of the 10% limitation. However, the $12,000 is carried over to 1993 and fully deducted in that year. The excess charitable contribution reduces the corporation's current E & P for 1992 by $12,000 and

---

2. § 312(k).

3. Reg. § 1.312–15(a)(2).

4. § 312(k)(3)(A).

5. See § 168(g)(2). The ADR midpoint life for most assets is set out in Rev.Proc. 87–56, 1987–2 C.B. 674. The recovery period is 5 years for automobiles and light-duty trucks and 40 years for real property. For assets with no class life, the recovery period is 12 years. Any amount expensed under § 179 is deducted over a period of 5 years in computing E & P. See § 312(k)(3)(B).

6. § 312(f)(1).

7. Under prior law, gains from installment sales were not included in E & P until recognized for purposes of computing taxable income for the year. Thus, gain deferred for purposes of computing taxable income was also deferred for purposes of computing E & P.

8. Under prior law, these costs were charged against E & P in the same manner as they were treated for purposes of computing taxable income.

Tax Purposes when using Taxable Income

1992
15000 char. dont.
8000) allowed ded. on Taxes
12,000

increases its current E & P for 1993, when the deduction is allowed, by a like amount. The increase in E & P in 1993 is necessitated by the fact that the charitable contribution carryover reduces the taxable income for that year (the starting point for computing E & P) and already has been taken into account in determining the E & P for 1992. ◆

──────── EXAMPLE 7 ────────

On January 2, 1990, X Corporation purchased equipment with an alternative recovery period of 10 years for $30,000. The equipment was then depreciated under MACRS. The asset was sold on July 2, 1992, for $27,000. For purposes of determining taxable income and E & P, cost recovery claimed on the machine and the machine's adjusted basis are summarized as follows:

	Cost Recovery	Adjusted Basis
Taxable income		
1990: $30,000 × 14.29%	$4,287	$25,713
1991: $30,000 × 24.49%	7,347	18,366
1992: $30,000 × 17.49% ÷ $\frac{1}{2}$ (half-year for year of disposal)	2,624	15,742
E & P		
1990: $30,000 ÷ 10-year recovery period ÷ $\frac{1}{2}$ (half-year for first year of service)	$1,500	$28,500
1991: $30,000 ÷ 10-year recovery period	3,000	25,500
1992: $30,000 ÷ 10-year recovery period ÷ $\frac{1}{2}$ (half-year for year of disposal)	1,500	24,000

Gain on the sale for purposes of determining taxable income and the increase (decrease) in E & P are computed as follows:

	Taxable Income	E & P
$27,000 – $15,742 (adjusted basis)	$11,258	
$27,000 – $24,000 (adjusted basis)		$3,000 ◆

──────── EXAMPLE 8 ────────

In 1992, X Corporation, a calendar year taxpayer, sells unimproved real estate (basis of $20,000) for $100,000. Under the terms of the sale, beginning in 1993, X will receive two annual payments of $50,000 each with interest of 9%. X Corporation does not elect out of the installment method. Although X's taxable income for 1992 will not reflect any of the gain from the sale, the corporation must increase E & P for 1992 by $80,000 (the deferred profit component). ◆

Summary of E & P Adjustments

Recall that E & P serves as a measure of the earnings of the corporation that are treated as available for distribution as taxable dividends to the shareholders. Initially, E & P is increased by the corporation's taxable income. However, various transactions for taxable income must be adjusted in determining the corporation's current E & P. These adjustments are reviewed in Concept Summary 4–1. Other items that affect E & P, such as property dividends, are covered later in the chapter and are not incorporated in the Concept Summary. The effect of stock redemptions on E & P is covered in Chapter 5.

The Source of the Distribution

In determining the source of a dividend distribution, the dividend is deemed to have been made first from current E & P and then from E & P accumulated since February 28, 1913.[9]

EXAMPLE 9

At the beginning of the current year, Y Corporation has a deficit in accumulated E & P of $30,000. For the year, it has current E & P of $10,000 and distributes $5,000 to its shareholders. The $5,000 distribution is treated as a taxable dividend since it is deemed to have been made from current E & P. This is the case even though Y Corporation still has a deficit in accumulated E & P at the end of the current year. ◆

Distributions made during the year may exceed the current year's E & P. In this case, the portion of each distribution considered to have been made from current E & P is the percentage that the total E & P for the year bears to the total distributions for that year. This allocation can be important if any of the shareholders sell their stock during the year and current distributions exceed current E & P.

EXAMPLE 10

As of January 1, 1992, Z Corporation has two *equal* shareholders, E and F, and accumulated E & P of $10,000. Current E & P for 1992 amounts to $30,000. On

---

CONCEPT SUMMARY 4–1
E & P ADJUSTMENTS

Nature of the Transaction	Effect on Taxable Income in Arriving at Current E & P
Tax-exempt income	Add
Federal income taxes	Subtract
Loss on sale between related parties	Subtract
Payment of premiums on insurance policy on life of corporate officer	Subtract
Collection of proceeds of insurance policy on life of corporate officer	Add
Excess charitable contribution (over 10% limitation)	Subtract
Deduction of excess charitable contribution in succeeding taxable year (increase E & P because deduction reduces taxable income while E & P was reduced in a prior year)	Add
Realized gain (not recognized) on an involuntary conversion	No effect
Percentage depletion (only cost depletion can reduce E & P)	Add
Accelerated depreciation (E & P is reduced only by straight-line, units-of-production, or machine hours depreciation)	Add
Deferred gain on installment sale (all gain is added to E & P in year of sale)	Add
Intangible drilling costs deducted currently (reduce E & P in future years by amortizing costs over 60 months)	Add
Mine exploration and development costs (reduce E & P in future years by amortizing costs over 120 months)	Add

---

9. Regulations relating to the source of a distribution are at Reg. § 1.316–2.

August 1, 1992, E sells all of her stock to G. During 1992, $40,000 is distributed to E and F ($20,000 to each) on July 1 and $40,000 to F and G ($20,000 to each) on December 1. The distributions are allocated as follows:

	Source of Distribution	
	Current E & P	Accumulated E & P
July 1 distribution ($40,000)	$15,000	$10,000
December 1 distribution ($40,000)	15,000	—

The tax consequences to the shareholders are as follows:

	Shareholder		
	E	F	G
July distribution ($40,000)			
Dividend income—			
From current E & P ($15,000)	$ 7,500	$ 7,500	$ –0–
From accumulated E & P ($10,000)	5,000	5,000	–0–
Return of capital ($15,000)	7,500	7,500	–0–
December distribution ($40,000)			
Dividend income—			
From current E & P ($15,000)	–0–	7,500	7,500
From accumulated E & P ($0)	–0–	–0–	–0–
Return of capital ($25,000)	–0–	12,500	12,500
Total dividend income	$12,500	$20,000	$ 7,500
Nontaxable return of capital (presuming sufficient basis in the stock investment)	$ 7,500	$20,000	$12,500

Note that the current E & P was allocated between both distributions, while the accumulated E & P was applied to and exhausted by the first distribution. ◆

Distinguishing between Current and Accumulated E & P

Accumulated E & P is the total of all previous years' current E & P as computed on the first day of each taxable year. Computation is made in accordance with the tax law in effect during that year. The factors that affect the computation of the current E & P for any one year have been discussed previously. Why must current and accumulated E & P be distinguished when it is clear that distributions are taxable if and to the extent that current *and* accumulated E & P exist?

1. When a deficit exists in accumulated E & P and a positive balance exists in current E & P, distributions are regarded as dividends to the extent of the current E & P. Refer to Example 9.
2. Current E & P is allocated on a pro rata basis to the distributions made during the year; accumulated E & P is applied (to the extent necessary) in chronological order beginning with the earliest distributions. Refer to Example 10.
3. Unless and until the parties can show otherwise, it is presumed that any distribution is covered by current E & P.
4. When a deficit exists in current E & P (a current loss develops) and a positive balance exists in accumulated E & P, the accounts are netted at the date of distribution. If the resulting balance is zero or a deficit, the

distribution is a return of capital. If a positive balance results, the distribution is a dividend to the extent of the balance. Any loss is allocated ratably during the year unless the parties can show otherwise.

The following example illustrates distinctions 3 and 4.

─────────────────────── EXAMPLE 11 ───────────────────────

Q Corporation uses a fiscal year of July 1 through June 30 for tax purposes. T, Q Corporation's only shareholder, uses a calendar year. As of July 1, 1992, Q Corporation has a zero balance in its accumulated E & P account. For fiscal year 1992–1993 the corporation suffers a $5,000 operating loss. On August 1, 1992, Q distributes $10,000 to T. The distribution is dividend income to T and must be reported as such when she files her income tax return for calendar year 1992 on or before April 15, 1993. Because T cannot prove until June 30, 1993, that the corporation had a deficit for fiscal 1992–1993, she must assume the $10,000 distribution was fully covered by current E & P. When T learns of the deficit, she can file an amended return for 1992 showing the $10,000 as a return of capital. ◆

─────────────────────── EXAMPLE 12 ───────────────────────

At the beginning of the current year, R Corporation (a calendar year taxpayer) has accumulated E & P of $10,000. During the year, the corporation incurs a $15,000 net loss from operations that accrued ratably. On July 1, R Corporation distributes $6,000 in cash to H, its sole shareholder. To determine how much of the $6,000 cash distribution represents dividend income to H, the balance of both accumulated and current E & P as of July 1 must be determined and netted. This is necessary because of the deficit in current E & P.

| | **Source of Distribution** | |
	Current E & P	Accumulated E & P
January 1		$10,000
July 1 ($\frac{1}{2}$ of $15,000 net loss)	($7,500)	2,500
July 1 distribution—($6,000):		
Dividend income: ($2,500)		
Return of capital: ($3,500)		

The balance in E & P on July 1 is $2,500. Thus, of the $6,000 distribution, $2,500 is taxed as a dividend, and $3,500 represents a return of capital. ◆

PROPERTY DIVIDENDS—IN GENERAL
◆

The previous discussion assumed that all distributions by a corporation to its shareholders were in the form of cash. Although most corporate distributions are cash, a corporation may distribute property as a dividend for various reasons. The shareholders may want a particular property that is held by the corporation. The corporation may be strapped for cash, but may not want to forgo distributing a dividend to its shareholders.

Generally, the distribution of property as a dividend is treated in the same manner as a cash distribution. However, the value of property distributed and the basis of that property to the corporation are seldom the same. Consequently, the distribution of a property dividend involves additional tax considerations. The following questions must be asked when property is distributed as a dividend:

1. What is the amount of the dividend distributed to the shareholder?
2. What is the basis of the property received by the shareholder?

3. Does the corporation recognize gain or loss upon the distribution?
4. What is the effect of the property distribution on the E & P of the corporation?

Property Dividends—Effect on the Shareholder

When a corporation distributes property rather than cash to a shareholder, the amount distributed is measured by the fair market value of the property on the date of distribution. Section 301(c) applies to such distributions. Thus, the portion of the distribution covered by existing E & P is a dividend, and any excess is treated as a return of capital.

If the fair market value of the property distributed exceeds the corporation's E & P and the shareholder's basis in the stock investment, a capital gain results. The amount distributed is reduced by any liabilities to which the distributed property is subject immediately before and immediately after the distribution and by any liabilities of the corporation assumed by the shareholder. [10] The basis in the distributed property is the fair market value of the property on the date of the distribution.

―――――――――――― EXAMPLE 13 ――――――――――――

P Corporation has E & P of $60,000. It distributes land with a fair market value of $50,000 (adjusted basis of $30,000) to its sole shareholder, T. The land is subject to a liability of $10,000, which T assumes. T has a taxable dividend of $40,000 [$50,000 (fair market value) − $10,000 (liability)]. The basis of the land to T is $50,000. ◆

―――――――――――― EXAMPLE 14 ――――――――――――

Ten percent of X Corporation is owned by Y Corporation. X Corporation has ample E & P to cover any distributions made during the year. One distribution made to Y Corporation consists of a vacant lot with adjusted basis of $5,000 and a fair market value of $3,000. Y Corporation has a taxable dividend of $3,000, and its basis in the lot becomes $3,000. ◆

Property that has depreciated in value is usually not suitable for distribution as a property dividend. Note what has happened in Example 14. The loss of $2,000 (adjusted basis $5,000, fair market value $3,000) disappears. X Corporation could have preserved the loss for itself if it had sold the lot and then distributed the $3,000 proceeds.

Property Dividends—Effect on the Corporation

A property distribution by a corporation to its shareholders poses two questions. Does the distribution result in recognized gain or loss to the corporation making the distribution? What effect will the distribution have on the corporation's E & P?

Recognition of Gain or Loss. All distributions of appreciated property cause gain to the distributing corporation.[11] In effect, the corporation that makes a property dividend is treated as if it had sold the property to the shareholder for its fair market value. However, the distributing corporation does not recognize loss on distributions of property with a tax basis in excess of fair market value.

―――――――――――――――――――――――――

10. § 301(b)(2).

11. Section 311 covers the taxability of a corporation on distributions.

———————————— EXAMPLE 15 ————————————

X Corporation distributes land (basis of $10,000 and fair market value of $30,000) to T, an individual shareholder. X Corporation recognizes a gain of $20,000. ◆

———————————— EXAMPLE 16 ————————————

Assume the property in Example 15 has a fair market value of $10,000 and a basis of $30,000. X Corporation does not recognize a loss on the distribution. ◆

If the distributed property is subject to a liability in excess of basis or the shareholder assumes such a liability, a special rule applies. The fair market value of the property for purposes of determining gain on the distribution is treated as not being less than the amount of the liability.

———————————— EXAMPLE 17 ————————————

Assume the land in Example 15 is subject to a liability of $35,000. X Corporation recognizes gain of $25,000 on the distribution. ◆

Effect of Corporate Distributions on E & P. In the event of a corporate distribution, the E & P account is reduced by the amount of money distributed or by the greater of the fair market value or the adjusted basis of property distributed, less the amount of any liability on the property.[12] E & P is increased by gain recognized on appreciated property distributed as a property dividend.[13]

———————————— EXAMPLE 18 ————————————

M Corporation distributes property (basis of $10,000 and fair market value of $20,000) to T, its shareholder. M Corporation recognizes a gain of $10,000, which is added to its E & P. E & P is then reduced by $20,000, the fair market value of the property. T has dividend income of $20,000. ◆

———————————— EXAMPLE 19 ————————————

Assume the same facts as in Example 18, except that the fair market value of the property is $15,000 and the adjusted basis in the hands of M Corporation is $20,000. Because loss is not recognized and the adjusted basis is greater than fair market value, E & P is reduced by $20,000. T reports dividend income of $15,000. ◆

———————————— EXAMPLE 20 ————————————

Assume the same facts as in Example 19, except that the property is subject to a liability of $6,000. E & P is now reduced by $14,000 [$20,000 (adjusted basis) − $6,000 (liability)]. T has a dividend of $9,000 [$15,000 (amount of the distribution) − $6,000 (liability)], and his basis in the property is $15,000. ◆

Under no circumstances can a distribution, whether cash or property, either generate a deficit in E & P or add to a deficit in E & P. Deficits can arise only through corporate losses.

———————————— EXAMPLE 21 ————————————

X Corporation had accumulated E & P of $10,000 at the beginning of the current tax year. During the year, it had current E & P of $15,000. At the end of the year, it distributed cash of $30,000 to its sole shareholder, A (an individual). X Corporation's E & P at the end of the year will be zero. The beginning E & P of $10,000 is increased

———

12. §§ 312(a), (b), and (c).   **13.** § 312(b).

by current E & P of $15,000 and is reduced $25,000 by the dividend distribution. The remaining $5,000 of the distribution to A does not reduce E & P because a distribution cannot generate a deficit in E & P. ◆

Skip

───────────────────────── EXAMPLE 22 ─────────────────────────

Assume X Corporation in Example 21 had an operating loss of $15,000 during the tax year (rather than current E & P of $15,000). Its E & P at the end of the year will be a deficit of $5,000. The operating loss generates a $5,000 deficit in E & P, computed as follows: $10,000 (beginning E & P) − $15,000 (operating loss) = $5,000 deficit in E & P. The $30,000 distribution to A does not increase the deficit in E & P because a distribution cannot add to a deficit. ◆

A distribution by a corporation to its shareholders can be treated as a dividend for Federal income tax purposes even though it is not formally declared or designated as a dividend. Also, it need not be issued pro rata to all sharehold-ers.[14] Nor must the distribution satisfy the legal requirements of a dividend as set forth by applicable state law. The key factor determining dividend status is a measurable economic benefit conveyed to the shareholder. This benefit, often described as a *constructive dividend*, is distinguishable from actual corporate distributions of cash and property in form only.

CONSTRUCTIVE DIVIDENDS
◆

Leads to constructive div.
1. debt : equity

2. excessive compensation
[IRS (unreasonable)]

3. personal use of
corp owned prop.
goes to seminar takes
convention
whole family

Constructive dividend situations usually arise in the context of closely held corporations. Here, the dealings between the parties are less structured, and frequently, formalities are not preserved. The constructive dividend serves as a substitute for actual distributions. Usually, it is intended to accomplish some tax objective not available through the use of direct dividends. The shareholders may be attempting to bail out corporate profits in a form deductible to the corporation. Recall that dividend distributions do not provide the distributing corporation with an income tax deduction, although they do reduce E & P. Alternatively, the shareholders may be seeking benefits for themselves while avoiding the recognition of income. Constructive dividends are, in reality, disguised dividends.

Do not conclude that all constructive dividends are deliberate attempts to avoid actual and formal dividends. Often, constructive dividends are inadvertent. Consequently, a dividend result may come as a surprise to the parties. For this reason, if for none other, an awareness of the various constructive dividend situations is essential to protect the parties from unanticipated tax consequences.

Types of Constructive Dividends

The most frequently encountered types of constructive dividends are summarized below.

Shareholder Use of Corporate-Owned Property. A constructive dividend can occur when a shareholder uses corporation property for personal purposes at no cost. Personal use of corporate-owned automobiles, airplanes, yachts, fishing camps, hunting lodges, and other entertainment facilities is commonplace in some closely held corporations. The shareholder has dividend income to the extent of the fair rental value of the property for the period of its personal use.

──────────────

14. See *Lengsfield v. Comm.*, 57–1 USTC ¶9437, 50 AFTR 1683, 241 F.2d 508 (CA–5, 1957).

Bargain Sale of Corporate Property to a Shareholder. Shareholders often purchase property from a corporation at a cost below the fair market value of the property. These bargain sales produce dividend income to the extent of the difference between the property's fair market value on the date of sale and the amount the shareholder paid for the property.[15] These situations might be avoided by appraising the property on or about the date of the sale. The appraised value should become the price to be paid by the shareholder.

Bargain Rental of Corporate Property. A bargain rental of corporate property by a shareholder also produces dividend income. Here the measure of the constructive dividend is the excess of the property's fair rental value over the rent actually paid. Again, appraisal data should be used to avoid any questionable situations.

Payments for the Benefit of a Shareholder. If a corporation pays an obligation of a shareholder, the payment is treated as a constructive dividend. The obligation involved need not be legally binding on the shareholder; it may, in fact, be a moral obligation.[16] Forgiveness of shareholder indebtedness by the corporation can create an identical problem.[17] Excessive rentals paid by a corporation for the use of shareholder property are also treated as constructive dividends.

Excessive Compensation. A salary payment of a shareholder-employee that is deemed to be unreasonable is frequently treated as a constructive dividend. As a consequence, it is not deductible by the corporation. In determining the reasonableness of salary payments, the following factors are considered:

- The employee's qualifications.
- A comparison of salaries with dividend distributions.
- The prevailing rates of compensation for comparable positions in comparable business concerns.
- The nature and scope of the employee's work.
- The size and complexity of the business.
- A comparison of salaries paid with both gross and net income.
- The taxpayer's salary policy toward all employees.
- For small corporations with a limited number of officers, the amount of compensation paid the employee in question in previous years.[18]

Loans to Shareholders. Advances to shareholders that are not bona fide loans are also deemed to be constructive dividends. Whether an advance qualifies as a bona fide loan is a question of fact to be determined in light of the particular circumstances. Factors considered in determining whether the advance is a bona fide loan include the following:

- Whether the advance is on open account or is evidenced by a written instrument.

---

15. Reg. § 1.301–1(j).

16. *Montgomery Engineering Co. v. U.S.*, 64–2 USTC ¶9618, 13 AFTR2d 1747, 230 F.Supp. 838 (D.Ct.N.J., 1964); *aff'd.* in 65–1 USTC ¶9368, 15 AFTR2d 746, 344 F.2d 966 (CA–3, 1965).

17. Reg. § 1.301–1(m).

18. *Mayson Manufacturing Co. v. Comm.*, 49–2 USTC ¶9467, 38 AFTR 1028, 178 F.2d 115 (CA–6, 1949).

- Whether the shareholder furnished collateral or other security for the advance.
- How long the advance has been outstanding.
- Whether any payments have been made.
- The shareholder's financial capability to repay the advance.
- The shareholder's use of the funds (e.g., payment of routine bills versus nonrecurring, extraordinary expenses).
- The regularity of the advances.
- The dividend-paying history of the corporation.

If a corporation succeeds in proving that an advance to a shareholder is a bona fide loan, the advance is not deemed to be a constructive dividend. But getting past this hurdle does not necessarily eliminate all constructive dividend treatment. The shareholder will still have a constructive dividend in the amount of any forgone interest. Interest-free or below-market loans by a corporation to a shareholder cause the shareholder to have a constructive dividend to the extent of "imputed interest." This is the difference between the rate the Federal government pays on new borrowings, compounded semiannually, and the interest charged on the loan.[19] The corporation is deemed to have made a dividend distribution to the shareholder to the extent of the forgone interest. The shareholder is then deemed to have made an interest payment to the corporation for the same amount. Although the shareholder may be permitted to deduct the deemed interest payment, the corporation has interest income. No corresponding deduction is allowed since the imputed interest element is a constructive dividend.

─────────────────── EXAMPLE 23 ───────────────────

T Corporation loans its principal shareholder, S, $100,000 on January 2, 1992. The loan is interest-free. On December 31, 1992, T Corporation is deemed to have made a dividend distribution to S in the amount of the imputed interest on the loan, determined by using the Federal rate and compounded semiannually. Assume the Federal rate is 10%. T Corporation is deemed to have paid a dividend to S in the amount of $10,250.

Although S has dividend income of $10,250, she may be permitted to offset the income with a $10,250 deemed interest payment to T Corporation. T Corporation has deemed interest income of $10,250, but has no corresponding deduction. The deemed payment from T Corporation to S is a nondeductible dividend. ◆

Loans to a Corporation by Shareholders. Shareholder loans to a corporation may be reclassified as equity because the debt has too many features of stock. Any interest and principal payments made by the corporation to the shareholder are treated as constructive dividends.

Tax Treatment of Constructive Dividends

Constructive distributions possess the same tax attributes as actual distributions.[20] Thus, a corporate shareholder would be entitled to the dividends received deduction of § 243. The constructive distribution would be a taxable dividend only to the extent of the corporation's current and accumulated E & P.

─────────────────────────────────────

19. See § 7872.

20. *Simon v. Comm.*, 57–2 USTC ¶9989, 52 AFTR 698, 248 F.2d

869 (CA–8, 1957).

The task of proving that the distribution constitutes a return of capital because of inadequate E & P rests with the taxpayer.[21]

Stock Dividends—§ 305

A shareholder's proportionate interest in a corporation does not change upon receipt of a stock dividend. Accordingly, such distributions were initially accorded tax-free treatment.[22] Subsequently, the test for taxability of a stock dividend was based on whether the proportionate interest of a shareholder changed following the distribution. The 1954 Code simply stated that stock dividends would not be taxable unless (1) the shareholder could elect to receive either stock or property or (2) the stock dividends were in discharge of preference dividends. In response, corporations devised various methods to distribute stock dividends that would change the shareholder's interest and still qualify as tax-free.[23]

The provisions of § 305 that currently govern the taxability of stock dividends are based on the proportionate interest concept. Stock dividends are not taxable if they are pro rata distributions of stock, or stock rights, on common stock. The general rule that stock dividends are nontaxable has five exceptions, summarized as follows:

1. Distributions payable either in stock or property.
2. Distributions resulting in the receipt of property by some shareholders and an increase in the proportionate interest of other shareholders in the assets or E & P of the distributing corporation.
3. Distributions that result in the receipt of preferred stock by some common stock shareholders and the receipt of common stock by other shareholders.
4. Distributions on preferred stock other than an increase in the conversion ratio of convertible preferred stock made solely to take account of a stock dividend or stock split with respect to stock into which the preferred is convertible.
5. Distributions of convertible preferred stock, unless it can be shown that the distribution will not result in a disproportionate distribution.

Note that the exceptions to nontaxability of stock dividends deal with various disproportionate distribution situations.

Holders of convertible securities are considered shareholders. As a result, payment of interest on convertible debentures cause stock dividends paid on common stock to be taxable. This result can be avoided if the conversion ratio or conversion price is adjusted to reflect the stock dividend.[24]

If stock dividends are not taxable, the corporation's E & P is not reduced.[25] If the stock dividends are taxable, the distributing corporation treats the distribution in the same manner as any other taxable property dividend.

If a stock dividend is taxable, basis to the shareholder-distributee is fair market value, and the holding period starts on the date of receipt. If a stock

21. *DiZenzo v. Comm.*, 65–2 USTC ¶9518, 16 AFTR2d 5107, 348 F.2d 122 (CA–2, 1965).

22. See *Eisner v. Macomber*, 1 USTC ¶32, 3 AFTR 3020, 40 S.Ct. 189 (USSC, 1920).

23. See "Stock Dividends," Senate Report 91–552, 1969–3 C.B. 519.

24. See Reg. § 1.305–3(d) for illustrations on how to compute required adjustments on conversion ratios or prices.

25. § 312(d)(1).

dividend is not taxable, § 307 requires that the basis of the stock on which the dividend is distributed be reallocated. If the dividend shares are identical to these formerly held shares, basis in the old stock is reallocated by dividing the taxpayer's cost in the old stock by the total number of shares. If the dividend stock is not identical to the underlying shares (e.g., a stock dividend of preferred on common), basis is determined by allocating the cost of the formerly held shares between the old and new stock according to the fair market value of each. The holding period includes the holding period of the formerly held stock.[26]

———————— EXAMPLE 24 ————————

A, an individual, bought 1,000 shares of stock two years ago for $10,000. In the current tax year, A receives 10 shares of common stock as a nontaxable stock dividend. A's basis of $10,000 is divided by 1,010. Each share of stock has a basis of $9.90 instead of the pre-dividend $10 basis. ◆

———————— EXAMPLE 25 ————————

Assume A received, instead, a nontaxable preferred stock dividend of 100 shares. The preferred stock has a fair market value of $1,000, and the common stock, on which the preferred is distributed, has a fair market value of $19,000. After the receipt of the stock dividend, the basis of the common stock is $9,500, and the basis of the preferred is $500, computed as follows:

Fair market value of common	$19,000
Fair market value of preferred	1,000
	$20,000
Basis of common: 19/20 × $10,000	$ 9,500
Basis of preferred: 1/20 × $10,000	$ 500

◆

Stock Rights

The rules for determining taxability of stock rights are identical to those for determining taxability of stock dividends. If the rights are taxable, the recipient has income to the extent of the fair market value of the rights. The fair market value then becomes the shareholder-distributee's basis in the rights.[27] If the rights are exercised, the holding period for the new stock is the date the rights (whether taxable or nontaxable) are exercised. The basis of the new stock is the basis of the rights plus the amount of any other consideration given.

If stock rights are not taxable and the value of the rights is less than 15 percent of the value of the old stock, the basis of the rights is zero. However, the shareholder may elect to have some of the basis in the formerly held stock allocated to the rights.[28] If the fair market value of the rights is 15 percent or more of the value of the old stock and the rights are exercised or sold, the shareholder must allocate some of the basis in the formerly held stock to the rights.

Assume the value of the stock rights is less than 15 percent of the value of the stock and the shareholder makes an election to allocate basis to the rights. The election is made by attaching a statement to the shareholder's return for the year in which the rights are received.[29]

26. § 1223(5).
27. Reg. § 1.305–1(b).

28. § 307(b)(1).
29. Reg. § 1.307–2.

—————————— EXAMPLE 26 ——————————

A corporation with common stock outstanding declares a nontaxable dividend payable in rights to subscribe to common stock. Each right entitles the holder to purchase one share of stock for $90. One right is issued for every two shares of stock owned. T owns 400 shares of stock purchased two years ago for $15,000. At the time of the distribution of the rights, the market value of the common stock is $100 per share, and the market value of the rights is $8 per right. T receives 200 rights. He exercises 100 rights and sells the remaining 100 rights three months later for $9 per right. T need not allocate the cost of the original stock to the rights because the value of the rights is less than 15% of the value of the stock ($1,600 ÷ $40,000 = 4%).

If T does not allocate his original stock basis to the rights, the tax consequences are as follows:

- Basis in the new stock is $9,000 ($90 × 100). The holding period of the new stock begins on the date the stock was purchased.
- Sale of the rights would produce long-term capital gain of $900 ($9 × 100). The holding period of the rights starts with the date the original 400 shares of stock were acquired.

If T elects to allocate basis to the rights, the tax consequences are as follows:

- Basis in the stock is $14,423 [$40,000 ÷ $41,600 (value of rights and stock) × $15,000 (cost of stock)].
- Basis in the rights is $577 [$1,600 (value of rights) ÷ $41,600 (value of rights and stock) × $15,000 (cost of stock)].
- When T exercises the rights, his basis in the new stock will be $9,288.50 [$9,000 (cost) + $288.50 (basis in 100 rights)].
- Sale of the rights would produce a long-term capital gain of $611.50 [$900 (selling price) − $288.50 (basis in the remaining 100 rights)]. ◆

The basis rules for stock dividends and stock rights are summarized in Figure 4–1.

Corporate Distributions

TAX PLANNING CONSIDERATIONS

In connection with the discussion of corporate distributions, the following points need reinforcement:

- Because E & P is the measure of dividend income, its periodic determination is essential to corporate planning. Thus, an E & P account should be established and maintained, particularly if the possibility exists that a corporate distribution might represent a return of capital.
- Accumulated E & P is the sum of all past years' current E & P. There is no statute of limitations on the computation of E & P. The IRS could, for example, redetermine a corporation's current E & P for a tax year long since passed. Such a change would affect accumulated E & P and would have a direct impact on the taxability of current distributions to shareholders.
- Taxpayers should be aware that manipulating distributions to avoid or minimize dividend exposure is possible.

—————————— EXAMPLE 27 ——————————

Q Corporation has accumulated E & P of $100,000 as of January 1, 1992. During 1992, it expects to have earnings from operations of $80,000 and to make a cash distribution of $60,000. Q Corporation also expects to sell an asset for a loss of $100,000. Thus, it anticipates incurring a deficit of $20,000 for the year. The best approach would be to

FIGURE 4–1   Basis of Nontaxable Stock Dividends and Stock Rights

Stock Dividends

Calculate FMV of old and new stock.

FMV of old stock	$xx,xxx
FMV of new stock	xx,xxx
Total value of stock	$xx,xxx

Allocate basis in old stock to old and new stock based on FMV of each.

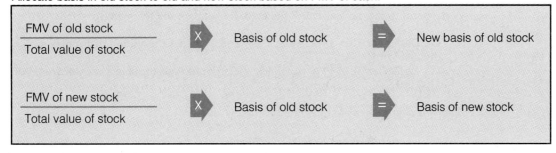

$$\frac{\text{FMV of old stock}}{\text{Total value of stock}} \quad X \quad \text{Basis of old stock} \quad = \quad \text{New basis of old stock}$$

$$\frac{\text{FMV of new stock}}{\text{Total value of stock}} \quad X \quad \text{Basis of old stock} \quad = \quad \text{Basis of new stock}$$

Stock Rights

Calculate FMV of old stock and stock rights.

FMV of old stock	$xx,xxx
FMV of stock rights	xx,xxx
Total value of stock and rights	$xx,xxx

If FMV of stock rights is at least 15% of FMV of stock, allocate basis in old stock between old stock and stock rights. If not, allocation is elective.

Allocate basis of old stock between old stock and stock rights based on FMV of each.

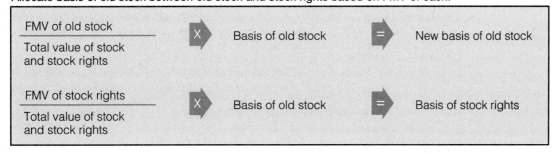

$$\frac{\text{FMV of old stock}}{\text{Total value of stock and stock rights}} \quad X \quad \text{Basis of old stock} \quad = \quad \text{New basis of old stock}$$

$$\frac{\text{FMV of stock rights}}{\text{Total value of stock and stock rights}} \quad X \quad \text{Basis of old stock} \quad = \quad \text{Basis of stock rights}$$

recognize the loss as soon as possible and immediately thereafter make the cash distribution to the shareholders. Suppose these two steps took place on January 1, 1992. Because the current E & P for 1992 will have a deficit, the accumulated E & P account must be brought up to date (refer to Example 12 in this chapter). Thus, at the time of the distribution, the combined E & P balance is zero [$100,000 (beginning balance in accumulated E & P) – $100,000 (existing deficit in current E & P)], and the $60,000 distribution to the shareholders constitutes a return of capital. Current deficits are allocated pro rata throughout the year unless the parties can prove otherwise. Here they can. ◆

EXAMPLE 28

After several unprofitable years, Y Corporation has a deficit in accumulated E & P of $100,000 as of January 1, 1992. Starting in 1992, Y Corporation expects to generate annual E & P of $50,000 for the next four years and would like to distribute this amount to its shareholders. The corporation's cash position (for dividend purposes) will correspond to the current E & P generated. Compare the following possibilities:

1. On December 31 of 1992, 1993, 1994, and 1995, Y Corporation distributes a cash dividend of $50,000.
2. On December 31 of 1993 and 1995, Y Corporation distributes a cash dividend of $100,000.

The two alternatives are illustrated as follows:

Year	Accumulated E & P (First of Year)	Current E & P	Distribution	Amount of Dividend
		Alternative 1		
1992	($ 100,000)	$50,000	$ 50,000	$50,000
1993	(100,000)	50,000	50,000	50,000
1994	(100,000)	50,000	50,000	50,000
1995	(100,000)	50,000	50,000	50,000
		Alternative 2		
1992	($ 100,000)	$50,000	$ –0–	$ –0–
1993	(50,000)	50,000	100,000	50,000
1994	(50,000)	50,000	–0–	–0–
1995	–0–	50,000	100,000	50,000

Alternative 1 leads to an overall result of $200,000 in dividend income, since each $50,000 distribution is fully covered by current E & P. Alternative 2, however, results in only $100,000 of dividend income to the shareholders. The remaining $100,000 is a return of capital. Why? At the time Y Corporation made its first distribution of $100,000 on December 31, 1993, it had a deficit of $50,000 in accumulated E & P (the original deficit of $100,000 is reduced by the $50,000 of current E & P from 1992). Consequently, the $100,000 distribution yields a $50,000 dividend (the current E & P for 1993) and $50,000 as a return of capital. As of January 1, 1994, Y Corporation's accumulated E & P now has a deficit balance of $50,000 (a distribution cannot increase a deficit in E & P). Add in $50,000 of current E & P from 1994, and the balance as of January 1, 1995, is zero. Thus, the second distribution of $100,000 made on December 31, 1995, also yields $50,000 of dividends (the current E & P for 1995) and $50,000 as a return of capital. ◆

Constructive Dividends

Tax planning can be particularly effective in avoiding constructive dividend situations. Shareholders should try to structure their dealings with the corporation on an arm's length basis. For example, reasonable rent should be paid for the use of corporate property, and a fair price should be paid for its purchase. The parties should make every effort to support the amount involved with appraisal data or market information obtained from reliable sources at or close to the time of the transaction. Dealings between shareholders and a closely held corporation should be as formal as possible. In the case of loans to shareholders, for example, the parties should provide for an adequate rate of interest, written evidence of the debt, and a realistic repayment schedule that is both arranged and followed.

If corporate profits are to be bailed out by the shareholders in a form deductible to the corporation, a balanced mix of the possible alternatives could lessen the risk of disallowance by the IRS. Rent for the use of shareholder property, interest on amounts borrowed from shareholders, or salaries for services rendered by shareholders are all feasible substitutes for dividend distributions. But overdoing any one approach may attract the attention of the IRS. Too much interest, for example, might mean the corporation is thinly capitalized, and some of the debt is really equity investment.

Much can be done to protect against the disallowance of corporate deductions for compensation that is determined to be unreasonable in amount. Example 29 is an illustration, all too common in a family corporation, of what *not* to do.

―――――――――――――――― EXAMPLE 29 ――――――――――――――――

Z Corporation is wholly owned by T. Corporate employees and annual salaries include Mrs. T ($15,000), T, Jr. ($10,000), T ($80,000), and E ($40,000). The operation of Z Corporation is shared about equally between T and Ms. E (an unrelated party). Mrs. T (T's wife) performed significant services for the corporation during the corporation's formative years but now merely attends the annual meeting of the board of directors. T, Jr. (T's son), is a full-time student and occasionally signs papers for the corporation in his capacity as treasurer. Z Corporation has not distributed a dividend for 10 years, although it has accumulated substantial E & P. What is wrong with this situation?

- Mrs. T's salary seems vulnerable unless proof is available that some or all of her $15,000 annual salary is payment for services rendered to the corporation in prior years (she was underpaid for those years).[30]
- T, Jr.'s, salary is also vulnerable; he does not appear to earn the $10,000 paid to him by the corporation. True, neither T, Jr., nor Mrs. T is a shareholder, but each one's relationship to T is enough of a tie-in to raise the unreasonable compensation issue.
- T's salary appears susceptible to challenge. Why is he receiving $40,000 more than E when it appears they share equally in the operation of the corporation?
- Z Corporation has not distributed dividends for 10 years, although it is capable of doing so. ◆

What could have been done to improve the tax position of the parties in Example 29? Mrs. T and T, Jr., are not entitled to a salary as neither seems to be performing services for the corporation. Paying them a salary simply aggravates the problem. The IRS is more apt to consider *all* the salaries to members of the family as being excessive under the circumstances. Mr. T should probably reduce his compensation to correspond to that paid Ms. E. He can then attempt to distribute corporate earnings to himself in some other form.

The problem raised in Example 29 could also be alleviated if the corporation did pay some dividends to Mr. T. The IRS has been successful in denying a deduction for salary paid to a shareholder-employee even when t̄ payment was reasonable ― situation where the corporation had not distributed any

――――――――――――――

30. See, for example, *R. J. Nicoll Co.*, 59 T.C. 37 (1972).

dividends.[31] Most courts, however, have not denied deductions for compensation solely because a dividend was not paid. A better approach is to compare an employee's compensation with the level of compensation prevalent in the particular industry.

The corporation can substitute *indirect* compensation for Mr. T. by paying expenses that benefit him personally but are nevertheless deductible to the corporation. For example, premiums paid by the corporation for sickness, accident, and hospitalization insurance for Mr. T are deductible to the corporation.[32] These premiums would not be taxable to Mr. T unless he receives payments in excess of his medical expenses.[33] The corporation could also pay for travel and entertainment expenses incurred by Mr. T on behalf of the corporation. Such expenditures must be primarily for the benefit of the corporation to be deductible. Mr. T would not have taxable income in the amount of the expenditures.[34]

In making indirect compensation payments to an employee-shareholder, be aware that the IRS may look to the total compensation package when testing for reasonableness. Indirect payments must not be overlooked.

EXAMPLE 30

Ms. T, the president and sole shareholder of T Corporation, is paid an annual salary of $100,000 by the corporation. Ms. T would like to draw funds from the corporation but is concerned that additional salary payments might cause the IRS to contend her salary is unreasonable. Ms. T does not want T Corporation to pay any dividends. She also wishes to donate $50,000 to her alma mater to establish scholarships for needy students. T Corporation could make the contribution on behalf of Ms. T. The payment clearly benefits Ms. T, but the amount of the contribution will not be taxed to her.[35] T Corporation can take a charitable contribution deduction for the payment. ◆

EXAMPLE 31

Assume in Example 30 that Ms. T has made an individual pledge to the university to provide $50,000 for scholarships for needy students. T Corporation satisfies Ms. T's pledge by paying the $50,000 to the university. The $50,000 will be taxed to Ms. T.[36] In this context, the $50,000 payment to the university may be treated as *indirect* compensation to Ms. T. In determining whether Ms. T's salary is unreasonable, both the *direct* payment of $100,000 and the *indirect* $50,000 payment will be considered. Ms. T's total compensation package is $150,000. ◆

PROBLEMS MATERIALS

DISCUSSION QUESTIONS

1. What is meant by the term *earnings and profits*? 4-33 Concept Summary 4-1
2. Why is it important to distinguish between current and accumulated E & P? 4-7a8
3. In determining Y Corporation's current E & P for 1992, how should the following transactions be handled in adjusting taxable income?

---

31. *McCandless Tile Service v. U.S.*, 70–1 USTC ¶9284, 25 AFTR2d 70–870, 422 F.2d 1336 (Ct. Cls., 1970). The court in *McCandless* concluded that a return on equity of 15% of net profits was reasonable.

32. Reg. § 1.162–10.

33. The medical reimbursement plan must meet certain

nondiscrimination requirements of § 105(h)(2).

34. Reg. § 1.62–2(c)(4).

35. *Henry J. Knott*, 67 T.C. 681 (1977).

36. *Schalk Chemical Co. v. Comm.*, 62–1 USTC ¶9496, 9 AFTR2d 1579, 304 F.2d 48 (CA–9, 1962).

a. Collection of an installment note receivable resulting from a 1991 sale. (Y Corporation did not elect out of the installment method.)
b. An NOL carryover from 1991 fully used in 1992.
c. An excess capital loss for 1992 that is not carried back.
d. Collection on a key employee life insurance policy upon the death of an executive.
e. Excess charitable contribution deduction on a donation made in 1992.

4. Describe the effect of a distribution in a year when the distributing corporation has

a. A deficit in accumulated E & P and a positive amount in current E & P.
b. A positive amount in accumulated E & P and a deficit in current E & P.
c. A deficit in both current and accumulated E & P.
d. A positive amount in both current and accumulated E & P.

5. Five years ago, a corporation determined its current E & P to be $100,000. In the current year, it makes a distribution of $200,000 to its shareholders. The IRS contends that the current E & P of the corporation five years ago really was $150,000.

a. Can the IRS successfully make this contention?
b. What difference would the additional $50,000 in E & P make?

6. If a corporation is chartered in a state that prohibits the payment of dividends that impair paid-in capital, is it possible for the corporation to pay a dividend that is a return of capital for tax purposes and yet comply with state law? Discuss.

7. The suggestion is made that any distributions to shareholders by a calendar year corporation should take place on January 1 before the corporation has developed any current E & P. Assess the validity of this suggestion.

8. T, an individual shareholder, receives a distribution from X Corporation and treats it as a return of capital. Upon audit by the IRS, he tells the agent: "Show me that X Corporation had adequate E & P to cover the distribution, and I will report the distribution as dividend income." Please comment.

9. X Corporation has no current or accumulated E & P. It distributes inventory (fair market value of $50,000 and basis of $10,000) to A, its sole shareholder. Does A recognize any dividend income? Explain.

10. A corporation with no E & P distributes a property dividend. Can it be said that the shareholders need not recognize any dividend income? Explain.

11. A corporation distributed property (adjusted basis of $100,000 and fair market value of $80,000) to its shareholders. Has the corporation acted wisely? Why or why not?

12. Does the distributing corporation recognize gain or loss when it distributes property as a dividend to its shareholders? Explain.

13. Discuss the effects of the following in generating or adding to a deficit in E & P:

a. A dividend distribution by the corporation
b. An operating loss of the corporation.

14. When are stock dividends taxable?
15. How are nontaxable stock rights handled for tax purposes? Taxable stock rights?
16. X Corporation sells its plant and equipment to its shareholders. Shortly thereafter, X enters into a long-term lease for the use of these assets. In connection with the possible tax ramifications of these transactions, consider the following:

a. The sale of the assets for less than their adjusted basis to X Corporation's shareholders.
b. The amount of rent X Corporation has agreed to pay.

17. Why is it important that an advance from a corporation to a shareholder be categorized as a bona fide loan? In resolving this issue, comment on the relevance of the following factors:

a. The corporation has never paid a dividend.
b. The advance is on open account.
c. The advance provides for 2% interest.
d. No date is specified for the repayment of the advance.

e. The shareholder used the advance to pay personal bills.

f. The shareholder repays the advance immediately after the transaction is questioned by the IRS on audit of the corporate income tax return.

18. How can shareholders bail out corporate profits in a manner that will provide the corporation with a deduction? What are the risks involved?

19. Whether compensation paid to a corporate employee is reasonable is a question of fact to be determined from the surrounding circumstances. How would the resolution of this problem be affected by each of the following factors?

a. The employee is not a shareholder but is related to the sole owner of the corporate employer.

b. The employee-shareholder never completed high school.

c. The employee-shareholder is a full-time college student.

d. The employee-shareholder was underpaid for her services during the formative period of the corporate employer.

e. The corporate employer pays a nominal dividend each year.

f. Year-end bonuses are paid to all shareholder-employees.

20. X Corporation has both individual and corporate shareholders. The individual shareholders want profits paid out in a form deductible to X Corporation (e.g., interest, rents) and not as dividends. Would the corporate shareholders be similarly motivated? Why or why not?

PROBLEMS

21. At the beginning of the year, T Corporation (a calendar year taxpayer) has accumulated E & P of $50,000. Its current E & P is $30,000. During the year, T Corporation distributes $90,000 ($45,000 each) to its equal shareholders, A and B. A has a basis of $8,000 in her stock, and B has a basis of $2,000 in his stock. How will the $90,000 distribution be treated for tax purposes?

22. At the beginning of the current year, X Corporation (a calendar year taxpayer) has accumulated E & P of $15,000. During the year, the corporation incurs a $20,000 net loss from operations that accrued ratably. On July 1, X Corporation distributes $10,000 to T, its sole shareholder. How much of the $10,000 is dividend income to T?

23. Complete the following schedule for each case:

	Accumulated E & P Beginning of Year	Current E & P	Cash Distributions (all on last day of year)	Amount Taxable	Return of Capital
a.	$ 40,000	($ 10,000)	$50,000	$30,000	$20,000
b.	(50,000)	30,000	40,000	30,000	10,000
c.	30,000	50,000	70,000	70,000	-0-
d.	60,000	(20,000)	45,000	40,000	5,000

e. Same as (d), except the distribution of $45,000 is made on June 30 and the corporation uses the calendar year for tax purposes. [45,000] [-0-]

24. Complete the following schedule for each case:

	Accumulated E & P Beginning of Year	Current E & P	Cash Distributions (all on last day of year)	Amount Taxable	Return of Capital
a.	$ 75,000	$ 20,000	$60,000	$60,000	$-0-
b.	20,000	40,000	45,000	45,000	-0-
c.	(90,000)	50,000	30,000	30,000	-0-
d.	60,000	(55,000)	40,000	5,000	35,000

e. Same as (d), except the distribution of $40,000 is made on June 30 and the corporation uses the calendar year for tax purposes. [32,500] [7500]

25. A had a basis of $10,000 in W Corporation stock that he sold to B on July 30, 1992, for $60,000. W Corporation had accumulated E & P of $25,000 on January 1, 1992,

[Handwritten top margin: A 10,000 / 15,000 / 5000   Acu 25,000 111 20,000   40,000 DI V Tax / 35,000 DI V Tax / 5,000 Returned Cap   Sale 60,000 basis / (5,000) basis / 55,000 Profit & taxable   B, 60000 Basis 10,000 DIV Tax / Rec 40,000 30,000 Return]

and current E & P (for 1992) of $20,000. During 1992, W Corporation made the following distributions: $40,000 cash to A on July 1, 1992, and $40,000 cash to B on December 30, 1992. How will the distributions be taxed to A and to B? What gain will A recognize on the sale of his stock to B?

26. T Corporation had accumulated E & P of $20,000 at the beginning of the current tax year. During the current tax year, it had current E & P of $30,000. At the end of the year, it distributed cash of $70,000 to its sole shareholder, A (an individual). What is X Corporation's E & P at the end of the year?

27. Assume in Problem 26 that T Corporation had an operating loss of $30,000 during the current tax year (rather than current earnings for E & P purposes of $30,000). It distributed cash of $70,000 to its sole shareholder, A, at the end of the year. What is X Corporation's E & P at the end of the year?

28. Indicate in each of the following independent situations the effect on taxable income and E & P, stating the amount of any increase (or decrease) as a result of the transaction. (In determining the effect on E & P, assume E & P has already been increased by current taxable income.)

Transaction	Taxable Income Increase (Decrease)	E & P Increase (Decrease)
a. Receipt of $15,000 tax-exempt income	No Effect	15,000
b. Payment of $15,150 Federal income taxes	No Effect	(15,150)
c. Collection of $100,000 on life insurance policy on corporate president	No Effect	100,000
d. Charitable contribution, $30,000, $20,000 allowable as a deduction in the current tax year	(20,000)	(10,000)
e. Deduction of remaining $10,000 charitable contribution in succeeding year	(10,000)	10,000
f. Realized gain on involuntary conversion of $200,000 ($30,000 of gain is recognized)	30,000	No Effect

[Handwritten notes near table: "the 30 was included for taxable income" "now 30" "already did the 10 now must add back" "already added"]

29. Indicate in each of the following independent situations the effect on taxable income and E & P, stating the amount of any increase (or decrease) as a result of the transaction. (In determining the effect on E & P, assume E & P has already been increased by current taxable income.)

Transaction	Taxable Income Increase (Decrease)	E & P Increase (Decrease)
a. Intangible drilling costs incurred in the current tax year and deductible from current taxable income in the amount of $50,000	_____	_____
b. Sale of unimproved real estate, basis of $200,000, fair market value of $800,000 (no election out of installment basis; payments in year of sale total $40,000)	_____	_____
c. Accelerated depreciation of $70,000 (straight-line would have been $40,000)	_____	_____
d. Sale of equipment to 100% owned corporation (adjusted basis was $120,000 and selling price was $50,000)	_____	_____

30. Equipment with a useful life of 7 years under MACRS and an ADR midpoint life of 10 years was purchased on January 3, 1991, at a cost of $100,000. A § 179 deduction to expense was not elected. The equipment had an adjusted basis of $52,475 on July 3, 1992, when it was sold for $70,000. What are the tax consequences on the sale, and what adjustment is made to E & P?

31. X Corporation sells property, adjusted basis of $200,000, fair market value of $180,000, to its sole shareholder for $160,000. How much loss can the corporation deduct as a result of this transaction? What is the effect on the corporation's E & P for the year of sale?

32. M Corporation has beginning E & P of $60,000. Its current taxable income is $30,000. During the year, it distributed land worth $100,000, adjusted basis of $30,000, to T, one of its individual shareholders. T assumes a liability on the property in the amount of $10,000. The corporation had tax-exempt interest income of $2,000 and received $40,000 on a term life insurance policy on the death of a corporate officer. Premiums on the policy for the year were $1,000.

    a. What is the amount of taxable income to T?
    b. What is the E & P of M Corporation after the property distribution?
    c. What is T's tax basis in the property received?
    (Note: Disregard the effect of the corporate income tax.)

33. X Corporation, with E & P of $300,000, distributes property worth $70,000, adjusted tax basis of $100,000, to Y, a corporate shareholder. The property is subject to a liability of $15,000, which Y assumes.

    a. What is the amount of dividend income to Y?
    b. What is Y's basis in the property received?
    c. How does the distribution affect X Corporation's E & P account?

34. Y Corporation had E & P of $20,000 when it made a current distribution of land with a cost of $40,000 and a fair market value of $90,000. Determine a sole shareholder's taxable income from the distribution.

35. A Corporation distributes inventory to its shareholders. Basis of the inventory is $16,000, and fair market value is $32,000. What is the effect of this distribution on the corporation's taxable income and on its E & P?

36. T Corporation distributes inventory to its shareholders with an adjusted basis of $15,000 and fair market value of $40,000. The inventory is subject to a bank lien of $45,000. What is the effect of this distribution on taxable income of the corporation?

37. X Corporation, a cash method, calendar year taxpayer, had the following income and expenses in the current year: income from services rendered, $40,000; salaries paid to employees, $20,000; tax-exempt interest, $5,000; dividends from a corporation in which X Corporation holds a 5% interest, $8,000; STCL on the sale of stock, $6,000; estimated Federal income taxes paid, $2,300. X Corporation purchased five-year MACRS property in the current year for $28,000; no § 179 election was made. The property has a seven-year class life. Compute taxable income and E & P for X Corporation.

38. At the beginning of its taxable year 1992, T Corporation had E & P of $50,000. T Corporation sold an asset at a loss of $50,000 on June 30, 1992. T Corporation incurred a total deficit for the calendar year 1992 of $55,000. Assume T Corporation made a distribution of $15,000 to its sole shareholder, A, an individual, on July 1, 1992. How will A be taxed on the $15,000?

39. X Corporation had a deficit of $60,000 in E & P at the beginning of its taxable year 1992. Its net profits for the period January 1, 1992, through June 30, 1992, were $75,000, but its E & P for the entire taxable year 1992 was only $5,000. If X Corporation made a distribution of $15,000 to its sole shareholder A, an individual, how would A be taxed on the distribution?

40. The stock in XY Corporation is owned equally by X, an individual, and Y Corporation. On January 1, 1992, XY had a deficit of $50,000. Its current E & P (for taxable year 1992) was $35,000. In 1992, XY distributed cash of $15,000 to both X and

Y Corporation. How will X and Y Corporation be taxed on the distribution? What is the accumulated E & P of XY Corporation at the end of 1992?

41. Y Corporation had $10,000 E & P at the beginning of 1992. In March of 1992, Y Corporation sold land with a basis of $100,000 to an unrelated third party for $300,000. In payment for the land, the purchaser paid $60,000 cash and gave Y Corporation a note in the amount of $240,000. The note will be paid in four installments of $60,000 each, the first installment being due March 1, 1993. Y reported the gain on the installment basis and accordingly reported only $40,000 of the gain from the sale in 1992. In addition to the gain on the sale of the land, Y Corporation had other income that resulted in an increase in E & P of $20,000. Y Corporation distributed $100,000 to its sole shareholder, A, an individual, on November 10, 1992. How will A be taxed on the $100,000?

42. XY Corporation is the sole shareholder of Y Corporation. T Corporation is a prospective buyer of Y Corporation but can only pay $300,000 of the $350,000 price XY wants for its stock in Y Corporation. Y Corporation has $50,000 cash on hand that it distributes to XY Corporation. XY Corporation then sells its stock to T Corporation for $300,000. What are the tax consequences to XY Corporation on the sale if XY Corporation has a basis of $100,000 in the Y Corporation stock? (Assume Y Corporation has sufficient E & P to cover the $50,000 distribution.)

43. X Corporation advances $60,000 as an interest-free loan to its shareholder, A (an individual). X Corporation can prove the advance is a bona fide loan. What are the tax consequences of the loan to X Corporation and to A?

44. T Corporation declared a dividend permitting its shareholders to elect to receive $10 per share or 2 additional shares of stock in the corporation for every 10 shares currently held. T Corporation has only common stock outstanding. Stock in T Corporation has a fair market value of $50 per share. All shareholders elect to receive stock. Will the shareholders have any taxable gain on the receipt of the stock?

45. X Corporation has two classes of common stock outstanding, Class A and Class B. During the current year, X Corporation distributed a preferred stock dividend to the Class A shareholders and a common stock dividend to the Class B shareholders. Is either of these distributions a taxable dividend to the shareholders? Explain.

46. A paid $30,000 for 15 shares of stock in XY Corporation five years ago. In November 1991, she received a nontaxable stock dividend of 5 additional shares in XY Corporation. She sells the 5 shares in March 1992 for $10,000. What is her gain, and how is it taxed?

47. AB Corporation declares a nontaxable dividend payable in rights to subscribe to common stock. One right and $60 entitles the holder to subscribe to one share of stock. One right is issued for each share of stock owned. T, a shareholder, owns 100 shares of stock that she purchased two years ago for $3,000. At the date of distribution of the rights, the market value of the stock was $80, and the market value of the rights was $20 per right. T received 100 rights. She exercises 60 rights and purchases 60 additional shares of stock. She sells the remaining 40 rights for $750. What are the tax consequences of these transactions to T?

48. T Corporation has a deficit in accumulated E & P of $50,000 as of January 1, 1992. Starting in 1992, T Corporation expects to generate annual E & P of $50,000 for the next four years and would like to distribute this amount to its shareholders. How should T Corporation distribute the $50,000 over the four-year period (for a total distribution of $200,000) to provide the least amount of dividend income to its shareholders (all individuals)?

RESEARCH PROBLEMS

RESEARCH PROBLEM 1   A, a wealthy individual, had substantial income in 1991. A owned 80% of the common (voting) stock in AB Corporation and 100% of the preferred stock. The preferred stock, 65,000 shares, had a call value of $50,000. AB Corporation was required to pay a dividend of $2 per share on the preferred stock before any dividends could be paid on the common stock. On March 10, 1991, AB Corporation declared a dividend of $2 per share on the preferred stock and $1 per share on the common stock. The dividend was payable on April 10, 1991, to shareholders of record as of April 1, 1991. On March 20, 1991, A gave all his preferred shares to his favorite charity, Y-Tech University. On April 10, 1991, AB Corporation paid Y-Tech a dividend of $130,000. On June 15, 1991, A offered to purchase the preferred shares from Y-Tech for the then value of the shares, $50,000. As Y-Tech had no desire to remain a shareholder in AB Corporation, it sold the stock to A for $50,000. On his 1991 tax return, A claimed a charitable contribution deduction of $180,000, the value of the preferred stock on the date of the gift. (The $180,000 value was reflected in the $50,000 call value of the stock plus the $130,000 dividend that had been declared on the stock.) A reported no income in connection with the transfer of the stock. Upon an audit of A's return in 1992, the IRS asserted a tax deficiency against A, contending that A had ordinary income of $130,000 as a result of the dividend payment to the charity. The IRS contended that the assignment of income doctrine caused the dividend income to be attributed to A. A contends that he should not be taxed on the dividend as Y-Tech University was "entitled" to the dividend payment. Should A be taxed on the dividend payment to the charity?

Research Problem 2   T is the president and majority shareholder of X Corporation. During 1989, T was paid a salary of $50,000 and received a year-end bonus of $200,000. Upon audit of X Corporation in 1990, the IRS disallowed $150,000 of the amount paid to T as being unreasonable. Under a repayment agreement, T reimbursed X Corporation for the $150,000 in 1991. On his 1989 return, T had included the $150,000 in gross income. On his 1991 return, he deducted none of the repayment but elected the option set forth in § 1341(a)(5). Thus, T claimed a credit for the amount of tax that was generated by the inclusion of the $150,000 on his 1989 return. Upon audit of his 1991 return in 1992, the IRS did not accept the credit approach but did permit a deduction of $150,000 for 1991. Because T was in a higher tax bracket in 1989, a deficiency resulted for 1991. T comes to you for advice. Should he challenge the tax deficiency for tax year 1991?

Research Problem 3   J, the principal shareholder of X Corporation, diverted sums totaling $60,000 from the corporation during tax year 1991. Upon audit of J's return, the IRS contended these sums were taxable income to J under § 61 of the Code. J disagrees, stating that such sums represent constructive dividends and are taxable only to the extent of X Corporation's E & P, which J argues had a deficit in 1990. The IRS contends that even if § 61 does not apply, the $60,000 would still be taxable income because X Corporation had income in 1991. X Corporation is on the cash basis. It had a deficit in its E & P account as of January 1, 1991. However, it had E & P in 1991 of $65,000. Its income tax liability for 1991 was $31,500. The IRS argues that $31,500 cannot be a charge against current E & P because the tax was not paid until 1992 and the corporation was on the cash basis. Consequently, the $60,000 would be taxable income to J in 1991, regardless of whether it is income under § 61 or under § 301. J comes to you for advice. What advice would you give him?

CHAPTER

5

CORPORATIONS: REDEMPTIONS AND LIQUIDATIONS

OBJECTIVES

Describe the various stock redemptions that qualify for sale or exchange treatment and thereby avoid dividend treatment.

Review the tax rules governing the distribution of stock and securities of a controlled corporation.

Contrast property dividends and stock redemptions with distributions in complete liquidation of a corporation.

Review the tax effect of a complete liquidation on the corporation being liquidated.

Review the tax effect on the shareholders of a corporation being liquidated.

Recognize the tax planning opportunities available to minimize the income tax result in the complete liquidation of a corporation.

OUTLINE

Chapter 4 considered the tax treatment of corporate distributions that are a return *on* a shareholder's investment. The distributions are treated as § 301 distributions and are taxed as dividends to the extent of the earnings and profits (E & P) of the corporation. Corporate distributions that are a return *of* a shareholder's investment receive more favorable tax treatment. The distributions are treated like a sale or exchange of the shareholder's investment. As a result, the shareholder does not recognize income to the extent of the basis in the stock, and any excess is treated as capital gain. To qualify for exchange treatment and not be taxed under § 301, a corporate distribution must meet the provisions of the specific applicable Code Section. If not, the distribution becomes a § 301 distribution.

Corporate distributions that receive the more favorable exchange treatment are the qualified stock redemption and the distributions made to a shareholder when a corporation terminates its existence. Even more favorable treatment is available to a parent corporation for a distribution of stock of a subsidiary. Under certain circumstances, the parent may distribute such stock tax-free to its shareholders.

Because corporate distributions that represent a return of the shareholder's investment have many tax ramifications, the transactions should be planned with a full understanding of the tax consequences. This chapter examines the tax implications of corporate distributions that are not dividend distributions.

STOCK REDEMPTIONS — IN GENERAL
◆

In a stock redemption, a corporation purchases its stock from a shareholder. A shareholder's sale of stock back to the corporation resembles a sale of the stock to an outsider, or third party. Consequently, a stock redemption will often be treated like a sale for tax purposes.

A stock redemption may have the same effect as a dividend. For example, if a shareholder owns all the stock of a corporation and sells half of that stock to the corporation, his or her ownership percentage in the corporation will not change. After the redemption, the shareholder still owns all the stock of the corporation. In this instance the stock redemption resembles a dividend distribution and is taxed as such.

Stock redemptions occur for several reasons. A shareholder may want to retire. Rather than the other shareholders purchasing his or her stock, the corporation simply redeems all of the retiring shareholder's shares. In this case, the remaining shareholders are not required to use their own funds to purchase the stock. When a shareholder dies, the corporation may wish to purchase the stock of the deceased shareholder from the estate. The corporation provides the funds, thus relieving the remaining shareholders of the need to furnish the purchase money. As an alternative to a redemption by the corporation, the surviving shareholders may purchase the stock of the withdrawing shareholder. If corporate funds are used for this purpose, the surviving shareholders may have dividend consequences.

STOCK REDEMPTIONS — EXCHANGE TREATMENT
◆

A successful stock redemption provides "exchange" treatment for the shareholder. Exchange treatment permits a shareholder to recover his or her capital investment tax-free and avoid dividend consequences. Exchange treatment generally results in capital gain or loss. A capital gain is beneficial for a shareholder who is in the highest tax bracket as the tax is limited to 28 percent. It also provides a benefit to a shareholder who has substantial capital losses. A capital loss on a stock redemption would not be beneficial, but a redemption that produces a capital loss is rare.

―――――――――――――――――――― EXAMPLE 1 ――――――――――――――――

X Corporation redeems a substantial portion of Ms. T's stock in a qualified stock redemption. X Corporation pays Ms. T $200,000 for stock she acquired several years ago at a cost of $150,000. Ms. T treats the $200,000 redemption proceeds as follows: $150,000 as a tax-free return of basis and $50,000 as a long-term capital gain. The $50,000 is taxed at a maximum rate of 28%. Assume Ms. T has capital losses of $40,000 and no other capital gains. She can offset the entire $40,000 capital loss against the capital gain. Otherwise, only $3,000 of her capital loss can be utilized. ◆

To determine what is a redemption for tax purposes, look to the Code. The label given to the transaction by the parties *or* by state law is not controlling. The applicable Code sections are §§ 302 and 303. Section 302 provides that if a corporation redeems its stock within the meaning of § 317 and pursuant to §§ 302(b)(1), (2), (3), or (4), the redemption is treated as a distribution in partial or full payment of a shareholder's stock. Section 303 provides that certain distributions of property to a shareholder in exchange for stock included in a decedent's estate are treated as a stock redemption.

Section 317 defines a stock redemption as an *exchange* between a corporation and its shareholder of the corporation's stock for property.

Historical Background and Overview

Before the 1954 Code, stock redemptions that constituted ordinary taxable dividends were distinguished from those qualifying for capital gain by the so-called dividend equivalency rule. When a redemption was essentially equivalent to a dividend, it did not qualify as a stock redemption. The entire amount received by the shareholder was subject to taxation as ordinary income to the extent of the corporation's E & P.

―――――――――――――――――――― EXAMPLE 2 ――――――――――――――――

A, an individual, owns 100% of the stock of X Corporation. X Corporation has E & P of $50,000. A sells one-half of his shares to the corporation for $50,000. His basis in one-half of the stock is $10,000, and he has held the stock for five years. If the sale of the stock to X Corporation qualified as a stock redemption, A would have a long-term capital gain of $40,000. However, the distribution is essentially equivalent to a dividend. A's percentage of ownership in the corporation has not changed. He is deemed to have received a taxable dividend of $50,000. ◆

Under the Code, the following major types of stock redemptions qualify for exchange treatment and therefore avoid dividend income consequences:

- Distributions not essentially equivalent to a dividend [§ 302(b)(1)].
- Distributions substantially disproportionate in terms of shareholder effect [§ 302(b)(2)].
- Distributions in complete termination of a shareholder's interest [§ 302(b)(3)].
- Distributions in partial liquidation of a corporation, but only to a noncorporate shareholder when (1) the distribution is not essentially equivalent to a dividend or (2) an active business is terminated [§ 302(b)(4)].
- Distributions to pay a shareholder's death taxes [§ 303].

Stock Attribution Rules

To deter the use of certain qualifying stock redemptions by related parties, § 318 imposes constructive ownership of stock (stock attribution) rules. In testing for a stock redemption, a shareholder may be required to take into account stock owned by related parties. Related parties include immediate family, specifically, spouses, children, grandchildren, and parents. Attribution also takes place *from* and *to* partnerships, estates, trusts, and corporations (50 percent or more ownership required in the case of corporations).

EXAMPLE 3

T, an individual, owns 30% of the stock in X Corporation, the other 70% being held by her children. For purposes of § 318, T is treated as owning 100% of the stock in X Corporation. She owns 30% directly and, because of the family attribution rules, 70% indirectly. ◆

EXAMPLE 4

C, an individual, owns 50% of the stock in Y Corporation. The other 50% is owned by a partnership in which C has a 20% interest. C is deemed to own 60% of Y Corporation: 50% directly and, because of the partnership interest, 10% indirectly. ◆

The stock attribution rules of § 318 do not apply to stock redemptions to pay death taxes. Under certain conditions, the *family* attribution rules (refer to Example 3) do not apply to stock redemptions in complete termination of a shareholder's interest.

Not Essentially Equivalent to a Dividend
Stock Redemption—§ 302(b)(1)

Section 302(b)(1) provides that a redemption is treated as a distribution in part or full payment in exchange for the stock if it is "not essentially equivalent to a dividend." Few objective tests exist to determine when a redemption is or is not essentially equivalent to a dividend. Section 302(b)(1) was added to provide specifically for redemptions of preferred stock.[1] Often, such stock is called in by the corporation without the shareholders exercising any control over the redemption. Some courts interpreted § 302(b)(1) to mean a redemption would be granted capital gain treatment if the redemption had a business purpose and no tax avoidance scheme existed to bail out dividends at favorable tax rates.[2] The real question was whether the stock attribution rules of § 318(a) applied to this provision. However, some courts appeared to be less concerned with the application of § 318(a) than with the presence of a business purpose for the redemption.

The question of the applicability of § 318 was presumably settled by the Supreme Court in *U.S. v. Davis.*[3] In *Davis*, a taxpayer and his family owned all of the common stock of a corporation. He made an additional contribution of $25,000 for 1,000 shares of preferred stock. The preferred stock was purchased to increase the company's working capital so that the company might qualify for a government loan. It was understood that the corporation would redeem the preferred stock after the loan was repaid. At that time, the corporation did indeed redeem the taxpayer's preferred stock for $25,000. The taxpayer did not report the $25,000 on his personal income tax return. He assumed it was a stock redemption under § 302 and did not exceed his stock basis.

The Supreme Court in *Davis* agreed with the IRS that the redemption was essentially equivalent to a dividend and was taxable as ordinary income under §§ 301 and 316. The Court stated that § 318(a) applies to § 302(b)(1). Conse-

---

1. See S.Rept. No. 1622, 83d Cong., 2d Sess., at 44.

2. See, for example, *Kerr v. Comm.*, 64–1 USTC ¶9186, 13 AFTR2d 386, 326 F.2d 225 (CA–9, 1964).

3. 70–1 USTC ¶9289, 25 AFTR2d 70–827, 90 S.Ct. 1041 (USSC, 1970).

quently, the taxpayer was deemed the owner of all the common stock. Because there was not ". . . a meaningful reduction of the shareholder's proportionate interest in the corporation," the redemption did not qualify under § 302(b)(1).[4]

Currently, a redemption will qualify under § 302(b)(1) as not being "essentially equivalent to a dividend" when there has been a meaningful reduction of the shareholder's proportionate interest in the redeeming corporation. The facts and circumstances of each case will determine whether a distribution in redemption of stock is essentially equivalent to a dividend within the meaning of § 302(b)(1).[5] Courts have considered a decrease in the redeeming shareholder's voting control to be the most significant indicator of a meaningful reduction.[6] Other factors considered are reductions in the rights of redeeming shareholders to share in corporate earnings or to receive corporate assets upon liquidation.[7] The "meaningful reduction" test is applied whether common stock or preferred stock is being redeemed.

EXAMPLE 5

A, an individual, owns 58% of the common stock of Y Corporation. After a redemption of part of A's stock, A owns 51% of the stock of Y Corporation. A would continue to have dominant voting rights in Y; thus, the redemption would be treated as "essentially equivalent to a dividend," and A would have ordinary income on the entire amount of the distribution. ◆

EXAMPLE 6

X Corporation redeems 2% of the stock of B, a minority shareholder. Before the redemption, B owned 10% of X Corporation. In this case, the redemption may qualify as "not essentially equivalent to a dividend." B experiences a reduction in her voting rights, her right to participate in current earnings and accumulated surplus, and her right to share in net assets upon liquidation. ◆

If a redemption is treated as an ordinary dividend, the shareholder's basis in the stock redeemed attaches to the remaining stock. According to the Regulations, this basis would attach to other stock held by the taxpayer (or to stock he or she owns constructively).[8]

EXAMPLE 7

H and W, husband and wife, each own 50 shares in X Corporation, representing 100% of the stock of X. All the stock was purchased for $50,000. The corporation redeems H's 50 shares. Assuming the rules governing the complete termination of a shareholder's interest under § 302(b)(3) would not apply, the redemption would be treated as a taxable dividend. H's basis in the stock, $25,000, would attach to W's stock so that W would have a basis of $50,000 in the 50 shares she currently owns in X Corporation. ◆

Substantially Disproportionate Redemptions—§ 302(b)(2)

A redemption of stock qualifies for capital gain treatment under § 302(b)(2) if two conditions are met:

4. Later cases have addressed the issue of whether family discord should be considered in the application of § 318 in factual situations similar to those in *U.S. v. Davis.* In *Robin Haft Trust,* 75–1 USTC ¶9209, 35 AFTR2d 75–650, 510 F.2d 43 (CA–1, 1975), the First Court of Appeals said yes; the attribution rules should not be mechanically applied. However, the IRS refused to follow the *Robin Haft Trust* case. In *David Metzger Trust,* 82–2 USTC ¶9718, 51 AFTR2d 83–376, 693 F.2d 459 (CA–5, 1982), the Fifth Court of

Appeals agreed with the IRS, stating that family discord should not be taken into account in applying the attribution rules.

5. Reg. § 1.302–2(b). See *Mary G. Roebling,* 77 T.C. 30 (1981).

6. See *Jack Paparo,* 71 T.C. 692 (1979), and *Blanche S. Benjamin,* 66 T.C. 1084 (1976).

7. See *Grabowski Trust,* 58 T.C. 650 (1972).

8. Reg. § 1.302–2(c).

1. The distribution must be substantially disproportionate. To be substantially disproportionate, the shareholder must own, after the distribution, less than 80 percent of his or her interest in the corporation before the redemption. For example, if a shareholder has a 60 percent ownership in a corporation that redeems part of the stock, the redemption is substantially disproportionate only if the percentage of ownership after the redemption is less than 48 percent (80 percent of 60 percent).

2. The shareholder must own, after the distribution, less than 50 percent of the total combined voting power of all classes of stock entitled to vote.

Figure 5–1 provides a graphic presentation of a redemption qualifying under § 302(b)(2).

In determining the percentage of ownership of the shareholder, the constructive ownership rules of § 318(a) apply.

FIGURE 5–1

Redemption Qualifying under § 302(b)(2)

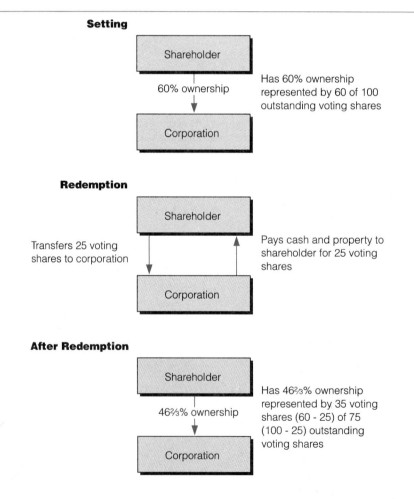

Setting

Shareholder

60% ownership

Corporation

Has 60% ownership represented by 60 of 100 outstanding voting shares

Redemption

Shareholder

Transfers 25 voting shares to corporation

Pays cash and property to shareholder for 25 voting shares

Corporation

After Redemption

Shareholder

46⅔% ownership

Corporation

Has 46⅔% ownership represented by 35 voting shares (60 - 25) of 75 (100 - 25) outstanding voting shares

Results Redemption is a qualified redemption under § 302(b)(2). It meets both conditions of § 302(b)(2):
1. Shareholder owns less than 50% of the total combined voting power in the corporation.
2. Shareholder owns less than 80% of the 60% ownership held prior to the redemption (80% x 60% = 48%).

———————————————— EXAMPLE 8 ————————————————

A, B, and C, unrelated individuals, own 30 shares, 30 shares, and 40 shares, respectively, in X Corporation. X Corporation has E & P of $200,000. The corporation redeems 20 shares of C's stock for $30,000. C paid $200 a share for the stock two years ago.

C's ownership in X Corporation before and after the redemption is as follows:

	Total Shares	C's Ownership	Ownership Percentage	80% of Original Ownership
Before redemption	100	40	40%	32% (80% × 40%)
After redemption	80	20	25% (20 ÷ 80)	

C's 25% ownership after the redemption meets both tests of § 302(b)(2). It is less than 50% of the total voting power and less than 80% of C's original ownership. The distribution qualifies as a stock redemption. C has a long-term capital gain of $26,000 [$30,000 − $4,000 (20 shares × $200)]. ◆

———————————————— EXAMPLE 9 ————————————————

Assume that B and C are father and son. The redemption described above would not qualify for exchange treatment. C is deemed to own the stock of B so that after the redemption, C would have 50 shares of a total of 80 shares, a more than 50% ownership. He would also fail the 80% test.

C's ownership in X Corporation is computed as follows:

	Total Shares	C's Direct Ownership	B's Ownership	C's Deemed Ownership	Ownership Percentage	80% of Original Ownership
Before redemption	100	40	30	70	70%	56% (80% × 70%)
After redemption	80	20	30	50	62.5% (50 ÷ 80)	

C's deemed ownership of 62.5% fails to meet either of the tests of § 302(b)(2). It is more than 50% ownership and more than 80% of C's original ownership. Thus, the distribution does not qualify as a stock redemption. C has a taxable dividend of $30,000. ◆

Complete Termination of a Shareholder's Interest Redemptions—§ 302(b)(3)

If a shareholder terminates his or her entire stock ownership in a corporation through a stock redemption, the redemption generally will qualify for exchange treatment under § 302(b)(3). Such a complete termination may not meet the substantially disproportionate rules of § 302(b)(2) if the constructive ownership rules of § 318(a)(1) are applied. The difference in the two provisions is that the constructive ownership rules of § 318(a)(1) do not apply to § 302(b)(3). This occurs only if both the following conditions are met:

1. The former shareholder has no interest, other than that of a creditor, in the corporation after the redemption (including an interest as an officer, director, or employee) for at least 10 years; and
2. The former shareholder files an agreement to notify the IRS of any acquisition within the 10-year period and to retain all necessary records pertaining to the redemption during this time period.

A shareholder can reacquire an interest in the corporation by bequest or inheritance, but in no other manner. The required agreement should be in the form of a separate statement signed by the shareholder and attached to the return for the year in which the redemption occurred. The agreement should state that the shareholder agrees to notify the appropriate District Director within 30 days of reacquiring an interest in the corporation within the 10 year period following the redemption.

A redeemed estate or trust may waive family attribution. This occurs if, after the redemption, neither the entity nor its beneficiaries hold an interest in the corporation or acquire such an interest within the 10-year period. All parties involved must file an agreement to be jointly and severally liable for any taxes due if a reacquisition occurs.[9]

EXAMPLE 10

D, a 40% shareholder in X Corporation, dies, and his will designates W as his sole beneficiary. The remaining interest in X Corporation is held as follows: 35% by X (D's son) and 25% by E (a key employee). After the executor of D's estate redeems all that is permissible under § 303 (the sum total of death taxes and administration expenses [see later discussion]), a 10% interest remains in the estate. The remaining 10% interest can be redeemed under § 302(b)(3) if both the entity (D's estate) and the beneficiary (W) terminate all interest in the corporation and do not reacquire an interest within a 10-year period. The parties (D's estate and W) must agree to be jointly and severally liable for any taxes due in the event of reacquisition. ◆

Redemptions in Partial Liquidation—§ 302(b)(4)

Sale or exchange treatment for each type of stock redemption [§§ 302(b)(1), (2), and (3)] discussed thus far depends on shareholder considerations. The application of § 302(b)(4) is determined by corporate conditions.

Under § 302(b)(4), noncorporate shareholders are allowed sale or exchange treatment for partial liquidations. These are defined in § 302(e) to include either of the following:

- A distribution not essentially equivalent to a dividend.
- A distribution pursuant to the termination of an active business.

To qualify as a partial liquidation, distribution must be made within the taxable year in which the plan is adopted or within the succeeding taxable year.

The not essentially equivalent to a dividend approach is determined at the corporate level. In this context, § 302 presents a true paradox for the reader. First, there is the not essentially equivalent to a dividend test of § 302(b)(1), which is applied at the shareholder level. Second, there is the not essentially equivalent to a dividend test of § 302(e), which looks to the effect of the distribution on the corporation. Thus, *identical terminology* in the same Code Section carries different meanings!

The not essentially equivalent to a dividend test presumably encompasses prior case law. This required a genuine contraction of the business of the corporation.

EXAMPLE 11

X Corporation owned a building with seven stories. Part of the building was rented, and part was used directly in X Corporation's business. A fire destroyed the two top floors, and X Corporation received insurance proceeds. For business reasons, X Corporation did not rebuild the two floors. With excess funds collected as insurance

---

9. § 302(c)(2)(C).

proceeds from the fire, the corporation purchased some stock from its shareholders. The distribution qualified as a partial liquidation.[10] ◆

The genuine contraction of a corporate business concept has been difficult to apply due to lack of objective tests. The IRS has ruled that proceeds from the sale of excess inventory distributed to shareholders in exchange for part of their stock will not qualify.[11] Because the genuine contraction of a corporate business test is so subjective, it should not be relied upon without a favorable ruling from the IRS.

In contrast, the complete termination of a business test sets out objective requirements. A distribution will qualify as a partial liquidation under the complete termination of a business test if:

- The corporation has more than one trade or business and at least two of the trades or businesses have been in existence for more than five years.
- The corporation terminates one trade or business that has been in existence for more than five years while continuing a remaining trade or business that has been in existence for more than five years.
- The trade or business that was terminated was not acquired in a taxable transaction within the five-year period.

The five-year requirement prevents the bailout of E & P by the acquisition and distribution of another business within a short period of time.

──────────────── EXAMPLE 12 ────────────────

X Corporation has been selling a single product to its customers. It loses its major customer, and a severe drop in sales results. The corporation reduces its inventory investment and has substantial cash on hand. It redeems 20% of its outstanding stock as a liquidating dividend. A, an individual shareholder, receives $10,000 for stock that cost $5,000 two years ago. The distribution will not qualify under § 302. The corporation had only one business activity, and the distribution is not a disproportionate redemption. The $10,000 is a taxable dividend to A assuming adequate E & P. The distribution would not qualify as a genuine contraction of a corporate business since it only reduces excess inventory. ◆

──────────────── EXAMPLE 13 ────────────────

X Corporation, the owner and operator of a wholesale grocery business, acquired a freight-hauling concern. The acquisition was by purchase and therefore constituted a taxable transaction. Three years later, the freight-hauling concern is distributed in kind on a pro rata basis to all of the shareholders of X Corporation. The distribution does not satisfy the requirements of § 302(e)(3) for two reasons. First, the business distributed had not been conducted for five years. Second, it was acquired by X Corporation in a taxable transaction. As the distribution was pro rata among the shareholders, none of the regular types of stock redemptions [i.e., §§ 302(b)(1), (2), or (3)] can be used. All other alternatives exhausted, X Corporation's distribution falls into the classification of a dividend distribution. ◆

Redemptions to Pay Death Taxes—§ 303

Section 303 provides an executor the opportunity to redeem stock in a closely held corporation when the stock represents a substantial amount of the gross estate of the shareholder-decedent. The purpose of the redemption is to provide

──────────────

10. *Joseph W. Imler*, 11 T.C. 836 (1948). **11.** Rev.Rul. 60–322, 1960–2 C.B. 118.

the estate with liquidity. Stock in a closely held corporation is generally not marketable. However, it could be redeemed if § 302 would not cause ordinary dividend treatment. Section 303, to an extent, alleviates this problem.

Section 303 is an exception to § 302(b). If a stock redemption qualifies under § 303, the rules of § 302(b) do not apply. The distribution will qualify as a stock redemption regardless of whether it is substantially disproportionate or not essentially equivalent to a dividend.

In a § 303 redemption, the redemption price generally equals the basis of the stock. Under § 1014, the income tax basis of property owned by a decedent becomes the property's fair market value on the date of death (or alternate valuation date if available and if elected). When this so-called step-up or step-down in basis that occurs at death (see Chapter 18) equals the redemption price, the exchange is free of any income tax consequences to the shareholder's estate.

Section 303 applies to a distribution made with respect to stock of a corporation when the value of the stock in the gross estate of a decedent exceeds 35 percent of the value of the adjusted gross estate. (For a definition of "gross estate" and "adjusted gross estate," see the Glossary of Tax Terms in Appendix C.)

EXAMPLE 14

The adjusted gross estate of D, decedent, is $900,000. The death taxes and funeral and administration expenses of the estate total $200,000. Included in the estate is stock in X Corporation, a closely held corporation, valued at $340,000. D had acquired the stock years ago at a cost of $60,000. X Corporation redeems $200,000 of the stock from D's estate. The redemption qualifies under § 303 and would not be a dividend to D's estate. Section 1014 applies to give the stock a step-up in basis. Consequently, there is no tax on the redemption. ◆

In determining whether the value of stock in a corporation exceeds 35 percent of the value of the adjusted gross estate of a decedent, the stock of two or more corporations is treated as the stock of a single corporation. Stock in corporations in which the decedent held a 20 percent or more interest is treated as stock in a single corporation for purposes of § 303.[12]

EXAMPLE 15

The adjusted gross estate of a decedent is $300,000. The gross estate includes stock in X and Y Corporations valued at $100,000 and $80,000, respectively. Unless the two corporations are treated as a single corporation, § 303 does not apply to a redemption of the stock. Assume the decedent owned all the stock of X Corporation and 80% of the stock of Y. Section 303 applies because 20% or more of the value of the stock of both corporations is included in the decedent's estate. The 35% test is met when the stock is treated as that of a single corporation. ◆

The use of § 303 is subject to time limitations. Section 303 applies only to redemptions made within 90 days after the expiration of the period of limitations for the assessment of the Federal estate tax. If a petition for a redetermination of an estate tax deficiency is timely filed with the U.S. Tax Court, the applicable period for a § 303 redemption is extended to 60 days after the decision of the Court becomes final.[13] Estates that have elected installment payments under § 6166 ("Extension of Time When the Estate Consists Largely of an Interest in a Closely Held Business") are allowed additional time to carry out the redemption.[14] The 15-year extension under § 6166 is discussed at length in Chapter 18.

---

12. § 303(b)(2)(B).

13. § 303(b)(1). The latter extension of time applies only to contests in the Tax Court. It does not apply to a petition

initiated solely for the purpose of extending the time period under § 303.

14. § 303(b)(1)(C).

Section 303 applies to the extent of the sum of the estate, inheritance, legacy, and succession taxes imposed by reason of the decedent's death. Also allowed are the funeral and administration expenses deductible to the estate.[15] Stock must be redeemed from a shareholder whose interest in the estate is reduced by the payment of these taxes and expenses.

Effect on the Corporation Redeeming Its Stock

Having considered the different types of stock redemptions that will receive exchange treatment, what is the tax effect to the corporation redeeming its stock? If the corporation uses property to carry out the redemption, is gain or loss recognized on the distribution? Furthermore, what effect does the redemption have on the corporation's E & P? These matters are discussed in the following paragraphs.

Recognition of Loss by the Corporation.   The purchase of stock, including the repurchase by an issuing corporation of its own stock, generally is treated as a capital transaction that does not give rise to a loss. All expenses a corporation incurs in redeeming its stock are nonamortizable capital expenditures. Stock purchase premiums are not deductible. Also not deductible are payments to a shareholder for an agreement not to reacquire stock in the corporation for a specified time as well as legal, accounting, transfer agent, brokerage, and appraisal fees.

Recognition of Gain by the Corporation.   Section 311 provides that corporations are taxed on all distributions of appreciated property whether in the form of a property dividend or a stock redemption.

─────────────────── EXAMPLE 16 ───────────────────

To carry out a stock redemption, Y Corporation transfers land (basis of $80,000, fair market value of $300,000) to a shareholder. Y Corporation has a recognized gain of $220,000 ($300,000 − $80,000). ◆

Effect on Earnings and Profits.   The E & P account of a corporation is reduced by a stock redemption in an amount not in excess of the ratable share of the E & P of the distributing corporation attributable to the stock redeemed.[16]

─────────────────── EXAMPLE 17 ───────────────────

X Corporation has 100 shares of stock outstanding. It redeems 30 shares for $100,000 at a time when it has paid-in capital of $120,000 and E & P of $150,000. The charge to E & P is 30% of the amount in the E & P account ($45,000), and the remainder of the redemption price ($55,000) is a reduction of the capital account. ◆

Stock redemptions that do not fall under any of the four major types provided for in the Code are treated as dividend distributions to the extent of E & P. Resourceful taxpayers, however, found two ways to circumvent the redemption provisions. Both involved structuring as a sale of the stock what was, in effect, a stock redemption or a dividend distribution. The widespread use of these approaches to obtain capital gain treatment available in the past led to the enactment of § 306, dealing with preferred stock bailouts, and § 304, dealing with transfers of stock to related corporations.

STOCK
REDEMPTIONS — NO
EXCHANGE TREATMENT
◆

─────────

15. § 303(a).   **16.** § 312(n)(7).

Preferred Stock Bailouts—§ 306

The Problem. Suppose a shareholder would like to bail out corporate profits as a long-term capital gain rather than as a dividend. Several possibilities exist:

- A sale of stock to the corporation that qualifies as a stock redemption under the four types provided for by § 302 or the one type allowed under § 303.
- A complete liquidation of the corporation under § 331.
- A sale of stock to third parties.

A stock redemption under § 302 is difficult to carry out successfully in the case of a family corporation unless the shareholder completely terminates his or her interest in the corporation. A redemption of stock under § 303 is not available until after the death of a shareholder. Partial liquidations are limited to peculiar circumstances and are hard to arrange. Complete liquidations are not feasible for going concerns with good present and future profit potential. Lastly, the sale of stock to third parties may not be desirable if a shareholder wishes to maintain the same voting power in the corporation.

Clever taxpayers devised the following scheme to bail out corporate profits:[17]

First, the corporation issues a nontaxable preferred stock dividend on common stock [§ 305(a)]. The preferred stock is nonvoting.

Second, the shareholder assigns to the preferred stock an appropriate portion of the basis of the common stock [§ 307(a)].

Third, the shareholder sells the preferred stock to a third party for the stock's fair market value. If the stock is a capital asset, the spread between the selling price and the assigned basis is capital gain. The holding period of the common stock can be counted [§ 1223(5)] to determine the nature of the gain—either short-term or long-term capital gain.

Fourth, the third party holds the preferred stock for a suitable period of time (at least more than one year) and then returns it to the corporation for redemption at a premium. If the requirements of § 302(b)(3) are met (complete termination of a shareholder's interest), the difference between the purchase price and the redemption proceeds (the premium) is taxed as long-term capital gain.

Note what has been accomplished. The original shareholder obtains the bailout of corporate profits as a long-term capital gain. No diminution in the control of the corporation occurs as the voting common stock has remained intact. The third party purchaser of the preferred stock is rewarded for its cooperation by the premium paid upon the later redemption of the stock.

The Solution of § 306. The tax avoidance possibilities of the preferred stock bailout approach led to § 306. This provision produces the following tax consequences:

- The shareholder has ordinary income on the sale (but not the receipt) of the preferred stock to a third party. The amount of the ordinary income is the fair market value of the preferred stock (on the date of distribution) that would have been a dividend had the corporation distributed cash in lieu of stock [§ 306(a)(1)]. Such income is *not a dividend* and has no effect on the issuing corporation's E & P.[18] In this respect, § 306 leads to a harsher result than does a taxable dividend distribution.

---

17. *Chamberlin v. Comm.*, 53–2 USTC ¶9576, 44 AFTR 494, 207 F.2d 462 (CA–6, 1953), *cert. den.*, 74 S.Ct. 516 (USSC, 1954).

18. Reg. § 1.306–1(b)(1).

- No loss is recognized on any sale of the preferred stock by the shareholder.
- If the shareholder does not sell the preferred stock to a third party but has it redeemed by the issuing corporation, a different rule applies. The redemption proceeds constitute dividend income to the extent of the corporation's E & P on the date of the redemption [§ 306(a)(2)].

─────────────────── EXAMPLE 18 ───────────────────

As of January 1 of the current year, Z Corporation has E & P of $150,000. T, the sole shareholder of Z Corporation, owns all of Z's common stock (100 shares) with a basis of $60,000. On that date, Z Corporation declares and pays a preferred stock dividend [nontaxable under § 305(a)] of 100 shares. After the dividend, the fair market value of one share of common is $2,000, and the fair market value of one share of preferred is $1,000. Two days later, T sells the 100 shares of preferred to V for $100,000. Section 306 produces the following results:

- After the distribution and before the sale, the preferred stock has a basis to T of $20,000 [($100,000 value of preferred ÷ $300,000 value of preferred and common) × $60,000 (the original basis of the common stock)].
- The sale of the preferred stock generates $100,000 of ordinary income to T. This would have been the amount of dividend income T would recognize had cash instead of preferred stock been distributed.
- The $20,000 basis allocated to the preferred stock is not lost but is returned to the common stock account.
- Z Corporation's E & P account is unaffected by either the stock distribution or its subsequent sale. ◆

─────────────────── EXAMPLE 19 ───────────────────

Assume the same facts as in Example 18 with this exception: Z Corporation's E & P is only $50,000 on the date the preferred stock is distributed. Under these circumstances, the $100,000 sale proceeds are accounted for as follows: $50,000 ordinary income under § 306, $20,000 applied against the basis of the preferred stock, and $30,000 capital gain. Whether the capital gain is long term or short term depends upon the holding period of the underlying common stock. ◆

What Is § 306 Stock?   Section 306 stock is stock other than common that (1) is received as a nontaxable stock dividend, (2) is received tax-free in a corporate reorganization or separation to the extent that either the effect of the transaction was substantially the same as the receipt of a stock dividend or the stock was received in exchange for § 306 stock, or (3) has a basis determined by reference to the basis of § 306 stock. Stock rights are treated as stock for these purposes. Stock acquired through the exercise of such rights is treated as § 306 stock to the extent of the fair market value of the rights at the time of their distribution. If a corporation has no E & P on the date of distribution of a nontaxable preferred stock dividend, the stock will not be § 306 stock.

Exceptions to § 306.   Section 306(b) excepts the following transactions from the general rule:

1. A shareholder sells *all* (both common and preferred) of the stock interest to an unrelated third party. To determine what is a related or an unrelated party, refer to the constructive ownership rules of § 318(a).
2. A corporation redeems *all* (both common and preferred) of the stock of a shareholder if the redemption qualifies under § 302(b)(3) (complete termination of a shareholder's interest).
3. Stock is turned in to the corporation pursuant to a complete liquidation or a qualified partial liquidation.

4. The transaction involves stock on which no gain or loss is recognized at disposal. For example, on the death of a shareholder, the preferred stock passes to the estate or heirs free of any taint.

5. The transfer is not in pursuance of a plan having as one of its principal purposes the avoidance of the Federal income tax. What this means is not entirely clear.[19] The Regulations refer to isolated dispositions of preferred stock by minority shareholders or a sale by a shareholder of all the preferred stock subsequent to a disposition of all the common stock.[20]

Most of the preceding exceptions can be understood by recalling the basic objective of the preferred stock bailout scheme. This is to bail out corporate profits at capital gain rates with no loss of control. This objective cannot be accomplished if, for example, *all* of the stock is sold to a third party or redeemed by the corporation (refer to exceptions 1 and 2).

--- EXAMPLE 20 ---

D makes a gift of § 306 stock to her son, S. The transfer will not trigger ordinary income to D because no gain is recognized on a gift. The stock will be § 306 stock in the hands of S. The § 306 ordinary income taint is transferred from D to S. ◆

--- EXAMPLE 21 ---

T transfers cash to a newly created corporation in return for all its stock (1,000 shares of common and 500 shares of preferred). The preferred stock will not be § 306 stock as it was not issued as a nontaxable dividend. ◆

Redemptions through Use of Related Corporations—§ 304

Without § 304, the rules of § 302 (detailing when a stock redemption is treated as a taxable dividend) could be circumvented if a shareholder had a controlling interest in more than one corporation. For example, a shareholder could sell the stock in X Corporation to Y Corporation and receive capital gain treatment. This would be the case regardless of whether or not the proportionate interest in X Corporation changed substantially as a result of the sale. Section 304 closes the loophole. When a shareholder sells stock of one corporation to a related corporation, the sale is treated as a redemption subject to §§ 302 and 303.

Section 304 applies when a corporation acquires stock in another corporation from a shareholder in exchange for property and the shareholder has at least a 50 percent ownership in both corporations. Section 317(a) defines property to mean money, securities, and any other property. Stock (or rights to acquire stock) in the corporation making the distribution is specifically excluded. This means that most tax-free corporate reorganizations involving the exchange of stock for stock will generally avoid the consequences of § 304.[21]

Control for the purpose of § 304 is defined as the ownership of stock possessing at least 50 percent of the total combined voting power of all classes of stock entitled to vote, or at least 50 percent of the total value of all classes of stock. Section 304 also applies if an individual has a 50 percent interest in a

---

19. *Fireoved v. U.S.*, 72–2 USTC ¶9485, 30 AFTR2d 72–5043, 462 F.2d 1281 (CA–3, 1972), and S.Rept. No. 1622, 83d Cong., 2d Sess.

20. Reg. § 1.306–2(b)(3).

21. *Caamano v. Comm.*, 89–2 USTC ¶9464, 64 AFTR 2d 89–5335, 879 F.2d 156 (CA–5, 1989), and *Bhada v. Comm.*, 90–1 USTC

¶50,001, 65 AFTR 2d 90–421, 892 F.2d 39 (CA–6, 1989), in which the courts concluded that stock in a subsidiary exchanged for parent corporation stock is not "property" for purposes of § 304. Thus, § 304 would not apply to the acquisition of subsidiary stock by the shareholders of a parent corporation in exchange for their parent stock.

corporation that has control (as defined above) of another corporation. For purposes of determining the 50 percent control, the constructive ownership rules of § 318(a) apply.[22]

Transfers Involving Brother-Sister Corporations.   If an individual controls two corporations[23] and transfers stock in one corporation to the other for property, the exchange is treated as a redemption of the stock of the *acquiring* corporation. If the distribution is treated as a dividend under § 301, the stock received by the acquiring corporation is treated as a contribution to the corporation's capital. In that event, basis of the stock to the acquiring corporation is the basis the shareholder had in the stock. The individual's basis in the stock of the acquiring corporation is increased by the basis of the stock surrendered. In applying the provisions of § 302(b) to the exchange, reference is made to the shareholder's ownership of stock in the issuing corporation and not to ownership of stock in the acquiring corporation.[24] The amount of dividend income is determined as if the property were distributed by the acquiring corporation to the extent of its E & P and then by the issuing corporation to the extent of its E & P.[25]

EXAMPLE 22

A owns 100 shares of B Corporation stock and 200 shares of S Corporation stock, representing 50% ownership in both corporations. A sells 20 shares of stock in B Corporation to S Corporation for $30,000. B Corporation has E & P of $100,000, and S Corporation has E & P of $20,000. The stock was purchased by A two years ago for $5,000. ◆

What are the results of the sale in Example 22? Section 304 applies to the transaction. The sale is treated as a redemption of the stock of S Corporation. If the redemption qualifies under § 302(b), A will have a long-term capital gain of $25,000 on the sale. If not, the transaction will be considered to be a dividend under § 301.

- To determine whether the sale qualifies as a stock redemption, refer to A's ownership in B Corporation before and after the redemption. Assuming the not essentially equivalent to a dividend provision of § 302(b)(1) is inapplicable, the substantially disproportionate redemption provisions of § 302(b)(2) are considered.
- A's ownership of B Corporation before and after the sale is determined as follows:

	Total Shares	A's Shares	S Corporation's Shares	A's Deemed Ownership	Ownership Percentage	80% of Original Ownership
Before sale	200	100		100	50%	40%
After sale	200	80	20	90*	45% (90 ÷ 200)	

*A constructively owns 50% of the 20 shares transferred to S Corporation because he has a 50% ownership in S Corporation. Thus, A owns 90 shares in B Corporation [80 + 10 (50% of 20) = 90].

- A's deemed ownership of 45% of the stock in B Corporation does not meet the 80% test of § 302(b)(2). A does not own less than 80% of his interest in B Corporation prior to the sale. The sale does not qualify as a redemption.

---

22. § 304(c)(3).

23. Control being determined under § 304 for these purposes.

24. Reg. § 1.304–2(a).

25. § 304(b)(2).

- Because the sale does not qualify as a stock redemption, A will have dividend income of $30,000. A's basis in his S Corporation stock will be increased by $5,000.
- S Corporation will have a basis of $5,000 in the B Corporation stock it acquired from A.

_____ EXAMPLE 23 _____

Assume A in Example 22 sells 60 (instead of 20) of his shares in B Corporation to S Corporation for $90,000. His basis in the 60 shares is $15,000. After the sale, A owns 70 shares in B Corporation, determined as follows:

	Total Shares	A's Shares	S Corporation's Shares	A's Deemed Ownership	Ownership Percentage	80% of Original Ownership
Before sale	200	100		100	50%	40%
After sale	200	40	60	70*	35%(70 ÷ 200)	

*A constructively owns 50% of the 60 shares transferred to S Corporation because of his 50% ownership of S Corporation. Thus, A owns 70 shares in B Corporation [40 + 30 (50% of 60) = 70].

A's deemed ownership of 35% of the stock in B Corporation meets both the 50% ownership and the 80% ownership tests of § 302(b)(2). Consequently, A has a long-term capital gain of $75,000. The basis of the stock in B Corporation received by S Corporation is $90,000. A's basis in the S Corporation stock remains the same. ◆

Transfers involving brother-sister corporations [§ 304(a)(1)] are summarized in Figure 5–2.

FIGURE 5–2

Redemptions Involving Brother-Sister Corporations

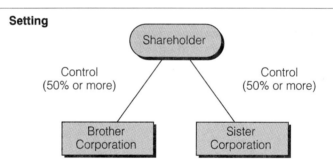

Setting

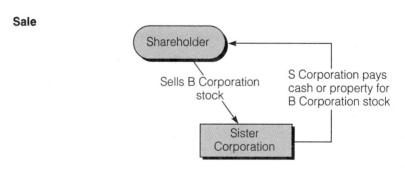

Sale

Result   Sale is recast and treated as if Sister Corporation redeemed its own stock.

Test of § 302 is applied to shareholder's ownership in Brother Corporation.

Parent-Subsidiary Situations.   If a subsidiary corporation acquires stock in its parent from a shareholder of the parent corporation and the parent owns at least 50 percent of the subsidiary's stock, § 304 applies to the transaction. However, the acquisition is treated as though the parent had *redeemed* its own stock.[26] The transaction is construed as a distribution from the subsidiary to the parent and a subsequent distribution from the parent to the individual shareholder.[27] The transfer is treated as a redemption of the parent corporation stock (rather than that of the acquiring corporation). If the transaction does not qualify as a stock redemption, the shareholder's basis in the stock sold to the subsidiary attaches to the remaining stock owned in the parent.

EXAMPLE 24

A, an individual, owns 50% of P Corporation, which, in turn, owns 50% of S Corporation. P Corporation has 200 shares of stock outstanding, 100 of which are owned by B (no relationship to A). A sells 20 of his 100 shares to S Corporation for $40,000. He purchased the 20 shares two years ago for $10,000. After the sale, A is considered to own 84 shares in P Corporation, determined as follows:

	Total Shares	A's Shares	S Corporation's Shares	A's Deemed Ownership	Ownership Percentage	80% of Original Ownership
Before sale	200	100		100	50%	40%
After sale	200	80	20	84*	42% (84 ÷ 200)	

*A constructively owns 4 shares in P Corporation because of S Corporation's ownership. P Corporation owns 10 of the 20 shares transferred to S Corporation because of its 50% ownership of S Corporation. A directly owns 40% of P Corporation after the sale (80 ÷ 200). Thus, A constructively owns 4 of the 10 shares constructively owned by P Corporation (10 × 40%).

A's 84 shares represent a 42% ownership in P Corporation, which does not meet the 80% ownership test of § 302(b)(2). Consequently, the $40,000 is treated as a dividend to A to the extent of the E & P of S Corporation and then to the extent of the E & P of P Corporation. The cost of the 20 shares, $10,000, attaches to A's basis in his remaining shares in P Corporation. P Corporation is deemed to have received a dividend from S Corporation in the amount of $40,000. ◆

Transfers involving parent-subsidiary situations [§ 304(a)(2)] are summarized in Figure 5–3.

DISTRIBUTION OF STOCK AND SECURITIES OF A CONTROLLED CORPORATION
◆

If a corporation has control [80 percent control as defined in § 368(c)] of another corporation, stock in the subsidiary corporation can be distributed to the shareholders of the parent corporation tax-free if certain requirements of § 355 are met. When a subsidiary is newly formed to perfect a corporate division, § 355 applies through § 368(a)(1)(D) (a corporate divisive reorganization discussed in Chapter 7). However, when a subsidiary already exists, § 355 alone applies. Although § 355 is discussed further in Chapter 7 in connection with the corporate reorganization provisions, it is mentioned here because, applied alone, it involves a transaction resembling a dividend or a stock redemption.

General Requirements of § 355

Section 355 applies only if the following conditions are met:

---

26. Reg § 1.304–3(a).   **27.** § 304(b)(2).

- A parent distributes to its shareholders at least an 80 percent controlling interest in its subsidiary. (The parent transfers its controlling interest in the subsidiary to the parent's shareholders.)
- Following the distribution, both the parent and the subsidiary continue to engage in a trade or business in which each had engaged for at least five years before the distribution.
- The parent has held stock in the subsidiary for at least five years prior to the distribution (unless the subsidiary stock was acquired in a nontaxable transaction).

The distribution can take the form of a spin-off, a split-off, or a split-up. (See the discussion of a spin-off, a split-off, and a split-up below.)

Section 355 requires that both the controlled corporation and the parent corporation be engaged in the active conduct of a trade or business for at least five years before the distribution. This requirement also appears in § 302(b)(4) with respect to partial liquidations. The five-year requirement was added to both §§ 302 (b)(4) and 355 to deter the bailout of E & P by the acquisition and distribution of another business within a short span of time.

If a corporation discontinues a trade or business that it has conducted for at least five years, it can distribute the assets pertaining to such business to the shareholders in exchange for their stock as a partial liquidation. The shareholders, however, must recognize capital gain. In the distributions of stock of a controlled corporation, pursuant to § 355, the shareholder recognizes no gain or loss.

FIGURE 5–3

**Redemptions Involving
Parent-Subsidiary Corporations**

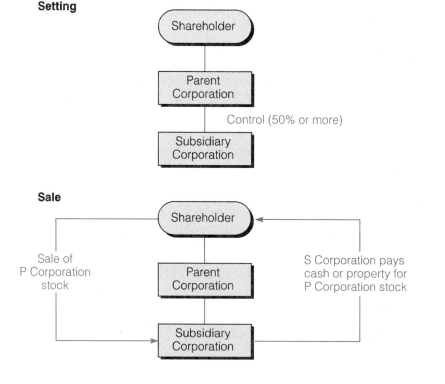

Setting

Sale

Result   Sale is recast and treated as if Parent Corporation redeemed its own stock.

Test of § 302 is applied to shareholder's ownership in Parent Corporation.

What constitutes an active trade or business is often the subject of litigation. The Regulations take the position that the holding of stock, securities, land, or other property, including casual sales of such properties, is not an active trade or business.[28] The problem of defining an active trade or business is discussed in more detail in Chapter 7 in connection with the application of § 355 to a divisive reorganization.

———————— EXAMPLE 25 ————————

X Corporation has operated an active business for the past 10 years. Six years ago it acquired all of the stock of Y Corporation, which has been engaged in an active business for 8 years. X Corporation distributes all the stock of Y Corporation to its shareholders. Both corporations continue to operate their separate businesses. Assuming a business reason exists for the distribution, the distribution qualifies under § 355, and the receipt of the Y Corporation stock is tax-free to the shareholders of X Corporation. This is a spin-off. ◆

A distribution under § 355 must not be used principally as a means of distributing the E & P of either the distributing corporation or the controlled corporation. If the stock or securities of the controlled corporation are sold shortly after the exchange, the sale is evidence that the transaction was used as a means of distributing E & P. A distribution made pursuant to § 355 must also have a business purpose. The purpose of the requirement is to limit § 355 to distributions made when the corporate structure must be readjusted for business reasons. This affects only a readjustment of continuing interests in property under modified corporate forms. Problems with the antitrust laws are an example of a business reason justifying the distribution of a subsidiary's stock to the parent's shareholders.

E & P of the distributing corporation is decreased by a distribution of stock in its subsidiary. The decrease is the *lesser of* the following:

1. An amount determined by multiplying the distributing corporation's E & P by a fraction. The numerator of the fraction is the fair market value of the subsidiary's stock, and the denominator is the fair market value of all the parent corporation's assets.
2. The net worth of the subsidiary.

If this decrease is more than the E & P of the subsidiary, the E & P account of the subsidiary is increased to equal the decrease. If the subsidiary's E & P exceeds the decrease in the E & P of the parent, the subsidiary's E & P account remains the same.

The parent corporation (but not its shareholders) recognizes gain in a § 355 distribution if the parent makes a "disqualified distribution" of stock or securities of a controlled subsidiary.

- A disqualified distribution occurs if any person, immediately after the distribution, holds "disqualified stock" in either the parent or the controlled subsidiary. The disqualified stock must constitute at least a 50 percent interest.
- The prohibited 50 percent interest includes either a 50 percent control of the combined voting power of all classes of voting stock or a 50 percent control of the total value of all classes of stock.

————————————

28. Regulations covering distributions of stock and securities of controlled corporations, including examples and limitations, are at Reg. §§ 1.355–1 to –5.

- Disqualified stock is stock in either the parent or the subsidiary "purchased" after October 9, 1990, and during the five-year period preceding the § 355 distribution.
- A purchase includes any transaction in which the acquiror's basis is not determined by reference to the transferor's basis. A purchase includes stock received in a § 351 transfer to the extent the transferor received the stock in exchange for cash, marketable stock, or debt of the transferor.

If a shareholder of a parent corporation purchases stock in the parent within a five-year period, the parent will recognize gain if it distributes at least 50 percent of the stock or securities in its subsidiary to that shareholder in exchange for the purchased stock or securities. In determining gain to the parent, the parent is treated as though it sells the subsidiary stock or securities at fair market value.

EXAMPLE 26

A purchased a 30% interest in P Corporation on December 1, 1991. On June 1, 1992, P Corporation distributes all its stock (90% interest) in S Corporation to its shareholders. P Corporation distributes 50% of its stock in S Corporation to A in exchange for her 30% interest in P Corporation. The remaining 50% interest in S Corporation is distributed to other shareholders in P Corporation. The distribution qualifies under § 355. Thus, the shareholders do not recognize gain on the exchange of their stock in P Corporation for stock in S Corporation. However, because the stock distributed to A is disqualified stock, P Corporation recognizes gain on that stock. P Corporation recognizes gain in the amount of the difference between its basis in the S Corporation stock and the stock's fair market value. ◆

The reason P Corporation is required to recognize gain in Example 26 is that the corporation used appreciated property to redeem its stock. If A's purpose in acquiring the P Corporation stock is to acquire the S Corporation stock, § 355 would provide a loophole in the concept of double taxation of corporate income. To avoid a tax on P Corporation's distribution of the stock in S Corporation, A must hold the P Corporation stock for more than five years prior to the distribution of the S Corporation stock.

Spin-Off, Split-Off, and Split-Up

A § 355 distribution takes the form of a spin-off, a split-off, or a split-up. A *spin-off* is a distribution of subsidiary stock to the shareholders of the parent corporation giving them control of the subsidiary. The shareholders of the parent do not surrender any of their stock for the subsidiary stock. This distribution resembles an ordinary dividend distribution. A *split-off* is identical to a spin-off, except that the shareholders in the parent corporation exchange some of their parent corporation stock for the subsidiary stock. It resembles a stock redemption. A *split-up* is the distribution of the stock of two subsidiaries to shareholders of the parent in complete liquidation of the parent.

EXAMPLE 27

P Corporation owns all the stock of S Corporation. Both P Corporation and S Corporation have actively conducted a business for the past 10 years. P Corporation distributes all its S Corporation stock equally to its two shareholders, A and B, individuals. A and B do not surrender any of their stock in P Corporation. The distribution qualifies as a tax-free spin-off. ◆

EXAMPLE 28

Assume in Example 27, that A and B exchange one-third of their stock in P Corporation for the stock in S Corporation. The distribution qualifies as a tax-free split-off. ◆

──────────────── EXAMPLE 29 ────────────────

P Corporation's only assets are the stock it owns in S Corporation and in T Corporation (100% in both). P Corporation distributes all the stock in S Corporation and in T Corporation to its shareholders, A and B. P Corporation then liquidates. The distribution is a split-up. ◆

Refer to Figure 7–9 in Chapter 7 for a graphic presentation of a spin-off, a split-off, and a split-up in connection with a "D" reorganization.

Tax Consequences of a § 355 Distribution at the Shareholder Level

If the requirements of § 355 are met, the shareholders of the parent corporation have no gain on the receipt of the stock in the subsidiary corporation. A shareholder can receive only stock or securities tax-free. If other property is received, it is boot and is subject to taxation under § 356.

To further qualify the exchange, a § 355 distribution is tax-free only if the principal amount of the securities surrendered is the same as the principal amount of the securities received. If the principal amount of the securities received is greater than the principal amount of the securities surrendered or if no securities are surrendered, the shareholder has boot. The amount of the boot is the fair market value of the excess principal amount determined on the date of the exchange.

──────────────── EXAMPLE 30 ────────────────

T, an individual, exchanges stock in X Corporation (the parent corporation) for stock and securities in Y Corporation (the subsidiary corporation) pursuant to § 355. The exchange is a tax-free split-off except to the extent of the securities received. The securities in Y have a principal amount of $1,000 and a fair market value of $950 on the date of the exchange. T has boot of $950. ◆

──────────────── EXAMPLE 31 ────────────────

Assume in Example 30 that T also surrenders securities in X for the securities in Y. The securities in X have a principal amount of $600. T has boot of $380, the fair market value of the excess principal of $400 ($950 ÷ $1,000 × $400 = $380). ◆

The basis of stock received by a shareholder pursuant to § 355 is determined by §§ 358(b) and (c). Basis of the stock held before the exchange is allocated among the stock of all classes held immediately after the transaction in proportion to the fair market value of the stock of each class.[29] The rule is the same regardless of whether a spin-off, split-off, or split-up is involved. Regarding a spin-off (where the shareholder receives stock in the subsidiary without surrendering stock in the parent), the distribution is treated as an exchange. A portion of the basis in the old stock is allocated to the new shares.

──────────────── EXAMPLE 32 ────────────────

A, an individual, has a basis of $7,000 in her 100 shares of stock in P Corporation. A receives 50 shares of stock in S Corporation pursuant to a distribution that qualifies under § 355. The stock in P Corporation has a value of $300 per share, and the stock in S Corporation has a value of $100 per share. A's basis in the P Corporation stock is allocated between the P Corporation stock and the S Corporation stock as follows:

──────────────

29. Reg § 1.358–2(a)(2).

Basis of P Corporation stock:

$$\$7,000 \times \frac{\$30,000 \text{ (fair market value of P Corporation stock)}}{\$35,000 \text{ (fair market value of P Corporation and S Corporation stock)}} = \$6,000$$

Basis of S Corporation stock:

$$\$7,000 \times \frac{\$5,000 \text{ (fair market value of S Corporation stock)}}{\$35,000 \text{ (fair market value of P Corporation and S Corporation stock)}} = \$1,000$$

◆

──────────────────── Example 33 ────────────────────

Assume in Example 32 that A exchanges 50 shares in P Corporation for the 50 shares in S Corporation. The remaining 50 shares in P Corporation have a basis of $5,250, and the basis of the 50 shares in S Corporation is $1,750, computed as follows:

Basis of P Corporation stock:

$$\$7,000 \times \frac{\$15,000 \text{ (fair market value of 50 remaining shares in P Corporation)}}{\$20,000 \text{ (fair market value of P Corporation stock and S Corporation stock)}} = \$5,250$$

Basis of S Corporation stock:

$$\$7,000 \times \frac{\$5,000 \text{ (fair market value of S Corporation stock)}}{\$20,000 \text{ (fair market value of P Corporation stock and S Corporation stock)}} = \$1,750$$

◆

If a distribution pursuant to § 355 fails to meet the requirements of this Section, the distribution becomes taxable. If a spin-off is involved, the stock distributed to the parent corporation's shareholders is treated as an ordinary dividend. If a split-off is involved, the distribution is treated as a stock redemption subject to the provisions of § 302. This determines whether it qualifies as a capital gain or whether it is treated as a dividend. If a split-up is involved, the transaction is treated as a complete liquidation of the parent corporation.

Every taxpayer who receives a distribution of stock or securities of a corporation controlled by a second corporation must attach a detailed statement to the return for the year in which the distribution is received. The statement must provide appropriate information to show the application of § 355. It must include a description of the stock and securities surrendered (if any) and received and the names and addresses of all the corporations involved in the transaction.[30]

LIQUIDATIONS—IN GENERAL
◆

When a stock redemption is carried out or a dividend is distributed, the assumption usually is that the corporation will continue as a separate entity. With complete liquidation, corporate existence terminates. A complete liquidation, like a qualified stock redemption, receives exchange treatment. However, the tax effects of a liquidation vary somewhat from those of a stock redemption.

The Liquidation Process

A complete liquidation exists for tax purposes when a corporation ceases to be a going concern. The corporation continues solely to wind up affairs, pay debts,

─────────────
30. Reg. § 1.355–5(b).

and distribute any remaining balance to shareholders.[31] Legal dissolution under state law is not required for the liquidation to be complete for tax purposes. A transaction will be treated as a liquidation even if the corporation retains a nominal amount of assets to pay remaining debts and preserve legal status.[32]

A liquidation may occur for several different reasons. The corporate business may have been unsuccessful. In some instances when a corporation has been profitable, the shareholders may decide to terminate the corporation to acquire its assets.

A liquidation occurs when another person or corporation wants to purchase the assets of the corporation. The purchaser may buy the stock of the shareholders and then liquidate the corporation to acquire the assets. On the other hand, the purchaser may buy the assets directly from the corporation. After the assets are sold, the corporation distributes the sales proceeds to its shareholders and liquidates. The different means used to liquidate a corporation produce varying tax results.

Liquidations and Other Distributions Compared

A property distribution, whether in the form of a dividend or a stock redemption, produces gain (but not loss) to the distributing corporation. For the shareholder, the fair market value of a property dividend produces ordinary income to the extent of the corporation's E & P. On the other hand, a stock redemption qualifying under § 302 or § 303 results in exchange treatment.

The tax effects to the corporation in a complete liquidation are similar to those in a stock redemption in that a liquidation also yields exchange treatment. Still a complete liquidation produces somewhat different tax consequences. With certain exceptions, a liquidating corporation recognizes gain *and* loss upon distribution of its assets. The shareholders receive exchange treatment on receipt of the property from the liquidating corporation. The distribution of assets is treated as payment for the shareholder's stock and results in either a gain or a loss.

Liquidations and stock redemptions parallel each other as to the effect of E & P. For the corporation undergoing liquidation, E & P has no tax impact on the gain or loss to be recognized by the shareholders. Section 301 (governing dividend distributions) specifically does not apply to complete liquidations.[33]

─────────────── EXAMPLE 34 ───────────────

Z Corporation, with E & P of $40,000, makes a cash distribution of $50,000 to its sole shareholder. Assume the shareholder's basis in the Z Corporation stock is $20,000 and the stock is held as an investment. If the distribution is not in complete liquidation or if it does not qualify as a stock redemption, the shareholder recognizes dividend income of $40,000 (the amount of Z Corporation's E & P) and treats the remaining $10,000 of the distribution as a return of capital. If the distribution is pursuant to a complete liquidation or qualifies as a stock redemption, the shareholder has a recognized capital gain of $30,000 [$50,000 (the amount of the distribution) − $20,000 (the basis in the stock)]. In the latter case, Z Corporation's E & P is of no consequence to the tax result. ◆

In the event the distribution results in a *loss* to the shareholder, an important distinction can exist between stock redemptions and liquidations. The distinc-

31. Reg. § 1.332–2(c).
32. Rev.Rul. 54–518, 1954–2 C.B. 142.
33. § 331(b).

tion arises because § 267 (disallowance of losses between related parties) applies to stock redemptions but not to liquidations.

─────────────────────── EXAMPLE 35 ───────────────────────

The stock of P Corporation is owned equally by three brothers, R, S, and T. When T's basis in his stock investment is $40,000, the corporation distributes $30,000 to him in cancellation of all his shares. If the distribution is a stock redemption, the $10,000 realized loss is not recognized.[34] T and P Corporation are related parties because T is deemed to own more than 50% in value of the corporation's outstanding stock. T's direct ownership is limited to 33⅓%, but through his brothers he owns indirectly another 66⅔% for a total of 100%. If the distribution qualifies as a complete liquidation, T's $10,000 realized loss is recognizable. ◆

With reference to the basis of noncash property received from the corporation, the rules governing liquidations and stock redemptions are identical. Section 334(a) specifies that the basis of such property distributed pursuant to a complete liquidation under § 331 shall be the fair market value on the date of distribution.

The tax consequences of a complete liquidation of a corporation are examined in this chapter from the standpoint of the effect on the distributing corporation and on the shareholder. Tax rules differ when a controlled subsidiary is liquidated. Thus, the rules relating to the liquidation of a controlled subsidiary receive separate treatment.

LIQUIDATIONS—EFFECT ON THE DISTRIBUTING CORPORATION
◆

For the corporation in the process of complete liquidation, §§ 336 and 337 control the tax results. The general rules relating to complete liquidations are covered in § 336, where gain or loss is recognized to the distributing corporation. However, for certain distributions of disqualified property and some distributions to related shareholders, loss is not recognized. Under § 337, a subsidiary corporation does not recognize gain or loss for distributions to a parent corporation that owns 80 percent or more of the stock of the subsidiary.

Background

Originally, a corporate distribution of property, whether a liquidating or a nonliquidating distribution, produced neither gain nor loss to the distributing corporation. This nonrecognition concept was referred to as the *General Utilities* rule.[35] Over the years, however, statutory and judicial modifications and interpretations significantly increased the number of recognition situations. For example, depreciation and the investment tax credit were recaptured on distributed assets. Further, under the tax benefit rule, a corporation had to include in income any assets distributed to the shareholders for which it had previously claimed a deduction. In addition, the assignment of income doctrine was applied to distributions in liquidation and to sales by the liquidating corporation. Gain resulted from the distribution or sale of LIFO inventory and installment notes receivable. The sale of inventory produced income to the corporation unless the inventory was sold in bulk to one person in one transaction. Due to the many modifications, a liquidating corporation was not shielded from recognition of *all* income.

34. *McCarthy v. Conley, Jr.*, 65–1 USTC ¶9262, 15 AFTR2d 447, 341 F.2d 948 (CA–2, 1965).

35. The doctrine was attributed to the 1935 Supreme Court decision in *General Utilities & Operating Co. v. Helvering*, 36–1 USTC ¶9012, 16 AFTR 1126, 56 S.Ct. 185 (USSC, 1935).

With the many statutory and judicial inroads, not much was left of the *General Utilities* doctrine when it was repealed in 1986. Only a few transfers still insulated the liquidating corporation from a recognition result. The protected transfers included the following: distributions in kind and sale of investment assets (e.g., marketable securities and land), distributions in kind and bulk sales of non-LIFO inventory, and the § 1231 element for assets used in a trade or business. With the repeal of the *General Utilities* rule, now a liquidating corporation, as a general rule, recognizes all gains and most losses on distributions of property.

General Rule

Section 336 provides that a liquidating corporation recognizes gain or loss on the distribution of property in complete liquidation. The property is treated as if it were sold to the distributee at the fair market value. Section 336, which repealed the *General Utilities* doctrine, strengthens the notion of double taxation that is inherent in operating a business in the corporate form. As a result, liquidating distributions are subject to tax both at the corporate level and at the shareholder level.

When property distributed in a complete liquidation is subject to a liability of the liquidating corporation, the fair market value of that property cannot be less than the amount of the liability.

─────────────── EXAMPLE 36 ───────────────

Pursuant to a complete liquidation, T Corporation distributes to its shareholders land held as an investment (basis of $200,000, fair market value of $300,000). The land is subject to a liability in the amount of $350,000. T Corporation has a gain of $150,000 on the distribution. ◆

Limitation on Losses. As a general rule, losses on the distribution of property in a complete liquidation are recognized. There are two exceptions, however. The first exception applies to certain distributions to related parties as defined under § 267. The second exception prevents a loss deduction on certain distributions of property with a built-in loss that was contributed to the corporation shortly before the adoption of a plan of liquidation. In this instance, the built-in loss may be disallowed as a deduction upon liquidation even if the distribution is to an unrelated party.

Because the abolition of the *General Utilities* rule opens the door for recognition of losses in a liquidation, Congress was concerned that taxpayers might attempt to create artificial losses at the corporate level. Taxpayers could accomplish this by contributing property with built-in losses to the corporation before a liquidation. Recall from Chapter 3 that in § 351 transfers (nontaxable transfers to a corporation in exchange for stock when the transferor is in control of the corporation) and contributions to capital, the transferor's income tax basis carries over to the transferee corporation. Thus, high basis, low fair market value property could be transferred to a corporation contemplating liquidation. The expectation would be that such built-in losses might neutralize expected gains from appreciated property distributed or sold in the liquidation process.

Section 336(d) closes the possibility of utilizing built-in losses to neutralize the gain upon liquidation. The deductibility of losses is limited in related-party situations (those covered by § 267) and in certain sales and distributions of built-in loss property to unrelated parties. A corporation and a shareholder are related parties if the shareholder owns (directly or indirectly) more than 50 percent in value of the corporation's outstanding stock.

Once the related-party situation is present, losses are disallowed on distributions to the related parties in either of the following cases: (1) the distribution is not pro rata, or (2) the property distributed is disqualified property. Disqualified property is property acquired by the liquidating corporation in a § 351 transaction or as a contribution to capital during a five-year period ending on the date of the distribution.

—————————————— EXAMPLE 37 ——————————————

Z Corporation's stock is held equally by three brothers. One year before Z's liquidation, the shareholders transfer property (basis of $150,000, fair market value of $100,000) to Z Corporation in return for stock (a § 351 transaction). In liquidation, Z Corporation transfers the property (still worth $100,000) to the brothers. Because § 267 applies (each brother owns directly and indirectly 100% of the stock) and disqualified property is involved, none of the $50,000 realized loss is recognized by Z Corporation. ◆

—————————————— EXAMPLE 38 ——————————————

Assume that Z Corporation stock is owned by A and B, who are unrelated. A owns 80% and B owns 20% of the stock in Z Corporation. Z Corporation has the following assets (none of which were acquired in a § 351 transaction or as a contribution to capital) that are distributed in complete liquidation of Z Corporation:

	Adjusted Basis	Fair Market Value
Cash	$600,000	$600,000
Equipment	150,000	200,000
Building	400,000	200,000

Assume Z Corporation distributes the equipment to B and the cash and the building to A. Z Corporation recognizes a gain of $50,000 on the distribution of the equipment. The loss of $200,000 on the building will be disallowed. This is because the distribution is not pro rata, and the loss property is distributed to a related party. ◆

—————————————— EXAMPLE 39 ——————————————

Assume that Z Corporation in Example 38 distributed the cash and equipment to A and the building to B. Again, Z Corporation recognizes the $50,000 gain on the equipment. However, it can now recognize the $200,000 loss on the building. The loss property is not distributed to a related party since B does not own more than 50% of the stock in Z Corporation. ◆

The loss limitation provisions are extended to distributions to *unrelated* parties when loss property is transferred to a corporation shortly before the corporation is liquidated. This second exception to the general rule that a corporation can recognize losses on a complete liquidation is imposed to prevent the doubling of losses, or the so-called "stuffing" of a corporation.

—————————————— EXAMPLE 40 ——————————————

Assume A, a shareholder in T Corporation, transfers property with a basis of $10,000, fair market value of $3,000, to T Corporation in a transaction that qualifies under § 351. A's basis in the additional stock acquired in T Corporation, in exchange for the property, is $10,000. T Corporation's basis in the property is also $10,000. A few months after the transfer, T Corporation adopts a plan of complete liquidation. Upon liquidation, T Corporation distributes the property to A. If T Corporation were permitted a loss deduction of $7,000, there would be a double loss because A would also recognize a loss of $7,000 upon receipt of the property [$10,000 (basis in A's stock) − $3,000 (fair market value of the property)]. To prevent the doubling of losses, § 336(d) prohibits T Corporation from taking a loss on the distribution even if A is an unrelated party. ◆

Losses are disallowed on a distribution to shareholders who are not related parties when the property distributed was acquired in a § 351 transaction or as a contribution to capital. Furthermore, it must have been contributed as part of a plan, whose principal purpose was to recognize loss by the corporation in connection with the liquidation. Such a purpose will be presumed if the transfer occurs within two years of the adoption of the plan of liquidation.

The prohibition against a loss deduction on distributions to unrelated parties is broader than the first exception, which disallows losses on certain distributions to related parties. The prohibition applies regardless of whether the shareholder is a related party under § 267. At the same time, however, the prohibition is narrower than the first exception since it applies only to property that had a built-in loss upon acquisition by the corporation and only as to the amount of the built-in loss.

EXAMPLE 41

On January 2, 1992, in a transaction that qualifies under § 351 T Corporation acquires property with a basis of $10,000, fair market value of $3,000. T Corporation adopts a plan of liquidation on July 1, 1992, and distributes the property to A, an unrelated party, on November 10, 1992, when the property is worth $1,000. T Corporation can recognize a loss of $2,000, the difference between the value of the property on the date of acquisition and the fair market value of the property on the date of distribution. Only the built-in loss of $7,000 [$10,000 (basis) − $3,000 (fair market value on date of acquisition)] is disallowed. ◆

EXAMPLE 42

Assume the property in Example 41 was worth $12,000 on the date T Corporation acquired the property. However, the property is worth only $2,000 when T Corporation distributes the property upon the complete liquidation of the corporation. If the distribution is to an unrelated shareholder, T Corporation will recognize the entire $8,000 loss [$10,000 (basis) − $2,000 (fair market value on date of distribution)]. However, if the distribution is to a related party, T Corporation cannot recognize any of the loss because the property is disqualified property (e.g., property acquired in a § 351 transaction within five years of the distribution). The loss limitation applies even though the property was worth more than its basis when it was transferred to the corporation. When the distribution is to a related party, the loss is disallowed even though the decline in value occurred entirely during the period the corporation held the property. However, if the property is distributed to an unrelated party, only the built-in loss (e.g., the loss that occurred prior to the transfer to the corporation) is disallowed. ◆

For liquidation loss purposes, the basis of disqualified property, which is later sold or distributed to an unrelated party, is reduced by the amount the property's basis on the contribution date exceeds the property's fair market value on that date.[36] Any subsequent decline in value to the point of the liquidating distribution results in a deductible loss (as long as the property is not distributed to a related party).

The loss limitation can apply regardless of how long the corporation has held the property prior to liquidation. If the property is held for two years or less, a tax avoidance purpose is presumed. Still, if there is a clear and substantial relationship between the contributed property and the business of the corporation, a loss will be permitted on the distribution of the property to an unrelated party. When there was a business reason for transferring the loss property to the liquidating corporation, a loss will also be permitted on the sale of the property.

---

36. § 336(d)(2).

─────────────── Example 43 ───────────────

Z Corporation's stock is held 60% by A and 40% by B. One year before Z's liquidation, property (basis of $150,000, fair market value of $100,000) is transferred to Z Corporation as a contribution to capital. There is no business reason for the transfer. In liquidation, Z Corporation transfers the property (now worth $90,000) to B. Because the distribution is to an unrelated party, the basis is reduced to $100,000 for liquidation purposes [$150,000 (carryover basis under § 362) − $50,000 (difference between carryover basis of $150,000 and fair market value of $100,000)]. A loss of $10,000 ($100,000 − $90,000) can be recognized. (If the property is distributed to A, a related party, even the $10,000 loss is disallowed.) ◆

─────────────── Example 44 ───────────────

Assume in Example 43, that the property is transferred to Z Corporation because a bank required the additional capital investment as a condition to making a loan to Z Corporation. Because there is a business purpose for the transfer, presumably the loss of $50,000 is recognized if the property is distributed to B in liquidation. If the property is distributed to A, a related party, the loss is disallowed. ◆

Distributions of loss property by a liquidating corporation are summarized in Figure 5–4.

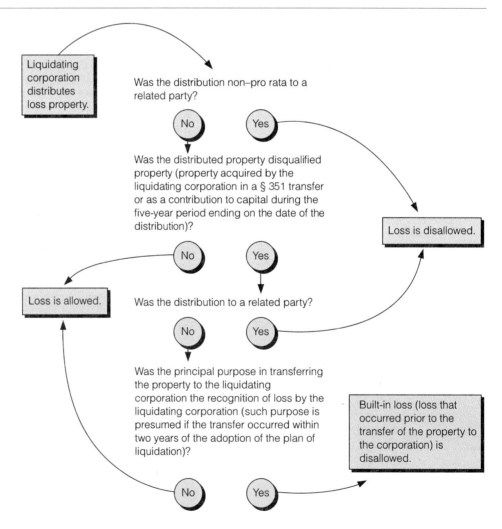

Figure 5–4
Distributions of Loss Property by a Liquidating Corporation

Expenses of Liquidation. The general expenses involved in liquidating a corporation are deductible to the corporation as business expenses under § 162. Examples include the legal and accounting cost of drafting a plan of liquidation and the cost of revoking the corporate charter. Liquidation expenses relating to the disposition of corporate assets are also deductible. Expenses relating to the sale of corporate assets, including a brokerage commission for the sale of real estate and a legal fee to clear title, are offset against the selling price of the assets.

─────────────── EXAMPLE 45 ───────────────

During its liquidation, R Corporation incurs the following expenses:

General liquidation expenses	$12,000
Legal expenses incurred in distributing property	200
Sales commissions to sell inventory	3,000
Brokerage fee on sale of real estate	8,000

R Corporation can deduct $12,200 ($12,000 + $200). The $3,000 commission and the $8,000 brokerage fee are applied against the selling price of the inventory and the real estate. ◆

Filing Requirements for Corporate Liquidations. A copy of the minutes of the shareholders' meeting in which the plan of liquidation was adopted must be attached to the income tax return for the liquidating corporation. A statement must be included listing the assets sold, with dates of sales given. The statement should include computations of gain or loss both realized and recognized on the sales. Form 966, Corporate Dissolution or Liquidation, must be filed with the IRS within 30 days after the adoption of the plan of liquidation. Notification of this type is required by some states. Information returns (Form 1099–DIV, transmitted to each shareholder and Form 1096, sent to the IRS) notify shareholders of their respective gains or losses.

The tax consequences to the shareholders of a corporation in the process of liquidation are governed by the general rule under § 331 and two exceptions under §§ 332 and 338 (relating to the liquidation of a subsidiary).

LIQUIDATIONS — EFFECT ON THE SHAREHOLDER
◆

The General Rule under § 331

In the case of a complete liquidation, the general rule under § 331(a)(1) provides for exchange treatment. Since § 1001(c) requires the recognition of gain or loss on the sale or exchange of property, the end result is to treat the shareholder as having sold his or her stock to the corporation being liquidated. The difference between the fair market value of the assets received from the corporation (less the income tax paid by the corporation) and the adjusted basis of the stock surrendered becomes the amount recognized. If the stock is a capital asset in the hands of the shareholder, capital gain or loss results. The burden of proof is on the taxpayer to furnish evidence on the adjusted basis of the stock. In the absence of such evidence, the stock is deemed to have a zero basis, and the full amount of the liquidation proceeds becomes the amount of the gain recognized.[37]

Section 334(a) provides that under the general rule of § 331, the income tax basis to the shareholder of property received in a liquidation is the property's fair market value on the date of distribution. The rule follows the same approach taken with stock redemptions that qualify for exchange treatment.

───────────

37. *John Calderazzo,* 34 TCM 1, T.C. Memo. 1975–1.

Special Rule for Certain Installment Obligations

Section 453(h) provides some relief from the bunching of gain problem encountered when a liquidating corporation sells its assets. The liquidating corporation must recognize all gain on such sales. The shareholders' gain on the receipt of notes obtained by the corporation on the sale of its assets may be deferred to the point of collection.[38] Such treatment requires the shareholders to allocate their bases in the stock among the various assets received from the corporation.

EXAMPLE 46

After a plan of complete liquidation has been adopted, X Corporation sells its only asset, unimproved land held as an investment. The land has appreciated in value and is sold to P (an unrelated party) for $100,000. Under the terms of the sale, X Corporation receives cash of $25,000 and P's notes for the balance of $75,000. The notes are payable over 10 years ($7,500 per year) and carry a 9% rate of interest. Immediately after the sale, X Corporation distributes the cash and notes to S, an individual and sole shareholder. S has an adjusted basis in the X Corporation stock of $20,000, and the installment notes have a value equal to the face amount ($75,000). These transactions have the following tax result:

- X Corporation recognizes gain on the sale of the land, measured by the difference between the $100,000 selling price and the basis X Corporation had in the land.
- S may defer the gain on the receipt of the notes to the point of collection.
- S must allocate the adjusted basis in the stock ($20,000) between the cash and the installment notes. Using the relative fair market value approach, 25% [$25,000 (amount of cash)/$100,000 (total distribution)] of $20,000 (adjusted basis in the stock), or $5,000, is allocated to the cash, and 75% [$75,000 (FMV of notes)/$100,000 (total distribution)] of $20,000 (adjusted basis in the stock), or $15,000, is allocated to the notes.
- S must recognize $20,000 [$25,000 (cash received) − $5,000 (allocated basis of the cash)] in the year of the liquidation.
- Since S's gross profit on the notes is $60,000 [$75,000 (contract price) − $15,000 (allocated basis of the notes)], the gross profit percentage is 80% [$60,000 (gross profit)/$75,000 (contract price)]. S must report a gain of $6,000 [$7,500 (amount of note) × 80% (gross profit percentage)] on the collection of each note over the next 10 years. The interest element is accounted for separately. ◆

If the shareholder receives distributions in more than one taxable year, basis reallocations may require the filing of amended returns.[39]

Special rules apply if the installment obligations arise from sales between certain related parties.[40]

LIQUIDATIONS—PARENT-SUBSIDIARY SITUATIONS

◆

Section 332 is an exception to the general rule that the shareholder recognizes gain or loss on a corporate liquidation. If a parent corporation liquidates a subsidiary corporation in which it owns at least 80 percent of the voting stock, no gain or loss is recognized for distributions to the parent.[41]

---

38. Section 453(h) does not apply to the sale of inventory property and property held by the corporation primarily for sale to customers in the ordinary course of its trade or business unless such property is sold in bulk to one person.

39. § 453(h)(2). For an example of such a possibility, see the Finance Committee Report on H.R. 6883 (reported with amendments on September 26, 1980), the Installment Sales Revision Act of 1980.

40. §§ 453(h)(1)(C) and (D). For this purpose, related parties are defined in § 1239(b).

41. § 337(a).

The requirements for application of § 332 are as follows:

- The parent must own at least 80 percent of the voting stock of the subsidiary and at least 80 percent of the total value of the subsidiary's stock.
- The subsidiary must distribute all its property in complete redemption of all its stock within the taxable year or within three years from the close of the tax year in which a plan was adopted and the first distribution occurred.
- The subsidiary must be solvent.[42]

If these requirements are met, § 332 becomes mandatory.

When a series of distributions occurs in the liquidation of a subsidiary corporation, the parent corporation must own the required amount of stock (80 percent) on the date a plan of liquidation is adopted. Such ownership must continue at all times until all property has been distributed.[43] If the parent fails to qualify at any time, the provisions for nonrecognition of gain or loss do not apply to any distribution.[44]

If a liquidation is not completed within one taxable year, for each taxable year that falls wholly or partly within the period of liquidation, the parent corporation shall file with its income tax return a waiver of the statute of limitations on assessment. The parent corporation may be forced to file a bond with the District Director to ensure prompt payment of taxes should § 332 not apply.[45]

For the taxable year in which the plan of liquidation is adopted and for all taxable years within the period of liquidation, the parent corporation must file with its return a statement of all facts pertaining to the liquidation.[46]

Tax Treatment When a Minority Interest Exists

A distribution to a minority shareholder in a § 332 liquidation is treated in the same manner as one made pursuant to a nonliquidating redemption. The distributing corporation recognizes gain (but not loss) on the property distributed to the minority shareholder.

─────────────── EXAMPLE 47 ───────────────

The stock of S Corporation is held as follows: 80% by P Corporation and 20% by T, an individual. S Corporation is liquidated on December 10, 1992, pursuant to a plan adopted on January 10, 1992. At the time of its liquidation, S Corporation has assets with a basis of $100,000 and fair market value of $500,000. S Corporation must recognize gain of $80,000 [($500,000 fair market value − $100,000 basis) × 20% minority interest]. The remaining gain of $320,000 is sheltered by § 337(a). ◆

The minority shareholder is subject to the general rule of § 331. Accordingly, the difference between the fair market value of the assets distributed and the basis of the minority shareholder's stock is the amount of gain or loss recognized. The tax basis of property received by the minority shareholder is the property's fair market value on the date of distribution.[47]

─────────────────

42. Reg. §§ 1.332–2(a) and (b).
43. The date of the adoption of a plan of complete liquidation could be crucial in determining whether § 332 applies. See, for example, *George L. Riggs, Inc.,* 64 T.C. 474 (1975).

44. Reg. § 1.332–2(a).
45. Reg. § 1.332–4(a).
46. Reg. § 1.332–6.
47. § 334(a).

Indebtedness of Subsidiary to Parent

If a subsidiary satisfies a debt owed to the parent with appreciated property, it must recognize gain on the transaction unless § 332 applies. When § 332 applies, the subsidiary does not recognize gain or loss upon the transfer of properties to the parent. This is the case even if some properties are transferred to satisfy the subsidiary's indebtedness to the parent.[48]

--------------------------------- EXAMPLE 48 ---------------------------------

S Corporation owes its parent, P Corporation, $20,000. It satisfies the obligation by transferring land (worth $20,000 with a tax basis of $8,000). Normally, S Corporation recognizes a gain of $12,000 on the transaction. However, if the transfer is made pursuant to a liquidation under § 332, S Corporation does not recognize a gain. ◆

The special provision noted above will not apply to the parent corporation. Realized gain or loss is recognized by the parent corporation on the satisfaction of indebtedness, even if property is received during liquidation of the subsidiary.

--------------------------------- EXAMPLE 49 ---------------------------------

P Corporation purchased bonds of its subsidiary, S Corporation, at a discount. Upon liquidation of the subsidiary pursuant to § 332, P receives payment in the face amount of the bonds. The transaction has no tax effect on S Corporation. However, P Corporation recognizes gain in the amount of the difference between its basis in the bonds and the amount received in payment. ◆

If a parent corporation does not receive at least partial payment for its stock in a subsidiary corporation upon liquidation of the subsidiary, § 332 will not apply.[49] The parent corporation has a bad debt deduction for the difference between the value of any properties received from the subsidiary and its basis in the subsidiary debt.

If the subsidiary is insolvent, the parent corporation will also have a loss deduction for its worthless stock in the subsidiary. The loss is ordinary if more than 90 percent of the subsidiary's gross receipts for all tax years were from sources other than passive sources.[50] Otherwise, the loss is a capital loss.

--------------------------------- EXAMPLE 50 ---------------------------------

P Corporation paid $100,000 for all the stock of S Corporation 15 years ago. At present, S has a deficit of $600,000 in E & P. If P liquidates S, § 332 will not apply because S is insolvent. P Corporation has a loss deduction for its worthless stock in S Corporation. If more than 90% of the gross receipts of S Corporation for all tax years were from sources other than passive sources, the loss is ordinary. Otherwise, it is a capital loss. Assume P also loaned S Corporation $50,000. Since the assets are not sufficient to pay the liabilities, P also has a loss on the note. Upon liquidation, the basis of the assets of S to P is the fair market value. P's loss is measured by the fair market value of S's assets less the liabilities payable to third parties less P's basis in the S stock and note. ◆

Basis of Property Received by the Parent Corporation—The General Rule of § 334(b)(1)

Unless a parent corporation elects under § 338, property received in a complete liquidation of its subsidiary under § 332 has the same basis it had in the hands

---

48. § 337(b).
49. Reg. § 1.332–2(b).

50. See § 165(g) and Reg. § 1.165–5. See the discussion in Chapter 3.

of the subsidiary.[51] The parent's basis in stock of the liquidated subsidiary disappears. This is so even if some of the property is transferred to the parent in satisfaction of debt owed the parent by the subsidiary.

──────────── EXAMPLE 51 ────────────

P, the parent corporation, has a basis of $20,000 in stock in S Corporation, a subsidiary in which it owns 85% of all classes of stock. P Corporation purchased the stock of S Corporation 10 years ago. In the current year, P Corporation liquidates S Corporation and acquires assets worth $50,000 with a tax basis to S Corporation of $40,000. P Corporation has a basis of $40,000 in the assets, with a potential gain upon sale of $10,000. P Corporation's original $20,000 basis in S Corporation's stock disappears. ◆

──────────── EXAMPLE 52 ────────────

P Corporation has a basis of $60,000 in stock in S Corporation, a subsidiary acquired 10 years ago. It liquidates S Corporation and receives assets worth $50,000 with a tax basis to S Corporation of $40,000. P Corporation has a basis of $40,000 in the assets it acquired from S Corporation. If it sells the assets, it has a gain of $10,000 in spite of the fact that its basis in S Corporation stock was $60,000. P Corporation's loss will never be recognized. ◆

Because the parent corporation takes the subsidiary's basis in its assets, the carryover rules of § 381 apply (see Chapter 7). The parent acquires a net operating loss of the subsidiary, any business credit carryover, capital loss carryover, and a carryover of the subsidiary's E & P. Section 381 applies to most tax-free reorganizations and to a tax-free liquidation under § 332 if the subsidiary's bases in its assets carry over to the parent.

Basis of Property Received by the Parent Corporation— The Exception of § 338

Background.   Under the general rule of § 332(b)(1), problems developed when a subsidiary was liquidated shortly after acquisition by a parent corporation.

1. When the basis of the subsidiary's assets was in excess of the purchase price of the stock, the parent received a step-up in basis in such assets at no tax cost. If, for example, the parent paid $100,000 for the subsidiary's stock and the basis of the assets transferred to the parent was $150,000, the parent enjoyed a $50,000 benefit without any gain recognition. The $50,000 increase in basis of the subsidiary's assets could have led to additional depreciation deductions and either more loss or less gain upon the later disposition of the assets by the parent.

2. If the basis of the subsidiary's assets was below the purchase price of the stock, the parent suffered a step-down in basis in such assets with no tax benefit. Return to Example 52, but change the situation slightly so that the subsidiary's stock is not held for 10 years. Instead, the subsidiary is liquidated shortly after acquisition. The basic inequity of the "no loss" situation now develops. But why would a corporation pay more for the stock in another corporation than the latter's basis in the assets? One reason is that the basis of the assets has no necessary correlation to the fair market value. Another possibility is that the acquiring corporation may have no choice in the matter if it really wants the assets. The shareholders in the acquired corporation may prefer to sell their stock rather than the assets of the corporation.

──────────────

51. § 334(b)(1) and Reg. § 1.334–1(b).

In the landmark decision of *Kimbell-Diamond Milling Co. v. Comm.*,[52] the courts finally resolved these problems. When a parent corporation liquidates a subsidiary shortly after the acquisition of its stock, the parent is really purchasing the assets of the subsidiary. Consequently, the basis of the assets should be the cost of the stock. Known as the "single transaction" approach, the basis determination is not made under the general rule of § 334(b)(1). The *Kimbell-Diamond* problem ultimately led to the enactment of § 338.

Requirements for Application.   Section 338 provides that an acquiring corporation may elect to treat the acquisition of stock in an acquired corporation as a purchase of the acquired corporation's assets. The election must be made by the fifteenth day of the ninth month beginning after the month in which the qualified stock purchase occurs. The election is irrevocable.

A purchasing corporation makes a qualified stock purchase if it acquires at least 80 percent of the voting power and at least 80 percent of the value of the acquired corporation within a 12-month period. The 12-month period begins with the first purchase of stock. The stock must be acquired in a taxable transaction (e.g., § 351 and other nonrecognition provisions do not apply). An acquisition of stock by any member of an affiliated group, including the purchasing corporation, is considered to be an acquisition by the purchasing corporation.

Tax Consequences.   If the parent makes a qualified election under § 338, the purchasing corporation has a basis in the subsidiary's assets equal to its basis in the subsidiary's stock. The subsidiary need not be liquidated.

Under § 338, the subsidiary corporation is deemed to have sold its assets for an amount equal to the purchasing corporation's grossed-up basis in the subsidiary's stock. This must be adjusted for liabilities of the subsidiary corporation. The grossed-up basis is the basis in the subsidiary stock multiplied by a fraction. The numerator of the fraction is 100 percent. The denominator is the percentage of value of the subsidiary's stock held by the purchasing corporation on the acquisition date.[53] The amount is allocated among the subsidiary's assets using the residual method described below.

The election of § 338 produces gain or loss to the subsidiary being purchased. The subsidiary is treated as having sold all of its assets at the close of the acquisition date in a single transaction at the fair market value.[54] The subsidiary is then treated as a new corporation that purchased all of the assets as of the beginning of the day after the acquisition date.

─────────────────────────── EXAMPLE 53 ───────────────────────────

S Corporation has an $800,000 basis in its assets and liabilities totaling $500,000. It has E & P of $200,000 and assets worth $2,000,000. P Corporation purchases 80% of the stock of S on March 10, 1992, for $1,200,000 [($2,000,000 less liabilities of $500,000) × 80%]. Because the purchase price of the S stock exceeds S's basis in its assets, and to eliminate S's E & P, P may choose to elect § 338 by December 15, 1992. S need not be liquidated for § 338 to apply. If P elects § 338, the tax consequences are as follows:

■ S is deemed to have sold its assets for an amount equal to the grossed-up basis in the S stock.

52. 14 T.C. 74 (1950), *aff'd.* in 51–1 USTC ¶9201, 40 AFTR 328, 187 F.2d 718 (CA–5, 1951), *cert. den.* 72 S.Ct. 50 (USSC, 1951).

53. § 338(b)(4).
54. § 338(a).

- The grossed-up basis in the S stock is computed as follows: The basis of the S stock is multiplied by a fraction, with 100% the numerator and 80% the denominator. The basis of the S stock, $1,200,000, is multiplied by 100/80. The result is $1,500,000, which is adjusted for S Corporation's liabilities of $500,000 for a deemed selling price of $2,000,000.
- The selling price of $2,000,000 less the basis of S's assets of $800,000 produces a recognized gain to S Corporation of $1,200,000. ◆

In that P did not purchase 100% of the stock of S, different results occur depending on whether or not S is liquidated. If S is not liquidated, it is treated as a new corporation as of March 11, 1992. The basis of S's assets is $2,000,000, and the E & P is eliminated. If S Corporation is liquidated, P Corporation has a basis of $1,600,000 in S's assets, representing 80% of S's assets. S's E & P does not carry over to P.

Note the results of the § 338 election. The assets of S Corporation receive a stepped-up basis but at a substantial tax cost. S Corporation must recognize all of its realized gain. Any tax liability S Corporation incurs on its recognized gain causes P Corporation to reduce the amount paid for the assets of S Corporation.

Allocation of Purchase Price. The new stepped-up basis of the assets of a subsidiary when a § 338 election is in effect is allocated among the assets by use of the residual method.[55] The amount of the purchase price that exceeds the aggregate fair market values of the tangible and identifiable intangible assets must be allocated to goodwill or going concern value. Neither goodwill nor going concern value can be amortized for tax purposes.

EXAMPLE 54

For $4,000,000, P Corporation acquires all of the stock of S Corporation and elects to liquidate under § 338. If the fair market value of S Corporation's physical assets is $3,500,000, P must allocate $500,000 of the purchase price either to goodwill or to going concern value. ◆

In Example 54, none of the purchase price has to be allocated to goodwill or going concern value if the physical assets are worth $4,000,000. However, the burden of proof of showing no residual amount is on the taxpayer and not on the IRS.

Consistency Requirement. A consistency requirement under § 338 prevents the acquiring corporation from choosing which of the acquired subsidiary corporations are to be covered by the § 338 election. The consistency period is a one-year period before and after the acquisition of the subsidiary. During this time, the parent is deemed to have made an election under § 338 if it makes a direct purchase of assets from the subsidiary or from an affiliate of the subsidiary.[56] Exceptions exist, such as for asset purchases in the ordinary course of a business.

EXAMPLE 55

P Corporation purchases all of the stock of T Corporation within a 12-month period. During that 12-month period, P Corporation purchases all of the assets of S Corporation, a subsidiary of T Corporation. P Corporation is deemed to have made a § 338 election as to T Corporation even though it did not actually make such an election. ◆

---

55. § 1060.   **56.** § 338(e).

In addition, during the consistency period, tax treatment of acquisitions of stock of two or more other companies that are members of an affiliated group must be consistent.[57]

─────────────── Example 56 ───────────────

P Corporation purchases all the stock in T Corporation and makes a timely election under § 338. If T Corporation owns all the stock in S Corporation, the § 338 election also applies to S Corporation. This results even if P Corporation never made an election as to S Corporation. If P Corporation does not make an election as to T Corporation, it cannot make the election as to S Corporation. ◆

A Comparison of §§ 334(b)(1) and 338. Under the general rule of § 334(b)(1), a subsidiary's basis in its assets carries over to the parent corporation upon liquidation. A subsidiary liquidation under §§ 332 and 334(b)(1) is completely tax-free (except for any minority interest). A liquidation under § 338, while tax-free to the parent, is taxable to the subsidiary. The subsidiary assets will have a stepped-up basis.

If a liquidation under § 332 qualifies under § 338 and a timely election is made, the holding period of the property received by the parent corporation begins on the date the parent acquired the subsidiary's stock. If the corporation is not liquidated, the holding period of the assets to the subsidiary would start anew on the day after the acquisition date. [58] In a liquidation under § 334(b)(1), the holding period of the subsidiary carries over to the parent.

A Summary of the Liquidation Rules. Sections 336, 337, and 338 set out the tax effects to a corporation that is liquidated. Section 336 provides the general rule that gain or loss is recognized. There are exceptions with respect to loss recognition when distributions are not made pro rata to related parties or when disqualified property is distributed.

Section 337 applies when a subsidiary corporation in which the parent has at least an 80 percent stock ownership is liquidated. Under § 337, the subsidiary corporation will not recognize gain or loss on distributions to the parent. With respect to distributions to a minority interest, § 336 provides that the subsidiary corporation will recognize gain, but not loss. Section 338 sets out an exception to § 337. If control (at least 80 percent) of a subsidiary corporation is acquired within a 12-month period, an election can be made under § 338. In that event, gain or loss is recognized to the subsidiary corporation.

Sections 331 and 332 set out the tax effects to the shareholders of a liquidated corporation. Section 331 provides the general rule that the shareholders have gain or loss on the liquidation. Section 332 applies to a parent corporation shareholder when § 337 is applicable. Under § 332, a parent corporation shareholder does not recognize gain or loss upon liquidation of its subsidiary.

Sections 334 and 338 provide the rules governing basis of assets acquired in a corporate liquidation. Section 334 provides the general rule that basis of the acquired assets will be the fair market value of the assets. There is an exception when a subsidiary is liquidated. A parent corporation holding at least an 80 percent stock ownership in the subsidiary will have a carryover basis in the subsidiary's assets. Section 338 applies only when an election is made in

─────────────────────────────

57. § 338(f).

58. § 338(a).

connection with the acquisition of at least an 80 percent interest in a subsidiary corporation within a 12-month period. When an election is made under § 338, the basis of the assets of the subsidiary is the basis the parent had in the stock of the subsidiary.

The rules regarding liquidations are set out in Concept Summary 5–1.

Stock Redemptions

TAX PLANNING CONSIDERATIONS

Several possibilities exist in connection with tax planning for stock redemptions:

- The § 302(b)(1) variety (not essentially equivalent to a dividend) provides minimal utility and should be relied upon only as a last resort. Instead, the redemption should be structured to fit one of the safe harbors. These include either § 302(b)(2) (substantially disproportionate), § 302(b)(3) (complete termination), or § 303 (to pay death taxes).
- For a family corporation in which all of the shareholders are related to each other, the only hope of a successful redemption may lie in the use of § 302(b)(3) or § 303. But in using § 302(b)(3), be careful that the family stock attribution rules are avoided. Here, strict compliance with § 302(c)(2)

CONCEPT SUMMARY 5–1
SUMMARY OF LIQUIDATION RULES

Effect on the Shareholder	Basis of Property Received	Effect on the Corporation
§ 331—The general rule provides for capital gain treatment on the difference between the FMV of property received and the basis of the stock in the corporation. (Gain on installment obligations resulting from sales of noninventory property or inventory property sold in bulk to one person by the corporation may, however, be deferred to the point of collection.)	§ 334(a)—Basis of assets received by the shareholder will be the FMV on the date of distribution (except for installment obligations in which gain is deferred to the point of collection).	§ 336—Gain or loss is recognized for distributions in kind and for sales by the liquidating corporation. Losses are not recognized for distributions to related parties (shareholders who own, directly or indirectly, more than 50% of the corporation's stock) if the distribution is not pro rata or if disqualified property is distributed. Losses may be disallowed on distributions of disqualified property even if made to unrelated parties.
§ 332—Liquidation of a subsidiary in which the parent owns 80% of the voting stock and 80% of the value of the subsidiary stock. No gain or loss is recognized to the parent corporation. Subsidiary must distribute all of its property within the taxable year or within three years from the close of the taxable year in which the plan is adopted.	§ 334(b)(1)—Property has the same basis as it had in the hands of the subsidiary. Parent's basis in the stock disappears. Carryover rules of § 381 apply.	§ 337—No gain or loss is recognized to the subsidiary on distributions to an 80% or more parent. Gain (but not loss) is recognized on distributions to minority shareholders.
	§ 338—Basis of assets takes the basis that the parent held in the stock in the subsidiary. Basis is allocated to assets using the residual method. Carryover rules of § 381 do not apply. (Subsidiary need not be liquidated.)	§ 338—Gain or loss is recognized to the subsidiary corporation.

(the withdrawing shareholder does not continue as an employee of the corporation, etc., and does not reacquire an interest in the corporation within 10 years) is crucial.

- The alternative to a successful stock redemption or partial liquidation is dividend treatment under § 301. But do not conclude that a dividend is always undesirable from a tax standpoint. Suppose the distributing corporation has little, if any, E & P or the distributee-shareholder is another corporation. In the latter situation, dividend treatment may be preferred due to the availability of the dividends received deduction.

- Recall that a stock redemption may be utilized successfully to provide needed funds to purchase the interest of a retiring or deceased shareholder. Rather than the remaining shareholders buying the stock of the retiring or deceased shareholder, the corporation redeems the stock from the shareholder or from the estate.

- A third party who wishes to purchase all the stock of a corporation can also use the stock redemption to obtain the needed purchase money. The third party purchases a small amount of stock from the shareholders. The corporation then redeems all the stock except that of the third party. The third party becomes the sole shareholder of the corporation, but the corporation furnished most of the needed purchase money.

- When using the § 303 redemption, the amount to be sheltered from dividend treatment is the sum of death taxes and certain estate administration expenses. Nevertheless, a redemption in excess of the limitation does not destroy the applicability of § 303. Even better, any such excess (if properly structured) might qualify under § 302. Thus, § 302 can be used to pick up where § 303 left off.

- The timing and sequence of a redemption should be carefully handled.

---------------------------------- EXAMPLE 57 ----------------------------------

P Corporation's stock is held as follows: R (60 shares), S (20 shares), and T (20 shares). R, S, and T are all individuals and are not related to each other. The corporation redeems 24 of R's shares. Shortly thereafter, it redeems 5 of S's shares. Does R's redemption qualify as substantially disproportionate? Taken in isolation, it would appear to meet the requirements of § 302(b)(2)—the 80% and 50% tests have been satisfied. Yet, if the IRS takes into account the later redemption of S's shares, R has not satisfied the 50% test; he still owns $36/71$ of the corporation after both redemptions. A greater time lag between the two redemptions places R in a better position to argue against collapsing the series of redemptions into one. ◆

Corporate Liquidations

With the repeal of the *General Utilities* rule, liquidating distributions are taxed at both the corporate and the shareholder level. When a corporation liquidates, it can, as a general rule, deduct losses on assets that have depreciated in value. These assets should not be distributed in the form of a property dividend before liquidation. If such assets are distributed as property dividends, the corporation receives no tax benefit from the potential loss. Barring certain exceptions, losses are recognized in complete liquidations.

Under the general rule of § 331, shareholders have recognized gain or loss equal to the difference between the liquidation proceeds and the basis of the stock given up. When the gain is large, a shareholder may consider shifting it to others. One approach is to give the stock to family members or donate it to charity. Whether or not this procedure will be successful depends on the timing of the transfer. If the donee of the stock is not in a position to prevent the liquidation of the corporation, the donor is deemed to have made an anticipatory assignment of income. As a result, the gain is still taxed to the donor. Hence, advance planning is crucial in arriving at the desired tax result.

Recall that § 453(h) provides some relief from the general rule of § 331 that the shareholder recognizes all gain upon receiving the liquidation proceeds. Assume corporate assets are sold after a plan of liquidation has been adopted. The assets are purchased with installment notes. The shareholders receiving the notes as liquidation distributions may be able to report the gain on the installment method. In that case, some gain can be deferred until the notes are collected.

The use of § 332 for the liquidation of a subsidiary is not elective. Nevertheless, some flexibility may be available:

- Whether § 332 applies depends on the 80 percent stock ownership test. Assuming the transaction has some substance, § 332 may be avoided if a parent corporation reduces its stock ownership in the subsidiary below this percentage. On the other hand, the opposite approach may be desirable. A parent can make § 332 applicable by acquiring enough additional stock in the subsidiary to meet the 80 percent test.
- Once § 332 becomes effective, less latitude is allowed in determining the parent's basis in the subsidiary's assets. If § 334(b)(1) applies, the subsidiary's basis carries over to the parent. If § 338 applies and a timely election is made, the parent's basis becomes the cost of the stock. (If the subsidiary is not liquidated, the basis of the assets to the subsidiary is the parent's cost of the stock.) Section 338 can be avoided by failing to make a timely election.
- If a timely election is made under § 338, the parent corporation's basis in the stock of the subsidiary is allocated among the assets of the subsidiary by use of the residual method.
- The residual method requires the parent corporation's basis in excess of the aggregate fair market value of the physical assets to be allocated to goodwill or going concern value (which cannot be amortized for tax purposes). For this reason, appraisal data relating to the physical assets should be obtained to minimize the amount the IRS may allocate to goodwill or going concern value. Recall that the burden of proof as to the value of the physical assets is on the taxpayer.
- A § 338 election should be carefully weighed as the election can be detrimental. Any stepped-up basis in the subsidiary's assets produces immediate taxable gain to the subsidiary.
- Some nontax considerations may affect the form of a liquidation. The sale of a corporation's assets may take one of two forms. In one form, the corporation's stock is sold, and the purchaser then liquidates the corporation. In the other form, the corporation's assets are sold, and the sales proceeds are distributed to the shareholders who then liquidate the corporation. Selling the stock presents fewer problems. The transfer of assets requires that title be changed and that creditors be notified. Some corporations hold valuable nontransferable trademarks or licenses. In this case, only a sale of stock can be used. On the other hand, a sale of assets may be preferable if minority shareholders refuse to sell their stock and the purchaser wants full control.
- A sale of stock poses fewer tax problems to the seller. The buyer may prefer a purchase of the assets of the corporation to receive a stepped-up tax basis. A purchase of the stock and an election under § 338 produce this result. However, there is a substantial tax cost since the purchased corporation must recognize a gain on the transaction. Still a purchase of

the stock can be beneficial to the purchaser when the purchased corporation has a basis in its assets in excess of the value of the assets. In this case, a purchase of the stock generally permits the purchaser to retain the higher basis.

PROBLEM MATERIALS

DISCUSSION QUESTIONS

1. Compare stock redemptions and liquidations with other corporate distributions in terms of the following:

   a. Recognition of gain to the shareholder.
   b. Recognition of gain or loss by the distributing corporation.
   c. Effect on the distributing corporation's E & P.

2. Compare stock redemptions with liquidations in terms of the following:

   a. Possible disallowance of a loss (§ 267) to a shareholder.
   b. Basis of noncash property received from the corporation.

3. Compare a stock redemption under §§ 302(b)(1), (2), and (3) with a stock redemption pursuant to a partial liquidation under § 302(b)(4).

4. Under what circumstances does § 303 apply to a stock redemption? What is the tax effect of the application of § 303?

5. "A § 303 stock redemption usually results in no gain or loss being recognized by the estate." Evaluate this statement.

6. A corporation distributes $100,000 to a shareholder in complete redemption of the shareholder's stock. Can the corporation reduce its E & P by this amount? Explain.

7. What is a preferred stock bailout?

8. T, a 30% shareholder in X Corporation, sells one-half of his preferred stock and one-half of his common stock to a third party. Is there any danger that § 306 could apply to the sale of the preferred stock? Why or why not?

9. It has been said that the operation of § 306 to a sale of preferred stock could have a harsher tax effect than if the corporation had distributed a taxable dividend in the first place. Explain.

10. What problems arise when a shareholder sells stock he or she owns in one corporation to a related corporation?

11. In order for a distribution by a corporation to qualify as a partial liquidation, the corporation must have been engaged in two active trades or businesses for at least five years before the distribution. Further, a distribution of subsidiary stock to shareholders of the parent corporation will not qualify for nonrecognition treatment under § 355 unless both the parent corporation and the subsidiary corporation have engaged in a trade or business for at least five years. What is the purpose of the five-year requirement?

12. Describe a spin-off, a split-off, and a split-up.

13. What losses are not recognized to the liquidating corporation in a complete liquidation?

14. What are related-party situations?

15. What is disqualified property in a liquidating distribution?

16. Can losses ever be recognized in a complete liquidation if disqualified property is involved? Explain.

17. Discuss the tax treatment of liquidation expenses in connection with the following:

    a. General liquidation expenses.
    b. Expenses relating to a distribution of assets in kind.
    c. Expenses relating to the sale of assets.

18. Explain the tax consequences to a shareholder of a corporation in the process of liquidation under the general rule of § 331.

19. In terms of the applicability of § 332, describe the effect of each of the following factors:

   a. The adoption of a plan of complete liquidation.
   b. The period of time in which the corporation must liquidate.
   c. The amount of stock held by the parent corporation.
   d. The solvency of the subsidiary being liquidated.

20. What are the tax consequences of a § 332 liquidation when a minority interest is involved?

21. Under § 332, how is the satisfaction by a subsidiary of a debt owed to its parent treated for tax purposes?

22. Could a liquidation of one corporation involve §§ 331 and 332?

23. Describe the problem that led to the enactment of § 338.

24. What are the requirements for the application of § 338?

25. Under what circumstances could the application of § 338 be beneficial to the parent corporation? Detrimental?

26. Explain the residual method of allocating basis to assets in a § 338 election.

27. Compare §§ 334(b)(1) and 338 with respect to the following:

   a. Carryover to the parent of the subsidiary's corporate attributes.
   b. Recognition by the subsidiary of gain or loss on distributions to its parent.

28. Will the application of § 331 to a liquidation always result in capital gain or loss being recognized by a shareholder? Why or why not?

29. "The E & P of the corporation being liquidated will disappear."

   a. Do you agree with this statement?
   b. Why or why not?

30. Is it possible to have a complete liquidation where the existence of the corporation being liquidated is not terminated? Elaborate.

Problems

31. X Corporation, with E & P of $1,000,000, distributes property with a basis of $100,000 and a fair market value of $250,000 to A, one of its three shareholders. Each of the shareholders has a one-third interest in the corporation.

   a. What are the tax consequences to X Corporation and to A if the distribution is a property dividend and A is an individual?
   b. What are the tax consequences in (a) if A is a corporation?
   c. What are the tax consequences to X Corporation and to A if the distribution is a qualified stock redemption and A is an individual? Assume A has a basis of $80,000 in the stock surrendered to X Corporation.
   d. What are the tax consequences in (c) if A is a corporation?

32. T Corporation has 400 shares of common stock outstanding. B owns 150 of the shares, B's mother owns 50 shares, B's brother owns 40 shares, and B's son owns 60 shares. X Corporation owns 50 shares. B owns 70% of the stock in X Corporation.

   a. In applying the stock attribution rules of § 318, how many shares does B own in T Corporation?
   b. Assume B owns only 30% of X Corporation. How many shares does B own, directly or indirectly, in T Corporation?
   c. Assume B owns 30% of BZ Partnership. The partnership owns 50 shares in T Corporation. How many shares does B own in T Corporation assuming the same facts as in (a) above?

33. V Corporation has 1,000 shares of common stock outstanding. The shares are owned by unrelated shareholders as follows: H, 400 shares; J, 400 shares; and K 200 shares. The corporation redeems 100 shares of the stock owned by K for $45,000. K

paid $100 per share for her stock two years ago. The E & P of V Corporation was $400,000 on the date of redemption. What is the tax effect to K of the redemption?

34. In Problem 33, assume H is the father of K. How would this affect the tax status of the redemption? What if H were K's brother instead of her father?

35. Y Corporation is owned by A, S (A's son), and D (A's daughter). A owns 50 shares in Y, S owns 25, and D owns 25. In the current year, Y Corporation redeems all of A's shares. Determine whether the redemption qualifies under § 302(b)(3) under the following circumstances:

   a. A acquires 25 shares in Y Corporation when S dies two years later and leaves his property to A.
   b. A does not file an agreement with her tax return to notify the IRS of any acquisition of stock in Y Corporation in the next 10 years.
   c. A remains as a director in Y Corporation.
   d. A resigns as director of Y Corporation; D becomes a director of Y Corporation to replace A.

36. X Corporation has 200 shares of common stock outstanding, owned as follows: A, 100 shares; B (unrelated to A), 50 shares; estate of F (A's father), 50 shares. Determine whether the following redemptions of X Corporation stock qualify for exchange treatment:

   a. X Corporation redeems the stock of the estate of F. A is the beneficiary of F's estate.
   b. X Corporation redeems all of A's 100 shares. A is the beneficiary of F's estate.
   c. X Corporation redeems all of A's 100 shares and all of the 50 shares of the estate of F.

37. A and B, individuals, own all the stock in X Corporation. Each has a basis of $50,000 in his 50 shares. X Corporation has accumulated E & P of $360,000.

   A wishes to retire in the current year and wants to sell his stock for $150,000, the fair market value. B would like to purchase A's shares and, thus, become the sole shareholder in X Corporation, but B is short of funds. What are the tax consequences to A, to B, and to X Corporation under the following circumstances?

   a. X Corporation distributes cash of $150,000 to B, and B uses the cash to purchase A's shares.
   b. X Corporation redeems all of A's shares for $150,000.

38. X Corporation, which has E & P of $6,000,000, manufactures widgets. In addition it operates a separate division that sells farm machinery. X Corporation also owns stock in several corporations that it purchased for investment purposes. The stock in X Corporation is held by A, an individual, and Y Corporation. Both A and Y Corporation own 100 shares in X Corporation purchased 10 years ago at a cost of $10,000 per share. Determine whether the following transactions qualify as partial liquidations under § 302(b)(4). In each transaction, determine the tax consequences to X Corporation, to Y Corporation, and to A, including the tax basis of any property received by the shareholders, A and Y Corporation.

   a. The division selling farm machinery was destroyed by fire. X Corporation decided to discontinue the business and distributed all the insurance collected as a result of the fire to A and to Y Corporation in redemption of 20 shares from each shareholder. The assets in the farm machinery division that were destroyed by fire had a basis to X Corporation of $1,000,000 and a fair market value of $5,000,000. The insurance recovery was $4,000,000.
   b. X Corporation has manufactured widgets and sold farm machinery for 10 years. It decided in the current year to discontinue selling farm machinery and distributed all the assets of the farm machinery division to A and Y Corporation, equally, in redemption of 20 shares from each shareholder. The assets in the farm machinery division had a basis of $1,000,000 to X Corporation and a fair market value of $5,000,000 on the date of the distribution.
   c. Assume that X Corporation had manufactured widgets for only 2 years but had sold farm machinery for the past 10 years. It distributed the farm machinery

equally to A and to Y Corporation as in (b) for half the shares A and Y Corporation held in X Corporation.

d. X Corporation distributed the stock it held in other corporations equally to A (an individual) and to Y Corporation in exchange for 10 shares of stock that A and Y Corporation held in X Corporation. The stock had a basis to X Corporation of $100,000 and a fair market value of $500,000 on the date of the distribution.

39. T Corporation was organized 10 years ago to construct family dwellings. Three years ago, it began selling furniture. Because of a glut in the real estate market, T Corporation discontinued its construction business. It sold all its assets used in the construction business for $500,000 and distributed the $500,000 to its equal share-holders, A, an individual, and B, a corporation, in exchange for one-half of the shares held by A and by B Corporation. A had a basis of $80,000 in his redeemed stock, and B Corporation had a basis of $100,000 in its redeemed stock. T Corporation has E & P of $1,000,000. What are the tax consequences of the redemption to A and to B Corporation?

40. The adjusted gross estate of D, decedent, is $1,000,000. D's estate will incur death taxes and funeral and administration expenses of $120,000. D's gross estate includes stock in X Corporation (fair market value of $120,000, basis to D of $10,000) and stock in Y Corporation (fair market value of $200,000, basis to D of $50,000). D owned 25% of the stock in X Corporation and 40% of the stock in Y Corporation. If X Corporation redeems all of D's stock from D's estate, will the redemption qualify under § 303? Why or why not?

41. The gross estate of D, decedent, includes stock in A Corporation and B Corporation valued at $150,000 and $250,000, respectively. The adjusted gross estate of D is $900,000. D owned 30% of A stock and 60% of B stock. Death taxes and funeral and administration expenses for D's estate were $100,000. D had a basis of $60,000 in the A stock and $90,000 in the B stock. What are the tax consequences to D's estate if A Corporation redeems one-third of D's stock for $50,000 and B Corporation redeems one-fifth of D's stock for $50,000?

42. The adjusted gross estate of D, a decedent, is $2,000,000. D's estate will incur death taxes and funeral and administration expenses of $400,000. D's gross estate includes stock in T Corporation (fair market value of $800,000 with a cost basis to D of $100,000). D owned 60% of the stock in T Corporation. His daughter, A, owns the other 40%. T Corporation redeems all of D's stock in T Corporation for $800,000. T Corporation has E & P of $1,500,000.

a. Assume A is D's heir. How will D's estate be taxed on the redemption?
b. Assume D's favorite charity is the sole beneficiary under his will. How will D's estate be taxed on the redemption?

43. On January 1, 1992, T Corporation had paid-in capital of $60,000 and E & P of $90,000. T Corporation had no current E & P (for 1992) as its deductions equaled its income for 1992. The 450 shares in T Corporation are owned equally by A, B, and C, unrelated individuals, each of whom paid $10,000 in 1985 for their stock in T Corporation. On June 1, 1992, T Corporation redeemed all the stock of C for $100,000 in a redemption that qualified under § 302(b)(3). On November 10, 1992, T Corporation paid $45,000 to A and $45,000 to B. What are the tax consequences of the stock redemption and the cash distributions to A, B, and C?

44. X Corporation has 500 shares of stock outstanding. It redeems 50 shares for $90,000 when it has paid-in capital of $300,000 and E & P of $400,000. What is the reduction in the E & P of X Corporation as a result of the redemption?

45. T Corporation has 1,000 shares of stock outstanding. It redeems 350 shares for $200,000 when it has paid-in capital of $100,000 and E & P of $700,000. What is the reduction in the E & P of T Corporation as a result of the redemption?

46. X Corporation has 100 shares of common stock outstanding owned as follows: A, 50 shares, and B (an unrelated party), 50 shares. A and B each paid $1,000 per share for the X Corporation stock 10 years ago. X Corporation has $100,000 accumulated E & P and $20,000 current E & P. X distributes land held as an investment (fair market value of $80,000, adjusted basis of $30,000) to A in redemption of 25 of A's shares.

a. What are the tax results to A on the redemption of A's stock in X Corporation?

b. What are the tax results to X Corporation on the redemption?

c. What is the E & P of X Corporation after the redemption?

47. C and D are the sole shareholders of TZ Corporation, which has E & P of $500,000. C and D each have a basis of $50,000 in their 100 shares of TZ stock. TZ Corporation issued a preferred stock dividend on the common shares of C and D. C and D each received 100 shares of preferred stock with a par value of $200 per share. Fair market value of one share of common was $300, and fair market value of one share of preferred was $200.

a. What are the tax consequences of the distribution to C and D?

b. What are the tax consequences to C if he later sells his preferred stock to A for $40,000? A is unrelated to C.

c. What are the tax consequences to D if she subsequently sells all her stock (both common and preferred) to B for $80,000? B is unrelated to D.

d. What are the tax consequences to C and his son, S, if C dies and bequeaths his stock to S, who later sells the preferred stock to A for $50,000? The preferred stock had a fair market value of $45,000 on the date of C's death.

e. What are the tax consequences to D if she makes a gift to her daughter of the preferred stock?

48. T owns 200 shares of X Corporation and 100 shares of Y Corporation, representing 100% ownership of X and 50% ownership of Y. T sells 60 shares of Y Corporation to X Corporation for $90,000. T purchased the stock in Y Corporation three years ago at a cost of $1,000 per share. What are the tax consequences of the sale, assuming X Corporation has E & P of $80,000 and Y Corporation has E & P of $100,000?

49. A, an individual, owns 50% of T Corporation, which in turn owns 70% of Y Corporation. A sells 60 of his 100 shares in T Corporation to Y Corporation for $30,000. A purchased the 60 shares two years ago for $10,000. What are the tax consequences of the sale assuming T Corporation has E & P of $120,000 and Y Corporation has E & P of $50,000?

50. T, an individual, owns 100% of X Corporation, which in turn owns 60% of W Corporation. X Corporation has E & P of $500,000, and W Corporation has E & P of $40,000. T sells 75 of her 200 shares in X Corporation to W Corporation for $100,000. T paid $500 per share for her stock in X Corporation five years ago. What are the tax consequences of the sale?

51. B owns 250 shares of stock in X Corporation and 200 shares of stock in Y Corporation, representing an 80% interest in both corporations. B sells 20 shares of Y stock to X Corporation for $20,000. The Y stock was acquired 10 years ago; the tax basis to B of these 20 shares is $2,000. B's share of the E & P of X Corporation is $10,000 on the date of sale; his share of the E & P of Y Corporation is $15,000. What are the tax consequences of this transaction?

52. A, an individual shareholder in P Corporation, exchanges stock in P (the parent corporation) for all the stock and some securities in S Corporation. The transaction meets the requirement of § 355. The stock in P that A exchanged had a fair market value of $200,000 and a tax basis of $40,000. The stock he received in S had a fair market value of $150,000; the securities had a fair market value of $50,000 and a principal amount of $56,000. What gain, if any, is recognized by A?

53. T Corporation has been engaged in the manufacture of farm equipment for over 5 years. The stock in T Corporation is held by W Corporation, which has sold automobiles for the past 10 years. W Corporation acquired the T Corporation stock 8 years ago. A shareholder dispute occurred in the previous year. In the current year with the dispute still unresolved, W Corporation distributes all its stock in T Corporation to its shareholders.

a. What are the tax consequences of the distribution to R, an individual shareholder, who receives stock in T Corporation worth $60,000? R does not surrender any of her stock in W Corporation.

b. What would be the tax consequences to R if T Corporation had been in existence for only two years before the distribution?

54. T, an individual, purchased a 25% interest in P Corporation on December 2, 1990, for $100,000. On November 30, 1992, P Corporation distributed its stock (100% interest) in S Corporation to its shareholders. P Corporation distributed 60%, or 600 shares, of its stock in S Corporation, valued at $110,000, in exchange for T's 25% interest in P Corporation. The remaining 40%, or 400 shares, of its stock in S Corporation was distributed to its other shareholders. P Corporation had a basis of $20 per share in its stock in S Corporation. What are the tax consequences of the distribution of the stock in S Corporation to P Corporation and to T?

55. Assume P Corporation, in Problem 54, distributed the stock in S Corporation to its shareholders on November 30, 1996. What are the tax consequences to P Corporation and to T?

56. T, an individual, has a basis of $12,000 in her 50 shares in P Corporation. T receives 100 shares of stock in S Corporation pursuant to a distribution that qualifies under § 355. The stock in P Corporation has a value of $1,000 per share, and the stock in S Corporation has a value of $500 per share. What basis will T have in the stock in S Corporation?

57. Assume, in Problem 56, that T exchanged 25 shares of her 50 shares of stock in P Corporation for the 100 shares of stock in S Corporation. What basis would T have in her remaining stock in P Corporation and in the stock in S Corporation?

58. T Corporation, with E & P of $100,000, distributes land with a basis of $70,000 and a fair market value of $200,000 to its sole shareholder, A. A has a $20,000 basis in her 2,000 shares in T Corporation. What are the tax consequences to T Corporation and to A under the following circumstances?

   a. The distribution was made pursuant to a complete liquidation of T Corporation. Assume the land was T Corporation's only asset and T has no liabilities.

   b. The distribution was made pursuant to a redemption of one-half of A's stock in T Corporation.

59. Z Corporation is owned equally by A and B, who are not related. Each has a stock basis of $90,000. Z Corporation has the following assets and no liabilities:

	Basis to Z Corporation	Fair Market Value
Cash	$ 10,000	$ 10,000
Inventory	40,000	60,000
Equipment ($20,000 depreciation has been taken)	10,000	50,000
Building	40,000	120,000
Land	10,000	20,000
Stock in TS Corporation (10% interest)	80,000	200,000
Total	$190,000	$460,000

Compute the tax liability to Z Corporation and the taxable gain to A and B if Z Corporation is liquidated in the current year after Z Corporation sells each asset for its fair market value and distributes the after-tax proceeds to A and B. Straight-line depreciation of $60,000 had been claimed on the building. The land was used in Z Corporation's business.

60. After a plan of complete liquidation has been adopted, Z Corporation sells its only asset, land, to T (an unrelated party) for $250,000. Under the terms of the sale, Z Corporation receives cash of $50,000 and T's note in the amount of $200,000. The note is payable in five years ($40,000 per year) and carries an interest rate of 9%. Immediately after the sale, Z Corporation distributes the cash and notes to A, an individual and sole shareholder of Z Corporation. A has a basis of $60,000 in the Z Corporation stock. What are the tax results to A if the choice is to defer as much gain as possible on the transaction? Assume the installment notes possess a value equal to the face amount.

61. S Corporation distributes to its shareholders land held as an investment (basis of $100,000, fair market value of $600,000) pursuant to a complete liquidation. The land is

subject to a liability of $700,000. How much gain does S Corporation have on a distribution of the land?

62. T Corporation's stock is held equally by F and D, father and daughter. One year before liquidation, F transfers property (basis of $200,000, fair market value of $60,000) to T Corporation in return for stock. In liquidation, T Corporation transfers the property to D. At the time of the liquidation, the property is worth $50,000. How much loss would T Corporation recognize on the distribution?

63. X Corporation's stock is held equally by three sisters, A, B, and C. The three sisters owned, as tenants in common, a tract of land on which a warehouse needed by the corporation was located. The land and warehouse had a basis of $325,000 and fair market value of $100,000. Three years prior to liquidation, A, B, and C transferred the land and warehouse to the corporation in return for stock. At the time of the liquidation, the land and warehouse were worth $60,000 and had a tax basis of $322,000. In liquidation, X Corporation transferred the land and warehouse equally to A, B, and C as tenants in common. How much loss would X Corporation recognize on the distribution?

64. T Corporation has the following assets:

	Basis to T Corporation	Fair Market Value
Cash	$ 300,000	$300,000
Inventory	100,000	300,000
Equipment	1,060,000	600,000
Building	400,000	760,000
Land	40,000	40,000

The inventory had been purchased by T Corporation; the remaining assets were acquired seven years ago. T Corporation adopted a plan of liquidation in January 1992 and distributed its assets that same year to its shareholders, A (70%) and B (30%). A and B are unrelated. What are the tax consequences to T Corporation under the following independent circumstances?

a. The assets are distributed to A and B in proportion to their stock interests (70% interest in each asset to A and 30% interest in each asset to B).

b. The equipment, building, and land are distributed to A, and the cash and inventory are distributed to B.

c. The equipment is distributed to B, and the remaining assets are distributed to A.

d. What is the result in (a) if the equipment had been transferred to T Corporation in a § 351 transaction 10 months before the liquidation when the equipment had a basis of $1,060,000 and a fair market value of $660,000?

65. On January 10, 1992, in a transaction that qualifies under § 351, X Corporation acquired land with a basis to the contributing shareholder of $400,000. The land had a value on that date of $250,000. X Corporation adopts a plan of liquidation on July 1, 1992. On December 10, 1992, when the value of the land has declined to $200,000, X Corporation distributes the land to A, a shareholder who owns 30% of the stock in X Corporation. X Corporation never used the land for any business purpose during the time it owned the land. How much loss can X Corporation recognize on the distribution of the land?

66. Assume in Problem 65, that X Corporation distributed the land to B, a shareholder who owns 60% of its stock. How much loss can X Corporation recognize on the distribution of the land?

67. Assume the land in Problems 65 and 66 had a value of $450,000 on the date it was contributed to X Corporation. However, on the date of distribution, its value was only $350,000. How much loss can X Corporation recognize on the distribution of the land to A? How much loss can X Corporation recognize if it distributes the land to B?

68. T Corporation acquired land in a § 351 exchange in 1990. The land had a basis of $600,000 and a fair market value of $650,000 on the date of the transfer. T

Corporation has two shareholders, A and B, unrelated individuals. A owns 80% of the stock in T Corporation and B owns 20%. T Corporation adopts a plan of liquidation in 1992. On this date the value of the land has decreased to $200,000. In distributing the land either to A or to B, or to both, as part of liquidating distributions from T Corporation, should T Corporation

a. distribute all the land to A?
b. distribute all the land to B?
c. distribute 80% of the land to A and 20% to B?
d. distribute 50% of the land to A and 50% to B?
e. sell the land and distribute the proceeds of $200,000 proportionately to A and to B?

69. Assume in Problem 68 that the plan of liquidation is not adopted until 1993. In addition, assume the land had a fair market value of $500,000 on the date of the transfer of the land to T Corporation. Its fair market value on the date of the liquidation has decreased to $200,000. How would your answers to Problem 68 change?

70. The stock of S Corporation is held as follows: 85% by P Corporation and 15% by T, an individual. S Corporation is liquidated on October 1, 1992, pursuant to a plan of liquidation adopted on January 15, 1992. At the time of its liquidation, S Corporation's assets had a basis of $2,000,000 and fair market value of $18,000,000. P Corporation has a basis of $800,000 in its S Corporation stock. The basis of the stock in S Corporation to T is $80,000.

a. How much gain, if any, must S Corporation recognize on the liquidation?
b. How much gain, if any, is recognized on receipt of property from S Corporation by P Corporation? By T?

71. At the time of its liquidation under § 332, S Corporation had the following assets and liabilities:

	Basis to S Corporation	Fair Market Value
Cash	$ 480,000	$ 480,000
Marketable securities	360,000	960,000
Unimproved land	600,000	1,200,000
Unsecured bank loan	(120,000)	(120,000)
Mortgage on land	(360,000)	(360,000)

P Corporation, the sole shareholder of S Corporation, has a basis in its stock investment of $1,440,000. At the time of its liquidation, S Corporation's E & P was $800,000.

a. How much gain (or loss) will S Corporation recognize if it distributes all of its assets and liabilities to P Corporation?
b. How much gain (or loss) will P Corporation recognize?
c. If § 334(b)(1) applies, what will be P Corporation's basis in the marketable securities it receives from S Corporation?
d. What will be P's basis in the unimproved land?

72. S Corporation, owned by two individual shareholders, has a basis of $450,000 (fair market value of $1,000,000) in its assets and has E & P of $80,000. Its liabilities total $100,000. P Corporation purchases 20% of all the stock of S Corporation for $180,000 on March 1, 1992; 15% for $135,000 on September 20, 1992; and 60% for $540,000 on December 1, 1992, or a total consideration of $855,000.

a. Is P Corporation entitled to make an election under § 338?
b. Assume P Corporation may make an election under § 338. Should P do so? When must P make such an election?
c. What are the tax consequences to S Corporation and to P Corporation if P Corporation makes a valid election under § 338 but does not liquidate S Corporation?

d. What is the tax result if S Corporation is liquidated four months after a valid § 338 election? A, an individual who holds the 5% minority interest in S Corporation, has a $10,000 basis in his stock in S. What is the tax result to A upon the liquidation?

73. S Corporation is wholly owned by A, an individual, who has a basis in the S stock of $100,000. S Corporation has the following assets and no liabilities:

	Basis to S Corporation	Fair Market Value
Inventory	$100,000	$160,000
Equipment (§ 1245 depreciation recapture potential of $200,000)	80,000	300,000
Building (no recapture potential)	60,000	400,000

P Corporation wants to buy the assets of S Corporation or the stock in S.

a. What are the tax results to S Corporation, to P Corporation, and to A under the following circumstances?

■ P purchases the S stock in 1992 for $860,000 and makes an election under § 338.
■ S Corporation adopts a plan of complete liquidation, sells all its assets to P Corporation, and distributes the cash of $860,000 to A.

b. Which alternative is preferable to P Corporation?

74. P Corporation paid $900,000 for all the stock of S Corporation 10 years ago. S Corporation's balance sheet is as follows:

Assets

Cash	$ 22,500
Inventory	67,500
Accounts receivable	45,000
Equipment	180,000
Land	225,000
	$ 540,000

Liabilities and Shareholders' Equity

Accounts payable	$ 360,000
Payable to P Corporation	540,000
Common stock	900,000
Deficit	(1,260,000)
	$ 540,000

What are the tax consequences to P Corporation if it liquidates S Corporation?

75. S Corporation is owned by T, an individual, who is interested in selling either his stock in S Corporation or S's assets. The financial statement of S Corporation as of December 31, 1991, is as follows:

Assets

	Basis to S Corporation	Fair Market Value
Cash	$ 30,000	$ 30,000
Accounts receivable	20,000	20,000
Inventory	30,000	50,000
Equipment (depreciation of $80,000 allowed)	100,000	200,000
Land	200,000	400,000
	$380,000	$700,000

Liabilities and Shareholders' Equity

Accounts payable	$ 80,000	$ 80,000
Mortgages payable	100,000	100,000
Common stock	50,000	520,000
Retained earnings	150,000	
	$380,000	$700,000

P Corporation is interested in purchasing S Corporation. Should P Corporation purchase the stock for $520,000 or the assets for $700,000? If stock is purchased for $520,000, what steps should P Corporation take to secure maximum tax benefits?

76. S Corporation is owned 90% by P Corporation. The parent is contemplating a liquidation of S Corporation and the acquisition of its assets. P Corporation purchased the stock of S from S's two individual shareholders a month ago on January 1, 1992, for $200,000. The financial statement of S Corporation as of January 1, 1992, is as follows:

Assets

	Basis to S Corporation	Fair Market Value
Cash	$ 20,000	$ 20,000
Inventory	40,000	30,000
Accounts receivable	80,000	50,000
Equipment	200,000	160,000
Land	260,000	140,000
	$600,000	$400,000

Liabilities and Shareholders' Equity

Accounts payable	$ 60,000	$ 60,000
Mortgages payable	100,000	100,000
Common stock	500,000	240,000
Retained earnings	(60,000)	
	$600,000	$400,000

The management of P Corporation asks your advice on the feasibility of an election under § 338. How will you advise your client?

RESEARCH PROBLEMS

RESEARCH PROBLEM 1   The stock of X Corporation is held 10% by Y and 90% by Z. W would like to purchase all of this stock but has the cash to pay for only 60%. X Corporation has enough cash on hand to redeem 40% of its shares. Consider and evaluate the following alternatives in terms of X Corporation, Y, Z, and W:

a. X Corporation redeems 40% of the shares from Z. W purchases the remaining 50% held by Z and the 10% owned by Y.

b. W borrows enough money from a bank to purchase all of Y's and Z's shares. Later, W has X Corporation redeem 40% of the shares purchased to pay off the bank loan.

c. X Corporation redeems all of Y's shares. W purchases 60% of the shares held by Z. X Corporation then redeems the remainder of Z's 30% interest.

d. X Corporation distributes 90% of its cash to Z and 10% to Y. This reduces the value of the stock to a level where W's cash is adequate to purchase all of Z's and Y's shares.

Partial list of research aids:

Television Industries, Inc. v. Comm., 60–2 USTC ¶9795, 6 AFTR2d 5864, 284 F.2d 322 (CA–2, 1960).

Zenz v. Quinlivan, 54–2 USTC ¶9445, 45 AFTR 1672, 213 F.2d 914 (CA–6, 1954).
U.S. v. Carey, 61–1 USTC ¶9428, 7 AFTR2d 1301, 289 F.2d 531 (CA–8, 1961).

RESEARCH PROBLEM 2   A, an individual, owned 80% of the common stock of XY Corporation. In 1990, when XY Corporation had E & P of $300,000, it issued a pro rata dividend of preferred stock on common stock. As a result of the distribution, A received 100 shares of preferred stock that he did not report as income. In 1991, A donated the preferred stock to his favorite charity, his alma mater. A deducted $100,000, the amount he determined to be the fair market value of the stock on the date of the gift, as a charitable contribution on his 1991 income tax return. A's adjusted gross income for 1991 was $500,000. Upon audit of A's return in 1992, the IRS disallowed the deduction contending that the preferred stock was § 306 stock. Thus, according to the IRS, the gift was subject to the provisions of § 170(e)(1)(A) of the Code. A seeks your advice.

RESEARCH PROBLEM 3   A owns 40% of X Corporation; his father owns the remaining 60%. A also owns 70% of Y Corporation, with the remaining 30% being owned by his wife. A terminates his entire interest in X Corporation through a stock redemption that he reports as a long-term capital gain pursuant to § 302(b)(3). Three years later, Y Corporation enters into a contract with X Corporation whereby Y Corporation is given exclusive management authority over X Corporation's operations. Upon audit, the IRS disallowed long-term capital gain treatment on the stock redemption in X Corporation contending that A acquired an interest in X within 10 years from the date of the redemption because of Y's management contract with X. What is the result?

RESEARCH PROBLEM 4   X Corporation is controlled by H. As part of a property settlement incident to a divorce between H and W, X Corporation agrees to redeem the shares held by W (H's ex-wife). Because of cash-flow problems, the stock is to be redeemed in annual increments over a period from 1989 to 1994. Although the agreement is mandatory in its terms, no redemptions were carried out in 1989 or 1990; however, redemptions were effected in 1991. W reports the gain on the redemption of her stock as a capital gain under § 302(b)(1) in 1991. The IRS contends the redemption in 1991 is a dividend, as there has not been a ''meaningful reduction'' in W's stock interests. W contends that although the redemption in 1991 does not represent a meaningful reduction, when the redemptions are taken as a whole, the effect of all the redemptions does satisfy the meaningful reduction test. What is the result?

RESEARCH PROBLEM 5   YZ Corporation was liquidated in 1991. In the year of liquidation, YZ Corporation reported taxable gain of $8,000,000, based upon a value in its assets of $10,000,000 and a basis of $2,000,000. After paying its tax liability of $2,720,000, YZ Corporation distributed its remaining assets, valued at $7,280,000 ($10,000,000 less the tax paid of $2,720,000), to its 10 shareholders. Shareholder A received $728,000 and reported a long-term capital gain in 1991 of $628,000 ($728,000 distribution – $100,000 stock basis). In 1992, the IRS audited YZ Corporation and determined that the corporation had an additional gain of $1,000,000 in the year of liquidation. The IRS assessed additional tax of $340,000 plus penalties and interest against YZ Corporation and then against A, based on transferee liability. A comes to you for advice. He is not certain where the other shareholders are located.

    a. If A is required to pay all of the tax liability, will he be entitled to deduct the amount paid as a loss?
    b. What is the nature of the loss—capital or ordinary?
    c. Would § 1341 apply?
    d. How can a shareholder be protected from the problem facing A?

RESEARCH PROBLEM 6   P Corporation, a supermarket development company, acquired 95% of all the stock in S Corporation in 1975 at a cost of $11,000,000. S Corporation owns and operates several grocery stores. In 1991, P Corporation became concerned that it was not in its best interest to operate grocery stores through a subsidiary corporation. As a result, on December 1, 1991, P sold all its stock in S Corporation to X Corporation for

$500,000 cash and a promissory note in the amount of $6,500,000. P then claimed a long-term capital loss of $4,000,000 [$7,000,000 (selling price of the S Corporation stock) − $11,000,000 (cost of the stock)]. P Corporation had a long-term capital gain of $5,000,000 in 1988 and carried back the $4,000,000 loss to offset this gain. As a result, P Corporation claimed it was entitled to a substantial tax refund. Shortly after P Corporation sold its S Corporation stock to X Corporation, S Corporation was merged into X Corporation and was liquidated. On January 15, 1992, P Corporation purchased 93% of the property formerly belonging to S Corporation from X Corporation in consideration of X Corporation canceling the note in the amount of $6,500,000.

The IRS audited P Corporation's income tax returns in 1992. It disallowed the long-term capital loss of $4,000,000, contending that P Corporation had, in effect, liquidated S Corporation. According to the IRS, because P Corporation would have owned at least 80% of the stock of S Corporation before and during the deemed liquidation, § 332 applied to the transaction. Under § 332, gains and losses on the liquidation of an 80% owned subsidiary are not recognized. What is the result to P Corporation?

ALTERNATIVE MINIMUM TAX AND CERTAIN PENALTY TAXES IMPOSED ON CORPORATIONS

OBJECTIVES

Describe the reason for the alternative minimum tax.

Explain the alternative minimum tax for corporations.

Discuss the adjusted current earnings adjustment.

Explain the purpose of the accumulated earnings tax and the personal holding company tax.

Define the "reasonable needs of the business" and explain their role in avoiding the accumulated earnings tax.

Explain the mechanics of the accumulated earnings tax.

Define the requirements for personal holding company status.

Discuss the mechanics of the personal holding company tax.

Compare the accumulated earnings tax with the personal holding company tax and show how each of these taxes can be avoided or controlled.

OUTLINE

In the early 1980s, the perception that many large corporations were not paying their fair share of Federal income tax was widespread. A study released in 1986 reported that 130 of the 250 largest corporations in the United States paid zero or less in Federal taxes in at least one year during the period 1981 through 1985 (e.g., Reynolds Metals, General Dynamics, Georgia Pacific, and Texas Commerce Bankshares). Political pressure subsequently led to the adoption of an alternative minimum tax (AMT) to ensure that corporations with substantial economic income pay a minimum amount of Federal taxes.

Corporations are now less able to use exclusions, deductions, and credits available under the law to pay no taxes. A separate tax system with a quasi-flat tax rate is applied each year to a corporation's economic income. If the tentative alternative minimum tax is greater than the regular corporate tax under § 11, then the corporation must pay the regular tax plus this excess, the alternative minimum tax.

After the introduction of the AMT, the controversial Citizens for Tax Justice group stated that the effective tax rate for corporations rose from 14.9 percent in 1986 to 22.1 percent in 1987. Yet 16 companies legally avoided paying any Federal income taxes during 1987 (e.g., General Motors, IBM, Greyhound, Hewlett-Packard, and Goodyear).

Small corporations have several techniques to minimize their tax liability. Chapter 12 discusses one major technique for minimization of the tax liability of closely held corporations: the S corporation election. However, some of the corporations that fall into the closely held category either may not qualify for the election or may find it unattractive. How can these other taxpayers transmit corporate earnings to the shareholders while producing a deduction for the corporation? One method is to reduce the amount of equity capital invested in a controlled corporation by increasing the debt obligations. In other words, convert dividends into interest payments deductible by the corporation. This method has limits. The IRS may contend that the capital structure is unrealistic and the debt is not valid. For these reasons, the IRS will disallow the corporate deduction for interest expense (refer to Chapter 3).

An alternative possibility is to convert the earnings of the closely held corporation into compensation to the officers, generally the major shareholders. The compensation is a deductible expense. If it were not for the reasonableness requirement, officer-shareholders could withdraw all corporate profits as salaries and eliminate the corporate tax (refer to Chapter 4). However, the reasonableness requirement prevents a corporation from deducting as salaries what are actually nondeductible dividends.

Another approach involves the lease of shareholder-owned property to the corporation. The corporation (the lessee) deducts the lease payment from gross income and saves taxes at the corporate level. The shareholders must recognize the rental payments as ordinary income. But there is an overall tax savings because the corporation obtains deductions for what are essentially dividend payments. However, the IRS may classify such payments as disguised dividends and disallow the rental deductions (refer to Chapter 4).

A fourth method is to accumulate the earnings at the corporate level. A temporary or permanent accumulation of earnings in a corporation results in a deferral of the second tax at the shareholder level. The corporation can invest the funds in tax-free vehicles or in other corporations to take advantage of the dividends received deduction. A *modest* tax benefit could result from accumulations at the corporate level. This benefit could occur because dividend income would be converted into long-term capital gain. Under the Revenue Reconciliation Act of 1990, long-term capital gains of noncorporate taxpayers cannot be taxed at a rate in excess of 28 percent. Dividend income is ordinary income and can be taxed at a rate as high as 31 percent.

Congress took steps to stem corporate accumulations as early as the first income tax law enacted under the Sixteenth Amendment. Today, in addition to the usual corporate income tax, an extra tax is imposed on earnings accumulated beyond the reasonable needs of the business. Also, a penalty tax may be imposed on undistributed personal holding company income.

This chapter indicates how corporations can reduce or eliminate the alternative minimum tax, which to a large degree taxes a company's economic income. Also, it demonstrates how closely held corporations can accumulate earnings without triggering the imposition of the accumulated earnings and personal holding company penalty taxes.

ALTERNATIVE MINIMUM TAX
◆

The alternative minimum tax (AMT) applicable to regular corporations is similar to the AMT applicable to individuals.[1] Many of the adjustments and tax preference items necessary to arrive at alternative minimum taxable income (AMTI) are the same. The rates and exemptions are different, but the objective is identical. The objective is to force taxpayers who are more profitable than their taxable income reflects to pay additional income taxes.

The formula for determining the AMT liability of corporate taxpayers appears in Figure 6–1 and follows the format of Form 4626 (Alternative Minimum Tax—Corporations).

AMT Adjustments

As Figure 6–1 indicates, the starting point for computing AMTI is the taxable income of the corporation before any net operating loss (NOL) deduction. Certain adjustments must be made to this amount. Unlike tax preference items, which are always additions, the adjustments may either increase or decrease taxable income.

The positive adjustments arise as a result of timing differences and are added back to the taxable income in computing AMTI. Since most preferences only defer taxes, a corporation may recoup AMT paid on tax preferences when the

---

FIGURE 6–1
AMT Formula for Corporations

Regular taxable income before NOL deduction
Plus/minus: AMT adjustments (except ACE adjustment)
Plus: Tax preferences
Equals: AMTI before AMT NOL deduction and ACE adjustment
Plus/minus: ACE adjustment
Equals: AMTI before AMT NOL deduction
Minus: AMT NOL deduction (limited to 90%)
Equals: Alternative minimum taxable income (AMTI)
Minus: Exemption
Equals: Alternative minimum tax base
Times: 20% rate
Equals: AMT before AMT foreign tax credit
Minus: AMT foreign tax credit (possibly limited to 90%)
Equals: Tentative minimum tax
Minus: Regular tax liability before credits minus regular foreign tax credit
Equals: Alternative minimum tax (AMT)

deferral of regular tax (that the preference created) is reversed and the regular tax is due. Once the preferences reverse themselves, they are deducted from taxable income to arrive at AMTI. This mechanism is called the *netting process*.

Although net operating losses are separately stated in Figure 6–1, they are actually negative adjustments. They are separately stated in Figure 6–1 and on Form 4626 as they may not exceed more than 90 percent of AMTI. Thus, such adjustments cannot be determined until all other adjustments and tax preference items are considered. The 90 percent limitation on NOLs assures that each corporate taxpayer pays at least a minimum tax of not less than 2 percent of its AMTI each year (10% times 20% rate). However, this 2 percent AMTI figure may be reduced by the exemption amount and credits, so a corporation may pay no AMT.

Other adjustments include the following:

- A portion of accelerated depreciation on property placed in service after 1986. For realty, the adjustment amount is the difference between accelerated and straight-line depreciation using a 40-year life. For personalty, the adjustment is the excess of accelerated depreciation over the amount determined using the 150 percent declining-balance method switching to straight-line.

--- EXAMPLE 1 ---

P Corporation placed an asset costing $10,000 in service on March 15, 1993. Based upon a three-year recovery class life, this personalty has the following effect upon the AMTI:

Year	Tax Deduction 200%	AMT Deduction 150%	Increase or (Decrease) AMT Adjustment
1993	$3,333	$2,500	$ 833
1994	4,445	3,750	695
1995	1,481	2,500	(1,019)
1996	741	1,250	(509)

- Since different depreciation methods are used for AMT and regular tax purposes, the adjusted bases for these depreciable assets are affected. When the bases are different and the asset is disposed of, a basis adjustment is necessary to reflect the difference in the AMT gain or loss *and* the regular tax gain or loss.

--- EXAMPLE 2 ---

Assume the same facts as in Example 1 except that the asset is sold at the end of the second year for $4,000. For regular tax purposes, the basis is $2,222 ($10,000 − $3,333 − $4,445), and the basis for AMT purposes is $3,750 ($10,000 − $2,500 − $3,750). Thus, the regular tax gain is $1,778 ($4,000 − $2,222), and the AMT gain is $250 ($4,000 − $3,750). Consequently, a $1,528 negative basis adjustment is required when computing AMT ($1,778 − $250). ◆

- Passive activity losses of certain closely held corporations and personal service corporations.
- The excess of mining exploration and development costs over what would have resulted if the costs had been capitalized and written off over 10 years.
- For contracts entered into on or after March 1, 1986, the requirement that the percentage of completion method be used for AMTI purposes. Thus, corporations using the completed contract method must make the appropriate adjustment.

- For AMTI purposes, denial to dealers of the use of the installment method in accounting for sales. Consequently, gain must be reflected in the year the property is disposed of.
- A portion of the difference between adjusted current earnings (ACE) and unadjusted AMTI (post-1989).
- A special energy deduction of (1) 75 percent of the preference portion of exploratory intangible drilling costs (IDC); (2) 15 percent of the preference portion of the remaining IDC; (3) 50 percent of the preference portion of the percentage depletion from marginal properties; and (4) a specified percentage of the energy-related portion of ACE.

Adjusted Current Earnings

The ACE rules are a separate parallel system to both AMT and taxable income. S corporations, real estate investment trusts, regulated investment companies, and real estate mortgage investment conduits are not subjected to the ACE provisions.

The purpose of the ACE adjustment is to ensure that the mismatching of financial statement income and taxable income will not produce inequitable results. The ACE adjustment is tax-based and can be a negative amount. AMTI is increased by 75 percent of the excess of ACE over unadjusted AMTI. Or, AMTI is reduced by 75 percent of the excess of unadjusted AMTI over ACE. This negative adjustment is limited to the aggregate of the positive adjustments under ACE for prior years reduced by the previously claimed negative adjustments. See Concept Summary 6–1. Thus, the ordering of the timing differences is crucial because any unused negative adjustment is lost forever. Unadjusted AMTI is AMTI without the ACE adjustment or the AMT NOL.[2]

<hr>

EXAMPLE 3

A calendar year corporation has the following data:

	1991	1992	1993
Unadjusted AMTI	$3,000	$3,000	$3,100
Adjusted current earnings	4,000	3,000	2,000

In 1991, since ACE exceeds unadjusted AMTI by $1,000, $750 (75% × $1,000) will be included as a positive adjustment to AMTI. No adjustment is necessary for 1992. Unadjusted AMTI exceeds ACE by $1,100 in 1993, so there is a potential negative adjustment to AMTI of $825. Since the total increases to AMTI for prior years equal $750 (and there are no negative adjustments), only $750 of the potential negative adjustment will reduce AMTI for 1993. Further, $75 of the negative amount is lost forever. Prior book income adjustments are ignored for limitation purposes. ◆

ACE should not be confused with current earnings and profits. Many items are treated in the same manner, but certain items that are deductible in computing E & P (but are not deductible in calculating taxable income) generally are not deductible in computing ACE (e.g., Federal income taxes). Concept Summary 6–2 compares the impact various transactions will have on the determination of ACE and E & P.

The starting point for computing ACE is AMTI. This is defined as regular taxable income after AMT adjustments (other than the NOL and ACE adjustments) and tax preferences.[3] The resulting figure is adjusted for the following items in order to determine ACE:

<hr>

2. §§ 56(g)(1) and (2).

3. § 56(g)(3).

- *Exclusion items.* These are income items (net of related expenses) that are included in earnings and profits, but will never be included in regular taxable income or AMTI (except on liquidation or disposal of a business). An example would be interest income from tax-exempt bonds. Thus, tax-exempt interest income and original issue discount (OID) on tax-exempt bonds are taxed at 15 percent (75% × 20%) by the AMT. Exclusion expense items do *not* include fines and penalties, disallowed golden parachute payments, and the disallowed portion of meal and entertainment expenses.
- *Depreciation.* The depreciation system is calculated using the alternative depreciation system in § 168(g). Thus, depreciation is based on acquisition costs using the straight-line method without regard to salvage value. The half-year or the mid-quarter convention is used for all property other than eligible real estate. The mid-month convention is used for eligible real estate. The recovery periods are 5 years for automobiles, 12 years for property with no class life, and 40 years for all residential rental property and nonresidential real property.

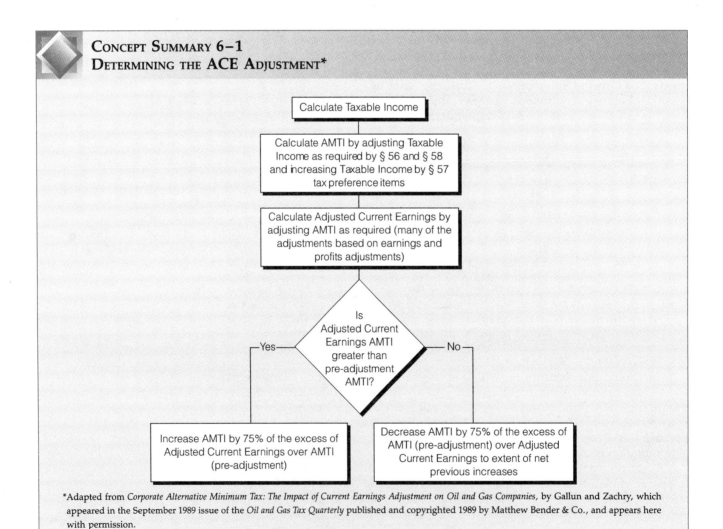

CONCEPT SUMMARY 6–1
DETERMINING THE ACE ADJUSTMENT*

Adapted from Corporate Alternative Minimum Tax: The Impact of Current Earnings Adjustment on Oil and Gas Companies, by Gallun and Zachry, which appeared in the September 1989 issue of the *Oil and Gas Tax Quarterly* published and copyrighted 1989 by Matthew Bender & Co., and appears here with permission.

- *Disallowed items.* A deduction is not allowed in computing ACE if it is never deductible in computing earnings and profits. Thus, the dividends received deduction and NOL deduction are not allowed. However, since the starting point for ACE is AMTI before the NOL, no adjustment is necessary for NOL. An exception does allow the 100 percent dividends received deduction if the payer corporation and recipient corporation are not members of the same affiliated group (a life insurance company or a foreign corporation) and an 80 percent deduction when a recipient corporation has at least 20 percent ownership of a payer corporation.[4] The exception does not cover dividends received from corporations where the ownership percentage is less than 20 percent. A corporation should therefore consider increasing ownership to the 20 percent minimum level.
- *Other adjustments.* The following adjustments, which are required for regular earnings and profits purposes, are necessary: intangible drilling costs, construction period carrying charges, circulation expenditures, mineral exploration and development costs, organization expenditures, LIFO inventory adjustments, installment sales, and long-term contracts.[5]
- *Special rules.* Other special rules apply to disallowed losses on exchange of debt pools, acquisition expenses of life insurance companies, depletion, and certain ownership changes.

CONCEPT SUMMARY 6–2
IMPACT UPON ACE AND E & P OF VARIOUS TRANSACTIONS

	Effect on Unadjusted AMTI in Arriving at ACE	Effect on Taxable Income in Arriving at E & P
Tax-exempt income (net of expenses)	Add	Add
Federal income tax	No effect	Subtract
Dividends received deduction (80% and 100%)	No effect	Add
Exemption amount of $40,000	No effect	No effect
Key employee insurance proceeds	Add	Add
Excess charitable contribution	No effect	Subtract
Capital losses	No effect	Subtract
Disallowed travel and entertainment expenses	No effect	Subtract
Penalties and fines	No effect	Subtract
Intangible drilling costs deducted currently	Add	Add
Deferred gain on installment sales	Add	Add
Realized (not recognized) gain on an involuntary conversion	No effect	No effect
Loss on sale between related parties	Subtract	Subtract
Gift received	No effect	No effect
Net buildup on life insurance policy	Add	Add

---

4. §§ 56(g)(4)(C)(i) and (ii).   5. §§ 312(n)(1) through (6).

———————————————— EXAMPLE 4 ————————————————

M Corporation makes the ACE adjustment calculation as follows:

AMTI		$278,000
Plus:		
Municipal bond interest	$21,000	
Installment gain	14,000	
70% dividends received deduction	30,000	
Income element in cash surrender life insurance	6,000	
Organization expense amortization	7,000	78,000
		$356,000
Less:		
Ace depreciation in excess of amount allowed for AMTI	$23,000	
Life insurance expense	1,000	24,000
Adjusted current earnings		$332,000
AMTI		−278,000
Base amount		$ 54,000
Times		.75
ACE adjustment (positive)		$ 40,500

◆

Tax Preferences

AMTI includes designated tax preference items. In many cases, this inclusion has the effect of subjecting nontaxable income to the AMT. Some of the most common tax preferences include the following:

- Amortization claimed on certified pollution control facilities.
- Accelerated depreciation on real property in excess of straight-line (placed in service before 1987).
- Tax-exempt interest on state and local bonds where the generated funds are not used for an essential function of the government.
- Percentage depletion claimed in excess of the adjusted basis of property.
- The excess of intangible drilling costs over 10-year amortization if in excess of 65 percent of net oil and gas income.
- Untaxed appreciation on property donated to charity. An exception is made for a tax year beginning in 1991 for tangible personal property. This includes long-term capital gain property whose use is related to the donee's purpose (e.g., a painting donated to an art museum). In this event, the untaxed appreciation is not an AMT preference.

———————————————— EXAMPLE 5 ————————————————

B Corporation contributes capital gain property (not tangible personal property) to a university. The property has a cost basis of $7,000, with a fair market value of $10,000. B qualifies for a $10,000 deduction for income tax purposes. There is a $3,000 tax preference item ($10,000 − $7,000) as a result of the appreciation. ◆

Computing Alternative Minimum Taxable Income

The following example illustrates the effect of tax preferences and adjustments in arriving at AMTI.

──────────────── EXAMPLE 6 ────────────────

For 1992, W Corporation (a calendar year taxpayer) had the following transactions:

Taxable income	$200,000
Mining exploration costs	50,000
Percentage depletion claimed (the property has a zero adjusted basis)	70,000
Donation of land held since 1980 as an investment (basis of $40,000 and fair market value of $50,000) to a qualified charity	50,000
Interest on City of Elmira (Michigan) bonds. The proceeds were used for nongovernmental purposes	20,000

W Corporation's AMTI for 1992 is determined as follows:

Taxable income		$200,000
Adjustments		
Excess mining exploration costs [$50,000 (amount expensed) − $5,000 (amount allowed over a 10-year amortization period)]		45,000
Tax preferences		
Excess depletion	$70,000	
Tax-exempt interest income	10,000	
Interest on bonds	20,000	100,000
AMTI		$345,000

◆

Exemption

The AMT is 20 percent of AMTI that exceeds the exemption amount. The exemption amount for a corporation is $40,000 reduced by 25 percent of the amount by which AMTI exceeds $150,000.

──────────────── EXAMPLE 7 ────────────────

Y Corporation has AMTI of $180,000. Since the exemption amount is reduced by $7,500 [25% × ($180,000 − $150,000)], the amount remaining is $32,500 ($40,000 − $7,500). Thus, Y Corporation's alternative minimum tax base (refer to Figure 6–1) is $147,500 ($180,000 − $32,500). ◆

Note that the exemption phases out entirely when AMTI reaches $310,000.

Minimum Tax Credit

The AMT is a separate tax system that is computed side-by-side with the regular tax. Along with the "netting concept," a minimum tax credit is available to eliminate the possibility of double taxation. Essentially, the AMT paid in one tax year may be carried forward indefinitely and used as a credit against the corporation's future *regular* tax liability that exceeds its tentative minimum tax. The minimum tax credit may not be carried back and may not be offset against any future *minimum* tax liability.

Unfortunately, the law does not cover the reverse situation (a preference item generates a regular tax in one year and results in an AMT in a later year). An example could be unearned income that is taxed in the year of receipt but is not recognized for book income purposes until the year earned. Consequently, it is entirely possible that the same income could be taxed twice.

─────────────────── EXAMPLE 8 ───────────────────

In Example 6, the AMTI exceeds $310,000, so there is no exemption amount. The tentative minimum tax is $69,000 (20% of $345,000). Assuming the regular tax liability in 1992 is $68,000 (34% of $200,000), the alternative minimum tax liability is $1,000 ($69,000 − $68,000). The amount of the minimum tax credit carryover is $1,000, which is all of the current year's AMT. ◆

Other Aspects of the AMT

Investment tax credit carryovers and other general business credits under the regular tax can offset 25 percent of AMT liability. Only 90 percent of foreign tax credits can be applied against AMT liability for years before April 1, 1990. This 90 percent limit does not apply to certain corporations meeting specified requirements for tax years beginning after March 31, 1990. The nonconventional fuel credit, drug testing credit, and Puerto Rico and U.S. possessions tax credit are available to offset the AMT.

In addition to paying their regular tax liability, corporations have to make estimated tax payments of the AMT liability. Even corporations that prepare quarterly financial statements may find this requirement adds to compliance costs. Unfortunately, the estimated tax payment dates will not coincide with the dates of the financial statements. Accordingly, estimating book income accurately for AMT purposes from the information usually available may be difficult.

For taxable years beginning after December 31, 1986, the tax law imposes an environmental tax on corporations with large amounts of AMTI. The tax is 0.12 percent on the excess of modified AMTI over $2,000,000.[6] Modified AMTI is AMTI determined without regard to any AMT NOL adjustment and the environmental tax deduction. No tax credits are allowed against the tax, and the corporation must include the tax in its quarterly estimated payments. A corporation may be subject to the environmental tax even though it owes no AMT (the regular corporate income tax is larger).

Both the AMT and the environmental tax can be computed and reported by completing Form 4626 [Alternative Minimum Tax—Corporations (Including Environmental Tax)].

PENALTY TAX ON UNREASONABLE ACCUMULATIONS
◆

In a corporate situation, income is taxed at the corporation level and again when the income is distributed or the stock is sold or exchanged. One method of optimizing the distribution of corporate earnings is to accumulate the earnings until the most advantageous time to distribute them to shareholders. While the earnings are being accumulated, the corporation can invest in dividend-paying stocks and take advantage of the 70 percent dividends received deduction. Also, for corporate income below $75,000, the corporate rate may be below the individual tax rate.

If the board of directors is aware of the tax problems of the shareholders, it can channel earnings into the shareholders' pockets with a minimum of tax cost by using any of several mechanisms. The corporation can distribute dividends only in years when the major shareholders are in lower tax brackets. Alternatively, dividend distributions might be curtailed causing the value of the stock to increase, in a manner similar to a savings account. Later, the shareholders can sell their stock in the year of their choice at an amount that reflects the increased retained earnings and receive capital gain treatment. In this manner, the capital gain could be postponed to years when less tax results (e.g., the shareholders

6. § 59A.

have capital losses to offset the gains). Alternatively, the shareholders can retain their shares. Upon death, the estate or heirs will receive a step-up in basis equal to the fair market value of the stock on date of death or, if elected, on the alternate valuation date. The increment in value represented by the step-up in basis will be largely attributable to the earnings retained by the corporation and will not be subject to income taxation.

Accumulating corporate earnings always entails problems, however. A penalty tax may be imposed on accumulated taxable earnings, or a personal holding company tax may be levied on certain accumulated passive income. Consider first the accumulated earnings tax. The tax law is framed to discourage the retention of earnings that are unrelated to the business needs of the company. Earnings retained in the business to avoid the imposition of the tax that would have been imposed on distributions to the shareholder are subject to a penalty tax.

────────────────────── EXAMPLE 9 ──────────────────────

T operated a consulting business as a sole proprietor in 1991. Assume she is in the 28% tax bracket in 1992, and she incorporates her business at the beginning of the year. Her business earns $120,000 in 1992, before her salary of $60,000. Since $60,000 of the income is accumulated, $6,800 of taxes are "saved" ($16,800 individual tax versus $10,000 corporate tax on the $60,000 accumulated). This accumulated savings could occur each year with the corporation reinvesting the saved taxes. Thus, without an accumulated earnings tax or personal holding company tax, T could use her corporation like a savings account. For example, the corporation could take advantage of the 70% dividends received deduction for dividend-paying stocks. With the top individual tax rate (31% for 1992) below the top corporate tax rate (34% for 1992), it is less attractive to hold investment property in a C corporation than in a flow-through entity (partnership, S corporation, or sole proprietor). Further, the earnings are still at the corporate level, and T might be in a higher individual rate when the accumulated earnings are distributed. ◆

The Element of Intent

Although the penalty tax is normally applied against closely held corporations, a corporation is not exempt from the tax merely because its stock is widely held.[7] For example, a Second Court of Appeals decision[8] imposed the tax upon a widely held corporation with over 1,500 shareholders. However, a much smaller group of shareholders actually controlled the corporation. As a practical matter, a widely held corporation that is not under the legal or effective control of a small group is unlikely to be suspected of accumulating earnings for the purpose of tax avoidance.

The key to imposition of the tax is not the number of the shareholders in the corporation but whether a shareholder group controls corporate policy. If such a group does exist and withholds dividends to protect its own tax position, an accumulated earnings tax (§ 531) problem might materialize.

When a corporation is formed or used to shield its shareholders from individual taxes by accumulating rather than distributing earnings and profits, the "bad" purpose for accumulating earnings is considered to exist under § 532(a). This subjective test, in effect, asks, Did the corporation and/or shareholder(s) *intend* to retain the earnings in order to avoid the tax on dividends? According to the Supreme Court, the tax avoidance motive need *not* be the dominant or controlling purpose to trigger application of the penalty tax; it need only be a contributing factor to the retention of earnings.[9] If a corporation accumulates

────────────

7. § 532(c).

8. *Trico Products v. Comm.*, 43–2 USTC ¶9540, 31 AFTR 394, 137 F.2d 424 (CA–2, 1943).

9. *U.S. v. The Donruss Co.*, 69–1 USTC ¶9167, 23 AFTR2d 69–418, 89 S.Ct. 501 (USSC, 1969).

funds beyond its reasonable needs, such action is determinative of the existence of a "bad" purpose, unless the contrary can be proven by the preponderance of the evidence. The fact that the business is a mere holding or investment company is *prima facie* evidence of this tax avoidance purpose.[10]

Imposition of the Tax and the Accumulated Earnings Credit

Contrary to its name, the accumulated earnings tax is not levied on the corporate accumulated earnings balance. It is imposed on the current year's addition to this balance not needed for a reasonable business purpose. The tax is not imposed upon S corporations, personal holding companies, foreign personal holding companies, tax-exempt organizations, and passive foreign investment companies. The tax is in addition to the regular corporate tax and the 20 percent alternative minimum tax. For taxable years beginning after December 31, 1987, the rate is 28 percent.

Most corporations are allowed a minimum $250,000 credit against accumulated taxable income, even when earnings are accumulating beyond reasonable business needs. However, certain personal service corporations in health, law, engineering, architecture, accounting, actuarial science, performing arts, and consulting are limited to a $150,000 accumulated earnings credit. Moreover, a nonservice corporation (other than a holding or investment company) may retain more than $250,000 ($150,000 for a service organization) of accumulated earnings if the company can justify the accumulation as necessary to meet the reasonable needs of the business.[11]

The accumulated earnings credit is the greater of the following:

1. The current earnings and profits for the tax year that are needed to meet the reasonable needs of the business (see the subsequent discussion) *less* the net long-term capital gain for the year (net of any tax). In determining the reasonable needs for any one year, the accumulated earnings and profits of past years must be taken into account.
2. The amount by which $250,000 exceeds the accumulated earnings and profits of the corporation at the close of the preceding tax year (designated the *minimum credit*).

──────────────── EXAMPLE 10 ────────────────

T Corporation, a calendar year manufacturing concern, has accumulated E & P of $120,000 as of December 31, 1991. For 1992, it has no capital gains and current E & P of $140,000. A realistic estimate places T Corporation's reasonable needs of the business for 1992 at $200,000.

The allowable credit is the greater of (1) or (2).

	(1)	(2)
Reasonable needs	$200,000	
Minimum credit		$250,000
Accumulated E & P	120,000	120,000
Potential credit	$ 80,000	$130,000

Thus, the credit becomes $130,000 (the greater of $80,000 or $130,000). ◆

---

10. § 533. See, for example, *H. C. Cockrell Warehouse Corp.*, 71 T.C. 1036 (1979).

11. §§ 535(c) and 537 and Reg. § 1.537–1.

Several observations can be made about the accumulated earnings credit. First, the minimum credit of $250,000 is of no consequence as long as the prior year's ending balance in accumulated E & P is $250,000 or more. Second, when the credit is based on reasonable needs, the credit is the amount that exceeds accumulated E & P. Third, a taxpayer must choose between the reasonable needs credit (item 1) and the minimum credit (item 2). Combining the two in the same year is not permissible. Fourth, although the § 531 tax is not imposed on accumulated E & P, the amount of the credit depends upon the balance of this account as of the end of the preceding year.

Reasonable Needs of the Business

If a corporation's funds are invested in assets essential to the needs of the business, the IRS will have a difficult time imposing the accumulated earnings tax. "Thus, the size of the accumulated earnings and profits or surplus is not the crucial factor; rather it is the reasonableness and nature of the surplus."[12] What are the reasonable business needs of a corporation? This is precisely the point upon which difficulty arises and which creates controversy with the IRS.

Justifiable Needs—In General.   The reasonable needs of a business include the business's reasonably anticipated needs.[13] These anticipated needs must be specific, definite, and feasible. A number of court decisions illustrate that indefinite plans referred to only briefly in corporate minutes merely provide a false feeling of security for the taxpayer.[14]

The Regulations list some legitimate reasons that could indicate that the earnings of a corporation are being accumulated to meet the reasonable needs of the business. Earnings may be allowed to accumulate to provide for bona fide expansion of the business enterprise or replacement of plant and facilities as well as to acquire a business enterprise through the purchase of stock or assets. Provision for the retirement of bona fide indebtedness created in connection with the trade or business (e.g., the establishment of a sinking fund for the retirement of bonds issued by the corporation) is a legitimate reason for accumulating earnings under ordinary circumstances. Providing necessary working capital for the business (e.g., to acquire inventories) and providing for investment or loans to suppliers or customers (if necessary to maintain the business of the corporation) are valid grounds for accumulating earnings.[15] Funds may be retained for self-insurance[16] and realistic business contingencies (e.g., lawsuits, patent infringement).[17] Accumulations to avoid an unfavorable competitive position[18] and to carry key employee life insurance policies[19] are justifiable. Accumulation for the possible loss of a key customer or client is a reasonable need of the business.[20]

The reasonable business needs of a company also include the post-death § 303 redemption requirements of a corporation.[21] Accumulations for such

---

12. *Smoot Sand & Gravel Corp. v. Comm.*, 60–1 USTC ¶9241, 5 AFTR2d 626, 274 F.2d 495 (CA–4, 1960).

13. § 537(a)(1).

14. See, for example, *Fine Realty, Inc. v. U.S.*, 62–2 USTC ¶9758, 10 AFTR2d 5751, 209 F.Supp. 286 (D.Ct. Minn., 1962).

15. Reg. § 1.537–2(b).

16. *Halby Chemicals Co., Inc. v. U.S.*, 67–2 USTC ¶9500, 19 AFTR2d 1589 (Ct.Cls., 1967).

17. *Dielectric Materials Co.*, 57 T.C. 587 (1972).

18. *North Valley Metabolic Laboratories*, 34 TCM 400, T.C.Memo, 1975–79.

19. *Emeloid Co. v. Comm.*, 51–1 USTC ¶66,013, 40 AFTR 674, 189 F.2d 230 (CA–3, 1951). Key employee life insurance is a policy on the life of a key employee that is owned by and made payable to the employer. Such insurance enables the employer to recoup some of the economic loss that could materialize upon the untimely death of the key employee.

20. *EMI Corporation*, 50 TCM 569, T.C.Memo. 1985–386 and *James H. Rutter*, 52 TCM 326, T.C.Memo. 1986–407.

21. The § 303 redemption to pay death taxes and administration expenses of a deceased shareholder is discussed in Chapter 5. See § 537(a).

purposes are limited to the amount needed (or reasonably anticipated to be needed) to redeem stock included in the gross estate of the decedent-shareholder.[22] This amount may not exceed the sum of the death taxes and funeral and administration expenses allowable under §§ 2053 and 2106.[23]

Section 537(b) provides that reasonable accumulations to pay future product liability losses represent a reasonable anticipated need of the business. Guidelines for the application of this change are prescribed in Proposed Regulations.

Justifiable Needs—Working Capital Requirements for Inventory Situations. For many years the penalty tax on accumulated earnings was based upon the concept of retained earnings. The courts generally looked at retained earnings alone to determine whether there was an unreasonable accumulation. However, a corporation may have a large retained earnings balance and yet possess no liquid assets with which to pay dividends. Therefore, the emphasis should more appropriately be placed upon the liquidity of a corporation. Does the business have liquid assets *not* needed that could be used to pay dividends? The courts did not begin to use this liquidity approach until 1960, however.

Over the years, greater recognition has been placed on the liquidity needs of the corporation. The reasonable needs of the business can be divided into two categories:

1. Working capital needed for day-to-day operations.
2. Expenditures of a noncurrent nature (extraordinary expenses).

The operating cycle of a business is the average time interval between the acquisition of materials (or services) entering the business and the final realization of cash. The courts seized upon the operating cycle because it had the advantage of objectivity for purposes of determining working capital. A normal business has two distinct cycles:

1. Purchase of inventory → the production process → finished goods inventory
2. Sale of merchandise → accounts receivable → cash collection

A systematic operating cycle formula was developed in *Bardahl Manufacturing Co.* and *Bardahl International Corp.*[24] The technique became known as the *Bardahl* formula.

The following is the standard formula used to determine the reasonable working capital needs for a corporation:

$$\text{Inventory cycle} = \frac{\text{Average inventory}}{\text{Cost of goods sold}}$$

Plus

$$\text{Accounts receivable cycle} = \frac{\text{Average accounts receivable}}{\text{Net sales}}$$

Minus

$$\text{Accounts payable cycle} = \frac{\text{Average accounts payable}^{25}}{\text{Purchases}}$$

Equals

A decimal percentage

22. §§ 537(a)(2) and (b)(1).
23. § 303(a).
24. *Bardahl Manufacturing Co.*, 24 TCM 1030, T.C.Memo. 1965–200; *Bardahl International Corp.*, 25 TCM 935,

T.C.Memo. 1966–182. See also *Apollo Industries, Inc. v. Comm.*, 66–1 USTC ¶9294, 17 AFTR2d 518, 358 F.2d 867 (CA–1, 1966).

25. The accounts payable cycle was developed in *Kingsbury Investments, Inc.*, 28 TCM 1082, T.C.Memo. 1969–205.

The formula assumes that working capital needs are computed on a yearly basis. However, this may not provide the most favorable result. A business that experiences seasonally based high and low cycles illustrates this point. For example, a construction company can justify a greater working capital need if computations are based on a cycle that includes the winter months only and not on an annual average.[26] In the same vein, an incorporated CPA firm would choose a cycle during the slow season.

Both of the original *Bardahl* decisions used the so-called peak cycle approach. Here the inventory and accounts receivable figures are the amounts for the month-end during which the total amounts in inventory and accounts receivable are the greatest. In fact, the *Bardahl International* decision specifically rejects the average cycle approach. However, some courts have rejected the peak cycle approach,[27] which probably should be used where the business of the corporation is seasonal.[28] Using peak amounts increases the numerators of the inventory and receivable fractions, while the denominators stay the same. The turnover periods increase, which, in turn, increases the operating cycle percentage. A higher percentage produces a larger necessary accumulation of working capital. This makes a corporation less likely to be subject to the accumulated earnings tax.

The decimal percentage derived above, when multiplied by the cost of goods sold plus general, administrative, and selling expenses (not including unpaid Federal income taxes and depreciation),[29] equals the working capital needs of the business. Paid estimated Federal income taxes are treated as operating expenses, but profit-sharing contributions and charitable contributions are not operating expenses.

If the statistically computed working capital needs plus any extraordinary expenses are more than the current year's net working capital, no penalty tax is imposed. Working capital is the excess of current assets over current liabilities. This amount is the relatively liquid portion of the total business capital that is a buffer for meeting obligations within the normal operating cycle of the business.

However, if working capital needs plus any extraordinary expenses are less than the current year's net working capital, the possibility of the imposition of a penalty tax does exist.[30]

In *Bardahl Manufacturing Corp.*, the costs and expenses used in the formula were those of the following year, whereas in *Bardahl International Corp.*, costs and expenses of the current year were used. Use of the subsequent year's expected costs seems to be the more equitable position, but a taxpayer may not use the higher of the current year or next year's costs over a number of years.

The IRS normally takes the position that the operating cycle should be reduced by the accounts payable cycle. The IRS maintains that the payment of such expenses may be postponed by various credit arrangements that will reduce the operating capital requirements. However, a number of court decisions have omitted such a reduction. In any case, a corporate tax planner should not have to rely on creditors to avoid the accumulated earnings penalty tax. The corporation with the most acute working capital problem will probably have a large accounts payable balance. If the formula for determining reasonable

26. See *Audits of Construction Contracts*, AICPA, 1965, p. 25.

27. See, for example, *W. L. Mead, Inc.*, 34 TCM 924, T.C.Memo. 1975–215.

28. *Magic Mart, Inc.*, 51 T.C. 775 (1969).

29. In *W. L. Mead, Inc.*, cited in Footnote 27, the Tax Court allowed depreciation to be included in the expenses of a service firm with no inventory. Likewise, in *Doug-Long, Inc.*, 72 T.C. 158 (1979), the Tax Court allowed a truck stop to include quarterly estimated tax payments in operating expenses.

30. *Electric Regulator Corp. v. Comm.*, 64–2 USTC ¶9705, 14 AFTR2d 5447, 336 F.2d 339 (CA–2, 1964) used "quick assets" (current assets less inventory).

working capital needs is used, a large accounts payable balance will result in a sizable reduction in the maximum working capital allowable before the tax is imposed. For tax planning purposes, a corporation should hold accounts payable at a reduced level.

--------------------------------------- EXAMPLE 11 ---------------------------------------

Q, an accountant for a local appliance store, is asked by his president to determine if the corporation is susceptible to the accumulated earnings tax. Q calculates, as a fraction of the year, the inventory cycle (.08), the receivables cycle (.12), and the payables cycle (.13). The three ratios are combined to determine the operating cycle ratio of .07 (.08 + .12 − .13 = .07). Since the operating expenses are $525,000, Q calculates the working capital needs to be $36,750 (.07 times $525,000).

Next Q calculates the actual working capital, using current assets at fair market value less current liabilities. Thus, $285,000 less $200,000 results in $85,000 of actual working capital. Comparing actual working capital ($85,000) with the working capital needs of $36,750, Q determines that the corporation has excess working capital of $48,250. If this appliance store has no other reasonable business needs, the corporation may be subject to the accumulated earnings tax. ◆

Justifiable Needs—Working Capital Requirements for Noninventory Situations. In a service business, inventories are not purchased, and part of the operating cycle in the *Bardahl* formula is missing. However, a service business incurs certain costs such as salaries and overhead for a period of time before billing customers for services. Some courts have used a rough rule of thumb to determine an inventory equivalent cycle. Under certain circumstances, a human resource accounting (HRA) approach may be used to determine the working capital needs of a noninventory corporation. The use of an HRA approach is based on the contention that the strength of a service business—and its major asset—is its highly educated, skilled technicians. Such individuals must be available both to attract clients and to execute projects efficiently. In the event of a business downturn, it would be foolish to abruptly discharge highly paid specialists, recruited and trained at considerable expense. The business decline might prove to be of brief duration.

One court[31] allowed an engineering firm to add to the IRS's *Bardahl*-calculated operating reserve the reasonable professional and technical payroll for an additional period of two months (or 60 days). The Court felt that this extra amount would ". . . allow sufficient reserve for one cycle of full operation plus a reasonable period (60 days) of curtailed operation to recapture business or, in the alternative, to face up to hard decisions on reducing the scope of the entire operation or abandoning it." Further, the Court expressed its opinion that a multiple of reasonable professional and technical salaries is a useful method for determining the amount to be included in an operating reserve. However, the Court did not indicate why it selected two months as the magic number. It can be anticipated that the courts will continue to evolve a *Bardahl*-like formula for noninventory corporations.

No Justifiable Needs. Certain situations do *not* call for the accumulation of earnings. For example, accumulating earnings to make loans to shareholders[32] or brother-sister corporations is not considered within the reasonable needs of the business.[33] Accumulations to retire stock without curtailment of the business

---

31. *Simons-Eastern Co. v. U.S.*, 73–1 USTC ¶9279, 31 AFTR2d 73–640, 354 F.Supp. 1003 (D.Ct. Ga., 1972). See also *Delaware Trucking Co., Inc.*, 32 TCM 105, T.C.Memo. 1973–29, and *Magic Mart, Inc.*, cited in Footnote 28.

32. Reg. §§ 1.537–2(c)(1), (2), and (3).

33. See *Young's Rubber Corp.*, 21 TCM 1593, T.C.Memo. 1962–300.

and for unrealistic business hazards (e.g., depression of the U.S. economy) are invalid reasons for accumulating funds.[34] The same holds true for accumulations made to carry out investments in properties or securities unrelated to the corporation's activity.[35]

Concept Summary 6–3 reviews the previous discussion regarding what does and does not constitute a reasonable need of the business.

─────────────────────────── EXAMPLE 12 ───────────────────────────

For a period of years, M, Inc., a trucking company, has considered the purchase of various vehicles and other facilities directly related to its business. It has, during the same time, also invested in oil and gas drilling projects (mostly wildcats). Despite substantial accumulated earnings, the corporation made no distributions of dividends during the same period of years. The Claims Court imposed the penalty tax because the plan to acquire vehicles and facilities was not supported by documents in existence or prepared during the taxable years at issue. Furthermore, accumulations to further the oil and gas investments were unjustified. The company was not in the oil and gas business, and the corporation was only a minor investor.[36] ◆

Measuring the Accumulation. Should the cost or fair market value of assets be used to determine whether a corporation has accumulated earnings and profits beyond its reasonable needs? This issue remains unclear. The Supreme Court has indicated that fair market value is to be used when dealing with marketable securities.[37] Although the Court admitted that the concept of earnings and profits does not include unrealized appreciation, it asserted that the current asset ratio must be considered in determining if accumulated earnings are reasonable. Thus, the Court looked to the economic realities of the situation and held that fair market value is to be used with respect to readily marketable securities. The Court's opinion did not address the proper basis for valuation of

---

CONCEPT SUMMARY 6–3
REASONABLE BUSINESS NEEDS

Legitimate Reasons	**Invalid Reasons**
Expansion of a business.	Loans to shareholders.
Replacement of capital assets.	Loans to brother-sister corporations.
Replacement of plant.	Future depression.
Acquisition of a business.	Unrealistic contingencies.
Working capital needs.	Investment in assets unrelated to the business.
Product liability loss.	Retirement of stock without a curtailment of the business.
Loans to suppliers or customers.	
Redemption under § 303 to pay death taxes and administration expenses of a shareholder.	
Realistic business hazards.	
Loss of a major customer or client.	
Reserve for actual lawsuit.	
To protect a family business from takeover by outsiders.	
Debt retirement.	
Self-insurance.	

---

34. *Turnbull, Inc. v. Comm.,* 67–1 USTC ¶9221, 19 AFTR2d 609, 373 F.2d 91 (CA–5, 1967), and Reg. § 1.537–2(c)(5).

35. Reg. § 1.537–2(c)(4).

36. *Cataphote Corp. of Miss. v. U.S.,* 75–2 USTC ¶9753, 36

AFTR2d 75–5990 (Ct.Cls., 1975).

37. *Ivan Allen Co. v. U.S.,* 75–2 USTC ¶9557, 36 AFTR2d 75–5200, 95 S.Ct. 2501 (USSC, 1975).

assets other than marketable securities. However, the IRS may assert that this rule should be extended to include other assets. Therefore, tax advisers and corporate personnel should regularly check all security holdings to guard against accumulations caused by the appreciation of investments.

——————————————— EXAMPLE 13 ———————————————

C Company had accumulated earnings and profits of approximately $2,000,000. Five years ago, the company invested $150,000 in various stocks and bonds. At the end of the current tax year, the fair market value of these securities approximates $2,500,000. Two of C Company's shareholders, father and son, own 75% of the stock. If these securities are valued at cost, current assets minus current liabilities are deemed to be equal to the reasonable needs of the business. However, if the marketable securities are valued at their $2,500,000 fair market value, the value of the liquid assets greatly exceeds the corporation's reasonable needs. Under the Supreme Court's economic reality test, the fair market value is used. Consequently, the corporation is subject to the § 531 penalty tax. ◆

Mechanics of the Penalty Tax

The taxable base of the accumulated earnings tax is a company's accumulated taxable income (ATI). Taxable income of the corporation is modified as follows:[38]

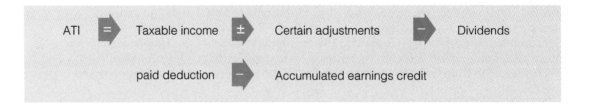

The "certain adjustments" include the following items (for a corporation not a mere holding or investment company):
As deductions—

1. Corporate income tax accrued.
2. Charitable contributions in excess of 10 percent of adjusted taxable income.
3. Capital loss adjustment.[39]
4. Excess of net long-term capital gain over net short-term capital loss, diminished by the capital gain tax and reduced by net capital losses from earlier years.

And as additions—

5. Capital loss carryovers and carrybacks.
6. Net operating loss deduction.
7. The dividends received deduction.

---

38. § 535(a).
39. This deduction (item 3) and item 4 are either/or deductions, since a corporation would not have both in the same year. For the capital loss adjustment, see § 535(b)(5).

The purpose of each of these adjustments is to produce an amount that more closely represents the dividend-paying capacity of the corporation. For example, the corporate income tax is deducted from taxable income because the corporation does not have this money to pay dividends. Conversely, the dividends received deduction is added to taxable income since the deduction has no impact upon the ability to pay a dividend. Note that item 4, in effect, allows a corporation to accumulate any capital gains without a penalty tax.

Payment of dividends reduces the amount of accumulated taxable income subject to the penalty tax. The dividends paid deduction includes those dividends paid during the tax year that the shareholders must report as ordinary income *and* any dividends paid within two and one-half months after the close of the tax year.[40] A nontaxable stock dividend under § 305(a) does not affect the dividends paid deduction. Further, a shareholder may file a consent statement to treat as a dividend the amount specified in the statement. A consent dividend is taxed to the shareholder even though it is not actually distributed. The consent dividend is treated as a contribution to the capital of the corporation (paid-in capital) by the shareholder.[41]

EXAMPLE 14

A nonservice closely held corporation that had no capital gains or losses in prior years has the following financial transactions for calendar year 1992:

Taxable income	$300,000
Tax liability	100,250
Excess charitable contributions	22,000
Short-term capital loss	(40,000)
Dividends received (less than 20% owned)	100,000
Research and development expenses	46,000
Dividends paid in 1992	40,000
Accumulated earnings (1/1/92)	220,000

Presuming the corporation is subject to the § 531 tax and has *no* reasonable business needs that justify its accumulations, the accumulated taxable income is calculated as follows:

Taxable income			$300,000
Plus: 70% dividends received deduction			70,000
			$370,000
Less: Tax liability	$100,250		
Excess charitable contributions	22,000		
Net short-term capital loss adjustment	40,000		
Dividends paid	40,000		
Accumulated earnings minimum credit ($250,000 – $220,000)	30,000	232,250	
Accumulated taxable income			$137,750

Thus, the accumulated earnings penalty tax for 1992 would be $38,570 ($137,750 × 28%). ◆

---

40. §§ 535(a), 561(a), and 563(a).

41. §§ 565(a) and (c)(2). The consent dividend procedure would be appropriate if the corporation is not in a position to make a cash or property distribution to its shareholders. The dividends paid deduction is discussed more fully later in the chapter.

———————————————— EXAMPLE 15 ————————————————

In Example 14, assume that the reasonable needs of the business of § 535(c) amount to $270,000 in 1992. The current year's accumulated earnings are now reduced by $50,000, rather than the $30,000, of accumulated earnings minimum credit. Accumulated taxable income is $117,750, and the penalty tax is $32,970. Note that the first $220,000 of accumulated earnings *cannot* be omitted in determining whether taxable income for the current year is reasonably needed by the enterprise. ◆

PERSONAL HOLDING COMPANY PENALTY TAX
◆

The personal holding company (PHC) tax was enacted to discourage the sheltering of certain types of passive income in corporations owned by high tax bracket individuals. These "incorporated pocketbooks" were frequently found in the entertainment and construction industries. For example, a taxpayer could shelter the income from securities in a corporation, which would pay no dividends, and allow the corporation's stock to increase in value. Like the accumulated earnings tax, the purpose of the PHC tax is to force the distribution of corporate earnings to the shareholders. However, in any one year, the IRS cannot impose both the PHC tax and the accumulated earnings tax.[42]

———————————————— EXAMPLE 16 ————————————————

Considerable tax savings could be achieved by incorporating a "pocketbook" if § 541 did not exist. Assume that investments that yield $50,000 a year are transferred to a corporation by a 31% income tax bracket shareholder. A tax savings of $8,000 will occur each year if no dividends are paid to the shareholder. With no corporation, there would be a total tax liability of $15,500, but with a corporation the tax liability is only $7,500 in 1992 (15% × $50,000). Further, if the yield of $50,000 is in the form of dividends, the corporate tax will be even less because of the dividends received deduction. ◆

Whether a corporation will be included within the statutory definition of a personal holding company for any particular year depends upon the facts and circumstances during that year.[43] Therefore, PHC status may be conferred even in the absence of any avoidance intent on the part of the corporation. In one situation,[44] a manufacturing operation adopted a plan of complete liquidation, sold its business, and invested the proceeds of the sale in U.S. Treasury bills and certificates of deposit. During the liquidating corporation's last tax year, 100 percent of the corporation's adjusted ordinary gross income was interest income. Since the corporation was owned by one shareholder, the corporation was a PHC, even though in the process of liquidation.

Certain types of corporations are expressly excluded from PHC status in § 542(c):

- Tax-exempt organization under § 501(a).
- Banks and domestic building and loan associations.
- Life insurance companies.
- Surety companies.
- Foreign personal holding companies.
- Lending or finance companies.
- Foreign corporations.
- Small business investment companies.

---

42. § 532(b)(1) and Reg. § 1.541–1(a).
43. *Affiliated Enterprises, Inc. v. Comm.*, 44–1 USTC ¶9178. 32 AFTR 153, 140 F.2d 647 (CA–10, 1944).

44. *Weiss v. U.S.*, 75–2 USTC ¶9538, 36 AFTR2d 75–5186 (D.Ct. Ohio, 1975). See also *O'Sullivan Rubber Co., v. Comm.*, 41–2 USTC ¶9521, 27 AFTR 529, 120 F.2d 845 (CA–2, 1941).

Without these exceptions, the business world could not perform necessary activities without a high rate of taxation. For example, a legitimate finance company should not be burdened by the PHC tax because it is performing a valuable business function of loaning money. In contrast, in the case of a classic incorporated pocketbook, the major purpose is to shelter the investment income from possible higher individual tax rates.

Definition of a Personal Holding Company

Two tests are incorporated within the PHC provisions:

1. Was more than 50 percent of the *value* of the outstanding stock owned by five or fewer individuals at any time during the *last half* of the taxable year?
2. Is a substantial portion (60 percent or more) of the corporate income (adjusted ordinary gross income) composed of passive types of income such as dividends, interest, rents, royalties, or certain personal service income?

If the answer to *both* of these questions is yes, the corporation is classified as a PHC. Once classified as a PHC, the corporation must pay a penalty tax in addition to the regular corporate income tax. The penalty tax is 28 percent.

Stock Ownership Test. To meet the stock ownership test, more than 50 percent *in value* of the outstanding stock must be owned, directly or indirectly, by or for not more than five individuals sometime during the last half of the tax year. Thus, if the corporation has nine or fewer shareholders, it automatically meets this test. If 10 unrelated individuals own an *equal* portion of the value of the outstanding stock, the stock ownership requirement is not met. However, if these 10 individuals do not hold equal value, the test is met.

The ownership test is based on fair market value and not on the number of shares outstanding. Fair market value is determined in light of all the circumstances and is based on the company's net worth, earning and dividend-paying capacity, appreciation of assets, and other relevant factors. If there are two or more classes of stock outstanding, the total value of all the stock is allocated among the various classes according to the relative value of each class.[45]

In determining the stock ownership of an individual, broad constructive ownership rules apply. Under § 544, the following attribution rules determine indirect ownership:

1. Any stock owned by a corporation, partnership, trust, or estate is considered to be owned proportionately by the shareholders, partners, or beneficiaries.
2. The stock owned by the members of an individual's family (brothers, sisters, spouse, ancestors, and lineal descendants) or by the individual's partner is considered to be owned by the individual.
3. If an individual has an option to purchase stock, the stock is regarded as owned by that person.[46]
4. Convertible securities are treated as outstanding stock.

---

45. Reg. § 1.542–3(c).
46. For examples of how these constructive ownership rules

operate, see Reg. §§ 1.544–2, –3(a), and –4.

—————————— EXAMPLE 17 ——————————

A and B, two individuals, are the equal beneficiaries of a trust that owns the entire capital stock of M Corporation. M Corporation owns all of the stock of N Corporation. All of the stock of M Corporation and N Corporation is considered to be owned equally by A and B by reason of indirect ownership under § 544(a)(1). ♦

—————————— EXAMPLE 18 ——————————

During the last half of the tax year, X Corporation has 1,000 shares of outstanding stock, 499 of which are held by various individuals having no relationship to one another and none of whom are partners. The remaining 501 shares are held by seven shareholders as follows:

H	100
H's spouse	50
H's brother	20
H's sister	70
H's father	120
H's son	80
H's daughter	61

Under the family attribution rules of § 544(a)(2), H owns 501 shares of X for purposes of determining stock ownership in a personal holding company. ♦

Attribution rules 2, 3, and 4 are applicable only for the purpose of classifying a corporation as a PHC and cannot be used to avoid the application of the PHC provisions. Basically, the broad constructive ownership rules make it difficult for a closely held corporation to avoid application of the stock ownership test. For example, convertible securities are treated as outstanding stock only if the effect of the inclusion is to make the corporation a PHC (and not to expand the total amount of stock in order to avoid PHC classification).

Gross Income Test. The gross income test is met if 60 percent or more of the corporation's adjusted ordinary gross income (AOGI) consists of certain passive income items (PHC income). AOGI is calculated by subtracting certain items from gross income (as defined by § 61).[47] The adjustments required to arrive at AOGI appear in Concept Summary 6–4.

CONCEPT SUMMARY 6–4
ADJUSTED ORDINARY GROSS INCOME DETERMINATION

Gross income

Less: a.   Capital gains.

b.   Section 1231 gains.

Equals: Ordinary gross income (OGI).

Less: c.   Depreciation, property taxes, interest expense, and rental expenses directly related to gross income from rents (not to exceed the income from rents).

d.   Depreciation, property and severance taxes, interest expense, and rental expenses directly related to gross income from mineral, oil, and gas royalties (not to exceed gross income from the royalties).

e.   Interest on a condemnation award, a judgment, a tax refund, and an obligation of the United States held by a dealer.

Equals: Adjusted ordinary gross income (AOGI).

—————————————

47. §§ 543(b)(1) and (2).

In Concept Summary 6–4, the deduction of items (a) and (b) from gross income results in the intermediate concept, ordinary gross income (OGI), the use of which is noted subsequently. The starting point, gross income, is not necessarily synonymous with gross receipts. In fact, for transactions in stocks, securities, and commodities, the term "gross income" includes only the excess of gains over any losses.[48]

PHC income includes income from dividends; interest; royalties; annuities;[49] rents; mineral, oil, and gas royalties; copyright royalties; produced film rents; computer software royalties; and amounts from certain personal service contracts.

EXAMPLE 19

M Corporation has four shareholders, and its AOGI is $95,000, consisting of gross income from a merchandising operation of $40,000, interest income of $15,000, dividend income of $25,000, and adjusted income from rents of $15,000. Total passive income is $55,000 ($15,000 + $25,000 + $15,000). Since 60% of AOGI ($57,000) is greater than the passive income ($55,000), the corporation is not a personal holding company. ◆

EXAMPLE 20

Assume in Example 19 that the corporation received $21,000 in interest income rather than $15,000. Total passive income is now $61,000 ($21,000 + $25,000 + $15,000). Since 60% of AOGI ($60,600) is less than passive income of $61,000, the corporation is a personal holding company. ◆

Most passive types of income such as dividends, interest, royalties, and annuities cause few classification problems. Certain income items, however, may or may not be classified as PHC income. Special rules apply to rent income, mineral, oil, and gas royalties, and personal service contracts.

Rent Income. Although rent income is normally classified as PHC income, it can be excluded from that category if two tests are met. The first test is met if a corporation's adjusted income from rents is 50 percent or more of the corporation's AOGI. The second test is satisfied if the total dividends for the tax year are equal to or greater than the amount by which the nonrent PHC income exceeds 10 percent of OGI.[50] Dividends for this purpose include those actually paid, those considered as paid on the last day of the tax year, and consent dividends (see the later discussion of the dividends paid deduction). The taxpayer must meet both tests for the rent income to be excluded from PHC income. (See Figure 6–4 later in the chapter.)

With respect to the 50 percent test, "adjusted income from rents" is defined as gross income from rents reduced by the deductions allowable under § 543(b)(3). The deductions are depreciation, property taxes, interest, and rent. Generally, compensation is not included in the term "rents" and is not an allowable deduction. The final amount included in AOGI as adjusted income from rents cannot be less than zero.

EXAMPLE 21

Assume that Z Corporation has rent income of $10,000 and the following business deductions:

---

48. Reg. § 1.542–2. See also Reg. § 1.543–2(b) where net gain on transactions in stocks and securities is not reduced by a net loss on commodities futures transactions.

49. § 543(a)(1).

50. § 543(a)(2).

Depreciation on rent property	$1,000
Interest on mortgage	2,500
Real property taxes	1,500
Salaries and other business expenses (§ 162)	3,000

The adjusted income from rents included in AOGI is $5,000 ($10,000 − $1,000 − $2,500 − $1,500). Salaries and other § 162 expenses do not affect the calculation of AOGI. ◆

A company deriving its income primarily from rental activities can avoid PHC status by merely distributing as dividends the amount of nonrental PHC income that exceeds 10 percent of its OGI.

───────────── EXAMPLE 22 ─────────────

During the tax year, N Corporation receives $15,000 in rent income, $4,000 in dividends, and a $1,000 long-term capital gain. Corporate deductions for depreciation, interest, and real estate taxes allocable to the rent income are $10,000. The company pays a total of $2,500 in dividends to its eight shareholders. To determine whether or not rent income is PHC income, OGI, AOGI, and adjusted income from rents must be calculated.

Rent income	$15,000
Dividends	4,000
Long-term capital gain	1,000
Gross income	$20,000
Deduct: Gains from sale or disposition of capital assets	1,000
OGI	$19,000
Deduct: Depreciation, interest, and real estate taxes	10,000
AOGI	$ 9,000

First, adjusted income from rents must be 50% or more of AOGI.

Rent income	$15,000
Deduct: Depreciation, interest, and real estate taxes	10,000
Adjusted income from rents	$ 5,000
50% of AOGI	$ 4,500

N Corporation has satisfied the first test.

Second, total dividends paid for the year are $2,500. This figure must be equal to or greater than the amount by which nonrent PHC income exceeds 10% of OGI.

Nonrent PHC income	$4,000
Less: 10% of OGI	1,900
Excess	$2,100

N Corporation meets both tests, and the adjusted income from rents is not PHC income. ◆

Mineral, Oil, and Gas Royalties.   As with rent income, adjusted income from mineral, oil, and gas royalties can be excluded from PHC income if certain tests are met.[51] First, adjusted income from the royalties must constitute 50 percent or more of AOGI. Second, nonroyalty PHC income may not exceed 10 percent of OGI. Note that this 10 percent test is not accompanied by the dividend escape clause previously described in relation to rent income. Therefore, corporations receiving income from mineral, oil, or gas royalties must be careful to minimize nonroyalty PHC income. Furthermore, adjusted income from rents and copyright royalties is considered to be nonroyalty PHC income whether or not treated as such by §§ 543(a)(2) and (4). Third, the company's business expenses under § 162 (other than compensation paid to shareholders) must be at least 15 percent of AOGI.

───────────────── EXAMPLE 23 ─────────────────

P Corporation has gross income of $4,000, which consists of gross income from oil royalties in the amount of $2,500, $400 of dividends, and $1,100 from the sale of merchandise. The total amount of the deductions for depletion, interest, and property and severance taxes allocable to the gross income from oil royalties equals $1,000. Deductions allowable under § 162 are $450. P Corporation's adjusted income from oil royalties will not be PHC income if the three tests are met. Therefore, OGI, AOGI, and adjusted income from oil royalties must be determined:

Oil royalties income	$2,500
Dividends	400
Sale of merchandise	1,100
Gross income (*and* OGI)	$4,000
Deduct: Depletion, interest, and property and severance taxes	1,000
AOGI	$3,000

Adjusted income from oil royalties must be 50% or more of AOGI.

Oil royalties income	$2,500
Deduct: Depletion, interest, and property and severance taxes	1,000
Adjusted income from oil royalties	$1,500
50% of AOGI	$1,500

The first test is met. Since nonroyalty PHC income is $400 (composed solely of the $400 of dividends) and this amount is not more than 10% of OGI, the second test is also satisfied. The third requirement is satisfied if deductible expenses under § 162 amount to at least 15% of AOGI.

§ 162 expenses	$450
15% of $3,000 (AOGI)	$450

P Corporation's adjusted income from oil royalties is not PHC income. ◆

────────────────────

51. § 543(a)(3).

As in the case of income from mineral, oil, and gas royalties and rents, copyright royalties and produced film rents are not categorized as PHC income if certain tests are met.[52]

Royalties received from licensing computer software are excluded from the definition of PHC income if the following conditions are satisfied:

- The corporation must be actively engaged in the business of developing computer software.
- The royalties must be at least 50 percent of OGI.
- Business-related deductions equal or exceed 25 percent of OGI.
- Passive income (other than computer software royalties) in excess of 10 percent of OGI must be distributed as a dividend.

Personal Service Contracts. Any amount from personal service contracts is classified as PHC income only if (1) some person other than the corporation has the right to designate, by name or by description, the individual who is to perform the services and (2) the person so designated owns, directly or indirectly, 25 percent or more in value of the outstanding stock of the corporation at some time during the taxable year.[53]

EXAMPLE 24

B, C, and D (all attorneys) are equal shareholders in X Company, a professional association engaged in the practice of law. E, a new client, retains X Company to pursue a legal claim. Under the terms of the retainer agreement, E designates B as the attorney who will perform the legal services. The suit is successful, and 30% of the judgment E recovers is paid to X Company as a fee. Since the parties have met all of the requirements of § 543(a)(7), the fee received by X Company is PHC income.[54] ◆

The result reached in Example 24 could have been avoided had B not been specifically named in the retainer agreement as the party to perform the services.

Calculation of the PHC Tax

To this point, the discussion has focused on the determination of PHC status. Once a corporation is classified as a PHC, the amount upon which the penalty tax is imposed must be computed. The tax base is called undistributed PHC income (UPHC income). Basically, this amount is taxable income, subject to certain adjustments, minus the dividends paid deduction. After the adjustments, UPHC income more clearly represents the corporation's dividend-paying capacity. Concept Summary 6–5 shows how this amount is determined.

Dividends Paid Deduction. Since the purpose of the PHC penalty tax is to force a corporation to pay dividends, five types of dividends paid deductions reduce the amount subject to the penalty tax. (See Figure 6–2.) First, dividends actually paid during the tax year ordinarily reduce UPHC income.[55] However, such distributions must be pro rata. They must exhibit no preference to any shares of stock over shares of the same class or to any class of stock over other classes outstanding.[56] The prohibition is especially harsh when portions of an

---

52. §§ 543(a)(4) and (5).
53. § 543(a)(7). For an application of the "right to designate," see *Thomas P. Byrnes, Inc.*, 73 T.C. 416 (1979).
54. The example presumes X Company will be treated as a

corporation for Federal tax purposes. As noted in Chapter 2, this is the usual result of professional association status.
55. §§ 561(a)(1) and 562.
56. § 562(c).

employee-shareholder's salary are declared unreasonable and classified as a disguised or constructive dividend.[57] In the case of a property dividend of appreciated property, the dividends paid deduction is the fair market value of the property (not adjusted basis).

CONCEPT SUMMARY 6–5
UNDISTRIBUTED PHC INCOME DETERMINATION

Taxable income

Plus:
   a. Dividends received deduction.

   b. Net operating loss (NOL), other than the NOL from the preceding year (computed without the dividends received deduction).

   c. Certain business expenses and depreciation attributable to nonbusiness property owned by the corporation that exceed the income derived from such property (unless taxpayer proves that the rent was the highest obtainable and the rental business was a bona fide business activity).*

Less:
   d. Federal income tax accrual (other than the PHC tax and the accumulated earnings tax).

   e. Excess charitable contributions beyond the 10% corporate limitation (with a maximum of the 20%, 30%, or 50% limitation imposed on individuals).**

   f. Excess of long-term capital gain over short-term capital loss (net of tax).

Equals: Adjusted taxable income.

Less: Dividends paid deduction.

Equals: Undistributed PHC income.

*§ 545(b).
**Reg. § 1.545–2.

Type of Dividend	Availability	Timing	Statutory Location	Effect on Shareholders
Current year	Both § 531 and § 541	By end of year.	§ 561(a)(1)	Reduction in ATI and UPHC income.
Two and one-half month grace period	Both § 531 and § 541	On or before the 15th day of the 3rd month after end of year.	§§ 563(a) and (b)	Reduction in ATI and UPHC income.
Consent dividend	Both § 531 and § 541	Not later than due date of the corporate tax return.	§ 565(a)	Treated as a dividend as of end of tax year and given back as a contribution to capital.
Dividend carryover	§ 541	Not later than due date of the corporate tax return.	§ 564	Reduction in UPHC income.
Deficiency dividend	§ 541	Within 90 days after determination of PHC tax deficiency.	§ 547	Treated as if dividend paid in offending year. No impact on interest and penalties.

FIGURE 6–2

Dividends Paid Deductions

---

57. Refer to Chapter 4 and *Henry Schwartz Corp.*, 60 T.C. 728 (1973).

━━━━━━━━━━━━━━━━ EXAMPLE 25 ━━━━━━━━━━━━━━━━

Three individuals are equal shareholders in a personal holding company. A property dividend is paid to the three shareholders in the following proportion: 25%, 35%, and 40%. This is not a pro rata distribution, and the dividends are not deductible from UPHC income. ◆

A two and one-half month grace period exists following the close of the tax year. Dividends paid during this period may be treated as paid during the tax year just closed. However, the amount allowed as a deduction from UPHC income cannot exceed either (1) the UPHC income for the tax year or (2) 20 percent of the total dividends distributed during the tax year.[58] Reasonable cause may not be used to overcome the 20 percent limitation even if the taxpayer relied upon incorrect advice given by an accountant.[59]

The consent dividend procedure[60] involves a hypothetical distribution of the corporate income taxed to the shareholders. Since the consent dividend is taxable, a dividends paid deduction is allowed. The shareholder's basis in his or her stock is increased by the consent dividend (a contribution to capital), and a subsequent actual distribution of the consent dividend might be taxed. The consent election is filed by the shareholders at any time not later than the due date of the corporate tax return. The consent dividend is considered distributed by the corporation on the last day of the tax year and is included in the gross income of the shareholder in the tax year in which or with which the tax year of the corporation ends. The disadvantage of this special election is that the shareholders must pay taxes on dividends they do not actually receive. However, if cash is not available for dividend distributions, the consent dividend route is a logical alternative.

━━━━━━━━━━━━━━━━ EXAMPLE 26 ━━━━━━━━━━━━━━━━

Q Corporation, a calendar year taxpayer solely owned by T, is a PHC. Dividends of $30,000 must be paid to avoid the PHC tax, but the company has a poor cash position. T elects the consent dividend treatment under § 565 and is taxed on $30,000 of dividends. The shareholder's basis in Q Corporation stock is increased by $30,000 as a result of this special election. Thus, the corporation does not incur the PHC tax, but T is taxed even though he receives no cash from the corporation with which to pay the tax. ◆

Even after a corporation has been classified as a PHC, a delayed dividend distribution made in a subsequent tax year can avoid the PHC penalty tax. This deficiency dividend provision[61] allows a dividend to be paid within 90 days after the determination of the PHC tax deficiency for a prior tax year. A determination occurs when a decision of a court is final, a closing agreement under § 7121 is signed, or a written agreement is signed between the taxpayer and a District Director. The dividend distribution *cannot be made* before the determination or after the running of the 90-day time period. Furthermore, the deficiency dividend procedure does not relieve the taxpayer of interest, additional amounts, or assessable penalties computed with respect to the PHC tax.

A dividend carryover from two prior years may be available to reduce the UPHC income. When the dividends paid by a company in its prior years exceed the company's UPHC income for those years, the excess may be deducted in the

---

58. §§ 563(b) and 543(a)(2)(B)(ii).

59. *Kenneth Farmer Darrow*, 64 T.C. 217 (1975).

60. Reg. § 1.565–1.

61. § 547.

current year. See § 564(b) for the computation of this dividend carryover and Figure 6–2 for a summary of dividends paid deductions.

Personal Holding Company Planning Model. Some of the complex PHC provisions may be developed into a flow chart format. Figures 6–3 and 6–4 provide a PHC planning model and the rules for the rent exclusion test.

Computations Illustrated. After the appropriate adjustments are made to corporate taxable income and the sum of the dividends paid is subtracted, the resulting figure is UPHC income. This is multiplied by the appropriate penalty tax rate to obtain the PHC tax. Although the tax revenue from the PHC tax is small, the consequences of this confiscatory tax can be severe. Taxpayers should monitor their corporations and take the necessary steps to avoid the tax.

FIGURE 6–3   **Personal Holding Company Planning Model**

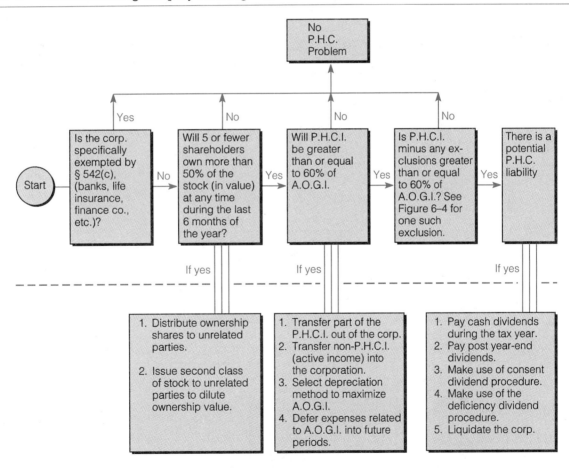

From "Understanding and Avoiding the Personal Holding Company Tax: A Tax Planning Model," by Pratt and Whittenburg, which appeared in the June 1975 issue of *Taxes — the Tax Magazine* published and copyrighted 1975 by Commerce Clearing House, Inc., and appears here with their permission.

——————————————— EXAMPLE 27 ———————————————

X Corporation had the following items of income and expense in the current year:

Dividend income (less than 20% owned)	$ 40,000
Rent income	150,000
Depreciation expense	40,000
Mortgage interest	30,000
Real estate taxes	30,000
Salaries	20,000
Dividends paid (three shareholders)	20,000
Corporate income tax liability (§ 11)	6,300

OGI is $190,000 ($40,000 + $150,000), and AOGI is $90,000 ($190,000 − $40,000 − $30,000 − $30,000). Taxable income is $42,000, computed as follows:

Rent income		$ 150,000
Dividend income		40,000
		$ 190,000
Less: Depreciation expense	$40,000	
Mortgage interest	30,000	
Real estate taxes	30,000	
Salaries	20,000	(120,000)
		$ 70,000
Less: Dividends received deduction ($40,000 × 70%)		(28,000)
Taxable income		$ 42,000

FIGURE 6–4   **Rent Exclusion Test**

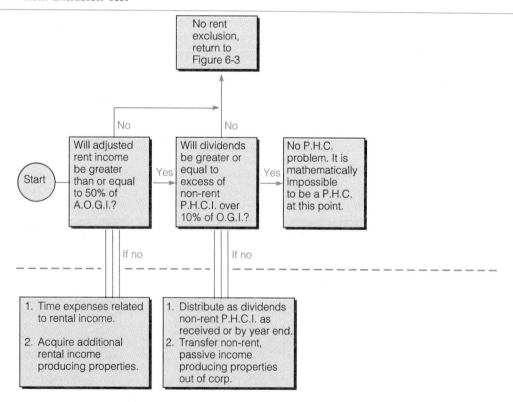

From "Understanding and Avoiding the Personal Holding Company Tax: A Tax Planning Model," by Pratt and Whittenburg, which appeared in the June 1975 issue of *Taxes — the Tax Magazine* published and copyrighted 1975 by Commerce Clearing House, Inc., and appears here with their permission.

The adjusted income from rents is $50,000 ($150,000 − $100,000). The corporation does meet the 50% rent income test, since $50,000 is greater than 50% of AOGI ($90,000 × 50% = $45,000). But the corporation did not pay at least $21,000 of dividends (nonrent PHC income $40,000 − $19,000 = $21,000). Therefore, the 10% rent income test is not met, and the rent income is classified as PHC income. Since all income is passive, X Corporation is a PHC. The PHC tax of $12,236 is calculated as follows:

Taxable income	$ 42,000
Plus: Dividends received deduction ($40,000 × 70%)	28,000
	$ 70,000
Less: § 11 tax	(6,300)
	$ 63,700
Less: Dividends paid	(20,000)
UPHC income	$ 43,700
	× .28
PHC tax liability	$ 12,236

◆

───────────────── EXAMPLE 28 ─────────────────

Assume in Example 27 that $22,000 of dividends are paid to the shareholders (instead of $20,000). In this case, the rent income is not PHC income because the 10% test is met ($22,000 is equal to or greater than the nonrent PHC income in excess of 10% of OGI). Thus, an increase of at least $2,000 in the dividends paid in Example 27 avoids the $12,236 PHC tax liability. ◆

A review of several important distinctions between the penalty tax on the unreasonable accumulation of earnings (§ 531) and the tax on personal holding companies (§ 541) sets the stage for the presentation of tax planning considerations applicable to these taxes.

COMPARISON OF §§ 531 AND 541

◆

- Unlike § 531, no element of intent is necessary for the imposition of the § 541 tax.[62] This makes § 541 a real trap for the unwary.
- The imposition of the § 541 tax is not affected by the past history of the corporation. Thus, it could be just as applicable to a newly formed corporation as to one that has been in existence for many years. This is not the case with the § 531 tax. Past accumulations have a direct bearing on the determination of the accumulated earnings credit. In this sense, younger corporations are less vulnerable to the § 531 tax since complete insulation generally is guaranteed until accumulations exceed $250,000.
- Although both taxes pose threats for closely held corporations, the stock ownership test of § 542(a)(2) makes this threat very explicit with regard to the § 541 tax. However, publicly held corporations can be subject to the § 531 tax if corporate policy is dominated by certain shareholders who are using the corporate form to avoid income taxes on dividends through the accumulation of corporate profits.[63]
- Sufficient dividend distributions can eliminate both taxes. In the case of § 531, however, such dividends must be distributed on a timely basis. Both taxes allow a two and one-half month grace period and provide for the

---

62. In light of the Supreme Court decision in *Donruss* (refer to Footnote 9 and the related text), what role, if any, will intent play in the future in helping taxpayers avoid the § 531 tax?

In this connection, see the dissenting opinion issued by Justice Harlan.

63. § 532(c).

consent dividend procedure.[64] Only the § 541 tax allows the deficiency dividend procedure.

■ Differences in reporting procedures arise because the § 541 tax is a self-assessed tax and the § 531 tax is not. For example, if a corporation is a personal holding company, it must file a Schedule PH along with its Form 1120 (the corporate income tax return) for the year involved. Failure to file the Schedule PH can result in the imposition of interest and penalties and also brings into play a special six-year statute of limitations for the assessment of the § 541 tax.[65] On the other hand, the § 531 tax is assessed by the IRS and consequently requires no reporting procedures on the part of the corporate taxpayer.

TAX PLANNING CONSIDERATIONS

Alternative Minimum Tax

Planning for the AMT is complicated by the fact that many of the procedures recommended run counter to what is done to reduce the regular corporate income tax. For example, depreciating most real estate over a period of 40 years avoids the AMT adjustment. In terms of minimizing the regular corporate tax liability, however, the preferable choice is the usual shorter period of 27.5 years.

Avoiding Preferences and Adjustments.

Investments in state and local bonds are attractive for income tax purposes because the interest is not included in gross income. Some of these bonds are issued to generate funds that are not used for an essential function of the government. The interest on such bonds is a tax preference item and could lead to the imposition of the AMT. When the AMT applies, investors should take this into account. Perhaps an investment in regular tax-exempt bonds or even fully taxed private-sector bonds might yield a higher after-tax rate of return.

For a corporation anticipating AMT problems, capitalizing rather than expensing certain costs can avoid generating preferences and adjustments. The decision should be based on the present discounted value of after-tax cash flows under the available alternatives. Costs that may be capitalized and amortized, rather than expensed, include circulation expenditures, mining exploration and development costs, and research and experimentation expenditures.

Controlling the Timing of Preferences and Adjustments.

In many situations, smaller corporations may be able to avoid the AMT by making use of the exemption. In order to do this, taxpayers should attempt to avoid bunching positive adjustments and tax preferences in any one year. When the expenditure is largely within the control of the taxpayer, timing to avoid bunching is more easily accomplished.

――――――――――――――――――――――――― EXAMPLE 29 ―――――――――――――――――――――――――

T Corporation, a calendar year accrual basis taxpayer, wants to contribute $15,000 to the Mission for the Homeless (a qualified charity). To carry out the donation, T Corporation will use marketable securities held as an investment for many years. The securities have a basis of $2,000 and a fair market value of $15,000. T Corporation, however, is in a dilemma. It does not know whether it will be subject to the AMT for

---

64. Under the § 531 tax, dividends paid within the first two and one-half months of the succeeding year *must* be carried back to the preceding year. In the case of the § 541 tax, the carryback is optional—some or all of the dividends can be

deducted in the year paid. The 20% limit on carrybacks applicable to § 541 [see § 563(a)] does not cover § 531 situations.

65. § 6501(f).

1992. Even worse, estimates are so close that some or all of the $13,000 tax preference from the charitable contribution could trigger the AMT. In late December of 1992, the board of directors of T Corporation authorizes the $15,000 contribution. ◆

What is accomplished in Example 29? T Corporation places itself in a position of maximum flexibility. By March 15, 1993, it should be able to assess more clearly how much, if any, of the charitable contribution generates an AMT for 1992. If none, then the full $15,000 can be paid on or before March 15, 1993, and deducted in 1992 (see Chapter 2). If some or all of the charitable contribution will cause an AMT result, this can be manipulated by deferring the payment until after March 15, 1993. Thus, the deduction and resulting tax preference amount are shifted to 1993.

Optimum Use of the AMT and Regular Corporate Income Tax Rate Difference. A corporation that cannot avoid the AMT in a particular year can often save taxes by taking advantage of the difference between the AMT and the regular tax rates. In general, a corporation that expects to be subject to the AMT should accelerate income and defer deductions for the remainder of the year. Since the difference between the regular tax and the AMT is 14 percent (34% − 20%), this strategy results in the income being taxed 14 percent less than it would be if reported in the next year. There is always the risk that the regular corporate rate may increase in future years.

If the same corporation expects to be subject to the AMT for the next year (or years), this technique must be reversed. The corporation should defer income and accelerate deductions. The strategy delays the date the corporation has to pay the tax.

EXAMPLE 30

X Corporation expects to be in the 34% tax bracket in 1993 but is subject to the AMT in 1992. In late 1992, X Corporation is contemplating selling a tract of unimproved land (basis of $20,000 and fair market value of $100,000). Under these circumstances, it is preferable to sell the land in 1992. The gain of $80,000 ($100,000 − $20,000) generates a tax of $16,000 [$80,000 (recognized gain) × 20% (AMT rate)]. However, if the land is sold in 1993, the resulting tax is $27,200 [$80,000 (recognized gain) × 34% (regular corporate income tax rate)]. A saving of $11,200 ($27,200 − $16,000) materializes by making the sale in 1992. ◆

EXAMPLE 31

Y Corporation is subject to the AMT in 1992 but expects to be limited to the regular tax in 1993. In late 1992, Y Corporation is considering donating $10,000 in cash to a special building fund of the Salvation Army (a qualified charitable organization). If the donation is made in 1992, Y will save only $2,000 [$10,000 (amount of the deduction) × 20% (AMT rate)]. Moreover, if the donation is postponed until 1993, the saving will be $3,400 [$10,000 (amount of the deduction) × 34% (regular corporate income tax rate)]. Thus $1,400 ($3,400 − $2,000) is saved by postponing the deduction until 1993. ◆

The Subchapter S Option. Corporations that make the S election will not be subject to the corporate AMT. As noted in Chapter 12, however, various AMT adjustments and preferences pass through to the individual shareholders. But one troublesome adjustment, the one involving the ACE adjustment, is eliminated since it does not apply to individual taxpayers. Furthermore, when converting to an S corporation, any unused minimum tax credit generated during a prior C corporation year may be used to offset any built-in gains tax paid.

Buy-Sell Agreements.   Corporate buy-sell agreements are usually structured either as a redemption where the corporation purchases its own stock or as cross purchases where the nonselling shareholders purchase the stock owned by the selling shareholder. Often these agreements are funded by insurance, and the proceeds of a life insurance policy owned by a corporation increases the ACE adjustment. The insurance proceeds will have an effective tax rate of 15 percent [75% (ACE percentage) × 20% (AMT rate)]. By using cross-purchase agreements, rather than redemption agreements, the tax on life insurance proceeds is avoided. If conversion of the redemption agreements is unwise, an S corporation election avoids the AMT on the insurance proceeds.

The § 531 Tax

The modification of capital gain rates has made most corporate distributions less attractive, and many companies prefer permanent rather than temporary deferral of accumulated earnings. Even with corporate rates higher than individual rates, a corporation can invest accumulated funds in tax-free securities or purchase high-yield corporate stocks to take advantage of the dividends received deductions. Thus, the threat of the accumulated earnings tax and the personal holding company tax continues to be a prime concern of many corporations.

Justifying the Accumulations.   The key defense against imposition of the § 531 tax is to show that the accumulations are necessary to meet the reasonable needs of the business. Several points should be kept in mind:

- To the extent possible, the justification for the accumulation should be documented. If, for example, the corporation plans to acquire additional physical facilities for use in its trade or business, the minutes of the board of directors' meetings should reflect the decision. Furthermore, such documentation should take place during the period of accumulation. This planning may require some foresight on the part of the taxpayer. Meaningful planning to avoid a tax problem should not be based on what happens after the issue has been raised by an agent as the result of an audit. In the case of a profitable closely held corporation that accumulates some or all of its profits, the parties should operate under the assumption that § 531 is always a potential issue. Recognition of a tax problem at an early stage is the first step in a satisfactory resolution.
- Multiple reasons for making an accumulation are not only permissible but invariably advisable. Suppose, for example, a manufacturing corporation plans to expand its plant. It would not be wise to stop with the cost of the expansion as the only justification for all accumulations. What about further justification based on the corporation's working capital requirements as determined under the *Bardahl* formula or some variation? Other reasons for making the accumulation may be present and should be recognized.
- The reasons for the accumulation should be sincere and, once established, pursued to the extent feasible.

──────────────── EXAMPLE 32 ────────────────

In 1988, the directors of W Corporation decide to accumulate $1,000,000 to fund the replacement of W's plant. Five years pass, and no steps are taken to begin construction. ◆

──────────────── EXAMPLE 33 ────────────────

In 1988, the directors of Y Corporation decide to accumulate $1,000,000 to fund the replacement of Y's plant. In the ensuing five-year period, the following steps are taken: a site selection committee is appointed (1988); a site is chosen (1989); the site (land) is purchased (1990); an architect is retained, and plans are drawn up for the new plant (1991); bids are requested and submitted for the construction of the new plant (1993). ◆

Compare Examples 32 and 33. Y Corporation is in a much better position to justify the accumulation. Even though the plant has not yet been replaced some five years after the accumulations began, the progress toward its ultimate construction speaks for itself. W Corporation may be hard pressed to prove the sincerity of its objective for the accumulations in light of its failure to follow through on the projected replacement.

▪ The amount of the accumulation should be realistic under the circumstances.

─────────────── EXAMPLE 34 ───────────────

W Corporation plans to replace certain machinery at an estimated cost of $500,000. The original machinery was purchased for $300,000 and, because $250,000 in depreciation was deducted for tax purposes, has a present book value of $50,000. How much of an accumulation can be justified for the replacement to avoid the § 531 tax? Initially, $500,000 seems to be the appropriate amount since this represents the estimated replacement cost of the machinery. But what about the $250,000 in depreciation that W Corporation already deducted? If it is counted again as part of a reasonable accumulation, a double tax benefit results. Only $250,000 [$50,000 (the unrecovered cost of the old machinery) + $200,000 (the additional outlay necessary)] can be justified as the amount for an accumulation.[66] ◆

─────────────── EXAMPLE 35 ───────────────

During the current year, a competitor files a $2,000,000 patent infringement suit against Z Corporation. Competent legal counsel advises Z Corporation that the suit is groundless. Under such conditions, the corporation can hardly justify accumulating $2,000,000 because of the pending lawsuit. ◆

▪ Since the § 531 tax is imposed on an annual basis, justification for accumulations may vary from year to year.[67]

─────────────── EXAMPLE 36 ───────────────

For calendar years 1991 and 1992, R Corporation was able to justify large accumulations due to a pending additional income tax assessment. In early 1993, the assessment is settled and paid. After the settlement, R Corporation can no longer consider the assessment as a reasonable anticipated need of the business. ◆

Danger of Loans to Shareholders. The presence of loans made by a corporation to its shareholders often raises the § 531 issue. If this same corporation has a poor dividend-paying record, it becomes particularly vulnerable. The avowed goal of the § 531 tax is to force certain corporations to distribute dividends. If a corporation can spare funds for loans to shareholders, it certainly has the capacity to pay dividends. Unfortunately, the presence of such loans can cause other tax problems for the parties.

---

66. *Battelstein Investment Co. v. U.S.*, 71–1 USTC ¶9227, 27 AFTR2d 71–713, 442 F.2d 87 (CA–5, 1971).

67. Compare *Hardin's Bakeries, Inc. v. Martin, Jr.*, 67–1 USTC ¶9253, 19 AFTR2d 647, 293 F.Supp. 1129 (D.Ct.Miss., 1967),

with *Hardin v. U.S.*, 70–2 USTC ¶9676, 26 AFTR2d 70–5852 (D.Ct. Miss., 1970), *aff'd., rev'd., rem'd.* by 72–1 USTC ¶9464, 29 AFTR2d 72–1446, 461 F.2d 865 (CA–5, 1972).

―――――――――――――――――――――――― Example 37 ――――――――――――――――――――――――

During the year in question, Q Corporation made advances of $120,000 to its sole shareholder, T. Although prosperous and maintaining substantial accumulations, Q Corporation has never paid a dividend. Under these circumstances, the IRS could move in either of two directions. The Service could assess the § 531 tax against Q Corporation for its unreasonable accumulation of earnings. Alternatively, the IRS could argue that the advances were not bona fide loans but, instead, taxable dividends.[68] The dual approach places the taxpayers in a difficult position. If, for example, they contend that the advance was a bona fide loan, T avoids dividend income but Q Corporation becomes vulnerable to the imposition of the § 531 tax.[69] On the other hand, a concession that the advance was not a loan hurts T but helps Q Corporation avoid the penalty tax. ◆

Role of Dividends.   The relationship between dividend distribution and the § 531 tax can be further clarified. First, can the payment of enough dividends completely avoid the § 531 tax? The answer must be *yes* due to the operation of § 535. This provision defines accumulated taxable income as *taxable income* (adjusted by certain items) *minus the sum of the dividends paid deduction and the accumulated earnings credit.* Since the § 531 tax is imposed on accumulated taxable income, no tax is due if the dividends paid and the accumulated earnings credit are large enough to offset taxable income. The payment of sufficient dividends, therefore, avoids the tax.[70] Second, can the payment of *some* dividends completely avoid the § 531 tax? As the question is worded, the answer must be *no*. Theoretically, even significant dividend distributions will not insulate a corporation from the tax.[71] From a practical standpoint, however, the payment of dividends indicates that the corporation is not being used exclusively to shield its shareholders from tax consequences. To the extent that this reflects the good faith of the parties and the lack of tax avoidance motivation, it is a factor the IRS considers with regard to the § 531 issue.

Role of the S Corporation Election.   An S corporation election circumvents the application of the § 531 tax.[72] However, the protection only covers the period of S corporation status and is not retroactive to years during which the entity was a regular corporation.

―――――――――――――――――――――――― Example 38 ――――――――――――――――――――――――

P Corporation, a calendar year taxpayer, makes a timely and proper election under Subchapter S effective for tax year 1993. Since its formation in 1980, P Corporation has accumulated significant earnings and has never paid a dividend. The election protects the corporation from the imposition of the § 531 tax for year 1993 and for any subsequent years it remains in effect. It does not, however, preclude the IRS from assessing the tax on P Corporation for those years open under the statute of limitations in which it qualified as a regular corporation. ◆

Avoiding the § 541 Tax

The classification of a corporation as a personal holding company requires the satisfaction of *both* the stock ownership and the gross income tests. Failure to meet either of these two tests avoids PHC status and the § 541 tax.

―――

68. Refer to the discussion of constructive dividends in Chapter 4.

69. *Ray v. U.S.*, 69–1 USTC ¶9334, 23 AFTR2d 69–1141, 409 F.2d 1322 (CA–6, 1969).

70. Such dividends must, however, be taxable to the shareholders. Nontaxable stock dividends issued under § 305(a) do not affect the dividends paid deduction.

71. In *Henry Van Hummell, Inc. v. Comm.*, 66–2 USTC ¶9610, 18 AFTR2d 5500, 364 F.2d 746 (CA–10, 1966), the § 531 tax was imposed even though the corporation paid out over 60% of its taxable income as dividends.

72. See Chapter 12.

- The stock ownership test can be handled through a dispersion of stock ownership. In this regard, however, watch the application of the stock attribution rules.
- Remember the following relationship when working with the gross income test:

$$\frac{\text{PHC income}}{\text{AOGI}} = 60\% \text{ or more}$$

Decreasing the numerator (PHC income) or increasing the denominator (AOGI) of the fraction reduces the resulting percentage. Keeping the percentage below 60 percent precludes classification as a personal holding company. To control PHC income, investments in low-yield growth securities are preferable to those that generate heavy interest or dividend income. Capital gains from the sale of such securities will not affect PHC status since they are not included in either the numerator or the denominator of the fraction. Investments in tax-exempt securities are attractive because the interest income, like capital gains, has no effect in applying the gross income test.

- Income from personal service contracts may, under certain conditions, be PHC income. Where a 25 percent or more owner of a PHC is specifically designated in a retainer agreement as the party to perform the services, the personal service contract income will be PHC income. See Example 24 earlier in the chapter.
- Rent income may or may not be PHC income. The relative amount of rent income is the key consideration. If

$$\frac{\text{Adjusted income from rents}}{\text{AOGI}} = 50\% \text{ or more}$$

and nonrent PHC income less 10 percent of OGI is distributed as a dividend, rent income is not PHC income. Maximizing adjusted income from rents clearly improves the situation for taxpayers. Since adjusted income from rents represents gross rents less attributable expenses, a conservative approach in determining such expenses is helpful. The taxpayer should minimize depreciation (e.g., choose straight-line over accelerated cost recovery method). This approach to the handling of expenses attributable to rental property is confusing to many taxpayers because it contradicts what is normally done to reduce income tax consequences.

- In some cases, it is possible to reduce PHC exposure by readjusting corporate structures.

──────────────────────── EXAMPLE 39 ────────────────────────

P Corporation carries on two principal activities: a rental business (approximately 49% of total gross receipts) and a finance operation (approximately 51% of total gross receipts). As currently constituted, P Corporation could well be classified as a personal holding company. (One cannot be sure without applying the stock ownership tests.) The gross income test is probably satisfied since interest income from the finance operation and rents from the rental business are PHC income.[73] The separation of these two activities into multiple corporations solves the problem.[74] The rents no

---

73. See, for example, *Hilldun Corp. v. Comm.*, 69–1 USTC ¶9319, 23 AFTR2d 69–1090, 408 F.2d 1117 (CA–2, 1969).

74. The separation could be carried out as a nontaxable reorganization. Refer to Chapter 7.

longer are PHC income due to the 50% or more of AOGI test. The finance operation is an excepted corporation to which the PHC tax does not apply.[75] ◆

In the same vein, business combinations (e.g., mergers and consolidations) or the filing of a consolidated return by an affiliated group of corporations can be used to dilute the PHC income of one corporation with the income from operations of another to avoid meeting the gross income test.

Corporations in the process of liquidation can be particularly susceptible to the PHC tax for two reasons. Operating income may be low because the corporation is in the process of winding up its business. If passive investment income remains at the level maintained during periods of normal operations or perhaps increases, the corporation might satisfy the gross income test.[76] In addition, the parties may never realize that the corporation was a PHC until it has been completely liquidated. At this point, the tax can no longer be neutralized through the issuance of a deficiency dividend.[77] The solution to the problem is to recognize the vulnerability of the corporation and keep it on the safe side of the gross income test. Good control can be obtained over the situation if the earlier corporate distributions in liquidation include those assets that generate PHC income.

PHC status need not carry tragic tax consequences if the parties are aware of the issue and take appropriate steps. Since the tax is imposed on UPHC income, properly timed dividend distributions neutralize the tax and avoid interest and penalties. Also, as long as a corporation holds PHC status, the § 531 tax cannot be imposed.

——————— EXAMPLE 40 ———————

X Corporation is owned entirely by two sisters, R and S (ages 86 and 88, respectively). X Corporation's major assets consist of investments in low-yield and high-growth securities, unimproved real estate, and tax-exempt bonds, all of which have a realizable value of $500,000. The basis of the stock in X Corporation to each sister is $50,000. ◆

The liquidation of X Corporation (a frequent solution to undesired PHC status) would be disastrous to the two sisters. As noted in the discussion of § 331 in Chapter 5, a liquidation results in the recognition of a capital gain of $400,000. In this case, therefore, it is preferable to live with PHC status. Considering the nature of the assets held by X Corporation, this may not be difficult to do. Keep in mind that the interest from the tax-exempt bonds is not PHC income. Should X Corporation wish to sell any of its investments, the long-term capital gain that results is not PHC income. The PHC tax on any other income (the dividends from the securities) can be controlled through enough dividend distributions to reduce UPHC income to zero. Furthermore, as long as X Corporation remains a PHC, it is insulated from the § 531 tax (the imposition of which would be highly probable in this case).

The liquidation of X Corporation should await the deaths of R and S and should be carried out by their estates or heirs. By virtue of the application of § 1014 (see Chapter 18), the income tax basis in the stock is stepped up to the fair market value of the stock on the date of death. Much, if not all, of the capital gain potential currently existing at the shareholder level is eliminated.

—————

75. Pursuant to § 542(c)(6), a lending or finance company is excepted under certain circumstances.

76. Investment or PHC income might increase if the corporation, pending complete dissolution, invested some or all of the

proceeds from the sale of its operating assets.

77. *Michael C. Callan*, 54 T.C. 1514 (1970), and *L. C. Bohart Plumbing & Heating Co., Inc.*, 64 T.C. 602 (1975).

PROBLEM MATERIALS

DISCUSSION QUESTIONS

1. Why did Congress enact the AMT?
2. For AMTI purposes, what is the difference between adjustments and tax preferences?
3. In arriving at AMTI, why are NOLs stated separately instead of being included with other adjustments?
4. How is the ACE adjustment calculated?
5. Does the AMT exemption favor smaller corporations over larger corporations? Why or why not?
6. What purpose is served by the AMT credit for prior year minimum tax?
7. Using the legend provided, classify the impact that each of the following items has upon taxable income or loss for purposes of determining AMTI:

Legend

I = increase in taxable income
D = decrease in taxable income
E = either an increase or a decrease in taxable income
N = no impact

a. Amortization claimed on certified pollution control facilities.
b. Adjusted current earnings (ACE) adjustment.
c. Excess mining exploration and development costs.
d. AMT net operating loss deduction.
e. Statutory exemption.
f. Accelerated depreciation on post-1986 property acquisitions.
g. Tax-exempt interest on private activity bonds.
h. LIFO inventory.
i. Excess percentage depletion.
j. Untaxed appreciation on charitable contribution.

8. Do situations arise when it would be advisable for a corporation to accelerate income into an AMT year? Explain.
9. Do situations arise where it would be advisable for a corporation to defer deductions from an AMT year to a non-AMT year (where only the regular corporate income tax applies)? Explain.
10. What corporations are statutorily excepted from the accumulated earnings tax?
11. List some valid business reasons for accumulating funds in a closely held corporation.
12. Explain the purpose(s) underlying the creation of the accumulated earnings penalty tax and the PHC tax.
13. A merger of two corporations could result in the imposition of the accumulated earnings tax on the surviving corporation. Is this possible? Explain.
14. Explain the *Bardahl* formula. How could it be improved?
15. Why might a corporation not wish to include Federal income taxes in the calculation of the *Bardahl* formula (the accounts payable turnover)?
16. How can human resource accounting be used in an accumulated earnings situation?
17. Can the IRS impose both the PHC tax and the accumulated earnings tax upon a construction company?
18. ATI = taxable income − certain adjustments + the dividends paid deduction − the accumulated earnings credit. Please comment.
19. In making the "certain adjustments" (refer to Question 18) necessary in arriving at ATI, which of the following items should be added (+), should be subtracted (−), or will have no effect (NE) on taxable income?

a. A nontaxable stock dividend distributed by the corporation to its shareholders.
b. Corporate income tax incurred and paid.
c. Charitable contributions paid in the amount of 10% of taxable income.
d. Deduction of a net operating loss carried over from a prior year.
e. The dividends received deduction.

20. If a corporation has an effective Federal income tax of 34% and also incurs an accumulated earnings tax of 28%, what is the aggregate tax rate?

21. Ms. J (a widow) and Mr. K (a bachelor) are both shareholders in H Corporation (closely held). If they elope during the year, what possible effect, if any, could it have on H Corporation's vulnerability to the PHC tax?

22. M Corporation is a consulting firm. Its entire outstanding stock is owned by three individuals. M Corporation enters into a contract with T Corporation to perform certain consulting services in consideration of which T is to pay M $35,000. The individual who is to perform the services is not designated by name or description in the contract, and no one but M has the right to designate such person. Does the $35,000 constitute PHC income?

23. Why is the designation of capital gain income still important for PHC purposes?

24. Which of the following income items could be PHC income?

a. Annuities.
b. Interest.
c. Rental income.
d. Sales of inventory.
e. Dividends.
f. Mineral royalties.
g. Copyright royalties.
h. Produced film rents.
i. Gain from sale of farmland.

25. D, a shareholder in H Corporation, dies, and under his will, the stock passes to his children. If H Corporation is a personal holding company, what effect, if any, will D's death have on the continuation of this status?

26. How are OGI and AOGI calculated?

27. The election to capitalize (rather than to depreciate) certain expenses to rental property could make a difference in determining whether or not the corporate lessor is a personal holding company. How could this be so?

28. If the 50% test as to rents is satisfied, the PHC tax cannot be imposed upon the corporation. Do you agree? Why or why not?

29. Ford Motor Corporation has no difficulty avoiding either the accumulated earnings tax or the PHC tax. Explain.

30. The payment of enough dividends can avoid either the accumulated earnings tax or the PHC tax. Explain.

31. Explain the deficiency dividend procedure for purposes of the accumulated earnings tax.

32. If a corporation has an effective Federal income tax of 34% and also incurs a PHC tax, what is the aggregate tax rate in 1992?

33. Relate the following points to the avoidance of the accumulated earnings tax:

a. Documentation of justification for the accumulation.
b. Multiple justifications for the accumulation.
c. Follow-up on the established justification for the accumulation.
d. Loans by the corporation to its shareholders.
e. The corporation's record of substantial dividend payments.
f. An S corporation election.
g. Human resource accounting.

34. Relate the following points to the avoidance of the PHC tax:

a. Sale of stock to outsiders.
b. An increase in AOGI.

   c. A decrease in PHC income.

   d. Long-term capital gains recognized by the corporation.

   e. Corporate investment in tax-exempt bonds.

   f. Income from personal service contracts.

   g. The choice of straight-line depreciation for rental property owned by the corporation.

   h. A merger of several corporations.

   i. The liquidation of a corporation.

35. Compare the accumulated earnings tax to the PHC tax on the basis of the following items:

   a. The element of intent.

   b. Applicability of the tax to a newly created corporation.

   c. Applicability of the tax to a publicly held corporation.

   d. The two and one-half month rule with respect to the dividends paid deduction.

   e. The availability of the deficiency dividend procedure.

   f. Procedures for reporting and paying the tax.

PROBLEMS

36. In each of the following independent situations, determine the tentative minimum tax:

	AMTI (before the exemption amount)
A Corp.	$140,000
B Corp.	160,000
C Corp.	330,000

37. For 1992, P Corporation (a calendar year taxpayer) had the following transactions:

Taxable income	$100,000
Accelerated depreciation on realty in excess of straight-line (placed in service in 1988)	150,000
Amortization of certified pollution control facilities	10,000
Tax-exempt interest on municipal bonds (funds were used for nongovernmental purposes)	30,000
Untaxed appreciation on property donated to charity	8,000
Percentage depletion in excess of the property's adjusted basis	70,000

   a. Determine P Corporation's AMTI for 1992.

   b. Determine the alternative minimum tax base (refer to Figure 6–1).

   c. Determine the tentative minimum tax.

   d. What is the amount of the AMT?

38. Q Corporation (a calendar year corporation) reports the following information for the years listed below:

	1991	1992	1993
Unadjusted AMTI	$3,000	$3,000	$6,000
Adjusted current earnings	5,000	3,000	2,000

Compute the ACE adjustment for each year.

39. Based upon the following facts, calculate accumulated current earnings (ACE):

Alternative minimum taxable income (AMTI)	$120,000
Municipal bond interest	62,000
Expenses related to municipal bonds	4,000
Key employee life insurance proceeds in excess of cash surrender value	200,000
Excess of FIFO over LIFO	14,000
Organization expense amortization	10,000
Cost of goods sold	822,000
Advertising expenses	76,000
ACE depreciation in excess of amount allowed for AMTI	28,000
Life insurance expense	17,000

40. Z Corporation, a calendar year taxpayer, has the following pre-adjusted alternative minimum taxable income (AMTI) and adjusted current earnings for 1991 through 1994:

	Pre-adjusted AMTI	ACE
1991	$80,000	$70,000
1992	60,000	90,000
1993	50,000	40,000
1994	50,000	10,000

Calculate Z's positive and negative adjustments, if any, for ACE.

41 Determine whether each of the following transactions is a preference (P), an adjustment (A), or not applicable (NA) for purposes of the corporate AMT:

a. Depletion in excess of basis.
b. Accelerated depreciation on property placed in service after 1986.
c. Mining exploration and development costs.
d. Adjusted current earnings.
e. Certain tax-exempt interest.
f. Untaxed appreciation on property donated to charity.
g. Dividends received deduction.

42. A calendar year consulting corporation has accumulated earnings and profits of $80,000 on January 1, 1992. For the calendar year 1992, the corporation has taxable income of $100,000. This corporation has no reasonable needs that justify an accumulation of its earnings and profits. Calculate the amount vulnerable to the accumulated earnings penalty tax.

43. A nonservice corporation has accumulated earnings and profits of $225,000 as of December 31, 1991. The company has earnings of $100,000 for the taxable year 1992 and has a dividends paid deduction of $30,000 (paid during the last half of the tax year). The corporation determines that the earnings for the tax year that may be retained for the reasonable needs of the business are $65,000 over the $250,000 minimum credit, and that it is entitled to a $6,000 deduction for net capital gain (after adjustment for attributable tax and prior capital losses). Calculate the accumulated earnings credit for the tax year ending December 31, 1992.

44. In 1992, P Corporation, a manufacturing company, retained $60,000 for its reasonable business needs. The company had a long-term capital gain of $20,000 and a net short-term capital loss of $15,000, with a resulting capital gain tax of $1,250. The accumulated earnings and profits at the end of 1991 was $260,000. On January 25, 1992, a taxable dividend of $90,000 was paid. Calculate the accumulated earnings credit for 1992.

45. A retail corporation had accumulated earnings and profits on January 1, 1992, of $250,000. Its taxable income for the year 1992 was $75,000. The corporation paid no dividends during the year. There were no other adjustments to determine accumulated taxable income. Assume that a court determined that the corporation is subject to the accumulated earnings tax and that the reasonable needs of the business required earnings and profits in the total amount of $266,500. Determine the accumulated earnings tax and explain your calculations.

46. A construction corporation is accumulating a significant amount of earnings and profits. Although the corporation is closely held, it is not a personal holding company. The following facts relate to the tax year 1992:

- Taxable income, $450,000.
- Federal income tax, $153,000.
- Dividend income from a qualified domestic corporation (less than 20% owned), $40,000.
- Dividends paid in 1992, $70,000.
- Consent dividends, $35,000.
- Dividends paid on 2/1/93, $5,000.
- Accumulated earnings credit, $10,000.
- Excess charitable contributions of $9,000 (the portion in excess of the amount allowed as a deduction in computing the corporate income tax).
- Net capital loss adjustment, $4,000.

Compute the accumulated earnings tax, if any.

47. The following facts relate to a closely held legal services corporation's 1992 tax year:

Net taxable income	$400,000
Federal income taxes	136,000
Excess charitable contributions	20,000
Capital loss adjustment	20,000
Dividends received (less than 20% owned)	140,000
Dividends paid	40,000
Accumulated earnings, 1/1/92	130,000

   a. Assume that this is not a personal holding company. Calculate any accumulated earnings tax.
   b. Can the deficiency dividend procedure be applicable to the accumulated earnings tax?

48. Which of the following purposes can be used by a corporation to justify accumulations to meet the reasonable needs of the business?

   a. X Corporation creates a reserve for a depression that might occur in 1995.
   b. P Corporation has an extraordinarily high working capital need.
   c. Q Corporation, a manufacturing company, invests in several oil and gas drilling funds.
   d. N, a hotel, is being sued because of a structural accident that injured 32 people.
   e. M Corporation is considering establishing a sinking fund to retire some bonds.
   f. Z Corporation carries six key employee life insurance policies.
   g. T Corporation makes loans to R Corporation, an unrelated party that is having financial problems and is a key customer.
   h. B Corporation agrees to retire 20% of its outstanding stock without curtailing its business.

49. A wholly owned motor freight corporation has permitted its earnings to accumulate. The company has no inventory but wishes to use the *Bardahl* formula to determine the amount of operating capital required for a business cycle. The following facts are relevant:

Yearly revenues	$3,300,000
Average accounts receivable	300,000
Yearly expenses	3,500,000
Average accounts payable	213,000

   a. Determine the turnover rate of average accounts receivable.
   b. Determine the number of days in the accounts receivable cycle.
   c. Determine the expenses for one accounts receivable cycle.
   d. Determine the number of days in the accounts payable cycle.
   e. Determine the operating capital needed for one business cycle.

f. Explain why the time allowed a taxpayer for the payment of accounts payable should be taken into consideration in applying the *Bardahl* formula.

50. Indicate in each of the following independent situations whether or not the corporation involved has any accumulated taxable income and, if so, the amount (assume the corporation is not a mere holding or investment company):

	F Corporation	G Corporation
Taxable income	$150,000	$500,000
Accrued Federal income taxes	41,750	170,000
Capital loss adjustment	1,000	
Net LTCG		42,000
Tax on LTCG		14,280
Contributions in excess of 10%	10,000	
NOL deduction	24,000	
70% dividends received deduction		35,000
Dividends paid deduction	4,000	8,000
Accumulated earnings credit	80,000	100,000

51. March is the longest operating cycle for U Corporation, which has reasonable business needs of $40,000 in addition to the working capital required for one operating cycle. Certain additional information is provided as follows:

Accounts receivable—March	$ 120,000
Inventory—March	160,000
Accounts payable—March	101,000
Cost of goods sold	1,000,000
Other expenses (less depreciation)	100,000
Depreciation	90,000
Sales	2,000,000
Dividends paid	7,000
Accumulated earnings (beginning)	180,000
Accrued Federal income taxes	220,000

Determine the operating cycle needs of U Corporation without considering accrued Federal income taxes as an operating expense.

52. N Corporation is having accumulated earnings problems but has no accounts receivable. C, the corporate controller, provides you with the following information:

Year-end balances:		
Current assets		
Cash	$ 25,000	
Inventory (average)	72,000	
	$ 97,000	
Current liabilities	17,000	
Working capital available	$ 80,000	
Income statement:		
Gross sales		$330,000
Less: Sales returns and allowances		30,000
		$300,000
Less: Cost of goods sold	$170,000	
Sales and administrative expenses	50,000	
Depreciation	15,000	
Income taxes	9,000	244,000
Net income		$ 56,000

Calculate the working capital *required* for the corporation if purchases total $120,000.

53. Determine whether the following factors or events will increase (+), decrease (–), or have no effect (NE) on the working capital needs of a corporation when calculating the *Bardahl* formula:

    a. Decrease in depreciation deduction.
    b. Use of peak inventory figure rather than average inventory.
    c. An increase in the annual cost of goods sold.
    d. Purchase of a tract of land for a future parking lot.
    e. Use of average receivables rather than peak receivables.
    f. An increase in annual net sales.
    g. An increase in accounts payable.
    h. An increase in the annual expenses.
    i. Gain on the sale of treasury stock.

54. The stock of P Corporation is owned as follows:

S Corporation (wholly owned by K)	100 shares
K's wife	100 shares
K's partner	100 shares
K's wife's sister	100 shares
A	50 shares
B	30 shares
C	20 shares
Unrelated individuals with 10 or fewer shares	500 shares
Total	1,000 shares

Do five or fewer individuals own more than 50% of P Corporation?

55. N Corporation, at some time during the last half of the taxable year, had 1,800 shares of outstanding stock, 450 of which were held by various individuals having no relationship to one another and none of whom were partners. The remaining 1,350 shares were held by 51 shareholders as follows:

Relationship	Shares		Shares		Shares		Shares		Shares	
An individual	A	100	B	20	C	20	D	20	E	20
His father	AF	10	BF	10	CF	10	DF	10	EF	10
His wife	AW	10	BW	40	CW	40	DW	40	EW	40
His brother	AB	10	BB	10	CB	10	DB	10	EB	10
His son	AS	10	BS	40	CS	40	DS	40	ES	40
His daughter by former marriage (son's half-sister) ..	ASHS	10	BSHS	40	CSHS	40	DSHS	40	ESHS	40
His brother's wife ...	ABW	10	BBW	10	CBW	10	DBW	160	EBW	10
His wife's father	AWF	10	BWF	10	CWF	110	DWF	10	EWF	10
His wife's brother ...	AWB	10	BWB	10	CWB	10	DWB	10	EWB	10
His wife's brother's wife	AWBW	10	BWBW	10	CWBW	10	DWBW	10	EWBW	110
His partner	AP	10	—	—	—	—	—	—	—	—

Is the stock ownership test of § 544 met for determining whether this corporation is a personal holding company?

56. A corporation has gross income of $20,000, which consists of $11,000 of rent income and $9,000 of dividend income. The corporation has $3,000 of rent income adjustments and pays $8,000 of dividends to its nine shareholders.

    a. Calculate adjusted income from rents.
    b. Calculate AOGI.
    c. Is the so-called 50% test met? Show calculations.

d. Is the 10% rent income test met? Show calculations.

e. Is the corporation a personal holding company?

57. Assume one change in the situation in Problem 56. Rent income adjustments are decreased from $3,000 to $2,000. Answer the same questions as in Problem 56.

58. X Corporation has $20,000 of interest income, $40,000 of gross income from rents, and $20,000 of personal service income (not PHC income). Expenses in the amount of $20,000 relate directly to the rent income. Assume there are eight shareholders and the 10% test is met. Is this corporation a PHC? Explain.

59. P Corporation has dividend income of $10,000, rent income of $60,000, and income from an operating business (not PHC income) of $40,000. Expenses in the amount of $14,000 relate directly to the rent income. Assume there are six shareholders and the 10% test is met. Is this corporation a PHC? Explain.

60. C Corporation has gross income of $165,000, which consists of gross income from rent of $100,000, $40,000 from the sale of merchandise, interest of $15,000, and income from annuities of $10,000. Deductions directly related to the rent income total $28,000.

a. Calculate OGI.

b. Calculate AOGI.

c. Calculate adjusted income from rent.

d. Does the rent income constitute PHC income? Explain.

e. Is this corporation a PHC (assuming there are seven shareholders)?

61. Assume the same facts as in Problem 60 except that $9,000 of dividends are paid to the shareholders. Answer the same questions as in Problem 60.

62. T is the sole owner of a corporation. The following information is relevant to the corporation's tax year just ended:

Capital gain	$ 20,000
Dividend income	30,000
Rent income	130,000
Rent expenses	40,000
Section 162 business expenses	15,000
Dividends paid	12,000

a. Calculate OGI.

b. Calculate AOGI.

c. Calculate adjusted income from rents.

d. Calculate nonrent PHC income.

e. Does this corporation meet the 50% rent income test? Explain.

f. Does this corporation meet the 10% rent income test? Explain.

g. Is this company a PHC?

h. Would your answers change if $15,000 of dividends are paid?

63. X Corporation has the following financial data for the tax year 1992:

Rent income	$430,000
Dividend income	2,900
Interest income	50,000
Operating income	9,000
Depreciation (rental warehouses)	100,000
Mortgage interest	125,000
Real estate taxes	35,000
Officers' salaries	85,000
Dividends paid	2,000

a. Calculate OGI.

b. Calculate AOGI.

   c. Does X Corporation's adjusted income from rents meet the 50% or more of AOGI test?
   d. Does X Corporation meet the 10% dividend test?
   e. How much in dividends could X Corporation pay within the two and one-half month grace period during 1993?
   f. If the 1992 corporate income tax return has not been filed, what would you suggest for X Corporation?

64. Using the legend provided, classify each of the following statements accordingly:

Legend

A = relates only to the tax on unreasonable accumulation of earnings (the § 531 tax)
P = relates only to the personal holding company tax (the § 541 tax)
B = relates to both the § 531 tax and the § 541 tax
N = relates to neither the § 531 tax nor the § 541 tax

   a. The tax is applied to taxable income after adjustments are made.
   b. The tax is a self-assessed tax.
   c. An accumulation of funds for reasonable business purposes will help avoid the tax.
   d. A consent dividend mechanism can be used to avoid the tax.
   e. If the stock of the corporation is equally held by 10 unrelated individuals, the tax cannot be imposed.
   f. Any charitable deduction in excess of the 10% limitation is allowed as a deduction before the tax is imposed.
   g. Gains from the sale or disposition of capital assets are not subject to the tax.
   h. A sufficient amount of rent income will cause the tax not to be imposed.
   i. A life insurance company would not be subject to the tax.
   j. A corporation with only dividend income would avoid the tax.

65. The PHC tax is computed on an amount called undistributed personal holding company (UPHC) income. To arrive at UPHC income, certain adjustments are made to taxable income. Determine whether the following independent items are positive (+), negative (–), or no adjustment (NA):

   a. Federal income taxes on the accrual basis.
   b. Tax-free interest from municipal bonds.
   c. Charitable deductions in excess of 10%.
   d. Net capital gain minus any taxes.
   e. Dividends paid during the taxable year.
   f. Dividends received deduction.
   g. NOL carryforward from three tax years ago.
   h. Consent dividends under § 565.

66. Indicate in each of the following independent situations whether or not the corporation involved is a PHC (assume the stock ownership test is met):

	A Corporation	B Corporation	C Corporation	D Corporation
Sales of merchandise	$ 8,000	$ –0–	$ –0–	$ 2,500
Capital gains	–0–	–0–	–0–	1,000
Dividend income	15,000	5,000	1,000	2,500
Gross rent income	10,000	5,000	9,000	15,000
Expenses related to rents	8,000	2,500	8,000	10,000
Dividends paid	–0–	–0–	–0–	500
Personal holding company? (Circle Y for yes or N for no.)	Y N	Y N	Y N	Y N

67. Indicate in each of the following independent situations whether or not the corporation involved is a PHC (assume the stock ownership test is met):

	E Corporation	F Corporation	G Corporation	H Corporation
Sales of merchandise	$ -0-	$3,000	$ -0-	$ -0-
Capital gains	-0-	-0-	1,000	-0-
Interest income	20,000	4,800	2,000	60,000
Gross rent income	80,000	1,200	20,000	50,000
Expenses related to rents	60,000	1,000	10,000	-0-
Dividends paid	12,000	-0-	-0-	20,000
Personal holding company? (Circle Y for yes or N for no.)	Y N	Y N	Y N	Y N

68. Calculate in each of the following independent situations the PHC tax liability in 1992:

	P Corporation	Q Corporation
Taxable income	$140,000	$580,000
Dividends received deduction	37,000	70,000
Contributions in excess of 10%	3,000	10,000
Federal income taxes	37,850	197,200
Net capital gain	70,000	40,000
Capital gain tax	25,350	13,600
NOL under § 172		12,000
Current year dividends	12,000	120,000
Consent dividends		20,000
Two and one-half month dividends	4,000	

RESEARCH PROBLEMS

RESEARCH PROBLEM 1 In 1993, X Corporation lost a Tax Court decision upholding the following deficiencies in income tax and accumulated earnings tax:

Year	Deficiency in Income Tax	Accumulated Earnings Tax
1981	$360,000	$ -0-
1982	200,000	450,000
1983	201,000	600,000

May X Corporation deduct the deficiency in income taxes for 1982 and 1983 from accumulated taxable income in order to determine the accumulated earnings tax in 1982 and 1983?

RESEARCH PROBLEM 2 Dr. B owns 90% of the stock of Dental Services, Inc. Dr. B performs medical services under an employment contract with the corporation. He is the only dentist employed and is the only officer of the corporation actively engaged in the production of income. Dental Services, Inc., furnishes office space and equipment and employs a dental hygienist and a receptionist to assist Dr. B.

   a. Various patients receive dental care from Dr. B. Does Dental Services have PHC income under § 543(a)(7)?
   b. Suppose Patient J secures an absolute binding promise from Dr. B that the dentist will personally perform a root canal operation and that the dentist has no right to substitute another dentist. Would your answer change?

RESEARCH PROBLEM 3   X owns 100% of both A and B Corporations. A Corporation's accumulated earnings for 1989, 1990, 1991, and 1992 were reflected almost entirely in liquid assets, which were used to obtain bonding on the construction work of the sister corporation, B. A Corporation itself undertook no construction work as a general contractor and paid no dividends during the three-year period. Both corporations entered into an indemnity agreement under which both would be liable to the bonding company for any loss suffered by the bonding company from the issuance of a bond to either of the corporations. A Corporation was merged into B Corporation in early January 1991. Assume that A Corporation would be subject to the accumulated earnings tax if the reasonable business needs of B Corporation are not considered. Would A Corporation be subject to the accumulated earnings tax in 1989, 1990, 1991, and 1992?

RESEARCH PROBLEM 4   X Corporation derived most of its income from contracts involving the personal services of its sole shareholder, B. In October 1992, B discovered that his trusted accountant, H, had embezzled almost $300,000 from the corporation during the calendar years ending in 1989, 1990, and 1991. H wrote the checks, prepared the books, and made the financial statements. The accountant also neglected to file corporate tax returns for the same years. X Corporation claimed theft losses on its tax returns for 1989, 1990, and 1991. The IRS disallowed them since embezzlement losses are properly deducted in the year of discovery.

Happily, the theft losses were claimed in 1992 and carried back to 1989, 1990, and 1991, thereby eliminating most of the corporate tax liability. But the corporation was a PHC during the years 1989, 1990, and 1991. B discovered that the PHC did not have a loss carryback (just a one-year carryforward). The disallowed theft loss deduction resulted in undistributed PHC income. B also discovered that § 545 does not provide for a §165(e) loss deduction in arriving at undistributed PHC income. Discuss B's dilemma.

RESEARCH PROBLEM 5   During early 1992, P Corporation's controller discovers that the corporation is a personal holding company for 1991. He decides to use the deficiency dividend procedure under § 547 for avoiding the PHC tax. The company is short of cash. Can a consent dividend qualify for deficiency dividend treatment? Should the controller make a full disclosure of the liability for the PHC tax on the 1991 corporate tax return by filing a Schedule PH?

RESEARCH PROBLEM 6   A, Inc., has six shareholders, and most of its income is from a grant of a trademark by A, Inc., to Pac Company. The contract grant can be summarized as follows:

a. The grant of the trademark by A, Inc., to Pac was exclusive, worldwide, and forever as long as Pac made the required production payments.

b. At such time as Pac had made production payments to A of $1,000,000, A was required to transfer legal title to the trademark to Pac (as distinguished from a mere option in Pac to acquire the title).

c. A had no right to terminate the agreement except upon the failure of Pac to make the required periodic payments. Furthermore, after the transfer of title to the trademark from A to Pac, the termination rights no longer applied even if Pac failed to make the required continuing payments.

d. Although Pac was not permitted to dispose of the portion of the business using the trademark "MYCLO" separately from a sale of Pac's entire business without A's prior approval, "said approval shall not be unreasonably withheld."

e. A retained the right to inspect the business operations of Pac to ensure continuing quality control.

f. A agreed that it would not use the trademark any further or engage in any business involving the products covered by the trademark that was conveyed to Pac.

If most of A, Inc., income is from the trademark, would A be subject to the PHC tax?

RESEARCH PROBLEM 7   V and S are equal shareholders of P Corporation. In 1992, the corporation received gross rent of $5,000 from a 30-unit apartment building it owned. The company incurred depreciation, interest, and property tax expenses in the amount of $900 that were attributable to the building. The company also received $500 rent from a duplex it leased to V and S. The company incurred depreciation, interest, and property tax expenditures in the amount of $200 (attributable to the duplex). The company also had $3,000 gross income from a bookstore it owned and operated, and the company received dividend income of $1,000 from R Corporation. Discuss.

CHAPTER

CORPORATIONS: REORGANIZATIONS

OBJECTIVES

Explain the utility for tax purposes of a corporate reorganization.

Summarize the general tax consequences of a corporate reorganization.

Describe in depth the statutory requirements for the different types of reorganizations.

Discuss the various administrative and judicial criteria for the different types of reorganizations.

Review the rules applicable to the carryover of corporate attributes.

Familiarize the reader with certain planning procedures available to insulate corporate reorganizations from adverse income tax consequences.

OUTLINE

Corporations are often involved in restructurings ranging from complicated mergers and acquisitions to recapitalizations and corporate divisions. The small, closely held corporation, as well as the corporate giant, can find itself a party to a corporate combination or corporate division. The mergers and acquisitions of the past were generally beneficial, resulting in substantial economic growth for the corporations involved.

In the past few years, the dramatic surge in takeover activity has been marked by intense battles for corporate control. Many mergers are the result of a friendly agreement between the two companies. However, some recent mergers have been unwelcome acquisitions triggered by so-called corporate raiders seeking to profit from hostile tender offers. A whole new vocabulary has emerged from the attempted hostile takeovers and the defensive measures adopted by merger candidates. Terms such as "greenmail," "golden parachute," "tin parachute," "poison pill," "white knight," "junk bond," and "Pac-Man" have special meanings in corporate finance. These terms are defined later in the chapter.

An example of a corporate-control transaction was the attempted takeover of Revlon by Pantry Pride. As a defensive measure, the board of directors of Revlon adopted a "poison pill" note plan. Under the plan, all shareholders of Revlon, except the person whose 20 percent stock accumulation caused the attempted takeover, were granted purchase rights to Revlon stock. In addition, a friendly bid was made by a "white knight," Forstmann Little. Certain Revlon financial data were then made available to Forstmann Little but not to Pantry Pride. In another example, the board of directors of Unocal Corporation adopted a defensive self-tender offer to counter Mesa Petroleum Company's hostile bid. Some corporations have given key executives "golden parachute" contracts, under which the executives will receive large benefits if they are terminated without sufficient cause after a merger. When Federated Department Stores of Cincinnati was taken over by Campeau, senior executives of Federated reportedly received in excess of $12 million.

Taxes play an important role in corporate restructurings. The type of compensation a target corporation's shareholders receive is dictated by tax provisions. For example, merger transactions and corporate divisions that are accomplished through the use of stock or securities as consideration are generally wholly or partly tax-free. If the acquired company's shareholders receive cash or other property, their gains are taxed at the time of the transaction. Most corporate acquisitions are structured so that they are tax-free and involve only stock-for-stock or assets-for-stock exchanges.

Courts originally concluded that even minor changes in the form of a corporation's structure would produce taxable gain to the shareholders involved.[1] Congress, however, soon determined that businesses should be permitted to proceed with necessary adjustments without being subject to taxation.[2] The theory for nonrecognition of gain on a corporate acquisition or a corporate division is similar to the theory underlying other nonrecognition transactions. Examples of other nonrecognition provisions include the like-kind exchange under § 1031 and the involuntary conversion of property under § 1033. Section 351 adopts the theory by providing for nonrecognition of gain upon the transfer of property to a controlled corporation. Sections 361 and 368 adopt the theory by providing for nonrecognition of gain in certain corporate restructures or "reorganizations." The Regulations state the underlying assumption behind the nonrecognition of gain or loss:

---

1. *U.S. v. Phellis*, 1 USTC ¶54, 3 AFTR 3123, 42 S.Ct. 63 (USSC, 1921).

2. Reg. § 1.368–1(b). See S.Rept. No. 275, 67th Cong., 1st Sess. (1921), at 1939–1 C.B. 181.

. . . the new property is substantially a continuation of the old investment still unliquidated; and, in the case of reorganizations, . . . the new enterprise, the new corporate structure, and the new property are substantially continuations of the old still unliquidated.[3]

Although the term *reorganization* is commonly associated with a corporation in financial difficulty, for tax purposes the term refers to a corporate adjustment or combination that is tax-free under § 368. To qualify as a tax-free reorganization, a corporate restructuring transaction must not only meet the specific requirements of § 368 but also must meet several general requirements. These are set out in the Regulations or are judicially imposed. For example, a tax-free reorganization must meet the *continuity of interest* and *continuity of business enterprise* tests set out in the Regulations. It must meet the judicial condition that it have a *sound business purpose,* and it can be denied tax-free status because of the court-imposed *step transaction* doctrine. There must be a *plan of reorganization,* and tax-free status is only available to *parties to the reorganization.* All of these concepts are discussed later in the chapter. The initial and most important consideration is whether the transaction qualifies for nonrecognition status under § 368.

Summary of the Different Types of Reorganizations

Section 368(a) of the Code specifies seven corporate restructures or *reorganizations* that will qualify as nontaxable exchanges. The planner of a nontaxable business combination must determine in advance that the proposed transaction falls specifically within one of these seven types. If the transaction fails to qualify, it will not be granted special tax treatment. In certain situations, the parties should obtain a letter ruling from the IRS that the proposed combination qualifies as a tax-free reorganization under § 368.

Section 368(a)(1) states that the term *reorganization* means the following:

A. A statutory merger or consolidation.
B. The acquisition by one corporation, in exchange solely for all or a part of its voting stock, of stock of another corporation. The exchange also can be solely for all or part of the voting stock of a corporation that is in control of the acquiring corporation. Immediately after the acquisition, the acquiring corporation must have control of the other corporation.
C. The acquisition by one corporation, in exchange solely for all or a part of its voting stock, of substantially all of the properties of another corporation. The exchange also can be solely for all or part of the voting stock of a corporation that is in control of the acquiring corporation. In determining whether the exchange is solely for stock, the assumption by the acquiring corporation of a liability of the other is disregarded. Likewise, the fact that the property acquired is subject to a liability is disregarded.
D. A transfer by a corporation of all or a part of its assets to another corporation if, immediately after the transfer, the transferor or one or more of the shareholders, or any combination thereof, is in control of the corporation to which the assets are transferred. "One or more of the shareholders" includes persons who were shareholders immediately

---

3. Reg. § 1.1011–2(c).

before the transfer. Pursuant to the plan, stock or securities of the corporation to which the assets are transferred must be distributed in a transaction that qualifies under § 354, § 355, or § 356.

E. A recapitalization.

F. A mere change in identity, form, or place of organization.

G. A transfer by a corporation of all or a part of its assets to another corporation in a bankruptcy or receivership proceeding. Pursuant to the plan, stock and securities of the transferee corporation must be distributed in a transaction that qualifies under § 354, § 355, or § 356.

These seven types of tax-free reorganizations are designated by their identifying letters: "Type A," "Type B," "Type C," and so on. Basically, excepting the recapitalization (E), the change in form (F), and the insolvent corporation (G) provisions, a tax-free reorganization is (1) a statutory merger or consolidation, (2) an exchange of stock for voting stock, (3) an exchange of assets for voting stock, or (4) a divisive reorganization (the so-called spin-off, split-off, or split-up).

Glossary of Terms

Familiarity with the corporate finance vocabulary can be helpful in understanding the reorganization provisions. The following terms often appear when corporate restructuring is discussed.

Acquiring Corporation.   The transferee corporation; the corporation that receives the assets of another corporation in a corporate acquisition or combination.

Asset Purchase.   In an asset purchase, the acquiring corporation buys only the assets (some or all) of the acquired corporation but does not assume all of the acquired corporation's liabilities. An asset purchase differs from a merger and from a stock purchase.

Exclusive Merger Agreement.   An agreement that prevents the corporations involved from negotiating or accepting competing offers pending submission of a merger agreement for shareholder approval.

Golden Parachutes.   Executive employment contracts that provide substantial postemployment compensation for corporate executives who lose their positions without sufficient cause after a merger.

Goodwill.   An intangible asset that represents the premium paid for the assets of an acquired corporation. It is the excess of the amount paid for the assets over their fair market value.

Greenmail.   The practice of purchasing a large block of stock while at the same time threatening a proxy battle or tender offer that will force the target corporation to buy back the stock at a premium. The term also refers to the payments made by the target corporation to purchase or redeem one shareholder's stock on terms that are not offered to all shareholders.

Junk Bonds.   High-yield securities used by parties initiating a tender offer. The bonds are speculative and are secured by the target company's assets. Repayment is usually dependent upon the cash flow of the target business. Often the acquiror contemplates the sale of the target company's assets. Lending institutions make loans or purchase these debt securities because of the high interest rates and high commitment fees that are promised.

Leveraged Buy-Out. A method of buying a corporation or a division of a corporation in which the buyer borrows most of the purchase price using the purchased assets as collateral for the loan. Often the buyers are managers of the divisions that are being sold.

Merger. A combination of two or more corporations into one surviving corporation. The surviving corporation acquires the assets and the liabilities of the merged corporations as a matter of law.

Other Property. Consideration other than stock or securities in a corporate combination or division. To the extent of "other property," the shareholders of the corporations involved have taxable gain.

Pac-Man. A defense to an unsolicited takeover bid in which the target corporation makes a counter tender offer for the stock of the raider corporation. The target corporation attempts to gain control of the raider before the raider gains control of the target. This is the "I'll eat you before you eat me" defense.

Poison Pill. A defensive weapon against a hostile takeover attempt. The target passes a resolution stating that common shareholders will be issued a pro rata dividend of stock or rights to acquire stock of the target if a raider obtains a certain percentage of the target's common stock. By diluting the target's stock, a poison pill makes a hostile acquisition too expensive for the raider. Under a poison pill plan, the target usually has the right to redeem the rights for a nominal price until the raider has acquired a specified amount of securities. Some plans permit redemption of the stock within a certain period after the acquisition.

Raider. A person or corporation that seeks to gain control of another corporation in an unwelcome acquisition.

Securities. Bonds and long-term notes. Short-term notes with a maturity date of 5 years or less are not securities. Notes with a maturity date between 5 and 10 years may or may not qualify as securities.

Self-Tender. A defensive measure to ward off a hostile takeover bid. The target corporation purchases its own shares for cash or debt securities at a price in excess of the raider's bid.

Shark Repellants. Different provisions employed by potential target corporations as defensive measures to discourage takeover bids. A corporation's charter or bylaws are amended to provide for staggered terms for members of the board of directors, supermajority provisions, cumulative voting, and fair price provisions.

Standstill Agreement. An agreement that limits the percentage of shares a particular shareholder may hold. The agreement generally prohibits a shareholder from making a tender offer for the corporation's stock during the term of the agreement. It may provide for a right of first refusal to the corporation to restrict the shareholder's ability to transfer his or her shares.

Target. The transferor corporation; the corporation that transfers business assets in a merger or acquisition.

Target Shareholders. Shareholders of the acquired or transferor corporation who receive stock in the acquiring, or transferee, corporation in a merger or acquisition.

Tender Offer. An offer made by an acquiring corporation to obtain stock of a target corporation in an unfriendly acquisition. The acquiring corporation agrees to pay a stated price above the then-existing market price for any of the target's shareholders' stock that is "tendered" to it before a particular date.

Tin Parachute. A management defensive measure to discourage a hostile takeover. The target company's executives negotiate contracts with the company's salaried employees under which the employees will receive severance pay, health and life insurance benefits, and outplacement services if they lose their jobs as a result of a proxy fight or a takeover.

White Knight. An acquiring company that is more friendly to the target. Often the target looks for a company to enter into a bidding war with the unfriendly acquiring company. The target generally grants an option to the friendly company, permitting it to purchase key assets or a large block of newly issued stock. This prevents the unfriendly corporation from acquiring a sufficient amount of the target's stock.

Summary of Tax Consequences in a Tax-Free Reorganization

Gain or Loss. In a corporate restructuring that qualifies as a tax-free reorganization, the acquiring corporation does not recognize gain or loss unless it transfers appreciated property along with its stock and securities to the target corporation.[4] No gain or loss is recognized to the target corporation on the exchange of property pursuant to a tax-free reorganization unless the target (1) fails to distribute *other property* received in the exchange or (2) distributes appreciated property to its shareholders.[5]

Generally, the security holders of the various corporations involved in a tax-free reorganization do not recognize gain or loss on the exchange of their stock and securities except when they receive cash or other consideration in addition to stock and securities.[6] As far as securities are concerned, gain is not recognized only if securities are surrendered in the same principal amount (or a greater principal amount) as the principal amount of the securities received.

If the security holders receive additional consideration, they recognize gain but not more than the sum of money and the fair market value of other property received. If a shareholder does not surrender any stock, the additional consideration will generally be treated as a dividend to the extent of the shareholder's share of the corporation's earnings and profits.[7] If the distribution is characterized as a dividend, any recognized gain is dividend income to the extent of the shareholder's share of earnings and profits. The remainder is treated as an exchange of property.

Basis. Property received by the acquiring corporation from the target corporation retains the basis it had in the hands of the target, increased by the amount of gain

---

4. § 1032.

5. §§ 361(a) and (b).

6. § 356(a).

7. § 356. Compare *Shimberg v. U.S.*, 78–2 USTC ¶9607, 42 AFTR2d 78–5575, 577 F.2d 283 (CA–5, 1978), with *Comm. v. Clark*, 89–1 USTC ¶9230, 63 AFTR2d 89–860, 109 S.Ct. 1455 (USSC, 1989). In *Comm. v. Clark*, the Supreme Court ruled that the question of whether the payment of boot in a shareholder exchange pursuant to a tax-free reorganization has the effect of a dividend distribution is answered by examining the effect of the exchange as a whole. Boot can be characterized as capital gain if the requirements of § 302 are met. In applying § 302, the Supreme Court held that stock ownership reduction is determined by reference to ownership in the acquiring corporation.

recognized to the target on the transfer.[8] The tax basis of stock and securities received by a shareholder pursuant to a tax-free reorganization will be the same as the basis of those surrendered. This will be decreased by the amount of boot received and increased by the amount of gain and dividend income, if any, recognized on the transaction.[9] Because of the substituted basis, the unrecognized gain or loss will be recognized when the new stock or securities are disposed of in a taxable transaction.

The basis rules are summarized in Figures 7–1 and 7–2. Examples 1 through 3 illustrate how the gain or loss and basis rules operate in actual practice.

--------------------------- EXAMPLE 1 ---------------------------

A, an individual, exchanges stock he owns in Target Corporation for stock in Acquiring Corporation plus $2,000 cash. The exchange is pursuant to a tax-free reorganization of both corporations. A paid $10,000 for the stock in Target two years ago. The stock in Acquiring has a fair market value of $12,000. A has a realized gain of $4,000 ($12,000 + $2,000 − $10,000), which is recognized to the extent of the boot received, $2,000. Assume the distribution has the effect of a dividend. If A's share of earnings and profits in Target is $1,000, that amount would be a taxable dividend. The remaining $1,000 would be treated as a gain from the exchange of property. A's basis in the Acquiring stock would be $10,000 [$10,000 (basis in stock surrendered) − $2,000 (boot received) + $2,000 (gain and dividend income recognized)]. ◆

--------------------------- EXAMPLE 2 ---------------------------

Assume A's basis in the Target stock was $15,000. A would have a realized loss of $1,000 on the exchange, none of which would be recognized. His basis in the Acquiring stock would be $13,000 [$15,000 (basis in stock surrendered) – $2,000 (boot received)]. ◆

--------------------------- EXAMPLE 3 ---------------------------

Target Corporation transfers assets with a fair market value of $800,000 and a basis of $100,000 to Acquiring Corporation for stock in Acquiring Corporation worth $800,000 in a qualifying ''D'' reorganization. Neither Target nor Acquiring Corporation would have a gain on the exchange. Target's basis in the Acquiring stock would be $100,000, and Acquiring's basis in the Target assets would be $100,000. (The stock in Acquiring Corporation will be distributed to Target's shareholders, who will have a substituted basis in the Acquiring stock.) If Acquiring Corporation transfers stock worth $700,000 and equipment worth $100,000 with a basis of $50,000, Acquiring will recognize a gain of $50,000 on the transfer. If Target fails to distribute the equipment, Target will have gain to the lesser of the gain realized or $100,000. If Target distributes the equipment, its shareholders and not Target will be taxed on the recognized gain occasioned by the receipt of the equipment. ◆

Target's basis in property transferred	$xx,xxx	**FIGURE 7–1**
Plus: Gain recognized to Target on the transaction	x,xxx	**Basis to Acquiring Corporation**
Equals: Basis of property to Acquiring Corporation	$xx,xxx	**of Property Received**

Basis of stock and securities transferred	$xx,xxx	**FIGURE 7–2**
Plus: Gain and dividend income recognized	x,xxx	**Basis to Target Shareholders of**
Minus: Money and fair market value of other property received	(x,xxx)	**Stock and Securities Received**
Equals: Basis of stock and securities received	$xx,xxx	

8. § 362(b).

9. § 358.

Type A

Although the terms are not analogous, "Type A" reorganizations include both mergers and consolidations. A *merger* has been defined as the union of two or more corporations in which one of the corporations retains its corporate existence and absorbs the other or others. The other corporations lose their corporate existence by operation of law. A *consolidation* occurs when a new corporation is created to take the place of two or more corporations.

EXAMPLE 4

Acquiring Corporation acquires all the properties of Target Corporation in exchange for 5,000 shares of stock in Acquiring Corporation. The Acquiring stock is distributed to Target's shareholders in complete liquidation of Target Corporation. This transaction qualifies as an "A" reorganization (assuming the requirements of state law are met). It is a statutory merger. ◆

EXAMPLE 5

Alpha and Beta Corporations are consolidated under state law into a new corporation, Zeta Corporation. Zeta stock is distributed to the shareholders of Alpha and Beta in complete liquidation of each. This is an "A" reorganization, a consolidation. ◆

The "Type A" reorganization is illustrated in Figure 7–3.

Advantages and Disadvantages.   The "A" reorganization allows more flexibility than the other types of reorganizations. Unlike both the "B" and "C" reorganizations, the consideration need not be voting stock. Further, the "A" reorganization allows money or property to change hands without disqualifying the business combination as a tax-free reorganization. The money or property will constitute boot, and some gain may be recognized. However, the receipt of this boot will not destroy the tax-free treatment of stock received as consideration.

If consideration other than stock is to be used, be careful not to run afoul of the *continuity of interest* test. This test, promulgated by the courts, requires that at least 50 percent of the consideration used in a reorganization be stock.

FIGURE 7–3

"A" Reorganization

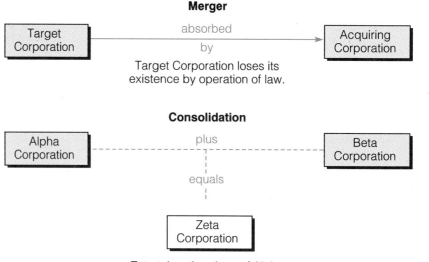

Merger

Target Corporation → *absorbed by* → Acquiring Corporation

Target Corporation loses its existence by operation of law.

Consolidation

Alpha Corporation --- *plus* --- Beta Corporation

equals

Zeta Corporation

Zeta takes the place of Alpha and Beta Corporations, which lose their corporate existence by operation of law.

Definite disadvantages should be considered before an "A" reorganization is carried out. Because the "A" reorganization is statutory, compliance with applicable state law is necessary to perfect the acquisition. In almost all states, shareholders of all corporations participating in a merger or consolidation have the right to dissent and have their shares appraised and bought. Meeting the demands of objecting shareholders can become so cumbersome that the parties may be forced to abandon the "A" reorganization. Because a majority of the shareholders of all corporations involved must approve the transaction, all of the problems inherent in shareholder meetings are present. These problems are magnified if the stock of either of the corporations is widely held.

Another disadvantage of the "A" reorganization is that the acquiring corporation is required to assume *all* liabilities of the target corporation. The surviving corporation assumes the liabilities of the target corporation as a matter of law. The legal procedure required to transfer assets and liabilities is not complex when a merger or consolidation occurs. Nevertheless, the fact that all liabilities (including unknown and contingent liabilities) pass to the transferee corporation is a distinct disadvantage.

The Use of a Subsidiary in a "Type A" Reorganization. Many of the problems of compliance with state law in the "Type A" reorganization can be reduced if a subsidiary becomes the acquiring corporation. When a subsidiary acquires the assets of another corporation and gives its own voting stock as consideration, most problems regarding the validity of the stock transfer are solved. However, the parent corporation may want the shareholders of the target corporation to hold the parent's stock rather than the stock of the subsidiary. This enables the parent to retain control over the subsidiary. The parent does not want to be the acquiring corporation because it does not want to assume the liabilities of the target corporation. If the subsidiary becomes the acquiring corporation, it will assume the liabilities of the target corporation. As a result, the assets of the parent will be protected.

A major problem of the "A" reorganization is the need to secure the approval of a majority of the shareholders of the acquiring corporation. Because the parent corporation is the majority shareholder, this problem is lessened.[10] Only the approval of the board of directors of the parent corporation need be obtained. Also eliminated is the possibility that the parent's shareholders might exercise their right to dissent. For these reasons, the use of a subsidiary corporation to effect the "A" reorganization offers advantages.

The exchange of a parent's stock by a subsidiary in a statutory merger qualifies the reorganization as a tax-free "A" reorganization if (1) no subsidiary stock is used and (2) the exchange would have been an "A" reorganization had the merger been into the parent.[11]

Under § 368(a)(2)(E), a so-called *reverse merger* is permitted. To qualify as a tax-free reorganization under this provision, the surviving corporation must hold, in addition to its own properties, substantially all of the properties of the merged corporation. The former shareholders of the surviving corporation must receive voting stock of the controlling corporation in exchange for control (80 percent) of the surviving corporation.

The following examples demonstrate the use of a subsidiary in an "A" reorganization.

---

10. The approval of a majority of the shareholders of the target corporation is still required.

11. § 368(a)(2)(D).

─────────────── EXAMPLE 6 ───────────────

Acquiring Corporation is a subsidiary of Parent Corporation. It also holds some stock in Parent. Acquiring transfers the Parent stock it owns to the shareholders of Target Corporation for substantially all the assets of Target. Target is liquidated. This is an "A" reorganization using parent company stock. If Parent Corporation is the only shareholder of Acquiring, the merger can be effected by securing approval of Parent's board of directors. Because the vote of Parent's shareholders is not required, considerable time and expense are avoided. Further, Parent's assets are protected from Target Corporation's creditors. ◆

─────────────── EXAMPLE 7 ───────────────

In a reverse merger, Target Corporation, rather than Acquiring Corporation, would survive. Further, the stock in Parent Corporation must be voting stock only. The shareholders of Target must surrender their stock representing 80% control of Target to Parent for its voting stock. Acquiring Corporation would transfer all its assets to Target and be liquidated. Target Corporation then becomes the subsidiary of Parent Corporation. ◆

The use of a subsidiary in an "A" reorganization and a reverse merger are illustrated in Figure 7–4.

A disadvantage of the reverse merger is the requirement that voting stock of the parent corporation be used and that at least 80 percent of the stock of the target corporation be obtained. These requirements severely limit the flexibility present in the regular "A" reorganization. Indeed, the provision corresponds more closely to a "Type B" reorganization than to a "Type A."

FIGURE 7–4

Use of a Subsidiary in an "A" Reorganization

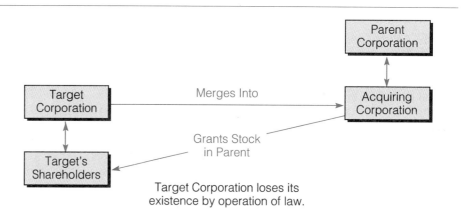

Target Corporation loses its existence by operation of law.

Reverse Merger

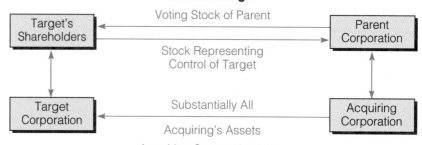

Acquiring Corporation loses its existence by operation of law. Target becomes the subsidiary of Parent.

Before attempting an "A" reorganization by using a subsidiary or the reverse merger provisions, state law must be checked. Because the "A" reorganization is a statutory merger, state law requirements must be met.

Type B

In a "Type B" reorganization, a corporation acquires the stock of another corporation solely in exchange for its voting stock. Immediately after the acquisition, the acquiring corporation must be in control of the target corporation. This is, in simple terms, a transaction in the form of an exchange of stock for voting stock. Voting stock must be the sole consideration, and the requirement is strictly construed.

─────────────── EXAMPLE 8 ───────────────

Acquiring Corporation exchanges 20% of its voting stock for stock representing 80% of all classes of stock in Target Corporation. The exchange qualifies as a "B" reorganization. Acquiring becomes the parent of Target. It should be noted that this type of reorganization precludes the use of boot. Consequently, gain is never recognized in a "B" reorganization. ◆

─────────────── EXAMPLE 9 ───────────────

If, in the previous example, Acquiring Corporation exchanges nonvoting preferred stock or bonds in addition to voting stock, the transaction does not qualify as a "B" reorganization. ◆

The "Type B" reorganization is illustrated in Figure 7–5.

The Eighty Percent Control Requirement. Stock may be acquired from the shareholders or directly from the corporation. If A Corporation has 100 shares outstanding, for example, B Corporation must acquire, in exchange for its voting stock, at least 80 of those shares. Alternatively, B could acquire 400 newly issued shares directly from A Corporation. It would then own 400 shares of 500 outstanding shares, an 80 percent ownership.

For control, the parent, or acquiring corporation, must have at least 80 percent of the total combined voting power of all classes of stock entitled to vote. Also, it must acquire at least 80 percent of the total number of shares of all other classes of stock of the corporation. The requirement does not mean that the acquiring corporation must actually "acquire" 80 percent of the target corporation. Rather, after the acquisition, it must have an 80 percent ownership. A previous cash purchase can be counted in determining the 80 percent ownership if the purchase was a separate transaction. It must not be part of the plan to gain control of the target corporation. The acquisition of stock of another corporation by the acquiring corporation solely for its voting

FIGURE 7–5
"B" Reorganization

Acquiring Corporation becomes the parent and Target Corporation, the subsidiary.

stock can be tax-free even though the acquiring corporation already owns stock of the other corporation.[12]

─────────────── EXAMPLE 10 ───────────────

Acquiring Corporation purchased 30% of Target for cash six years ago. It acquires another 50% in the current year through the issuance of voting stock. It seems unlikely that the acquisition of Target's stock for cash six years ago was part of the plan to gain control of Target in the current year. Thus, even though some of the shares of Target were acquired with cash, the requirements of a "B" reorganization are still satisfied. ◆

─────────────── EXAMPLE 11 ───────────────

What if Acquiring Corporation purchased 30% of Target's stock for cash three months ago? Now the acquisition of the additional 50% of Target's stock for voting stock seems to be part of a continuing effort to gain control of Target. The acquisition of the remaining stock for voting stock will probably not be tax-free. ◆

The Use of a Subsidiary in a "Type B" Reorganization. In the "Type B" as in the "Type A" reorganization, voting stock of the acquiring corporation's parent may be used. The following example demonstrates the use of a subsidiary in a "B" reorganization.

─────────────── EXAMPLE 12 ───────────────

P Corporation is the parent of Acquiring Corporation. Acquiring Corporation also owns some stock in P. It exchanges stock (voting stock only) in P for control of the stock in Target Corporation. This qualifies as a "B" reorganization. Target will become the subsidiary of Acquiring Corporation. ◆

The use of a parent's stock by a subsidiary in a "Type B" reorganization is illustrated in Figure 7–6.

The "Solely for Voting Stock" Requirement. The "B" reorganization is limited in that the *sole* consideration must be voting stock. Voting stock plus some other consideration does not meet the statutory requirement.[13] This limitation on consideration is a great disadvantage of the "B" reorganization.

Absent the voting stock problem, the stock for voting stock acquisition has the advantage of simplicity. Generally, the shareholders of the target corporation act

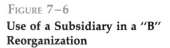

FIGURE 7–6

Use of a Subsidiary in a "B" Reorganization

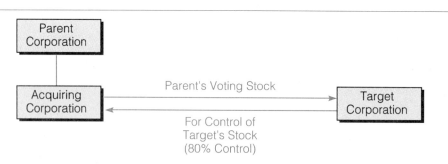

Target Corporation becomes the subsidiary of Acquiring Corporation.

─────────────────────

12. Reg. § 1.368–2(c).

13. *Helvering v. Southwest Consolidated Corporation*, 41–1 USTC

¶9402, 27 AFTR 160, 119 F.2d 561 (CA–5, 1941), *rev'd.* in 42–1 USTC ¶9248, 28 AFTR 573, 62 S.Ct. 546 (USSC, 1942).

individually in transferring their stock, so the affairs of the corporation itself are not directly involved. Consequently, no formal action is required of the shareholders of the target corporation. Similarly, no formal action is required of the shareholders of the acquiring corporation. This assumes there are sufficient treasury or unissued shares to effect the transaction without any formal shareholder action to increase authorized shares.[14] Thus, much of the shareholder problem present in the "A" reorganization is eliminated.

There can be disadvantages to a "B" reorganization. Assuming the acquiring corporation does not obtain 100 percent control of the target corporation, problems may arise with respect to the minority interest remaining in the target.

"Type A" and "Type B" Reorganizations Compared. A "Type A" reorganization is an assets-for-stock exchange. A "Type B" reorganization is a stock-for-stock exchange. In a "Type A" reorganization, the target corporation is liquidated; in a "Type B" reorganization, the target corporation becomes the subsidiary of the acquiring corporation.

―――――――――――――― EXAMPLE 13 ――――――――――――――

Target has assets with an adjusted basis of $400,000 and liabilities of $100,000. Its common stock consists of 2,000 shares with a par value of $100 per share. It has no other classes of stock and has E & P of $100,000. Target's assets are worth $500,000. Acquiring Corporation acquires the assets of Target in a tax-free "A" reorganization. Acquiring will have a basis of $400,000 in Target's assets. [Property received from a target corporation has a carryover basis to the acquiring corporation. Basis in the hands of the target corporation carries over to the acquiring corporation. See § 362(b).] ◆

―――――――――――――― EXAMPLE 14 ――――――――――――――

If Acquiring Corporation in Example 13 acquires Target by exchanging with Target's shareholders 30% of its voting stock (worth $320,000) for 1,600 shares of Target stock, the reorganization qualifies as a "B" reorganization. Target becomes the subsidiary of Acquiring. Acquiring's basis in the Target stock is the basis Target's shareholders had in the stock. Again § 362(b) applies. However, Target's shareholders will have a substituted basis in the Acquiring stock (their basis in the Acquiring stock will be the basis they had in the Target stock). (Basis for the shareholders of Target is determined under § 358, which provides for a substituted basis rather than a carryover basis as under § 362.) ◆

Type C

In the "Type C" reorganization, the acquiring corporation acquires substantially all of the assets of the target corporation solely in exchange for voting stock. It is basically an exchange of assets for voting stock.

A transaction will not qualify as a "C" reorganization unless the target corporation distributes to its shareholders the stock, securities, and other properties it receives in the reorganization as well as any of its own properties.[15]

―――――――――――――― EXAMPLE 15 ――――――――――――――

Acquiring Corporation transfers voting stock representing a 30% interest in the corporation to Target Corporation for substantially all of the assets of Target. After the

---

14. Though shareholders in the "B" reorganization normally do not act through the corporation, this is subject to legal or other restrictions on transfers of shares.

15. § 368(a)(1)(G).

exchange, Target's only assets are the voting stock in Acquiring Corporation. This exchange qualifies as a "C" reorganization if Target distributes the voting stock to its shareholders. ◆

The "Type C" reorganization is illustrated in Figure 7–7.

"Type A" and "Type C" Reorganizations Compared. The "Type C" reorganization has almost the same consequences as the "Type A," but the rule with respect to consideration is more exacting for the "Type C." However, the "C" reorganization is preferable to the "A" in many circumstances. In the "C" reorganization, unlike the "A," the acquiring corporation assumes only the liabilities it chooses to assume. It is normally not liable for unknown or contingent liabilities. Further, in some states, only the approval of the shareholders in the target corporation is required in the "C" reorganization. This considerably diminishes the magnitude of the problem involved in the "A" reorganization. Generally, only the shareholders of the target corporation enjoy dissenters' rights in a "C" reorganization. These rights must be recognized in both the target and the acquiring corporation in a statutory merger or consolidation.

The "C" reorganization can also be carried out by the use of a subsidiary, as demonstrated in the following examples.

EXAMPLE 16

Parent Corporation is in control of Acquiring Corporation. Acquiring also owns some stock in Parent. It transfers the Parent stock (voting stock) to Target Corporation for substantially all of the assets of Target. Target is then liquidated. The transaction qualifies as a "C" reorganization. ◆

EXAMPLE 17

The acquiring corporation could be the parent corporation even though the subsidiary ultimately acquires the assets of Target Corporation. Parent Corporation could acquire the assets of Target for its voting stock and then transfer the assets to its subsidiary. ◆

Figure 7–8 illustrates how a subsidiary corporation can use its parent's stock in carrying out a "Type C" reorganization.

Consideration in the "Type C" Reorganization. Consideration in the "C" reorganization normally consists of voting stock, as in the "B" reorganization. However, there are exceptions to this rule. Section 368(a)(2)(B) provides that cash and other property do not disrupt the tax-free status of the reorganization if at least 80 percent of the fair market value of all the property of the target corporation is obtained by the use of voting stock. An assumption of the liabilities of the target corporation is disregarded in determining whether the transaction is solely for voting stock.[16]

FIGURE 7–7
"C" Reorganization

Acquiring Corporation becomes the
parent and Target Corporation, the subsidiary.
Target Corporation must distribute all its assets to its shareholders.

---

16. § 368(a)(1)(C).

The "C" reorganization has a slight degree of freedom in reference to consideration, while the "B" does not. But in making the statutory computation that *other property* does not exceed 20 percent of the fair market value of the property transferred, a restriction is imposed. Liabilities assumed by the acquiring corporation are treated as *other property* if the corporation receives other consideration. Liabilities assumed by the acquiring corporation normally exceed 20 percent of the fair market value of the assets acquired. Thus, the provision relaxing the requirement of *solely* for voting stock is limited in application. The following examples illustrate the problem.

─────────────── EXAMPLE 18 ───────────────

Target Corporation transfers assets with a fair market value of $200,000 to Acquiring Corporation for voting stock valued at $160,000 and cash of $40,000. No liabilities are assumed. Target distributes the cash and stock to its shareholders, and liquidates. The transaction qualifies as a "C" reorganization since *other property* received is exactly 20% of $200,000. ◆

─────────────── EXAMPLE 19 ───────────────

Assume in Example 18 that Target transferred assets for stock valued at $140,000, cash of $40,000, and the assumption of $20,000 of its liabilities by Acquiring. Liabilities would be counted as *other property* since Target also received cash. *Other property* amounts to $60,000, which exceeds 20% of the fair market value of Target Corporation's assets. The transaction does not qualify as a "C" reorganization. ◆

─────────────── EXAMPLE 20 ───────────────

Assume Acquiring Corporation gives Target Corporation voting stock worth $120,000 and assumes $80,000 of Target Corporation's liabilities. The transaction qualifies as a "C" reorganization. Liabilities assumed by the acquiring corporation are disregarded as no additional consideration (other than stock) is used. ◆

Asset Transfers. The "C" reorganization requires that substantially all of the assets of the target corporation be transferred. Numerous problems arise in determining whether the *substantially all* requirement has been met. There is no statutory definition of "substantially all." To obtain a favorable ruling from the IRS, assets representing at least 90 percent of the fair market value of the net assets and at least 70 percent of the fair market value of the gross assets held by the target corporation must be transferred.[17] Smaller percentages than this rule

FIGURE 7–8

Use of a Subsidiary in a "C" Reorganization

After the reorganization, Target Corporation's only asset would be Acquiring's voting stock. Acquiring's stock must be distributed to Target's shareholders.

─────────────

17. Rev.Rul. 77–37, 1977–2 C.B. 568, amplified by Rev.Proc. 86–42, 1986–2 C.B. 722.

of thumb adopted by the IRS may still qualify. However, the parties will have to rely on case law to obtain a favorable decision.[18]

The results of a statutory merger and an asset acquisition are almost identical if the target corporation is liquidated in a "C" reorganization. In both situations, the acquiring corporation receives the assets of the target. As all the properties of the target corporation must be distributed, the target corporation generally is liquidated in a "C" reorganization. The shareholders of the target will receive stock in the acquiring corporation. The methods used to achieve these almost identical results as well as the legal consequences of the two are quite different. These differences make the choice of the preferable form of acquisition important.

Type D

The first three types of tax-free corporate reorganizations are designed for corporate combinations. The "D" reorganization is different in that it is generally a mechanism for corporate division. However, the "D" reorganization can also be a corporate combination.

There are two types of "D" reorganizations. In the acquisitive "D" reorganization, an acquiring corporation transfers all or substantially all of its assets to a target corporation in exchange for control of the target. In the divisive "D" reorganization, an acquiring corporation transfers part of its assets for controlling stock of the target. The controlling stock of the target is distributed to the shareholders of the acquiring corporation. Thus, in a "D" reorganization, the target corporation transfers a controlling interest in its stock rather than transferring its assets. The acquiring corporation transfers assets in a "D" reorganization.

Acquisitive "D" Reorganization.   Section 354 applies to a "D" reorganization that is a corporate combination. The Section requires that substantially all the property of one corporation be transferred to the second corporation for control (50 percent) of the second corporation. All stock and other property received by the transferor corporation must be distributed to the transferor's shareholders. If any assets remain in the transferor corporation, the requirements of § 354 are not met. This transaction can also meet the requirements of a "C" reorganization. If a transaction can be both a "C" and a "D" reorganization, § 368(a)(2)(A) provides that it be treated as a "D" reorganization.

–––––––––––––––––––––––––– EXAMPLE 21 ––––––––––––––––––––––––––

Acquiring Corporation wishes to acquire Target Corporation, but Target Corporation holds a nontransferable license. Thus, Target must be the surviving corporation. Acquiring transfers all its assets to Target for 80% of the stock of Target Corporation. Acquiring Corporation then distributes all the Target stock to its shareholders and is liquidated. The transaction qualifies as a "D" reorganization. ◆

–––––––––––––––––––––––––– EXAMPLE 22 ––––––––––––––––––––––––––

Parent Corporation transfers all its assets to a newly formed subsidiary corporation. The subsidiary stock is then distributed to Parent's shareholders, and Parent is liquidated. The transaction qualifies as a "D" reorganization. It is equivalent to an "F" reorganization. In essence, it is a new corporate shell around an old body. ◆

––––––––––––––––––

18. See, for example, *National Bank of Commerce of Norfolk v. U.S.,*   Va., 1958).
58–1 USTC ¶9278, 1 AFTR2d 894, 158 F.Supp. 887 (D.Ct.

Divisive "D" Reorganization. The more typical "D" reorganization involves a corporation division. Shareholders of a corporation may wish to divide corporate assets and split up the business of a corporation for many reasons. Antitrust problems may arise. The shareholders may have differences of opinion. Family planning may enter the picture.

A corporate division can be accomplished in several ways. The old corporation can be liquidated and the assets distributed to the various shareholders. Those wishing to continue the business in corporate form can then establish a new corporation. Assets can be transferred to a controlled corporation tax-free under § 351. However, there are problems upon liquidation of the old corporation. Shareholders will normally recognize gain upon the liquidation, and § 336 will generate tax at the corporate level. Consequently, this route may not be the best. A stock redemption under § 302, either a substantially disproportionate distribution or a qualified partial liquidation, is another possibility. However, gain will normally be recognized both at the shareholder level and at the corporate level.

The better alternative is to effect a split-up under § 368(a)(1)(D) and distribute stock and securities in the new corporation pursuant to § 355. Utilizing the "D" reorganization, the shareholders of a corporation can divide the corporation tax-free.

Section 355, discussed in Chapter 5, provides for a tax-free distribution by a parent corporation of stock in its subsidiary. That Section is utilized in conjunction with § 368 to provide for a tax-free corporate division. A corporation can transfer part of its assets to a newly formed subsidiary followed by a tax-free distribution of the stock in the subsidiary to its shareholders.

EXAMPLE 23

A and B, individuals, are the sole shareholders of Manufacturing Corporation. Manufacturing was organized 10 years ago and has been actively engaged in development, manufacturing, and sales of two products, widgets and bolts. Considerable friction has developed between A and B, who wish to divide the business. A wants the assets used for the manufacture of widgets, and B wants to continue the manufacture of bolts. A new corporation, Developer, is formed. All the assets relating to the manufacture of widgets are transferred to Developer. All the stock in Developer is distributed to A in exchange for all of A's stock in Manufacturing. After the reorganization, B will own all the stock in Manufacturing, and A will own all the stock in Developer. By virtue of § 355, neither gain nor loss will be recognized to either A or B upon the exchange of A's stock in Manufacturing for all the stock in Developer. Gain or loss is not recognized to Manufacturing under § 361. Developer receives the assets of Manufacturing tax-free under § 1032 (a corporation does not recognize gain or loss on the receipt of money or property in exchange for its stock). ◆

Spin-Offs, Split-Offs, and Split-Ups. To qualify as a tax-free reorganization, the transferor corporation must obtain stock representing control (80 percent) in the transferee corporation. The stock must be distributed to its shareholders pursuant to § 355. Section 355 permits stock to be received tax-free by shareholders in a qualifying spin-off, split-off, or split-up. Consequently, the stock received in the new corporation must be distributed to the shareholders of the transferor corporation either as a spin-off or as a split-off. In a spin-off, the shareholders do not surrender any stock in the distributing corporation. In a split-off, the shareholders do surrender stock in the distributing corporation in exchange for stock in the new corporation. In a split-up, the assets of one corporation are transferred to two or more new corporations. Stock in the new corporations is distributed to the transferor's shareholders. The transferor corporation is liquidated. The spin-off, split-off, and split-up are illustrated in Figure 7–9.

EXAMPLE 24

A owns 200 shares of R Corporation stock with a basis of $40,000 (value of $60,000). In a "D" reorganization (a spin-off), she receives a distribution of 50 shares of S Corporation stock valued at $20,000. A surrenders none of her R stock. The basis she had in her R stock is allocated to the R stock and S stock using the fair market value of each. Thus, $20,000/$80,000 of the $40,000 basis, or $10,000, will be allocated to the S stock, and $60,000/$80,000 of the $40,000 basis, or $30,000, will be allocated to the R stock. ◆

FIGURE 7–9

"D" Reorganization

Spin-Off

Alpha's shareholders receive stock representing control of Beta without surrendering any stock in Alpha.

Split-Off

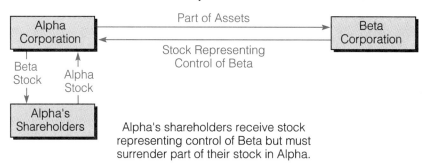

Alpha's shareholders receive stock representing control of Beta but must surrender part of their stock in Alpha.

Split-Up

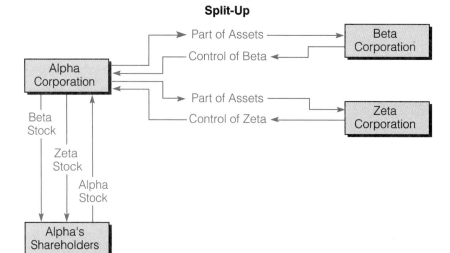

A part of Alpha's assets are transferred to Beta; the remainder of the assets are transferred to Zeta. Stock in Beta and Zeta is transferred to Alpha's shareholders for their stock in Alpha, and Alpha is liquidated.

───────────── EXAMPLE 25 ─────────────

Assume that a split-off occurred in Example 24. A surrenders 100 shares of R stock for 50 shares of S stock. Again, her basis of $40,000 will be allocated between the R and S stock using the fair market value of each. The fair market value of the retained R stock is $30,000. Thus, $30,000/$50,000 of the $40,000, or $24,000, will be allocated to the R stock A retained, and $20,000/$50,000 of the $40,000, or $16,000, will be allocated to the S stock. ◆

───────────── EXAMPLE 26 ─────────────

A and B, individuals, are the sole shareholders of Books, a publishing corporation. Books was organized six years ago and has been actively engaged in publishing both books and periodicals. Because of antitrust problems, Books wishes to divide the business. Two new corporations are formed, Books II and Periodicals. All the assets relating to the book-publishing business are transferred to Books II. All assets relating to the publishing of periodicals are transferred to Periodicals. A exchanges all her stock in Books for the stock in Books II. B exchanges all his stock in Books for the stock in Periodicals. Books is liquidated. The transaction qualifies as a "D" reorganization. It is a split-up. Neither A nor B recognizes gain on the exchange. A's basis in her stock in Books becomes the basis for her stock in Books II. B's basis in his stock in Books becomes his basis for his stock in Periodicals. ◆

Requirements of § 355. Under the "D" reorganization provisions in § 368, the requirements of § 355 must be met if the transfer is to be considered tax-free. All the requirements of § 355 discussed in Chapter 5 come into play. Stock representing control [control being 80 percent as defined in § 368(c)(1)] of the transferee corporation must be distributed to the shareholders of the transferor corporation. The assets transferred (plus those retained) must represent an active business that has been owned and conducted by the transferor corporation for at least five years before the transfer. A distribution under § 355 must not be used principally as a device for the distribution of the E & P of either the distributing corporation or the controlled corporation.

Note that control in a "D" reorganization has different meanings depending upon whether the reorganization is a corporate combination or a corporate division. If a corporate combination, control is ownership of at least 50 percent of the total voting stock *or* 50 percent of the total *value* of all classes of stock.[19] If the reorganization is a corporate division, control is ownership of at least 80 percent of the total voting stock *and* at least 80 percent of the total *number* of shares of all other classes of stock.[20]

───────────── EXAMPLE 27 ─────────────

R Corporation has been engaged in the manufacture of certain products. It also owns investment securities. It transfers the investment securities to a newly formed corporation and distributes the stock of the new corporation to its shareholders. The transaction does not qualify as a "D" reorganization. The holding of investment securities does not constitute a trade or business. The shareholders of R Corporation will be taxed on the receipt of the stock. ◆

───────────── EXAMPLE 28 ─────────────

Assume R Corporation has a separate research department. It transfers the research department to a new corporation and distributes the stock of the new corporation to its shareholders. The activities of the research department do not constitute a trade or business. The transaction does not qualify as a "D" reorganization. ◆

---

19. § 368(a)(2)(H).   **20.** § 368(c).

──────────────── EXAMPLE 29 ────────────────

R Corporation manufactures a single product, but it has had two plants for the past 10 years. It transfers one plant and related activities to a new corporation and distributes the stock of the new corporation to its shareholders. The activities of each plant constitute a trade or business. The transaction qualifies as a "D" reorganization. ◆

──────────────── EXAMPLE 30 ────────────────

Assume one of the plants in Example 29 has been in existence for only two years. R Corporation transfers one plant and related activities to a new corporation and distributes the stock of the new corporation to its shareholders. Though the activities of each plant constitute a trade or business, one has not been in existence for at least five years. Consequently, the transaction does not qualify as a "D" reorganization. It does not matter which plant is transferred. Both, the one transferred and the one retained, must have been in existence for at least five years before the transfer. ◆

As noted in Chapter 5, § 355 requires a business purpose for the transfer and the absence of a tax avoidance scheme. The distribution of stock and securities need not be pro rata, however, if all the other requirements of § 355 are satisfied.[21]

──────────────── EXAMPLE 31 ────────────────

A and B, individuals, own all the stock of R Corporation, which has operated two active businesses for the past 10 years. R transfers the assets representing one business to a newly formed corporation, S Corporation. The stock of S is distributed to B only, in exchange for a part of B's stock in R Corporation. The transaction qualifies as a "D" reorganization. ◆

Type E

The "Type E" reorganization is a recapitalization—a major change in the character and amount of outstanding capital stock or paid-in capital of a corporation. The transaction is significant only as far as shareholders who exchange stock or securities are concerned. The corporation itself receives no property and should have no tax problems.

The following types of exchanges qualify for nonrecognition treatment as an "E" reorganization: bonds for stock, stock for stock, and bonds for bonds.[22] When a corporation discharges its bonds by issuing stock, the exchange qualifies as an "E" reorganization. A corporation can exchange its common stock for preferred stock or its preferred stock for common stock tax-free. The exchange of bonds for other bonds is tax-free if the securities surrendered are in the same principal amount (or a greater principal amount) as the principal amount of the securities received.

──────────────── EXAMPLE 32 ────────────────

A corporation with $100,000 par value bonds outstanding issues preferred shares to the bondholders instead of liquidating the bonds for cash. The exchange qualifies as an "E" reorganization. ◆

──────────────── EXAMPLE 33 ────────────────

The stock in R Corporation is owned one-half by F and one-half by F's sons, A and B. F wishes to retire and relinquish control of the corporation. He exchanges his common voting stock for nonvoting preferred stock. The exchange qualifies as an "E" reorganization. However, any difference in value between stock received and stock surrendered could be treated as compensation or as a gift. ◆

---

21. Reg. § 1.355–3(a).　　　　　　　　　　**22.** Reg. § 1.368–2(e).

EXAMPLE 34

R Corporation exchanges a new issue of common stock with no rights for its outstanding preferred stock. The preferred stock possessed certain priorities with reference to the amount and time of payment of dividends and the distribution of the corporate assets upon liquidation. The exchange qualifies as an "E" reorganization. ◆

If a corporation exchanges common or preferred stock for its outstanding preferred stock that has dividends in arrears, the exchange qualifies as an "E" reorganization. However, if there is an increase in the proportionate interest of the preferred shareholders in the assets or E & P of the corporation, § 305 will trigger dividend income to the shareholders. The amount treated as a dividend is the lesser of:

- The amount by which the greater of (1) the fair market value or (2) the liquidation preference of the stock received in the exchange exceeds the issue price of the preferred stock surrendered, or
- The amount of the dividend in arrears.

The exchange of stock for bonds does not qualify as an "E" reorganization. The receipt of the bonds is treated as boot, taxable under § 356, unless bonds are also surrendered in either the same or a greater principal amount than the bonds received.

Type F

The "Type F" reorganization is "a . . . mere change in identity, form or place of organization, however effected."[23] The IRS has ruled that if a reorganization qualifies as an "A," "C," or "D" reorganization and as an "F" reorganization, "Type F" reorganization treatment will predominate.[24]

EXAMPLE 35

X Corporation changes its name to Y Corporation. This is an "F" reorganization. ◆

EXAMPLE 36

X Corporation, a corporation organized in New Mexico, incorporates Y Corporation in Delaware and transfers all its assets to Y in exchange for all of Y's stock. X is to be liquidated. Its shareholders surrender all their X stock for a pro rata distribution of the Y stock. This transaction can be an "A," a "C," or a "D" reorganization. It also satisfies the requirements of an "F" reorganization. Consequently, it will be treated as an "F" reorganization. ◆

The surviving corporation in an "F" reorganization is the same corporation as its predecessor. Consequently, the tax characteristics of the predecessor carry over to the successor. Such a reorganization is a mere change in identity or form, and net operating losses can be carried back as well as forward.

An "F" reorganization is restricted to a *single* operating corporation. An "F" reorganization will not jeopardize the status of § 1244 stock, nor will it terminate a valid Subchapter S election.[25] There is no significant change in stock ownership in the "F" reorganization.[26]

---

23. § 368(a)(1)(F).

24. Rev.Rul. 57–276, 1957–1 C.B. 126.

25. Reg. § 1.1244(d)–3(d)(1) and Rev. Rul. 64–250, 1964–2 C.B. 333.

26. Rev.Rul. 66–284, 1966–2 C.B. 115.

Type G

The Bankruptcy Act of 1980 created the "G" reorganization. In this type of reorganization, all or a part of the assets of a debtor corporation are transferred to an acquiring corporation in a bankruptcy or similar proceeding in a Federal or state court. The stock or securities of the acquiring corporation must be distributed in a transaction that qualifies under § 354, § 355, or § 356. The debtor corporation's creditors must receive voting stock of the acquiring corporation for debt representing 80 percent or more of the total fair market value of the debt of the debtor corporation.

A "G" reorganization need not comply with state merger laws. Nor must the former shareholders control the acquiring corporation after the exchange as in the "D" reorganization. To satisfy the distribution requirement, some of the debtor corporation's security holders (creditors) must receive stock or securities in the acquiring corporation. There are no restrictions on the type of consideration used, but the reorganization must meet the continuity of interest test discussed later in the chapter. The creditors of the debtor corporation (and any shareholders who receive consideration for their stock) are treated as owners of the debtor corporation for purposes of the test.

Comparison of Types of Reorganizations

The advantages and disadvantages of the various types of reorganizations are summarized in Concept Summary 7–1.

A discussion of reorganizations must consider certain basic conditions that pervade the entire field. Various judicially created doctrines—sound business purpose, continuity of interest, and continuity of business enterprise—have become basic requirements for the tax-free status of corporate reorganizations. The courts have also formulated the so-called step transaction doctrine to determine the tax status of a reorganization effected through a series of related transactions. In addition, a plan of reorganization is required. In essence, these doctrines have imposed additional requirements for tax-free status of corporate reorganizations.

Sound Business Purpose

Even if the statutory requirements of a reorganization have been literally followed, a transaction will not be tax-free unless it exhibits a business purpose.[27] The requirement that a reorganization must exhibit a business purpose is a judicially created doctrine.[28] Moreover, the Regulations have followed the courts in recognizing this requirement.[29]

The test of business purpose, and whether it may reflect the shareholder's purpose rather than that of the corporation, is not well-defined. In one case, the Court implied that the benefit to the corporation must be direct and substan-

27. *Gregory v. Helvering*, 35–1 USTC ¶9043, 14 AFTR 1191, 55 S.Ct. 266 (USSC, 1935).

28. The doctrine as developed in the *Gregory* case became a precedent for all transactions that might be shams devised merely for tax avoidance purposes. It brought about the

principle of substance over form. The IRS and the courts will look through the form of a transaction to determine what really took place. All business transactions must have a sound business purpose.

29. Reg. § 1.368–1(c).

CONCEPT SUMMARY 7–1
SECTION 368: CORPORATE REORGANIZATIONS

Reorganization	Type	Advantages	Disadvantages
A	Merger or consolidation.	1. No requirement that consideration be voting stock.	1. State law must be followed—dissenters' rights and required shareholder meetings may present problems.
		2. As much as 50% of consideration can be cash without tax consequences for receipt of stock (cash and other property will be taxed).	2. All liabilities of target corporation are assumed by acquiring corporation as a matter of law.
	Subsidiary "A."	1. As parent is majority stockholder, problem of securing approval of majority shareholder is removed.	1. For "reverse merger," must have 80% control of target corporation.
		2. Subsidiary, rather than parent, will assume liabilities of target corporation.	2. For "reverse merger," only voting stock of the parent may be used.
B	Stock-for-stock exchange.	1. Stock may be acquired from shareholders.	1. *Only* voting stock of acquiring corporation may be used.
		2. Procedures to effect reorganization are not complex.	2. Must have 80% control of a target corporation.
			3. May have minority interest remaining in target corporation.
C	Assets-for-stock exchange.	1. Less complex as to state law than "A."	1. *Substantially all* assets of target corporation must be transferred.
		2. Cash or property can be used as consideration if less than 20% of fair market value of property transferred.	2. Liabilities count as *other property* for 20% rule if any consideration other than stock and liabilities is used.
			3. The target corporation must distribute the stock, securities, and other properties it receives in the reorganization to its shareholders.
D	Normally corporate division (spin-off, split-off, or split-up).	1. Permits corporate division without tax consequences if no *boot* is involved.	1. Requirements of § 354, § 355, or § 356 must be met.
E	Recapitalization.	1. Allows for major change in makeup of shareholders' equity.	1. Be careful that provisions of § 305 are not violated.
F	Change in identity, form, or place of organization.	1. Survivor is treated as same entity as predecessor; thus, tax attributes of predecessor can be carried back as well as forward.	
G	Court-approved reorganization of debtor corporation.	1. Creditors can exchange notes for stock tax-free.	
		2. State merger laws need not be followed.	

tial.[30] In more recent cases, courts have conceded that it is sometimes impossible to draw a line between the purpose of the corporation and the purpose of the shareholders.[31]

Cases indicate that the business purpose doctrine does not operate in reverse. It is normally the revenue agent who asserts lack of business purpose to deny tax-free status to a corporate reorganization. Occasionally, however, the taxpayer may want the transaction to be taxable in order to receive a step-up in basis in assets or to recognize a loss. Taxpayers have attempted to employ the business purpose doctrine to prevent the transaction from being considered a reorganization. In those instances, however, the courts have required the taxpayers to abide by the form of the transaction and have agreed with the IRS that a reorganization was involved.[32] One reason for giving the IRS this advantage is that the taxpayer is initially in command of tax consequences. Generally, *business purpose* is devised in the offices of the taxpayer's attorneys. Consequently, taxpayers should not be allowed to benefit from the option of producing or failing to produce documentation of a sufficient purpose.

Continuity of Interest

The continuity of interest doctrine is founded in the basic philosophy of the tax-free reorganization. If a shareholder or corporation has substantially the same investment after a corporate exchange as before, no tax should be imposed upon the transaction. For the "A" reorganization, however, the Code imposes no limitations on consideration. Consequently, a purchase of the properties of one corporation could qualify as a reorganization even though the consideration was cash or short-term notes.[33] Without some restrictions on consideration, the reorganization provisions would be an avenue for tax avoidance. Thus, courts imposed what has been termed the *continuity of interest* test. To qualify for tax-free status, the seller must acquire an equity interest in the purchasing corporation.[34]

The IRS has attempted to define exactly how much equity shareholders of the target corporation must receive in the acquiring corporation. For purposes of issuing an advance ruling, the IRS will deem the test met if shareholders of the target corporation, in the aggregate, receive stock in the acquiring corporation equal in value to at least 50 percent of all formerly outstanding stock of the target corporation.[35] Not all shareholders of the target corporation need to have a proprietary interest in the surviving corporation. The requirement is applied to the total consideration given in the acquisition. It would be met if one or more of the target corporation's shareholders retain a sufficient proprietary interest in the continuing corporation.

─────────────── EXAMPLE 37 ───────────────

Target Corporation, with 50 shareholders, merges into Acquiring Corporation pursuant to state statute. Under the merger plan, the shareholders of Target can elect to

30. *Bazley v. Comm.*, 47–1 USTC ¶9288, 35 AFTR 1190, 67 S.Ct. 1489 (USSC, 1947).

31. *Estate of Parshelsky v. Comm.*, 62–1 USTC ¶9460, 9 AFTR2d 1382, 303 F.2d 14 (CA–2, 1962).

32. *Survaunt v. Comm.*, 47–2 USTC ¶9344, 35 AFTR 1557, 162 F.2d 753 (CA–8, 1947).

33. The use of short-term notes was first disallowed in *Cortland Specialty Co. v. Comm.*, 3 USTC ¶980, 11 AFTR 857, 60 F.2d 937 (CA–2, 1932), *cert. den.* 53 S.Ct. 316 (USSC, 1933). In *Cortland*, the Court stated that there must be some continuity of interest on the part of the transferor corporation or its

shareholders to secure tax exemption.

34. *Pinellas Ice & Cold Storage v. Comm.*, 3 USTC ¶1023, 11 AFTR 1112, 53 S.Ct. 257 (USSC, 1933), and *LeTulle v. Scofield*, 40–1 USTC ¶9150, 23 AFTR 789, 60 S.Ct. 313 (USSC, 1940). In *LeTulle*, a corporation transferred all its assets to another corporation for cash and bonds. The Court held that the transaction was not a tax-free reorganization if the transferor's only retained interest was that of a creditor. This concept is now in the Regulations. See Reg. § 1.368–2(a).

35. Rev.Proc. 74–26, 1974–2 C.B. 478, § 3.02, updated by Rev.Proc. 77–37, 1977–2 C.B. 568.

receive either cash or stock in Acquiring. Thirty of the shareholders (holding 40% of Target's outstanding stock) elect to receive cash; the remaining 20 shareholders of Target (holding 60% of the stock) elect to receive stock in Acquiring. This plan satisfies the continuity of interest test. The shareholders receiving cash will be taxed on the transaction. Those receiving stock will not. ◆

EXAMPLE 38

A and B, individuals, each hold 50% of the stock of Target Corporation. Target merges into Acquiring Corporation. A receives cash for his stock in Target, while B receives stock in Acquiring. This should also qualify as a tax-free merger. B receives stock in Acquiring equal in value to at least 50% of the formerly outstanding stock in Target. A will be taxed on the transaction, but B will not. ◆

The continuity of interest requirement presents problems mainly for the "A" reorganization. The other reorganization provisions have *statutory* limitations on consideration.

Continuity of Business Enterprise

The Regulations refer to a "continuity of business enterprise under the modified form" as a prerequisite for a tax-free reorganization.[36] The requirement is an expansion of the sound business purpose principle.[37] However, it is a separate test. Originally, it was interpreted to mean that the acquiring corporation must conduct business activities of the same type as the target corporation.[38] Amendments to the Regulations provide that this test is satisfied only if the transferee continues the historic business of the transferor. If the business is not continued, the transferee must use a significant portion of the assets of the transferor in its business.[39]

Step Transaction

The court-imposed step transaction doctrine is employed to determine whether a reorganization is tax-free when a series of related transactions is involved. The courts look at the conditions before and after the change in ownership. Assuming the transactions in the series are related, all will be considered as one for tax purposes. In one case, the Court advanced a test for determining whether a series of steps is to be treated as a single indivisible transaction.[40] The Court stated that the test is one of mutual interdependence: "Were the steps so interdependent that the legal relations created by one transaction would have been fruitless without a completion of the series?"

The step transaction presents complications for reorganizations when *unwanted* assets are involved. If the target corporation attempts to dispose of its unwanted assets before a reorganization, the doctrine could be used to defeat tax-free status of the reorganization. The result is that substantially all of the properties are not transferred. The *substantially all* requirement is present in the "C" reorganization, the "D" reorganization, and the subsidiary "A" reorganization. Assuming application of the step transaction is appropriate, a prior nontaxable disposition of unwanted assets and a later reorganization are treated as a single transaction. Consequently, the acquiring corporation has failed to acquire substantially all of the target corporation's assets.

---

36. Reg. § 1.368–1(b).

37. *Gregory v. Helvering*, cited in Footnote 27.

38. Rev.Rul. 56–330, 1956–2 C.B. 204.

39. Reg. § 1.368–1(d).

40. *American Bantam Car Co.*, 11 T.C. 397 (1948), *aff'd.* in 49–2

USTC ¶9471, 38 AFTR 820, 177 F.2d 513 (CA–3, 1949), *cert. den.* 70 S.Ct. 622 (USSC, 1950). If the steps are not related, the doctrine is not applicable. See *Esmark, Inc.*, 90 T.C. 171 (1988).

———————————————————— EXAMPLE 39 ————————————————————

Acquiring Corporation wants to acquire certain, but not all, of the assets of Target Corporation. A direct conveyance of the desired property to Acquiring Corporation will not be a tax-free reorganization since the unwanted assets are a substantial portion of Target's total assets. A valid "C" reorganization is not possible as substantially all of Target's assets will not be conveyed. A possible solution would be to organize a new corporation, transfer the unwanted assets to the new corporation for all of its stock, and distribute the stock to Target's shareholders. The remaining assets in Target Corporation would then be transferred to Acquiring Corporation in return for stock. What has been accomplished?

- The first transfer would be tax-free under § 351 as a transfer to a corporation in exchange for at least 80 percent of the new company's stock.
- The second transfer of Target's remaining assets to Acquiring Corporation in return for stock is a tax-free "C" reorganization. What could go wrong with the results? ◆

In a case[41] with facts similar to those in Example 39, a court agreed with the IRS that the first transfer was equivalent to a retention of assets by Target Corporation. If the unwanted assets had remained in Target, the transfer to Acquiring Corporation would not have met the *substantially all* test. A transfer to cause the reorganization provisions to be available in situations such as in Example 39 was held to be unwarranted tax avoidance.

Example 39 involved two nontaxable events. If unwanted assets are sold to an unrelated purchaser in a taxable transaction, a later transfer of the remaining assets for stock might qualify as a "C" reorganization. Further, a dividend distribution to shareholders of the transferor corporation should not affect the tax-free nature of a subsequent reorganization.

The IRS generally views any transaction occurring within one year of the reorganization as part of the acquisition. This assumes there is no proof the transaction was, in fact, unrelated.[42] The application of the step transaction doctrine to such a transaction makes the continuity of interest test significant in a "B" or "C" reorganization. This occurs when the shareholders of the transferor corporation immediately dispose of stock received in the transferee corporation. In the case of an "A" reorganization, the application of the doctrine can cause an otherwise tax-free reorganization to be treated as a purchase. Such a result is possible if the shareholders do not retain their equity interests for a reasonable period of time.

Plan of Reorganization and Parties Thereto

Section 361 states that a *party to a reorganization* recognizes neither gain nor loss if it exchanges property under a *plan of reorganization* for stock or securities in another corporation also a *party to the reorganization*. Section 354 provides that gain or loss will not be recognized if stock or securities in a corporation that is a party to the reorganization are exchanged solely for stock or securities in the same corporation or in another corporation also a party to the reorganization. Section 368 does not mention *plan of reorganization,* and the term is not defined in the Code. The Regulations state that "plan of reorganization" refers to a

---

41. *Helvering v. Elkhorn Coal Co.*, 38–1 USTC ¶9238, 20 AFTR 1301, 95 F.2d 732 (CA–4, 1938), *cert. den.* 59 S.Ct. 65 (USSC, 1938).

42. In Rev.Rul. 69–48, 1969–1 C.B. 106, the IRS applied the step transaction doctrine to transactions that were 22 months apart.

consummated transaction specifically defined as a reorganization under § 368.[43] The Regulations take the position that the term limits (rather than enlarges) the definition of *reorganization*. Only those exchanges or distributions that are directly a part of transactions described in § 368 produce nonrecognition of gain or loss.

The requirement that there be a plan of reorganization implies that a formal, written document is essential. The Regulations refer to the adoption of a plan of reorganization.[44] Though the courts have not required a written plan, it is preferable that the parties execute a formal document. This will set forth the rights of all parties and list the steps required to carry out the exchange.

The parties to a reorganization are defined in §§ 368(b)(1) and (2). Parties to a reorganization include a corporation resulting from the reorganization and both corporations in an acquisition by one corporation of stock or properties of another. Also included is the parent of the acquiring corporation when parent stock is exchanged for property in an "A," "B," or "C" reorganization.

EXAMPLE 40

A parent corporation, P, uses stock of its subsidiary, S, as consideration for the acquisition of assets in Target Corporation. The transaction will not qualify as a tax-free reorganization because S is not a party to the reorganization. Refer to Figures 7–4, 7–6, and 7–8. Parent stock can be exchanged by a subsidiary in a reorganization, but a parent that is a party to a reorganization cannot use subsidiary stock to effect a reorganization. The parent must use its own stock. ◆

Assumption of Liabilities

A corporate reorganization normally results in a continuation of the business activities of the previous corporations, and liabilities are seldom liquidated. The acquiring corporation will either assume the liabilities of the acquired organization or take property subject to liabilities. In a regular sale or purchase of properties, the assumption of liabilities by the purchaser is part of the selling price.[45] As noted in Chapter 3, in some nonrecognition transactions, assumption of liabilities is considered boot and is taxable. This is not true in a § 351 transaction because of § 357. In a tax-free reorganization pursuant to §§ 357 and 368(a)(1)(C), assumed liabilities are, for the most part, disregarded in computing taxable gain to the transferor corporation.

Section 368(a)(1) discusses the acquisition of another corporation's properties solely in exchange for all or a part of the acquirer's voting stock. It specifically states that the assumption of a liability of the acquired corporation will be disregarded. Congress added the provision to the predecessor of § 368(a)(1)(C) to eliminate any *solely for voting stock* problem in the "C" reorganization. However, § 368(a)(1)(B) contains no similar provision. Any assumption of a liability by the transferor corporation in a "B" reorganization presumably will violate the *solely for voting stock* requirement. Normally, the assumption of liabilities is not present in a "B" reorganization as the "Type B" is simply a change in stock ownership.

Special Situations

The dramatic increase in unfriendly takeover attempts in the past few years has presented a whole new array of complex issues and options with which directors

---

43. Reg. § 1.368–2(g).
44. Reg. § 1.368–3(a).

45. *Crane v. Comm.*, 47–1 USTC ¶9217, 35 AFTR 776, 67 S.Ct. 1047 (USSC, 1947).

of target corporations must contend. Many companies have taken various measures to discourage unfriendly takeover attempts. These defensive measures include staggering the terms of the board of directors over several years instead of having the entire board up for election at one time. This makes it more difficult for the acquiring corporation to elect its own board of directors in order to gain control.

Some corporations have given key employees golden parachute contracts that will pay them large benefits if they are terminated after an unfriendly merger. Poison pills, tin parachutes, self-tender offers, Pac-Man defenses, exclusive merger agreements, and standstill agreements are some of the more recent defensive weapons adopted to ward off hostile takeover attempts. (See the glossary at the beginning of the chapter for a definition of these terms.)

Members of the board of directors of a target corporation face complex legal issues when they adopt defensive measures. Are the directors serving their own interests and not considering the benefits that might accrue to the target's shareholders if a takeover attempt is successful? Directors of the target corporation must take some position in a hostile takeover attempt; they cannot remain neutral. In considering the available alternatives, directors must adopt measures that are beneficial to the corporation. Their own private interests cannot be considered.

Congress has entered the corporate control arena by adding several new provisions to tax some of the measures adopted in unfriendly merger transactions. One such provision is § 5881, which imposes a 50 percent tax on any gain realized, even though not recognized, by anyone receiving greenmail. Recall that the term *greenmail* refers to payments made to one shareholder of a target corporation to redeem or purchase the shareholder's stock in the target on terms that are not offered to all shareholders. Section 5881 is applicable in the following circumstances:

- Consideration is transferred by a target corporation, or any person acting in concert with the target corporation, to acquire, either directly or indirectly, the stock of a shareholder in the target corporation.
- The shareholder in the target corporation has held the target stock for less than two years prior to that shareholder making, or threatening to make, a public tender offer. A public tender offer is any tender offer that is required to be filed or registered with any Federal or state securities agency.
- The consideration transferred to the shareholder was not made available to other shareholders of the target corporation.

Gain realized by a white knight, the friendly bidder who enters the bidding war in response to the target corporation's attempt to find a more compatible acquiring company, may also be subject to the tax under § 5881.

─────────────────── Example 41 ───────────────────

A corporate raider, R, buys 20% of the stock of Target Corporation, or 15,000 shares, in the open market on November 10, 1991, for $10 per share. R then makes a public tender offer to the remaining shareholders of Target to buy their shares in Target for $14 per share. Target's directors seek a white knight to ward off a hostile takeover by R. Knight, a corporation that is friendly to Target, agrees to purchase Target stock. In 1992, Knight offers Target's shareholders $15 per share to be paid in the form of stock in Knight Corporation. Then, in order to prevent any disagreements with R, Knight offers to pay R $16 per share in voting stock in Knight for the 15,000 shares R purchased. After purchasing R's 15,000 shares, or 20% of Target's shares, Knight acquires an additional 45,000 shares, or 60% of Target's shares, for a total of 80% of the stock in Target. The consideration given Target shareholders is voting stock in Knight Corporation. The transaction qualifies as a ''B'' reorganization because control of Target was obtained solely for voting stock in Knight.

■ The transaction raises another question: Is the exchange of R's stock in Target for voting stock in Knight greenmail that is subject to the 50 percent excise tax under § 5881?

■ Because R was paid more than other Target shareholders and because he held the Target stock for less than two years prior to making a public tender offer, R is subject to the tax. Recall that the tax is applicable to gain *realized* even though the gain is not *recognized*. Further, § 5881 is applicable to Knight's purchase of R's stock because acquisitions of stock by persons acting in concert with the target corporation are covered under § 5881.

■ If the exchange is greenmail, R must pay a penalty tax of $45,000 (50% of realized gain of $90,000). R paid $150,000 for the Target stock (15,000 shares at $10 per share) and realized $240,000 on the exchange (15,000 shares at $16 per share). The penalty tax under § 5881 is applicable to the total gain realized, not just the excess of the price paid R over the price paid other shareholders.

■ Note that had R transferred the Target stock for $15 per share, the price other shareholders received, he would have escaped the 50 percent penalty tax. His consideration at $15 per share would be $225,000. After paying the $45,000 penalty tax under § 5881, R's consideration for the exchange, at $16 per share, is only $195,000 ($240,000 − $45,000). ◆

EXAMPLE 42

Assume in Example 41, that after R made his public tender offer, Knight purchased 20,000 shares in Target for $14 per share. Knight then also makes a public tender offer for the remaining shares in Target at $15 per share. A year later because of antitrust problems, Target redeems Knight's 20,000 shares for $16 per share. Target does not make the same offer to its remaining shareholders. Knight may be subject to the § 5881 penalty tax. The question of whether § 5881 applies to a proposed friendly takeover is left open. If Knight is subject to § 5881, the penalty tax would be $20,000, or 50% of Knight's gain of $40,000. Knight paid $280,000 for the Target stock (20,000 shares at $14 per share). The stock was redeemed by Target for $320,000 (20,000 shares at $16 per share) for a gain of $40,000 [$320,000 (redemption price) less $280,000 (cost of the stock)]. ◆

Tax problems arise in other contexts when unfriendly mergers, or measures to ward off hostile takeovers, occur. For example, golden parachutes that fall under the prohibition of § 280G are not deductible to the extent of the *excess parachute payment*. Further, the person receiving a golden parachute is subject to an excise tax of 20 percent[46] of the excess payment in addition to income and Social Security taxes. In addition, the use of a poison pill to ward off hostile takeovers can cause the corporation involved to be barred from acquiring another corporation in a tax-free ''B'' or ''C'' reorganization.

EXAMPLE 43

A is president of Target Corporation. His average salary for the past five years was $150,000. In 1992, Target Corporation is taken over, and A loses his position. Pursuant to an employment contract, A is paid $1,000,000 in 1992. A parachute payment has occurred because the $1,000,000 payment exceeds $450,000 (three times the base amount of $150,000, A's average salary for the past five years). The excess of the $1,000,000 payment over the base amount of $150,000, or $850,000, is not deductible to Target Corporation under § 280G. Further, A is subject to an excise tax of $170,000 ($850,000 × 20%) under § 4999. ◆

---

46. § 4999.

───────────────── EXAMPLE 44 ─────────────────

Parent Corporation adopts a poison pill as a preventive measure in case a corporate raider attempts a hostile takeover. Parent's shareholders are given rights to purchase one preferred share for each share of Parent's voting stock. Later, Parent becomes interested in acquiring Target Corporation because Parent believes that combining the two businesses will increase sales and produce greater market penetration. Parent issues 10% of its voting stock to the shareholders of Target Corporation in exchange for 80% of the stock in Target. The shareholders of Target are also given rights to purchase one preferred share in Parent for each share of voting stock acquired in the exchange. The IRS may take the position that the rights are boot.[47] Thus, the exchange may not qualify as a "B" reorganization since the consideration for the exchange was not solely voting stock in Parent. ◆

───────────────── EXAMPLE 45 ─────────────────

Assume, in Example 44, that Target transferred substantially all its assets to Parent for Parent's voting stock, an assumption of Target's liabilities by Parent, and the issuance of the rights. If the IRS is correct that the rights are boot, all the liabilities assumed by Parent, in addition to the value of the rights, cannot exceed 20% of the consideration, or the transfer will not qualify as a "C" reorganization. ◆

CARRYOVER OF CORPORATE TAX ATTRIBUTES
◆

In General

Determining the tax features of an acquired corporation to be carried over to the acquiring or successor corporation is a significant problem in a corporate acquisition and in the liquidation of a subsidiary corporation. Some tax features of an acquired corporation (the carryover of losses, tax credits, and deficits) will be welcomed by a successor corporation. Others may prove less welcome. It is immaterial whether the acquiring corporation desires to carry over the attributes of its acquired predecessor inasmuch as the carryover rules, if applicable, are mandatory.

The carryover rules should be carefully considered in every corporate acquisition; they may, in fact, determine the form of the acquisition. This is particularly true in the liquidation of a subsidiary pursuant to § 332. The carryover rules apply in the liquidation of a controlled subsidiary under § 332 if the basis of the transferred assets carries over to the parent. If basis of assets is determined under the single transaction approach of § 338, the carryover rules do not apply.

Theory of Carryovers. Before the enactment of § 381, case law determined the tax benefits of an acquired corporation that could be carried over to the successor. With respect to net operating losses, general theory held that only the corporation sustaining the loss could take the deduction. As a result, the form of a corporate acquisition largely determined whether a tax loss could be carried over to the acquiring corporation. If a statutory merger or consolidation occurred, the courts permitted the carryover of the predecessor corporation's deductions. Since the assets and liabilities of the two corporations were amalgamated by operation of law, a carryover was justified. Carryovers were not permitted in other forms of corporate acquisitions.[48]

The courts held that although a credit balance in earnings and profits of the target corporation would carry over to the successor corporation, a deficit would

───────────────────────

47. See Ltr.Ruls. 8808081 and 8925087.

48. *New Colonial Ice Co. v. Helvering*, 4 USTC ¶1292, 13 AFTR

1180, 54 S.Ct. 788 (USSC, 1934).

not.[49] The rule was designed to prevent any earnings and profits from escaping taxation.

Section 381 now determines which tax benefits of an acquired corporation can be carried over to the successor, but it does not apply to all transactions. In instances where it does not apply, case law is still applicable.

Allowance of Carryovers. Section 381 provides for the carryover of various specific tax attributes from one corporation to another in certain tax-free liquidations and reorganizations. It permits the successor corporation "... to step into the 'tax shoes' of the predecessor corporation."[50]

Section 381(c) lists the tax features of an acquired corporation that can be carried over to a successor corporation. Section 381 does not apply to any other items. Only the following transactions are covered: the "A," "C," "F," nondivisive "D," and "G" reorganizations. It also covers the liquidation of a controlled subsidiary under § 332 where the subsidiary's basis in its assets carries over to the parent.

Net Operating Loss Carryovers

A net operating loss (NOL) carryover, as determined under § 172, is permitted as a deduction of the successor corporation under § 381(c)(1). However, the amount of the carryover is limited.

Limitations on Carryovers. Several Code Sections limit the amount of an NOL carryover. Sections 381(c)(1)(B) and 382 limit the aggregate deduction the successor corporation can obtain from NOLs of the predecessor corporation or corporations. Section 269 will deny the deduction altogether if a tax avoidance scheme exists. Section 384 limits the amount of preacquisition loss an acquiring corporation can use to offset built-in gains of the acquired corporation.

Limitation of Carryover for Year of Transfer. Under § 381(c)(1)(B), the amount of an NOL that can be carried to the first tax year ending after the transfer date is limited to a percentage representing the remaining days in that tax year. For example, if two calendar year corporations merged on July 1, only a portion of an NOL of the acquired corporation can be used to offset income for that tax year. The amount is limited to one-half of the taxable income of the acquiring corporation. The limitation applies only for the purpose of computing the NOL deduction of the successor corporation for the successor's first taxable year ending after the date of the transfer. The limitation does not apply in determining the portion of any NOL that may be carried to any taxable year of the successor corporation after the first taxable year.

─────────────────────── EXAMPLE 46 ───────────────────────

Target Corporation merges into Acquiring Corporation on December 16, 1991. Target Corporation had an NOL of $73,000, while Acquiring Corporation had taxable income of $100,000 for 1991. Only $4,110 ($100,000 × 15/365 = $4,110) of the $73,000 NOL can be used to offset Acquiring's taxable income. Acquiring would have taxable income of $95,890 ($100,000 − $4,110). The remainder of the loss carryover from Target Corporation, $68,890, can be carried forward to offset Acquiring's 1992 taxable income.

49. *Comm. v. Sansome*, 3 USTC ¶978, 11 AFTR 854, 60 F.2d 931 (CA–2, 1931), *cert. den.* 53 S.Ct. 291 (USSC, 1932), and *Comm. v. Phipps*, 49–1 USTC ¶9204, 37 AFTR 827, 69 S.Ct. 616 (USSC, 1949).

50. S. Rept. 1622, 83d Cong., 2d Sess. (1954).

If the merger had taken place on December 31, there would have been no NOL deduction for 1991 ($100,000 × 0/365 = $0). The entire loss of $73,000 can be carried to 1992. ◆

The taxable years to which an NOL can be carried back or forward are in the Code section that contains the general rules for NOLs.[51]

Timing is important if an NOL carryover is possible. The taxable year of the transferor corporation will end on the date of distribution or transfer (except in the case of an "F" reorganization).[52] Section 381(c)(1)(A) states that NOL carryovers are carried to the first taxable year of the acquiring corporation ending after the date of the transfer, subject to the limitation noted above. If the transfer is not completed by the last day of the taxable year of both corporations, the first rule will apply. This will produce a short taxable year for the loss corporation (it will end on the date of transfer) that will be counted as a full year for purposes of the 15-year carryover period. The portion of the taxable year of the acquiring corporation beginning on the date of transfer will count as a full year in computing the carryover period. Thus, a full year could be lost. For example, a transferor corporation's NOL for 1992 would be spread over only 14 years if it is merged into a calendar year transferee corporation on any day in 1992 other than December 31. Two taxable years would occur in 1992 so the carryover would apply to years 1992 through 2006.

Ownership Changes. Section 382 imposes limitations on the carryover of an NOL if there is (1) an *owner shift* or (2) an *equity structure shift*. If neither an owner shift nor an equity structure shift occurs, § 382 is not applicable, and no limitation is placed on the amount of the NOL carryover. If either an owner shift or an equity structure shift occurs, the NOL carryover is subject to what is termed a § 382 *limitation*.

- An owner shift is any change in the respective ownership of stock by a 5 percent shareholder. The change is determined by looking to a testing period that is the shorter of the prior three years or the period following the most recent ownership change.
- Stock changes do not include stock acquired by gift, death, or divorce or pursuant to certain employee stock ownership plan (ESOP) transactions. Holdings of nonvoting preferred stock are not considered in determining whether an ownership change has occurred.
- All less-than-5 percent shareholders are treated as a single 5 percent shareholder.
- If a 50 percent shareholder treats his or her stock as being worthless during a tax year and holds it at year-end, the shareholder is considered to have acquired the stock on the first day of the succeeding year. This rule applies in determining whether there has been a more-than-50 percent change in stock ownership.

  - The shareholder is regarded as not having owned the stock previously.
  - As a result, a claim of a worthless stock deduction by a 50 percent shareholder can cause an owner shift.

51. § 172(b)(1). See Reg. § 1.381(c)(1)–1(e)(3) for the application of this Section to corporate reorganizations.

52. § 381(b)(1). In the "F" reorganization, the transferor corporation's year does not end on the transfer date.

Carryovers are considered as though there had been no reorganization. An NOL could thus be carried back as well as forward.

■ An equity structure shift is a tax-free reorganization other than a divisive reorganization or an "F" reorganization.

■ If either the owner shift or the equity structure shift causes a more-than-50 percent change in the ownership of the loss corporation, the NOL carryover is subject to the § 382 limitation.

■ The § 382 limitation provides that the taxable income of the new loss or the surviving corporation may be reduced each year by the NOL carryover. The reduction is available only to the extent of the value of the loss corporation's stock on the date of the ownership change multiplied by the long-term tax exempt rate.

 ■ The long-term tax-exempt rate is the highest of the Federal long-term rates in effect in the three-calendar-month period before the stock change.

 ■ Information regarding the Federal long-term rate is available on a monthly basis in Revenue Rulings published by the IRS in the *Internal Revenue Bulletin*.[53]

■ The objective of the § 382 limitation is to restrict the use of NOLs to a hypothetical future income stream.

 ■ The income stream is to be measured by the yield that would have been received had the value of the stock been invested in long-term securities.

 ■ The real reason for the tie-in to the long-term exempt rate is to approximate the rate at which the old loss corporation could have used its NOL.

■ Any § 382 limitation not used because of insufficient taxable income may be carried forward to future years.

■ Thus, § 382 does not disallow an NOL. It merely limits the amount of NOL carryover that the new loss or surviving corporation can utilize on an annual basis.

■ If the value of the old loss corporation is large relative to its NOL carryovers, § 382 will not cause a problem. Only if the old loss corporation has a small fair market value relative to its NOL carryovers will § 382 seriously limit the amount of the carryover.

EXAMPLE 47

The stock of L Corporation is publicly traded, and no shareholder holds 5% or more of the stock. During the three-year period between January 1, 1989, and January 1, 1992, numerous trades are made involving the stock of L Corporation, but no person (or persons) becomes a 5% shareholder (either directly or indirectly) and increases his or her (or their) ownership by more than 50 percentage points. No ownership change takes place that will result in § 382 limitations to any NOL carryovers. No ownership shift has occurred since the less-than-5% shareholders are aggregated. They own 100% before the trades and 100% after the trades. ◆

EXAMPLE 48

U Corporation, a calendar year taxpayer, has a more-than-50% ownership change on January 1, 1992. At this point, it has an NOL carryover of $500,000. Also, the value of the U Corporation stock is $1,000,000, and the long-term tax-exempt rate is 10%. U Corporation's § 382 limitation for 1992 is $100,000 ($1,000,000 × 10%). If in calendar

---

53. Although the long-term tax-exempt rate will be readily available in determining the § 382 limitation, ascertaining the value of the acquired corporation's stock could prove troublesome.

year 1992, U Corporation has taxable income of $70,000 (before any NOL carryover), $70,000 of the loss can be used. The $30,000 remaining portion ($100,000 − $70,000) can be carried over and will increase the § 382 limitation for 1993 to $130,000 ($30,000 + $100,000). ◆

EXAMPLE 49

On July 1, 1992, Target Corporation is merged into Acquiring Corporation in an "A" reorganization. At the time of the merger, Target Corporation had an NOL of $100,000. Pursuant to the merger, the shareholders of Target Corporation receive 40% of the stock of Acquiring Corporation. An equity structure shift (an "A" reorganization) has taken place. There has been a more-than-50% change over the lowest percentage of Target Corporation stock owned by the shareholders at any time during the testing period. If the value of Target Corporation is $50,000 and the applicable rate is 10%, the § 382 limitation on Target Corporation's NOL is $5,000 ($50,000 × 10%). ◆

EXAMPLE 50

Assume in Example 49 that the shareholders of Target Corporation receive 50% of the stock of Acquiring Corporation. There has not been a more-than-50% change over the lowest percentage of Target Corporation owned by the shareholders during the testing period. The entire $100,000 will carry over with no § 382 limitation. ◆

EXAMPLE 51

On July 1, 1992, Y Corporation is owned by two unrelated shareholders, C (70%) and D (30%). Y Corporation redeems all of C's stock in exchange for nonvoting preferred stock. Following this recapitalization, an ownership change in Y Corporation has occurred. The percentage of Y stock owned by D during the testing period has increased by more than 50 percentage points. For this purpose, the preferred stock issued to C is not counted. Any NOL that Y Corporation might have will be subject to the § 382 limitation. ◆

An owner shift or an equity structure shift often does not occur on the last day of the tax year. In that case, the annual § 382 limitation is allocated based on the number of days in the tax year before and after the change.

A new loss or surviving corporation must satisfy the continuity of business enterprise requirement for a two-year period following any ownership change or equity structure shift. If it fails to do so, any NOL carryforward will be disallowed completely.

To prevent the parties from increasing the value of the loss corporation, certain capital contributions (including § 351 transfers) are to be disregarded if they are tax motivated. Capital contributions (including § 351 transfers) are presumed to be tax motivated if they occur within the two years preceding the ownership change.

If at least one-third of the fair market value of a corporation's assets consists of nonbusiness assets, an adjustment is necessary. The value of the loss corporation is reduced by the excess of the value of the nonbusiness assets over the corporation's indebtedness attributable to such assets. Nonbusiness assets include any assets held for investment, including cash, marketable securities, and investments in subsidiaries.

Built-In Gains and Losses. The corporation having an NOL may be the acquiring corporation. If an acquired corporation has a built-in gain, § 384 applies. The acquiring corporation with an NOL is prevented from offsetting the loss against any built-in gain of the acquired corporation that is recognized during the five-year period following the acquisition. Section 384 applies if a loss corporation acquires control of a gain corporation. It is applicable to an "A", "C", or "D" reorganization.

1. A built-in gain exists if the fair market value of the acquired corporation's assets exceeds the aggregate adjusted bases of its assets immediately before the transfer.[54]
2. If an asset was not held by the acquired corporation immediately before the acquisition or if the gain is attributable to an increase in the value of the asset after the acquisition, the gain will not be treated as built-in gain.
3. Any net unrealized built-in losses of the loss corporation that are recognized during the five-year recognition period are preacquisition losses. These losses also may not be offset by any built-in gain from the acquired corporation.
   a. A built-in loss of the loss corporation exists to the extent the aggregate adjusted bases of the loss corporation's assets exceed the asset value immediately before the acquisition.
   b. If an asset was not held by the loss corporation immediately before the acquisition, the loss will not be treated as a preacquisition loss.
   c. Any loss that results in a reduction in the value of the corporation's assets after the acquisition is not a preacquisition loss.

────────────────── EXAMPLE 52 ──────────────────

Loss Corporation has an NOL carryforward of $300,000 and a built-in loss of $100,000. It acquires Target Corporation in an ''A'' reorganization in 1992. That same year, an asset acquired from Target Corporation with an adjusted basis of $10,000 is sold for $80,000. The $70,000 gain on the sale may not be offset by Loss Corporation's NOL. ◆

────────────────── EXAMPLE 53 ──────────────────

Assume Target Corporation in Example 52 has built-in gain of $100,000 on the date of the acquisition. In 1992, Loss Corporation sells assets acquired from Target Corporation for $400,000. The assets have an adjusted basis of $250,000. The amount treated as built-in gain that cannot be offset by Loss Corporation's NOL is limited to $100,000. Loss Corporation may use its loss to offset $50,000 of the recognized gain on the sale. Any additional gain recognized on assets acquired from Target Corporation can be offset by Loss Corporation's NOL because all the unrealized built-in gain has been recognized. ◆

────────────────── EXAMPLE 54 ──────────────────

Assume Loss Corporation in Example 52 sells one of its assets for $60,000. The asset had an adjusted basis of $90,000 and a value of $70,000 on the date of the acquisition of the assets of Target Corporation. Loss Corporation will recognize a total loss of $30,000, but only $20,000 is treated as preacquisition loss. ◆

Earnings and Profits

The Supreme Court held in an early case[55] that the earnings and profits of an acquired corporation carries over to a successor corporation. However, the Court later held that a successor corporation was not permitted to apply a deficit in the acquired corporation's earnings and profits against its own earnings and profits.[56] There was confusion in applying these general rules. Section 381(c)(2) clarifies these rules with respect to the carryover of earnings and profits of a predecessor corporation. Earnings and profits of a predecessor corporation is deemed to have been received by the successor corporation as of the date of the

────────────────────────

54. The special rule for built-in gains does not apply if the amount of the built-in gain (or built-in loss) does not exceed the lesser of (a) 15% of the value of the corporation's assets or (b) $10,000,000. For this purpose, value is computed by

excluding cash and marketable securities. See § 382(h)(3)(B).

55. *Comm. v. Sansome*, cited in Footnote 49.

56. *Comm. v. Phipps*, cited in Footnote 49.

distribution or transfer. A deficit may be used to offset earnings and profits accumulated by the successor corporation only after the date of the transfer. Thus, both earnings and profits and deficits carry over, but deficits reduce earnings and profits only after the date of transfer.

If one corporation has accumulated earnings and profits and the other has a deficit, the deficit can be used only to offset earnings and profits accumulated after the date of the transfer. The acquiring corporation has two separate earnings and profits accounts after the date of the transfer. One account contains the total accumulated earnings and profits as of the date of the transfer. The other contains the total deficits as of the date of the transfer.[57] The deficit in one account may not be used to reduce accumulated earnings and profits in the other account.

Capital Loss Carryovers

Section 381(c)(3) prescribes the same limitations for the carryover of capital losses of the predecessor corporation as those imposed on the carryover of NOLs. The taxable year of the acquiring corporation is the first taxable year ending after the date of transfer. The capital loss carryover is a short-term capital loss to the acquiring corporation. The amount deductible in the year of transfer is limited to a percentage of the net capital gains of the successor corporation computed with reference to the number of days remaining in the tax year.

EXAMPLE 55

Target Corporation has a capital loss in the amount of $30,000. Target transfers all its assets to Acquiring Corporation on July 1. Acquiring Corporation files its return on the basis of a calendar year. Acquiring Corporation has net capital gains (computed without regard to any capital loss carryovers) for that year of $40,000. The amount of capital loss carryover available in the current year is $20,000 ($40,000 × 1/2). ◆

Section 382(b), which limits the carryover of an NOL if there is an owner shift or an equity structure shift, is applicable to the capital loss carryover. The limitation is computed in the same manner as the limitation on an NOL.

Method of Accounting

The acquiring corporation must use the method of accounting used by the acquired corporation on the date of transfer unless the acquired and the acquiring corporations employ different methods. If different methods are used, the acquiring corporation must continue the different methods if it operates the business of the acquired corporation as a separate and distinct unit after the reorganization.[58]

Other Carryovers

Numerous other carryover items are prescribed by § 381. The successor corporation determines depreciation on acquired assets in the same manner as did the predecessor corporation. Should installment obligations pass to a transferee corporation in a reorganization, the transferee corporation will report the income from the obligations on the installment method. If there is an involuntary conversion, the successor corporation is treated as the predecessor.

---

57. Reg. § 1.381(c)(2)–1(a)(5).

58. § 381(c)(4) and Reg. § 1.381(c)(4)–1(c)(4).

Section 383 limits the amount of unused foreign tax credits and other credits that may be carried over if an owner shift or an equity structure shift causes a more-than-50 percent change in the ownership of the loss corporation. The limitation under § 383 is applied to these credits in the same manner as it is applied to capital loss carryovers.

Though the carryover items under § 381 are numerous, the others have limited applicability and are not discussed in this text.

Disallowance of Carryovers

Irrespective of § 381, the IRS can utilize § 269 to disallow the carryover of tax benefits if a tax avoidance scheme is apparent. Section 269 states that if a corporation acquires property of another corporation primarily to evade or avoid Federal income tax by securing the benefit of a deduction, credit, or other allowance that the acquiring corporation would not otherwise enjoy, the item will be disallowed. Whether or not the principal purpose is the evasion or avoidance of taxes becomes a question of fact. If the business of the loss corporation is promptly discontinued after a corporate reorganization, the IRS may use § 269 in an attempt to disallow the loss carryover.

Section 269 may be applied to disallow an NOL carryover even though the carryover might be limited under § 382.[59]

─────────────────── EXAMPLE 56 ───────────────────

Target Corporation, which has an NOL of $100,000, is merged into Acquiring Corporation. Acquiring acquires Target for the principal purpose of utilizing the NOL. After the merger, the former shareholders of Target own 10% of the fair market value of the stock in Acquiring. Under § 382, the loss is limited to the value of the Acquiring stock multiplied by the long-term exempt rate. However, under § 269, none of the loss can be used by Acquiring. ◆

Concept Summary 7–2 summarizes the carryover rules.

Assessing the Possible Alternatives

TAX PLANNING CONSIDERATIONS

The various types of corporate reorganizations should not be considered in isolation. Often the parties involved can achieve the desired tax result through more than one type of reorganization.

─────────────────── EXAMPLE 57 ───────────────────

X Corporation operates two businesses, each of which has been in existence for five years. One business is a manufacturing operation, the other is a wholesale distributorship. Z Corporation wishes to acquire only the former business and not to purchase all the assets of X Corporation. X Corporation has an NOL, a deficit in earnings and profits, and a basis in its assets in excess of their fair market value. ◆

What course of action might be advisable to transfer the manufacturing operation from X to Z with the least, if any, tax consequences? Compare the following three possibilities:

1. X Corporation transfers the manufacturing operation to Z Corporation in return for some of the latter's stock.

─────────────────────────

59. Reg. § 1.269–6.

2. X Corporation forms Y Corporation and transfers the wholesale distributorship to it in return for all of Y's stock. The Y stock is then distributed to X's shareholders. This portion of the arrangement is a nontaxable spin-off. X Corporation now transfers the manufacturing operation to Z Corporation in exchange for some of the latter's stock.

CONCEPT SUMMARY 7–2
SUMMARY OF CARRYOVER RULES

Tax attributes carry over under § 381 in tax-free liquidations under § 332 (when § 338 is not elected) and in tax-free reorganizations, as follows:

1. Net operating losses and capital losses.

   A. Year of transfer.
   Section 381(c)(1)(B) limits the amount of the loss in the year of transfer to the taxable income of the surviving corporation (capital gain in the case of a carryover of a capital loss) multiplied by a percentage representing the remaining days in the year of transfer.

   B. Ownership changes.

   - Section 382 imposes an annual limitation on the amount of loss carryover if an owner shift or an equity structure shift occurs.

     - An owner shift is a more-than-50 percent change in the ownership of shareholders owning 5 percent or more of the corporate stock.
     - An equity structure shift is a tax-free reorganization, other than an "F," in which a more-than-50 percent change occurs in the ownership of the loss corporation.

   - The § 382 limitation provides that the annual carryover may not exceed the value of the old loss corporation's stock on the date of the transfer multiplied by the Federal long-term rate.
   - The Federal long-term rate is the highest of the Federal long-term rates in the three-calendar-month period before the stock change.

   C. Built-in gains and losses.

   - Except for a *de minimis* exception, an NOL and a built-in loss of an acquiring corporation will not offset a built-in gain of an acquired corporation for a period of five years following the date of the acquisition.
   - A built-in gain or built-in loss is measured by the difference between the fair market value of an asset and its tax basis immediately before the acquisition.

2. Earnings and profits.

   A. E & P of an acquired corporation carries over.
   B. If either corporation has a deficit in E & P, the surviving corporation will have two E & P accounts.
   C. One account will contain the total accumulated E & P as of the date of the transfer. The other will contain the total deficit as of the date of the transfer.
   D. The deficit in one account may not be used to reduce the accumulated E & P in the other account.

3. Method of accounting.

   A. The acquiring corporation will use the method of accounting used by the acquired corporation.
   B. If the acquired corporation and the acquiring corporation used different methods, the acquiring corporation continues the different methods if the business of the acquired corporation is operated as a separate and distinct unit after the acquisition.

4. Other tax attributes.

   A. Depreciation and cost recovery methods carry over.
   B. The installment method of reporting carries over.
   C. The surviving corporation is treated as the predecessor for purposes of involuntary conversions.

3. The nontaxable spin-off described in possibility 2 is followed by Z Corporation's acquisition of all the X Corporation stock in exchange for some of Z's stock. The end result is that X Corporation becomes a subsidiary of Z Corporation.

Possibility 1 probably will not fit within the definition of a "C" reorganization because substantially all of the assets are not transferred by X Corporation in return for Z Corporation stock. The manufacturing operation (the "wanted" assets) is transferred, the wholesale distributorship ("unwanted" assets) is not.

Possibility 2 suffers from these same shortcomings. If the spin-off is disregarded, the transaction becomes an unsuccessful attempt to carry out a "C" reorganization (possibility 1). Disregarding the spin-off is the natural result of following the step transaction doctrine.[60]

Possibility 3 follows a different approach. It starts with the spin-off of the *unwanted* assets and concludes with Z Corporation obtaining the *wanted* assets by purchasing the X stock. Taken by itself, this last step satisfies the stock-for-stock requirement of a "B" reorganization. If, however, the step transaction doctrine is applied and the spin-off is disregarded, the Y Corporation stock distributed to X's shareholders might be considered as property *other than voting stock* in Z Corporation. The IRS has not chosen to take this position and probably will recognize the nontaxability of a spin-off of *unwanted* assets followed by a "B" reorganization.[61]

Resolving Shareholder Disputes

The use of a split-off under the "D" reorganization should not be overlooked as a means of resolving shareholder disputes.

───────────────────── EXAMPLE 58 ─────────────────────

Target Corporation was organized 10 years ago and since that time has operated retail and wholesale businesses. Target's two shareholders, R and S, each manage one of the businesses. Due to a difference of opinion between R and S over corporate policy, R and S decide to separate the two businesses. ◆

Presuming R and S plan to continue operating each business in the corporate form, any tax consequences on the division can be avoided by pursuing a "D" reorganization. Target Corporation could form Acquiring Corporation by transferring to it one of the businesses, say, the wholesale operation, in return for all the Acquiring stock. Next the Acquiring stock is distributed to the manager of the wholesale business, R, in exchange for all of his stock in Target Corporation. After the nontaxable split-off, S has the retail business through his sole ownership in Target Corporation, and R has control of the wholesale operation through the ownership of Acquiring Corporation.

Reorganizations Compared with Stock Redemptions and Liquidations

Example 58 is an opportunity to review certain other possibilities discussed in previous chapters.

─────────────────────

60. *Helvering v. Elkhorn Coal Co.*, cited in Footnote 41.

61. Rev.Rul. 70–434, 1970–2 C.B. 83.

1. If, for example, one of the shareholders, say, S, wishes to continue operating in the corporate form while the other does not, the stock redemption approach can be used (refer to Chapter 5). R could exchange all of his stock in Target Corporation for the wholesale business. This would qualify as a complete termination of a shareholder's interest under § 302(b)(3) and as a partial liquidation under § 302(b)(4). R will recognize a capital gain or loss measured by the difference between the fair market value of the wholesale business and his basis in the Target stock surrendered. As noted in Chapter 5, gain is recognized by Target Corporation because of the redemption.

2. If both shareholders are indifferent about whether the businesses should continue to operate in the corporate form, a complete liquidation of Target Corporation may be appropriate. The liquidation is carried out by making a distribution in kind of the wholesale business to R and of the retail business to S. As was true in the stock redemption alternative, the shareholders recognize a capital gain or loss measured by the difference between the fair market value of the property received and the basis of the stock given up. Gain is recognized by Target Corporation because of the liquidation (refer to Chapter 5).

The stock redemption and liquidation approaches produce gain at both the corporate level and the shareholder level. The "D" reorganization postpones the recognition of *any* gain on the division of the businesses. In a purely tax-free exchange, no change will take place in income tax basis. Thus, S's basis in the Target Corporation stock remains the same, while R's basis in the Target stock surrendered carries over to the new Acquiring Corporation stock received. At the corporate level, Target retains the same basis it had in the retail business, and Acquiring assumes Target's basis in the wholesale operation.

Carryover Considerations.   The tax differences between corporate reorganizations and liquidations are significant in other respects.

───────────────────────────── Example 59 ─────────────────────────────

P Corporation wants to acquire the assets of S Corporation. These assets have a basis to S Corporation of $300,000 and a fair market value of $200,000. S Corporation has incurred losses in its operations during the past several years and possesses unabsorbed NOLs. P Corporation plans to continue the business conducted by S, hoping to do so on a profitable basis. ◆

To carry out the acquisition planned by P Corporation, the tax consequences of various available alternatives must be assessed. In this connection, consider the following:

1. Using cash and/or other property, P Corporation purchases the assets directly from S Corporation. Following the purchase, S Corporation liquidates and distributes the cash and/or property to its shareholders.

2. P Corporation purchases all of the stock in S Corporation from its shareholders. Shortly thereafter, P liquidates S.

3. Utilizing an "A" reorganization, S Corporation merges into P Corporation. In exchange for their stock, the shareholders of S Corporation receive stock in P Corporation.

4. Under a "C" reorganization, S Corporation transfers all of its assets to P Corporation in return for the latter's voting stock. S distributes the P stock to its shareholders.

A satisfactory solution must center around the preservation of S Corporation's favorable tax attributes—the high basis in the assets and the NOL carryovers. Alternative 1 is highly unsatisfactory. The purchase price (probably $200,000) becomes the basis of the assets in the hands of P Corporation. Further, any unused NOLs will disappear upon the liquidation of S Corporation. S Corporation has a realized loss of $100,000 [$300,000 (basis in the assets) − $200,000 (sale proceeds)] from the sale of its assets. Yet the realized loss may generate little, if any, tax savings to S Corporation. In view of S Corporation's past history (unabsorbed NOL carryovers), it appears doubtful that the company will generate much income in the year of sale.

Alternative 2 suffers from the same shortcomings as alternative 1. When a subsidiary is liquidated under § 332, the basis of property received by the parent corporation is determined under either § 334(b)(1) or § 338 (assuming it applies and a timely election is made). In this case, if the parent elects under § 338, the assumed cost of the S Corporation stock ($200,000) becomes P's basis in the assets received from S (refer to Chapter 5). Consequently, the $100,000 built-in loss S Corporation has in its assets disappears and benefits neither P nor S. Likewise, S Corporation's unused NOL carryovers disappear.

If an election under § 338 is not made, the general rule of § 334(b)(1) applies for basis determination purposes. S Corporation's basis in its assets carries over to P Corporation. What P Corporation paid for the S stock becomes irrelevant. Other tax attributes of S Corporation (e.g., NOLs) will, under certain circumstances, carry over to P Corporation. Section 269 (dealing with the disallowance of any deduction or credit when the acquisition was made to evade or avoid income tax) could present a problem, however. Section 269(b) specifically applies to a liquidation within two years after the acquisition date of a qualified stock purchase when an election is not made under § 338. Section 269(b)(1)(D) provides that if the principal purpose of the liquidation is the evasion or avoidance of income tax by securing the benefit of a deduction, credit, or other allowance, the items involved may be disallowed.

Alternatives 3 and 4 should accomplish the same tax result as not electing under § 338 but with less tax risk. Presuming P Corporation can establish a business purpose for the "A" or "C" reorganization, § 269 can be avoided.

The preservation of favorable tax attributes, such as the NOL carryover and any capital loss or investment credit carryovers, should be considered in the context of the sale of a small corporation.

EXAMPLE 60

X Corporation, worth $200,000, has an NOL of $150,000. The stock in X Corporation is owned by two individuals: A, 55%, and B, 45%. A wants to sell his interest in X Corporation and retire. But what happens to the NOL if A sells his entire interest? There would be a more-than-50% change in the ownership of X Corporation. Therefore, the § 382 limitation would be $200,000 times the long-term tax-exempt rate. Assume the rate is 10%. The loss of $150,000 would now be limited to $20,000 annually. Can a sale be structured so that the NOL is not so limited? ◆

An owner shift is determined by looking to a three-year testing period. A could sell 15 percent of his stock in Year 1, 15 percent in Year 2, 15 percent in Year 3, and 10 percent in Year 4. Note that in neither of the three-year testing periods (Years 1 through 3 or Years 2 through 4) is there a more-than-50 percent change in the ownership of X Corporation. Thus, there is no § 382 limitation. X Corporation can deduct the entire $150,000 NOL sooner rather than later.

The Role of the Letter Ruling

When feasible, the parties contemplating a corporate reorganization should apply for and obtain from the IRS a letter ruling concerning the income tax effect of the transaction(s). Assuming the parties carry out the transfers as proposed in the ruling request, a favorable ruling provides, in effect, an insurance policy. If the tax implications are significant, as they often are with corporate reorganizations, the advantage of obtaining prior IRS approval is clear. The pros and cons of letter rulings and how they are obtained are discussed in Chapter 16.

PROBLEM MATERIALS

DISCUSSION QUESTIONS

1. What is the theory underlying nonrecognition of gain or loss in a corporate reorganization?

2. Briefly explain the seven forms of corporate reorganizations that qualify for nonrecognition treatment.

3. How does the receipt of boot affect the tax-free status of a corporate reorganization?

4. What are the advantages of effecting a business combination through a "Type A" reorganization?

5. What problems exist in effecting a business combination through a "Type A" reorganization?

6. How can the use of a subsidiary corporation in a "Type A" reorganization solve some of the problems inherent in such a reorganization?

7. What is a reverse merger?

8. What is the principal limitation of the "Type B" reorganization?

9. In what instances will a "Type C" reorganization be more beneficial than a "Type A" reorganization?

10. X Corporation transfers all of its assets to a newly formed corporation, Y, for all of Y's stock. The Y stock is exchanged with X's shareholders for all of their stock in X. X is then liquidated. Does the exchange qualify as a tax-free reorganization? Explain.

11. What is the difference between a spin-off pursuant to § 355 and a spin-off coupled with a "Type D" reorganization?

12. In what instances is a "Type D" reorganization accompanied by transfer of only part of the assets of the transferor corporation beneficial?

13. When is the receipt of bonds tax-free in a "Type E" reorganization?

14. Why can a "Type F" reorganization give the surviving corporation more tax benefits in certain instances than can an "A" or a "C" reorganization?

15. How does the business purpose requirement affect a tax-free reorganization?

16. What is the continuity of interest test?

17. What is the continuity of business enterprise test?

18. How does the step transaction doctrine affect the tax consequences of corporate combinations?

19. Does the assumption of liabilities of an acquired corporation by the acquiring corporation trigger gain recognition to the acquired corporation?

20. What is greenmail? When is the concept of greenmail applicable to a white knight?

21. What is a golden parachute? When does a golden parachute result in a penalty tax for the recipient?

22. What is the tax status of a golden parachute to the payor corporation?

23. How can a poison pill affect a "B" or a "C" reorganization?

24. What reorganizations are not covered by the carryover provisions of § 381?

25. What is the status of an NOL carryover if the assets of the loss corporation are purchased by another corporation?

26. How does an owner shift affect an NOL carryover?

27. How does an equity structure shift affect an NOL carryover?

28. What is the § 382 limitation on an NOL?

29. How does the long-term tax-exempt rate affect an NOL?

30. If a corporation having an NOL acquires a profitable corporation, can the NOL of the acquiring corporation be used to offset gain of the acquired corporation? Explain.

31. How will a deficit in earnings and profits of an acquired corporation carry over to offset earnings and profits of the acquiring corporation?

32. Do capital loss carryovers survive in a tax-free reorganization?

33. X Corporation is interested in acquiring the assets of Y Corporation. Y has a basis of $400,000 in its assets (fair market value of Y's assets is $250,000). Y has incurred substantial losses in the last few years and has a $175,000 NOL carryover. X believes that by making some changes in operations it could make Y a successful corporation. What is the best alternative for tax purposes for acquiring either the assets or the stock of Y Corporation?

PROBLEMS

34. What type of reorganization is effected in the following transactions?

    a. XY Corporation acquires all the assets of T Corporation in exchange for newly issued nonvoting preferred stock of XY Corporation. T Corporation distributes the preferred stock in XY Corporation to its shareholders in exchange for their common stock in T Corporation. T is then dissolved.

    b. P Corporation transfers P voting stock to S Corporation in exchange for preferred stock in S Corporation. P owns 85% of the voting stock in S Corporation. S exchanges the voting stock in P Corporation with shareholders in T Corporation holding 95% of the stock in T Corporation.

    c. The shareholders of X and Y Corporations agree to form W Corporation. All the assets of X and Y Corporations are transferred to W Corporation in exchange for common stock in W Corporation. The common stock in W Corporation is then distributed to the shareholders of X and Y Corporations in exchange for all their stock in X and Y. X and Y Corporations are then dissolved.

    d. Assume in (c) that the shareholders of X and Y Corporations receive stock in W Corporation worth $400,000 and long-term bonds worth $200,000.

    e. Assume in (c) that the shareholders of X and Y Corporations receive stock in W Corporation worth $100,000 and long-term bonds worth $300,000.

    f. S Corporation transfers voting stock in P Corporation, its parent, to A Corporation for substantially all of A's assets. A then distributes the P stock to its shareholders.

    g. S Corporation transfers all its assets to X Corporation. P, the parent of S, transfers its voting stock to the shareholders of X for 80% control of X Corporation. S Corporation is then liquidated.

    h. X Corporation transfers assets worth $300,000 to Y Corporation for voting stock worth $200,000, the assumption of liabilities in the amount of $40,000, and cash of $60,000.

    i. A Corporation has been actively engaged in two businesses for the past 10 years. It transfers assets of one business to a newly formed corporation and distributes stock in the new corporation, representing control of the corporation, to the shareholders of A.

    j. A Corporation manufactures a single product but has two plants. One plant was established three years ago; the other has been in existence since the corporation was organized eight years ago. A transfers the older plant to a new corporation and distributes stock in the new corporation to half its shareholders in exchange for all of their A stock.

   k. Common shares in A Corporation are owned by father and son. The father exchanges his common stock in A for newly issued nonvoting cumulative preferred stock.

   l. A, a New York corporation, incorporates B in Delaware and transfers all its assets to B in exchange for B's stock. A is subsequently liquidated.

   m. A parent corporation exchanges stock in its subsidiary for substantially all of the assets of X Corporation.

35. **a.** T, a shareholder of X Corporation, exchanges his X Corporation stock for stock in Y Corporation. The exchange is pursuant to a tax-free reorganization of X and Y. T paid $50,000 for his stock in X Corporation three years ago. The X stock is worth $100,000, and the stock T receives in Y is worth $80,000. What is T's basis in the Y Corporation stock?

   b. Assume T receives $20,000 cash in addition to the Y stock. What are the tax consequences to T, and what basis does he have in the Y Corporation stock?

36. A, an individual, exchanges stock he owns in T Corporation for stock in J Corporation and additionally receives $30,000 cash. The exchange is pursuant to a tax-free reorganization of both corporations. A paid $40,000 five years ago for the stock in T Corporation. The stock in J Corporation has a fair market value of $100,000. A's share of E & P of T Corporation is $15,000. How will A treat this transaction for tax purposes?

37. Assume the same facts as in Problem 36, except that A paid $140,000 (instead of $40,000) for his stock in T Corporation. How would A treat the transaction for tax purposes?

38. Target Corporation has assets with a fair market value of $4,000,000, adjusted basis of $1,000,000, and liabilities of $500,000. It transfers assets worth $3,700,000 in a "C" reorganization to Y Corporation in exchange for voting stock in Y Corporation and Y Corporation's assumption of its liabilities. Target Corporation retained a building worth $300,000, basis of $150,000. Target Corporation distributes the voting stock in Y Corporation and the building to A, its sole shareholder. How much gain will Target Corporation recognize on the reorganization?

39. Assume in Problem 38 that the consideration Y Corporation gives for all the assets of Target Corporation is voting stock worth $3,200,000, a building worth $300,000, basis of $150,000, and the assumption of Target Corporation's liabilities. Target distributes the stock and the building to its sole shareholder, A. Will either Target Corporation or Y Corporation recognize any gain on the reorganization?

40. P Corporation owned all the stock of S Corporation. S Corporation was merged into W Corporation in a statutory merger in which the shareholders of W Corporation received voting stock in P Corporation and cash for all their stock in W Corporation.

   a. Does the transaction qualify as an "A" reorganization?

   b. Assume that the shareholders in W Corporation exchanged 70% of their stock in W Corporation for voting stock in P Corporation. Will the exchange qualify as an "A" reorganization?

41. Pursuant to a plan of reorganization, X Corporation's shareholders deposit all their stock in X with X Corporation. X then exchanges its shareholders' stock with Y Corporation for 30% of the voting stock of Y. X Corporation delivers the Y stock to its shareholders.

   a. What are the tax results of the transaction?

   b. Assume Y also transferred 10% of its nonvoting preferred stock to X, with X then delivering the preferred stock as well as the voting stock to its shareholders. What is the tax result?

42. P Corporation transfers part of its voting stock to Y Corporation's only shareholders, A and B, who then transfer all their stock in Y to S Corporation, a subsidiary of P. Does this qualify as a tax-free reorganization? Why or why not?

43. Target Corporation has assets with a basis of $600,000 (fair market value of $900,000) and liabilities of $200,000. Its common stock consists of 20,000 shares at a par value of $15 per share. Target has E & P of $100,000. Acquiring Corporation exchanges with Target's shareholders 1,000 shares of its voting stock (worth $560,000) for 16,000 shares of common stock in Target. What are the tax results of the exchange?

44. S Corporation owns 20% of the voting stock of its parent, P Corporation. P owns 100% of S Corporation. S Corporation acquired 40% of the stock of T Corporation three years ago in a cash tender offer. P would like to acquire control of T Corporation in a tax-free reorganization. Can this be done? Explain.

45. T Corporation transfers assets with a fair market value of $100,000 to Z Corporation and receives voting stock valued at $80,000 and cash of $20,000. No liabilities are assumed. T distributes the cash and the stock in Z to its shareholders and is liquidated. Does this transaction qualify as a tax-free reorganization?

46. X Corporation transfers assets with a fair market value of $300,000 to Y Corporation and receives voting stock valued at $200,000 and cash of $40,000. Y Corporation assumes $60,000 of X Corporation's liabilities. X distributes the cash and stock in Y and is liquidated. Would this transaction qualify as a "C" reorganization?

47. A and B formed XY Corporation in January 1988 by each investing $50,000 in cash and receiving 5,000 shares of $10 par value common stock in XY. XY acquired operating assets with the $100,000 cash and continued in business until December 31, 1992, at which time the basis in its assets was $80,000. XY Corporation had an NOL carryover of $20,000 as of the end of that tax year. On December 31, 1992, XY transferred all its assets to C Corporation for $100,000 worth of stock in C and $20,000 cash. XY then distributed the C stock and $20,000 cash to its shareholders, A and B, in exchange for A's and B's stock in XY. XY was then liquidated. A received $60,000 worth of C stock, and B received $40,000 of stock and the $20,000 cash. The C stock transferred to XY represented a 55% ownership in C. What are the tax consequences of the transaction to C, XY, A, and B?

48. Target Corporation has assets worth $300,000 and liabilities of $40,000. X Corporation wants to acquire all of Target's assets in a "C" reorganization.

    a. If X Corporation assumes all of Target's liabilities, how much cash may X Corporation pay Target's shareholders in addition to distributing X Corporation's voting stock to them?

    b. How much cash may X Corporation pay Target's shareholders if Target's liabilities total $80,000 and X Corporation assumes all Target's liabilities?

49. Target Corporation transfers assets with a tax basis of $200,000, fair market value of $300,000, to Acquiring Corporation for voting stock in Acquiring worth $260,000 and $40,000 cash. Target distributes the cash and the Acquiring stock to its shareholder, and is liquidated. What are the tax consequences of the transfer? What are the basis of the assets to Acquiring and the basis of the Acquiring Corporation stock to Target?

50. Assume the same facts as Problem 49, except the consideration given by Acquiring consists of voting stock worth $200,000 and the assumption of $100,000 of Target Corporation's liabilities. What are the tax consequences and the bases of the assets and stock transferred?

51. X Corporation transfers 30% of its voting stock to Y Corporation for Y's assets worth $2,000,000. X also assumes liabilities of Y in the amount of $500,000. Y transfers the X stock to its shareholders for their Y stock. Y Corporation is then liquidated. Does this qualify as a tax-free reorganization? Suppose X transferred its voting stock plus $500,000 cash for Y's assets worth $2,000,000. Y distributes the cash and voting stock to its shareholders and is liquidated. Does this qualify as a tax-free reorganization?

52. X Corporation wishes to acquire control of T Corporation. X Corporation transfers 200 shares of newly issued voting stock to the shareholders of T Corporation in exchange for all their stock in T Corporation. However, X Corporation also pays reorganization expenses and attorney's fees incurred by the shareholders of T Corporation in connection with the transaction. Does the transaction qualify as a tax-free reorganization? Explain.

53. X Corporation has assets with a basis of $400,000. X transfers the assets (worth $800,000) to Y Corporation for voting stock valued at $640,000, cash of $60,000, and the assumption of $100,000 of X's liabilities. X distributes the voting stock in Y and the cash of $60,000 to A, its sole shareholder, and liquidates. A had a basis of $80,000 in his stock in X. What are the tax consequences of the transfer to X, Y, and A?

54. T Corporation has two shareholders, C and D, both individuals. C and D purchased their stock in T Corporation 10 years ago at a cost of $50,000 each. T Corporation has been manufacturing Product A and Product B for the past 10 years. T also has a separate research department. In 1991, T Corporation transfers all the assets used in manufacturing Product A to W, a newly formed corporation, for all the stock in W Corporation. The assets transferred to W Corporation have a net value of $600,000 and a tax basis of $200,000. T Corporation distributes all the stock in W Corporation to C in exchange for all of C's stock in T Corporation. The stock in W Corporation has a value of $600,000. T Corporation will continue to manufacture Product B.

    a. What gain, if any, will T Corporation recognize on the transfer of these assets to W Corporation in exchange for all the stock in W Corporation?
    b. What gain, if any, will C recognize on the exchange of the stock in T Corporation for the stock in W Corporation?
    c. What basis will C have in the stock in W Corporation?

55. Assume T Corporation, in Problem 54, has manufactured Product B for only two years.

    a. What gain, if any, will T Corporation recognize on the transfer of the Product A manufacturing assets to W Corporation in exchange for all the stock in W Corporation?
    b. What gain, if any, will C recognize on the exchange of the stock in T Corporation for the stock in W Corporation?
    c. What basis will C have in the stock in W Corporation?

56. Assume T Corporation, in Problem 54, transferred the assets used in the research department to W Corporation for all the stock in W Corporation. These assets also have a net value of $600,000 and a tax basis of $200,000.

    a. What gain, if any, will T Corporation recognize on the transfer of these assets to W Corporation in exchange for all the stock in W Corporation?
    b. What gain, if any, will C recognize on the exchange of the stock in T Corporation for the stock in W Corporation?
    c. What basis will C have in the stock in W Corporation?

57. C, an individual shareholder in T Corporation, has 50 shares of stock in T Corporation that she purchased two years ago for $60 per share. The stock is now worth $200 per share. Pursuant to a tax-free split-off, C received 100 shares of stock in W Corporation in exchange for 10 shares in T Corporation. The stock in W Corporation was worth $20 per share. What are the tax consequences of the exchange to C?

58. X Corporation has 1,000 shares of $100 par value preferred stock and 2,000 shares of $100 par value common stock outstanding. A, a highly valued employee of X, owns 200 shares of preferred stock and 400 shares of common, or 20% of each. B owns the remaining shares, or 80% of each. To retain A in the corporation, B agrees to surrender 1,000 of his shares of common stock for 1,000 newly issued shares of preferred stock to give A a 40% ownership in X. Will this transaction qualify as a tax-free reorganization? Why or why not? What are some possible tax problems that could arise?

59. T Corporation has 150 shares of common stock outstanding. C owns 100 shares, and 50 shares are owned by D, C's daughter. C and D have a basis of $500 in each share in T Corporation; each share has a fair market value of $2,000. T Corporation adopts a plan of recapitalization on August 10, 1991, whereby each shareholder may exchange one share of common stock for five shares of nonvoting preferred stock, fair market value of $400 per share. C exchanges her 100 shares of common stock for 500 shares of nonvoting preferred stock and relinquishes control of T Corporation. What are the tax consequences to C?

60. T, an individual, is a 10% shareholder in X Corporation. X Corporation, with E & P of $150,000 and assets worth $750,000, is merged into Y Corporation. T receives cash of $5,000, common stock in Y Corporation worth $60,000, and preferred stock in Y worth $10,000. T's basis in her X Corporation stock was $14,000. Assuming that the merger qualifies as an "A" reorganization, what are the tax consequences to T? To X Corporation? To Y Corporation?

61. Target Corporation has assets with a basis of $200,000 and a fair market value of $300,000, liabilities of $40,000, and E & P of $160,000. Acquiring Corporation, with E & P of $100,000, acquires all the assets of Target Corporation in a "C" reorganization. Acquiring assumes Target's liabilities and transfers voting stock worth $260,000 to Target in exchange for all of Target's assets. Target distributes the voting stock in Acquiring to its two shareholders, A and B, and liquidates. A and B have an aggregate basis of $30,000 in their Target stock. What are the tax consequences to A and B? To Target Corporation? To Acquiring Corporation?

62. X Corporation is merged into Y Corporation in a statutory merger. X Corporation had 5,000 shares of common stock outstanding, with a fair market value of $100 a share. One of X's shareholders exchanges his X stock (50 shares) for which he paid $80 per share for five 10% debenture bonds in Y Corporation (face value *and* fair market value of $1,000 per bond). What are the tax consequences to the shareholder?

63. Assume the shareholder in Problem 62 exchanges his stock for 100 shares of stock in W Corporation. Y Corporation was holding the W stock as an investment. The stock was worth $50 per share.

64. T, an individual, owns all the stock in Z Corporation. T has a basis of $50,000 in the Z Corporation stock, which currently has a fair market value of $300,000. Z Corporation is merged into W Corporation. What are the tax consequences to T in the following transactions when T exchanges her stock in Z Corporation for stock in W Corporation?

   a. T receives a .5% interest in W Corporation.
   b. T receives W Corporation preferred stock worth $100,000 and bonds of W Corporation with a principal amount of $250,000 and a fair market value of $200,000 payable in 15 years.
   c. T receives voting stock in W Corporation worth $200,000 and cash of $100,000.

65. X Corporation has assets worth $1,000,000 and liabilities totaling $200,000. Y Corporation is interested in acquiring either the assets or the stock of X Corporation. X Corporation wants the acquisition to be tax-free. Discuss whether the parties can arrange an "A," "B," or "C" reorganization under the following circumstances:

   a. Dissenting shareholders in X Corporation own 15% of the stock in X Corporation.
   b. Dissenting shareholders in X Corporation own 35% of the stock in X Corporation.

66. T Corporation transfers assets with a net value of $1,000,000, basis of $400,000, to Acquiring Corporation in exchange for voting stock in S Corporation, a subsidiary of Acquiring Corporation. The stock in S Corporation has a value of $1,000,000 and represents a 10% interest in S Corporation. Acquiring Corporation holds the remaining 90% interest in S Corporation. What gain, if any, will T Corporation recognize on the exchange of its assets for voting stock in S Corporation?

67. On June 1, 1991, a corporate raider, R, buys 20% of the stock of Target Corporation, or 10,000 shares, in the open market for $15 per share. R then threatens to make a public tender offer to Target's remaining shareholders to buy their shares for $18 per share. Upon learning of the threatened public tender offer, Target's board of directors offers the remaining shareholders $19 per share for their stock. On December 1, 1992, to eliminate R as a shareholder, the board of directors offers to pay R $20 per share. R accepts the offer and sells the 10,000 shares he had purchased at $15 per share for $20 per share. What gain will R have on the sale of the stock after any penalties he is required to pay?

68. Assume in Problem 67 that Target Corporation offers to pay all its shareholders, including R, $19 per share after R's threatened public tender offer. What gain would R have if he accepts the offer and sells the 10,000 shares for $19 per share?

69. T is president of Target Corporation. T's average annual salary for the past five years was $200,000. In 1992, Acquiring Corporation gains control of Target Corporation in a hostile takeover, and T loses his position. Pursuant to an employment contract with Target Corporation, T is paid $1,500,000 in 1992.

   a. What are the tax consequences to T of the $1,500,000 payment?
   b. Can Target Corporation, which is now controlled by Acquiring Corporation, deduct the $1,500,000 payment?

70. X Corporation merges into Y Corporation on June 30, 1992. Both corporations have a calendar year. X has an NOL of $300,000. Y's taxable income for 1992 is $360,000. How much of the loss can be used to offset Y's 1992 taxable income? (Assume § 382 is not applicable.)

71. T Corporation is merged into X Corporation on January 1, 1992. At the time of the merger, T Corporation had an NOL of $150,000. Pursuant to the merger, the shareholders of T Corporation receive 30% of the stock of X Corporation. T Corporation has a value of $100,000 on the date of the merger, and the long-term tax-exempt rate is 10%. How much of T Corporation's NOL can be used to offset X Corporation's taxable income of $500,000 in 1992?

72. Assume the shareholders in Problem 71 receive 60% of the stock of X Corporation. How much of T Corporation's NOL can be used to offset X Corporation's taxable income in 1992?

73. XY Corporation is owned equally by 10 shareholders and has an NOL of $200,000. Determine whether the § 382 loss limitation will apply in the following transactions:

   a. Six of the shareholders sell their stock to a third party, A.
   b. Four of the shareholders sell their stock to a third party, A.
   c. Assume in (b) that XY Corporation redeems the stock of three other shareholders in the following year.

74. X Corporation has an NOL of $400,000. The NOL was incurred in 1990. X Corporation has assets worth $300,000 and liabilities of $200,000 on January 1, 1992, when Y Corporation acquires all the assets of X Corporation in a statutory merger. Y Corporation exchanged stock worth $100,000 for the assets of X Corporation. The stock in Y Corporation was distributed to the shareholders of X Corporation. The shareholders in X Corporation acquired a 10% interest in Y Corporation. The tax-exempt rate on January 1, 1992, was 8%.

   a. If Y Corporation continues the business of X Corporation, how much of X's NOL can be used to offset Y Corporation's taxable income in 1992?
   b. How much of the $400,000 NOL of X Corporation will Y Corporation be able to use in future years assuming Y Corporation has adequate taxable income in each year after 1992?
   c. How much of the NOL of X Corporation will Y Corporation be able to use if Y Corporation does not continue the business of X Corporation?
   d. Assume that the assets of X Corporation (worth $300,000) include equipment with a value of $50,000 that was transferred to X Corporation in 1990. How much of the NOL of X Corporation can be used to offset Y Corporation's taxable income in 1992?
   e. Assume the assets of X Corporation consist of marketable securities worth $125,000. Indebtedness attributable to the marketable securities is $75,000. How much of the NOL of X Corporation can be used to offset Y Corporation's taxable income in 1992?

75. Loss Corporation has an NOL of $300,000. On January 2, 1992, Target Corporation, a profitable corporation, is merged into Loss Corporation in a tax-free "A" reorganization. The shareholders of Target receive 40% of the stock in Loss Corporation. Target Corporation had a building with a basis of $80,000 and fair market value of $500,000 that was transferred to Loss. On March 1, 1992, Loss

Corporation sells the building for $500,000. How much of the gain on the sale can be offset by Loss Corporation's NOL if Loss Corporation had a net worth of $200,000 on January 2, 1992, and the tax-exempt rate on January 2, 1992, is 10%?

76. Target Corporation, which has an NOL of $400,000, is merged into Acquiring Corporation in an "A" reorganization. Acquiring Corporation acquires Target for the principal purpose of utilizing the NOL. After the merger, the former shareholders of Target own 60% of the fair market value of the stock in Acquiring. The value of Target stock on the date of the merger is $100,000, and the long-term tax-exempt rate is 8%. How much of the NOL can be used by Acquiring Corporation?

77. Target Corporation has a capital loss in the amount of $80,000. On July 1,1992, Target Corporation transfers all its assets to Acquiring Corporation for 55% of the stock in Acquiring Corporation. Acquiring Corporation files its return on the basis of a calendar year. In 1992, Acquiring Corporation has net capital gains (computed without regard to any capital loss carryovers) of $100,000. How much of the $80,000 capital loss carried over from Target Corporation can be used to offset the capital gains?

78. T Corporation had accumulated E & P of $70,000 on January 1, 1992, when it merged into W Corporation. W Corporation had an accumulated deficit in E & P of $10,000 on January 1, 1992. In 1992 W Corporation had an NOL of $60,000, producing a current deficit in E & P of $60,000. On December 30, 1992, W Corporation distributed $30,000 to its shareholders. How will the shareholders of W Corporation be taxed on the $30,000 distribution? May the NOL of $60,000 incurred in 1992 be carried back to offset the taxable income of T Corporation for the past three years?

79. X Corporation has a deficit in E & P of $60,000. It acquires the assets of Y Corporation in a statutory merger. Y has E & P of $300,000. After the merger, X distributes $180,000 to its shareholders. How will the $180,000 be treated for tax purposes?

80. X Corporation uses the cash method of accounting for computing taxable income for its service business. X acquires the assets of Y Corporation in a statutory merger. Y has been using the accrual method of accounting for its retail boat business. X continues both the retail and service operations after the merger as separate businesses. What accounting method must be used to compute taxable income?

81. T Corporation, worth $700,000, has an NOL of $200,000. The stock in T Corporation is owned by two individuals: C, 55%, and D, 45%. C wants to sell her interest in T Corporation to D. The long-term tax-exempt rate is 8%.

   a. If C sells her entire interest in T Corporation to D in 1992, how much of its NOL may T Corporation deduct thereafter?

   b. How should the sale of C's interest to D be structured to produce the best tax results to T Corporation?

RESEARCH PROBLEMS

RESEARCH PROBLEM 1 N Insurance Company acquired S Insurance Company in a tax-free reorganization. S Insurance Company had an NOL carryover of $200,000. S Insurance Company acquired stock in N Insurance Company as consideration for the transfer of its assets to N. It did not liquidate and retained the stock in N as its principal asset. N Insurance Company deducted S Insurance Company's NOL carryover on its income tax return. The IRS disallowed the deduction under Reg. § 1.382(b)–1(a)(2). The Regulation states that shareholders of a loss corporation do not own stock in the acquiring corporation for purposes of determining the amount of an NOL of the acquired corporation that can be carried over to the acquiring corporation unless that stock has actually been distributed to the individual shareholders. N Insurance Company contends that it is entitled to all the loss carryover because the stock it transferred to S represented 50% of the value of all of its outstanding stock and it had no control over the disposition of that stock by S Insurance Company. N Insurance Company seeks your advice. What would you advise the corporation?

RESEARCH PROBLEM 2 P owned all the stock of XY Corporation on May 1, 1991. XY Corporation operated several fast-food restaurants. W Corporation was interested in acquiring the restaurants operated by XY Corporation and thus proposed a merger of XY Corporation into W Corporation. W Corporation entered into a contract with XY Corporation and P on May 1, 1991, in which P would exchange all of his stock in XY Corporation for unregistered stock in W Corporation. The assets of XY Corporation would be transferred to W Corporation, and XY Corporation would be liquidated. Under the terms of the contract, P would be employed by W Corporation. The contract included a covenant by P not to compete in the restaurant business with W Corporation for a period of two years. The contract also gave P a right to have the stock in W Corporation registered. Because stock in W Corporation was publicly traded, the unregistered stock could not be sold for a period of two years under SEC rules. In June of 1991, P purchased three fast-food restaurants in nearby cities and began to operate the restaurants by employing members of his family. The directors of W Corporation terminated P's employment as a result of P's breach of the covenant not to compete. P then demanded that W Corporation register the stock P received in the exchange so that P might sell the stock. W Corporation registered the stock on February 1, 1992, at which time P sold all his stock in W Corporation.

Upon audit of the tax returns of XY Corporation and P for 1991, the IRS contended that the exchange of P's stock in XY Corporation for the stock in W Corporation was a taxable exchange. The IRS contended that the step transaction doctrine should be applied to the exchange since P sold all the stock he acquired in W Corporation for cash less than a year later. P contended that the parties intended that the exchange be a tax-free "A" reorganization and that the sale of the stock in W Corporation was caused by subsequent events not related to the original transaction. Does the exchange of stock in XY Corporation for stock in W Corporation qualify as an "A" reorganization?

RESEARCH PROBLEM 3 The former shareholders of R Corporation exchanged all their shares in R for voting stock in M Corporation. The agreement provided that a sufficient number of shares in M, valued at $20 per share, would be issued to the shareholders of R to equal the value of R shares. In the event the purchase price was not evenly divisible by shares at $20 per share, the difference would be paid in cash. The value of shares was not so divisible. Therefore, each shareholder was paid an additional $40 in lieu of fractional shares. The shareholders of R did not report any gain on their income tax returns with respect to the stock exchange. The IRS contends each shareholder has a taxable gain based on the difference between the fair market value of shares in M plus the $40 cash and the tax basis of the stock in R. The IRS is of the opinion the exchange is not nontaxable. It is an exchange for stock and cash and hence does not qualify as a "B" reorganization. The shareholders seek your advice. What would you advise?

RESEARCH PROBLEM 4 A state-chartered savings and loan association merges with a Federal savings and loan association. The shareholders of the state-chartered savings and loan exchange their guaranty stock in the savings and loan for passbook savings accounts and certificates of deposit in the Federal savings and loan association. The savings accounts and certificates of deposit were the only form of equity in the Federal savings and loan association. Does the merger qualify as an "A" reorganization? Why or why not?

RESEARCH PROBLEM 5 T Corporation had a large NOL. A, an individual who was the sole shareholder and president of W Corporation, purchased all the stock of T on January 10. On December 15 of the same year, W adopted a plan to merge T and W. After the merger on January 5 of the following year, T was liquidated. W Corporation offset the NOL of T against its income from operations in the later year. Upon audit of W's return, the IRS disallowed the carryover of T's loss to W. A seeks your advice. A's argument is that she was the sole shareholder of both T and W on the date of the merger. Thus, the provisions of § 382 provide that all the loss of T can be carried over to W. What would you advise A?

RESEARCH PROBLEM 6 Target Corporation manufactures and sells chemical products in the United States and foreign countries. In 1991, a holding company, P Corporation, whose subsidiaries sell food products, made a tender offer to buy all of Target's stock. The shareholders of Target agreed to dispose of their stock in Target if the transfer qualified as a tax-free reorganization. P Corporation decided to transfer all of the stock of one of its subsidiaries to the shareholders of Target Corporation in exchange for all their stock in Target. The subsidiary was then merged into Target Corporation. Thus, the acquisition qualified as a tax-free ''A'' reorganization, a reverse merger. After the reverse merger, Target Corporation deducted its legal fees and investment banking fees incurred in connection with the merger. Upon audit in 1992, the IRS disallowed the deduction of such fees contending that the fees should be capitalized. What result?

CHAPTER

8

CONSOLIDATED TAX RETURNS

OBJECTIVES

Present the fundamental concepts relating to consolidated tax returns.

Identify the sources of the rules controlling consolidated taxable income.

Identify major advantages and disadvantages of filing consolidated tax returns.

Describe the corporations that are eligible to file on a consolidated basis.

Explain the compliance aspects of the consolidated return election.

Illustrate the computation of consolidated taxable income.

Apply the rules that relate to intercompany transactions within a consolidated group.

Demonstrate the computations of deductions and credits that are derived on a consolidated basis.

Identify various limitations that restrict the use of losses and credits of group members that were derived in separate-return years.

Discuss the computation of the parent's investment basis in a subsidiary, including those subsidiaries that generate net lifetime taxable losses.

Describe several tax planning opportunities that are available to groups that make the consolidation election.

OUTLINE

To this point, the discussion has centered on the computation of the tax liability of individual corporations under the regular tax calculation, along with specific penalty taxes and the alternative minimum tax. This is an appropriate approach to the study of corporate taxation, as more than 90 percent of all U.S. corporations (almost 4 million) are closely held (i.e., either by a small group of operators/investors or by members of the same family).

Nevertheless, a majority of the assets held by businesses are owned by about 100,000 large corporate conglomerates. These corporations conduct the bulk of the country's "big business" and generate most of the taxable income earned by corporate taxpayers.

Motivations to Consolidate

Corporate conglomerates are present in every aspect of life. The local dairy or bakery is likely to be owned by General Mills or General Foods. Oil and insurance companies own movie-making corporations. Professional sports teams are corporate cousins of the newspapers and television/radio stations that carry their games. The same corporate group that produces night lights for a child's nursery may manufacture control equipment for bombers and other elements of the Defense Department's arsenal.

What tax incentives lead to the creation of such seemingly strange corporate bedfellows? Much of the answer to this question can be found in the rules that control the filing of consolidated tax returns. In general terms, the IRS allows certain corporate groups to be treated as a single entity for Federal income tax purposes. This enables the group to use available tax exemptions and brackets optimally among its members and to shelter the income of profitable members with the losses of other members. Thus, through the consolidated return rules, corporate taxpayers have an opportunity to manage the combined tax liability of the members of the group.

The consolidated return rules may be available to a taxpayer as a result of any or all of the following business decisions:

■ Consolidated returns may be the result of a merger, acquisition, or other corporate combination (discussed in Chapter 7 of this text).

_____ EXAMPLE 1 _____

When D Corporation acquires all of the stock of E Corporation, a new corporate group, D and E Corporation, is formed. The two group members can elect to file their tax return on a consolidated basis. ♦

■ A group of business taxpayers may be restructured to comply with changes in regulatory requirements, meet the demands of a competitive environment, or gain economies of scale and operate more efficiently in a larger arrangement. Consequently, an election to file a consolidated return becomes available.

_____ EXAMPLE 2 _____

R Corporation, a retailer, acquires W Corporation, a wholesaler, in an effort to control its flow of inventory in unstable economic times. The two group members can elect to file their tax returns on a consolidated basis. ♦

■ The taxpayers may be seeking to gain tax and other financial advantages that are more readily available to corporate combinations.

EXAMPLE 3

Over the next three years, M Corporation will be selling a number of its business assets at a loss. If N Corporation acquires all of the stock of M and the group elects to file its tax returns on a consolidated basis, N will be able to combine its gains from the sale of business property with M's losses in computing the group's consolidated § 1231 gain/loss for the year. ◆

Source and Philosophy of Consolidated Return Rules

Some form of consolidated corporate tax return has been allowed for Federal purposes since World War I. At that time, the Treasury became suspicious that conglomerates were shifting taxable income to a number of smaller entities to avoid the high marginal rates of the excess profits tax that had been imposed to finance the war effort. Thus, the consolidated return rules can be seen as perhaps the earliest effort of the IRS to limit the tax benefits available to multiple corporations.

EXAMPLE 4

Assume that the marginal Federal income tax rate is 10% on the first $100,000 of taxable income and 15% on any taxable income in excess of $100,000. The additional five percentage points constitute a war profits tax, and the revenue they raise is used for the war effort.

Further assume that the tax law includes no restrictions on the tax computations of related corporations. A corporation with annual taxable income of $1 million can eliminate its entire exposure to the war profits tax by splitting its business evenly among 10 separate corporations. ◆

At various times since World War I, Congress has modified the pertinent Regulations and imposed a higher tax rate on consolidated groups to increase the cost of making the consolidation election. During the Great Depression, when it feared "too much" income was being sheltered within consolidated groups, Congress suspended the application of the rules for most taxpayers. On other occasions, complex limitations were placed upon the use and timing of positive tax benefits, such as net operating loss carryovers, that were acquired in a corporate consolidation. Congress imposed these limits to discourage profitable corporations from "trafficking" in businesses that had generated net losses.

Currently, Congress has delegated most of its legislative authority involving consolidated returns to the Treasury. As a result, the majority of the rules that affect consolidated groups are found in the Regulations. The Code provisions dealing with consolidated returns are strictly definitional in nature and broad in scope,[1] while the related Regulations dictate the computational and compliance requirements of the group.[2]

The length and detail of these Regulations make the consolidated return rules among the most complex in the entire Federal income tax law. For the most part, the underlying purpose of the rules remains one of organizational neutrality; that is, a group of closely related corporations should have neither a tax advantage nor a disadvantage relative to taxpayers who file separate corporate returns.

The derivation of a set of consolidated financial statements for a conglomerate and the computation of its consolidated taxable income correspond only slightly. The equity approach followed for financial accounting purposes has a role in the

---

1. §§ 1501–1505.

2. Reg. §§ 1.1501–1, 1.1502–0 through 1.1502–100, 1.1503–1 through 1.1503–2T, and 1.1504–1.

consolidated return rules, but exceptions to accounting conventions are both critical and numerous. Thus, a knowledge of financial accounting consolidation procedures will not necessarily be of great assistance in computing consolidated taxable income, nor will a lack of familiarity with accounting conventions be a hindrance.

EXAMPLE 5

Dividends paid by SubCo to its 100% owner, Parent Corporation, are eliminated from the separate taxable income computations of both group members in deriving consolidated taxable income. This treatment parallels the eliminating entry that is made in developing the group's consolidated financial statements. ◆

EXAMPLE 6

SubCo sells an asset to its 100% owner, Parent Corporation, at a tax and accounting gain of $100,000. The asset appreciates by another $20,000 before Parent sells it to an unrelated party, Outsider Corporation.

No tax or accounting gain is reported by the group members until the ultimate sale by Parent to Outsider. In constructing the consolidated financial statements, Parent realizes a $120,000 gain. For tax purposes, however, SubCo is assigned $100,000 of the gain, and Parent recognizes only "its" $20,000. ◆

International Perspectives

The United States is one of the few Western countries that allows consolidated returns. Most of its trading partners allow their taxing authority to recompute the taxable income of the members of a conglomerate,[3] but require the members to file separate tax returns. This is especially true for group members that are incorporated outside the host country. Thus, in the view of these more restrictive countries, the ability of a taxpayer to shelter taxable income among multiple corporations and jurisdictions should be eliminated. Although U.S. rules also preclude most foreign corporations from joining in a consolidated return,[4] there appears to be no current trend toward the abolition of the consolidated return rules for domestic corporations.

ASSESSING CONSOLIDATED RETURN STATUS
◆

As Concept Summary 8–1 illustrates, all of the members of a corporate group must meet three broad requirements to be eligible to elect to file consolidated income tax returns: (1) The corporations must meet the statutory ownership requirements to be classified as an affiliated group.[5] (2) The corporations must be eligible to make a consolidation election.[6] (3) The group must meet various tax accounting and compliance requirements in making and maintaining the election.[7]

In making the election to file consolidated tax returns, the related taxpayers must weigh the advantages and disadvantages of such an election..

The potential advantages of filing consolidated returns include the following:

- The operating and capital loss carryovers on one group member may be used to shelter the corresponding income of other group members.
- The taxation of all intercompany dividends may be eliminated.
- Recognition of income from certain intercompany transactions can be deferred.

---

3. This is similar to the powers assigned to the IRS under § 482.
4. § 1504(b)(3).

5. §§ 1504(a)(1) and (2).
6. This a negative definition, rooted in §§ 1504(b) through (f).
7. See especially Reg. §§ 1.1502–75, –76, and –77.

- Certain deductions and credits may be optimized by using consolidated amounts in computing pertinent limitations (e.g., the deductions for charitable contributions and dividends received, and foreign tax credits).
- The tax basis of investments in the stock of subsidiaries is increased by the amount of positive subsidiary earnings and profits (E & P).
- The alternative minimum tax (AMT) attributes of all group members can be used in deriving consolidated alternative minimum taxable income (AMTI). This can reduce the adjusted current earnings (ACE) adjustment and other AMT preferences and adjustments.
- The share holdings of all group members can be used in meeting other statutory requirements.[8]
- The adjusted ordinary income of all group members can be used in avoiding the personal holding company tax.
- Current-year operating losses of one group member can be used to defer or reduce the (regular or AMT) estimated tax payments of the entire group.

Consolidated returns also have a number of potential disadvantages, including the following:

- The election is binding on all subsequent tax years of the group members, unless either the makeup of the affiliated group changes or the IRS consents to a revocation of the election.

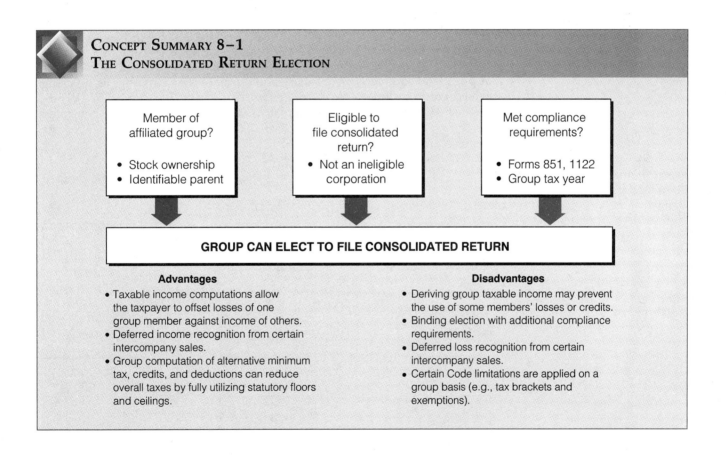

CONCEPT SUMMARY 8–1
THE CONSOLIDATED RETURN ELECTION

Member of affiliated group?	Eligible to file consolidated return?	Met compliance requirements?
• Stock ownership • Identifiable parent	• Not an ineligible corporation	• Forms 851, 1122 • Group tax year

GROUP CAN ELECT TO FILE CONSOLIDATED RETURN

Advantages	Disadvantages
• Taxable income computations allow the taxpayer to offset losses of one group member against income of others. • Deferred income recognition from certain intercompany sales. • Group computation of alternative minimum tax, credits, and deductions can reduce overall taxes by fully utilizing statutory floors and ceilings.	• Deriving group taxable income may prevent the use of some members' losses or credits. • Binding election with additional compliance requirements. • Deferred loss recognition from certain intercompany sales. • Certain Code limitations are applied on a group basis (e.g., tax brackets and exemptions).

---

8. E.g., for purposes of the § 165(g) deduction for losses from worthlessness of securities and the corporate control requirement of § 351(a).

- Capital and operating losses of one group member are applied against the corresponding income of the other group members even when assigning the losses to separate return years would produce a greater tax benefit. The benefit might be due, for instance, to rate discounts or changes in tax rates.
- Recognition of losses from certain intercompany transactions is deferred.
- Using consolidated amounts in computing the limitations may decrease the amounts of certain deductions and credits.
- The tax basis of investments in the stock of subsidiaries is decreased by the amount of negative subsidiary E & P and by distributions from E & P.
- The requirement that all group members use the parent's tax year creates short tax years for the subsidiaries. As a result, a subsidiary's income may be bunched and one of the years of its charitable contribution and loss carryforward period may be lost.
- Recognition of legal and other rights of minority shareholders may be more restrictive in the context of a consolidated group.
- Additional administrative costs may be incurred in complying with the consolidated return Regulations.

ELECTING CONSOLIDATED RETURN STATUS
◆

As Concept Summary 8–1 illustrated, the election to file on a consolidated basis is restricted to groups of corporations that (1) meet the stock ownership criteria of an affiliated group, (2) are statutorily eligible to make such an election, and (3) satisfy various compliance requirements in making and maintaining the election.

Controlled and Affiliated Groups

The Code includes two definitions of groups of multiple corporations, namely, the *controlled group*[9] and the *affiliated group*.[10] Broadly speaking, a controlled group refers to both parent-subsidiary and brother-sister corporations, while an affiliated group includes only parent-subsidiary groups (see Figure 8–1). Thus, the affiliated group definition essentially describes a subset of the controlled

FIGURE 8–1
Controlled and Affiliated Groups

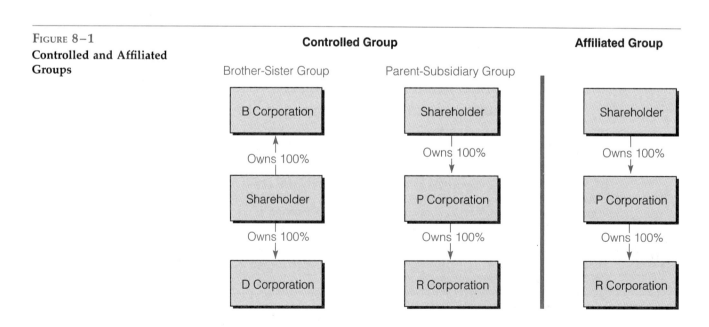

Controlled Group

Brother-Sister Group   Parent-Subsidiary Group

Affiliated Group

9. §§ 1563(a)(1) and (2).   10. § 1504.

group specification; rules that apply to controlled groups are effective for nearly all affiliated groups, but not vice versa.

Controlled Groups. As Chapter 2 explained, a controlled group is treated as one corporation for purposes of assigning a number of tax benefits, including the following:

- Discounted marginal tax rates on the first $75,000 of taxable income.[11]
- The $150,000 or $250,000 accumulated earnings credit.[12]
- The $40,000 exemption in computing AMTI.[13]
- The $2 million exemption in computing the environmental superfund tax.[14]

In addition, members of a controlled group must defer the recognition of any realized loss on intercompany sales until a sale is made at a gain to a nongroup member.[15] Similarly, any gain on the sale of depreciable property between members of a controlled group is recognized as ordinary income.[16]

These restrictions are imposed to limit taxpayers' ability to minimize a group's tax liability by creating multiple corporations. Each member of the group is assigned an equal share of the above benefits every taxable year, unless all members consent to some other apportionment method.

A *parent-subsidiary controlled group* exists when one corporation owns at least 80 percent of the voting power of another corporation or holds shares representing at least 80 percent of the value.[17] Multiple tiers of subsidiaries and chains of ownership are allowed, as long as the group has an identifiable parent corporation (i.e., after attribution, at least 80 percent of one corporation must be owned by another).

--------------------------------- EXAMPLE 7 ---------------------------------

In the following figure, a parent-subsidiary controlled group exists in the first ownership structure, but not in the second (inadequate ownership level) or third (no identifiable parent).

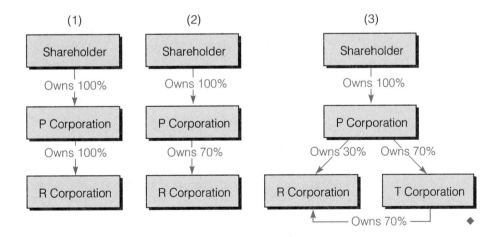

---

11. §§ 11(b)(1) and 1561(a)(1).

12. §§ 535(c)(2) and (3) and 1561(a)(2).

13. §§ 55(d)(2) and 1561(a)(3).

14. §§ 59A(a) and 1561(a)(4).

15. §§ 267(a)(1), (b)(3), and (f).

16. §§ 1239(a) and (c).

17. § 1563(a)(1). For this purpose, stock ownership is attributed from partnerships to their partners, and from estates and trusts to their beneficiaries, if that ownership represents at least 5% of corporate voting power or value. In addition, all stock options are considered to be exercised by their holders. §§ 1563(d)(1) and (e)(1) through (3).

A *brother-sister controlled group* exists when five or fewer individuals, trusts, or estates own at least 80 percent of the voting power, or hold shares representing at least 80 percent of the value, of two or more corporations.[18] In addition, the aggregate common ownership of the identified shareholders must exceed 50 percent of the voting power or value of the corporation's shares. For this purpose, a shareholder's common ownership equals his or her lowest level of holdings with respect to all of the corporations. These common ownership values are aggregated among all of the identified shareholders; for a brother-sister controlled group, the sum must exceed 50 percent. See Chapter 2 for a more detailed discussion of these rules.

Affiliated Groups. An *affiliated group* exists when one corporation owns at least 80 percent of the voting power of another corporation and holds shares representing at least 80 percent of its value.[19] This definition is very similar to that of the parent-subsidiary controlled group. Again, multiple tiers and chains of corporations are allowed as long as the group has an identifiable parent corporation.

The following are the most important differences between parent-subsidiary controlled groups and affiliated groups:

- An affiliated group must have 80 percent of the voting power *and* value of the members of the group, whereas a controlled group needs only 80 percent of the voting power *or* value. This difference can be important when preferred stock or other shares with voting or liquidation limitations are involved.
- The stock attribution rules that must be applied to a controlled group are not required for an affiliated group. Thus, in an affiliated group, the identifiable parent corporation itself must own at least 80 percent of the voting power and value of the shares of at least one subsidiary.
- The corporations must meet the stock ownership tests of the affiliated group rule on *every day* of the tax year, whereas the corresponding controlled group tests are applied only on the last day of the year.[20]

Members of an affiliated group are allowed to either (1) claim on their separately filed tax returns a 100 percent dividends received deduction for payments passing between them[21] or (2) elect to file income tax returns on a consolidated basis.

─────────────────────────── EXAMPLE 8 ───────────────────────────

In the first ownership structure in the accompanying figure, P, R, T, and V form an affiliated group, with P as the parent, under the stock ownership rules. V cannot be included in a consolidated return, however, so the consolidation election is available only to P, R, and T. In the second structure, P, R, and T form an affiliated group, and all of them can be included in a properly executed consolidated return. P is the identifiable parent of the group. R and T essentially form a brother-sister group below P.

─────────────────────────────

18. § 1563(a)(2). For this purpose, stock ownership is attributed from corporations to their shareholders, from partnerships to their partners, and from estates and trusts to their beneficiaries, if that ownership represents at least 5% of corporate voting power or value. Moreover, with some exceptions, share ownership is attributed to and from

spouses, children, and grandchildren. In addition, all stock options are considered to be exercised by their holders. §§ 1563(d)(2) and (e).

19. §§ 1504(a)(1) and (2).

20. §§ 1501 and 1563(b)(1).

21. § 243(b)(1).

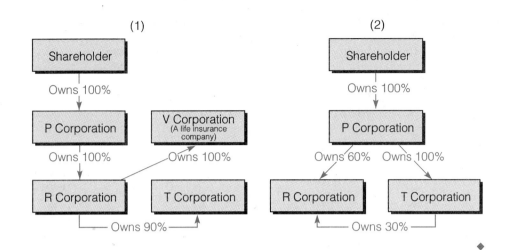

Eligibility for the Consolidation Election

The Code lists a number of corporations that may *not* use a consolidated return to report their taxable income.[22] Thus, these corporations cannot be used to meet the stock ownership tests, and their taxable incomes cannot be included in a consolidated return.[23] Of the entities that are ineligible for consolidated return status, the following are most frequently encountered:

- Corporations established outside the U.S. or in a U.S. possession.
- Tax-exempt (charitable) corporations.[24]
- Insurance companies.
- S corporations.[25]
- Partnerships, trusts, estates, and any other noncorporate entities.

Compliance Requirements

An eligible entity that meets the stock ownership test can be included in a consolidated group if several compliance requirements are met.

The Initial Consolidated Return.   Under the Regulations, the first consolidated tax return must include the following:

- The Form 1120 for the tax year of the consolidated group should include the taxable results of the operations of all of the members of the consolidated group. This return is filed in lieu of the separate returns of the group members.[26] The identified group then continues to file on a consolidated basis until an eligible group no longer exists, or an election to "un-consolidate" is made.[27]

22. § 1504(b).

23. A few other, infrequently encountered corporations are also prohibited from filing on a consolidated basis. These include domestic international sales corporations and possessions corporations, regulated investment companies and real estate investment trusts. §§ 1504(b)(4) through (7). Narrow exceptions are available, however, under which certain insurance companies, exempt organizations, and 100%-owned Canadian or Mexican subsidiaries can be included in a consolidated return. §§ 1504(c) through (e).

24. This includes any entity that is exempt from tax under § 501.

See Chapter 14 for a discussion of the qualification of charitable organizations for exempt status.

25. Section 1361(b)(2)(A) implies that an entity must choose between S corporation and consolidated return status.

26. Reg. § 1.1502–75(a)(1).

27. Reg. § 1.1502–75(c). The IRS permits such an election only rarely, on the parent's assertion of (1) a good-cause reason to disengage from consolidated status or (2) a substantial change in the tax law that adversely affects the consolidated tax liability.

■ A Form 1122 should be attached to the first consolidated tax return for all of the subsidiaries included in the group.[28] This form represents a consent by all of the entities to be included in the consolidated group.

The election must be made no later than the extended due date of the parent's return for the year. Only in the case of an inadvertent error can the election to consolidate be rescinded once this extended due date passes.[29]

EXAMPLE 9

Parent Corporation owns 100% of the stock of SubCo. Both corporations use calendar tax years and file separate returns. The entities wish to file on a consolidated basis starting with the tax return for 1993. Parent Corporation does not file to obtain an extended due date for its 1993 return.

If the consolidation election is to be effective, Parent must file a Form 1120 that includes the taxable income of the two corporations by March 15, 1994. SubCo must execute a Form 1122 and attach it to the consolidated Form 1120. ◆

EXAMPLE 10

Continue with the facts of the previous example. Parent Corporation files a complete consolidated Form 1120 on March 1, 1994. On March 5, 1994, the Supreme Court issues a decision that will have considerable adverse effect on the group's 1995–1999 taxable incomes. If Parent and SubCo file separate 1993 returns by March 15, 1994 (or by some later date if an extension to file is obtained in a timely fashion), the IRS will ignore the consolidation election.

If Parent and SubCo fail to file separate returns in this manner, the election to consolidate will be in force for all future years, or until the IRS approves Parent's application to revoke it. ◆

An application to terminate the consolidation election must be filed at least 90 days prior to the extended due date of the consolidated return.[30] Generally, when a subsidiary leaves an ongoing consolidated group, it must wait five years before it can reenter the group.[31]

Subsequent Consolidated Returns. Each succeeding consolidated tax return must include Form 851, Affiliations Schedule, reproduced in Appendix B of this text. This report identifies all of the corporations in the electing group, summarizes pertinent shareholdings and stock ownership changes that occurred during the tax year, and lists the estimated tax payments made by the group members for the year.

Consolidated tax returns are due on the fifteenth day of the third month following the close of the group's tax year (this is March 15 for a calendar year taxpayer). A six-month extension to file the return can be obtained by executing Form 7004, but an estimated payment of the remaining tax liability for the group must accompany the extension application.

Liability for Taxes. Group members are jointly and severally liable for the entire consolidated tax liability.[32] This rule applies to interest and penalties imposed as a result of audits as well as to tax liabilities. Furthermore, the IRS is not bound to follow internal agreements among group members in apportioning the liability.[33]

---

28. Reg. § 1502–75(b). A specimen Form 1122 is included in Appendix B of this text.

29. Reg. §§ 1.1502–75(b)(3) and 301.9100–1T(a).

30. Reg. § 1.1502–75(c)(1)(i).

31. § 1504(a)(3).

32. Reg. § 1.1502–6(a).

33. Reg. § 1.1502–6(c).

—————————————— EXAMPLE 11 ——————————————

Parent Corporation, a calendar year taxpayer, acquired 100% of the stock of calendar year SubCo on December 20, 1993. The group filed on a consolidated basis from that date until December 31, 1995, when all of the SubCo stock was sold to Foreign Corporation.

A 1995 IRS audit determined that Parent owed an additional $10 million in Federal income taxes, relating to a sale it made on December 30, 1993. By mid-1996, however, Parent's cash-flow difficulties had brought it close to bankruptcy and forced it to cease activities.

Due to the consolidation election, the IRS can assess the delinquent taxes from SubCo (and Foreign Corporation) in 1995.[34] Under the Code, SubCo is liable for the full amount of any consolidated tax liability, even when it is not the source of the income that led to the tax. ◆

Starting with the third consolidated return year, estimated tax payments must be made on a consolidated basis.[35] Prior to that year, estimates can be computed and paid on either a separate or consolidated basis.

Regular tax liability is computed applying the graduated tax rates to consolidated taxable income, following the requirements of controlled group status. In this regard, contributions to the actual payment of the tax liability often are arranged to correspond to contributions to consolidated taxable income. Benefits accruing from the graduated corporate tax rates are apportioned equally among the group members unless all members consent to some other method through an annual election.

—————————————— EXAMPLE 12 ——————————————

Parent Corporation owns 100% of the stock of SubCo, and the two corporations file a consolidated tax return. Over the course of a five-year period, the corporations generate the following taxable income/(loss). The low marginal rates that apply to the group's first $75,000 of taxable income might be assigned as follows:

Year	Parent's Taxable Income	SubCo's Taxable Income	Low Brackets Assigned to Parent	Low Brackets Assigned to SubCo
1*	$ 100,000	$ (10,000)	$37,500	$37,500
2**	100,000	(10,000)	75,000	–0–
3	50,000†	10,000	65,000	10,000
4	(15,000)†	10,000	65,000	10,000
5	100,000	100,000	37,500	37,500

  * No election to consolidate is made by group members; brackets are allocated equally between them.
  ** The indicated election was made for each of the following years.
  † The taxpayer believes that Parent's taxable income is more likely to be adjusted on audit. ◆

Alternative minimum tax (AMT) liability is computed on the basis of consolidated AMTI.[36] The group is allowed only one $40,000 AMT exemption, which is phased out also using consolidated AMTI. Similarly, the AMT adjustment for adjusted current earnings (ACE), which is 75 percent of the excess of ACE over pre-ACE AMTI, is computed using consolidated amounts. Thus, the ACE adjustment of the group may be smaller than the aggregate of the ACE adjustments for the members if they had not consolidated.

—————————

34. The assessment will be limited to SubCo's allocable share of the tax (here, probably zero) if it occurs after the sale of the shares to Foreign Corporation. Reg. § 1.1502–6(b).

35. Reg. § 1.1502–5(a)(1).

36. See Chapter 6 for a full discussion of the AMT computations.

--------- EXAMPLE 13 ---------

If Parent Corporation and SubCo, its 100%-owned subsidiary, file separately, their pre-ACE AMTI, adjusted current earnings, and ACE adjustments are as follows:

Parent's Separate Adjusted Current Earnings	Parent's Separate Pre-ACE AMTI	SubCo's Separate Adjusted Current Earnings	SubCo's Separate Pre-ACE AMTI
$1,000,000	$400,000	$400,000	$500,000

The corporations incurred no intercompany transactions that would alter the computation of these amounts on a consolidated basis.

When the ACE adjustment is computed on a consolidated basis, SubCo's "unused" excess AMTI is offset against Parent's adjusted current earnings, and the aggregate ACE adjustment is reduced by $75,000.

Separate Computations	Consolidated Computations
Parent's ACE adjustment: .75 × ($1,000,000 − $400,000) = $450,000	Consolidated ACE adjustment: .75 × ($1,400,000 − $900,000) = $375,000
SubCo's ACE adjustment: .75 × ($400,000 − $500,000) = $ −0−	◆

Tax Accounting Periods and Methods. All the members of a consolidating group must use the parent's tax year.[37] As a result, the group may be required to file a short-year return for the first year a subsidiary is included in the consolidated return, so that the parent's year-end can be adopted.[38] There are two "30-day" exceptions to this short-year rule, which can be elected by the subsidiary when appropriate:[39]

- If the subsidiary is acquired within the first 30 days of its separate tax year, its entire tax year can be included in the consolidated return.
- If the subsidiary is acquired when 30 or fewer days are remaining in the parent's tax year, the subsidiary can be excluded entirely from the consolidated return for the acquisition year.

--------- EXAMPLE 14 ---------

Parent Corporation acquires 100% of the stock of SubCo on October 1, 1993. Both parties intend for the group to file a consolidated tax return immediately upon the acquisition. Parent uses a calendar tax year, while SubCo has been using a March 31 tax year.

The first consolidated return is due on March 15, 1994 (ignoring filing extensions). The 1993 consolidated return includes the entire year's results for Parent and the postacquisition results of SubCo. SubCo must also file a separate return, reporting its results for the period April 1, 1993, through September 30, 1993. ◆

--------- EXAMPLE 15 ---------

Continue with the facts of the previous example, except that SubCo was acquired on April 5, 1993. If SubCo elects, it need not file a short-period (April 1–April 4) return. Instead, all of SubCo's taxable results occurring after March 31, 1993, are included in the consolidated return.

37. Reg. § 1.1502–76(a)(1).
38. Reg. § 1.1502–76(b)(2).

39. Reg. § 1.1502–76(b)(5).

Alternatively, if SubCo were acquired on December 20, 1993, it could elect to file a separate return for the periods April 1, 1992, through March 31, 1993, and April 1 through December 31, 1993. Consolidated return status would effectively begin on January 1, 1994. ◆

When a mid-year acquisition occurs, both short years are used in tracking the carryforward period of unused losses and credits.[40] Short-year income and deductions are apportioned between the pre- and postacquisition periods. The apportionment may either be done on a daily basis or as the items are recorded for financial accounting purposes, at the election of the corporation being acquired.[41]

───────────────── EXAMPLE 16 ─────────────────

All of the stock of calendar year SubCo is acquired by Parent Corporation on July 15, 1993. The corporations elect to file a consolidated return immediately upon the acquisition.

SubCo had generated a long-term capital loss in its 1990 tax year. As of January 1, 1994, only one year remains in the carryforward period for the capital loss. ◆

───────────────── EXAMPLE 17 ─────────────────

Continue with the facts of the previous example. According to SubCo's financial accounting records, $400,000 of its $1,000,000 accounting and taxable income for the year was generated after the acquisition. At SubCo's election, either $400,000 (the "books" apportionment method) or $465,753 [(170 postacquisition days/365 days) × $1,000,000 income] (the "daily" method) can be included in the first consolidated return. ◆

Members of a consolidated group can continue to use the tax accounting methods that were in place prior to the consolidation election.[42] Thus, the members of a consolidated group may use different accounting methods.[43] On the other hand, since the $5 million gross-receipts test with respect to use of the cash method of accounting is applied on a consolidated basis,[44] some of the group members may need to switch from the cash to the accrual method of tax accounting.

Upon acquiring a subsidiary, the parent corporation records a stock basis on its tax balance sheet equal to the acquisition price. At the end of every consolidated return year, the parent records one or more adjustments to this stock basis, as in the financial accounting "equity" method. This treatment prevents double taxation of gain (or deduction of loss) upon the ultimate disposal of the subsidiary's shares.[45] The adjustments are recorded on the last day of the consolidated return year or on the (earlier) date of the disposal of the shares.[46]

STOCK BASIS OF SUBSIDIARY
◆

40. Reg. § 1.1502–76(d).

41. Reg. § 1.1502–76(b)(4).

42. Reg. § 1.1502–17(a).

43. A series of complex adjustments to inventory values are required where a group member (1) filed a separate return in the preceding tax year; (2) sold inventory assets to another group member in that year, and the goods remained unsold at the end of the separate-return year; and (3) otherwise was eligible to file on a consolidated basis with the purchaser for that year. Reg. § 1.1502–18(b). These adjustments override the usual intercompany transaction rules discussed later in

the chapter. Essentially, built-in gain from such inventory is recognized immediately upon the consolidation.

44. §§ 448(a)(1) and (c)(2). If the members of the consolidated group are treated as personal service corporations, however, their gross receipts are not aggregated, unless the parent so elects; by using this election in an optimal manner, the cash method may be available to some or all of the members. §§ 448(d)(2) and (d)(4)(C).

45. This procedure parallels the accounting for equity basis in a partnership or S corporation. See Chapters 10 and 12.

46. Reg. § 1.1502–32(a).

In this regard, positive adjustments include the following:

- An allocable share of the subsidiary's undistributed E & P for the year.
- An allocable share of the consolidated operating or capital loss of a subsidiary that could not utilize the loss through a carryback to a prior year.

Negative adjustments to stock basis include the following:

- An allocable share of the subsidiary's deficit in E & P for the year.
- An allocable share of any carryover operating or capital losses that are deducted on the consolidated return and have not previously reduced stock basis.
- Dividends paid by the subsidiary to the parent out of E & P.

EXAMPLE 18

Parent Corporation acquired all of the stock of SubCo on January 1, 1993, for $1,000,000. The parties immediately elected to file consolidated tax returns. SubCo had a deficit in E & P of $100,000 in 1993, but it generated $40,000 taxable income in 1994 and $65,000 in 1995. SubCo paid a $10,000 dividend in mid-1995.

Parent has the following stock bases in SubCo on the last day of each of the indicated years:

1993	$900,000
1994	$940,000
1995	$995,000

◆

When accumulated deficits in the subsidiary's postacquisition E & P exceed the acquisition price, an *excess loss account* is created.[47] This account (1) allows the consolidated return to recognize the losses of the subsidiary in the current year and (2) enables the group to avoid the need to reflect a negative stock basis on its tax-basis balance sheet. If the subsidiary stock is sold to a nongroup member while an excess loss account exists, the seller recognizes the balance of the account as capital gain income.[48]

EXAMPLE 19

Parent Corporation acquired all of the stock of SubCo on January 1, 1993, for $100,000. As a result of SubCo's operations, the group records the following amounts:

Year	Operating Gain/(Loss)	Stock Basis	Excess Loss Account
1993	$(40,000)	$60,000	$ –0–
1994	(80,000)	–0–	20,000
1995	30,000	10,000	–0–

If Parent sells the SubCo stock for $50,000 at the end of 1994, Parent recognizes a $70,000 capital gain ($50,000 amount realized − $0 adjusted basis in stock + $20,000 recovery of excess loss account). If the sale takes place at the end of 1995, the capital gain is $40,000.[49] ◆

---

47. Reg. § 1.1502–19. This is preferable to the treatment of excessive losses by partnerships and S corporations, where loss deductions are suspended until sufficient equity basis is created.

48. Reg. §§ 1.1502–19(a)(1) and (2). For this purpose, stock redemptions, worthlessness of the stock, and termination of the consolidation election all trigger recognition of income to

the extent of the excess loss account. Reg. § 1.1502–19(b). If the subsidiary is insolvent, the gain is recognized as ordinary income. Reg. § 1.1502–19(a)(2)(ii).

49. Technically, the 1995 subsidiary income first is used to eliminate the excess loss account (i.e., before it creates new stock basis). Reg. § 1.1502–32(e)(3).

To limit the recognition effects of an excess loss account, the group may elect to reduce the parent's basis of any remaining stock or indebtedness of the subsidiary that is held after the triggering disposition.[50] After the bases of these other investments have been reduced to zero, the seller must recognize the balance of the excess loss account.

In a chain of more than one tier of subsidiaries, the computation of the stock basis amounts starts with the lowest-level subsidiary, then proceeds up the ownership structure to the parent's holdings. In this regard, there is no such concept as consolidated E & P. Rather, each entity accounts for its own increments to E & P (and those of its subsidiaries) on an annual basis, immediately recognizing within E & P any gain or loss on intercompany transactions and reducing E & P by an allocable share of the consolidated tax liability.[51]

Derivation of annual consolidated taxable income involves more than a mere summing of the members' separate taxable income amounts. As Figure 8–2 shows, a number of additional steps are required for several reasons: (1) a few intercompany transactions are directly eliminated from the computation; (2) several transactions are accounted for on a consolidated basis and are therefore removed from the members' computations and treated using group amounts; and (3) certain transactions receive special deferral treatment under the Code, so they are removed from further computations until the deferral period ends.

COMPUTING CONSOLIDATED TAXABLE INCOME
◆

FIGURE 8–2   **Computing Consolidated Taxable Income**

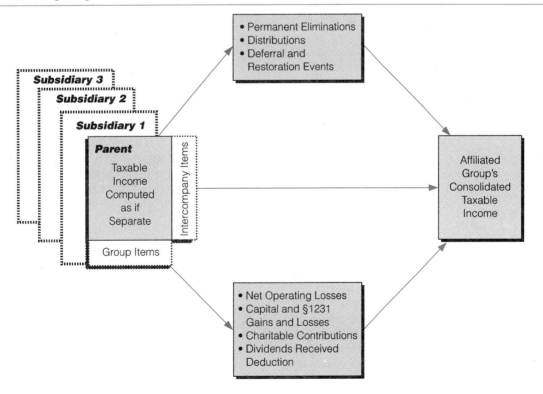

---

50. Reg. § 1.1502–19(a)(6).
51. Reg. § 1.1502–33(d). In the absence of an election to use some other allocation method, the consolidated tax liability is allocated to each group member in proportion to its contribution to consolidated taxable income. § 1552(a). Reg. §§ 1.1552–1(a)(2) and (3)(i).

Specifically, each group member splits several items off from its separately computed taxable income. Thus, consolidated taxable income becomes a combination of the revised separate taxable incomes and the resulting income/loss from group items and deferral/restoration events.

Computational Procedure

The remainder of this chapter will follow the computational procedure suggested in Figure 8–2.[52] Figure 8–3 presents a skeleton worksheet for this computational procedure. Additional information would be added to the worksheet for every additional subsidiary. In each case, the starting point for this procedure is the separate taxable incomes of all the group members.

———————————————— EXAMPLE 20 ————————————————

Parent Corporation owns 100% of the stock of SubCo. This year, Parent's taxable income amounted to $100,000, while SubCo generated a $40,000 taxable loss. There were no transactions between the two corporations, and they incurred no capital or § 1231 gains/losses, charitable contributions, dividend income, or other items that are accounted for on a group basis. Accordingly, consolidated taxable income was $60,000.

	Separate Taxable Income	Adjustments	Postadjustment Amounts
Parent information	$100,000	_____	$100,000
SubCo information	(40,000)	_____	(40,000)
Group-basis transactions	_____	_____	_____
Deferral/restoration events	_____	_____	_____
Consolidated taxable income			$ 60,000

* Permanent eliminations.
** Group-basis transaction.
†Deferral/restoration event.

◆

Typical Intercompany Transactions

General Rules.   When one member of a consolidated group engages in a transaction with another member of the group, an intercompany transaction occurs. In contrast to the financial accounting treatment of most such transactions, the most commonly encountered items *remain in* the members' separate taxable incomes and therefore cancel each other out on a consolidated basis.[53]

FIGURE 8–3
Consolidated Taxable Income Worksheet

	Separate Taxable Income	Adjustments	Postadjustment Amounts
Parent information	_____	_____	_____
Subsidiary information	_____	_____	_____
Group-basis transactions	_____	_____	_____
Deferral/restoration events	_____	_____	_____
Consolidated taxable income			_____

* Permanent eliminations.
** Group-basis transaction.
† Deferral/restoration event.

————————————————

52. Inventory adjustments, recovery of excess loss accounts, and treatment of depletion deductions, among other items, also are included at an appropriate point in these computations.

53. Reg. § 1.1502–13(b)(1).

For instance, when one group member performs services for another member during the year, the purchaser of the services incurs a deductible expenditure, while the service provider generates includible income. The net result is a zero addition to consolidated taxable income.[54]

This two-step procedure prevents the group from avoiding any § 267 loss disallowances. Furthermore, when the members involved in the transaction are using different tax accounting methods, the payor's deduction for the expenditure is deferred until the year in which the recipient recognizes the related gross income.[55]

───────────────── EXAMPLE 21 ─────────────────

In the current year, Parent Corporation provided consulting services to its 100%-owned subsidiary, SubCo, under a contract that requires no payments to Parent until next year. Both parties use the accrual method of tax accounting. The services that Parent rendered are valued at $100,000. In addition, Parent purchased $15,000 of supplies from SubCo.

Including these transactions, Parent's taxable income for the year amounted to $500,000. SubCo reported $150,000 separate taxable income. The group is not required to make any eliminating adjustments. The members' deductions incurred offset the income included by the other party to the intercompany transaction. The consolidated taxable income includes both Parent's $15,000 deduction for supplies and SubCo's $15,000 gross receipts therefrom, so the consolidated taxable income computation *de facto* results in an elimination similar to the kind made in financial accounting.

	Separate Taxable Income	Adjustments	Postadjustment Amounts
Parent information	$500,000	_____	$500,000
SubCo information	150,000	_____	150,000
Group-basis transactions	_____	_____	_____
Deferral/restoration events	_____	_____	
Consolidated taxable income			$650,000

* Permanent eliminations.
** Group-basis transaction.
† Deferral/restoration event.

───────────────── EXAMPLE 22 ─────────────────

Continue with the facts of the previous example, except that Parent is a cash basis taxpayer. Since Parent will not recognize the $100,000 of service income earned in the current year until the next tax period, SubCo's related deduction also is deferred until the following year. Thus, the intercompany item—SubCo's deduction—must be eliminated from consolidated taxable income. Additional recordkeeping is required to keep track of this intercompany transaction (and all others like it), so that the deduction is claimed in the appropriate year.

	Separate Taxable Income	Adjustments	Postadjustment Amounts
Parent information	$500,000	_____	$500,000
SubCo information	150,000	+ $100,000 due to use of different tax accounting methods	250,000
Group-basis transactions	_____	_____	_____
Deferral/restoration events	_____	_____	
Consolidated taxable income			$750,000

* Permanent eliminations.
** Group-basis transaction.
† Deferral/restoration event.

54. Reg. §§ 1.1502–13(a)(1)(i) and (b)(1).

55. §§ 267(a)(2) and (b)(3); Reg. § 1.1502–13(b)(2).

Several other rules also apply to intercompany transactions. Certain deferral/restoration events require adjusting computations among tax years; these provisions are addressed in a later section of the chapter. Dividends received from other group members are eliminated from the recipients' separate taxable incomes, and no dividends received deduction is allowed.[56] When the distribution is comprised of noncash assets, the subsidiary payor realizes (and defers) any gain on the distributed property, and the (eliminated) dividend amount equals the fair market value of the asset.[57]

EXAMPLE 23

Parent Corporation received a $50,000 cash dividend from 100%-owned SubCo in the current year. Including this item, Parent's separate taxable income amounted to $200,000, and SubCo reported $240,000 separate taxable income.

Parent cannot claim a dividends received deduction for this payment, but the dividend is eliminated in computing consolidated taxable income. No elimination is required for SubCo, as dividend payments are nondeductible.

	Separate Taxable Income	Adjustments	Postadjustment Amounts
Parent information	$200,000	− $100,000 dividend received from SubCo*	$100,000
SubCo information	240,000		240,000
Group-basis transactions			
Deferral/restoration events			
Consolidated taxable income			$340,000

* Permanent eliminations.
** Group-basis transaction.
† Deferral/restoration event.

Realized gains and losses from other intercompany transactions involving stock or debt of group members are treated as deferral events, which are discussed later in the chapter.[58] Several other permanent eliminations are delineated in the Regulations.[59]

Members' Net Operating Losses. Most often, the election to file consolidated returns is motivated by the parent corporation's desire to gain access to the positive tax attributes of the subsidiary corporation, especially its net operating losses (NOLs). Congress has enacted a number of provisions, however, to discourage corporate acquisitions that are solely tax motivated. These include §§ 381 and 382, which limit the current-year and overall use of NOL carryovers by parties in a tax-favored reorganization (see Chapter 7 of this text), and §§ 269 and 482, which allow the IRS to reallocate income and deduction items of related parties that allegedly distort taxable income.

The usual corporate NOL computations are available to the losses of the consolidated group. Excessive losses are carried back 3 years and then forward 15 years, although the parent may elect to forgo the carryback deductions for all members of the group.[60] The NOL is derived after removing any consolidated charitable contribution deduction and capital gain or loss from consolidated

---

56. Reg. § 1.1502–14(a)(1). If the distribution exceeds the payor's E & P, the stock basis of the payor is reduced. When the basis reaches zero, an excess loss account is created. Reg. § 1.1502–14(a)(2). Dividends received from nongroup members may result in a dividends received deduction; they constitute a group-basis item (discussed later in the chapter).

57. §§ 301(b)(1) and (d); 311(b)(1); Reg. §§ 1.1502–14(c)(1) and –14T; Ltr. Rul. 8922096.

58. Reg. §§ 1.1502–14(b) through (e).

59. Reg. §§ 1.1502–15 through 19.

60. Prop.Reg. § 1.1502–21(b)(3)(i).

taxable income. These items are removed because they have their own carryover periods and rules.[61] The consolidated dividends received deduction remains a part of the consolidated NOL.[62]

─────────────────── EXAMPLE 24 ───────────────────

Parent Corporation and SubCo have filed consolidated returns since both entities were incorporated in 1991. Neither group member incurred any capital gain or loss transactions during 1991–1994, nor did they make any charitable contributions. Taxable income computations for the members include the following:

Year	Parent's Taxable Income	SubCo's Taxable Income	Consolidated Taxable Income
1991	$100,000	$ 40,000	$140,000
1992	100,000	(40,000)	60,000
1993	100,000	(140,000)	?
1994	100,000	210,000	?

The 1993 consolidated loss of $40,000 can be carried back to offset 1991 consolidated taxable income. Alternatively, Parent can elect to carry the loss forward to 1994, forgoing any carryback computation. This might be appropriate given an increase in statutory tax rates effective for 1994 or an application of the AMT in 1991 and 1992. ♦

Complications arise, however, when the corporations enter or depart from a consolidated return election, so that members' operating losses are either incurred in a "separate return year" and deducted in a "consolidated return year," or vice versa. Congress has imposed a variety of restrictions on the availability of such deductions to discourage profitable corporations from acquiring unprofitable entities simply in order to file immediate refund claims based on loss and credit carryforwards. Figure 8–4 summarizes the applicable limitations.

FIGURE 8–4   Limitations on Use of Net Operating Losses

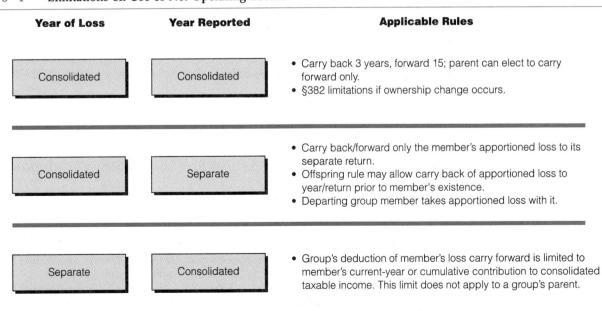

Year of Loss	Year Reported	Applicable Rules
Consolidated	Consolidated	• Carry back 3 years, forward 15; parent can elect to carry forward only. • §382 limitations if ownership change occurs.
Consolidated	Separate	• Carry back/forward only the member's apportioned loss to its separate return. • Offspring rule may allow carry back of apportioned loss to year/return prior to member's existence. • Departing group member takes apportioned loss with it.
Separate	Consolidated	• Group's deduction of member's loss carry forward is limited to member's current-year or cumulative contribution to consolidated taxable income. This limit does not apply to a group's parent.

────────────────────

61. For instance, there is no election available that would enable the parent to forgo the net capital loss carryback.

62. Reg. § 1.1502–21(f).

In any case where the members of a consolidated group change over time, the taxpayer must apportion the consolidated NOL among the group members. When more than one group member generated a loss for the consolidated year, the following formula is used to apportion the loss among the electing group's members:

$$\frac{\text{Member's separate NOL}}{\text{Members' aggregate NOLs}} \quad \text{X} \quad \text{Consolidated NOL} \quad = \quad \frac{\text{Member's}}{\text{apportioned NOL}}$$

─────────────── EXAMPLE 25 ───────────────

Parent Corporation and SubCo have filed consolidated returns since 1992. Both entities were incorporated in 1991. Neither group member incurred any capital gain or loss transactions during 1991–1994, nor did they make any charitable contributions. Taxable income computations for the members include the following:

Year	Parent's Taxable Income	SubCo's Taxable Income	Consolidated Taxable Income
1991*	$100,000	$ 40,000	N/A
1992**	100,000	(40,000)	$60,000
1993**	100,000	(140,000)	?
1994**	100,000	210,000	?

* Separate return year.
** Consolidated return year.

In 1993, SubCo can carry back the entire $40,000 consolidated NOL to its separate 1991 tax year, because it is solely responsible for generating the loss. SubCo will file for the refund of taxes that result from the carryback, and it alone will receive the refund.[63]

Alternatively, Parent could elect to forgo the carryback of the 1993 consolidated loss, thereby preserving the loss deduction for the group's subsequent years. In that case, the 1994 tax reduction would be claimed by filing the 1994 consolidated tax return, and Parent would receive the refund. ◆

─────────────── EXAMPLE 26 ───────────────

Parent Corporation, SubOne, and SubTwo have filed consolidated returns since 1992. All of the entities were incorporated in 1991. None of the group members incurred any capital gain or loss transactions during 1991–1994, nor did they make any charitable contributions. Taxable income computations for the members include the following:

Year	Parent's Taxable Income	SubOne's Taxable Income	SubTwo's Taxable Income	Consolidated Taxable Income
1991*	$100,000	$100,000	$ 40,000	N/A
1992**	100,000	100,000	(40,000)	$160,000
1993**	100,000	(60,000)	(120,000)	?
1994**	100,000	100,000	210,000	?

* Separate return year.
** Consolidated return year.

If Parent does not elect to forgo the carryback of the $80,000 1993 consolidated NOL, both subsidiaries can carry losses back to the 1991 separate return years and receive separate refunds. SubOne can carry back a $26,667 loss [(SubOne's NOL $60,000/aggregate NOLs $180,000) × Consolidated NOL $80,000], and SubTwo can carry back a $53,333 loss. ◆

─────────────────────────────

63. Reg. § 1.1502–78(b)(1) and (c), Example 4.

Under the so-called offspring rule, the consolidated group can use a carryback loss that is apportioned to a member of the electing group, even though that member was not in existence in the carryback year.[64] If the member joined the group immediately upon its incorporation, but cannot use an apportioned loss in the carryback period because it was not in existence, that loss is still available to the group.[65]

——————————————— EXAMPLE 27 ———————————————

Parent Corporation, SubOne, and SubTwo have filed consolidated returns since 1992. The first two entities were incorporated and consolidated in 1991, and SubTwo came into existence in 1992 through an asset spin-off from Parent. None of the group members incurred any capital gain or loss transactions during 1991–1994, nor did they make any charitable contributions. Taxable income computations for the members include the following:

Year	Parent's Taxable Income	SubOne's Taxable Income	SubTwo's Taxable Income	Consolidated Taxable Income
1991*	$100,000	$ 40,000	–	$140,000
1992*	100,000	100,000	$ (40,000)	160,000
1993*	100,000	(60,000)	(120,000)	?
1994*	100,000	100,000	210,000	?

* Consolidated return year.

If Parent does not elect to forgo the carryback of the $80,000 1993 consolidated NOL, SubOne can carry its $26,667 loss back to 1991. SubTwo's $53,333 share of the loss can also be carried back to 1991 and used by the consolidated group. Under the offspring rule, SubTwo is treated as being a member of the group for the entire *group* carryback period because its existence is rooted in Parent's assets. ◆

When a corporation leaves a consolidated group, it takes with it any apportioned share of any unused loss carryforwards, to be used on its subsequent separate returns.

——————————————— EXAMPLE 28 ———————————————

Parent Corporation, SubOne, and SubTwo have filed consolidated returns since 1991, the year in which all of the entities were incorporated. None of the group members incurred any capital gain or loss transactions during 1991–1994, nor did they make any charitable contributions. Taxable income computations for the members include the following:

Year	Parent's Taxable Income	SubOne's Taxable Income	SubTwo's Taxable Income	Consolidated Taxable Income
1991*	$100,000	$100,000	$ 40,000	$240,000
1992*	100,000	100,000	(40,000)	160,000
1993*	100,000	(60,000)	(120,000)	?
1994**	100,000	100,000	210,000	N/A

* Consolidated return year.
** Separate return year.

———————————————

64. Reg. 1.1502–79(a)(2).
65. Prop.Reg. 1.1502–21(b)(2)(ii)(B) restricts the use of this

loss to the parent, if the carryback year is a separate return year for the parties.

Parent elects to forgo any loss carryback for the group's 1993 operations. On the first day of the 1994 tax year, a foreign investor purchases all of the stock of SubTwo. On its 1994 separate return, SubTwo can deduct its $53,333 share of the 1993 NOL carryforward.[66] ◆

When an NOL is carried forward from a separate return year onto a consolidated return, another set of limitations applies.[67] The consolidated return can include an NOL carryforward from the member's separate return limitation year (SRLY) period only to the extent of the lesser of its (1) current-year or (2) cumulative positive contribution to current-year consolidated income.[68]

The SRLY limitations never apply to the electing group's identifiable parent.[69] Nor do they apply to a member that met all of the eligibility and stock ownership tests for consolidated return status, but never was included in a consolidation election.[70]

EXAMPLE 29

Parent Corporation and SubCo have filed consolidated returns since 1992. Both entities were incorporated in 1991. Neither group member incurred any capital gain or loss transactions during 1991–1994, nor did they make any charitable contributions. Taxable income computations for the members include the following:

Year	Parent's Taxable Income	SubCo's Taxable Income	Consolidated Taxable Income
1991*	$100,000	$(40,000)	N/A
1992**	100,000	(10,000)	$90,000
1993**	100,000	15,000	?
1994**	100,000	70,000	?

* Separate return year.
** Consolidated return year.

The thrust of the SRLY rules is to presume that Parent acquired SubCo so that it could deduct losses from a separate return year against consolidated income. Accordingly, none of SubCo's separate return loss from 1991 can be deducted in computing 1992 consolidated taxable income; the deduction is limited to the lesser of SubCo's current-year (zero) or cumulative (zero) contribution to consolidated taxable income.

In computing 1993 consolidated taxable income, the SubCo SRLY loss deduction is limited to $5,000, the lesser of SubCo's current-year ($15,000) or cumulative ($5,000) contribution to consolidated taxable income. ◆

EXAMPLE 30

Parent Corporation and SubCo have filed consolidated returns since 1992. Both entities were incorporated in 1991. Neither group member incurred any capital gain or loss transactions during 1991–1994, nor did they make any charitable contributions. Taxable income computations for the members include the following:

---

66. SubTwo cannot take the entire $120,000 NOL that is attributable to it. Reg. §§ 1.1502–79(a)(1)(ii) and (b)(2)(ii). Losses and carryovers must first be absorbed within the current consolidated return year before any loss apportionment occurs.

67. Reg. § 1.1502–21(c), known as the "separate return limitation year (SRLY)" rules. The SRLY rules apply to capital loss and credit carryforwards as well.

68. Prop.Reg. § 1.1502–21(c).

69. Reg. § 1.1502–1(f)(2)(i), known as the "lonely parent" rule.

70. Reg. § 1.1502–1(f)(2)(ii).

Year	Parent's Taxable Income	SubCo's Taxable Income	Consolidated Taxable Income
1991*	$ (40,000)	$100,000	N/A
1992**	(100,000)	(10,000)	($110,000)
1993**	20,000	165,000	?
1994**	100,000	70,000	?

* Separate return year.
** Consolidated return year.

The 1993 consolidated return can include a deduction for Parent's entire 1991 NOL of $40,000. The deduction is not limited to the lesser of Parent's current-year ($20,000) or cumulative (zero) contribution to consolidated taxable income. ◆

Computation of Group Items

Several income and deduction items are derived on a consolidated-group basis. Therefore, statutory limitations and allowances are applied to the group as though it were a single corporation. This computational convention allows the group members to match various types of gains and losses and to increase specific limitations, which are required by the Code, in a manner that optimizes the overall tax benefit.

Specifically, the following items are computed on a group basis:

- Net capital gain/loss.[71]
- Section 1231 loss.[72]
- Casualty/theft loss.
- Charitable contributions.[73]
- Dividends received deduction.[74]
- Net operating loss.

Following the computational procedure of Figures 8–2 and 8–3, all of the group-basis items are removed from each member's separate taxable income. Then, using the consolidated taxable income figure to that point, statutory limitations are applied to the aggregate income and expenditures of the group, and group-basis gains, losses, income, and deductions are derived.

────────────────────── EXAMPLE 31 ──────────────────────

Parent Corporation's current-year taxable income included $300,000 net income from operations and a $50,000 net long-term capital gain. Parent also made a $40,000 contribution to State University. Accordingly, its separate taxable income amounted to $315,000:

Income from operations	$300,000
Capital gain income	+ 50,000
Charitable contribution (maximum)	− 35,000
Separate taxable income	$315,000

71. Net capital losses are nondeductible against ordinary income by the group. Unused losses are carried back three years, then forward five years, and are treated as short-term capital losses. § 1212(a) and Reg. § 1.1502–22.

72. Net § 1231 gains are treated as long-term capital gains, while net losses produce ordinary deductions. § 1231(a) and Reg. § 1.1502–23.

73. Limited to 10% of consolidated taxable income, with a five-year carryforward period. §§ 170(b)(2) and (d)(2), and Reg. § 1.1502–24.

74. The deduction is 70% of the dividend amount, increased to 80% if the recipient owns at least 20% of the shares of the payor corporation, and to 100% if the recipient owns at least 80% of the shares of the nonconsolidated payor corporation. § 243 and Reg. § 1.1502–26. The deduction may be limited when group taxable income is low. See Chapter 2.

SubCo generated $170,000 income from operations and incurred a $45,000 short-term capital loss. Thus, its separate taxable income was $170,000, and aggregate separate taxable income for the group amounted to $485,000.

Upon consolidation, a larger amount of Parent's charitable contribution becomes deductible, and its capital gain is almost fully sheltered from current-year tax.

	Separate Taxable Income	Adjustments	Postadjustment Amounts
Parent information	$315,000	− $50,000 capital gain income**	$300,000
		+ $35,000 charitable contribution deduction**	
SubCo information	170,000	$45,000 short-term capital loss**	170,000
Group-basis transactions		+ $5,000 net long-term capital gain	−35,000
		− $40,000 charitable contribution deduction (maximum for group is $47,500)	
Deferral/restoration events			
Consolidated taxable income			$435,000

* Permanent eliminations
** Group-basis transaction.
† Deferral/restoration event.

◆

Computing these items on a group basis does not always result in a reduction of aggregate group taxable income. Nevertheless, the possibility of using the group-basis computations may affect transactions by group members late in the tax year when it becomes apparent that planning opportunities may be available. It may also encourage the taxpayer to seek fellow group members that bring complementary tax attributes to the consolidated return.

──────────────── EXAMPLE 32 ────────────────

Parent Corporation owns 15% of the stock of Outsider Corporation throughout the year. Outsider paid a $150,000 dividend to Parent during the year. Parent also generated $400,000 of taxable operating income and sold a § 1231 asset at a $10,000 gain. Parent's separate taxable income is computed as follows:

Operating income	$400,000
Dividend income	+150,000
§ 1231 gain	+ 10,000
Dividends received deduction (70%)	−105,000
Separate taxable income	$455,000

As a 10% owner of the corporation, SubCo received a $100,000 dividend from Outsider. SubCo's operations produced a $20,000 net taxable loss for the year, and it sold a § 1231 asset at a $4,000 loss. Thus, SubCo's separate taxable income is computed as follows:

Operating income	$(20,000)
Dividend income	+100,000
§ 1231 loss	− 4,000
Dividends received deduction[75]	− 53,200
Separate taxable income	$ 22,800

---

75. Limited to 70% of taxable income before the deduction.
§ 246(b)(1).

A consolidated return increases the group's dividends received deduction,[76] but it wastes the opportunity to claim SubCo's § 1231 loss as an ordinary deduction.

	Separate Taxable Income	Adjustments	Postadjustment Amounts
Parent information	$455,000	− $150,000 dividend received from Outsider**	$400,000
		− $10,000 § 1231 gain**	
		+ $105,000 dividends received deduction**	
SubCo information	$ 22,800	− $100,000 dividend received from Outsider**	(20,000)
		+ $4,000 § 1231 loss	
		+ $53,200 dividends received deduction	
Group-basis transactions		+ $250,000 dividend received from Outsider	+81,000
		− $175,000 dividends received deduction (70% × $250,000)	
		+ $6,000 § 1231 gain	
Deferral/restoration events			
Consolidated taxable income			$461,000

* Permanent elimination.
** Group-basis transaction.
† Deferral/restoration event

◆

Other items computed on a consolidated basis include the general business credit, any recapture of that credit, the foreign tax credit, the percentage depletion deduction, and all of the elements of alternative minimum taxable income.

Deferral and Restoration Events

A special class of intercompany transactions receives deferral treatment under the Regulations.[77] The gain or loss realized on these transactions is removed from consolidated taxable income until a *restoration event* occurs. The purpose of these rules is to prevent group members from accelerating loss deductions that relate to sales of assets within the group. Generally, the loss will be deductible only when control of the asset leaves the electing group.

Deferral/restoration treatment applies to sales of assets or the performance of services among group members. The entire deferred gain or loss is restored to the consolidated taxable income computation when, say, the asset is transferred outside the group through a subsequent sale. Full gain or loss restoration also can be triggered when the transferor of the property leaves the group or the consolidation election is terminated. Generally, the restored gain or loss is recognized in the same manner as it would have been on the initial transfer.[78] Asset basis and holding periods "start over," reflecting the purchaser's intermediary acquisition.[79] The installment method is not available for any deferral/restoration transaction.[80]

---

76. The group cannot apply an 80% rate for the dividends received deduction, despite the fact that aggregate group ownership in Outsider Corporation now exceeds 20%. See Reg. § 1.1502–26(a)(1)(i).

77. Reg. §§ 1.1502–13(c) through (h) and –13T.

78. Sections 267 and 1239 may convert other types of gain into ordinary income. See especially Reg. §§ 1.267(f)–1T and –2T and 1.1239–1(a) and (b)(3).

79. Reg. § 1.1502–13(g).

80. Reg. § 1.1502–13(c)(1)(ii).

——————————————————— EXAMPLE 33 ———————————————————

Parent Corporation sold a plot of land to SubCo in the current year for $100,000. Parent had acquired the land 10 years ago for $40,000. The consolidated return also reflects the operating results of the parties: Parent generated a $10,000 gain, and SubCo produced a $100,000 gain.

This intercompany transaction is a deferral/restoration event: Parent's $60,000 realized gain is deferred through an elimination in the computation of consolidated taxable income. SubCo's basis in the land is $100,000, and its holding period in the land begins with this year's purchase. The $60,000 gain is recognized when SubCo sells the land to Outsider Corporation.

	Separate Taxable Income	Adjustments	Postadjustment Amounts
Parent information	$ 70,000	_____	$70,000
SubCo information	100,000	_____	100,000
Group-basis transactions			
Deferral/restoration events		− $60,000 gain on intercompany sale to SubCo†	− 60,000
Consolidated taxable income			$110,000

* Permanent elimination.
** Group-basis transaction.
† Deferral/restoration event.

SubCo sold the land to Outsider for $110,000 in a year in which its operating income totaled $60,000 (exclusive of the sale of the land), and Parent's operating income amounted to $170,000.

	Separate Taxable Income	Adjustments	Postadjustment Amounts
Parent information	$170,000	_____	$170,000
SubCo information	70,000	_____	70,000
Group-basis transactions			
Deferral/restoration events		+ $60,000 restored gain on Parent's sale to SubCo†	+ 60,000
Consolidated taxable income			$300,000

* Permanent elimination.
** Group-basis transaction.
† Deferral/restoration event.

◆

Any deferred gain or loss on a transfer is recognized upon the earliest restoration event to occur. Other potential restoration events include the following:

- The acquiring group member claims a cost recovery deduction for the asset.[81]
- A nongroup member's installment note is transferred among group members (e.g., with the transferred asset itself).
- The transferred inventory is written down from its purchase price to fair market value.[82]

---

81. Reg. §§ 1.1502–13(d)(1) and −13T(l). The deferred gain is restored to consolidated taxable income over a period of years, using the ACRS, MACRS, or other cost recovery method that the acquiring group member employs. Thus,

the present value of the tax on this restored gain is reduced when the purchaser uses slower methods of cost recovery.

82. Reg. § 1.1502–13(f)(1)(viii).

Generally, the deferral/restoration rules are attractive to the group when intercompany sales take place at a gain. When such sales generate losses, however, the mandatory nature of the rules may become burdensome. Consequently, the Regulations allow an election that overrides the deferral/restoration rules. With the election, all intercompany gains and losses are immediately includible or deductible.[83] The election remains in force until the IRS consents to its revocation.

Choosing Consolidated Return Partners

**TAX PLANNING
CONSIDERATIONS**

Taxpayers should optimize their overall tax benefits when choosing consolidated return partners. Within the limitations of the rules discussed earlier in the chapter, target corporations might include those with appropriate amounts of the following:

- Loss and credit carryovers.
- Passive activity income, loss, or credits.
- Gains that can be deferred through intercompany sales.
- Contributions to consolidated ACE adjustments.
- Excess limitation amounts (e.g., with respect to charitable contributions).
- Section 1231 gains, losses, and look-back profiles.

Consolidation versus 100 Percent Dividends Received Deduction

When adequate ownership is held, a 100 percent dividends received deduction is available for payments received from subsidiaries with whom a consolidated return is *not* filed. Thus, this tax benefit is still available when the taxpayer wishes to affiliate with an insurance company, foreign entity, or other ineligible corporation. A taxpayer that cannot find potential group partners with the desired level of complementary tax attributes may also take advantage of this benefit.

**CONCEPT SUMMARY 8–2
THE CONSOLIDATED TAX RETURN**

1. Groups of corporations form for a variety of tax and nontax reasons. The election to file Federal income tax returns on a consolidated basis allows certain group members to use their positive tax attributes (e.g., loss or credit carryovers) to offset negative tax attributes (e.g., taxable income) of other members.

2. Consolidated tax returns are limited to eligible corporations that satisfy stock ownership tests and meet various compliance requirements. For instance, all group members must conform their tax years to that of the parent of the group. Group members may use different tax accounting methods, however.

3. Group members are jointly and severally liable for the overall tax liability of the group. For the most part, computations of estimated tax liabilities must be made on a consolidated basis.

4. The stock basis of a subsidiary is derived from the acquisition price of the stock, increased by the taxable income (or decreased by the losses) of the subsidiary, and decreased by dividend distributions. An excess loss account is created when aggregate losses of the subsidiary exceed both the purchase price and ensuing income amounts. The excess loss account is recaptured as capital gain when the subsidiary stock is disposed of.

5. In computing consolidated taxable income, certain items, such as charitable contributions and § 1231 gains and losses, are computed on a consolidated basis, while other gains and losses are deferred until later tax periods. The group is subject to severe restrictions in using any operating losses of a subsidiary that has been acquired or disposed of.

---

83. Reg. § 1.1502–13(c)(3).

Protecting the Group Member's Liability for Tax Payments

Because all group members are responsible for consolidated tax liabilities, interest, and penalties, target subsidiaries and their (present and potential) shareholders should take measures to protect their separate interests.

EXAMPLE 34

Return to the facts of Example 11. Exposure by SubCo and its successive shareholders to tax (and all other) liabilities of Parent Corporation should be minimized by including appropriate clauses in purchase contracts and related documents. For instance, (1) Foreign Corporation could alter its negotiating position so that it pays less to acquire the SubCo stock; (2) SubCo might attempt to recover any Parent taxes that it pays through courts other than the Tax Court; and (3) SubCo might make a 30-day election to limit its years of exposure to 1994 and 1995. ◆

A short tax year may be created when a member with a nonmatching tax year joins or leaves the group. When this occurs, the group should consider measures to limit the ensuing negative tax consequences. For instance, additional income can be accelerated into the short year of acquisition. This will reduce any loss carryforwards when the carryover period effectively is shortened due to the takeover. The group should also make suitable income-allocation elections in assigning income to the short year. Finally, group estimated tax payments should be computed using both consolidated and separate liability amounts to determine the more beneficial method. In this way, only the minimum quarterly tax payments will be made, and the benefits of the time value of money will be maximized.

Electing to Postpone Recognition of the Excess Loss Account

An election to reduce the investment basis of remaining subsidiary stock and debt (i.e., upon disposition of shares when an excess loss account exists) may be attractive when the remaining shares are not likely to be sold in the near future. In that case, the present value of the tax on any resulting increased gain will be low. The election may also be used to offset any recognition of the postponed gain upon debt repayments or stock sales when future operating losses are anticipated. The election generally is not attractive when operating loss carryforwards are available in the current year. These can be used to shelter the gain recognized on recovery of the excess loss account.

EXAMPLE 35

Parent Corporation owns preferred stock of SubCo with a basis of $10,000. Parent's basis in its common stock investment in SubCo has been eliminated through SubCo's operating losses; in fact, Parent holds a $6,000 excess loss account for SubCo.

Parent sells the SubCo common for $9,000. Thus, it must recognize a $15,000 capital gain on the sale. Alternatively, Parent can elect to recognize only a $9,000 gain on the sale and to reduce its basis in the SubCo preferred to $4,000. ◆

Election to Override Deferral and Restoration Rules

The election to make all intercompany transactions includible or deductible upon completion of the intragroup transaction may be especially attractive in the following circumstances: (1) due to market or other conditions, the transfers generate realized losses that the taxpayer wishes to deduct; (2) the transactions occur frequently, making recordkeeping burdensome (particularly for cost recovery assets that are exchanged in midrecovery life); and (3) intercompany transactions produce ordinary income under §§ 1239, 1245, or some other provision in years for which sufficient operating loss carryforwards are available.

Recall, however, that the § 267(f) rules may further limit the seller's ability to deduct a loss from a sale to a fellow *controlled* group member.[84] In fact, such a loss remains nondeductible even when the purchasing group member disengages from the consolidation election, but remains a member of a controlled group with the internal seller.

—————————————— EXAMPLE 36 ——————————————

SubCo purchased an asset from Parent Corporation last year, with Parent incurring a $10,000 realized loss that was nondeductible under the deferral/restoration rules. This year, SubCo sold the asset to Foreign Corporation, also a 100%-owned subsidiary of Parent. Foreign cannot be a member of the affiliated group because it is not incorporated in the United States. The sale is not a restoration event, however, because Foreign is a member of a controlled group with the other two entities. ◆

PROBLEM MATERIALS

DISCUSSION QUESTIONS

1. Why is it appropriate to study the complex consolidated return rules?

2. What is the general function of the consolidated return rules?

3. Under which business or tax circumstances might the taxpayer be eligible to elect to file a consolidated tax return?

4. Where can one find the various elements of the consolidated tax return rules?

5. Describe the three basic requirements that must be met before a corporation can join in a consolidated tax return.

6. Summarize the advantages and disadvantages of filing consolidated tax returns.

7. What broad requirements must a group of corporations meet if it desires to file tax returns on a consolidated basis?

8. Define the following terms: parent-subsidiary controlled group, brother-sister controlled group, affiliated group.

9. What are the major differences between affiliated groups and parent-subsidiary controlled groups?

10. Identify several corporations that are ineligible to file tax returns on a consolidated basis.

11. What compliance requirements must be met on a group's first consolidated tax return?

12. What compliance requirements must be met by a group on successive consolidated tax returns?

13. How does the Code restrict the use of tax accounting periods and methods by the members of a consolidated group?

14. How does a parent corporation compute the basis of its stock investment in a subsidiary?

15. How and why does consolidated taxable income differ from the sum of the separate taxable incomes of the members of the consolidated group?

—————————————————————

84. Reg. § 1.267(f)–2T(c).

16. Which items of taxable income are computed on a consolidated basis? How are these computations made?

17. How does the computation of consolidated taxable income differ from the procedures used for financial accounting purposes? Why do such differences exist?

18. What is the purpose of the rules that limit the deductibility of group members' NOLs on a consolidated tax return?

19. How do the Regulations treat deferral/restoration intercompany transactions?

20. Identify several restoration events.

PROBLEMS

21. SubCo sold an asset to Parent at a tax and accounting gain of $200,000. The asset appreciated by another $30,000 before Parent sold it to an unrelated party, Outsiders, Inc.

    a. Compute the realized financial accounting and recognized taxable income of the group members for these transactions, indicating the date upon which the gain is triggered and the member that includes the gain.

    b. Same as (a), except that the asset declines in value by $30,000 while it is in Parent's hands.

22. Parent Corporation owns 100% of the stock of SubCo, and the two corporations file a consolidated tax return. Over the course of a five-year period, the corporations generate the following taxable income/(loss). Indicate how you would assign the taxpayers' low marginal rates that apply to the group's first $75,000 of taxable income.

Year	Parent's Taxable Income	SubCo's Taxable Income	Low Brackets Assigned to Parent	Low Brackets Assigned to SubCo
1	$100,000	$(10,000)	?	?
2	(10,000)	100,000	?	?
3	80,000	10,000	?	?
4	100,000	10,000	?	?
5	300,000	300,000	?	?

23. Parent Corporation acquired 100% of the stock of SubCo on September 15, 1993. Both parties intend for the group to file a consolidated tax return immediately upon the acquisition. Parent uses a calendar tax year. SubCo has been using a March 31 tax year.

    a. When is the group's first consolidated tax return due? What operating periods are included in the return?

    b. Same as (a), except that the acquisition occurred on December 14, 1993.

24. Calendar year Parent Corporation acquired all of the stock of SubCo on January 1, 1993, for $100,000. The subsidiary's operating gains and losses are shown below. In addition, a $20,000 dividend is paid at the end of 1994.

    Complete the following chart, indicating the appropriate stock basis and excess loss account amounts.

Year	Operating Gain/(Loss)	Stock Basis	Excess Loss Account
1993	$(45,000)	?	?
1994	(70,000)	?	?
1995	40,000	?	?

25. In the current year, Parent Corporation provided advertising services to its 100%-owned subsidiary, SubCo, under a contract that requires no payments to Parent

until next year. Both parties use the accrual method of tax accounting and a calendar tax year. The services that Parent rendered were valued at $130,000. In addition, Parent received $25,000 of interest payments from SubCo, relative to an arm's length note between them.

Including these transactions, Parent's taxable income for the year amounted to $500,000. SubCo reported $50,000 separate taxable income. Use the computational worksheet of Figure 8–3 to derive the group's consolidated taxable income.

26. Parent Corporation, SubOne, and SubTwo have filed consolidated returns since 1992. All of the entities were incorporated in 1991. None of the group members incurred any capital gain or loss transactions during 1991–1994, nor did they make any charitable contributions. Taxable income computations for the members include the following:

Year	Parent's Taxable Income	SubOne's Taxable Income	SubTwo's Taxable Income	Consolidated Taxable Income
1991*	$100,000	$100,000	$ 40,000	N/A
1992**	100,000	100,000	(40,000)	$160,000
1993**	100,000	(80,000)	(240,000)	?
1994**	100,000	100,000	210,000	?

* Separate return year.
** Consolidated return year.

   a. How much of the 1993 loss is apportioned to SubOne and SubTwo? How is this loss treated in generating a refund of prior tax payments?

   b. Why would Parent consider electing to forgo the carryback of the 1993 consolidated NOL?

27. The group of Parent Corporation, SubOne, and SubTwo has filed a consolidated return since 1992. The first two entities were incorporated in 1991, and SubTwo came into existence in 1992 through an asset spin-off from Parent. Taxable income computations for the members are shown below. None of the group members incurred any capital gain or loss transactions during 1991–1994, nor did they make any charitable contributions. Describe the treatment of the group's 1993 consolidated NOL.

Year	Parent's Taxable Income	SubOne's Taxable Income	SubTwo's Taxable Income	Consolidated Taxable Income
1991*	$200,000	$ 70,000	—	$270,000
1992*	100,000	20,000	$ (40,000)	80,000
1993*	100,000	(90,000)	(180,000)	?
1994*	100,000	100,000	210,000	?

* Consolidated return year.

28. Parent Corporation and SubCo have filed consolidated returns since 1992. Both entities were incorporated in 1991. Taxable income computations for the members are shown below. Neither group member incurred any capital gain or loss transactions during 1991–1994, nor did they make any charitable contributions.

Compute the group's 1992, 1993, and 1994 loss carryforward deductions related to SubCo's 1991 NOL.

Year	Parent's Taxable Income	SubCo's Taxable Income	Consolidated Taxable Income
1991*	$100,000	$(60,000)	N/A
1992**	100,000	(30,000)	$70,000
1993**	100,000	12,000	?
1994**	100,000	70,000	?

* Separate return year.
** Consolidated return year.

29. Parent Corporation's current-year taxable income included $100,000 net income from operations and a $50,000 net long-term capital gain. Parent also made a $40,000 contribution to State University. SubCo produced $70,000 income from operations and incurred a $65,000 short-term capital loss.

Use the computational worksheet of Figure 8–3 to derive the group members' separate taxable incomes and the group's consolidated taxable income.

30. Parent Corporation sold a plot of undeveloped land to SubCo this year for $100,000. Parent had acquired the land several years ago for $20,000. The consolidated return also reflects the operating results of the parties: Parent generated $130,000 income, and SubCo produced a $20,000 loss.

a. Use the computational worksheet of Figure 8–3 to derive the group members' separate taxable incomes and the group's consolidated taxable income.

b. Same as (a), except that SubCo sold the land to Outsider Corporation for $110,000 in a subsequent year, when its operating income totaled $30,000 (exclusive of the sale of the land), and Parent's operating income amounted to $90,000.

RESEARCH PROBLEMS

RESEARCH PROBLEM 1   Parent Corporation purchased all of the stock of SubCo in the current year. The parties intend to file their Federal income tax returns on a consolidated basis, effective immediately.

One of the assets on SubCo's balance sheet was an investment in undeveloped land, acquired by SubCo seven years ago for $50,000. The land now is worth $20,000, and Parent would like to sell the land in the current year to offset its other § 1231 gains that would be fully taxable on the consolidated return.

It is likely that SubCo will continue to generate small NOLs for the next five years until the additional investment associated with being a member of a conglomerate enables SubCo to turn a profit.

Advise Parent on the deductibility of this loss in the current year.

Partial list of research aids:

Reg. § 1.1502–15.
Prop.Reg. § 1.1502–15.

RESEARCH PROBLEM 2   Parent Corporation, a member of a calendar year consolidated group with SubCo, acquired a computer system from LastMicro on January 4, 1991, for $50,000. On January 5, 1993, it sold the system to SubCo for $35,000.

Compute (a) the cost recovery deductions available to SubCo as it uses the system in its business through 1999, and (b) the timing and magnitude of the restored Parent gain that is recognized by the group on its consolidated return.

Partial list of research aids:

Reg. § 1.1502–13T(l).

CHAPTER

9

TAXATION OF INTERNATIONAL TRANSACTIONS

OBJECTIVES

Describe the provisions of the foreign tax credit.

Explain the rules for sourcing income and allocating deductions.

Review U.S. taxation of nonresident aliens and foreign corporations.

Discuss U.S. taxation of foreign-source income of U.S. citizens and residents.

Summarize the U.S. tax law regarding controlled foreign corporations.

Describe the tax consequences of transferring ownership to foreign persons.

Discuss the tax treatment of foreign currency transactions.

OUTLINE

The U.S. government is not prohibited from taxing income earned outside the United States by U.S. persons, nor is it precluded from taxing income earned in the United States by non-U.S. persons. When the United States and another country both tax the income from an international transaction, double taxation may result. Knowledge of the laws and concepts applied by the United States in taxing international transactions, however, will aid taxpayers in arranging their transactions to minimize or eliminate double taxation.

This chapter covers U.S. Federal taxation of (1) transactions involving U.S. persons and foreign investment and (2) transactions involving foreign persons and U.S. investment. Additionally, tax planning suggestions are offered to aid taxpayers in minimizing the taxation of international transactions.

Significant Terminology

Some important terms with regard to U.S. international taxation include the following:

- *Effectively connected*. Income with this designation is taxed differently than passive income that is not effectively connected with a U.S. trade or business.
- *Nonresident alien*. Both of the designations, nonresident and alien, must apply to an individual if that person is to be classified as a non-U.S. person for Federal income tax purposes.
- *Controlled foreign corporation*. U.S. control of a foreign corporation can affect tax treatment under a number of tax law provisions. The designation of controlled foreign corporation (CFC) originated in Subpart F of the Internal Revenue Code.

As previously noted, the United States retains the right to tax its citizens and residents on their worldwide taxable income. This approach can result in double taxation and presents a potential problem to U.S. persons who invest abroad.

--- EXAMPLE 1 ---

R, a U.S. resident, has a business in Mexico. This business earns him taxable income of $75,000 in 1992. He pays income tax of $20,000 on these earnings to the Mexican tax authorities. He also must include the $75,000 in gross income for U.S. tax purposes. Ignoring any foreign taxes he might pay, assume he would owe $21,000 in U.S. income taxes on this foreign-source income. This results in total taxes on the $75,000 of $41,000, or 55%. ◆

To reduce the possibility of double taxation, the U.S. Congress enacted the foreign tax credit (FTC) provisions. Under these provisions, a qualified taxpayer is allowed a tax credit for foreign income taxes paid. The credit is a dollar-for-dollar reduction of U.S. income tax liability.

--- EXAMPLE 2 ---

R, in Example 1 above, takes an FTC of $20,000, reducing his U.S. tax liability on the foreign-source income to $1,000. Therefore, R's total taxes on the $75,000 are $21,000. ◆

The Credit Provisions

The Direct Credit. Section 901 provides a direct FTC to U.S. taxpayers who pay or incur a foreign income tax. For purposes of the direct credit, only the taxpayer who bears the legal incidence of the foreign tax is eligible for the credit. R, in Example 1 above, would be eligible for the direct credit.

The Indirect Credit. If a U.S. corporation operates in a foreign country through a branch, the direct credit is available for foreign taxes paid. If, however, a U.S. corporation operates in a foreign country through a foreign subsidiary, the direct credit is not available for foreign taxes paid by the foreign corporation. Section 902 attempts to equate branch and subsidiary operations by allowing an indirect credit. The indirect credit is available to U.S. corporate taxpayers who receive actual or constructive dividends from foreign corporations that have paid a foreign tax on earnings. These foreign taxes are deemed paid by the corporate shareholders in the same proportion as the dividends actually or constructively received bear to the foreign corporation's post-1986 undistributed earnings.[1] Section 78 requires a domestic corporation that chooses the FTC for deemed-paid foreign taxes to *gross up* dividend income by the amount of deemed-paid taxes.

EXAMPLE 3

D, a domestic corporation, owns 50 percent of F, a foreign corporation. D receives a dividend of $120,000 from F. F's foreign taxes paid on post-1986 earnings were $500,000. F's post-1986 earnings (after taxes) total $1,200,000. D's deemed-paid foreign taxes for FTC purposes are $50,000:

Cash dividend from F	$120,000
Deemed-paid foreign taxes:	
$500{,}000 \times \dfrac{\$120{,}000}{\$1{,}200{,}000} =$	50,000
Gross income to D	$170,000

D must include the $50,000 in gross income for the gross-up adjustment if the FTC is elected. ◆

Certain ownership requirements must be met before the indirect credit is available to a domestic corporation. The domestic corporation must own 10 percent or more of the voting stock of the foreign corporation. The credit is also available for deemed-paid foreign taxes of second- and third-tier foreign corporations if the 10 percent ownership requirement is met at the second- and third-tier level. Further, a 5 percent indirect ownership requirement must be met from tier to tier. The § 902 ownership requirements are summarized in Figure 9-1.

FTC Limitations. To prevent foreign taxes from being credited against U.S. taxes levied on U.S.-source taxable income, the FTC is subject to a limitation. Section 904 provides that the FTC for any taxable year shall not exceed the lesser of the actual foreign taxes paid or accrued, or the U.S. taxes (before the FTC) on foreign-source taxable income (the general limitation). The general limitation formula is as follows:

$$\frac{\text{U.S. tax}}{\text{before FTC}} \times \frac{\text{Foreign-source taxable income}^{2}}{\text{Worldwide taxable income}}$$

---

1. For dividends attributable to pre-1987 earnings, the deemed-paid foreign taxes are to be determined on a year-by-year basis. For transition rules concerning the carryforward and carryback of deficits between post-1986 and pre-1987 E & P, see IRS Notice 87-54, 1987-2 C.B. 363.

For other FTC transition rules, see IRS Notice 87-6, 1987-1 C.B. 417.

2. For FTC purposes, the taxable income of an individual, estate, or trust is computed without any deduction for personal exemptions. § 904(b)(1).

—————————————— EXAMPLE 4 ——————————————

T, a U.S. resident, invests in foreign securities. His worldwide taxable income for 1992 is $120,000, consisting of $100,000 in salary from a U.S. employer and $20,000 of income from foreign sources. Foreign taxes of $6,000 were withheld by foreign tax authorities. Assume that T's U.S. tax before the FTC is $33,600. His FTC for 1992 is $5,600 [$33,600 × ($20,000/$120,000)]. Thus, his net U.S. tax liability is $28,000. ◆

As Example 4 illustrates, the limitation can prevent the total amount of foreign taxes paid in high tax jurisdictions from being credited. Taxpayers could overcome this problem, however, by generating additional foreign-source income that is subject to no, or low, foreign taxation.

—————————————— EXAMPLE 5 ——————————————

Compare Domestic Corporation's FTC situation when the corporation has only $500,000 of highly taxed foreign-source income with the situation where Domestic also has $100,000 of low-taxed foreign-source interest income.

	Only Highly Taxed Income	With Low-Taxed Interest
Foreign-source income	$500,000	$600,000
Foreign taxes	275,000	280,000
U.S.-source income	700,000	700,000
U.S. taxes (34%)	408,000	442,000
FTC limitation	170,000*	204,000**

*$408,000 × ($500,000/$1,200,000).

**$442,000 × ($600,000/$1,300,000).

Domestic's foreign taxes increase by only $5,000, while its FTC limitation increases by $34,000. ◆

FIGURE 9–1
Section 902 Ownership Requirements

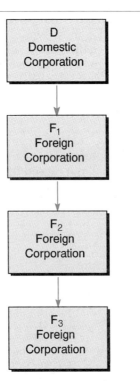

D must own directly at least 10% of the voting stock of F_1 and must own indirectly at least 5% of the voting stock of F_2 and F_3.

F_1 must own directly at least 10% of the voting stock of F_2.

F_2 must own directly at least 10% of the voting stock of F_3.

There is no provision for a credit for deemed-paid foreign taxes from a foreign corporation below the third tier.

To prevent the *cross-crediting* of foreign taxes illustrated in Example 5, Congress has enacted legislation providing for several separate limitation *baskets*. These provisions require that a separate limitation be calculated for certain categories of foreign-source taxable income and the foreign taxes attributable to such income. Currently, § 904(d) provides separate limitation baskets for the following:

- Passive income.
- High withholding tax income.
- Financial services income.
- Shipping income.
- Dividends from each noncontrolled § 902 corporation.
- Dividends from a domestic international sales corporation (DISC) or former DISC to the extent they are treated as foreign-source income.
- Taxable income attributable to foreign trade income under § 923(b).
- Distributions from a foreign sales corporation (FSC) or former FSC out of E & P attributable to foreign trade income or qualified interest and carrying charges under § 263(c).

All other foreign-source income is included in a general (or overall) limitation basket. These separate limitations are diagramed in Concept Summary 9–1.

A separate limitation under § 907 applies to foreign taxes paid on foreign oil and gas extraction income. This limitation is applied before consideration of the general limitation. Special provisions define the various categories of income, particularly with regard to the possibility that a certain item of income could fall in more than one basket, such as passive income and high withholding tax interest.

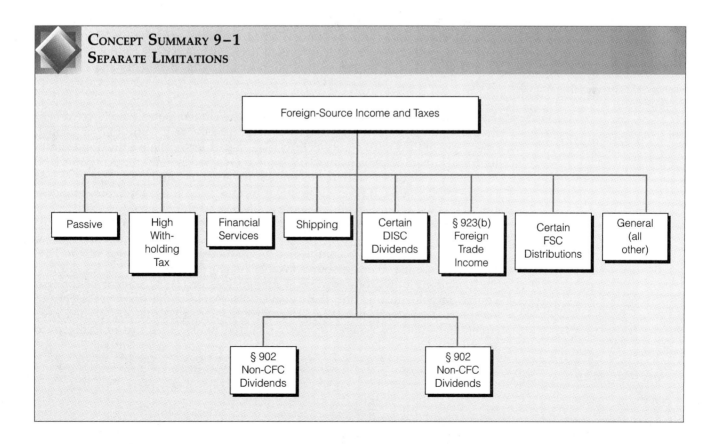

CONCEPT SUMMARY 9–1
SEPARATE LIMITATIONS

Foreign-Source Income and Taxes

Passive | High With-holding Tax | Financial Services | Shipping | Certain DISC Dividends | § 923(b) Foreign Trade Income | Certain FSC Distributions | General (all other)

§ 902 Non-CFC Dividends

§ 902 Non-CFC Dividends

In addition, there are *look-through* rules in the case of controlled foreign corporations (CFCs). These rules require the U.S. shareholder receiving, for example, dividend income to *look through* to the source (classification) of the income at the CFC level.

─────────────────────────── EXAMPLE 6 ───────────────────────────

D, a domestic corporation, receives foreign-source dividend income from three noncontrolled § 902 foreign corporations, X, Y, and Z. D's worldwide taxable income is $3,300,000, and its U.S. tax liability before the FTC is $1,122,000. The FTC is determined as follows:

Payor	Dividend	Foreign Taxes Paid and Deemed Paid	FTC Limitation	FTC
X	$ 50,000	$ 4,000	$17,000*	$ 4,000**
Y	100,000	40,000	34,000	34,000
Z	150,000	7,500	51,000	7,500
	$300,000	$51,500		$45,500

*$1,122,000 × ($50,000/$3,300,000).

**Lesser of $4,000 or $17,000.

Without the separate basket limitation, D would have an FTC of $51,500 ($4,000 + $40,000 + $7,500). ◆

The limitations can result in unused (noncredited) foreign taxes for the tax year. Section 904 provides for a two-year carryback and five-year carryover of excess foreign taxes. The taxes can be credited in years when the formula limitation for that year exceeds the foreign taxes attributable to the same tax year. The carryback and carryover provision is available only within the separate baskets. In other words, excess foreign taxes in one basket cannot be carried over unless there is an excess limitation in the same basket for the carryover year.

Foreign Losses. Citizens and residents of the United States who have foreign investments or operations that are held directly (e.g., through a branch operation) or through a conduit entity (e.g., a partnership) have the opportunity to offset foreign losses against U.S.-source income, thereby reducing the U.S. income tax due on U.S.-source income. If the foreign country in which the loss is generated (sourced) taxes subsequent income from these foreign operations, the FTC could reduce or eliminate any U.S. tax on the income.

To overcome this loss of tax revenue to the United States, tax law provides that the overall foreign losses should be recaptured as U.S.-source income for FTC purposes.[3] This is accomplished by reducing the numerator of the FTC limitation formula. Foreign-source taxable income is reduced by the lesser of (1) the remaining unrecaptured overall foreign loss or (2) 50 percent of foreign-source taxable income for the taxable year (unless the taxpayer elects to recapture a greater percentage). Unrecaptured foreign losses are carried over indefinitely until recaptured. Losses incurred before 1976 are not subject to recapture.

---

3. § 904(f)(1).

The Tax Reform Act of 1986, which increased the number of FTC limitation baskets, requires that, where a taxpayer has foreign losses in some baskets and foreign income in others, the foreign losses be allocated proportionately among the income baskets. Furthermore, where losses of one basket (classification) were allocated against income in another basket, subsequent income in this prior loss category basket must be recharacterized as income of the basket that the prior losses offset.[4] The taxpayer must also make basket adjustments and be subject to the recharacterization provision when there is a U.S. loss and foreign-source income.

The overall foreign loss recapture provisions required for the FTC will recapture the losses when the U.S. taxpayer subsequently earns foreign-source income. However, these provisions will not necessarily reach the situation where overall foreign losses have been incurred and the U.S. taxpayer disposes of the trade or business property used predominantly outside the United States before any or all of the loss is recaptured.

The statutory solution to this problem is that the U.S. taxpayer will have U.S.-source income in the amount of the lesser of the fair market value of the property less its adjusted basis, or the remaining amount of unrecaptured foreign losses. Note that in this case the foreign-source income in the numerator of the FTC limitation is reduced by the lesser of 100 percent of the gain on disposition or the remaining unrecaptured overall foreign loss. The basket recharacterization rules apply for this purpose. Section 904(f)(3) can create taxable income because it applies to such dispositions whether or not they are otherwise taxable dispositions. Thus, *disposition* includes a gift of the property and incorporation of a foreign branch. The property disposition provision, however, does not apply to stock.

The Alternative Minimum Tax FTC.   For purposes of the alternative minimum tax, the FTC is limited to the lesser of the credit for regular tax purposes or 90 percent of the tentative minimum tax before the credit.[5] The 10 percent cutback is calculated on the tentative minimum tax without regard to the alternative tax NOL deduction. The general FTC limitation is calculated by using alternative minimum taxable income rather than taxable income in the denominator of the formula and the tentative minimum tax rather than the regular tax. The source of alternative minimum taxable income must be determined for the purpose of foreign-source taxable income.

Other Considerations.   In order for a foreign levy to qualify for the FTC, it must be a tax, and its predominant character must be that of an income tax in the U.S. sense.[6] A levy is a tax if it is a compulsory payment, as contrasted with a payment for a specific economic benefit such as the right to extract oil. A tax's predominant character is that of an income tax in the U.S. sense if it reaches realized net gain and is not dependent on being credited against the income tax of another country (not a *soak-up* tax). Persons whose foreign taxes are partially creditable because only a portion of the foreign levy is considered an income tax in the U.S. sense are dual capacity taxpayers.[7] A tax that is levied in lieu of an income tax is also creditable.[8]

4. Reg. § 1.904(f)–13T provides transition rules for recapture in taxable years beginning after 1986 of overall foreign losses incurred in taxable years beginning before 1987.

5. § 59. A "small corporation" exception is available.

6. Reg. § 1.901–2.

7. Reg. § 1.901–2A.

8. § 903 and Reg. § 1.903–1.

─────────────────── Example 7 ───────────────────

D, a domestic corporation, receives oil extraction income from operations in a foreign country. The tax laws of the foreign country levy a 50% tax on extraction income and a 30% tax on all other taxable income derived within the country. If D pays $700,000 in taxes to the foreign country with regard to its extraction income, only $420,000 [$700,000 × (30% ÷ 50%)] of that amount is creditable as an income tax. ◆

─────────────────── Example 8 ───────────────────

X, a domestic corporation, generates $2 million of taxable income from operations in F, a foreign country. Under F's tax laws, a tax is levied on income generated in F by foreign residents only in cases in which the country of residence (such as the United States) allows a tax credit for foreign taxes paid. X will not be allowed an FTC for taxes paid to F because the foreign tax is a soak-up tax. ◆

Certain foreign taxes that meet the definition of creditable may not be creditable for other reasons. Section 901(j) prohibits a credit for taxes paid to foreign governments that the United States does not recognize even though the taxes otherwise meet the definition of creditable. Furthermore, where a person, or a member of a controlled group that includes such a person, participates in or cooperates with an unapproved international boycott during the taxable year, the FTC is reduced. Section 901 provides for the otherwise allowable FTC to be reduced by multiplying by the international boycott factor.[9]

For purposes of the FTC, foreign taxes are attributable to the year in which they are paid or accrued. For taxpayers using the cash method of accounting for tax purposes, an election to take the FTC in the year in which the foreign taxes accrue is available under § 905. Such an election is binding on the taxpayer for the year in which it is made and for all subsequent years. Taxes paid in a foreign currency are translated to U.S. dollars for FTC purposes at the exchange rate in effect when the taxes are actually paid.[10] Any adjustment of foreign taxes paid by a foreign corporation is translated at the rate in effect at the time of adjustment. However, any refund or credit is translated at the rate in effect at the time the foreign taxes were originally paid.

The FTC is elective for any particular tax year. Any Internal Revenue Code (Code) provision that reads "[i]f the taxpayer chooses" (such as § 901) signifies an elective provision. If the taxpayer does not "choose" to take the FTC, § 164 allows a deduction for foreign taxes paid or incurred. However, a taxpayer cannot take a credit and a deduction for the same foreign income taxes.[11] A taxpayer can take a deduction in the same year as an FTC for foreign taxes that are not creditable (e.g., soak-up taxes).

Possessions Corporations

To encourage the economic development of U.S. possessions, a credit provision was enacted for income from operations in U.S. possessions. Domestic corporations may elect to receive a § 936 credit against U.S. taxes. The credit is equal to 34 percent of possession-source taxable income and qualified investment income whether any tax is paid or due to the possession. This is referred to as a *tax-sparing* credit. No additional credit or deduction is allowed for income taxes actually paid to the possession. A number of pharmaceutical companies, including Eli Lilly Co., have used subsidiaries with operations in Puerto Rico to take advantage of this and local tax benefits.

─────────────────────────────────

9. §§ 908 and 999.
10. §§ 986(b) and 987.

11. § 275.

The credit is allowed against the U.S. tax attributable to foreign-source taxable income from the active conduct of a trade or business in a U.S. possession. It is also allowed on the sale or exchange of substantially all the assets used by the domestic corporation in that active trade or business and on qualified possession-source investment income. The credit is not allowed against certain taxes such as the accumulated earnings tax under § 531 and the personal holding company tax under § 541.

In order to elect the credit, the domestic corporation must meet certain conditions. Eighty percent or more of its gross income for the three-year period immediately preceding the taxable year for which the credit is taken must be derived from sources within a U.S. possession. In addition, 75 percent or more of its gross income for that period must have been derived from the active conduct of a trade or business within a U.S. possession. The credit is not available for income received in the United States unless it is possession-source income received from an unrelated person and is attributable to an active trade or business conducted in a possession.

Specific rules apply regarding intangible property income. The credit is not available for such income. Intangible property income is includible in taxable income by a domestic corporation as U.S.-source income. However, all of its shareholders who are U.S. persons may elect to include their pro rata share of that income in their gross income as U.S.-source income.

EXAMPLE 9

A qualified possessions corporation has the following foreign-source income on which it pays the following foreign taxes:

Taxable Income	Source	Foreign Taxes
$400,000 active trade or business income	Possession	$40,000
50,000 qualified investment income	Possession	–0–
10,000 passive nonqualified income	Possession	–0–
40,000 investment income	Nonpossession	16,000

Assume that the taxpayer's worldwide taxable income is $500,000 and its U.S. tax before the FTC is $170,000. The § 936 possessions corporation credit is $153,000 (34% × $450,000), and the § 901 FTC is $13,600, the lesser of $16,000 or $13,600 [$170,000 × ($40,000/$500,000)]. ◆

The sourcing of income within or without the United States has a direct bearing on a number of tax provisions. The numerator of the FTC limitation formula is foreign-source taxable income. Generally, nonresident aliens and foreign corporations are subject to Federal taxation only on U.S.-source income. The foreign earned income exclusion is available only for foreign-source income.

Income Sourced within the United States

The determination of the source depends on the type of income realized. This makes the classification of income an important consideration (e.g., income from the sale of property versus income for the use of property). A detailed discussion of the characterization of income, however, is beyond the scope of this chapter. Section 861 contains source rules for most types of income. Other rules pertaining to the source of income are found in §§ 862–865.

Interest. Interest income received from the U.S. government, or the District of Columbia, and from noncorporate U.S. residents or domestic corporations is sourced within the United States. There are a few exceptions to this rule, most notably, certain interest received from a resident alien individual or domestic corporation. This exception applies where an 80 percent foreign business requirement is met. Interest received on amounts deposited with a foreign branch of a U.S. corporation is also treated as foreign-source income if the branch is engaged in the commercial banking business.

─────────────── EXAMPLE 10 ───────────────

J holds a bond issued by X, a domestic corporation. For the immediately preceding three tax years, 82% of X's gross income was active foreign business income. The interest income that J receives for the tax year from X Corporation is foreign-source income.[12] ◆

Dividends.   Dividends received from domestic corporations (other than certain possessions corporations) are sourced within the United States. Generally, dividends paid by a foreign corporation are foreign-source income. An exception to this rule applies, however, if 25 percent or more of a foreign corporation's gross income for the immediately preceding three tax years was effectively connected with the conduct of a U.S. trade or business. In this case, the dividends received in the taxable year are U.S.-source income to the extent of the proportion of gross income that was effectively connected with the conduct of a U.S. trade or business for the immediately preceding three-year period. Dividends from foreign sales corporations (FSCs) and domestic international sales corporations (DISCs) can be treated as U.S.-source income.

─────────────── EXAMPLE 11 ───────────────

T receives dividend income from the following corporations for the tax year:

Amount	Corporation	Effectively Connected Income for Past 3 Years	Active Foreign Business Income for Past 3 Years	U.S.-Source Income
$500	X, domestic	85%	15%	$500
600	Y, domestic	13%	87%	600
300	Z, foreign	80%	20%	240

The 80% active foreign business requirement would affect only interest income received from X Corporation and Y Corporation, not dividend income. Since Z Corporation is a foreign corporation meeting the 25% test, 80% of the dividend from Z Corporation is U.S.-source income. ◆

Personal Services Income.   The source of income from personal services is determined by the location in which the services are performed (within or without the United States). A limited *commercial traveler* exception is available. In order for personal services income to avoid being classified as U.S.-source income, the following requirements must be met:

- The services must be performed by a nonresident alien who is in the United States for 90 days or less during the taxable year;
- The compensation may not exceed $3,000 in total for the services performed in the United States; and

─────────────────────────────

12. § 861(c). As is subsequently discussed, certain interest income, even though U.S.-source income, is not taxable if earned by nonresident aliens or foreign corporations.

■ The services must be performed on behalf of

■ a nonresident alien, foreign partnership, or foreign corporation that is not engaged in a U.S. trade or business, or

■ an office or place of business maintained in a foreign country or possession of the United States by an individual who is a citizen or resident of the United States, a domestic partnership, or a domestic corporation.

─────────────────── EXAMPLE 12 ───────────────────

M, a nonresident alien, is an engineer employed by a foreign oil company. M spent four weeks in the United States arranging the purchase of field equipment for his company. His salary for the four weeks was $3,500. Even though the oil company is not engaged in a U.S. trade or business, and M was in the United States for less than 90 days during the taxable year, the income is U.S.-source income because it exceeds $3,000. ◆

The issue of whether income is derived from the performance of personal services is important in determining the income's source. It has been held that a corporation can perform personal services [13] and that, in the absence of capital as an income-producing factor, personal services income can arise even though there is no recipient of such services. [14] If payment is received for services performed partly within and partly without the United States, the income must be allocated for source purposes on some reasonable basis, such as days worked. [15]

Rents and Royalties. The source of income received for the use of tangible property is the country in which the property producing the income is located. The source of income received for the use of intangible property (e.g., patents, copyrights, secret processes and formulas) is the country in which the property producing the income is used.

Sale or Exchange of Property. Income from the disposition of U.S. real property interests is U.S.-source income. The definition of a U.S. real property interest is discussed subsequently in regard to the Foreign Investment in Real Property Tax Act (FIRPTA). Generally, the location of real property determines the source of any income derived from the property.

The source of income from the sale of personal property (property other than real property) depends on several factors including whether the property was produced by the seller, the type of property sold (e.g., inventory or a capital asset), and the residence of the seller. The general rule under § 865 provides that the income, gain, or profit from the sale of personal property is sourced according to the residence of the seller. Income from the sale of purchased inventory, however, is sourced in the country in which the sale takes place. [16]

When the seller has produced the property, the income must be apportioned between the country of production and the country of sale. [17] The regulations

─────────────

13. See *British Timken Limited*, 12 T.C. 880 (1949), and Rev.Rul. 60–55, 1960–1 C.B. 270.

14. See *Robida v. Comm.*, 72–1 USTC ¶ 9450, 29 AFTR2d 72–1223, 460 F.2d 1172 (CA–9, 1972). The taxpayer was employed in military PXs around the world. He had large slot machine winnings and claimed the foreign earned income exclusion. The IRS challenged the exclusion on the grounds that the winnings were not earned income because there was no recipient of Robida's services. The Court, however, found, that in the absence of capital, the winnings were earned income.

15. Reg. § 1.861–4(b).

16. § 861(a)(6). The sale is deemed to take place where title passes. See Reg. § 1.861–7(c) regarding title passage. This is an area of tax law in which there has been considerable conflict. See, for example, *Kates Holding Company, Inc.*, 79 T.C. 700 (1982) and *Miami Purchasing Service Corporation*, 76 T.C. 818 (1981).

17. § 863(b)(2).

provide guidelines for allocating income between production and sales.[18] If the manufacturer or producer regularly sells to wholly independent distributors, this can establish an *independent* factory or production price that can be used to determine the split between production and sales income. However, if an independent price has not been established, taxable income from production and sales must be apportioned. One-half of the income is apportioned between U.S. and foreign sources in proportion to the value of the taxpayer's property within and without the United States that was used to produce the income. The remaining one-half is apportioned between U.S. and foreign sources in proportion to the taxpayer's gross sales (within and without the United States) of the property produced and sold.

Losses from the sale of personal property are sourced according to the source of any income that may have been generated by the property prior to its disposition. This provision discourages the manipulation of the source of losses for tax purposes.

There are several exceptions to the general rule for the sourcing of income from the sale of personal property:

1. Gain on the sale of depreciable personal property is sourced according to prior depreciation deductions to the extent of the deductions.
2. Gain attributable to an office or fixed place of business maintained outside the United States by a U.S. resident is foreign-source income.
3. Gain attributable to an office or fixed place of business maintained in the United States by a nonresident alien is U.S.-source income. This exception does not apply to a sale of inventory where a foreign office materially participates in the sale.
4. Gain on the sale of intangibles is sourced according to prior amortization deductions to the extent of the deductions. Contingent payments, however, are sourced as royalty income.
5. Gain from the sale of goodwill is sourced where the goodwill was generated.
6. Gain from the sale of stock of an 80 percent-owned foreign affiliate may be foreign-source income. This is the result if the affiliate is engaged in an active trade or business and the stock is sold in the foreign country in which the affiliate derives more than 50 percent of its gross income for the immediately preceding three-year period.

Transportation and Communication Income. Income from transportation beginning *and* ending in the United States is U.S.-source income. Fifty percent of the income from transportation beginning *or* ending in the United States is U.S.-source income, unless the U.S. point is only an intermediate stop. This rule does not apply to personal services income unless the transportation is between the United States and a possession.[19] Income from space and ocean activities conducted outside the jurisdiction of any country is sourced according to the residence of the person conducting the activity.

International communication income derived by a U.S. person is sourced 50 percent within the United States in cases where transmission is between the United States and a foreign country. International communication income derived by foreign persons is foreign-source income unless it is attributable to an office or other fixed place of business within the United States. In that case, it is U.S.-source income.

---

18. Reg. § 1.863–3.　　　　　　　　　　　　　**19.** §§ 863(c) and (d).

U.S.-Owned Foreign Corporations. To prevent the manipulation of the source of certain types of income received from related persons, income received from U.S.-owned foreign corporations can be classified as U.S.-source income for purposes of the FTC limitation.[20] The following types of income can be so reclassified:

1. Amounts included in the gross income of U.S. shareholders under Subpart F.
2. Undistributed foreign personal holding company income included in gross income by U.S. shareholders.
3. Amounts included in gross income as currently taxed income of a qualified electing fund.
4. Interest.
5. Dividends.

A foreign corporation is *U.S.-owned* for this purpose if 50 percent or more of the total combined voting power or total value of the stock of the foreign corporation is held directly or indirectly by U.S. persons. A U.S. corporation is treated as a U.S.-owned foreign corporation if dividend or interest income paid by the corporation is classified as foreign-source income under the sourcing provisions. Only interest and dividends properly allocable to U.S.-source earnings are treated as U.S.-source income for the taxable year.

EXAMPLE 13

F, a U.S.-owned foreign corporation, pays $100,000 in dividends to U.S. shareholders for the tax year. For the same period, F's E & P from U.S. sources is $150,000, and total E & P from all sources is $250,000. Dividend income of $60,000 [$100,000 × ($150,000/$250,000)] is classified as U.S.-source income for purposes of the FTC limitation. ◆

This rule does not apply to dividends and interest for tax years in which less than 10 percent of the payor foreign corporation's E & P is attributable to U.S.-source income.

Income Sourced without the United States

The provisions for sourcing income without the United States are not as detailed and specific as those for determining U.S.-source income. Basically, § 862 provides that if interest, dividends, compensation for personal services, income from the use or sale of property, and other income is not U.S.-source income, then it is foreign-source income.

Allocation and Apportionment of Deductions

The United States levies a tax on *taxable income.* Deductions and losses, therefore, must be allocated and apportioned between U.S.- and foreign-source gross income to determine U.S.- and foreign-source taxable income. A detailed discussion of Treasury Regulation § 1.861–8, which provides the basis for this allocation and apportionment, is beyond the scope of this chapter. Briefly, the regulation calls for deductions directly related to an activity or property to be allocated to classes of income. This is followed by apportionment between the

---

20. § 904(g).

statutory and residual groupings on some reasonable basis. For FTC purposes, foreign-source income is the statutory grouping, and U.S.-source income is the residual grouping.

─────────────────────────── EXAMPLE 14 ───────────────────────────

ABC, Inc., a domestic corporation has $2,000,000 gross income and a $50,000 expense, all related to real estate activities. The expense is allocated and apportioned as follows:

| | Gross Income | | | Apportionment | |
	Foreign	U.S.	Allocation	Foreign	U.S.
Sales	$1,000,000	$500,000	$37,500*	$25,000	$12,500**
Rentals	400,000	100,000	12,500	10,000	2,500
			$50,000	$35,000	$15,000

*$50,000 × ($1,500,000/$2,000,000).

**$37,500 × ($500,000/$1,500,000).

If it could be shown that $45,000 of the expense was directly related to sales income, the $45,000 would be allocated to that class of gross income, with the remainder allocated ratably. ◆

Specific rules apply to interest expenses. Their allocation and apportionment are based on the theory that money is fungible. With limited exceptions, interest expense is attributable to all the activities and property of the taxpayer regardless of the specific purpose for incurring the debt on which interest is paid.[21] Section 864(e)(2) generally provides that taxpayers must allocate and apportion interest expense on the basis of assets, using either the fair market value or the tax book value of the assets.[22] Once the fair market value is used, the taxpayer must continue to use this method. Special rules apply in allocating and apportioning interest expense in the case of an affiliated group of corporations.

─────────────────────────── EXAMPLE 15 ───────────────────────────

X, a domestic corporation, generates U.S.-source and foreign-source gross income for 1992. X's assets (tax book value) are as follows:

Generating U.S.-source income	$18,000,000
Generating foreign-source income	5,000,000
	$23,000,000

X incurs interest expense of $800,000 for 1992. Using the asset method and the tax book value, interest expense is apportioned to foreign-source income as follows:

$$\frac{\$5,000,000 \text{ (foreign assets)}}{\$23,000,000 \text{ (total assets)}} \times \$800,000 = \underline{\$173,913}$$

◆

Specific rules also apply to research and development expenditures, certain stewardship expenses, legal and accounting fees and expenses, income taxes, and losses.

───────────────────────────

21. Reg. § 1.861–10T(b) describes circumstances where interest expense can be directly allocated to specific debt. This exception to the fungibility concept is limited to cases in which specific property is purchased or improved with nonrecourse debt.

22. Reg. § 1.861–9T.

A deduction not definitely related to any class of gross income is ratably allocated to all classes of gross income and apportioned between U.S.- and foreign-source income.

Section 482 Considerations

Taxpayers may be tempted to manipulate the source of income and the allocation of deductions arbitrarily to minimize taxation. This manipulation is more easily accomplished between or among related persons. The IRS uses § 482 to counter such actions. The provision gives the IRS the power to reallocate gross income, deductions, credits, or allowances between or among organizations, trades, or businesses owned or controlled directly or indirectly by the same interests. This can be done whenever the IRS determines that reallocation is necessary to prevent the evasion of taxes or to reflect income more clearly. Section 482 is a "one-edged" sword available only to the IRS. The taxpayer cannot invoke it to reallocate income and expenses.[23]

The reach of § 482 is quite broad. It is the IRS's position that a corporation and its sole shareholder who works full-time for the corporation can be treated as two separate trades or businesses for purposes of § 482.[24] Two unrelated shareholders who each owned 50 percent of a corporation were held to be acting in concert for their common good and, thus, together controlled the corporation.[25]

Section 482 is supplemented by legislative regulations that provide rules for safe harbor charges in regard to loans, services, and the use of tangible property. The regulations provide little specific guidance in the area of intangibles. Several court decisions in recent years have addressed this issue.[26]

The regulations also provide three specific methods for determining an arm's length price on the sale of tangible property: the comparable uncontrolled price method, the resale price method, and the cost plus method. These methods are to be relied on in the order given. The regulations also allow for various undefined methods when none of these methods is appropriate.

After 1986, payments made by related parties for the sale or use of intangible property must be commensurate with the income attributable to the intangibles. Furthermore, the basis or inventory cost of imported property purchased from a related party cannot exceed the value declared for customs duty purposes.[27]

On October 19, 1988, the Treasury released its *Study of Intercompany Pricing* (the "White Paper"). It concluded that the market-based approach to intercompany pricing reflected in the current § 482 regulations cannot be applied effectively due to the integration of the tangible property and the marketing and manufacturing intangibles in income generation. The Treasury concluded that the market-based approach should be supplemented by an alternative pricing approach that considers the return earned in the marketplace on a firm's factors of production. The Treasury has been working closely with the IRS to develop proposed regulations to implement certain suggestions made in the White Paper. Treasury officials have commented, however, that there is no quick solution to the pricing issues addressed in the White Paper.

23. Reg. § 1.482–1(b)(3).

24. Rev.Rul. 88–38, 1988–1 C.B. 246. But see *Foglesong v. Comm.*, 82–2 USTC ¶9650, 50 AFTR2d 82–6016, 691 F.2d 848 (CA–7, 1982), *rev'g.* 77 T.C. 1102 (1981).

25. See *B. Forman Company, Inc. v. Comm.*, 72–1 USTC ¶9182, 29 AFTR2d 72–405, 453 F.2d 1144 (CA–2, 1972).

26. See *Eli Lilly & Company and Subsidiaries v. Comm.*, 88–2 USTC ¶9502, 62 AFTR2d 88–5569, 856 F.2d 855 (CA–7, 1988), *aff'g.* in part, *rev'g.* in part, and *rem'g.* 84 T.C. 996 (1985); *Bausch & Lomb, Inc., & Consolidated Subsidiaries*, 92 T.C. 525 (1989); and *G. D. Searle*, 88 T.C. 252 (1987).

27. § 1059A.

Generally, only the U.S.-source income of nonresident aliens (NRAs) and foreign corporations is subject to U.S. taxation. This reflects the reach of U.S. tax jurisdiction. The constraint, however, does not prevent the United States from also taxing the foreign-source income of NRAs and foreign corporations, when that income is effectively connected with the conduct of a U.S. trade or business.[28] The income of NRAs and foreign corporations subject to U.S. taxation can be divided into two classifications: *effectively connected* and *noneffectively connected* income. In some respects foreign corporations enjoy preferential income tax treatment compared with NRA individuals. In addition, NRA individuals can be subject to the Federal estate and gift tax.

Nonresident Alien Individuals

An NRA individual is an individual who is not a citizen or resident of the United States. Citizenship is determined under the immigration and naturalization laws of the United States.[29] Basically, the citizenship statutes are broken down into two categories: nationality at birth and nationality through naturalization.

Residency. For many years, the definition of residency for Federal income tax purposes was very subjective, requiring an evaluation of a person's intent and actions with regard to the length and nature of stay in the United States. In 1984, Congress enacted a more objective test of residency. Under § 7701(b), a person is a resident of the United States for income tax purposes if he or she meets either the "green card" test or the substantial presence test. If either of these tests is met for the calendar year, the individual is deemed a U.S. resident for the year.[30]

An alien issued a green card is considered a U.S. resident on the first day he or she is physically present in the United States after issuance. The green card is Immigration Form I–551. Newly issued cards are now rose (off-pink), but the form is still referred to as the "green card." Status as a U.S. resident remains in effect until the green card has been revoked or the individual has abandoned lawful permanent resident status.

The substantial presence test will apply to an alien without a green card. It is a mathematical test involving physical presence in the United States. An individual who is physically present in the United States for at least 183 days during the calendar year is a U.S. resident for income tax purposes. This 183-day requirement can also be met over a three-year period that includes the two immediately preceding years and the current year. For this purpose, each day of the current calendar year is counted as a full day, each day of the first preceding year as one-third day, and each day of the second preceding year as one-sixth day.

EXAMPLE 16

N, an alien, was present in the United States for 90 days in 1990, 180 days in 1991, and 110 days in 1992. For Federal income tax purposes, N is a U.S. resident for 1992 since her physical presence for the three-year period consisted of 185 days [(90 days × ⅙) + (180 days × ⅓) + (110 days × 1)]. ◆

Several exceptions are provided under the substantial presence test. Commuters from Mexico and Canada who are employed in the United States, but return home each day, are excepted. Also excepted are individuals who are

---

28. §§ 871, 881, and 882.

29. Title 8, Aliens and Nationality, *United States Code.*

30. See also Prop.Reg. § 301.7701(b).

prevented from leaving the United States due to a medical condition that arose while in the United States. Some individuals are exempt from the substantial presence test, including foreign government-related individuals (e.g., diplomats), qualified teachers, trainees and students, and certain professional athletes.

If an individual meets the substantial presence requirement under the three-year test period, but was not in the United States for at least 31 days in the current calendar year, the individual is not a resident under the substantial presence test. If the requirement is met under the three-year test period, but the individual was not present in the United States for 183 days in the current year, classification as a U.S. resident for the year can be avoided. This is accomplished by showing a closer connection (for example, home, family, social and professional ties) to another country. This exception will apply only if the individual's tax home[31] is in a foreign country and the person has taken no steps toward establishing permanent residence in the United States. Under the substantial presence test, residence begins the first day the individual is physically present in the United States and ends the last day of physical presence for the calendar year. This assumes the substantial presence test is not satisfied for the next calendar year. Nominal presence of 10 days or less can be ignored in determining whether the substantial presence test is met.

The application of the income tax treaties that the United States has in force with other countries depends on the residence of the taxpayer. Most of the treaties have "tie breaker" provisions for situations in which a person may qualify as a resident of both treaty countries under each country's laws. Certain treaties override § 7701(b) for the purpose of income tax status (as resident or nonresident), but may not override residence under § 7701(b) for purposes of other tax provisions (e.g., the sourcing of income).

Nonresident Aliens Not Engaged in a U.S. Trade or Business.   Section 871(a) subjects certain U.S.-source income that is not effectively connected with the conduct of a U.S. trade or business to a 30 percent tax. This income includes dividends, interest, rents, royalties, certain compensation, premiums, annuities, and other fixed, determinable, annual or periodic (FDAP) income. This tax generally is levied by a withholding mechanism that requires the payors of the income to withhold 30 percent of gross amounts.[32] This method eliminates the problems of assuring payment by nonresidents, determining allowable deductions, and, in many instances, the filing of tax returns by nonresidents. NRAs are allowed a deduction for casualty and theft losses with regard to property located within the United States, a deduction for qualified charitable contributions, and one personal exemption. Residents of countries contiguous to the United States are allowed dependency exemptions as well. Interest received from certain portfolio debt investments, even though U.S.-source income, is exempt from taxation. Interest earned on deposits with banking institutions is also exempt as long as it is not effectively connected with the conduct of a U.S. trade or business.

Capital gains not effectively connected with the conduct of a U.S. trade or business are exempt from tax as long as the NRA individual was not present in the United States for 183 days or more during the taxable year. If an NRA has not established a taxable year, the calendar year will be treated as the taxable year. NRAs are not permitted to carry forward capital losses.[33]

---

31. Tax home has the same meaning as under § 911(d)(3), but without regard to whether the individual's place of abode is in the United States.

32. §§ 873 and 1441.
33. § 871(a)(2).

Even though an NRA is not *actually* engaged in the conduct of a U.S. trade or business, any gains from the sale of U.S. real property interests are treated as effectively connected income. This is discussed in more detail subsequently. Furthermore, the taxpayer can elect to treat income from certain passive real estate activities (for example, a net lease arrangement) as effectively connected income. This allows the taxpayer to deduct any expenses incurred in earning the income attributable to the real estate in determining taxable income. Once made, the election is irrevocable.

Nonresident Aliens Engaged in a U.S. Trade or Business.   As long as FDAP income and capital gains are not effectively connected income, the tax treatment of these income items is the same for NRAs engaged in a U.S. trade or business as for NRAs who are not so engaged. Effectively connected income, however, is taxed at the same rates that apply to U.S. citizens and residents, and deductions for expenses attributable to that income are allowed.

Two important definitions determine the U.S. tax consequences to NRAs with U.S.-source income: "the conduct of a U.S. trade or business" and "effectively connected income." Section 864 and the accompanying regulations contain guidelines for making these determinations. General criteria for determining if a U.S. trade or business exists include the location of production activities, management, distribution activities, and other business functions. Trading in commodities and securities ordinarily will not constitute a trade or business. Dealers, however, need to avoid maintaining a U.S. trading office and trading for their own account. Corporations (other than certain personal holding companies) that are not dealers can trade for their own account as long as their principal office is located outside the United States. There are no restrictions on individuals who are not dealers. An NRA individual who performs services in the United States for a foreign employer is not engaged in a U.S. trade or business.

A U.S. trade or business is a prerequisite to having effectively connected income. Section 864(c) provides a dual test for determining if income, such as FDAP income and capital gains, is effectively connected income. Income is effectively connected with a U.S. trade or business if it is derived from assets used in, or held for use in, the trade or business (asset-use test) or if the activities of the trade or business were a material factor in the production of the income (business-activities test).

─────────────── EXAMPLE 17 ───────────────

N, an NRA, operates a U.S. business. During the year, excess cash funds accumulate. N invests these funds on a short-term basis so that they remain available to meet business needs. Any income earned from these investments is effectively connected income under the asset-use test. ◆

A partnership having any effectively connected taxable income allocable under § 704 to foreign partners must withhold tax equal to the *applicable percentage* of the income allocated to foreign partners.[34] The applicable percentage is 31 percent for noncorporate foreign partners and 34 percent for foreign corporate partners. The withheld tax paid by the partnership is treated as a credit against the foreign partner's tax liability. The withholding tax paid by the partnership is treated as distributed to the foreign partner on the earlier of the

───────────

34. § 1446.

date that the taxes are actually paid or the last day of the partnership tax year in which the tax was paid.

Estate and Gift Taxes. The value of property situated in the United States is included in a deceased NRA's gross estate for U.S. estate tax purposes.[35] Thus, the question of situs (location) of property owned by the decedent at the time of death is important.

Generally, the situs of real property is not subject to conflict. One probably would not question the conclusion that a piece of land in Kansas is situated in the United States. Also, the situs of tangible personal property is easily determined (e.g., jewelry in a safe deposit box located in a bank in New York City). Specific rules are provided for certain intangible property. Stock owned and held by an NRA at the time of death is deemed situated in the United States only if it was issued by a domestic corporation.[36] Debt obligations of a U.S. person or the United States, a state or any political subdivision thereof, or the District of Columbia are deemed property situated within the United States. However, the proceeds of life insurance on the life of an NRA are not property situated within the United States.[37] Furthermore, amounts on deposit in U.S. banks are not property situated within the United States if the interest income earned on the deposits is foreign-source income. A similar rule applies to portfolio debt obligations where the interest income earned on the debt is exempt from U.S. income taxation.

The tax rates applicable to the taxable estate of a deceased NRA are found in § 2001(c) and are the same as those applicable to the taxable estate of a U.S. citizen or resident. Section 2102(c) allows a unified credit against the estate tax imposed on an NRA's taxable estate of only $13,000. In fact, the credit is not *unified* since, for gift tax purposes, taxable gifts made by NRAs are subject to the same rates imposed on U.S. citizens and residents,[38] but a unified credit against the gift tax is not allowed to NRAs.[39] The gift tax is imposed only on an NRA's transfer of tangible property[40] situated in the United States.[41] The marital deduction is not available to NRAs. It is also not available to U.S. persons (or their estates) on transfers to noncitizen spouses.[42] However, a $100,000 annual gift tax exclusion is allowed on transfers to a noncitizen spouse.[43] Under a limited exception for estate tax purposes, the marital deduction is available if the property passes to a qualified domestic trust[44] or to a spouse who is a U.S. resident on the date of death of the decedent and becomes a U.S. citizen before the estate tax return is filed.

For purposes of the estate and gift tax, an individual is a *nonresident* if his or her domicile is not within the United States at the time of death or on the date the gift is transferred.[45] A person acquires a domicile in a place by living there with no definite present intention to change domicile at a later date. In other words, *action* and *intent* are required to establish domicile. Intent is more often subject to question than action. It is easy to determine whether an individual has actually lived and acquired permanent physical ties, such as a personal residence, in the United States. Some factors that the courts have considered in determining intent are participation in local affairs, payment of taxes, voting status, location of personal property, and statements concerning residence.

---

35. § 2103.
36. § 2104(a).
37. § 2105.
38. § 2502.
39. § 2505.
40. § 2501(a)(2).

41. § 2511.
42. § 2056.
43. § 2523.
44. § 2056A.
45. Reg. § 20.0–1.

Foreign Corporations

Definition. The classification of an entity as a foreign corporation for U.S. tax purposes is an important consideration. Section 7701(a)(5) defines a foreign corporation as one that is not domestic. A domestic corporation is a corporation that is created or organized in the United States.

The IRS looks at the corporate characteristics outlined in the regulations under § 7701 to determine whether a foreign entity should be treated as an association taxable as a corporation. See the discussion of these characteristics in Chapter 2. In determining the presence or absence of any of these characteristics, the IRS looks at the rights and duties of the foreign entity under the laws of the jurisdiction in which it resides. Classification of the foreign entity as a corporation, an association taxable as a corporation, a partnership, or some other form of entity can affect the U.S. tax consequences with regard to the entity and its owners. For example, stock in a foreign corporation is not included in the U.S. gross estate of an NRA individual even where all the assets of the corporation are located in the United States. Also, individuals expecting the pass-through of losses of a foreign partnership will be denied those losses if the foreign entity is deemed to be an association taxable as a corporation for U.S. tax purposes.

Income Not Effectively Connected with a U.S. Trade or Business. Under § 881, U.S.-source FDAP income of foreign corporations is taxed by the United States in the same manner as that of NRA individuals—at a flat 30 percent rate. Basically, foreign corporations qualify for the same exemptions from U.S. taxation regarding interest and dividend income as do NRA individuals. The U.S.-source capital gains of foreign corporations are exempt from the Federal income tax if they are not effectively connected with the conduct of a U.S. trade or business.

Effectively Connected Income. Section 882 subjects foreign corporations conducting a trade or business within the United States to Federal income taxation on effectively connected income. Additionally, any U.S.-source income other than noneffectively connected FDAP and capital gains is deemed effectively connected, for example, casual sales of items by the home office.[46] For such purposes, foreign corporations are subject to the same tax rates as domestic corporations.

Branch Profits Tax. In addition to the income tax imposed under § 882 on effectively connected income of a foreign corporation, a tax equal to 30 percent of the *dividend equivalent amount* for the taxable year is imposed on any foreign corporation.[47]

The objective of the branch profits tax is to afford equal tax treatment to income generated by a domestic corporation controlled by a foreign corporation and to income generated by other U.S. operations controlled by foreign corporations. If the foreign corporation operates through a U.S. subsidiary (a domestic corporation), the income of the subsidiary is taxable by the United States when derived and is also subject to a withholding tax when repatriated (returned as dividends to the foreign parent). Before the branch profits tax was enacted, a foreign corporation with a branch in the United States paid only the initial tax on its U.S. earnings; remittances were not taxed.

---

46. Reg. § 1.864–4(b), Example (3).   **47.** § 884.

The dividend equivalent amount (DEA) is the foreign corporation's effectively connected earnings for the taxable year, adjusted for increases and decreases in the corporation's U.S. net equity (investment in the U.S. operations). The DEA is limited to current E & P and post-1986 accumulated E & P that is effectively connected, or treated as effectively connected, with the conduct of a U.S. trade or business. It does not include E & P that has been previously subject to the branch profits tax. E & P for this purpose does not include income otherwise exempt from U.S. taxation, certain FSC income, gain on sale of stock of a domestic corporation that is a U.S. real property holding corporation, and income that the taxpayer elects to treat as effectively connected under Subpart F. U.S. net equity is the sum of money and the aggregate adjusted basis of assets and liabilities directly connected to U.S. operations that generate effectively connected income. A decrease in net equity as the result of a deficit for the tax year is not subject to the branch profits tax.

─────────────── EXAMPLE 18 ───────────────

F, a foreign corporation, has a U.S. branch operation with the following tax results and other information for 1992:

E & P effectively connected with a U.S. trade or business	$2,000,000
U.S. corporate tax (at 34%)	680,000
Remittance to home office	1,000,000
Increase in U.S. net equity	320,000*

*$2,000,000 − $680,000 U.S. taxes − $1,000,000 remittance.

The DEA and branch profits tax are computed as follows:

After-tax E & P effectively connected with a U.S. trade or business (1992)	$1,320,000
Less increase in U.S. net equity	(320,000)
DEA	$1,000,000
Branch profits tax rate	× 30%
Branch profits tax	$ 300,000

The 30 percent rate of the branch profits tax may be reduced or eliminated by a treaty provision. A lower rate specified in a treaty applies where the treaty provides for a branch profits tax or withholding on dividends paid by a corporation resident in the treaty country. The rate reduction will not apply if the foreign corporation is not a qualified resident of the treaty country (for example, a foreign corporation owned by persons nonresident in the treaty country). The branch profits tax does not apply where prohibited by treaty under a nondiscrimination clause. If a foreign corporation is subject to the branch profits tax, no other tax is levied on the dividend actually paid by the corporation during the taxable year.[48]

The Foreign Investment in Real Property Tax Act

Under prior law, NRAs and foreign corporations could avoid U.S. taxation on gains from the sale of U.S. real estate if the gains were treated as capital gains

───────────────

48. Section 884(e)(3) states that no tax will be imposed by §§ 871(a), 881(a), 1441, or 1442.

and were not effectively connected with the conduct of a U.S. trade or business. Furthermore, the United States has a number of income tax treaties that allow for an annual election to treat real estate operations as a trade or business. Persons who were residents of the treaty countries could take advantage of the election for tax years prior to the year of sale and then revoke the election for the year in which the sale took place. In the mid-1970s, midwestern farmers put pressure on Congress to eliminate what they saw as a tax advantage that would allow nonresidents to bid up the price of farmland. This and other concerns regarding the foreign ownership of U.S. real estate led to enactment of the Foreign Investment in Real Property Tax Act (FIRPTA) of 1980.

Under FIRPTA, gains and losses realized by NRAs and foreign corporations from the sale or other disposition of U.S. real property interests are treated as effectively connected with the conduct of a U.S. trade or business even where those persons are not actually so engaged. NRA individuals must pay a tax equal to at least 21 percent of the lesser of their alternative minimum taxable income or net U.S. real property gain for the taxable year.[49]

For purposes of § 897, losses of individual taxpayers are taken into account only to the extent they are deductible under § 165(c) (business losses, losses on transactions entered into for profit, and losses from casualties and thefts).

U.S. Real Property Interest (USRPI). Any direct interest in real property situated in the United States and any interest in a domestic corporation (other than solely as a creditor) are U.S. real property interests (USRPIs). This definition applies unless the taxpayer can establish that a domestic corporation was not a U.S. real property holding corporation (USRPHC) during the shorter of the period after June 18, 1980, during which the taxpayer held an interest in the corporation, or for the five-year period ending on the date on which the interest was disposed of (the base period). A domestic corporation is not a USRPHC if it holds no USRPIs on the date of disposition of its stock and if any USRPIs held by the corporation during the base period were disposed of in a transaction in which gain, if any, was fully recognized. This exception also applies if the USRPI disposed of by the corporation was stock of a second USRPHC that ceased to be a USRPHC by way of a taxable disposition of its USRPIs .

───────────────────────────── Example 19 ─────────────────────────────

From January 1, 1987, through January 1, 1992, F (a foreign investor) holds shares in D, a U.S. corporation. During this period, D holds two parcels of U.S. real estate and stock of S, another U.S. corporation. S also owns U.S. real estate. The two parcels of real estate held directly by D were disposed of on December 15, 1988, in a like-kind exchange in which D acquired foreign realty. S disposed of its U.S. real estate in a taxable transaction on January 1, 1992. An interest in D will be treated as a USRPI because D did not recognize gain on the December 15, 1988, exchange of the USRPIs. If D's ownership of U.S. real estate had been limited to its indirect ownership through S, as of January 2, 1992, an interest in D would not constitute a USRPI. This result would occur because S disposed of its USRPIs in a taxable transaction in which gain was fully recognize   ◆

A USRPHC is any corporation (whether foreign or domestic) where the fair market value of the corporation's USRPIs equals or exceeds 50 percent of the

─────────────────────────

49. § 897. The Revenue Reconciliation Act of 1990 increased the AMT rate for individuals to 24% for taxable years beginning after 1990. It is expected that a technical correction will increase the § 897 rate of 21% to 24%.

aggregate of fair market value of certain specified assets. These assets are the corporation's USRPIs, its interests in real property located outside the United States, plus any other of its assets that are used or held for use in a trade or business. Stock regularly traded on an established securities market is not treated as a USRPI where a person holds no more than 5 percent of such stock.

Gain on a disposition of stock of a foreign real property holding corporation is not subject to tax under § 897. However, gain on a disposition of a USRPI by such a foreign corporation is subject to § 897. An exception to this gain recognition is provided for cases in which the basis of property in the hands of the distributee is the same as the adjusted basis to the distributing corporation. This exception only applies if the distributee would be subject to U.S. income taxation on a subsequent disposition of the property. Furthermore, a foreign corporation can elect to be treated as a domestic corporation under an income tax treaty that contains an antidiscrimination clause.[50]

Withholding Provisions.   The tax law requires any purchaser or agent acquiring a USRPI from a foreign person to withhold 10 percent of the amount realized on the disposition.[51] The amount withheld must be submitted along with Form 8288 within at least 20 days after the transfer. The amount withheld need not exceed the transferor's maximum tax liability with regard to the transfer. A domestic partnership, trust, or estate with a foreign partner, foreign grantor treated as owner, or foreign beneficiary must withhold 34 percent (or 31 percent where allowed by the IRS) of the gain allocable to that person on a disposition of a USRPI. Foreign corporations are also subject to withholding provisions on certain distributions.

Failure to withhold can subject the purchaser or the purchaser's agent to interest on any unpaid amount.[52] A civil penalty of 100 percent of the amount required to be withheld and a criminal penalty of up to $10,000 or five years in prison can be imposed for willful failure to withhold.[53]

Certain exemptions from withholding are provided. An agent for the purchaser or seller is liable for withholding only an amount equal to the compensation he or she received for handling the transaction.

Special Provisions

Taxpayers Married to Nonresident Aliens.   Section 6013(g) allows a citizen or resident of the United States, who is married to an NRA at the close of the taxable year, to elect to file a joint return with the NRA spouse. Both spouses must consent to the election, and, once made, the election applies for the current year and all subsequent years unless revoked. Such an election results in the treatment of the NRA as a U.S. resident for income tax purposes. The election subjects the NRA's worldwide taxable income to U.S. taxation.

Dual Resident Taxpayers.   Under § 6013(h), a taxpayer who is a dual resident (an NRA for a portion of the tax year and a U.S. resident for a portion of the tax year) can elect to file a joint return if he or she is a U.S. resident at the close of the taxable year and is married to a U.S. citizen or resident. Both spouses must consent to the election, which can be made only one time. The election also

---

50. The branch profits tax applies to a foreign corporation engaged in a U.S. trade or business even where the corporation has made an election under § 897(i) to be treated as a U.S. corporation.

51. § 1445.

52. §§ 6601, 6621, and 6651.

53. §§ 6672 and 7202.

subjects the dual resident's worldwide taxable income for the entire tax year to U.S. taxation.

Community Income. Section 879 sets forth the tax treatment of community income in the case of a married couple where one or both persons are NRAs. Earned income, other than trade or business income and a partner's distributive share of partnership income, is treated as income of the spouse who rendered the personal services. Trade or business income is treated as income of the husband. However, if the wife exercises substantially all of the management and control of a trade or business, all the gross income and deductions attributable to the trade or business are treated as hers. A partner's distributive share of partnership income is treated as that of the partner. Other community income derived from separate property owned by one spouse is treated as that spouse's income. All other community income is treated as the applicable community property law provides.

EXAMPLE 20

H, a U.S. citizen, is married to W, an NRA. H and W do not elect to file a joint return. Under the laws of F, their country of residence, dividends from stock owned jointly by married couples are considered the property of the husband. If H and W receive dividends on stock they own jointly, H must include the entire dividend in gross income for U.S. tax purposes even where it is foreign-source income. ◆

Expatriation to Avoid Tax. An NRA individual who lost U.S. citizenship within 10 years immediately preceding the close of the current tax year is subject to U.S. taxation under § 877. An exception is made if the loss of citizenship did not have as one of its principal purposes the avoidance of the U.S. income, estate, or gift tax. Under § 877, only U.S.-source taxable income is subject to tax and only if the tax under § 877 is greater than the tax that the expatriate would otherwise owe with regard to U.S.-source taxable income. For purposes of § 877, gain on the sale or exchange of property (other than stock or debt obligations) located in the United States is U.S.-source income. Gain on the sale or exchange of stock issued by a domestic corporation and debt obligations of U.S. persons or of the United States, a state or political subdivision thereof, or the District of Columbia also is subject to § 877. This source rule also applies to the sale or exchange of property that takes its basis in whole or in part by reference to the property described above.

Tax Treaties

Income Tax. Over 40 income tax treaties between the United States and other countries are in effect.[54] These treaties generally provide *taxing rights* with regard to the taxable income of residents of one treaty country who have income sourced in the other treaty country. For the most part, neither country is prohibited from taxing the income of its residents.[55] The treaties generally provide for primary taxing rights that require the other treaty partner to allow a credit for the taxes paid on income that is taxed under the primary taxing rights of one treaty partner and is also taxed by the other treaty partner.

EXAMPLE 21

T, a resident of F, a country with which the United States has an income tax treaty, earns income attributable to a permanent establishment (e.g., place of business) in the

---

54. *Treaties and Other International Acts Series* (TIAS), U.S. Government Printing Office.

55. *Convention between the United States of America and the French Republic with Respect to Taxes on Income and Property,* Art. 22(4)(a).

United States. Under the treaty, the United States has primary taxing rights with regard to this income. F can also require that the income be included in gross income and subject to F's income tax, but must allow a credit for the taxes paid to the United States on the income. ◆

Primary taxing rights usually depend on the residence of the taxpayer or the presence of a permanent establishment in a treaty country to which the income is attributable. Generally, a permanent establishment is a branch, office, factory, workshop, warehouse, or other fixed place of business.

The United States developed a Model Income Tax Treaty[56] as the starting point for negotiating income tax treaties with other countries. The most controversial of the articles in the model treaty is Article 16, Limitation On Benefits. This article is meant to prevent what is known as *treaty shopping.* Treaty shopping occurs when an entity resident in a treaty country takes advantage of the provisions of the treaty even though the majority of the owners of the entity are not residents of the treaty country. Article 16 disallows treaty benefits to an entity unless more than 75 percent of the beneficial interest in the entity is owned, directly or indirectly, by one or more individual residents of the same treaty country in which the entity is resident. The entity cannot be a conduit for meeting liabilities, such as interest or royalty payments, to persons who are not residents in either treaty country and who are not U.S. citizens. The United States' negotiating position with regard to Article 16 of the Model Income Tax Treaty has led to the termination of some treaties.[57]

Several code provisions override the income tax treaties to some extent, for example, § 884 (the branch profits tax) and § 897 (FIRPTA). Taxpayers who take a "treaty-based" position contrary to the Internal Revenue Code must disclose that position on their tax return.[58] Penalties are imposed for failure to disclose.[59] Taking a treaty-based position requires the filing of a tax return even in cases where a return would not otherwise be required.

The U.S. Treasury Department is currently considering the impact of the Tax Reform Act of 1986 on tax treaties that have been negotiated. Several international trade organizations have expressed concern that treaty override provisions inhibit treaty negotiations and international trade.

Estate and Gift Tax. The United States has estate tax treaties with fewer than 20 countries. Some of these treaties are combined estate and gift tax treaties. Like the income tax treaties, they provide primary taxing rights and a credit for taxes paid to the treaty country with the primary taxing rights. Primary taxing rights generally reside with the country where the property is located (older treaties) or the country of domicile of the donor or decedent (newer treaties). Primary taxing rights regarding real property and property of a permanent establishment for the most part reside with the country in which the property is situated.

Citizens and residents of the United States are subject to Federal taxation on their worldwide taxable income. U.S. taxpayers who operate in a foreign country as a sole proprietor, or through a foreign branch or foreign partnership, must include foreign-source income in gross income for U.S. tax purposes. They are allowed a deduction for related expenses and losses. The beneficiary of a

U.S. TAXPAYERS ABROAD

---

56. Treasury Department Model Income Tax Treaty (June 16, 1981).

57. U.S.–Netherlands Antilles and U.S.–Aruba income tax treaties as of January 1, 1988.

58. § 6114.

59. § 6712.

foreign trust includes only distributions of trust income in gross income for U.S. tax purposes, unless the trust is a grantor trust with a U.S. grantor. In that case, the income is taxed directly to the grantor for U.S. tax purposes.[60] An FTC is available for foreign income taxes paid.

Income tax treaties can reduce or eliminate the taxation of the income by the foreign country party to the treaty. Since, under the treaty, the United States reserves the right to tax its citizens and residents, relief from double taxation is achieved with the FTC. In addition to the FTC, several other tax provisions involve certain foreign-source income of U.S. citizens and residents.

The Foreign Earned Income Exclusion—§ 911

To allow U.S. multinational entities to be competitive in the world market, Congress enacted legislation granting an exclusion (from U.S. gross income) for a certain amount of qualified foreign earned income. This exclusion was meant to allow multinational entities to employ U.S. citizens and residents for foreign operations without having to pay them a wage or salary far in excess of that paid to nationals of the particular foreign country or countries. The United States taxes worldwide taxable income of its citizens and residents. Consequently, without the exclusion, the tax burden on a U.S. taxpayer working abroad could be much greater than that on a native of the foreign country.

Currently, § 911 allows a foreign earned income exclusion for (1) a qualified housing cost amount and (2) foreign earned income not in excess of $70,000. The exclusion is elective and is made by filing Form 2555 with the income tax return, or with an amended return, for the first taxable year for which the election is to be effective. An election once made remains in effect for that year and for all subsequent years unless revoked. If the election is revoked for any taxable year, the taxpayer may not make the election again (without consent of the IRS) until the sixth taxable year following the taxable year for which revocation was first effective.[61]

Qualified Individuals.　The exclusion is available to an individual whose tax home is in a foreign country and who is either (1) a U.S. citizen and bona fide resident of a foreign country or countries or (2) a citizen or resident of the United States who, during any 12 consecutive months, is physically present in a foreign country or countries for at least 330 full days. *Tax home* has the same meaning as under § 162(a)(2) relating to travel expenses while away from home. The issue of whether a stay abroad is temporary can be troublesome. If the stay abroad is deemed to be temporary, the taxpayer's tax home has not shifted to the foreign country. In Revenue Ruling 83–82, the IRS held that an individual who worked in another city for 16 months was temporarily away from home.[62]

Only whole days count for the physical presence test. The taxpayer has some flexibility in choosing the 12-month period.

--- Example 22 ---

C, a U.S. citizen, arrived in Ireland from Boston at 3 P.M. on March 28, 1991. C remained in Ireland until 8 A.M. on March 1, 1992, at which time she departed for the United States. Among other possible 12-month periods, C is present in a foreign country an aggregate of 330 full days during each of the following 12-month periods: March 1, 1991, through February 28, 1992, and March 29, 1991, through March 28, 1992.[63] ◆

---

60. § 677.
61. Reg. § 1.911–7.

62. 1983–1 C.B. 45.
63. Reg. § 1.911–2(d).

Some factors considered in establishing a bona fide foreign residence are intention of the taxpayer, establishment of the taxpayer's home temporarily in a foreign country for an indefinite period, participation in community activities, and, in general, assimilation into the foreign environment.[64] Section 911 is not available to a U.S. citizen or resident who resides and/or works in a foreign country in contravention of an executive order. These include countries with which the United States has broken diplomatic ties, such as Iran and Cuba. However, an individual who is required to leave a foreign country before meeting the bona fide residence or physical presence test may obtain a waiver on establishing that the requirements would have been met under normal conditions. Circumstances that trigger this exception include war, civil unrest, and similar adverse conditions that prevent the normal conduct of business.

If spouses both earn foreign earned income, each may be eligible for the foreign earned income exclusion. Each spouse is subject to a separate limitation, even when the couple files a joint return. Community property laws are ignored, and the income is treated as that of the spouse who actually performed the services.

The General Exclusion. The foreign earned income (general) exclusion is available for foreign earned income and is limited to the lesser of (1) $70,000 or (2) foreign earned income less the housing cost amount exclusion. The exclusion is available for the tax year in which income would be taken into account for tax purposes. The limitation, however, is determined for the tax year in which the services were performed. Income received after the close of the taxable year following the taxable year in which the services were performed does not qualify for the exclusion.

EXAMPLE 23

T, a U.S. resident, is present in a foreign country for all of 1991. T earns $100,000 from the performance of personal services. T returns to the United States on January 1, 1992, and remains there. Of the $100,000 foreign earned income, T receives $60,000 in 1991 and $40,000 in 1992. T can take a foreign earned income exclusion of $60,000 for 1991 and $10,000 for 1992 ($70,000 statutory limit minus the $60,000 excluded for 1991). If T did not receive the $40,000 until 1993, no exclusion would be allowed for 1993 because the $40,000 was received after the close of the taxable year following the taxable year in which the services were performed. ◆

The statutory amount must be prorated on a daily basis where the taxpayer does not qualify for the exclusion for the full tax year. If T, in Example 23 above, qualified for only 11 months of the year, the statutory amount would be $64,055 [$70,000 × (334 days/365 days)].

Amounts paid by the United States, or any agency of the United States, to an employee do not qualify for the exclusion. Such persons usually are not subject to the income tax of the country where they work. Hence, relief from double taxation is not necessary since it does not exist.

The Housing Cost Amount. The housing cost amount is equal to the qualified housing expenses of an individual for the tax year less a base amount. The base amount is 16 percent of the salary of an employee of the United States for Step 1 Grade GS–14. The base amount is determined on a daily basis. For 1991, the base amount for a full year was $8,385. For a qualified individual employed

---

64. *Sochurek v. Comm.*, 62–1 USTC ¶9293, 9 AFTR2d 883, 300 F.2d 34 (CA–7, 1962).

overseas for 250 days of the year, the applicable base amount would be $5,743 [$8,385 × (250 days/365 days)].

Qualified housing expenses include reasonable expenses paid or incurred during the taxable year for housing for the individual (and spouse and dependents where appropriate) in a foreign country. Qualified housing expenses are those provided by an employer and include utilities and insurance, but not interest and taxes deductible under § 163 or § 164. Under certain conditions, housing expenses for a second household will be allowed for a spouse and dependents.

If the taxpayer is an employee, all housing expenses are treated as provided by the employer. However, only housing expenses for which the employer actually incurs a cost are included in the taxpayer's gross income as foreign earned income. The housing cost amount exclusion is limited to foreign earned income.

EXAMPLE 24

C, a U.S. citizen, works as an engineer for a U.S. multinational company in Bahrain. C is a bona fide resident of Bahrain for the entire calendar and tax year and earns a salary of $80,000. In addition, C's employer provides housing costs in the amount of $16,000. If the base amount is $8,385 and C elects both exclusions, the housing cost amount exclusion is $7,615 ($16,000 − $8,385), and the foreign earned income exclusion is $70,000 (the lesser of foreign earned income of $96,000 minus the $7,615 housing cost amount exclusion, or the $70,000 statutory limit). C's taxable income will include $18,385 of foreign earned income ($80,000 + $16,000 − $7,615 − $70,000). ◆

A self-employed individual is not eligible to exclude housing expenses, but can elect to deduct them. It is possible that an individual could have housing expenses that must be allocated between employer-provided amounts and amounts incurred by the individual as a self-employed person. The § 911 regulations provide guidelines for such a situation. The deduction for housing expenses is limited to the lesser of the housing cost amount or foreign earned income less the foreign earned income exclusion.

FOREIGN CORPORATIONS CONTROLLED BY U.S. PERSONS
◆

To minimize current tax liability, taxpayers often attempt to defer the recognition of taxable income. One way of trying to defer income recognition is to shift the income-generating activity to a foreign entity that is not within the U.S. tax jurisdiction. A foreign corporation is the most suitable entity for such an endeavor since, unlike a partnership, it is not a conduit through which income is taxed directly to the owner.

Realizing that the above tax planning device would hinder the collection of Federal tax revenues, Congress enacted §§ 951–964 in the Revenue Act of 1962. This and subsequent legislation have led to the present provisions for corporations controlled by U.S. persons.

Controlled Foreign Corporations

Subpart F, §§ 951–964 of the Code, provides that certain types of income generated by controlled foreign corporations (CFCs) are currently included in gross income by its U.S. shareholders. For Subpart F to apply, the foreign corporation must have been a CFC for an uninterrupted period of 30 days or more during the taxable year. When this is the case, U.S. shareholders must include in gross income their pro rata share of Subpart F income and increase in earnings that the CFC has invested in U.S. property for the tax year. This rule applies to U.S. shareholders who own stock in the corporation on the last day of the tax year on which the corporation is a CFC. The gross income inclusion must be made for their taxable year in which or with which the taxable year of the corporation ends.

―――――――――――― EXAMPLE 25 ――――――――――――

F, a calendar year corporation, is a CFC for all of 1992. X, a U.S. resident, owns 60% of F's one class of stock for the entire year. Subpart F income is $100,000, investment in U.S. property has not increased, and no distributions have been made during the year. X, a calendar year taxpayer, must include $60,000 in gross income as a constructive dividend for 1992. ◆

―――――――――――― EXAMPLE 26 ――――――――――――

F is a CFC until July 1, 1993. T, a U.S. citizen, owns 30% of its one class of stock for the entire year. T must include $14,877 [$100,000 × 30% × (181 days/365 days)] in gross income as a constructive dividend for 1993. ◆

Section 957 defines a CFC as any foreign corporation in which more than 50 percent of the total combined voting power of all classes of stock entitled to vote or the total value of the stock of the corporation is owned by U.S. shareholders on any day during the taxable year of the foreign corporation. For purposes of determining if a foreign corporation is a CFC, a *U.S. shareholder* is defined as a U.S. person who owns, or is considered to own, 10 percent or more of the total combined voting power of all classes of voting stock of the foreign corporation. Stock owned directly, indirectly, and constructively is counted. The foreign subsidiaries of most multinational U.S. parent corporations are CFCs.

Under § 958, indirect ownership involves stock held through a foreign entity, such as a foreign corporation, foreign partnership, or foreign trust. This stock is considered as actually owned proportionately by the shareholders, partners, or beneficiaries. The constructive ownership rules under § 318(a), with certain modifications, apply in determining if a U.S. person is a U.S. shareholder, in determining whether a foreign corporation is a CFC, and for certain related-party provisions of Subpart F. Some of the modifications include the following:

- Stock owned by a nonresident alien individual is not considered constructively owned by a U.S. citizen or resident alien individual.
- If a partnership, estate, trust, or corporation owns, directly or indirectly, more than 50 percent of the voting power of a corporation, it is deemed to own all of its stock.
- The threshold for corporate attribution is 10 percent rather than 50 percent.

―――――――――――― EXAMPLE 27 ――――――――――――

Shareholders of Foreign Corporation	Voting Power	Classification
A	30%	U.S. person
B	9%	U.S. person
C	41%	Foreign person
D	20%	U.S. person

B is A's son. A, B, and D are U.S. *shareholders*. A owns 39%, 30% directly and 9% constructively through B. B also owns 39%, 9% directly and 30% constructively through A. Thus, B is a U.S. shareholder. D owns 20% directly. F is a CFC because

U.S. shareholders own 59% of the voting power. If B were not related to A or to any other U.S. persons who were shareholders, B would not be a U.S. shareholder, and F would not be a CFC. ◆

U.S. shareholders must include their pro rata share of the applicable income in their gross income only to the extent of their actual ownership. Stock held indirectly is considered actually owned for this purpose.

─────────────────────── EXAMPLE 28 ───────────────────────

B, in Example 27 above, would recognize only 9% of the Subpart F income as a constructive dividend. A would recognize 30% and D would recognize 20%. If B were a foreign corporation, wholly owned by A, A would recognize 39% as a constructive dividend. If C owned only 40% of the stock and E, a U.S. person, owned 1% and was not related to any of the other shareholders, E would not be a *U.S. shareholder* and would not have to include any of the Subpart F income in gross income. ◆

Subpart F Income. Subpart F income consists of the following:

- Insurance income (§ 953).
- Foreign base company income (§ 954).
- International boycott factor income (§ 999).
- Illegal bribes.
- Income derived from a § 901(j) foreign country.

Insurance income is income attributable to any insurance or annuity contract in connection with property in, or liability arising out of activity in, or the lives or health of residents of a country other than the country under the laws of which the CFC is created or organized. The income includes that from the reinsurance of such property, activity, or persons, and any arrangement with another corporation whereby the other corporation assumes these risks in exchange for the CFC's insurance of risks not described above.

If the foreign corporation is a *captive insurance company,* the U.S. shareholders must include any related-person insurance income in gross income as a constructive dividend if the U.S. shareholders own 25 percent or more of the voting power of the foreign corporation. For this purpose, any U.S. person owning *any* stock of the foreign corporation is deemed a *U.S. shareholder.* Related-person insurance income is that attributable to insurance or reinsurance where the primary insured is a U.S. shareholder or a person related to a U.S. shareholder. Corporations in which such persons own less than 20 percent of the voting power and value are excluded, as are corporations for which the related-person insurance income for the taxable year is less than 20 percent of its total insurance income. Moreover, a foreign corporation can elect to treat its related-person insurance income as effectively connected with a U.S. trade or business and avoid Subpart F with regard to this income. By making the election, the CFC waives the right to any income tax treaty benefits with regard to the related-person insurance income.

Foreign Base Company Income. There are five categories of foreign base company income (FBCI):

- Foreign personal holding company income.
- Foreign base company sales income.
- Foreign base company services income.
- Foreign base company shipping income.
- Foreign base company oil-related income.

Each of these income categories is defined in § 954. A *de minimis* rule provides that if the total amount of a foreign corporation's FBCI and gross insurance income for the taxable year is less than the lesser of 5 percent of gross income or $1 million, none of its gross income will be treated as FBCI for the tax year. The *de minimis* rule does not apply to other types of income under Subpart F, such as increases in investment in U.S. property. However, if a foreign corporation's FBCI and gross insurance income exceed 70 percent of total gross income, all the corporation's gross income for the tax year is treated as FBCI or insurance income.

FBCI and insurance income subject to high foreign taxes are not included under Subpart F if the taxpayer establishes that the income was subject to an effective rate, imposed by a foreign country, of more than 90 percent of the maximum corporate rate under § 11. For 1991, this rate must be greater than 30.6 percent (90% × 34%).

Foreign personal holding company (FPHC) income is gross income that consists of the following:

- Dividends, interest, royalties, rents, and annuities.
- Excess gains over losses from the sale or exchange of property (including an interest in a trust or partnership) that gives rise to FPHC income as described above or that does not give rise to any income.
- Excess gains over losses from transactions in any commodities (other than bona fide hedging transactions as part of an active business as a producer, processor, merchant, or handler of commodities, or foreign currency gains or losses under § 988).
- Excess of foreign currency gains over foreign currency losses attributable to § 988 foreign currency transactions (other than any transaction directly related to the business needs of the CFC).
- Any income equivalent to interest.

FPHC income does not include rents and royalties derived in the active conduct of a trade or business and received from an unrelated person or any export financing interest that is derived in the conduct of a banking business. FPHC income also does not include rent and royalty income received from a related person for the use of property within the foreign country in which the CFC is organized. Also excluded are dividends and interest income received from related persons that are created or organized in the same foreign country as the CFC and have a substantial part of their trade or business assets located in the foreign country. These exceptions will not apply where the interest, rent, or royalty reduces the payor's Subpart F income.

Foreign base company (FBC) sales income is income derived from the purchase of personal property from or on behalf of a related person, or from the sale of personal property to or on behalf of a related person.

─────────────────── EXAMPLE 29 ───────────────────

F, a CFC owned 100% by X, a U.S. corporation, will generate FBC sales income in any one of the following situations:

- Purchase of widgets from anyone as commission agent for X Corporation.
- Purchase of widgets from X Corporation and sale to anyone.
- Purchase of widgets from anyone and sale to X Corporation.
- Sale of widgets to anyone as commission agent for X Corporation. ◆

An exception applies to property that is manufactured, produced, grown, or extracted in the country in which the CFC was organized or created and also to property sold for use, consumption, or disposition within that country. Certain income derived by a branch of the CFC in another country can be deemed FBC sales income. This would be the case if the effect of using the branch is the same as if the branch were a wholly owned subsidiary.[65]

FBC services income is income derived from the performance of services for or on behalf of a related person and performed outside the country in which the CFC was created or organized. Income from services performed before and in connection with the sale of property by a CFC that has manufactured, produced, grown, or extracted such property is not FBC services income.

FBC shipping income includes several classifications of income, including dividends and interest received from a foreign corporation, to the extent that income is attributable to, or is derived from or in connection with, the shipping activity. Thus, income attributable to the use of any aircraft or vessel in foreign commerce, the performance of services directly related to the use of such aircraft or vessel, or sale or exchange of any such aircraft or vessel is FBC shipping income.

FBC oil-related income is income, other than extraction income, derived in a foreign country in connection with the sale of oil and gas products and sold by the CFC or a related person for use or consumption within the country in which the oil or gas was extracted. Only corporations with production of at least 1,000 barrels per day are treated as deriving FBC oil-related income.

Distributions of Previously Taxed Income.   Under § 959, distributions from a CFC are treated as being first from E & P attributable to increases in investment in U.S. property previously taxed as a constructive dividend, second from E & P attributable to previously taxed Subpart F income other than that described above, and last from other E & P. Thus, distributions of previously taxed income are not taxed as a dividend but reduce E & P.

─────────────────────────── Example 30 ───────────────────────────

ABC, Inc., a U.S. shareholder that owns 100% of F, a CFC, receives a $100,000 distribution from F. F's E & P is composed of the following amounts:

- $50,000 attributable to previously taxed increases in investment in U.S. property.
- $30,000 attributable to previously taxed Subpart F income.
- $40,000 attributable to other E & P.

ABC has a taxable dividend of only $20,000, all attributable to other E & P. The remaining $80,000 is previously taxed income. F's E & P is reduced by $100,000. The remaining E & P of F is all attributable to other E & P. ♦

A U.S. shareholder's basis in CFC stock is increased by constructive dividends included in income under Subpart F and decreased by subsequent distributions of previously taxed income. Under § 960, U.S. corporate shareholders who own at least 10 percent of the voting stock of a foreign corporation are allowed an indirect FTC for foreign taxes deemed paid on constructive dividends included in gross income under Subpart F. The indirect credit also is available for Subpart F income attributable to second- and third-tier foreign corporations as long as the 10 percent ownership requirement is met from tier to tier. Deemed-paid taxes for which an indirect FTC is allowed under § 960 are not creditable under § 902 when actual distributions of previously taxed income are made.

Dispositions of Stock of a CFC.   The Subpart F provisions provide for the current taxation of Subpart F income of a CFC to U.S. shareholders to the extent

─────────────

65. Reg. § 1.954–3(b).

of their pro rata share. This, however, does not reach the earnings of the CFC that are not included in the taxable income of the shareholders under Subpart F (e.g., active trade or business income not involving related persons). Section 1248 prevents the gain from the disposition of CFC stock from escaping taxation as ordinary income to the extent that it previously had not been taxed.

Section 1248(a) requires that gain on the sale or other disposition of stock of a CFC by a U.S. shareholder be treated as dividend income to the extent of the transferor's share of undistributed nonpreviously taxed E & P of the corporation.

The various constructive dividend possibilities for CFC income appear in Concept Summary 9–2.

The Accumulated Earnings Tax

The accumulated earnings tax applies to a foreign corporation only to the extent that the corporation had U.S.-source taxable income and foreign-source taxable income effectively connected with a U.S. trade or business. Any distribution of E & P (and any interest payment) to a U.S.-owned foreign corporation may be treated as derived from U.S. sources under § 535 for purposes of the accumulated earnings tax. This is the result if 10 percent or more of the E & P of the distributor foreign corporation for the taxable year is derived from sources within the United States or is effectively connected with the conduct of a trade or business within the United States. This provision applies to distributions received directly or through one or more other entities. See Chapter 6 for details regarding the accumulated earnings tax.

The Personal Holding Company (PHC) Tax

If a foreign corporation is a personal holding company (PHC), only its U.S.-source taxable income and foreign-source taxable income effectively connected with a U.S. trade or business are subject to the PHC tax *and* only if the foreign corporation is not a foreign PHC. The accumulated earnings tax and the PHC tax are referred to as penalty taxes since they are applied in addition to any regular corporate income tax. See Chapter 6 for a detailed discussion of the PHC tax.

The Foreign Personal Holding Company (FPHC) Tax

The major distinction between the FPHC tax and the PHC tax is that the FPHC tax is levied on the U.S. shareholders of an FPHC rather than on the corporation. Section 551 requires that a pro rata share of the undistributed FPHC income (a deemed dividend) be included in the gross income of U.S. persons who are shareholders of the FPHC. Only persons who are shareholders on the last day in the taxable year in which a *U.S. group* existed must include this deemed dividend in gross income. The undistributed FPHC income for the taxable year is limited to current E & P. The amount taxable as a deemed dividend to a U.S. shareholder is treated as a contribution to the capital of the corporation and increases the shareholder's basis in the corporation's stock.

A foreign corporation is an FPHC if it meets two requirements. First, 60 percent or more of the gross income of the foreign corporation for the taxable year must be FPHC income. This percentage drops to 50 percent or more after the 60 percent requirement has been met for a tax year. The percentage remains at 50 percent until the foreign corporation does not meet the 50 percent test for three consecutive years or does not meet the stock ownership requirement for an entire tax year.

Second, more than 50 percent of the total combined voting power or the total value of the stock of the corporation must be owned, directly or indirectly, by five or fewer individuals who are U.S. persons (the U.S. group) at any time during the taxable year. Attribution rules for determining constructive ownership are provided in § 554. Furthermore, stock held through a domestic or foreign entity is considered owned proportionately by its partners, beneficiaries, or shareholders. The amount of the deemed dividend included in gross income by the U.S. shareholders is equal to each shareholder's pro rata share of undistributed FPHC income for the portion of the year the stock ownership test was satisfied. A U.S. shareholder need not be a member of the U.S. group in order to incur taxation.

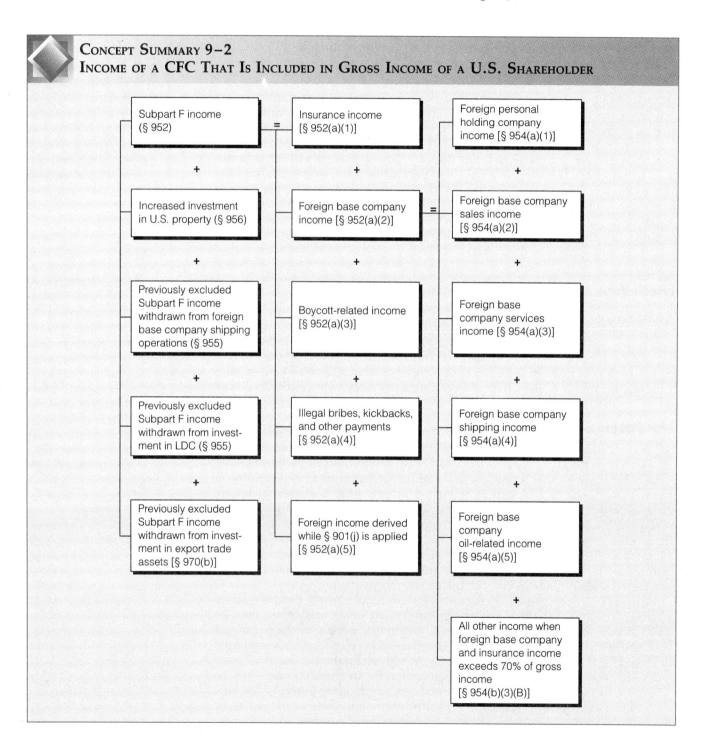

CONCEPT SUMMARY 9–2
INCOME OF A CFC THAT IS INCLUDED IN GROSS INCOME OF A U.S. SHAREHOLDER

Subpart F income (§ 952)

= Insurance income [§ 952(a)(1)]

Foreign personal holding company income [§ 954(a)(1)]

+

+

+

Increased investment in U.S. property (§ 956)

Foreign base company income [§ 952(a)(2)]

= Foreign base company sales income [§ 954(a)(2)]

+

+

+

Previously excluded Subpart F income withdrawn from foreign base company shipping operations (§ 955)

Boycott-related income [§ 952(a)(3)]

Foreign base company services income [§ 954(a)(3)]

+

+

+

Previously excluded Subpart F income withdrawn from investment in LDC (§ 955)

Illegal bribes, kickbacks, and other payments [§ 952(a)(4)]

Foreign base company shipping income [§ 954(a)(4)]

+

+

+

Previously excluded Subpart F income withdrawn from investment in export trade assets [§ 970(b)]

Foreign income derived while § 901(j) is applied [§ 952(a)(5)]

Foreign base company oil-related income [§ 954(a)(5)]

+

All other income when foreign base company and insurance income exceeds 70% of gross income [§ 954(b)(3)(B)]

─────────────────────── EXAMPLE 31 ───────────────────────

S, Mrs. S, T, Mrs. T, and T, Jr., (the U.S. group) each own 11 shares of the 100 outstanding shares of F, a foreign corporation. M, an unrelated U.S. person, owns 5 shares, and NRAs own the remaining 40 shares. If F is an FPHC for the entire tax year, all of the U.S. shareholders hold their shares all year, and undistributed FPHC income for the tax year is $100,000, each U.S. shareholder includes his or her pro rata share of the $100,000 in gross income as a dividend for the taxable year. M includes $5,000 in gross income. ◆

Undistributed FPHC income is taxable income adjusted in a manner similar to the adjustments made in arriving at undistributed PHC income (see Chapter 6). However, capital gains are not eliminated. FPHC income consists of passive income such as the following:

- Dividends.
- Interest.
- Royalties.
- Gains from the sale or exchange of securities.
- Certain income derived from a trust or estate or sale of an interest in a partnership, trust, or estate.
- Certain personal service contract income.
- Certain rents constituting less than 50 percent of the foreign corporation's gross income.

Dividends paid and deemed paid under § 561 for the taxable year can reduce the amount taxable as undistributed FPHC income. In addition, income otherwise qualifying as FPHC income is ignored if it is received from a related corporation. U.S. shareholders of a CFC that is also an FPHC are not taxed on the same income under Subpart F and the FPHC provisions. Income falling within both provisions is taxed only under Subpart F.[66]

Constructive dividends of undistributed FPHC income are limited to current E & P and reduce the E & P of the FPHC. Previously taxed income is not considered with regard to these constructive dividends. Therefore, subsequent distributions of E & P can result in dividend income.

─────────────────────── EXAMPLE 32 ───────────────────────

For the current tax year, E & P and undistributed FPHC income treated as a constructive dividend to U.S. shareholders are both equal to $100,000. This constructive dividend reduces current E & P to zero. However, accumulated E & P is $50,000. If an actual distribution is made during the subsequent tax year when current E & P is zero, the distribution is treated as a dividend to the extent of accumulated E & P. ◆

A FPHC distribution made in the first two and one-half months of the FPHC's tax year may be treated as made during the preceding tax year. This is allowed only to the extent that the distribution does not exceed undistributed FPHC income for the year immediately preceding the year of actual distribution.

Passive Foreign Investment Companies

A foreign corporation with numerous U.S. persons as shareholders may not meet the definition of a CFC or an FPHC (e.g., each unrelated shareholder holds no more than 5 percent of the stock). However, such a foreign corporation may

─────────────────────

66. § 951(d).

be a passive foreign investment company (PFIC). Under § 1296(a), a foreign corporation is a PFIC if either (1) 75 percent or more of its annual gross income is passive or (2) 50 percent or more of its assets (by value) produce passive income.[67] A PFIC does not include a foreign investment company that has elected under § 1247 to distribute income currently.

If the foreign corporation is a PFIC, when U.S. shareholders receive an excess distribution or dispose of their shares, they must pay an interest charge for the tax deferral they have had on their share of corporate earnings. If the foreign corporation is a qualified electing fund (QEF), however, shareholders can elect to recognize their share of the income of the corporation as it is earned and avoid the interest charge. Throwback rules apply to distributions from and sales of stock of PFICs that are not QEFs. This can cause the interest charge to be compounded.

EXAMPLE 33

X, a U.S. person, purchases shares in a non-QEF PFIC on January 1, 1989, for $10,000 and sells the shares on December 31, 1993, for $15,000. The $5,000 gain is allocated back over the five years, 1989–1993, $1,000 to each year. U.S. tax liability is calculated for each amount for the applicable year. X owes the tax due for 1989 plus interest on the tax due compounded for four years. Tax for 1990 through 1993 is determined in the same manner. ◆

The QEF route includes reporting requirements to keep the IRS informed of the fund's income, its character, and the ownership of outstanding stock. If the QEF election is made, the shareholders give up the confidentiality they might otherwise have maintained with regard to their ownership in the corporation.

An excess distribution is a distribution that exceeds by 125 percent the average amount of distributions on the PFIC stock for the three immediately preceding taxable years. The § 902 indirect FTC is allowed. Furthermore, a 10 percent corporate shareholder of a QEF is eligible for the § 960 credit (the credit available for the foreign taxes paid on constructive dividends under Subpart F). If tax has been withheld on the distribution, this is taken into consideration. QEF income previously taxed under § 1291 can be distributed tax-free. Generally Subpart F and the FPHC provisions take precedence over the PFIC provisions.

Foreign Sales Corporations

Prior to 1985, the Domestic International Sales Corporations (DISC) provisions (§§ 991–997) allowed for a deferral of the tax on a portion of the export income of a DISC until actual repatriation of the earnings. Over the years, Congress cut the amount of export income on which deferral was allowed. As the result of charges by the General Agreement on Trade and Tariffs (whose members include some of the United States' major trading partners) that the DISC provisions were a prohibited *export subsidy*, the DISC provisions were curtailed. As an alternative, the Foreign Sales Corporation (FSC) provisions (§§ 921–927) were enacted. The major short-term benefit of converting an export operation from a DISC to an FSC was that deferred DISC income that was forgiven would never be subject to U.S. taxation. The only remaining DISCs are interest charge ones—the price of deferral is an annual interest charge on the deferred taxes.[68] Only export sales up to $10 million qualify for deferral. Amounts in excess of $10 million are deemed distributed.

Most large multinational firms prefer CFCs to FSCs because they establish a more permanent active foreign presence, as in manufacturing. Mid-sized companies, such as Convex, often use FSCs, however, as do companies with very high profit margins (e.g., 50 to 60 percent).

---

67. A foreign corporation may elect to make this determination based on the adjusted bases of its assets.

68. § 995(f).

FSCs are not allowed a tax deferral on export income. Instead, a certain percentage (about 15 or 16 percent depending on taxpayer status) of export income is exempt from U.S. taxation (exempt foreign trade income). Pricing methods are provided for determining exempt foreign trade income.

In order for a foreign corporation to elect FSC status, it must meet a foreign presence requirement. An exception to this requirement is provided if the foreign corporation's export receipts do not exceed $5 million (the small FSC exception). The foreign presence requirement includes maintaining a foreign office, operating under foreign management, keeping a permanent set of books at the foreign office, conducting foreign economic processes (e.g., selling activities), and being a foreign corporation.[69] Recall that a foreign corporation is one organized or created under the laws of a foreign country or any U.S. possession. The FSC provisions, however, require that the foreign corporation be incorporated in a country with which the United States has agreed to exchange information or in a U.S. possession. In addition, the corporation must have no more than 25 shareholders at any time during the taxable year and have no preferred stock outstanding at any time during the taxable year.

Most FSCs operate as commission FSCs. Rather than buying the item produced by the parent and then reselling it, they receive a commission for "arranging sales." The maximum profit allowed the FSC cannot exceed the greater of the following:

- 23 percent of combined taxable income (CTI) of the related exporter and the FSC.
- 1.83 percent of foreign trade gross receipts (not exceeding 46 percent of CTI).
- Taxable income using § 482 arm's length pricing provisions.[70]

The first two methods are known as the "administrative pricing rules." The following illustration shows the tax deferral available with a commission FSC.

─────────────── EXAMPLE 34 ───────────────

In 1990, an FSC was incorporated in a U.S. possession by DOMI, the U.S. parent. The FSC operates as a commission FSC for DOMI's export sales of product X.

DOMI's gross sales	$ 80,000
Cost of goods sold	(44,000)
DOMI's gross income from sales	$ 36,000
Expenses attributable to export sales	(9,500)
Net income from sales before FSC considerations	$ 26,500
Expenses paid by FSC	(2,000)
CTI	$ 24,500
FSC's profit under CTI method (23%)	$ 5,635
FSC's profit under gross receipts method (1.83% of gross receipts)	$ 1,464

Since the CTI method results in more profit to the FSC than the gross receipts method *and* does not exceed 46% of CTI, the FSC is allowed to earn a profit of $5,635. The FSC's commission is determined as follows:

Maximum profit allowed	$5,635
Expenses incurred by FSC	2,000
FSC commission	$7,635

---

69. § 922.   70. § 925.

The tax attributable to FSC activity is calculated as follows:

Commission income	$7,635	
$\frac{8}{23}$ of commission income		$2,656
Expenses incurred by FSC	$2,000	
$\frac{8}{23}$ of FSC's expenses		(696)
Taxable income		$1,960
U.S. tax (at 34%)		$ 666

The exempt foreign trade income is $3,675 [($7,635 − $2,000) × 15/23]. This is equal to 15% of $24,500. ◆

Other Considerations

The Revenue Reconciliation Act of 1989 limits deductions of interest expense by certain foreign-controlled U.S. corporations. While primarily aimed at these foreign-controlled entities, this provision also can apply to U.S. parent corporations paying interest to their foreign subsidiaries. This rule is referred to as the "earnings stripping" provision since it will only apply if the payor's debt-to-equity ratio exceeds 1.5 to 1 and a high proportion of earnings is paid out as interest expense. Disallowed amounts can be carried over to future years.

The 1989 Act also requires that the tax years of CFCs and FPHCs conform to that of a more-than-50 percent U.S. owner. Additionally, a CFC is allowed to use a tax year ending such that no more than one month's deferral of income recognition is provided to the majority U.S. shareholder.

TRANSFERRING OWNERSHIP TO A FOREIGN PERSON
◆

This chapter has illustrated a number of tax motives for investing or operating overseas through a foreign entity. To originate investment through, or transfer investment to, a foreign entity, the U.S. taxpayer must make some sort of transfer to the foreign entity. This may be in the form of a cash investment, or it may be the transfer of all the assets of a U.S. entity.

──────────── EXAMPLE 35 ────────────

S, a U.S. citizen, exchanges $500,000 for 50% of the stock of Z, a newly formed foreign corporation. ◆

──────────── EXAMPLE 36 ────────────

ABC Company, a U.S. partnership, transfers its assets to a newly formed foreign corporation in exchange for 100% of its stock. The stock is transferred to ABC's partners in complete liquidation of the partnership. ◆

──────────── EXAMPLE 37 ────────────

XYZ, Inc., a U.S. corporation, transfers all of the assets of its foreign branch to a newly formed foreign corporation in exchange for 100% of its stock. ◆

In each of the above cases, U.S. property has been exchanged for foreign property. In situations where potential taxable income is transferred to a corporation outside the U.S. Federal tax jurisdiction, taxation may be incurred on the transfer. The tax result of transferring property to a foreign corporation depends on the income potential of the property and the character of the property in the hands of the transferor or transferee. Generally, the tax treatment of outbound transfers such as those described in Examples 35 through 37 is covered under § 367(a) or § 1491.

Section 367

Outbound Transfers. The tax treatment of transfers of property by a U.S. person to a foreign corporation is prescribed in § 367(a). These *outbound* transfers include (1) transfer of property to a CFC under § 351, (2) liquidation of a domestic subsidiary into a foreign parent corporation under § 332, (3) acquisition of stock in a domestic corporation by a foreign corporation in a "B" reorganization, and (4) acquisition of a domestic corporation's assets by a foreign corporation in a "C" reorganization.

In order for the transferee foreign corporation to be considered a corporation in connection with any of the above transfers, the transferor must comply with the regulations under § 367(a).[71] These regulations require that the transferor recognize any gain realized on the transfer. The character of any gain recognized depends on the character of the property transferred. A transfer by a U.S. person of an interest in a partnership to a foreign corporation is treated as a transfer of that person's pro rata share of the assets of the partnership.

Several exceptions apply to the effect that only the gain in what have been termed *tainted* assets is subject to taxation under § 367(a). Excluded from the tainted asset category are property to be used by the foreign corporation in the active conduct of a trade or business outside the United States and stock or securities of a foreign corporation that is a party to the exchange or reorganization. Certain property to be used by the foreign corporation in the active conduct of a trade or business outside the United States, however, is *tainted and*, thus, subject to § 367. In effect, a *deemed sale* is treated as having occurred when the following assets are transferred:

- Inventory (raw goods, work-in-process, and finished goods).
- Installment obligations and accounts receivable.
- Foreign currency or other property denominated in foreign currency.
- Property leased by the transferor unless the transferee is the lessee.

In addition to gain on the *tainted* assets listed above, any *U.S. depreciation* (§§ 1245 and 1250) and other type recapture potential (e.g., §§ 617, 1252, and 1254) in the assets transferred must be recognized to the extent of gain realized. This provision applies only to appreciated assets for which the depreciation or other deduction has resulted in a tax benefit. The U.S. depreciation is the portion of the depreciation attributable to use of the property in the United States.

The exception from *tainted* classification also does not apply to certain property to be leased by the transferee, to be sold in the reasonably foreseeable future, and oil and gas working interests to be farmed out or transferred for a nonoperating interest within three years of the § 367(a) transfer.

The transfer of intangibles is treated separately as a transfer pursuant to a sale for contingent payments.[72] These amounts are treated as received by the transferor over the life of the intangible and are U.S.-source ordinary income. They must be taken into income by the transferor and must be commensurate with the income attributable to the intangible. A subsequent disposition by the transferee will trigger income recognition to the initial transferor under § 367.

Specific provisions apply for the transfer of stock and securities under § 367(a). An active trade or business reason for the transfer of domestic or foreign corporate stock will generally prevent current gain recognition. The

---

71. See Reg. §§ 1.367(a)–1T through –6T. **72.** § 367(d)(2).

presence of other conditions, such as the transfer of stock or securities of a foreign corporation that is a party to the exchange, can also result in deferral of gain recognition.

Inbound and Offshore Transfers.   As previously illustrated, one objective of Federal tax law is to prevent E & P that has accumulated in U.S.-owned foreign corporations from escaping U.S. taxation. Section 367(b) covers the tax treatment of inbound and offshore transfers with regard to stock of a CFC. Examples of inbound transactions are liquidation of a foreign corporation into a domestic parent under § 332, acquisition of the stock of a foreign corporation by a domestic corporation in a ''B'' reorganization, and acquisition of the assets of a foreign corporation by a domestic corporation in a ''C'' or ''D'' reorganization. Offshore transfers include a foreign corporate ''B'' acquisition of a first- or lower-tier foreign corporation in exchange for stock of a non-CFC; foreign corporate ''B,'' ''C,'' or ''D'' acquisition of a foreign corporation in exchange for CFC stock; and a foreign § 351 transfer of stock or other property in a foreign corporation having a U.S. shareholder.

This subsection is brief and is supported by a complex set of regulations. Basically, U.S. persons directly or indirectly a party to an inbound or offshore transfer involving stock of a CFC must recognize dividend income to the extent of their pro rata share of the previously untaxed E & P of the foreign corporation. Exceptions allowing deferral are available except in those cases where, after the transfer, all or a portion of the E & P would be out of the reach of U.S. tax authorities.

EXAMPLE 38

USA, Inc., a domestic corporation, owns all the stock of F_1, a foreign corporation. F_1 owns all of the stock of F_2, a foreign corporation. F_1 transfers all of its assets to F_3, a foreign corporation, in exchange for 40% of F_3's stock. F_1 is then liquidated with USA, Inc., receiving F_3 stock in exchange for its F_1 stock. F_3 is not a CFC. USA, Inc., realizes a gain of $250,000 on the transaction. USA must include the E & P with respect to its ownership in F_1 and F_2 before the exchange in gross income as a dividend. USA's basis in the F_3 stock is the basis it had in the F_1 stock exchanged plus any gain recognized.[73] ◆

Section 1491

Section 367 covers only certain otherwise tax-free outbound transfers to foreign corporations. A U.S. person can transfer appreciated property to a foreign person (one outside the U.S. tax jurisdiction) in a transfer that is not covered by § 367(a) [e.g., a transfer to a foreign partnership]. Congress has dealt with such situations in § 1491.

Under § 1491, a U.S. person who transfers appreciated property to a foreign corporation as paid-in surplus or as a contribution to capital to a foreign partnership, or to a foreign estate or trust, must pay an excise tax on the transfer. The tax is equal to 35 percent of the excess of the fair market value of the property over the sum of its adjusted basis and any gain recognized to the U.S. person on the transfer. Section 1491 does not apply where the transfer falls under § 367 or the transferor elects tax treatment similar to § 367 before the transfer. Furthermore, under § 1057, the transferor can elect to treat the transfer as a sale or exchange at fair market value and recognize gain equal to the excess of the fair market value over the adjusted basis of the property in the hands of the transferor.

---

73. Temp.Reg. § 7.367(b)–7(c).

The tax imposed by § 1491 is self-assessed and must be paid by the transferor at the time of the transfer. The transfer is reported by filing Form 926 (and paying any tax due) with the District Director to whom the taxpayer's income tax return is required to be filed.

The § 1491 tax is an excise tax. The significance of this distinction is that the transferee does not increase the basis of the property by the appreciation subject to the excise tax. The parties to the transfer can overcome this result if the transferor elects § 1057 treatment.

EXAMPLE 39

T, a U.S. person, transfers property with an adjusted basis of $80,000 and a fair market value of $150,000 to a foreign partnership. Under § 1491, T must pay an excise tax of $24,500 [35% × ($150,000 − $80,000)] on the transfer. The partnership's basis in the property is $80,000. If T elects to treat the transfer as a sale or exchange under § 1057, he will recognize gross income of $70,000 ($150,000 − $80,000) on the transfer, and the partnership's basis in the property will be $150,000. ◆

FOREIGN CURRENCY TRANSACTIONS
◆

Changes in the relative value of a foreign currency and the U.S. dollar (the foreign exchange rate) affect the dollar value of foreign property held by the taxpayer, the dollar value of foreign debts, and the dollar amount of gain or loss on a transaction denominated in a foreign currency.

EXAMPLE 40

D, a domestic corporation, purchases merchandise for resale from F, a foreign corporation, for 50,000K. On the date of purchase, 1K (a foreign currency) is equal to $1 U.S. (1K:$1). At this time, the account payable is $50,000. On the date of payment by D (the foreign exchange date), the exchange rate is 1.25K:$1. In other words, the foreign currency has devalued in relation to the U.S. dollar, and D will pay F 50,000K, which cost D only $40,000. D must record the purchase of the merchandise at $50,000 and recognize a foreign currency gain of $10,000 ($50,000 − $40,000). ◆

Taxpayers may find it necessary to translate amounts denominated in foreign currency into U.S. dollars for any of the following purposes:

- Purchase of goods, services, and property.
- Sale of goods, services, and property.
- Collection of foreign receivables.
- Payment of foreign payables.
- FTC calculations.
- Recognizing income or loss from foreign branch activities.

The foreign currency exchange rates, however, have no effect on the transactions of a U.S. person who arranges all international transactions in U.S. dollars.

EXAMPLE 41

X, a domestic corporation, purchases goods from F, a foreign corporation, and pays for these goods in U.S. dollars. F then exchanges the U.S. dollars for the currency of the country in which it operates. X has no foreign exchange considerations with which to contend. If X purchased goods from F and was required to pay F in a foreign currency, X would have to exchange U.S. dollars for the foreign currency in order to make payment. If the exchange rate had changed from the date of purchase to the date of payment, X would have a foreign currency gain or loss on the currency exchange. ◆

Tax Issues

The following are the major tax issues that must be considered in the taxation of foreign currency exchange:

1. The character of the gain or loss (ordinary or capital).
2. The date of recognition of any gain or loss.
3. The source (U.S. or foreign) of the foreign currency gain or loss.

─────────────────────── EXAMPLE 42 ───────────────────────

Batch, Inc., a domestic corporation, purchases computer parts for resale from Chips, a foreign corporation, for 125,000K. On the date of purchase, .75K (a foreign currency) is equal to $1 U.S. (.75K:$1). On the date of payment by Batch (the foreign exchange date), the exchange rate is .8K:$1. In other words, Batch paid 125,000K, which cost Batch $156,250 in U.S. dollars (125,000K/.8K). Batch, however, must record the purchase of the computer parts for inventory purposes at $166,667 (125,000K/.75K) and recognize a foreign currency gain of $10,417 ($166,667 − $156,250). ◆

Before 1987, there was little statutory authority dealing with the taxation of foreign currency transactions. The IRS rulings and the court decisions on the subject were not consistent. The Tax Reform Act of 1986 provided statutory rules for most business transactions involving foreign currency exchange. Many personal transactions involving foreign currency exchange are not covered by these provisions, however, and the law developed prior to the 1986 Act still applies. For individuals, the post-1986 statutory provisions apply only to the extent that allocable expenses qualify as trade or business expenses under § 162 or expenses of producing income under § 212.[74]

The following concepts are important when dealing with the tax aspects of foreign exchange:

1. Foreign currency is treated as property other than money.
2. Gain or loss on the exchange of foreign currency is considered separately from the underlying transaction (e.g., the purchase or sale of goods).
3. No gain or loss is recognized until a transaction is closed.

─────────────────────── EXAMPLE 43 ───────────────────────

If, in Example 42 above, the foreign exchange rate on the date of purchase was .75K:$1, 1.2K:$1 on a date between the purchase and payment dates, and .75K:$1 on the payment date, Batch realizes no foreign currency gain or loss. The transaction was not closed at the time of the foreign exchange rate fluctuation. ◆

Functional Currency

Prior to 1987, the Code contained no provisions for determining tax results when foreign operations could be recorded in a foreign currency. However, in 1981, the Financial Accounting Standards Board adopted FAS 52 on foreign currency translation. FAS 52 introduced the *functional currency* approach (the currency of the economic environment in which the foreign entity operates generally is to be used as the monetary unit to measure gains and losses). The 1986 Act adopted this approach for the most part.

Under § 985, all income tax determinations are to be made in the taxpayer's functional currency. Generally, a taxpayer's functional currency will be the U.S.

─────────────────────────────

74. § 988(e). This applies to expenses deductible under § 212 other than that part dealing with expenses incurred in   connection with taxes.

dollar. In certain circumstances, a qualified business unit (QBU) may be required to use a foreign currency as its functional currency. A QBU is a separate and clearly identified unit of a taxpayer's trade or business (e.g., a foreign branch). A corporation is a QBU. An individual is not a QBU; however, a trade or business conducted by an individual may be a QBU.[75]

Section 988 Transactions

The disposition of a nonfunctional currency can result in a foreign currency gain or loss under § 988. Section 988 transactions include those in which gain or loss is determined with regard to the value of a nonfunctional currency, such as the following:

1. Acquisition of (or becoming obligor under) a debt instrument.
2. Accruing (or otherwise taking into account) any item of expense or gross income or receipts that is to be paid or received at a later date.
3. Entering into or acquiring any forward contract, futures contract, option or similar investment position unless such position is a regulated futures contract or nonequity option that would be marked-to-market under § 1256.[76]
4. Disposition of nonfunctional currency.

Section 988 generally treats exchange gain or loss falling within its provisions as ordinary income or loss. Certain exchange gain or loss will be apportioned in the same manner as interest expense.[77] Capital gain or loss treatment may be elected with regard to forward contracts, futures contracts, and options that constitute capital assets in the hands of the taxpayer. These capital assets cannot be part of a straddle or marked-to-market under § 1256 and must meet certain identification requirements.

As under pre-1987 law, a closed or completed transaction is required. The residence of the taxpayer generally determines the source of a foreign exchange gain or loss. For this purpose, the residence of a QBU is the country in which its principal place of business is located.

Branch Operations

Where a QBU (a foreign branch, in this case) uses a foreign currency as its functional currency, the profit or loss must be computed in the foreign currency each year and translated into U.S. dollars for tax purposes. Section 987 requires use of the profit and loss method for this purpose. This method requires that the entire amount of profit or loss, without taking remittances into account, be translated using a weighted-average exchange rate for the taxable year. Exchange gain or loss is recognized on remittances from the QBU. This is done by comparing the U.S. dollar amount of the remittance at the exchange rate in effect on the date of remittance with the U.S. dollar value (at the appropriate weighted-average rate) of a pro rata portion of post-1986 accumulated earnings of the branch. This gain or loss is ordinary and is sourced according to the income to which the remittance is attributable.

---

75. Reg. § 1.989(a)–1(b).
76. Section 988(c)(1)(D)(ii) provides for an election to bring positions in regulated futures contracts and nonequity options that would be marked-to-market under § 1256 within

the provisions of § 988. The election, once made, is binding for all future years. Special provisions apply with regard to qualified funds as defined under § 988(c)(1)(E)(iii).
77. Temp.Reg. § 1.861–9T(b).

─────────────── EXAMPLE 44 ───────────────

D, a domestic corporation, began operation of a QBU (foreign branch) in 1989. The functional currency of the QBU is the K. The QBU's profits for 1989–1991 are as shown.

	Income (in Ks)	Exchange Rate	Income in U.S. Dollars
1989	200K	1K:$1	$200
1990	200K	1.25K:$1	160
1991	200K	1.6K:$1	125
	600K		$485

The income is taxed to D in the year earned regardless of whether any remittances take place. ◆

Distributions from Foreign Corporations

An actual distribution of E & P from a foreign corporation is included in income by the U.S. recipient at the exchange rate in effect on the date of distribution. Thus, no exchange gain or loss is recognized. Deemed dividend distributions under Subpart F must be translated at the weighted-average exchange rate for the CFC's tax year to which the deemed distribution is attributable. Exchange gain or loss can result when an actual distribution of this previously taxed income is made. The gain or loss is the difference in the exchange rates on the date the deemed distribution is included in income and the date of the actual distribution.

─────────────── EXAMPLE 45 ───────────────

In 1991, the QBU (see Example 44) remits 300K to D when the exchange rate is 1.6K:$1. D has a foreign currency loss of $55, determined as follows:

		Difference
$62.50* from 1989 at 1K:$1 =	$100.00**	($ 37.50)
$62.50 from 1990 at 1.25K:$1 =	80.00	(17.50)
$62.50 from 1991 at 1.6K:$1 =	62.50	–0–
	$242.50	($ 55.00)

*[300K × (200K/600K)] at rate of 1.6K:$1 = $62.50.

**[300K × (200K/600K)] at rate of 1K:$1 = $100.

The loss is an ordinary loss for 1991. It is sourced by reference to the post-1986 accumulated earnings (1989–1991).[78] The results would generally be the same if this was a distribution of previously taxed Subpart F income. ◆

For FTC purposes, foreign taxes are translated at the exchange rate in effect when the foreign taxes were paid. For purposes of the indirect FTC, any adjustment of foreign taxes paid by the foreign corporation is translated at the rate in effect at the time of adjustment. Any refund or credit is translated at the rate in effect at the time of original payment of the foreign taxes.

─────────────────────

78. See the *General Explanation of the Tax Reform Act of 1986* ("Blue Book"), prepared by the Staff of the Joint Committee on Taxation, p. 1110.

─────────────── EXAMPLE 46 ───────────────

F, a foreign subsidiary of D, a U.S. corporation, has pre-tax income of 300K. F pays 100K in foreign taxes. The exchange rate was .5K:$1 when the income was earned and the foreign taxes paid. None of the income is Subpart F income. If the 200K net earnings are distributed when the exchange rate is .4K:$1, the deemed-paid taxes are $200 [($500/$500) × $200]. The effective tax rate is 40%. ◆

The U.S. tax provisions in the international area include numerous reporting requirements. Furthermore, civil and criminal penalties for noncompliance can apply.[79]

Form 5471 must be filed annually by a U.S. person who controls a foreign corporation. This is an information return that must include information such as the name, principal place of business, and nature of the business of the foreign corporation and any transactions between the U.S. person and the foreign corporation during the tax year. The form must be filed with the U.S. person's income tax return.[80] The officers, directors, and 10 percent shareholders of a foreign personal holding company also are required to file a Form 5471.[81] A Form 926 must be filed when a U.S. person makes certain transfers to a foreign corporation or makes certain distributions to a non-U.S. person.[82]

A domestic corporation that is 25 percent or more foreign owned must file an information return and maintain certain records where they will be accessible to the IRS.[83] Additionally, any foreign corporation carrying on a trade or business in the United States must file an information return and maintain records in a similar manner.[84] Form 5472 is used for these purposes.

DISCs, former DISCs, FSCs, and former FSCs must maintain records and file an information return.[85] U.S. persons who acquire or dispose of an interest in a foreign partnership must file an information return disclosing information regarding the transfer.[86] Creation of, or a transfer to, a foreign trust by a U.S. person necessitates the filing of a Form 3520.[87] Furthermore, any U.S. beneficiary of a foreign trust who is subject to tax on trust income under § 679 must file an annual return.[88] Information returns are also required in connection with foreign investment in U.S. real property interests.[89]

These provisions have led to complaints that the reporting requirements overlap significantly and that the extensive information required is expensive and difficult to obtain. The Treasury has been attempting to reduce the overlap.

REPORTING REQUIREMENTS
◆

Tax legislation tends progressively to reduce the ability to plan transactions and operations in a manner that minimizes tax liability. However, taxpayers who are not limited by the constraints of a particular transaction or operation can use the following suggestions to plan for the maximum tax benefits.

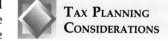 **TAX PLANNING CONSIDERATIONS**

The Foreign Tax Credit Limitation and Sourcing Provisions

The FTC limitation is partially based on the amount of foreign-source taxable income in the numerator of the limitation ratio. Consequently, the sourcing of

─────────────

79. See, for example, §§ 6677, 6679(a), and 7203.
80. § 6038.
81. § 6035.
82. § 6038B.
83. § 6038A.
84. § 6038C.

85. § 6011(c).
86. § 6046A.
87. § 6048.
88. § 6048(c).
89. § 6039C.

income is extremely important. Income that is taxed by a foreign tax jurisdiction benefits from the FTC only to the extent that it is classified as foreign-source income under U.S. tax law. Thus, elements such as the place of title passage that affect the sourcing of income should be considered carefully before a transaction is undertaken.

A taxpayer who can control the timing of income and loss recognition will want to avoid recognizing losses in years in which the loss will be apportioned among the FTC limitation baskets. Otherwise, the foreign taxes for which a credit is allowed for the tax year will be reduced.

--- EXAMPLE 47 ---

D, a U.S. person, has U.S.-source taxable income of $200,000, worldwide taxable income of $300,000, and a U.S. tax liability (before FTC) of $84,000. D receives foreign-source taxable income, pays foreign income taxes, and has an FTC as shown:

Basket	Amount	Foreign Taxes	FTC Limitation	FTC
Passive	$ 20,000	$ 800	$ 5,600	$ 800
General	50,000	20,500	14,000	14,000
Non-CFC § 902 corporation #1	15,000	3,000	4,200	3,000
Non-CFC § 902 corporation #2	15,000	4,500	4,200	4,200
	$100,000	$28,800		$22,000

If D had a foreign-source loss of $10,000 that would fall in the shipping limitation basket, the FTC would be reduced by $1,820. The U.S. tax liability before the FTC would be $81,200; 50% of the loss would be apportioned to the general limitation basket reducing the FTC limitation for this basket to $12,600 [$81,200 × ($45,000/ $290,000)]; and 15% would be apportioned to the non-CFC § 902 corporation #2 basket, reducing the FTC limitation for this basket to $3,780 [$81,200 × ($13,500/ $290,000)]. D would avoid this result if he could defer recognition of the loss to a tax year in which it would not have a negative effect on the FTC. ◆

When negotiating the terms of the sale of an intangible, such as a patent, the taxpayer may be able to influence the source of the gain on the sale by controlling the amount of consideration that is contingent on the productivity or use of the intangible by the purchaser. Under § 865, contingent payments are sourced in the same manner as royalty income (where the intangible will be used). If the intangible will be used outside the United States, the greater the portion of the sales price that is contingent, the greater the foreign-source income. This will benefit the U.S. seller as long as any taxation of the contingent payments by the foreign tax authorities does not exceed the U.S. tax on those amounts.

The Foreign Corporation as a Tax Shelter

An NRA who is able to hold U.S. investments through a foreign corporation can accomplish much in the way of avoiding U.S. taxation. Any capital gains (other than dispositions of U.S. real property interests) are not subject to U.S. taxation. This assumes that they are not effectively connected with a U.S. trade or business and are not gains from commodity transactions entered into by a foreign corporation with its principal place of business in the United States. The NRA can dispose of the stock of a foreign corporation that holds U.S. real property and not be subject to taxation under § 897 (FIRPTA). Furthermore, the stock of a foreign corporation is not included in the U.S. gross estate of a deceased NRA even if all the assets of the foreign corporation are located in the United States.

Caution is advised where the foreign corporation may generate income effectively connected with the conduct of a U.S. trade or business. The income may be taxed at a higher rate than if the NRA individually generated the income. The trade-off between a higher U.S. tax on this income and protection from the U.S. estate tax and § 897 must be weighed.

Planning under Subpart F

The *de minimis* rule[90] allows a CFC to avoid the classification of income as FBC income or insurance income and prevents the U.S. shareholder from having to include it in gross income as a constructive dividend. Thus, a CFC with total FBC income and insurance income in an amount close to the 5 percent or $1 million level should monitor income realization to assure that the *de minimis* rule applies for the tax year. At least as important is avoiding the classification of all the gross income of the CFC as FBC income or insurance income. This happens when the sum of the FBC income and gross insurance income for the taxable year exceeds 70 percent of total gross income.

Careful timing of increases in investment in U.S. property can reduce the potential for constructive dividend income to U.S. shareholders. The gross income of U.S. shareholders attributable to increases in investment in U.S. property is limited to the E & P of the CFC.[91] E & P that is attributable to amounts that either in the current year or a prior tax year have been included in gross income as Subpart F income is not taxed again when invested in U.S. property.

The Foreign Earned Income Exclusion

The tax benefit of the foreign earned income exclusion depends on the tax the income will incur in the country in which earned and the year in which received. If the foreign country levies little or no tax on the income, the U.S. taxpayer will be able to exclude the housing cost amount plus up to $70,000 of foreign earned income and pay little or no tax on the income to the foreign tax jurisdiction. Since foreign earned income qualifies for the exclusion only if received in the year in which earned or the immediately succeeding tax year, the timely payment of such income is necessary.

In high tax jurisdictions, the taxpayer may benefit more from taking the foreign tax credit than from excluding the earnings from gross income. The taxpayer earning income in a high tax jurisdiction should compare the tax result of taking the exclusion with the tax result of forgoing either or both exclusions for the FTC. If U.S. taxes on the income are eliminated under all options and the taxpayer has excess foreign taxes to carry back or carry forward, then the FTC generally is more beneficial than the exclusion.

Taxpayers must also carefully monitor their trips to the United States when attempting to qualify for the exclusion under the physical presence test. Taxpayers who are attempting to establish a bona fide foreign residence must make sure that their ties to the foreign country predominate over their ties to the United States for the period for which bona fide foreign residence is desired.

---

90. § 954(b)(3).　　　　　　　　　　　91. §§ 959(a)(1) and (2).

Tax Treaties

The value of treaty benefits should never be overlooked by a taxpayer planning to perform services in a foreign country, to enter into a transaction with a foreign person or in a foreign country, or to conduct operations in a foreign country. Such persons should review the appropriate tax treaties carefully to apprise themselves of any benefits that may be available. International treaties not expressly labeled tax treaties also may contain provisions that are beneficial to U.S. or foreign persons entering into international transactions.[92]

Nonresident Aliens and U.S. Resident Status

An NRA who does not want worldwide income subject to U.S. taxation should not acquire a green card unless he or she has decided that U.S. resident status is worth the price of U.S. income taxation on a worldwide basis. Furthermore, an NRA who does not intend to become a U.S. resident for the tax year should avoid being physically present in the United States under any of the conditions that would lead to U.S. resident status for income tax purposes. Even if a person becomes a U.S. resident for income tax purposes, this does not necessarily mean that domicile has been changed to the United States. A resident alien can avoid the U.S. estate and gift tax in part at least by avoiding U.S. domicile. The showing of an intention to retain domicile in a foreign country suffices to retain foreign domicile for U.S. estate and gift tax purposes. Thus, to avoid U.S. domicile, the NRA or resident alien must maintain sufficient ties with a foreign country.

PROBLEM MATERIALS

DISCUSSION QUESTIONS

1. What factors must a taxpayer consider in determining whether a foreign tax is creditable for FTC purposes?

2. What income tax consequences need to be considered by a corporate shareholder who takes the indirect credit?

3. What are some of the tax consequences affected by the sourcing of income as within or without the United States?

4. How is U.S.-source income determined if an NRA receives a $12,000 check for the performance of personal services partly within and partly without the United States?

5. What are the basic considerations in allocating interest expense between U.S.- and foreign-source income for deduction purposes?

6. What requirements must be met and what tax consequences should be considered by a taxpayer and NRA spouse in making the election to file a joint return?

7. What is the difference in the definition of "residency" for U.S. income tax purposes and for U.S. estate tax purposes?

8. How can an NRA individual holding U.S. property (e.g., land and buildings) at the time of death avoid the U.S. estate tax?

---

92. *Arthur A. Amaral*, 90 T.C. 802 (1988).

9. Why can stock of a foreign corporation held by NRA individuals be considered a tax shelter for U.S. tax purposes?

10. Why is a foreign corporation a preferred vehicle for the holding of U.S. real property by NRAs and foreign corporations?

11. Describe "treaty shopping."

12. Why does the United States allow an exclusion for foreign earned income, but not for foreign unearned income such as dividends from foreign corporations?

13. Why is the § 936 possessions corporation credit referred to as a "tax-sparing" credit?

14. How does the tax law prevent Subpart F income from being taxed more than once to the U.S. shareholders?

15. Can a foreign corporation owned 100 percent by U.S. persons be

    a. A CFC, but not an FPHC?
    b. An FPHC, but not a CFC?
    c. A PFIC, but not a CFC or an FPHC?

16. When would the accumulated earnings tax or the personal holding company tax be applied to a foreign corporation?

17. What is the objective of §§ 367(a) and 1491? Do the two provisions overlap to cause double taxation?

18. When would a U.S. corporation conducting international transactions *not* have to consider foreign exchange consequences?

19. Describe the effect of gain or loss on the exchange of foreign currency being considered separate from the underlying transaction (e.g., purchasing or selling goods).

20. When would the U.S. recipient of a constructive dividend (for example, under Subpart F) have a foreign exchange gain or loss?

PROBLEMS

21. For the tax year, J, a U.S. resident individual, has worldwide taxable income (without regard to personal exemptions) of $160,000, consisting of $120,000 U.S.-source income and $40,000 foreign-source dividend income. J's U.S. income tax liability before the FTC is $46,000, and the foreign tax paid on the dividend income is $10,000. What is J's FTC for the tax year?

22. D, a domestic calendar year corporation, has worldwide taxable income consisting of $400,000 U.S.-source income and a $100,000 foreign-source dividend received from F, a § 902 noncontrolled foreign corporation. F's post-1986 E & P after taxes is $2,000,000. F's foreign income taxes attributable to the E & P are $1,100,000.

    a. What is the amount of D's deemed-paid foreign taxes with regard to the dividend from F?
    b. What is D's FTC for the tax year?

23. How would the answers to Problem 22 change if the foreign tax authorities withheld $30,000 in taxes on the dividend from F, and D received only $70,000 with regard to the dividend?

24. Given the following two separate ownership structures, may X Corporation claim an FTC due to foreign taxes paid by F Corporation although X does not own any of F's stock? D, E, and F are foreign corporations.

    a. X owns 40% of D Corporation, D Corporation owns 40% of E Corporation, and E Corporation owns 50% of F Corporation.
    b. The same as (a) except that E Corporation owns 30% of F Corporation rather than 50%.

25. World, Inc., a U.S. multinational corporation, has the following taxable income and pays the following taxes for 1992:

Category	Amount	Source	Foreign Taxes
Manufacturing	$100,000	Foreign	$ 40,000
	500,000	U.S.	–0–
Interest	50,000	Foreign	2,000
	20,000	U.S.	–0–
Dividends	40,000	Foreign*	10,000
	30,000	U.S.	–0–
Shipping	260,000	Foreign	130,000

*This is comprised of $20,000 from each of two § 902 noncontrolled foreign corporations. The foreign taxes attributable to the dividends were $8,000 and $2,000, respectively.

U.S. taxes before FTC = $340,000.

a. What is World's FTC allowed for the tax year?
b. Are there any excess foreign taxes or excess limitations and, if so, how are they treated for FTC purposes?

26. T, a U.S. resident, received the following dividend and interest income for 1992. What is the source (U.S. or foreign) of each income item?

   a. $5,000 dividend income from C, a domestic corporation, that has gross income from the active conduct of a foreign trade or business for the immediately preceding three-year period of $1,700,000. C's total gross income for the same period was $2,000,000.
   b. $10,000 dividend from G, a foreign corporation, that has gross income effectively connected with the conduct of a U.S. trade or business for the immediately preceding three-year period of $500,000. G's total gross income for the same period was $1,500,000.
   c. $800 interest from N, an NRA individual, on a loan made by T to N.
   d. $15,000 interest on X Corporation bonds. X is a domestic corporation that derived $1,800,000 of its gross income for the immediately preceding three-year period from the active conduct of a foreign trade or business. X's total gross income for this same period was $2,100,000.
   e. $2,000 interest from a savings account in a Chicago bank.

27. T, a resident of France, is sent to the United States by F Corporation, a foreign employer, to arrange the purchase of some machine tools. T spends three weeks in the United States. This is T's only trip to the United States during the year. T's gross monthly salary is $3,500. T's pay check is deposited in his French bank account while he is in the United States. The salary is attributable to 15 U.S. and 6 French working days. T's foreign employer has a U.S. trade or business. What is the amount of T's U.S.-source income?

28. Determine the source of income from the following sales:

   a. Sale of widgets (inventory) purchased by a U.S. resident in Florida and sold to a Canadian company, title passing in Canada.
   b. Sale of widgets (inventory) manufactured in Texas by a U.S. resident and sold to a German company, title passing in Germany.
   c. Sale of machinery that had been used exclusively in a foreign trade or business by a domestic corporation to an unrelated foreign corporation, title passing in Japan.
   d. Sale of IBM stock by R, an NRA individual, sale taking place on the New York Stock Exchange.

29. Determine the source of income (U.S. or foreign) in each of the following situations:

   a. A commercial building located in Houston is purchased by a foreign corporation, closing taking place in Tokyo.
   b. N, an NRA, is an employee of a foreign corporation. During the tax year, he works in the United States for five weeks as part of his job with the foreign corporation. He is paid $450 per week.

c. T, a U.S. citizen, works for D, a U.S. corporation. Her salary for the tax year is $45,000. She worked 225 days in the United States and 25 days in a foreign country.

d. Sale of depreciable property by X, a domestic corporation, for $150,000. The property had an adjusted basis of $80,000 at the time of sale. Depreciation deductions of $100,000 had been taken on the property, $75,000 against foreign-source income and $25,000 against U.S.-source income.

30. F, a foreign corporation resident in country M, is owned 100% by X, a domestic corporation. F, therefore, is a CFC. Determine F's Subpart F income (before expenses and cost of goods sold) for the tax year, given the following items of income:

a. $200,000 from the sale of merchandise (purchased from X) to customers in country N.

b. $120,000 insurance income from the insurance of the risks of G, another foreign corporation owned by X and resident in country P.

c. $75,000 commissions from the sale of merchandise on behalf of X to residents of country M for use within M.

d. $80,000 from the sale of merchandise to X. The merchandise was purchased from an unrelated manufacturer resident in country P.

e. $300,000 from performance on a construction contract entered into by X. The services were performed by F's personnel in country P.

31. T, a U.S. shareholder, owns 15% of the only class of stock of F, a CFC. F is a CFC until July 1 of the current tax year. T has held the stock since F was organized and continues to hold it for the entire year. T and F are both calendar year taxpayers. If F's Subpart F income for the tax year is $100,000, E & P is $150,000, and no distributions have been made for the tax year, what is the amount, if any, that T must include in gross income under Subpart F for the tax year?

32. The following individual U.S. persons own stock in F, a foreign personal holding company. If undistributed FPHC income is $150,000 for the tax year, how much of this amount must each U.S. person include in income as a constructive dividend?

Mr. Green	15
Mrs. Green	10
Green, Jr.	5
Mr. Smith	15
Mrs. Smith	15
Ms. Jones, unrelated to the Greens and the Smiths	9

Nonresident aliens own the remaining 31 shares.

33. P, a foreign corporation, is a PFIC for the current tax year. R, a U.S. resident and shareholder, receives a distribution of $20,000 from P. P's total E & P is $200,000. The average amount of distributions on the PFIC stock attributable to R's interest for the immediately preceding three tax years was $5,000.

a. Does R receive an excess distribution?

b. If so, how much?

c. How is the excess distribution, if any, treated for tax purposes?

34. N, a citizen and resident of country A, comes to the United States for the first time on February 1, 1992, and remains until June 10 of the same year, at which time N returns to A. N comes back to the United States on September 11, 1992, and remains until November 30, 1992, when N again returns to country A. N does not possess a green card. Is N a U.S. resident for 1992 under the substantial presence test? If so, is there any way that N can overcome the presumption of residence?

35. A, an NRA, has the following U.S.-source income for 1992. Determine A's U.S. tax liability assuming that A is single, has no § 165 losses, and makes no charitable contributions.

Capital gain*	$15,000
Dividend from D Corporation**	10,000
Interest from U.S. bank account***	4,000
Net income from U.S. trade or business	50,000

*Not effectively connected to the U.S. business.

**A owns 30% of the stock of D, a U.S. corporation.

***The interest is attributable to the deposit of idle funds of the U.S. trade or business.

36. W, a U.S. resident, is married to H, an NRA. W has taxable income of $70,000 for the tax year. H, who is retired, receives foreign-source investment income of $20,000 for the tax year. Can W and H file a joint return? If so, should they?

37. N, a deceased NRA, owned the following property at the date of his death. What amount, if any, is included in N's gross estate for U.S. estate tax purposes?

Property	Location	Value at Death
Stock of D, a domestic corporation	Safe deposit box in London	$200,000
Jewelry	Safe deposit box in Miami	150,000
Condominium	Miami	300,000
Stock of F, a foreign corporation	Safe deposit box in Miami	100,000
Cash	Bank in Miami	50,000
	Bank in London	80,000
Personal residence	London	250,000
Other personal property	Miami	40,000
	London	150,000

38. F, a foreign corporation, operates a trade or business in the United States. F's U.S.-source taxable income effectively connected with this trade or business is $300,000 for the current tax year. F's current E & P is $250,000. F's net U.S. equity at the beginning of the year was $1.5 million and at the end of the year was $1.4 million. F is resident in a country with which the United States does not have an income tax treaty. What is the effect of the branch profits tax on F for the current tax year?

39. F, an NRA, is a partner in a domestic partnership, Realty For Sale. The partnership sells a U.S. real property interest for a gain of $1,200,000 (amount realized is $2,500,000, and basis is $1,300,000). F's pro rata share of the gain is $600,000. Does such a transaction call for any action on the part of the partnership with regard to F's share of the gain? Explain.

40. Assume that T, a U.S. citizen, becomes a bona fide resident of F, a foreign country, on March 28, 1991, and remains a resident until January 1, 1993. T is on the calendar year and cash tax basis in the United States. T earns a salary of $73,000 in 1992, but receives $60,000 of this amount in 1992 and $13,000 in 1993. T has no other foreign-source income in either year. How much of her salary is excludible under § 911 for 1992? How much for 1993? What would be the result if T received the $13,000 in 1994?

41. Calculate net taxable foreign-source earned income using the housing cost amount exclusion and the general exclusion for foreign-source earned income, given the following facts:

Total foreign-source earned income	$130,000*
Housing expenses paid by employer	35,000
Tax year	1992

*Includes the $35,000.

For ease of calculation, use $8,500 as the base amount for purposes of the housing cost amount exclusion.

42. Referring back to Problem 41, calculate both exclusions under the assumption that the taxpayer was a qualified resident of the foreign country for only 11 months of the tax year.

43. In which of the following situations must an "information" return be filed with the IRS:

   a. A U.S. person owns 55% of a foreign corporation.
   b. A U.S. person owns 25% of a domestic corporation.
   c. A non-U.S. person owns 25% of a domestic corporation.
   d. A non-U.S. person owns 55% of a foreign corporation.

44. To which of the following transfers would § 1491 apply, assuming that the transferor made no special election?

   a. Transfer of oil and gas royalty interest from a U.S. person to a foreign trust.
   b. Transfer of oil and gas royalty interest from a U.S. person to a CFC in a transaction that qualified under § 351.
   c. Transfer of stock of a U.S. publicly held corporation by a U.S. person to an uncontrolled foreign corporation.
   d. Transfer of patent from a U.S. partnership to a foreign partnership.

45. Referring to § 367, identify the assets for which gain must be recognized by a U.S. person on transfer to a newly formed foreign corporation, to be organized and resident in the Cayman Islands, assuming the fair market value of the assets exceeds their adjusted basis.

   a. Accounts receivable of a cash basis service company.
   b. 5,000 shares of Exxon Corporation stock.
   c. All rights to the films *U.S. Depreciation* and *Outbound Transfer.*
   d. Widgets, gadgets, and doodads that are items manufactured and normally held for sale by the U.S. transferor.
   e. 800,000K, a foreign currency.
   f. Section 1231 assets to be devoted by the foreign corporation to the active conduct of its trade or business in the Cayman Islands.

46. Assume that D, a domestic corporation, organizes a foreign branch in 1990. The branch is a QBU and uses the K (a foreign currency) as its functional currency. The following income and taxes resulted in 1990–1992:

	Income	Foreign Taxes	Exchange Rate
1990	150K/$300	40K/$80	.5K:$1
1991	160K/$200	56K/$70	.8K:$1
1992	140K/$140	45K/$45	1K:$1

Assuming the maximum corporate rate of 34% applies for U.S. tax purposes, determine the net U.S. tax for each year, with respect to the branch income.

47. Referring back to Problem 46, assume that in 1992, 300K is remitted to the home office of D in the United States. Does this remittance trigger a foreign currency gain or loss? If so, what is its character (ordinary or capital)?

48. D, a U.S. corporation, contracts to buy a supply of rubber from a Malaysian company. The rubber is purchased on 90-day credit terms. The contract was for 80,000 tons of rubber at 1,200,000M$. D paid for the rubber 90 days after purchase. At the date of purchase, the exchange rate was 5M$:$1. Ninety days later the exchange rate was 4M$:$1.

   a. At what cost should D record the rubber purchase?
   b. How much, in U.S. dollars, did D have to pay 90 days after purchase for the rubber?
   c. Was there any recognizable gain or loss on payment? If so, how much and what is its character?

49. P, a U.S. corporation, and N, its commission foreign sales corporation (FSC), have the following profit picture with regard to P's export product. Using the administrative pricing rules, calculate N's taxable income.

P's gross sales	$80,000
P's gross income from sales	35,000
P's net income from sales before FSC considerations	25,000
Expenses incurred by FSC	2,500

50. Under which of the following circumstances can the foreign-source income of a U.S. person be re-sourced as U.S.-source income for purposes of the FTC?

   a. The income is dividends from a U.S.-owned foreign corporation.
   b. The income is highly taxed by the foreign country.
   c. The taxpayer has an overall foreign loss.
   d. A treaty reduces the foreign withholding rate from 30 to 15%.

RESEARCH PROBLEMS

RESEARCH PROBLEM 1   Marla was born in the United States to wealthy parents. She spent a large part of her childhood and adulthood traveling in Europe, especially in Spain. She eventually married a Spanish nobleman who begged her to acquire Spanish citizenship. As a Christmas gift in 1991, she informed him that she had applied for Spanish citizenship and been accepted. She was a Spanish citizen. When Marla talked with her U.S. tax attorney earlier in 1991, she had learned that taking Spanish citizenship would automatically rescind her U.S. citizenship. Furthermore, her U.S. tax treatment would change. She would be taxed as a nonresident alien. Early in 1992, Marla asks her U.S. attorney to sell several stocks for her that will result in capital gain income. Since she is a nonresident alien, these gains are exempt from U.S. taxation. Will the provisions of § 877 apply to these gains?

Partial list of research aids:

Cecil B. Furstenberg, 83 T.C. 755 (1984).

RESEARCH PROBLEM 2   George and Fred are both U.S. citizens who work on offshore oil rigs in territorial waters of country F. George works a shift of 28 days followed by 28 days off. On his off-duty days, he flies to his home in Florida where his wife and children live. George's employment prohibits him from living onshore in country F during his rest period. Fred works two out of every three weeks during the same period. He spends his free time in Z, the capital of country F, where he leases an apartment. He has a checking account and a savings account in Z. He also has an automobile, a boat, and other durable goods that he purchased in Z. He does not have a family in the United States, but has a girlfriend in Z. The issue is whether or not George and/or Fred have established a bona fide residence in a foreign country for purposes of the § 911 foreign earned income exclusion.

Partial list of research aids:

Robert C. Bujol, 53 TCM 762, T.C.Memo. 1987–230.
Kurt Van Yost, 44 TCM 1071, T.C.Memo. 1982–516.
Chesley O. James, 55 TCM 1112, T.C.Memo. 1988–266.

RESEARCH PROBLEM 3   J, a U.S. citizen, lives in Switzerland. He is an artist who sells his paintings throughout the world. As a U.S. citizen, he is subject to taxation on his worldwide income. J seeks to take a foreign earned income exclusion with regard to the income he receives from the sales of the paintings. An IRS agent questions the claim that the income from sale of the paintings is "earned" income for purposes of the exclusion. How would you advise J?

Partial list of research aids:

Mark Tobey, 60 T.C. 227 (1973), *acq.* 1979–1 C.B. 1.

RESEARCH PROBLEM 4 T, a citizen and resident of country B, comes to the United States for the first time on June 1, 1991, and remains until December 15, 1991, when he returns to country B. On April 1, 1992, T returns to the United States with green card permanent resident status and remains until November 10, 1992, when he surrenders his green card and returns to country B. T does not qualify as a U.S. resident for 1993. For what period(s) does T qualify as a U.S. resident for income tax purposes during 1991 and 1992?

Partial list of research aids:

Prop.Reg. § 301.7701(b)–4(e).

RESEARCH PROBLEM 5 F, a CFC incorporated in foreign country A, manufactures goods in A. It derives all of its gross income from the sale of these goods by its branch X in country B. The sales income is attributable 80% to sales made to Y, an unrelated party, for use in country C and 20% to sales made to Z for use in country D. The total gross income from sales of $900,000 is allocated to branch X. F derives total gross income of $4,000,000, consisting of $3,900,000 from manufacturing operations and $100,000 of dividends, which are includible in foreign base company income. How would the 10% and 70% tests for purposes of Subpart F affect F's U.S. shareholders? How would the branch sales affect Subpart F income?

Partial list of research aids:

Reg. § 1.954–1(d)(4).
Reg. § 1.954–3(b).

PART

FLOW-THROUGH ENTITIES

Unlike C corporations, some business entities are taxed under the conduit principle. Generally, this means that the tax attributes of various transactions are retained as they flow through the entity to the owners. With limited exceptions, no tax is imposed at the entity level. Part III discusses two types of flow-through entities—partnerships and corporations that make the Subchapter S election.

CHAPTER

PARTNERSHIPS: FORMATION, OPERATION, AND BASIS

OBJECTIVES

Define a partnership and identify its governing concepts.

Explain the computational process for partnership income (loss).

Discuss the tax effects of a partnership formation, including property contributions.

Illustrate how debt affects the adjusted basis of partners' interests.

Explain how partnership organization and syndication costs are treated.

Specify how a partnership tax year is determined.

Explain the tax problems involved when a partner engages in transactions with the partnership.

Provide insights as to when and how a partnership can best be used.

OUTLINE

Forms of Doing Business—Federal Tax Consequences

The status of a corporation as a separate tax entity presents several important disadvantages. The attribute that many observers perceive as most detrimental to the incorporation of a business is the potential for the double taxation of the corporation's income. Under the belief that shareholders receive taxable income from the corporation only in the form of dividend distributions, these observers maintain that every dollar of corporate taxable income is subject to Federal income tax on at least two levels. When the dollar is earned by the corporation, it is subject to the corporate income tax. Then, what is left of the dollar after the corporate tax is paid is subject again to income tax at the shareholder level when it is distributed as a dividend.

Several provisions of the Internal Revenue Code are designed to counteract this potential for double taxation. The dividends received deduction can be interpreted as a measure to offset the effects of double taxation (or triple taxation, in the case of intercorporate shareholdings). The shareholder of a closely held corporation may find greater opportunities for avoiding the double taxation of corporate income by effectively using statutory and judicially approved income-splitting techniques. These often take the form of a payment of a reasonable salary to the shareholder-employee, interest to a shareholder-creditor, and rent to a shareholder-lessor. In addition, the Code allows generous tax-favored contributions to deferred compensation plans, which can delay the recognition of income from salarylike payments for many years. This greatly reduces the present value of the tax that must be paid.

This chapter begins an analysis of two other statutory provisions that are meant to counteract the possibilities for the double taxation of corporate income, namely, partnerships and S corporations. In each case, the owner of a trade or business elects to avoid treating the enterprise itself as a separate taxable entity. The owners of the business are taxed on a proportionate share of the entity's taxable income at the end of each of its taxable years, regardless of the magnitude of distributions that the owners received during the year. The entity serves merely as an information provider to the IRS with respect to the proportionate income shares that its owners have received. In this manner, the tax falls directly upon the owners of the enterprise, and no double taxation occurs.

The recent surge in popularity of partnerships and S corporations can be traced to two major factors. Foremost among these is the owners' opportunity to obtain a lower tax rate. Since the maximum rate for individuals is 31 percent, as opposed to 34 percent for C corporations, the use of a flow-through entity can reduce the applicable tax liability. Moreover, if an individual has investments that produce passive losses, he or she may wish to invest in a flow-through entity that produces passive income. Taxpayers who invested in tax shelter loss generators were caught short when the passive activity limitation (PAL) rules were enacted. To counteract these rules, the taxpayers sought activities whose positive passive income could offset passive tax shelter losses.

Since partnerships and S corporations are so widespread, a study of related tax problems will prove useful to students, business owners, and consultants. This chapter primarily addressses partnership formations and operations. Chapter 11 focuses on dispositions of partnership interests, partnership distributions, and optional basis adjustments. Chapter 12 is concerned with S corporations. Chapter 13 includes a comparative analysis of the various forms by which business can be conducted.

Tax Consequences of Partnership Activities

A partnership is not a taxable entity.[1] Rather, the taxable income or loss of the partnership, and any other receipts or expenditures that receive special tax treatment on the partners' tax returns, flow through to the partners at the end of the entity's tax year.[2] Each partner receives his or her allocable share of the partnership's ordinary income for the year, as well as of any other such specially treated items. As a result, the partnership itself pays no Federal income tax on its income, but the partners' own individual tax liabilities are affected by the activities of the entity.

―――――――――――――― EXAMPLE 1 ――――――――――――――

A is a 40% partner in the ABC Partnership. Both A's and the partnership's tax years end on December 31. In 1992, the partnership generates $200,000 of ordinary taxable income. However, because the partnership needs capital for expansion and debt reduction, A makes no cash withdrawals during 1992. He meets his living expenses by reducing his investment portfolio. A is taxed on his $80,000 allocable share of the partnership's 1992 income, even though he received no property distributions from the entity during 1992. ◆

[handwritten: basis increases by 80,000 due to this]

[handwritten: must use schedule K]

[handwritten: all taxed monies are then capital taxable distribution is when basis becomes 0]

When income flows through to a partner from the entity, his or her basis in the partnership increases accordingly. When a partner receives the flow-through of a loss, basis is reduced. The profits- and loss-sharing ratios that are included in the partnership agreement usually determine the allocation of partnership ordinary taxable income among the partners.[3]

―――――――――――――― EXAMPLE 2 ――――――――――――――

Assume the same facts as in Example 1, except that the partnership recognizes a 1992 taxable loss of $100,000. A's 1992 adjusted gross income is reduced by $40,000 because his proportionate share of the loss flows through to him from the partnership. He claims a $40,000 partnership loss for the year and reduces the basis in his partnership interest by the same amount. ◆

[handwritten: basis is reduced by 40,000]

Many items of income and expense retain their tax character as they flow through to the partners. Generally, if an item of income or expense could affect a partner's taxable income in a special manner if it retained its character, then that character applies to the partner.[4] The item is withheld from the computation of the entity's ordinary taxable income and is reported separately by the partnership to the partners and to the IRS. All other items are netted at the partnership level before they flow through to the partners.

―――――――――――――― EXAMPLE 3 ――――――――――――――

B is a 25% partner in the SS Partnership. The cash basis entity collected sales income of $60,000 during 1992 and incurred $15,000 in business expenses. In addition, it sold a corporate bond for a $9,000 long-term capital gain. Finally, the partnership made a $1,000 contribution to the local Performing Arts Fund drive. The fund is a qualifying charity. SS and all of its partners use a calendar tax year.

B receives ordinary taxable income from the partnership for 1992 of $11,250 [($60,000 − $15,000) × 25%]. She also receives a flow-through of a $2,250 long-term capital gain and a $250 charitable contribution deduction. The ordinary income

―――――――――――――

1. § 701.
2. § 702.

3. § 704(a).
4. § 703(a)(1).

increases B's gross income outright, and the capital gain and charitable contribution are combined with her other similar activities for the year as though she had incurred them herself. These items could be treated differently on the individual tax returns of the various partners (e.g., because a partner may be subject to a percentage limitation on his or her charitable contribution deduction for 1992), so they are withheld from the computation of ordinary partnership income and flow through to the partners separately. ◆

Other items that are allocated separately to the partners[5] include recognized gains and losses from property transactions; dividend income; tax preferences and adjustments for the alternative minimum tax; expenditures that qualify for the jobs credit and the foreign tax credit; expenses that would be itemized by the partners or other nonbusiness deductions; and other items that are specially allocated to certain partners by the partnership agreement. If a special allocation is to be recognized for tax purposes, however, it must produce economic consequences in addition to tax savings for the partner receiving the allocation.[6]

Example 4

When the GH Partnership was formed, G contributed cash and H contributed some City of Helena bonds that she had held for investment purposes. The partnership agreement allocates all of the tax-exempt interest income from the bonds to H as an inducement for her to remain a partner. This is a special allocation of an item to a partner that is acceptable for income tax purposes; it reflects the differing economic circumstances that underlie the partners' contributions to the capital of the entity. Since H would have received the exempt income if she had not joined the partnership, she can retain the tax-favored treatment via the special allocation. ◆

Example 5

Assume the same facts as in Example 4. Three years after it was formed, GH purchased some City of Butte bonds. The municipal bond interest income flows through to the partners as a separately stated item, so it retains its tax-exempt status. However, the partnership agreement allocates all of this income to G because he is subject to a higher marginal income tax bracket than is H. This allocation is not effective for income tax purposes, as it has no purpose other than the reduction of the partner's income tax liability. ◆

Conceptual Basis for Partnership Taxation

The unique tax treatment of partners and partnerships can be traced to two legal concepts that evolved long ago: the *aggregate* or *conduit concept* and the *entity concept*. Both concepts have been used in civil and common law, and their influence can be seen in practically every related tax rule.

Aggregate or Conduit Concept. The aggregate or conduit concept treats the partnership as a channel through which income, credits, deductions, etc., flow to the partners for their own tax consideration. Under this concept, the partnership is regarded as a collection of taxpayers joined in an agency relationship with one another. The imposition of the income tax on individual partners reflects the influence of this doctrine. The aggregate concept has influenced the tax treatment of other pass-through units, such as S corporations (Chapter 12) and certain trusts (Chapter 9).

---

5. § 702(a).   6. § 704(b).

Entity Concept. The entity concept treats partners and partnerships as separate units and gives the partnership its own tax "personality" by (1) requiring a partnership to file an information tax return and (2) treating partners as separate and distinct from the partnership in certain transactions between a partner and the entity. A partner's recognition of capital gain or loss on the sale of his or her partnership interest illustrates this doctrine.

Combined Concepts. Rules that contain a blend of both the entity and aggregate concepts include provisions concerning the formation, operation, and liquidation of a partnership.

What Is a Partnership?

A partnership is an association of two or more persons to carry on a trade or business, with each contributing money, property, labor, or skill, and with all expecting to share in profits and losses.[7] For Federal income tax purposes, a partnership includes a syndicate, group, pool, joint venture, or other unincorporated organization, through which any business, financial operation, or venture is carried on. The entity must not be otherwise classified as a corporation, trust, or estate. If a partnership is used for the following purposes, however, it may elect to be excluded from the partnership rules:

- Investment motivations, rather than the active conduct of a trade or business.
- Joint production, extraction, or use of property.
- Underwriting, selling, or distributing a specific security issue.[8]

When a partnership is used to conduct a service business, such as public accounting, law, medicine, etc., very likely it will be a *general partnership,* so that creditors are protected by partnership and partner assets. On the other hand, the *limited partnership* form will likely be used for real estate development activities, so that investors are protected against losses in excess of their investment. A limited partnership is comprised of a general partner and numerous limited partners. Unless special rules apply, only the general partners are liable to creditors; each limited partner's risk of loss is restricted to his or her equity investment in the entity.

Partner's Gain or Loss on Contributions to Entity

When a taxpayer transfers property to an entity in exchange for valuable consideration, a taxable exchange normally results. Typically, both the taxpayer and the entity will realize and recognize gain or loss on the exchange. The gain or loss recognized by the transferee is the difference between the fair market value of the consideration received and the adjusted basis of the property transferred.

Generally, however, neither the partner nor the partnership recognizes a gain or loss that is realized when a partner contributes property to a partnership in exchange for a partnership interest. Instead, the realized gain or loss is deferred.[9] There are two reasons for this treatment. First, Congress is not

---

7. § 7701(a)(2).

8. § 761(a).

9. § 721.

interested in hindering the creation of valid economic entities by requiring gain recognition when a partnership is created. Requiring that gain be recognized on such transfers would make the formation of some partnerships economically unfeasible. Second, because the partnership interest received is typically not a liquid asset, the partner may not easily be able to find the cash to pay the tax. Thus, the deferral of the gain recognizes the economic realities of the business world and follows the wherewithal to pay principle of taxation.

EXAMPLE 6

A transfers two assets to the AB Partnership, on the day that the entity is created, in exchange for a 60% profit and loss interest. This 60% partnership interest is worth $60,000. She contributes cash of $40,000 and retail display equipment (basis to her as a sole proprietor, $8,000; fair market value, $20,000). Since an exchange has occurred between two entities, A will realize a $12,000 gain on this transaction. The gain realized is the fair market value of the partnership interest of $60,000 less the basis of the assets that A surrendered to the partnership [$40,000 (cash) + $8,000 (equipment)].

Under § 721, A does not recognize the $12,000 realized gain in the year of contribution. A might have been pressed for cash if she had been required to recognize the $12,000 gain. All that she received from the partnership was an illiquid partnership interest; she received no cash with which to pay any resulting tax liability. ◆

EXAMPLE 7

Assume the same facts as in Example 6, except that the equipment A contributed to the partnership had an adjusted basis of $25,000. She has a $5,000 realized loss [$60,000 − ($40,000 + $25,000)], but she cannot deduct any of this loss. Realized losses, as well as realized gains, are deferred by § 721.

If it were not essential that the partnership receive A's display equipment rather than similar equipment purchased from an outside supplier, A should have sold the equipment to a third party. This would have allowed her to deduct a $5,000 loss in the year of the sale. A, then, could have contributed $60,000 cash (including the proceeds from the sale) for her interest in the partnership, and the partnership would have funds to purchase similar equipment. ◆

EXAMPLE 8

Assume the same facts as in Example 6. Five years after the partnership was created, A contributes another piece of equipment to the entity from her sole proprietorship. This property has a basis of $35,000 and a fair market value of $50,000. A can defer the recognition of this $15,000 realized gain. Section 721 is effective whenever a partner makes a contribution to the capital of the partnership. ◆

The nonrecognition provisions of § 721 may not always apply, however. If the transfer consists of appreciated stocks and securities and the partnership is an investment partnership, it is likely that the realized gain on the stocks and securities will be recognized by the contributing partner at the time of contribution.[10] This provision prevents multiple investors from using the partnership form to diversify their investment portfolios on a tax-free basis.

Also, the nonrecognition provisions of § 721 will not defer the tax on a transaction that is essentially an exchange of properties.[11]

EXAMPLE 9

Two individuals, A and B, own land and stock, respectively. A would like to have B's stock, and B wants A's land. If A and B both contribute their property to a newly formed AB Partnership in exchange for interests in the partnership, the tax on the

---

10. § 721(b).

11. Reg. § 1.731–1(c)(3).

transaction would appear to be deferred under § 721. The tax on a subsequent distribution by the partnership of the land to B and the stock to A would also appear to be deferred under § 731 (discussed later in the chapter). According to a literal interpretation of the statutes, no taxable exchange has occurred. A and B will find, however, that this type of tax subterfuge is not permitted. The IRS will disregard the passage of the properties through the partnership and will hold, instead, that A and B exchanged the land and stock directly. Thus, the transactions will be treated as any other taxable exchange. ◆

A final exception occurs when a partner receives his or her interest in the partnership as compensation for services rendered to the partnership. This is not a tax-deferred transaction. Services are not included in the definition of property that can be transferred to a partnership on a tax-free basis. Instead, the partner performing the services recognizes ordinary compensation income equal to the fair market value of the partnership interest received.[12]

The partnership may deduct the amount included in the partner's income if the services are of a deductible nature. If the services are not deductible to the partnership, they must be capitalized to an asset account. For example, architectural plans created by a partner will be capitalized to the structure built with those plans. Alternatively, day-to-day management services performed by a partner for the partnership are usually deductible by the partnership.

―――――――――――――――― EXAMPLE 10 ――――――――――――――――

When they formed the BCD Partnership, B, C, and D each received a one-third interest in the entity. D became a one-third partner to compensate him for the accounting and tax-planning services that he rendered during the formation of the partnership. The value of a one-third interest in the partnership (for each of the parties) is $20,000. D must recognize $20,000 of compensation income. This treatment resembles the results that would occur if the partnership had paid D $20,000 for his services and D had immediately contributed that amount to the entity for a one-third ownership interest. ◆

Basis Calculations Relative to Contributed Property

When a partner contributes an asset to the capital of a partnership, the entity assigns a carryover basis to the property.[13] The entity's basis in the asset is equal to the basis the partner held in the property prior to its transfer to the partnership. This basis is increased by the amount of any gain that the partner recognized as a result of the formation of an investment company partnership. Thus, two assets are created out of one when a partnership is formed, namely, the property in the hands of the new entity and the new asset (the partnership interest) in the hands of the partner. Both assets are assigned a basis that is derived from the partner's existing basis in the contributed property.

To understand the logic of these rules, consider what Congress was attempting to accomplish in this deferral transaction. Earlier, it was observed that gain or loss is deferred when property is contributed to a partnership in exchange for a partnership interest. This deferral is implemented through the calculation of the partnership's basis in the transferred property and the partner's basis for his or her partnership interest. These basis amounts will be the amounts necessary to allow for the recognition of the deferred gain or loss if the property or the partnership interest is subsequently disposed of in a taxable transaction. This treatment is similar to the treatment of assets transferred to a controlled corporation[14] and the treatment of like-kind exchanges.[15]

―――――――――――――――――

12. § 83(a).
13. § 723.

14. § 351.
15. § 1031.

EXAMPLE 11

On June 1, 1992, J transfers property of the JKL Partnership in exchange for a one-third interest in the partnership. The property has an adjusted basis to J of $10,000 and a fair market value of $30,000 on June 1. J has a realized gain on the exchange of $20,000 ($30,000 − $10,000) but, under § 721, does not recognize any of the gain. J's basis for his partnership interest is the amount necessary to recognize the $20,000 deferred gain if his partnership interest is subsequently sold for its $30,000 fair market value. This amount, $10,000, is referred to as *substituted* basis. The basis of the property contributed to the partnership is the amount necessary to allow for the recognition of the $20,000 deferred gain if the property is subsequently sold for its $30,000 fair market value. This amount, also $10,000, is referred to as *carryover* basis. ◆

The holding period for the contributed asset also carries over to the partnership. Thus, the partnership's holding period for the asset includes the period during which the partner owned the asset individually.

Depreciation Method and Period. If depreciable property is contributed to the partnership, the partnership is usually required to use the same cost recovery method and life used by the partner. The partnership merely "steps into the shoes" of the partner and continues the same cost recovery calculations. If the property is not MACRS or ACRS property, the partnership must treat the property as used property for depreciation purposes. The partnership may not immediately expense any part of the basis of the § 179 property it receives from the transferor partner.

Receivables, Inventory, and Losses. To prevent ordinary income from being converted into capital gain, gain or loss is treated as ordinary if it occurs on the disposal of either of the following:[16]

- Contributed receivables that were unrealized in the contributing partner's hands at the contribution date. Such receivables include the right to receive payment for goods or services delivered (or to be delivered) at the contribution date.
- Contributed property that was inventory in the contributor's hands on the contribution date, *when the disposal occurs within five years of this date.* Inventory includes all property except capital and real or depreciable business assets.

Income to the partnership

To prevent a capital loss from being converted into an ordinary loss, capital treatment is assigned to a loss on the disposal of the following:

- Contributed property that was capital loss property in the contributor's hands on the contribution date, *when the disposal occurs within five years of this date.*

EXAMPLE 12

T operates a cash basis retail electronics and television store as a sole proprietor. R is an enterprising individual who likes to invest in small businesses. On January 2 of the current year, T and R form the TR Partnership. Their partnership contributions are as follows:

---

16. § 724. For this purpose, § 724(d)(2) waives the holding period requirement in defining § 1231 property.

	Adjusted Basis	Fair Market Value
From T:		
Receivables	$ –0–	$ 2,000
Land used as parking lot*	1,200	3,000
Inventory	2,500	5,000
From R:		
Cash	10,000	10,000

*Parking lot had been held for five months at contribution date.

Within 30 days of forming the partnership, TR collects the receivables and sells the inventory for cash. It uses the land for the next 10 months as a parking lot, then sells it for $3,500 cash. TR realized the following income in the current year from these transactions:

- Ordinary income of $2,000 from collecting receivables.
- Ordinary income of $2,500 from sale of inventory.
- § 1231 gain of $2,300 from sale of land.

The land takes a carryover holding period. Thus, it is classified as long term at the sale date. ◆

──────────────── EXAMPLE 13 ────────────────

Assume the same facts as Example 12, except for the following:

- The land contributed by T was held for investment and had a fair market value of $800 at the contribution date.
- TR used the land as a parking lot for 11 months and sold it for $650.

TR realizes the following income and loss from these transactions:

- Ordinary income of $2,000 from collecting receivables.
- Ordinary income of $2,500 from sale of inventory.
- Capital loss of $400 from sale of land.
- § 1231 loss of $150 from sale of land.

Since the land was sold within five years of the contribution date, the built-in $400 of the realized loss is a capital loss. The post-contribution loss of $150 is a § 1231 loss, since TR used the property in its business. ◆

Throughout this chapter and the next, reference is made to the partnership's inside basis and the partner's outside basis. *Inside basis* refers to the aggregate adjusted basis of partnership assets, as determined from the partnership's tax accounts. *Outside basis* represents the actual dollars that the partner has invested in the partnership. Each partner owns a share of the partnership's inside basis and maintains his or her own records of outside basis. In many cases—especially on formation of the partnership—the total of all partners' outside basis will equal the partnership's inside basis. Differences between inside and outside basis arise when a partner's interest is sold to another person for more or less than the selling partner's inside basis. The buying partner's outside basis equals the price paid for the interest, but his or her share of the entity's inside basis is derived from historical cost.

Concept Summary 10–1 reviews the rules that apply to partnership asset contribution and basis adjustments.

Tax Accounting Elections

A newly formed partnership must make numerous tax accounting elections. These elections are formal decisions on how a particular transaction or tax attribute should be handled. Most of these elections must be made by the partnership rather than by the partners individually.[17] The *partnership* makes the elections involving the following items:

- Inventory method.
- Cost or percentage depletion method, excluding oil and gas wells.
- Accounting method (cash, accrual, or hybrid).
- Capitalizing or expensing of fixed assets.
- Cost recovery methods and assumptions.
- Tax year (when an IRS-specified year is not followed).
- Amortization of organizational costs and period.
- Amortization of start-up expenditures and period.
- Optional basis adjustments for property.
- Section 179 deductions for certain tangible personal property.
- Nonrecognition treatment for involuntary conversions gains.
- Election out of partnership rules.

Each partner is bound by the decisions made by the partnership relative to these elections. If the partnership fails to make an election, a partner cannot compensate for this error by making the election individually.

While most elections must be made by the partnership, the partners are required to make three specific elections individually.[18] These elections involve relatively narrow tax issues. Each *partner* individually makes the election on the following issues:

- Income from discharge of indebtedness.
- Cost or percentage depletion method for oil and gas wells.
- Deductions and credits for foreign countries and U.S. possessions.

CONCEPT SUMMARY 10–1
PARTNERSHIP FORMATION AND BASIS COMPUTATION

1. The *entity concept* treats partners and partnerships as separate units. The nature of gains and losses is determined at the partnership level.
2. The *aggregate concept* is used to connect partners and partnerships. It allows income, gains, losses, credits, deductions, etc. to flow through to the partners for separate tax reporting.
3. Sometimes both the *aggregate* and *entity* concepts apply, but one usually dominates. When land used as a parking lot is sold for a gain within five years of its contribution date, and the land was held by the contributing partner as inventory, the resulting gain is ordinary (aggregate concept).
4. Generally, partners or partnerships do not recognize gain or loss when property is contributed for capital interests.
5. Partners contributing property for partnership interests generally take the contributed property's adjusted basis for their *outside basis* in their partnership interest. The partners are said to take a substituted basis in their partnership interest.
6. The partnership will generally continue to use the contributing partner's basis for the *inside basis* in property it receives. The contributed property is said to take a carryover basis.
7. The holding period of a partner's interest includes that of contributed property when the property was a § 1231 asset or capital asset in the partner's hands. Otherwise, the holding period starts on the day the interest is acquired. The holding period of an interest acquired by a cash contribution starts at acquisition.
8. The partnership's holding period for contributed property includes the contributing partner's holding period.

---

17. § 703(b).   **18.** §§ 703(b)(1), (2), and (3).

Organization and Syndication Costs

Amounts paid or incurred to organize a partnership or promote the sale of a partnership interest are not deductible. However, the Code permits a ratable amortization of some of these costs.[19]

Organization Costs.   The partnership may elect to amortize organization costs ratably over a period of 60 months or more, starting with the month in which it began business. The election must be made by the due date (including extensions) of the partnership return for the year it began business.

Organization costs include expenditures that are (1) incident to the creation of the partnership; (2) chargeable to a capital account; and (3) of a character that, if incident to the creation of a partnership with an ascertainable life, would be amortized over that life. These expenditures include accounting fees and legal fees incident to the partnership's organization. To be amortizable, the expenditures must be incurred within a period that starts a reasonable time before the partnership begins business. The period ends with the due date (without extensions) of the tax return for the initial tax year.

Cash method partnerships are not allowed to deduct *in the year incurred* the portion of organization costs that are paid after the end of the first year. The partnership can deduct, in the year of payment, the portion of the expenditures that would have been deductible in a prior year, if they had been paid before that year's end.

Costs incurred for the following items are not organization costs:

- Acquiring assets for the partnership.
- Transferring assets to the partnership.
- Admitting partners, other than at formation.
- Removing partners, other than at formation.
- Negotiating operating contracts.
- Syndication costs.

EXAMPLE 14

The calendar year ABC Partnership was formed on May 1 of the current year and immediately started business. ABC incurred $720 in legal fees for drafting the partnership agreement and $480 in accounting fees for tax advice of an organizational nature. The legal fees were paid in October of the current year. The accounting fees were paid in January of the following year. The partnership selected the cash method of accounting and elected to amortize its organization costs.

On its first tax return, ABC deducts $96 of organization costs [($720 legal fees/60 months) × 8 months]. No deduction was taken for the accounting fees since they were paid the following year. On its tax return for next year, ABC deducts organization costs of $304 {[($720 legal fees/60 months) × 12 months] + [($480 accounting fees/60 months) × 20 months]}. The $64 of accounting fees [($480/60) × 8] that could have been deducted on ABC's first tax return if they had been paid by the end of that year are also deducted in the second year. ◆

Syndication Costs.   Unlike organization costs, syndication costs are capitalized without an amortization election. These costs include the following expenditures incurred for promoting and marketing partnership interests:

---

19. § 709.

- Brokerage fees.
- Registration fees.
- Legal fees paid to the underwriter, placement agent, and issuer (general partner or the partnership) for security advice or advice on the adequacy of tax disclosures in the prospectus or placement memo for securities law purposes.
- Accounting fees related to offering materials.
- Printing costs of prospectus, placement memos, and other selling materials.

Fees for tax advice about partnership operations and forecasts used to plan operations and structure transactions are not syndication costs. These costs should be deductible either as organization costs or as general business start-up expenditures. In either case, they can be amortized over a period of 60 months or more.

Taxable Year of the Partnership

In computing a partner's taxable income for a specific year, the partner's distributive share of partnership income and guaranteed payments for the partnership year that ends with or within the partner's taxable year must be included.

When all partners use the calendar year, it is beneficial in present value terms if the partnership adopts a fiscal year ending with January 31. Why? As Figure 10–2 illustrates, when the adopted year ends on January 31, the reporting of income from the partnership and payment of related taxes can be deferred an additional 11 months. For instance, income earned by the partnership in March 1992 is not taxed to the partners until January 31, 1993, and the related individual tax return is not due until April 15, 1994. Even though each partner may be required to file quarterly tax returns and make estimated tax payments, some deferral is still possible.

Under the general rules for determining a partnership's tax year, the partners' tax years should be considered in the order presented in Figure 10–1.[20]

─────────────── Example 15 ───────────────

A and B will be equal partners in the AB Partnership. A uses the calendar year, and B uses the fiscal year ending August 31. Since neither A nor B will be a majority partner,

Figure 10–1 Required Tax Year of Partnership	In Order, Partnership Must Use	Requirements
	Majority partners' tax year	■ Own more than 50% of capital *and* profits.
		■ Have a common tax year.
	Principal partners' tax year	■ All of those who own more than 5% of capital *or* profits.
		■ Have a common tax year.
	Year with smallest amount of income deferred	■ "Least aggregate deferral" method.

20. § 706(b).

and since as principal partners they will not have the same tax year, the general rules indicate that the partnership's required tax year must be determined by the "least aggregate deferral" method. The following computations support August 31 as AB's tax year, since the 2 months of deferral using that year-end is less than the 4 months of deferral when December 31 is used.

Test for 12/31 Year-End

Partner	Year Ends	Profit Interest		Months of Deferral		Product
A	12/31	50%	×	–0–	=	0.0
B	8/31	50%	×	8	=	4.0
Aggregate number of deferral months						4.0

Test for 8/31 Year-End

Partner	Year Ends	Profit Interest		Months of Deferral		Product
A	12/31	50%	×	4	=	2.0
B	8/31	50%	×	–0–	=	0.0
Aggregate number of deferral months						2.0

[handwritten: Must choose the lessor of the two]

When the tax years described in Figure 10–1 are undesirable to the entity, three other alternative tax years can be used instead.

- Elect a tax year so that taxes on partnership income are deferred for not more than *three months* from the required tax year. Then, have the partnership maintain with the IRS a prepaid, non-interest-bearing deposit of estimated taxes deferred. *[handwritten: Very hard to calculate]*
- Follow IRS procedures to obtain approval for using a *natural business tax year*. The IRS has stated that a natural business year exists when 25 percent or more of the partnership's gross receipts were recognized during the last 2 months of the same 12-month period for three consecutive years.[21] New partnerships cannot use this justification because they lack the required three-year history. *[handwritten: a seasonal business can usually do this]*

FIGURE 10–2

Deferral Benefit When Fiscal Year Is Used and All Partners Are on the Calendar Year

Partnership Fiscal Year Ending   1/31/92

September 1991 | October | November | December | January 1992 | February | March | April | May | June | July | August | September | October | November | December

1/1/92 ... 12/31/92

Partners on Calendar Year

21. Rev.Proc. 74–33, 1974–2 C.B. 489; Rev.Rul. 87–57, 1987–2 C.B. 117; and Rev.Proc. 87–32, 1987–1 C.B. 396.

- Establish to the IRS's satisfaction that a *business purpose* exists for a different tax year (a natural business year at the end of a peak season or shortly thereafter, such as a Maine or Minnesota fishing resort that closes every fall). It is difficult to obtain IRS approval when using the business purpose exception.

To use the three-month-or-less deferral rule, the partnership must file an election on Form 8716 by the *earlier of* the following:

- The fifteenth day of the fifth month following the month that includes the first day of the tax year for which the election is effective (e.g., for a June 30 fiscal year, this is November 15).
- The due date (without extensions) of the partnership return resulting from the election.

Required tax deferral deposits are computed at the highest individual tax rate plus one percentage point. The first payment is due on April 15 (plus extensions) of the calendar year following the calendar year in which the first tax year begins. Future payments are also due on April 15 (plus extensions). When the required tax deferral deposit increases, the partnership makes additional payments. When it decreases, the partnership can get a refund. In summary, the partnership maintains an annually adjusted prepaid tax deferral balance with the IRS.[22]

OPERATIONS OF THE PARTNERSHIP
◆

An individual, corporation, trust, estate, or partnership can become a partner in a partnership. Since a partnership is a tax-reporting, rather than a taxpaying, entity for purposes of its Federal (and state) income tax computations, income, deductions, credits, and alternative minimum tax (AMT) preferences and adjustments can be reported and taxed on any of a number of income tax forms (e.g., Forms 1040 [individuals], 1041 [fiduciaries, see Chapter 19], 1120 [C corporations], and 1120S [S corporations]).

A partnership is subject to all other taxes, in the same manner as any other business. Thus, the partnership files returns and pays the outstanding amount of pertinent sales taxes, property taxes, and unemployment, Social Security, and other payroll taxes.

Measuring and Reporting Income

The partnership's Form 1065 organizes and reports the transactions of the entity for the tax year, and each of the partnership's tax items is reported on Schedule K of that return. Each partner, and the IRS, receives a Schedule K–1 that reports the partner's allocable share of partnership income, credits, and preferences for the year. As required by § 6031, Form 1065 is due on the fifteenth day of the fourth month following the close of the partnership's tax year; for a calendar year partnership, this is April 15.

Income Measurement.   The measurement and reporting of partnership income require a two-step approach. Certain items must be segregated and reported separately on the partnership return and each partner's Schedule K–1.

---

22. §§ 444 and 7519.

Items that are not separately reported are netted at the partnership level. Items passed through separately include the following:

- Short- and long-term capital gains and losses.
- Section 1231 gains and losses.
- Charitable contributions.
- Portfolio income items (dividends, interest, and royalties).
- Immediately expensed tangible personal property.
- Items allocated differently from the general profit and loss ratio.
- Recovery of items previously deducted (tax benefit items).
- AMT preference and adjustment items.
- Passive activity items (rental real estate income or loss).
- Expenses related to portfolio income.
- Intangible drilling and development costs.
- Taxes paid to foreign countries and U.S. possessions.
- Nonbusiness and personal items (e.g., alimony, medical, and dental).[23]

The reason for separately reporting the preceding items is rooted in the aggregate or conduit concept. Here, items that affect various exclusions, deductions, and credits at the partner level must pass through without loss of identity so that the proper tax for each partner may be determined.[24]

A partnership is not allowed the following deductions:

- Personal exemptions.
- Taxes paid to foreign countries or U.S. possessions.
- Net operating losses.
- Alimony, medical expense, moving expense, and individual retirement savings.
- Depletion of oil and gas interests.
- Dividends received deduction.

─────────────────────── EXAMPLE 16 ───────────────────────

Z is a one-third partner in the XYZ Partnership. This year, the entity entered into the following transactions:

Fees received	$100,000
Salaries paid	30,000
Cost recovery deductions	11,000
Supplies, repairs	3,000
Payroll taxes paid	9,000
Contribution to art museum	5,000
Short-term capital gain recognized	12,000
Net income from passive rental operations	7,000
Dividends received	1,500
City of Albuquerque bond interest received	2,300
AMT adjustment—installment sale	(44,000)
Payment of Y's alimony obligations	4,000

The entity experienced a $20,000 net loss from operations last year, its first year of operations.

───────────────────

23. § 702(a).   **24.** § 702(b).

The two-step computational process that is used to determine partnership income is applied in the following manner:

Nonseparately Stated Items (Ordinary Income)

Fee income	$100,000
Salary deduction	−30,000
Cost recovery deductions	−11,000
Supplies, repairs	− 3,000
Taxes paid	− 9,000
Ordinary income	$ 47,000

Separately Stated Items

Charitable contributions	$ 5,000
Short-term capital gain	12,000
Passive income (net rent income)	7,000
Portfolio income (dividends received)	1,500
Exempt income (bond interest)	2,300
AMT adjustment—installment sale	(44,000)

§ 179 Not in here

Each of the separately stated items passes through proportionately to each partner and is included on the appropriate schedule or netted with similar items that the partner generated for the year. Thus, in determining what his tax liability will be on his Form 1040, Z includes a $1,667 charitable contribution, a $4,000 short-term capital gain, $2,333 of passive rent income, $500 of dividend income, and a $14,667 negative adjustment in computing alternative minimum taxable income. Z treats these items as if he had generated them himself. In addition, Z reports $15,667 as his share of the partnership's ordinary income, the combination of the nonseparately stated items.

The partnership is not allowed a deduction for last year's $20,000 net operating loss—this item was passed through to the partners' own income tax returns for the previous year. Moreover, no deduction is allowed for personal expenditures (payment of Y's alimony), and no personal exemption is allowed on the Form 1065. ◆

Withdrawals. Capital withdrawals by partners during the year do not affect the partnership's income measuring and reporting process. These items are treated as distributions made on the last day of the partnership's tax year. Furthermore, when withdrawals exceed the partners' shares of partnership income, the excess may generate additional gross income, unless repayment is required.[25]

Penalties. Each partner's share of partnership items should be reported on his or her individual tax return in the same manner as presented on the Form 1065. If a partner treats an item differently, the IRS must be notified of the inconsistent treatment.[26] A partnership with 10 or fewer partners, where each partner's share of partnership items is the same for all items, is automatically excluded from this rule.[27] If a partner fails to comply with this requirement because of negligence or intentional disregard of rules or regulations, a negligence penalty may be added to the tax due.

To encourage the filing of a partnership return, a penalty is imposed on the partnership of $50 per month (or fraction thereof), but not to exceed five

25. § 731(a)(1).
26. § 6222.
27. § 6231(a)(1)(B).

months, for failure to file a complete and timely information return without reasonable cause.[28] Every general partner is personally liable for the penalty.

Partnership Allocations

Each previous example in this chapter has assumed that the partner has the same percentage interest in capital, profits, and losses. Thus, a partner who owns a 25 percent interest in partnership capital has been assumed to own 25 percent of partnership profits and 25 percent of partnership losses.

Economic Effect.   A partner does not have to have identical percentage shares of all capital, profits, and losses. The partnership agreement can provide that any partner may share capital, profits and losses in different ratios. For example, a partner could have a 25 percent capital sharing ratio, yet be accorded 30 percent of the profits and 20 percent of the losses of the partnership. Such *special* allocations are permissible if they follow certain rules contained in the Regulations under § 704(b).[29] Although these rules are too complex to discuss in detail, the general outline of one of these rules—the *economic effect* test—can be easily understood.

We will always assume equal partnership

In general, the economic effect test requires the following:

1. An allocation of income to a partner must increase the partner's capital account, and an allocation of deduction or loss must decrease the partner's capital account.
2. When the partner's interest is liquidated, the partner must receive assets that have a fair market value equal to the balance in his or her capital account.
3. A partner with a negative capital account must restore that account upon liquidation of his or her interest. Restoration of a negative capital account can best be envisioned as a contribution of cash to the partnership equal to the negative balance.

These requirements are designed to ensure that a partner bears the economic burden of a loss or deduction allocation and receives the economic benefit of an income allocation.

———————————————— EXAMPLE 17 ————————————————

A and B each contribute $20,000 cash to the newly formed AB Partnership. The partnership uses the cash to acquire a depreciable asset for $40,000. The partnership agreement provides that the depreciation will be allocated 90% to A and 10% to B. Other items of partnership income, gain, loss, or deduction will be allocated equally between the partners. Upon liquidation of the partnership, property will be distributed to the partners in accordance with their capital account balances. Any partner with a negative capital account must restore the capital account upon liquidation. Assume the first-year depreciation on the equipment is $4,000. Also, assume nothing else happens in the first year that affects the partners' capital accounts.

A's capital account will be $16,400 ($20,000 − $3,600), and B's capital account will have a balance of $19,600 ($20,000 − $400) after the first year of partnership operations. The Regulations require that a hypothetical sale of the asset for its $36,000 adjusted basis on the last day of the year and an immediate liquidation of the partnership should result in A and B receiving distributions equal to their capital accounts. According to the partnership agreement, A will receive $16,400, and B will

———————————————————————————————————

28. § 6098.   29. Reg. § 1.704–1(b).

receive $19,600 of the cash in the liquidating distribution. A, therefore, bears the economic burden of $3,600 depreciation since he contributed $20,000 to the partnership and would receive only $16,400 upon liquidation. Likewise, B's economic burden is $400 since he would receive only $19,600 of his original $20,000 investment. The agreement, therefore, has economic effect.

If the partnership agreement had provided that A and B should each receive $18,000 of the liqudiation proceeds, the "special" allocation of the depreciation would be defective. The IRS would require that the depreciation be allocated equally ($2,000 each) to the two partners. ◆

Precontribution Gain or Loss. Despite the flexibility that special allocations can provide, allocations of income, gain, loss, and deductions relative to contributed property may not be so allocated under the rules described above. Instead, precontribution gain or loss must be allocated among the partners to take into account the variation between the basis of the property and its fair market value on the date of contribution.[30] For nondepreciable property, this means that *built-in* gain or loss on the date of contribution must be allocated to the contributing partner when the property is eventually disposed of by the partnership in a taxable transaction.

EXAMPLE 18

M and X formed an equal profit and loss sharing partnership. M contributed cash of $10,000, and X contributed land purchased two years ago and held for investment. The land had an adjusted basis and fair market value at the contribution date of $6,000 and $10,000, respectively. For accounting purposes, the partnership recorded the land at its fair market value of $10,000. For tax purposes, the partnership took a carryover basis in the land of $6,000. After using the land as a parking lot for five months, MX sold it for $10,600. No other transactions took place.

The accounting and tax gain from the land sale are computed as follows:

	Accounting	Tax
Amount realized	$10,600	$10,600
Adjusted basis	10,000	6,000
Gain realized	$ 600	$ 4,600
Gain at contribution date to X	–0–	4,000
Remaining gain (split equally)	$ 600	$ 600

this goes to X as it was his at the beginning

M recognizes $300 of the gain ($600 postcontribution gain ÷ 2), and X recognizes $4,300 [$4,000 built-in gain + ($600 ÷ 2)]. ◆

Concept Summary 10–2 reviews the tax reporting rules for partnership activities.

Basis of Partnership Interest

Previously, this chapter discussed how to compute a partner's adjusted basis when the partnership is formed. It was noted that the partner's adjusted basis in the newly formed partnership usually equals (1) his or her adjusted basis in any property he or she contributed to the partnership plus (2) the fair market value of any services the partner performed for the partnership.

A partnership interest also may be acquired after the partnership has been formed. The method of acquisition controls how the partner's adjusted basis is

---

30. § 704(c)(1)(A).

computed. If the partnership interest is purchased from another partner, the purchasing partner's basis is the amount paid (cost basis) for the partnership interest. The basis of a partnership interest acquired by gift is generally the donor's basis for the interest plus, in certain cases, some or all of the transfer tax paid by the donor. The basis of a partnership interest acquired through inheritance is usually the fair market value of the interest on the date the partner dies.

After the partnership begins its activities, the partner's basis is adjusted for numerous items. The following operating results increase a partner's adjusted basis:

Increase by Profits decreases by Losses

- The partner's proportionate share of partnership income (including capital gains and tax-exempt income).
- The partner's proportionate share of any increase in partnership liabilities.

The following operating results decrease the partner's adjusted basis in the partnership:

- The partner's proportionate share of partnership deductions and losses (including capital losses).
- The partner's proportionate share of nondeductible expenses.
- The partner's proportionate share of any decrease in partnership liabilities.[31]

CONCEPT SUMMARY 10–2
TAX REPORTING OF PARTNERSHIP ACTIVITIES

Event	Partnership Level	Partner Level
1. Compute partnership ordinary income.	Form 1065, Line 22, Page 1.	Schedule K–1 (Form 1065), Line 1, Page 1.
	Schedule K, Form 1065, Line 1, Page 3.	Each partner's share is passed through for separate reporting.
		Each partner's basis is increased.
2. Compute partnership ordinary loss.	Form 1065, Line 22, Page 1.	Schedule K–1 (Form 1065), Line 1, Page 1.
	Schedule K, Form 1065, Line 1, Page 3.	Each partner's share is passed through for separate reporting.
		Each partner's basis is decreased.
		The amount of a partner's loss deduction may be limited.
		Losses that may not be deducted are carried forward for use in future years.
3. Separately reported items like portfolio income, capital gain and loss, and § 179 deductions.	Schedule K, Form 1065, various lines, Page 3.	Schedule K–1 (Form 1065), various lines, Pages 1 and 2. Each partner's share is passed through for separate reporting.
4. Net earnings from self-employment.	Schedule K, Form 1065, Line 15, Page 3.	Schedule K–1, (Form 1065), Line 15, Page 2.

---

31. §§ 705 and 752.

Under no circumstances can the partner's adjusted basis for the partnership interest be reduced below zero.

Increasing the partner's adjusted basis for his or her share of partnership taxable income is logical since the partner has already been taxed on the income. By increasing the partner's basis, the Code ensures that the partner will not be taxed again on the income when he or she sells the interest or receives a distribution from the partnership.

It is also logical that the tax-exempt income should increase the partner's basis. If the income is exempt in the current period, it should not contribute to the recognition of gain when the partner either sells his or her interest or receives a distribution.

Example 19

K is a one-third partner in the KLM Partnership. His proportionate share of the partnership income during the current year consists of $20,000 of ordinary taxable income and $10,000 of tax-exempt income. The adjusted basis of K's partnership interest before adjusting for his share of income is $35,000, and the fair market value of the interest before considering the income items is $50,000.

The unrealized gain inherent in K's investment in the partnership is $15,000 ($50,000 − $35,000). K's proportionate share of the income items should increase the fair market value of the interest to $80,000 ($50,000 + $20,000 + $10,000). By increasing the adjusted basis of K's partnership interest to $65,000 ($35,000 + $20,000 + $10,000), the Code ensures that the unrealized gain inherent in K's partnership investment remains at $15,000. This makes sense because the $20,000 of ordinary taxable income is taxed to K this year and should not be taxed again when K either sells his interest or receives a distribution. Similarly, the exempt income is exempt this year and should not increase K's gain when he either sells his interest or receives a distribution from the partnership. ◆

Decreasing the partner's adjusted basis for his or her share of deductible losses, deductions, and noncapitalizable, nondeductible expenditures is logical for the same reasons. An item that is deductible currently should not contribute to creating a loss when the partnership interest is sold or a distribution is received from the partnership. Similarly, a noncapitalizable, nondeductible expenditure should never be deductible nor contribute to a loss when a subsequent sale or distribution transaction occurs.

Liability Sharing. A partner's adjusted basis is also affected by his or her share of partnership debt. Under § 752, increases in a partner's share of debt are treated as contributions by the partner to the partnership.[32] Decreases in a partner's share of debt are treated as distributions from the partnership to the partner (distributions are discussed in Chapter 11). Partnership debt includes any partnership obligation that creates an asset; results in a deductible expense; or results in a nondeductible, noncapitalizable item at the partnership level. This definition includes most debt that would be considered a liability under financial accounting rules except for accounts payable of a cash basis partnership and certain contingent liabilities.

Two types of partnership debt exist. *Recourse debt* is partnership debt for which the partnership or at least one of the partners is personally liable. This liability can exist, for example, through the operation of state law or through personal guarantees that a partner makes to the creditor. Personal liability of a party related to a partner (under attribution rules) is treated as the personal liability of the partner. *Nonrecourse debt* is debt for which no party is personally liable. Lenders of nonrecourse debt generally require that collateral be pledged against the loan. Upon default, the lender can claim only the collateral, not the partners' personal assets.

------

32. Reg. § 1.752–1.

How liabilities are shared among the partners depends upon when the liability was incurred. If the debt was created before January 29, 1989, the rules are relatively straightforward. Recourse debt is shared among the partners in accordance with their loss sharing ratios while nonrecourse debt is shared among the partners in accordance with the way they share partnership profits. Although questions can arise about the calculation of the profit or loss sharing ratios and the treatment of personal guarantees of debt, the rules for sharing this earlier debt are generally easy to apply.

The rules for sharing partnership debt created after January 29, 1989, are much more complex. A complete analysis of these rules is beyond the scope of this text. The basic principles contained in these rules, however, can be easily understood.

Recourse debt created after January 29, 1989, is shared in accordance with a *constructive liquidation* scenario. This scenario assumes that most partnership assets become worthless and are sold for this worthless value. The losses on the sales are then allocated among the partners according to their loss sharing ratios. These losses reduce the partners' capital accounts. Any partner with a negative balance in his or her capital account will be treated as contributing cash to the partnership to restore that negative balance to zero. The liabilities are deemed to be paid with the cash that would be contributed by the partners, and, immediately thereafter, the partnership is treated as being liquidated. The amount of cash that each partner would contribute under this scenario to restore his or her negative capital account is the amount that the partner shares in partnership liabilities.

--------------------------------- EXAMPLE 20 ---------------------------------

On January 1 of the current year, A and B each contribute $20,000 cash to the newly created AB General Partnership. Each partner has a 50% interest in partnership capital, profits, and losses. The first year of partnership operations resulted in the following balance sheet as of December 31:

	Basis	Fair Market Value
Cash	$12,000	$12,000
Receivables	7,000	7,000
Land and buildings	50,000	50,000
	$69,000	$69,000
Recourse payables	$30,000	$30,000
A, capital	19,500	19,500
B, capital	19,500	19,500
	$69,000	$69,000

The recourse debt is shared in accordance with the constructive liquidation scenario. All of the partnership assets are deemed to be worthless and are sold for that worthless amount. This creates a loss of $69,000 ($12,000 + $7,000 + $50,000), which is allocated equally between the two partners. The $34,500 loss allocated to each partner creates negative capital accounts of $15,000 each for A and B. If the partnership were actually liquidated, each partner would contribute $15,000 cash to the partnership; the cash would be used to pay the partnership recourse payables; and the partnership would be liquidated. Because each partner would be required to contribute $15,000 to pay the liabilities, each shares in $15,000 of the recourse payables. Accordingly, A and B will each have an adjusted basis for their partnership interests of $34,500 ($19,500 + $15,000) on December 31. ◆

--------------------------------- EXAMPLE 21 ---------------------------------

Assume the same facts as in Example 20, except that the partners will allocate partnership losses 60% to A and 40% to B. The constructive liquidation scenario will result in the $69,000 loss being allocated $41,400 to A and $27,600 to B. As a result, A's capital account will have a negative balance of $21,900, and B's account will have a negative balance of $8,100. Each partner will be deemed to contribute cash equal to these negative capital accounts, and the cash would be used to pay the recourse liabilities under the liquidation scenario. Accordingly, A and B will share $21,900 and $8,100, respectively, in the recourse debt. ◆

Nonrecourse debt created after January 29, 1989, generally is shared among the partners in the same way they share deductions related to the debt. An exception to the general rule occurs, however, for debt where a minimum gain exists or where § 704(c) [precontribution gain or loss] principles must be applied. The minimum gain exception is beyond the scope of this text. The following example illustrates the § 704(c) exception.

--- EXAMPLE 22 ---

Y contributes an asset to the partnership in exchange for a one-third interest in the capital, profits, and losses of the partnership. The asset has an adjusted basis to Y of $24,000 and a fair market value on the contribution date of $50,000. The asset is encumbered by a nonrecourse note (created June 15, 1992) of $35,000. The Regulations provide that the first $11,000 of the nonrecourse debt is allocated to Y under § 704(c) principles. The § 704(c) amount is the excess of the $35,000 nonrecourse debt transferred over the $24,000 adjusted basis of the contributed property. The remaining $24,000 nonrecourse debt is shared according to the deduction sharing ratio, of which Y's share is $8,000. Therefore, Y shares in $19,000 ($11,000 + $8,000) of the nonrecourse debt. ◆

Other Factors Affecting Basis Calculations. The partner's basis is also affected by (1) postacquisition contributions of cash or property to the partnership; (2) postacquisition distributions of cash or property from the partnership; and (3) special calculations that are designed to allow the full deduction of percentage depletion for oil and gas wells. Postacquisition contributions of cash or property affect basis in the same manner as contributions made upon the creation of the partnership. Postacquisition distributions of cash or property reduce basis. The details of the postacquisition distribution rules are discussed in Chapter 11.

--- EXAMPLE 23 ---

E is a one-third partner in the M Partnership. On January 1, 1992, E's basis in his partnership interest was $50,000. During 1992, the calendar year, accrual basis partnership generated ordinary taxable income of $200,000. It also received $60,000 of interest income from City of Buffalo bonds, and it paid $2,000 in nondeductible bribes to local law enforcement officials, so that the police would not notify the IRS about the products that the entity had imported without paying the proper $15,000 in tariffs. On July 1, 1992, E contributed $20,000 cash and a computer (zero basis to him) to the partnership. E's monthly draw from the partnership is $3,000; this is not a guaranteed payment. The only liabilities that the partnership has incurred are trade accounts payable. On January 1, 1992, the trade accounts payable totaled $45,000; this account balance was $21,000 on January 1, 1993.

E's basis in the partnership on December 31, 1992, is $112,000, computed as follows:

Beginning balance	$ 50,000
Share of ordinary partnership income	66,667
Share of exempt income	20,000
Share of nondeductible expenditures	(667)
E's basis in noncash capital contribution	–0–
Additional cash contributions	20,000
Capital withdrawal	(36,000)
Share of net decrease in partnership liabilities	(8,000)
	$112,000

◆

———————————— EXAMPLE 24 ————————————

Assume the same facts as in Example 23. If E withdraws cash of $112,000 from the partnership on January 1, 1993, the withdrawal reduces his basis to zero. He has recognized his share of the partnership's corresponding income throughout his association with the entity, via the annual flow-through of his share of the partnership's income and expense items. In addition, the $20,000 municipal bond interest retains its nontaxable character in this distribution. E receives such assets as a part of his capital withdrawal because his basis was increased in 1992 when the partnership received the interest income. ◆

Generally, a partner is required to compute his or her adjusted basis only at the end of the partnership year. This spares the partner the inconvenience of making day-to-day calculations of basis. When a partnership interest is sold, exchanged, or retired, however, the partner must compute his or her adjusted basis as of the date the transaction occurs. Computation of the gain or loss requires an accurate calculation of the partner's adjusted basis on the transaction date.

Partner's Adjusted Basis—Special Rule. Sometimes partners may not be able to calculate the adjusted basis of their interest according to the rules outlined above. The partnership records may have been lost or stolen, or the partnership interest may have been received from a donor who failed to maintain accurate records. Fortunately, a special rule comes to the rescue. The rule states that a partner's adjusted basis may be simply his or her proportionate dollar interest in the adjusted basis of partnership property. It may be used when

1. the partner cannot practicably compute his or her basis under the general rules outlined above; or
2. the IRS is satisfied that the calculation of basis under the special rule will not vary substantially from the basis that would have been computed under the general rules.[33]

———————————— EXAMPLE 25 ————————————

P received a gift of a partnership interest from her father 10 years ago. P is going to sell her partnership interest during the current year and asks her tax adviser how to calculate her adjusted basis for the interest. The adviser determines that it is impossible to compute her adjusted basis in the more direct manner preferred by the Code. P has never calculated her adjusted basis previously, and her father's records were destroyed in a fire several years before his death last year. P does know, however, that her one-third interest in the adjusted basis of partnership property is $25,000. Therefore, upon the special rule, P's adjusted basis for her partnership interest is deemed to be $25,000. ◆

Figure 10-3 summarizes the rules for computing a partner's basis for his or her partnership interest.

TUES

Loss Limitations

Partnership losses flow through to the partners for use on their tax returns. However, the amount and nature of the losses that may be used by a partner for tax computational purposes may be limited. When limitations apply, all or a portion of the losses are held in suspension until a triggering condition occurs. At that later date, the losses can be used to determine the partner's tax liability.

---

33. § 705(b).

Three different limitations may apply to partnership losses that are passed through to a partner. The first is the overall limitation contained in § 704(d). This limitation allows losses only to the extent the partner has adjusted basis for his or her partnership interest. Losses that are deductible under the overall limitation may then be subject to the at-risk limitation of § 465. Losses are only deductible under this provision if the partner has at-risk basis for his or her partnership interest. Any losses that survive this second limitation may be subject to a third limitation, the passive loss rules of § 469. Only losses that make it through these applicable limitations are deductible on the partner's tax return.

EXAMPLE 26

A is a partner in a partnership that does not invest in real estate. On January 1, 1992, A's adjusted basis for her partnership interest is $50,000, and her at-risk basis is $35,000. Her share of losses from the partnership for 1992 is $60,000, all of which is passive. She has one other passive income-producing investment that produced $25,000 of passive income during 1992.

A will be able to deduct $25,000 of partnership losses on her Form 1040 for 1992. Her deductible loss is calculated as follows:

Applicable Provision	Deductible Loss	Suspended Loss
Overall limitation	*Basis →* $50,000	$10,000 *carryover*
At-risk limitation	35,000	15,000 *carryover*
Passive loss limitation	25,000	10,000 *carryover*
Passive losses are ded only to Passive Income		35,000 *carryover*

A can deduct only $50,000 under the overall limitation. Of this $50,000, only $35,000 is deductible under the at-risk limitation. Under the passive loss limitation, passive losses can only be deducted against passive income. Thus, A can deduct only $25,000 on her return in 1992. ◆

Overall Limitation. A partner's deduction of flow-through partnership losses is limited by the overall limitation to the adjusted basis of the partner's ownership interest at the end of the partnership year, before considering any losses for that year. Distributions and gains recognized during the year are taken into account before losses are applied against basis.

Losses that cannot be deducted because of this rule are suspended and carried forward (never back) for use against future increases in the partner's interest basis. Such increases might result from additional capital contributions, additional debts, or future income.

FIGURE 10–3

Partner's Basis in Partnership Interest

Price paid for interest as an original contribution to the partnership or to a partner or former partner (including share of partnership debt) or gift or inherited basis

+ Since interest acquired, partner's share of partnership's

■ Debt increase

■ Income items

■ Exempt income items

■ Excess of depletion deductions over adjusted basis of property subject to depletion

+ Partner's contributions

− Since interest acquired, partner's share of partnership's

■ Debt decrease

■ Loss items

■ Nondeductible items not chargeable to a capital account

■ Special depletion deduction for oil and gas wells

− Partner's distributions and withdrawals

The basis of a partner's interest can never be negative.

But must keep track of any carryover losses on some type of worksheet.

—————————— EXAMPLE 27 ——————————

C and D do business as the CD Partnership, sharing profits and losses equally. All parties use the calendar year. At the start of the current year, the basis of C's partnership interest is $25,000. The partnership sustained an operating loss of $80,000 in the current year and earned a profit of $70,000 in the next year. For the current year, only $25,000 of C's $40,000 allocable share of the partnership loss (one-half of $80,000 loss) can be deducted under the overall limitation. As a result, the basis of C's partnership interest is zero as of January 1 of the following year, and C must carry forward the remaining $15,000 of partnership losses. ◆

—————————— EXAMPLE 28 ——————————

Assume the same facts as in Example 27. Since the partnership earned a profit of $70,000 for the next calendar year, C reports net partnership income of $20,000 ($35,000 distributive share of income less the $15,000 carryforward loss). The basis of C's partnership interest becomes $20,000. ◆

In Example 27, C's entire $40,000 share of the current year partnership loss could have been deducted under the overall limitation in the current year if C had contributed an additional $15,000 or more in capital by December 31. Alternatively, if the partnership had incurred additional debt of $30,000 or more by the end of the current year, C's basis would have been increased to permit the loss to be deducted in that year. Thus, if partnership losses are projected for a given year, careful tax planning can ensure their deductibility under the overall limitation.

At-Risk Limitation. The at-risk rules generally limit the loss deduction of individuals and closely held corporations from business and income-producing activities to amounts that are economically invested in the enterprise (adjusted basis of contributed property, cash contributions, recourse debt, and the earnings share that has not been withdrawn or used to absorb losses).[34] A closely held corporation exists when five or fewer individuals own more than 50 percent of the entity's stock under appropriate attribution and ownership rules.

Some or all of the partners are personally liable for partnership recourse debt. This debt is included in the adjusted basis of the partners who will have to pay this debt from their own resources if the partnership fails to pay the creditor. In general, these partners will also include the debt in their at-risk basis.

No partner, however, carries any financial risk on nonrecourse debt. Therefore, as a general rule, partners cannot include nonrecourse debt in their at-risk basis even though that debt is included in the adjusted basis of their partnership interest. There is an exception to this general rule, however, that applies in many cases. Real estate nonrecourse financing provided by a bank, retirement plan, or similar party or by a Federal, state, or local government generally is deemed to be at risk.[35] Consequently, although the general rule provides that nonrecourse debt is not at risk, the overriding exception may provide that it is deemed to be at risk.

When determining a partner's loss deduction, the overall limitation rule is invoked first (the deduction is limited to the partner's interest basis at the end of the partnership year). Then, the at-risk provisions are applied to see if the remaining loss is still deductible. Suspended losses are carried forward until a partner has a sufficient amount at risk in the activity to absorb them.[36]

---

34. § 465(a).

35. § 465(b)(6).

36. § 465(a)(2).

EXAMPLE 29

U invests $5,000 in the CC Limited Partnership as a general partner. Shortly thereafter, the partnership acquires the master recording of a well-known vocalist for $250,000 ($50,000 from the partnership and $200,000 secured from a local bank via a *recourse* mortgage). U's share of the recourse debt is $10,000, and his interest basis is $15,000 ($5,000 cash investment + $10,000 debt share). Since the debt is recourse, U's at-risk amount is also $15,000. U's share of partnership losses in the first year of operations (due principally to depreciation of the master recording) is $11,000. U is entitled to deduct $11,000 of partnership losses because this amount is less than both his interest basis and at-risk amount. ◆

EXAMPLE 30

Assume the same facts as in Example 29, except that the bank loan is nonrecourse in nature (the partners have no direct liability under the terms of the loan in the case of a default). U's interest basis in the entity still is $15,000, but he can deduct only $5,000 of the flow-through loss, as the amount that he has at risk in the investment does not include the nonrecourse debt. ◆ *This time the At Risk basis was NOT Increased by the debt.*

Passive Activity Rules.   A partnership loss share also may be disallowed under the passive activity rules. Although these rules are not applicable per se to partnerships, they most assuredly affect how and when a partner's loss can be deducted. The rules require taxpayers to separate their activities into three groups:

- *Active.* Earned income, such as salary and wages; income or loss from a trade or business in which the taxpayer materially participates; and guaranteed payments from a partnership for services.
- *Portfolio.* Annuity income, interest, dividends, guaranteed payments from a partnership for interest on capital, royalties not derived in the ordinary course of a trade or business, and gains and losses from disposal of investment assets.
- *Passive.* Income from a trade or business in which the taxpayer does not materially participate on a regular, continuous, and substantial basis,[37] or income from a rental activity.

Material participation in an activity is determined annually, as proven by the taxpayer. Thus, a Maine vacation resort operator investing in a California grape farm or an electrical engineer employed in Virginia investing in an Iowa corn and hog farm may have difficulty proving material participation in the activities (regular, continuous, and substantial involvement with daily operations).

Rent income from real or personal property generally is passive income, regardless of the taxpayer's level of participation. Exceptions are made for rent income from activities where substantial services are provided (hotel, motel, or other transient lodging and income from equipment rentals to various users for short periods).

Usually, passive activity losses can be offset only against passive activity income.[38] In determining the net passive activity loss for a year, generally losses and income from all passive activities are aggregated. The amount of suspended losses carried forward from a particular activity is determined by the ratio of the net loss from that activity to the aggregate net loss from all passive activities for the year. A special rule for rental real estate (discussed in the following section) allows a limited $25,000 offset against nonpassive income.[39]

37. §§ 469(c)(1) and (2).

38. § 469(a)(1).

39. § 469(i).

A taxpayer making a taxable disposition of an entire interest in a passive activity generally takes a full deduction for suspended losses in the year of disposal.[40] Suspended losses are deductible against income in the following order: income or gain from the passive activity, net income or gain from all passive activities, and other income. When a passive activity is transferred in a nontaxable exchange (e.g., a like-kind exchange or contribution to a partnership), suspended losses are deductible only to the extent of recognized gains. Remaining losses are deducted on disposal of the property received in the exchange.

─────────────── EXAMPLE 31 ───────────────

B has several investments in passive activities that generate aggregate losses of $10,000 in the current year. B wants to deduct all of these losses in the current year. To assure a loss deduction, she needs to invest in some passive activities that generate income. One of her long-time friends, an entrepreneur in the women's apparel business, is interested in opening a new apparel store in a nearby community. B is willing to finance a substantial part of the expansion but doesn't want to get involved with day-to-day operations. B also wants to limit any possible loss to her initial investment.

After substantial discussions, B and her friend decide to form a limited partnership, which will own the new store. B's friend will be the general partner, and B will be a limited partner. B invests $100,000, and her friend invests $50,000 and sweat equity (provides managerial skills and know-how). Each has a 50% interest in profits and losses. In the first year of operations, the store generates a profit of $30,000. Since B's share of the profit ($15,000) is passive activity income, it can be fully utilized against any passive activity losses. Thus, via her share of the apparel store profits, B assures a full deduction of her $10,000 of passive activity losses. ◆

Rental Real Estate Losses. Up to $25,000 of passive losses from rental real estate can be offset by individuals against active and portfolio income in any one year. The $25,000 maximum is reduced by 50 percent of the difference between the taxpayer's modified adjusted gross income (AGI) and $100,000. Thus, when the taxpayer's AGI reaches $150,000, the offset is eliminated.

The offset is available to those who actively (rather than materially) participate in rental real estate activities. Active participation is an easier test to meet. Unlike material participation, it does not require regular, continuous, and substantial involvement with the activity. However, the individual must own at least 10 percent of the fair market value of all interests in the rental property and either contribute to the activity in a significant and bona fide way regarding management decisions or actively participate in arranging for others to make such decisions.

─────────────── EXAMPLE 32 ───────────────

X invests $10,000 cash in the AXE Limited Partnership in the current year for a 10% limited interest in capital and profits. Shortly thereafter, the partnership purchases rental real estate subject to a nonconvertible qualified nonrecourse mortgage of $150,000 obtained from a commercial bank. X has no other passive loss activities during the current year.

X does not participate in any of AXE's activities. X's share of losses from AXE's first year of operations is $27,000. Before considering the loss, X's basis in the partnership interest is $25,000 [$10,000 cash + (10% × $150,000 debt)], and the loss deduction is limited to this amount. X's AGI before considering the loss is $60,000. The debt is exempted from the at-risk provisions, and it seems that X should be allowed to deduct the $25,000 loss share from portfolio or active income. However, the loss may not be offset against this income, since X is not an active participant for the $25,000 passive activity loss deduction. ◆

─────────────

40. § 469(g).

Many types of transactions may occur between a partnership and one of its partners. The partner may contribute property to the partnership, perform services for the partnership, or receive distributions from the partnership. The partner may borrow money from or lend money to the partnership. Property may be bought and sold between the partner and the partnership. Several of these transactions were discussed earlier in the chapter. The remaining types of partner-partnership transactions are the focus of this section.

Tues

Guaranteed Payments

If a partnership makes a payment to a partner in his or her capacity as a partner, the payment may be a draw against the partner's share of partnership income; a return of some or all of the partner's original capital contribution; or a guaranteed payment. A *guaranteed payment* is a payment for services performed by the partner or for the use of the partner's capital. The payment may not be determined by reference to partnership income. Guaranteed payments are usually expressed as a fixed-dollar amount or as a percentage of capital that the partner has invested in the partnership.

EXAMPLE 33

P, R, and S formed the PRS Partnership in 1992. According to the partnership agreement, P is to perform services for the partnership and receive a $21,000 distribution from the entity every year, payable in 12 monthly installments. R is to receive an amount that is equal to 18% of his capital account, as it is computed by the firm's accountant at the beginning of the year, payable in 12 monthly installments. S is the partnership's advertising specialist. He withdraws 3% of the partnership's net income every month for his personal use. P and R have received guaranteed payments from the partnership, but S has not. ◆

Guaranteed payments resemble the salary, interest, or rental expense payments of other businesses and receive similar treatment under partnership tax law.[41] Thus, in contrast to the provision that usually applies to withdrawals of assets by partners from their partnerships, guaranteed payments are deductible by the entity, and on the last day of the partnership's tax year, the recipients must report such income separately from their usual partnership allocations.

Separate Line Item on k1

EXAMPLE 34

Continue with the situation that was introduced in Example 33. For calendar year 1992, P received the $21,000 that was provided by the partnership agreement, R's guaranteed payment for 1992 was $18,000, and S withdrew $20,000 under his personal expenditures clause. Before considering these amounts, the partnership's ordinary income for 1992 was $650,000.

The partnership can deduct its payments to P and R, so the final amount of its 1992 ordinary income is $611,000 ($650,000 − $21,000 − $18,000). Thus, each of the equal partners is allocated $203,667 of ordinary partnership income for their 1992 individual income tax returns ($611,000 ÷ 3). In addition, P must report $21,000 of salary income, and R must include the $18,000 interest in his 1992 gross income. S's partnership draw is deemed to have come from his allocated $203,667 (or from the accumulated partnership income that was taxed to him in prior years) and is not taxed separately to him. ◆

EXAMPLE 35

Assume the same facts as in Example 34, except that S's withdrawals total $1,000, and ordinary partnership income (before considering the partners' distributions) was

---

41. § 707(c).

$30,000. The deductions for the guaranteed payments reduce the final ordinary income of the partnership to a $9,000 loss ($30,000 − $21,000 − $18,000). Thus, P's individual income tax return includes her $21,000 salary and the $3,000 partnership loss. R's gross income includes the $18,000 interest and his allocable $3,000 partnership loss. S's return merely includes his $3,000 share of the partnership loss. Guaranteed payments, like any other deductible expenses of a partnership, can create an ordinary loss for the entity. In this manner, the partners can allocate a higher or lower proportion of the tax benefits among them. ◆

EXAMPLE 36

Assume the same facts as in Example 33, except that the partnership's tax year ends on March 31, 1993. The total amount of the guaranteed payments is taxable to the partners on that date. Thus, even though P received 9 of her 12 payments for fiscal 1992 in calendar 1992, all of her salary is recognized in 1993. Similarly, all of R's interest income is taxable to him in 1993 and not when it is received. The deduction for, and the gross income from, guaranteed payments are allowed on the same date that all of the other income and expense items relative to the partnership are allocated to the partners (on the last day of the entity's tax year). ◆

Other Transactions between a Partner and a Partnership

Certain transactions between a partner and the partnership are treated as if the partner were an outsider, dealing with the partnership at arm's length.[42] Loan transactions, rental payments, and sales of property between the partner and the partnership are generally treated in this manner. In addition, payments for services are treated this way when the services are short-term technical services that the partner also provides for parties other than the partnership.

EXAMPLE 37

A, a one-third partner in the ABC Partnership, owns a tract of land that the partnership wishes to purchase. The land has a fair market value of $30,000 and an adjusted basis to A of $17,000. If A sells the land to the partnership, he will recognize a $13,000 gain on the sale, and the partnership will take a $30,000 cost basis in the land. If the land had a fair market value of $10,000 on the sale date, A would recognize a $7,000 loss. ◆

The timing of a payment by an accrual basis partnership to a cash basis service partner depends upon whether the payment is a guaranteed payment or a payment to a partner who is treated as an outsider. A guaranteed payment is includible in the partner's income when properly accrued by the partnership, even though the payment may not be made to the partner until the next taxable year. Conversely, the partner's method of accounting controls if the payment is treated as made to an outsider. Thus, the partnership cannot recognize the payment on its books until it actually makes the payment to the partner.

EXAMPLE 38

C, a cash basis taxpayer, is a partner in the accrual basis ABC Partnership. On December 31, 1992, the partnership accrues but does not pay $10,000 for deductible services that C performed for the partnership during the year. Both C and the partnership are calendar year taxpayers.

If the $10,000 accrual is a guaranteed payment, the partnership deducts the services in its calendar year ended December 31, 1992, and C includes the $10,000 in her

---

42. § 707(a).

income for the 1992 calendar year. The fact that C is a cash basis taxpayer and does not actually receive the cash in 1992 is irrelevant.

Conversely, if the payment is classified as a payment to an outsider, the partnership cannot deduct the payment until C actually receives the cash. If, for example, C receives the cash on March 25, 1993, the partnership deducts the payment and C recognizes the income on that date. ◆

An exception applies to sales of property between an individual and a partnership when the person owns, directly or indirectly, more than 50 percent of partnership capital or profits. This exception provides that no loss can be recognized on the transaction.[43] The disallowed loss may not vanish entirely, however. If the transferee eventually sells the property at a gain, the disallowed loss reduces the gain that the transferee would otherwise recognize.

Example 39

W sells land (adjusted basis to him, $30,000; fair market value, $45,000) to a partnership in which he controls a 60% capital interest. The partnership pays him $20,000 for the land. W cannot deduct his $10,000 realized loss. The sale apparently was not at arm's length, but the taxpayer's intentions are irrelevant. W and the partnership are related parties, and the loss is disallowed.

When the partnership sells the land to an outsider at a later date, it receives a sales price of $44,000. The partnership can offset the recognition of its realized gain on the subsequent sale ($44,000 sales proceeds − $20,000 adjusted basis = $24,000) by the amount of the prior disallowed loss ($30,000 − $20,000 = $10,000). Thus, it recognizes a $14,000 gain on its sale of the land. ◆

Using a similar rationale, any gain that is realized on a sale or exchange between a partner and a partnership in which the partner controls a capital or profit interest of 50 percent or more must be recognized as ordinary income, unless the asset is a capital asset in the hands of the purchaser.[44]

Example 40

Z purchases some land (adjusted basis, $30,000; fair market value, $45,000) from a partnership in which he controls a 90% profit interest, for $45,000. The land was a capital asset to the partnership. If Z holds the land for investment purposes, the partnership recognizes a $15,000 capital gain. However, if Z is a land developer and the property is not a capital asset to him, the partnership must recognize $15,000 ordinary income from the same sale, even though the property was a capital asset to the entity. ◆

Partners as Employees

A partner generally does not qualify as an employee for tax purposes. Thus, a partner receiving guaranteed payments will not be regarded as an employee for purposes of withholding taxes or for qualified pension and profit sharing plans. Moreover, since a partner is not an employee of his or her partnership, the entity cannot deduct its payments for the partner's fringe benefits. In fact, the partner's distributive share of ordinary partnership income is subject to the Federal self-employment tax.[45]

Concept Summary 10–3 reviews partner-partnership transactions.

---

43. § 707(b).
44. § 707(b)(2).

45. § 1402(a).

CONCEPT SUMMARY 10–3
PARTNER-PARTNERSHIP TRANSACTIONS

1. Partners can transact business with their partnerships in a nonpartner capacity. These transactions include such things as the sale and exchange of property, rentals, etc.
2. Losses are disallowed between a partner or related party and a partnership when the partner or related party owns more than a 50% interest in the partnership's capital or profits. When there is income from a related party sale, it is ordinary if the property is a capital asset to the transferor, but not to the transferee.
3. Guaranteed payments to partners generally are deductible to the partnership in determining the partnership's taxable income (ordinary income) and includible in the receiving partner's gross income for the partnership year that ends with or within the partner's tax year under the partnership's method of accounting.

Choosing Partnership Taxation

TAX PLANNING
CONSIDERATIONS

Concept Summary 10–4 enumerates various factors that the owners of a business should consider in deciding whether to use a C corporation, S corporation, or partnership as a means of doing business. The reader should refer back to this listing when he or she finishes reading Chapters 11 (advanced partnership topics) and 12 (S corporations). Chapter 13 includes a more elaborate discussion of the tax effects of various forms of conducting business.

Formation and Operation of a Partnership

Potential partners should be cautious in transferring assets to a partnership, so that they are not required to recognize any gain upon the creation of the entity. The exceptions to the nonrecognition provisions of § 721 are relatively straightforward and resemble the corresponding portions of § 351. However, any partner can make a tax-deferred contribution of additional assets to the entity after the inception of the partnership. This possibility is not available to less-than-controlling shareholders in a corporation.

The partners should anticipate the tax benefits and pitfalls that are presented in Subchapter K and should take appropriate actions to resolve any resulting problems. Typically, all that is needed is an appropriate provision in the partnership agreement (e.g., with respect to differing allocation percentages for gains and losses). Recall, however, that a special allocation of income, expense, or credit items in the partnership agreement must satisfy certain requirements before it will be respected by the IRS.

Transactions between Partners and Partnerships

Partners should be careful when engaging in transactions with the partnership to ensure that no negative tax results occur. A partner who owns a majority of the partnership generally should not sell property at a loss to the partnership, since the loss will be disallowed. Similarly, a majority partner typically would not want to sell a capital asset to the partnership at a gain, if the asset is to be used by the partnership as other than a capital asset. The gain on this transaction is taxed as ordinary income to the selling partner rather than as capital gain.

As an alternative to selling property to a partnership, the partner may want to lease it to the partnership. The partner will recognize rent income, and the partnership will have a rent expense. If the partner needs more cash immediately, the partner may wish to sell the property to an outside third party who will lease the property to the partnership for a fair rental.

The timing of payments by accrual basis partnerships to cash basis partners will vary depending on whether the payment is a guaranteed payment or is treated as a payment to an outsider. If the payment is a guaranteed payment, the timing will occur when the partnership properly accrues the payment. Conversely, if the payment is treated as a payment to an outsider, the actual date the payment is made will control the timing of the transaction.

Preserving Cost Recovery Deductions on Contributed Property

If the contributed property is subject to depreciation recapture, ordinary income results. Unless the partnership is considered the original user of depreciable property, it will not be allowed to deviate from the contributing partner's recovery period or method. Thus, consideration should be given to retaining ownership of the property and leasing it to the partnership.

CONCEPT SUMMARY 10–4
ADVANTAGES AND DISADVANTAGES OF THE PARTNERSHIP FORM

The partnership form may be attractive when one or more of the following factors is present:

- The entity is generating net taxable losses and/or valuable tax credits, which will be of use directly to the owners.
- The entity does not generate material amounts of tax preference and adjustment items, which would increase the alternative minimum tax liabilities of its owners.
- The entity is generating net passive income, which its owners can use to claim immediate deductions for net passive losses that they have generated from other sources.
- Other means by which to reduce the effects of the double taxation of business income (e.g., compensation to owners, interest, and rental payments) have been exhausted.
- Given the asset holdings and distribution practices of the entity, the possibility of liability under the accumulated earnings and personal holding company taxes is significant.
- Restrictions relative to S corporation status (e.g., the 35-shareholder maximum or the restriction to one class of outstanding stock) are not attractive, perhaps because of elaborate executive compensation arrangements or an anticipated public offering of stock.
- The owners wish to make special allocations of certain income or deduction items. Such allocations are not possible under the C or S corporation forms.
- The owners anticipate liquidation of the entity within a period of less than 10 years. Such transactions would generate entity-level recognized gains relative to appreciated property sold or distributed because of the liquidation and could make the entity subject to S corporation penalty taxes.
- Adequate basis amounts in the partnership exist; these facilitate the deduction of flow-through losses and the assignment of an adequate basis to assets distributed in-kind to the partners.

The partnership form may be less attractive when one or more of the following factors is present:

- The entity is generating net taxable income, which will be taxed directly to the owners who do not necessarily receive any funds with which to pay the tax.
- The type of income that the entity is generating (e.g., business and portfolio income) is not as attractive to its owners as net passive income would be because the owners could use net passive income to offset the net passive losses that they have generated on their own.
- Congress enacts tax legislation raising the maximum marginal tax rate applicable to individuals above that applicable to C corporations.

Drafting the Partnership Agreement

Although a written partnership agreement is not required, many rules governing the tax consequences to partners and their partnerships refer to such an agreement. Remember that a partner's distributive share of income, gain, loss, deduction, or credit is determined in accordance with the partnership agreement. Consequently, if taxpayers operating a business in partnership form want a measure of certainty as to the tax consequences of their activities, a carefully drafted partnership agreement is crucial. An agreement that sets forth the obligations, rights, and powers of the partners should prove invaluable in settling controversies among them and provide some degree of certainty as to the tax consequences of the partners' actions.

PROBLEM MATERIALS

DISCUSSION QUESTIONS

1. What is a partnership for Federal income tax purposes? *10-5*

2. Distinguish between the entity concept and the aggregate or conduit concept of a partnership. *10-4 &5*

3. How is the basis of a contributing partner's interest determined? *10-3*

4. If appreciated property is contributed to a partnership in exchange for a partnership interest, what basis does the partnership take in the property? *Ex 11*

5. Why is a partnership required to file any tax return? *10-4 &5 and 14 &15*

6. What is the purpose of the three rules that implement the economic effect test? *Example 17*

7. What effect does the contribution of property subject to a liability have on the basis of the contributing partner's interest? What is the effect on the basis of the other partners' interests? *FIGURE 10-3*

8. To what extent can partners deduct their distributive shares of partnership losses? What happens to any unused losses? *Examples 26 - 28*

9. Discuss the applicability of the at-risk rules to a partnership and its partners. *Pg 10-25 & Ex. 29*

10. What are guaranteed payments? *Ex 33 to 36*

11. Compare the nonrecognition of gain or loss provision on contributions to a partnership with the similar provision with respect to corporate formation. What are the major differences and similarities? *10-31 C/S 10-4 & Chapter 3*

PROBLEMS

12. D is an attorney who is financially quite successful. M is a real estate developer who has little cash for investment. The two decide to buy some real estate. D will contribute the money to buy the properties and have veto power over which properties to purchase. M will make all other decisions. Profits and losses from the operation will be shared equally. *10-5*

    a. Is this a partnership for tax purposes? Why or why not?
    b. Would your answer change if D had no veto power and was to receive a guaranteed 10% annual return on her money?

13. L and K form an equal partnership with a cash contribution of $50,000 from L and a property contribution (adjusted basis of $30,000 and a fair market value of $50,000) from K. *Example 11 & C/S 10-1*

    a. How much gain, if any, must L recognize on the transfer? Must K recognize any gain?
    b. What is L's interest basis in the partnership?

c. What is K's interest basis in the partnership?

d. What basis does the partnership take in the property transferred by K?

14. The cash basis AB Partnership incurred the following organization and syndication costs in calendar 1992:

Attorney fees for preparing partnership agreement	$2,100
Printing costs for preparing documents that were used to help sell the partnership interests	4,000
Accounting fees for tax advice of an organizational nature	2,400

The attorney fees and printing costs were incurred and paid in 1992. The accounting fees were incurred in December 1992 and paid in February 1993. If the partnership begins business in July 1992, how much of the organization costs can be amortized in 1992? In 1993?

15. R, P, and M form an equal partnership on January 1 of the current year. Each partner and RPM use the cash method of accounting. For reporting purposes, R uses a calendar year, P uses an August 31 fiscal year, and M uses a June 30 fiscal year.

a. What is RPM's required tax year under the least aggregate deferral method?

b. Assuming that RPM cannot establish a natural business year that differs from your answer in (a), what tax year can RPM elect that provides the partners with the *greatest* aggregate additional deferral?

16. X and Y are equal members of the XY Partnership. They are real estate investors who formed the partnership two years ago with equal cash contributions. XY then purchased a piece of land.

On January 1 of the current year, to acquire a one-third interest in the entity, Z contributed to the partnership some land he had held for investment, fair market value of $20,000. Z purchased the land three years ago for $25,000. No special allocation agreements were in effect before or after Z was admitted to the partnership. The XYZ Partnership holds all land for investment.

Immediately before Z's property contribution, the balance sheet of the XY Partnership was as follows:

	Basis	FMV		Basis	FMV
Land	$5,000	$40,000	X, capital	$2,500	$20,000
			Y, capital	2,500	20,000
	$5,000	$40,000		$5,000	$40,000

a. At the contribution date, what are Z's date basis and basis of interest in the XYZ Partnership?

b. On June 30 of the current year, the partnership sold the land contributed by Z for $20,000. How much is the recognized gain or loss, and how is it allocated among the partners?

c. Prepare a balance sheet for the XYZ Partnership immediately after the land sale.

17. Assume the same facts as in Problem 16, with the following exceptions.

■ The fair market value of the land contributed by Z declined after Z joined the partnership.

■ XYZ sold the land contributed by Z for $17,000.

a. How much is the recognized gain or loss, and how is it allocated among the partners?

b. Prepare a balance sheet for the XYZ Partnership immediately after the land sale, along with schedules that support the amount in each partner's capital account.

18. Assume the same facts as in Problem 16, with the following exceptions.

■ The fair market value of the land not contributed by Z declined after Z joined the partnership.

■ XYZ sold the land for $17,000.

a. How much is the recognized gain or loss, and how is it allocated among the partners?

b. Prepare a balance sheet for the XYZ Partnership immediately after the land sale, along with schedules that support the amount in each partner's capital account.

19. E and Z are equal partners in the accrual basis EZ Partnership. At the beginning of the current year, E's capital account has a balance of $10,000, and the partnership has recourse debts of $30,000 payable to unrelated parties. All partnership recourse debt is shared equally between the partners. The following information about EZ's operations for the current year is obtained from the partnership's records.

Taxable income	$48,000
Tax-exempt interest income	5,000
§ 1231 gain	6,200
Long-term capital gain	500
Long-term capital loss	100
Short-term capital loss	250
Charitable contribution to Girl Scouts	800
Cash distribution to E	10,000

50%

figure 10-3

Assume that year-end partnership debt payable to unrelated parties is $24,000.

a. What is E's basis in the partnership at the beginning of the year?
b. What is E's basis in the partnership at the end of the current year?

20. L, B, and R form the LBR Partnership on January 1 of the current year. In return for a 30% interest, L transfers property (basis of $24,000, fair market value of $37,500) subject to a nonrecourse liability of $15,000. The liability is assumed by the partnership. B transfers property (basis of $37,500, fair market value of $22,500) for a 30% interest, and R transfers cash of $30,000 for the remaining 40% interest.

a. How much gain must L recognize on the transfer?
b. What is L's basis of interest in the partnership?
c. How much loss may B recognize on the transfer?
d. What is B's basis of interest in the partnership?
e. What is R's basis of interest in the partnership?
f. What basis does the LBR Partnership take in the property transferred by L?
g. What is the partnership's basis in the property transferred by B?

Example 22

21. Assume the same facts as in Problem 20, except that the property contributed by L has a fair market value of $67,500 and is subject to a nonrecourse mortgage of $45,000.

a. How much gain must L recognize on the transfer?
b. What is L's basis of interest in the partnership?
c. What is B's basis of interest in the partnership?
d. What is R's basis of interest in the partnership?
e. What basis does the LBR Partnership take in the property transferred by L?

Example 22

22. J and K established the JK General Partnership on December 31 of the current year. The capital accounts are properly maintained, and each partner has to restore any deficit in his capital account. The partnership agreement provides that J will be allocated 90% of the partnership income, gains, losses, deductions, and credits until he has been allocated income and gains equal to his previous allocations of losses and deductions. Thereafter, all partnership items will be allocated equally. Each partner contributed $20,000 cash to the partnership in exchange for his partnership interest. The partnership used the $40,000 cash to help purchase a parcel of land for $100,000. The other $60,000 of financing for the land was obtained from a local bank. In addition to using the land as collateral, both partners are also personally liable on the note. How will the note be shared between the partners for purposes of computing each partner's adjusted basis for his partnership interest?

Ex: 20 & 21

23. The MGP General Partnership was created on January 1, 1992, by having M, G, and P each contribute $10,000 cash to the partnership in exchange for a one-third interest

Ex: 20 & 21

in partnership income, gains, losses, deductions, and credits. On December 31, 1992, the partnership balance sheet reads as follows:

	Basis	FMV
Assets	$40,000	$55,000
Recourse debt	$12,000	$12,000
M, capital	11,000	16,000
G, capital	11,000	16,000
P, capital	6,000	11,000
	$40,000	$55,000

P's capital account is less than M and P's capital accounts because P has withdrawn more cash than the other partners.

How do the partners share the recourse debt as of December 31, 1992?

24. A is a partner in the calendar year AD Partnership, which is not involved in real estate. Her share of the AD Partnership's losses for the current year is $50,000. Immediately before considering the deductibility of this loss, A's adjusted basis for her partnership interest is $40,000, and her at-risk basis for the interest is $28,000. A is also a partner in another partnership that allocated $13,000 of income to her. A works full-time in the other partnership but has never performed any services for the AD Partnership. Based upon this information, how much of the $50,000 loss can A deduct on her current calendar year return?

25. As of January 1 of last year, the outside basis and at-risk basis of D's 25% interest in the DEF Partnership were $24,000. D and the partnership use the calendar year for tax purposes. The partnership incurred an operating loss of $100,000 for last year and a profit of $8,000 for the current year. D is a material participant in the partnership.

    a. How much loss, if any, may D recognize for last year?
    b. How much net reportable income must D recognize for the current year?
    c. What is D's interest in the partnership as of January 1 of the current year?
    d. What is D's interest in the partnership as of January 1 of the next year?
    e. What year-end tax planning would you suggest to ensure that D can deduct his share of partnership losses?

26. FM and FT are equal partners in the calendar year F & F Partnership. FM uses a fiscal year ending June 30, and FT uses a calendar year. FM is paid an annual calendar year salary of $50,000. For the last calendar year, F & F's taxable income was $40,000. For the current calendar year, the partnership's taxable income is $50,000.

    a. What is the aggregate amount of income from the partnership that FM must report for his tax year that ends within the current calendar year?
    b. What is the aggregate amount of income from the partnership that FT must report for the current calendar year?
    c. If FM's annual salary is increased to $60,000 starting on January 1 of the current calendar year and the taxable income of the partnership for the last year and the current year are the same (i.e., $40,000 and $50,000), what is the aggregate amount of income from the partnership that FM must report for his tax year that ends within the current calendar year?

27. N, an equal partner in the MN Partnership, is to receive a payment of $20,000 for services plus 50% of the partnership's profits or losses. After deducting the $20,000 payment to N, the partnership has a loss of $12,000.

    a. How much, if any, of the $12,000 partnership loss will be allocated to N?
    b. What is the net income from the partnership that N must report on his personal income tax return?

28. D is a 50% owner of Philadelphia Cheese Treets, Inc., a C corporation. She receives a $5,000 monthly salary from the corporation, and Cheese Treets generates $200,000 taxable income for its tax year ending January 31, 1993.

a. How do these activities affect D's 1992 adjusted gross income?
b. Same as (a), except that Cheese Treets is a partnership. Treat D's salary as a guaranteed payment.

29. Four Lakes Partnership is owned by four sisters. A holds a 70% interest; each of the others owns 10%. A sells investment property to the partnership for its fair market value of $54,000 (basis of $72,000).

a. How much loss, if any, may A recognize?
b. If the partnership later sells the property for $81,000, how much gain must it recognize?
c. If A's basis in the investment property were $20,000 instead of $72,000, how much, if any, capital gain would she recognize on the sale?

E/: 39 & 40

30. Indicate whether the following statements are true or false.

a. Since a partnership is not a taxable entity, it is not required to file any type of tax return. *10-14*
b. Each partner can choose a different method of accounting and depreciation computation in determining his or her gross income from the entity. *10-9 & 10*
c. A partnership may not choose a tax year that is different from that of all of its principal partners. *10-13*
d. Generally, a transfer of appreciated property to a partnership results in recognized gain to the contributing partner at the time of the transfer. *F → § 721*
e. The period of time that a partner held the asset prior to its transfer to the partnership is included in the holding period of the asset for the partnership. *10-8*
f. A partner can carry forward, for an unlimited period of time, any operating losses that exceed his or her basis in the entity, provided the partner retains an ownership interest in the partnership. *10-24*
g. When a partner renders services to the entity in exchange for an unrestricted interest, he or she does not recognize any gross income. *10-7*
h. Losses on sales between a partner and the partnership always are non-deductible. *10-30*

31. For each of the following independent statements, indicate whether the tax attribute is applicable to regular corporations (C), partnerships (P), both business forms (B), or neither business form (N):

a. Restrictions are placed on the type and number of owners.
b. Business income is taxable to the owners rather than to the entity.
c. Distributions of earnings to the owners result in a tax deduction to the entity.
d. The characteristics of an entity's income flow through to the owners.
e. Capital gains are subject to tax at the entity level.
f. Organization costs can be amortized over a period of 60 months or more.

COMPREHENSIVE TAX RETURN PROBLEM

Marilyn Pearson (222–54–7580), Lowell Dries (759–85–4486), and Rebecca Wright (423–70–8476) are equal partners in PDW, a general partnership that provides public relations services to various small businesses. PDW's Federal I.D. number is 94–8423590. The partnership uses the cash method of accounting and adopted the calendar year for reporting. It began business operations on January 15, 1988. Its current address is 2986 Vulcan Drive, Birmingham, AL 35203. The partnership has total assets of $210,000 on December 31, 1991. The following information was taken from the partnership's income statement for the current year:

Receipts	
Fees collected	$160,200
Taxable interest	900
Tax-exempt interest	600
Long-term capital loss	(3,000)
Short-term capital gain	1,000

Payments	
Contribution to Birmingham U.—FMV	4,900
Employee salaries	39,000
Equipment rental	9,000
Office rentals paid	24,000
Salary, Rebecca Wright, managing partner	13,000
Entertainment and travel, subject to 20% rule	10,000
Payroll taxes	4,500
Depreciation	3,600
Repairs	2,100

The contribution to Birmingham University consisted of stock that the partnership had purchased in January 1991 for $4,500. The partnership claimed $3,600 depreciation for both tax and financial accounting purposes. Assume none of the depreciation creates a tax preference. Net income per books is $50,000. On January 1, 1991, each partner's financial and tax accounting capital account was $12,000. No additional capital contributions were made in 1991, and each partner withdrew $20,000 cash from the partnership during the year. The entity had $18,000 of recourse liabilities on hand on December 31, 1991, which the partners shared equally.

None of the partners, all U.S. citizens, sold any portion of their interests in the partnership during 1991. The partnership's operations are entirely restricted to the Birmingham metropolitan area. The partnership had no foreign operations, no foreign bank accounts, and no interest in any foreign trusts.

The IRS's business code for the partnership operations is 8740. The tax return is filed in Memphis, TN. PDW does not own an interest in any other partnership. The partnership is not classified as a tax shelter or as a publicly traded partnership.

a. Prepare Form 1065 and Schedule K for PDW Partnership, leaving blank any items where insufficient information has been provided. Omit Schedules A, D, and L and line 15 on Schedule K.

b. Prepare Schedule K–1 for Rebecca Wright, the designated Tax Matters Partner, who lives at 2022 Chandy Road, Homewood, AL 35209. Omit line 15 on her Schedule K–1.

RESEARCH PROBLEMS

RESEARCH PROBLEM 1   Mark and John each contributed $10,000 cash to form a limited partnership. Mark is the general partner, and John is the limited partner. The partnership used the $20,000 cash to make a down payment on a building. The rest of the building's $200,000 purchase price was financed with an interest-only nonrecourse loan of $180,000, which was obtained from an independent third-party bank. The partnership shares all partnership items equally between the partners except for the MACRS deductions and building maintenance, which are allocated 70% to John and 30% to Mark. The partnership definitely wishes to satisfy the "economic effect" requirements of Reg. § 1.704–1 and Reg. § 1.704–2 and will reallocate MACRS, if necessary, to satisfy the requirements of the Regulations. Mark has an unlimited obligation to restore his capital account while John is subject to a qualified income offset provision. Assume all partnership items, except for MACRS, will net to zero throughout the first three years of the partnership operations. Also, assume that each year's MACRS deduction will be $10,000 (to simplify the calculations).

Evaluate the allocation of MACRS in each of the three years under Reg. § 1.704–1 and Reg. § 1.704–2.

RESEARCH PROBLEM 2   Ann, Beverly, and Claude formed the ABC Partnership on January 1, 1991, with each contributing land or buildings held for investment with a $100,000 fair market value. Ann's basis in her land was zero, as she had received it as a gift from her mother when its fair market value was zero. Beverly had paid $40,000 for her property, and Claude had paid $30,000.

Creation of the partnership was Ann's idea, as she wanted to dispose of her piece of land, but was aware of the steep income tax price for doing so. Her plan, devised without consulting you (her regular tax adviser) but in response to a presentation on the "Oprah Winfrey Show," was to use the partnership to purge herself of exposure to this recognized gain. Her potential buyer, Claude, would take Ann's land as a tax-favored § 731 partnership distribution, and the equity in Claude and Beverly's buildings could be used to secure a mortgage. Much of the cash proceeds from the mortgage would be distributed to Ann, but spread over several years. By that time, she would have built up some partnership basis, so the distributions would not be fully taxable, and an important deferral of the remaining tax liabilities would have been accomplished.

Finally, several months *after* the contributions have taken place, Ann approaches you for advice. Comment on the possibilities of success for her plan.

PARTNERSHIPS: DISTRIBUTIONS, TRANSFER OF INTERESTS, AND TERMINATIONS

OBJECTIVES

Explain the effects of nonliquidating distributions.

Explain the effects of liquidating distributions.

Discuss the tax consequences that result from the sale or exchange of a partnership interest.

Compare the disposition of a partnership interest by gift and by death.

Explain the effect of the optional adjustments to basis.

Discuss the events that can cause a partnership to terminate.

Describe the special constraints that exist in a family partnership.

OUTLINE

After a partnership is established, many of its day-to-day transactions create no unusual tax problems. Revenue earned and expenses paid by the partnership are typically handled for tax purposes in the same manner as they are handled for individuals. Certain transactions involving partners or partnerships, however, can have some surprising results. For example, when a partnership interest is sold or exchanged for more or less than its basis, capital gain or loss may be recognized. However, under certain conditions, the disposal of a partnership interest creates ordinary income, *even when* the overall result is a loss. Moreover, ordinary income can arise when a partnership simply distributes assets to its partners. Here, either the receiving partner or the partnership can have ordinary income.

This chapter also discusses the taxation of partnership distributions. Unlike corporate distributions that may result in dividend income to the shareholder, most proportional distributions of partnership property create no recognized gain or loss to the distributee partner. Instead, the distributee partner's realized gain or loss is deferred until the partner subsequently disposes of the distributed property in a taxable transaction.

In addition, this chapter addresses optional adjustments to the basis of partnership property, partnership terminations, and special problems associated with family and limited partnerships.

DISTRIBUTIONS FROM A PARTNERSHIP
◆

Draw from comes from Inetial basis Partial Liquidation

The tax treatment of distributions from a partnership to a partner was introduced in Chapter 10 in the context of routine cash withdrawals (or "draws") and distributions from a continuing partnership to a partner who will remain a member of the partnership. As a result, the partner's outside basis is reduced by the amount of the cash received. The partnership's inside basis in assets is similarly reduced.

Partners may also receive distributions of property from the partnership. All distributions from a partnership to a partner fall into two distinct categories: liquidating distributions and nonliquidating distributions. Liquidating distributions are of two types. Liquidating distributions made by a continuing partnership to a retiring partner or a deceased partner's successor first must be categorized under the rules of § 736. These rules will be discussed later in this chapter. Liquidating distributions to partners from a liquidating partnership will be discussed later in this section.

Nonliquidating distributions are all distributions that are not liquidating distributions and are not otherwise classified under the law (e.g., guaranteed payments, interest, rents paid to partners by the partnership). Nonliquidating distributions are of two types: draws or partial liquidations. A *draw* is a distribution of a partner's share of current or accumulated partnership profits that have been taxed to the partner in current or prior taxable years of the partnership. A *partial liquidation* is a distribution that reduces the partner's interest in partnership capital but does not liquidate the partner's entire interest in the partnership. Both types of nonliquidating distributions will be discussed in this section.

--------- EXAMPLE 1 ---------

K joins the calendar year KLM Partnership on January 1, 1992, by contributing $40,000 cash to the partnership in exchange for a one-third interest in partnership capital, profits, and losses. K's distributive share of partnership income for the year is $25,000. On December 31, 1992, the partnership makes a cash distribution to K. A distribution of $25,000 or less to K will be classified as a draw. A distribution of more than $25,000 and less than $65,000 will be classified as a partial liquidation of K's capital. If the partnership were to liquidate on December 31, 1992, and distribute $65,000 to K, the liquidating distribution would be handled under the rules to be discussed in this section. However, if the partnership continues in existence, the $65,000 liquidating distribution to K must first be classified under § 736 (discussed later in the chapter). ◆

Nonliquidating Distributions

In general, neither the partner nor the partnership recognizes gain or loss when a nonliquidating distribution occurs.[1] The partner generally takes a carryover basis for the assets distributed. In addition, the distributee partner's outside basis is reduced (but not below zero) by the amount of cash and the adjusted basis of property distributed to the partner by the partnership.[2]

There are two reasons for this favorable tax treatment. First, because a partner pays taxes on his or her share of the income earned by the partnership, this income should not be taxed again when it is distributed to the partner. In addition, Congress has decided that the distribution of cash or property to a partner is generally not a transaction worthy of current taxation, even if the distribution exceeds the partner's share of partnership income. Note that this treatment is much more favorable than the dividend treatment accorded a shareholder in a C corporation.

──────────────── EXAMPLE 2 ────────────────

J is a one-fourth partner in the SP Partnership. His basis in his partnership interest is $40,000 on December 31, 1992. The fair market value of the interest is $70,000. The partnership distributes $25,000 cash to him on that date. The distribution is not taxable to J or the partnership. The distribution reduces J's adjusted basis in the partnership to $15,000 ($40,000 − $25,000), and the fair market value of his partnership interest should, arguably, be reduced to $45,000 ($70,000 − $25,000). ◆

──────────────── EXAMPLE 3 ────────────────

Assume the same facts as in Example 2, except that, in addition to the $25,000 cash, the partnership distributes land with an adjusted basis to the partnership of $13,000 and a fair market value of $30,000 on the date of distribution. The distribution is not taxable to J or the partnership. J reduces his basis in the partnership to $2,000 [$40,000 − ($25,000 + $13,000)] and takes a carryover basis of $13,000 in the land. The fair market value of J's remaining interest in the partnership should, arguably, be reduced to $15,000 [$70,000 − ($25,000 + $30,000)].

If J had sold his partnership interest for $70,000 rather than receiving the distributions, he would have realized and recognized gain of $30,000 ($70,000 selling price − $40,000 outside basis). Because he has not recognized any gain or loss on the distribution of cash and land, he should still have the $30,000 of deferred gain to recognize at some point in the future. This is exactly what will happen. If J were to sell the cash, land, and remaining partnership interest on January 1, 1993, the day after the distribution, he would realize and recognize gains of $17,000 ($30,000 − $13,000) on the land and $13,000 ($15,000 − $2,000) on the partnership interest. These gains total $30,000, which is exactly the amount of gain he would have recognized if the distribution had not been made and the original partnership interest had been sold. ◆

A partner recognizes gain from a nonliquidating distribution only to the extent that the cash (or "deemed" cash under the liability-sharing rules) received exceeds the outside basis of the partner's interest in the partnership.[3]

────────────────

1. § 731(a)(1).
2. § 732(a)(1).

3. § 731(a)(1).

—————————————————— EXAMPLE 4 ——————————————————

K is a one-third partner in the SF Partnership. Her basis in this ownership interest is $50,000 on December 31, 1992, after accounting for the calendar year entity's 1992 operations and for K's 1992 capital contributions and withdrawals. On December 31, 1992, the partnership distributes $60,000 cash to K. K must recognize a $10,000 gain from this distribution by the partnership ($60,000 cash received − $50,000 basis in her partnership interest). Most likely, K will recognize this distribution as a capital gain.[4] ◆

When the inside basis of the distributed assets exceeds the distributee partner's outside basis, the Code requires that the assets be deemed distributed in a certain order. Cash is treated as being distributed first, unrealized receivables and inventory second, and all other assets last. If the remaining outside basis is insufficient to cover the entire inside basis of the assets in either the second or third class, that remaining outside basis is allocated pro rata among the assets within that class in accordance with the relative inside bases of the assets.[5]

—————————————————— EXAMPLE 5 ——————————————————

Assume the same facts as in Example 4, except that the partnership distributes cash of $12,000; cash basis receivables with an inside basis of $0 and fair market value of $10,000; and two parcels of land to K. The partnership has a basis of $15,000 in one of these parcels and $45,000 in the other. Each parcel has a fair market value of $50,000.

Step 1. Determine the order in which these assets are distributed. According to the Code, the cash is treated as being distributed first, the unrealized receivables second, and the two parcels of land last.

Step 2. Determine whether K recognizes any gain on the distribution. Since the $12,000 cash that K received does not exceed the basis for her partnership interest, she recognizes none of the $72,000 gain that she realized on the transfer [$122,000 amount realized ($12,000 + $10,000 + $50,000 + $50,000) − $50,000 basis in the partnership interest].

Step 3. Determine the basis K takes in each distributed asset and the effect of the distribution on her outside basis. K first assigns a $12,000 basis to the cash and a $0 carryover basis to the unrealized receivables. Her remaining $38,000 [$50,000 − ($12,000 + $0)] outside basis is allocated, pro rata, to the two parcels of land. This pro rata allocation of the remaining outside basis occurs because the partnership's $60,000 ($15,000 + $45,000) adjusted basis in the property exceeds K's $38,000 remaining outside basis in her partnership interest immediately before the distribution of the land.

K assigns the $38,000 outside basis to the land parcels pro rata to their adjusted inside bases to the partnership (and not according to their relative fair market values). K takes a $9,500 basis in the first parcel of land, computed as follows:

$$\$38,000 \times \frac{\$15,000}{\$60,000} = \underline{\underline{\$9,500}}$$

She takes a basis of $28,500 in the second parcel of land, computed as follows:

$$\$38,000 \times \frac{\$45,000}{\$60,000} = \underline{\underline{\$28,500}}$$

◆

---

4. § 731(a). If the partnership holds any "hot assets," however, some or all of the $10,000 gain would be recognized as ordinary income. See § 751(b) and the related discussion of

ordinary income ("hot") assets later in this chapter.

5. § 732 and Reg. § 1.732–1(c)(1).

—————————— EXAMPLE 6 ——————————

Assume the same facts as in Example 5, and that K sells both of the parcels early in 1993 at their fair market values, receiving proceeds of $100,000 ($50,000 + $50,000) and collecting $10,000 for the cash basis receivables. Now she recognizes all of the $72,000 gain that she deferred upon receiving the property from the partnership [$100,000 amount realized − $38,000 adjusted basis for the two parcels ($9,500 + $28,500) plus $10,000 received − $0 basis for the receivables]. ◆

Review the tax results of Example 5. Although K does not have to recognize any of the gain that she realizes from the distribution, she has a zero outside basis for her partnership interest. This zero basis will not be attractive to K if she anticipates that the partnership will generate net losses in the near future. Since her tax basis in the entity is zero, she will be unable to deduct her share of the losses when they flow through to her on the last day of the partnership's tax year.

The low basis that K has assigned to the parcels of land is of no tax detriment to her if she does not intend to sell the land in the near future. Since land does not generate cost recovery deductions, the substituted basis will be used only to determine K's gain or loss upon her disposition of the asset in a taxable sale or exchange.

Concept Summary 11–1 reviews the rules that apply to nonliquidating partnership distributions.

Liquidating Distributions

Liquidating distributions consist of a single distribution or a series of distributions that result in the termination of the partner's entire interest in the partnership. If the partnership continues in existence after the partner's interest is liquidated, the rules of § 736 govern the classification of the liquidating payments. These rules will be discussed later in the chapter. Other rules apply,

---

 CONCEPT SUMMARY 11–1
NONLIQUIDATING DISTRIBUTIONS

1. Generally, neither the distributee partner nor the partnership recognizes any gain or loss on a nonliquidating distribution. However, if the cash distributed exceeds the distributee partner's outside basis, he or she recognizes gain.
2. The distributee partner usually takes the same basis for the distributed property that it had to the partnership. However, where the inside basis of distributed property exceeds the partner's outside basis, the basis taken by the distributed property cannot exceed that outside basis.
3. Gain recognized by the distributee partner on a nonliquidating distribution is generally capital in nature.

Calculations

1. Partner's outside basis. _____
2. Less: Cash distributed to partner, including reduction in share of liabilities. _____
3. Gain recognized by partner (excess of Line 2 over Line 1). _____
4. Partner's remaining outside basis (Line 1 − Line 2). If less than $0, enter $0. _____
5. Partner's basis in unrealized receivables and inventory distributed (enter lesser of Line 4 or the inside basis of the unrealized receivables and inventory). _____
6. Basis available to allocate to other property distributed (Line 4 − Line 5). _____
7. Inside basis of other property distributed. _____
8. Basis to partner of other property distributed (enter lesser of Line 6 or Line 7). _____
9. Partner's remaining outside basis (Line 6 − Line 8). _____

however, if the partner's interest is liquidated because the partnership is also liquidating. This section examines the latter type of liquidating distribution.

When a partnership liquidates, the liquidating distributions to a partner usually consist of an interest in several or all of the partnership assets. As with nonliquidating distributions, the Code requires that these assets be treated in a certain order. Cash is considered first. The cash distributed reduces the liquidated partner's outside basis dollar for dollar. The partner's remaining outside basis is then allocated to unrealized receivables and inventory in an amount equal to the partnership's adjusted basis in that property. If the partnership's bases in the unrealized receivables and inventory exceed the partner's remaining outside basis, the remaining outside basis is allocated to the unrealized receivables and inventory in the ratio of their inside bases to the partnership. Finally, if the liquidating partner has any remaining outside basis, that basis is allocated pro rata to any other assets received according to their inside bases to the partnership.[6] Note that these rules are similar to those that apply to a nonliquidating distribution.

The partnership does not recognize gain or loss in a liquidating distribution. However, a partner who receives a distribution from a liquidating partnership may recognize either gain or loss. Gain is recognized only if cash distributed to the partner exceeds his or her outside basis in the partnership. The amount of gain is the difference between the money received and the partner's outside basis. This gain rule is the same as the rule that governs the recognition of gain on nonliquidating distributions.

EXAMPLE 7

When T's basis in her partnership interest is $25,000, she receives cash of $15,000 and a proportionate share of inventory and buildings in a distribution that liquidates her entire partnership interest. The inventory has a basis to the partnership of $20,000 and a fair market value of $30,000. The building's basis is $8,000, and the fair market value is $12,000. The building was depreciated under the straight-line method. Under these circumstances, T recognizes no gain or loss. After reducing T's basis by the cash received, the remaining $10,000 is allocated to the inventory. The basis of the inventory in T's hands is $10,000, and the basis of the building is zero.

Of the inventory's original basis in the hands of the partnership, $10,000 appears to have been *lost* in the liquidating distribution. The partnership may be able to "save" this portion of the inventory's basis by making an election to adjust the basis of its remaining inventory upward. This concept is discussed later in the chapter. ◆

EXAMPLE 8

Assume the same facts as in Example 7, except that there was no inventory and T received two buildings (both of which were depreciated under the straight-line method). Building 1 had a basis of $6,000 to the partnership, and Building 2 had a basis of $9,000. Again, no gain or loss is recognized. The $10,000 basis of T's interest after reduction for the cash received is allocated to the buildings in the ratio of their bases to the partnership. T's basis in Building 1 is $4,000 ($6/15 \times $10,000$), and her basis in Building 2 is $6,000 ($9/15 \times $10,000$). ◆

The distributee partner may also recognize a *loss* on a liquidating distribution. The partner recognizes a loss if both of the following are true:

1. The partner receives *only* money, unrealized receivables, and inventory.
2. The partner's outside basis in the partnership interest exceeds the partnership's inside basis for the assets distributed. This excess amount is the loss recognized by the distributee partner.[7]

---

6. §§ 731 and 732.　　　　　　　　　　　　7. § 731(a)(2).

The word "only" is important. A distribution of any other property will postpone recognition of the loss.

--------------------------------- EXAMPLE 9 ---------------------------------

When R's basis is $40,000, he receives a liquidating distribution of $7,000 cash and a proportionate share of inventory having a partnership basis of $3,000 and a fair market value of $10,000. After the distribution, R is no longer a partner. Since R cannot allocate to the inventory more than $3,000 of the $33,000 remaining basis after reduction for cash, he recognizes a $30,000 capital loss on the liquidation. The basis of the inventory is $3,000. ◆

--------------------------------- EXAMPLE 10 ---------------------------------

Assume the same facts as in Example 9, except that R receives $44,000 cash in addition to the inventory. Under these circumstances, R recognizes $4,000 capital gain (cash of $44,000 less $40,000 basis), and the inventory is assigned a zero basis. ◆

--------------------------------- EXAMPLE 11 ---------------------------------

Assume the same facts as in Example 9, except that R also receives the desk he used in the partnership. The desk has an adjusted basis of $100 to the partnership. Applying the rules outlined above to this revised fact situation produces the following results:

Step 1. Cash of $7,000 is distributed to R and reduces his outside basis to $33,000.
Step 2. Inventory is distributed to R. He takes a $3,000 carryover basis in the inventory and reduces his outside basis in the partnership to $30,000.
Step 3. The desk is distributed to R. Since the desk is not cash, an unrealized receivable, or inventory, he cannot recognize a loss. Therefore, R has an adjusted basis of $30,000 for the desk. ◆

What can R do with a $30,000 desk? If he continues to use it in a trade or business, he can depreciate it. Once he has established a business use to him, he could sell the desk and recognize a large § 1231 loss. If the loss is isolated in the year of the sale, it is an ordinary loss. Also, a theft of the desk would produce a business loss that is deductible as an ordinary loss. Thus, with proper planning, no liquidated partner should be forced to recognize a capital loss.

Gain realized by the withdrawing partner on the subsequent disposition of inventory is ordinary income, unless the disposition occurs more than five years after the distribution.[8] The withdrawing partner's holding period for all other property received in a liquidating distribution includes the partnership's related holding period.

Concept Summary 11–2 delineates the rules that apply to liquidating partnership distributions.

LIQUIDATING DISTRIBUTIONS TO RETIRING OR DECEASED PARTNERS

Payments made by an ongoing partnership in complete liquidation of a retiring partner's interest are classified as either *income* or *property* payments by § 736. Payments made to a successor to the interest of a deceased partner are similarly classified by § 736.[9] Although these payments can be made in cash, property, or both cash and property, this discussion will assume that all payments are made in cash. It is critical to observe that § 736 only classifies the payments. Other Code sections provide the rules for computing the tax effects of these payments.

---

8. § 735(a)(2).

9. A successor is typically the estate of the deceased or the party who inherits the decedent's interest.

Property Payments

Cash payments made by the partnership in exchange for a partner's pro rata interest in partnership assets are commonly referred to as *property payments* or, alternatively, as § 736(b) payments. It is useful to think of these cash payments as having been made by the partnership in lieu of distributing a pro rata share of each partnership asset to the partner.

A partner who gives up a pro rata share of any partnership asset expects the cash payment to reflect his or her share of the asset's fair market value. Therefore, when determining the amount of § 736(b) payments, it is necessary to determine the fair market value of the partner's share of each asset.

Cash payments made for the partner's pro rata share of each partnership asset are classified as § 736(b) payments with the following exceptions:

- Payments made for the partner's pro rata share of unrealized receivables.
- Payments made for the partner's pro rata share of the partnership goodwill. This exception only applies to payments for goodwill that exceed the partner's pro rata share of the partnership's inside basis for goodwill. In addition, the exception only applies if the partnership agreement does not state that the payments are for goodwill.
- Certain annuities and lump-sum payments made to retiring partners or deceased partner's successors.

CONCEPT SUMMARY 11–2
LIQUIDATING DISTRIBUTIONS WHEN THE PARTNERSHIP ALSO LIQUIDATES

1. Generally, neither the distributee partner nor the partnership recognizes gain or loss when a partnership liquidates. However, a partner recognizes gain if the cash received exceeds his or her outside basis. A distributee partner recognizes loss when only money, unrealized receivables, and inventory are received and the partner's outside basis is greater than the inside basis of the assets distributed.

2. Distributed assets must be treated as being distributed in a certain order. Cash is distributed first, inventory and unrealized receivables second, and all other assets last. Assets in the last category take a substituted basis equal to the distributee partner's remaining outside basis.

3. Gain or loss recognized by a distributee partner in a distribution that liquidates a partnership is generally capital in nature.

Calculations

1. Partner's outside basis. _____
2. Less: Cash distributed to partner. _____
3. Gain recognized by partner (excess of Line 2 over Line 1). _____
4. Partner's remaining outside basis (Line 1 − Line 2). _____
5. Partner's basis in unrealized receivables and inventory distributed (enter lesser of Line 4 or the inside basis of the unrealized receivables and inventory). _____
6. Basis to partner of other property distributed (Line 4 − Line 5). _____
7. Loss recognized by partner (if no other property was distributed, enter amount from Line 6). _____
8. Partner's remaining outside basis. _____$0_____

These exceptions are classified as § 736(a) payments. In addition, inventory that is substantially appreciated is subject to special treatment. This discussion will assume that no substantially appreciated inventory exists.[10]

EXAMPLE 12

The ABC Partnership has the following balance sheet on December 31, 1992:

	Adjusted Basis	Fair Market Value
Cash	$36,000	$36,000
Unrealized receivables	–0–	18,000
Land	9,000	27,000
	$45,000	$81,000
A, capital	$15,000	$27,000
B, capital	15,000	27,000
C, capital	15,000	27,000
	$45,000	$81,000

Partner A is retiring from the partnership. She will receive $36,000 cash, none of which is stated to be for goodwill. The payment A receives for her interest in the cash and land will be a § 736(b) property payment. This payment consists of $12,000 paid for the cash (⅓ × $36,000) and $9,000 paid for A's share of the fair market value of the land (⅓ × $27,000). The remaining cash of $15,000 is for her interest in the unrealized receivables and unstated goodwill and is a § 736(a) payment, which is discussed in Example 14. ◆

The Code provides that, in general, § 736(b) cash payments are treated first as a return of the partner's outside basis in the partnership.[11] Once the entire basis is returned, any additional amounts are taxed to the partner as capital gain. If the cash distributions are not sufficient to return the partner's entire outside basis, the shortfall is taxed to the partner as a capital loss.[12]

EXAMPLE 13

Assume the same facts as in Example 12. If A's outside basis is $15,000, she will recognize capital gain of $6,000 [($12,000 + $9,000) − $15,000] on the distribution. However, if A's outside basis is $25,000, she will recognize a $4,000 capital loss on the distribution [($12,000 + $9,000) − $25,000]. ◆

Income Payments

All payments that are not classified as § 736(b) property payments are categorized as § 736(a) income payments. In other words, any cash payments made in excess of the value of the retiring or deceased partner's proportionate interest in partnership property (including stated goodwill) will be taxed as § 736(a) income payments.

EXAMPLE 14

Assume the same facts as in Example 12. The $6,000 cash payment ($18,000 × ⅓) for A's pro rata share of the unrealized receivables is classified as a § 736(a) income payment. In addition, the remaining payment of $9,000 is treated as unstated goodwill

---

10. See Concept Summary 11–5 for an illustration involving substantially appreciated inventory.

11. §§ 736(b) and 731(a)(1).
12. § 731(a)(2).

and, therefore, as a § 736(a) income payment. The $9,000 remaining payment is computed as follows:

Total distribution		$36,000
Pro rata share of FMV of:		
Cash	$12,000	
Unrealized receivables	6,000	
Land	9,000	27,000
§ 736(a) remaining payment		$ 9,000

Note that if the partnership agreement had stated that this remaining payment was for goodwill, it would have been a § 736(b) payment. ◆

Section 736(a) income payments are further classified into two categories. Payments that are *not* determined by reference to partnership income are treated as guaranteed payments.[13] They are fully taxable as ordinary income to the distributee partner and are fully deductible by the continuing partnership.

Section 736(a) income payments that are determined by reference to partnership income are treated as distributive shares of that income.[14] They are taxed to the distributee partner according to their character to the partnership. Thus, for example, they may be taxed as capital gain as well as ordinary income.[15] Since this capital gain and ordinary income are allocated to the liquidated partner, the payments reduce the amount of partnership capital gain and ordinary income allocated to the remaining partners.[16]

Example 15

Assume the same facts as in Example 12 and review the analysis in Example 14. Because the $15,000 § 736(a) income payment ($6,000 + $9,000) is not determined by reference to partnership income, the payment is classified as a guaranteed payment. It is included as ordinary income on A's tax return and is deductible by the partnership. ◆

Series of Payments

When liquidating cash distributions are spread over a number of years, it is necessary to find and classify the payments for income items and for partnership property. If the partners have dealt at arm's length and specifically agreed to the allocation and timing of each class of payment, the agreement normally controls.

Example 16

Partner X retires from the equal XYZ Partnership at a time when partnership debt totals $90,000. All of the partners agree that X's interest in partnership property, exclusive of unrealized receivables and goodwill, is worth $105,000. To totally liquidate X's interest, X is to be paid $15,000 in cash per year for 10 years, and the remaining partners will assume X's share of partnership liabilities.

The total consideration for X's partnership interest is $180,000 (cash of $150,000 plus $30,000 debt assumption). If the partners agree that the assumption of X's share of liabilities and the first $75,000 of cash payments made by the partnership are to be treated as consideration for X's interest in partnership property (exclusive of unrealized receivables and goodwill), this agreement controls for tax purposes.

In the first five years, the $105,000 (including the assumption of partnership debts) is treated as liquidating payments for partnership property. X recognizes a gain when

---

13. § 736(a)(2).
14. § 736(a)(1).

15. §702(b).
16. Reg. § 1.736–1(a)(4).

these payments exceed the basis of his interest, but the partnership is not entitled to any deduction. In each of the next five years, X recognizes ordinary income of $15,000 from the payments. The partnership deducts $15,000 each year as a guaranteed payment.

Year	Total Payments	Income Payments	Property Payments
1	$ 45,000	$ –0–	$ 45,000
2	15,000	–0–	15,000
3	15,000	–0–	15,000
4	15,000	–0–	15,000
5	15,000	–0–	15,000
Subtotal	$105,000	$ –0–	$105,000
6	15,000	15,000	–0–
7	15,000	15,000	–0–
8	15,000	15,000	–0–
9	15,000	15,000	–0–
10	15,000	15,000	–0–
Total	$180,000	$75,000	$105,000

If the partners do not enter into a specific agreement as to the timing of payments for the two classes, a pro rata part of each payment is treated as a payment for partnership property, and the balance is treated as an income payment.

─────────────── EXAMPLE 17 ───────────────

Assume the same facts as in Example 16, except that the partners agree to a value of $120,000 (instead of $105,000) for X's interest in partnership property, exclusive of unrealized receivables and goodwill. Further assume that there is no specific agreement as to the timing of the payments for each class, except that the liabilities are assumed immediately. In this situation, all payments are allocated between income payments and payments for partnership property.

One-third ($60,000/$180,000) of each payment is for income items, and two-thirds ($120,000/$180,000) is for partnership property.

Year	Total Payments	Income Payments	Property Payments
1	$ 45,000	$15,000	$ 30,000
2	15,000	5,000	10,000
3	15,000	5,000	10,000
4	15,000	5,000	10,000
5	15,000	5,000	10,000
6	15,000	5,000	10,000
7	15,000	5,000	10,000
8	15,000	5,000	10,000
9	15,000	5,000	10,000
10	15,000	5,000	10,000
Total	$180,000	$60,000	$120,000

Concept Summary 11–3 reviews the rules for liquidating distributions when the partnership continues.

CONCEPT SUMMARY 11–3
LIQUIDATING DISTRIBUTIONS WHEN THE PARTNERSHIP CONTINUES

1. Payments made by an ongoing partnership to a liquidating partner are classified as § 736(a) income payments or as § 736(b) property payments.
2. Section 736(b) property payments are payments made for the liquidated partner's share of partnership assets.
3. However, payments made for the liquidated partner's share of unrealized receivables, certain goodwill that is not provided for in the partnership agreement, and certain annuity payments are classified as § 736(a) income payments.
4. Section 736(a) income payments are the payments mentioned in Item 3 above and all other payments that are not classified as § 736(b) property payments.
5. Section 736(b) property payments are taxed as a return of the partner's outside basis. Any excess cash received over the partner's outside basis is taxed as capital gain.
6. Section 736(a) income payments are further classified as either guaranteed payments or distributive shares. Guaranteed payments are taxable as ordinary income to the partner and are deductible by the partnership. Distributive shares retain the same tax character to the partner as they had to the partnership. Distributive shares are excludible from the continuing partners' tax returns.

SALE OF A PARTNERSHIP INTEREST
◆

A partner's investment in a partnership can be sold or exchanged, in whole or in part. The transaction can be between the partner and a third party or between the partner and the partnership in a manner similar to the sale of shares of corporate stock. Since the entity and aggregate concepts are both applied to the sale of a partnership interest, the resulting gain or loss may be divided into capital gain or loss and ordinary income.

General Rules

Generally, the sale or exchange of a partnership interest results in capital gain or loss, measured by the difference between the amount realized and the selling partner's adjusted basis in the partnership.[17]

Liabilities. In computing the amount realized and the adjusted basis of the interest sold, the selling partner considers pertinent partnership liabilities. The effect of changes in partnership liabilities on the partners' basis was discussed in Chapter 10. The purchasing partner includes any assumed indebtedness as a part of the consideration paid for the partnership interest.[18]

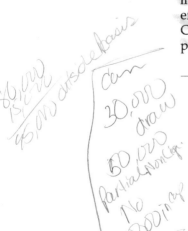

───────────── EXAMPLE 18 ─────────────

C originally contributed $50,000 in cash for a one-third interest in the CDE Partnership. During the time C was a partner, his share of partnership income was $90,000, and he withdrew $60,000 cash. C's capital account balance is now $80,000, and partnership liabilities are $45,000, of which C's share is $15,000. C's outside basis is $95,000 ($80,000 capital account plus $15,000 share of partnership debts).

C sells his partnership interest to F for $110,000 cash, with F assuming C's share of partnership liabilities. The total amount realized by C is $125,000 ($110,000 cash received plus $15,000 of partnership debts transferred to F). C's gain on the sale is $30,000 ($125,000 realized less adjusted basis of $95,000). ◆

───────────── EXAMPLE 19 ─────────────

Assume the same facts as in Example 18. What is F's outside basis in the new DEF Partnership? Since F did not contribute money or other property to the partnership,

17. § 741.   **18.** §742.

his outside basis is $125,000 (cash paid of $110,000 plus assumed partnership debt of $15,000). ◆

Tax Years That Close. When a partner disposes of an entire investment in the entity, the partnership's tax year closes for that partner as of the sale date. If the partnership uses an IRS-approved fiscal year and the partner uses a calendar year, income bunching may occur. The selling partner's distributive share of partnership income for the closed tax year is reported in his or her tax year that includes the sale date.

──────────────── EXAMPLE 20 ────────────────

Assume the same facts as in Example 18, except that the CDE Partnership had earned income of $12,000 as of the date C's interest was sold. Since the partnership year closes with respect to C, $4,000 of partnership income is reported in C's tax year that includes the sale date. In addition, C also reports his income share from the last partnership year that may have closed in this tax year. C's capital account and outside basis are increased by $4,000, and his recognized gain on the sale is reduced correspondingly. ◆

Effect of Hot Assets

A major exception to capital gain or loss treatment on the sale or exchange of a partnership interest arises when a partnership has hot assets. In general, *hot assets* are assets that when collected or disposed of would otherwise cause the partnership to recognize ordinary income. When a partner sells his or her interest in a partnership, two types of hot assets must be considered: unrealized receivables and substantially appreciated inventory.

An amount realized from the sale of a partnership interest that is attributable to *unrealized receivables* or *substantially appreciated inventory* is treated as being from the sale of a noncapital asset.[19] The purpose of this rule is to prevent the conversion of ordinary income into capital gain through the sale of a partnership interest.

Unrealized Receivables. The term *unrealized receivables* generally includes receivables from the sales of ordinary income property and rights to payments for services.[20] Sometimes the method of accounting, the nature of the property, or the property's holding period affects whether an item is an unrealized receivable. Under the cash method of accounting, trade receivables from inventory sales and from services (including related notes receivable) are included; under the accrual method, they are not. The gain element in installment receivables from the sale of capital assets or § 1231 assets is excluded. However, any portion of the gain that would be ordinary income is a hot asset.[21]

──────────────── EXAMPLE 21 ────────────────

The cash basis RB Partnership owns only a $7,200 receivable for rendering health care advice. Its basis in the receivable is zero because no income has been recognized. This item is a hot asset because ordinary income will be generated when RB collects on the account. ◆

──────────────── EXAMPLE 22 ────────────────

The accrual basis TAS Partnership has a long-term depreciable business asset with an adjusted basis of $15,000 and a market value of $30,000. Depreciation recapture

───────────────────────

19. § 751(a).
20. § 751(a)(1).

21. § 751(c).

potential is $10,000. In this case, TAS holds a $10,000 unrealized receivable with a zero basis and a $20,000 non-hot asset with an adjusted basis of $15,000. If TAS sold the asset for $30,000, it would recognize $10,000 of ordinary income and $5,000 of § 1231 gain. ◆

Recapture   *Hot asset*

─────────────────────────── EXAMPLE 23 ───────────────────────────

XYZ is a cash basis calendar year partnership that provides educational consulting services. Its three equal partners are full-time employees of a local university. None of the partners contributed property for a capital interest. They did, however, agree to share profits and losses equally, since all services provided by the partnership are rendered equally by the partners. The partnership's balance sheet included the following items at the end of last year.

	Adjusted Basis per Books	Market Value
Receivable for services rendered		
Total	$–0–	$30,000
Capital accounts		
X	$–0–	$10,000
Y	–0–	10,000
Z	–0–	10,000
Total	$–0–	$30,000

Z has accepted a position at another university and wants to sell her interest to R for its fair market value. X and Y agree to accept R as a partner. On January 5 of the current year, R pays Z $10,000 in cash for the partnership interest. At the sale date, and at the end of the last year, XYZ had no debts outstanding.

The hot asset rule applies to the sale. Although the sale of a partnership interest generally results in a capital gain or loss, the $10,000 gain on the sale of Z's interest (selling price of $10,000 less outside basis of zero) is ordinary. If Z had remained in the partnership and the partnership had collected the receivable, Z would have realized ordinary income of $10,000 ($30,000 × ⅓). Under the hot asset rule, the ordinary income is assigned to the partner who earned it. ◆

─────────────────────────── EXAMPLE 24 ───────────────────────────

C's interest in the equal ABC Partnership is sold to D for $17,000 cash. On the sale date, the partnership's cash basis balance sheet reflects the following:

Assets

	Adjusted Basis per Books	Market Value
Cash	$10,000	$10,000
Accounts receivable (for services)	–0–	30,000
Non-hot assets	14,000	20,000
Total	$24,000	$60,000

Hot Assets Ordinary Income

Liabilities and Capital

	Adjusted Basis per Books	Market Value
Liabilities	$ 9,000	$ 9,000
Capital accounts		
A	5,000	17,000
B	5,000	17,000
C	5,000	17,000
Total	$24,000	$60,000

The hot asset rule applies to the sale because the partnership has unrealized receivables. The total amount realized by C is $20,000 (cash price of $17,000 plus $3,000 of debt assumed by D). C's one-third interest includes $10,000 of market value in the receivables. Consequently, $10,000 of the $20,000 realized from the sale is considered as received in exchange for C's interest in the receivables. The remaining $10,000 is treated as received in exchange for a capital asset.

C's basis is $8,000 (capital account of $5,000 plus $3,000 debt share). No portion of this basis can be attributed to the unrealized receivables; they have a zero basis to the partnership. Thus, the full $10,000 received for the receivables is ordinary income ($10,000 less related zero basis).

C's entire basis of $8,000 is treated as being in non-hot assets and is applied against the remaining $10,000 received from the sale (amount realized of $20,000 less $10,000 allocated to hot assets). Thus, C also incurs a $2,000 capital gain ($10,000 less related $8,000 basis). ◆

─────────────── EXAMPLE 25 ───────────────

Assume the same facts as in Example 24, except that C's basis in his partnership interest is $10,000. Under these circumstances, C's capital gain or loss is zero. C still has $10,000 of ordinary income because of the unrealized receivables.

If C's basis in the partnership interest is $11,000 (instead of $10,000), an unusual result occurs. Although it appears that C has a $9,000 long-term capital gain ($20,000 amount realized less $11,000 basis), such is not the case. Rather, the receivables generate $10,000 of ordinary income, and C's $9,000 overall gain is accounted for with an additional long-term capital *loss* of $1,000. ◆

Substantially Appreciated Inventory. The term *substantially appreciated inventory* includes all partnership property except money, capital assets, and § 1231 assets. Specifically, the term includes inventory and similar noncapital and non-Section 1231 assets. Receivables of an accrual partnership are included in the definition of inventory, since they are neither capital assets nor § 1231 assets.[22]

This definition is broad enough to include all items considered to be unrealized receivables. The disadvantage of their inclusion can be seen when one determines whether the inventory is substantially appreciated. Since unrealized receivables are included at a zero basis in the substantial appreciation tests, they improve the partner's chances of incurring ordinary income.

Inventory items are substantially appreciated if, at the time of their sale or distribution, their aggregate fair market value exceeds 120 percent of their total adjusted basis to the partnership *and* if their fair market value is more than 10 percent of the fair market value of all partnership property other than money. In applying these tests, inventory items are evaluated as a group, rather than individually. If substantial appreciation of the entire inventory has occurred, each item is treated as substantially appreciated, even if a specific item has not appreciated.

─────────────── EXAMPLE 26 ───────────────

J's interest in the JKL Partnership is sold to M for $17,000 cash. On the sale date, the partnership balance sheet reflects the following:

	Adjusted Basis per Books	Market Value
Cash	$10,000	$10,000
Inventory	21,000	30,000
Non-hot assets	14,000	20,000
	$45,000	$60,000
J, capital	$15,000	$20,000
K, capital	15,000	20,000
L, capital	15,000	20,000
	$45,000	$60,000

─────────────────

22. § 751(d)(2).

The inventory is substantially appreciated. The appreciation is 143% ($30,000 ÷ $21,000), which is above the 120% threshold. In addition, the $30,000 fair market value of the inventory exceeds 10% of the fair market value of all partnership property, excluding cash [$30,000 > (.10 × $50,000)].

J's share of the inside basis of the inventory is $7,000 ($21,000 × $\frac{1}{3}$). J is deemed to have sold this share of inventory for $10,000 ($30,000 × $\frac{1}{3}$), thereby creating ordinary income of $3,000 on the sale of the hot asset. J recognizes the $3,000 ordinary income and $2,000 of capital gain from the rest of the sale:

only on sales gain have to worry about Hot Assets

5000 dollar gain altogether

Remaining sales price ($20,000 gross sales price − $10,000 allocated to hot asset sale)	$10,000
Remaining outside basis ($15,000 original outside basis − $7,000 allocated to hot asset sale)	(8,000)
Capital gain	$ 2,000

Tax Reporting. When a partnership owns hot assets, partners who sell or exchange a partnership interest must promptly notify the partnership of the transfers. After notification is received, the partnership must file an information return with the IRS for the calendar year in which the transfers took place. The return lists the names and addresses of the transferors and transferees. In addition, each person whose name is shown on the return is furnished the name and address of the partnership making the return and the information shown on it concerning him or her.

Concept Summary 11–4 enumerates the rules that generally apply to sales of partnership interests.

COMPREHENSIVE EXAMPLES
◆

Just Review yourself

The preceding examples in this chapter have attempted to introduce the concepts involved in liquidating or selling an entire interest in a partnership. The comprehensive examples in Concept Summary 11–5 are designed to compare the various calculations involved in both types of transactions.

Several points should be noted in reviewing these examples. Although the inventory account, by itself, is not substantially appreciated, it must be combined with the receivables when calculating the two tests for substantial appreciation. This is necessary because the Code's definition of inventory is expanded to include unrealized receivables.

CONCEPT SUMMARY 11–4
SALE OF A PARTNERSHIP INTEREST

1. A partnership interest is a capital asset and generally results in capital gain or loss on disposal.
2. The basis of a partner's interest includes a share of the partnership's debt.
3. The outside bases of the selling and buying partner, as well as the pertinent selling price and purchase price, include an appropriate share of partnership debt.
4. When hot assets are present, ordinary income is recognized on the disposal of a partner's interest.
5. Hot assets consist of unrealized receivables and substantially appreciated inventory.
6. Unrealized receivables include amounts earned by a cash basis taxpayer from services rendered and inventory sales. They also include depreciation recapture potential that would result if an asset were sold at a gain. The basis of these receivables usually is zero.
7. Substantially appreciated inventory includes all partnership property except cash, capital assets, and § 1231 assets. Inventory is substantially appreciated when its aggregate fair market value exceeds both 120% of its adjusted basis *and* 10% of the fair market value of all partnership property exclusive of cash. Substantially appreciated inventory also includes unrealized receivables.

Q sells his one-third interest in QPD, a cash basis calendar year partnership, to V for $10,000 cash. The balance sheet of QPD immediately before the sale is as follows:

	Adjusted Basis per Books	Market Value
Cash	$3,000	$3,000
Land	3,000	6,000
Receivable	–0–	7,000
Inventory	12,000	14,000
Total	$18,000	$30,000
Capital accounts		
Q	$6,000	$10,000
P	6,000	10,000
D	6,000	10,000
Total	$18,000	$30,000

If the hot asset rule is to apply, the partnership must have unrealized receivables, substantially appreciated inventory, or both. The receivable qualifies as a hot asset by itself, but the *inventory standing alone does not pass the two tests for substantial appreciation*. However, when the receivable is added to the inventory, the aggregate fair market value of the assets is $21,000 (account receivable $7,000 + inventory $14,000), and the two tests are passed. Thus, the inventory is a hot asset.

Appreciation Test

	Market Value	Adjusted Basis
Receivable	$7,000	$ –0–
Inventory	14,000	12,000
Total	$21,000	$12,000
		×120%
		$14,400

Test passed because
$21,000 > $14,400

Balance Sheet Test

	Market Value
All assets	$30,000
Less: Cash	3,000
Noncash assets	$27,000
	×10%
	$2,700

Test passed because
$21,000 > $2,700

Now classify QPD's property as either hot assets or non-hot assets.

	Hot Assets	Non-Hot Assets	Market Value	Q's One-Third Share
Cash		$3,000	$3,000	$1,000
Land		3,000	6,000	2,000
Receivable	$ –0–		7,000	2,333
Inventory	12,000		14,000	4,667
Total	$12,000	$6,000	$30,000	
Q's one-third share	$4,000	$2,000	$10,000	

Q allocates the $10,000 amount realized from the sale between the hot assets and non-hot assets and then compares the allocated amounts with his share of the related adjusted basis. As a result, Q recognizes $3,000 ordinary income and $1,000 capital gain.

Q's One-Third Share	Hot Assets	Non-Hot Assets	Totals
Amount realized	$7,000	$3,000	$10,000
Adjusted basis	4,000	2,000	6,000
Gain/loss recognized	$3,000	$1,000	$4,000
	Ordinary income	*Capital gain*	

Continue with the same facts, except that now Q's interest in QPD is liquidated with a $10,000 cash payment.

Q is treated as receiving an income payment of $2,333 for the unrealized receivables, thereby creating ordinary income. The remaining $7,667 portion of the payment ($10,000 − $2,333) is for Q's interest in partnership property. It includes $4,667 for Q's interest in substantially appreciated inventory with a $4,000 basis. Here, Q has ordinary income of $667 ($4,667 − $4,000). The remaining $3,000 portion of the payment ($10,000 − $2,333 − $4,667) is for Q's interest in the other partnership property. Since Q's remaining basis in it is only $2,000 ($6,000 − $0 for the receivables − $4,000 for the inventory), Q has a capital gain of $1,000 ($3,000 − $2,000).

Payments for Income Items	Cash Received	Q's Basis	Income
Unrealized receivables	$ 2,333	$ –0–	$2,333
Goodwill	–0–	–0–	–0–
Total	$ 2,333	$ –0–	$2,333
Payments for Partnership Property			
Substantially appreciated inventory	$ 4,667	$4,000	$ 667
Remaining partnership property	3,000	2,000	1,000
Total	$ 7,667	$6,000	$1,667
Aggregate amounts	$10,000	$6,000	$4,000

Also note that Q's $4,000 basis for the hot assets includes his one-third share of the $12,000 inside basis for the hot assets. Accordingly, Q's ordinary income is not the $7,000 fair market value of the hot assets deemed sold but the $7,000 fair market value less the $3,000 proportionate basis.

In the liquidating transaction, note that although the test for substantially appreciated inventory includes the unrealized receivables, the cash paid for the receivables is a § 736(a) income payment while the cash paid for the inventory is a § 736(b) property payment. Payments for both hot assets create ordinary income to the recipient.

Finally, it is not appropriate to conclude that there are no tax differences between a sale and a liquidation. "Comparing Sales to Liquidations" in the Tax Planning Considerations section of this chapter discusses several of these differences.

EXCHANGE OF A PARTNERSHIP INTEREST
◆

Partnership property or a partnership interest may be involved in an exchange rather than a sale. For example, a partnership may incorporate, or partners in different entities may swap interests. The tax consequences of an exchange usually are the same as for a sale. Certain exchanges, however, can qualify as nontaxable events.

Transfers to Controlled Corporations

The controlled corporation rules of § 351 provide that gain or loss is not recognized on the transfer of property to a corporation solely in exchange for stock in that corporation if, immediately after the exchange, the shareholders are in control of the corporation to which the property was transferred.

The transfer of a partnership interest to a corporation is treated as a nontaxable exchange if the conditions of the controlled corporation rules are met. All items of partnership income or loss, deduction, or credit attributable to the transferred interest are apportioned between the transferor partner and the corporation. Moreover, if the partnership interest transferred represented 50 percent or more of the total interest in capital and profits, the partnership is terminated. Partnership termination is discussed later in the chapter. When gain is recognized on the transfer of a partnership interest to a controlled corporation, determining its character requires an allocation similar to that presented in Concept Summary 11–5 in connection with the sale of a partnership interest.

Incorporation Methods. If partners decide to incorporate the business, at least three alternative methods are available:

- Each partner's interest is transferred to the corporation in exchange for stock under the usual § 351 rules. As a result, the partnership terminates, and the corporation owns all partnership assets. The corporation takes a substituted basis for the assets, and the old partners have a substituted basis for the stock.
- The partnership transfers all of its assets to the corporation in exchange for stock and the assumption of partnership liabilities. The stock then is distributed to the partners in proportion to their partnership interests. The corporation takes a carryover basis for the assets, and the old partners have a substituted basis for the stock.
- The partnership makes a pro rata distribution of all of its assets and liabilities to its partners in complete liquidation. The partners then transfer their undivided interests in the assets and liabilities to the corporation in exchange for stock under § 351. The corporation's basis for the assets is the substituted basis of those assets to the partners. The partners have a substituted basis for the stock.

Assuming that existing partnership debt does not exceed the basis of transferred assets, none of the three incorporation methods generates a recognized gain or loss. They do, however, cause different tax results. Moreover, if the resulting corporation intends to elect S status (see Chapter 12), the partners will not want to preclude that election by their own actions. Thus, selecting the appropriate incorporation method is crucial.

If the corporation plans to issue small business stock (§ 1244 stock), the stock must be issued directly to the partners and not to the partnership. Otherwise, ordinary loss benefits of the stock will be forfeited. Consequently, when a partnership is to be incorporated with § 1244 stock, the partnership should use the last method listed above and make a pro rata distribution of its assets and liabilities to its partners in a complete liquidation. The partners should then transfer these items to the corporation under the § 351 rules.

Like-Kind Exchanges

Another attempt to achieve nonrecognition treatment involves the exchange of an interest in one partnership for an interest in another. If the exchanged interests could qualify as like-kind property, no gain or loss would be recognized.

The like-kind exchange rules do not apply to the exchange of interests in different partnerships.[23] However, these rules can apply to exchanges of interests in the same partnership.[24]

Gift

Generally, the donor of a partnership interest recognizes neither gain nor loss. If the donor's entire interest is transferred, all items of partnership income, loss,

OTHER DISPOSITIONS

◆

---

23. § 1031(a)(2)(D).

24. Rev.Rul. 84–52, 1984–1 C.B. 157.

deduction, or credit attributable to the interest are prorated between the donor and donee.

However, if the partnership uses the cash method of accounting and has accounts receivable at the time of transfer, the gift may be considered an anticipatory assignment of income. Similarly, if the partnership holds installment notes receivable, the gift of an interest may be considered a taxable disposition of the notes.[25] If the donor's share of partnership liabilities exceeds the donor's basis in the partnership, the gift is treated as part gift and part sale.

Death of a Partner

Unless the partners have a buy-sell agreement providing for a deceased partner's interest to be sold immediately to the remaining partners for a formula or fixed price, the partnership's tax year does not close when a partner dies.[26] Furthermore, the transfer of a partnership interest to a deceased partner's estate or other successor is not considered a sale or exchange. Also, the death of a partner does not result in a taxable disposition of installment obligations held by the partnership.[27]

In professional partnerships, local law may prohibit an estate or other successor from continuing as a partner (beyond a certain time period). In all cases, the remaining partners may wish to buy out or liquidate the deceased partner's interest in the partnership. Community property laws may complicate these transactions.

OPTIONAL ADJUSTMENTS TO PROPERTY BASIS
◆

When a partner purchases a partnership interest, the purchase price reflects what the acquiring partner believes the interest in the partnership is worth. This price reflects, to a large extent, the value the partner placed on the partnership assets. Because the value of the assets probably differs from their inside bases, a discrepancy exists between the partner's outside basis and his or her share of the inside basis of partnership assets.

The inside basis of the partnership property cannot be adjusted to reflect the purchase price paid by the partner unless the partnership makes a special optional adjustment election.[28] When the election is not made, the statute produces some inequitable results.

EXAMPLE 27

A partnership owns a building with an adjusted basis of $450,000 and a fair market value of $900,000. T, an individual, buys a one-third interest in the partnership for $300,000 (an amount equal to one-third of the value of the building). Although the price T paid for the interest was based on fair market value, the building's depreciation continues to be determined on the partnership's related adjusted basis of $450,000, of which T's share is only $150,000. ◆

EXAMPLE 28

In contrast, assume that the building in Example 27 had an adjusted basis of $600,000 and a fair market value of $300,000. Assume also that T purchased the one-third interest for $100,000 (an amount equal to one-third of the value of the building). Although the purchase price was based on fair market value, T obtains the benefit of *double* depreciation deductions since these deductions are calculated on the adjusted basis of the depreciable property ($600,000), which is twice the property's market value. ◆

---

25. § 453B(a).

26. § 706(c)(2)(A)(ii).

27. § 453B(c).

28. § 743(a).

A result similar to that presented in Example 28 can take place when a partnership purchases a partner's interest with a cash payment that is less than the retiring partner's share of the adjusted basis of the partnership assets. Here, the partnership does not reduce the adjusted basis of its assets for the excess share *not* paid to the retiring partner. If some of the remaining assets are depreciable, the remaining partners receive larger depreciation deductions (based on their old share of these assets, plus deductions based on the excess share *not* paid to the retiring partner).

To prevent or alleviate the results presented in Examples 27 and 28, an optional adjustment election is available, under which the basis of partnership assets may be adjusted following either a sale or exchange of an interest or a distribution of partnership property.[29]

Sale or Exchange of an Interest

If the optional adjustment election is in effect and a partner's interest is sold to or exchanged with a third party, a partner dies, or a partnership interest is distributed, the partnership adjusts the basis of its assets as illustrated in the following tables.[30]

The partnership *increases* the adjusted basis of partnership property as follows:

Transferee's outside basis in the partnership	$ xxx
Less: Transferee's share of the inside basis of all partnership property	(xxx)
Increase	$ xxx

The partnership *decreases* the adjusted basis of partnership property as follows:

Transferee's share of the inside basis of all partnership property	$ xxx
Less: Transferee's outside basis in the partnership	(xxx)
Decrease	$ xxx

In both cases, the adjustment affects the basis of partnership property with respect to the transferee only. When the optional adjustment results in a step-up of depreciable property, the transferee partner generally must depreciate the optional adjustment as if it were a newly acquired asset. The transferee partner, therefore, shares in the depreciation taken by the partnership on the original asset and reports all of the depreciation taken on the basis created by the optional adjustment.

For most other calculations involving property for which an optional adjustment has been made, the partner's basis in the property is his or her share of the inside basis for the property plus or minus the partner's optional basis adjustment.

──────────────── EXAMPLE 29 ────────────────

R is a member of the RST Partnership, and all partners have equal interests in capital and profits. The partnership has made an optional basis adjustment election. R's

─────────────

29. § 743(a).

30. § 743(b).

interest is sold to U for $76,000. The balance sheet of the partnership at the date of the sale shows the following:

| | Assets | |
	Adjusted Basis per Books	Market Value
Cash	$ 15,000	$ 15,000
Depreciable assets	150,000	213,000
Total	$165,000	$228,000
	Capital	
Capital accounts		
R	$ 55,000	$ 76,000
S	55,000	76,000
T	55,000	76,000
Total	$165,000	$228,000

The adjustment is the difference between the basis of the transferee's interest in the partnership and the transferee's share of the adjusted basis of partnership property. The basis of U's interest is $76,000. U's share of the adjusted basis of partnership property is $55,000. U's optional adjustment that is added to the basis of partnership property is $21,000.

Transferee's interest basis in partnership	$ 76,000
Less: Transferee's share of adjusted basis of all partnership property	(55,000)
Increase	$ 21,000

◆

Partnership Distributions

Optional adjustments to basis are also available to the partnership when property is distributed to a partner. If an optional basis adjustment election is in effect, the basis of partnership property upon a distribution to a partner is *increased* by the following:[31]

- Any gain recognized by a distributee partner.
- The excess of the adjusted basis of any distributed property to the partnership over the adjusted basis of that property in the hands of the distributee.

Conversely, the basis of partnership property is *decreased* by the following:

- Any loss recognized by a distributee partner.
- In the case of a liquidating distribution, the excess of the distributee's adjusted basis of any distributed property over the basis of that property to the partnership.

─────────────── EXAMPLE 30 ───────────────

R has a partnership basis of $50,000 and receives a building with an adjusted basis to the partnership of $120,000 in termination of his interest. The building's basis in R's hands is $50,000. If an optional basis adjustment election is in effect, the partnership increases the basis of its remaining property by $70,000.

─────────────

31. § 734(b).

Partnership's adjusted basis in distributed property	$120,000
Less: Distributee's basis in distributed property	(50,000)
Increase	$ 70,000

──────────────── EXAMPLE 31 ────────────────

Assume the same facts as in Example 30, except that the partnership's basis in the building was $40,000. R's basis in the building is still $50,000, and the partnership reduces the basis of its remaining property by $10,000.

Distributee's basis in distributed property	$ 50,000
Less: Partnership's adjusted basis in distributed property	(40,000)
Decrease	$ 10,000

Although these rules may seem confusing at first reading, understanding the theory on which they are based will help to clarify the situation. In general, the inside basis for all partnership assets equals the outside basis for all of the partners' interests. When this equality exists either before or after a distribution, no adjustment to the basis of partnership property is necessary. However, when the equality does not exist after the distribution, an adjustment can bring the inside and outside bases back into equality. This is the adjustment that is made by the two increases and the two decreases described above.

──────────────── EXAMPLE 32 ────────────────

Assume the ABC Partnership has an inside basis of $12,000 for its asset. A, B, and C each have outside bases of $4,000 for their partnership interests. If the partnership liquidates partner A's interest with a $5,000 cash distribution, the resulting balance sheet will be unbalanced as follows:

$$
\begin{array}{ccc}
\$12,000 & = & \$12,000 \\
(5,000) & \neq & (4,000) \\
\hline
\$ 7,000 & \neq & \$ 8,000
\end{array}
$$

This unbalanced situation can be eliminated by adding $1,000 to the inside basis of the formula. Note that this is the same amount as the gain that A will recognize on the distribution ($5,000 cash − $4,000 outside basis = $1,000 gain). Therefore, by adding the amount of A's gain to the inside basis of the partnership assets, the inside basis = outside basis formula is back in balance.

$$
\begin{array}{ccc}
\$ 7,000 & \neq & \$ 8,000 \\
+1,000 & & \\
\hline
\$ 8,000 & = & \$ 8,000
\end{array}
$$

Note that if the partnership liquidated A's interest with a distribution of land having a $5,000 inside basis, the same unbalanced situation would occur. Although this transaction will not create any recognized gain for A, the $1,000 optional adjustment is the excess of the $5,000 inside basis of any distributed property over the $4,000 substituted basis of that property in the hands of the distributee ◆

The two optional adjustment decreases can also be explained by this type of analysis.

The Basis Adjustment Election

A basis adjustment election can be made for any year in which a transfer or distribution occurs by attaching a statement to a timely filed partnership return (including extensions).[32] An election is binding for the year for which it is made and for all subsequent years, unless the IRS consents to its revocation. Permission to revoke generally is granted for business reasons, such as a change in the nature of the business or an increase in the frequency of interest transfers. Permission is not granted if it appears the primary purpose is to avoid downward adjustments to basis otherwise required under the election.

TERMINATION OF A PARTNERSHIP

◆

When does a partnership's final tax year end? Technically, it ends when the partnership terminates, which occurs on either of the following events:

- No part of the business continues to be carried on by any of the partners in a partnership.
- Within a 12-month period, there is a sale or exchange of 50 percent or more of the partnership's capital and profits.[33]

A partnership's tax year can close when the partnership incorporates or when one partner in a two-party partnership buys out the other partner, thereby creating a sole proprietorship. A termination can also occur, of course, when the partnership ceases operations and liquidates.

A partnership tax year generally does not close upon the death of a partner, the entry of a new partner, or the liquidation of a partner in other than a two-party partnership. A partnership tax year also does not close upon the sale or exchange of an existing partnership interest unless the transaction results in 50 percent or more of the partnership capital and profits being sold within a 12-month period.

EXAMPLE 33

Partner R, who held a one-third interest in the RST Partnership, died on November 20 of the last calendar year. The partnership uses an approved fiscal year ending September 30. R used a calendar year. The partnership agreement does not contain a buy-sell provision that is triggered upon the death of a partner. Thus, the partnership's tax year does not close with R's death. Instead, income from the fiscal year ending September 30 of the current calendar year will be taxed to R's estate or other successor. Income from the fiscal year ending September 30 of the last year must be reported on R's final income tax return, which covers the period from January 1 to November 20.

CONCEPT SUMMARY 11–6
OPTIONAL BASIS ADJUSTMENT RULES

1. A partnership (not the transferee) can elect to adjust the basis of its assets when a partner's interest is sold to a third party (including another partner), a partner dies, a partnership interest is distributed, or partnership property is distributed to a partner.
2. Once the election is made, it stays in effect until the IRS consents to its revocation.
3. A partnership may not want to make a basis adjustment election because it applies to all pertinent transactions (a partnership must adjust the basis of its properties downward as well as upward).

---

32. § 754.   33. § 708(b)(1).

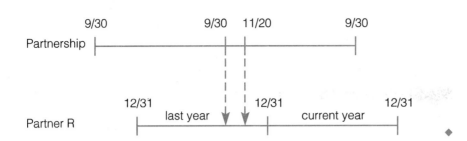

A *technical* termination of a partnership occurs when the partnership business operations continue but the partnership terminates because there has been a sale or exchange of the requisite 50 percent capital and profits interests within 12 months. The terminated partnership is deemed to liquidate by distributing its assets and liabilities to the partners. A new partnership is immediately formed by having the partners recontribute the assets and liabilities to the new partnership. A technical termination has several consequences:

- Potential bunching of income to partners when the partnership and the partners have different tax years.
- Changes in the basis of partnership assets when they are distributed to the partners in liquidation of the old partnership. Recall that some or all of the assets will take a substituted (not carryover) basis in a liquidating distribution.
- Section 704(c) problems (precontribution gain, loss, etc.) may result for some or all of the partners on the contribution of the partnership assets to the new partnership.
- The old partnership's favorable tax year will be lost and may not be able to be reelected by the new partnership.

─────────────── EXAMPLE 34 ───────────────

The XYZ Partnership balance sheet on December 31, 1992, reads as follows:

	Adjusted Basis	Market Value
Cash	$30,000	$30,000
Inventory	9,000	9,000
Capital asset	21,000	45,000
	$60,000	$84,000
X, capital	$20,000	$28,000
Y, capital	20,000	28,000
Z, capital	20,000	28,000
	$60,000	$84,000

On December 31, X sells her partnership interest to A for $28,000, and Y sells his partnership interest to B for $30,000. B paid more than A simply because B did not bargain as well. The sale of the two interests results in a "technical" termination of the partnership. The old XYZ Partnership terminates and distributes its assets pro rata to each of the partners, Z, A, and B. Each partner then immediately recontributes his or her pro rata share of the assets to the new partnership. While the liquidating distribution transaction will not change the basis of the cash or inventory to the partners, each partner will take a substituted basis in one-third of the capital asset. Therefore, Z's basis in the capital asset will be $7,000; A's basis will be $15,000; and B's basis will be $17,000. The partnership will have to account for each partner's built-in gain or loss on his one-third portion of the capital asset under § 704(c). If the XYZ

Partnership had a favorable tax year, that year would be lost with the termination of XYZ. The ZAB Partnership will have to justify the tax year it adopts the same as any new partnership formed on December 31, 1992. ◆

Family Partnerships

Family partnerships are owned and controlled primarily by members of the same family. Such partnerships may be established for a variety of reasons. A daughter may have a particular expertise that, coupled with her parents' abilities, will allow them to establish a successful business. Often, however, the primary reason for establishing a family partnership is the desire to save taxes. If the parents are in higher marginal tax brackets than the children, family tax dollars are saved by funneling some of the parents' income to the children.

With such potential tax savings possible, why do so few family partnerships exist? One reason is that valid family partnerships are hard to establish for tax purposes. A basic tenet of tax law is that income must be taxed to the person who performs the services or owns the capital that generates the income. A parent, therefore, cannot transfer a profits interest to a child and expect the transfer to be recognized for tax purposes.

Because of the concern that family partnerships are being established primarily for tax avoidance purposes, a family member is recognized as a partner only in the following cases:

- Capital is a material income-producing factor in the partnership, and the family member's capital interest is acquired in a bona fide transaction (even if by gift or purchase from another family member) in which ownership and control are received.
- Capital is not a material income-producing factor, but the family member contributes substantial or vital services.[34]

Capital. If a partnership derives a substantial portion of its gross income from the use of capital, such as inventories or investments in plant, machinery, or equipment, the capital is considered to be a material income-producing factor. Ordinarily, capital is not a material income-producing factor if the partnership's income consists principally of fees, commissions, or other compensation for personal services performed by partners or employees.

Children as Partners. When capital is a material income-producing factor and a partnership interest is transferred by gift or sale to a child who is under age 14 and is eligible to be claimed as a dependent by the parent-partner, the child's distributive share of income in excess of $1,200 generally is taxed at the parent's tax rate, unless the income share constitutes earned income. Regardless of age, if the child provides bona fide services to a partnership and the income share constitutes earned income, the parent-partner's tax rate is avoided, and the child's full standard deduction (to the extent of the earned income) can be used.

─── EXAMPLE 35 ───

X operates a first-floor-window-washing business in a summer lakeside resort city. Relatively small amounts of capital are required to operate the sole proprietorship (buckets, sponges, squeegees, etc.). During the summer, X normally hires middle and high school students to wash windows. X's 13-year-old daughter and 12-year-old son

---

34. § 704(e).

want to work in the business during the summer to earn money for spending and for college. Each obtains the necessary summer work permit. X creates the XDS Partnership and gives each child a 5% interest.

X figures that if her children were paid an hourly rate, about 5% of XDS's profits would be distributed to them as wages. X believes that an ownership interest will help the children learn what running a profitable business entails and prepare them for an active business life after their education is completed.

Since capital is not a material income-producing factor in the business, and the children's profit percentages approximate what they would earn if they were paid an hourly rate, all of the income is classified as earned income. Thus, the kiddie tax is avoided. ◆

Gift of Capital Interest. If a family member acquires a capital interest by gift in a family partnership in which capital is a material income-producing factor, only part of the income may be allocated to this interest. First, the donor of the interest is allocated an amount of partnership income that represents reasonable compensation for services to the partnership. Then, the remaining income generally is divided among the partners. An interest purchased by one family member from another is considered to be created by gift for this purpose.[35]

———————— EXAMPLE 36 ————————

A partnership in which a 50% interest was transferred by gift between a parent and child generated a profit of $90,000. Capital is a material income-producing factor. The parent performed services valued at $20,000. The child performed no services. Under these circumstances, $20,000 is allocated to the parent as compensation. Of the remaining $70,000 of income attributable to capital, at least 50%, or $35,000, is allocated to the parent. ◆

Limited Liability Companies

The limited liability company (LLC) is a new form of entity that combines partnership taxation with limited personal liability for all owners of the entity. Several states have passed legislation permitting the establishment of LLCs, and many more states have legislation pending.

An LLC offers the following advantages over a limited partnership:

- None of the owners of an LLC are personally liable for the entity's debts. General partners in a limited partnership have personal liability for these debts.
- Limited partners cannot participate in the management of the partnership. All owners of an LLC can participate in the entity's management.

An LLC also offers the following advantages over an S corporation:

- LLCs can have more than 35 owners.
- Any taxpayers, including corporations, nonresident aliens, other partnerships, and trusts can be owners of an LLC. S corporation shareholders are limited to individuals, estates of individuals, and certain trusts.
- The transfer of property to an LLC in exchange for an ownership interest in the entity is governed by partnership tax provisions rather than corporate tax provisions. Thus, the transferors need not satisfy the 80

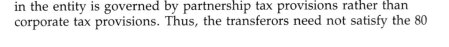

---

35. § 704(e)(3).

percent control requirement needed for tax-free treatment under the corporate tax statutes.

- The S corporation taxes on built-in gains and passive income do not apply to LLCs.
- An LLC can own 80 percent of the stock of another operating corporation. An S corporation cannot.
- An owner's basis in an LLC includes the owner's share of all LLC liabilities under § 752. Only certain S corporation liabilities are included in the S corporation shareholder's basis.
- An LLC may make special allocations under § 704(b), while S corporations must allocate income, loss, etc. on a per share/per day basis.
- The optional adjustments to basis election can be made for the benefit of the LLC and its owners. Such adjustments are not possible in an S corporation.

Although no state is likely to adopt a limited liability statute that is identical in every respect to the legislation of other states, LLC statutes will probably differ only slightly from state to state.

When taxpayers have asked the IRS to rule on the status of an LLC as a partnership for tax purposes, all of the rulings have been favorable.[36] In each instance, the LLC was not taxed as an association (corporation) because it failed to meet the corporate tests of continuity of life and free transferability of interests.

Sales and Exchanges of Partnership Interests

Delaying Ordinary Income. A partner planning to dispose of a partnership interest in a taxable transaction might consider either an installment sale or a pro rata distribution of his or her share of hot assets, followed by a sale of the remaining interest in the partnership. Although the subsequent disposition of the hot assets usually results in ordinary income, the partner can spread the income over more than one tax year by controlling the disposal dates in this manner.

Basis Adjustment for Transferee. If a partnership interest is acquired by purchase, the partner may want to condition the acquisition on the partnership's promise to make an election to adjust the basis of partnership assets. Making the election will result in the basis in the partner's ratable share of partnership assets being adjusted to reflect the difference between the purchase price and the selling partner's share of these assets. Failure to do so could result in the loss of future depreciation deductions or could convert ordinary losses into capital losses.

Planning Partnership Distributions

General Rules. In planning for any partnership distributions, taxpayers should be alert to the following possibilities:

- When gain recognition is undesirable, ascertain that cash distributions from a partnership, including any debt assumptions, do not exceed the basis of the receiving partner's interest.

---

36. For example, see Rev.Rul. 88–76, 1988–2 C.B. 360.

- When a partner is to receive a liquidating distribution and the full basis of the interest will not be recovered, to preserve the partner's loss recognition, be certain that the only assets received by the partner are cash, unrealized receivables, and inventory.
- Current and liquidating distributions result in ordinary income recognition for either the receiving partner or the partnership if hot assets are present. When such income is undesirable, be certain that the partner's interest in hot assets is not changed as a result of the distribution.
- A partner who purchases an interest in a partnership from another partner may want the partnership to make an optional basis adjustment election. This should occur before the purchase takes place.
- Maximize distributions of passive income to partners who are generating passive activity losses from other sources, so as to accelerate their loss deductions.
- When the partnership agreement initially is drafted, consider the importance of the provisions that relate to liquidating distributions of partnership income and property. The arm's length requirement will be met, and the specifics of the agreement will be followed by the IRS if these points are addressed early in the life of the entity. Accordingly, the timing of partner income and partnership deductions can be determined, and an effective plan of succession can be carried out.

Valuation Problems. Both the IRS and the courts usually consider the value of a partner's interest or any partnership assets agreed upon by all partners to be correct. Thus, in planning the sale or liquidation of a partnership interest, one should document the results of the bargaining process. To avoid valuation problems on liquidation, include a formula or agreed-upon procedure in the partnership agreement or in a related buy-sell agreement.

Comparing Sales to Liquidations

When a partner disposes of his or her entire interest in a partnership for a certain sum, the before-tax result of a sale of that interest to another partner or partners will be the same as the liquidation of the interest under § 736. In other words, if both transactions result in the same amount of pre-tax dollars, the partner should be ambivalent about which form the transaction takes unless one form offers tax savings that the other does not.

The tax consequences of a sale of a partnership interest and a liquidation of a partner's interest by an ongoing partnership may differ considerably. One difference occurs when the payment for that interest is extended over several years. When a partner sells the partnership interest to another partner, the selling partner can postpone the recognition of income under the installment sale rules. These rules are very restrictive and require that gain and income be recognized at least as quickly as the proportionate share of the receivable is collected. Under § 736, the § 736(b) payments for partnership property can be made before the income payments under § 736(a). Furthermore, the § 736(b) payments can be treated as a return of basis first with gain recognized only after the distributee partner has received amounts equal to his or her basis. This treatment results in a deferral of gain and income recognition under § 736 that is not available under the installment sale provisions.

The partner who purchases a partnership interest often pays an amount that can be attributed, in part, to partnership goodwill. This purchased goodwill is included in the purchasing partner's outside basis for his or her partnership interest. However, since neither the partner nor the partnership can amortize

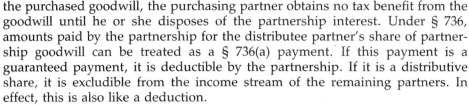

the purchased goodwill, the purchasing partner obtains no tax benefit from the goodwill until he or she disposes of the partnership interest. Under § 736, amounts paid by the partnership for the distributee partner's share of partnership goodwill can be treated as a § 736(a) payment. If this payment is a guaranteed payment, it is deductible by the partnership. If it is a distributive share, it is excludible from the income stream of the remaining partners. In effect, this is also like a deduction.

Recapture income (§§ 1245, 1250, etc.) is an unrealized receivable. Section 736 classifies unrealized receivables as income payments. When the partnership pays a liquidating partner for his or her share of recapture potential in the partnership assets, that amount may be deducted by the partnership as a guaranteed payment or excluded from the remaining partners' income streams if it is a distributive share. When a partner purchases an interest in the partnership, the amount paid for a share of the recapture potential is included in his or her cost basis for the partnership. The partner is not allowed an immediate deduction for this amount.

Finally, a partnership will terminate if 50 percent or more of the total interest in partnership capital and profits is sold within a 12-month period. A liquidation under § 736, however, is not considered a sale or exchange under this rule. Therefore, a partnership can liquidate a partner's interest without terminating the partnership, even though that individual is a 98 percent partner in partnership capital and profits immediately before the liquidating distribution.

A sale and a liquidation of a partnership interest also differ in other respects that are beyond the scope of this text. The point to remember is that differences exist that may result in considerable after-tax savings for the partners. Careful planning can result in a properly structured transaction.

Other Partnership Issues

Choice of Entity.   The partnership liquidation rules demonstrate the general superiority of the partnership form to that of the C corporation at this stage of the life of the business.

- The partnership can effectively claim deductions for its payment for goodwill. Goodwill is not deductible by corporations.
- The liquidation itself is not a taxable event. Under the rules that apply to corporations, however, liquidating distributions and sales in preparation for a distribution are fully taxable.
- Tax liability relative to the liquidation is generated at the partner level, but only upon a recognition event. The timing of this event is virtually under the control of the (ex-)partner. In this manner, the tax obligations can be optimized (i.e., they can be placed into the most beneficial tax year and rate bracket).

Family Partnerships.   Make certain that very young and elderly members of a family partnership contribute services to the entity, so as to justify their income-shifting allocations. These services can comprise the most routine facets of the business, including clerical and duplication functions, monitoring and operating copy and fax machines, and ongoing maintenance of the indoor and outdoor landscaping environments. Although no more than a market level of compensation can be assigned for this purpose, the services themselves constitute evidence of the active role that the partner plays in the operations of the entity.

Since there is no equivalent of the kiddie tax for elderly taxpayers, retention of the founding members of the partnership past the nominal retirement age often facilitates the income-shifting goals of the family.

PROBLEM MATERIALS

CHAPTER 11
PARTNERSHIPS: DISTRIBUTIONS,
TRANSFER OF INTERESTS,
AND TERMINATIONS
◆
11–31

DISCUSSION QUESTIONS

1. Discuss the various types of distributions from a partnership and the tax consequences of each. *Concept Summaries 11-1, 11-2 & 11-3*

2. Distinguish between § 736 income and property payments. What are the tax consequences of such payments to the remaining partners and the partnership? *Ex 12-15*

3. If liquidation payments are to be spread over a number of years, how are the payments to be allocated between income payments and property payments? *Ex 16 & 17*

4. Under what circumstances is a loss recognized by a withdrawing partner whose entire interest is liquidated in a proportionate distribution of assets? *Ex 9 and § 731(a)(2)*

5. What is the character of a gain or loss recognized on the sale or exchange of a partnership interest? *Ex 21 to 26*

6. Discuss the possible collateral effects of a sale or exchange of a partnership interest. *Ex 18 & 34 Reg §1.708-1(b)(ii)*

~~7.~~ 7. What are unrealized receivables of a partnership? Substantially appreciated inventory items? *11-18 & 15*

8. Under what circumstances will the transfer of a partnership interest to a controlled corporation for stock result in taxable gain? *11-19*

9. Distinguish between the basis adjustments allowed for sales and exchanges and for distributions. Why are such adjustments allowed? When could an unfavorable result occur? *Ex. 27-32*

10. Which taxpayer makes the optional adjustment to basis election and what are the consequences of this election? *11-23 & 24*

11. Describe the various types of events that can cause a partnership termination. Which of these can cause a "technical" termination? *11-24 & 25*

12. What is a family partnership? Under what circumstances can a family member be a partner in such a partnership? What income allocation is required? *11-26 & 27*

13. Discuss the advantages of a limited liability company over an S Corporation. If a limited liability company incurs debt from an independent third-party bank, how do you think that debt should be treated under the liability sharing rules discussed in Chapter 10? *11-27 & 28*

14. A retiring partner often can choose between selling his partnership interest to the other partners or selling it to the partnership. Explain why the method selected may make a difference for tax purposes. *11-29 & 30*

PROBLEMS

15. When B's outside basis in the BCD Partnership is $25,000, the partnership distributes to her $7,000 cash and a parcel of land (fair market value of $30,000; inside basis to the partnership of $12,000). B remains a partner in the partnership, and the partnership contains no hot assets.

Ex 2-5

   a. Determine the recognized gain or loss to the partnership as a result of this distribution. *0*

   b. Determine the recognized gain or loss to B as a result of this distribution. *0*

   c. Determine B's basis in the land and BCD Partnership after the distribution. *Examples 2-5   12,000 Land   6,000 P/S*

   25000
   (7000)
   18,000
   (12,000)
   6,000

16. In each of the following independent cases, indicate:

Ex (2-6)

   ■ Whether the partner recognizes gain or loss.
   ■ Whether the partnership recognizes gain or loss.
   ■ The partner's adjusted basis for the property distributed.
   ■ The partner's outside basis in the partnership after the distribution.

   a. R received $31,000 cash in partial liquidation of her interest in the partnership. R's outside basis for her partnership interest immediately before the distribution was $30,000.

b. S received $6,000 cash and land with an inside basis to the partnership of $12,000 in partial liquidation of her interest. S's outside basis for her partnership interest immediately before the distribution was $16,000.

c. Assume the same facts as in (b), except that S's outside basis for her partnership interest immediately before the distribution was $35,000.

d. M received $4,000 cash and two tracts of land in partial liquidation of her partnership interest. The two tracts have adjusted bases to the partnership of $8,000 and $24,000, respectively. Each tract has a $20,000 fair market value. M's outside basis for her partnership interest immediately before the distribution was $20,000.

17. The basis of L's partnership interest is $17,080. L receives a pro rata liquidating distribution consisting of $9,760 cash and his share of inventory with a basis of $12,200 to the partnership and a fair market value of $18,300. Assume the partnership also liquidates.

a. How much gain or loss, if any, must L recognize as a result of the distribution?

b. What basis will L take in the inventory?

c. If the inventory is sold two years later for $18,000, what are the tax consequences to L?

d. What are the tax consequences to the partnership as a result of the liquidating distribution?

e. Would your answer to (b) change if this had been a nonliquidating distribution?

18. Assume the same facts as in Problem 17, except that L's basis in the partnership is $24,400 instead of $17,080.

a. How much gain or loss, if any, must L recognize on the distribution?

b. What basis will L take in the inventory?

c. What are the tax consequences to the partnership?

d. Would your answer to (a) or (b) change if this had been a nonliquidating distribution?

19. D's partnership basis is $64,500. In a pro rata distribution in liquidation of the partnership, D receives $12,900 cash and two parcels of land with bases of $17,200 and $12,900 to the partnership. The partnership held both parcels of land for investment, and the parcels had fair market values of $32,250 and $43,000. Assume the partnership also liquidates.

a. How much gain or loss, if any, must D recognize on the distribution?

b. What basis will D take in each parcel?

c. If the land had been held as inventory by the partnership, what effect, if any, would it have on your responses to (a) and (b)?

20. Assume the same facts as in Problem 19, except that D received $21,500 cash and an old truck having a basis of $430 to the partnership and a fair market value of $215.

a. How much loss, if any, may D recognize on the distribution?

b. What basis will D take in the truck?

c. Suppose D's son drives the truck for personal use for one year before selling it for $100. How much loss may D recognize on the sale of the truck? What tax planning procedure could have prevented this result?

21. Use the approach introduced in Concept Summary 11–2 to derive the realized and recognized gain or loss for the two owners of the dissolving AB Partnership, and the bases of the distributed assets, given the following facts:

	Partner A (2/3)	Partner B (1/3)
Interest basis	$50,000	$15,000
Cash received	20,000	10,000
Inventory received		
Market value	6,000	3,000
Basis to AB	3,000	1,500

Depreciation recapture potential		
Amount	8,000	4,000
Basis to AB	–0–	–0–
Building received		
Market value	90,000	45,000
Basis to AB	72,000	36,000

(handwritten: this recap is ordinary gain ◆ anything over that is a capital gain)

22. X sells his interest in the equal HEX Partnership to Y for $47,000 cash and the assumption of X's share of partnership liabilities. On the sale date, the partnership's cash basis balance sheet reflects the following:

(handwritten: Concept summary 11-5)

	Adjusted Basis	Fair Market Value
Cash	$51,000	$ 51,000
Accounts receivable	–0–	60,000
Capital assets	9,000	39,000
Total	$60,000	$150,000

	Adjusted Basis	Fair Market Value
Note payable	$ 9,000	$ 9,000
Capital accounts		
H	17,000	47,000
E	17,000	47,000
X	17,000	47,000
Total	$60,000	$150,000

a. What is the total amount realized by X on the sale?
b. How much, if any, ordinary income must X recognize on the sale?
c. How much capital gain to X?
d. What is Y's basis in the partnership interest acquired?
e. If the partnership makes an election to adjust the bases of the partnership assets to reflect the sale, what adjustment is made?

(handwritten: C/S 11-5, EX-19, EX 29)

23. Assume in Problem 22 that X's partnership interest is not sold to an outsider. Instead, the partnership makes a liquidating distribution of $47,000 cash to X, and the remaining partners assume X's share of the liabilities. How much gain or loss must X recognize?

(handwritten: C/S 1/5, §736)

24. The balance sheet of the NOP Partnership on December 31, 1992, is as follows:

	Basis	FMV
Cash	$15,000	$15,000
Accounts receivable	–0–	9,000
Land	24,000	57,000
	$39,000	$81,000
N, capital	$13,000	$27,000
O, capital	13,000	27,000
P, capital	13,000	27,000
	$39,000	$81,000

(handwritten: EX. 12)

P decides to retire from the partnership. He is to be paid cash in liquidation of his interest according to the following schedule:

December 31, 1992	$9,000
December 31, 1993	$9,000
December 31, 1994	$9,000

P's outside basis for his partnership interest is $13,000. The partnership has never made a § 754 election. P acquired his interest in the partnership in 1986.

What are the alternatives available to P and the partnership regarding the taxation of the distributions? Compute the amount of § 736(a) and § 736(b) payment under these alternatives.

25. At the end of the current year, K, an equal partner in the four-person KLOM Partnership, has an outside basis of $18,000 in the partnership, including a $40,000 share of partnership debt. At the end of the current year, K's share of the partnership's § 1245 recapture potential is $12,000. The partnership did not have any taxable income or loss in the current year, and all parties use the calendar year. Describe the income tax consequences to K in each of the following situations that take place at the end of the current year:

   a. K sells the partnership interest to T for $25,000 cash and the assumption of the appropriate share of partnership liabilities.   C/S 11-5 & EX. 21 to 23
   b. K dies after a lengthy illness on December 31 of the current year. K's widow takes his place in the partnership.   11-20

26. Briefly discuss how your responses in Problem 25 would change if the KLOM Partnership had $88,000 of unrealized receivables at the end of the current year, including § 1245 recapture potential.   EX 24

27. In each of the following liquidating distributions, determine the amount and character of any gain or loss to be recognized by each partner and the basis of each asset (other than cash) received. Indicate the amount of any optional basis adjustments available to the distributing partnership. Assume the partnership also liquidates.

   EX. 7, 30 & 32

   a. R has a partnership basis of $18,000 and receives a distribution of $25,000 in cash.
   b. S has a partnership basis of $9,000 and receives $3,000 cash and a capital asset with a basis to the partnership of $4,000 and a fair market value of $12,000.
   c. T has a partnership basis of $15,000 and receives $4,000 cash, inventory with a basis to the partnership of $8,000, and a capital asset with a partnership basis of $10,000. The inventory and capital asset have fair market values of $5,000 and $7,000, respectively.

28. L, a partner in the cash basis LAM Partnership, has a 30% interest in partnership profits and losses. The partnership's balance sheet at the end of the current year is as follows:

	Basis	**FMV**		**Basis**	**FMV**
Cash	$ 25,000	$ 25,000	L, capital	$ 54,000	$135,000
Receivables	–0–	240,000	A, capital	63,000	157,500
Land	155,000	185,000	M, capital	63,000	157,500
Totals	$180,000	$450,000	Totals	$180,000	$450,000

L sells her interest in the LAM Partnership to J at the end of the current year for cash of $135,000.

   a. How much income must L report on her tax return for the current year from the sale, and what is its nature?   EX. 23
   b. If the partnership did not make an optional basis adjustment election, what are the type and amount of income that J must report in the next year when the receivables are collected?

c. If the partnership did make an optional basis adjustment election, what are the type and amount of income that J must report in the next year when the receivables are collected (assuming no other transactions in the next year)? The land (which is used in the LAM Partnership's business) is sold for $205,000? *EX 29 1.755-1(b)?*

29. For each of the following independent fact patterns, indicate whether a termination of the partnership has occurred for tax purposes. Assume no other partnership interests have been sold either one year before or one year after the transactions described.

   a. M sells her interest in capital and profits of the MPQ Partnership. She owns a 68% interest in capital and a 48% interest in the partnership profits.

   b. L and H are equal partners in the L & M Partnership. L dies on January 15, 1992. H purchases L's interest from his estate on March 15, 1992. Answer for January 15, 1992.

   c. Answer (b), for March 15, 1992.

   d. F, a 58% partner in the F & D Partnership gives his entire interest to his son on July 1, 1992.

   e. A, B, and C are equal partners in the ABC Partnership. On January 22, 1992, A sells his entire interest to D. On December 29, 1992, B sells a 15% interest to E. On January 25, 1993, C sells his interest to F. *11-24 & 11-25*

30. Reconsider the fact situation presented in Example 29. Construct the STU balance sheet for the end of the day on which the optional basis adjustment is made with respect to U's purchase.

31. P and C, parent and child, operate a local apparel shop as a partnership. The PC Partnership earned a profit of $20,000 in the current year. C's equal partnership interest was acquired by purchase from the parent. Assume that capital is a material income-producing factor and that P manages the day-to-day operations of the shop without any help from C. Reasonable compensation for P's services would be $8,000.

   a. How much of the partnership income is allocated to P?

   b. What is the maximum amount of partnership income that can be allocated to C?

   c. Assuming that C is five years old, has no other income, and is claimed as a dependency exemption by the parent, how is the C's income from the partnership taxed? *§ 1(g) §63(c)(5)*

RESEARCH PROBLEMS

RESEARCH PROBLEM 1 The ABC Partnership agreement was drafted in 1984. While the agreement covered many issues, it did not contain a provision explaining how a retiring partner would be paid for his or her share of partnership goodwill. In 1992, the partnership executed an agreement entitled "Amendment of Limited Partnership Agreement," which provided that A was to receive $100,000 cash from the partnership on July 1, 1992. The payment was to be made to retire A's interest in the partnership. Of that amount, $30,000 is in return for A's one-third interest in the fair market value of the net assets of the partnership. The other $60,000 was referred to as "a guaranteed payment, or a payment for goodwill."

The IRS agent says that the "Amendment of Limited Partnership Agreement" is not clear and, therefore, chooses to treat the payment for goodwill as ordinary income to A and deductible by the partnership. Assume this approach maximizes the tax revenue for the government. Assuming you would prefer return of basis and capital gain treatment for A, what authority can you obtain to support your position?

RESEARCH PROBLEM 2 The accrual basis KB Partnership had a § 754 election in effect when one of its partners sold a portion of her partnership interest and incurred a $50,000 gain. Complete the chart below, following the basis allocation rules dictated by § 755, and indicate the amount of the total adjustment to be allocated to each of the assets on the balance sheet of the new KGB Partnership. Offer KGB any tax planning advice that results from the application of these rules.

Item	Fair Market Value	Basis before § 754 Adjustment	Allocated Adjustment	Basis to KGB after Adjustment
Cash	$ 15,000	$ 15,000		
Receivables	28,000	31,000		
Inventory	57,000	45,000		
Marketable securities held for investment for four years	42,000	50,000		
Depreciable equipment	110,000	88,000		
Land held for speculation	75,000	104,000		
Partnership goodwill	5,000	–0–		

CHAPTER

S CORPORATIONS

OBJECTIVES

Provide an in-depth discussion of the rules governing S corporation status.

Describe the corporations that qualify for the S election.

Discuss how the election must be made and, once made, how it can be lost.

Explain the effect of the S election on the corporation and its shareholders.

Describe the situations where S status is desirable or undesirable.

OUTLINE

GENERAL CONSIDERATIONS

◆

[handwritten margin notes: S is a tax Election states consern states is a corporation is a corporation PA has S corp for State tax]

Since the top individual tax rates are less than the top corporate tax rate of 34 percent, both Subchapters S and K of the Code have taken on added importance. Most businesses have reevaluated the desirability of using a C corporation as a means of conducting a trade or business in favor of a flow-through entity, such as an S corporation or a partnership. One major consequence of the 1986 increase in corporate taxes was a predictable increase in the number of S corporation elections.

Subchapter S of the Internal Revenue Code of 1986 allows certain corporations to receive unique treatment for Federal income tax purposes.[1] Although this election essentially results in the S corporation receiving tax treatment that resembles that of a partnership, the entity is still a corporation under state law and for many other tax purposes. Special provisions pertain to the entity, however, under the operational provisions of §§ 1361–1379.

An S corporation is largely a tax-reporting, rather than a tax-paying, entity. In this respect, the entity is treated much like a partnership. As in the partnership conduit concept, the taxable income of an S corporation flows through to the shareholders, regardless of whether the income is distributed in the form of actual dividends. There is, in general, no S corporation corporate-level tax, and the income is taxed to the shareholders immediately. The S corporation is not subject to the alternative minimum tax, accumulated earnings tax, or personal holding company tax. Certain S corporations may, however, be subject to an excess passive investment income tax or a built-in gains tax.

EXAMPLE 1

Assume that an entity earns $300,000 in 1992. Assume also that the applicable marginal individual tax rate is 31%, the applicable marginal corporate tax rate is 34%, and all after-tax income is distributed currently.

	C Corporation	S Corporation or Partnership
Earnings	$ 300,000	$300,000
Less: Corporate tax	(102,000)	–0–
Available for distribution	$ 198,000	$300,000
Less: Tax at shareholder level	(61,380)	(93,000)
Available after-tax earnings	$ 136,620	$207,000

[handwritten: 199750; 61423; 137828; issue bonuess NO corp taxes; 69172]

The flow-through business entity generates an extra $70,380 of after-tax earnings compared to a C corporation. Moreover, the flow-through business entity avoids the corporate alternative minimum tax (AMT) and the AMT ACE adjustment (refer to Chapter 6). The C corporation might be able to reduce this disadvantage by paying out its earnings as compensation, rents, or interest expense. Tax at the owner level can also be avoided by not distributing after-tax earnings. ◆

The entity's losses are allocated to the shareholders, who deduct them on their individual tax returns. The nature of a closely held sports organization makes an S election advantageous. H. R. "Bum" Bright, for example, purchased the Dallas Cowboys in 1984 for $85 million. Before the sale of the Cowboys to Jerry Jones in 1989, the team's record plummeted, along with attendance. With

---

1. Under the tax law, a Subchapter S corporation is called an "S corporation." A regular corporation that has not elected S status is designated a "C corporation." C corporations are those governed by Subchapter C of the Code (§§ 301–386).

an S election, Bright could have taken advantage of these losses on his personal tax return, except that he had a similar run of bad luck as the largest shareholder in First Republic Bank Corporation.

Other corporate transactions that flow through separately under the conduit concept include net long-term capital gains and losses, charitable contributions, tax-exempt interest, foreign tax credits, and business credits. Each shareholder of an S corporation separately takes into account his or her pro rata share of certain items of income, deductions, and credits (see Figure 12–1). Under § 1366(b), the character of any item of income, expense, gain, loss, or credit is determined at the corporate level. These tax items pass through as such to each shareholder, based on the prorated number of days during the relevant S year that each held stock in the corporation.

Subchapter S in Perspective

Subchapter S permits certain corporations to avoid the corporate income tax and enables them to pass through operating losses to their shareholders. It represents an attempt to achieve a measure of tax neutrality in resolving the difficult problem of whether a business should be conducted as a sole proprietorship, partnership, or corporation.

In dealing with Subchapter S, certain observations should be kept in mind.

1. S corporation status is an elective provision. Failure to make the election will mean that the rules applicable to the taxation of corporations ← 2553? (Subchapter C status) and shareholders will apply (refer to Chapter 2).
2. S corporations are regular corporations in the legal sense. The S election affects only the Federal income tax consequences of electing corporations. In fact, a few states, including Michigan and New Jersey, do not recognize the S election at all and subject such corporations to the state corporate income tax and any other state corporate taxes that are imposed. See Chapter 15 for a discussion of multistate income tax effects.

FIGURE 12–1   Flow-Through of Separate Items of Income and Loss to S Corporation Shareholders

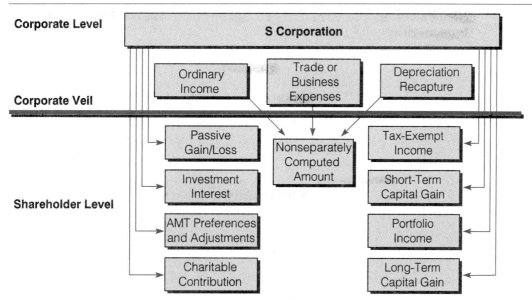

3. Federal income tax law treats S corporations neither as partnerships nor as regular corporations. The tax treatment resembles partnership taxation, but involves a unique set of tax rules. However, Subchapter C controls unless Subchapter S otherwise provides a pertinent tax effect.

4. Because Subchapter S is an elective provision, strict compliance with the applicable Code requirements generally has been demanded by both the IRS and the courts. Any unanticipated deviation from the various governing requirements may therefore lead to an undesirable and often unexpected tax result (e.g., the loss of the S election).

In summary, an S corporation may be subject to the following taxes:

■ Preelection built-in gains tax.
■ Passive investment income penalty tax.

An S corporation is *not* subject to the following taxes:

■ Corporate income tax.
■ Accumulated earnings tax.
■ Personal holding company tax.
■ Alternative minimum tax.
■ Environmental excise tax on AMT income.[2]

QUALIFICATION FOR S CORPORATION STATUS
◆

Definition of a Small Business Corporation

A small business corporation must possess the following characteristics:

■ Is a domestic corporation (is incorporated or organized in the United States).
■ Is not otherwise ineligible for the election.
■ Has no more than 35 shareholders. *KEY*
■ Has as its shareholders only individuals, estates, and certain trusts.
■ Does not have a nonresident alien shareholder.
■ Issues only one class of stock.

No maximum or minimum dollar sales or capitalization restrictions apply to an S corporation.

--------------------------------- EXAMPLE 2 ---------------------------------

Two individuals decide to incorporate their business and make an S election. They note that the definition of "small" in § 1361(b)(1) relates chiefly to the number of shareholders and not to the size of the corporation. With only two shareholders, they clearly meet the definition of a small business corporation with respect to the S election. Once they make the election, the corporation will not be subject to a corporate income tax.

During their shareholders' meeting, the individuals review § 1244(c)(1) to decide whether to issue § 1244 stock. (See Chapter 3 for a discussion of § 1244 stock.) In sharp contrast to § 1361(b)(1), this "small business corporation" definition looks to the extent of the capitalization of the corporation. The individuals agree that the two provisions are not mutually exclusive, because § 1244 stock allows them to receive ordinary *loss* treatment on future stock sales or on bankruptcy. The shareholders vote to issue § 1244 stock. ◆

---

2. Rev.Rul. 89–82, 1989–1 C.B. 23.

Ineligible Corporation. Banks, insurance companies, Puerto Rico or possessions corporations, and members of an affiliated group (see Chapter 8) are not eligible to make an S election. Thus, an S corporation cannot own 80 percent or more of the stock of another corporation. Under certain conditions, however, a corporation can establish one or more inactive affiliates, in the event that such companies may be needed in the future. The "affiliated group" prohibition does not apply as long as none of the affiliated corporations engages in business or produces gross income.[3]

EXAMPLE 3

T Corporation is formed in Texas to develop and promote a new fast-food franchise system, namely, the "Texas Chicken Delight." If the entity is successful in Texas, the shareholders of T will expand the operation to New Mexico, Oklahoma, Arkansas, and Louisiana. With this in mind and with a view toward protecting the name and product identification of the parent corporation, T Corporation forms subsidiaries in each of these states. Although T Corporation and its subsidiaries now constitute an affiliated group, T can still qualify as an S corporation as long as the subsidiaries remain inactive and generate no gross income. If any of the subsidiaries begin conducting business, T Corporation can no longer maintain its S election. ◆

Number of Shareholders Limitation. An electing corporation is limited to 35 shareholders. This number corresponds to the private placement exemption under Federal securities law. In testing for the 35-shareholder limitation, a husband and wife are treated as one shareholder as long as they remain married. Furthermore, the estate of a husband or wife and the surviving spouse are treated as one shareholder in § 1361(c)(1).

EXAMPLE 4

H and W (husband and wife) jointly own 10 shares in S Corporation, with the remaining 90 shares outstanding owned by 34 other unmarried persons. H and W are divorced; pursuant to the property settlement approved by the court, the 10 shares held by H and W are divided between them (5 to each). Before the divorce settlement, S Corporation had only 35 shareholders. After the settlement, it has 36 shareholders and no longer qualifies as a small business corporation. ◆

Type of Shareholder Limitation. All of an S corporation's shareholders must be either individuals, estates, or certain trusts.[4] Stated differently, none of the shareholders may be partnerships, corporations, or nonqualifying trusts. The justification for this limitation is related to the 35-shareholder restriction. If, for example, a partnership with 40 partners could be a shareholder, could it not be said that the corporation has at least 40 owners? If this interpretation were permitted, the 35-shareholder restriction could be easily circumvented by indirect ownership. Keep in mind, though, that an S corporation can be a partner in a partnership, and it can own stock of another corporation or all the stock of an inactive subsidiary corporation.

a small portion *less than 80%*

The tax law permits a voting trust arrangement. Moreover, other exceptions mitigate the rule that a trust cannot be a shareholder in an S corporation. Since these exceptions are of limited applicability, they are not discussed in this text.

An S corporation may be a general partner in a partnership. Thus, in such a partnership arrangement, all equity holders (S shareholders and partners) have

---

3. § 1361(c)(6).   **4.** § 1361(b)(1)(B).

both the limited liability of corporate ownership and the pass-through tax treatment of an S corporation. Essentially, the group is free from the 35-shareholder limitation.[5]

EXAMPLE 5

To obtain more financial capital, P, an S corporation with 35 shareholders, places most of its assets into a limited partnership; P is the only general partner. Ten other individuals and two corporations invest as limited partners in the partnership. P is to receive 65% of the profits. Now 45 individuals and two corporations own the previous business. The partnership arrangement avoids double taxation and offers limited liability for its 47 owners. ◆

Nonresident Alien Prohibition. None of an S corporation's shareholders can be nonresident aliens.[6] In a community property jurisdiction where one of the spouses is married to a nonresident alien, this rule can be a trap for the unwary.[7] A resident alien or a nonresident U.S. citizen can be an S corporation shareholder, however.

The probable reason for discrimination against nonresident alien individuals is administrative. It would be difficult to collect the shareholder-level tax from people outside the U.S. taxing jurisdiction. However, as business becomes increasingly international in scope, this prohibition may be subject to criticism.

One Class of Stock Limitation. An S corporation can have only one class of stock issued and outstanding.[8] Congress apparently felt that the capital structure of a small business corporation should be kept relatively simple. Allowing more than one class of stock (e.g., common and preferred) would complicate the pass-through to the shareholders of various corporate tax attributes. Authorized and unissued stock or treasury stock of another class does not disqualify the corporation. Likewise, unexercised stock options, phantom stock, stock appreciation rights, warrants, and convertible debentures often do not constitute a second class of stock, and differences in voting rights among shares of common stock are permitted.[9]

Safe harbor rules provide that "straight debt" is not treated as a second class of stock and does not disqualify an S election.[10] The characteristics of straight debt include the following:

- The debtor is subject to a written, unconditional promise to pay on demand or on a specified date a sum certain in money.
- The interest rate and payment date are not contingent on corporate profit, management discretion, or similar factors.
- The debt is not convertible into stock.
- The creditor is an individual (other than a nonresident alien), an estate, or qualified trust.

Essentially, an S corporation has one class of stock unless deliberate actions are taken to circumvent the requirement. Facts and circumstances determine the proper tax treatment of business transactions. For example, a second class of

---

5. G.C.M. 36966 (December 27, 1976); Ltr.Rul. 8711020 (12/86).

6. § 1361(b)(1)(C).

7. See, for example, *Ward v. U.S.*, 81–2 USTC ¶9519, 48 AFTR2d 81–5942, 661 F.2d 226 (Ct. Cls., 1981), where the Court found that the stock was owned as community property. Since the taxpayer-shareholder (a U.S. citizen) was married to a citizen and resident of Mexico, the nonresident

alien prohibition was violated. If the taxpayer-shareholder had held the stock as separate property, the S election would have been valid.

8. § 1361(b)(1)(D).

9. § 1361(c)(4).

10. § 1361(c)(5)(A).

stock does not exist where the IRS recharacterizes a payment of excessive compensation as a dividend distribution.

Making the Election

If the corporation satisfies the definition of a small business corporation, the next step to achieving S status is a valid election. Key factors include who must make the election and when the election must be made.

Who Must Elect.   The election is made by filing Form 2553, and all shareholders must consent.[11] For this purpose, both husband and wife must file consents if they hold the stock as joint tenants, tenants in common, tenants by the entirety, or community property. Since a husband and wife generally are considered as one shareholder for purposes of the 35-shareholder limitation, this inconsistency in treatment has led to considerable taxpayer grief—particularly in community property states where the spouses may not realize that their stock is jointly owned as a community asset.

EXAMPLE 6

Three shareholders, A, B, and C, incorporate in January and file Form 2533. Shareholder C is married and lives in California. A is single and B is married; they live in North Carolina. A, B, and C must consent to the S election. Because C is married and lives in a community property state, C's spouse must also consent to the election. Since North Carolina is not a community property state, B's spouse need not consent to the S election. ◆

The consent of a minor shareholder can be made by the minor or a legal or natural guardian (e.g., parent). If the stock is held under a state Uniform Gifts to Minors Act, the custodian of the stock may consent for the minor, but only if the custodian is also the minor's legal or natural guardian. The minor is not required to issue a new consent when he or she comes of age and the custodianship terminates.[12]

When the Election Must Be Made.   To be effective for the following year, the election can be made at any time during the current year. To be effective for the current year, the election must be made on or before the fifteenth day of the third month of that year. An election can be effective for a short tax year of less than two months and 15 days, even if it is not made until the following tax year.[13]

EXAMPLE 7

In 1992, X Corporation, a calendar year C corporation, decides to become an S corporation beginning January 1, 1993. An election made at any time during 1992 accomplishes this objective. If, however, the election is made in 1993, it must be made on or before March 15, 1993. An election after March 15, 1993, will not make X Corporation an S corporation until 1994. ◆

Although no statutory authority exists for obtaining an extension of time for filing an S election, a shareholder may obtain an extension of time to file a consent, if a timely election is filed, reasonable cause is given, and the interests of the government are not jeopardized.[14]

---

11. § 1362(a)(2). But see Example 10 for a situation where a nonshareholder may be required to consent.

12. Rev.Rul. 71–287, 1971–2 C.B. 317.

13. § 1362(b).

14. Rev.Rul. 60–183, 1960–1 C.B. 625; *Pestcoe*, 40 T.C. 195 (1963); Temp.Reg. § 18.1362–2(e).

─────────────── EXAMPLE 8 ───────────────

X and Y decide to convert their C corporation into a calendar year S corporation for 1993. At the end of February before the election is filed, Y travels to the Ukraine in the former Soviet Union and forgets to sign a consent to the election. Y will not return to the United States until June and cannot be reached by fax. X files the S election on Form 2553, and also requests an extension of time to file Y's consent to the election. X indicates the reasonable cause for the extension (i.e., shareholder out of the country). Since the government's interest will not be jeopardized, the IRS probably will grant Y an extension of time to file the consent. X must file the election on Form 2553 on or before the fifteenth day of the third month (i.e., March 15) for the election to be effective for January 1, 1993. ◆

An election cannot be made for an entity that does not yet exist.[15] For a newly created corporation, the question may arise as to when the 2½-month election period begins to run. Reg. § 1.1372–2(b)(1) specifies that the first month begins at the earliest occurrence of any of the following events: (1) when the corporation has shareholders, (2) when it acquires assets, or (3) when it begins doing business.[16]

─────────────── EXAMPLE 9 ───────────────

Several individuals acquire assets on behalf of T Corporation on June 29, 1992, and begin doing business on July 3, 1992. They subscribe to shares of stock, file articles of incorporation for T Corporation, and become shareholders on July 7, 1992. The S election must be filed no later than 2½ months from June 29, 1992 (on or before September 12) to be effective for 1992. ◆

Where an S corporation's first taxable year begins after the first day of a month, the first month of the 2½-month period starts with the first day of the tax year and ends after the close of the day *before* the numerically corresponding day of the succeeding month.[17]

Even if the 2½-month rule is met, a current election will not be valid until the following year under either of the following conditions:

▪ The eligibility requirements were not met during any part of the taxable year before the date of election.
▪ Persons who were shareholders during any part of the taxable year before the election date, but were not shareholders when the election was made, did not consent.

These rules prevent the allocation of income or losses to preelection shareholders who either were ineligible to hold S corporation stock or did not consent to the election.

─────────────── EXAMPLE 10 ───────────────

As of January 15, 1992, the stock of X Corporation (a calendar year C corporation) was held equally by three individual shareholders: U, V, and Z. On that date, Z sells his interest to U and V. On March 14, 1992, U and V make the S election by filing Form 2553. X cannot become an S corporation until 1993. Although the election was timely filed, Z did not consent. Had all the shareholders (U, V, and Z) signed Form 2553 during the year, S status would have taken effect as of January 1, 1992. ◆

Once an election is made, it need not be renewed. It remains in effect unless otherwise lost.

---

15. See, for example, *T.H. Campbell & Bros., Inc.*, 34 TCM 695, T.C.Memo. 1975–149; Ltr.Rul. 8807070.

16. For support of Reg. § 1.1372–2(b)(1) see, for example, *Nick A. Artukovich*, 61 T.C. 100 (1973).

17. Reg. 1.1362–(3).

Loss of the Election

An S election terminates if one of the Code's eligibility rules is violated. In addition, an S election can be lost in any of the following ways:

- A new shareholder owning more than one-half of the stock affirmatively refuses to consent to the election.
- Shareholders owning a majority of shares (voting and nonvoting) voluntarily revoke the election.
- The number of shareholders exceeds the maximum allowable limitation.
- A class of stock other than voting or nonvoting common stock is created.
- A subsidiary (other than a nonoperating entity) is acquired.
- The corporation fails the passive investment income limitation.
- A nonresident alien becomes a shareholder.

Voluntary Revocation. Section 1362(d)(1) permits a voluntary revocation of the election if shareholders owning a majority of shares consent. A revocation filed up to and including the fifteenth day of the third month of the tax year is effective for the entire tax year, unless a prospective effective date is specified. A revocation made after the fifteenth day of the third month of the tax year is effective on the first day of the following tax year. However, if a prospective date is specified, the termination is effective as of the specified date.

EXAMPLE 11

The shareholders of T Corporation, a calendar year S corporation, elect to revoke the election on January 5, 1992. Assuming the election is duly executed and timely filed, T becomes a regular corporation for calendar year 1992. If the election is not made until June 1992, T is not a C corporation until calendar year 1993. ◆

A revocation that designates a prospective effective date results in the splitting of the year into a short S corporation taxable year and a short C corporation taxable year. The day *before* the day on which the revocation occurs is treated as the last day of a short S corporation taxable year, and the day on which the revocation occurs is treated as the first day of the short regular corporate taxable year. The corporation allocates the income or loss for the entire year on a pro rata basis (weighted daily allocation).

EXAMPLE 12

Assume the same facts as in Example 11, except that T designates July 1, 1992, as the revocation date. Accordingly, June 30, 1992, is the last day of the S corporation taxable year. The C taxable year runs from July 1, 1992, to December 31, 1992. Any income or loss for the entire year is allocated between the short years on a pro rata basis. ◆

Rather than elect a pro rata allocation, the corporation can elect (with the consent of *all* who were shareholders at any time during the S short year) to report the income or loss on each return on the basis of income or loss as shown on the corporate permanent records. Under this method, items are attributed to the short S and C corporation years according to the time they were incurred (as reflected in the entity's accounting records).[18]

---

18. §§ 1362(e)(1), (2) and (3).

Cessation of Small Business Corporation Status. A corporation not only must be a small business corporation to make the S election but also must continue to qualify as such to keep the election. In other words, meeting the definition of a small business corporation is a continuing requirement for maintaining the S status. In the case of such an involuntary termination, the loss of the election applies as of the date on which the disqualifying event occurs.[19]

———————————— EXAMPLE 13 ————————————

T Corporation has been a calendar year S corporation for three years. On August 13, 1992, one of its 35 unmarried shareholders sells *some* of her stock to an outsider. T now has 36 shareholders, and it ceases to be a small business corporation. For 1992, T is an S corporation through August 12, 1992, and a C corporation from August 13 through December 31, 1992. ◆

Passive Investment Income Limitation. The Code provides a passive investment income limitation for an S corporation that possesses accumulated earnings and profits from years in which the entity was a C corporation. If such a corporation has passive income in excess of 25 percent of its gross receipts for three consecutive taxable years, the S election is terminated as of the beginning of the following taxable year.[20]

———————————— EXAMPLE 14 ————————————

For 1989, 1990, and 1991, B Corporation, a calendar year S corporation, derived passive income in excess of 25% of its gross receipts. If B holds accumulated earnings and profits from years in which it was a C corporation, its S election is terminated as of January 1, 1992. ◆

Such damaging C corporation earnings and profits could be acquired by an S corporation from a regular corporation where earnings and profits carry over under § 381 (e.g., due to a merger), or they could be earned in years before the S election. S corporations themselves never generate earnings and profits.[21]

Although this definition of passive investment income appears to parallel that of personal holding company income (refer to Chapter 6), the two types of income are not identical. For example, long-term capital gain from the sale of securities would be passive investment income but would not be personal holding company income. Moreover, there are no relief provisions for rent income similar to the personal holding company rules. The inclusion of gains from the sale of securities within the definition of passive investment income generally has made it difficult, if not impossible, for corporations that deal chiefly in security transactions to achieve S status if harmful C corporation earnings and profits exist.

Rents present a unique problem. Although rents are classified by the Code as passive investment income, Reg. § 1.1372–4(b)(5)(vi) states that rents do not fall into this category if the corporation (landlord) renders significant services to the occupant (tenant). This exception is similar to the material participation test for passive activity income of § 469.

———————————— EXAMPLE 15 ————————————

T Corporation owns and operates an apartment building. Although the corporation provides utilities for the building, maintains the lobby in the building, and furnishes

———

19. § 1362(d)(2)(B).
20. § 1362(d)(3)(A)(ii).

21. § 1362(d)(3)(B).

trash collection for the tenants, this does not constitute the rendering of significant services for the occupants.[22] Thus, the rents paid by the tenants of the building are passive investment income to T. ◆

─────────────── EXAMPLE 16 ───────────────

Assume the facts as in Example 15, with one addition—T also furnishes maid services to its tenants. Now the services rendered are significant in that they go beyond what one might normally expect the landlord of an apartment building to provide. Under these circumstances, the rental income no longer constitutes passive investment income. ◆

Reelection after Termination. After the election has been terminated, § 1362(g) enforces a five-year waiting period before a new election can be made. The Code does, however, allow the IRS to make exceptions to this rule and permit an earlier reelection by the corporation in two situations:[23]

- There is a more than 50 percent change in ownership after the first year for which the termination is applicable.
- The event causing the termination was not reasonably within the control of the S corporation or its majority shareholders.

─────────────── EXAMPLE 17 ───────────────

K, the sole owner of an S corporation, voluntarily terminates the S election in February 1992. Unless consent for a new election is given by the Commissioner, the successor corporation cannot make another S election until 1997. The Commissioner probably would not allow an early reelection. The same result would occur if the election was involuntarily terminated in 1992 and the precipitating event was within the control of the corporation or shareholder K. ◆

─────────────── EXAMPLE 18 ───────────────

Suppose, in Example 17, that K sells 80% of her stock to M in 1993. Since there was a more than 50% change in ownership, the successor corporation may be able to obtain a consent from the IRS for an early S election. ◆

Since an S corporation is largely a tax-reporting, rather than a tax-paying, entity, the entity is treated much like a partnership. As in the partnership conduit concept, the taxable income of an S corporation flows through to the shareholders, whether or not such income is distributed in the form of actual dividends. Likewise, losses of the entity are allocated to the shareholders, who deduct them on their individual tax returns. Other corporate transactions that flow through separately under the conduit concept include net long-term capital gains and losses, charitable contributions, tax-exempt interest, foreign tax credits, and business credits.

Similar to the partnership rules, each shareholder of an S corporation takes into account separately his or her pro rata share of certain items of income, deductions, and credits. Under § 1366(b), the character of any item of income, expense, gain, loss, or credit is determined at the corporate level. These tax items pass through as such to each shareholder, based on the prorated number of days during the relevant S year that each held stock in the corporation.

OPERATIONAL RULES
◆

───────────────

22. *Bramlette Building Corp., Inc.,* 52 T.C. 200 (1969), *aff'd.* in 70–1 USTC ¶9361, 25 AFTR2d 70–1016, 424 F.2d 751 (CA–5, 1970).

23. § 1362(f); Reg. § 1.1372–5(a); Rev.Rul. 78–274, 1978–2 C.B. 220.

Choice of Tax Year

Since S corporation shareholders report their shares of S items as of the entity's year-end, the selection of a corporate tax year is an important tax decision. An S corporation may use a calendar year or a fiscal year; for tax deferral purposes, a corporate fiscal year ending January 31 and a calendar year shareholder would be ideal.

EXAMPLE 19

An S corporation is organized on October 5, 1992. Its Subchapter S ordinary income for the next 15 months is as follows:

October 5–December 31, 1992	$ 30,000
January 1993	20,000
February–September 30, 1993	180,000
October–December 31, 1993	60,000

If the S corporation elects a calendar year, the shareholders recognize $30,000 of income in 1992. But if a January 31 fiscal year is used, the calendar year shareholders recognize no income for 1992. Furthermore, only $50,000 is taxable to the shareholders in 1993. This deferral of income caused Congress to require most S corporations to use calendar years. If this S corporation could select a September 30 fiscal year, no income is taxable to the shareholders in 1992, and only $230,000 is taxable in 1993. ◆

S corporations must conform to the taxable years of their shareholders (the calendar year in most instances). There are two exceptions to this general rule. First, an S corporation may use a taxable year for which it can establish a business purpose.[24] Second, an S corporation may make a one-time election under § 444 to keep or establish a fiscal year, provided that a corporate-level payment is made on any income deferred by the shareholders.

An S corporation can establish an acceptable business purpose for a fiscal year in three ways:

- The fiscal year is a natural business year.
- The fiscal year serves an acceptable business purpose.
- An existing S corporation meets certain grandfathering requirements. [25]

Meeting the natural business year exception involves a simple quantitative test. If 25 percent or more of a corporation's gross receipts for the 12-month period is recognized in the last 2 months of that period, and the requirement has been met for three consecutive 12-month periods, the S corporation may adopt, retain, or change to a noncalendar year. If the entity is to establish a natural business year, it must have at least a 47-month gross receipts history.

EXAMPLE 20

An S corporation's gross receipts total $100,000 for each of the last three calendar years. If the corporation recognizes at least $25,000 of its gross receipts in April and May for three consecutive years, the S corporation may adopt, retain, or change to a May 31 year-end. The following diagram illustrates the test for the May 31 year-end.

---

24. § 1378(a).

25. Rev. Proc. 87–32, 1987–2 C.B. 396.

First 10 months		April	May
If > $75,000, does not qualify for May 31 year-end		If $25,000 or more, qualifies for May 31 year-end	

◆

Other business purposes may be used to establish that a fiscal year is acceptable to the IRS. However, the fiscal year must be close to the entity's natural business year (e.g., the entity barely fails the 25 percent test). The IRS lists the following factors that do *not* constitute a valid business purpose:[26]

- The use of a particular fiscal year for regulatory or financial accounting purposes.
- Personnel practices of the corporation.
- Tax deferral for the shareholders.
- Use of a fiscal year for administrative purposes (e.g., awarding bonuses or promotions).
- Use of model years, price lists, or other items that change on a noncalendar annual basis.

In general, a taxable year under the § 444 election may not result in a deferral period of more than three months. However, an S corporation in existence before 1987 may elect to retain its previous taxable year for years after 1986, even though such a year results in a deferral period exceeding three months.[27]

The penalty for a fiscal year under § 444 is that the S corporation must make a required payment on April 15 for any tax year for which the election is in effect. This required payment is equal to the highest rate of tax under § 1 plus one percentage point. Thus, for election years beginning in 1992, the required payment rate is 32 percent (31% + 1%). Such payments are not deductible by the S corporation (or by any person) for Federal income tax purposes. They are refundable deposits that do not earn interest and do not pass through to the S shareholders.[28]

EXAMPLE 21

X was a C corporation in 1986 with a September 30 fiscal year. During 1987, X elects S status and is unable to meet the business purpose exception for maintaining a fiscal year. For X to maintain a fiscal year, it must elect under § 444 and make a required payment under § 7519 by April 15. A failure to make this payment will result in the termination of the § 444 election, effective for the year in which the failure occurred.

An electing corporation need not make a required payment until the amount for the current and all preceding election years exceeds $500. If X Corporation had made an S election in 1986, § 444 would not be available. However, the entity would be allowed to change to a taxable year under § 444 by treating the deferral period of the tax year being changed as the same as the deferral period of the last tax year of the C corporation. ◆

The payment required from an S corporation under a § 444 election should approximate the tax that would be payable if a calendar year were used.

---

26. Rev.Rul. 87–57, 1987–2 C.B. 117.

27. Reg. § 1.444–1T(b).

28. § 7519.

Although the § 444 election is complex, an S corporation may have valid business reasons to select a fiscal year. A company may have difficulty closing the books, preparing statements, and issuing its Schedules K–1 on a timely basis under a calendar year.

Computation of Taxable Income

Subchapter S taxable income or loss generally is determined in a manner similar to the tax rules that apply to partnerships, except that the amortization of organizational expenditures under § 248 is an allowable deduction.[29] Further-more, an S corporation can deduct salaries and payroll taxes. Finally, S corporations must recognize any gains (but not losses) under § 1363(d) on distributions of appreciated property to the shareholders.

Certain deductions not allowable for a partnership also are not allowable for an S corporation, including the standard deduction, personal exemption, alimony deduction, personal moving expenses, and expenses for the care of certain dependents. Furthermore, provisions of the Code governing the computation of taxable income applicable only to corporations, such as the dividends received deduction, do not apply.[30]

In general, S corporation items are divided into (1) nonseparately computed income or losses and (2) separately stated income, losses, deductions, and credits that uniquely could affect the tax liability of any shareholders. In essence, nonseparate items are lumped together into an undifferentiated amount that constitutes Subchapter S taxable income or loss. For example, any net gains from the recapture provisions of § 1245 and §§ 1250 through 1255 constitute nonseparately computed income. Likewise, any § 291 recapture amount constitutes nonseparately computed income.

Each shareholder is allocated a pro rata portion of this nonseparately computed amount (see Example 23). Under § 1366(a)(1), for a shareholder who dies during the year, the share of the pro rata items up to the date of death is reported on the shareholder's final individual income tax return (see Example 24). Tax accounting and other elections are generally made at the corporate level, except for elections that shareholders may make separately (e.g., foreign tax credit election).

The following items, among others, are separately stated on Schedule K of the Form 1120S, and each shareholder takes into account his or her pro rata share (the share is passed through on a Schedule K–1):[31]

- Tax-exempt income.[32]
- Long-term and short-term capital gains and losses.
- Section 1231 gains and losses.
- Charitable contributions.
- Passive gains, losses, and credits under § 469.
- Certain portfolio income.
- Section 179 expense deduction.
- Tax preferences.
- Depletion.

- Foreign income or losses.
- Wagering gains or losses.
- Nonbusiness income or loss (§ 212).
- Recoveries of tax benefit items.
- Intangible drilling costs.
- Investment interest, income, and expenses.
- Total property distributions.
- Total dividend distributions from accumulated earnings and profits.

---

29. § 1363(b).

30. § 703(a)(2).

31. §§ 1366(a) and (b).

32. Tax-exempt income passes through to the shareholders and increases their tax basis in the stock.

This pro rata method assigns an equal amount of each of the S items to each day of the year. If a shareholder's stock holding changes during the year, this per-day method assigns the shareholder a pro rata share of each item for *each* day the stock is owned:

S Corporation item	X	Percentage of shares owned	X	Percentage of year owned	=	Amount of item to be reported

This per-day method must be used unless the shareholder disposes of his or her entire interest in the entity.[33]

If a shareholder's interest is completely terminated during the tax year, all shareholders may elect to treat the S taxable year as two taxable years, with the first year ending on the date of the termination. Under this election, an interim closing of the books is undertaken, and the owners report their shares of the S corporation items as they occurred during the year.[34]

EXAMPLE 22

The following is the income statement for B, an S corporation:

Sales		$ 40,000
Less cost of sales		(23,000)
Gross profit on sales		$ 17,000
Less: Interest expense	$1,200	
Charitable contributions	400	
Advertising expenses	1,500	
Other operating expenses	2,000	(5,100)
		$ 11,900
Add: Tax-exempt interest	$ 300	
Dividend income	200	
Long-term capital gain	500	
	$1,000	
Less: Short-term capital loss	(150)	850
Net income per books		$ 12,750

Subchapter S taxable income for B is calculated as follows, using net income for book purposes as a starting point:

Net income per books			$12,750
Separately computed items			
Deduct: Tax-exempt interest		$ 300	
Dividend income		200	
Long-term capital gain		500	
		$(1,000)	
Add: Charitable contributions	$400		
Short-term capital loss	150	550	
Net effect of separately computed items			(450)
Subchapter S taxable income			$12,300

---

33. §§ 1366(a)(1) and 1377(a)(1).   **34.** § 1377(a)(2).

The $12,300 of Subchapter S taxable income, as well as the separately computed items, are divided among the shareholders based upon their stock ownership. ◆

——————————— Example 23 ———————————

Assume in Example 22 that shareholder P owned 10% of the stock for 100 days and 12% for the remaining 265 days. Using the required per-day allocation method, P's share of the S corporation items is as follows:

	Schedule K Totals	P's Share 10%	12%	P's Schedule K–1 Totals
Subchapter S taxable income	$12,300	$337	$1,072	$1,409
Tax-exempt interest	300	8	26	34
Dividend income	200	5	17	22
LTCG	500	14	44	58
Charitable contributions	400	11	35	46
STCL	150	4	13	17

P's share of the Subchapter S taxable income is the total of $12,300 × (.10 × 100/365) plus $12,300 × (.12 × 265/365), or $1,409. P's Schedule K–1 totals flow through to his Form 1040. ◆

——————————— Example 24 ———————————

If, in Example 22, P dies after owning the stock 100 days, his share of the S corporation items are reported on the final Form 1040. Thus, only the items in the column labeled 10% in Example 23 would be reported on P's final tax return. S corporation items that occur after the shareholder's death most likely would appear on the Form 1041 (the estate's income tax return). ◆

Tax Treatment of Distributions to Shareholders

The rules governing distributions to S shareholders blend the entity and conduit approaches. A distribution to a shareholder of a C corporation is treated as ordinary dividend income to the extent of earnings and profits, as a nontaxable return of capital until the stock basis reaches zero, and as a sale or exchange thereafter. To accommodate both preelection and postelection earnings, effectively a dormant C corporation exists within the distribution framework of an S corporation.

The amount of any distribution to an S corporation shareholder is equal to the cash plus the fair market value of any other property distributed. Either of two sets of distribution rules applies, depending upon whether the electing corporation has accumulated earnings and profits (e.g., from Subchapter C years).

A distribution by an S corporation having no accumulated earnings and profits is not includible in gross income to the extent that it does not exceed the shareholder's adjusted basis in stock. When the amount of the distribution exceeds the adjusted basis of the stock, the excess is treated as a gain from the sale or exchange of property (capital gain in most cases).

——————————— Example 25 ———————————

P, a calendar year S corporation, has no accumulated earnings and profits. During 1992, J, an individual shareholder, receives a cash dividend of $12,200 from P Corporation. J's basis in his stock is $9,700. J recognizes a capital gain from the cash distribution of $2,500, the excess of the distribution over the stock basis ($12,200 – $9,700). The remaining $9,700 is tax-free, but it reduces J's basis in the stock to zero. ◆

An S corporation should maintain an accumulated adjustments account (AAA). Essentially, the AAA is a cumulative total of undistributed net income items for S corporation taxable years beginning after 1982. The AAA is adjusted in a similar fashion to the shareholder's stock basis, except there is no adjustment for tax-exempt income and related expenses and no adjustment for Federal taxes attributable to a C corporation tax year. Further, any decreases in stock basis have no impact on AAA when the AAA balance is negative.

The AAA is a corporate account,[35] whereas the shareholder basis in the stock investment is calculated at the shareholder level. Therefore, the AAA (unlike the stock basis) can have a negative balance. The AAA is determined at the end of the year of a distribution rather than at the time the distribution is made. When more than one distribution occurs in the same year, a pro rata portion of each distribution is treated as having been made out of the AAA. The AAA is important in maintaining the treatment of a property distribution as tax-free. This AAA procedure provides the mechanism for taxing the income of an S corporation only once.

A shareholder has a proportionate interest in the AAA regardless of the size of his or her stock basis.[36] However, since the AAA is a corporate account, no connection exists between the prior accumulated S corporation income and any particular shareholder. Thus, the benefits of AAA can be shifted from one shareholder to another. For example, when an S shareholder transfers stock to another shareholder, any AAA on the purchase date is fully available to the purchaser. Similarly, issuing additional stock to a new shareholder in an S corporation having AAA dilutes the account relative to the existing shareholders.

The treatment of a cash distribution from an S corporation with accumulated earnings and profits is summarized as follows:

1. Tax-free up to the amount in the AAA (limited to stock basis).
2. Any previously taxed income (PTI)[37] in the corporation under prior-law rules on a tax-free basis. However, PTI probably cannot be distributed in property other than cash [according to Reg. § 1.1375–4(b), effective under prior law].
3. The remaining distribution constitutes a dividend to the extent of accumulated earnings and profits. With the consent of all of its shareholders, an S corporation may elect to have a distribution treated as made from accumulated earnings and profits rather than from the AAA. This is known as an *AAA bypass election*. Otherwise, no adjustments are made to accumulated earnings and profits during S years except for distributions taxed as dividends, and adjustments from redemptions, liquidations, reorganizations, and divisions. For example, accumulated earnings and profits can be acquired in a reorganization.
4. Any residual amount is applied against the shareholder's remaining basis in the stock.[38] Such amount is considered to be a return of capital, which is not taxable. In this context, basis is reduced by the fair market value of the distributed asset.
5. Distributions that exceed the shareholder's tax basis for the stock are taxable as capital gains.

---

35. § 1368(e)(1)(A).

36. § 1368(c).

37. §§ 1368(c)(1) and (e)(1). Before 1983, an account similar to AAA was in place, namely, previously taxed income (PTI). Any S corporations in existence before 1983 might have PTI, which currently may be distributed tax-free.

38. § 1368(c).

─────────────────────── Example 26 ───────────────────────

T, a calendar year S corporation, distributes a $1,200 cash dividend to its only shareholder, X, on December 31, 1992. The shareholder's basis in the stock is $100 on December 31, 1991, and the corporation has no accumulated earnings and profits. For 1992, T Corporation had $1,000 of nonseparately computed income from operations, $500 capital loss, and $400 of tax-exempt income.

X must report $1,000 of income and $500 of deductions. The tax-exempt income is not taxed to the shareholder. X's stock basis is increased by the $400 tax-exempt income and the $1,000 taxable income, and it is decreased by the $500 of deductions. The results of current operations affect the shareholder's basis before the application of the distribution rule.

Immediately before the cash dividend, X's stock basis is $1,000. Thus, $1,000 of the cash dividend is tax-free ($500 from the AAA and $500 from the remaining stock basis). Since X's stock basis drops to zero, the additional $200 of the distribution is a $200 gain from the sale or exchange of stock ($1,200 − $1,000). X's AAA and stock basis are both zero as of December 31, 1992, determined as follows:

	Corporate AAA	X's Stock Basis
Balance, 1/1/92	–0–	$ 100
Income	$1,000	1,000
Loss	(500)	(500)
Tax-exempt income	—	400
Subtotal	$ 500	$ 1,000
Distribution	(500)	(1,000)
Balance, 12/31/92	$ –0–	$ –0–

─────────────────────── Example 27 ───────────────────────

Assume the same facts as in Example 26, except that T had Subchapter C earnings and profits of $750. T has an AAA of $500 ($1,000 − $500), which does not include the tax-exempt income. X's basis in the stock immediately before the distribution is $1,000 since X's basis is increased by the tax-exempt income. Therefore, X is not taxed on the first $500, which is a recovery of the AAA. The next $700 is a taxable dividend from the accumulated earnings and profits account. (Refer to the first column, step 3, of Concept Summary 12–1.)

Concept Summary 12–1
Classification Procedures for Distributions from an S Corporation*

Where Earnings and Profits Exist	Where No Earnings and Profits Exist
1. Tax-free to the extent of accumulated adjustments account.**	
2. Any PTI from pre-1983 tax years can be distributed tax-free.	
3. Ordinary dividend from accumulated earnings and profits.***	
4. Tax-free reduction in basis of stock.	1. Nontaxable to the extent of adjusted basis in stock.
5. Excess treated as gain from the sale or exchange of stock (capital gain in most cases).	2. Excess treated as gain from the sale or exchange of property (capital gain in most cases).

*A distribution of appreciated property by an electing corporation results in recognized gain that first is allocated to and reported by the shareholders.

**Once stock basis reaches zero, any distribution from AAA is treated as a gain from the sale or exchange of stock. Thus, basis is an upper limit on what a shareholder may receive tax-free.

***An AAA bypass election is available to pay out accumulated E & P before reducing the AAA [§ 1368(e)(3)].

X's basis in the stock is $500 ($1,000 − $500). Although the taxable portion of the distribution does not reduce X's basis in the stock, the nontaxable AAA distribution does. ◆

Schedule M–2. Schedule M–2 on page 4 of Form 1120S (reproduced below) contains a column labeled "Other adjustments account." Essentially, this account includes items not used in the calculation of the AAA, such as tax-exempt income and any related nondeductible expenses. However, distributions from this account are not taxable. Once the earnings and profits account reaches zero, distributions fall under the two-tier system: (1) nontaxable to the extent of basis, then (2) capital gain. Moreover, there is no need for an "other adjustments account" when a corporation has no accumulated earnings and profits.

--- EXAMPLE 28 ---

During 1992, S Corporation records the following items:

Accumulated adjustments account, beginning of year	$ 8,500
Prior-taxed income, beginning of year	6,250
Ordinary income	25,000
Tax-exempt interest	4,000
Key employee life insurance proceeds received	5,000
Payroll penalty expense	2,000
Charitable contributions	3,000
Unreasonable compensation	5,000
Premiums on key employee life insurance	2,000
Distributions to shareholders	16,000

S Corporation's Schedule M–2 for the current year appears as follows:

Schedule M-2	Analysis of Accumulated Adjustments Account, Other Adjustments Account, and Shareholders' Undistributed Taxable Income Previously Taxed (See instructions.)		
		(a) Accumulated adjustments account	(b) Other adjustments account	(c) Shareholders' undistributed taxable income previously taxed
1	Balance at beginning of tax year . . .	8,500		6,250
2	Ordinary income from page 1, line 21 . .	25,000		
3	Other additions		9,000**	
4	Loss from page 1, line 21.	( )		
5	Other reductions	(10,000*)	(2,000)	
6	Combine lines 1 through 5	23,500	7,000	
7	Distributions other than dividend distributions .	16,000	-	
8	Balance at end of tax year. Subtract line 7 from line 6	7,500	7,000	6,250

*$2,000 (payroll penalty) + $3,000 (charitable contributions) + $5,000 (unreasonable compensation).
**$4,000 (tax-exempt interest) + $5,000 (life insurance proceeds). ◆

Any distribution of *cash* by the corporation with respect to the stock during a post-termination transition period of approximately one year is applied against and reduces the adjusted basis of the stock, to the extent that the amount of the distribution does not exceed the AAA.[39] Thus, a terminated S corporation should make a cash distribution during the one-year period following termination to the extent of all previously undistributed net income items for all S tax years. Since only cash distributions reduce the AAA during this post-termination period, the C corporation should not make any property distributions. Most likely, the entity should sell any property and distribute the proceeds.

---

39. §§ 1371(e) and 1377(b).

─────────────────────── **Example 29** ───────────────────────

The sole shareholder of P, a calendar year S corporation during 1991, elects to terminate the S election, effective January 1, 1992. As of the end of 1991, P has an AAA of $1,300. P's sole shareholder, Q, can receive a nontaxable distribution of cash during a post-termination transition period of approximately one year to the extent of P's AAA. Although a cash dividend of $1,300 during 1992 would be nontaxable to Q, it would reduce the adjusted basis of Q's stock. ◆

Alternative Minimum Tax.   An S corporation is not directly subject to the alternative minimum tax (AMT). Under the conduit approach, all tax preference items flow through the S corporation to be included in the shareholders' AMT calculations. The allocation of the tax preference items is based upon the pro rata daily allocation method, unless the corporation has elected the interim closing-of-the-books method. Each shareholder includes the proper portion of each tax preference item in his or her AMT calculations. For a list of tax preference items, see Chapter 6.

An S corporation has the advantage of calculating tax preference items using individual, rather than corporate, rules. Thus, the S corporation has no accumulated current earnings (ACE) adjustment. For corporations with large ACE adjustments, an S election can be quite attractive. Recall, though, that the 24 percent individual AMT rate is higher than the corresponding corporate rate.

─────────────────────── **Example 30** ───────────────────────

During 1992, an S corporation has a positive AMT adjustment for mining exploration costs of $45,000, an excess depletion tax preference of $70,000, and untaxed appreciation on a charitable contribution of stock of $10,000. The ACE adjustment is $80,000. If T is a 10% shareholder, T is assigned 10% of $45,000, $70,000, and $10,000 as tax preference items ($4,500 + $7,000 + $1,000), but T generates no ACE adjustment. ◆

An S corporation is allowed to use the amount of any AMT credit carryover arising in a C corporation tax year as an offset against the built-in gains tax.

Corporate Treatment of Certain Property Distributions

An S corporation recognizes a gain on any distribution of appreciated property (other than in a reorganization) in the same manner as if the asset had been sold to the shareholder at its fair market value.[40] The corporate gain is passed through to the shareholders. There is an important reason for this rule. Without it, property might be distributed tax-free (other than for certain recapture items) and later sold without income recognition to the shareholder, because the stepped-up basis equals the asset's fair market value. The character of the gain—capital gain or ordinary income—depends upon the type of asset being distributed.

The S corporation does not recognize a loss for assets that are worth less than their basis. Furthermore, when such property is distributed, the shareholder's basis in the asset is equal to the asset's fair market value. Thus, the potential loss is postponed until the shareholder sells the stock of the S corporation. Since loss property receives a step-down in basis without any loss recognition by the S corporation, such dividend distributions should be avoided. See Concept Summary 12–2.

───────────────

40. § 311(b).

─────────── EXAMPLE 31 ───────────

Q, an S corporation for 10 years, distributes a tract of land held as an investment to its majority shareholder. The land was purchased for $22,000 many years ago and is currently worth $82,000. Q recognizes a capital gain of $60,000, which increases the AAA by $60,000. Then the property dividend reduces AAA by $82,000 (the fair market value). The tax consequences are the same for appreciated property, whether it is distributed to the shareholders and they dispose of it, or the corporation sells the property and distributes the proceeds to the shareholders.

If the land were purchased for $80,000 many years ago and is currently worth $30,000, the $50,000 realized loss is not recognized at the corporate level, and the shareholder receives a $30,000 basis in the land. The $50,000 realized loss disappears from the corporate level. Since loss is not recognized on the distribution of property that has declined in value, the AAA is not reduced. To recognize the loss on such property, the property must be sold by the S corporation. ◆

─────────── EXAMPLE 32 ───────────

Assume the same facts as in Example 31, except that Q is a C corporation or a partnership. Assume the partner's basis in the partnership is $25,000. The tax consequences may be summarized as follows:

| | Appreciated Property | | |
	S Corporation	C Corporation	Partnership
Entity gain/loss	$60,000	$60,000	$ –0–
Owner's gain/loss	60,000	60,000	–0–
Owner's basis	82,000	82,000	25,000

| | Property That Has Declined in Value | | |
	S Corporation	C Corporation	Partnership
Entity gain/loss	$ –0–	$ –0–	$ –0–
Owner's gain/loss	–0–	–0–	–0–
Owner's basis	30,000	30,000	25,000

◆

CONCEPT SUMMARY 12–2
DISTRIBUTION OF PROPERTY

	Appreciated Property	Depreciated Property
S corporation	Realized gain is recognized to the corporation, which passes it through to the shareholders. Such gain increases a shareholder's stock basis, generating a market value basis in the property. On the distribution, the shareholder's stock basis is reduced by the FMV of the property (but not below zero).	Realized loss is not recognized. The shareholder assumes an FMV basis in the property. Loss is postponed indefinitely.
C corporation	Realized gain is recognized under § 311(b) and increases E & P (net of tax). The shareholder assumes an FMV basis and has an FMV taxable dividend.	Realized loss is not recognized.
Partnership	No gain to the partnership or partner. Basis to the partner is limited to the partner's basis in the partnership.	Realized loss is not recognized.

Shareholder's Tax Basis

The calculation of the initial tax basis of stock in an S corporation is similar to that for the basis of stock in a C corporation and depends upon the manner in which the shares are acquired (e.g., gift, inheritance, purchase). When a shareholder transfers to an S corporation property that is encumbered by a mortgage, the assumed liability reduces the shareholder's basis in the stock. Once the initial tax basis is determined, various transactions during the life of the corporation affect the shareholder's basis in the stock. Although each shareholder is required to compute his or her own basis in the S shares, neither Form 1120S nor Schedule K–1 provides a place for deriving this amount. See Concept Summary 12–3.

A shareholder's basis is increased by further stock purchases and capital contributions. Operations during the year also cause the following upward adjustments to basis:[41]

- Nonseparately computed income.
- Separately stated income items (e.g., nontaxable income).
- Depletion in excess of basis in the property.

The following items cause a downward adjustment to basis (but not below zero):

- Nonseparately computed loss.
- Separately stated loss and deduction items.
- Distributions not reported as income by the shareholder (an AAA distribution).
- Nondeductible expenses of the corporation.

A shareholder's basis in the stock can never be reduced below zero. Any further downward adjustment (losses or deductions) in excess of the stock basis is

Know

CONCEPT SUMMARY 12–3
ADJUSTMENTS TO STOCK BASIS AND AAA

	Stock Basis*	AAA
Original basis (e.g., purchase, inheritance, gift)	Increase	No effect
Stock purchases	Increase	No effect
Taxable income items	Increase	Increase
Nontaxable income	Increase	No effect
Capital gains	Increase	Increase
Deductible expenses	Decrease	Decrease
Expenses related to tax-exempt income	Decrease	No effect
Losses (ordinary and capital)	Decrease	Decrease
Depletion in excess of basis	Increase	Increase
Depletion (not in excess of basis)	Decrease	Decrease
Corporate distributions (FMV)	Decrease**	Decrease**

*Can never go below zero.
**Only by tax-free distributions under § 1367(a)(2)(A), and only after the income and loss adjustments.

---

41. § 1367(a).

applied to reduce (but not below zero) the shareholder's basis in any indebtedness from the electing corporation. Any excess of losses or deductions over both bases is *suspended* until there are subsequent bases. Once the basis of any debt is reduced, it is later increased (only up to the original amount) by the subsequent *net* increase resulting from *all* positive and negative basis adjustments. The debt basis is adjusted before any increase is made in the stock basis.[42] A distribution below stock basis does not reduce any debt basis. If a loss and a distribution occur in the same year, the loss reduces the basis before the distribution.[43]

—————————————————— EXAMPLE 33 ——————————————————

T, a sole shareholder, has a $7,000 stock basis and a $2,000 basis in a loan that she made to a calendar year S corporation at the beginning of 1992. Subchapter S net income during 1992 is $8,200. The corporation incurred a short-term capital loss of $2,300 and received $2,000 of tax-exempt interest income. Cash of $15,000 is distributed to T on November 15, 1992. As a result, T's basis in her stock is zero, and her loan basis is still $2,000 at the end of 1992, since only losses and deductions (and not distributions) reduce the debt basis. T recognizes a $100 gain ($15,000 − $14,900). See Concept Summaries 12–2 and 12–3.

	Corporate AAA	T's Stock Basis	T's Loan Basis
Beginning balance	$ –0–	$ 7,000	$2,000
S net income	$ 8,200	8,200	–0–
Tax-exempt income	–0–	2,000	–0–
STCL	(2,300)	(2,300)	–0–
Subtotal	$ 5,900	$14,900	$2,000
Distribution ($15,000)	5,900 this is in this 14,900	–0–	
Ending balance	$ –0–	$ –0–	$2,000

Although stock basis cannot be reduced below zero, the $100 excess distribution does not reduce T's loan basis. ◆

The basis rules for an S corporation are somewhat similar to the rules for determining a partner's interest basis in a partnership. However, a partner's basis in the partnership interest includes the partner's direct investment plus a ratable share of any partnership liabilities.[44] Conversely, corporate borrowing has no effect on the stock basis of an S corporation shareholder. If a partnership borrows from a partner, the partner receives a basis increase as if the partnership had borrowed from an unrelated third party.[45] In a similar fashion, an S corporation shareholder has a tax basis in any loan made by the shareholder to the S corporation. Although S losses may be applied against such loan basis, partnership losses do not reduce a partner's loan basis.

Treatment of Losses

Net Operating Loss. One major advantage of an S election is the ability to pass through any net operating loss (NOL) of the corporation directly to the shareholders. Under § 1366(a)(1)(A), a shareholder can deduct such a loss for

---

42. § 1367(b)(2).
43. §§ 1366(d)(1)(A) and 1368(d)(1).

44. § 752(a).
45. Reg. § 1.752–1(e).

the year in which the S corporation's tax year ends. The corporation is not entitled to any deduction for the NOL. The individual shareholder's loss is deducted as a deduction *for* AGI. A shareholder's basis in the stock is reduced to the extent of any pass-through of the NOL, and the shareholder's AAA is reduced by the same deductible amount.[46]

--------- Example 34 ---------

An S corporation incurs a $20,000 NOL for the current year. At all times during the tax year, the stock was owned equally by the same 10 shareholders. Each shareholder is entitled to deduct $2,000 *for* AGI for the tax year in which the corporate tax year ends. ◆

Net operating losses are allocated among shareholders in the same manner. NOLs are allocated on a daily basis to all shareholders.[47] Transferred shares are considered to be held by the transferee (not the transferor) on the date of the transfer.[48]

Deductions for an S corporation's NOL pass-through cannot exceed a shareholder's adjusted basis in the stock *plus* the basis of any loans made by the shareholder to the corporation. If a taxpayer is unable to prove the tax basis, the NOL pass-through can be denied.[49] In essence, a shareholder's stock or loan basis cannot go below zero. As noted previously, once a shareholder's adjusted stock basis has been eliminated by an NOL, any excess NOL is used to reduce the shareholder's basis for any loans made to the corporation (but never below zero). The basis for loans is established by the actual advances made to the corporation and not by indirect loans.[50] If the shareholder's basis is insufficient to allow a full flow-through and there is more than one type of loss (e.g., in the same year, the taxpayer incurs both a passive loss and a net capital loss), the flow-through amounts are determined on a pro rata basis.

Except in the Eleventh Circuit, the fact that a shareholder has guaranteed a loan made to the corporation by a third party has no effect upon the shareholder's loan basis unless payments have actually been made as a result of the guarantee.[51] If the corporation defaults on an indebtedness and the shareholder makes good on the guarantee, the shareholder's indebtedness basis is increased to that extent.[52] Such a subsequent increase in basis has no influence on the results of a prior year in which an NOL exceeded a shareholder's adjusted basis. See Concept Summary 12–3 for adjustments to stock basis and AAA.

A shareholder's share of an NOL may be greater than both the basis, in the stock and the basis of the indebtedness. A shareholder is entitled to carry forward a loss to the extent that the loss for the year exceeds both the stock basis and the loan basis. Any loss carried forward may be deducted *only* by the same shareholder if and when the basis in the stock of or loans to the corporation is restored.[53]

Any loss carryover remaining at the end of a one-year post-termination transition period is lost forever.[54] The post-termination transition period ends on

---

46. § 1368(e)(1)(A).

47. § 1377(a)(1).

48. Reg. § 1.1374–1(b)(3).

49. See *Donald J. Sauvigne*, 30 TCM 123, T.C.Memo. 1971–30.

50. *Ruth M. Prashker*, 59 T.C. 172 (1972); *Frederick G. Brown v. U.S.*, 83–1 USTC ¶9364, 52 AFTR2d 82–5080, 706 F.2d 75 (CA–6, 1983).

51. See, for example, *Estate of Leavitt*, 90 T.C. 206 (1988), *aff'd.* 89–1 USTC ¶9332, 63 AFTR2d 89–1437, 875 F.2d 420 (CA–4, 1989); *Selfe v. U.S.*, 86–1 USTC ¶9115, 57 AFTR2d 86–464, 778 F.2d 769 (CA–11, 1985); *James K. Calcutt*, 91 T.C. 14 (1988).

52. Rev.Rul. 70–50, 1970–1 C.B. 178.

53. § 1366(d).

54. § 1377(b).

the later of (1) one year after the effective date of the termination of the S election or the due date for the last S return (whichever is later) or (2) 120 days after the determination that the corporation's S election had terminated for a previous year. Thus, if a shareholder has a loss carryover, he or she should increase the stock or loan basis and flow through the loss before disposing of the stock.

––––––––––––––––––––––––––– EXAMPLE 35 –––––––––––––––––––––––––––

T, an individual, has a stock basis of $4,000 in an S corporation. He has loaned $2,000 to the corporation and has guaranteed another $4,000 loan made to the corporation by a local bank. Although his share of the S corporation's NOL for the current year is $9,500, T may deduct only $6,000 of the NOL on his individual tax return. T may carry forward $3,500 of the NOL, to be deducted when the basis in his stock or loan to the corporation is restored. T has a zero basis in both the stock and the loan after the flow-through of the $6,000 NOL. ◆

Net operating losses from C corporation years cannot be utilized at the corporate level (except with respect to built-in gains), nor can they be passed through to the shareholders. Further, the carryforward period continues to run during S status.[55] Consequently, it may not be appropriate for a corporation that has unused NOLs to make the S election. When a corporation is expecting losses in the future, an S election should be made before the loss year.

If a loan's basis has been reduced and is not restored, income is recognized when the loan is repaid. If the corporation issued a note as evidence of the debt, repayment constitutes an amount received in exchange for a capital asset, and the amount that exceeds the shareholder's basis is entitled to capital gain treatment.[56] However, if the loan is made on open account, the repayment constitutes ordinary income to the extent that it exceeds the shareholder's basis in the loan. Each repayment must be prorated between the gain portion and the repayment of the debt.[57] Thus, a note should be given to assure capital gain treatment for the income that results from a loan's repayment.

Since the basis rule requires that corporate income be used to restore debt basis before it can be used to restore stock basis, a double tax on current income can result. Any current income distributed, after both debt and stock basis have been reduced to zero, is taxed as capital gain because it is considered a return of capital, but only to the extent of stock basis. To avoid this double tax, shareholders should consider forgiving debt that the S corporation owes them. Such a forgiveness is considered a contribution of capital, with a resulting increase in the shareholder's stock basis.

With a note it will be capital income. If no note ordinary income

Passive Losses and Credits. Section 469 provides that net passive losses and credits are not deductible when incurred and must be carried over to a year when there is passive income. Thus, one must be aware of three major classes of income, losses, and credits—active, portfolio, and passive. S corporations are not directly subject to the limits of § 469, but corporate rental activities are inherently passive, and other activities of an S corporation may be passive unless a shareholder materially participates in operating the business. An S corporation may engage in more than one such activity. If the corporate activity is rental or the shareholder does not materially participate, any passive losses or credits flow through. The shareholders are able to apply them only against

55. § 1371(b).
56. *Joe M. Smith*, 48 T.C. 872 (1967), *aff'd.* and *rev'd.* in 70–1 USTC ¶9327, 25 AFTR2d 70–936, 424 F.2d 219 (CA–9, 1970),

and Rev.Rul. 64–162, 1964–1 C.B. 304.
57. Rev.Rul. 68–537, 1968–2 C.B. 372.

income from other passive activities at the shareholder level. A passive activity loss is the amount by which passive deductions exceed any passive gross income.

Regular, continuous, and substantial involvement in the S corporation is necessary to meet the material participation requirement. The existence of material participation is determined at the shareholder level. There are seven tests for material participation, including a need to participate in the activity for more than 500 hours during the taxable year.[58]

EXAMPLE 36

N is a 50% owner of an S corporation engaged in a passive activity under § 469 in 1992. N, a nonparticipating shareholder, receives a salary of $6,000 for services as a result of the passive activity. This deduction creates a $6,000 passive loss at the corporate level. N has $6,000 of earned income as a result of the salary. The $6,000 salary creates a $6,000 deduction/passive loss, which flows through to the shareholders. N's $3,000 share of the loss may not be deducted against the $6,000 earned income. Under § 469(e)(3), earned income is not taken into account in computing the income or loss from a passive activity. ◆

At-Risk Rule. The at-risk rules generally apply to S corporation shareholders. Essentially, the amount at risk is determined separately for each shareholder. The amount of the corporation's losses that are passed through and deductible by the shareholders is not affected by the amount the corporation has at risk. A shareholder usually is considered at risk with respect to an activity to the extent of cash and the adjusted basis of other property contributed to the electing corporation, any amount borrowed for use in the activity for which the taxpayer has personal liability for payment from personal assets, and the net fair market value of personal assets that secure nonrecourse borrowing.[59] The § 1366(d) limitations and at-risk limitations are applied before the passive activity limitations.[60]

EXAMPLE 37

Shareholder A has a basis of $35,000 in his S corporation stock. He takes a $15,000 nonrecourse loan from a local bank and lends the proceeds to the S corporation. He now has a stock basis of $35,000 and a debt basis of $15,000. However, due to the at-risk limitation, he can deduct only $35,000 of losses from the S corporation. ◆

CONCEPT SUMMARY 12–4
TREATMENT OF LOSSES

Step 1.   Allocate total loss to the shareholder on a daily basis, based upon stock ownership.

Step 2.   If the shareholder's loss exceeds his or her stock basis, apply any excess to adjusted basis of indebtedness to the shareholder. Losses from distributions do not reduce debt basis.

Step 3.   Where loss exceeds the debt basis, any excess is suspended and carried over to succeeding tax years.

Step 4.   In succeeding tax years, any net increase (resulting from *all* positive and negative basis adjustments) restores the debt basis first, up to its original amount.

Step 5.   Once debt basis is restored, any net increase remaining is used to increase stock basis.

Step 6.   Any suspended loss from a previous year now reduces stock basis first and debt basis second.

Step 7.   If the S election terminates, any suspended loss carryover may be deducted during the post-termination transition period to the extent of the *stock* basis at the end of such period. Any loss remaining at the end of this period is lost forever.

---

58. Reg. § 1.469–5T(a).

59. The at-risk rules and their significance for income tax

purposes are discussed in Chapter 11.

60. Reg. § 1.469–2T(d)(6).

Tax on Preelection Built-in Gains

Because Congress was concerned that certain C corporations would elect S status to avoid the corporate income tax on the sale or exchange of appreciated property (avoid a tax on built-in gains), it completely revamped § 1374. A C corporation converting to S status after 1986 generally incurs a corporate-level tax on any built-in gains when the S corporation disposes of an asset in a taxable disposition within 10 years after the date on which the S election took effect.

General Rules. The built-in gains tax is applied to any unrealized gain attributable to appreciation in the value of an asset (e.g., real estate, cash basis receivables, goodwill) or other income items while held by the C corporation. The highest corporate tax rate (applicable to that type of income) is applied to the lesser of (1) the recognized built-in gains of the S corporation for the tax year or (2) the amount that would be the taxable income of the corporation for that tax year if it were a C corporation. Any built-in gain that escapes taxation due to the taxable income limitation is carried forward to future tax years. Then it is treated as recognized built-in gain. Thus, given a low or negative taxable income in any year when built-in gain assets are sold, the taxpayer defers the payment of the built-in gains penalty tax liability. The total amount of gain that ever is recognized is limited to the aggregate net built-in gains of the corporation at the time it converted to S status. Thus, it may be advisable to obtain an independent appraisal when converting a C corporation to an S corporation. Certainly, a memorandum should be prepared listing the fair market values of all assets, along with the methods used to arrive at the values.

––––––––––––––––––– EXAMPLE 38 –––––––––––––––––––

M is a former C corporation whose first S corporation year began on January 1, 1992. At such time, M had two assets: X, with a value of $1,000 and a basis of $400, and Y, with a value of $400 and a basis of $600. Thus, net unrealized built-in gains as of January 1, 1992, are $400. If asset X is sold for $1,000 during 1992 and asset Y is retained, the recognized built-in gain is limited to $400. ◆

––––––––––––––––––– EXAMPLE 39 –––––––––––––––––––

Assume the same facts in Example 38, except that taxable income in 1992 is $300. The built-in gains tax is assessed only on $300. However, the $100 recognized built-in gain that circumvents the tax in 1992 is carried forward and treated as recognized built-in gain in 1993. There is no statutory limit on the carryforward period, but the gain would effectively expire at the end of the 10-year recognition period applicable to all built-in gains (except for installment sales after March 25, 1990).[61] ◆

Gains on sales or distributions of all assets by an S corporation are presumed to be built-in gains unless the taxpayer can establish that the appreciation accrued after the conversion. This § 1374 tax is avoided if the S election was made before 1987.[62]

To the extent that a tax is imposed on any built-in gain, under § 1366(f)(2), such tax reduces proportionately the amount of any gain or loss item that passes through to the shareholder. Postconversion appreciation is subject to the regular S corporation pass-through rules.

––––––––––––––––––– EXAMPLE 40 –––––––––––––––––––

M Corporation elects S status, effective for calendar year 1991. As of January 1, 1991, one of M's assets has a basis of $50,000 and a fair market value of $110,000. Early

––––––––––––––––––

61. § 1374(d)(7); Notice 90–27, I.R.B. 1990–15. **62.** § 1362.

in 1992, the asset is sold for $135,000. M incurs a realized gain of $85,000, of which $60,000 is subject to the § 1374 penalty tax of 34%. The entire $85,000 gain is subject to the corporate pass-through rules (reduced by the built-in gains tax itself), but only $25,000 of the gain fully bypasses the corporate income tax. ◆

Normally, tax attributes of a C corporation do not carry over to a converted S corporation. For purposes of the tax on built-in gains, however, certain carryovers are allowed. An S corporation can offset these gains by related attributes from prior C corporation years such as unexpired net operating losses or capital losses. In a similar manner, AMT credit carryovers (arising in a C corporation tax year) and business credit carryforwards are allowed to offset the built-in gains tax.

———————————————— EXAMPLE 41 ————————————————

Assume the same facts as in Example 40, except that M also had a $10,000 net operating loss carryover when it elected S status. The NOL reduces M's built-in gain from $60,000 to $50,000. Thus, only $50,000 is subject to the § 1374 penalty tax. ◆

———————————————— EXAMPLE 42 ————————————————

An S corporation has a built-in gain of $100,000 and taxable income of $90,000. The built-in gains tax liability is calculated as follows:

Lesser of taxable income and built-in gain	$ 90,000
Less: NOL carryforward from C year	(12,000)
Capital loss carryforward from C year	(8,000)
Tax base	$ 70,000
Highest corporate tax rate	.34
Tentative tax	$ 23,800
Less: Business credit carryforward from C year	(4,000)
AMT credit carryforward from C year	(3,000)
Built-in gains tax liability	$ 16,800

The $10,000 realized (but not taxed) built-in gain in excess of taxable income may be carried forward to the next years, as long as the next year is within the 10-year recognition period. ◆

Concept Summary 12–5 summarizes the calculation of the built-in gains tax. The term *disposition* includes not only sales or exchanges but also other income-recognition events in which a taxpayer disposes of or relinquishes a

CONCEPT SUMMARY 12–5
CALCULATION OF BUILT-IN GAINS TAX LIABILITY

Step 1. Select the smaller of built-in gains or taxable income.*
Step 2. Deduct unexpired net operating losses and capital losses from a C corporation tax year.
Step 3. Multiply the tax base obtained in step 2 by the top corporate tax rate.
Step 4. Deduct any business credit carryforwards and alternative minimum tax credit carryovers arising in a C corporation tax year from the amount obtained in step 3.
Step 5. The corporation pays any tax resulting in step 4.

*Any net recognized built-in gain in excess of taxable income may be carried forward to the next year, as long as the next year is within the 10-year recognition period.

right to claim or receive income.[63] For example, if a cash basis C corporation with accounts receivable converts to S status, the corporate-level tax will be applied to the fair market value of the receivables when they are collected. Similarly, the completion of a long-term contract by a converted S corporation using the completed contract method might be subject to this rule.

A like-kind exchange or reorganization exchange of built-in gain property may not avoid the corporate-level tax. Property received in exchange for built-in gain property in carryover or substituted basis transactions inherits the built-in gain and recognition period applicable to the original property.

─────────────── EXAMPLE 43 ───────────────

An S corporation transfers a built-in gain asset in a § 1031 like-kind exchange. The property received in exchange inherits the amount of built-in gain attributable to the transferred property along with the remainder of the original recognition period. The corporation can avoid this built-in gain tax if it sells the exchange property more than 10 years after converting to S status. ◆

The § 1374 tax is applied to the net recognized built-in gain of the former C corporation on the date of conversion to S status. Thus, loss assets on the date of conversion reduce the recognized built-in gain and any potential tax under § 1374.[64] However, the IRS indicates that contributions of loss property within two years before the earlier of the date of conversion or the date of filing an S election are presumed to have a tax avoidance motive and will not reduce the corporation's net unrealized built-in gain. Other losses incurred by the electing corporation during the year will offset any built-in gains in arriving at net recognized gains.

─────────────── EXAMPLE 44 ───────────────

B owns all of the stock of an S corporation, which in turn owns two assets on the S conversion date: asset 1 (basis of $5,000 and FMV of $4,000) and asset 2 (basis of $1,000 and FMV of $5,000). The S corporation has a potential net realized built-in gain of $3,000 (i.e., the built-in gain of $4,000 in asset 2 reduced by the built-in loss of $1,000 in asset 1). If both assets are sold in the same tax year, the loss is netted against the gain. ◆

Advisably, the taxpayer should maximize built-in losses at the conversion date and minimize the built-in gain assets. For example, a cash basis S corporation can accomplish this by reducing receivables, accelerating payables, and accruing compensation costs. To reduce or defer the penalty tax, the taxpayer might also minimize taxable income in any year when built-in gain assets are sold. Finally, realized built-in losses reduce the § 1374 tax liability only if they occur in a year when built-in gains also are realized.

The total amount of built-in gain tax is reduced by the portion of excess net passive income subject to the § 1375 tax that is attributable to the gain.

LIFO Recapture Tax. When a corporation uses the FIFO method for its last year before making the S election, any built-in gain is recognized and taxed as the inventory is sold. This is not true for a LIFO-basis corporation, unless it invades the LIFO layer during the 10-year period. To preclude deferral of gain recognition under LIFO, the law requires a LIFO recapture amount upon making an S election.

─────────────────────

63. § 1374(d)(5); see also Announcement 86–128, I.R.B. No. 51, 22.

64. § 1374(c)(2) and (d)(1).

A C corporation using LIFO for its last year before making an S election must include in income the excess of the inventory's value under FIFO over the LIFO value. The increase in tax liability resulting from LIFO recapture is payable in four equal installments, with the first payment due on or before the due date for the corporate return for the last C corporation year (without regard to any extensions). The remaining three installments must be paid on or before the due dates of the succeeding corporate returns. No interest is due if payments are made by the due dates. The basis of the LIFO inventory is adjusted to take into account this LIFO recapture amount.

Example 45

Q Corporation converts to S corporation status for 1993. Q used the LIFO inventory method in 1992 and had an ending LIFO inventory of $110,000 (with a FIFO value of $190,000). Q must add $80,000 of LIFO recapture amount to its 1992 taxable income, resulting in an increased tax liability of $27,200 ($80,000 × 34%). Thus, Q must pay one-fourth ($6,800) with its 1992 corporate tax return. The three succeeding installments of $6,800 each must be paid with Q's next three tax returns. ◆

Passive Investment Income Penalty Tax

A tax is imposed on the excess passive income of S corporations that possess accumulated earnings and profits from Subchapter C years. The tax rate is the highest corporate rate for the year. It is applied to the portion of the corporation's net passive income that bears the same ratio to the total net passive income for the tax year as excess gross passive income bears to the total gross passive income for the year. However, the amount subject to the tax may not exceed the taxable income of the corporation computed under § 1374(d)(4).[65]

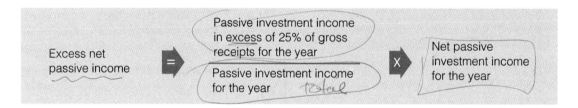

For this purpose, passive investment income means gross receipts derived from royalties, rents, dividends, interest, annuities, and sales and exchanges of stocks and securities.[66] Only the net gain from the disposition of capital assets (other than stocks and securities) is taken into account in computing gross receipts. Net passive income means passive income reduced by any deductions directly connected with the production of such income. Any tax resulting from the application of § 1375 reduces the amount the shareholders must take into income.

The excess net passive income cannot exceed the corporate taxable income for the year before considering any net operating loss deduction or the special deductions allowed by §§ 241–250 (except the organization expense deduction of § 248).

Example 46

At the end of 1992, B Corporation, an electing S corporation, has gross receipts totaling $264,000 (of which $110,000 is passive investment income). Expenditures directly con-

----

65. §§ 1375(a) and (b).

66. § 1362(d)(3)(D)(i).

nected to the production of the passive investment income total $30,000. Therefore, B Corporation has net passive investment income of $80,000 ($110,000 − $30,000), and the amount by which its passive investment income for tax year 1992 exceeds 25% of its gross receipts is $44,000 ($110,000 passive investment income less $66,000). Excess net passive income (ENPI) is $32,000, calculated as follows:

$$\text{ENPI} = \frac{\$44,000}{\$110,000} \times \$80,000 = \$32,000$$

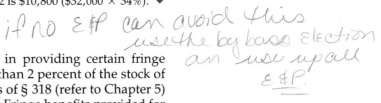

B Corporation's passive investment income tax for 1992 is $10,800 ($32,000 × 34%). ◆

Fringe Benefit Rules

An S corporation cannot deduct its expenditures in providing certain fringe benefits to an employee-shareholder owning more than 2 percent of the stock of the S corporation. The constructive ownership rules of § 318 (refer to Chapter 5) are used in applying the 2 percent ownership test.[67] Fringe benefits provided for such a shareholder-employee constitute gross income for him or her. Such recognition occurs upon the receipt of the following benefits, among others:

- Excludible group term life insurance.
- The $5,000 death benefit exclusion.
- An excludible accident and health plan.
- Excludible meals and lodging furnished for the convenience of the employer.
- Workers' compensation payments on behalf of the shareholder-employee.[68]

─────────────── EXAMPLE 47 ───────────────

P, an S corporation, pays for the medical care of two shareholder-employees during the current year. T, an individual owning 2% of the stock, receives $1,700 for this purpose. S, an individual owning 20% of the stock, receives $3,100. P deducts the $1,700 as a business expense. The $3,100 paid on behalf of S is not deductible by the corporation because S owns more than 2% of the stock. S can deduct the $3,100, but only to the extent that personal medical expenses are allowable as an itemized deduction under § 213. ◆

─────────────── EXAMPLE 48 ───────────────

Assume the same facts as in Example 47, except that T is related to another 1% shareholder. Under the constructive ownership rules of § 318, T also is a greater than 2% shareholder and is subject to the same limitations as S. ◆

Other Operational Rules

Oil and Gas Producers. Oil and gas producers seldom choose S status. The election by a C corporation of Subchapter S is treated as a transfer of oil and gas properties under § 613A(c)(13)(C). Therefore, as of the date of the election, neither the shareholders nor the electing corporation is allowed to claim percentage depletion on production from proven oil or gas wells.

Miscellaneous Rules. Several other points may be made about the possible effects of various Code provisions on S corporations:

───────────────

67. §§ 1372(a) and (b). **68.** Rev.Rul. 72–596, 1972–2 C.B. 395.

■ An S corporation is required to make estimated tax payments with respect to any recognized built-in gain, excess passive investment income, and investment tax credit recapture.

■ An S corporation may own stock in another corporation, but an S corporation may not have a corporate shareholder. An S corporation is not eligible for a dividends received deduction.

■ An S corporation is not subject to the 10 percent of taxable income limitation applicable to charitable contributions made by a C corporation.

■ Foreign taxes paid by an electing corporation pass through to the shareholders and should be claimed as either a deduction or a credit (subject to the applicable limitations).[69] However, an electing corporation is not eligible for the foreign tax credit with respect to taxes paid by a foreign corporation in which the S corporation is a shareholder.

■ Any family member who renders services or furnishes capital to an electing corporation must be paid reasonable compensation. Otherwise, the IRS can make adjustments to reflect the value of such services or capital.[70] This rule may make it more difficult for related parties to shift Subchapter S taxable income to children or other family members.

EXAMPLE 49

F and M each own one-third of a fast-food restaurant, and their 14-year-old son owns the other shares. Both parents work full-time in the restaurant operations, but the son works infrequently. Neither parent receives a salary during 1992, when the taxable income of the S corporation is $160,000. The IRS can require that reasonable compensation be paid to the parents to prevent the full one-third of the $160,000 from being taxed to the son. Otherwise, this would be an effective technique to shift earned income to a family member to reduce the total family tax burden. With the § 1(i) "kiddie" tax treatment of the unearned income of children, though, this shifting technique becomes much more valuable. ◆

■ The depletion allowance is computed separately by each shareholder. Each shareholder is treated as having produced his or her pro rata share of the production of the electing corporation, and each is allocated a respective share of the adjusted basis of the electing corporation as to oil or gas property held by the corporation.[71]

■ An S corporation is placed on the cash method of accounting for purposes of deducting business expenses and interest owed to a cash basis related party.[72] Thus, the timing of the shareholder's income and the corporate deduction must match.

■ The 20 percent basic research credit is not available to an S corporation. As a further limitation, this credit may offset only the tax attributable to the S shareholder's interest in the trade or business that generated the credit.

■ Although § 1366(a)(1) provides for a flow-through of S corporation items to a shareholder, it does not apply to self-employment income.[73] Thus, a shareholder's portion of S corporation income is not self-employment income and is not subject to the self-employment tax. Compensation for services rendered to an S corporation is, however, subject to FICA taxes.

■ A few states (namely, Connecticut, Michigan, New Hampshire, New Jersey, Tennessee) and the District of Columbia do not recognize the S

---

69. § 1373(a).
70. § 1366(e). In addition, beware of an IRS search for the "real owner" of the stock, under Reg. § 1.1373–1(a)(2).

71. § 613A(c)(13).
72. § 267(b).
73. Rev.Rul. 59–221, 1959–1 C.B. 225.

election.[74] Thus, some or all of the entity's income may be subject to a state-level income tax. Refer to related material in Chapter 15.

■ An S corporation is subject to the unified audit and litigation procedures under § 6241. Only a single-shareholder S corporation is exempt from this rule.[75]

When the Election Is Advisable

**TAX PLANNING
CONSIDERATIONS**

*this is
good
if time
Read*

Effective tax planning with S corporations begins with the determination of whether the election is appropriate. In light of changes made by TRA of 1986, the taxpayer may wish to reevaluate the desirability of using a C corporation as a means of conducting a trade or business. In this context, one should consider the following factors:

■ Are losses from the business anticipated? If so, the S election may be highly attractive because these losses pass through to the shareholders.

■ What are the tax brackets of the shareholders? If the shareholders are in high individual income tax brackets, it may be desirable to avoid S corporation status and have profits taxed to the corporation at lower C rates (e.g., 15 percent or 25 percent).

■ When the immediate pass-through of Subchapter S taxable income is avoided, profits of the corporation may later be taken out by the shareholders as capital gain income through stock redemptions, some liquidating distributions, or sales of stock to others; received as dividend distributions in low tax bracket years; or negated by a partial or complete step-up in basis upon the death of the shareholder.[76] On the other hand, if the shareholders are in low individual income tax brackets, the pass-through of corporate profits has less effect, and the avoidance of the corporate income tax becomes the paramount consideration. Under these circumstances, the S election could be highly attractive. Although an S corporation usually escapes Federal taxes, it may not be immune from state and local taxes imposed on corporations or from several Federal penalty taxes.

■ Does a C corporation have a net operating loss carryover from a prior year? Such a loss cannot be used in an S year (except for purposes of the built-in gains tax). Even worse, S years count in the 15-year carryover limitation. Thus, even if the S election is made, one might consider terminating the election before the carryover limitation expires. Such a termination would permit the loss to be utilized by what is now a C corporation.

■ Both individuals and C corporations are subject to the alternative minimum tax. Many of the tax preference and adjustment items are the same, but some apply only to corporate taxpayers while others are limited to individuals. The minimum tax adjustment relating to accumulated current earnings could create havoc with some C corporations (refer to Chapter 6). S corporations themselves are not subject to this tax.

■ Some C corporations must convert from the cash method to the accrual method of accounting (refer to Chapter 2).

■ S corporations and partnerships have lost some of the flexibility in the choice of their accounting period (see also Chapter 10).

---

74. Boucher, Raabe, and Taylor, *Multistate S Corporation Tax Guide* (Panel Publishers, 1993).

75. *Blanco Investments & Land Ltd.*, 89 T.C. 1169 (1987). Reg.

§ 301.6241–1T(c)(2)(i). For a different opinion, see *Miller v. Comm.*, 710 F.Supp. 1377 (N.D. Ga., 1989).

76. See the discussion of § 1014 in Chapter 18.

- By taxing C corporations on nonliquidating and liquidating distributions of appreciated property (refer to Chapter 5), the effect of double taxation is reinforced.
- The modifications made to § 382 (refer to Chapter 7) have imposed severe restrictions on the carryover of net operating losses.
- Since the S election may or may not provide the shareholders with tax advantages, one must consider all of the provisions that will affect the owners.

───────────────── EXAMPLE 50 ─────────────────

T has a basis of $500,000 in his business assets, including some land, which is subject to a liability of $700,000. T transfers all of the assets of the business to a newly formed corporation, X, in exchange for all of the stock in X Corporation. X elects to be taxed as an S corporation. X incurs ordinary losses as follows: Year 1, $50,000; Year 2, $80,000; Year 3, $90,000. T deducts the losses to offset income from other sources. X is audited in Year 3.

- The IRS asserts that T must recognize a $200,000 gain upon the incorporation of X under § 357(c), because the liabilities exceed T's basis in the assets. T's basis in the X stock is zero: $500,000 (basis of T's assets) − $700,000 (liabilities assumed by X) + $200,000 (gain recognized to T).
- Because T's basis in the X stock is zero, T is not entitled to deduct any of the losses for Year 1, Year 2, or Year 3.
- Because T was actively involved in his business, had he not incorporated, he could have offset total losses of $220,000 against other ordinary income. He would also have eliminated the $200,000 gain upon the incorporation of his business. Thus, the incorporation and S election caused T to generate additional income for tax purposes of $420,000. ◆

The choice of the form of doing business often is dictated by other factors. For example, many businesses cannot qualify for the S election—due to the possibility of a public offering or a need for substantial capital inflow—or would find the partnership form more practical. Therefore, freedom of action based on tax considerations may not be an attainable goal. Several tax attributes of partnerships, S corporations, and regular corporations are examined more fully in Chapter 13.

Making a Proper Election

Once the parties have decided the election is appropriate, it becomes essential to ensure that the election is made properly.

- Make sure all shareholders consent. If any doubt exists concerning the shareholder status of an individual, it would be wise to have such party issue a consent anyway.[77] Too few consents will be fatal to the election; the same cannot be said for too many consents.
- Be sure that the election is timely and properly filed. Either hand carry the election to an IRS office or send it by certified or registered mail. A copy of the election should become part of the corporation's permanent files.
- Regarding the preceding, be careful to ascertain when the timely election period begins to run for a newly formed corporation. Keep in mind that an election made too soon (before the corporation is in existence) is worse than one made too late. If serious doubts exist concerning when this

---

77. See *William B. Wilson*, 34 TCM 463, T.C. Memo. 1975–92.

period begins, more than one election might be considered a practical means of guaranteeing the desired result.

- It still is beneficial for an S corporation to issue § 1244 stock (refer to Chapter 3). This type of stock allows the original shareholder to obtain an ordinary deduction for a loss on the sale or worthlessness of the stock rather than receive long-term capital loss treatment. Shareholders have nothing to lose and everything to gain by complying with § 1244.

Preserving the Election

Recall how an election can be lost and that a five-year waiting period generally is imposed before another S election is available. To preserve an election, the following points should be kept in mind:

- As a starting point, all parties concerned should be made aware of the various transactions that lead to the loss of an election.
- Watch for possible disqualification as a small business corporation. For example, the divorce of a shareholder, accompanied by a property settlement, could violate the 35-shareholder limitation. The death of a shareholder could result in a nonqualifying trust becoming a shareholder. The latter circumstance might be avoided by utilizing a buy/sell agreement or binding the deceased shareholder's estate to turn in the stock to the corporation for redemption or, as an alternative, to sell it to the surviving shareholders.[78]
- Make sure a new majority shareholder (including the estate of a deceased shareholder) does not file a refusal to continue the election.
- Watch for the passive investment income limitation. Avoid a consecutive third year with excess passive income if a corporation has accumulated Subchapter C earnings and profits. In this connection, assets that produce passive investment income (e.g., stocks and bonds, certain rental assets) might be retained by the shareholders in their individual capacities and thereby kept out of the corporation.
- Do not transfer stock to a nonresident alien.
- Do not create an active affiliate or issue a second class of stock.

Planning for the Operation of the Corporation

Operating an S corporation to achieve optimum tax savings for all parties involved requires a great deal of care and, most important, an understanding of the applicable tax rules.

Accumulated Adjustment Account. Although the corporate-level accumulated adjustments account (AAA) is used primarily by an S corporation with accumulated earnings and profits (AEP) from a Subchapter C year, all S corporations should maintain an accurate record of the AAA. Because there is a grace period for distributing the AAA after termination of the S election, the parties must be in a position to determine the balance of the account.

─────────────── EXAMPLE 51 ───────────────

Y, an S corporation during 1991, has no accumulated earnings and profits from a Subchapter C year. Over the years, Y made no attempt to maintain an accurate

---

78. See the discussion in Chapter 18 for the treatment of buy/sell agreements. Most such agreements do not create a second class of stock. Rev.Rul. 85–161, 1985–2 C.B. 191; *Portage* *Plastics Co. v. U.S.*, 72–2 USTC ¶9567, 30 AFTR2d 72–5229, 470 F.2d 308 (CA–7, 1973).

accounting for the AAA. In 1992, the S election is terminated, and Y has a grace period for distributing the AAA tax-free to its shareholders. A great deal of time and expense may be necessary to reconstruct the AAA balance in 1992. ◆

Tax-exempt income is not included in gross income and does not increase AAA. For an S corporation with AEP, tax-exempt income usually is a bad investment. Any subsequent distribution of tax-exempt income exceeds the AAA balance and is treated as dividend income to the extent of any AEP.

When AEP is present, a negative AAA may cause double taxation of S corporation income. With a negative AAA, a distribution of current income restores the negative AAA balance to zero, but is considered to be a distribution in excess of AAA and is taxable as a dividend to the extent of AEP.

The AAA bypass election may be used to avoid the accumulated earnings tax or personal holding company tax in the year preceding the first tax year under Subchapter S. This bypass election allows the AEP to be distributed instead.

Example 52

Z, an S corporation during 1991, has a significant amount in its AEP account. The shareholders expect to terminate the election in 1992, when they will be subject to low income tax rates. Since the new C corporation may be subject to the accumulated earnings penalty tax in 1992, the shareholders may wish to use the AAA bypass election to distribute some or all of the AEP. Of course, any distributions of the AEP account in 1991 would be taxable to the shareholders. ◆

A net loss allocated to a shareholder reduces the AAA. This required adjustment should encourage an electing corporation to make annual distributions of net income to avoid the reduction of an AAA by a future net loss.

Salary Structure. The amount of salary paid to a shareholder-employee of an S corporation can have varying tax consequences and should be considered carefully. Larger amounts might be advantageous if the maximum contribution allowed under the retirement plan has not been reached. Smaller amounts may be beneficial if the parties are trying to shift taxable income to lower-bracket shareholders, lessen payroll taxes,[79] curtail a reduction of Social Security benefits, or reduce losses that do not pass through because of the basis limitation. Many of the problems that arise in this area can be solved with proper planning. Most often, such planning involves making before-the-fact projections of the tax positions of the parties involved.

The IRS can require that reasonable compensation be paid to family members who render services or provide capital to the S corporation. Section 1366(e) allows the IRS to make adjustments in the items taken into account by family-member shareholders to reflect the value of services or capital provided by such parties. Refer to Example 49.

Loss Considerations. A net loss in excess of tax basis may be carried forward and deducted only by the same shareholder in succeeding years. Thus, before disposing of the stock, a shareholder should increase the basis of such stock/loan to flow through the loss. The next shareholder does not obtain the carryover loss.

Any unused carryover loss in existence upon the termination of the S election may be deducted only in the next tax year and is limited to the individual's *stock* basis (not loan basis) in the post-termination year.[80] The shareholder may wish to purchase more stock, to increase the tax basis in order to absorb the loss.

---

79. In this regard, see Rev.Rul. 74–44, 1974–1 C.B. 287. **80.** § 1366(d)(3).

The NOL provisions create a need for sound tax planning during the last election year and the post-termination transition period. If it appears that the S corporation is going to sustain a net operating loss or use up any loss carryover, each shareholder's basis should be analyzed to determine if it can absorb the share of the loss. If basis is insufficient to absorb the loss, further investments should be considered before the end of the post-termination transition year. Such investments can be accomplished through additional stock purchases from the corporation, or from other shareholders, to increase basis. This action will ensure the full benefit from the NOL or loss carryover.

EXAMPLE 53

A calendar year C corporation has an NOL in 1991 of $20,000. The corporation makes a valid S election in 1992 and has another $20,000 NOL in that year. At all times during 1992, the stock of the corporation was owned by the same 10 shareholders, each of whom owned 10% of the stock. T, one of the 10 shareholders, has an adjusted basis at the beginning of 1992 of $1,800. None of the 1991 NOL may be carried forward into the S year. Although T's share of the 1992 NOL is $2,000, the deduction for the loss is limited to $1,800 in 1992 with a $200 carryover. ◆

Avoiding the Passive Investment Income Tax. Too much passive investment income may cause an S corporation to incur a § 1375 penalty tax and/or terminate the S election. Several planning techniques can be used to avoid both of these unfavorable events. Where a small amount of AEP exists, an AAA bypass election may be appropriate to purge the AEP, thereby avoiding the § 1375 tax altogether. Alternatively, the corporation might reduce taxable income below the excess net passive income; similarly, passive investment income might be recognized in years in which there is a net operating loss. In addition, the tax can be avoided if the corporation manufactures gross receipts. By increasing gross receipts without increasing passive investment income (PII), the amount of PII in excess of 25 percent of gross receipts is reduced.

EXAMPLE 54

An S corporation has paid a § 1375 penalty tax for two consecutive years. In the next year, the corporation has a large amount of AAA. If the AEP account is small, a bypass election may be appropriate to purge the corporation of the AEP. Without any AEP, no § 1375 tax applies, and the S election is not terminated. Any distribution of AEP to the shareholders constitutes taxable dividends, however.

Another alternative is to manufacture a large amount of gross receipts without increasing PII (merge with a grocery store). If the gross receipts from the grocery store are substantial, the amount of the PII in excess of 25 percent of gross receipts is reduced. ◆

Managing the Built-In Gains Tax. A taxable income limitation encourages an S corporation to create deductions or accelerate deductions in the years that built-in gains are recognized. Although the postponed built-in gain is carried forward to future years, the time value of money makes the postponement beneficial. For example, payment of compensation, rather than a distribution, creates a deduction that reduces taxable income and postpones the built-in gains tax.

EXAMPLE 55

M, an S corporation, has built-in gain of $110,000 and taxable income of $120,000 before payment of salaries to its two shareholders. If M pays at least $110,000 in salaries to the shareholders (rather than a distribution), taxable income will drop to zero, and the built-in gain will be postponed. Thus, M needs to keep the salaries as high as possible, to postpone the built-in gains tax in future years and reap a benefit from the time value of money. Of course, paying the salaries may increase the payroll tax burden if the salaries are below FICA and FUTA limits. ♦

Giving built-in gain property to a charitable organization does not trigger the built-in gains tax. However, the built-in gain may be a preference item at the shareholder level for purposes of the alternative minimum tax. Built-in *loss* property may be sold in the same year that built-in gain property is sold to reduce or eliminate the built-in gains tax. Generally, the taxpayer should sell built-in loss property in a year when an equivalent amount of built-in gain property is sold. Otherwise, the built-in loss could be wasted.

Example 56

X Corporation elects S status effective for calendar year 1991. As of January 1, 1991, X's only asset has a basis of $40,000 and a fair market value of $100,000. If this asset is sold for $120,000 in 1992, X recognizes an $80,000 gain, of which $60,000 is subject to the corporate built-in gains tax. The other $20,000 of gain is subject to the S corporation pass-through rules and bypasses the corporate income tax.

Unless the taxpayer can show otherwise, any appreciation existing at the sale or exchange is presumed to be preconversion built-in gain. Therefore, X incurs a built-in gain of $80,000 unless it can prove that the $20,000 gain developed after the effective date of the election. ♦

Controlling Adjustments and Preference Items. The individual alternative minimum tax (AMT) affects more taxpayers than ever before, because the tax base has expanded and the difference between regular tax rates and the individual AMT rate has been narrowed. In an S corporation setting, tax preferences flow through proportionately to the shareholders, who, in computing the individual AMT, treat the preferences as if they were directly realized.

A flow-through of tax preferences can be a tax disaster for a shareholder who is an "almost-AMT taxpayer." Certain steps can be taken to protect such a shareholder from being pushed into the AMT. For example, a large 1992 donation of appreciated property by an S corporation could adversely affect an "almost-AMT taxpayer." Certain adjustment and preference items are subject to elections that can remove them from a shareholder's AMT computation. Certain positive adjustments can be removed from a shareholder's AMTI base if the S corporation elects to capitalize and amortize certain expenditures over a prescribed period of time. These expenditures include excess intangible drilling and development expenditures, research and experimental costs, mining exploration and development expenditures, and circulation expenses.

Other corporate choices can protect an "almost-AMT shareholder." Using a straight-line method of cost recovery (rather than an accelerated method) can be beneficial to certain shareholders. Many of these decisions and elections, however, may generate conflicts of interest when some shareholders are not so precariously situated and would not suffer from the flow-through of adjustments and tax preference items.

Allocation of Tax Items. If a shareholder dies or stock is transferred during the taxable year, tax items may be allocated under the pro rata approach or the per-books method. Absent the per-books election, a shareholder's pro rata share of tax items is determined by assigning an equal portion of each item to each day of the tax year and then dividing that portion pro rata among the shares outstanding on the transfer day. With the consent of all persons who were shareholders during the entire taxable year, an S corporation can elect to allocate tax items according to the permanent records using normal tax accounting rules.

The allocation is made as if the taxable year consists of two taxable years. The first portion ends on the date of termination. On the day the shares are transferred, the shares are considered owned by the shareholder who acquired the shares. The selected method may be beneficial to the terminating shareholder and harmful to the acquiring shareholder. An election might result in a higher allocation of losses to a taxpayer who is better able to utilize the losses. In the case of the death of a shareholder, a per-books election prevents the income and loss allocation to a deceased shareholder from being affected by postdeath events.

—————————————— EXAMPLE 57 ——————————————

A, the owner of all of the shares of an S corporation, transfers all of the stock to B at the middle of the tax year. There is a $100,000 net operating loss for the entire tax year, but $30,000 of the loss occurs during the first half of the year. Absent a per-books election, $50,000 of the loss would be allocated to A, with $50,000 allocated to B. If the corporation makes the per-books election, B will receive $70,000 of the loss. Of course, B may have a difficult time convincing A to consent to the election. ◆

—————————————— EXAMPLE 58 ——————————————

M, a calendar year S corporation, is equally owned by J and K. J dies on June 29 (not a leap year). M has income of $250,000 for January 1 through June 29 and $750,000 for the remainder of the year. Absent the per-books election, the income is allocated by assigning an equal portion of the annual income of $1 million to each day (or $2,739.73 per day) and allocating the daily portion among the shareholders. J is allocated 50% of the daily income for the 180 days from January 1 to June 29, or $246,575.70 ($2,739.73/2 × 180). J's estate would be allocated 50% of the income for the 185 days from June 30 to December 31, or $253,425.02 ($2,739.73/2 × 185).

If the per-books election is made, the income of $250,000 from January 1 to June 29 is divided equally between J and K, so that each is allocated $125,000. The income of $750,000 from June 30 to December 31 is divided equally between J's estate and K, or $375,000 to each. ◆

Termination Aspects. It is always advisable to avoid accumulated earnings and profits in an S corporation. There is the ever-present danger of terminating the election because of excess passive investment income in three consecutive years. Further, there is the § 1375 penalty tax on excess passive net income. Thus, one should try to eliminate such AEP through a dividend distribution or liquidation of the corporation with a subsequent reincorporation. If the AEP account is small, to eliminate the problem, all the shareholders may consent under § 1368(e)(3) to have distributions treated as made first from AEP rather than from the AAA (the AAA bypass election).

One should issue straight debt to avoid creating a second class of stock and establish an instrument with a written unconditional promise to pay on demand or on a specific date a sum certain in money with a fixed interest rate and payment date.

If the shareholders of an S corporation decide to terminate the election other than through voluntary revocation, they should make sure that the disqualifying act possesses substance. When the intent of the parties is obvious and the act represents a technical noncompliance rather than a real change, the IRS may be able to disregard it and keep the parties in S status.[81]

Liquidation of an S Corporation. S corporations are subject to many of the same liquidation rules applicable to C corporations (refer to Chapter 5). In

——————————————

81. See *Clarence L. Hook,* 58 T.C. 267 (1972).

#1 Advantages
PP. 12-2 & 12-4
12-32
Chapter 2-2-10
12-7 (2nd term)
12-4
12-3 & Fig 12-1
12-3 & 12-11 Fig 12-1

Disadvantages
12-2
12-4
12-31
12-34 & 35
12-3 & 33
12-25, 26 Fig 12-1
12-6
12-12 & 12-13
12-25

general, the distribution of appreciated property to S shareholders in complete liquidation is treated as if the property were sold to the shareholders in a taxable transaction. Unlike a C corporation, however, the S corporation incurs no incremental tax on the liquidation gains, because such gains flow through to the shareholders subject only to the built-in gains tax of § 1374. Any corporate gain increases the shareholder's stock basis by a like amount and reduces any gain realized by the shareholder when he or she receives the liquidation proceeds. Thus, an S corporation usually avoids the double tax that is imposed on C corporations.

With respect to loss property, a liquidation is more favorable than a nonliquidating distribution. Recall that a loss is not recognized for nonliquidating property distributions. With certain exceptions, an S corporation does recognize a loss on the liquidating distribution of depreciated property.

PROBLEM MATERIALS

DISCUSSION QUESTIONS

1. What are the major advantages and disadvantages of an S election?

2. Which of the following items could be considered to be disadvantageous (or potential hazards) for S elections?

    a. The dividends received deduction is lost. *EX: 46*
    b. Foreign tax credit is not available. *12-14 & 32*
    c. Net operating loss at the corporate level cannot be utilized. *12-23 — 25*
    d. Constructive dividends are not actually distributed. *12-2*
    e. A locked-in AAA occurs after termination. *C/S 12-1*
    f. An AAA is a personal right that cannot be transferred. *12-17 false statement*
    g. Basis in stock is increased by constructive dividends. *12-22 & 23*
    h. A trust is treated as a shareholder. *12-5*
    i. Salaries of certain shareholders are not high enough. *12-36*

3. Which, if any, of the following will prevent a corporation from making a valid S corporation election?

    a. There are 26 shareholders. *12-4 & 5*
    b. One shareholder is a resident alien. *12-4 & 6*
    c. One of the shareholders is a partnership. *12-5*
    d. There is a net operating loss during the year. *C/S 12-4*
    e. One-half of the common stock does not have voting rights. *12-6*
    f. One of the shareholders is an estate. *12-5*
    g. One of the shareholders is a minor. *12-7*

4. On February 23, 1992, the two 50% shareholders of a calendar year corporation decide to elect to be an S corporation. One of the shareholders had purchased her stock from a previous shareholder on January 18, 1992. Discuss any potential problems. *EX: 10*

5. Q is the sole owner of a calendar year S corporation that manufactures water heaters. On March 9, Q realizes that the corporation is going to make a very large profit. Discuss how Q can terminate his corporation's S election. *EX: 11-13*

6. In which of the following situations is a termination of the calendar year S corporation election effective as of the first day of the following tax year?

    a. A partnership becomes a shareholder on April 2. *Ex 13*
    b. There is a failure of the passive investment income limitation. *EX 14*
    c. A new 45% shareholder affirmatively refuses to consent to the S election. *EX 11*

12-9

If Stated 1/1 of Following yr.

d. Shareholders owning 57% of the outstanding stock file a formal revocation on February 23. *Ex. 13*

e. A second class of stock is issued on March 3.

f. The electing corporation becomes a member of an affiliated group on March 10. *Ex 3 p-9*

7. An S corporation recently had its S election involuntarily terminated. Must the corporation wait five years before making a new election? *EX. 17 & 18*

8. K is considering creating an S corporation for her interior decorating business. She has a friend who has an S corporation with a January 31 fiscal year. K wishes to set up a similar fiscal year. Advise K. *EX 19 & 20*

9. In the current year, an S corporation distributes land worth $88,000 to a 33% shareholder. The land cost $22,000 three years ago. Discuss any tax impact on the corporation or the shareholder from this distribution. The corporation has no accumulated earnings and profits, and the stock basis is $102,000. *Examples 22, 31 & 43* *each shareholder must report a pro rata portion of this gain on their indv. tax return*

10. Y's basis in his S corporation is $5,500, but he anticipates that his share of the net operating loss for this year will be $7,400. The tax year is not closed. Advise Y. *EX. 35*

11. How do the passive loss limitations of § 469 affect an S corporation? *EX 36*

12. Discuss planning opportunities under the § 1374 built-in gains tax. *ex 38 — 43*

13. One of your clients is considering electing S status. T, Inc., is a six-year-old company with two equal shareholders who paid $30,000 each for their stock. In 1992, T, Inc., has a $90,000 NOL carryforward. Estimated income is $40,000 for 1993 and approximately $25,000 for each of the next three years. Should T, Inc., make an S election for 1992? *12-2, 12-3 & 12-25*

PROBLEMS

14. An S corporation's profit and loss statement for 1992 shows net profits of $90,000 (book income). The corporation has three equal shareholders. From supplemental data, you obtain the following information about the corporation for 1992:

EX. 22

Selling expense	$11,500
Tax-exempt interest	2,000
Dividends received	9,000
Section 1231 gain	6,000
Section 1245 gain	10,000
Recovery of bad debts	3,400
Capital losses	(6,000) *add this back*
Salary to owners (each)	9,000
Cost of goods sold	95,000

a. Compute Subchapter S taxable income or loss for 1992.

b. What would be one shareholder's portion of taxable income or loss? *Example 22*

15. N, a calendar year S corporation is equally owned by R and T. T dies on April 1 (not a leap year), and the estate selects a March 31 fiscal year. N Corporation has $400,000 of income for January 1 through March 31 and $600,000 for the remainder of the year.

a. Determine how income is allocated to R and T under the pro rata approach.

b. Determine how income is allocated to R and T under the per-books method. *Examples 23 & 24*

16. P has been the sole shareholder of a calendar year S corporation since 1981. At the end of 1992, P's stock basis is $15,500, and she receives a distribution of $17,000. Corporate-level accounts are as follows: *undistributed net Income* *tax free up to the Amt in the AAA (limited to stock basis)*

AAA	$6,000
PTI	9,000 *Previously taxed Income*
AEP	500 *Accumulated earnings & profit*

How is P taxed on the distribution? *Concept Summary 12-1*

17. P owned 10% of the outstanding stock of a calendar year S corporation. P sold all of his stock to Q on July 1, 1992. At the end of 1992, the total AAA was $800,000 before

Example 23 & Concept Summary 12-1

considering any distributions, and the amount in the accumulated earnings and profits account was $800,000. The corporation made a distribution of $600,000 to the shareholders on April 1, 1992, which included a distribution of $60,000 to P. On October 1, 1992, another distribution of $600,000 was made to the shareholders, including $60,000 to Q. Determine the amounts taxable to P and Q.

18. A calendar year S corporation has $60,000 of accumulated earnings and profits. Q, the sole shareholder, has an adjusted basis in her stock of $50,000 with zero in the AAA. Determine the tax aspects if a $60,000 salary is paid to Q.

19. Assume the same facts as in Problem 18, except that Q receives a dividend of $60,000.

20. Using the categories in the following legend, classify each transaction as a plus (+) or minus (–) on Schedule M–2 of Form 1120S:

Legend

PTI	= Shareholders' undistributed taxable income previously taxed
AAA	= Accumulated adjustments account
OAA	= Other adjustments account
NA	= No direct effect on Schedule M

a. Receipt of tax-exempt interest income.
b. Unreasonable compensation determined.
c. Ordinary income.
d. Distribution of nontaxable income (PTI) from 1981.
e. Nontaxable life insurance proceeds.
f. Expenses related to tax-exempt securities.
g. Charitable contributions.
h. Gifts in excess of $25.
i. Nondeductible fines.
j. Organizational expenses.

21. Individuals A and B form an S corporation, with A contributing cash of $100,000 for a 50% interest and B contributing appreciated ordinary income property with an adjusted basis of $10,000 and a FMV of $100,000.

a. Determine B's initial basis in his stock, assuming that he receives a 50% interest.
b. The S corporation sells the property for $100,000. Determine A's and B's stock basis after the sale.
c. Determine A's and B's gain or loss if the company is liquidated.

22. M, a calendar year S corporation, has two unrelated shareholders, each owning 50% of the stock. Both shareholders have a $400,000 stock basis as of January 1, 1992. At the beginning of 1992, M has AAA of $300,000 and accumulated earnings and profits of $600,000. During 1992, M has operating income of $100,000. At the end of the year, M distributes securities worth $1 million, with an adjusted basis of $800,000. Determine the tax effects of these transactions.

23. Assume the same facts as in Problem 22, except that the two shareholders consent under § 1368(e)(3) to distribute accumulated earnings and profits first.

24. An S corporation's Form 1120S shows taxable income of $70,000 for 1992. P, an individual, owns 40% of the stock throughout the year. The following information is obtained from the corporate records:

Salary paid to P	$52,000
Tax-exempt insurance proceeds	3,000
Charitable contributions	6,000
Dividends received from a foreign corporation	5,000
Long-term capital loss	6,000
Section 1245 gain	11,000
Refund of prior state income taxes	5,000
Cost of goods sold	72,000

Short-term capital loss	7,000
Selling expenses	18,000
Long-term capital gains	14,000
Advertising expenses	11,000
P's beginning stock basis	$21,000
P's additional stock purchases	7,000
P's beginning AAA	19,000
P's loan to corporation	20,000

   a. Compute book income or loss. *example 22*
   b. Compute P's ending stock basis. *Examples 26 & 27 & C/S 12-3*
   c. Calculate ending corporate AAA. *Concept Summary 12-3*

25. At the beginning of 1992, M, a 50% shareholder of a calendar year S corporation, has a stock basis of $22,000. During the year, the corporation has taxable income of *+* $32,000. The following data are obtained from supplemental sources:

Dividends received *+*	$12,000
Tax-exempt interest *+ stock-only*	18,000
Short-term capital gain *+*	6,000
Section 1245 gain	10,000
Section 1231 gain *+*	7,000
Charitable contributions *=*	5,000
Political contributions *=*	8,000
Long-term capital loss *—*	12,000
Dividends to M *—*	6,000
Advertising expense	13,000
Beginning AAA	42,000

   a. Compute M's ending stock basis. *examples 26 & 27*
   b. Compute ending AAA. *C/S 12-3*

26. For each of the following independent statements, indicate whether the transaction will increase (+), decrease (–), or have no effect (NE) on the adjusted basis of a shareholder's stock in an S corporation: *Examples 28 & 29 Concept Summary 12-3*

   a. Tax-exempt income. *↑*
   b. Long-term capital gain. *+*
   c. Net operating loss. *—*
   d. Section 1231 gain. *+*
   e. Excess of percentage depletion over the basis of the property. *+*
   f. Separately computed income. *+*
   g. Nontaxable return-of-capital distribution by the corporation. *—*
   h. Charitable contributions. *—*
   i. Business gift in excess of $25. *—*
   j. Section 1245 gain. *+*
   k. Dividends received by the S corporation. *+*
   l. Short-term capital loss. *—*
   m. Recovery of a bad debt. *+*
   n. Long-term capital loss. *—*

27. A calendar year S corporation has a taxable loss of $80,000 and a capital loss of $20,000 for 1993. M, an individual, owns 40% of the corporate stock and has a $21,000 basis in the stock. Determine the amount of the taxable loss and capital loss, if any, that flow through to M. *Concept Summary 12-4*

28. N, an individual, owns 30% of the stock of an S corporation throughout 1992 and lends the corporation $6,000 during the year. N's stock basis in the corporation at the end of the year is $22,000. If the corporation sustains a $110,000 operating loss during the year, what amount, if any, is N entitled to deduct with respect to the operating loss? *Concept Summary 12-4*

◆ *Rev. Rul*

12–44 *68-537*

Cited in footnotes57
& Concept Summary 12-4

29. T is the sole owner of a C corporation, which incurred a $47,000 net operating loss in 1991. An S election became effective January 1992, and the S corporation incurred another $56,000 net operating loss. During 1992, T loaned the company $20,000, and her stock basis (before considering the NOL) was $40,000.

a. Determine the tax consequences of these events.

b. What are the tax effects if the S corporation repays half of the loan in 1993?

30. B is a 30% shareholder of an S corporation that has a $120,000 net operating loss for a nonleap year. On February 3, B sold all of his stock to C for $63,000. C owns her stock for the rest of the year. B's stock basis at the beginning of the year is $52,000.

Concept Summary

12-4

a. What amount, if any, of the NOL will pass through to B and C?

b. What gain, if any, is taxable to B on the sale of his stock?

31. During February 1989, W, Inc., a C corporation, elects to become an S corporation at a time when its building and land are worth $2.2 million. The adjusted basis of the land is $200,000, and the basis of the building is $400,000. The company has some securities valued as of February at $260,000 (with an $80,000 cost basis). You are both the firm's accountant and a 40% shareholder. What happens at both the corporate and shareholder level in the following events?

Example 40

a. In November 1992, W, Inc., moves into a new building and sells the land and old building for $2.3 million (total tax basis of $500,000).

Ex: 42 →b. The company sells one-half of the securities in February 1993 for $145,000.

32. N Corporation elects S status effective for tax year 1990. As of January 1, 1990, N's assets were appraised as follows:

	Adjusted Basis	Fair Market Value
Cash	$ 16,010	$ 16,010
Accounts receivable	–0–	55,400
Inventory (FIFO)	70,000	90,000
Investment in land	110,000	195,000
Building	220,000	275,000
Goodwill	–0–	93,000

Example 42

In the following situations, calculate any § 1374 tax, assuming that the highest corporate rate is 34%:

a. During 1990, N Corporation collects $45,000 of the accounts receivable and sells 80% of the inventory for $96,000.

b. In 1992, N Corporation sells the land held for investment for $197,000.

c. In 1996, the building is sold for $310,000.

33. A cash basis S corporation has the following assets and liabilities on January 1, 1992, the date its S election is made:

Example 40 to 45

	Adjusted Basis	Fair Market Value
Cash	$ 200,000	$ 200,000
Accounts receivable	–0–	100,000
Equipment	110,000	100,000
Land	1,800,000	2,500,000
Accounts payable	–0–	110,000

During 1992, the S corporation collects the accounts receivable and pays the accounts payable. The land is sold for $3 million, and the taxable income for the year is $600,000. Calculate any § 1374 penalty tax.

Example 46

34. During 1992, an S corporation has operating revenues of $400,000, taxable interest of $400,000, operating expenses of $260,000, and deductions attributable to the interest of $150,000. Calculate any § 1375 penalty tax.

Example 46

35. At the end of 1992, an S corporation has gross receipts of $190,000 and gross income of $170,000. The corporation has accumulated earnings and profits of $22,000 and taxable income of $35,000. It has passive investment income of $100,000, with $30,000 of expenses directly related to the production of passive investment income. Calculate the excess net passive income and any § 1375 penalty tax.

36. P is an accrual basis S corporation with three shareholders. The AAA is $74,000 at the beginning of 1992. P Corporation's three shareholders have the following stock ownership and basis at the beginning of 1992: A (50%), $50,000; B (30%), $20,000; and C (20%), $10,000. P Corporation has the following income and expenses during 1992:

concept
summary
12-3

Interest income	$ 10,000
Operating income	200,000
Tax-exempt income	10,000
Cost of goods sold	160,000
Shareholders' salaries	30,000
Other salaries	40,000
Other expenses	50,000

Calculate each shareholder's stock basis at the end of 1992.

COMPREHENSIVE TAX RETURN PROBLEM

Jay Mitchell (243–58–8695) and Stan Marshall (221–51–8695) are 70% and 30% owners of Dana, Inc. (73–8264911), a service company located in Dime Box, Texas. The company's S corporation election was made on January 15, 1991. The following information was taken from the income statement for 1991:

Tax-exempt interest	$ 1,000
Gross rents	5,000
Gross royalties	10,000
Service income	110,000
Salaries and wages	55,000
Repairs	2,000
Officers' compensation	15,000
Bad debts	5,000
Rent expense	5,000
Taxes	5,000
Expenses relating to tax-exempt income	500
Charitable contributions	2,000
Payroll penalties	1,500
Advertising expenses	5,000
Other deductions	10,000

A partially completed comparative balance sheet appears as follows:

	Beginning of the Year	End of the Year
Cash	$6,000	$ 6,500
Accounts receivable	2,000	4,000
Loan to Jay Mitchell	–0–	2,000
Total	$8,000	$12,500
Accounts payable	$2,000	$ 1,800
Other current liabilities	–0–	1,200
Capital stock	6,000	6,000
Retained earnings	–0–	?
Previously taxed income	–0–	?
Accumulated adjustments account	–0–	?
Other adjustments account	–0–	?
Total liabilities/shareholders' equity	$8,000	$12,500

The corporation distributed $16,500 to the two shareholders during the year. From the available information, prepare Form 1120S and Schedule K–1 for Jay Mitchell. If any information is missing, make realistic assumptions.

RESEARCH PROBLEMS

RESEARCH PROBLEM 1 An East Coast health care management consulting partnership wants to merge with its largest West Coast competitor. The partners of both entities want to conduct business as an S corporation, to secure additional limited liability against potential professional malpractice suits, to meet market demands for "portable" health care services for an increasingly mobile public, to place structural restrictions on the combined entity so as to discourage future hostile takeover attempts, and to facilitate the operation of a stock option plan that will provide profit-maximization incentives for its upper management.

Because of restrictions under applicable state laws, the combination of the two groups will take the following form: the new entity will file articles of incorporation, the shares will be distributed to the partnerships proportionate to their respective asset contributions, and all the partnerships' assets will be transferred into the new corporation through a series of § 351 transfers. Thus, the partners of the two existing entities will receive distributions of shares in the new S corporation in complete liquidation of their partnership interests. When this restructuring of the two partnerships is completed, an S election for the new corporation will be made in a timely fashion.

All of the technical requirements for making an S election (e.g., with respect to number and type of shareholders and type of outstanding shares of stock) will be satisfied by the combined partnerships under the proposed plan of consolidation, except one: the partnerships themselves momentarily will hold shares in the new corporation. Since a partnership is an ineligible shareholder under the provisions of Subchapter S, will the S election be invalidated and the consolidation plan foiled?

RESEARCH PROBLEM 2 On February 24, the two shareholders of Mercer, Inc., Sidney Marvin and William Pestcoe, held a shareholder meeting at their business office. They decided to terminate the S election prospectively, as of July 1 of the current year. They were expecting a large amount of income in the last half of the tax year. Pestcoe prepared the necessary statement of revocation, obtained Marvin's signature, signed it himself, and intended to mail it to the IRS the next day.

Pestcoe was stricken with a coronary occlusion during the night and was confined in the hospital for 19 days. He failed to mail the revocation until July 16. The revocation statement indicated that the election would be terminated in July.

When Marvin learned of the slipup in August, he became worried. On August 27, he "gave" a share of the S corporation's stock to his cousin, a nonresident alien. He did not inform the IRS of the transfer. Is this organization still an S corporation?

RESEARCH PROBLEM 3 Felder Company, a calendar year corporation, is owned by a husband and wife who are having marital problems and living apart. On March 9, 1993, both shareholders held a shareholder meeting at their attorney's office and agreed to elect S corporation status. The lawyer prepared Form 2553 and gave it to the husband, H, on March 11. When H could not locate his wife by March 13, he mailed a letter asking for an extension of time for filing Form 2553. He was able to locate his wife on the evening of March 15. She signed Form 2553, and H mailed it at a nearby post office by 11:00 P.M. The envelope, however, was eventually postmarked on March 16. To protect his position, H hand delivered a copy of Form 2553 to the District Director on March 16. When is the S election effective?

RESEARCH PROBLEM 4 A client comes to your office and indicates that she wishes to make an S election for her corporation. She wishes to have a Qualified Subchapter S Trust (QSST) as one of the shareholders. Prepare a report addressing the timing aspects of the S election and the QSST election.

PART

IV

ADVANCED TAX PRACTICE CONSIDERATIONS

Besides coping with the procedural aspects of tax administration and practice, a specialist in taxation may be confronted with a variety of technical subjects. Some of these include tax considerations in choosing a form for operating a business, the unique rules applicable to tax-exempt entities, and multistate dealings. The following chapters, therefore, reflect a cross section of the myriad problems often encountered in tax practice.

COMPARATIVE FORMS OF DOING BUSINESS

OBJECTIVES

Identify the principal legal and tax forms for conducting a business.

Be aware of the relative importance of nontax factors in making business decisions.

Distinguish between the forms for conducting a business according to whether they are subject to single taxation or double taxation.

Discuss techniques for avoiding double taxation and for controlling the entity tax.

Describe the applicability and the effect of the conduit or the entity concept on the following:

- Recognition at time of contribution to the entity.
- Basis of ownership interest.
- Results of operations.
- Recognition at time of distribution.
- Passive activity losses.
- At-risk rules.
- Special allocations.

Analyze the effect of the disposition of a business on the owners and the entity for each of the forms for conducting a business.

OUTLINE

Principal Forms

The principal *legal* forms for conducting a business entity are a sole proprietorship, partnership, or corporation.[1] From a *Federal income tax* perspective, these same forms are available with the corporate form being divided into two types (S corporation and C or regular corporation). In most instances, the legal form and the tax form are the same. In some cases, however, the IRS may attempt to tax a business entity as a form different from its legal form. This reclassification normally takes one of two possible approaches:

1. The IRS ignores the corporate form and taxes the owners directly (the corporate entity lacks substance).
2. The IRS ignores the partnership form and taxes the partnership as if it were a corporation.

The IRS may try to reclassify a corporation for several reasons. Historically, attempts by the IRS to ignore the corporate form were logical because the corporate rates were lower than the individual rates (e.g., 46 percent for the corporation versus 50 percent for the individual). Currently, the maximum corporate rate of 34 percent (or 39 percent during the phase-out of the 15 percent and 25 percent rates) is higher than the individual rate of 31 percent, so on the surface this reason no longer appears to be valid. However, the specific rates for a particular individual taxpayer may be higher than the corporate rates. For example, an individual may be in the 31 percent bracket, and the corporation may be in either the 15 percent or the 25 percent bracket. Another reason for taxing the owners directly is to make them ineligible for favorable taxation of certain fringe benefits (see the subsequent discussion in Favorable Treatment of Certain Fringe Benefits).

In the case of a partnership, reclassification of a partnership as if it were a corporation can subject the business entity to double taxation. In addition, the resultant loss of conduit status eliminates the ability to pass partnership losses through to the tax returns of the partners. For example, see the discussion of *associations* in Chapter 2.

The taxpayer generally is bound for tax purposes by the legal form that is selected. The major statutory exception to this is the ability of an S corporation to receive tax treatment similar to that of a partnership.[2] A less important statutory exception allows certain partnerships to elect not to be taxed as a partnership.[3]

An individual conducting a sole proprietorship files Schedule C of Form 1040. If more than one trade or business is conducted, a separate Schedule C is filed for each trade or business. A partnership files Form 1065. A corporation files Form 1120, and an S corporation files Form 1120S.

Limited Liability Company

A limited liability company is a hybrid business form that combines the corporate characteristic of limited liability for the owners with the tax character-

---

1. A business entity can also be conducted in the form of a trust or estate. These two forms are not discussed in this chapter. See the discussion of the income taxation of trusts and estates in Chapter 19. A few states (e.g., Virginia) have enacted legislation permitting a business entity to be conducted as a limited liability company. Since the number of states involved is small, this chapter includes only a brief discussion of this form.

2. §§ 1361 and 1362.

3. § 761.

istics of the partnership. Among the states that permit this legal form for conducting a business entity are Colorado, Florida, Kansas, Texas, Wyoming, and Virginia. This legal form generally is not available to entities that provide professional services (e.g., accountants, attorneys, architects, and physicians).

As previously discussed, the tax form for a business entity may be different from the legal form. The mere passage of a state law providing for an entity called a limited liability company does not ensure that the entity will be taxed as a partnership.

The association issue was discussed in Chapter 2. Under § 7701(a)(3) and the related Regulations, a business entity will be considered an association and taxed as a corporation if it possesses a majority of the following characteristics: continuity of life, centralized management, limited liability, and free transferability of interests.

The tax status of the limited liability company was uncertain until the IRS issued Revenue Ruling 88–76.[4] Under this ruling, a Wyoming limited liability company was classified as a partnership for tax purposes. The key to this result was the avoidance of association status. Since a limited liability company will always possess the characteristic of limited liability, it is imperative to avoid at least two of the three remaining characteristics for association status.

NONTAX FACTORS
◆

Tax factors are only one of many factors to consider in making any business decision. The substantial reduction in tax rates brought about by TRA of 1986 makes taxation less significant. Above all, any business decision should make economic sense.

―――――――――――――― EXAMPLE 1 ――――――――――――――

T is considering investing $10,000 in a limited partnership. He projects that he will be able to deduct the $10,000 within the next two years (his share of partnership losses). Since T's marginal tax rate is 31%, the deductions will produce a positive cash flow effect of $3,100 ($10,000 × 31%). However, there is a substantial risk that T will not recover any of his original investment. If this occurs, his negative cash flow from the investment in the limited partnership is $6,900 ($10,000 − $3,100). T must decide if the investment makes economic sense. ◆

Capital Formation

The ability of an entity to raise capital is a factor that must be considered. A sole proprietorship is subject to obvious limitations. Compared to the sole proprietorship, the partnership has a greater opportunity to raise funds through the pooling of owner resources.

―――――――――――――― EXAMPLE 2 ――――――――――――――

A and B decide to form a partnership, AB. A contributes cash of $200,000, and B contributes land with an adjusted basis of $60,000 and a fair market value of $200,000. The partnership is going to construct an apartment building at a cost of $800,000. AB pledges the land and the building to secure a loan of $700,000. ◆

The limited partnership provides even greater potential than the general partnership form because a limited partnership can secure funds from investors (limited partners).

―――――――――――――

4. Rev.Rul. 88–76, 1988–2 C.B. 360.

Most popular real estate

General partnerships the How they benefit

Personal service can be different

EXAMPLE 3

C and D form a limited partnership, CD. C contributes cash of $200,000, and D contributes land with an adjusted basis of $60,000 and a fair market value of $200,000. The partnership is going to construct a shopping center at a cost of $5 million. Included in this cost is the purchase price of $800,000 for land adjacent to that contributed by D. Thirty limited partnership interests are sold for $100,000 each to raise $3 million. Nonrecourse creditor financing of $2 million is obtained with the shopping center (including the land) being pledged. ◆

The § 465 at-risk provision and the § 469 passive activity loss provision both have reduced the tax attractiveness of investments in real estate, particularly in the limited partnership form. In effect, the tax consequences have a critical effect on the economic consequences.[5]

Of the different forms of business entities, the corporate form offers the greatest ease and potential for obtaining owner financing because it can issue additional shares of stock. The ultimate examples of this form are the large public companies that are listed on the stock exchanges.

Limited Liability

Only the corporation has limited liability under state law. This absence of personal liability on the part of the owners is the most frequently cited advantage of the corporate form.

EXAMPLE 4

A, B, and C each invest $25,000 for all the shares of stock of the ABC Corporation. ABC obtains creditor financing of $100,000. ABC is the defendant in a personal injury suit resulting from an accident involving one of ABC's delivery trucks. The court awards a judgment of $2.5 million to the plaintiff. The award exceeds ABC's insurance coverage by $1.5 million. Even though the judgment will probably result in the bankruptcy of ABC, the shareholders will have no personal liability for the unpaid corporate debts. ◆

Limited liability is not available to all corporations. For many years, state laws did not permit professional individuals (e.g., accountants, attorneys, architects, and physicians) to incorporate. Even though professionals are now permitted to incorporate, the statutes do not provide unlimited liability with respect to the performance of professional services.

Even if state law provides for limited liability, the shareholders of small corporations may have to forgo this benefit. Quite often, such a corporation may be unable to obtain external financing (e.g., a bank loan) unless the shareholders guarantee the loan.

The limited partnership form provides limited liability to the limited partners. Their liability is limited to the amount invested plus any additional amount that they agreed to invest. However, the general partner (or partners) has unlimited liability.

EXAMPLE 5

A, the general partner, invests $250,000 in ABC, a limited partnership. B and C, the limited partners, each invest $50,000. While the potential loss for B and C is limited to $50,000 each, A's liability is unlimited. ◆

---

5. See the related discussions in Chapters 10 and 11. For a comprehensive discussion of these provisions, see Chapter 7 in *West's Federal Taxation: Individual Income Taxes.*

Indirectly, it may be possible to provide the general partner with limited liability by having a corporation as the general partner. See Figure 13–1. Structured this way, the general partner (the corporation) has limited its liability under the corporate statutes. Therefore, individual A is protected from personal liability by being merely the shareholder of Corporation A. The potential exists, however, that unless this approach is very carefully structured, the IRS will treat the limited partnership as an association and therefore taxable as a corporation.[6]

Overall Impact on Entity and Owners

Both the sole proprietorship and the partnership are subject to single taxation. This result occurs because the owner(s) and the entity generally are not considered separate for tax purposes. Thus, the tax liability is levied at the owner level rather than at the entity level.

On the other hand, the corporate form is subject to double taxation. This is frequently cited as the major tax disadvantage of the corporate form. Under double taxation, the entity is taxed on the earnings of the corporation, and the owners are taxed on distributions to the extent they are made from corporate earnings.

The S corporation provides a way to attempt to avoid double taxation and to subject the earnings to a lower tax rate (individual tax rates rather than corporate tax rates). However, the S corporation provisions impose restrictions on ownership structure with respect to the number and type of shareholders. In addition, statutory exceptions subject the entity to taxation in certain circumstances. To the extent these exceptions apply, double taxation may result. Finally, the distribution policy of the S corporation may produce difficulties with respect to the *wherewithal to pay* concept.

SINGLE VERSUS DOUBLE TAXATION
◆

─────────── EXAMPLE 6 ───────────

T, Inc., has been operating as an S corporation since it began its business two years ago. For both of the prior years, T incurred a tax loss. T has taxable income of $75,000 for 1992 and expects that its earnings will increase each year in the foreseeable future. Part of this earnings increase will result from T's expansion into other communities in the state. Since most of this expansion will be financed internally, no dividend distributions will be made to the shareholders.

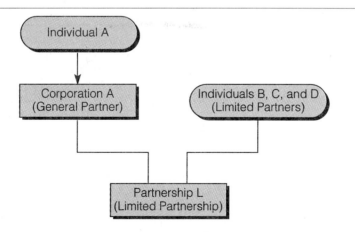

FIGURE 13–1
Limited Partnership with a Corporate General Partner

---

6. See the discussions of associations in Chapter 2 and limited partnerships in Chapter 11. Also see Rev.Proc. 89–12, 1989–1 C.B. 798 and Rev.Rul. 88–76, 1988–2 C.B. 360.

Long term goals is a factor

Assuming all of the shareholders of T are in the 31% tax bracket, their tax liability for 1992 will be $23,250 ($75,000 × 31%). Although the S corporation election will avoid double taxation, the shareholders will have a wherewithal to pay problem. In addition, the actual tax liability for 1992 would have been less if T, Inc., had not been an S corporation [(15% × $50,000) + (25% × $25,000) = $13,750]. ◆

Because no distribution

The data in Example 6 can be used to illustrate two additional tax concepts. First, the current wherewithal to pay problem could be resolved by terminating the S corporation election. The tax liability would then be imposed at the corporate level. Since the corporation does not intend to make any dividend distributions, double taxation at the present time would be avoided. Terminating the election will also reduce the overall shareholder-corporation tax liability by $9,500 ($23,250 − $13,750).[7] Second, tax decisions on the form of business organization should consider more than the current taxable year. If the S election is terminated, another election will not be available for five years. Assuming that the projections are valid and the corporate profits will continue to increase each year, the higher corporate tax rates (34% versus 31%) will produce a greater tax liability at the corporate level than would have been produced at the shareholder level if the S election had been retained. Thus, the decision to revoke the election should have at least a five-year time frame. Perhaps a better solution would be to retain the election and distribute enough dividends to the S corporation shareholders to enable them to pay the shareholder tax liability.

Two other variables that relate to the adverse effect of double taxation are the timing and form of corporate distributions. If no distributions are made in the short run, then only single taxation occurs in the short run.[8] To the extent that double taxation does occur in the future, the cash-flow effect should be discounted to the present. Second, when the distribution is made, is it in the form of a dividend or a return of capital (a stock redemption or a complete liquidation)?

─────────────────── **EXAMPLE 7** ───────────────────

T Corporation has taxable income of $100,000 for 1992. T's tax liability is $22,250. All of T's shareholders are in the 31% bracket. If dividends of $77,750 are distributed in 1992, the shareholders will have a tax liability of $24,102 ($77,750 × 31%). The combined corporation-shareholder tax liability is $46,352 ($22,250 + $24,102) for a combined effective tax rate of 46.4%. ◆

─────────────────── **EXAMPLE 8** ───────────────────

helps reduce double taxation →

Assume the same facts as in Example 7, except the form of the distribution is a stock redemption and the basis for the redeemed shares is $57,750. The shareholders have a recognized gain of $20,000 and a tax liability of $6,200 ($20,000 × 31%). The combined corporation-shareholder tax liability is $28,450 ($22,250 + $6,200) for a combined effective tax rate of 28.5%. ◆

The differences in the tax consequences in Examples 7 and 8 are even more obvious when illustrated in bar graph form.

─────────────

7. The absence of distributions to shareholders could create an accumulated earnings tax problem under § 531. However, as long as earnings are used to finance expansion, the "reasonable needs" provision will be satisfied, and the corporation will avoid any accumulated earnings tax.

8. This assumes there is no accumulated earnings tax problem. See the subsequent discussion of distributions in Minimizing Double Taxation.

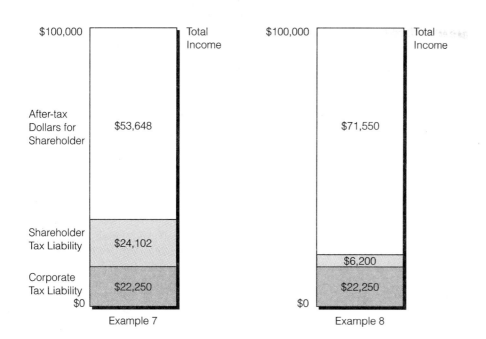

Example 7   Example 8

Alternative Minimum Tax

All of the forms of business are directly or indirectly subject to the alternative minimum tax (AMT).[9] For the sole proprietorship and the corporation, the effect is direct (the AMT liability calculation is attached to the tax form that reports the entity's taxable income—Form 1040 or Form 1120). For the partnership and the S corporation, the effect is indirect (the tax preferences and adjustments are passed through from the entity to the owners, and the AMT liability calculation is not attached to the tax form that reports the entity's taxable income—Form 1065 or Form 1120S).

When compared with the other forms of business, the corporation appears to have a slight advantage. The corporate AMT rate of 20 percent is less than the individual AMT rate of 24 percent. An even better perspective is provided by comparing the AMT rate with the maximum regular rate for both the individual and the corporation. For the individual, the AMT rate is 77 percent (24%/31%) of the maximum regular rate. The AMT rate for the corporation is 59 percent (20%/34%) of the maximum regular rate. Therefore, on the basis of comparative rates, the corporation does have an advantage.

The apparent corporate AMT rate advantage may be more than offset by the AMT adjustment that applies only to the corporation. This is the adjustment for adjusted current earnings (ACE). The amount of the adjustment is 75 percent of the excess of ACE over unadjusted alternative minimum taxable income. If unadjusted alternative minimum taxable income exceeds ACE for the tax year, the adjustment is negative.[10]

If the ACE adjustment is continually going to cause the corporation to be subject to the AMT, the owners should consider electing S corporation status if the eligibility requirements can be satisfied. Since the S corporation does not have this item as an adjustment, it may be possible to reduce the tax liability.

---

9. § 55.

10. §§ 56(c)(1) and (f). See the discussion of the corporate AMT in Chapter 6.

State Taxation

In selecting a form for doing business, the determination of the tax consequences should not be limited to Federal income taxes. Consideration should also be given to state income taxes, and, if applicable, local income taxes.[11]

The S corporation provides a good illustration of this point. Suppose that the forms of business being considered are a limited partnership or a corporation. An operating loss is projected for the next several years. The owners decide to operate the business in the corporate form. The principal nontax criterion for the decision is the limited liability attribute of the corporation. The owners have agreed to consent to an S corporation election. Thus, the corporate losses can be passed through to the shareholders to deduct on their individual tax returns. However, assume that state law does not permit the S corporation election on the state income tax return. Thus, the owners will not receive the tax benefits of the loss deductions that would have been available on their state income tax returns if they had chosen the limited partnership form. As a result of providing limited liability to the owner who would have been the general partner for the limited partnership, the loss deduction at the state level is forgone.

CONTROLLING THE ENTITY TAX

◆

Of the four forms of business entities, it appears at first glance that only the corporation needs to be concerned with controlling the entity tax. If control is defined in the narrow sense of double taxation, then this issue is restricted to the corporate form. However, from the broader perspective of controlling the tax liability related to the profits of the business entity, whether imposed at the entity or owner level, all four business forms are encompassed.

Techniques that can be used to minimize the current period tax liability include the following:

1. Distribution policy.
2. Recognizing the interaction between the regular tax liability and the alternative minimum tax liability.
3. Utilization of special allocations.
4. Favorable treatment of certain fringe benefits.
5. Minimizing double taxation.

Some of the techniques apply to all four forms of business entities. Others apply to only one of the four forms. Even those that apply to all do not minimize taxes equally for all forms. Since the first three techniques are discussed elsewhere in this chapter, only the last two are discussed here.

Favorable Treatment of Certain Fringe Benefits

Ideally, a fringe benefit produces the following tax consequences:

- Deductible by the entity (employer) that provides the fringe benefit.
- Excludible from the gross income of the taxpayer (employee) who receives the fringe benefit.

---

11. See the discussion of multistate corporate taxation in Chapter 15.

From the perspective of the owner or owners of an entity, when the entity provides such favorably taxed fringe benefits to an owner, the benefits are paid for with *before-tax* dollars.

─────────────── EXAMPLE 9 ───────────────

T, the owner of T Ranch, Inc., a corporation in the 34% tax bracket, is provided with meals and lodging that qualify for exclusion treatment under § 119. The annual cost of the meals and lodging to T Ranch, Inc., is $10,000. Since the cost is deductible in calculating the taxable income of T Ranch, Inc., on Form 1120, the after-tax cost to T Ranch, Inc., is only $6,600 [$10,000 − (34% × $10,000)]. Since the $10,000 is excluded in calculating T's gross income, there is no additional tax cost at the owner level. If T had paid for the meals and lodging himself, no deduction would have been permitted because these expenditures are nondeductible personal expenditures. Thus, from T's perspective, the receipt of excludible meals and lodging of $10,000 is equivalent to receiving a distribution from the corporation of $14,493 [$10,000/(100% − 31%)], assuming T is in the 31% tax bracket. ◆

Not all favorably taxed fringe benefits receive exclusion treatment. Although not as attractive to the recipient, another approach provided in the Code is deferral treatment (e.g., pension plans and profit sharing plans).

Example 9 illustrates how certain fringe benefits can be used to benefit the owner of an entity and at the same time have a beneficial impact on the combined tax liability of the entity and the owner. In recognition of this, Congress has enacted various nondiscrimination provisions that generally negate favorable tax treatment if the fringe benefit program is discriminatory. In addition, the Code includes several statutory provisions that make the favorably taxed fringe benefit treatment available only to *employees* (e.g., group term life insurance, meal and lodging exclusion).[12]

The IRS defines the term *employee* restrictively. For the owner of a business entity to be treated as an employee, the entity must be a corporation.[13] For this purpose, an S corporation is treated as a partnership, and a greater than 2 percent shareholder is treated as a partner.[14]

Classification of an owner as a nonemployee produces two negative results. First, the deduction for the cost of the fringe benefit to the entity is disallowed at the entity level. Second, the owner whose fringe benefit has been paid for by the entity must include the cost of the fringe benefit in gross income.

Minimizing Double Taxation

Only the corporate form is potentially subject to double taxation. Several techniques are available for eliminating or at least reducing the second layer of taxation:

1. Making distributions to the shareholders that are deductible to the corporation.
2. Not making distributions to the shareholders.
3. Making distributions that qualify for return of capital treatment at the shareholder level.
4. Making the S corporation election.

───────────────

12. §§ 79 and 119.
13. Reg. § 1.79–0(b). The IRS has not been completely successful with respect to this position.
14. § 1372(a).

*Salaries &
bonuses
are hard to
prove unreasonable*

*Keeping in good
proportion*

*reclassed plus to
thin capitalization*

Making Deductible Distributions. Use of the first technique requires careful advance planning. Typical distribution forms that will result in a deduction to the corporation are (1) salary payments to shareholder-employees, (2) lease rental payments to shareholder-lessors, and (3) interest payments to shareholder-creditors. Recognizing the tax benefit of this technique, the IRS scrutinizes these types of transactions carefully. All three types are evaluated in terms of *reasonableness*.[15] In addition, the interest payments may result in the IRS raising the *thin incorporation* issue and reclassifying some or all of the debt as equity.[16] IRS success with either approach will raise the specter of double taxation.

--- EXAMPLE 10 ---

T owns all the stock of T, Inc., and is also the chief executive officer. T, Inc.'s taxable income before salary payments to T is as follows:

1990	$ 80,000
1991	50,000
1992	250,000

During the year, T receives a monthly salary of $3,000. In December of each year, T reviews the operations for the year and determines the year-end bonus to be paid to the key officers (only T for bonus purposes). T's yearly bonuses are as follows:

1990	$ 44,000
1991	14,000
1992	214,000

The obvious purpose of T, Inc.'s bonus program is to reduce the corporate taxable income to zero and thereby avoid double taxation. The examination of T, Inc.'s tax return by the IRS would likely result in a deduction disallowance for unreasonable compensation. ◆

--- EXAMPLE 11 ---

T and U each contribute $20,000 to TU, Inc., for all the stock of TU, Inc. In addition, they each loan $80,000 to TU, Inc. The loan is documented by formal notes, the interest rate is 12%, and the maturity date is 10 years from the date of the loan.

The notes provide the opportunity for the corporation to make payments of $9,600 each year to both T and U and for the payments not to be subject to double taxation. That is, the interest payments are includible in the gross income of T and U, but are deductible by TU, Inc., in calculating its taxable income. At the time of repayment in 10 years, neither T nor U will have any gross income from the repayment since the $80,000 amount realized is equal to the basis for the note of $80,000 (return of capital concept).

If the IRS succeeded in reclassifying the notes as equity, T and U's includible gross income of $9,600 each would remain the same (interest income would be reclassified as dividend income). However, because the dividend payments are not deductible by TU, Inc., the corporation's taxable income would increase by $19,200 ($9,600 × 2). To make matters worse, the repayment of the notes in 10 years would not qualify for return of capital treatment and would likely result in dividend income treatment for T and U. ◆

15. § 162(a)(1). *Mayson Manufacturing Co. v. Comm.*, 49–2 USTC ¶9467, 38 AFTR 1028, 178 F.2d 115 (CA–6, 1949); *Harold's Club v. Comm.*, 65–1 USTC ¶9198, 15 AFTR2d 241, 340 F.2d 861 (CA–9, 1965).

16. § 385; Rev.Rul. 83–98, 1983–2 C.B. 40; *Bauer v. Comm.*, 84–2 USTC ¶9996, 55 AFTR2d 85–433, 748 F.2d 1365 (CA–9, 1984).

Not Making Distributions.   Double taxation will not occur unless the corporation makes (actual or deemed) distributions to the shareholders. A closely held corporation that does not make distributions will eventually encounter an accumulated earnings tax problem unless the reasonable needs requirement is satisfied. When making distribution policy decisions each year, the board of directors should be apprised of any potential accumulated earnings tax problem and take the appropriate steps to eliminate it. The accumulated earnings tax rate of 28 percent is the same as the maximum tax bracket on capital gains for individual taxpayers.[17]

─────────────────────────── EXAMPLE 12 ───────────────────────────

According to an internal calculation made by T Corporation, its accumulated taxable income is $400,000. The board of directors would prefer not to declare any dividends, but is considering a dividend declaration of $400,000 to avoid the accumulated earnings tax. All of the shareholders are in the 31% bracket.

If a dividend of $400,000 is declared, the tax cost to the shareholders is $124,000 ($400,000 × 31%). If a dividend is not declared and the IRS assesses the accumulated earnings tax, the tax cost to the corporation for the accumulated earnings tax would be $112,000 ($400,000 × 28%).

To make matters worse, the corporation will have incurred the accumulated earnings tax cost without being successful in getting funds out of the corporation to the shareholders. If the unwise decision were now made to distribute the remaining $288,000 ($400,000 − $112,000) to the shareholders, the additional tax cost at the shareholder level would be $89,280 ($288,000 × 31%). Therefore, the combined shareholder-corporation tax cost would be $201,280 ($112,000 + $89,280). This is 162% ($201,280/$124,000) of the tax cost that would have resulted from an initial dividend distribution of $400,000. ◆

Assuming that the accumulated earnings tax can be avoided (e.g., a growth company whose reasonable needs justify its no dividend policy), a policy of no distributions to shareholders can avoid forever the second layer of taxation. This will occur if the shares of stock are bequeathed to the taxpayer's beneficiaries. As a result of the step-up in basis rules for inherited property, the basis of the stock for the beneficiaries will be the fair market value at the date of the decedent's death rather than the decedent's basis.

Return of Capital Distributions.   The magnitude of the effect of double taxation can be reduced if the corporate distributions to the shareholders can qualify for return of capital rather than dividend treatment. For an ongoing corporation, the stock redemption provisions offer an opportunity to reduce the includible gross income at the shareholder level. The corporate liquidation provisions can be used if the business entity will cease to operate in corporate form.

─────────────────────────── EXAMPLE 13 ───────────────────────────

T Corporation makes a distribution of $400,000 to its shareholders. A and B, two of the shareholders, each receive $25,000. The form of the distribution permits the shareholders to surrender a certain number of shares of stock. The potential exists that the distribution can qualify for stock redemption treatment at the shareholder level. A satisfies the requirements for a substantially disproportionate distribution under § 302. B does not because he is in control of the corporation after the distribution (he owns 60% of the stock). Assuming A's basis for the shares redeemed is $20,000, A has

─────────────────────────

17. § 531. See the discussion of the accumulated earnings tax in
    Chapter 6.

a capital gain of $5,000 ($25,000 − $20,000). B has dividend income of $25,000. He must allocate his stock basis among his remaining shares. ◆

Electing S Corporation Status.   Electing S corporation status generally eliminates double taxation by making the corporation a tax reporter rather than a taxpayer. Therefore, the only tax levy is at the shareholder level. Factors to consider in making this election include the following:

- Are all the shareholders willing to consent to the election?
- Can the qualification requirements under § 1361 be satisfied at the time of the election?
- Since the qualification requirements become maintenance requirements, can these requirements continue to be satisfied?
- For what period will the conditions that make the election beneficial continue to prevail?
- Will the corporate distribution policy create wherewithal to pay problems at the shareholder level?

--- EXAMPLE 14 ---

T Corporation commenced business in January 1992. The two shareholders are U and V, both of whom are in the 31% tax bracket. According to the available projections, the following operating results are expected to occur for the first five years of operations:

1992	$ (50,000)
1993	400,000
1994	600,000
1995	800,000
1996	1,000,000

The corporation plans to expand rapidly. Therefore, no distributions will be made to shareholders. In addition, beginning in 1993, preferred stock will be offered to a substantial number of investors to help finance the expansion.

If the S corporation election is made for 1992, the $50,000 loss can be passed through to U and V's tax returns. Therefore, the cash flow effect would be $15,500 ($50,000 × 31%). Assume that the election is either revoked or is involuntarily terminated at the beginning of 1993 as a result of the issuance of the preferred stock. The corporate tax liability for 1993 would be $136,000 ($400,000 × 34%).

If the S corporation election is not made for 1992, the $50,000 loss will be a net operating loss. The amount can be carried forward to reduce the corporate taxable income to $350,000 ($400,000 − $50,000). The resultant tax liability is $119,000 ($350,000 × 34%).

Should the S corporation election be made for just the one-year period? The answer is unclear. With an assumed after-tax rate of return to U and V of 10%, the value of the $15,500 one year hence is $17,050 ($15,500 × 110%). Even considering the time value of money, the combined corporation/shareholder negative cash-flow effect of $118,950 ($136,000 − $17,050) in the case of an S election is about the same as the $119,000 corporate tax liability that would result for a regular corporation. The negative cash flow is even greater when related accounting and/or legal fees are considered. ◆

CONDUIT VERSUS ENTITY TREATMENT
◆

Under the *conduit* concept, the entity is viewed merely as an extension of the owners. Under the *entity* concept, the entity is regarded as being separate and distinct from its owners. The effects that these different approaches have on the following are examined for the partnership, corporation, and S corporation:

- Recognition at time of contribution to the entity.
- Basis of ownership interest.
- Results of operations.
- Recognition at time of distribution.
- Passive activity losses.
- At-risk rules.
- Special allocations.

The sole proprietorship is not analyzed separately because the owner and the business are in essence the same. In one circumstance, however, a tax difference does occur. Recognition does not occur when an owner contributes an asset to a sole proprietorship. Thus, the basis generally is a carryover basis. However, if the asset is a personal use asset, the sole proprietorship's basis is the *lower of* the adjusted basis or the fair market value at the date of contribution. Also note that if a personal use asset is contributed to a partnership or corporation, this *lower of* rule applies.

Effect on Recognition at Time of Contribution to the Entity

Since the conduit approach applies for the partnership, § 721 provides for no recognition on the contribution of property to the partnership in exchange for a partnership interest. Section 721 protects both a contribution associated with the formation of the partnership and later contributions. The partnership has a carryover basis for the contributed property, and the partners have a carryover basis for their partnership interests.[18]

Since the entity approach applies for the corporation, the transfer of property to a corporation in exchange for its stock is a taxable event. However, if the § 351 control requirement is satisfied, no gain or loss is recognized. In this case, both the corporate property and the shareholders' stock will have a carryover basis.[19] This control requirement makes it more likely that shareholders who contribute appreciated property to the corporation after the formation of the corporation will recognize gain.

To the extent that the fair market value of property contributed to the entity at the time of formation is not equal to the property's adjusted basis, a special allocation may be desirable. With a special allocation, the owner contributing the property receives the tax benefit or detriment for any recognized gain or loss that subsequently results because of the initial difference between the adjusted basis and the fair market value. For the partnership, this special allocation treatment is mandatory. No such allocation is available for the corporate form, since the gain or loss is recognized at the corporation level rather than at the shareholder level. For the S corporation, no such allocation is available. The recognized gain or loss will be reported on the shareholders' tax returns based on their stock ownership.

──────────── EXAMPLE 15 ────────────

T contributes land with an adjusted basis of $10,000 and a fair market value of $50,000 for a 50% ownership interest. At the same time, U contributes cash of $50,000 for the remaining 50% ownership interest. Because the entity is unable to obtain the desired zoning, it subsequently sells the land for $50,000.

If the entity is a corporation, T will have a realized gain of $40,000 ($50,000 − $10,000) and a recognized gain of $0 resulting from the contribution. His basis for his

18. See the pertinent discussion in Chapter 10, including Example 23.

19. See the pertinent discussion in Chapter 3, including Examples 1 and 2.

stock will be $10,000, and the corporation will have a basis for the land of $10,000. The corporation will have a realized and recognized gain of $40,000 ($50,000 − $10,000) when it sells the land. Thus, what should have been T's recognized gain becomes the corporation's taxable gain. There is no way that the corporation can directly allocate the recognized gain to T. The corporation could distribute the land to T and let him sell the land, but the distribution may be taxable to T as a dividend, and gain may be recognized at the corporate level on the distribution.

If the entity is a partnership, the tax consequences will be the same as they were in the corporate illustration except for the $40,000 recognized gain on the sale of the land. The partnership will have a realized and recognized gain of $40,000 ($50,000 − $10,000). However, even though T's share of profits and losses is only 50%, all of the $40,000 recognized gain will be allocated to him. If the entity is an S corporation, the tax consequences will be the same as in the corporate illustration except that T will report $20,000 of the recognized gain on his tax return and the other shareholder will report $20,000 also. ◆

Effect on Basis of Ownership Interest

In a partnership, since the partner is the taxpayer, profits and losses of the partnership affect the partner's basis for his or her partnership interest. Likewise, the partner's basis is increased by his or her share of partnership liability increases and is decreased by his or her share of partnership liability decreases. This liability effect enables the partner to benefit from the leverage concept. Accordingly, the partner's basis changes frequently.[20]

For the corporate entity, the corporation is the taxpayer. Therefore, the shareholder's basis for the stock is not affected by corporate profits and losses or corporate liability increases or decreases.

The treatment of an S corporation shareholder falls in between that of the partner and the corporate shareholder. The S corporation shareholder's stock basis is increased by the share of profits and decreased by the share of losses, but it is not affected by corporate liability increases or decreases. Thus, unlike the partner, the S corporation shareholder does not benefit from the leverage concept.

───────────────────── EXAMPLE 16 ─────────────────────

T contributes cash of $100,000 to an entity for a 30% ownership interest. The entity borrows $50,000 and repays $20,000 of this amount by the end of the taxable year. The profits for the year are $90,000.   50−20 = 30000(30%) = 9000

If the entity is a partnership, T's basis at the end of the period will be $136,000 ($100,000 investment + $9,000 share of net liability increase + $27,000 share of profits). If T is a corporate shareholder instead, his stock basis will be $100,000 ($100,000 original investment). If the corporation is an S corporation, T's stock basis will be $127,000 ($100,000 + $27,000). ◆

Effect on Results of Operations

The entity concept is responsible for producing potential double taxation for the corporate form (the corporation is taxed on its earnings, and the shareholders are taxed on the distribution of earnings). Thus, from the perspective of taxing the results of operations, the entity concept appears to be a disadvantage for the corporation. Furthermore, the maximum corporate tax rate (34 percent) exceeds the maximum individual tax rate (31 percent). However, whether the entity concept actually produces disadvantageous results depends on the following:

───────────────────────

20. §§ 705 and 752.

- Whether the corporation generates positive taxable income.
- The tax rates that apply for the corporation and for the shareholders.
- The distribution policy of the corporation.

As discussed previously, techniques exist for getting cash out of the corporation to the shareholders without incurring double taxation (e.g., compensation payments to shareholder-employees, lease rental payments to shareholder-lessors, and interest payments to shareholder-creditors). Since these payments are deductible to the corporation, they reduce corporate taxable income. If the payments can be used to reduce corporate taxable income to zero, the corporation will have no tax liability.

The maximum corporation tax bracket does exceed the maximum individual tax bracket. However, in a specific situation, the corporate tax rates that apply may be less than the applicable individual rates. This opportunity for the corporation to be subject to a lower tax rate is not available for personal service corporations. There, the only rate available is 34 percent.[21]

As previously discussed, double taxation can occur only if distributions are made to the shareholders. Thus, if no distributions are made and if the entity can avoid the accumulated earnings tax (e.g., based on the statutory credit or the reasonable needs adjustment) and the personal holding company tax (e.g., the corporation primarily generates active income), only one current level of taxation will occur. If distributions do occur in the future with respect to current earnings, the resultant tax liability should be discounted for the interim period. If the distribution can qualify for return of capital treatment (stock redemption or liquidation) rather than dividend treatment, the shareholder tax liability will be decreased. Ideally, taxation of the earnings at the shareholder level can be avoided permanently if the stock passes through the decedent shareholder's estate.

The entity concept does result in the earnings components losing their identity when they are passed through to shareholders in the form of dividends. This may produce a negative result for net long-term capital gains, as the potential 28% rate ceiling is lost. Since capital gains lose their identity when passed through in the form of dividends, they cannot be used to offset capital losses at the shareholder level. An even more negative result is produced when dividends are paid out of tax-exempt income (tax-exempt income is excludible in calculating corporate taxable income, but is included in calculating current earnings and profits). Thus, what should not be subject to taxation is taxed because of the entity concept.

Both the partnership and the S corporation use the conduit concept in reporting the results of operations. Any item that is subject to special treatment on the taxpayer-owners' tax return is reported separately to the owners. Other items are netted and reported as taxable income. Thus, taxable income merely represents those income and deduction items that are not subject to special treatment.[22]

Many of the problems that the entity concept may produce for the corporate form are not present for the partnership or S corporation. Included in this category are double taxation, problems with the reasonableness requirement, and loss of identity of the income or expense item at the owner level.

Only the partnership completely applies the conduit concept in reporting the results of operations. In several circumstances, the S corporation is subject to taxation at the corporate level, including the tax on built-in gains and the tax on

---

21. § 11(b)(2).   **22.** §§ 701, 702, 1363, and 1366.

certain passive investment income.[23] This limited application of the entity concept necessitates additional planning to attempt to avoid taxation at the corporate level.

Effect on Recognition at Time of Distribution

The application of the conduit concept results in distributions not being taxed to the owners. The application of the entity concept produces the opposite result. Therefore, distributions can be made to partners or to S corporation shareholders tax-free, whereas the same distribution would produce dividend income treatment for corporate shareholders.

In this regard, a distinction must be made between distributions of earnings and other distributions for the S corporation. The S corporation generally is treated as a conduit with respect to its operations. However, as previously discussed, in several cases the entity concept is applied, and the S corporation becomes a taxpayer rather than merely a tax reporter. In effect, the conduit concept applies to S corporation operations unless otherwise specified in Subchapter S of the Code. Since distributions of earnings are included in the operations category, they are subject to conduit treatment through the application of the Accumulated Adjustments Account (AAA).[24] Distributions in excess of earnings qualify for return of capital treatment.

A combination entity/conduit concept applies to property distributions to S corporation shareholders. As discussed above, the conduit concept applies with respect to the shareholder. However, if the property distributed is appreciated property, § 311(b) provides that the realized gain is recognized at the corporate level (same treatment as a regular corporation). This gain recognition is an application of the entity concept. Then, however, the conduit concept is applied to the pass-through of the gain to the shareholders.

EXAMPLE 17

W, an S corporation, is equally owned by P and Q. W distributes two parcels of land to P and Q. W has a basis for each parcel of $10,000. Each parcel has a fair market value of $15,000. The distribution results in a $10,000 ($30,000 − $20,000) recognized gain for W. P and Q each report $5,000 of the gain on their individual income tax returns. ◆

if previously a c corp

Stock redemptions and complete liquidations are not covered by the provisions of Subchapter S. Therefore, the tax consequences of an S corporation stock redemption are determined under the regular corporate provisions in § 302, while those for a complete liquidation are determined under the regular corporate provisions in § 336.

Effect on Passive Activity Losses   *Sep Stated Item*

The passive activity loss rules apply to the partnership and to the S corporation, but apply to the corporation only for personal service corporations and closely held corporations. A *closely held corporation* is defined as one that meets the stock ownership requirement under the personal holding company provisions. That is, more than 50 percent of the value of the outstanding stock at any time during the last half of the taxable year is owned by or for not more than five individuals. The definition of a personal service corporation is modified slightly from the standard definition under § 269A. A corporation is classified as a § 469 *personal service corporation* only if the following requirements are satisfied:

---

23. §§ 1374 and 1375.   **24.** § 1368.

- The principal activity of the corporation is the performance of personal services.
- The services are substantially performed by owner-employees.
- Owner-employees own more than 10 percent in value of the stock of the corporation.

The **general passive activity loss rules** apply to the personal service corporation. Therefore, passive activity losses cannot be offset against either active income or portfolio income. For the closely held corporation, the application of the passive activity rules is less harsh. Although passive activity losses cannot be offset against portfolio income, they can be offset against active income.

The statutory language of § 469(a)(2), which describes the taxpayers subject to the passive activity loss rules, does not mention either the partnership or the S corporation. Instead, it mentions the individual taxpayer. Since the conduit concept applies, the passive activity results are separately stated at the partnership or S corporation level and are passed through to the partners or shareholders with the identity maintained.

Effect on At-Risk Rules

The at-risk rules of § 465 apply to both the partnership and the S corporation. Although the statutory language of § 465(a) mentions neither, the conduit concept that applies to both entities results in the application of § 465. Section 465 also applies to closely held corporations (defined the same as under the passive activity loss rules). However, exceptions are available for closely held corporations that are actively engaged in equipment leasing or are defined as qualified C corporations.

The application of the at-risk rules produces a harsher result for the partnership than for the S corporation. This occurs because the partnership, in the absence of § 465, would have a greater opportunity to use the leveraging concept.

EXAMPLE 18

T is the general partner, and U and V are the limited partners in the TUV limited partnership. T contributes land with an adjusted basis of $40,000 and a fair market value of $50,000 for his partnership interest, and U and V each contribute cash of $100,000 for their partnership interests. They agree to share profits and losses equally. To finance construction of an apartment building, the partnership obtains $600,000 of nonrecourse financing [not qualified nonrecourse financing under § 465(b)(6)] using the land and the building as the pledged assets. Each partner's basis for his partnership interest is as follows:

	T	U	V
Contribution	$ 40,000	$100,000	$100,000
Share of nonrecourse debt	200,000	200,000	200,000
Basis	$240,000	$300,000	$300,000

Without the at-risk rules, U and V could pass through losses up to $300,000 each even though they invested only $100,000 and have no personal liability for the nonrecourse debt. However, the at-risk rules limit the loss pass-through to the at-risk basis, which is $100,000 for U and $100,000 for V. Note that the at-risk rules also can affect the general partner. Since T is not at risk for the nonrecourse debt, his at-risk basis is $40,000. If the mortgage were recourse debt, his at-risk basis would be $640,000 ($40,000 + $600,000). Thus, as a result of the at-risk rules, leveraging is available only for recourse debt for partners who have potential personal liability. ◆

—————————————————— EXAMPLE 19 ——————————————————

Assume the same facts as in Example 18, except that the entity is an S corporation and T receives 20% of the stock and U and V each receive 40%. The basis for their stock is as follows:

T	$ 40,000
U	100,000
V	100,000

The nonrecourse debt does not affect the calculation of stock basis. The stock basis for each shareholder would remain the same even if the debt were recourse debt. Only direct loans by the shareholders increase the ceiling on loss pass-through (basis for stock plus basis for loans by shareholders). ◆

Effect of Special Allocations

An advantage of the conduit concept over the entity concept is the ability to make special allocations. Special allocations are not permitted for the corporate form. However, indirectly, the corporate form may be able to achieve results similar to those produced by special allocations through payments to owners (e.g., salary payments, lease rental payments, and interest payments) and through different classes of stock (e.g., preferred, common). However, even in these cases, the breadth of the treatment and the related flexibility are less than that which can be achieved under the conduit concept.

Although the S corporation is a conduit, it is treated more like a corporation than a partnership with respect to special allocations. This treatment results from the application of the per share and per day rule in § 1377(a). Although the S corporation is limited to one class of stock, it can still use the payments to owners procedure. However, the IRS has the authority to reallocate income among members of a family if fair returns are not provided for services rendered or capital invested.[25]

—————————————————— EXAMPLE 20 ——————————————————

The stock of an S corporation is owned by F (50%), S (25%), and D (25%). S and D are the adult children of F. F is in the 31% bracket, and S and D are in the 15% bracket. Only F is an employee of the corporation. He is paid an annual salary of $20,000, whereas employees with similar responsibilities in other corporations earn $100,000. The corporation generates earnings each year of approximately $200,000.

It appears that the reason F is paid a low salary is to enable more of the earnings of the S corporation to be taxed to S and D, who are in lower tax brackets. Thus, the IRS could use its statutory authority to allocate a larger salary to F. ◆

The partnership has many opportunities to use special allocations, including the following:

- The ability to share profits and losses differently from the share in capital.
- The ability to share profits and losses differently.
- The special allocation required under § 704(c) for the difference between the adjusted basis and the fair market value of contributed property.
- The special allocation of any item permitted under § 704(a) if the substantial economic effect rule of § 704(b) is satisfied.

25. § 1366(e).

- The optional adjustment to basis permitted under § 734 that results from partnership distributions.
- The optional adjustment to basis permitted under § 743 that results from an acquisition by purchase, taxable exchange, or inheritance.

A key factor in evaluating the tax consequences of disposing of a business is whether the disposition is viewed as the sale of an ownership interest or as a sale of assets. Generally, the tax consequences are more favorable if the transaction is treated as a sale of the ownership interest.

DISPOSITION OF A BUSINESS OR AN OWNERSHIP INTEREST
◆

Sole Proprietorship

Regardless of the form of the transaction, the sale of a sole proprietorship is treated as the sale of individual assets. Thus, gains and losses must be calculated separately. Classification as capital gain or ordinary income depends on the nature and holding period of the individual assets. Ordinary income property such as inventory will result in ordinary gains and losses. Section 1231 property such as land, buildings, and machinery used in the business will produce § 1231 gains and losses (subject to depreciation recapture under §§ 1245 and 1250). Capital assets such as investment land and stocks qualify for capital gain or loss treatment.

If the amount realized exceeds the fair market value of the identifiable assets, the excess is identified with goodwill, which is a capital asset. From the purchaser's perspective, classification of the excess as goodwill produces negative tax consequences in that the goodwill cannot be amortized. One way to avoid this negative result is to identify the excess with a covenant not to compete.

EXAMPLE 21

S sells her sole proprietorship to P for $600,000. The identifiable assets are as follows:

	Adjusted Basis	Fair Market Value
Inventory	$ 20,000	$ 25,000
Accounts receivable	40,000	40,000
Machinery and equipment*	125,000	150,000
Buildings**	175,000	250,000
Land	40,000	100,000
	$400,000	$565,000

*Potential § 1245 recapture of $50,000.
**Potential § 1250 recapture of $20,000.

The sale will produce the following results for S:

	Gain (Loss)	Ordinary Income	§ 1231 Gain	Capital Gain
Inventory	$ 5,000	$ 5,000		
Accounts receivable	–0–			
Machinery and equipment	25,000	25,000		
Buildings	75,000	20,000	$ 55,000	
Land	60,000		60,000	
Goodwill	35,000			$35,000
	$200,000	$50,000	$115,000	$35,000

can be covenant not to compete

If the sale is structured this way, P cannot deduct the $35,000 paid for goodwill. If, however, P paid the $35,000 to S for a covenant not to compete for a period of seven years, P could deduct $5,000 each year. However, this would result in S's $35,000 capital gain being reclassified as ordinary income.

Partnership

The sale of a partnership can be structured as the sale of assets or as the sale of an ownership interest. If the transaction takes the form of an asset sale, it will be treated the same as for a sole proprietorship (described above). The sale of an ownership interest is treated as the sale of a capital asset under § 741 (subject to ordinary income potential under § 751 for unrealized receivables and substantially appreciated inventory). Thus, if capital gain treatment can produce beneficial results for the taxpayer (e.g., has capital losses to offset or will benefit from using the alternative tax on net capital gains), the sale of an ownership interest is preferable.

From the buyers' perspective, the form does not produce different tax consequences. If the transaction is an asset purchase, the basis for the assets will be the amount paid for them. Assuming the buyers intend to continue to operate in the partnership form, the assets can be contributed to a partnership under § 721. Therefore, the owners' basis for their partnership interests will be equal to the purchase price for the assets. Likewise, if ownership interests are purchased, the owners' basis will be the purchase price, and the partnership's basis for the assets will be the purchase price since the original partnership will have terminated.[26]

A problem may arise if an individual purchases a partnership interest from another partner and the amount paid exceeds the new partner's pro rata share of the partnership's basis for the assets. If the new partner does not acquire at least a 50 percent capital and profits interest, the old partnership may not terminate.[27]

--- EXAMPLE 22 ---

P purchases S's partnership interest for $100,000. P acquires both a 20% capital interest and a 20% interest in profits and losses. At the purchase date, the assets of the partnership are as follows:

	Adjusted Basis	Fair Market Value
Cash	$ 10,000	$ 10,000
Inventory	30,000	35,000
Accounts receivable	15,000	15,000
Machinery and equipment	70,000	90,000
Buildings	100,000	150,000
Land	175,000	200,000
	$400,000	$500,000

In effect, P paid $100,000 for his 20% share of partnership assets ($500,000 × 20%). His basis for his partnership interest will reflect the purchase price of $100,000. However, P's proportionate share of the partnership assets is based on the partnership's adjusted basis for the assets of $400,000 (i.e., $400,000 × 20% = $80,000). Since P's acquisition of his ownership interest from S did not result in a termination of the partnership, the partnership's adjusted basis for the assets does not change. There-

---

26. § 708(b)(1)(B).   27. §§ 708(b)(1)(A) and (B).

fore, if the partnership were to liquidate all of its assets immediately for $500,000, P's share of the recognized gain of $100,000 ($500,000 − $400,000) would be $20,000 ($100,000 × 20%). This result occurs in spite of the fact that P paid fair market value for his partnership interest.

The Code does provide an opportunity to rectify this inequity to P. If the partnership elects the optional adjustment to basis under § 754, the operational provisions of § 743 will result in P having a special additional basis for each of the appreciated partnership assets. The amount is the excess of the amount P effectively paid for each of the assets over his pro rata share of the partnership's basis for the assets.

	Amount Paid (20% Share)	Pro Rata Share of Adjusted Basis	Special Basis Adjustment
Cash	$ 2,000	$ 2,000	$ −0−
Inventory	7,000	6,000	1,000
Accounts receivable	3,000	3,000	−0−
Machinery and equipment	18,000	14,000	4,000
Buildings	30,000	20,000	10,000
Land	40,000	35,000	5,000
	$100,000	$80,000	$20,000

Therefore, if the partnership sells the inventory, P's share of the ordinary income is $1,000 ($5,000 × 20%). He then reduces this amount by his special additional basis of $1,000. Thus, the net effect, as it equitably should be, is $0 ($1,000 − $1,000). ◆

As Example 22 illustrates, the optional adjustment to basis election under § 754 provides a way to avoid the aforementioned problem. However, four additional factors need to be considered. First, the election must be made by the partnership, not just by the acquiring partner. Therefore, the acquiring partner should obtain a written agreement from the other partners indicating they will consent to the § 754 election. Second, the election is a continuing election. Thus, while the election will benefit an acquiring partner if the partnership assets are appreciated at the date of acquisition, it will produce detrimental consequences (i.e., a negative special basis adjustment) if the adjusted basis exceeds the fair market value of the assets at the acquisition date. Third, the election not only activates the operational provisions of § 743, it also activates the operational provisions of § 734 with respect to partnership distributions. Fourth, if the members of the partnership change frequently, recordkeeping can become complex.

Corporation

The sale of the business can be structured as either an asset sale or a stock sale. The stock sale has the dual advantage to the seller of being less complex both as a legal transaction and as a tax transaction. It also has the advantage of providing a way to avoid double taxation. Finally, the gain on the sale of the stock is a capital gain to the shareholder.

―――――――――――――― EXAMPLE 23 ――――――――――――――

P and Q each own 50% of the stock of PQ, Inc. They have owned the business for 10 years. P's basis for his stock is $40,000, and Q's basis for her stock is $60,000. They agree to sell the stock to R for $300,000. P has a long-term capital gain of $110,000 ($150,000 − $40,000), and Q has a long-term capital gain of $90,000 ($150,000 − $60,000). R has a basis for her stock of $300,000. PQ, Inc.'s basis for its assets does not change as a result of the stock sale. ◆

Structuring the sale of the business as a stock sale may produce detrimental tax results for the purchaser. As Example 23 illustrates, the basis of the corporation's assets is not affected by the stock sale. If the fair market value of the stock exceeds the corporation's adjusted basis for its assets, the purchaser is denied the opportunity to step up the basis of the assets to reflect the amount in effect paid for them through the stock acquisition. Note that this is similar to the problem at the partnership level if the § 754 election is not made.

For an asset sale, the seller of the business can be either the corporation or the shareholders. If the seller is the corporation, the corporation sells the business (the assets), pays any debts not transferred, and makes a liquidating distribution to the shareholders. If the sellers are the shareholders, the corporation pays any debts that will not be transferred and makes a liquidating distribution to the shareholders; then the shareholders sell the business.

Regardless of the approach used for an asset sale, double taxation will occur. The corporation is taxed on the actual sale of the assets and is taxed as if it had sold the assets when it makes the liquidating distribution of the assets to the shareholders who then sell the assets. The shareholders are taxed when they receive cash or assets distributed in-kind by the corporation.

The asset sale resolves the purchaser's problem of not being able to step up the basis of the assets to their fair market value. The basis for each asset will be the amount paid for it. In order to operate in corporate form (assuming the purchaser is not a corporation), the purchaser will need to transfer the property to a corporation in a § 351 transaction.

From the perspective of the seller, the ideal form of the transaction is a stock sale. Conversely, from the purchaser's perspective, the ideal form is an asset purchase. Prior to TRA of 1986, the corporate liquidation provisions tended to equate the tax consequences of these two forms.

Neither the new § 336 nor the revised § 338 permits double taxation to be avoided. Therefore, the bargaining ability of the seller and the purchaser to structure the sale as a stock sale or an asset sale, respectively, has become more critical than prior to TRA of 1986.

Rather than selling the entire business, an owner may sell his or her ownership interest. Since the form of the transaction is a stock sale, the results for the selling shareholder will be the same as if all the shareholders had sold their stock (i.e., capital gain or capital loss to the shareholder).

S Corporation

Since the S corporation is a corporation, it is subject to the provisions for a corporation discussed previously. Either an asset sale at the corporate level or a liquidating distribution of assets produces recognition at the corporate level. However, under the conduit concept applicable to the S corporation, the recognized amount is taxed at the shareholder level. Therefore, double taxation is avoided directly (only the shareholder is involved) for a stock sale and indirectly (the conduit concept ignores the involvement of the corporation) for an asset sale.

After TRA of 1986 eliminated the corporate liquidation rules that had generally enabled corporations to avoid double taxation, the potential existed for the S corporation election to be made prior to the liquidation of a corporation to avoid double taxation. Recognizing this potential, Congress enacted the built-in gain rules of § 1374 to close this loophole. Thus, if § 1374 applies, taxation will occur at the corporate level, and double taxation will result.

See Concept Summary 13–1 for a summary of the tax consequences of the disposition of a business.

CONCEPT SUMMARY 13–1
TAX TREATMENT OF DISPOSITION OF A BUSINESS

		Tax Consequences	
Form of Entity	Form of Transaction	Seller	Buyer
Sole proprietorship	Sale of individual assets.	Gain or loss is calculated separately for the individual assets. Classification as capital or ordinary depends on the nature and holding period of the individual assets. If amount realized exceeds the fair market value of the identifiable assets, the excess is allocated to goodwill (except to the extent identified with a covenant not to compete), which is a capital asset.	Basis for individual assets is the allocated cost. Prefers that any excess of purchase price over the fair market value of identifiable assets be identified with a covenant not to compete, since goodwill cannot be amortized.
	Sale of the business.	Treated as if a sale of the individual assets (as above).	Treated as if a purchase of the individual assets (as above).
Partnership	Sale of individual assets.	Treatment is the same as for the sole proprietorship.	Treatment is the same as for the sole proprietorship. If the intent is to operate in partnership form, the assets can be contributed to a partnership under § 721.
	Sale of ownership interest.	Partnership interest is treated as the sale of a capital asset under § 741 (subject to ordinary income potential under § 751 for unrealized receivables and substantially appreciated inventory).	Basis for new partner's ownership interest is the cost. The new partnership's basis for the assets is also the pertinent cost (i.e., contributed to the partnership under § 721), since the original partnership will have terminated.
Corporation	Sale of corporate assets by corporation (i.e., corporation sells assets, pays debts, and makes liquidating distribution to the shareholders).	Double taxation occurs. Corporation is taxed on the sale of the assets with the gain or loss determination and the classification as capital or ordinary treated the same as for the sole proprietorship. Shareholders calculate gain or loss as the difference between the stock basis and the amount received from the corporation in the liquidating distribution. Capital gain or loss usually results, since stock typically is a capital asset.	Basis for individual assets is the allocated cost. If the intent is to operate in corporate form, the assets can be contributed to a corporation under § 351.
	Sale of corporate assets by the shareholders (i.e., corporation pays debts and makes liquidating distribution to the shareholders).	Double taxation occurs. At the time of the liquidating distribution to the shareholders, the corporation is taxed as if it had sold the assets. Shareholders calculate gain or loss as the difference between the stock basis and the fair market value of the assets received from the corporation in the liquidating distribution. Capital gain or loss usually results, since stock typically is a capital asset.	Same as above.

Form of Entity	Form of Transaction	Tax Consequences Seller	Buyer
	Sale of corporate stock.	Enables double taxation to be avoided. Since the corporation is not a party to the transaction, there are no tax consequences at the corporate level. Shareholders calculate gain or loss as the difference between the stock basis and the amount received for the stock. Capital gain or loss usually results, since stock typically is a capital asset.	Basis for the stock is its cost. The basis for the corporate assets is not affected by the stock purchase.
S corporation	Sale of corporate assets by corporation.	Recognition occurs at the corporate level on the sale of the assets with the gain or loss determination and the classification as capital or ordinary treated the same as for the sole proprietorship. Conduit concept applicable to the S corporation results in the recognized amount being taxed at the shareholder level. Double taxation associated with the asset sale is avoided, because the shareholder's stock basis is increased by the amount of gain recognition and decreased by the amount of loss recognition. Shareholders calculate gain or loss as the difference between the stock basis and the amount received from the corporation in the liquidating distribution. Capital gain or loss usually results, since stock typically is a capital asset.	Basis for individual assets is the allocated cost. If the intent is to operate in corporate form (i.e., as an S corporation), the assets can be contributed to a corporation under § 351.
	Sale of corporate assets by the shareholders.	At the time of the liquidating distribution to the shareholders, recognition occurs at the corporation level as if the corporation had sold the assets. The resultant tax consequences for the shareholders and the corporation are the same as for the sale of corporate assets by the S corporation.	Same as above.
	Sale of corporate stock.	Same as the treatment for the sale of stock of a regular corporation.	Same as the treatment for the purchase of stock of a regular corporation.

OVERALL COMPARISON OF FORMS OF DOING BUSINESS

◆

See Concept Summary 13–2 for a detailed comparison of the tax consequences of the following forms of doing business: sole proprietorship, partnership, S corporation, and corporation.

	Sole Proprietorship	Partnership*	S Corporation**	Regular Corporation***
Restrictions on type or number of owners	One owner. The owner must be an individual.	Must have at least 2 owners.	Only individuals, estates, and certain trusts can be owners. Maximum number of shareholders limited to 35.	None, except some states require a minimum of 2 shareholders.
Incidence of tax	Sole proprietorship's income and deductions are reported on Schedule C of the individual's Form 1040. A separate Schedule C is prepared for each business.	Entity not subject to tax. Partners in their separate capacity subject to tax on their distributive share of income. Partnership files Form 1065.	Except for certain built-in gains and passive investment income when earnings and profits are present from Subchapter C tax years, entity not subject to Federal income tax. S corporation files Form 1120S. Shareholders are subject to tax on income attributable to their stock ownership.	Income subject to double taxation. Entity subject to tax, and shareholder subject to tax on any corporate dividends received. Corporation files Form 1120.
Highest tax rate	31 percent at individual level.	31 percent at partner level.	31 percent at shareholder level.	39 percent at corporate level plus 31 percent on any corporate dividends at shareholder level.
Choice of tax year	Same tax year as owner.	Selection generally restricted to coincide with tax year of majority partners or principal partners, or to calendar year.	Restricted to a calendar year unless IRS approves a different year for business purposes or other exceptions apply.	Unrestricted selection allowed at time of filing first tax return.
Timing of taxation	Based on owner's tax year.	Partners report their share of income in their tax year with or within which the partnership's tax year ends. Partners in their separate capacities are subject to payment of estimated taxes.	Shareholders report their shares of income in their tax year with or within which the corporation's tax year ends. Generally, the corporation uses a calendar year, but see "Choice of tax year" above. Shareholders may be subject to payment of estimated taxes. Corporation may be subject to payment of estimated taxes for the taxes imposed at the corporate level.	Corporation subject to tax at close of its tax year. May be subject to payment of estimated taxes. Dividends will be subject to tax at the shareholder level in the tax year received.

	Sole Proprietorship	Partnership*	S Corporation**	Regular Corporation***
Basis for allocating income to owners	Not applicable (only one owner).	Profit and loss sharing agreement. Cash basis items of cash basis partnerships are allocated on a daily basis. Other partnership items are allocated after considering varying interests of partners.	Pro rata share based on stock ownership. Shareholder's pro rata share is determined on a daily basis, according to the number of shares of stock held on each day of the corporation's tax year.	Not applicable.
Contribution of property to the entity	Not a taxable transaction.	Generally, not a taxable transaction.	Is a taxable transaction unless the § 351 requirements are satisfied.	Is a taxable transaction unless the § 351 requirements are satisfied.
Character of income taxed to owners	Retains source characteristics.	Conduit—retains source characteristics.	Conduit—retains source characteristics.	All source characteristics are lost when income is distributed to owners.
Basis for allocating a net operating loss to owners	Not applicable (only one owner).	Profit and loss sharing agreement. Cash basis items of cash basis partnerships are allocated on a daily basis. Other partnership items are allocated after considering varying interests of partners.	Prorated among shareholders on a daily basis.	Not applicable.
Limitation on losses deductible by owners	Investment plus liabilities.	Partner's investment plus share of liabilities.	Shareholder's investment plus loans made by shareholder to corporation.	Not applicable.
Subject to at-risk rules	Yes, at the owner level. Indefinite carryover of excess loss.	Yes, at the partner level. Indefinite carryover of excess loss.	Yes, at the shareholder level. Indefinite carryover of excess loss.	Yes, for closely held corporations. Indefinite carryover of excess loss.
Subject to passive activity loss rules	Yes, at the owner level. Indefinite carryover of excess loss.	Yes, at the partner level. Indefinite carryover of excess loss.	Yes, at the shareholder level. Indefinite carryover of excess loss.	Yes, for closely held corporations and personal service corporations. Indefinite carryover of excess loss.
Tax consequences of earnings retained by entity	Taxed to owner when earned and increases his or her investment in the sole proprietorship.	Taxed to partners when earned and increases their respective interests in the partnership.	Taxed to shareholders when earned and increases their respective basis in stock.	Taxed to corporation as earned and may be subject to penalty tax if accumulated unreasonably.
Nonliquidating distributions to owners	Not taxable.	Not taxable unless money received exceeds recipient partner's basis in partnership interest. Existence of § 751 assets may cause recognition of ordinary income.	Generally not taxable unless the distribution exceeds the shareholder's AAA or stock basis. Existence of accumulated earnings and profits could cause some distributions to be dividends.	Taxable in year of receipt to extent of earnings and profits or if exceeds basis in stock.

	Sole Proprietorship	Partnership*	S Corporation**	Regular Corporation***
Distribution of appreciated property	Not taxable.	No recognition at the partnership level.	Recognition at the corporate level to the extent of the appreciation. Conduit—amount of recognized gain is passed through to shareholders.	Taxable at the corporate level to the extent of the appreciation.
Splitting of income among family members	Not applicable (only one owner).	Difficult—IRS will not recognize a family member as a partner unless certain requirements are met.	Rather easy—gift of stock will transfer tax on a pro rata share of income to the donee. However, IRS can make adjustments to reflect adequate compensation for services.	Same as an S corporation, except that donees will be subject to tax only on earnings actually or constructively distributed to them. Other than unreasonable compensation, IRS generally cannot make adjustments to reflect adequate compensation for services and capital.
Organizational costs	Start-up expenditures are amortizable over 60 months.	Amortizable over 60 months.	Same as partnership.	Same as partnership.
Charitable contributions	Limitations apply at owner level.	Conduit—partners are subject to deduction limitations in their own capacities.	Conduit—shareholders are subject to deduction limitations in their own capacities.	Limited to 10 percent of taxable income before certain deductions.
Alternative minimum tax	Applies at owner level. AMT rate is 24 percent.	Applies at the partner level rather than at the partnership level. AMT preferences and adjustments are passed through from the partnership to the partners.	Applies at the shareholder level rather than at the corporate level. AMT preferences and adjustments are passed through from the S corporation to the shareholders.	Applies at the corporate level. AMT rate is 20 percent.
ACE adjustment	Does not apply.	Does not apply.	Does not apply.	The adjustment is made in calculating AMTI. The adjustment is 75 percent of the excess of adjusted current earnings over unadjusted AMTI. If the unadjusted AMTI exceeds adjusted current earnings, the adjustment is negative.
Tax preference items	Apply at owner level in determining alternative minimum tax.	Conduit—passed through to partners who must account for such items in their separate capacities.	Conduit—passed through to shareholders who must account for such items in their separate capacities.	Subject to alternative minimum tax at corporate level.

	Sole Proprietorship	Partnership*	S Corporation**	Regular Corporation***
Capital gains	Taxed at owner level using maximum 28 percent rate.	Conduit—partners must account for their respective shares.	Conduit, with certain exceptions (a possible penalty tax)—shareholders must account for their respective shares.	Taxed at corporate level using maximum 34 percent rate. No other benefits.
Capital losses	Only $3,000 of capital losses can be offset each tax year against ordinary income. Indefinite carryover.	Conduit—partners must account for their respective shares.	Conduit—shareholders must account for their respective shares.	Carried back three years and carried forward five years. Deductible only to the extent of capital gains.
§ 1231 gains and losses	Taxable or deductible at owner level. Five-year lookback rule for § 1231 losses.	Conduit—partners must account for their respective shares.	Conduit—shareholders must account for their respective shares.	Taxable or deductible at corporate level only. Five-year lookback rule for § 1231 losses.
Foreign tax credits	Available at owner level.	Conduit—passed through to partners.	Generally conduit—passed through to shareholders.	Available at corporate level only.
§ 1244 treatment of loss on sale of interest	Not applicable.	Not applicable.	Available.	Available.
Basis treatment of entity liabilities	Includible in interest basis.	Includible in interest basis.	Not includible in stock basis.	Not includible in stock basis.
Built-in gains	Not applicable.	Not applicable.	Possible corporate tax.	Not applicable.
Special allocations to owners	Not applicable (only one owner).	Available if supported by substantial economic effect.	Not available.	Not applicable.
Availability of fringe benefits to owners	None.	None.	None unless a 2 percent or less shareholder.	Available within antidiscrimination rules.
Effect of liquidation/redemption/reorganization on basis of entity assets	Not applicable.	Usually carried over from entity to partner unless a § 754 election is made, excessive cash is distributed, or more than 50 percent of the capital interests are transferred within 12 months.	Taxable step-up to fair market value.	Taxable step-up to fair market value.
Sale of ownership interest	Treated as the sale of individual assets. Classification of recognized gain or loss depends on the nature of the individual assets.	Treated as the sale of a partnership interest. Recognized gain or loss is classified as capital under § 741, subject to ordinary income treatment under § 751.	Treated as the sale of corporate stock. Recognized gain is classified as capital gain. Recognized loss is classified as capital loss, subject to ordinary loss treatment under § 1244.	Treated as the sale of corporate stock. Recognized gain is classified as capital gain. Recognized loss is classified as capital loss, subject to ordinary loss treatment under § 1244.

*Refer to Chapters 10 and 11 for additional details on partnerships.
**Refer to Chapter 12 for additional details on S corporations.
***Refer to Chapters 2 through 9 for additional details on regular corporations.

Selection of the proper business form can result in both nontax and tax advantages. Both of these factors should be considered in making the selection decision. A proper business form at one point in time may not be the proper business form at a different time. Thus, this choice should be reviewed periodically.

TAX PLANNING CONSIDERATIONS

In looking at the tax attributes, consideration should be given to the tax consequences of the following:

- Contribution of assets to the entity by the owners at the time the entity is created and at later dates.
- Taxation of the results of operations.
- Distributions to owners.
- Disposition of an ownership interest.
- Termination of the entity.

PROBLEM MATERIALS

DISCUSSION QUESTIONS

1. What are the principal legal forms for conducting a business entity? What are the principal Federal income tax forms for doing so?

2. The legal form of conducting a business entity is not always the same as the tax form. Discuss two instances in which the IRS may attempt to tax an entity in a form different from its legal form.

3. A corporation is one of the legal forms that can be used to conduct a business. Discuss why the corporate form is divided into S corporations and C corporations for Federal income tax purposes.

4. Discuss the business and tax advantages of a limited liability company.

5. Compare the partnership and corporate business forms in terms of each of the following nontax factors:

   a. Capital formation.
   b. Limited liability.

6. Several taxpayers would like to conduct a business in partnership form under which all of the owners have limited liability. Can a partnership be structured in such a way that this objective is accomplished? If so, are there any related tax pitfalls?

7. Classify each of the following entity forms with respect to whether it is subject to single or double taxation:

   - Sole proprietorship.
   - Partnership.
   - C corporation.
   - S corporation.

8. T is considering electing S corporation status for his newly created corporation. His motives for doing so are to avoid double taxation and to have the earnings of the corporation taxed at the lower individual rates (31% individual rate versus 34% corporate rate). Will the S election produce the results that T expects?

9. A corporation expects to incur losses for its first year of operations and to earn a profit thereafter. The shareholders are considering whether to elect S corporation status. Discuss the factors that should be considered in making the decision.

10. Which taxpayer is subject to the higher tax rate for the AMT, an individual or a corporation? What AMT adjustment applies only to corporations?

11. Is it possible to avoid the effect of the alternative minimum tax by organizing the entity in a business form that is not directly subject to the AMT (partnership or S corporation)?

12. "A favorably taxed fringe benefit is one that is deductible by the employer who provides it and is excludible from the gross income of the employee who receives it." Discuss the extent to which this statement is correct. 13-9

13. Discuss the difference, if any, in the tax treatment of certain fringe benefits for the owner-employee of a corporation and the owner-employee of a sole proprietorship. 13-9

14. T is the sole shareholder of X, Inc., a C corporation. The corporation normally has taxable income of approximately $500,000. Discuss the tax consequences to T and to X, Inc., of a salary payment to T of $100,000 versus a dividend distribution of $100,000 to T. 13-10

15. What techniques can the shareholders of a C corporation use to avoid double taxation by reducing corporate taxable income? What response can the IRS then use? 13-10

16. T is considering contributing $100,000 to TUV, Inc. However, a business acquaintance suggests that he invest only $60,000 and lend $40,000 to the corporation. Are there any tax benefits to following this advice? Are there any tax pitfalls? 13-10

17. X Corporation has been operating for 10 years. X's taxable income each year has been approximately $100,000. X has not made any dividend distributions during this period and does not intend to do so in the near future. What negative result may occur because of this policy? Describe a set of circumstances for X under which this negative result would not occur. 13 - 11 & 12

18. For the corporate entity, what is a return of capital distribution and what are the tax consequences to the shareholder? 13-11

19. T and U are considering organizing their business either as a partnership or as a corporation. Distinguish between the effects of the conduit concept and the entity concept with respect to the recognition of gain or loss at the time of the transfer of assets to the entity. Is it possible to organize the business as a corporation and not have the entity concept apply? 13-13

20. Why are special allocations either permitted or required for the partners in a partnership, yet are not permitted for the shareholders in a corporation? 13-13

21. Entity liabilities have an effect on the calculation of a partner's basis for his or her partnership interest. Yet entity liabilities do not have any effect on a corporate shareholder's calculation of his or her stock basis. What is the reason for this difference in tax treatment? 13-14

22. In calculating the basis of a partner's interest in the partnership, the partner's basis is increased by his or her share of the partnership liabilities. Since the S corporation is taxed similarly to a partnership, is the same adjustment made in calculating an S corporation shareholder's basis for his or her stock? 13-14

23. What effect do profits and losses have on the following?

    a. Partner's basis for partnership interest.
    b. C corporation shareholder's basis for stock. 13-14
    c. S corporation shareholder's basis for stock.

24. Why is it impossible for a personal service corporation to be taxed at a lower statutory rate than the shareholders of the corporation? 13-15

25. The conduit concept applies to the S corporation. Are there any circumstances in which the S corporation is a taxpayer rather than merely a tax reporter? 13-15 & 16

26. Distributions of earnings of a C corporation are taxed at the shareholder level as dividend income. Why are the earnings of an S corporation that are distributed to shareholders not treated as dividend income by the shareholders? 13-16

27. Distinguish between the tax treatment of a distribution of earnings and other distributions of an S corporation. 13-17

28. What types of corporations are subject to the passive activity loss rules? 13-16 & 17

29. A partner's ability to pass through and deduct his or her share of the partnership loss is limited by his or her partnership interest basis. Why does the Code further limit the loss pass-through and deduction with the at-risk basis? What effect do the passive activity loss rules have on this area? 13-17 & 18

30. Discuss the tax consequences for a partner who sells her partnership interest. How is the basis of the new partner's ownership interest determined? 13-20

31. Q, Inc., R, Inc., and U, Inc., have taxable income as follows:

Corporation	Taxable Income
Q	$ 85,000
R	150,000
U	350,000

Using the 15%, 25%, 34%   *is the average rate*

  a. Calculate the marginal tax rate and the effective tax rate for each of the corporations.
  b. Explain why the marginal tax rate for a corporation can exceed 34%, but the effective tax rate cannot do so.

32. Y, an unmarried taxpayer, is going to establish a manufacturing business. He anticipates that the business will be profitable immediately, due to a patent that he holds. He anticipates that profits for the first year will be about $500,000 and will increase at a rate of about 20% per year for the foreseeable future. He will be the sole owner of the business. Advise Y on the form of business entity he should select.

33. L, Inc., will begin operations on January 1. Earnings for the next five years are projected to be relatively stable at about $100,000 per year. The shareholders of L, Inc., are in the 31% tax bracket.

  a. Assume that L, Inc., will reinvest its after-tax earnings in the growth of the company. Should L, Inc., operate as a C corporation or as an S corporation
  b. Assume that L, Inc., will distribute its after-tax earnings each year to its shareholders. Should L, Inc., operate as a C corporation or as an S corporation?

34. CD, Inc., is a closely held corporation that is owned by 15 shareholders. Selected financial information provided by CD, Inc., is as follows:

Net income before income taxes	$ 400,000
Retained earnings	1,500,000
Adjusted current earnings	300,000
Alternative minimum taxable income (unadjusted)	340,000

  a. Calculate CD, Inc.'s ACE adjustment.
  b. Assuming that net income before income taxes is a loss of $400,000, calculate CD, Inc.'s ACE adjustment.
  c. Assume that CD, Inc., is not closely held (e.g., 10,000 shareholders). Calculate the ACE adjustment.

Covenant not to compete to takeover goodwill

35. E and F are negotiating with G to purchase the business that G operates in corporate form (G, Inc.). The assets of G, Inc., are as follows:

	Basis	FMV
Cash	$ 20,000	$ 20,000
Accounts receivable	50,000	50,000
Inventory	100,000	110,000
Furniture and fixtures	150,000	170,000*
Building	200,000	250,000**
Land	40,000	150,000

560,000   *150,000 good will*   *750,000*

*Potential depreciation recapture under § 1245 is $45,000.   *If gain exceed then cap if less ordinary*
**The straight-line method was used to depreciate the building. The balance in the accumulated depreciation account is $340,000.

G's basis for the stock of G, Inc., is $560,000. G is in the 31% tax bracket, and G, Inc., is in the 34% tax bracket.

  a. Assume that E and F purchase the stock of G, Inc., from G and that the purchase price is $900,000. Determine the tax consequences to E and F, G, Inc., and G.
  b. Assume that E and F purchase the assets from G, Inc., and that the purchase price is $900.000. Determine the tax consequences to E and F, G, Inc., and G.

c. Assume that the purchase price is $550,000 because the fair market value of the building is $150,000 and the fair market value of the land is $50,000. E and F purchase the stock of G, Inc., from G. Determine the tax consequences to E and F, G, Inc., and G.

36. J and K are unmarried brothers who own and operate a farm. They live on the farm and take their meals on the farm for the "convenience of the employer." The fair market value of their lodging is $12,000, and the fair market value of their meals is $8,000. The meals are prepared for them by the farm cook who prepares their meals along with those of the three other farm employees.

   a. Determine the tax consequences of the meals and lodging to J and K if the farm is incorporated.
   b. Determine the tax consequences of the meals and lodging to J and K if the farm is not incorporated.

37. A business entity's taxable income before the cost of certain fringe benefits paid to owners and other employees is $400,000. The amounts paid for these fringe benefits are as follows:

	Owners	Other Employees
Group term life insurance	$15,000	$45,000
Meals and lodging incurred for the convenience of the employer	25,000	20,000
Pension plan	30,000*	70,000

*H.R. 10 (Keogh) plan for partnership and S corporation.

The business entity is equally owned by four owners.

   a. Calculate the taxable income of the business entity if the entity is a partnership, a corporation, or an S corporation.
   b. Determine the effect on the owners for each of the three business forms.

38. D, Inc., has taxable income of $200,000 before paying salaries to the two shareholder-employees, A and B. D, Inc., follows a policy of distributing all after-tax earnings to the shareholders.

   a. Determine the tax consequences for D, Inc., A, and B if the corporation pays salaries to A and B as follows:

Option 1		Option 2	
A	$120,000	A	$45,000
B	80,000	B	30,000

   b. Is D, Inc., likely to encounter any tax problems associated with either option?

39. E, Inc., has taxable income of $300,000. E has been in business for many years and long ago used up the accumulated earnings credit. Assume that E has no additional "reasonable needs of the business" for the current tax year.

   a. Determine the total potential tax liability for E, Inc., if it declares no dividends.
   b. Determine the total potential tax liability for E, Inc., if it declares and pays dividends equal to the after-tax earnings.

40. C and D each own 50% of the stock of CD, Inc. When the corporation was organized, C contributed cash of $90,000, and D contributed land with an adjusted basis of $60,000 and a fair market value of $115,000. CD, Inc., assumed D's $25,000 mortgage on the land. In addition to the capital contributions, C and D each loaned the corporation $50,000. The maturity date of the loan is in 10 years, and the interest rate is 12%, the same as the Federal rate.

   a. Determine the tax consequences to C and D and CD, Inc., of the initial contribution of assets, the shareholder loans, and the annual interest payments if the loans are classified as debt.
   b. If the loans are reclassified as equity.

41. P contributes land (currently zoned as agricultural land) to an entity in which he has a 90% ownership interest after the contribution. P's basis for the land is $40,000, and the fair market value is $60,000. Since the entity is unsuccessful in obtaining commercial zoning for the land, the entity sells the land six months later for $65,000.

   a. Determine the tax consequences to the entity and to P from the sale of the land if the entity is a partnership.
   b. Determine the tax consequences to the entity and to P from the sale of the land if the entity is a C corporation.
   c. Determine the tax consequences to the entity and to P from the sale of the land if the entity is an S corporation.

42. T contributes $25,000 to a business entity in exchange for a 20% ownership interest. During the first year of operations, the entity earns a profit of $150,000. At the end of that year, the entity has liabilities of $60,000.

   a. Calculate T's basis for his stock if the entity is a corporation.
   b. Calculate T's basis for his stock if the entity is an S corporation.
   c. Calculate T's basis for his partnership interest if the entity is a partnership.

43. An entity engages in the following transactions during the taxable year:

   ▪ Sells stock held for three years as an investment for $30,000. The adjusted basis of the stock is $20,000.
   ▪ Sells land used in the business for $65,000. The land had been used as a parking lot and originally cost $40,000.
   ▪ Receives tax-exempt interest on municipal bonds of $5,000.
   ▪ Receives dividends on IBM stock of $8,000.

   Describe the effect of these transactions on the entity and the owners of the entity if the entity is:

   a. A partnership.
   b. A C corporation.
   c. An S corporation.

44. P is a partnership that is owned by J and K. J's basis for her partnership interest is $60,000, and K's basis is $80,000. P distributes $50,000 to J and $60,000 to K.

   a. Determine the tax consequences of the distribution to J, K, and P.
   b. Assume that P is a C corporation rather than a partnership. P, Inc.'s earnings and profits are $200,000. J's basis for her stock is $60,000, and K's stock basis is $80,000. Determine the tax consequences of the distribution to J, K, and P, Inc.

45. X, Inc., distributes land to T in a transaction that qualifies as a stock redemption. X's basis for the land is $10,000, and the fair market value is $25,000. T surrenders shares of stock that have a basis of $16,000. After the redemption, T owns 10% of the stock of X, Inc.

   a. Determine the tax consequences to X, Inc., and T if X, Inc., is a regular corporation.
   b. Determine the tax consequences to X, Inc., and T if X, Inc., is an S corporation.

46. P, a personal service corporation, has the following types of income and losses for 1992:

Active income	$90,000
Portfolio income	20,000
Passive activity losses	50,000

   a. Calculate P's taxable income for 1992.
   b. Assume that instead of being a personal service corporation, P is a closely held corporation. Calculate P's taxable income for 1992.

47. D contributes $50,000 to a business entity in exchange for a 10% ownership interest. The business entity incurs a loss of $900,000 for 1992. The entity liabilities at the end of 1992 are $700,000. Of this amount, $150,000 is for recourse debt, and $550,000 is for nonrecourse debt.

a. Assume the business entity is a partnership. How much of D's share of the loss can be deducted on her 1992 individual tax return? What is D's basis for her partnership interest at the end of 1992?

b. Assume the business entity is a corporation. How much of D's share of the loss can be deducted on her 1992 individual tax return? What is D's basis for her stock at the end of 1992?

48. R contributes land to a business entity in January 1992 for a 30% ownership interest. R's basis for the land is $60,000, and the fair market value is $100,000. The business entity was formed three years ago by P and Q, who have equal ownership. The entity is unsuccessful in getting the land rezoned from agricultural to residential. In October 1992, the land is sold for $110,000.

a. Determine the tax consequences of the sale of the land for the business entity and the three owners if the organization form is a corporation.

b. Determine the tax consequences of the sale of the land for the business entity and the three owners if the organization form is an S corporation.

c. Determine the tax consequences of the sale of the land for the business entity and the three owners if the organization form is a partnership.

49. T is the owner of a sole proprietorship. The entity has assets as follows:

	Basis	FMV
Cash	$10,000	$10,000
Accounts receivable	–0–	25,000
Office furniture and fixtures*	15,000	17,000
Building**	75,000	90,000
Land	60,000	80,000

*Potential depreciation recapture under § 1245 of $5,000.
**The straight-line method of depreciation has been used to depreciate the building.

T sells the business for $250,000 to Z.

a. Determine the tax consequences to T, including the classification of any recognized gain or loss.

b. Determine the tax consequences to Z.

c. Advise Z on how the purchase agreement could be modified to produce more beneficial tax consequences for her.

50. G and H own the GH Partnership. They have conducted the business in partnership form for 10 years. Each has a basis for his partnership interest as follows:

G	$100,000
H	150,000

GH Partnership has the following assets:

	Basis	FMV
Cash	$ 10,000	$ 10,000
Accounts receivable	30,000	28,000
Inventory	25,000	26,000
Building*	100,000	150,000
Land	250,000	400,000

*The straight-line method has been used to depreciate the building. Accumulated depreciation is $70,000.

G and H sell their partnership interests to K and L for $307,000 each.

a. Determine the tax consequences of the sale to G, H, and GH Partnership.

b. From a tax perspective, should it matter to K and L whether they purchase G and H's partnership interests or the partnership assets from GH Partnership?

CHAPTER

EXEMPT ENTITIES

OBJECTIVES

Identify the different types of exempt organizations.

Differentiate between the tax consequences of public charities and private foundations.

Discuss the taxes imposed on the prohibited transactions of private foundations.

Explain the tax on unrelated business income and debt-financed income.

Explain the reporting requirements for exempt organizations.

Identify planning opportunities for exempt organizations.

OUTLINE

Ideally, any entity that generates profit would prefer not to be subject to the Federal income tax. All of the types of entities discussed in Chapter 13 are subject to the Federal income tax at one (e.g., sole proprietorship, partnership, and S corporation forms generally are only subject to single taxation) or more (e.g., C corporation form is subject to double taxation) level(s). However, entities classified as exempt organizations may be able to escape Federal income taxation altogether.

Churches are among the types of organizations that are exempt from Federal income tax. Nevertheless, one must be careful not to conclude that anything labeled a church will qualify for exempt status.

During the 1970s and 1980s, a popular technique for attempting to avoid Federal income tax was the establishment of so-called mail-order churches. For example, in one typical scheme, a nurse obtained a certificate of ordination and a church charter from an organization that sold such documents.[1] The articles of incorporation stated that the church was organized exclusively for religious and charitable purposes, including a religious mission of healing the spirit, mind, emotions, and body. The nurse was the church's minister, director, and principal officer. Taking a vow of poverty, she transferred all her assets, including a house and car, to the church. The church assumed all of the nurse's liabilities, including the mortgage on her house and her credit card bills. The nurse continued to work at a hospital and deposited her salary in the church's bank account. The church provided her with a living allowance sufficient to maintain or improve her previous standard of living. She was also permitted to use the house and car for personal purposes.

The IRS declared that such organizations were shams and not bona fide churches. For a church to be tax-exempt under § 501(c)(3), none of its net earnings may be used to the benefit of any private shareholder or individual. In essence, the organization should serve a public rather than a private interest. While the courts have consistently upheld the IRS position, numerous avoidance schemes such as this have been attempted.

As discussed in Chapter 1, the major objective of the Federal tax law is to raise revenue. If revenue raising were the only objective, however, the Code would not contain provisions that permit certain organizations to be either partially or completely exempt from Federal income tax. As Chapter 1 pointed out, social considerations may also affect the tax law. This objective bears directly on the decision by Congress to provide for exempt organization tax status. The House Report on the Revenue Act of 1938 explains:[2]

> The exemption from taxation of money or property devoted to charitable and other purposes is based upon the theory that the Government is compensated for the loss of revenue by its relief from the financial burden which would otherwise have to be met by appropriations from public funds, and by the benefits resulting from the promotion of the general welfare.

Recognizing this social consideration objective, Subchapter F (Exempt Organizations) of the Code (§§ 501–528) provides the authority under which certain organizations are exempt from Federal income tax. Exempt status is not open-ended in that two general limitations exist. First, the nature or scope of the

---

1. Rev.Rul. 81–94, 1981–1 C.B. 330.

2. See 1939–1 (Part 2) C.B. 742 for reprint of H.R. No. 1860, 75th Congress, 3rd Session.

organization may result in it being only partially exempt from tax.[3] Second, the organization may engage in activities that are subject to special taxation.[4]

An organization qualifies for exempt status *only* if it fits into one of the categories provided in the Code. Examples of qualifying exempt organizations and the specific statutory authority for their exempt status are listed in Concept Summary 14-1.[5]

TYPES OF EXEMPT ORGANIZATIONS
◆

CONCEPT SUMMARY 14-1
TYPES OF EXEMPT ORGANIZATIONS

Statutory Authority	Brief Description	Examples or Comments
§ 501(c)(1)	Corporations that are instrumentalites of the United States.	Commodity Credit Corporation, Federal Deposit Insurance Corporation, Federal Land Bank.
§ 501(c)(2)	Corporations holding title to property for and paying income to exempt organizations.	Corporation holding title to college fraternity house.
§ 501(c)(3)	Religious, charitable, educational, scientific, literary, etc., organizations.	Boy Scouts of America, Red Cross, Salvation Army, Episcopal Church, United Fund, University of Richmond.
§ 501(c)(4)	Civic leagues.	Garden club, tenants' association promoting tenants' legal rights in entire community, anti-abortion organization, League of Women Voters.
§ 501(c)(5)	Labor, agricultural, and horticultural organizations.	Teachers' association, organization formed to promote effective agricultural pest control, organization formed to test soil and to educate community members in soil treatment, garden club.
§ 501(c)(6)	Business leagues, chambers of commerce, real estate boards, etc.	Chambers of commerce, American Plywood Association, medical association peer review board, organization promoting acceptance of women in business and professions.
§ 501(c)(7)	Social clubs.	Country club, rodeo and riding club, press club, bowling club, college fraternities.
§ 501(c)(8)	Fraternal beneficiary societies.	Must operate under the lodge system *and* must provide for the payment of life, sickness, accident, or other benefits to members or their dependents.
§ 501(c)(9)	Voluntary employees' beneficiary associations.	Purpose is to provide for the payment of life, sickness, accident, or other benefits to members, their dependents, or their designated beneficiaries.

---

3. See the subsequent discussion of Unrelated Business Taxable Income.
4. See the subsequent discussions of Prohibited Transactions and Taxes Imposed on Private Foundations.
5. Section § 501(a) provides for exempt status for organizations described in §§ 401 and 501. The orientation of this chapter is

toward organizations that conduct business activities. Therefore, the exempt organizations described in § 401 (qualified pension, profit sharing, and stock bonus trusts) are outside the scope of the chapter and are not discussed. Likewise, organizations described in § 501 that are not involved in the conduct of business activities are excluded.

Statutory Authority	Brief Description	Examples or Comments
§ 501(c)(10)	Domestic fraternal societies.	Must operate under the lodge system; must not provide for the payment of life, sickness, accident, or other benefits; and must devote the net earnings exclusively to religious, charitable, scientific, literary, educational, and fraternal purposes.
§ 501(c)(11)	Local teachers' retirement fund associations.	Only permitted sources of income are amounts received from (1) public taxation, (2) assessments on teaching salaries of members, and (3) income from investments.
§ 501(c)(12)	Local benevolent life insurance associations, mutual or cooperative telephone companies, etc.	Local cooperative telephone company, local mutual water company, local mutual electric company.
§ 501(c)(13)	Cemetery companies.	Must be operated exclusively for the benefit of lot owners who hold the lots for burial purposes.
§ 501(c)(14)	Credit unions.	Excludes Federal credit unions that are exempt under § 501(c)(1).
§ 501(c)(15)	Mutual insurance companies.	Mutual fire insurance company, mutual automobile insurance company.
§ 501(c)(16)	Corporations organized by farmers' cooperatives for financing crop operations.	Related farmers' cooperative must be exempt from tax under § 521.
§ 501(c)(19)	Armed forces members' posts or organizations.	Veterans of Foreign Wars (VFW), Reserve Officers Association.
§ 501(c)(20)	Group legal service plans.	Group legal service plan provided by a corporation for its employees.
§ 501(d)	Religious and apostolic organizations.	Communal organization. Members must include pro rata share of the net income of the organization in their gross income as dividends.
§ 501(e)	Cooperative hospital service organizations.	Centralized purchasing organization for exempt hospitals.
§ 501(f)	Cooperative service organization of educational institutions.	Organization formed to manage universities' endowment funds.

REQUIREMENTS FOR EXEMPT STATUS
◆

Exempt status frequently requires more than mere classification in one of the categories of exempt organizations. Many of the organizations that qualify for exempt status share the following characteristics:

1. The organization serves some type of *common good*.[6]
2. The organization is *not* a *for profit* entity.[7]
3. *Net earnings* do not benefit the members of the organization.[8]
4. The organization does not exert *political influence*.[9]

Serving the Common Good

The underlying rationale for all exempt organizations is that they serve some type of *common good*. However, depending on the type of the exempt organization, the term *common good* may be interpreted broadly or narrowly. If interpreted

---

6. See, for example, §§ 501(c)(3) and (4).
7. See, for example, §§ 501(c)(3), (4), (6), (13), and (14).
8. See, for example, §§ 501(c)(3), (6), (7), (9), (10), (11), and (19).
9. See, for example, § 501(c)(3).

broadly, the group being served is the general public or some large subgroup thereof. If interpreted narrowly, the group is the specific group referred to in the statutory language. One of the factors in classifying an exempt organization as a private foundation is the size of the group it serves.

Not for Profit Entity

The organization may not be organized or operated for the purpose of making a profit. For some types of exempt organizations, the *for-profit prohibition* appears in the statutory language. For other types, the prohibition is implied.

Net Earnings and Members of the Organization

What uses are appropriate for the net earnings of a tax-exempt organization? The logical answer would seem to be that the earnings should be used for the exempt purpose of the organization. However, where the organization exists for the good of a specific group of members, such an open-ended interpretation could permit net earnings to benefit specific group members. In addition, even where the organization exists for the common good, unreasonable payments could be made to insiders and others for goods and services. Therefore, the Code specifically prohibits certain types of exempt organizations from using their earnings in this way. In these cases, the statutory language is, or is similar to, the following:

> . . . no part of the net earnings . . . inures to the benefit of any private shareholder or individual. . .[10]

In some cases, the statutory prohibition appears in the Regulations rather than in the Code. In other instances, a statutory prohibition is unnecessary because the definition of the exempt organization in the Code effectively prevents such use. For example, the Code defines domestic fraternal societies as follows:

> . . . the net earnings of which are devoted exclusively to religious, charitable, scientific, literary, educational, and fraternal purposes. . .[11]

Political Influence

Religious, charitable, educational, etc., organizations are generally prohibited from attempting to influence legislation or participate in political campaigns. Participation in political campaigns includes both participation *on behalf of* a candidate and participation *in opposition to* a candidate.

Only in limited circumstances are such exempt organizations permitted to attempt to influence legislation. See the subsequent discussion under Prohibited Transactions.

TAX CONSEQUENCES OF EXEMPT STATUS: GENERAL
◆

An organization that is appropriately classified as one of the types of exempt organizations is generally exempt from Federal income tax. Four exceptions to this general statement exist, however. If the exempt organization engages in a *prohibited transaction*, it will be subject to tax. Second, if the organization is a so-called *feeder organization*, it is subject to tax. Third, if the organization is classified as a *private foundation*, it may be partially subject to tax.

---

10. § 501(c)(6). 11. § 501(c)(10)

Finally, an exempt organization is subject to tax on its *unrelated business taxable income*.

In addition to being exempt from Federal income tax, an exempt organization may be eligible for other benefits, including the following:

- The organization may be exempt from state income tax, state franchise tax, sales tax, or property tax.
- The organization may receive discounts on postage rates.
- Donors of property to the exempt organization may qualify for charitable contribution deductions on their Federal and state income tax returns.

Prohibited Transactions

The Code contains a separate section on prohibited transactions (§ 503). However, this Section should not be viewed as all-inclusive. If the organization fails to continue to qualify as one of the types of exempt organizations, it will have effectively engaged in a prohibited transaction.

Engaging in a prohibited transaction can produce two potential results. First, it can result in part or all of the organization's income being subject to Federal income tax. Even worse, the organization may forfeit its exempt status. The distinction between these two different tax consequences is highly important. Prohibited transactions will be discussed in the following sequence:

1. Failure to continue to qualify as one of the types of exempt organizations.
2. Election not to forfeit exempt status associated with lobbying activities.
3. Violation under § 503 (prohibited transactions).

Failure to Continue to Qualify. Organizations initially qualify for exempt status only if they qualify as a type of exempt organization under § 501. The initial qualification requirements then effectively become maintenance requirements. Failure to satisfy these maintenance requirements results in the loss of exempt status.

Election Not to Forfeit Exempt Status for Lobbying. Organizations exempt under § 501(c)(3) (religious, charitable, educational, etc., organizations) generally are prohibited from attempting to influence legislation (lobbying activities) or from participating in political campaigns.[12] Since this is both a qualification and a maintenance requirement, its violation can result in the forfeiture of exempt status.

Certain § 501(c)(3) exempt organizations are permitted to engage in lobbying activities on a limited basis.[13] Eligible for such treatment are most § 501(c)(3) exempt organizations (educational institutions, hospitals, and medical research organizations; organizations supporting government schools; organizations publicly supported by charitable contributions; certain organizations that are publicly supported by various sources including admissions, sales, gifts, grants, contributions, or membership fees; and certain organizations that support certain types of public charities). Specifically excluded from eligibility are churches or an integrated auxiliary of a church, and private foundations. Organizations not permitted to engage in lobbying activities are referred to as *disqualified organizations*.

---

12. § 501(c)(3).   **13.** § 501(h).

Qualifying § 501(c)(3) organizations must make an *affirmative election* to be eligible to participate in lobbying activities on a limited basis. If the election is made, a ceiling is placed on lobbying expenditures. Exceeding the ceiling is a violation of a maintenance requirement and thus can lead to the forfeiture of exempt status. Even when the ceiling is not exceeded, a tax may be imposed on some of the lobbying expenditures (discussed subsequently).

Two terms are key to the calculation of the ceiling amount: *lobbying expenditures* and *grass roots expenditures.* Lobbying expenditures are made for the purpose of influencing legislation through either of the following:

- Attempting to affect the opinions of the general public or any segment thereof.
- Communicating with any legislator or staff member or with any government official or staff member who may participate in the formulation of legislation.

Grass roots expenditures are made for the purpose of influencing legislation through attempting to affect the opinions of the general public or any segment thereof.

A statutory ceiling is imposed on both lobbying expenditures and grass roots expenditures. The ceiling on lobbying expenditures is computed as follows:

150% × Lobbying nontaxable amount = Lobbying expenditures ceiling

The ceiling on grass roots expenditures is computed as follows:

150% × Grass roots nontaxable amount = Grass roots expenditures ceiling

The election by a § 501(c)(3) organization to be eligible to make lobbying expenditures on a limited basis is not without adverse tax consequences. The election also subjects the exempt organization to tax on the *excess lobbying expenditures* as follows:[14]

25% × Excess lobbying expenditures = Tax liability

The excess lobbying expenditures are the greater of the following:[15]

- Excess of the lobbying expenditures for the taxable year over the lobbying nontaxable amount.
- Excess of the grass roots expenditures for the taxable year over the grass roots nontaxable amount.

The *lobbying nontaxable amount* is the lesser of (1) $1,000,000 or (2) the amount determined in Figure 14–1.[16] The *grass roots nontaxable amount* is 25 percent of the lobbying nontaxable amount.[17]

———————————— EXAMPLE 1 ————————————

F, a qualifying § 501(c)(3) organization, incurs lobbying expenditures for the taxable year of $500,000 and grass roots expenditures of $0. Exempt purpose expenditures for

---

14. § 4911(a)(1).

15. § 4911(b).

16. § 4911(c)(2).

17. § 4911(c)(4).

the taxable year are $5,000,000. F elects to be eligible to make lobbying expenditures on a limited basis.

Applying the data in Figure 14–1, the lobbying nontaxable amount is $400,000 [$225,000 + 5% ($5,000,000 − $1,500,000)]. The ceiling on lobbying expenditures is $600,000 (150% × $400,000). Therefore, the $500,000 of lobbying expenditures are within the permitted ceiling of $600,000. However, the election results in the imposition of tax on the excess lobbying expenditures of $100,000 ($500,000 lobbying expenditures − $400,000 lobbying nontaxable amount). The resulting tax liability is $25,000 ($100,000 × 25%). ◆

A § 501(c)(3) organization that makes disqualifying lobbying expenditures is subject to a tax on the lobbying expenditures for the taxable year. A tax may also be levied on the organization's management. The rate of the tax on the organization is 5 percent, and the rate on management is also 5 percent. The tax is imposed on management only if the managers knew that making the expenditures was likely to result in the organization no longer qualifying under § 501(c)(3), and if the managers' actions were willful and not due to reasonable cause. The tax does not apply to private foundations (see the subsequent discussion of private foundations).[18] Concept Summary 14–2 summarizes the rules on influencing legislation.

Violation under § 503. Section 503 results in the exempt organization losing its exempt status, at least temporarily, if it engages in a prohibited transaction. Since none of the exempt organizations subject to § 503 treatment are among the types of exempt organizations being examined in this chapter, § 503 is not discussed further.[19]

Feeder Organizations

A *feeder organization* carries on a trade or business for the benefit of an exempt organization and remits its profits to the exempt organization. Such organizations are not exempt from Federal income tax. This provision is intended to prevent an entity whose primary purpose is to conduct a trade or business for profit from escaping taxation merely because all of its profits are payable to one or more exempt organizations.[20]

Figure 14–1 **Calculation of Lobbying Nontaxable Amount**	**Exempt Purpose Expenditures**	**Lobbying Nontaxable Amount Is**
	Not over $500,000	20% of exempt purpose expenditures*
	Over $500,000 but not over $1,000,000	$100,000 + 15% of the excess of exempt purpose expenditures over $500,000
	Over $1,000,000 but not over $1,500,000	$175,000 + 10% of the excess of exempt purpose expenditures over $1,000,000
	Over $1,500,000	$225,000 + 5% of the excess of exempt purpose expenditures over $1,500,000

*Exempt purpose expenditures generally are the amounts paid or incurred for the taxable year to accomplish the following purposes: religious, charitable, scientific, literary, educational, fostering national or international amateur sports competition, or the prevention of cruelty to children or animals.

18. § 4912.
19. §§ 503(a) and (c).

20. § 502(a).

Three types of activities are *not* subject to the feeder organization rules:[21]

- An activity that generates rent income that would be excluded from the definition of the term *rent* for purposes of the unrelated business income tax (discussed subsequently).
- Activities that normally would constitute a trade or business, but where substantially all the work is performed by volunteers.
- Activities that normally would constitute the trade or business of selling merchandise, but where substantially all the merchandise has been received as contributions or gifts.

Tax Consequences of Private Foundation Status

Certain exempt organizations are classified as private foundations. This classification produces two negative consequences. First, the classification may have an adverse impact on the contributions received by the donee exempt organization. Contributions may decline because the tax consequences for donors may not be as favorable as they would be if the exempt organization were not a private foundation.[22] Second, the classification may result in taxation at the exempt organization level. The reason for this less beneficial tax treatment is that private foundations define common good more narrowly and therefore have more restricted donor support. In other words, § 501(c)(3) organizations that are not classified as private foundations—the so-called *public charities*—generally do have broad public support (or actively function in a supporting relationship to such organizations).

Definition of a Private Foundation. The Code defines a private foundation by enumerating the § 501(c)(3) exempt organizations that are not private foundations. Thus, only § 501(c)(3) exempt organizations so enumerated are *not* private foundations. In this regard, the following § 501(c)(3) organizations are *outside* the definition of a private foundation:[23]

CONCEPT SUMMARY 14–2
EXEMPT ORGANIZATIONS AND INFLUENCING LEGISLATION

Factor	Tax Result
Type to which applicable	§ 501(c)(3) organization.
Effect of influencing legislation	Subject to tax on lobbying expenditures under § 4912.
	Forfeit exempt status under § 501(c)(3).
	Not eligible for exempt status under § 501(c)(4).
Effect of electing § 501(h) treatment	Limited ability to make lobbying expenditures.
	Subject to tax under § 4911.

---

21. § 502(b).
22. § 170(e)(1)(B)(ii).

23. § 509(a).

1. Churches; educational institutions; hospitals and medical research organizations; charitable organizations receiving a major portion of their support from the general public or the United States, a state, or a political subdivision thereof that is operated for the benefit of a college or university; and governmental units [favored activities category].
2. Organizations that are broadly supported by the general public (excluding disqualified persons), by governmental units, or by organizations described in (1) above.
3. Organizations organized and operated exclusively for the benefit of organizations described in (1) or (2) [a supporting organization].
4. Organizations organized and operated exclusively for testing for public safety.

To meet the broadly supported requirement in (2) above, both the following tests must be satisfied:

- External support test.
- Internal support test.

Under the *external support test,* the organization *normally* must receive more than one-third of its support each taxable year from the three groups listed in (2) in the form of the following:

- Gifts, grants, contributions, and membership fees.
- Gross receipts from admissions, sales of merchandise, performance of services, or the furnishing of facilities in an activity that is not an unrelated trade or business for purposes of the unrelated business income tax (discussed subsequently). However, such gross receipts from any person or governmental agency in excess of the greater of $5,000 or 1 percent of the organization's support for the taxable year are not counted.

The *internal support test* limits the amount of support *normally* received from the following sources to one-third of the organization's support for the taxable year:

- Gross investment income (gross income from interest, dividends, rents, and royalties).
- Unrelated business taxable income (discussed subsequently) minus the related tax.

For this purpose, the term *normally* refers to the tests being satisfied for the four taxable years preceding the current taxable year. Satisfying the test for the current taxable year will result in the subsequent taxable year being treated as satisfying the test.[24]

EXAMPLE 2

P, a § 501(c)(3) organization, received the following support during the taxable year:

Governmental unit A for services rendered	$30,000
Governmental unit B for services rendered	20,000
General public for services rendered	20,000
Gross investment income	15,000
Contributions from individual substantial contributors (disqualified persons)	15,000

---

24. Reg. § 1.509(a)–3(c).

For purposes of the *external support test,* the support from governmental unit A is counted only to the extent of $5,000 (greater of $5,000 or 1% of $100,000 support). Likewise, for governmental unit B, only $5,000 is counted as support. Thus, the total countable support is only $30,000 ($20,000 from the general public + $5,000 + $5,000), and the related percentage is only 30% ($30,000/$100,000). The $15,000 received from disqualified persons is excluded from the numerator but is included in the denominator. Thus, P fails the test for the taxable year.

In calculating the *internal support test,* only the gross investment income of $15,000 is included in the numerator. Thus, the test is satisfied ($15,000/$100,000 = 15%) for the taxable year.

Since P did not satisfy both tests (it failed the external support test), it does not qualify as an organization that is broadly supported. ◆

The intent of the two tests is to exclude from private foundation status those § 501(c)(3) organizations that are responsive to the general public rather than to the private interests of a limited number of donors or other persons.

Examples of § 501(c)(3) organizations that are properly classified as private foundations receiving broad public support include the United Fund, the Girl Scouts, university alumni associations, symphony orchestras, and the PTA.

Taxes Imposed on Private Foundations

In general, a private foundation is exempt from Federal income tax. However, because it is a private foundation rather than a more broadly, publicly supported organization, it may be subject to the following taxes, which are levied only on private foundations:[25]

- Tax based on investment income.
- Tax on self-dealing.
- Tax on failure to distribute income.
- Tax on excess business holdings.
- Tax on investments that jeopardize charitable purposes.
- Tax on taxable expenditures.

These taxes restrict the permitted activities of private foundations. The taxes may be imposed on the private foundation and the foundation manager, and they may be imposed in the form of both an initial tax and an additional tax. The initial taxes (first-level), with the exception of the tax based on investment income, are imposed because the private foundation engages in so-called *prohibited transactions.* Such transactions include both certain actions and certain failures to act. The additional taxes (second-level) are imposed only if the prohibited transactions are not corrected within a statutory time period. The additional taxes are effectively waived (not assessed or abated or refunded) if the prohibited transactions are modified during a statutory correction period.[26] See Concept Summary 14–3 for additional details. The tax on a failure to distribute income will be used to illustrate how expensive these taxes can be and the related importance of avoiding the imposition of such taxes.

Both an initial (first-level) tax and an additional (second-level) tax may be imposed on a private nonoperating foundation for failure to distribute a sufficient portion of its income. The initial tax is imposed at a rate of 15 percent on the undistributed income for the taxable year that is not distributed by the end of the following taxable year. The initial tax will continue to be imposed on such undistributed income for each year until the IRS assesses the tax.

---

25. §§ 4941–4945.   26. § 4961.

The additional tax is imposed at a rate of 100 percent on the amount of the inadequate distribution that is not distributed by the assessment date. The additional tax is effectively waived if the undistributed income is distributed within 90 days after the mailing of the deficiency notice for the additional tax. Extensions of this period may be obtained.

Undistributed income is the excess of the distributable amount (in effect, the amount that should have been distributed) over qualifying distributions made by the entity. The distributable amount is the excess of the minimum investment return over the sum of the (1) unrelated business income tax and (2) the excise tax based on net investment income under § 4940. The minimum investment return is 5 percent of the excess of the fair market value of the foundation's assets over the unpaid debt associated with acquiring or improving these assets. The foundation's assets employed directly in carrying on the foundation's exempt purpose are not used in making this calculation.

─────────────────────── EXAMPLE 3 ───────────────────────

P, a private foundation, has undistributed income of $80,000 for its taxable year 1989. It distributes $15,000 of this amount during 1990 and an additional $45,000 during 1991. The IRS deficiency notice is mailed to P on August 5, 1992. The initial tax is $12,750 [($65,000 × 15%) + ($20,000 × 15%)].

At the date of the deficiency notice, no additional distributions have been made with respect to the 1989 undistributed income. Therefore, since the remaining

CONCEPT SUMMARY 14–3
TAXES IMPOSED ON PRIVATE FOUNDATIONS

Type of Tax	Code Section	Purpose	Private Foundation Initial Tax	Private Foundation Additional Tax	Foundation Manager Initial Tax	Foundation Manager Additional Tax
On investment income	§ 4940	Audit fee to defray IRS expenses.	2%*			
On self-dealing	§ 4941	Engaging in transactions with disqualified persons.	5%**	200%**	2.5%†	50%†
On failure to distribute income	§ 4942	Failing to distribute adequate amount of income for exempt purposes.	15%	100%		
On excess business holdings	§ 4943	Investments that enable the private foundation to control unrelated businesses.	5%	200%		
On jeopardizing investments	§ 4944	Speculative investments that put the private foundation's assets at risk.	5%	25%	5%††	5%†
On taxable expenditures	§ 4945	Expenditures that should not be made by private foundations.	10%	100%	2.5%††	50%†

*May be possible to reduce the tax rate to 1%. In addition, an exempt operating foundation [see §§ 4940(d)(2) and 4942(j)(3)] is not subject to the tax.
**Imposed on the disqualified person rather than the foundation.
†Subject to a statutory ceiling of $10,000.
††Subject to a statutory ceiling of $5,000.

undistributed income of $20,000 has not been distributed by August 5, 1992, an additional tax of $20,000 ($20,000 × 100%) is imposed.

If P distributes the $20,000 of undistributed income for 1989 within 90 days of the IRS deficiency notice, the additional tax will be waived. Without this distribution, however, the foundation will owe $32,750 in taxes. ◆

UNRELATED BUSINESS INCOME TAX
◆

As explained in the previous section, private foundations are subject to excise taxes for certain actions or failures to act. One of these excise taxes penalizes the private foundation for using the foundation to gain control of unrelated businesses (tax on excess business holdings). However, the term *unrelated business* for purposes of that excise tax is different from the term *unrelated business* as used in the discussion of the unrelated business income tax that follows.

The general objective of the tax on unrelated business income is to tax such income as if the entity were subject to the corporate income tax. Thus, the tax rates that are used are those applicable to a corporate taxpayer.[27] In general, *unrelated business income* is income from activities not related to the exempt purpose of the exempt organization, and the tax is levied because the organization is engaging in substantial commercial activities.[28] Without such a tax, nonexempt organizations (regular taxable business entities) would be at a substantial disadvantage when trying to compete with the exempt organization. Thus, the unrelated business income tax is intended to neutralize the exempt entity's tax advantage.[29]

―――――――――――― EXAMPLE 4 ――――――――――――

C is an exempt private foundation. Its exempt activity is to maintain a restoration of eighteenth-century colonial life (houses, public buildings, taverns, businesses, and craft demonstrations) that is visited by over 1 million people each year. A fee is charged for admission to the "restored area." In addition to this "museum" activity, C operates two hotels and three restaurants that are available to the general public. The earnings from the hotel and restaurant business are used to defray the costs of operating the "museum" activity.

The "museum" activity is not subject to the Federal income tax, except to the extent of any tax liability for any of the aforementioned excise taxes that are levied on private foundations. However, even though the income from the hotel and restaurant business is used for exempt purposes, such income is unrelated business income and is subject to the tax on unrelated business income. ◆

The tax on unrelated business income applies to all organizations that are exempt from Federal income tax under § 501(c), except those exempt under § 501(c)(1). In addition, the tax applies to state colleges and universities (educational institutions above the secondary level operated by any governmental agency or political subdivision thereof).[30]

A materiality exception generally exempts an entity from being subject to the unrelated business income tax if such income is insignificant. See the later discussion of the $1,000 statutory deduction generally available to all exempt organizations.

Unrelated Trade or Business

For an exempt organization to be subject to the tax on unrelated business income, the following factors must be present:[31]

―――――――――――――――――――

27. § 511(a)(1).
28. § 512(a)(1).
29. Reg. § 1.513-1(b).

30. § 511(a)(2) and Reg. § 1.511-2(a)(2).
31. § 513(a) and Reg. § 1.513-2(a).

- The organization conducts a trade or business.
- The trade or business is not substantially related to the exempt purpose of the organization.
- The trade or business is regularly carried on by the organization.

The first two factors are discussed below, and the third factor is discussed under Unrelated Business Income.

The Code specifically excepts the following activities from classification as an unrelated trade or business. That is, even if all of the above factors are present, the activity will not be classified as an unrelated trade or business.[32]

- The individuals performing substantially all the work of the trade or business do so without compensation (e.g., an orphanage operates a retail store for sales to the general public, and all the work is done by volunteers).
- The trade or business consists of selling merchandise, and substantially all of the merchandise has been received as gifts or contributions (e.g., thrift shops).
- For § 501(c)(3) organizations and for state colleges or universities, the trade or business is conducted primarily for the convenience of the organization's members, students, patients, officers, or employees (e.g., a laundry operated by the college for laundering dormitory linens and students' clothing, a college bookstore).
- For local associations of employees under § 501(c)(4), the trade or business consists of selling to association members, at their usual place of employment, work-related clothing and equipment and items normally sold through vending machines, snack bars, or food dispensing facilities. However, the association must have been organized before May 27, 1969.

Definition of Trade or Business. Trade or business, for this purpose, is broadly defined. It includes any activity conducted for the production of income through the sale of merchandise or the performance of services. An activity need not generate a profit to be treated as a trade or business. The activity may be part of a larger set of activities conducted by the organization, some of which may be related to the exempt purpose. Such inclusion in a larger set does not result in the activity losing its identity as an unrelated trade or business.[33]

─────────────────────────── EXAMPLE 5 ───────────────────────────

H is an exempt hospital that operates a pharmacy. The pharmacy provides medicines and supplies to the patients in the hospital (i.e., it contributes to the conduct of the hospital's exempt purpose). In addition, the pharmacy sells medicines and supplies to the general public. The activity of selling to the general public constitutes a trade or business for purposes of the unrelated business income tax. ◆

Not Substantially Related to the Exempt Purpose. Exempt organizations frequently conduct unrelated trades or businesses to provide income to help defray the costs of conducting the exempt purpose (see the hotel and restaurant business in Example 4). Providing financial support for the exempt purpose will not prevent an activity from being classified as an unrelated trade or business and thereby being subject to the tax on unrelated business income.

Determining whether a trade or business is substantially related to the accomplishment of an organization's exempt purpose requires an examination

---

32. § 513(a).

33. Reg. § 1.513–1(b).

of the relationship, if any, between the trade or business and the accomplishment of the exempt purpose. Not only must the trade or business contribute to the accomplishment of the exempt purpose, but it must also contribute *importantly* to that end. To be related to the accomplishment of the exempt purpose, the conduct of the business activities must be causally related to the exempt purpose. Whether a causal relationship exists and its importance are determined by examining the facts and circumstances. One must consider the size and extent of the activities in relation to the nature and extent of the exempt function that the activities serve. [34]

EXAMPLE 6

D, an exempt organization, operates a school for training children in the performing arts. As an essential part of that training, the children perform for the general public. The children are paid at the minimum wage for the performances, and D derives gross income by charging admission to the performances.

The income from admissions is not income from an unrelated trade or business, because the performances by the children contribute importantly to the accomplishment of the exempt purpose of providing training in the performing arts. ◆

EXAMPLE 7

Assume the facts are the same as in Example 6, except that four performances are conducted each weekend of the year. Assume that this number of performances far exceeds that required for training the children. Thus, the part of the income derived from admissions for these excess performances is income from an unrelated trade or business. ◆

The trade or business may sell merchandise that has been produced as part of the accomplishment of the exempt purpose. The sale of such merchandise is normally treated as substantially related. However, if the merchandise is not sold in substantially the same state it was in at the completion of the exempt purpose, the gross income subsequently derived from the sale of the merchandise is income from an unrelated trade or business.[35]

EXAMPLE 8

H, an exempt organization, conducts programs for the rehabilitation of the handicapped. One of the programs includes training in radio and television repair. H derives gross income by selling the repaired items. The income is substantially related to the accomplishment of the exempt purpose. ◆

An asset or facility used in the exempt purpose may also be used in a nonexempt purpose. Income derived from the use in the nonexempt purpose is income from an unrelated trade or business. Related expense allocations for assets and employees used in both an exempt and a nonexempt purpose are to be made on a reasonable basis.[36]

EXAMPLE 9

M, an exempt organization, operates a museum. As part of the exempt purpose of the museum, educational lectures are given in the museum's theater during the operating hours of the museum. In the evening, when the museum is closed, the theater is leased to an individual who operates a movie theater. The lease income received from the individual who operates the movie theater is income from an unrelated trade or business. ◆

---

34. Reg. § 1.513–1(d).
35. Reg. § 1.513–1(d)(4)(ii).

36. Reg. § 1.513–1(d)(4)(iii).

Special Rule for Bingo Games. A special provision applies in determining whether income from bingo games is from an unrelated trade or business. Under this provision, a *qualified bingo game* is not an unrelated trade or business. However, in order to be a qualified bingo game, both of the following requirements must be satisfied:[37]

- The bingo game is legal under both state and local law.
- Commercial bingo games (conducted for a profit motive) ordinarily are not permitted in the jurisdiction.

EXAMPLE 10

B, an exempt organization, conducts weekly bingo games. The laws of the state and municipality in which B conducts the bingo games expressly provide that bingo games may be conducted by exempt organizations. The laws do not permit bingo games to be conducted by profit-oriented entities. Since both of the requirements for bingo games are satisfied, the bingo games conducted by B are not an unrelated trade or business. ◆

EXAMPLE 11

B, an exempt organization, conducts weekly bingo games in City X and City Y. State law expressly permits exempt organizations to conduct bingo games. State law also provides that profit-oriented entities may conduct bingo games in City X, which is a resort community. Several businesses regularly conduct bingo games there.

The bingo games conducted by B in City Y are not an unrelated trade or business. However, the bingo games that B conducts in City X are an unrelated trade or business because commercial bingo games are regularly permitted to be conducted there. ◆

Special Rule for Distribution of Low-Cost Articles. If an exempt organization distributes low-cost items and the distributions are incidental to the organization's solicitation for charitable contributions, such distributions may not be considered an unrelated trade or business. A low-cost article is one that costs $5 (to be indexed) or less. Examples of such items are pens, stamps, stickers, stationery, and address labels. If more than one item is distributed to a person during the calendar year, the costs of the items are combined. The following requirements must be satisfied for the distributions to be *incidental*:[38]

- The person receiving the low-cost article did not request it.
- The person receiving the low-cost article receives it without having given express consent.
- The distribution of the article is accompanied by a request for a charitable contribution.
- The person receiving the low-cost article is notified at the time of receipt that the article may be retained even if a charitable contribution is not made.

Special Rule for Rental or Exchange of Membership Lists. If an exempt organization conducts a trade or business that consists of either exchanging with or renting to other exempt organizations the organization's donor or membership list (mailing lists), the activity is not an unrelated trade or business.[39]

37. § 513(f).
38. § 513(h)(1)(A).

39. § 513(h)(1)(B).

Other Special Rules. Other special rules are used in determining whether each of the following activities is an unrelated trade or business:[40]

- Qualified public entertainment activities (e.g., a state fair).
- Qualified convention and trade show activities.
- Certain services provided at cost or less by a hospital to other small hospitals.
- Certain pole rentals by telephone or electric companies.

Unrelated Business Income

If an exempt organization conducts an unrelated trade or business, taxation will result only if the exempt organization regularly conducts the activity and the business produces unrelated business income.

Regularly Carried on by the Organization. An activity will not be classified as unrelated business income unless it is regularly carried on by the exempt organization. The purpose of this provision is to assure that only activities that are actually competing with taxable organizations are subject to the unrelated business income tax. Accordingly, factors to be considered in applying the *regularly carried on* test include the frequency of the activity, the continuity of the activity, and the manner in which the activity is pursued. In other words, is the activity generally being conducted similarly to the conduct of the activity by a taxable organization?[41]

--- EXAMPLE 12 ---

E, an exempt organization, owns land that is located next to the state fairgrounds. During the 10 days of the state fair, E uses the land as a parking lot and charges individuals attending the state fair for parking there. Under these circumstances, the activity is not regularly carried on. ◆

--- EXAMPLE 13 ---

F, an exempt organization, has its offices in the downtown area. It owns a parking lot adjacent to its offices on which its employees park during the week. On Saturdays, it rents the spaces in the parking lot to individuals shopping or working in the downtown area. In this case, F is conducting a business activity on a year-round basis, even though it is only for one day per week. Thus, an activity is regularly being carried on. ◆

Unrelated Business Income Defined. Unrelated business income is generally the income derived from the unrelated trade or business, reduced by the deductions directly connected with the conduct of the unrelated trade or business.[42]

Unrelated Business Taxable Income

General Tax Model. The model for unrelated business taxable income appears in Figure 14–2.

Positive adjustments:[43]

1. A charitable contribution deduction is permitted without regard to whether the charitable contributions are associated with the unrelated

---

40. §§ 513(d), (e), and (g).
41. § 512(a)(1) and Reg. § 1.513–1(c).

42. § 512(a)(1).
43. §§ 512(a)(1) and (b) and Reg. § 1.512(b)–1.

trade or business. However, to the extent the charitable contributions deducted in calculating net unrelated business income (see Figure 14–2) exceed 10 percent of unrelated business taxable income (without regard to the charitable contribution deduction), the excess is treated as a positive adjustment.

─────────────── EXAMPLE 14 ───────────────

E, an exempt organization, has unrelated business taxable income of $100,000 (excluding the charitable contribution deduction). Total charitable contributions (all associated with the unrelated trade or business) are $13,000. Assuming that the $13,000 is deducted in calculating net unrelated business income, the excess of $3,000 [$13,000 − 10% ($100,000)] is a positive adjustment in calculating unrelated business taxable income. ◆

2. Unrelated debt-financed income [including debt-financed income associated with items (1) through (4) in the subsequent discussion of negative adjustments] net of the unrelated debt-financed deductions (see the subsequent discussion of Unrelated Debt-Financed Income).
3. Certain interest, annuity, royalty, and rent income received by the exempt organization from an organization it controls (80 percent test) is included in unrelated business taxable income. These amounts are included regardless of whether the activity on the part of the controlling organization is a trade or business or is regularly conducted. Therefore, to the extent these amounts are not included in net unrelated business income (see Figure 14–2), a positive adjustment is required in calculating unrelated business taxable income. This provision overrides the modifications for these types of income (discussed subsequently under negative adjustments).

Negative adjustments:

1. Income from dividends, interest, and annuities net of all deductions directly related to producing such income.
2. Royalty income, regardless of whether it is measured by production, gross income, or taxable income from the property, net of all deductions directly related to producing such income. However, if the income is from a working interest and the exempt organization is responsible for its share of the development costs, the resulting income is not considered to be royalty income.
3. Rent income from real property and from certain personal property net of all deductions directly related to producing such income. Personal property rents are included in the negative adjustment only if the personal property is leased with the real property. In addition, the amount of the personal property rent income must be incidental (determined at the time the personal property is placed in service by the lessee) when compared with the total rent income under the lease. Under the Regulations, personal property rent income is not incidental if it exceeds 10 percent of total rent income under the lease. However, none

───

FIGURE 14–2
Tax Formula for Unrelated Business Taxable Income

Gross unrelated business income
− Deductions
= Net unrelated business income
± Modifications
= Unrelated business taxable income

of the rent income (from real property and personal property) is treated as a negative adjustment if either of the following conditions is present:

a. More than 50 percent of the rent income under the lease is from personal property.

b. Rent income is calculated completely, or in part, based on the profits of the lessee (unless the calculation is based on a fixed percentage of sales or receipts).

───────────────────── EXAMPLE 15 ─────────────────────

E, an exempt organization, leases land and a building (realty) and computers (personalty) housed in the building. The lease identifies $46,000 of the rent as being for the land and building and $4,000 for the computers. Expenses that are properly allocable to the land and building are $10,000. The net rent income from the land and building of $36,000 ($46,000 – $10,000) and the income from the computers of $4,000 are treated as negative adjustments. ◆

───────────────────── EXAMPLE 16 ─────────────────────

Assume the facts are the same as in Example 15, except the rent income from the land and building is $35,000 and that from the computers is $15,000. Since the rent income from the computers is not incidental, it is not treated as a negative adjustment. ◆

───────────────────── EXAMPLE 17 ─────────────────────

Assume the facts are the same as in Example 15, except the rent income from the land and building is $20,000 and that from the computers is $30,000. Since over 50% of the rent income under the lease is from the computers, neither the rent income from the land and building nor that from the computers is treated as a negative adjustment. ◆

If the lessor of real property provides significant services to the lessee, the income, for this purpose, is not rent income.

4. Gains and losses from the sale, exchange, or other disposition of property *except for* inventory.

───────────────────── EXAMPLE 18 ─────────────────────

Assume E, the owner of the land, building, and computers in Example 15 sells these assets for $450,000. The adjusted basis of these assets is $300,000. The recognized gain of $150,000 is treated as a negative adjustment in calculating unrelated business taxable income (it is included in gross unrelated business income and then is deducted as a modification). ◆

5. Certain research income net of all deductions directly related to producing such income.

6. The charitable contribution deduction is permitted without regard to whether the charitable contributions are associated with the unrelated trade or business. Therefore, to the extent that the charitable contributions exceed those deducted in calculating net unrelated business income (see Figure 14–2), the excess is treated as a negative adjustment in calculating unrelated business taxable income. The total deductions for charitable contributions may not exceed 10 percent of unrelated business taxable income (without regard to the charitable contribution deduction) [see positive adjustment (1)].

───────────────────── EXAMPLE 19 ─────────────────────

E, an exempt organization, has unrelated business taxable income of $100,000 (excluding the charitable contribution deduction). The total charitable contributions are $9,000, of which $7,000 (those associated with the unrelated trade or business) have been deducted in calculating net unrelated business income. Therefore, the remaining $2,000 of charitable contributions is deducted as a negative adjustment in calculating unrelated business taxable income. ◆

7. A specific deduction of $1,000 is permitted.

Unrelated Debt-Financed Income

In the formula for calculating the tax on unrelated business income (see Figure 14–2), unrelated debt-financed income is one of the positive adjustments. Examples of income from debt-financed property include the rental of real estate, rental of tangible personal property, and investments in corporate stock, including gains from the disposition of such property. Gains from unrelated business income property are also included to the extent the gains are not otherwise treated as unrelated business income.

Definition of Debt-Financed Income. *Debt-financed income* is the gross income generated from debt-financed property. *Debt-financed property* is all property of the exempt organization that is held to produce income and on which there is acquisition indebtedness *except* for the following:[44]

1. Property for which substantially all the use is for the achievement of the exempt purpose of the exempt organization.
2. Property whose gross income is otherwise treated as unrelated business income.
3. Property whose gross income is from the following sources and is not otherwise treated as unrelated business income:

    a. Income from research performed for the United States or a Federal governmental agency, or a state or a political subdivision thereof.
    b. For a college, university, or hospital, income from research.
    c. For an organization that performs fundamental (as distinguished from applied) research for the benefit of the general public, income from research.

4. Property used in a trade or business that is treated as not being an unrelated trade or business under one of the statutory exceptions (see page 14–14).

For purposes of the first exception, the phrase *substantially all* means that the use in the exempt purpose must be at least 85 percent of the use of the property by the exempt organization. If the 85 percent test is not satisfied, but a portion of the use of the property is for the exempt purpose, then that portion of the property is not debt-financed property.[45]

EXAMPLE 20

F, an exempt organization, owns a five-story office building on which there is acquisition indebtedness. Three of the floors are used for F's exempt purpose. The two other floors are leased to X Corporation. In this case, the *substantially all* test is not satisfied. Therefore, 40% of the office building is debt-financed property, and 60% is not. ◆

---

44. § 514(b).

45. Reg. § 1.514(b)–1(b)(1) (ii).

In addition to the four above exceptions, a special rule provides that certain land that is acquired to be used for an exempt purpose within 10 years (property acquired for prospective exempt use) may be excluded from being debt-financed property. To qualify for exclusion under this special rule, the following requirements must be satisfied: [46]

1. The exempt organization acquires real property for the principal purpose of using the land (substantially all its use) for the achievement of the exempt purpose of the exempt organization.
2. Such use is to commence within 10 years of the acquisition date.
3. At the acquisition date, the acquired property is located in the *neighborhood* of other property of the exempt organization for which substantially all the use is for the achievement of the exempt purpose of the exempt organization.

Even if the third requirement is not satisfied, the land may still be excluded from debt-financed property if the acquired land is converted to use for the achievement of the exempt purpose of the organization within the 10-year period. Qualification under this provision will result in a refund of taxes previously paid. If the exempt organization is a church, the 10-year period becomes a 15-year test, and the neighborhood requirement is waived.

Definition of Acquisition Indebtedness. In general terms, acquisition indebtedness is debt sustained by the exempt organization in association with the acquisition of property (but see the earlier discussion of exclusions from the definition of property for this purpose). More precisely, *acquisition indebtedness* consists of the unpaid amounts of the following for debt-financed property:[47]

1. Debt incurred in acquiring or improving the property.
2. Debt incurred before the property was acquired or improved, but which would not have been incurred without the acquisition or improvement.
3. Debt incurred after the property was acquired or improved, but which would not have been incurred without the acquisition or improvement. The incurrence must also have been reasonably foreseeable at the time of acquisition or improvement.

─────────────── EXAMPLE 21 ───────────────

F, an exempt organization, acquires land for $100,000. To finance the acquisition, F mortgages the land and receives loan proceeds of $80,000. F leases the land to X Corporation. The mortgage is acquisition indebtedness. ◆

─────────────── EXAMPLE 22 ───────────────

G, an exempt organization, makes improvements to an office building that it rents to X Corporation. Excess working capital funds are used to finance the improvements. G is later required to mortgage its laboratory building, which it uses for its exempt purpose, to replenish the working capital. The mortgage is acquisition indebtedness. ◆

Portion of Debt-Financed Income and Deductions Treated as Unrelated Business Taxable Income. Once the amount of the debt-financed income and deductions is determined, one must ascertain what portion of the debt-financed

---

46. § 514(b)(3).
47. § 514(c)(1). Under a special rule, educational organizations can exclude certain debt incurred for real property acquisitions from classification as acquisition indebtedness.

income and deductions constitutes unrelated debt-financed income and deductions. Unrelated debt-financed income increases unrelated business taxable income, and unrelated debt-financed deductions decrease unrelated business taxable income (see the earlier discussion under Unrelated Business Taxable Income).

The calculation is made for each debt-financed asset. The gross income from the property is multiplied by the following percentage:[48]

$$\frac{\text{Average acquisition indebtedness for the property}}{\text{Average adjusted basis of the property}} = \text{Debt/basis percentage}$$

This percentage has a statutory ceiling of 100 percent. If debt-financed property is disposed of during the taxable year at a gain, average acquisition indebtedness in the formula is replaced with highest acquisition indebtedness. *Highest acquisition indebtedness* is defined as the largest amount of acquisition indebtedness with respect to the property for the 12-month period preceding the date of disposition.[49]

Deductions directly related to the debt-financed property and the income from it are allowed. However, depreciation deductions are limited to the amount calculated using the straight-line method. Once the allowable deductions are determined, this amount is multiplied by the debt/basis percentage.[50]

--------------------------------- EXAMPLE 23 ---------------------------------

F, an exempt organization, owns an office building that it leases to X Corporation for $120,000 per year. The average acquisition indebtedness is $300,000, and the average adjusted basis is $500,000. Since the office building is debt-financed property, the unrelated debt-financed income is calculated as follows:

$$\frac{\$300,000}{\$500,000} \times \$120,000 = \$72,000$$

◆

Average Acquisition Indebtedness. The *average acquisition indebtedness* for a debt-financed property is the average amount of the outstanding debt for the taxable year (ignoring interest) during the portion of the year the property is held by the exempt organization. This amount is calculated by summing the outstanding debt on the first day of each calendar month the property is held by the exempt organization. Then this total is divided by the number of months the property is held by the organization. A partial month is treated as a full month.[51]

--------------------------------- EXAMPLE 24 ---------------------------------

On August 12, F, an exempt organization, acquires an office building that is debt-financed property for $500,000. The initial mortgage on the property is $400,000. The principal amount of the debt on the first of each month is as follows:

Month	Principal Amount
August	$ 400,000
September	380,000
October	360,000
November	340,000
December	320,000
Total	$1,800,000

---

48. § 514(a)(1).
49. § 514(c)(7).
50. § 514(a)(3).
51. § 514(c)(7) and Reg. § 1.514(a)–1(a)(3).

The average acquisition indebtedness is $360,000 ($1,800,000 ÷ 5 months). August is treated as a full month. ◆

Average Adjusted Basis. The *average adjusted basis* of debt-financed property is calculated by summing the adjusted basis of the property on the first day during the taxable year the property is held by the exempt organization and the adjusted basis on the last day during the taxable year the property is so held and dividing by two.[52]

─────────────────────── EXAMPLE 25 ───────────────────────
Assume the facts are the same as in Example 24. In addition, during the taxable year, depreciation of $5,900 is deducted. The average adjusted basis is $497,050 [($500,000 + $494,100) ÷ 2]. ◆

Concept Summary 14–4 summarizes the rules concerning the unrelated business income tax.

Obtaining Exempt Organization Status

Not all exempt organizations are required to obtain IRS approval for their exempt status. Among those required by statute to do so are organizations exempt under §§ 501(c)(3), 501(c)(9), and 501(c)(20).[53] Even in these cases, exceptions are provided (e.g., churches).

CONCEPT SUMMARY 14–4
UNRELATED BUSINESS INCOME TAX

Purpose	To tax the entity on unrelated business income as if it were subject to the corporate income tax.
Applicable tax rates	Corporate tax rates.
Exempt organizations to which applicable	All organizations that are exempt under § 501(c) except corporations that are instrumentalities of the United States.
Requirements for being subject to the tax	The organization conducts a trade or business; the trade or business is not substantially related to the exempt purpose of the organization; and the trade or business is regularly carried on by the organization.
Exceptions to being covered by the tax	1. All the work is performed by volunteers.
	2. Substantially all of the merchandise being sold has been received by gift.
	3. For § 501(c)(3) organizations, the business is conducted primarily for the benefit of the organization's members, students, patients, officers, or employees.
	4. For a local association of employees under § 501(c)(4), the trade or business consists of selling to association members, at their usual place of employment, work-related clothing and equipment and items normally sold through vending machines, snack bars, or food dispensing facilities.
$1,000 provision	If the gross income from an unrelated trade or business is less than $1,000, it is not necessary to file a return associated with the unrelated business income tax.

───────────────

52. § 514(a)(1) and Reg. § 1.514(a)–1(a)(2).

53. §§ 508(a) and 508(c).

Even when not required to obtain IRS approval, most exempt organizations do apply for exempt status. Typically, an organization does not want to assume that it qualifies for exempt status and describe itself in that way to the public only to have the IRS rule later that it does not qualify. Organizations exempt under § 501(c)(3) use Form 1023 [Application for Recognition of Exemption under Section 501(c)(3)]. Form 1024 [Application for Recognition of Exemption under Section 501(a)] is used for most other types of exempt organizations.

Annual Filing Requirements

Most exempt organizations are required to file an annual information return.[54] The return is filed on Form 990 (Return of Organization Exempt from Income Tax). The following exempt organizations are not required to file Form 990:[55]

- Corporations that are instrumentalities of the United States.
- Churches.
- Organizations whose annual gross receipts do not exceed $25,000.
- Private foundations.

Private foundations are required to file Form 990–PF (Return of Private Foundation). The due date for the return is the fifteenth day of the fifth month after the end of the taxable year.

Exempt organizations that are subject to the unrelated business income tax may be required to file Form 990–T (Exempt Organization Business Income Tax Return). The return must be filed if the organization has gross income of at least $1,000 from an unrelated trade or business. The due date for the return is the fifteenth day of the fifth month after the end of the taxable year.

If an exempt organization is subject to any of the excise taxes imposed on private foundations, Form 4720 (Return of Certain Excise Taxes on Charities and Other Persons) must be filed. The return is filed with the private foundation's Form 990–PF.

TAX PLANNING CONSIDERATIONS

Exempt organizations can provide two potential tax benefits. First, the entity may be exempt from Federal income tax. Second, contributions to the entity may be deductible by the donor.

An organization that qualifies as an exempt organization may still be subject to certain types of Federal income tax, including the following:

- Tax on prohibited transactions.
- Tax on feeder organizations.
- Tax on private foundations.
- Tax on unrelated business income.

Therefore, classification as an exempt organization should not be interpreted to mean that the organization need not be concerned with any Federal income tax. Such a belief can result in the organization engaging in transactions that produce a substantial tax liability.

An organization will be exempt from taxation only if it fits into one of the categories enumerated in the Code. Thus, particular attention must be given to

---

54. § 6033(a)(1).

55. § 6033(a)(2).

the qualification requirements. Since these requirements, in effect, become maintenance requirements, these requirements must continue to be satisfied to avoid termination of exempt status.

Only certain types of organizations are required to obtain IRS approval for exempt status. Even if the organization is not required to do so, obtaining IRS approval is normally a prudent course of action. Assuming that the organization is exempt and later being notified by the IRS that it does not qualify can produce two adverse consequences. First, the organization will be liable for Federal income tax. Second, contributions that have been made by donors to the organization will not qualify as deductible charitable contributions under § 170. Form 1023 or Form 1024 normally is used to apply for exempt organization status.

Exempt organizations that can qualify as public charities receive more beneficial tax treatment than do those that qualify as private foundations. Thus, if possible, the organization should be structured to qualify as a public charity. The following are some of the disadvantages that can result when an exempt organization is classified as a private foundation:

- Taxes may be imposed on the private foundation.
  - Tax based on investment income.
  - Tax on self-dealing.
  - Tax on failure to distribute income.
  - Tax on excess business holdings.
  - Tax on investments that jeopardize charitable purposes.
  - Tax on taxable expenditures.
- Donors may receive less favorable tax deduction treatment under § 170 than they would if the exempt organization were not a private foundation.

One method of avoiding private foundation status is to have a tax-exempt purpose that results in the organization not being one of the § 501(c)(3) organizations that are classified as private foundations (the *organization* approach). If this is not feasible, it may be possible to operate the organization so that it receives broad public support and thereby avoids private foundation status (the *operational* approach).

If the organization is a private foundation, care must be exercised to avoid the assessment of tax liability on prohibited transactions. This objective can best be achieved by establishing controls that prevent the private foundation from engaging in transactions that will trigger the imposition of the taxes. If an initial tax is assessed, corrective actions should be implemented to avoid the assessment of an additional tax.

If the exempt organization conducts an unrelated trade or business, it may be subject to tax on the unrelated business income. Worse yet, the unrelated trade or business could result in the loss of exempt status if the IRS determines that the activity is the primary purpose of the organization. Thus, caution and planning should be used to eliminate the latter possibility and to minimize the former.

One approach that can be used to avoid the imposition of the tax on unrelated business income at the exempt organization level is to establish a taxable subsidiary to conduct the unrelated trade or business. The establishment of a subsidiary enables the revenues and expenses of the exempt organization to be clearly delineated from those of the unrelated trade or business. When the subsidiary remits its after-tax profits to the exempt organization in the form of dividends, the dividends will not be taxable to the exempt organization. In addition, having a taxable subsidiary conduct the unrelated trade or business avoids the possibility that the IRS will consider the unrelated business income to be an excessive percentage of the total revenues of the exempt organization. Such a view can lead to the IRS questioning the exempt organization's right to retain its exempt status.

Rental activities illustrate the necessity of careful planning to avoid including the income from the activity in calculating unrelated business taxable income. The income from the rental of real property by an exempt organization is not part of unrelated business taxable income. However, five circumstances can negate this beneficial result:

1. If personal property is leased with the real property and more than 50 percent of the rent income under the lease is from personal property, all the rent income is included in calculating unrelated business taxable income.
2. If rent income from real property is calculated completely, or in part, based on the profits of the lessee (unless the calculation is based on a fixed percentage of sales or receipts), the rent income is included in calculating unrelated business taxable income.
3. If the lessor of real property provides significant services to the lessee, the income is not treated as rent income and thus is included in the computation of unrelated business taxable income.
4. If the rent income is received from an organization that the exempt organization controls (80 percent), the income is included in calculating unrelated business taxable income.
5. To the extent the rent income is classified as unrelated debt-financed income, it is included in calculating unrelated business taxable income.

PROBLEM MATERIALS

DISCUSSION QUESTIONS

1. Are all churches exempt from Federal income tax?
2. Why are certain organizations either partially or completely exempt from Federal income tax?
3. What are the four general requirements for exempt status?
4. Under what circumstances may an exempt organization be subject to Federal income tax?
5. Religious organizations are generally prohibited from attempting to influence legislation or participating in political campaigns. Therefore, a church cannot participate in a political campaign on behalf of a candidate. Can a church participate in a political campaign *in opposition* to a political candidate?
6. Is a qualifying exempt organization ever subject to Federal income tax?
7. How can a § 501(c)(3) organization engage in lobbying without engaging in a prohibited transaction?
8. X is a hospital that is exempt from Federal income tax under § 501(c)(3). X has made the required election to be permitted to engage in lobbying activities on a limited basis. X incurs lobbying expenditures, none of which are grass roots expenditures. Describe the tax to which X may be subject due to its lobbying activities.
9. What is a feeder organization, and why is it not exempt from Federal income tax?
10. What types of activities are not subject to the tax imposed on feeder organizations?
11. What is a private foundation, and what are the disadvantages of an exempt organization being classified as a private foundation?

12. Describe the internal support test for a private foundation.

13. What types of taxes may be levied on a private foundation? Why are the taxes levied?

14. A private foundation has net investment income of $50,000, yet its tax liability on net investment income is zero. Explain.

15. Describe the tax on excess business holdings including the purpose, rates, and on whom it is levied.

16. What is the purpose of the tax on unrelated business income?

17. What exempt organizations are subject to the tax on unrelated business income?

18. Can an exempt organization avoid the unrelated business income tax by using the profits generated from the unrelated trade or business to support the exempt purpose of the organization?

19. Under what circumstances can an exempt organization conduct bingo games and not have the income be treated as unrelated business income?

20. Under what circumstances can an exempt organization distribute low-cost articles and not have the activity be classified as an unrelated trade or business?

21. Passive income (e.g., interest, royalties, and annuities) generally is not unrelated business income. Under what circumstances do such items increase the amount of unrelated business taxable income?

22. What effect does unrelated debt-financed income have on unrelated business income?

23. Define each of the following with respect to unrelated debt-financed property:

   a. Debt-financed income.
   b. Debt-financed property.
   c. Acquisition indebtedness.
   d. Average acquisition indebtedness.
   e. Average adjusted basis.

24. T is the treasurer of the City Garden Club, a new garden club. A friend, who is the treasurer of the garden club in a neighboring community, tells T that it is not necessary for the garden club to file a request for exempt status with the IRS. Has T received correct advice?

25. What form should an organization use to file an application for exempt status?

26. Under what circumstances is an exempt organization not required to file an annual informational return on Form 990?

27. H, an exempt hospital, has gross income from an unrelated trade or business of $900. Is H required to file Form 990-T and pay tax on the unrelated business taxable income?

PROBLEMS

28. E, a § 501(c)(3) educational institution, makes lobbying expenditures of $100,000. E incurs exempt purpose expenditures of $400,000 in carrying out its educational mission.

   a. Determine the tax consequences to E if it does not elect to be eligible to participate in lobbying activities on a limited basis.
   b. Determine the tax consequences to E if it does elect to be eligible to participate in lobbying activities on a limited basis.

29. F, a § 501(c)(3) medical research organization, makes lobbying expenditures of $1.2 million. F incurs exempt purpose expenditures of $20 million in carrying out its medical research mission.

   a. Determine the tax consequences to F if it does not elect to be eligible to participate in lobbying activities on a limited basis.
   b. Determine the tax consequences to F if it does elect to be eligible to participate in lobbying activities on a limited basis.

30. P, a § 501(c)(3) organization, received support from the following sources:

Governmental unit A for services rendered	$ 4,000
General public for services rendered	60,000
Gross investment income	30,000
Contributions from disqualified persons	20,000
Contributions from other than disqualified persons	86,000

    a. Does P satisfy the test for receiving broad public support?
    b. Is P a private foundation?

31. X, a private foundation, has the following items of income and deductions:

Interest income	$10,000
Rent income	50,000
Dividend income	15,000
Royalty income	5,000
Unrelated business income	30,000
Rent expenses	12,000
Unrelated business expenses	7,000

X is not an exempt operating foundation and is not eligible for the 1% tax rate.

    a. Calculate the net investment income.
    b. Calculate the tax on net investment income.
    c. What is the purpose of the tax on net investment income?

32. P, a private foundation, has been in existence for 10 years. During this period, P has been unable to satisfy the requirements for classification as a private operating foundation. At the end of 1991, it had undistributed income of $100,000. Of this amount, $40,000 was distributed in 1992, and $60,000 was distributed during the first quarter of 1993. The IRS deficiency notice was mailed on August 1, 1994.

    a. Calculate the initial tax for 1991, 1992, and 1993.
    b. Calculate the additional tax for 1994.

33. F is the foundation manager of P, a private foundation. D, a substantial contributor to P, engages in an act of self-dealing with P. F is aware that the act is an act of self-dealing. The amount involved is $130,000.

    a. Calculate the amount of the initial tax.
    b. Calculate the amount of the additional tax if the act of self-dealing is not corrected within the correction period.

34. The board of directors of P, a private foundation, consists of A, B, and C. They vote unanimously to provide a $100,000 grant to D, a business associate of each of the directors. The grant is to be used for travel and education and does not qualify as a permitted grant to individuals (i.e., it is a taxable expenditure under § 4945). Each director knows that D was selected for the grant because she is a friend of the organization and that the grant is a taxable expenditure.

    a. Calculate the initial tax imposed on the private foundation.
    b. Calculate the initial tax imposed on the foundation manager (i.e., board of directors).

35. A museum that is an exempt organization operates a gift shop. The annual operations budget of the museum is $2.5 million. Gift shop sales generate a profit of $750,000. Another $500,000 of endowment income is generated. Both the income from the gift shop and the endowment income are used to support the exempt purpose of the museum. The balance of $1.25 million required for annual operations is provided through admission fees.

    a. Calculate the amount of unrelated business income.
    b. Assume that the endowment income is reinvested rather than being used to support annual operations. Calculate the amount of unrelated business income.

36. H, an exempt organization, has unrelated business income of $800 and unrelated business expenses of $300. Calculate the amount of the unrelated business income tax.

37. F, an exempt organization, has unrelated business taxable income of $400,000 (excluding the deduction for charitable contributions). During the year, it makes charitable contributions of $45,000, of which $38,000 are associated with the unrelated trade or business.

   a. Calculate unrelated business taxable income.
   b. Assume that the charitable contributions are $39,000, of which $38,000 is associated with the unrelated trade or business. Calculate unrelated business taxable income.

38. P, an exempt hospital, is going to operate a pharmacy that will be classified as an unrelated trade or business. P establishes the pharmacy as a wholly owned subsidiary. During the current year, the subsidiary generates taxable income and pays dividends of $50,000 to P.

   a. What are the tax consequences to the subsidiary?
   b. What are the tax consequences to P?

39. G, an exempt organization, leases a factory building, machinery, and equipment to Y Corporation. Under the lease, the annual rent for the building is $150,000, and the rent for the machinery and equipment is $200,000. Depreciation on the building is $5,500, and depreciation on the machinery and equipment is $40,000.

   a. Calculate the amount of unrelated business taxable income to G.
   b. Assume that the rent income from the machinery and equipment is only $20,000 and the related depreciation is $4,000. Calculate the amount of unrelated business taxable income to G.

40. T, an exempt organization, leases an office building to W Corporation for $150,000. T previously had used the building as its headquarters. Now, however, T has constructed a new headquarters building, enabling it to lease the first building to W. Calculate the amount of unrelated business income and the effect on unrelated business taxable income.

41. C, an exempt organization, leases office equipment to X Corporation for $200,000. C purchased the office equipment specifically for the purpose of leasing it to X.

   a. Determine the effect of the lease on unrelated business taxable income.
   b. Assume that, instead of purchasing new office equipment to lease to X, C leased surplus office equipment that it no longer needed for its operations. Determine the effect of the lease on unrelated business taxable income.

42. D, an exempt organization, sells the following assets during the taxable year:

Asset	Gain (Loss)	Use
Building A	$ 40,000	In exempt purposes
Building B	(15,000)	Leased to T Corporation
Building C	30,000	In exempt purposes

Determine the effect of these transactions on unrelated business taxable income.

43. J, an exempt organization, owns a building that cost $600,000. Depreciation of $250,000 has been deducted. The building is mortgaged for $400,000. The mortgage was incurred at the acquisition date. The building contains 10,000 square feet of floor space. J uses 7,000 square feet of the building in carrying on its exempt purpose and leases the remaining 3,000 square feet to L Corporation. Is the building debt-financed property?

44. T, an exempt organization, leases a building to Q Corporation. The annual rent income is $150,000, and the annual depreciation expense is $30,000. A mortgage was used to finance the initial acquisition of the building by T. Average acquisition indebtedness is $800,000. The adjusted basis of the building at the beginning of the taxable year is $900,000.

a. Calculate the unrelated debt-financed income and deductions.

b. Assume that, rather than leasing the building, T uses it in the performance of its exempt purpose. Calculate the unrelated debt-financed income and deductions.

45. K, an exempt organization, acquires a building for $800,000 on September 1, 1992. The principal amount of the related mortgage on the first day of the following months is as follows:

September	$600,000
October	595,000
November	590,000
December	585,000

Depreciation deducted during 1992 was $7,400. K leases the building to L Corporation.

a. Calculate the average acquisition indebtedness for the building.
b. Calculate the average adjusted basis for the building.
c. Calculate the debt/basis percentage.

RESEARCH PROBLEMS

RESEARCH PROBLEM 1 The ACAA, an athletic association that is exempt under § 501(c)(3), supervises the conduct of regional and national athletic events. The most prominent event and biggest revenue generator is the men's basketball tournament. The tournament includes 64 teams and is conducted at various sites throughout the country over a three-week period.

Through an agent, the ACAA publishes programs for the tournament and sells them to spectators. About 35% of the pages in the programs are advertisements sold by the agent to local and national companies. The ACAA has consistently treated the advertising revenue from the programs as exempt income under § 501(c)(3). An IRS agent has taken the position that the advertising revenue is income from an unrelated trade or business. Determine the appropriate treatment for the advertising revenue.

Partial list of research aids:

National Collegiate Athletic Association, 92 T.C. 456 (1989).

RESEARCH PROBLEM 2 State University has operated a television station since 1950. The station operates under a commercial license and is an affiliate of ABC. In addition to the regular network programming, the television station broadcasts educational programming in the form of in-school classroom instruction, educational extension programming, and closed circuit educational programming. The station is also used in the training of students who are enrolled in degree programs as preparation for careers in the television industry.

State University maintains that the television station is substantially related to the purpose for which the university was granted exempt status under § 501(c)(3). The only purpose for operating the television station is to contribute to the achievement of the educational goals of the university.

Determine if the television station is subject to the tax on unrelated business income.

CHAPTER

MULTISTATE CORPORATE TAXATION

OBJECTIVES

Establish fundamental concepts relating to state income taxation.

Illustrate the computation of a multistate corporation's state tax liability.

Define nexus and its role in state income taxation.

Emphasize the importance of Public Law 86–272.

Describe the nature and treatment of business and nonbusiness income.

Distinguish between allocation and apportionment of a multistate corporation's taxable income.

Discuss the sales, payroll, and property apportionment factors.

Introduce the unitary method of state taxation.

Discuss the states' income tax treatment of S corporations.

Examine other commonly encountered state and local taxes on businesses.

Recognize the tax planning opportunities available to minimize a corporation's state and local tax liability.

OUTLINE

Although most of this text concentrates on the effects of the Federal income tax law upon the computation of a taxpayer's annual tax liability, a variety of tax bases apply to most business taxpayers. For instance, a multinational corporation may be subject to tax in a number of different countries (see Chapter 9). Similarly, the taxpayer may be subject to a county-level wheel tax on its business vehicles, a state sales or use tax on many of its asset purchases, and state and local income or franchise taxes on its net income or on the privilege of doing business in the taxing jurisdiction. Indeed, estimates are that at least one-third of the tax dollars paid by business taxpayers go to state and local authorities.

What determines the application of state and local taxes in today's business environment? The following examples illustrate some of the complexities involved.

- The taxpayer's manufacturing, wholesaling, sales, retailing, and credit operations may each be centered in a different state to take advantage of various economic development incentives created by politicians.
- Mail-order and other catalog operations blur the traditional jurisdictional boundaries for buyer and seller alike. Often advertising campaigns boast "no sales tax payable."
- Similarly, the ability to transfer sales and purchase orders, pricing information, and other data via telephone lines and satellite transmissions may tempt the taxpayer to overlook traditional applications of the property and sales tax base. For instance, is computer software tangible (and subject to property tax) or intangible property? Which state's property tax should apply to a satellite?
- In addition to flying over virtually the entire country, the major airlines depart from and land in the majority of the states. Which state's income tax should apply to the ticket income? Should sales or income tax apply to sales of liquor while the plane is airborne?
- Local political concerns lead to a multiplicity of tax rules as politicians attempt to serve their constituents by introducing a variety of special tax incentives. This variety can be confusing, however. Taxpayers may have difficulty determining whether they qualify for energy or investment tax credits, S corporation status, exemptions from sales tax liability or income tax withholding, or passive loss relief at the local level.
- Each jurisdiction in which the entity is subject to tax represents a geometrical increase in compliance responsibilities. For instance, how many tax returns must be filed by a three-person S corporation operating in 15 states?
- Various states and localities have adopted revenue-raising statutes that vary in sophistication and operate on different time schedules. For instance, although fewer than half the states have adopted an alternative minimum tax, more jurisdictions are likely to adopt these taxes in the near future. Thus far, states that have imposed the tax have tended to select different bases. In addition, the aggressiveness with which departments of revenue enforce their tax statutes varies from state to state. Accordingly, the taxpayer must deal with a patchwork of germane taxing provisions in an environment that is often uncertain.

This chapter reviews the basic tax concepts that are predominant among most states that impose a tax based on net income and discusses the major areas in which tax planning can reduce a corporation's state tax burden.

Most of this chapter is devoted to a discussion of state taxes that are based on income. Each state is free to identify its corporate tax by a different term. Not all of the states that impose a tax on corporate income call the tax an "income tax." Rather, some states refer to their tax on corporate income as a franchise tax,[1] a business tax, a license tax, or a business profits tax.

OVERVIEW OF CORPORATE STATE INCOME TAXATION
◆

Forty-six states and the District of Columbia impose a tax based on a corporation's taxable income. Since each state is free to create its own tax provisions, the tax practitioner could be faced with 47[2] entirely different state tax provisions. Fortunately, however, to simplify the filing of tax returns and increase compliance with state tax laws, the majority of states "piggyback" onto the Federal income tax base. This means they have adopted *en masse* part or all of the Federal provisions governing the definition of income and the allowance of various exemptions, exclusions, and deductions.

Computing State Taxable Income

In more than 40 of the states that impose a corporate income tax, the starting point in computing state taxable income is taxable income as reflected on the Federal corporate income tax return (Form 1120). These states typically use either taxable income before the net operating loss and special deductions (line 28) or taxable income itself (line 30). Those states whose computation of state taxable income is not coupled to the Federal tax return have their own state-specific definitions of gross and taxable income. Nonetheless, even these states typically adopt most Federal income and deduction provisions.

Although Federal tax law plays a significant role in the computation of state taxable income, there is a wide disparity in both the methods used to determine a state's taxable income and the tax rates imposed on that income. Accordingly, when a corporation's business is transacted or conducted in only one state, computing state taxable income is relatively simple because that state's income tax is imposed upon the entire net income of the corporation. However, few middle- or large-sized corporations restrict their operations to only one state. Increasing the number of states in which a corporation is subject to tax leads to an exponential rise in the complexity of determining the corporation's state income tax liability.

The formula used by a multistate corporation to determine its tax liability in a typical state is illustrated in Figure 15–1.

Operational Implications

Generally, the accounting period and methods used by a corporation for state tax purposes must be the same as those used on the Federal return. Accordingly, if the corporation changes any of its methods of accounting for Federal income tax purposes, it must change its methods similarly for state tax purposes.

As the starting point for computing state taxable income often is directly related to the Federal taxable income amount, most states also "piggyback" onto the IRS's audit process. Consequently, virtually all of the states require notification, usually within 90 days, of the final settlement of a Federal income tax audit. State authorities then adjust the originally calculated state tax liability appropriately.

---

1. Although a franchise tax in some states is a business privilege tax based on a corporation's capital stock or net worth, several states use the term for the tax that they impose on a corporation's net income.

2. Although the District of Columbia is not a state, it operates in much the same manner as a state and imposes a tax based on income. Four states impose no corporate income tax at all: Nevada, South Dakota, Washington, and Wyoming. Corporations, however, are subject to a business and occupation tax in Washington.

State Modifications

Federal taxable income generally is used as the starting point in computing the state's income tax base, but numerous state adjustments or modifications are often necessary to (1) reflect differences between state and Federal tax statutes; (2) remove income that a state is constitutionally prohibited from taxing; and (3) eliminate the recovery of income for which the state did not permit a deduction on an earlier tax return.

The required modifications to Federal income vary significantly among the states. Accordingly, this section discusses the most common additions and subtractions that the states require. Figure 15–2 includes the most frequently encountered modifications; those denoted by a block are required by a majority of the states. In computing the taxable income for a given state, only a selected number of these modifications may be applicable.

────────────────────────── EXAMPLE 1 ──────────────────────────

X Corporation is subject to tax only in State A. The starting point in computing A taxable income is Federal taxable income. Modifications then are made to reflect, among other provisions, the exempt status of interest on A obligations, dividends received from in-state corporations, and the disallowance of a deduction for state income taxes. X generated the following income and deductions.

Sales	$1,500,000
Interest on Federal obligations	50,000
Interest on municipal obligations of State B	100,000
Dividends received from 50% owned State A corporations	200,000
Total income	$1,850,000
Expenses related to Federal obligations	$ 1,000
Expenses related to municipal obligations	5,000
State income tax expense	50,000
Depreciation allowed for Federal tax purposes (the deduction allowed for state purposes is $300,000)	400,000
Other allowable deductions	1,000,000
Total deductions	$1,456,000

FIGURE 15–1
Computing Corporate State Income Tax Liability

	Starting point in computing taxable income*
±	State modification items
	State tax base
±	Total net allocable (loss)/income (nonbusiness income)
	Total apportionable income/(loss) (business income)
×	State's apportionment percentage
	Income apportioned to the state
±	Income/(loss) allocated to the state
	State taxable income/(loss)
×	State tax rate
	Gross income tax liability for state
−	State's tax credits
	Net income tax liability for the state

*Most states use either line 28 or line 30 of the Federal corporate income tax return (Form 1120). In other states, the corporation is required to identify and report each element of income and deduction on the state return.

X's taxable income for Federal and state purposes is $139,000 and $295,000, respectively.

Federal Taxable Income

Sales	$1,500,000
Interest on Federal obligations	50,000
Dividends received from domestic corporations	200,000
Total income	$1,750,000
Expenses related to Federal obligations	$ 1,000
State income tax expense	50,000
Depreciation	400,000
Other allowable deductions	1,000,000
Total deductions	$1,451,000
Taxable income before special deductions	$ 299,000
Less: Dividends received deduction (80% × $200,000)	160,000
Federal taxable income	$ 139,000

FIGURE 15–2
Common State Modifications

- Interest income received on state and municipal obligations and any other interest income that is exempt from Federal income tax. For this purpose, some states exempt interest earned on their own obligations.

- Expenses deducted in computing Federal taxable income that are directly or indirectly related to U.S. obligations.

- Income-based franchise and income taxes imposed by any state and the District of Columbia that were deducted in computing Federal taxable income.

- The amount by which the Federal deductions for depreciation, amortization, or depletion exceed those permitted by the state. This adjustment is not necessary in states that have continuously conformed to the Federal depreciation, amortization, and depletion provisions.

- The amount by which the state gain or loss from the disposal of assets differs from the Federal gain or loss. Due to the difference in permitted depreciation methods and state provisions that did not require a corporation to reduce the basis of the property on which it had claimed a Federal investment tax credit, a corporation's assets may have different Federal and state tax bases. This adjustment is not necessary if the state and Federal basis provisions are identical.

- Adjustments required as a result of different elections being made for state and Federal purposes. Examples of such elections include the methods under which income from installment sales or long-term contracts are determined.

  Federal net operating loss deduction. This modification is not required by states in which the starting point in the computation of taxable income is Federal income before special deductions.

Subtraction Modifications

- Interest on U.S. obligations or obligations of U.S. instrumentalities to the extent included in Federal taxable income but exempt from state income taxes under U.S. law. Although a state is prohibited from imposing an income tax on U.S. government obligations, a state may impose an income-based franchise tax on that interest income.

- Expenses that are directly or indirectly related to the state and municipal interest that is taxable for state purposes.

- Refunds of franchise and income taxes imposed by any state and the District of Columbia, to the extent included in Federal taxable income.

- The amount by which the state deductions for depreciation, amortization, or depletion exceed the deductions permitted for Federal tax purposes.

- Adjustments required as a result of different elections being made for state and Federal purposes. Examples of such elections include the methods under which income from installment sales or long-term contracts is determined.

  Dividends received from certain out-of-state corporations.

  Net operating loss deduction as determined for state tax purposes.

  Deduction for Federal income tax paid. Currently, only a few states permit such a deduction.

  Dividends received from certain domestic corporations, to the extent included in Federal income.

State A Taxable Income

Federal taxable income	$139,000
Addition Modifications	
Interest on State B obligations	100,000
State income tax expense	50,000
Excess depreciation deduction allowed for Federal purposes ($400,000 − $300,000)	100,000
Expenses related to Federal obligations	1,000
Subtraction Modifications	
Expenses related to State B obligations	(5,000)
Dividends from in-state corporations included in Federal taxable income ($200,000 − $160,000)	(40,000)
Interest on Federal obligations	(50,000)
State A taxable income	$295,000

─────────────── EXAMPLE 2 ───────────────

Continue with the facts of Example 1, except that the $100,000 of municipal interest was generated from State A obligations. The computation of Federal taxable income is unaffected by this change. Since A exempts interest on its own obligations from taxation, X's A taxable income is $200,000.

State A Taxable Income

Federal taxable income	$139,000
Addition Modifications	
State income tax expense	50,000
Excess depreciation deduction allowed for Federal purposes ($400,000 − $300,000)	100,000
Expenses related to Federal obligations	1,000
Subtraction Modifications	
Dividends from in-state corporations included in Federal taxable income ($200,000 − $160,000)	(40,000)
Interest on Federal obligations	(50,000)
State A taxable income	$200,000

UDITPA and the Multistate Tax Commission

The Uniform Division of Income for Tax Purposes Act (UDITPA) is a model law relating to the assignment of income among the states for corporations that maintain operations in more than one state (multistate corporations). Many states have adopted the provisions of UDITPA, either by joining the Multistate Tax Compact or by modeling their laws after the provisions of UDITPA.

The Multistate Tax Commission (MTC), which is appointed by the member states of the Multistate Tax Compact, writes regulations and other rules that interpret UDITPA. When a new MTC rule or regulation is created, the member states propose its adoption to their respective legislatures. The majority of member states adopt the regulations with no exceptions or only minor changes.

Many of the states that are not members of the Multistate Tax Compact also model their laws after UDITPA and the MTC regulations.

Jurisdiction to Impose Tax: Public Law 86–272

The state in which a business is incorporated has the jurisdiction to tax the corporation, regardless of the volume of business activity that it conducts within the state. Whether a state can tax the income of a business that is incorporated in another state usually depends on the relationship between the state and the corporation. When a corporation's income is derived partly from property that is owned, or a business that is conducted, in other states, the states in which the income is generated can claim some of that income for tax purposes. If a corporation is to be subject to a tax in a state other than its state of incorporation, sufficient *nexus* must be established with the state.

Nexus describes the degree of business activity that must be present before a taxing jurisdiction has the right to impose a tax on an entity's income. The measure of the relationship that is necessary to create nexus is defined by state statute. Typically, sufficient nexus is present when a corporation derives income from sources within the state, owns or leases property in the state, employs personnel in the state, or has capital there. At one time, however, it was unclear whether a corporation had nexus with a state in which it only solicited orders for the sale of inventory.

The dominant historical theory on this issue was that interstate activities conducted by a corporation within a state could not be subjected to a tax on the privilege of doing business.[3] Imposition of an income tax on interstate activities was held to be in violation of the Commerce Clause of the U.S. Constitution. In 1959, the philosophy of the Supreme Court changed dramatically; the Court held that the Commerce Clause was not violated by a net income tax on foreign (out-of-state) corporations if the following criteria were satisfied:[4]

- The tax was not discriminatory.
- The tax was fairly apportioned to the state.
- The local activities in the taxing state established sufficient nexus.

Due to the strong business opposition to these Supreme Court decisions, Congress quickly enacted Public Law 86–272[5] to limit the states' right to impose an income tax on interstate activities. This law prohibits a state from taxing a business whose only connection with the state is to solicit orders for sales of tangible personal property that is sent outside the state for approval or rejection. If approved, the orders are filled and shipped by the business from a point outside the state. The immunity afforded by this statute does not apply to any taxpayer incorporated within the taxing state. Taxpayers who merely register to do business in the state are generally immune under the statute, however.

Under Public Law 86–272, though, only the sale of tangible personal property is immune from taxation. Leases, rentals, and other dispositions of tangible personal property are not protected activities. Moreover, sales, leases, rentals, or other dispositions of real property and intangible property, as well as sales of services, do not receive immunity under Public Law 86–272. In this regard, each

---

3. *Freeman v. Hewitt*, 67 S.Ct. 274 (1946); *Spector Motor Service, Inc. v. O'Connor*, 71 S.Ct. 508 (1956).

4. *Northwestern States Portland Cement Company v. Minnesota* and *Williams v. Stockham Valves & Fittings, Inc.*, 79 S.Ct. 357 (1959).

5. 15 U.S.C. 381–385.

state constructs its own definition of tangible and intangible property. In addition, since property ownership is not a protected activity, providing a company-owned automobile to an out-of-state salesperson may create nexus with a state, even though the salesperson merely solicits sales orders.

An activity is immune from taxation if it consists merely of solicitation. However, the term "solicitation" is not defined by the statute; therefore, each state is free to select its own definition. Some states have concluded that any activity beyond the mere solicitation of orders will subject an out-of-state corporation to tax. Under such an interpretation, any of the following (common but substantively) minimal activities within the state could establish nexus:

- Listing the company in the telephone directory.
- Conducting training seminars or classes for salespersons or customers' personnel.
- Handling of customer complaints by sales representatives.
- Repairing or maintaining the company's products (even if performed only occasionally and at no charge to the customer).
- Setting up promotional items by sales personnel.

The MTC has issued a statement of "Information Concerning Practices of Multistate Tax Commission States under Public Law 86–272." Figure 15–3 summarizes the activities that the MTC has identified as being directly related to solicitation (protected activities) and activities unrelated to solicitation (which establish income tax nexus for the entity).

Independent Contractors.   Public Law 86–272 extends immunity to certain in-state activities conducted by an independent contractor that would not be permitted if performed directly by the taxpayer. Generally, an independent contractor may engage in the following limited activities without establishing nexus: (1) soliciting sales; (2) making sales; and (3) maintaining a sales office. The maintenance of inventory by the independent contractor under consignment or any other type of arrangement with the principal normally results in the loss of immunity.

For purposes of applying the independent contractor provisions, a sales representative who works with a single principal is not considered to be an independent contractor and, instead, is subject to the same limitations as employees. In addition, for the special rules to apply in some states, independent contractors must hold themselves out as soliciting orders for more than one principal.

ALLOCATION AND APPORTIONMENT OF INCOME
◆

A corporation that conducts business activities in more than one state must determine the portion of its net income that is subject to tax by each state. A corporation that has established sufficient nexus with another state generally must both *allocate* and *apportion* its income.

Apportionment is a means by which a corporation's business income is divided among the states in which it conducts business. Under an apportionment procedure, a corporation determines allowable income and deductions for the company as a whole and then apportions some of its net income to a given state, according to an approved formula.

Allocation is a method under which specific components of a corporation's income, net of related expenses, are directly assigned to a certain state.

Allocation differs from apportionment in that allocable income is assigned to one state, whereas apportionable income is divided among several states. Nonapportionable (nonbusiness) income generally includes

■ Income or losses derived from the sale of nonbusiness real or tangible property, or
■ Income or losses derived from rentals and royalties from nonbusiness real or tangible personal property.

This income normally is assigned to the state where the property that generated the income or loss is located.

As Figure 15–1 indicated, total allocable (nonapportionable) income or loss typically is removed from corporate net income before the state's apportionment percentage is applied. The nonapportionable income or loss assigned to a state then is combined with the income apportionable to that state to arrive at total income subject to tax in the state.

———————————————— EXAMPLE 3 ————————————————

C Corporation conducts business in States N, O, P, and Q. C's $900,000 taxable income is comprised of $800,000 of apportionable income and $100,000 of allocable income

---

Under the Multistate Tax Commission's interpretation, the following activities will not create nexus under P.L. 86–272.

■ Advertising campaigns or sales activities; incidental and minor advertising.
■ Carrying free samples only for display or distribution.
■ Owning or furnishing automobiles to salespersons.
■ Passing inquiries or complaints on to the home office.
■ Checking customers' inventories for reorder.
■ Maintaining a sample or display room for two weeks or less during the year.
■ Soliciting sales by an in-state resident employee, provided that the employee does not maintain a place of business in the state, including an office in the home.

The Multistate Tax Commission has stated that the following activities are considered sufficient to establish nexus in the taxing jurisdiction.

■ Making repairs or providing maintenance.
■ Collecting delinquent accounts; investigating credit worthiness.
■ Installation or supervision of installation.
■ Conducting training classes, seminars, or lectures.
■ Providing engineering services.
■ Approving or accepting order, or handling customer complaints.
■ Repossessing property.
■ Picking up or replacing damaged or returned property.
■ Hiring, training, or supervising personnel.
■ Providing shipping information and coordinating deliveries.
■ Maintaining a sample or display room in excess of two weeks (14 days).
■ Carrying samples for sale, exchange, or distribution in any manner for consideration or other value.
■ Owning, leasing, maintaining, or otherwise using any of the following facilities or property in the state: repair shop; parts department; employment office; purchasing office; warehouse; meeting place for directors, officers, or employees; stock of goods; telephone answering service; or mobile stores (i.e., trucks with driver-salespersons).
■ Owning, leasing, maintaining, or using real property or fixtures.
■ Consigning tangible personal property to any person, including an independent contractor.
■ Maintaining an office for an employee, including an office in the home.

FIGURE 15–3
Practices of MTC States under Public Law 86–272

generated from transactions conducted in State Q. C's sales, property, and payroll are evenly divided among the four states, and all of the states employ the identical apportionment formula. Accordingly, $200,000 of C's income is taxable in each of States N, O, and P. C is subject to income tax on $300,000 of income in State Q.

Apportionable income		$800,000
Apportionment percentage (apportionable income is divided equally among the four states)		×25%
Income apportioned to each state		$200,000

	State N	State O	State P	State Q
Income apportioned	$200,000	$200,000	$200,000	$200,000
Income allocated	–0–	–0–	–0–	100,000
Taxable income	$200,000	$200,000	$200,000	$300,000

The Apportionment Procedure

Apportionment assumes that the production of business income is linked to business activity, and the laws of each state define a number of factors believed to indicate the amount of corporate activity conducted within the state. However, apportionment often does not provide a uniform division of an organization's income based on its business activity because each state is free to choose the type and number of factors that it believes are indicative of the business activity conducted within its borders. Therefore, a corporation may be subject to state income tax on more or less than 100 percent of its income. In a recent case, more than 135 percent of a corporation's Federal taxable income was apportioned to the two states in which it conducted business. The Massachusetts Appellate Tax Board held that the "minor overlapping" of the measures of net income that result when other states impose a tax on a corporation using a somewhat different net income apportionment formula is only "an inconsequential result of honest state efforts" to fairly apportion a corporation's income.[6]

An equally incongruous consequence of apportionment may result when the operations in a state result in a loss.

EXAMPLE 4

X Corporation's operations include two manufacturing facilities, located in States A and B, respectively. The plant located in A generated $500,000 of income, and the plant located in B generated a loss of $200,000. Therefore, X's total taxable income is $300,000.

By applying the statutes of each state, X determines that its apportionment factors for A and B are .65 and .35, respectively. Accordingly, X's income is apportioned to the states as follows.

Income apportioned to State A: .65 × $300,000 = $195,000

Income apportioned to State B: .35 × $300,000 = $105,000

X is subject to tax in B on $105,000 of income, even though the operations conducted in that state resulted in a loss. ◆

---

6. *Statler Industries, Inc. v. Comm. of Revenue*, Massachusetts Appellate Tax Board, Docket Nos. 142503, 142504, 142505; September 1, 1988.

Business and Nonbusiness Income

Once it has been established that more than one state has the right to impose a tax on a corporation's income, the corporation's income must be divided among the states possessing such a right. Generally, the first step in ascertaining the taxable income that is attributable to a state is to divide the corporation's income into two classes: *business income* and *nonbusiness income.*

Business income is assigned among the states by using an apportionment formula. In contrast, nonbusiness income may either be apportioned or allocated to the state in which the income-producing asset is located. For instance, income derived from the rental of nonbusiness real property generally is allocated to the state in which the property is located. If the corporation is not taxed in the state in which the income-producing asset is located, most states allocate the income to the state in which the corporation is *commercially domiciled.* Commercial domicile is the principal place from which the corporation's trade or business is directed or managed.[7]

The classification as business or nonbusiness income may also have an effect on the organization's apportionment formula. Allocable income, along with the payroll expense and property directly related to generating that income, generally is excluded from both the numerator and the denominator of the apportionment formula.

─────────────── EXAMPLE 5 ───────────────

TNT Corporation, a manufacturer of explosive devices, is a multistate taxpayer that has nexus with States P and Q. During the taxable year, TNT's net sales of explosive devices were $900,000; $600,000 were made in P and $300,000 were made in Q. The corporation also received $90,000 from the rental of nonbusiness real property located in P.

Both states employ a three-factor apportionment formula under which sales, property, and payroll are equally weighted. However, the states do not agree on the definition of apportionable income. The tax provisions of P provide that nonbusiness rent income is allocable and business income is apportionable, while Q requires a corporation to apportion all of its (business and nonbusiness) income. The sales factor (the ratio of in-state sales to total sales) for each of the states is computed as follows:

$$\text{State P:} \quad \frac{\$600{,}000 \text{ (sales in State P)}}{\$900{,}000 \text{ (total sales)}} = 66.67\%$$

$$\text{State Q:} \quad \frac{\$300{,}000 \text{ (sales in State Q)}}{\$990{,}000 \text{ (total sales)}^*} = 30.30\%$$

*Since rent income is treated as business income, rents are included in the denominator of the sales factor.

◆

─────────────── EXAMPLE 6 ───────────────

Continue with the facts of Example 5, except that the rent income was generated from property located in Q, rather than from property located in P. Although the sales factor for P remains the same, the sales factor for Q changes.

$$\text{State P:} \quad \frac{\$600{,}000 \text{ (sales in State P)}}{\$900{,}000 \text{ (total sales)}} = 66.67\%$$

$$\text{State Q:} \quad \frac{\$390{,}000 \text{ (sales in State Q)}}{\$990{,}000 \text{ (total sales)}} = 39.39\%$$

─────────

7. UDITPA § 1(b).

Due to the composition of the sales factor in the two states, TNT's income never is perfectly apportioned: the aggregate of the sales factors is either more or less than 100%. ◆

Defining Business Income

As with most other income tax provisions, the states have defined business and nonbusiness income in various ways. Under UDITPA, business income is defined as [8]

> . . . income arising from transactions and activity in the regular course of the taxpayer's trade or business and includes income from tangible and intangible property if the acquisition, management, and disposition of the property constitute integral parts of the taxpayer's regular trade or business operations.

The Multistate Tax Commission (MTC) adds that

> In general all transactions and activities of the taxpayer which are dependent upon or contribute to the operations of the taxpayer's economic enterprise as a whole constitute the taxpayer's trade or business and will be transactions and activity arising in the regular course of, and will constitute integral parts of, a trade or business. [9]

The taxpayer's accounting and organizational labels (e.g., as manufacturing income, interest, dividends, royalties, gains, operating income) are "no aid in determining whether income is business or nonbusiness income." Moreover, the taxpayer's income is presumed to be business income unless it is clearly classifiable as nonbusiness income. [10]

Business income arises from the taxpayer's regular course of business or constitutes an integral part of the taxpayer's regular business. [11] In determining whether an item of income is (apportionable) business income, state courts have developed a variety of approaches to determine what constitutes a taxpayer's "regular course of business." [12]

The question of whether the acquisition, management, and disposition of property constitute an integral part of the taxpayer's regular trade or business frequently arises with respect to investment income. The most commonly encountered criteria focus on one or more of the following factors:

- The purpose of acquiring or holding the investment.
- The source of the funds used to acquire the investment.
- The use of the income generated from the investment.

Where the asset that generated the income is or was used in the taxpayer's regular business, such as manufacturing equipment, the income generally is business income. If profits from the taxpayer's regular business are used to acquire the investment, the income may be business income. [13] Similarly,

8. UDITPA § 1(a).
9. MTC Reg. IV.1.(a).
10. MTC Reg. IV.1.(a).
11. MTC Reg. IV.1.(a).
12. *Atlantic Richfield Co. v. State of Colorado and Joseph F. Dolan*, 601 P.2d 628 (Colo.S.Ct., 1979); *Appeal of A. Epstein and Sons,*

Inc., (Cal.State Bd. of Equalization, 1984).
13. *Cincinnati, New Orleans and Texas Pacific Railway Co. and Southern Railroad Co. v. Kentucky Department of Revenue,* 684 S.W.2d 303 (Ky.Ct.App., 1984); a contrary conclusion was reached in *Petition of Becton, Dickinson and Company* (N.Y. State Tax Comm., 1982).

business income exists where the investment income is used as working capital or to satisfy ordinary business expenses.[14]

A few states, including Connecticut and New Jersey, fail to distinguish between business and nonbusiness income. In these states, all of a corporation's income is deemed to be business income and subject to apportionment.

EXAMPLE 7

X Corporation is subject to income tax in several states. X earned $2,500,000 from the sales of its products and $1,000,000 from the sale of assets that were unrelated to X's regular business operations.

In the states that distinguish between business and nonbusiness income, $2,500,000 of X's income is apportioned to the state according to the state's apportionment formula. The gain on the sale of the nonbusiness assets is allocated to the state in which the assets were located. In the states that subject a corporation's entire income to apportionment, $3,500,000 ($2,500,000 + $1,000,000) is apportioned to the states in which the taxpayer conducts business. ◆

Nonbusiness Income

Nonbusiness income is defined as "all income other than business income."[15] Thus, nonbusiness income is the corporation's income that is unrelated to its regular business operations. Usually, nonbusiness income comprises passive and portfolio income, such as dividends, interest, rents, royalties, and certain capital gains. However, passive or portfolio income may be classified as business income when the acquisition, management, and disposition of the underlying property constitute an integral part of the taxpayer's regular business operation.

In addition, some states consider the relationship between the parties in determining the appropriate classification of the income. When the payer and payee are part of a *unitary* business (as defined later in this chapter), the income normally is classified as business income.

EXAMPLE 8

X Corporation owns and operates two manufacturing facilities, one in State A and the other in State B. Due to a temporary decline in the corporation's sales, X has rented 10% of its A facility to an unaffiliated corporation. X generated $100,000 net rent income and $900,000 income from manufacturing.

Both A and B classify such rent income as allocable nonbusiness income. By applying the statutes of each state, as discussed in the next section, X determines that its apportionment factors are .40 for A and .60 for B. X's income attributable to each state is determined as follows:

Income Subject to Tax in State A

Taxable income	$1,000,000
Less: Allocable income	(100,000)
Apportionable income	$ 900,000
Times: Apportionment factor	40%
Income apportioned to State A	$ 360,000
Plus: Income allocated to State A	100,000
Income subject to tax in State A	$ 460,000

---

14. *Howard Johnson Co. v. Department of Revenue* (Ill.Cir.Ct., 1982); *Montgomery Ward & Co., Inc. v. Commissioner of Taxation,* 151 N.W.2d 294 (Minn. S.Ct., 1967); *Sperry and Hutchinson Co. v.* *Department of Revenue,* 527 P.2d 729 (Ore. S.Ct., 1974).

15. UDITPA § 1(e).

Income Subject to Tax in State B

Taxable income	$1,000,000
Less: Allocable income	(100,000)
Apportionable income	$ 900,000
Times: Apportionment factor	60%
Income apportioned to State B	$ 540,000
Plus: Income allocated to State B	–0–
Income subject to tax in State B	$ 540,000

♦

EXAMPLE 9

Continue with the facts of Example 8, but assume that B does not distinguish between business and nonbusiness income. Thus, all of X's income is apportionable.

X properly determines that its apportionment factors are .40 for A and .58 for B. Since the apportionment factors used by the two states are derived differently, X's income that is subject to tax does not equal 100%.

Income Subject to Tax in State A	$ 460,000

Income Subject to Tax in State B	
Apportionable income	$1,000,000
Times: Apportionment factor	58%
Income apportioned to State B	$ 580,000

Due to differences in the states' definitions of apportionable and allocable income, $1,040,000 of X's $1,000,000 Federal taxable income is subject to state income taxation. ♦

Apportionment Factors: Elements and Planning

Business income is apportioned among the states by determining the appropriate apportionment percentage for each state that has a right to tax the entity. To determine the apportionment percentage for each state, a ratio is established for each of the factors included in the state's apportionment formula. Each ratio is calculated by comparing the level of a specific business activity within a state to the total corporate activity of that type. The ratios then are summed, averaged, and appropriately weighted (if required) to determine the corporation's apportionment percentage for a specific state.

Although apportionment formulas vary among jurisdictions, most states use a three-factor formula that equally weights sales, property, and payroll. However, approximately 15 states use a modified three-factor formula, where the sales factor is assigned a double weight. The use of a double-weighted sales factor tends to pull a larger percentage of an out-of-state corporation's income into the taxing jurisdiction of the state, because the corporation's major activity within the state—the sales of its products—is weighted more heavily than are its payroll and property activities. Double weighting the sales factor, however, provides tax relief for corporations that are domiciled in the state. Those corporations generally own significantly more property and incur more payroll costs (factors that are given less weight in the apportionment formula) within the state than do out-of-state corporations.

This discussion applies generally to manufacturing entities. Certain industries, such as financial institutions, insurance companies, air and motor carriers, pipeline companies, and public utilities, typically are required to use special apportionment formulas.

———————————————— EXAMPLE 10 ————————————————

C Corporation realized $500,000 of taxable income from the sales of its products in States A and B. C's activities in both states establish nexus for income tax purposes. C's sales, payroll, and property among the states include the following:

	State A	State B	Total
Sales	$1,250,000	$750,000	$2,000,000
Property	2,500,000	–0–	2,500,000
Payroll	1,500,000	–0–	1,500,000

If State B uses an equally weighted three-factor apportionment formula, $62,500 of C's taxable income is apportioned to State B.

Sales ($750,000/$2,000,000)	=	37.5%
Property ($0/$2,500,000)	=	–0–
Payroll ($0/$1,500,000)	=	–0–
Sum of apportionment factors		37.5%
Average	÷	3
Apportionment factor for State B		12.5%
Taxable income		× $500,000
Income apportioned to State B		$ 62,500

If State B uses a double-weighted sales factor in its three-factor apportionment formula, $93,750 of C's taxable income is apportioned to B.

Sales ($750,000/$2,000,000)	= 37.5% × 2 =	75%
Property ($0/$2,500,000)	=	–0–
Payroll ($0/$1,500,000)	=	–0–
Sum of apportionment factors		75%
Average	÷	4
Apportionment factor for State B		18.75%
Taxable income		× $500,000
Income apportioned to State B		$ 93,750

When a state uses a double-weighted sales factor, typically a larger percentage of an out-of-state corporation's income is subject to tax in the state. Here, an additional $31,250 ($93,750 − $62,500) of C's income is subject to tax in B. ◆

A single-factor apportionment formula consisting solely of a sales factor is even more detrimental to an out-of-state corporation than an apportionment factor that double weights the sales factor. Currently, only Iowa, Nebraska, and Texas require the use of a single-factor apportionment formula. Figure 15–4 indicates the variety of apportionment formulas that are applied by the states.

———————————————— EXAMPLE 11 ————————————————

PPR Corporation, a retailer of paper products, owns retail stores in States A, B, and C. A uses a three-factor apportionment formula under which the sales, property, and payroll factors are equally weighted. B uses a three-factor apportionment formula under which sales are double weighted. C employs a single-factor apportionment factor, based solely on sales.

PPR's operations generated $800,000 of apportionable income, and its sales and payroll activity and average property owned in each of the three states are as follows:

	State A	State B	State C	Total
Sales	$500,000	$400,000	$300,000	$1,200,000
Payroll	100,000	125,000	75,000	300,000
Property	150,000	250,000	100,000	500,000

$280,000 of PPR's apportionable income is assigned to A.

Sales ($500,000/$1,200,000)	=	41.67%
Payroll ($100,000/$300,000)	=	33.33%
Property ($150,000/$500,000)	=	30.00%
Sum of apportionment factors		105.00%
Average	÷	3
Apportionment factor for State A		35.00%

FIGURE 15-4   **Apportionment Factor Weights—Manufacturing Enterprises**

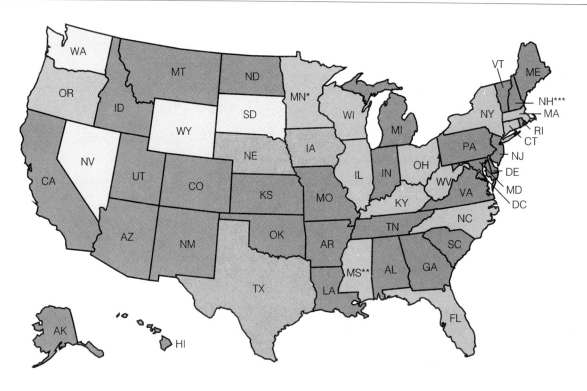

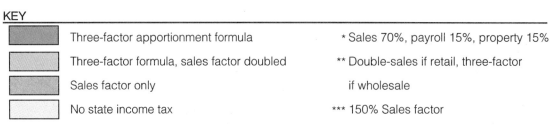

KEY

▨ Three-factor apportionment formula	* Sales 70%, payroll 15%, property 15%
▨ Three-factor formula, sales factor doubled	** Double-sales if retail, three-factor
▨ Sales factor only	if wholesale
▢ No state income tax	*** 150% Sales factor

Apportionable income	× $800,000	
Income apportioned to State A	$280,000	

$316,640 of PPR's apportionable income is assigned to B.

Sales ($400,000/$1,200,000) = 33.33% × 2	=	66.66%
Payroll ($125,000/$300,000)	=	41.67%
Property ($250,000/$500,000)	=	50.00%
Sum of apportionment factors		158.33%
Average	÷	4
Apportionment factor for State B		39.58%
Apportionable income	×	$800,000
Income apportioned to State B		$316,640

$200,000 of PPR's apportionable income is assigned to C.

Sales ($300,000/$1,200,000)	=	25.00%
Sum of apportionment factors		25.00%
Average	÷	1
Apportionment factor for State C		25.00%
Apportionable income	×	$800,000
Income apportioned to State C		$200,000

Summary

Income apportioned to State A	$280,000
Income apportioned to State B	316,640
Income apportioned to State C	200,000
Total income apportioned	$796,640

Due to the variations in the apportionment formulas employed by the various states, only 99.58% ($796,640/$800,000) of PPR's income is apportioned to the states in which it is subject to tax. ◆

The Sales Factor

The sales factor is a fraction, whose numerator is the corporation's total sales in the state during the tax period. The denominator is the corporation's total sales everywhere during the tax period. Gross sales for this purpose generally are net of returns, allowances, and discounts. Moreover, interest income, service charges, carrying charges, and time-price differential charges incidental to the sales are included in the sales factor. Federal and state excise taxes and state sales taxes are included in the factor, if these taxes are either passed on to the buyer or included in the selling price of the goods.

Since the sales factor is a component in the formula used to apportion a corporation's business income to a state, only sales that generate business income are includible in the fraction. The "sales" factor actually resembles a "receipts" factor since it also generally includes business income from the sale of inventory or services, interest, dividends, rentals, royalties, sales of assets, and other business income. Income on Federal obligations, however, is not included in the sales factor. When the sale involves capital assets, some states require that the gross proceeds, rather than the net gain or loss, be included in the fraction.

Some of the states have adopted the MTC Regulations, which provide exceptions to UDITPA's general rule under which all business gross receipts are to be included in the sales factor.[16] For instance, incidental or occasional asset sales and sales of intangible assets are excluded from gross receipts under these Regulations.

In determining the numerator of the sales factor, most states follow UDITPA's "ultimate destination concept," under which sales are assumed to take place at the point of delivery, as opposed to the location at which the shipment originates.

EXAMPLE 12

X Corporation, whose only manufacturing plant is located in State A, sells its product to residents of A through its local retail store. X also ships its product to customers in States B and C. The products that are sold to residents of A are assigned to A, while the products that are delivered to B and C are assigned to B and C, respectively. ◆

Dock Sales. "Dock sales" occur where a purchaser uses its owned or rented vehicles, or a common carrier with whom it has made arrangements, to take delivery of the product at the seller's shipping dock. Most states apply the destination test to dock sales in the same manner as it is applied to other sales. Thus, if the seller makes dock sales to a purchaser that has an in-state location to which it returns with the product, the sale is assigned to the purchaser's and seller's state. Where the seller makes dock sales to a purchaser that returns with the product to its out-of-state location, the sale is assigned to the state in which the purchaser delivers the goods.

Throwback Rule. Out-of-state sales that are not subject to tax in the destination state are pulled back into the origination state if that state has adopted a *throwback* rule. This rule is an exception to the destination test. The rule provides that, when a corporation is not subject to tax in the destination state or the purchaser is the U.S. government, the sales are treated as in-state sales of the origination state, and the actual destination of the product is disregarded. Consequently, when the seller is immune from tax in the destination state under Public Law 86–272, the sales are considered to be in-state sales of the origination state if that state has a throwback provision.

EXAMPLE 13

XYZ Corporation's entire operations are located in State A. Seventy percent ($700,000) of XYZ's sales are made in A, and the remaining 30% ($300,000) are made in State B. XYZ's solicitation of sales in B is limited to mailing a monthly catalog to its customers in that state. However, XYZ employees do pick up and replace damaged merchandise in State B.

The pickup and replacement of damaged goods establishes nexus with A. XYZ's activities in B are sufficient (as determined by A's law) to subject XYZ to a positive tax, based on its income. Therefore, XYZ is permitted to apportion its income between A and B. However, B's interpretation of activities necessary to create nexus is less strict than that imposed by A; in B, the mere pickup and replacement of damaged goods does not subject a corporation's income to tax.

XYZ's taxable income is $900,000. Both A and B impose a 10% corporate income tax and include only the sales factor in their apportionment formulas. If A has not adopted a throwback rule, XYZ's effective state income tax rate is 7%.

---

16. MTC Reg. IV.18.(c).

	Apportionment Factors	Net Income	Tax Rate	Tax
State A	70%	$900,000	10%	$63,000
State B	*	900,000	10%	–0–
Total tax liability				$63,000
Effective state income tax rate: $63,000/$900,000 =				7%

*As determined under B's laws, XYZ's income is not apportionable to State B, because insufficient nexus is present.

If A has adopted a throwback rule, XYZ will not benefit from its lack of nexus with B because the sales in B are considered to be in-state sales of A. Thus, XYZ's effective tax rate is 10%.

	Apportionment Factors	Net Income	Tax Rate	Tax
State A	100%	$900,000	10%	$90,000
State B	–0–	900,000	10%	–0–
Total tax liability				$90,000
Effective state income tax rate: $90,000/$900,000 =				10%
Tax increase due to throwback provision ($90,000 − $63,000)				$27,000

The Payroll Factor

The payroll factor is determined by comparing the compensation paid for services rendered within a state to the total compensation paid by the corporation. Generally, the payroll factor is a fraction, whose numerator is the total amount that a corporation paid or accrued for compensation in a state during the tax period. The denominator is the total amount paid or accrued by the corporation for compensation during the tax period. For purposes of the payroll factor, compensation includes wages, salaries, commissions, and any other form of remuneration paid or accrued to employees for personal services. Compensation may also include the value of board, rent, housing, lodging, and other benefits or services furnished to employees by the taxpayer in return for personal services, if these amounts constitute Federal gross income.

Payments made to an independent contractor or any other person who is not properly classifiable as an employee generally are excluded from the numerator and denominator of the payroll factor. Some states exclude from the payroll factor any compensation paid to corporate officers.

Several states have amended their statutes to provide that earnings that are included in a cash or deferred compensation plan, excluded from Federal gross income under § 401(k), are to be included in the numerator and the denominator of the payroll factor. Accordingly, the total compensation that is included in the denominator of a corporation's payroll factor may vary among the states in which the corporation's income is apportioned.

─────────────── EXAMPLE 14 ───────────────

X Corporation's sales office and manufacturing plant are located in State A. X also maintains a manufacturing plant and sales office in State C. For purposes of apportionment, A defines payroll as all compensation paid to employees, including contributions to § 401(k) deferred compensation plans. Under the statutes of C, neither compensation paid to officers nor contributions to § 401(k) plans are included in the payroll factor. X incurred the following personnel costs.

	State A	State C	Total
Wages and salaries for employees other than officers	$350,000	$250,000	$600,000
Salaries for officers	150,000	100,000	250,000
Contributions to § 401(k) plans	30,000	20,000	50,000
Total	$530,000	$370,000	$900,000

The payroll factor for State A is computed as follows:

$$\frac{\$530,000}{\$900,000} = 58.89\%$$

Since C defines payroll as excluding compensation paid to officers and contributions to § 401(k) plans, the payroll factor for C is computed as follows:

$$\frac{\$250,000}{\$600,000} = 41.67\%$$

The aggregate of X's payroll factors is 100.56% (58.89% + 41.67%). In certain cases, the sum of a corporation's payroll factors may be significantly more or less than 100%. ◆

The compensation of an employee normally cannot be split between two or more states during the year, unless he or she is transferred or changes positions during the year. Instead, each employee's compensation is allocated to only one state. Under UDITPA, compensation is treated as paid in the state (it is included in the numerator of the payroll factor) in which the services are primarily performed.

When an employee's services are performed in more than one state, his or her compensation is attributed to the employee's base of operations or, if there is no base of operations in any state in which some part of the service is performed, to the place from which the services are directed or controlled. When no services are performed in the state that serves as the base of operations or the place from which the services are directed, the employee's compensation is attributed to his or her state of residency.[17]

─────────────── EXAMPLE 15 ───────────────

X Corporation has its headquarters and a manufacturing plant in State A. P, a resident of State Y, works at the A manufacturing plant. P's compensation is included in the numerator of the payroll factor of A, as the service is performed entirely in A. ◆

Only compensation that is related to the production of apportionable income is included in the payroll factor. Accordingly, in those states that distinguish between business and nonbusiness income, compensation that is related to the operation, maintenance, protection, or supervision of nonbusiness income is not includible in the payroll factor.

─────────────── EXAMPLE 16 ───────────────

C Corporation, a manufacturer of automobile parts, is subject to tax in States X and Y. C incurred the following payroll costs:

	State X	State Y	Total
Wages and salaries for officers and personnel of manufacturing facilities	$450,000	$350,000	$800,000
Wages and salaries for personnel involved in nonbusiness rental activities	50,000	–0–	50,000

───────────────────────

17. UDITPA § 14.

If both states distinguish between business and nonbusiness income in determining apportionable income and include officers' compensation in the payroll factor, C's payroll factors are computed as follows:

Payroll factor for State X: $450,000/$800,000 = 56.25%

Payroll factor for State Y: $350,000/$800,000 = 43.75%　◆

———————————————— EXAMPLE 17 ————————————————

Continue with the facts of Example 16, but assume that Y defines apportionable income as the corporation's total income (business and nonbusiness income). C's payroll factor for X remains unchanged, but its payroll factor for Y is reduced.

Payroll factor for State X: $450,000/$800,000 = 56.25%

Payroll factor for State Y: $350,000/$850,000* = 41.18%

*$800,000 (compensation related to business income) + $50,000 (compensation related to nonbusiness income).　◆

Compensation related to the operation, maintenance, protection, or supervision of property used in the production of both apportionable and nonapportionable income or losses generally is prorated between business and nonbusiness sources.

———————————————— EXAMPLE 18 ————————————————

C Corporation, a manufacturer of paper products, operates paper mills in States A and B. In addition, the corporation owns rental real property in A. C incurred the following compensation expenses:

	State A	State B	Total
Wages and salaries for mill employees	$1,200,000	$1,500,000	$2,700,000
Wages and salaries for administrative staff	600,000	500,000	1,100,000
Compensation of officers	800,000	400,000	1,200,000

Ten percent of the time spent by the administrative staff located in A and 5% of the time spent by officers located in A are devoted to the operation, maintenance, and supervision of the nonbusiness rental property. Both states exclude such rent income from the definition of apportionable income. C's payroll factors for A and B are 51.02% and 48.98%, respectively.

Payroll factor for State A

$$\frac{\$2,500,000\ [\$1,200,000\ +\ 90\%(\$600,000)\ +\ 95\%(\$800,000)]}{\$4,900,000\ [\$2,700,000\ +\ 90\%(\$600,000)\ +\ \$500,000\ +\ 95\%(\$800,000)\ +\ \$400,000]} = 51.02\%$$

Payroll factor for State B

$$\frac{\$2,400,000\ (\$1,500,000\ +\ \$500,000\ +\$400,000)}{\$4,900,000\ [\$2,700,000\ +\ 90\%(\$600,000)\ +\ \$500,000\ +\ 95\%(\$800,000)\ +\ \$400,000]} = 48.98\%$$

◆

The Property Factor

The property factor generally is a fraction, whose numerator is the average value of the corporation's real and tangible personal property owned and used or rented and used in the state during the taxable year. The denominator is the average value of all of the corporation's real and tangible property owned or rented and used during the taxable year, wherever it is located. In this manner, a state's property factor reflects the extent of total property usage by the taxpayer in the state.

For this purpose, real and tangible property includes land, buildings, machinery, inventory, equipment, and other real and tangible personal property, other than coins or currency.[18] Other types of property that may be included in the factor are construction in progress (as it does not yet contribute to the production of income), offshore property, outer space property (satellites), and partnership property.

In the case of property that is in transit between locations of the taxpayer or between a buyer and seller, the assets are included in the numerator of the destination state. With respect to mobile or movable property, such as construction equipment, trucks, and leased electronic equipment, which is both in- and outside the state during the tax period, the numerator of a state's property factor is determined on the basis of the total time that the property was within the state. However, automobiles assigned to a traveling employee are included in the numerator of the property factor of the state to which the employee's compensation is assigned under the payroll factor or the state in which the automobile is licensed.[19]

Space satellites used in the communication industry generally are included in the numerator of the property factor based on the ratio of earth stations serviced. For example, if a satellite is being serviced by earth stations located in San Francisco, Chicago, New York, and Houston, 25 percent of the cost of the satellite will be included in the numerator of the property factor for each of the four corresponding states.

Property owned by the corporation typically is valued at its average original or historical cost plus the cost of additions and improvements, but without adjusting for depreciation. Some states allow property to be included at net book value or adjusted tax basis. The value of the property usually is determined by averaging the values at the beginning and end of the tax period. Alternatively, some states allow or require the amount to be calculated on a monthly basis if annual computation results in or require substantial distortions.

EXAMPLE 19

X Corporation, a calendar year taxpayer, owns property in States A and B. Both A and B require that the average value of assets be included in the property factor. A requires that the property be valued at its historical cost, and B requires that the property be included in the property factor at its net book value.

Account Balances at January 1, 1994

	State A	State B	Total
Inventories	$150,000	$100,000	$250,000
Building and machinery (cost)	200,000	400,000	600,000
Accumulated depreciation for building and machinery	(150,000)	(50,000)	(200,000)
Land	50,000	100,000	150,000
Total	$250,000	$550,000	$800,000

---

18. MTC Reg. IV.10.(a).

19. MTC Reg. IV.10.(d).

Account Balances at December 31, 1994

	State A	State B	Total
Inventories	$250,000	$200,000	$450,000
Building and machinery (cost)	200,000	400,000	600,000
Accumulated depreciation for building and machinery	(175,000)	(100,000)	(275,000)
Land	50,000	100,000	150,000
Total	$325,000	$600,000	$925,000

State A Property Factor

Historical Cost	January 1, 1994	December 31, 1994	Average
Property in State A	$ 400,000*	$ 500,000**	$ 450,000
Total property	1,000,000†	1,200,000††	1,100,000

*$150,000 + $200,000 + $50,000.
**$250,000 + $200,000 + $50,000.
†$250,000 + $600,000 + $150,000.
††$450,000 + $600,000 + $150,000.

$$\text{Property factor for State A: } \frac{\$450,000}{\$1,100,000} = 40.91\%$$

State B Property Factor

Net Book Value	January 1, 1994	December 31, 1994	Average
Property in State B	$550,000	$600,000	$575,000
Total property	800,000	925,000	862,500

$$\text{Property factor for State B: } \frac{\$575,000}{\$862,500} = 66.67\%$$

Due to the variations in the property factors, the aggregate of X's property factors equals 107.58%. ◆

Leased property, when included in the property factor, is valued at eight times its annual rental, less any subrentals. For this purpose, annual rentals may include payments, such as real estate taxes and insurance, made by the lessee in lieu of rent.

———————————————— EXAMPLE 20 ————————————————

X Corporation is subject to tax in States D and G. Both states require that leased or rented property be included in the property factor at eight times the annual rental costs, and that the average historical cost be used for other assets. Information regarding X's property and rental expenses follows.

Average Historical Cost

Property located in State D	$ 750,000
Property located in State G	450,000
Total property	$1,200,000

Lease and Rental Expenses

State D	$ 50,000
State G	150,000
Total	$ 200,000

State D Property Factor

$$\frac{\$1,150,000\ [\$750,000\ +\ 8(\$50,000)]}{\$2,800,000\ [\$1,200,000\ +\ 8(\$200,000)]} = 41.07\%$$

State G Property Factor

$$\frac{\$1,650,000\ [\$450,000\ +\ 8(\$150,000)]}{\$2,800,000\ [\$1,200,000\ +\ 8(\$200,000)]} = 58.93\%$$

Only property that is used in the production of apportionable income is includible in the numerator and denominator of the property factor. In this regard, idle property and property that is used in producing nonapportionable income generally are excluded. However, property that is temporarily idle or unused generally remains in the property factor.

A corporation may benefit by storing inventory in a low- or no-tax state (a desired state) because the average property value in the state in which the manufacturing operation is located is reduced significantly. When the manufacturing operation is located in a high-tax state, the establishment of a distribution center in a low- or no-tax state may reduce the overall state tax liability.

--- EXAMPLE 21 ---

XYZ Corporation realized $200,000 of taxable income from selling its product in States A and B. XYZ's manufacturing plant, product distribution center, and warehouses are located in A. The corporation's activities within the two states are as follows:

	State A	State B	Total
Sales	$500,000	$200,000	$700,000
Property	300,000	50,000	350,000
Payroll	100,000	10,000	110,000

XYZ is subject to tax in A and B. Both states utilize a three-factor apportionment formula that equally weights sales, property, and payroll; however, A imposes a 10% corporate income tax, while B levies a 3% tax. XYZ incurs a total income tax liability of $17,575.

	Apportionment Formulas	
	State A	State B
Sales	$500,000/$700,000 = 71.43%	$200,000/$700,000 = 28.57%
Property	$300,000/$350,000 = 85.71%	$50,000/$350,000 = 14.29%
Payroll	$100,000/$110,000 = 90.91%	$10,000/$110,000 = 9.09%
Total	248.05%	51.95%
Apportionment factor (totals/3):	82.68%	17.32%
Income apportioned to the state ($200,000 × apportionment factor)	$165,360	$34,640
Tax rate	10%	3%
Tax liability	$ 16,536	$ 1,039
Total tax liability	$17,575	

--- EXAMPLE 22 ---

Continue with the facts of Example 21, and further assume that XYZ's product distribution center and warehouse operations were acquired for $200,000 and the payroll of these operations is $20,000. Ignoring all nontax considerations, XYZ could reduce its tax liability by $3,514 (a 20% reduction) by moving its distribution center, warehouses, and applicable personnel to B.

	State A	State B	Total
Sales	$500,000	$200,000	$700,000
Property	100,000	250,000	350,000
Payroll	80,000	30,000	110,000

Apportionment Formulas

	State A	State B
Sales	$500,000/$700,000 = 71.43%	$200,000/$700,000 = 28.57%
Property	$100,000/$350,000 = 28.57%	$250,000/$350,000 = 71.43%
Payroll	$80,000/$110,000 = 72.73%	$30,000/$110,000 = 27.27%
Total	172.73%	127.27%

	State A		State B
Apportionment factor (totals/3):	57.58%		42.42%
Income apportioned to the state ($200,000 × apportionment factor)	$115,160		$84,840
Tax rate	10%		3%
Tax liability	$ 11,516		$ 2,545
Total tax liability		$14,061	
Tax imposed before move to State B		17,575	
Tax reduction due to move		$ 3,514	

◆

EFFECTS OF THE UNITARY
THEORY
◆

The unitary theory developed in response to the early problems that the states faced in attributing the income of a multistate business among the states in which the business was conducted. Originally, this theory was applied to justify apportionment of the income of multiple operating divisions within a single company. Over the years, however, the concept has been extended to require the combined reporting of certain affiliated corporations.

When two affiliated corporations are subject to tax in different states, each entity must file a return and report its income in the state in which it conducts business. Each entity reports its income separately from that of its affiliated corporations. In an effort to minimize overall state income tax, multistate entities have attempted to legally separate the parts of the business that are carried on in the various states.

─────────────────── EXAMPLE 23 ───────────────────

A Corporation owns a chain of retail stores located in several states. To enable each store to file and report the income earned only in that state, each store was organized as a separate subsidiary in the state in which it did business. In this manner, each store is separately subject to tax only in the state in which it is located. ◆

Since most states attempt to allocate as much income to in-state sources as possible, several states have adopted the *unitary* approach to computing state taxable income. Under this method, a corporation is required to file a combined or consolidated return that includes the results from all of the operations of the related corporations, not just from those that transacted business in the state. In this manner, the unitary method allows a state to apply formula apportionment to a firm's nationwide or worldwide unitary income. To include the activities of the corporation's subsidiaries in the apportionment formula, the state must subjectively determine that the subsidiaries' activities are an integral part of a unitary business and, as a result, are subject to apportionment.

What Is a Unitary Business?

A unitary business operates as a unit and cannot be segregated into independently operating divisions. The operations are integrated, and each division depends on or contributes to the operation of the business as a whole. It is not necessary that each unit operating within a state contribute to the activities of all divisions outside the state. The unitary theory ignores the separate legal existence of the entities and focuses instead on practical business realities. Accordingly, the separate entities are treated as a single business for state income tax purposes, and the apportionment formula is applied to the combined income of the unitary business.

The courts have developed three tests to define a unitary business: the three unities test, the contribution or dependency test, and the factors of profitability test. The *three unities test* requires the presence of unity of ownership, unity of operations, and unity of use. Unity of ownership generally is satisfied where 50 percent or more of the corporation's stock is owned directly or indirectly by another corporation within the group. Unity of operation is evidenced by the performance of certain functions, such as central purchasing, advertising, accounting and legal services, training, and management, by one of the corporations on behalf of the entire group. Unity of use is associated with executive forces and general systems of operations and is evidenced by major policy decisions that are made by centralized management, intercompany financing or product flow, and services that are provided by an affiliate to other affiliates.

EXAMPLE 24

Continue with the facts of Example 23. The parent corporation manufactured no goods, but conducted central management, purchasing, distributing, advertising, and administrative departments. The subsidiaries carried on a purely intrastate business, and they paid for the goods and services received at the parent company's cost, plus overhead. The parent company and the subsidiaries constitute a unitary business, due to their unitary operations (purchasing, distributing, advertising, and administrative functions). Accordingly, in states that have adopted the unitary method, the income and apportionment factors of the entire unitary group must be combined and apportioned to the states in which at least one member of the group has nexus. ◆

The *contribution* or *dependency test* focuses on whether the operation of the in-state business depends on, or contributes to, the corporation's out-of-state business. Examples of activities that may be considered as contributing factors include substantial borrowing on out-of-state operations to finance in-state operations, transfers of top-level executives from out-of-state operations, and transfers of manufacturing equipment and materials from out-of-state operations.

The *factors of profitability test* includes functional integration, centralization of management, and economies of scale. Functional integration includes product flow between affiliates and centralized functions such as advertising, accounting, purchasing, manufacturing, and financing. Components of centralized management include interlocking directorates, interchange of personnel at upper management levels, and required parent company approval on major policy decisions. A vertically integrated business generally can easily satisfy the contribution or dependency test and the factors of profitability test.

EXAMPLE 25

X Corporation organized its departments as separate corporations on the basis of function: mining copper ore, refining the ore, and fabricating the refined copper into consumer products. Regardless of the fact that the various steps in the process are operated substantially independently of each other with only general supervision from X's executive offices, X is engaged in a single unitary business. Its various divisions are engaged in different steps in a large, vertically structured enterprise. The need by one business segment for the products or raw materials provided by another satisfies the contribution or dependency test. The flow of products between the affiliates also provides evidence of functional integration, which generally requires some form of central decision or policy making that will satisfy the factors of profitability test. ◆

Notice that the application of the unitary theory is based on a series of subjective observations about the organization and operation of the taxpayer's businesses, whereas the availability of Federal controlled and affiliated group status is based on objective, mechanical ownership tests.

Tax Effects of the Unitary Theory

Use of the unitary approach by a state eliminates several of the planning techniques that could be used to shift income between corporate segments to avoid or minimize state taxes. In addition, the unitary approach usually results in a larger portion of the corporation's income being taxable in states where the compensation, property values, and sales prices are high relative to other states. This occurs because the larger in-state costs (numerators in the apportionment formula) include in the tax base a larger portion of the taxable income within the state's taxing jurisdiction. This has an adverse effect upon the corporation's overall state tax burden if the states in which the larger portions are allocated impose a high tax rate relative to the other states in which the business is conducted.

The presence of a unitary business is favorable when losses of unprofitable affiliates may be offset against the earnings of profitable affiliates. It also is favorable when income earned in a high-tax state may be shifted to low-tax states due to the use of combined apportionment factors.

EXAMPLE 26

X Corporation owns two subsidiaries, A and B. A, located in State K, generated taxable income of $700,000. During this same period, B located in State M, generated a loss of $400,000. If A and B are independent corporations, A is required to pay K tax on $700,000 of income. However, if the corporations constitute a unitary business, the income, as well as the apportionment factors, of the two entities are combined. As a result, the combined income of $300,000 ($700,000 − $400,000) is apportioned to unitary states K and M. ◆

EXAMPLE 27

C Corporation, a wholly owned subsidiary of Z Corporation, generated $1,000,000 taxable income. C's activities and sales are restricted to State P, which imposes a 10% income tax. Z's income for the taxable period is $1,500,000. Z's activities and sales are restricted to State Q, which imposes a 5% income tax. Both states use a three-factor apportionment formula that equally weights sales, payroll, and property. Sales, payroll, and average property for each of the corporations are as follows:

	C Corporation	Z Corporation	Total
Sales	$3,000,000	$7,000,000	$10,000,000
Payroll	2,000,000	3,500,000	5,500,000
Property	2,500,000	4,500,000	7,000,000

If the corporations are independent entities, the overall state income tax liability is $175,000.

State P (10% × $1,000,000)	=	$100,000
State Q (5% × $1,500,000)	=	75,000
Total state income tax		$175,000

If the corporations are members of a unitary business, the income and apportionment factors are combined in determining the income tax liability in unitary states P and Q. As a result of the combined reporting, the overall state income tax liability is reduced by $7,475.

State P Income Tax

Total apportionable income			$2,500,000
Apportionment formula			
Sales ($3,000,000/$10,000,000)	=	30.00%	
Payroll ($2,000,000/$5,500,000)	=	36.36%	
Property ($2,500,000/$7,000,000)	=	35.71%	
Total		102.07%	
Average (102.07% ÷ 3)			× 34.02%
State P taxable income			$ 850,500
Tax rate			× 10%
State P tax liability			$ 85,050

State Q Income Tax

Total apportionable income			$2,500,000
Apportionment formula			
Sales ($7,000,000/$10,000,000)	=	70.00%	
Payroll ($3,500,000/$5,500,000)	=	63.64%	
Property ($4,500,000/$7,000,000)	=	64.29%	
Total		197.93%	
Average (197.93% ÷ 3)			× 65.98%
State Q taxable income			$1,649,500
Tax rate			× 5%
State Q tax liability			$ 82,475
Total state income tax, if unitary ($85,050 + $82,475)			$ 167,525
Total state income tax, if nonunitary			175,000
Tax reduction from combined reporting			$ 7,475

The results of unitary reporting would have been detrimental if Q had imposed a higher rate of tax than P, because a larger percentage of the corporation's income is attributable to Q when the apportionment factors are combined. ◆

By identifying the states that have adopted the unitary method and the criteria under which a particular state defines a unitary business, a taxpayer may reduce its overall state tax by restructuring its corporate relationships to create or guard against a unitary relationship. For instance, an independent business enterprise can be made unitary by exercising day-to-day operational control and by centralizing functions, such as marketing, financing, accounting, and legal services. Figure 15–5 indicates the states that have adopted the unitary theory in determining taxable income.[20]

Water's Edge Election

The Supreme Court has affirmed the constitutionality of a state's authority to require worldwide combined reporting of a U.S. parent company with the

FIGURE 15–5   **Adoption of Unitary Theory**

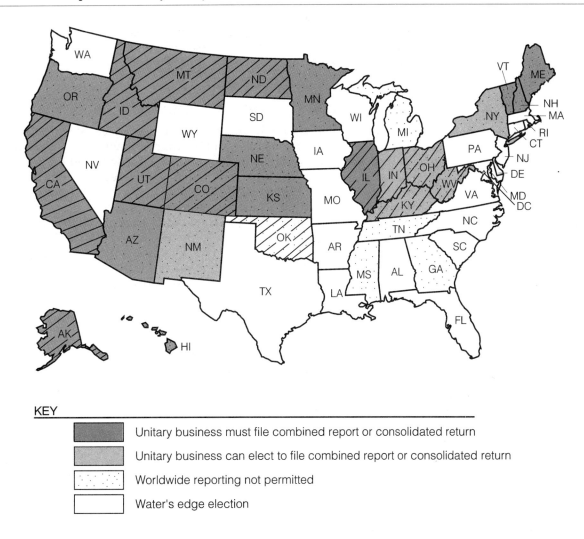

KEY

▨	Unitary business must file combined report or consolidated return
░	Unitary business can elect to file combined report or consolidated return
⁖	Worldwide reporting not permitted
☐	Water's edge election

---

20. For responding states with an income tax, tax year 1991. See Raabe and Boucher, eds., *Multistate Corporate Tax Guide* (Greenvale, N.Y.: Panel Publishers, Inc., 1992).

income of its foreign subsidiaries.[21] A series of cases in California has addressed this application of the unitary theory. These cases question whether such tax computations are unconstitutional in that they may affect the conduct of U.S. foreign policy and violate the Foreign Commerce Clause.[22] The cited cases currently are on appeal; consequently, the future of California's worldwide combined reporting requirement is uncertain.

As a result of pressure from the business community, the Federal government, and foreign countries, most of the states that impose an income tax on a unitary business's worldwide operations permit a multinational business to elect *water's edge* unitary reporting as an alternative to worldwide unitary filing.

The water's edge provision permits a multinational corporation to elect to limit the reach of the state's taxing jurisdiction to activities occurring within the boundaries of the United States. The decision to make a water's edge election may have a substantial effect on the tax liability of a multinational corporation. For instance, a water's edge election usually cannot be revoked for a number of years without permission from the appropriate tax authority. Moreover, corporations making this election may be assessed an additional tax for the privilege of excluding foreign entities from the combined report.[23]

Consolidated and Combined Returns

As discussed in Chapter 8, an affiliated group of corporations may file a consolidated return if all members of the group consent. Once such a return has been filed, the group must continue to file on a consolidated basis as long as it remains in existence, or until permission to file separate returns has been obtained. The consolidated return essentially treats the controlled corporations as a single taxable entity. Thus, the affiliated group pays only one tax, based upon the combined income of its members after certain adjustments (e.g., net operating losses) and eliminations (e.g., intercompany dividends and inventory profits).

Several states permit affiliated corporations to file a consolidated return if such a return has been filed for Federal purposes. The filing of a consolidated return is mandatory in only a few states.

Usually, only corporations that are subject to tax in the state can be included in a consolidated return, unless specific requirements are met or the state permits the inclusion of corporations without nexus.

In contrast, several states, including Illinois and Montana, allow or require the filing of a *combined* return, which eases the compliance burdens associated with a multistate unitary taxpayer. The combined group includes unitary members with nexus in one or more of the states accepting the combined return. The computations reflect apportioned and allocated income of the unitary members, resulting in a summary of the taxable income of the entities in each of

21. *Container Corporation of America v. Franchise Tax Board*, 103 S.Ct. 2933 (1983).

22. *Colgate-Palmolive Co. v. Franchise Tax Board*, 233 Cal. App. 3d 855, 284 Cal. Rptr. 780 (Cal.Ct. App. 1991), worldwide combined reporting of U.S. parent with foreign subsidiaries is not unconstitutional; *Barclay's Bank International v. Franchise Tax Board*, 232 Cal.App. 3d 1187, 275 Cal. Rptr. 626 (Cal.Ct. App. 1990), combined reporting of foreign parent with U.S. subsidiaries is unconstitutional; *Alcan Aluminum Corp. v. Franchise Tax Board*, Ca.Sup.Ct., Sacramento County (June 1991), combined reporting of foreign parent with U.S. subsidiaries is not unconstitutional.

23. For instance, California requires an annual election fee (in addition to the regular tax) equal to the larger of (a) .03% times the sum of (1) the taxpayer's 1986 California property and payroll (if a 12-month income year) and (2) the taxpayer's California sales for the current year, reduced by (3) post-1986 amounts expended for investment in new plants or facilities in California and (4) the amount expended for new employees in California; or (b) .01% times the sum of California sales, property, and payroll for the year.

the states. The combined return chiefly permits the unitary taxpayer to develop the summary of assigned taxable incomes, which is accepted by (and disclosed to) all of the states.

The majority of the 46 states that impose a corporate income tax have special provisions, similar to the Federal law, that govern the taxation of S corporations. As of 1992, only a few states—Connecticut, Michigan, New Hampshire, New Jersey, Tennessee, and Texas—and the District of Columbia do not provide special (no corporate-level tax) treatment for Federal S corporations.[24] In addition, Massachusetts imposes a corporate-level tax on S corporations that have gross receipts in excess of $6,000,000. In each of these states, an S corporation generally is subject to tax in the same manner as a regular (Subchapter C) corporation. Accordingly, if a multistate S corporation operates in any of these states, it is subject to state income tax and does not realize one of the primary benefits of S status—the avoidance of double taxation. Other potential tax-related benefits of the S election, including the pass-through of net operating losses and the reduction in the rate of tax imposed on individual and corporate taxpayers, may be curtailed.

--------------------------------- EXAMPLE 28 ---------------------------------

X, an S corporation, has established nexus in States A and B. A recognizes S status, while B does not. X generated $600,000 of ordinary business income and $100,000 of dividends that were received from corporations in which X owns 50% of the stock. X's State B apportionment percentage is 50%.

For B tax purposes, X must first compute its income as though it were a regular corporation and then apportion the resulting income to B. Assuming that B has adopted the Federal provisions governing the dividends received deduction, X's income, determined as though it were a C corporation, is $620,000 [$600,000 + (100% − 80%) × $100,000]. Accordingly, X is subject to corporate income tax in B on $310,000 ($620,000 × 50% apportionment percentage) of taxable income. ◆

Most states impose a different tax rate for corporate and individual taxpayers. Assuming that the state recognizes the entity's S status, if the corporation is generating income and the state corporate tax rate is higher than the rate imposed on individuals, an S election will reduce the overall state tax liability. Where the state has a graduated tax rate structure, the difference between the corporate and the individual tax rate must be analyzed in light of the amount of the corporation's income and the marginal tax rate under which the shareholders fall.

Eligibility

All of the states that recognize S status permit a corporation to be treated as an S corporation for state purposes only if the corporation has a valid Federal S election in place. Generally, the filing of a Federal S election is sufficient to render the corporation an S corporation for state tax purposes. In most states, an entity that is an S corporation for Federal tax purposes automatically is treated as an S corporation for state tax purposes. However, where an entity is an S corporation for Federal tax purposes, only a few states permit the entity to *elect out* of its S status for state purposes.

---

24. See Boucher, Raabe, and Taylor, *Multistate S Corporation Tax Guide* (Greenvale, N.Y.: Panel Publishers Inc., 1993) for additional details concerning the eligibility and operations requirements of S corporations at the state level.

Some states impose other eligibility requirements that must be satisfied before the corporation's S status will be recognized. Several states require that a copy of the Federal election be filed with the state. A few states require the corporation to make a special state S election. A number of states, including Alabama and Georgia, require that all nonresident shareholders consent to the S election and agree to report and pay any state income tax on their pro rata shares of S corporation income.

Corporate-Level Tax

Although S corporations generally are not taxable entities, Federal income tax liability may arise if the corporation has excess passive investment income or built-in gains. Several states have adopted similar provisions, and, therefore, an S corporation is exempt from the related state income tax only to the extent that it is exempt from corresponding Federal income taxes. In the majority of these states, the imposition of Federal income taxes generates a corporate-level tax for state purposes to the extent that corporate income is allocated or apportioned to the state.

EXAMPLE 29

A, an S corporation, has nexus with States X and Y, both of which recognize S status. X imposes a corporate-level tax on S corporations to the extent that the corporation is subject to Federal income tax. A's Federal excessive passive income is $60,000. The amount of income subject to tax in X depends on whether the passive income is classified as business or nonbusiness income and on A's apportionment percentage for X.

If the passive income is business income and A's State X apportionment percentage is 50%, A is subject to a corporate-level tax in X on $30,000 of passive income ($60,000 × 50%).

If the passive income is nonbusiness income that is allocated to Y, A is not subject to a corporate-level tax in X because none of the corporation's passive income is assigned to that state. ◆

A number of states deviate from the Federal S corporation provisions and provide that an S corporation is entirely exempt from state income tax only if all of its shareholders are residents of the state. In these states, an S corporation is taxed on the portion of its income that is attributable to nonresident shareholders. Some of these states, permit the S corporation to escape corporate-level tax on this income if its nonresident shareholders sign a form under which they agree to pay state tax on their share of the corporation's income. Moreover, a few states require the corporation to withhold taxes on the nonresident shareholders' portions of the entity's income.

EXAMPLE 30

ARGO, an S corporation, is subject to income tax only in Delaware. On the last day of its taxable year, 40% of ARGO's stock is held by nonresident shareholders. To the extent that ARGO's stock is held by resident shareholders, the corporation is not subject to income tax. Accordingly, ARGO is not subject to tax on 60% of its income.

The corporation *is* subject to tax on the remaining 40% of its income. Thus, ARGO computes the corporate income tax that it would be required to pay if it were a C corporation; the resulting tax then is multiplied by the percentage of stock held by nonresident shareholders. Consequently, ARGO pays 40% of the tax that it would be required to pay had it been a C corporation. ◆

Treatment of Multistate S Corporation Shareholders

An S corporation is required to apportion and allocate its income in the same manner as a regular corporation. Similarly, an S corporation generally is required to file a state income tax return in each state in which it has established nexus. To enable its shareholders to determine their income that is subject to state income tax, the corporation must report the amount of state income that is passed through to its shareholders. The income reported on the shareholders' income tax returns varies depending on whether the shareholder is a resident or nonresident of the state in which the return is filed.

Generally, resident shareholders of an S corporation are required to report their share of the corporation's entire income to their state of residency, regardless of the fact that the corporation's income is apportioned to several states. In addition, the shareholders must report their share of the corporation's income apportioned or allocated to other states and file nonresident income tax returns in the other states in which the corporation conducts business. To mitigate the impact of double state taxation, the shareholder generally is permitted to claim on his or her resident tax return an income tax credit for taxes that he or she paid to another state on the corporation's income.

An S corporation usually must report a nonresident shareholder's pro rata share of the corporation's income that is apportioned or allocated to the state. The nonresident shareholder is required to file a return and pay the resulting income tax to the state or states in which the corporation's income is apportioned and allocated. In states that require the corporation to pay a corporate-level tax on the income attributable to nonresident shareholders, the nonresident shareholders are not required to file a return. The corporation has already paid the income tax on that income.

―――――――――――――― EXAMPLE 31 ――――――――――――――

X, equally owned by E and F, is a multistate S corporation that apportions its income to States M and O. E is a resident of M, and F is a resident of O. X reported $300,000 of ordinary business income. Forty percent of X's income is apportioned to M, and the remainder is apportioned to O.

On his M resident income tax return, E reports $150,000 ($300,000 × 50% stock ownership) income, his share of the corporation's entire income. E also reports income of $90,000 ($300,000 × 60% apportionment percentage × 50% ownership interest) on an O nonresident tax return. E is allowed an income tax credit on his M return for the taxes that are paid to O.

On her O resident income tax return, F reports $150,000 ($300,000 × 50% stock ownership) income, her share of the corporation's entire income. F also reports income of $60,000 ($300,000 × 40% apportionment percentage × 50% ownership interest) on an M nonresident tax return. F is allowed an income tax credit on her O return for the taxes that are paid to M. ◆

In most of the jurisdictions that do not recognize S status, shareholders of S corporations are not subject to state income tax on their pro rata share of the corporation's undistributed income. However, the shareholders may be subject to tax on actual distributions from the corporation. In this manner, the distributions received are treated in the same manner as dividends received from a C corporation.

Composite Tax Return

In an effort to decrease compliance burdens and simplify the filing process for nonresident shareholders of S corporations, several states allow an S corporation to file a single income tax return and pay the resulting tax on behalf of some or all of its nonresident shareholders. State requirements for the filing of a composite or "block" return vary substantially.

State and Local Sales and Use Taxes

Forty-five states, and the District of Columbia, impose a consumers' sales tax on retail sales of tangible personal property for use or consumption. In many of these states, in-state localities, including cities, towns, school districts, or counties, also have the power to levy a sales tax. A consumers' sales tax is a tax imposed directly on the purchaser who acquires the asset at retail; the tax is measured by the price of the sale. The vendor or retailer merely acts as a collection agent for the state.

The use tax, which may be imposed either as a separate tax or as an extension of the sales tax, is designed to complement the sales tax. The purpose of the use tax is to prevent consumers from evading sales tax by purchasing goods outside the state for in-state use and to provide an equitable sales environment between in-state and out-of-state retailers.

All of the states exempt certain items, such as prescriptions and medical devices, from the tax. Several states provide that selected services are subject to tax.

Sales and use taxes are imposed on the final consumer of the taxable item. Sales by manufacturers, producers, and processors usually are exempt from the tax because these transactions are made in anticipation of a resale. Hence, sales to retailers who will resell the item to the ultimate consumer generally are exempt from the sales tax.

Certain sales to manufacturers, producers, and processors also are exempt in the majority of states. The exemptions applicable to such taxpayers usually include one or more of the following:

- Containers and other packing, packaging, and shipping materials actually used to transfer merchandise to customers of the purchaser.
- Tangible personal property that becomes an ingredient or component part of an article of tangible personal property destined for sale.
- Tangible personal property (other than fuel or electricity) that is consumed or destroyed or loses its identity in the manufacture of tangible personal property destined for sale.
- Machines and specific processing equipment and repair parts or replacements exclusively and directly used in manufacturing tangible personal property.

In most states, equipment used to transport materials to and from the manufacturing process and to store raw materials and finished products is not entitled to a sales tax exemption. This raises the question of the point at which the manufacturing process begins and ends.

───────────────────────────── EXAMPLE 32 ─────────────────────────────

X Corporation installs a railroad track that runs from the raw material storage area to the assembly line and acquires several railroad cars to transport the materials. Since the railroad track and cars are used for transportation purposes, rather than the direct manufacturing of the product, their acquisition is subject to sales tax. ◆

───────────────────────────── EXAMPLE 33 ─────────────────────────────

Continue with the facts of Example 32, except that heating the raw materials speeds up the fabrication process and makes it more flexible. If the railroad cars are heated, the manufacturing process generally is considered to have started at the time the raw materials are placed into the cars. Accordingly, the railroad track and cars are exempt from the sales tax. ◆

The Supreme Court has held that the regular solicitation of sales by independent brokers establishes sufficient nexus to require a nonresident seller to register and collect the use tax, even though the seller does not have regular employees, agents, and an office or other place of business in the state.[25] As a result, a corporation may be required to collect sales and use taxes in a state, where it is immune from the imposition of an income tax.

When conducting income tax planning, the tax adviser must be aware of the impact that sales and use taxes may have on a transaction that might otherwise be tax-free. For example, although the transfer of property to a controlled corporation in exchange for its stock generally is not subject to corporate income taxes, several states provide that such transfers constitute sales for sales and use tax purposes. Consequently, the transfers will be subject to sales or use taxes. Similarly, a corporate reorganization may be structured to avoid the imposition of income taxes, but under the sales and use tax statutes of several states, such transfers will be considered to be sales and, accordingly, will be subject to sales and use taxes.

Local Property Taxes

Property taxes, a major source of revenue at the city and county level, are referred to as *ad valorem* taxes because they are based on the value of property that is located in the state on a specific date. Generally, that date fixes taxable ownership, situs (location), and the valuation of the property. Nonetheless, to avoid tax evasion, personal property that is temporarily outside the state may be taxed at the domicile of the owner.

Property taxes can take the form of either real property taxes or personal property taxes. All states apply different tax rates and means of assessment to the two classes of property. The methods of assessing the value of the real and tangible property also vary in different taxing jurisdictions.

Although a personal property tax may be imposed on both intangible and tangible property, most states limit the tax to tangible property. The distinction between the various items of personal property is important because special rates or exemptions apply to certain types of property. For instance, inventory constitutes tangible personal property, but is exempt from taxation in some states. Moreover, in the states that do include inventory in the personal property tax base, the amount included in the tax base is measured by the average inventory on hand during the preceding year, rather than the inventory on hand on a specific date.

To encourage the shipment or storage of inventory in the state, approximately 40 states have adopted a *free port* provision, exempting certain inventory from property tax. The requirements necessary to satisfy the free port laws vary from state to state. In general, however, goods stored temporarily in a state escape property tax if one or more of the following conditions are met: (1) the goods have an out-of-state origin and/or destination; (2) the goods are stored in a public or other facility that is not owned by the consignee or consignor; and (3) the goods remain in their original packages.

────────────────── EXAMPLE 34 ──────────────────

A Corporation, a manufacturer of tangible personal property, is located in State C. Personal property, including inventory, is subject to tax in C. D, a neighboring state, has adopted a free port law that allows the taxpayer to escape property taxation on

─────────────

25. *Scripto, Inc. v. Carson,* 80 S.Ct. 619 (1960).

certain inventory. Accordingly, A can reduce its property tax in C by storing its inventory in a public warehouse in D. To determine whether the move will optimize the corporation's overall costs, the reduction in property tax must be compared with the additional costs, such as transportation and warehouse costs, of maintaining the D warehouse. ◆

Other Taxes

States may impose a variety of other state and local taxes on corporations, including incorporation or entrance fees or taxes; gross receipt taxes; stock transfer taxes; realty transfer and mortgage recording taxes; license taxes; and franchise taxes based on net worth or capital stock.

An incorporation or entrance fee or tax is an excise tax for the corporate privilege conferred on the business. At the time the business is incorporated, the state generally imposes a fee or tax for the privilege of conducting business within the state as a corporation. Similarly, an out-of-state corporation usually must pay an entrance fee or tax before it can transact business in a state other than its state of incorporation.

Some states base the incorporation or entrance tax on the par value of the authorized stock. To prevent tax evasion, a few of these states impose a similar fee or tax on subsequent increases in the corporation's authorized stock. Where the incorporation fee or tax is based on the amount of authorized stock, the tax may be based on the total amount of the stock, even though the corporation conducts business in several states.

A license tax is an excise tax on the privilege of engaging in a certain business, occupation, or profession. A state may impose business, occupational, or professional license taxes as a means of generating revenue or regulating the activities of the business, occupation, or profession for the public welfare.

Stock and realty transfer and mortgage recording taxes are nonrecurring taxes that are imposed at the time of recording or transfer. Stock transfer taxes are imposed on the transfer of shares or certificates of stock of domestic and foreign corporations. The tax typically is based on the number of shares transferred and the par or market value of the stock. Generally, the following stock transfers are exempt from the transfer tax: original issues, surrenders for reissue in smaller denominations, surrenders for reissuance to executor or administrator, deposits of stock as security for a loan, and transfers to a broker for sale or purchase.

The basis of the realty transfer tax usually is measured by the consideration paid or to be paid for the realty. The mortgage recording tax may be based on the actual consideration given, the value of the property, or the debt to be secured by the instrument.

Typically, a capital stock tax is an excise tax imposed on a domestic corporation for the privilege of existing as a corporation or imposed on an out-of-state corporation, either for the privilege of doing business or for the actual transaction of business within the state. This annual tax is usually based on the book value of the corporation's net worth, including capital, surplus, and retained earnings. In a few states, a corporation is subject to a franchise tax only to the extent that the tax exceeds the corporate income tax, but in the majority of states, the entity is subject to both taxes.

The majority of capital stock taxes are apportioned if the corporation does business or maintains an office in another state. In some states, however, the tax is levied on the entire authorized or issued capital stock of a domestic corporation, even though the corporation may be engaged in business in other states. For corporations based in other states, the tax is imposed only on the capital that is employed in the state as determined by an apportionment formula.

―――――――――――――――――――――――― EXAMPLE 35 ――――――――――――――――――――

The balance sheet of X, a domestic corporation of State A, at the end of its taxable year is as follows:

Cash	$100,000
Equipment (net of $50,000 accumulated depreciation)	150,000
Building (net of $75,000 accumulated depreciation)	225,000
Land	125,000
Total assets	$600,000
Accounts payable and other short-term liabilities	$100,000
Long-term liabilities	200,000
Capital stock	50,000
Paid-in capital in excess of par value	50,000
Retained earnings	200,000
Total liabilities and equity	$600,000

A imposes a 2% franchise tax based on the entire net worth of a domestic corporation. X is subject to a franchise tax in A of $6,000 ($600,000 assets – $300,000 liabilities = $300,000 net worth × 2% rate). ◆

―――――――――――――――――――――――― EXAMPLE 36 ――――――――――――――――――――

Continue with the facts of Example 35, except that A subjects a domestic corporation to tax only on the capital that is employed in the state. X properly determines its A apportionment percentage as 20%. In this case, X's A franchise tax liability is $1,200 ($300,000 net worth × 20% apportionment percentage = $60,000 capital employed in A × 2% rate). ◆

The definition of doing business in a state for capital stock purposes differs from that employed for income tax purposes. Public Law 86–272 does not protect solicitation activities from the imposition of a capital stock tax; accordingly, a corporation may find itself subject to a capital stock tax even though it is immune from income tax in the state.[26]

Capital stock tax liabilities can be significant for capital-intensive taxpayers to the extent that they reinvest a large portion of retained earnings (the tax base) in productive assets. If all nontax factors are equal, a taxpayer with sizable exposure to a capital stock tax should consider (1) funding expansion with debt, rather than retained earnings; (2) funding subsidiary operations with debt, rather than direct capital contributions; and (3) regularly paying dividends to parent companies that are domiciled in tax-favored states, such as Delaware. See the discussion of Passive Investment Holding Companies later in the chapter.

TAX PLANNING CONSIDERATIONS

The inconsistencies in the tax laws and rates among the states not only complicate state tax planning, but also provide the nucleus of pertinent planning opportunities. Although several tax planning devices are available to a corporation that does business in only one state, most planning techniques are directed toward corporations that do business or maintain property in more than one state. All suggested tax planning strategies should be reviewed in light of practical business considerations and the additional administrative and other costs that may be incurred since simply minimizing state taxes may not be prudent from a business perspective.

―――――――――――

26. *Clairol, Inc. v. Commonwealth,* 513 Pa. 74, 518 A.2d 1165 (1986).

Redirection of Corporate Activities

Traditional state tax planning involves a review of a corporation's activities within the various states to identify activities that can be redirected so as to reduce the organization's overall state tax liability. These planning techniques include legally manipulating the percentage of income that is apportioned among the states by minimizing the apportionment factors in certain states. However, the potential tax reductions generated under this approach may not be cost-effective for a corporation whose income is widely distributed among a large number of states that impose a tax on income.

Typically, the techniques applied in state income taxation are intertwined, so altering an organization's activities or entities may have a significant impact on several aspects of its overall tax liability. In determining which activities should be altered, carefully analyze the effects each change will have upon the corporation's total tax liability to ensure that the tax saved in one state is not offset or exceeded by an increase in the tax incurred in another state.

CONCEPT SUMMARY 15–1
PRINCIPLES OF MULTISTATE CORPORATE TAXATION

1. Taxability of an organization's income in a state other than the one in which it is incorporated depends on the laws, regulations, and judicial interpretations of the other state; the nature and level of the corporation's activity in, or contacts with, that state; and, to a limited extent, the application of P.L. 86–272.

2. Each state has adopted its own multistate income tax laws, regulations, methods, and judicial interpretations; consequently, the nonuniformity of state income taxing provisions provides a multitude of planning techniques that allow a multistate corporation to reduce its overall state tax liability legally.

3. The apportionment procedure is used to assign the income of a multistate taxpayer to the various states in which business is conducted. Generally, nonbusiness income is allocated, rather than apportioned, directly to the state in which the nonbusiness income-generating assets are located.

4. The various state apportionment formulas offer planning opportunities in that more or less than 100% of the taxpayer's income may be subjected to state income tax. When a loss is generated in one of the states, an unexpected assignment of income may result.

5. Most states employ an equally weighted three-factor apportionment formula. In some states, the sales factor is doubled, and occasionally only the sales factor is used in apportioning multistate taxable income. Generally, the greater the relative weight assigned to the sales factor, the greater the tax burden on out-of-state taxpayers.

6. The sales factor is based upon the destination concept except where a throwback rule applies. The payroll factor generally includes compensation that is included in Federal gross income, but some states include excludible fringe benefits. An employee's compensation usually is not divided among states. The property factor is derived using the average undepreciated historical costs for the assets and eight times the rental value of the asset.

7. The unitary theory requires the taxpayer to include worldwide activities and holdings in the apportionment factors. A water's edge election can limit these amounts to U.S. transactions.

8. Federal S corporations often receive tax-favored treatment in the states, but some jurisdictions limit these incentives to resident shareholders. Combined returns can facilitate the reporting burdens of the S corporation and its nonresident shareholders.

9. State and local jurisdictions assess sales, use, property, and other *ad valorem* or transfer taxes. Various exemptions from these taxes (e.g., for inventory and manufacturing purchases) are available in most jurisdictions.

10. State and local tax planning often involves modifications in the legal, functional, or technical means by which the taxpayer conducts business, but they should be undertaken only after considering their nontax effects. Establishing nexus in a low- or no-tax state often optimizes the multistate tax liability, while eliminating nexus in high-tax, nonunitary states can accomplish the same objective. Holding companies for investment assets can take advantage of the states' exemptions for certain interest and dividend income.

Selecting the Optimal State in Which to Be Taxed

Because the states employ different definitions of the amount and type of activity necessary to establish nexus, a company has some latitude in selecting the states with which it desires to be taxed. When a corporation has only a limited connection with an undesired (high-tax) state, it may abandon that activity by electing an alternative means of accomplishing the same result. For example, if providing a sales representative with a company-owned automobile constitutes nexus in an undesired state, the company could eliminate its connection with that state by reimbursing sales personnel for traveling expenses, instead of providing a company vehicle. Similarly, when nexus is caused by conducting training sessions or seminars in the state, the corporation could bypass this connection. This can be done by sending the sales representatives or customers' personnel to a nearby state in which nexus clearly has been established, or in which the activity would not constitute nexus.

In addition, when sufficient activity originates from the repair and maintenance of the corporation's products or the activities performed by the sales representatives within the state, the organization could incorporate the service or sales divisions. This would invalidate a nonunitary state's right to tax the parent corporation's income; only the income of the service or sales divisions would be subject to tax. However, this technique will be successful only if the incorporated division is a *bona fide* business operation. Therefore, the pricing of any sales or services between the new subsidiary and the parent corporation must be at arm's length, and the operations of the new corporation preferably should result in a profit.

Although most planning techniques are employed to disconnect a corporation's activities from an undesirable state, they can also be utilized to create nexus in a desirable state. For example, when the presence of a company-owned vehicle will create nexus in a desirable state, the corporation could provide its sales representatives in that state with company vehicles, rather than reimbursing or providing increased compensation for automobile expenses.

Establishing nexus in a state is advantageous, for instance, when that state has a lower tax rate than the state in which the income currently is taxed.

─────────────── EXAMPLE 37 ───────────────

XYZ Corporation generates $500,000 of taxable income from selling goods; specifically, 40% of its product is sold in State A and 60% in State B. Both states levy a corporate income tax and include only the sales factor in their apportionment formulas. The tax rate in A is 10%; B's rate is only 3%. XYZ's manufacturing operation is located in A; therefore, the corporation's income is subject to tax in that state. Currently, XYZ is immune from tax under Public Law 86–272 in B. Since A has adopted a throwback provision, XYZ incurs $50,000 of state income taxes.

	Apportionment Formula	Net Income	Tax Rate	Tax
State A	100/100	$500,000	10%	$50,000
State B	0/100	500,000	3%	–0–
Total tax liability				$50,000

Because B imposes a lower tax rate than A, XYZ substantially reduces its state tax liability if sufficient nexus is created with B.

	Apportionment Formula	Net Income	Tax Rate	Tax
State A	40/100	$500,000	10%	$20,000
State B	60/100	500,000	3%	9,000
Total tax liability				$29,000

Restructuring Corporate Entities

One of the major objectives of state tax planning is to design the proper mix of corporate entities. An optimal mix of entities often generates the lowest combined state income tax for the corporation. Ideally, the income from all of the entities will be subject to a low tax rate or no tax at all. However, this generally is not possible. Consequently, the goal of designing a good corporate combination often is to situate the highly profitable entities in states that impose a low (or no) income tax.

Matching Tax Rates and Corporate Income. When the corporation must operate in a high-tax state, divisions that generate losses also should be located there. Alternatively, unprofitable or less profitable operations can be merged into profitable operations to reduce the overall income subject to tax in the state. An ideal candidate for this type of merger may be a research and development subsidiary that is only marginally profitable, but is vital to the parent corporation's strategic goals. By using computer simulation models, a variety of different combinations can be tested to determine the optimal corporate structure.

Passive Investment Holding Companies. The creation of a passive investment subsidiary is another restructuring technique utilized to minimize a corporation's state tax burden. Nonbusiness or passive income generally is allocated to the state in which the income-producing asset is located, rather than apportioned among the states in which the corporation does business. Therefore, significant tax savings may be realized when nonbusiness assets are located in a state that either does not levy an income tax or provides favorable tax treatment for passive income. The corporation need not be domiciled in the state to benefit from these favorable provisions. Instead, the tax savings can be realized by forming a subsidiary holding company to hold the intangible assets and handle the corporation's investment activities. The subsidiary holding company technique usually produces the desired result in any no-tax state. Delaware, however, often is selected for this purpose due to its other corporate statutory provisions and favorable political, business, and legal climate.

Delaware does not impose an income tax upon a corporation whose only activity within the state is the maintenance and management of intangible investments and the collection and distribution of income from such investments or from tangible property physically located in another state. Consequently, trademarks, patents, stock, and other intangible property can be transferred to a Delaware corporation whose activity is limited to collecting passive income. The assets can be transferred to the subsidiary without incurring a Federal income tax under § 351 (see Chapter 3).

However, to receive the desired preferential state tax treatment, the holding company's activities within the state must be sufficient to establish nexus in the state. The holding company should avoid performing any activity outside the state that may result in establishing nexus with another state. In addition, the formation of the subsidiary must be properly implemented to assure the legal substance of the operation. The holding company must have a physical office, and it must function as an independent operation. Ensuring nexus and proper formation is not difficult since numerous consulting organizations are available to furnish new holding companies with all of the elements necessary to fulfill these requirements.

Because the subsidiary's activities are confined to Delaware (or some other no- or low-tax state), and its operations generate only passive income, its income will not be taxed in any nonunitary state. Moreover, most states exclude dividends from taxation or otherwise treat them favorably; therefore, the earnings of a passive investment subsidiary can be distributed as a dividend to the parent at a minimal tax cost. If the state in which the parent is located does not levy the full income tax on dividends received, the entire measure of passive income may escape taxation. Formation of an investment subsidiary also may favorably affect the parent corporation's apportionment formula in nonunitary states because the passive income earned by the subsidiary will be excluded from the numerator of its sales factor.

—————————————————— EXAMPLE 38 ——————————————————

XYZ Corporation generates $800,000 of taxable income; $600,000 is income from its manufacturing operations, and $200,000 dividend income was earned from passive investments. All of XYZ's sales are made, and assets are kept, in State A, which imposes a 10% corporate income tax and permits a 100% deduction for dividends that are received from subsidiaries. The corporation is not subject to tax in any other state. Consequently, XYZ incurs $80,000 of income tax (tax base $800,000 × tax rate 10%).

If XYZ creates a passive investment subsidiary in State B, which does not impose an income tax upon a corporation whose only activity within the state is the maintenance and management of passive investments, XYZ's tax liability is reduced by $20,000 (a 25% decrease). Since passive income is nonbusiness income (which is allocated for state tax purposes to the state in which it is located), the income earned from its passive investments is not subject to tax in A.

	State A (XYZ Corporation)	State B (Passive Investment Subsidiary)
Taxable income	$600,000	$200,000
Tax rate	10%	–0–*
Tax liability	$ 60,000	$ –0–
Total tax liability		$ 60,000
Tax imposed without restructuring		80,000
Tax reduction due to use of subsidiary		$ 20,000

*State B does not impose an income tax on a passive investment corporation.

The income earned by the subsidiary from its passive investments can be distributed to XYZ as a dividend without incurring a tax liability because A allows a 100% deduction for dividends that are received from subsidiary corporations. ◆

These desired results, however, will not be fully available in states that view the entire corporate operation as being unitary. Since those states require combined reporting, the income earned by the passive investment subsidiary is included in the corporation's apportionable or allocable income.

Other Parent-Subsidiary Techniques. By using *bona fide* intercompany financing and allocations among subsidiaries, the income of out-of-state subsidiaries may be minimized or maximized, depending upon the tax rates imposed by the states. When the parent is located in a high-tax state, increasing the income of a subsidiary that is located in a low- or no-tax state reduces the corporation's overall state tax liability. When the parent is located in a low- or no-tax state, the overall state tax is reduced by decreasing the income of a subsidiary located in a high-tax state. This planning technique is not successful in unitary states because the income of the entire affiliated group is subject to apportionment by the state.

Establishing a passive investment subsidiary or incorporating separate divisions or operations within specific states also reduces the corporation's overall state tax liability. This would be the case if the corporation is subject to a tax based upon the value of capital stock or net worth employed in the state. Substantial reductions in state tax liabilities can be realized by forming a separate corporation that employs only the minimum amount of capital in those states that impose a capital stock or net worth tax. The operations within the selected state are then limited to the separate corporation. Since the parent's entire capital stock or net worth will not be apportioned to those states, the tax base for the imposition of this tax may be greatly reduced.

Subjecting the Corporation's Income to Apportionment

When a multistate organization is domiciled in a high-tax state, some of its apportionable income is eliminated from the tax base in that state. In light of the high tax rate, this may result in significant tax savings. Apportioning income will be especially effective where the income that is attributed to the other states is not subject to income tax. The income removed from the taxing jurisdiction of the domicile state entirely escapes state income taxation when the state to which the income is attributed (1) does not levy a corporate income tax; (2) requires a higher level of activity necessary to subject an out-of-state company to taxation than that adopted by the state of domicile; or (3) is prohibited under Public Law 86–272 from taxing the income (assuming that the domicile state has not adopted a throwback provision). Thus, the right to apportion income may provide substantial benefits because the out-of-state sales will be excluded from the numerator of the sales factor and may not be taxed in another state.

However, to acquire the right to apportion its income, the organization must have sufficient activities in, or contacts with, one or more other states. Whether the type and amount of activities and/or contacts are considered adequate is determined by the domicile state's nexus rules. When the company's activities in or contacts with another state would, if carried on by an out-of-state corporation within the domicile state, subject the out-of-state corporation to tax, the company is entitled to apportion its income. The corporation's right to apportion its income is based entirely upon this criterion; the fact that the corporation actually is or is not paying tax, or whether the corporation is even taxable in another state, generally is disregarded. Therefore, a corporation should analyze its current activities in, and contacts with, other states to determine which, if any, activities or contacts could be redirected so that the corporation will be granted the right to apportion its income.

Planning with Apportionment Factors

Sales Factor.   The sales factor yields the greatest planning opportunities for a multistate corporation. In-state sales include those to purchasers with a destination point in that state; sales delivered to out-of-state purchasers are included in the numerator of the sales factor of the destination state. However, to be permitted to exclude out-of-state sales from the sales factor of the origination state, the seller generally must substantiate the shipment of goods to an out-of-state location. Therefore, the destinations of sales that a corporation makes and the means by which the goods are shipped must be carefully reviewed. Possibly, the corporation's overall state tax can be reduced by establishing a better recordkeeping system or by manipulating the numerator of the sales factor by changing the delivery location or method.

For example, a corporation may substantially reduce its state tax if the delivery location of its sales is changed from a state in which the company is taxed to one in which it is not. This technique may not benefit the corporation if the state in which the sales originate has adopted the throwback rule.

Property Factor.   Because most fixed assets are physically stationary in nature, the property factor is not so easily manipulated. Nonetheless, significant tax savings can be realized by establishing a leasing subsidiary in a low- or no-tax state. If the property is located in a state that does not include leased assets in the property factor, the establishment of a subsidiary from which to lease the property eliminates the assets from the property factor in the parent's state. This technique allows the corporation to change the character of the property from "owned" (which increases the tax base) to merely "used" (which is excluded from the property factor).

Permanently idle property generally is excluded from the property factor. Accordingly, a corporation should identify and remove such assets from the property factor to ensure that the factor is not distorted. It is equally important to identify and remove nonbusiness assets from the property factor in states that distinguish between business and nonbusiness income.

───────────────── EXAMPLE 39 ─────────────────

Z Corporation's property holdings were as follows:

	State A	Total
Equipment (average historical cost)	$1,200,000	$2,000,000
Accumulated depreciation (average)	800,000	1,000,000

Twenty percent of the equipment in State A is fully depreciated and is idle property. Assuming that A includes property in the factor at historical cost, Z's property factor is 54.55% [($1,200,000 − $240,000 idle property)/ ($2,000,000 − $240,000)]. If the idle property is not removed from the property factor, Z's property factor in A is incorrectly computed as 60% ($1,200,000/$2,000,000). ◆

Although the value of a taxpayer's property generally is determined by averaging the values at the beginning and end of the tax period, some states permit or require the average value to be calculated on a monthly basis if annual computation results in a substantial distortion. When the taxpayer experiences substantial variations in the property that is owned during the tax period, a monthly computation (where permitted) may be appropriate.

───────────────── EXAMPLE 40 ─────────────────

X Corporation, a calendar year taxpayer, is a manufacturer of swimwear with facilities located in several states. Since the swimwear usually is shipped to customers in mid-January, the inventory value is at its peak at the beginning and the end of the tax period. If the state permits, X may benefit from determining its average property value on a monthly basis. ◆

───────────────── EXAMPLE 41 ─────────────────

A Corporation, a calendar year taxpayer, has established nexus with numerous states. On January 2, A sold one of its two facilities in State X. The cost of this facility was $800,000.

On January 1, A owned property with a cost of $3,000,000, $1,500,000 of which was located in X. On December 31, A owned property with a cost of $2,200,000, $700,000 of which was located in X. If A's property factor in X is determined by averaging the beginning and end of year amounts, the property factor is 42.31%.

$$\text{State X: } \frac{\$1,500,000 + \$700,000}{2} = \$1,100,000$$

$$\text{Total: } \frac{\$3,000,000 + \$2,200,000}{2} = \$2,600,000$$

$$\frac{\$1,100,000}{\$2,600,000} = 42.31\%$$

If A's average property owned in X is determined on a monthly basis, its applicable property factor becomes 33.82%.

$$\text{State X: } \frac{\$1,500,000 + (11 \times \$700,000)}{12} = \$766,667$$

$$\text{Total: } \frac{\$3,000,000 + (11 \times \$2,200,000)}{12} = \$2,266,667$$

$$\frac{\$766,667}{\$2,266,667} = 33.82\%$$
◆

Payroll Factor. The payroll factor provides limited planning potential, unless several corporate employees spend substantial periods of time outside their state of employment or the corporation is able to relocate highly paid employees to low- or no-tax states. Use of an independent contractor who works for more than one principal, however, can be beneficial under certain circumstances. Since the commissions paid to independent contractors are excluded from the payroll factor, the taxpayer may reduce its payroll factor in a high-tax state.

--------- EXAMPLE 42 ---------

X Corporation's total payroll costs are $1,400,000. Of this amount, $1,000,000 was attributable to State A, a high-tax state. X's payroll factor in A is 71.43% ($1,000,000/$1,400,000).

Assuming that $200,000 of the A compensation had been paid to sales representatives and that X replaced its sales force with independent contractors, X's payroll factor in A would be reduced to 66.67% [($1,000,000 − $200,000)/($1,400,000 − $200,000)]. ◆

PROBLEM MATERIALS

DISCUSSION QUESTIONS

1. What is UDITPA? Why is it significant in the scheme of state taxation?
2. What is the general formula for the computation of state corporate income tax?
3. What is nexus? Why is it important in determining state taxable income?
4. Discuss the importance of Public Law 86–272.
5. What is the difference between allocation and apportionment?
6. Distinguish between business and nonbusiness income.
7. Why is the distinction between business and nonbusiness income important?
8. Under what assumption were apportionment procedures established? Does apportionment provide a uniform division of an organization's income?
9. What factors constitute the general three-factor apportionment formula?

10. When may the sum of a corporation's state apportionment formulas be more or less than 100%?

11. Discuss the general rule for including sales in the numerator of the sales factor.

12. How does the use of a double-weighted sales factor affect a taxpayer that does not have any physical facilities in a state in which it does business?

13. What is the throwback rule? When is it applicable? Why was such a rule adopted?

14. What is a dock sale?

15. Discuss the general rule for including compensation in the numerator of the payroll factor.

16. How are rental or lease payments generally treated for purposes of determining a state's property factor?

17. Discuss the unitary approach to state taxation.

18. Discuss the state treatment of S corporations. How may state treatments vary from the Federal provisions governing S corporations?

19. What is an ad valorem tax? Give an example of an ad valorem tax to which you are subject.

20. Identify the planning opportunities presented by the ability of a corporation to terminate or create nexus.

21. Discuss the planning opportunities presented by establishing a passive investment subsidiary.

PROBLEMS

22. Y Corporation is subject to tax only in State A. Y generated the following income and deductions:

Federal taxable income	$500,000
State A income tax expense	50,000
Depreciation allowed for Federal tax purposes	100,000
Depreciation allowed for state tax purposes	75,000

Federal taxable income is the starting point in computing State A taxable income. In addition, state income taxes are not deductible for state income tax purposes. Determine Y's State A taxable income.

23. A Corporation is subject to tax only in State X. A generated the following income and deductions:

Federal taxable income	$1,000,000
State X income tax expense	200,000
Depreciation allowed for Federal tax purposes	300,000
Depreciation allowed for state tax purposes	400,000
Interest on Federal obligations	50,000
Interest on State X obligations	100,000
Expenses related to State X obligations	10,000

The starting point in computing the State X income tax base is Federal taxable income. In addition, state income taxes are not deductible for state income tax purposes.

a. Determine A's State X taxable income, assuming that interest on X obligations is exempt from X income tax.

b. Determine A's taxable income, assuming that interest on X obligations is subject to X income tax.

24. A Corporation owns and operates two facilities that manufacture paper products. One of the facilities is located in State D, and the other is located in State E. A generated $1,500,000 of taxable income, comprised of $1,200,000 of income from its manufacturing facilities and a $300,000 gain from the sale of nonbusiness property, located in E. E does not distinguish between business and nonbusiness income, but

D limits apportionable income to business income. A's activities within the two states are outlined below.

	State D	State E	Total
Sales of paper products	$4,500,000	$3,800,000	$8,300,000
Property	3,600,000	2,500,000	6,100,000
Payroll	1,200,000	900,000	2,100,000

Both D and E utilize a three-factor apportionment formula, under which sales, property, and payroll are equally weighted. Determine the amount of A's income that is subject to income tax by each state.

25. Assume the same facts as Problem 24, except that, under the statutes of both D and E, a corporation's income subject to apportionment is limited to business income.

26. X Corporation generated $200,000 of taxable income from selling its product in States A and B. For the taxable year, the corporation's activities within the two states were as follows:

	State A	State B	Total
Sales	$500,000	$200,000	$700,000
Property	300,000	50,000	350,000
Payroll	100,000	10,000	110,000

X has determined that it is subject to tax in both A and B. Both states utilize a three-factor apportionment formula that equally weights sales, property, and payroll. The rates of corporate income tax imposed in A and B are 10% and 8%, respectively. Determine X's state income tax liability.

27. X Corporation has nexus in States A and B. X's activities for the year are summarized below.

	State A	State B	Total
Sales	$1,200,000	$ 800,000	$2,000,000
Property:			
Average cost	500,000	300,000	800,000
Average accumulated depreciation	(300,000)	(100,000)	(400,000)
Payroll	450,000	150,000	600,000
Rent expense	10,000	25,000	35,000

Determine the apportionment factors for A and B, assuming that A uses a three-factor apportionment formula under which sales, property (net depreciated basis), and payroll are equally weighted, and B employs a single-factor formula that consists solely of sales. State A has adopted UDITPA with respect to the inclusion of rent payments in the property factor.

28. Assume the facts of Problem 27, except that A uses a single-factor apportionment formula that consists solely of sales, and B uses a three-factor apportionment formula that equally weights sales, property (at historical cost), and payroll. State B does not include rent payments in the property factor.

29. Assume the facts of Problem 27, except that both states employ a three-factor formula, under which sales are double weighted. The basis of the property factor in A is historical cost, while the basis of this factor in B is the net depreciated basis. Neither A nor B includes rent payments in the property factor.

30. CARE Co., a calendar year taxpayer, was incorporated this year. CARE's entire first-year operations consisted of renovating two old manufacturing facilities that it had acquired, obtaining raw materials, ordering and installing equipment, hiring personnel, and producing several of CARE's products. However, the corporation sold no products during the year.

CARE's operations generated a net operating loss of $1,500,000. The corporation has income tax nexus in the two states (K and B) in which its manufacturing facilities are located. Determine the amount of CARE's net operating loss that is apportioned to each state, assuming that K employs a three-factor apportionment formula that equally weights sales, property, and payroll. B uses a three-factor formula under which sales are double weighted.

	State K	State B	Total
Average property (historical cost)	$1,100,000	$900,000	$2,000,000
Payroll	800,000	600,000	1,400,000

31. Although XYZ Corporation's manufacturing facility, distribution center, and retail store are located in State K, XYZ sells its products to residents located in States K, M, and N. Sales to residents of K are conducted through XYZ's retail store. Sales to residents of M are obtained by XYZ's sales representative who has the authority to accept and approve sales orders. Residents of N are able to purchase XYZ's product only if they arrange to take delivery of the product at XYZ's shipping dock. XYZ's sales were as follows:

Sales to residents of State K	$1,300,000
Sales to residents of State M	800,000
Sales to residents of State N	300,000

XYZ's activities within the three states are limited to those described above. All of the states have adopted a throwback provision and utilize a three-factor apportionment formula under which sales, property, and payroll are equally weighted. Determine XYZ's sales factors for K, M, and N.

32. A Corporation is subject to tax in States G, H, and I. A's compensation expense includes the following:

	State G	State H	State I	Total
Salaries and wages for nonofficers	$200,000	$300,000	$100,000	$600,000
Officers' salaries	–0–	–0–	200,000	200,000

States G and H include officers' salaries in the payroll factor. Officers' salaries are excluded in determining the payroll factor for State I. Compute A's payroll factors for G, H, and I.

33. CAR Corporation, a calendar year taxpayer, has manufacturing facilities in States A and B. A summary of CAR's property holdings follows.

	Beginning of Year		
	State A	State B	Total
Inventory	$ 300,000	$ 200,000	$ 500,000
Plant and equipment	2,200,000	1,500,000	3,700,000
Accumulated depreciation: plant and equipment	(1,200,000)	(500,000)	(1,700,000)
Land	500,000	600,000	1,100,000
Rental property*	900,000	300,000	1,200,000
Accumulated depreciation: rental property	(200,000)	(50,000)	(250,000)

	End of Year		
	State A	State B	Total
Inventory	$ 400,000	$ 100,000	$ 500,000
Plant and equipment	2,500,000	1,200,000	3,700,000
Accumulated depreciation: plant and equipment	(1,500,000)	(450,000)	(1,950,000)
Land	600,000	400,000	1,000,000
Rental property*	900,000	300,000	1,200,000
Accumulated depreciation: rental property	(300,000)	(100,000)	(400,000)

*Unrelated to CAR's regular business operations.

Determine the property factors for CAR Corporation, assuming that the statutes of both A and B provide that average historical cost of business property is to be included in the property factor.

34. Assume the facts of Problem 33, except that the statutes of A provide that the average historical cost of business property is to be included in the property factor, while the statutes of B provide that the average depreciated basis of business property is included in the property factor.

35. **a.** Assume the facts of Problem 33, except that nonbusiness income is apportionable in B.

   b. Assume the facts of Problem 34, except that nonbusiness income is apportionable in A and in B.

36. Employee K, a resident of State B, performs consulting services for XYZ Corporation, which is located in State A. K does not perform any services in A or C. XYZ has taxable income of $800,000. The corporation's activities this year include the following:

	State A	State B	State C	Total
Sales	$2,000,000	$ –0–	$1,000,000	$3,000,000
Property	500,000	–0–	50,000	550,000
Payroll	800,000	200,000*	100,000	1,100,000

*Compensation paid to K.

Both A and B have adopted UDITPA and utilize a three-factor apportionment formula, under which sales are double weighted. Determine the amount of XYZ's income that is apportionable to A and B, assuming that XYZ does not have sufficient nexus with B to be subject to income tax.

37. **a.** Assume the facts of Problem 36, except that K's base of operations is in A.

   b. Assume the facts of Problem 36, except that K's services are directed by XYZ's main office, which is located in A, and a portion of K's services are performed in A.

38. A Corporation's entire operations are located in State X. Although sales are made to State M residents who pick up the goods at A's shipping dock located in X, A does not have nexus with M. A's sales are as follows:

	State X	State M
Sales	$1,300,000	$500,000

   a. Determine A's sales factor for X and M, assuming that *neither* state has adopted a throwback rule.

   b. Determine A's sales factor for X and M, assuming that *both* states have adopted a throwback rule.

39. X Corporation incurs payroll expenses in States A, B, and C. For apportionment purposes, State A defines payroll as all compensation paid to employees, other than officers, including contributions to § 401(k) deferred compensation plans. State B includes compensation paid to all employees in its payroll factor, but does not include § 401(k) contributions. Under the statutes of State C, neither compensation paid to officers nor contributions to § 401(k) plans are included in the payroll factor.

   X incurred the following personnel costs. Determine X's payroll factor for States A, B, and C.

	State A	State B	State C
Wages for employees other than officers	$200,000	$300,000	$100,000
Officers' salaries	50,000	50,000	–0–
Contributions to § 401(k) plans*	40,000	60,000	20,000

*No § 401(k) contributions were made for X's officers.

40. X Corporation operates manufacturing facilities in State G and State H. In addition, the corporation owns non business rental property in H. X incurred the following compensation expenses:

	State G	State H	Total
Manufacturing wages	$375,000	$200,000	$575,000
Administrative wages	95,000	65,000	160,000
Officers' salaries	180,000	80,000	260,000

Twenty percent of the time spent by the administrative staff located in H and 10% of the time spent by officers located in H are devoted to the operation, maintenance, and supervision of the rental property. State G includes all income in the definition of apportionable income, while State H excludes non-business income from apportionable income. Both states include officers' compensation in the payroll factor. Determine X's payroll factors for State G and State H.

41. X, an S corporation, is subject to tax only in State A. On Schedule K of its Federal Form 1120S, X reported ordinary income of $600,000 from its business, taxable interest of $200,000, and charitable contributions of $100,000. A does not recognize S status, but it does follow the Federal provisions with respect to the determination of taxable income for a corporation. Determine X's State A taxable income.

42. A, which has been an S corporation since inception, is subject to tax in States Y and Z. On Schedule K of its Federal Form 1120S, A reported ordinary income of $500,000 from its business, taxable interest income of $10,000, capital loss of $30,000, and $40,000 of dividend income from a corporation in which A owns 30%.

Both states apportion a corporation's income by use of a three-factor formula that equally weights sales, payroll, and the average cost of property; both states treat interest and dividends as business income. In addition, both Y and Z follow Federal provisions with respect to the determination of taxable income for a corporation. Y recognizes S status, but Z does not. Based on the following information, determine the amount of taxable income on which A will pay tax in Y and Z.

	State Y	State Z
Sales	$1,000,000	$800,000
Property (average cost)	500,000	200,000
Payroll	800,000	300,000

43. X Corporation, a wholly owned subsidiary of XYZ Corporation, generated a $500,000 taxable loss. X's activities and sales are restricted to State A, which imposes an 8% income tax. XYZ's income for the taxable period is $1,000,000. XYZ's activities and sales are restricted to State B, which imposes an 11% income tax. Both states use a three-factor apportionment formula that equally weights sales, payroll, and property, and both have adopted the unitary theory. Sales, payroll, and average property for each corporation are as follows:

	X Corporation	XYZ Corporation	Total
Sales	$2,500,000	$4,000,000	$6,500,000
Property	1,000,000	2,500,000	3,500,000
Payroll	800,000	1,200,000	2,000,000

X and XYZ have been found to be members of a unitary business. Determine the overall state income tax for the unitary group.

44. K Corporation is subject to State A's franchise tax. The tax is imposed at a rate of 3% of the corporation's net worth that is apportioned to the state by use of a two-factor (sales and property equally weighted) formula. The property factor includes real and tangible personal property, valued at historical cost as of the end of the taxable year.

Forty percent of K's sales are attributable to A, and $300,000 of the cost of K's tangible personal property is located in A.

Determine the A franchise tax payable by K this year, given the following end-of-the-year balance sheet.

Cash		$500,000
Equipment	$1,000,000	
Accumulated depreciation	−300,000	700,000
Furniture and fixtures	$200,000	
Accumulated depreciation	−50,000	150,000
Intangible assets		350,000
Total assets		$1,700,000
Accounts and taxes payable		$600,000
Long-term debt		350,000
Common stock		1,000
Additional paid-in capital		249,000
Retained earnings		500,000
Total liabilities and equity		$1,700,000

CHAPTER 16

TAX ADMINISTRATION AND PRACTICE

OBJECTIVES

Summarize the organization and structure of the IRS.

Examine the various administrative pronouncements issued by the IRS and explain how they can be used in tax practice.

Summarize the administrative powers of the IRS, including the examination of taxpayer records, the assessment and demand process, and collection procedures.

Review the audit process, including how returns are selected for audit and the various types of audits conducted by the IRS.

Explain and illustrate the taxpayer appeal process, including various settlement options available.

Explain how interest on a deficiency or a refund is determined and when it is due.

Discuss the various penalties that can be imposed on acts of noncompliance by taxpayers.

Review the rules governing the statute of limitations on assessments and on refunds.

Summarize the statutory and nonstatutory prohibitions and guides for those engaged in tax practice.

OUTLINE

Few events arouse so much fear in the typical individual or corporation as the receipt of a letter from the Internal Revenue Service (IRS), notifying the taxpayer that prior years' tax returns are to be the subject of an audit. Almost immediately, calls are made to the tax adviser. Advice is sought as to what to reveal (or not reveal) in the course of the audit, how to delay or avoid the audit, and how friendly one should be with the auditor when he or she ultimately does arrive.

Indeed, many tax practitioners' reputations with their clients have been made or broken by the way they are observed to behave under the pressure of an audit situation. The strategy and tactics of audits—including such seemingly unimportant issues as whether the tax adviser brings donuts or other refreshments to the audit session, the color of his or her suit and tie, and the negotiation techniques—are the subject of both cocktail party banter and scholarly review.

In actuality, the practitioner can render valuable services to the taxpayer in an audit context, thereby assuring that tax payments for the disputed years are neither under- nor overreported, as part of an ongoing tax practice. In this regard, the adviser must appreciate (1) the elements of the Treasury's tax administration process and opportunities for appeal within the structure of the IRS, (2) the extent of the negative sanctions that can be brought to bear against taxpayers whose returns are found to have been inaccurate, and (3) ethical and professional constraints on the advice given and actions taken by the tax adviser on behalf of the client, within the context of an adversarial relationship with the IRS.

TAX ADMINISTRATION
◆

The Treasury has delegated the administration and enforcement of the tax laws to its agency, the IRS. In this process, the Service is responsible for providing adequate information, in the form of publications and forms with instructions, to taxpayers so that they can comply with the laws in an appropriate manner. The IRS also has the responsibilities of identifying delinquent tax payments and carrying out assessment and collection procedures under the restrictions of due process and other constitutional guarantees.

In meeting these responsibilities, the Service conducts audits of selected tax returns. Fewer than 1 percent of all individual tax returns are subjected to audit in a given tax year. However, certain types of both taxpayers and income—including, for instance cash-oriented businesses, real estate transactions, and estate- and gift-taxable transfers—are subject to much higher probabilities of audit.

Recently, however, much of the IRS's effort has been devoted to developing statutory and administrative requirements relative to information reporting and document matching. For instance, when a taxpayer engages in a like-kind exchange or sells a personal residence, various parties to the transaction are required to report the nature and magnitude of the transaction to the IRS. Later the Treasury's computers determine whether the transaction has been reported properly by comparing the information reported by the third parties with the events included on the relevant taxpayers' returns for the year.

In addition, the IRS has been placing increasing pressure on the community of tax advisers. Severe penalties may be assessed on those who have prepared the appropriate return when the Service's interpretation of applicable law conflicts with that of the preparer.

Organizational Structure of the IRS

The structure of the National Office of the IRS is illustrated in Figure 16–1. The IRS Commissioner, a presidential appointee, has organized the functions of the agency into three broad categories: (1) operations (the middle set of boxes in the figure), under which the day-to-day activities of the Service are conducted on a regional basis, augmented by assistant commissioners who engage in support and specialty areas, such as those relating to international and retirement-plan transactions, (2) information collection and processing (the boxes at the right); and (3) management and planning, including matters of internal personnel and finance.

Some of the most important responsibilities of the National Office are summarized in Figure 16-2. Operational duties are carried out by the offices of the Regional Commissioners as shown in Figure 16-3. Geographically, these functions are divided among more than 60 Districts, where face-to-face informational and audit work is carried out. Functionally, these duties are distributed among 10 Service Centers, where returns are received and processed by IRS clerical personnel.

IRS Procedure—Letter Rulings

Taxpayer dealings with the IRS commonly involve the issuance and receipt of informational publications, forms with instructions, and other direct correspon-

FIGURE 16-1   **IRS National Office Organization**

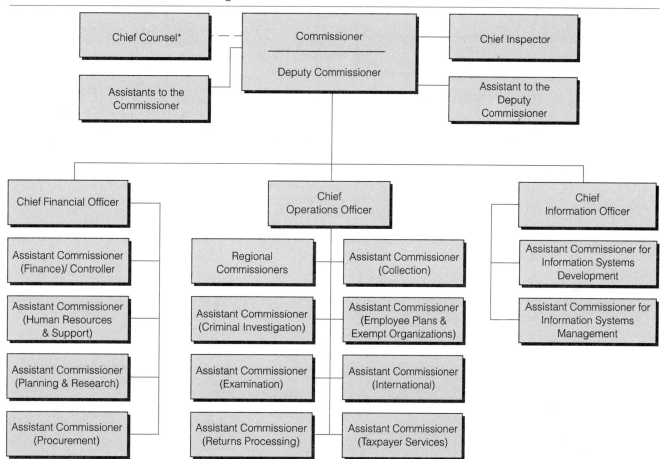

*Chief Counsel is part of the Legal Division, Department of the Treasury

dence. When a tax issue is controversial or a transaction involves considerable tax dollars, the taxpayer often wishes to obtain either assurance or direction from the IRS as to the treatment of the event. The letter ruling process is an effective means of dealing directly with the IRS while in the planning stages of a large or otherwise important transaction.

Rulings that are issued by the National Office represent a written statement of the position of the IRS concerning the tax consequences of a course of action contemplated by the taxpayer. Letter (individual) rulings do not have the force and effect of law, but they do provide guidance and support for taxpayers in similar transactions. The IRS will issue rulings only on uncompleted, actual

---

FIGURE 16–2

Organization of the IRS National Office

	Duties
Commissioner of Internal Revenue	Presidential appointee; establishes policy, supervises the activities of the entire IRS organization, and acts in an advisory capacity to the Treasury on legislative matters.
Deputy Commissioner	Chief operating officer; assists the Commissioner in planning, directing, coordinating, and controlling policies, programs, and other activities and in developing issues and objectives for strategic management of the IRS; supervises the Chief Financial Officer, Chief Operations Officer, Chief Information Officer, and Assistants to the Commissioner and Senior Deputy Commissioner.
Chief Financial Officer	National spokesperson for the planning and management of resources functions; establishes practices, procedures, standards, and controls for the financial system of the IRS.
Chief Operations Officer	Adviser to the Commissioner and Deputy Commissioner on policy and operational matters affecting field functions: approval and examination of employee plans and exempt organizations, investigation of criminal fraud, examination of tax returns, collection of delinquent accounts, and the tax information program.
Chief Information Officer	Spokesperson for the functions of strategic technology planning, data administration, technology standards, and telecommunications; establishes policies and standards affecting these functions and the development and acquisition of computer hardware and software.

FIGURE 16–3

Organization of the IRS Field Organization

	Duties
Regional Commissioners (7)	Establish regional standards, programs, and policies; have final settlement authority in the administrative appeal procedure for disputed tax deficiencies.
District Directors (63)	Come into direct contact with taxpayers; collect delinquent taxes; perform audit work, including the selection of taxpayers for audit; issue determination letters to taxpayers.
Service Centers (10)	Process tax returns.

(rather than hypothetical) transactions or on transactions that have been completed before the filing of the tax return for the year in question.

In certain circumstances, the IRS will not issue a ruling. It ordinarily will not rule in cases that essentially involve a question of fact.[1] For example, no ruling will be issued to determine whether compensation paid to employees is reasonable in amount and therefore allowable as a deduction.[2]

A letter ruling represents the current opinion of the IRS on the tax consequences of a transaction with a given set of facts. IRS rulings are not unchangeable. They are frequently declared obsolete or are superseded by new rulings in response to tax law changes. However, revocation or modification of a ruling is usually not applied retroactively to the taxpayer who received the ruling, if he or she acted in good faith in reliance upon the ruling and if the facts in the ruling request were in agreement with the completed transaction. The IRS may revoke any ruling if, upon subsequent audit, the agent finds a misstatement or omission of facts or substantial discrepancies between the facts in the ruling request and the actual situation.

A ruling may be relied upon only by the taxpayer who requested and received it and must be attached to the tax return for the year in question.

Issuance of letter rulings benefits both the IRS and the taxpayer. The IRS ruling policy is an attempt to promote a uniform application of the tax laws. In addition, other benefits may accrue to the government through the issuance of rulings. Rulings may reduce the volume of litigation or number of disputes with revenue agents that would otherwise result, and they make the IRS aware of the significant transactions being consummated by taxpayers. A fee is charged for processing a ruling request.

From the taxpayer's point of view, an advance ruling reduces the uncertainty of potential tax consequences resulting from a proposed course of action. Taxpayers frequently request a letter ruling before the consummation of a tax-free corporate reorganization. This is due to the severe tax consequences that would result if the reorganization were subsequently deemed to be taxable. Liquidations, stock redemptions, and transfers to controlled corporations under § 351 are other sensitive areas in which taxpayers want confirmation.

Letter rulings that are of both sufficient importance and general interest may be published as Revenue Rulings (in anonymous form) and thus made available to all taxpayers. As noted in Chapter 1, Revenue Rulings are released weekly in the *Internal Revenue Bulletin* and later consolidated in permanent form in the *Cumulative Bulletin*.

In general, all unpublished letter rulings, determination letters, and technical advice memoranda are open to public inspection with identifying details and certain confidential information deleted. Letter rulings and technical advice memoranda are published by Research Institute of America and Commerce Clearing House and can be obtained through the electronic document retrieval services, WESTLAW, LEXIS, and RIATAX (formerly PHINet). The general availability of such materials assists in the conduct of tax research and planning.

IRS Procedure—Additional Issuances

In addition to issuing unpublished letter rulings and published rulings and procedures, the IRS issues determination letters and technical advice memoranda.

---

1. Rev.Proc. 92–1, I.R.B. No. 1, 9.   2. Rev.Proc. 92–3, I.R.B. No. 1, 39.

A determination letter is issued by the District Director for a completed transaction when the issue involved is covered by judicial or statutory authority, regulations, or rulings. Determination letters are issued for various death, gift, income, excise, and employment tax matters.

———————————————— EXAMPLE 1 ————————————————

T Corporation recently opened a car clinic and has employed numerous mechanics. The corporation is not certain if the mechanics are to be treated as employees or as independent contractors for withholding and payroll tax purposes. T Corporation may request a determination letter from the appropriate District Director. ◆

———————————————— EXAMPLE 2 ————————————————

Assume the same facts as in Example 1. T Corporation would like to establish a pension plan that qualifies for the tax advantages of §§ 401 through 404. To determine whether the plan qualifies, T Corporation can request and obtain a determination letter from the IRS. ◆

———————————————— EXAMPLE 3 ————————————————

A group of physicians plans to form an association to construct and operate a hospital. The determination letter procedure is appropriate to ascertain the group's status—either subject to the Federal income tax or tax-exempt. ◆

A technical advice memorandum is rendered by the National Office to the District Director and/or Regional Commissioner in response to the specific request of an agent, Appellate Conferee, or District Director. The taxpayer may ask that a request for a technical advice memorandum be made if an issue in dispute is not treated by the law or precedent and/or published rulings or Regulations. Technical advice memoranda art also appropriate when there is reason to believe that the tax law is not being administered consistently by the IRS. For example, a taxpayer may inquire why an agent proposes to disallow a certain expenditure when agents in other districts permit the deduction. Technical advice requests arise from the audit process, whereas ruling requests are issued before any IRS audit.

Administrative Powers of the IRS

Examination of Records.   The Code authorizes the IRS to examine the taxpayer's books and records as part of the process of determining the correct amount of tax due. The IRS is also authorized to summon those persons responsible to appear and to produce the necessary books and records.[3] Taxpayers are required to maintain certain recordkeeping procedures and retain those records that are necessary to facilitate the audit. Therefore, the taxpayer and not the IRS has the burden of proof of substantiating any item on the tax return that is under examination. The files, workpapers, and other memoranda of a tax practitioner may be subpoenaed, since the courts have not extended to CPAs the privileged communication status that physicians and attorneys sometimes possess with respect to their clients.

Assessment and Demand.   The Code permits the IRS to assess a deficiency and to demand payment for the tax.[4] However, no assessment or effort to collect the tax may be made until 90 days after the issuance of a statutory notice of a deficiency (a 90-day letter). The taxpayer is therefore given 90 days to file a

---

3. § 7602.   4. § 6212.

petition to the U.S. Tax Court, effectively preventing the deficiency from being assessed or collected pending the outcome of the case.[5]

This assessment procedure has certain exceptions:

- The IRS may issue a deficiency assessment without waiting 90 days if mathematical errors on the return incorrectly state the tax at less than the true liability.
- If the IRS believes the assessment or collection of a deficiency is in jeopardy, it may assess the deficiency and demand immediate payment.[6] The taxpayer can avoid (stay) the collection of the jeopardy assessment by filing a bond for the amount of the tax and interest. This action prevents the sale of any property that has been seized by the IRS.

Following assessment of the tax, the IRS will issue a notice and demand for payment. The taxpayer is usually given 30 days after the notice and demand for payment to pay the tax.

IRS Collection Procedures. If the taxpayer neglects or refuses to pay the tax after the receipt of the 30-day notice and demand letter, a lien in favor of the IRS develops upon all property (whether realty or personalty, tangible or intangible) belonging to the taxpayer. This lien, commonly referred to as a statutory lien, is not valid until the IRS files Form 668 (Notice of Federal Tax Lien Under Internal Revenue Laws).

The levy power of the IRS is very broad. It allows the IRS to garnish (attach) wages and salary and to seize and sell all nonexempt property *by any means*. The IRS can make successive seizures on any property owned by the taxpayer until the levy is satisfied.[7]

In exceptional cases, an extension in the payment of a deficiency will be granted to prevent undue hardship.[8]

If property is transferred and the tax is not paid, the subsequent owners of the property may be liable for the tax. This pursuit of the tax liability against succeeding owners is referred to as transferee liability. For example, if an estate is insolvent and unable to pay the estate tax, the executor or the beneficiaries may be liable for the payment.[9]

The Audit Process

Selection of Returns for Audit. The IRS utilizes mathematical formulas to select tax returns that are most likely to contain errors and yield substantial amounts of additional tax revenues upon audit. The IRS does not openly disclose all of its audit selection techniques. However, the following observations can be made regarding the probability of a return's selection for audit:

- Certain groups of taxpayers are subject to audit more frequently than others. These groups include individuals with gross income in excess of $50,000, self-employed individuals with substantial business income and deductions, and cash businesses where the potential for tax evasion is high.

---

5. § 6213.
6. § 6861.
7. The taxpayer can keep certain personal and business property and a minimal amount of his or her income as a

subsistence allowance, even if a lien is outstanding. § 6334.
8. § 6161(b).
9. § 6901.

─────────────── EXAMPLE 4 ───────────────

T owns and operates a liquor store on a cash-and-carry basis. As all of T's sales are for cash, T might well be a prime candidate for an audit by the IRS. Cash transactions are easier to conceal than those made on credit. ◆

- If a taxpayer has been audited in a past year and the audit led to the assessment of a substantial deficiency, a return visit by the IRS can be expected.
- An audit might materialize if information returns (e.g., Form W–2, Form 1099) are not in substantial agreement with the income reported on the taxpayer's return. Over the years, the IRS has been able to correlate an increasing number of information returns with the returns filed by taxpayers. Obvious discrepancies do not necessitate formal audits but usually can be handled by correspondence with the taxpayer.
- If an individual's itemized deductions are in excess of norms established for various income levels, the probability of an audit is increased. Certain deductions (e.g., casualty and theft losses, business use of the home, tax-sheltered investments) are sensitive areas, since the IRS realizes that many taxpayers will determine the amount of the deduction incorrectly or may not be entitled to the deduction at all.
- The filing of a refund claim by the taxpayer may prompt an audit of the return.
- Certain returns are chosen on a random sample basis (known as the Taxpayer Compliance Measurement Program [TCMP]) to develop, update, and improve the mathematical formulas used in selecting returns. TCMP is a long-range research project designed to measure and evaluate taxpayer compliance characteristics. TCMP audits are tedious and time-consuming since the taxpayer generally is asked to verify most or all items on the tax return.
- Information is often obtained from other sources (e.g., other government agencies, news items, informants). The IRS can pay rewards to persons who provide information that leads to the detection and punishment of those who violate the tax laws. The rewards are paid at the discretion of a District Director and will not exceed 10 percent of the taxes, fines, and penalties recovered as a result of such information.[10]

─────────────── EXAMPLE 5 ───────────────

T reports to the police that burglars broke into his home while he was out of town and took a shoe box containing $25,000 in cash, among other things. A representative of the IRS reading the newspaper account of the burglary might well wonder why someone kept such a large amount of cash in a shoe box at home. ◆

─────────────── EXAMPLE 6 ───────────────

After 15 years, B is discharged by her employer, Dr. F. Shortly thereafter, the IRS receives a letter from B informing it that Dr. F keeps two sets of books, one of which substantially understates his cash receipts. ◆

Many individual taxpayers mistakenly assume that if they do not hear from the IRS within a few weeks following the filing of the return or if they have received a refund check, no audit will be forthcoming. As a practical matter, most individual returns are examined within two years from the date of filing. If not, they generally remain unaudited. All large corporations are subject to

─────────────

10. § 7623 and Reg. § 301.7623–1.

annual audits; in many instances, tax years remain open for long periods, since the taxpayer may agree to extend the statute of limitations pending settlement of unresolved issues.

Verification and Audit Procedures.   The tax return is initially checked for mathematical accuracy. A check is also made for deductions, exclusions, etc., that are clearly erroneous. An obvious error would be the failure to comply with the 7.5 percent limitation on the deduction for medical expenses. In such cases, the Service Center merely sends the taxpayer revised computations and a bill for the corrected amount of tax if the error results in additional tax liability. Taxpayers usually are able to settle such matters through direct correspondence with the IRS without the necessity of a formal audit.

Office audits are conducted by a representative of the District Director's Office, either in the office of the IRS or through correspondence. Individual returns with few or no items of business income are usually handled through the office audit procedure. In most instances, the taxpayer is required merely to substantiate a deduction, credit, or item of income that appears on the return. An individual may have claimed medical expenses that are larger than normal for taxpayers with comparable income. The taxpayer will be asked to present documentation in the form of canceled checks, invoices, etc., for the items in question. Note the substantiation procedure here that is absent from the mathematical check and simple error discovery process mentioned previously.

The *field audit* procedure is commonly used for corporate returns and for returns of individuals engaged in business or professional activities. This type of audit generally involves a more complete examination of a taxpayer's transactions. In contrast, an office audit usually is directed toward fewer items and is narrower in scope.

A field audit is conducted by IRS agents at the office or home of the taxpayer or at the office of the taxpayer's representative. Tax firms commonly meet with IRS agents in the firm's office during the field audit of a corporate client. The agent's work may be facilitated by a review of certain tax workpapers and discussions with the taxpayer's representative about items appearing on the tax return.

Upon a showing of good cause, a taxpayer may request and obtain a reassignment of his or her case from an office to a field audit. The inconvenience and expense involved in transporting records and other supporting data to the agent's office may constitute good cause for reassignment.

Prior to or at the initial interview, the IRS must provide the taxpayer with an explanation of the audit process that is the subject of the interview and describe the taxpayer's rights under that process. If the taxpayer clearly states at any time during the interview that he or she wishes to consult with an attorney, CPA, or enrolled agent or any other person permitted to represent the taxpayer before the IRS, then the IRS representative must suspend the interview.[11]

Any officer or employee of the IRS must, upon advance request, allow a taxpayer to make an audio recording of any in-person interview with the officer or employee concerning the determination and collection of any tax. The recording of IRS audit conferences may have significant legal implications. For example, if any IRS employee recklessly or intentionally disregards regulatory rules in the collection of Federal tax, the taxpayer can bring a civil action for damages in a Federal District Court.[12]

Settlement with the Revenue Agent.   Following an audit, the IRS agent may either accept the return as filed or recommend certain adjustments. The

11. § 7521(b).   12. § 7433.

Revenue Agent's Report (RAR) is reviewed by the agent's group supervisor and the Review Staff within the IRS. In most instances, the agent's proposed adjustments are approved. However, it is not uncommon for the Review Staff or group supervisor to request additional information or to raise new issues.

Agents must adhere strictly to IRS policy as reflected in published rulings, Regulations, and other releases. The agent cannot settle an unresolved issue based upon the probability of winning the case in court. Usually, issues involving factual questions can be settled at the agent level, and it may be advantageous for both the taxpayer and the IRS to reach agreement at the earliest point in the settlement process. For example, it may be to the taxpayer's advantage to reach agreement at the agent level and avoid any further opportunity for the IRS to raise new issues.

A deficiency (an amount in excess of tax shown on the return or tax previously assessed) may be proposed at the agent level. The taxpayer may wish to pursue to a higher level the disputed issues upon which this deficiency is based. The taxpayer's progress through the appeal process is discussed in subsequent sections of this chapter.

If agreement is reached upon the proposed deficiency, the taxpayer signs Form 870 (Waiver of Restrictions on Assessment and Collection of Deficiency in Tax). One advantage to the taxpayer of signing Form 870 at this point is that interest stops accumulating on the deficiency 30 days after the form is filed.[13] When this form is signed, the taxpayer effectively waives his or her right to receive a statutory notice of deficiency (90-day letter) and to subsequently petition the Tax Court. In addition, it is no longer possible for the taxpayer to go to the Appeals Division. The signing of Form 870 at the agent level generally closes the case. However, since Form 870 does not have the effect of a closing agreement, even after the taxpayer pays the deficiency, he or she may subsequently sue for refund of the tax in a Federal District Court or in the Claims Court. The IRS is not restricted by Form 870 and may assess additional deficiencies if deemed necessary.

The Taxpayer Appeal Process

If agreement cannot be reached at the agent level, the taxpayer receives a copy of the Revenue Agent's Report and a transmittal letter, which is commonly referred to as the 30-day letter. The taxpayer has 30 days to request an administrative appeal. If an appeal is not requested, a statutory notice of deficiency will be issued (90-day letter). Figure 16–4 illustrates the taxpayer's alternatives when a disagreement with the IRS persists.

A taxpayer who wishes to appeal must make an appropriate request to the Appeals Division. The request must be accompanied by a written protest, except in the following cases:

- The proposed tax deficiency does not exceed $10,000 for any of the tax periods involved in the audit.
- The deficiency resulted from a correspondence or office audit (i.e., not as a result of a field audit).

The Appeals Division is authorized to settle all tax disputes based on the hazards of litigation. Since the Appeals Division has final settlement authority until a statutory notice of deficiency (90-day letter) has been issued, the taxpayer may be able to obtain a negotiated settlement. In addition, an overall favorable

13. § 6601(c).

settlement may be reached by "trading" disputed issues. The Appeals Division occasionally may raise new issues if the grounds are substantial and of significant tax impact.

Both the Appeals Division and the taxpayer have the right to request technical advice memoranda from the National Office of the IRS. A technical advice memorandum that is favorable to the taxpayer is binding on the Appeals Division. Even if the technical advice memorandum is favorable to the IRS, the Appeals Division may nevertheless settle the case based on the hazards of litigation.

—————————————— EXAMPLE 7 ——————————————

At the time of the audit of T, the corporation that T controls had advances outstanding to T in the amount of $80,000. The IRS field agent held that these advances were constructive dividends to T (refer to the discussion in Chapter 4). Some facts point toward this result (e.g., the corporation is closely held, T has made no repayments, and the loan balance has increased over several years). Other facts, however, appear to indicate that these advances are bona fide loans (e.g., the advances are evidenced by a written instrument that provides for interest, T has the independent means of repayment, and the corporation has a good dividend-paying record).

FIGURE 16–4   **Income Tax Appeal Procedure**

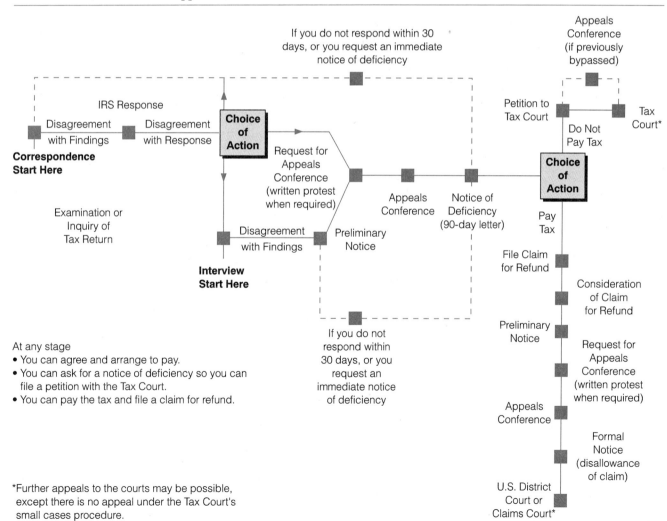

The Appeals Division and T's representative assess the hazards of litigation as being 50% for each side. Thus, if T chose to take the issue to court, she would have an even chance of winning or losing her case. Based on this assessment, both sides agree to treat $40,000 of the advance as a dividend and $40,000 as a bona fide loan. The agreement enables T to avoid $40,000 of dividend income (the loan portion) and saves her the cost of litigating the issue.

Thus, by going to the Appeals Division, T obtains a satisfactory settlement otherwise unobtainable from the agent. ◆

If agreement cannot be reached with the Appeals Division, the IRS issues a statutory notice of deficiency (90-day letter), which gives the taxpayer 90 days to file a petition with the Tax Court. After the case has been docketed in the Tax Court, the taxpayer has the opportunity to arrange for possible pretrial settlement with the Regional Counsel of the IRS (the attorney who will represent the United States in the Tax Court trial). The Appeals Division settlement power is transferred to the Regional Counsel when the case is docketed for a Tax Court trial after the issuance of the statutory notice of deficiency.

Taxpayers who file a petition with the U.S. Tax Court have the option of having their case heard before the informal Small Cases Division if the amount of the deficiency or claimed overpayment does not exceed $10,000.[14] If the Small Cases Division is used, neither party may appeal the case. The decisions of the Small Cases Division are not published or otherwise available as precedents for other cases.

The economic costs of a settlement offer from the Appeals Division should be weighed against the costs of litigation and the probability of winning the case. The taxpayer should also consider the impact of the settlement upon the tax liability for future periods in addition to the years under audit.

If a settlement is reached with the Appeals Division, the taxpayer is required to sign Form 870AD. Interest stops running on the deficiency when the Appeals Division accepts the Form 870AD. The IRS considers this settlement to be binding upon both parties unless fraud, malfeasance, concealment, or misrepresentation of material fact has occurred. The question of whether this settlement form is binding upon the taxpayer (whether settlement prevents the taxpayer from filing a subsequent refund claim and suit for refund) has been litigated with conflicting results.[15]

Offers in Compromise and Closing Agreements

The Code provides specific authority for the IRS to negotiate a compromise if the taxpayer's ability to pay the tax is doubtful.[16] If the taxpayer is financially unable to pay the total amount of the tax, a Form 656 (Offer in Compromise) must be filed with the District Director or the IRS Service Center.

The IRS investigates the claim by evaluating the taxpayer's financial ability to pay the tax. In some instances, the compromise settlement will include an agreement for final settlement of the tax through payments of a specified percentage of the taxpayer's future earnings. This settlement procedure usually entails lengthy periods of negotiation with the IRS and is used only in extreme cases.

The IRS has statutory authority to enter into a written agreement allowing taxes to be paid on an installment basis if that arrangement will facilitate

---

14. § 7463(a).

15. Compare *Stair v. U.S.*, 75–1 USTC ¶9463, 35 AFTR2d 75–1515, 516 F.2d 560 (CA–2, 1975), with *Unita Livestock*

Corp. v. U.S., 66–1 USTC ¶9193, 17 AFTR2d 254, 355 F.2d 761 (CA–10, 1966).

16. § 7122.

collection. The agreement may be modified or terminated because of (1) inadequate information or jeopardy; (2) subsequent change in financial condition; or (3) failure to pay any installment when due or to provide requested information.[17]

If the amount of tax liability involved is uncertain, a closing agreement may be appropriate. The IRS has identified situations in which closing agreements will be issued:[18]

1. An executor or administrator requires a determination of the tax liability either to facilitate the distribution of estate assets or to relieve himself or herself of fiduciary responsibility.
2. A liquidating corporation needs a determination of tax liability to proceed with the process of dissolution.
3. A taxpayer wishes to close returns on an annual basis.
4. Creditors demand evidence of the tax liability.

A closing agreement is binding on both the taxpayer and the IRS, except upon a subsequent showing of fraud, malfeasance, or misrepresentation of a material fact.[19] The closing agreement may be used when disputed issues carry over to future years. It may also be employed to dispose of a dispute involving a specific issue for a prior year or a proposed transaction involving future years. If, for example, the IRS is willing to make substantial concessions in the valuation of assets for death tax purposes, it may require a closing agreement from the recipient of the property to establish the income tax basis of the assets.

Interest

An important consideration for the taxpayer during negotiations with the IRS is the interest that accrues upon overpayments, deficiency assessments, and unpaid taxes. A taxpayer can effectively stop the accrual of interest upon a deficiency assessment by signing Form 870 and paying the tax. After taking this action, the taxpayer can sue in a Federal District Court or the Claims Court to recover the amount of the tax payment.

Determination of the Interest Rate. Several years ago, Congress recognized that the interest rates applicable to Federal tax underpayments (deficiencies) and overpayments (refunds) should be closer to the rates applied in the business world. Currently, the Code provides for the rates to be determined quarterly. [20] Thus, the rates that are determined during January are effective for the following April through June.

IRS interest is based on the Federal short-term rates published periodically by the IRS in Revenue Rulings. They are based on the average market yield on outstanding marketable obligations of the United States with remaining maturity of three years or less.

Underpayments are subject to the Federal short-term rates plus three percentage points, and overpayments carry the Federal short-term rates plus two percentage points. Consequently, the rate for tax deficiencies is one percentage point higher than the rate for tax refunds. For the second quarter of 1992, interest on tax deficiencies was set at 8 percent, and interest on refunds was 7 percent. In previous years, interest rates have ranged from a low of 6 percent to a high of 20 percent.

---

17. § 6159.
18. Rev.Proc. 68–16, 1968–1 C.B. 770.

19. § 7121(b).
20. § 6621.

In cases of deficiency assessments or claims for refund, interest is computed in accordance with the rates in effect during the period involved. For assessments where the statute of limitations is not applicable (e.g., no return was filed or fraud was involved—see the discussion later in the chapter), determining the interest element can be quite difficult.

Computation of the Amount of Interest. Interest is compounded daily.[21] Depending on the interest rate applicable, the daily compounding approach conceivably could double the principal amount over a period of five to eight years.

Tables for determining the daily compounded amount are available from the IRS. The tables ease the burden of those who prepare late returns where additional taxes are due.[22]

IRS Deficiency Assessments. Interest usually accrues from the unextended due date of the return until 30 days after the taxpayer agrees to the deficiency by signing Form 870. If the taxpayer does not pay the amount shown on the IRS's "notice and demand" (tax bill) within 30 days, interest again accrues on the deficiency.

Refund of Taxpayer's Overpayments. If the overpayment is refunded to the taxpayer within 45 days after the date the return is filed or is due, no interest is allowed. Interest is authorized, however, when the taxpayer files an amended return or makes a claim for refund of a prior year's tax (e.g., when net operating loss or investment tax credit carrybacks result in refunds of a prior year's tax payments).

In the past, when interest rates were sometimes as high as 20 percent, many taxpayers found it advantageous to delay filing various tax returns that led to refunds. Thus, the IRS was placed in the unfortunate role of providing taxpayers with a high-yield savings account. Under current law, however, taxpayers applying for refunds receive interest as follows:

- When a return is filed after the due date, interest on any overpayment accrues from the date of filing. However, no interest will be due if the IRS makes the refund within 45 days of the date of filing.

———————————————— EXAMPLE 8 ————————————————

T, a calendar year taxpayer, files her return for 1991 on December 1, 1992. The return reflects an overwithholding of $2,500. On June 8, 1993, T receives a refund of her 1991 overpayment. Under these circumstances, the interest on T's refund began to accrue on December 1, 1992 (not April 15, 1992). ◆

———————————————— EXAMPLE 9 ————————————————

Assume the same facts as in Example 8, except that the refund is paid to T on January 5, 1993 (rather than June 8, 1993). No interest is payable by the IRS, since the refund was made within 45 days of the filing of the return. ◆

- In no event will interest accrue on an overpayment unless the return that is filed is in "processible form." Generally, this means that the return must contain enough information to enable the IRS to identify the taxpayer and to determine the tax (and overpayment) involved.

———————

21. § 6622.

22. Rev.Proc. 83–7, 1983–1 C.B. 583.

■ In the case of a carryback (e.g., net operating loss, capital loss, certain tax credits), interest on any refund begins to accrue on the due date of the return (disregarding extensions) for the year in which the carryback arises. Even then, however, no interest accrues until a return is filed or, if already filed, the IRS pays the refund within 45 days.

─────────────────────── EXAMPLE 10 ───────────────────────

X Corporation, a calendar year taxpayer, incurs a net operating loss during 1992 that it can carry back to tax year 1989 for a refund. On December 27, 1993, it files a claim for refund. The earliest that interest can begin to accrue in this situation is March 15, 1993, but since the return was not filed until December 27, 1993, the later date controls. If, however, the IRS pays the refund within 45 days of December 27, 1993, no interest need be paid. ◆

Taxpayer Penalties

To promote and enforce taxpayer compliance with the U.S. voluntary self-assessment system of taxation, Congress has enacted a comprehensive array of penalties with respect to the tax system.

Tax penalties may involve both criminal and civil offenses. Criminal tax penalties are imposed only after the usual criminal process, in which the taxpayer is entitled to the same constitutional guarantees as nontax criminal defendants. Normally, a criminal penalty provides for imprisonment. Civil tax penalties are collected in the same manner as other taxes and usually provide only for monetary fines. Criminal and civil penalties are not mutually exclusive; therefore, both types of sanctions may be imposed on a taxpayer.

The Code characterizes tax penalties as additions to tax; thus, they cannot subsequently be deducted by the taxpayer.

Ad valorem penalties are additions to tax that are based upon a percentage of the owed tax. *Accessable penalties,* on the other hand, typically include a flat dollar amount. Assessable penalties are not subject to review by the Tax Court, but ad valorem penalties are subject to the same deficiency procedures that apply to the underlying tax.

Failure to File and Failure to Pay. For a failure to file a tax return by the due date (including extensions), a penalty of 5 percent per month (up to a maximum of 25 percent) is imposed on the amount of tax shown as due on the return.[23] If the failure to file is attributable to fraud, the penalty becomes 15 percent per month, to a minimum of 75 percent of the tax.[24]

For a failure to pay the tax due as shown on the return, a penalty of one-half of 1 percent per month (up to a maximum of 25 percent) is imposed on the amount of the tax. The penalty is doubled if the taxpayer fails to pay the tax after receiving a deficiency assessment.

In all of these cases, a fraction of a month counts as a full month. These penalties relate to the net amount of the tax due.

─────────────────────── EXAMPLE 11 ───────────────────────

T, a calendar year self-employed taxpayer, prepays $18,000 for income taxes during 1991. Her total tax liability for 1991 proves to be $20,000. Without obtaining an extension from the IRS, she files her Form 1040 in early August 1992 and encloses a check for the balance due of $2,000. The failure to file and the failure to pay penalties apply to the $2,000 (not the $20,000). ◆

───────────

23. § 6651(a).   **24.** § 6651(f).

During any month in which both the failure to file penalty and the failure to pay penalty apply, the failure to file penalty is reduced by the amount of the failure to pay penalty.

EXAMPLE 12

R files his tax return 10 days after the due date. Along with the return, he remits a check for $3,000, which is the balance of the tax he owes. Disregarding any interest liabilities, R's total penalties are as follows:

Failure to pay penalty (½ of 1% × $3,000)		$ 15
Plus:		
Failure to file penalty (5% × $3,000)	$150	
Less failure to pay penalty for the same period	15	
Failure to file penalty		135
Total penalties		$150

The penalties for one full month are imposed even though R was delinquent by only 10 days. Unlike the method used to compute interest, any part of a month is treated as a whole month. ◆

Because the existing penalty for failure to file may not be a sufficient deterrent when the tax due is small or the delay in filing is short, the law was amended to provide for a minimum penalty. The minimum penalty is the *lesser* of $100 or the amount of tax still due and applies only if the return is not filed within 60 days (with allowed extensions) of its due date.

When the minimum failure to file penalty applies, the amount of the failure to file penalty (when applicable) is not reduced by the failure to pay penalty. Rather, both penalties apply concurrently, and the combined total is due and owing.

EXAMPLE 13

T, a calendar year individual taxpayer, files her 1992 return 70 days after its due date. T did not obtain an extension of time for filing her return, and the return reflects additional income tax due of $300.

The regular penalty for T's delinquency would have been $45 (as determined under the procedure used in Example 12 using three months). Due to the minimum penalty, T's failure to file penalty will be $100. To this must be added a failure to pay penalty of $4.50 [1.5% (0.5% per month for three months) × $300], for total penalties of $104.50. ◆

These penalties can be avoided if the taxpayer can show that the failure to file and/or failure to pay was due to reasonable cause and not due to willful neglect. The Code is silent on what constitutes reasonable cause, and the Regulations do little to clarify this important concept.[25] Court decisions, however, do set some specific criteria, summarized as follows:

■ Reasonable cause was found where the taxpayer relied on the advice of a *competent* tax adviser given in good faith, the facts were fully disclosed to the adviser, and he or she considered that the specific question represented reasonable cause.[26] No reasonable cause was found, however,

---

25. Reg. § 301.6651–1(c)(1) likens reasonable cause to the exercise of "ordinary business care and prudence" on the part of the taxpayer.

26. *Estate of Norma S. Bradley,* 33 TCM 70, T.C.Memo. 1974–17.

where the taxpayer delegated the filing task to another, even when that person was an accountant or an attorney.[27]

- Among the reasons not qualifying as reasonable cause were lack of information on the due date of the return,[28] illness that did not incapacitate a taxpayer from completing a return,[29] refusal of the taxpayer's spouse to cooperate for a joint return,[30] and ignorance or misunderstanding of the tax law.[31]
- Reasonable cause for failure to pay is presumed under the automatic four-month extension (Form 4868) when the additional tax due is no greater than 10 percent of the tax liability shown on the return.

Accuracy-Related Penalties.   Major civil penalties relating to the accuracy of tax return data, including misstatements stemming from taxpayer negligence and improper valuation of income and deductions, are coordinated under the umbrella term *accuracy-related penalties*.[32] This consolidation of related penalties into a single levy eliminates the possibility that multiple penalties will be stacked (i.e., when more than one type of penalty applies to a single understatement of tax).

The accuracy-related penalties each amount to 20 percent of the portion of the tax underpayment that is attributable to one or more of the following infractions: (1) negligence or disregard of rules and regulations;[33] (2) substantial understatement of tax liability; (3) substantial valuation overstatement; and, (4) substantial valuation understatement. The penalties apply only where the taxpayer fails to show either a reasonable cause for the underpayment or a good faith effort to comply with the tax law.

Negligence.   For purposes of this accuracy-related penalty, *negligence* includes any failure to make a reasonable attempt to comply with the provisions of the tax law. The penalty also applies to any disregard (whether careless, reckless, or intentional) of rules and regulations.[34] The penalty can be avoided upon a showing of reasonable cause and that the taxpayer acted in good faith.[35]

The negligence penalty is applicable to *all* taxes, but does not apply when fraud is involved.

A negligence penalty might be assessed when the taxpayer fails to report gross income, overstates deductions, or fails to keep adequate records with which to comply with the law. When the taxpayer takes a nonfrivolous position on the return that is contrary to a published pronouncement of the IRS, the penalty is waived if the taxpayer has disclosed the disputed position in an attachment to the return.

Substantial Understatement of Tax Liability.   The understatement penalty is designed to strike at middle- and high-income taxpayers who play the so-called audit lottery.[36] Some taxpayers take questionable and undisclosed positions on their tax returns in the hope that the return will not be selected for audit. Disclosing the positions would have called attention to the return and increased the probability of audit.

---

27. *U.S. v. Boyle*, 85–1 USTC ¶13,602, 55 AFTR2d 85–1535, 105 S.Ct. 687 (USSC, 1985).

28. *Beck Chemical Equipment Co.*, 27 T.C. 840 (1957).

29. *Jacob Gassman*, 26 TCM 213, T.C.Memo. 1967–42, and *Babetta Schmidt*, 28 T.C. 367 (1957). Compare *Estate of Kirchner*, 46 B.T.A. 578 (1942).

30. *Electric and Neon, Inc.*, 56 T.C. 1324 (1971).

31. *Stevens Brothers Foundation, Inc.*, 39 T.C. 93 (1965).

32. § 6662.

33. Section 6653 represents prior law relative to civil negligence.

34. § 6662(c).

35. § 6664(c)(1).

36. § 6662(b)(2).

A substantial understatement of a tax liability transpires when the understatement exceeds the larger of 10 percent of the tax due or $5,000 ($10,000 for a C corporation). The understatement to which the penalty applies is 10 percent of the difference between the amount of tax required to be shown on the return and the amount of tax actually shown on the return.

The penalty can be avoided under any of the following circumstances:

■ The taxpayer has *substantial authority* for the treatment.[37]
■ The relevant facts affecting the treatment are adequately disclosed in the return or in a statement attached to the return.
■ The taxpayer has reasonable cause and acts in good faith.

Substantial authority is to be tested by looking to the taxpayer's position and not to the contrary authority. However, the existence of substantial authority does not necessarily mean that a taxpayer will prevail in a particular conflict with the IRS. Rather, the taxpayer merely has a defense to the imposition of the substantial understatement of tax liability penalty.

Penalty for Overvaluation. The objective of the overvaluation penalty is to deter taxpayers from inflating values (or basis), usually of charitable contributions of property, to reduce income taxes. The following are the penalty's main features:[38]

■ The penalty is 20 percent of the tax that would have been paid had the correct valuation (or basis) been used.[39]
■ The penalty applies only when the valuation (or basis) used is 200 percent or more of the correct valuation (or basis).
■ The penalty applies only to the extent that the resulting income tax underpayment exceeds $5,000 ($10,000 for C corporations).

─────────────────────── Example 14 ───────────────────────

In 1985, T (a calendar year taxpayer) purchased a painting for $10,000. In early 1993, when the painting is worth $18,000 (as later determined by the IRS), T donates the painting to an art museum. Based on the appraisal of a cousin who is an amateur artist, T deducts $40,000 for the donation on a timely filed return for 1993. Since T was in the 31% tax bracket, overstating the deduction by $22,000 results in a tax underpayment of $6,820 for 1993.

T's penalty for overvaluation is $1,364 [20% × $6,820 (the underpayment that resulted from using $40,000 instead of $18,000)]. ◆

The substantial valuation overstatement penalty can be avoided if the taxpayer can show reasonable cause and good faith. However, when the overvaluation involves *charitable deduction property*, the taxpayer must show two *additional* facts:

■ The claimed value of the property is based on a qualified appraisal made by a qualified appraiser.
■ The taxpayer made a good faith investigation of the value of the contributed property.[40]

─────────────────────────────

37. Review the discussion related to Footnote 53 in Chapter 1 of this text.
38. § 6662(b)(3).

39. For gross valuation mistatements (i.e., 400% or more), the penalty increases to 40%. § 6662(h).
40. § 6664(c)(2).

Based on these criteria, T in Example 14 would be unlikely to avoid the penalty. A cousin who is an amateur artist does not meet the definition of a qualified appraiser. Likewise, T has not made a good faith investigation of the value of the contributed property.

Penalty for Undervaluation.   When attempting to minimize the income tax, it is to the benefit of taxpayers to *overvalue* deductions. When attempting to minimize transfer taxes (estate and gift taxes), however, executors and donors may be inclined to *undervalue* the assets transferred. A lower valuation reduces estate and gift taxes. An accuracy-related penalty is imposed for substantial estate or gift tax valuation understatements.[41]

The penalty is 20 percent of the transfer tax that would have been due had the correct valuation been used on Form 706 (estate tax return) or Form 709 (gift tax return). The penalty only applies if the value of the property claimed on the return is 50 percent or less of the amount determined to be correct. The threshold amount for the application of the penalty is transfer tax liability in excess of $5,000. Thus, the penalty does not apply if the additional estate or gift tax due is $5,000 or less.

As with other accuracy-related penalties, reasonable cause and good faith on the part of the taxpayer is a defense.

Civil Fraud Penalty.   A 75 percent civil penalty is imposed on any underpayment resulting from fraud on the part of the taxpayer.[42] For this penalty, the burden of proof *is upon the IRS* to show by a preponderance of the evidence that the taxpayer had a specific intent to evade a tax.

Once the IRS has initially established that fraud has occurred, the taxpayer then bears the burden of proof to show by a preponderance of the evidence the portion of the underpayment that is not attributable to fraud.

Although the Code and the Regulations do not provide any assistance in ascertaining what constitutes civil fraud, it is clear that mere negligence on the part of the taxpayer (however great) will not suffice. In this regard, the particular facts involved must be considered. Fraud has been found in cases of manipulation of the books,[43] substantial omissions from income,[44] and erroneous deductions.[45]

The penalty is imposed only on the portion of the underpayment attributable to fraud.

─────────────── EXAMPLE 15 ───────────────

T underpaid his income tax for 1993 by $90,000. The IRS can prove that $60,000 of the underpayment was due to fraud. T can prove by a preponderance of the evidence that $30,000 of the underpayment was not due to fraud. The civil fraud penalty is $45,000 (75% × $60,000). ◆

If the underpayment of tax is partially attributable to negligence and partially attributable to fraud, the negligence penalty does not apply to any portion of the underpayment on which a fraud penalty is imposed.

41. § 6662(b)(5).

42. § 6663. As noted later in the chapter, fraudulent returns carry no statute of limitations.

43. *Dogget v. Comm.,* 60–1 USTC ¶9342, 5 AFTR2d 1034, 275 F.2d 823 (CA–4, 1960).

44. *Harvey Brodsky,* 21 TCM 578, T.C.Memo. 1962–105.

45. *Lash v. Comm.,* 57–2 USTC ¶9725, 51 AFTR 492, 245 F.2d 20 (CA–1, 1957).

Criminal Penalties. In addition to civil fraud penalties, the Code contains numerous criminal sanctions that carry various monetary fines and/or imprisonment. The difference between civil and criminal fraud often is one of degree. A characteristic of criminal fraud is the presence of willfulness on the part of the taxpayer. Thus, § 7201, dealing with attempts to evade or defeat a tax, contains the following language:

> Any person who *willfully* attempts in any manner to evade or defeat any tax imposed by this title or the payment thereof shall, in addition to other penalties provided by law, be guilty of a felony and, upon conviction thereof, shall be fined not more than $100,000 ($500,000 in the case of a corporation), or imprisoned not more than five years, or both, together with the costs of prosecution. [Emphasis added.]

As to the burden of proof, the IRS must show that the taxpayer was guilty of willful evasion "beyond the shadow of any reasonable doubt." Recall that in the civil fraud area, the standard applied to measure culpability is "by a preponderance of the evidence."

Failure to Pay Estimated Taxes. A penalty is imposed for a failure to pay estimated income taxes. The penalty applies to individuals and corporations and is based on the rate of interest in effect for deficiency assessments.[46] The penalty also applies to trusts and certain estates that are required to make estimated tax payments. The penalty is not imposed if the tax due for the year (less any amounts withheld) is less than $500. For employees, an equal part of withholding is deemed paid on each due date.

The penalty generally can be avoided if the quarterly payments were based on one-fourth of the lesser of 90 percent (93 percent for corporations) of the current year's tax or 100 percent of the preceding 12-month year's tax (even if none was due). Quarterly payments are to be made on or before the fifteenth day of the fourth month (April 15 for a calendar year taxpayer), sixth month, ninth month, and the first month of the following year. Corporations must make the last quarterly payment by the twelfth month of the same year. High-income individuals and large corporations can use the prior-year exception only on the first-quarter installment.

The penalty is levied on the amount of the underpayment for the period of the underpayment. Payments of estimated tax are credited against unpaid installments in the order in which the installments are required to be paid.

EXAMPLE 16

Mrs. T, who had no income tax withheld, made the following payments of estimated tax during 1993:

April 15, 1993	$1,400
June 17, 1993	2,300
September 16, 1993	1,500
January 15, 1994	1,800

Mrs. T's actual tax for 1993 is $8,000. Her tax in 1992 was $10,000. Therefore, each installment should have been at least $1,800 [($8,000 × 90%) × 25%].

Of the payment on June 17, $400 is credited to the unpaid balance of the first quarterly installment due on April 15, thereby effectively stopping the underpayment penalty for the first quarterly period. Of the remaining $1,900 payment on June 17,

---

46. §§ 6654 and 6655.

$100 is credited to the September 16 payment, resulting in this third quarterly payment being $200 short. Then $200 of the January 15 payment is credited to the September 16 shortfall, ending the period of underpayment for that portion due. The January 15, 1994, installment is now underpaid by $200, and a penalty will apply from January 15, 1994, to April 15, 1994 (unless paid sooner). ◆

In computing the penalty, Form 2210 (Underpayment of Estimated Tax by Individuals) or Form 2220 (Underpayment of Estimated Tax by Corporations) is used.

False Information with Respect to Withholding. The Federal income tax system is based on a pay-as-you-go approach, an important element of which involves withholding procedures on wages. One way employees might hope to avoid the operation of the withholding procedure would be to falsify the information provided to the employer on Form W–4 (Employee Withholding Allowance Certificate). For example, by overstating the number of exemptions, income tax withholdings could be cut or completely eliminated.

To encourage compliance, the tax law imposes a civil penalty of $500 when a taxpayer claims withholding allowances based on false information. The criminal penalty for willfully failing to supply information or for willfully supplying false or fraudulent information in connection with wage withholding is a fine of up to $1,000 and/or up to one year of imprisonment.[47]

Failure to Make Deposits of Taxes and Overstatements of Deposits. When the business is not doing well or cash-flow problems develop, employers have a great temptation to "borrow" from Uncle Sam. One way this can be done is to fail to pay over to the IRS the amounts that have been withheld from the wages of employees for FICA and income tax purposes. The IRS does not appreciate being denied the use of these funds and has a number of weapons at its disposal to discourage the practice, including the following:

- A penalty of up to 15 percent of any underdeposited amount not paid unless it can be shown that the failure is due to reasonable cause and not to willful neglect.[48]
- Various criminal penalties.[49]
- A 100 percent penalty if the employer's actions are willful.[50] The penalty is based on the amount of the tax evaded, not collected, or not accounted for or paid over. Since the penalty is assessable against the "responsible person" of the business, more than one party may be vulnerable (e.g., the president and treasurer of a corporation). Although the IRS may assess the penalty against several persons, it cannot collect more than the 100 percent due.

In addition to these penalties, the actual tax due must be remitted. An employer remains liable for the amount that should have been paid over even if the withholdings have not been taken out of the wages of its employees.[51]

Statutes of Limitations

A statute of limitations defines the period of time during which one party may pursue against another party a cause of action or other suit allowed under the

---

47. §§ 6682 and 7205.

48. § 6656.

49. See, for example, § 7202 (willful failure to collect or pay

over a tax).

50. § 6672.

51. § 3403.

governing law. Failure to satisfy any requirement provides the other party with an absolute defense should he or she see fit to invoke the statute. Inequity would result if there were no statute limiting action. Permitting the lapse of an extended period of time between the initiation of a claim and its pursuit could place the defense of the claim in jeopardy. Witnesses may have died or disappeared; records or other evidence may have been discarded or destroyed.

In terms of Federal tax consequences, it is important to distinguish between the statute of limitations on assessments by the IRS and the statute applicable to refund claims by a taxpayer.

Assessment and the Statute of Limitations. In general, any tax that is imposed must be assessed within three years of the filing of the return (or, if later, the due date of the return).[52] Some exceptions to this three-year limitation follow:

- If no return is filed or a fraudulent return is filed, assessments can be made at any time. There is, in effect, no statute of limitations.
- If a taxpayer omits an amount of gross income in excess of 25 percent of the gross income stated on the return, the statute of limitations is increased to six years. The courts have interpreted this extended period of limitations rule to include only items affecting income and not the omission of items affecting cost of goods sold.[53] In addition, gross income includes capital gains in the *gross* income amount (not reduced by capital losses).

————————————— EXAMPLE 17 —————————————

During 1988, T (an individual taxpayer) had the following income transactions (all of which were duly reported on his timely filed return):

Gross receipts		$ 480,000
Less cost of goods sold		(400,000)
Net business income		$ 80,000
Capital gains and losses—		
Capital gain	$36,000	
Capital loss	12,000	24,000
Total income		$ 104,000

T retains your services in 1993 as a tax consultant. It seems that he inadvertently omitted some income on his 1988 return and he wishes to know if he is "safe" under the statute of limitations. The six-year statute of limitations would apply, putting T in a vulnerable position only if he omitted more than $129,000 on his 1988 return [($480,000 + $36,000) × 25%]. ◆

- The statute of limitations may be extended by mutual consent of the District Director and the taxpayer.[54] This extension covers a definite period and is made by signing Form 872 (Consent to Extend the Time to Assess Tax). The extension is frequently requested by the IRS when the lapse of the statutory period is imminent and the audit has not been completed. In some situations, the extensions may apply only to unresolved issues. This practice often is applied to audits of corporate taxpayers and explains why many corporations have "open years."

---

52. §§ 6501(a) and (b)(1).
53. *The Colony, Inc. v. Comm.*, 58–2 USTC ¶9593, 1 AFTR2d 1894,

78 S.Ct. 1033 (USSC, 1958).
54. § 6501(c)(4).

Special rules relating to assessment are applicable in the following situations:

- Taxpayers (corporations, estates, etc.) may request a prompt assessment of the tax.
- The period for assessment of the personal holding company tax is extended to six years after the return is filed only if certain filing requirements are met.
- If a partnership or trust files a tax return (a partnership or trust return) in good faith and a later determination renders it taxable as a corporation, the return is deemed to be the corporate return for purposes of the statute of limitations.
- The assessment period for capital loss, net operating loss, and investment credit carrybacks is generally related to the determination of tax in the year of the loss or unused credit rather than in the carryback years.

If the tax is assessed within the period of limitations, the IRS has 10 years from the date of assessment to collect the tax.[55] However, if the IRS issues a statutory notice of deficiency to the taxpayer, who then files a Tax Court petition, the statute is suspended on both the deficiency assessment and the period of collection until 60 days after the decision of the Tax Court becomes final.[56]

Refund Claims and the Statute of Limitations.   To receive a tax refund, the taxpayer is required to file a valid refund claim. The official form for filing a claim is Form 1040X for individuals and Form 1120X for corporations. A refund claim must follow certain procedural requirements. If it does not, the claim may be rejected with no consideration of its merit. These procedural requirements include the following:

- A separate claim must be filed for each taxable period.
- The grounds for the claim must be stated in sufficient detail.
- The statement of facts must be sufficient to permit the IRS to evaluate the merits of the claim.

The refund claim must be filed within three years of the filing of the tax return or within two years following the payment of the tax if this period expires on a later date.[57] In most instances, the three-year period is relevant for determining running of the statute of limitations. Certain exceptions included in the Code can inadvertently reduce the benefits of the refund claim.[58]

─────────────────── EXAMPLE 18 ───────────────────

On March 10, 1990, T filed his 1989 income tax return reflecting a tax of $10,500. On July 10, 1991, he filed an amended 1989 return showing an additional $3,000 of tax that was then paid. On May 18, 1993, he filed a claim for refund of $4,500.

Assuming T is correct concerning the claim for refund, how much tax can he recover? The answer is only $3,000. Because the claim was not filed within the three-year period, T is limited to the amount he actually paid during the last two years.

T is entitled to interest on the $3,000 from July 10, 1991 (the date of the overpayment), to a date not more than 30 days before the date of the refund check (subject to the 45-day rule discussed earlier in the chapter). ◆

───────────────

55. § 6502(a).

56. § 6503(a)(1).

57. §§ 6511(a) and 6513(a).

58. § 6511(b).

─────────────────── EXAMPLE 19 ───────────────────

D had $10,000 withheld in 1989. Because she had a sizable amount of itemized deductions, D assumed she had no further tax to pay for the year. For this reason and because of the exigencies of business, and without securing an extension, she did not file her 1989 return until June 9, 1990. Actually, the return showed a refund of $600, which D ultimately received. On May 3, 1993, D filed a $4,000 claim for refund of her 1989 taxes. How much, if any, of the $4,000 may D recover? None. Although the time limitation was met (the claim was filed within three years of the filing of the return), the amount limitation was not. A refund cannot exceed the amount paid within three years preceding the filing of the claim, and for this purpose, D's withholdings were deemed paid as of April 15, 1990.

Had D requested and obtained an extension covering the filing of her 1989 return, the claim for refund would have been timely, and taxes paid would have exceeded the refund claimed. ◆

The tax law sets forth special rules for claims relating to bad debts and worthless securities. A seven-year period of limitations applies in lieu of the normal three-year rule.[59] The extended period is provided in recognition of the inherent difficulty of identifying the exact year in which a bad debt or security becomes worthless.

Refund claims relative to capital or net operating loss carrybacks may be filed within three years after the time for filing the tax return (including extensions) for the year of the loss. The IRS will accelerate the processing of a refund from a net operating loss carryback if Form 1045 (applicable to individuals) or Form 1139 (applicable to corporations) is utilized. But this special procedure is available only if the form is filed within the year following the year of the loss. In other cases, a Form 1040X or Form 1120X should be used.

A taxpayer whose refund claim is rejected by the IRS generally may file a suit for refund six months after the filing of the claim.[60] This suit is filed in a Federal District Court or in the Claims Court.

Mitigation of the Statute of Limitations. The Code contains a set of complex rules designed to preclude either the IRS or a taxpayer from taking advantage of the statute of limitations when doing so would be inequitable.[61] These Sections prevent the statute from being used as a means of obtaining a double benefit by maintaining an inconsistent position.

The Tax Practitioner

Definition. What is a tax practitioner? What service does the practitioner perform? To begin defining the term *tax practitioner*, one should consider whether the individual is qualified to practice before the IRS. Generally, practice before the IRS is limited to CPAs, attorneys, and persons who have been enrolled to practice before the IRS (called *enrolled agents* [*EAs*]). In most cases, are admitted to practice only if they successfully pass a special examination administered by the IRS. CPAs and attorneys are not required to take this examination and are automatically admitted to practice if they are in good standing with the appropriate licensing board regulating their profession.

Persons other than CPAs, attorneys, and EAs may, however, be allowed to practice before the IRS in limited situations. Circular 230 (issued by the Treasury

---

59. § 6511(d)(1).
60. § 6532(a)(1).

61. §§ 1311 through 1315.

Department and entitled "Rules Governing the Practice of Attorneys and Agents Before the Internal Revenue Service") permits the following notable exceptions:

- A taxpayer may always represent himself or herself. A person also may represent a member of his or her immediate family if no compensation is received for such services.
- Regular full-time employees may represent their employers.
- Corporations may be represented by any of their bona fide officers.
- Partnerships may be represented by any of the partners.
- Trusts, receiverships, guardianships, or estates may be represented by their trustees, receivers, guardians, or administrators or executors.
- A taxpayer may be represented by whoever prepared the return for the year in question. However, such representation cannot proceed beyond the agent level.

───────────────────── EXAMPLE 20 ─────────────────────

T, an individual, is currently undergoing audit by the IRS for tax years 1990 and 1991. She prepared the 1990 return herself but paid Z Company, a bookkeeping service, to prepare the 1991 return. Z may represent T in matters concerning only 1991. However, even for 1991, Z would be unable to represent T at an Appeals Division proceeding. T could, of course, represent herself, or she could retain a CPA, attorney, or EA to represent her in matters concerning both years under examination. ◆

Rules Governing Tax Practice. Circular 230 further prescribes the rules governing practice before the IRS. The following rules are imposed on CPAs, attorneys, and EAs:

- A requirement to make known to a client any error or omission the client may have made on any return or other document submitted to the IRS.
- A duty to submit records or information lawfully requested by the IRS.
- An obligation to exercise due diligence as to accuracy in the preparation and filing of tax returns.
- A restriction against unreasonably delaying the prompt disposition of any matter before the IRS.
- A restriction against charging the client "an unconscionable fee" for representation before the IRS.
- A restriction against representing clients with conflicting interests.

Anyone can prepare a tax return or render tax advice, regardless of his or her educational background or level of competence. Likewise, nothing prevents the "unlicensed" tax practitioner from advertising his or her specialty, directly soliciting clients, or otherwise violating any of the standards of conduct controlling CPAs, attorneys, and EAs. Nevertheless, some restraints do govern all parties engaged in rendering tax returns for the general public.

- If the party holds himself or herself out to the general public as possessing tax expertise, he or she could be liable to the client if services are performed in a negligent manner. At a minimum, the practitioner would be liable for any interest and penalties the client incurs because of the practitioner's failure to exercise due care.
- If someone agrees to perform a service (e.g., preparation of a tax return) and subsequently fails to do so, the aggrieved party may be in a position to obtain damages for breach of contract.

- The IRS requires all persons who prepare tax returns for a fee to sign as preparer of the return.[62] Failure to comply with this requirement could result in penalty assessment against the preparer.
- The Code prescribes various penalties for the deliberate filing of false or fraudulent returns. These penalties are applicable to a tax practitioner who either was aware of the situation or actually perpetrated the false information or the fraud.[63]
- Penalties are prescribed for tax practitioners who disclose to third parties information they have received from clients in connection with the preparation of tax returns or the rendering of tax advice.[64]

───────────────────── EXAMPLE 21 ─────────────────────

T operates a tax return preparation service. His brother-in-law, B, has just taken a job as a life insurance salesman. To help B find contacts, T furnishes B with a list of the names and addresses of all of his clients who report adjusted gross income of $10,000 or more. T is subject to penalties. ◆

- All nonattorney tax practitioners should avoid becoming engaged in activities that constitute the unauthorized practice of law. If they engage in this practice, action could be instituted against them in the appropriate state court by the local or state bar association. What actions constitute the unauthorized practice of law are undefined, and the issue remains an open question upon which reasonable minds can differ.

Preparer Penalties.   The Code also provides for the following penalties:

1. A $250 penalty for understatements due to unrealistic positions.[65] Unless adequate disclosure is made, the penalty is imposed if two conditions are satisfied:

    - Any part of any understatement of tax liability on any return or claim for refund is due to a position that did not have a realistic possibility of being sustained on its merits.
    - Any person who was an income tax return preparer for that return or claim knew (or should have known) of this position.

    The penalty can be avoided by showing reasonable cause and by showing that the preparer acted in good faith.

2. A $1,000 penalty for willful and reckless conduct.[66] The penalty applies if any part of the understatement of a taxpayer's liability on a return or claim for refund is due to either of two causes:

    - The preparer's willful attempt to understate the taxpayer's tax liability in any manner.
    - Any reckless or intentional disregard of rules or regulations by the preparer.

    Adequate disclosure can avoid the penalty. If both this penalty and the unrealistic position penalty (see item 1 above) apply to the same return, the total penalty cannot exceed $1,000.

---

62. Reg. § 1.6065–1(b)(1). Rev.Rul. 84–3, 1984–1 C.B. 264, contains a series of examples illustrating when a person will be deemed to be a preparer of the return.

63. § 7206.

64. § 7216.

65. § 6694(a).

66. § 6694(b).

3. A $1,000 ($10,000 for corporations) penalty per return or document is imposed against persons who aid in the preparation of returns or other documents that they know (or have reason to believe) would result in an understatement of the tax liability of another person.[67] Aiding does not include clerical assistance in the preparation process.

   If this penalty applies, neither the unrealistic position penalty (item 1) nor the willful and reckless conduct penalty (item 2) applies.

4. A $50 penalty is assessed against the preparer for failure to sign a return or furnish the preparer's identifying number.[68]

5. A $50 penalty is assessed if the preparer fails to furnish a copy of the return or claim for refund to the taxpayer.

6. A $500 penalty may be assessed if a preparer endorses or otherwise negotiates a check for refund of tax issued to the taxpayer.

Ethical Considerations—"Statements on Responsibilities in Tax Practice"

Tax practitioners who are CPAs, attorneys, or EAs must abide by the codes or canons of professional ethics applicable to their respective professions. The various codes and canons have much in common with and parallel the standards of conduct set forth in Circular 230.

In the belief that CPAs engaged in tax practice required further guidance in the resolution of ethical problems, the Tax Committee of the AICPA began issuing periodic statements on selected topics. The first of these "Statements on Responsibilities in Tax Practice" was released in 1964. All were revised in August 1988. The most important statements that have been issued to date are discussed below.[69]

Statement No. 1: Positions Contrary to IRS Interpretations. Under certain circumstances, a CPA may take a position that is contrary to that taken by the IRS. In order to do so, however, the CPA must have a good faith belief that the position has a realistic possibility of being sustained administratively or judicially on its merits if challenged.

The client should be fully advised of the risks involved and the penalties that may result if the position taken by the CPA is not successful. The client should also be informed that disclosure on the return may avoid some or all of these penalties.

In no case should the CPA exploit the audit lottery approach. That is, the CPA should not take a questionable position based on the probabilities that the client's return will not be chosen by the IRS for audit. Furthermore, the CPA should not "load" the return with questionable items in the hope that they might aid the client in a later settlement negotiation with the IRS.

Statement No. 2: Questions on Returns. A CPA should make a reasonable effort to obtain from the client, and provide, appropriate answers to all questions on a tax return before signing as preparer. Reasonable grounds may exist for omitting an answer. For example, reasonable grounds may include the following:

---

67. § 6701.
68. § 6695.

69. For an additional discussion of tax ethics, see Raabe, Whittenburg, and Bost, *West's Federal Tax Research*, 2d ed. (St. Paul: West Publishing Co., 1990), Chapter 1.

- The information is not readily available, and the answer is not significant taxwise.
- The meaning of the question as it applies to a particular situation is genuinely uncertain.
- The answer to the question is voluminous.

The fact that an answer to a question could prove disadvantageous to the client does not justify omitting the answer.

Statement No. 3: Procedural Aspects of Preparing Returns. In preparing a return, a CPA may in good faith rely without verification on information furnished by the client or by third parties. However, the CPA should make reasonable inquiries if the information appears to be incorrect, incomplete, or inconsistent. In this regard, the CPA should refer to the client's returns for prior years whenever appropriate.

EXAMPLE 22

A CPA normally can take a client's word for the validity of dependency exemptions. But suppose a recently divorced client wants to claim his three children (when he does not have custody) as dependents. You must act in accordance with § 152(e)(2) in preparing the return, and this will require evidence of a waiver by the custodial parent. Without this waiver, you should not claim the dependency exemptions on your client's tax return. ◆

EXAMPLE 23

While preparing a client's income tax return for 1993, you review his income tax return for 1992. In comparing the dividend income reported on the 1992 Schedule B with that received in 1993, you note a significant decrease. Further investigation reveals the variation is due to a stock sale in 1993 that was unknown to you until now. Thus, the review of the 1992 return has unearthed a transaction that should be reported on the 1993 return. ◆

If the Code or the Regulations require certain types of verification (as is the case with travel and entertainment expenditures), the CPA must advise the client of these rules. Further, inquiry must be made to ascertain whether the client has complied with the verification requirements.

Statement No. 4: Estimates. A CPA may prepare a tax return using estimates received from a taxpayer if it is impracticable to obtain exact data. The estimates must be reasonable under the facts and circumstances as known to the CPA. When estimates are used, they should be presented in such a manner as to avoid the implication of greater accuracy than exists.

Only in cases of unusual circumstances should the CPA disclose the use of estimates. Examples of unusual circumstances include the death or illness of the taxpayer, unavailability of an information return (e.g., a K–1 from a partnership), or destruction of taxpayer records.

Statement No. 5: Recognition of Administrative Proceeding. Many positions that a CPA must take depend upon the facts and circumstances of the situation. Usually in these cases, the tax law sets forth a standard that is vague, and its satisfaction is a matter of individual judgment. As facts may vary from year to year, so may the position taken by a CPA. In these types of situations, the CPA is not bound by an administrative or judicial proceeding involving a prior year.

EXAMPLE 24

Upon audit of T Corporation's income tax return for 1992, the IRS disallowed $20,000 of the $100,000 salary paid to its president and sole shareholder on the grounds that it is unreasonable [§ 162(a)(1)]. You are the CPA who has been engaged to prepare T's income tax return for 1993. Again the corporation paid its president a salary of $100,000 and chose to deduct this amount. Because you are not bound in 1993 by what the IRS deemed reasonable for 1992, the full $100,000 can be claimed as a salary deduction. ◆

Other problems that require a CPA's use of judgment include reclassification of corporate debt as equity (the thin capitalization possibility) and corporate accumulations beyond the reasonable needs of the business (the penalty tax under § 531).

Statement No. 6: Knowledge of Error. A CPA should promptly advise a client upon learning of an error in a previously filed return or upon learning of a client's failure to file a required return. The advice can be oral or written and should include a recommendation of the corrective measures, if any, to be taken. The error or other omission should not be disclosed to the IRS without the client's consent.

If the past error is material and is not corrected by the client, the CPA may be unable to prepare the current year's tax return. This situation might occur if the error has a carryover effect that prevents the CPA from determining the correct tax liability for the current year.

EXAMPLE 25

In preparing a client's 1993 income tax return, you discover the final inventory for 1992 was materially understated. First, you should advise the client to file an amended return for 1992 reflecting the correct amount in final inventory. Second, if the client refuses to make this adjustment, you should consider whether the error will preclude you from preparing a substantially correct return for 1993. Because this will probably be the case (the final inventory for 1992 becomes the beginning inventory for 1993), you should withdraw from the engagement.

If the client corrects the error, you may proceed with the preparation of the tax return for 1993. You should assure yourself that the error is not repeated. ◆

Statement No. 8:[70] Advice to Clients. In providing tax advice to a client, the CPA must use judgment to assure that the advice reflects professional competence and appropriately serves the client's needs. No standard format or guidelines can be established to cover all situations and circumstances involving written or oral advice by the CPA.

The CPA may communicate with the client when subsequent developments affect previous advice on significant matters. However, the CPA cannot be expected to assume responsibility for initiating the communication, unless he or she is assisting a client in implementing procedures or plans associated with the advice. The CPA may undertake this obligation by specific agreement with the client.

The foregoing statements merely represent guides to action and are not part of the AICPA's Code of Professional Ethics. But because the statements are representative of standards followed by members of the profession, a violation might indicate a deviation from the standard of due care exercised by most CPAs. The standard of due care is at the heart of any suit charging negligence that is brought against a CPA.

Strategy in Seeking an Administrative Ruling

TAX PLANNING
CONSIDERATIONS

Determination Letters. In many instances, the request for an advance ruling or a determination letter from the IRS is a necessary or desirable planning strategy.

---

70. Statement No. 7 has been omitted since it is conceptually similar to Statement No. 6.

The receipt of a favorable ruling or determination reduces the risk associated with a transaction when the tax results are in doubt. For example, the initiation or amendment of a pension or profit sharing plan should be accompanied by a determination letter from the District Director. Otherwise, on subsequent IRS review, the plan may not qualify, and the tax deductibility of contributions to the plan will be disallowed. In some instances, the potential tax effects of a transaction are so numerous and of such consequence that proceeding without a ruling is unwise.

Letter Rulings. In some cases, it may not be necessary or desirable to request an advance ruling. For example, it is generally not desirable to request a ruling if the tax results are doubtful and the company is committed to complete the transaction in any event. If a ruling is requested and negotiations with the IRS indicate that an adverse determination will be forthcoming, it is usually possible to have the ruling request withdrawn. However, the National Office of the IRS may forward its findings, along with a copy of the ruling request, to the District Director. In determining the advisability of a ruling request, the taxpayer should consider the potential exposure of other items in the tax returns of all "open years."

A ruling request may delay the consummation of a transaction if the issues are novel or complex. Frequently, a ruling can be processed within six months, although in some instances a delay of a year or more may be encountered.

Technical Advice Memoranda. A taxpayer in the process of contesting a proposed deficiency with the Appeals Division should consider requesting a

CONCEPT SUMMARY 16–1
TAX ADMINISTRATION AND PRACTICE

1. The Internal Revenue Service (IRS) enforces the tax laws of the United States. Its organization reflects its various responsibilities relative to taxpayer interaction, litigation and collection, and internal functions.
2. The IRS issues various pronouncements, communicating its position on certain tax issues. These pronouncements promote the uniform enforcement of the tax law among taxpayers and among the internal divisions of the IRS. Taxpayers should seek such rulings and memoranda when the nature or magnitude of a pending transaction requires a high degree of certainty in the planning process.
3. IRS audits can take several forms. Taxpayers are selected for audit based on the probable return to the Treasury from the process. Offers in compromise and closing agreements can be a useful means of completing an audit without resorting to litigation.
4. Certain IRS personnel are empowered to consider the hazards of litigation in developing a settlement with the taxpayer during the audit process.
5. The IRS pays interest to taxpayers on overpaid taxes, starting essentially 45 days after the due date of the return, at two percentage points over the Federal short-term rate. Interest paid to the IRS on underpayments is computed at three points over this Federal rate, starting essentially on the due date of the return. Interest for both purposes is compounded daily.
6. The Treasury assesses penalties when the taxpayer fails to file a required tax return or pay a tax. Penalties also are assessed when an inaccurate return is filed due to negligence or other disregard of IRS rules. Tax preparers are subject to penalties for assisting a taxpayer in filing an inaccurate return, failing to follow IRS rules in an appropriate manner, or mishandling taxpayer data or funds.
7. Statutes of limitations place outer boundaries on the timing and amounts of proposed amendments to completed tax returns that can be made by the taxpayer or the IRS.
8. Tax practitioners must operate under constraints imposed on them by codes of ethics or pertinent professional societies and by Treasury Circular 230. These rules also define the parties who can represent others in an IRS proceeding.

technical advice memorandum from the National Office of the IRS. If the memorandum is favorable to the taxpayer, it is binding on the Appeals Division. The request may be particularly appropriate when the practitioner feels that the agent or Appeals Division has been too literal in interpreting an IRS ruling.

Considerations in Handling an IRS Audit

As a general rule, a taxpayer should attempt to settle disputes at the earliest possible stage of the administrative appeal process. It is usually possible to limit the scope of the examination by furnishing pertinent information requested by the agent. Extraneous information or fortuitous comments may result in the opening of new issues and should be avoided. Agents usually appreciate prompt and efficient responses to inquiries, since their performance may in part be judged by their ability to close or settle assigned cases.

To the extent possible, it is advisable to conduct the investigation of field audits in the practitioner's office, rather than the client's office. This procedure permits greater control over the audit investigation and facilitates the agent's review and prompt closure of the case.

Many practitioners feel that it is generally not advisable to have clients present at the scheduled conferences with the agent, since the client may give emotional or gratuitous comments that impair prompt settlement. If the client is not present, however, he or she should be advised of the status of negotiations. The client makes the final decision on any proposed settlement.

The tax practitioner's workpapers should include all research memoranda, and a list of resolved and unresolved issues should be continually updated during the course of the IRS audit. Occasionally, agents will request access to excessive amounts of accounting data in order to engage in a so-called fishing expedition. Providing blanket access to working papers should be avoided. Workpapers should be carefully reviewed to minimize opportunities for the agent to raise new issues not otherwise apparent. It is generally advisable to provide the agent with copies of specific workpapers upon request. An accountant's workpapers are not privileged and may be subpoenaed by the IRS.

In unusual situations, a Special Agent may appear to gather evidence in the investigation of possible criminal fraud. When this occurs, the taxpayer should be advised to seek legal counsel to determine the extent of his or her cooperation in providing information to the agent. It is frequently desirable for the tax adviser to consult personal legal counsel in such situations. If the taxpayer receives a Revenue Agent's Report (RAR), it generally indicates that the IRS has decided not to initiate criminal prosecution proceedings. The IRS usually does not take any action upon a tax deficiency until the criminal matter has been resolved. If, for whatever reasons, the criminal action is dropped, the 75 percent civil fraud penalty normally will be assessed.

Litigation Considerations

During the process of settlement with the IRS, the taxpayer must assess the economic consequences of possible litigation. Specifically, the probability of winning in court should be weighed against the costs of settlement (legal and court costs). In some instances, taxpayers become overly emotional and do not give adequate consideration to the economic and psychological costs of litigation.

Signing Form 870 or Form 870–AD precludes the use of the Tax Court as a forum for future litigation. In that event, the taxpayer's only recourse is to pay the taxes and sue for a refund upon denial of a claim for refund. The Tax Court was established to provide taxpayers an opportunity to litigate issues without first paying the tax on the deficiency. Some taxpayers, however, prefer to litigate the case in a Federal District Court or the Claims Court, since the payment of tax effectively stops the running of interest on the deficiency.

In selecting a proper tax forum, consideration should be given to the decisions of the various courts in related cases. The Tax Court will follow the decisions of Courts of Appeals if the court is one to which the taxpayer may appeal.[71] For example, if an individual is in the jurisdiction of the Fifth Court of Appeals and that court has issued a favorable opinion on the same issue that currently confronts the taxpayer, the Tax Court will follow this opinion in deciding the taxpayer's case, even if previous Tax Court decisions have been adverse.

If the issue involves a question in which equity is needed, strategy may dictate the choice of a Federal District Court (where a jury trial is obtainable) or the Claims Court, which has frequently given greater weight to equity considerations than to strict legal precedent.

Penalties

Penalties are imposed upon a taxpayer's failure to file a return or pay a tax when due. These penalties can be avoided if the failure is due to reasonable cause and not due to willful neglect. Reasonable cause, however, has not been liberally interpreted by the courts and should not be relied upon in the routine type of situation.[72] A safer way to avoid the failure to file penalty is to obtain from the IRS an extension of time for filing the return.

Since it is not deductible for income tax purposes, the penalty for failure to pay estimated taxes can become quite severe. Often trapped by the provision are employed taxpayers with outside income. Such persons may forget about the outside income and place undue reliance on the amount withheld from wages and salaries as being adequate to cover their liability. Not only does April 15 provide a real shock (in terms of the additional tax owed) for these persons, but a penalty situation may have evolved. One possible way for an employee to mitigate this problem (presuming the employer is willing to cooperate) is described in the following example:

--- EXAMPLE 26 ---

T, a calendar year taxpayer, is employed by X Corporation and earns (after withholding) a monthly salary of $4,000 payable at the end of each month. T also receives income from outside sources (interest, dividends, and consulting fees). After some quick calculations in early October of 1993, T determines that he has underestimated his tax liability for 1993 by $7,500 and will be subject to the penalty for the first two quarters of 1993 and part of the third quarter. T, therefore, completes a new Form W–4 in which he arbitrarily raises his income tax withholding by $2,500 a month. X accepts the Form W–4, and as a result, an extra $7,500 is paid to the IRS on T's account for the payroll period from October through December 1993.

T avoids penalties for the underpayment for the first three quarters because withholding of taxes is allocated over the year involved. Thus, a portion of the additional $7,500 withheld in October–December is assigned to the January 1–April 15 period, the April 16–June 15 period, etc.[73] Had T merely paid the IRS an additional $7,500 in October, this would not have affected the penalty for the earlier quarters. ◆

---

71. *Jack E. Golsen*, 54 T.C. 742 (1970).

72. *Dustin v. Comm.*, 72–2 USTC ¶9610, 30 AFTR2d 72–5313, 467

F.2d 47 (CA–9, 1972), *aff'g.* 53 T.C. 491 (1969).

73. § 6654(g).

Statute of Limitations on Refund Claims

Avoiding the Statute of Limitations. A refund claim must be filed within the statutory period of limitations (usually within three years from the time the return was filed). The failure to file a refund claim within this period prevents the taxpayer from recovering previous overpayments of tax.

Suppose a matter is pending that, upon being resolved, could have an impact on a taxpayer's own situation. Although the taxpayer may not be personally involved in the controversy, a favorable outcome would result in a refund. By the time the issue is settled, however, any refund claim might be barred by the statute of limitations. To prevent this from happening, the taxpayer should consider filing what is known as a "protective claim for refund." This will keep the statute of limitations from running until the IRS acts upon the claim. The IRS will refrain from either approving or denying the claim until the pending matter is decided.

A protective claim for refund also may be advisable in situations where the controversy has not reached the litigation stage.

--------- **EXAMPLE 27** ---------

X Corporation is a shareholder in Y Corporation. Over the years, X has made advances to Y, and both parties have treated the transactions as bona fide loans. Annually, therefore, Y has been deducting interest expense, and X has been recognizing interest income.

Upon audit of Y, the IRS is threatening to disallow Y's interest expense deduction on the grounds that the advances were not loans but represented contributions to capital. Consequently, the purported interest payments are really nondeductible dividend distributions.

Based on these facts, X might be well advised to file protective claims for refund for all open years. These claims would be predicated on the assumption that if dividends are the ultimate result, X should be allowed a dividends received deduction. ◆

Voluntary Extension of the Statute of Limitations. If the IRS is unable to complete its audit within the period before the expiration of the statute of limitations, the taxpayer may be asked to agree to an extension of time for assessment by signing Form 872 (Consent to Extend the Time to Assess Tax). It may be unwise to agree to this extension since the IRS may subsequently assess a larger overall deficiency. Failure to agree to the extension of time, however, could force the IRS to issue a statutory notice of deficiency. This could cause the statutory notice to be unduly weighted against the taxpayer since it may contain many adjustments that otherwise could have been resolved had the IRS been permitted more time to consider the matter.

PROBLEM MATERIALS

DISCUSSION QUESTIONS

1. Why is it necessary for a tax practitioner to be familiar with the IRS organization and its administrative appeal procedures?

2. Why does the IRS issue rulings solely on uncompleted actual transactions or upon transactions that have been completed before the filing of the tax return?

3. During the course of your research of a tax problem, you find that another company received a favorable unpublished (letter) ruling approximately two years ago based on facts similar to your situation. What degree of reliance may be placed upon this ruling?

4. Under what circumstances might the request for an advance ruling be considered a necessity? Are there situations in which a ruling should not be requested? Why?

5. In what situations might a taxpayer seek a determination letter?

6. What purpose does a request for a technical advice memorandum serve?

7. A taxpayer is fearful of filing a claim for refund for a prior year because she is convinced that the claim will cause the IRS to audit that year's return. Please comment.

8. In March 1993, T receives a refund check from the IRS for the amount of overpayment she claimed when she filed her 1992 return in January. Does this mean that her 1992 return will not be audited? Explain.

9. Comment on the following:

   a. An RAR.
   b. Form 870.
   c. The 30-day letter.
   d. The 90-day letter.

10. Can an IRS agent settle cases based on the hazards of litigation?

11. Is it possible or desirable to "trade" unresolved issues with the Appeals Division?

12. How may the running of interest on a deficiency assessment be stopped?

13. V, a calendar year taxpayer, files her 1992 income tax return on February 9, 1993, on which she claims a $1,200 refund. If V receives her refund check on May 2, 1993, will it include any interest? Explain.

14. Why may it be desirable to settle with an agent rather than to continue by appealing to a higher level within the IRS?

15. For the completion and filing of his 1992 income tax return, R retains the services of a CPA. Because of a particularly hectic tax season, the CPA does not complete and file the return until June 1993. Does this exculpate R under the reasonable cause exception from the failure to file and pay penalties? Would it make any difference if R were entitled to a refund for 1992?

16. What bearing should the interest rate currently in effect have on each of the following situations?

   a. Whether a taxpayer litigates in the U.S. Tax Court or the Claims Court.
   b. The penalty for underpayment of estimated taxes.

17. Describe each of the following items:

   a. A closing agreement.
   b. An offer in compromise.

18. Certain individuals have stated that the preparation of a tax return by a qualified professional lends credibility to the return. Therefore, CPAs and attorneys should act in an impartial manner in the preparation of tax returns and should serve the overall enforcement needs of society for the administration of tax justice. Should a tax professional be an "umpire" or an "advocate"? Explain.

19. T, a vice president of Z Corporation, prepared and filed the corporate Form 1120 for 1991. This return is being audited by the IRS in 1993.

   a. May T represent Z Corporation during the audit?
   b. Can T's representation continue beyond the agent level (e.g., before the Appeals Division)?

20. During the course of an audit, the IRS agent requests a mutual extension of the statute of limitations for certain tax years. The agent states that this action is necessary to permit the completion of the audit. What are some of the pros and cons of signing Form 872?

PROBLEMS

21. Compute the failure to pay and failure to file penalties for J, who filed his 1991 income tax return on October 20, 1992, paying the $1,000 amount due. On April 1, 1992, J had received a four-month extension of time in which to file his return. He has no reasonable cause for failing to file his return by August 15 or for failing to pay the tax that was due on April 15, 1992. J's failure to comply with the tax laws was not fraudulent.

22. Indicate whether each of the following statements is true or false:

    a. The government never pays a taxpayer interest on an overpayment of tax.
    b. Penalties may be included as a itemized deduction on an individual's tax return, but net of the 2% of AGI floor.
    c. An extension of time for filing a return results in an automatic extension of the time in which the tax may be paid.
    d. The IRS can compromise on the amount of tax liability if there is doubt as to the taxpayer's ability to pay.
    e. The statute of limitations for assessing a tax never extends beyond three years from the filing of a return.
    f. There is no statute of limitations relative to a taxpayer's claim for a refund.

23. Define and illustrate the following terms or concepts:

    a. Fraud.
    b. Negligence.
    c. Reasonable cause.
    d. Civil penalty.
    e. Criminal penalty.

24. When can the taxpayer effect an "installment plan" paying for his or her delinquent taxes and associated interest and penalties?

25. Discuss which penalties, if any, might be imposed on the tax adviser in each of the following independent circumstances. In this regard, assume that the tax adviser

    a. suggested to the client various means by which to acquire excludible income.
    b. suggested to the client various means by which to conceal cash receipts from gross income.
    c. suggested to the client means by which to improve her cash flow by delaying for six months or more the deposit of the employee's share of Federal employment taxes.
    d. kept in his own safe deposit box the concealed income of item (c).
    e. failed, because of pressing time conflicts, to conduct the usual review of the client's tax return. The IRS later discovered that the return included fraudulent data.
    f. failed, because of pressing time conflicts, to conduct the usual review of the client's tax return. The IRS later discovered a mathematical error in the computation of the personal exemption.

26. T, a calendar year taxpayer, does not file her 1992 return until June 4, 1993. At this point, she pays the $3,000 balance due on her 1992 tax liability of $30,000. T did not apply for and obtain any extension of time for filing the 1992 return. When questioned by the IRS on her delinquency, T asserts: "If I was too busy to file my regular tax return, I was too busy to request an extension."

    a. Is T liable for any penalties for failure to file and for failure to pay?
    b. If so, compute the penalties.

27. X, a cash basis, calendar year taxpayer, filed his 1992 return 65 days after the due date. X never extended his return, and he paid the taxes that were due. What penalty will X incur and how much will he have to pay if his additional tax is $500? Disregard the additional interest X will have to pay.

28. Assume the same facts as in Problem 27, except that the additional income tax due was $80 (rather than $500). Based on these new facts and disregarding the interest element, how much more does X owe the IRS?

29. R, a calendar year individual taxpayer, files her 1991 return on January 11, 1993. R did not obtain an extension for filing her return, and the return reflects additional income tax due of $3,800.

   a. What are R's penalties for failure to file and to pay?
   b. Would your answer to (a) change if R, before the due date of the return, had retained a CPA to prepare the return and it was the CPA's negligence that caused the delay?

30. Z underpaid her taxes by $15,000. Of this amount $7,500 was due to negligence on Z's part. Determine the amount of Z's negligence penalty.

31. T underpaid his taxes by $250,000. A portion of the underpayment was attributable to negligence ($50,000) *and* to civil fraud ($150,000). What are T's total penalties?

32. A made a charitable contribution of property that he valued at $20,000. He deducted this amount as an itemized deduction on his tax return. The IRS can prove that the real value of the property is $8,000. A is in the 31% income tax bracket. Determine A's overvaluation penalty.

33. In 1986, T Corporation purchased 10% of the stock in X Corporation for $100,000. In 1988, X Corporation made a cash distribution to its shareholders of $500,000 ($50,000 of which was received by T Corporation). Since all parties were convinced that X Corporation had no earnings and profits at the time of the distribution, no dividend income was recognized by any of the shareholders.

   After the statute of limitations had expired, the IRS correctly determined that the distribution was fully covered by earnings and profits and should have been reported by the shareholders as dividend income. In 1992, T Corporation sells its stock investment in X Corporation for $250,000.

   a. How much gain should T Corporation recognize as a result of the sale?
   b. If T Corporation recognizes a gain of $150,000 as a result of the sale, does the IRS have any recourse?

34. When T accepted employment in 1993 with X Corporation, he completed a Form W–4 listing 14 exemptions. Since T was single and had no dependents, he misrepresented his situation on Form W–4. What penalties, if any, might the IRS impose upon T?

35. What is the applicable statute of limitations in each of the following independent situations?

   a. No return was filed by the taxpayer.
   b. In 1990, T incurred a bad debt loss that she failed to claim.
   c. On his 1990 return, a taxpayer inadvertently omitted a large amount of gross income.
   d. Same as (c), except that the omission was deliberate.
   e. For 1990, a taxpayer innocently overstated her deductions by a large amount.

36. During 1989, T (an individual calendar year taxpayer) had the following transactions, all of which were properly reported on a timely filed return:

Gross receipts		$ 960,000
Cost of goods sold		(800,000)
Gross profit		$ 160,000
Capital gains and losses—		
Capital gain	$ 72,000	
Capital loss	(24,000)	48,000
Total income		$ 208,000

   a. Presuming the absence of fraud on T's part, how much of an omission from gross income would be required to make the six-year statute of limitations apply?

b. Would it matter in your answer to (a) if cost of goods sold had been inadvertently overstated by $100,000?

37. On April 2, 1990, X filed his 1989 income tax return, which showed a tax due of $40,000. On June 1, 1992, X filed an amended return for 1989 that showed an additional tax of $12,000. X paid the additional amount. On May 18, 1993, X files a claim for a refund of $18,000.

a. If X's claim for a refund is correct, how much tax will he recover?
b. What will be the period that interest will run in regard to X's claim for a refund?

38. Ms. T had $40,000 withheld in 1989. Due to a sizable amount of itemized deductions, she figured that she had no further tax to pay for the year. For this reason and because of personal problems, and without securing an extension, she did not file her 1989 return until July 1, 1990. Actually, the return showed a refund of $2,400, which Ms. T ultimately received. On May 10, 1993, Ms. T filed a $16,000 claim for refund of her 1989 taxes.

a. How much, if any, of the $16,000 may Ms. T recover?
b. Would it have made any difference if Ms. T had requested and secured from the IRS an extension of time for filing her 1989 tax return?

39. R's Federal income tax returns (Form 1040) for the past three years (1990–1992) were prepared by the following persons:

Preparer	1990	1991	1992
R	X		
S		X	
T			X

S is R's next-door neighbor and owns and operates a pharmacy. T is a licensed CPA and is engaged in private practice. In the event R is audited and all three returns are examined, comment on who may represent R before the IRS at the agent level. Who may represent R before the Appeals Division?

40. Indicate whether the following statements are true or false (Note: SRTP = Statements on Responsibilities in Tax Practice):

a. When a CPA has reasonable grounds for not answering an applicable question on a client's return, a brief explanation of the reason for the omission should not be provided, because it would flag the return for audit by the IRS.
b. If a CPA discovers during an IRS audit that his or her client has a material error in the return under examination, he or she should immediately withdraw from the engagement.
c. If the client tells you that she had contributions of $500 for unsubstantiated cash donations to her church, you should deduct an odd amount on her return (e.g., $499), because an even amount ($500) would indicate to the IRS that her deduction was based on an estimate.
d. Basing an expense deduction on the client's estimates is not acceptable under the SRTP.
e. If a CPA knows that his or her client has a material error in a prior year's return, he or she should not, without the client's consent, disclose the error to the IRS.
f. If a CPA's client will not correct a material error in a prior year's return, the CPA should not prepare the current year's return for the client.

RESEARCH PROBLEMS

RESEARCH PROBLEM 1   For tax years 1982–1986, T filed fraudulent income tax returns. In 1988, however, he filed nonfraudulent amended returns and paid the additional basic taxes shown on the returns. In 1993, the IRS issued notices of deficiency, asserting liability under § 6653(b) for additions to tax on account of fraud. T invoked the three-year statute of limitations as a defense to the assessment. Which side will prevail? Why?

RESEARCH PROBLEM 2   B became a CPA in 1975 and has practiced public accounting since 1976. In 1993, he was hired by the accounting firm of GW who had, among other clients, R Corporation and R (the sole shareholder of R Corporation). In 1993, B was assigned the accounts of R Corporation and R and was designated to be the preparer of their 1992 income tax returns.

In the past, GW had adopted the practice of sending to its individual income tax clients a data questionnaire that was to be completed by the client and returned to the firm or used by the client as a guide in collecting the information necessary for the firm to prepare the returns. B did not use such a questionnaire when he prepared R's individual income tax return. Instead, the information necessary was supplied to B by R Corporation's bookkeeper. The information was reconciled by B with R's prior return, processed, and eventually timely filed with the IRS. B also prepared and filed the Form 1120 for R Corporation based on a trial balance sheet submitted by the same bookkeeper.

Unknown to B, R Corporation (due to high interest rates) had changed its borrowing policy. Instead of financing its operations through banking institutions, the credit source became R. Thus, an interest deduction of $15,000 was claimed on R Corporation's Form 1120 but was not reported as income on R's Form 1040. When B prepared the returns for the same clients for tax year 1993, the same procedure was followed. Thus, for the omitted interest income, history repeated itself.

When the IRS caught the oversight, it assessed the $100 tax preparer penalty against B for both tax years. How should this matter be resolved?

RESEARCH PROBLEM 3   The heirs of an estate engaged an attorney to handle its probate and relied upon him to perform all necessary acts. In turn, the attorney arranged to have an assistant of his named administrator and depended upon him to timely file the death tax return. The return was not timely filed, and no explanation was presented for the failure to do so. Is the estate liable for the addition to tax under § 6651(a)?

PART

FAMILY TAX PLANNING

Family tax planning has as its objective the minimization of *all* taxes imposed on the family unit. Carrying out this objective requires familiarity with the rules applicable to transfers by gift and by death. These rules must then be applied to reduce the transfer tax burden. Also to be considered are the income tax consequences of the transfers made. Finally, entities created as a result of these transfers (trusts and estates) are subject to unique income tax rules.

CHAPTER

17
The Federal Gift and Estate Taxes

18
Family Tax Planning

19
Income Taxation of Trusts and Estates

THE FEDERAL GIFT AND ESTATE TAXES

OBJECTIVES

Illustrate the mechanics of the unified transfer tax.

Establish which persons are subject to this tax.

Review the formulas for the Federal gift and estate taxes.

Explain which transfers are subject to the Federal gift or estate tax.

Describe the exclusions and the deductions available in arriving at a taxable gift or a taxable estate.

Illustrate the computation of the Federal gift or estate tax by making use of all available credits.

OUTLINE

TRANSFER TAXES— IN GENERAL

◆

Until now, this text has dealt primarily with the various applications of the Federal income tax. Also important in the Federal tax structure are various excise taxes that cover transfers of property. Sometimes called transaction taxes, excise taxes are based on the value of the property transferred, not on the income derived from the property. Two such taxes—the Federal estate tax and the Federal gift tax—are the central focus of Chapters 17 and 18.

Before the enactment of the Tax Reform Act of 1976, Federal law imposed a tax on the gratuitous transfer of property in one of two ways. If the transfer occurred during the owner's life, it was subject to the Federal gift tax. If, however, the property passed by virtue of the death of the owner, the Federal estate tax applied. Both taxes were governed by different rules including separate sets of tax rates. As Congress felt that lifetime transfers of wealth should be encouraged, the gift tax rates were lower than the estate tax rates.

The Tax Reform Act of 1976 significantly changed the approach taken by the Federal estate and gift taxes. Much of the distinction between life and death transfers was eliminated. Instead of subjecting these transfers to two separate tax rate schedules, the Act substituted a unified transfer tax that covers all gratuitous transfers. Thus, gifts are subject to a gift tax at the same rates as those applicable to transfers at death. In addition, current law eliminates the prior exemptions allowed under each tax and replaces them with a unified tax credit.

Nature of the Taxes

The Federal estate tax dates from 1916 and, like many taxes, was originally enacted to generate additional revenue in anticipation of this country's entry into World War I. The tax is designed to tax transfers at death. It may also have some application to lifetime transfers that become complete upon the death of the donor or to certain gifts made within three years of death.

The estate tax differs in several respects from the typical inheritance tax imposed by many states and some local jurisdictions. First, the Federal estate tax is imposed on the decedent's entire estate. It is a tax on the right to pass property at death. Inheritance taxes are taxes on the right to receive property at death and are therefore levied on the heirs. Second, the relationship of the heirs to the decedent usually has a direct bearing on the inheritance tax. In general, the more closely related the parties, the larger the exemption and the lower the applicable rates.[1] Except for transfers to a surviving spouse that may result in a marital deduction, the relationship of a decedent to his or her heirs has no effect on the Federal estate tax.

The Federal gift tax, enacted later, was designed to make the income and estate taxes more effective. Congress felt that individuals should not be able to give away property—thereby shifting the income tax consequences to others and avoiding estate taxes—without incurring some tax liability. The result is the Federal gift tax, which covers inter vivos (lifetime) transfers.

The Federal gift tax is imposed on the right to transfer property by one person (the donor) to another (the donee) for less than full and adequate consideration. The tax is payable by the donor.[2] If the donor fails to pay the tax when due, the donee may be held liable for the tax to the extent of the value of the property received.[3]

---

1. For example, one state's inheritance tax provides an exemption of $50,000 for surviving spouses, with rates ranging from 5% to 10% on the taxable portion. In contrast, an exemption of only $1,000 is provided for strangers (persons unrelated to the deceased), with rates ranging from 14% to 18% on the taxable portion. Other exemptions and rates between these extremes cover beneficiaries variously related to the decedent.

2. § 2502(c).

3. § 6324(b).

Persons Subject to the Tax. To determine whether a transfer is subject to the Federal gift tax, first ascertain if the donor is a citizen or resident of the United States. If the donor is not a citizen or a resident, it is important to determine whether the property involved in the gift was situated within the United States.

The Federal gift tax is applied to all transfers by gift of property wherever located by individuals who, at the time of the gift, were citizens or residents of the United States. The term "United States" includes only the 50 states and the District of Columbia; it does not include U.S. possessions or territories.[4] For a U.S. citizen, the place of residence at the time of the gift is immaterial.

For individuals who are neither citizens nor residents of the United States, the Federal gift tax is applied only to gifts of property situated within the United States.[5] A gift of intangible personal property (stocks and bonds) usually is not subject to the Federal gift tax when made by nonresident aliens.[6]

A gift by a corporation is considered a gift by the individual shareholders. A gift to a corporation is generally considered a gift to the individual shareholders. In certain cases, however, a gift to a charitable, public, political, or similar organization may be regarded as a gift to the organization as a single entity.[7]

The Federal estate tax is applied to the entire estate of a decedent who, at the time of his or her death, was a resident or citizen of the United States.[8] If the decedent was a U.S. citizen, the residence at death makes no difference.

If the decedent was neither a resident nor a citizen of the United States at the time of death, the Federal estate tax will be imposed on the value of any property located within the United States. In that case, the tax determination is controlled by a separate subchapter of the Internal Revenue Code.[9] In certain instances, the tax consequences outlined in the Internal Revenue Code may have been modified by death tax conventions (treaties) between the United States and various foreign countries.[10] Further coverage of this area is beyond the scope of this text. The following discussion is limited to the tax treatment of decedents who were residents or citizens of the United States at the time of death.[11]

Formula for the Gift Tax. Like the income tax, which uses taxable income (not gross income) as a tax base, the gift tax usually does not apply to the full amount of the gift. Deductions and the annual exclusion may be allowed to arrive at an amount called the *taxable gift*. However, unlike the income tax, which does not consider taxable income from prior years, *prior taxable gifts* must be added in arriving at the tax base to which the unified transfer tax is applied. Otherwise, the donor could start over again each year with a new set of progressive rates.

─────────────────── EXAMPLE 1 ───────────────────

D makes taxable gifts of $500,000 in 1985 and $500,000 in 1992. Presuming no other taxable gifts and *disregarding the effect of the unified tax credit*, D must pay a tax of $155,800 (see Appendix A, page A–8) on the 1985 transfer and a tax of $345,800 on the

---

4. § 7701(a)(9).

5. § 2511(a).

6. §§ 2501(a)(2) and (3). But see § 2511(b) and Reg. §§ 25.2511–3(b)(2), (3), and (4) for exceptions.

7. Reg. §§ 25.0–1(b) and 25.2511–1(h)(1). But note the exemption from the Federal gift tax for certain transfers to political organizations discussed later.

8. § 2001(a).

9. Subchapter B (§§ 2101 through 2108) covers the estate tax treatment of decedents who are neither residents nor citizens. Subchapter A (§§ 2001 through 2056A) covers the estate tax treatment of those who are either residents or citizens.

10. At present, the United States has death tax conventions with the following countries: Australia, Austria, Denmark, Germany, Finland, France, Greece, Ireland, Italy, Japan, Netherlands, Norway, Republic of South Africa, Sweden, Switzerland, and the United Kingdom. The United States has gift tax conventions with Australia, Austria, France, Japan, and the United Kingdom.

11. Further information concerning Subchapter B (§§ 2101 through 2108) can be obtained from the relevant Code Sections (and the related Treasury Regulations). See also the Instructions to Form 706NA (U.S. Estate Tax Return of Nonresident Not a Citizen of the U.S.).

1992 transfer (using a tax base of $1,000,000). If the 1985 taxable gift had not been included in the tax base for the 1992 gift, the tax would have been $155,800. The correct tax liability of $345,800 is more than twice $155,800! ◆

Because the gift tax is cumulative in effect, a credit is allowed against the gift taxes paid (or deemed paid) on prior taxable gifts included in the tax base. The deemed paid credit is explained later in the chapter.

─────────────────── EXAMPLE 2 ───────────────────

Assume the same facts as in Example 1. D will be allowed a credit of $155,800 against the gift tax of $345,800. Thus, D's gift tax liability for 1992 becomes $190,000 ($345,800 − $155,800). ◆

The annual exclusion before 1982 was $3,000. It was changed to $10,000 to allow larger gifts to be exempt from the Federal gift tax. The increase improves taxpayer compliance and eases the audit function of the IRS. It also recognizes the inflationary trend in the economy.

The formula for the gift tax is summarized below. (Note: Section [§] references are to the portion of the Internal Revenue Code involved.)

Determine whether the transfers are or are not covered by referring to §§ 2511 through 2519; list the fair market value of only the covered transfers		$xxx,xxx
Determine the deductions allowed by § 2522 (charitable) and § 2523 (marital)	$xx,xxx	
Claim the annual exclusion (per donee) under § 2503(b), if available	10,000	xx,xxx
Taxable gifts [as defined by § 2503(a)] for the current period		$ xx,xxx
Add: Taxable gifts from prior years		xx,xxx
Total of current and past taxable gifts		$ xx,xxx
Compute the gift tax on the total of current and past taxable gifts by using the rates in Appendix A		$ x,xxx
Subtract: Gift tax paid or deemed paid on past taxable gifts and the unified tax credit		xxx
Gift tax due on transfers during the current period		$ xxx

Formula for the Federal Estate Tax. The Federal unified transfer tax at death, commonly known as the Federal estate tax, is summarized below. (Note: Section [§] references are to the portion of the Internal Revenue Code involved.)

Gross estate (§§ 2031–2046)		$xxx,xxx
Subtract:		
Expenses, indebtedness, and taxes (§ 2053)	$xx	
Losses (§ 2054)	xx	
Charitable bequests (§ 2055)	xx	
Marital deduction (§§ 2056 and 2056A)	xx	x,xxx
Taxable estate (§ 2051)		$ xx,xxx
Add: Post-1976 taxable gifts [§ 2001(b)]		x,xxx
Tax base		$xxx,xxx
Tentative tax on total transfers [§ 2001(c)]		$ xx,xxx
Subtract:		
Unified transfer tax on post-1976 taxable gifts (gift taxes paid)	$xx	
Other tax credits (including the unified tax credit) (§§ 2010–2016)	xx	x,xxx
Estate tax due		$ xxx

The reason post-1976 taxable gifts are added to the taxable estate to arrive at the tax base goes back to the scheme of the unified transfer tax. Starting in 1977, all transfers, whether lifetime or by death, are treated the same. Consequently, taxable gifts made after 1976 must be accounted for upon the death of the donor. Note that the double tax effect of including these gifts is mitigated by allowing a credit against the estate tax for the gift taxes previously paid.

Role of the Unified Tax Credit. Before the unified transfer tax, the gift tax allowed a $30,000 specific exemption for the lifetime of the donor. A comparable $60,000 exemption was allowed for estate tax purposes. The purpose of these exemptions was to allow donors and decedents to transfer modest amounts of wealth without being subject to the gift and estate taxes. Unfortunately, inflation took its toll, and more taxpayers became subject to these transfer taxes than Congress believed was appropriate. The congressional solution was to rescind the exemptions and replace them with the unified tax credit.[12]

To curtail revenue loss, the credit was phased in as follows:

Year of Death	Amount of Credit	Amount of Exemption Equivalent
1977	$ 30,000	$120,667
1978	34,000	134,000
1979	38,000	147,333
1980	42,500	161,563
1981	47,000	175,625
1982	62,800	225,000
1983	79,300	275,000
1984	96,300	325,000
1985	121,800	400,000
1986	155,800	500,000
1987 & thereafter	192,800	600,000

The *exemption equivalent* is the amount of the transfer that will pass free of the gift or estate tax by virtue of the credit.

───────────────────── EXAMPLE 3 ─────────────────────

In 1992, D makes a taxable gift of $600,000. Presuming she has made no prior taxable gifts, D will not owe any gift tax. Under the tax rate schedules (see Appendix A, page A–8), the tax on $600,000 is $192,800, which is the exact amount of the credit allowed.[13] ◆

The Tax Reform Act of 1976 allowed donors one last chance to use the $30,000 specific exemption on lifetime gifts. If, however, the exemption was used on gifts made after September 8, 1976 (and before January 1, 1977), the unified tax credit must be reduced by 20 percent of the exemption utilized.[14] The credit must be adjusted whether the gift tax or the estate tax is involved. No adjustment is necessary for post-1976 gifts since the specific exemption was no longer available for such transfers.

---

12. §§ 2010 and 2505.

13. The rate schedules are contained in § 2001(c).

14. §§ 2010(c) and 2505(c).

EXAMPLE 4

Net of the annual exclusion, D, a widow, made gifts of $10,000 in June 1976 and $20,000 in December 1976. Assume D has never used any of her specific exemption and chooses to use the full $30,000 to cover the 1976 gifts. Under these circumstances, the unified tax credit will be reduced by $4,000 (20% × $20,000). The use of the specific exemption on transfers made before September 9, 1976, has no effect on the credit. ◆

Valuation for Estate and Gift Tax Purposes

The value of the property on the date of its transfer generally determines the amount that will be subject to the gift tax or the estate tax. Under certain conditions, however, an executor can elect to value estate assets on the alternate valuation date.

The alternate valuation date election was designed as a relief provision to ease the economic hardship that could result when estate assets decline in value over the six months after the date of death. If the election is made, all assets of the estate are valued six months after death *or* on the date of disposition if this occurs earlier.[15] The election covers *all* assets in the gross estate and cannot be applied to only a portion of the property.

EXAMPLE 5

D's gross estate consists of the following property:

	Value on Date of Death	Value Six Months Later
Land	$ 800,000	$ 840,000
Stock in X Corporation	900,000	700,000
Stock in Y Corporation	500,000	460,000
Total	$2,200,000	$2,000,000

If D's executor elects the alternate valuation date, the estate must be valued at $2,000,000. It is not permissible to value the land at its date of death value ($800,000) and choose the alternate valuation date for the rest of the gross estate. ◆

EXAMPLE 6

Assume the same facts as in Example 5 except that the executor sells the stock in Y Corporation for $480,000 four months after D's death. If the alternate valuation date is elected, the estate must be valued at $2,020,000. As to the stock in Y Corporation, the value on its date of disposition controls because that date occurred prior to the six months' alternate valuation date. ◆

The alternate valuation date election is not available unless the estate must file a Form 706 (Estate Tax Return). When an estate is required to file a Form 706 is discussed later in this chapter.

The election of the alternate valuation date must decrease the value of the gross estate *and* decrease the estate tax liability.[16] The reason for this last requirement is that the income tax basis of property acquired from a decedent will be the value used for estate tax purposes (discussed further in Chapter 18).[17] Without a special limitation, the alternate valuation date could be elected solely to add to income tax basis.

15. § 2032(a).
16. § 2032(c).

17. § 1014(a).

EXAMPLE 7

H's gross estate comprises assets with a date of death value of $1,000,000 and an alternate valuation date value of $1,100,000. Under H's will, all of his property passes outright to W (H's wife). Because of the marital deduction, no estate tax results regardless of which value is used. But if the alternate valuation date could be elected, W would have an income tax basis of $1,100,000 in the property acquired from H. ◆

The alternate valuation date cannot be elected in Example 7 for two reasons, either of which would suffice. First, the alternate valuation date will not decrease H's gross estate. Second, the election will not decrease H's estate tax liability. Thus, H's estate must use the date of death valuation of $1,000,000. As a result, W's income tax basis in the property received from H is $1,000,000.

Another valuation option available for estate tax purposes is the special use valuation method. Election of this method is limited to certain situations involving interests in closely held businesses (usually farms). Special use valuation is discussed in Chapter 18.

Key Property Concepts

When property is transferred either by gift or by death, the form of ownership can have a direct bearing on any transfer tax consequences. Understanding the different forms of ownership is necessary for working with Federal gift and estate taxes.

Undivided Ownership.   Assume D and Y own an undivided but equal interest in a tract of land. Such ownership can fall into any of four categories: joint tenancy, tenancy by the entirety, tenancy in common, or community property.

If D and Y hold ownership as joint tenants or tenants by the entirety, the right of survivorship exists. This means that the last tenant to survive receives full ownership of the property. Thus, if D predeceases Y, the land belongs entirely to Y. None of the land will pass to D's heirs or will be subject to administration by D's executor. A tenancy by the entirety is a joint tenancy between husband and wife.

If D and Y hold ownership as tenants in common or as community property, death does not defeat an owner's interest. Thus, if D predeceases Y, D's one-half interest in the land will pass to his or her estate or heirs.

Community property interests arise from the marital relationship. Normally, all property acquired after marriage, except by gift or inheritance, by husband and wife residing in a community property state becomes part of the community. The following states have the community property system in effect: Louisiana, Texas, New Mexico, Arizona, California, Washington, Idaho, Nevada, and Wisconsin. All other states follow the common law system of ascertaining the rights of spouses to property acquired after marriage.

Partial Interests.   Interests in assets can be divided in terms of rights to income and principal. Particularly when property is placed in trust, it is not uncommon to carve out various income interests that must be accounted for separately from the ultimate disposition of the property itself.

EXAMPLE 8

Under D's will, a ranch is to be placed in trust, life estate to S, D's son, with remainder to S's children (D's grandchildren). Under this arrangement, S is the life tenant and, as such, is entitled to the use of the ranch (including any income) during his life. Upon S's death, the trust terminates, and its principal passes to S's children. Thus, S's children receive outright ownership in the ranch when S dies. ◆

General Considerations

Requirements for a Gift. For a gift to be complete under state law, the following elements must be present:

- A donor competent to make the gift.
- A donee capable of receiving and possessing the property.
- Donative intent on behalf of the donor.
- Actual or constructive delivery of the property to the donee or the donee's representative.
- Acceptance of the gift by the donee.

Whether transfers are gifts under state law is important in applying the Federal gift tax. But state law does not always control. For example and with reference to the element of donative intent, the Regulations make it clear that this is not an essential factor in the application of the Federal gift tax.[18]

EXAMPLE 9

B (age 24) consents to marry D (age 62) if D transfers $200,000 of his property to her. The arrangement is set forth in a prenuptial agreement, D makes the transfer, and B and D are married. D lacked donative intent, and in most states no gift has been made from D to B. Nevertheless, the transfer is subject to the Federal gift tax. ◆

The key to the result reached in Example 9 and to the status of other types of transfers is whether full and adequate consideration in money or money's worth was given for the property transferred.[19] Although consideration is present in Example 9 (property for marriage) for purposes of state law, the consideration is not sufficient for the Federal gift tax. Under Reg. § 25.2512–8, "A consideration not reducible to a value in money or money's worth, as love and affection, promise of marriage, etc., is to be wholly disregarded, and the entire value of the property transferred constitutes the amount of the gift."

Incomplete Transfers.   The Federal gift tax does not apply to transfers that are incomplete. Thus, if the transferor retains the right to reclaim the property or has not really parted with the possession of the property, a taxable event has not taken place.

EXAMPLE 10

D creates a trust, income payable to S for life, remainder to R. Under the terms of the trust instrument, D can revoke the trust at any time and repossess the trust principal and the income earned. No gift takes place on the creation of the trust; D has not ceased to have dominion and control over the property. ◆

EXAMPLE 11

Assume the same facts as in Example 10, except that one year after the transfer, D relinquishes his right to terminate the trust. At this point, the transfer becomes complete and the Federal gift tax applies. ◆

Business versus Personal Setting. In a business setting, full and adequate consideration is apt to exist. Reg. § 25.2512–8 provides that "a sale, exchange, or other transfer of property made in the ordinary course of business (a

---

18. Reg. § 25.2511–1(g)(1).

19. § 2512(b).

transaction that is bona fide, at arm's length, and free of any donative intent) will be considered as made for an adequate and full consideration in money or money's worth." If the parties are acting in a personal setting, however, a gift usually is the result.

─────────────────────── EXAMPLE 12 ───────────────────────

D loans money to S in connection with a business venture. About a year later, D forgives part of the loan. D probably has not made a gift to S if D and S are unrelated parties.[20] ◆

─────────────────────── EXAMPLE 13 ───────────────────────

Assume the same facts as in Example 12, except that D and S are father and son and no business venture is involved. If the loan itself was not, actually a disguised gift, the later forgiveness will probably be treated as a gift. ◆

Do not conclude that the presence of *some* consideration may be enough to preclude Federal gift tax consequences. Again, the answer may rest on whether the transfer occurred in a business setting.

─────────────────────── EXAMPLE 14 ───────────────────────

D sells S some real estate for $40,000. Unknown to D, the property contains valuable mineral deposits and is really worth $100,000. D may have made a bad business deal, but he has not made a gift to S of $60,000. ◆

─────────────────────── EXAMPLE 15 ───────────────────────

Assume the same facts as in Example 14, except that D and S are father and son. In addition, D is very much aware of the fact that the property is worth $100,000. D has made a gift to S of $60,000. ◆

Certain Excluded Transfers. Transfers to political organizations are exempt from the application of the Federal gift tax.[21] This provision in the Code made unnecessary the previous practice whereby candidates for public office established multiple campaign committees to maximize the number of annual exclusions available to their contributors. As noted later, an annual exclusion of $10,000 (previously $3,000) for each donee passes free of the Federal gift tax.

The Federal gift tax does not apply to tuition payments made to an educational organization (e.g., a college) on another's behalf. Nor does it apply to amounts paid on another's behalf for medical care.[22] In this regard, the law is realistic since it is unlikely that most donors would recognize these items as transfers subject to the gift tax.

Lifetime versus Death Transfers. Be careful to distinguish between lifetime (inter vivos) and death (testamentary) transfers.

─────────────────────── EXAMPLE 16 ───────────────────────

D buys a U.S. savings bond, which he registers as follows: "D, payable to S upon D's death." No gift is made when D buys the bond; S has received only a mere expectancy (i.e., to obtain ownership of the bond at D's death). Anytime before his death, D may redeem or otherwise dispose of the bond and cut off S's interest. On D's death, no gift

─────────────────────────────

20. The forgiveness could result in taxable income to S under § 61(a)(12).

21. § 2501(a)(5).
22. § 2503(e).

is made because the bond passes to S by testamentary disposition. As noted later, the bond will be included in D's gross estate as property in which the decedent had an interest (§ 2033). ◆

EXAMPLE 17

D purchases an insurance policy on his own life (face value of $100,000) and designates S as the beneficiary. Until his death, D remains the owner of the policy and pays all premiums. In accordance with the reasoning in Example 16, no gift to S is made either when the policy is purchased or when D pays the premiums. On D's death, the $100,000 proceeds pass to S as a testamentary and not a lifetime transfer. As mentioned later, the insurance proceeds are included in D's gross estate under § 2042(2). ◆

Transfers Subject to the Gift Tax

Whether a transfer is subject to the Federal gift tax depends upon the application of §§ 2511 through 2519 and the Regulations thereunder.

Gift Loans. To understand the tax ramifications of gift loans, an illustration is helpful.

EXAMPLE 18

Before his daughter (D) leaves for college, F lends her $300,000. D signs a note that provides for repayment in five years. The loan contains no interest element, and neither F nor D expects any interest to be paid. Following F's advice, D invests the loan proceeds in income-producing securities. During her five years in college, D uses the income from the investments to pay for college costs and other living expenses. On the maturity date of the note, D repays the $300,000 she owes F. ◆

In a gift loan arrangement, the following consequences ensue:

- F has made a gift to D of the interest element. The amount of the gift is determined by the difference between the amount of interest charged (in this case, none) and the market rate (as determined by the yield on certain U.S. government securities).
- The interest element is included in F's gross income and is subject to the Federal income tax.
- D may be allowed an income tax deduction as to the interest element. This result may benefit D only if she is in a position to itemize her deductions *from* adjusted gross income.

The Code defines a gift loan as "any below-market loan where the foregoing [*sic*] of interest is in the nature of a gift."[23] Unless tax avoidance was one of the principal purposes of the loan, special limitations apply if the gift loan does not exceed $100,000. In such a case, the interest element may not exceed the borrower's net investment income.[24] Furthermore, if the net investment income does not exceed $1,000, it is treated as zero. Under a $1,000 *de minimis* rule, the interest element is to be disregarded.

Certain Property Settlements (§ 2516). Normally, the settlement of certain marital rights is not regarded as being for consideration and is subject to the

---

23. § 7872(f)(3).
24. Net investment income has the same meaning given to the term by § 163(d). Generally, net investment income is

investment income (e.g., interest, dividends) less related expenses.

Federal gift tax.[25] As a special exception to this general approach, Congress enacted § 2516. Under this provision, transfers of property interests made under the terms of a written agreement between spouses in settlement of their marital or property rights are deemed to be for adequate consideration. These transfers are exempt from the Federal gift tax if a final decree of divorce is obtained within the three-year period beginning on the date one year before the parties entered into the agreement. Likewise excluded are transfers to provide a reasonable allowance for the support of minor children (including legally adopted children) of a marriage. The agreement need not be approved by the divorce decree.

Disclaimers (§ 2518).   A disclaimer is a refusal by a person to accept property that is designated to pass to him or her. The effect of the disclaimer is to pass the property to someone else.

───────────────── EXAMPLE 19 ─────────────────

D dies without a will and is survived by a son, S, and a grandson, GS. At the time of his death, D owned real estate that, under the applicable state law, passes to the closest lineal descendant, S in this case. If, however, S disclaims his interest in the real estate, state law provides that the property passes to GS. At the time of D's death, S has considerable property of his own, and GS has none. ◆

Why might S want to consider issuing a disclaimer as to his inheritance and have the property pass directly from D to GS? By doing so, an extra transfer tax might be avoided. If the disclaimer does not take place (i.e., S accepts the inheritance) and the property eventually passes to GS (either by gift or by death), the later transfer will be subject to the application of either the gift tax or the estate tax.

For many years, whether a disclaimer would be effective in avoiding a Federal transfer tax depended on the application of state law. To illustrate by using the facts of Example 19, if state law determined that the real estate was deemed to have passed through S despite his disclaimer after D's death, the Federal gift tax would apply. In essence, S would be treated as if he had inherited the property from D and then given it to GS. As state law was not always consistent in this regard and sometimes was not even known, the application or nonapplication of Federal transfer taxes could depend on where the parties lived. To remedy this situation and provide some measure of uniformity, §§ 2046 (relating to disclaimers for estate tax purposes) and 2518 were added to the Code.

In the case of the gift tax, when the requirements of § 2518 are met and S issues a timely lifetime disclaimer (refer to Example 19), the property is treated as if it goes directly from D to GS. Since the property is not regarded as having passed through S (regardless of what state law holds), it is not subject to the Federal gift tax.

The tax law also permits the avoidance of the Federal gift tax in cases of a partial disclaimer of an undivided interest.

───────────────── EXAMPLE 20 ─────────────────

Assume the same facts as in Example 19, except that S wishes to retain one-half of the real estate for himself. If S makes a timely disclaimer of an undivided one-half interest in the property, the Federal gift tax will not apply to the portion passing to GS. ◆

Other Transfers Subject to Gift Tax.   Other transfers that may carry gift tax consequences (e.g., the exercise of a power of appointment, the creation of joint ownership) are discussed and illustrated in connection with the Federal estate tax.

───────────────

25. See Reg. § 25.2512–8 and Example 9 in this chapter.

Annual Exclusion

In General. The first $10,000 of gifts made to any one person during any calendar year (except gifts of future interests in property) is excluded in determining the total amount of gifts for the year.[26] The annual exclusion is applied to all gifts of a present interest made during the calendar year in the order in which they are made until the $10,000 exclusion per donee is exhausted. For a gift in trust, each beneficiary of the trust is treated as a separate person for purposes of the exclusion.

A *future interest* is defined as one that will come into being (as to use, possession, or enjoyment) at some future date. Examples of future interests include such rights as remainder interests that are commonly encountered when property is transferred to a trust. A *present interest* is an unrestricted right to the immediate use, possession, or enjoyment of property or of the income.

EXAMPLE 21

During the current year, D makes the following cash gifts: $8,000 to R and $12,000 to S. D may claim an annual exclusion of $8,000 with respect to R and $10,000 with respect to S. ◆

EXAMPLE 22

By a lifetime gift, D transfers property to a trust with a life estate (with income payable annually) to R and remainder upon R's death to S. D has made two gifts: one to R of a life estate and one to S of a remainder interest. (The valuation of each of these gifts is discussed in Chapter 18.) The life estate is a present interest and qualifies for the annual exclusion. The remainder interest granted to S is a future interest and does not qualify for the exclusion. Note that S's interest does not come into being until some future date (on the death of R). ◆

Although Example 22 indicates that the gift of an income interest is a present interest, this is not always the case. If a possibility exists that the income beneficiary may not receive the immediate enjoyment of the property, the transfer is of a future interest.

EXAMPLE 23

Assume the same facts as in Example 22, except that the income from the trust need not be payable annually to R. It may, at the trustee's discretion, be accumulated and added to the principal. Since R's right to receive the income from the trust is conditioned on the trustee's discretion, it is not a present interest. No annual exclusion will be allowed. The mere possibility of diversion is enough. It would not matter if the trustee never exercised the discretion to accumulate and did, in fact, distribute the trust income to R annually. ◆

Trust for Minors. Section 2503(c) offers an important exception to the future interest rules just discussed. Under this provision, a transfer for the benefit of a person who has not attained the age of 21 years on the date of the gift may be considered a gift of a present interest. This is true even though the minor is not given the unrestricted right to the immediate use, possession, or enjoyment of the property. For the exception to apply, the following conditions must be satisfied:

- Both the property and its income may be expended by or for the benefit of the minor before the minor attains the age of 21.

---

26. § 2503(b).

- Any portion of the property or its income not expended by the time the minor reaches the age of 21 shall pass to the minor at that time.
- If the minor dies before attaining the age of 21, the property and its income will be payable either to the minor's estate or as the minor may designate under a general power of appointment (discussed later in the chapter).

The exception allows a trustee to accumulate income on behalf of a minor beneficiary without converting the income interest to a future interest.

―――――――――――――――――――― EXAMPLE 24 ――――――――――――――――――――

D places property in trust, income payable to S until he reaches 21, remainder to S or S's estate. Under the terms of the trust instrument, the trustee is empowered to accumulate the trust income or apply it toward S's benefit. In either event, the accumulated income and principal must be paid to S whenever he reaches 21 years of age or to whomever S designates in his will if he dies before reaching such age. The conditions of § 2503(c) are satisfied, and D's transfer qualifies for the annual exclusion. S's interest is a present interest. ◆

Deductions

In arriving at taxable gifts, a deduction is allowed for transfers to certain qualified charitable organizations. On transfers between spouses, a marital deduction may be available. Since both the charitable and marital deductions apply in determining the Federal estate tax, these deductions are discussed later in the chapter.

Computing the Federal Gift Tax

The Unified Transfer Tax Rate Schedule. The top rates of the unified transfer tax rate schedule originally reached as high as 70 percent (see Appendix A, page A–5). For consistency with the maximum income tax rate applicable to individuals, which, until recently, was 50 percent, the top unified transfer tax rate was lowered to this amount. But the reduction was phased in, and the maximum of 50 percent is not scheduled to be reached until 1993 (see Appendix A, page A–9). For transfers (by gift or death) made from 1984 through 1992, the top rate is 55 percent (see Appendix A, page A–8). As noted later in the chapter, the benefits of the graduated rates are to be phased out for larger gifts beginning after 1987. Keep in mind that the unified transfer tax rate schedule applies to all transfers (by gift or death) after 1976. Different rate schedules apply for pre-1977 gifts (see Appendix A, page A–11) and pre-1977 deaths (see Appendix A, page A–10).

The Deemed Paid Adjustment. Review the formula for the gift tax (earlier in the chapter) and note that the tax base for a current gift includes *all* past taxable gifts. The effect of the inclusion is to force the current taxable gift into a higher bracket due to the progressive nature of the unified transfer tax rates (refer to Example 1). To mitigate such double taxation, the donor is allowed a credit for any gift tax previously paid (refer to Example 2).

Limiting the donor to a credit for the gift tax *actually paid* on pre-1977 taxable gifts would be unfair. Pre-1977 taxable gifts were subject to a lower set of rates (see Appendix A, page A–11) than those in the unified transfer tax rate schedule. As a consequence, the donor is allowed a *deemed paid* credit on pre-1977 taxable gifts. This is the amount that would have been due under the unified transfer tax rate schedule had it been applicable. Post-1976 taxable gifts do not need the deemed paid adjustment since the same rate schedule is involved in all gifts.

───────────────── EXAMPLE 25 ─────────────────

In early 1976, T made taxable gifts of $500,000, upon which a Federal gift tax of $109,275 (see Appendix A, page A–11) was paid. Assume T makes further taxable gifts of $700,000 in 1992. The unified transfer tax on the 1992 gifts would be determined as follows:

Taxable gifts made in 1992		$ 500,000
Add: Taxable gifts made in 1976		700,000
Total of current and past taxable gifts		$1,200,000
Unified transfer tax on total taxable gifts per Appendix A, page A–8 [$345,800 + (41% × $200,000)]		$ 427,800
Subtract:		
Deemed paid tax on pre-1977 taxable gifts per Appendix A, page A–8	$155,800	
Unified tax credit for 1992	192,800	(348,600)
Gift tax due on the 1992 taxable gift		$ 79,200

Note that the gift tax actually paid on the 1976 transfer was $109,275. Nevertheless, the deemed paid credit allowed T on the gift is $155,800, considerably more than what was paid. ◆

The Election to Split Gifts by Married Persons. To understand the reason for the gift-splitting election of § 2513, consider the following situations:

───────────────── EXAMPLE 26 ─────────────────

H and W are husband and wife and reside in Michigan, a common law state. H has been the only breadwinner in the family, and W has no significant property of her own. Neither has made any prior taxable gifts or has used the $30,000 specific exemption previously available for pre-1977 gifts. In 1992, H makes a gift to S of $1,220,000. Presuming the election to split gifts did not exist, H's gift tax is as follows:

Amount of gift	$1,220,000
Subtract: Annual exclusion	(10,000)
Taxable gift	$1,210,000
Gift tax on $1,210,000 per Appendix A, page A–8 [$345,800 + (41% × $210,000)]	$ 431,900
Subtract: Unified tax credit for 1992	(192,800)
Gift tax due on the 1992 taxable gift	$ 239,100

◆

───────────────── EXAMPLE 27 ─────────────────

Assume the same facts as in Example 26, except that H and W always have resided in California. Even though H is the sole breadwinner, income from personal services generally is community property. Consequently, the gift to S probably involves community property. If this is the case, the gift tax is as follows:

	H	W
Amount of the gift (50% × $1,220,000)	$ 610,000	$ 610,000
Subtract: Annual exclusion	(10,000)	(10,000)
Taxable gifts	$ 600,000	600,000
Gift tax on $600,000 per Appendix A, page A–8	$ 192,800	$ 192,800
Subtract: Unified tax credit for 1992	(192,800)	(192,800)
Gift tax due on the 1992 taxable gifts	$ –0–	$ –0–

◆

As the results of Examples 26 and 27 indicate, married donors residing in community property jurisdictions possessed a significant gift tax advantage over those residing in common law states. To rectify this inequity, the Revenue Act of 1948 incorporated into the Code the predecessor to § 2513. Under this Section, a gift made by a person to someone other than his or her spouse may be considered, for Federal gift tax purposes, as having been made one-half by each spouse. Returning to Example 26, H and W could treat the gift passing to S as being made one-half by each of them. They may do this in spite of the fact that the cash belonged to H. As a result, the parties are able to achieve the same tax consequence as was outlined in Example 27.

To split gifts, the spouses must be legally married to each other at the time of the gift. If they are divorced later in the calendar year, they may still split the gift if neither marries anyone else during that year. They both must indicate on their separate gift tax returns their consent to have all gifts made in that calendar year split between them. In addition, both must be citizens or residents of the United States on the date of the gift. A gift from one spouse to the other spouse cannot be split. Such a gift might, however, be eligible for the marital deduction.

The election to split gifts is not necessary when husband and wife transfer community property to a third party. It is available, however, if the gift consists of the separate property of one of the spouses. Generally, separate property is property acquired before marriage and property acquired after marriage by gift or inheritance. The election, then, is not limited to residents of common law states.

Procedural Matters

Having determined which transfers are subject to the Federal gift tax and the various deductions and exclusions available to the donor, the procedural aspects of the tax should be considered. The following sections discuss the return itself, the due dates for filing and paying the tax, and other related matters.

The Federal Gift Tax Return. For transfers by gift, a Form 709 (U.S. Gift Tax Return) must be filed whenever the gifts for any one calendar year exceed the annual exclusion or involve a gift of a future interest. A Form 709 need not be filed, however, for transfers between spouses that are offset by the unlimited marital deduction regardless of the amount of the transfer.[27]

─────────────── EXAMPLE 28 ───────────────

In 1992, D makes five gifts, each in the amount of $10,000, to his five children. If the gifts do not involve future interests, a Form 709 need not be filed to report the transfers. ◆

─────────────── EXAMPLE 29 ───────────────

During 1992, M makes a gift of $20,000 cash of her separate property to her daughter. To double the amount of the annual exclusion allowed, F (M's husband) is willing to split the gift. Since the § 2513 election can be made only on a gift tax return, a form must be filed even though no gift tax will be due as a result of the transfer. Useful for this purpose is Form 709–A (U.S. Short Form Gift Tax Return). This form is available to simplify the gift-splitting procedure. ◆

Presuming a gift tax return is due, it must be filed on or before the fifteenth day of April following the year of the gift.[28] As is the case with other Federal taxes, when the due date falls on Saturday, Sunday, or a legal holiday, the date for filing the return is the next business day. Note that the filing requirements for

---

27. § 6019(a)(2).   28. § 6075(b).

Form 709 have no correlation to the accounting year used by a donor for Federal income tax purposes. Thus, a fiscal year taxpayer must follow the April 15 rule for any reportable gifts.

Extensions of Time and Payment of Tax. If sufficient reason is shown, the IRS is authorized to grant reasonable extensions of time for filing the return.[29] Unless the donor is abroad, no extension longer than six months may be granted. The application must be made before the due date of the return and must contain a full report of the causes for the delay. For a calendar year taxpayer, an extension of time for filing an income tax return also extends the time for filing Form 709. An extension of time to file the return does not extend the time for payment of the tax.

The tax shown on the gift tax return is to be paid by the donor at the time and place fixed for the filing of the return.[30] A reasonable extension of time, not to exceed six months (unless the donor is abroad), may be granted by the IRS at the request of the donor for the payment of the tax shown on the return.[31]

Interest must be paid on any amount of tax that is not paid on or before the last date prescribed for the payment of the tax.[32] In addition, a penalty will be imposed unless the failure to pay was for reasonable cause. A penalty is also imposed for failure to file a gift tax return.[33] These penalties are discussed in Chapter 16.

CONCEPT SUMMARY 17–1
FEDERAL GIFT TAX PROVISIONS

1. The Federal gift tax applies to all gratuitous transfers of property made by U.S. citizens or residents. In this regard, it does not matter where the property is located.
2. In the eyes of the IRS, a gratuitous transfer is one not supported by full and adequate consideration. If the parties are acting in a business setting, such consideration usually exists. If, however, purported sales are between family members, a gift element may be suspected.
3. If one party lends money to another and intends some or all of the interest element to be a gift, the arrangement is categorized as a gift loan. To the extent that the interest provided for is less than the market rate, three tax consequences result. First, a gift has taken place between the lender and the borrower as to the interest element. Second, income may result to the lender. Third, an income tax deduction may be available to the borrower.
4. Property settlements can escape the gift tax if a divorce occurs within a prescribed period of time.
5. A disclaimer is a refusal by a person to accept property designated to pass to that person. The effect of a disclaimer is to pass the property to someone else. If certain conditions are satisfied, the issuance of a disclaimer will not be subject to the Federal gift tax.
6. Except for gifts of future interests, a donor is allowed an annual exclusion of $10,000. The future interest limitation does not apply to certain trusts created for minors.
7. The election to split a gift enables a married couple to be treated as two donors. The election doubles the annual exclusion and makes the unified tax credit available to the nonowner spouse.
8. The election to split gifts is not necessary if the property is jointly owned by the spouses. That is the case when the property is part of the couple's community.
9. In determining the tax base for computing the gift tax, all prior taxable gifts must be added to current taxable gifts. Thus, the gift tax is cumulative in nature.
10. Gifts are reported on Form 709 or Form 709–A. The return is due on April 15 following the year of the gift.

---

29. § 6081.

30. § 6151.

31. § 6161(a)(1).

32. § 6601.

33. §§ 6651(a)(1) and (2).

The following discussion of the estate tax coincides with the formula that appeared earlier in the chapter. The key components in the formula are the gross estate, the taxable estate, the tax base, and the credits allowed against the tentative tax. This formula can be summarized as follows:

Gross estate	−	Deductions allowed	=	Taxable estate	+	Post-1976 taxable gifts	=	Tax base
Tentative tax on total transfers	−	Tax credits	=	Estate tax due				

Gross Estate

Simply stated, the gross estate comprises all property subject to the Federal estate tax. This depends on the provisions of the Internal Revenue Code as supplemented by IRS pronouncements and the judicial interpretations of Federal courts.

In contrast to the gross estate, the probate estate is controlled by state (rather than Federal) law. The probate estate consists of all of a decedent's property subject to administration by the executor or administrator of the estate. The administration is supervised by a local court of appropriate jurisdiction (usually designated as a probate court). An executor (or executrix) is the decedent's personal representative appointed under the decedent's will. When a decedent dies without a will or fails to name an executor in the will (or that person refuses to serve), the local probate court appoints an administrator (or administratrix).

The probate estate is frequently smaller than the gross estate. It contains only property owned by the decedent at the time of death and passing to heirs under a will or under the law of intestacy (the order of distribution for those dying without a will). As noted later, such items as the proceeds of many life insurance policies become part of the gross estate but are not included in the probate estate.

All states provide for an order of distribution in the event someone dies without a will. After the surviving spouse, who receives some or all of the estate, the preference is usually in the following order: down to lineal descendants (e.g., children, grandchildren), up to lineal ascendants (e.g., parents, grandparents), and out to collateral relations (e.g., brothers, sisters, aunts, and uncles).

Property Owned by the Decedent (§ 2033). Property owned by the decedent at the time of death is included in the gross estate. The nature of the property or the use to which it was put during the decedent-owner's lifetime has no significance as far as the estate tax is concerned. Thus, personal effects (such as clothing), stocks, bonds, furniture, jewelry, works of art, bank accounts, and interests in businesses conducted as sole proprietorships and partnerships are all included in the deceased owner's gross estate. No distinction is made between tangible and intangible, depreciable and nondepreciable, business and personal assets.

The application of § 2033 can be illustrated as follows:

--------------------------- EXAMPLE 30 ---------------------------

D dies owning some City of Denver bonds. The fair market value of the bonds plus any interest accrued to the date of D's death is included in D's gross estate. Although interest on municipals is normally not taxable under the Federal income tax, it is property owned by D at the time of death. However, any interest accrued after death is not part of D's gross estate. ◆

EXAMPLE 31

D dies on April 8, 1992, at a time when she owns stock in X Corporation and Y Corporation. On March 2 of this year, both corporations authorized a cash dividend payable on May 1. For X Corporation, the dividend was payable to shareholders of record as of April 1. Y Corporation's date of record is April 10. D's gross estate includes the following: the stock in X Corporation, the stock in Y Corporation, and the dividend on the X Corporation stock. It does not include the dividend on the Y Corporation stock. ◆

EXAMPLE 32

D dies holding some promissory notes issued to him by his son. In his will, D forgives these notes, relieving the son of the obligation to make any payments. The fair market value of these notes will be included in D's gross estate. ◆

EXAMPLE 33

D died while employed by Z Corporation. Under an informal but nonbinding company policy, Z Corporation awards half of D's annual salary to D's widow as a death benefit. Presuming that D had no vested interest in and that the widow had no enforceable right to the payment, none of it will be included in his gross estate.[34] ◆

Dower and Curtesy Interests (§ 2034).   In its common law (nonstatutory) form, dower generally gave a surviving widow a life estate in a portion of her husband's estate (usually the real estate he owned) with the remainder passing to their children. Most states have modified and codified these common law rules, and the resulting statutes often vary between jurisdictions. In some states, for example, by statute, a widow is entitled to outright ownership of a percentage of her deceased husband's real estate and personal property. Curtesy is a similar right held by the husband in his wife's property that takes effect in the event he survives her. Most states have abolished the common law curtesy concept and have, in some cases, substituted a modified statutory version.

Dower and curtesy rights are incomplete interests and may never materialize. Thus, if a wife predeceases her husband, her dower interest in her husband's property is lost.

EXAMPLE 34

D dies without a will, leaving an estate of $900,000. Under state law, W (D's widow) is entitled to one-third of D's property. The $300,000 W receives will be included in D's gross estate. Depending on the nature of the interest W receives in the $300,000, this amount could qualify D's estate for a marital deduction. (This possibility is discussed at greater length later in the chapter. For the time being, however, the focus is on what is or is not included as part of the decedent's gross estate.) ◆

Adjustments for Gifts Made within Three Years of Death (§ 2035).   At one time, all taxable gifts made within three years of death were included in the donor's gross estate unless it could be shown that the gifts were not made in contemplation of death. The prior rule was designed to preclude tax avoidance since the gift tax and estate tax rates were separate and the former was lower than the latter. When the gift and estate tax rates were combined into the unified

---

34. *Barr's Estate*, 40 T.C. 227 (1963).

transfer tax, the reason for the rule for gifts in contemplation of death largely disappeared. The three-year rule has, however, been retained for the following items:

- Inclusion in the gross estate of any gift tax paid on gifts made within three years of death. Called the *gross-up* procedure, it prevents the gift tax amount from escaping the estate tax.
- Any property interests transferred by gift within three years of death that would have been included in the gross estate by virtue of the application of § 2036 (transfers with a retained life estate), § 2037 (transfers taking effect at death), § 2038 (revocable transfers), and § 2042 (proceeds of life insurance). All except § 2037 are discussed later in the chapter.

―――――――――――――――――― EXAMPLE 35 ――――――――――――――――――

Before his death in 1992, D made the following taxable gifts:

Year of Gift	Nature of the Asset	Fair Market Value		Gift Tax Paid
		Date of Gift	Date of Death	
1986	X Corporation stock	$100,000	$150,000	$ –0–
1990	Policy on D's life	40,000 (cash value)	200,000 (face value)	–0–
1991	Land	400,000	410,000	8,200

D's *gross estate* includes $208,200 [$200,000 (life insurance proceeds) + $8,200 (gross-up for the gift tax on the 1991 taxable gift)] as to these transfers. Referring to the formula for the estate tax (see page 17–4), the other post-1976 taxable gifts are added to the *taxable estate* (at the fair market value on the date of the gift) in arriving at the tax base. D's estate is allowed a credit for the $8,200 gift tax paid on the 1991 transfer. ◆

The three-year rule also applies in testing for qualification under § 303 (stock redemptions to pay death taxes and administration expenses), § 2032A (special valuation procedures), and § 6166 (extensions of time to pay death taxes). All these provisions are discussed in Chapter 18.

Transfers with a Retained Life Estate (§ 2036). Code §§ 2036 through 2038 were enacted on the premise that the estate tax can be avoided on lifetime transfers only if the decedent does not retain control over the property. The logic of this approach is somewhat difficult to dispute. One should not be able to escape the tax consequences of property transfers at death while remaining in a position to enjoy some or all of the fruits of ownership during life.

Under code § 2036, the value of any property transferred by the deceased during lifetime for less than adequate consideration must be included if either of the following was retained:

- The possession or enjoyment of, or the right to the income from, the property.
- The right, either alone or in conjunction with any person, to designate the persons who shall possess or enjoy the property or the income.

"The possession or enjoyment of, or the right to the income from, the property," as it appears in § 2036(a)(1), is considered to have been retained by the decedent to the extent that such income, etc., is to be applied toward the discharge of a legal obligation of the decedent. The term "legal obligation" includes a legal obligation of the decedent to support a dependent during the decedent's lifetime.[35]

The practical application of § 2036 can be explained by turning to two illustrations.

EXAMPLE 36

F's will passes all of F's property to a trust, income to D for his life (D is given a life estate). Upon D's death, the principal goes to R (R is granted a remainder interest). On D's death, none of the trust property is included in his gross estate. Although D held a life estate, § 2036 is inapplicable because D was not the transferor (F was) of the property. Section 2033 (property owned by the decedent) causes any income distributions D was entitled to receive at the time of his death to be included in his gross estate. ◆

EXAMPLE 37

By deed, D transfers the remainder interest in her ranch to S, retaining for herself the right to continue occupying the property until death. Upon D's death, the fair market value of the ranch will be included in D's gross estate. Furthermore, D is subject to the gift tax. The amount of the gift is the fair market value of the ranch on the date of the gift less the portion applicable to D's retained life estate. (See Chapter 18 for the way this gift is determined.) ◆

Revocable Transfers (§ 2038). Another type of lifetime transfer that is drawn into a decedent's gross estate is covered by § 2038. The gross estate includes the value of property interests transferred by the decedent (except to the extent that the transfer was made for full consideration) if the enjoyment of the property transferred was subject, at the date of the decedent's death, to any power of the decedent to *alter, amend, revoke, or terminate* the transfer. This includes the power to change the beneficiaries or the power to accelerate or increase any beneficiary's enjoyment of the property.

The capacity in which the decedent could exercise the power is immaterial. If the decedent gave property in trust, making him- or herself the trustee with the power to revoke the trust, the property is included in his or her gross estate. If the decedent named another person as trustee with the power to revoke, but reserved the power to later appoint him- or herself trustee, the property is also included in his or her gross estate. If, however, the power to alter, amend, revoke, or terminate was held at all times solely by a person other than the decedent and the decedent did not reserve a right to assume these powers, the property is not included in the decedent's gross estate.

The Code and the Regulations make it clear that one cannot avoid inclusion in the gross estate under § 2038 by relinquishing a power within three years of death.[36] Recall that § 2038 is one of several types of situations listed as exceptions to the usual rule excluding gifts made within three years of death from the gross estate.

In the event § 2038 applies, the amount includible in the gross estate is the portion of the property transferred that is subject, at the decedent's death, to the decedent's power to alter, amend, revoke, or terminate.

The classic § 2038 situation results from the use of a revocable trust.

---

35. Reg. § 20.2036–1(b)(2).

36. § 2038(a)(1) and Reg. § 20.2038–1(e)(1).

─────────────────── EXAMPLE 38 ───────────────────

G creates a trust, life estate to her children, remainder to her grandchildren. Under the terms of the trust, G reserves the right to revoke the trust and revest the trust principal and income in herself. As noted in Example 10, the creation of the trust does not result in a gift because the transfer is not complete. However, if G dies still retaining the power to revoke, the trust is included in her gross estate under § 2038. ◆

More subtle applications of § 2038 result from the use of a state Uniform Gifts to Minors Act. The Uniform Gifts to Minors Act permits the ownership of securities to be transferred to a minor with someone designated as custodian. The custodian has the right to sell the securities, collect any income, and otherwise act on behalf of the minor without court supervision. The custodianship arrangement is convenient and inexpensive. Under state law the custodianship terminates automatically when the minor reaches a specified age (usually age 21). If the custodian also has the power to terminate the arrangement, § 2038 could create estate tax problems.

─────────────────── EXAMPLE 39 ───────────────────

D transfers securities to S under the state's Uniform Gifts to Minors Act naming himself as the custodian. Under the Act, the custodian has the authority to terminate the custodianship at any time and distribute the proceeds to the minor. D dies four years later before the custodianship is terminated. Although the transfer is effective for income tax purposes, it runs afoul of § 2038.[37] Under this Section, the fair market value of the securities on the date of D's death is included in D's gross estate for Federal estate tax purposes. ◆

─────────────────── EXAMPLE 40 ───────────────────

Assume the same facts as in Example 39, except that D dissolves the custodianship (thereby turning the securities over to S) within three years of death. The fair market value of the securities on the date of D's death is included in D's gross estate.[38] ◆

─────────────────── EXAMPLE 41 ───────────────────

Assume the same facts as in Example 39, except that S comes of age and the custodianship terminates before D's death. Nothing is included in D's gross estate upon D's death. ◆

─────────────────── EXAMPLE 42 ───────────────────

G transfers securities to S under the state's Uniform Gifts to Minors Act naming D as the custodian. Nothing relating to these securities is included in D's gross estate upon D's death during the term of the custodianship. Section 2038 is not applicable because D was not the transferor. G's death during the custodianship causes no estate tax consequences; G has retained no interest or control over the property transferred. ◆

In application, the provisions related to incomplete transfers (§§ 2036 and 2038) tend to overlap. It is not unusual to find that either or both of these Sections apply to a particular transfer.

───────────────

37. If the minor is under the age of 14, net unearned income may be taxed at the parents' income tax rate. Net unearned income generally is passive income (e.g., dividends, interest) in excess of $1,200. §§ 1(i) and (j).

38. § 2035(d)(2).

Annuities (§ 2039). Annuities can be divided by their origin into commercial and noncommercial contracts. Noncommercial annuities are issued by private parties and, in some cases, charitable organizations that do not regularly issue annuities. Both varieties have much in common, but noncommercial annuities present special income tax problems and are not treated further in this discussion.

Reg. § 20.2039–1(b)(1) defines an annuity as representing "one or more payments extending over any period of time." According to the Regulation, the payments may be equal or unequal, conditional or unconditional, periodic or sporadic. Most commercial contracts fall into one of four general patterns:

1. *Straight-life annuity.* The insurance company promises to make periodic payments to X (the annuitant) during his or her life. Upon X's death, the company has no further obligation under the contract.
2. *Joint and survivor annuity.* The insurance company promises to make periodic payments to X and Y during their lives with the payments to continue, usually in a diminished amount, for the life of the survivor.
3. *Self and survivor annuity.* The company agrees to make periodic payments to X during his or her life and, upon X's death, to continue these payments for the life of a designated beneficiary. This and the preceding type of annuity are frequently used by married persons.
4. *Refund feature.* The company agrees to return to the annuitant's estate or other designated beneficiary a portion of the investment in the contract in the event of the annuitant's premature death.

In the case of a straight-life annuity, nothing is included in the gross estate of the annuitant at death. Section 2033 (property in which the decedent had an interest) does not apply because the annuitant's interest in the contract is terminated by death. Section 2036 (transfers with a retained life estate) does not cover the situation; a transfer made for full consideration is specifically excluded from § 2036 treatment. A commercial annuity is presumed to have been purchased for full consideration unless some evidence exists to indicate that the parties were not acting at arm's length.

EXAMPLE 43

D purchases a straight-life annuity that will pay him $6,000 a month when he reaches age 65. D dies at age 70. Except for the payments he received before his death, nothing relating to this annuity will affect D's gross estate. ◆

In the case of a survivorship annuity (classifications 2 and 3), the estate tax consequences under § 2039(a) are usually triggered by the death of the first annuitant. The amount included in the gross estate is the cost from the same company of a comparable annuity covering the survivor at his or her attained age on the date of the deceased annuitant's death.

EXAMPLE 44

Assume the same facts as in Example 43, except that the annuity contract provides for W to be paid $3,000 a month for life as a survivorship feature. W is 62 years of age when D dies. Under these circumstances, D's gross estate includes the cost of a comparable contract that provides an annuity of $3,000 per month for the life of a person (male or female, as the case may be) age 62. ◆

Full inclusion in the gross estate of the survivorship element is subject to an important exception under § 2039(b). The amount includible is to be based on the proportion of the deceased annuitant's contribution to the total cost of the contract. This is expressed by the following formula:

| Decedent's contribution to purchase price / Total purchase price of the annuity | X | Value of the annuity (or refund) at decedent's death | = | Amount includible in the deceased annuitant's gross estate |

$$\frac{\text{Decedent's contribution to purchase price}}{\text{Total purchase price of the annuity}} \times \text{Value of the annuity (or refund) at decedent's death} = \text{Amount includible in the deceased annuitant's gross estate}$$

———————————— EXAMPLE 45 ————————————

Assume the same facts as in Example 44, except that D and W are husband and wife and have always lived in a community property state. The premiums on the contract were paid with community funds. Since W contributed half of the cost of the contract, only half of the amount determined under Example 44 is included in D's gross estate. ◆

The result reached in Example 45 is not unique to community property jurisdictions. The outcome would have been the same in a noncommunity property state if W had furnished half of the consideration from her own funds.

Joint Interests (§§ 2040 and 2511).   Recall that joint tenancies and tenancies by the entirety are characterized by the right of survivorship. Thus, upon the death of a joint tenant, title to the property passes to the surviving tenant. None of the property is included in the *probate* estate of the deceased tenant. In the case of tenancies in common and community property, death does not defeat an ownership interest. Further, the deceased owner's interest is part of the probate estate.

The Federal *estate tax treatment* of tenancies in common or of community property follows the logical approach of taxing only the portion of the property included in the deceased owner's probate estate. Thus, if D, X, and Z are tenants in common in a tract of land, each owning an equal interest, and D dies, only one-third of the value of the property is included in the gross estate. This one-third interest is also the same amount that will pass to D's heirs.

———————————— EXAMPLE 46 ————————————

D, X, and Z acquire a tract of land, ownership listed as tenants in common, each party furnishing $20,000 of the $60,000 purchase price. When the property is worth $90,000, D dies. If D's undivided interest in the property is 33⅓%, the gross estate *and* probate estate each include $30,000. ◆

Unless the parties have provided otherwise, each tenant is deemed to own an interest equal to the portion of the original consideration he or she furnished. The parties in Example 46 could have provided that D would receive an undivided half interest in the property although he contributed only one-third of the purchase price. In that case, X and Z have made a gift to D when the tenancy was created, and D's gross estate and probate estate each include $45,000.

For certain joint tenancies, the tax consequences are different. All of the property is included in the deceased co-owner's gross estate unless it can be proven that the surviving co-owners contributed to the cost of the property.[39] If

———

39. § 2040(a).

a contribution can be shown, the amount to be excluded is calculated by the following formula:

$$\frac{\text{Surviving co-owner's contribution}}{\text{Total cost of the property}} \times \text{Fair market value of the property}$$

In computing a survivor's contribution, any funds received as a gift *from the deceased co-owner* and applied to the cost of the property cannot be counted. However, income or gain from gift assets can be counted.

If the co-owners receive the property as a gift *from another,* each co-owner is deemed to have contributed to the cost of his or her own interest.

The preceding rules can be illustrated as follows.

--------------------------- EXAMPLE 47 ---------------------------

D and Y (father and son) acquire a tract of land, ownership listed as joint tenancy with right of survivorship. D furnished $40,000 and Y $20,000 of the $60,000 purchase price. Of the $20,000 provided by Y, $10,000 had previously been received as a gift from D. When the property is worth $90,000, D dies. Because only $10,000 of Y's contribution can be counted (the other $10,000 was received as a gift from D), Y has furnished only one-sixth ($10,000/$60,000) of the cost. Thus, D's gross estate must include five-sixths of $90,000, or $75,000. This presumes Y can prove that he did in fact make the $10,000 contribution. In the absence of such proof, the full value of the property will be included in D's gross estate. D's death makes Y the immediate owner of the property by virtue of the right of survivorship. None of the property is part of D's probate estate. ◆

--------------------------- EXAMPLE 48 ---------------------------

F transfers property to D and Y as a gift listing ownership as joint tenancy with the right of survivorship. Upon D's death, one-half of the value of the property is included in the gross estate. Since the property was received as a gift and the donees are equal owners, each is considered to have furnished half of the consideration. ◆

To simplify the joint ownership rules for *married persons,* § 2040(b) provides for an automatic inclusion rule upon the death of the first joint-owner spouse to die. Regardless of the amount contributed by each spouse, one-half of the value of the property is included in the gross estate of the spouse who dies first. The special rule eliminates the need to trace the source of contributions and recognizes that any inclusion in the gross estate is neutralized by the marital deduction.

--------------------------- EXAMPLE 49 ---------------------------

In 1986, H purchases real estate for $100,000 using his separate funds and listing title as "H and W, joint tenants with the right of survivorship." H predeceases W six years later when the property is worth $300,000. If H and W are husband and wife, H's gross estate includes $150,000 (½ of $300,000) as to the property. ◆

--------------------------- EXAMPLE 50 ---------------------------

Assume the same facts as in Example 49, except that W (instead of H) dies first. Presuming the value at the date of death to be $300,000, W's gross estate includes $150,000 as to the property. In this regard, it is of no consequence that W did not contribute to the cost of the real estate. ◆

In both Examples 49 and 50, inclusion in the gross estate of the first spouse to die will be neutralized by the unlimited marital deduction allowed for estate tax purposes (see the discussion of § 2056 later in the chapter). Under the right of survivorship, the surviving joint tenant obtains full ownership of the property. The marital deduction generally is allowed for property passing from one spouse to another.

Whether a *gift* results when property is transferred into some form of joint ownership depends on the consideration furnished by each of the contributing parties for the ownership interest acquired.

──────────── EXAMPLE 51 ────────────

D and S purchase real estate as tenants in common, each furnishing $40,000 of the $80,000 cost. If each is an equal owner in the property, no gift has occurred. ◆

──────────── EXAMPLE 52 ────────────

Assume the same facts as in Example 51, except that of the $80,000 purchase price, D furnishes $60,000 and S furnishes only $20,000. If each is an equal owner in the property, D has made a gift to S of $20,000. ◆

──────────── EXAMPLE 53 ────────────

M purchases real estate for $240,000, the title to the property being listed as follows: "M, D, and S as joint tenants with the right of survivorship." If under state law the mother (M), the daughter (D), and the son (S) are deemed to be equal owners in the property, M will be treated as having made gifts of $80,000 to D and $80,000 to S. ◆

Several important *exceptions* exist to the general rule that gift treatment is triggered by the creation of a joint ownership with disproportionate interests resulting from unequal consideration. First, if the transfer involves a joint bank account, there is no gift at the time of the contribution.[40] If a gift occurs, it is when the noncontributing party withdraws the funds provided by the other joint tenant. Second, the same rule applies to the purchase of U.S. savings bonds. Again, any gift tax consequences are postponed until the noncontributing party appropriates some or all of the proceeds for his or her individual use.

──────────── EXAMPLE 54 ────────────

D deposits $200,000 in a bank account under the names of D and S as joint tenants. Both D and S have the right to withdraw funds from the account without the other's consent. D has not made a gift to S when the account is established. ◆

──────────── EXAMPLE 55 ────────────

Assume the same facts as in Example 54. At some later date, S withdraws $50,000 from the account for her own use. At this point, D has made a gift to S of $50,000. ◆

──────────── EXAMPLE 56 ────────────

D purchases a U.S. savings bond that he registers in the names of D and S. After D dies, S redeems the bond. No gift takes place when D buys the bond. In addition, S's redemption is not treated as a gift since the bond passed to her by testamentary disposition (S acquired the bond by virtue of surviving D) and not through a lifetime transfer. However, the fair market value of the bond is included in D's gross estate under § 2040. ◆

Powers of Appointment (§§ 2041 and 2514). A power of appointment is a power to determine who shall own or enjoy, presently or in the future, the property subject to the power. It must be created by another and does not

───────────

40. Reg. § 25.2511–1(h)(4).

include a power created or retained by the decedent when he or she transferred his or her own property. The term *power of appointment* includes all powers that are in substance and effect powers of appointment regardless of the terminology used in a particular instrument and regardless of local property law. If, for example, a trust instrument provides that the income beneficiary may appropriate or consume the principal of the trust, this right is a power of appointment over the principal even though those words are not used.

Powers of appointment fall into one of two classifications: *general* and *special*. A general power of appointment is one in which the decedent could have appointed himself, his creditors, his estate, or the creditors of his estate. In contrast, a special power enables the holder to appoint to others but *not* to herself, her creditors, her estate, or the creditors of her estate. Assume, for example, that D has the power to designate how the principal of the trust will be distributed among X, Y, and Z. At this point, D's power is only a special power of appointment. If D is given the further right to appoint the principal to himself, what was a special power of appointment becomes a general power.

Three things can happen to a power of appointment: exercise, lapse, and release. Exercising the power involves appointing the property to one or all of the parties designated. A lapse occurs upon failure to exercise a power. Thus, if a holder, D, fails to indicate how the principal of a trust will be distributed among X, Y, and Z, D's power of appointment will lapse, and the principal will pass in accordance with the terms of the trust instrument. A release occurs if the holder relinquishes a power of appointment.

A release must be distinguished from a disclaimer. In the former situation, the act follows after the acceptance of the power. If the designated holder decides he or she does not want the power, he or she may disclaim (refuse) and avoid the tax consequences that accompany a release. To constitute a disclaimer, the refusal must be made on a timely basis, be unequivocal, and be effective under applicable law.

Powers of appointment have the following transfer tax consequences:

1. No tax implications result from the exercise, lapse, or release of a special power of appointment.
2. The exercise, lapse, or release of a general power of appointment created after October 21, 1942, during life or upon the death of the holder causes the fair market value of the property (or income interest) subject to the power to be a gift or to be included in the holder's gross estate.
3. In connection with (2), a lapse of a general power is subject to gift or estate taxation only to the extent that the value of the property that could have been appointed exceeds the greater of either $5,000 or 5 percent of the aggregate value of the property out of which the appointment could have been satisfied.
4. In connection with (2), a holder is not considered to have had a general power of appointment if he or she had a right to consume or invade for his or her own benefit, as long as that right is limited by an ascertainable standard. The standard must relate to his or her health, education, support, or maintenance. A power to use the property for the "comfort, welfare, or happiness" of the holder is not an ascertainable standard and therefore is a general power of appointment.

The following examples illustrate these rules.

——————————————— EXAMPLE 57 ———————————————

F, D's father, leaves his property in trust, life estate to D and remainder to whichever of D's children D decides to appoint in her will. D's power is not a general power of appointment because she cannot exercise it in favor of herself. Thus, regardless of whether D exercises the power or not, none of the trust property subject to the power is included in her gross estate. ◆

─────────────── EXAMPLE 58 ───────────────

Assume the same facts as in Example 57. In addition to having the testamentary power to designate the beneficiary of the remainder interest, D is given a power to direct the trustee to pay to D from time to time as much of the principal as she might request "for her support." Although D now has a power that she can exercise in favor of herself, it is not a general power of appointment. The power is limited to an ascertainable standard. Thus, none of the property subject to these powers is subject to the gift tax or is included in D's gross estate at D's death. ◆

Life Insurance (§ 2042).   Under § 2042, the gross estate includes the proceeds of life insurance on the decedent's life if (1) they are receivable by the estate, (2) they are receivable by another for the benefit of the estate, or (3) the decedent possessed an incident of ownership in the policy.

Life insurance on the life of another owned by a decedent at the time of his or her death is included in his or her gross estate under § 2033 (property in which the decedent had an interest) and not under § 2042. The amount includible is the replacement value of the policy.[41] Under these circumstances, inclusion of the face amount of the policy is inappropriate as the policy has not yet matured.

─────────────── EXAMPLE 59 ───────────────

At the time of his death, D owned a life insurance policy on the life of S, face amount of $100,000 and replacement value of $25,000, with W as the designated beneficiary. Since the policy has not matured at D's death, § 2042 is inapplicable. However, § 2033 (property in which the decedent had an interest) compels the inclusion of $25,000 (the replacement value) in D's gross estate. If D and W owned the policy as community property, only $12,500 is included in D's gross estate. ◆

The term *life insurance* includes whole life policies, term insurance, group life insurance, travel and accident insurance, endowment contracts (before being paid up), and death benefits paid by fraternal societies operating under the lodge system.[42]

As just noted, proceeds of insurance on the life of the decedent receivable by the executor or administrator or payable to the decedent's estate are included in the gross estate. The estate need not be specifically named as the beneficiary. Assume, for example, the proceeds of the policy are receivable by an individual beneficiary and are subject to an obligation, legally binding upon the beneficiary, to pay taxes, debts, and other charges enforceable against the estate. The proceeds are included in the decedent's gross estate to the extent of the beneficiary's obligation. If the proceeds of an insurance policy made payable to a decedent's estate are community assets and, under state law, one-half belongs to the surviving spouse, only one-half of the proceeds will be considered as receivable by or for the benefit of the decedent's estate.

Proceeds of insurance on the life of the decedent not receivable by or for the benefit of the estate are includible if the decedent at his or her death possessed any of the incidents of ownership in the policy. In this connection, the term *incidents of ownership* not only means the ownership of the policy in a technical legal sense but also, generally speaking, the right of the insured or his or her

─────────────────────

41. Reg. § 20.2031–8(a)(1).
42. Reg. § 20.2042–1(a)(1). As to travel and accident insurance,

see *Comm. v. Estate of Noel*, 65–1 USTC ¶12,311, 15 AFTR2d 1397, 85 S.Ct. 1238 (USSC, 1965).

estate to the economic benefits of the policy. Thus, it also includes the power to change beneficiaries, revoke an assignment, pledge the policy for a loan, or surrender or cancel the policy.[43]

EXAMPLE 60

At the time of death, D was the insured under a policy (face amount of $100,000) owned by S with W as the designated beneficiary. The policy was originally taken out by D five years ago and immediately transferred as a gift to S. Under the assignment, D transferred all rights in the policy except the right to change beneficiaries. D died without having exercised this right, and the policy proceeds are paid to W. Under § 2042(2), the retention of an incident of ownership in the policy (e.g., the right to change beneficiaries) by D causes $100,000 to be included in the gross estate. ◆

Assuming that the deceased-insured holds the incidents of ownership in a policy, how much will be included in the gross estate if the insurance policy is a community asset? Only one-half of the proceeds becomes part of the deceased spouse's gross estate.

In determining whether a policy is *community property* or what portion of it might be so classified, state law controls. The states appear to follow one of two general approaches. Under the inception of title approach, the classification depends on when the policy was originally purchased. If purchased before marriage, the policy is separate property regardless of how many premiums were paid after marriage with community funds. However, if the noninsured spouse is not the beneficiary of the policy, he or she may be entitled to reimbursement from the deceased-insured spouse's estate for half of the premiums paid with community funds. The inception of title approach is followed in at least three states: Louisiana, Texas, and New Mexico.

Some community property jurisdictions classify a policy using the tracing approach: the nature of the funds used to pay premiums controls. Thus, a policy paid for 20 percent with separate funds and 80 percent with community funds will be 20 percent separate property and 80 percent community property. The point in time when the policy was purchased makes no difference. Conceivably, a policy purchased after marriage with the premiums paid exclusively with separate funds would be classified entirely as separate property. The tracing approach appears to be the rule in California and Washington.

Merely purchasing a life insurance contract with someone else designated as the beneficiary does not constitute a *gift*. As long as the purchaser still owns the policy, nothing has really passed to the beneficiary. Even on the death of the insured-owner, no gift takes place. The proceeds paid to the beneficiary constitute a testamentary and not a lifetime transfer. But consider the following possibility:

EXAMPLE 61

D purchases an insurance policy on his own life that he transfers to S. D retains no interest in the policy (such as the power to change beneficiaries). In these circumstances, D has made a gift to S. Furthermore, if D continues to pay the premiums on the transferred policy, each payment will constitute a separate gift. ◆

Under certain conditions, the death of the insured may represent a gift to the beneficiary of part or all of the proceeds. This occurs when the owner of the policy is not the insured.

---

43. Reg. § 20.2042–1(c)(2).

─────────────────────── EXAMPLE 62 ───────────────────────

D owns an insurance policy on the life of S, with T as the designated beneficiary. Up until the time of S's death, D retained the right to change the beneficiary of the policy. The proceeds paid to T by the insurance company by reason of S's death constitute a gift from D to T.[44] ◆

─────────────────────── EXAMPLE 63 ───────────────────────

H and W live in a community property state. With community funds, H purchases an insurance policy with a face amount of $100,000 on his own life and designates S as the revocable beneficiary. On H's death, the proceeds of the policy are paid to S. If under state law H's death makes the transfer by W complete, W has made a gift to S of $50,000. Since the policy was held as community property, W is the owner of only one-half of the policy. Furthermore, one-half of the proceeds of the policy ($50,000) is included in H's gross estate under § 2042. ◆

Taxable Estate

After the gross estate has been determined, the next step is to determine the taxable estate. By virtue of § 2051, the taxable estate is the gross estate less the following: expenses, indebtedness, and taxes (§ 2053); losses (§ 2054); charitable transfers (§ 2055); and the marital deduction (§§ 2056 and 2056A). As previously noted, the charitable and marital deductions also have gift tax ramifications (§§ 2522 and 2523).

Expenses, Indebtedness, and Taxes (§ 2053). A deduction is allowed for funeral expenses; expenses incurred in administering property; claims against the estate; and unpaid mortgages and other charges against property, whose value is included in the gross estate (without reduction for the mortgage or other indebtedness).

Expenses incurred in administering community property are deductible only in proportion to the deceased spouse's interest in the community.[45]

Administration expenses include commissions of the executor or administrator, attorney's fees of the estate, accountant's fees, court costs, and certain selling expenses for disposition of estate property.

Claims against the estate include property taxes accrued before the decedent's death, unpaid income taxes on income received by the decedent before he or she died, and unpaid gift taxes on gifts made by the decedent before death.

Amounts that may be deducted as claims against the estate are only for enforceable personal obligations of the decedent at the time of death. Deductions for claims founded on promises or agreements are limited to the extent that the liabilities were contracted in good faith and for adequate and full consideration. However, a pledge or subscription in favor of a public, charitable, religious, or educational organization is deductible to the extent that it would have constituted an allowable deduction had it been a bequest.[46]

Deductible funeral expenses include the cost of interment, the burial plot or vault, a gravestone, perpetual care of the grave site, and the transportation expense of the person bringing the body to the place of burial. If the decedent had, before death, acquired cemetery lots for him- or herself and family, no deduction is allowed, but the lots are not included in the decedent's gross estate under § 2033 (property in which the decedent had an interest).

44. *Goodman v. Comm.*, 46–1 USTC ¶10,275, 34 AFTR 1534, 156 F.2d 218 (CA–2, 1946).

45. *U.S. v. Stapf*, 63–2 USTC ¶12,192, 12 AFTR2d 6326, 84 S.Ct. 248 (USSC, 1963).

46. § 2053(c)(1)(A) and Reg. § 20.2053–5.

Losses (§ 2054). Section 2054 permits an estate tax deduction for losses from casualty or theft incurred during the period when the estate is being settled. As is true with casualty or theft losses for income tax purposes, any anticipated insurance recovery must be taken into account in arriving at the amount of the deductible loss. Unlike the income tax, however, the deduction is not limited by a floor ($100) or a percentage amount (the excess of 10 percent of adjusted gross income). If the casualty occurs to property after it has been distributed to an heir, the loss belongs to the heir and not to the estate. If the casualty occurs before the decedent's death, it should be claimed on the appropriate Form 1040. The fair market value of the property (if any) on the date of death plus any insurance recovery is included in the gross estate.

As is true of certain administration expenses, a casualty or theft loss of estate property can be claimed as an income tax deduction on the fiduciary return of the estate (Form 1041). But the double deduction prohibition of § 642(g) applies, and claiming the income tax deduction requires a waiver of the estate tax deduction.

Transfers to Charity (§§ 2055 and 2522). A deduction is allowed for the value of property in the decedent's gross estate that is transferred by the decedent through testamentary disposition to (or for the use of) any of the following:

1. The United States or any of its political subdivisions.
2. Any corporation or association organized and operated exclusively for religious, charitable, scientific, literary, or educational purposes, as long as no benefit inures to any private individual and no substantial activity is undertaken to carry on propaganda or otherwise attempt to influence legislation or participate in any political campaign on behalf of any candidate for public office.
3. A trustee or trustees of a fraternal society, order, or association operating under the lodge system if the transferred property is to be used exclusively for religious, charitable, scientific, literary, or educational purposes, and no substantial activity is undertaken to carry on propaganda or otherwise attempt to influence legislation or participate in any political campaign on behalf of any candidate for public office.
4. Any veterans' organization incorporated by an Act of Congress (or any of its subdivisions) as long as no benefit inures to any private individual.

The organizations just described are identical to those that qualify for the Federal gift tax deduction under § 2522. With the following exceptions, they are also the same organizations that will qualify a donee for an income tax deduction under § 170:

- Certain nonprofit cemetery associations qualify for income tax but not death and gift tax purposes.
- Foreign charities may qualify under the estate and gift tax but not under the income tax.

No deduction is allowed unless the charitable bequest is specified by a provision in the decedent's will or the transfer was made before death and the property is subsequently included in the gross estate. Generally speaking, a deduction does not materialize when an individual dies intestate (without a will). The amount of the bequest to charity must be mandatory and cannot be left to someone else's discretion. It is, however, permissible to allow another person—such as the executor of the estate—to choose which charity will receive the specified donation. Likewise, a bequest may be expressed as an alternative and still be effective if the noncharitable beneficiary disclaims (refuses) the intervening interest before the due date for the filing of the estate tax return (nine months after the decedent's death plus any extensions of time granted for filing).

Marital Deduction (§§ 2056, 2056A, and 2523). The marital deduction originated with the Revenue Act of 1948 as part of the same legislation that permitted married persons to secure the income-splitting advantages of filing joint income tax returns. The purpose of these statutory changes was to eliminate the major tax variations that could develop between taxpayers residing in community property and common law states. The marital deduction was designed to provide equity in the estate and gift tax areas.

In a community property state, for example, no marital deduction generally was allowed, since the surviving spouse already owned one-half of the community and that portion was not included in the deceased spouse's gross estate. In a common law state, however, most if not all of the assets often belonged to the breadwinner of the family. When that spouse died first, all of these assets were included in his or her gross estate. Recall that a dower or curtesy interest (regarding a surviving spouse's right to some of the deceased spouse's property), does not reduce the gross estate. To equalize the situation, therefore, a marital deduction, usually equal to one-half of all separate assets, was allowed upon the death of the first spouse.

Ultimately, Congress decided to dispense with these historical justifications and recognize husband and wife as a single economic unit. Consistent with the approach taken under the income tax, spouses are considered as one for transfer tax purposes. By making the marital deduction unlimited in amount, neither the gift tax nor the estate tax is imposed on outright interspousal transfers of property. Unlike prior law, the unlimited marital deduction even includes one spouse's share of the community property transferred to the other spouse.

Under § 2056, the marital deduction is allowed only for property that is included in the deceased spouse's gross estate *and* that passes or has passed to the surviving spouse. Property that *passes* from the decedent to the surviving spouse includes any interest received as (1) the decedent's heir or donee; (2) the decedent's surviving tenant by the entirety or joint tenant; (3) the appointee under the decedent's exercise (or lapse or release) of a general power of appointment; or (4) the beneficiary of insurance on the life of the decedent.

——————————————— EXAMPLE 64 ———————————————

At the time of his death in the current year, D owned an insurance policy on his own life (face amount of $100,000) with W (his wife) as the designated beneficiary. D and W also owned real estate (worth $250,000) as tenants by the entirety (D had furnished all of the purchase price). As to these transfers, $225,000 ($100,000 + $125,000) is included in D's gross estate, and this amount represents the property that passes to W for purposes of the marital deduction.[47] ◆

Under certain conditions, disclaimers of property by the surviving spouse in favor of some other heir affect the amount that passes and reduce the marital deduction. Thus, if W is entitled to $400,000 of H's property but disclaims $100,000 in favor of S, the remainderperson under the will, the $100,000 passes from H to S and not from H to W. Disclaimers by some other heir in favor of the surviving spouse may have the opposite effect. Suppose W, as remainderperson, will receive $300,000 under H's will, but the will also provides that S is to

——————————————

47. Inclusion in the gross estate falls under § 2042 (proceeds of life insurance) and § 2040 (joint interests). Although D provided the full purchase price for the real estate, § 2040(b) requires inclusion of only one-half of the value of the property when one spouse predeceases the other.

receive a specific bequest of $100,000. If S issues a timely disclaimer in favor of W, the amount passing from H to W for purposes of the marital deduction is increased from $300,000 to $400,000.

A similar problem arises when a property interest passing to the surviving spouse is subject to a mortgage or other encumbrance. In this case, only the net value of the interest after reduction by the amount of the mortgage or other encumbrance qualifies for the marital deduction. To allow otherwise would result in a double deduction since a decedent's liabilities are separately deductible under § 2053.

EXAMPLE 65

In his will, H leaves real estate (fair market value of $200,000) to his wife. If the real estate is subject to a mortgage of $40,000 (upon which H was personally liable), the marital deduction is limited to $160,000 ($200,000 − $40,000). The $40,000 mortgage is deductible under § 2053 as an obligation of the decedent (H). ◆

However, if the executor is required under the terms of the decedent's will or under local law to discharge the mortgage out of other assets of the estate or to reimburse the surviving spouse, the payment or reimbursement is an additional interest passing to the surviving spouse.

EXAMPLE 66

Assume the same facts as in Example 65, except that H's will directs that the real estate is to pass to H's wife free of any liabilities. Accordingly, H's executor pays off the mortgage by using other estate assets and distributes the real estate to H's wife. The marital deduction now becomes $200,000. ◆

Federal estate taxes or other death taxes paid out of the surviving spouse's share of the gross estate are not included in the value of property passing to the surviving spouse. Therefore, it is usually preferable for the deceased spouse's will to provide that death taxes be paid out of the portion of the estate that does not qualify for the marital deduction.

Certain interests in property passing from the deceased spouse to the surviving spouse are referred to as *terminable interests*. Such an interest will terminate or fail after the passage of time, upon the happening of some contingency, or upon the failure of some event to occur. Examples are life estates, annuities, estates for terms of years, and patents. A terminable interest will not qualify for the marital deduction if another interest in the same property passed from the deceased spouse to some other person. By reason of the passing, that other person or his or her heirs may enjoy part of the property after the termination of the surviving spouse's interest.[48]

EXAMPLE 67

H's will places H's property in trust, life estate to W, remainder to S or his heirs. The interest passing from H to W does not qualify for the marital deduction. It will terminate on W's death, and S or his heirs will then possess or enjoy the property. ◆

EXAMPLE 68

Assume the same facts as in Example 67, except that the trust was created by H during his life. No marital deduction is available for gift tax purposes for the same reason as in Example 67.[49] ◆

---

48. §§ 2056(b)(1) and 2523(b)(1).

49. Both Examples 67 and 68 contain the potential for a qualified

terminable interest property (QTIP) election discussed later in this section.

─────────────────── EXAMPLE 69 ───────────────────

During his life, H purchased a joint and survivor annuity providing for payments to himself for life and then to W for life should she survive him. All payments cease on the death of H or W, whoever dies later. If H dies first, the value of the survivorship annuity included in his gross estate under § 2039(a) and passing to W will qualify for the marital deduction. W's interest in the annuity will terminate on W's death, but it is not a terminable interest. No other person may possess or enjoy the property after W's death. ◆

The justification for the terminable interest rule can be illustrated by examining the possible result of Examples 67 and 68. Without the rule, H could have passed property to W at no cost because of the marital deduction. Yet, on W's death, none of the property would have been included in W's gross estate. Section 2036 (transfers with a retained life estate) would not apply to W since she was not the original transferor of the property. The marital deduction should not be available in situations where the surviving spouse can enjoy the property and still pass it to another without tax consequences. The marital deduction merely postpones the transfer tax on the death of the first spouse and operates to shift any such tax to the surviving spouse.

The terminable interest rule can be avoided under a *power of appointment exception*.[50] Under the exception, a property interest passing from the deceased spouse to the surviving spouse qualifies for the marital deduction (and not be considered a terminable interest) under the following conditions:

1. The survivor is entitled for life to all of the income from the entire interest.
2. Such income is payable annually or at more frequent intervals.
3. The survivor has the power to appoint the entire interest. This power may be exercised in favor of the survivor (or his or her estate).
4. Such power may be exercised by the survivor alone and in all events (although it may be limited to exercise either during life or by will).
5. No part of the interest is subject to a power in any other person to appoint to anyone other than the surviving spouse.

Conditions 3 and 4 require the surviving spouse to be the holder of a general power of appointment over the property. The exercise, release, or lapse of the power during the survivor's life or at death will be subject to either the gift or the death tax.[51] Thus, if Examples 67 and 68 are modified to satisfy the preceding conditions, the life estate passing from H to W is not a terminable interest and will qualify for the marital deduction.

As previously noted, the purpose of the terminable interest rule is to ensure that property not taxed to the transferor-spouse (due to the marital deduction) will be subject to the gift or estate tax upon disposition by the transferee-spouse.

Consistent with the objective of the terminable interest rule, another exception offers an alternative means for obtaining the marital deduction. Under this provision, the marital deduction is allowed for transfers of *qualified terminable interest property* (commonly referred to as QTIP). This is defined as property that passes from one spouse to another by gift or at death and for which the transferee-spouse has a qualifying income interest for life.

For a donee or a surviving spouse, a qualifying income interest for life exists under the following conditions:

───────────────

50. For the estate tax, see § 2056(b)(5). The gift tax counterpart is in § 2523(e).

51. §§ 2514 and 2041.

- Such person is entitled for life to all of the income from the property (or a specific portion of it), payable at annual or more frequent intervals.
- No person (including the spouse) has a power to appoint any part of the property to any person other than the surviving spouse during his or her life.[52]

If these conditions are met, an election can be made to claim a marital deduction as to the qualified terminable interest property. For estate tax purposes, the executor of the estate makes the election on Form 706 (the Federal estate tax return). For gift tax purposes, the donor spouse makes the election on Form 709 (the Federal gift tax return). The election is irrevocable.

If the election is made, a transfer tax will be imposed upon the qualified terminable interest property when the transferee-spouse disposes of it by gift or upon death. If the disposition occurs during life, the gift tax applies measured by the fair market value of the property as of that time.[53] If no lifetime disposition takes place, the fair market value of the property on the date of death (or alternate valuation date if applicable) is included in the gross estate of the transferee-spouse.[54]

EXAMPLE 70

In 1992, H dies and provides in his will that certain assets (fair market value of $400,000) are to be transferred to a trust under which W (H's wife) is granted a life estate with the remainder passing to their children upon W's death. Presuming all of the preceding requirements are satisfied and H's executor so elects, H's estate will receive a marital deduction of $400,000. ◆

EXAMPLE 71

Assume the same facts as in Example 70, with the further stipulation that W dies in 1998 when the trust assets are worth $900,000. This amount is included in W's gross estate. ◆

Because the estate tax will be imposed on assets not physically included in the probate estate, the law allows the liability for those assets to be shifted to the heirs. The amount to be shifted is determined by comparing the estate tax liability both with and without the inclusion of the qualified terminable interest property. This right of recovery can be canceled by a provision in the deceased spouse's will.[55]

The major difference between the power of appointment and the QTIP exceptions to the terminable interest rules relates to the control the surviving spouse has over the principal of the trust. In the power of appointment situation, the surviving spouse can appoint the principal to him- or herself (or to his or her estate). Only if this power is not exercised will the property pass as specified in the deceased spouse's will. In the QTIP situation, however, no such control exists as to the surviving spouse. If the QTIP election is made, the principal must pass as prescribed by the transferor (the donor in the case of a lifetime transfer or the decedent in the case of a death transfer).

In the case of a nonresident alien whose spouse is a U.S. citizen, the marital deduction is allowed for estate and gift tax purposes. Property passing to a surviving spouse who is not a U.S. citizen is not eligible for the estate tax martial

---

52. §§ 2523(f) and 2056(b)(7).
53. § 2519.

54. § 2044.
55. § 2207A(a).

deduction.[56] Similarly, no gift tax marital deduction is allowed where the spouse is not a U.S. citizen. However, the annual exclusion for these gift transfers is increased from $10,000 to $100,000.[57]

For the estate tax, an exception exists for certain transfers to a surviving spouse who is not a U.S. citizen.[58] If the transfer is to a *qualified domestic trust*, the marital deduction is allowed. A qualified domestic trust must meet the following conditions:[59]

- The trust instrument provides that all trustees be U.S. citizens or domestic corporations.
- The surviving spouse is entitled to all income from the trust payable at least annually.
- The trust must be subject to the estate tax upon the death of the surviving spouse.
- The executor makes an irrevocable election for the trust on the deceased spouse's estate tax return.

The reason for the qualified domestic trust exception is to guarantee that the marital deduction property will not escape estate taxes on the death of the surviving spouse. This would be possible if the property and spouse are outside the jurisdiction of the U.S. tax laws.

Computing the Federal Estate Tax

Once the taxable estate has been determined, post-1976 taxable gifts are added to arrive at the tax base. Note that pre-1977 taxable gifts do not enter into the computation of the tax base.

EXAMPLE 72

D dies in 1992, leaving a taxable estate of $800,000. During her life, D made taxable gifts as follows: $50,000 in 1975 and $100,000 in 1982. For estate tax purposes, the Federal estate tax base becomes $900,000 determined as follows: $800,000 (taxable estate) + $100,000 (taxable gift made in 1982). ◆

With the unified transfer tax rate schedule contained in § 2001(c), the tentative tax on the tax base is computed. Using the facts in Example 72, the tax on $900,000 is $306,800 [$248,300 + (39% × $150,000)]—see Appendix A, page A–8.

See the discussion below for the phase-out of the unified tax credit and the graduated tax rates for certain large estates.

All available estate tax credits are subtracted from the tentative estate tax to arrive at the estate tax (if any) that is due.

Estate Tax Credits

Unified Tax Credit (§ 2010). Recall from previous discussion of this credit that the amount of the credit allowed depends upon the year of the transfer. Returning to Example 72, the credit allowed on the gift in 1982 would be $62,800. Since the exemption equivalent of this amount is $225,000 (refer to the table preceding Example 3), no gift tax is due on the transfer. On D's death in 1992,

---

56. § 2056(d)(1).
57. § 2523(i).

58. § 2056(d)(2).
59. § 2056A.

however, the unified tax credit is $192,800, which is less than the tentative tax of $306,800 (refer to the discussion following Example 72). Disregarding the effect of any other estate tax credits, D's estate owes a tax of $114,000 [$306,800 (tentative tax on a tax base of $900,000) − $192,800 (unified tax credit for 1992)].

An adjustment to the unified tax credit will be necessary if any portion of the specific exemption was utilized on gifts made after September 8, 1976, and before January 1, 1977. In this regard, refer to Example 4.

Under the Revenue Act of 1987, the benefit of the unified tax credit and the graduated unified tax rates is phased out for taxable transfers exceeding a certain amount. The gift and estate tax liability for taxable transfers in excess of $10 million is increased by 5 percent of the excess until the benefit of the credit and graduated brackets is recaptured.

Credit for State Death Taxes (§ 2011). The Code allows a limited credit for the amount of any death tax actually paid to any state (or to the District of Columbia) attributable to any property included in the gross estate. Like the credit for foreign death taxes paid, this provision mitigates the harshness of subjecting the same property to multiple death taxes.

The credit allowed is limited to the lesser of the amount of tax actually paid or the amount provided for in a table contained in § 2011(b). (See Appendix A, page A–12.) The table amount is based on the adjusted taxable estate, which for this purpose is the taxable estate less $60,000. No credit is allowed if the adjusted taxable estate is $40,000 or less.

EXAMPLE 73

D's taxable estate is $98,000, and the state of appropriate jurisdiction imposes a death tax of $1,500 on this amount. Since the adjusted taxable estate is $38,000 ($98,000 − $60,000), none of the $1,500 paid qualifies for the death tax credit. ◆

EXAMPLE 74

D's taxable estate is $200,000, and the state of appropriate jurisdiction imposes a death tax of $3,000 on this amount. Because the adjusted gross estate is $140,000 ($200,000 − $60,000), the table amount limits the death tax credit to $1,200. ◆

As Examples 73 and 74 illustrate, the credit allowed by § 2011 may be less than the amount of state death taxes paid. The reverse is possible but usually is not the case. Most states make sure that the minimum tax payable to the jurisdiction is at least equal to the credit allowed by the table. Sometimes this result is accomplished by a soak-up or sponge tax superimposed on the regular inheritance tax. Thus, if the regular inheritance tax yields $2,500, but the maximum credit allowed by the table is $3,200, a soak-up tax would impose an additional $700 in state death taxes. In other states, the state death tax liability depends entirely upon the amount allowed for Federal death tax purposes under the table. In the previous illustration, the state death tax would be an automatic $3,200.

Credit for Gift Taxes (§ 2012). A credit is allowed against the estate tax for any Federal gift tax paid on a gift of property subsequently included in the donor-decedent's gross estate.

EXAMPLE 75

In 1965, D transfers a remainder interest in a farm to her children, retaining for herself a life estate. As a result of the transfer, D incurred and paid a Federal gift tax of $45,000. D dies in 1992 when the property is worth $400,000. Under § 2036 (retention of a life estate), the farm is included in D's gross estate. Thus, a double tax effect results. To mitigate this effect, § 2012 allows D's estate a credit for some or all of the $45,000 in gift taxes previously paid. ◆

The adjustments needed to work out the amount of the credit can become somewhat complicated and are not discussed further.[60]

Only taxable gifts made after 1976 are added to the donor's taxable estate in arriving at the base for the application of the unified transfer tax at death. To the extent these gifts have exceeded the unified tax credit and have generated a tax, the tax is credited against the transfer tax due at death.

Credit for Tax on Prior Transfers (§ 2013).   Suppose D owns some property that he passes at death to S. Shortly thereafter, S dies and passes the property to R. Assuming both estates are subject to the Federal estate tax, the successive deaths result in a multiple effect. To mitigate the possible multiple taxation that might result, § 2013 provides relief in the form of a credit for a death tax on prior transfers. In the preceding hypothetical case, S's estate may be able to claim as an estate tax credit some of the taxes paid by D's estate.

The credit is limited to the lesser of the following amounts:

1. The amount of the Federal estate tax attributable to the transferred property in the transferor's estate.
2. The amount of the Federal estate tax attributable to the transferred property in the decedent's estate.

To apply the limitations, certain adjustments must be made that are not covered in this text.[61] However, it is not necessary for the transferred property to be identified in the present decedent's estate or for it to be in existence at the time of the present decedent's death. It is sufficient that the transfer of property was subjected to the Federal estate tax in the estate of the transferor and that the transferor died within the prescribed period of time.

If the transferor dies within two years after or before the present decedent's death, the credit is allowed in full (subject to the preceding limitations). If the transferor died more than two years before the decedent, the credit is a certain percentage: 80 percent if the transferor died within the third or fourth year preceding the decedent's death, 60 percent if within the fifth or sixth year, 40 percent if within the seventh or eighth year, and 20 percent if within the ninth or tenth year.

EXAMPLE 76

Under D's will, S inherits property. One year later S dies. Assume the estate tax attributable to the inclusion of the property in D's gross estate was $15,000 and the estate tax attributable to the inclusion of the property in S's gross estate is $12,000. Under these circumstances, S's estate claims a credit against the estate tax of $12,000 (refer to limitation 2). ◆

EXAMPLE 77

Assume the same facts as in Example 76, except that S dies three years after D's death. The applicable credit is now 80% of $12,000, or $9,600. ◆

Credit for Foreign Death Taxes (§ 2014).   A credit is allowed against the estate tax for any estate, inheritance, legacy, or succession tax actually paid to a foreign

---

60. They are illustrated and explained in the instructions to Form 706 and in Reg. § 20.2012–1.

61. See the instructions to Form 706 and Reg. §§ 20.2013–2 and –3.

country. For purposes of this provision, the term *foreign country* means not only states in the international sense but also possessions or political subdivisions of foreign states and possessions of the United States.

The credit is allowed for death taxes paid with respect to (1) property situated within the foreign country to which the tax is paid, (2) property included in the decedent's gross estate, and (3) the decedent's estate. No credit is allowed for interest or penalties paid in connection with foreign death taxes.

The credit is limited to the lesser of the following amounts:

1. The amount of the foreign death tax attributable to the property situated in the country imposing the tax and included in the decedent's gross estate for Federal estate tax purposes.
2. The amount of the Federal estate tax attributable to particular property situated in a foreign country, subject to death tax in that country, and included in the decedent's gross estate for Federal estate tax purposes.

Both of these limitations may require certain adjustments to arrive at the amount of the allowable credit. These adjustments are illustrated in the Regulations and are not discussed in this text.[62] In addition to the credit for foreign death taxes under the provisions of Federal estate tax law, similar credits are allowable under death tax conventions with a number of foreign countries.[63] If a credit is allowed either under the provisions of law or under the provisions of a convention, the credit that is most beneficial to the estate should be claimed.

Procedural Matters

A Federal estate tax return, if required, is due nine months after the date of the decedent's death.[64] The time limit applies to all estates regardless of the nationality or residence of the decedent. Not infrequently, an executor will request and obtain from the IRS an extension of time for filing Form 706 (estate tax return).[65]

For the estate of a citizen or resident of the United States dying after 1976, Form 706 must be filed by the executor or administrator under the following conditions:[66]

Year of Death	Gross Estate in Excess of
1977	$120,000
1978	134,000
1979	147,000
1980	161,000
1981	175,000
1982	225,000
1983	275,000
1984	325,000
1985	400,000
1986	500,000
1987 & thereafter	600,000

---

62. Reg. §§ 20.20–2 and –3.

63. For the list of countries with which the United States has death tax conventions, refer to Footnote 10.

64. § 6075(a).

65. § 6081.

66. § 6018(a).

The filing requirements parallel the exemption equivalent amounts of the unified tax credit available for each year (refer to the table preceding Example 3). The filing requirements may be lower when the decedent has made taxable gifts after 1976 or has utilized any of the $30,000 specific gift tax exemption after September 8, 1976.

──────────────── EXAMPLE 78 ────────────────

D dies in 1992, leaving a gross estate of $595,000. If D did not make any post-1976 taxable gifts or use the specific gift tax exemption after September 8, 1976, his estate need not file Form 706. ◆

──────────────── EXAMPLE 79 ────────────────

Assume the same facts as in Example 78, except that D made a taxable gift of $20,000 in 1980. Since the filing requirement now becomes $580,000 [$600,000 (the regular filing requirement for 1992) − $20,000 (the post-1976 taxable gift)], D's estate must file Form 706. ◆

Form 706 must be filed with the IRS Service Center serving the district in which the decedent lived at the time of death. The return must be accompanied by various documents related to the determination of tax liability. For example, a statement on Form 712 must be obtained from the appropriate insurance company for each insurance policy listed on the return.

Penalties are imposed for willful failure to make and file a timely return and for willful attempts to evade or defeat payment of tax.[67]

THE GENERATION SKIPPING TRANSFER TAX
◆

In order to prevent partial avoidance of Federal gift and estate taxes on large transfers, the tax law imposes an additional generation skipping transfer tax.

The Problem

Previously, by structuring the transaction carefully, it was possible to bypass a generation of transfer taxes.

──────────────── EXAMPLE 80 ────────────────

Under his will, GF creates a trust, life estate to F (GF's son) and remainder to GD (GF's granddaughter) upon F's death. GF will be subject to the Federal estate tax, but no tax results on F's death. F held a life estate, but § 2036 does not apply. F was not the grantor of the trust. Nor does § 2033 (property owned by the decedent) come into play because F's interest disappeared upon his death. The ultimate result is that the property in trust skips a generation of transfer taxes. ◆

──────────────── EXAMPLE 81 ────────────────

GM gives assets to GS (her grandson). Called a direct skip, the gift would circumvent any transfer taxes that would have resulted had the assets been channeled through GS's parents. ◆

The Solution

The generation skipping transfer tax (GSTT) is imposed when a younger generation is bypassed in favor of a later generation.[68] The GSTT applies to

───────────────────

67. See, for example, §§ 6651, 6672, and 7203.

68. The generation skipping transfer tax provisions are

contained in §§ 2601–2663 of the Code.

lifetime transfers by gift and to transfers by death. The tax rate imposed is the highest rate under the gift and estate tax schedule— 55 percent through 1992 and 50 percent thereafter. Consequently, the GSTT does not permit the use of the graduated rate structure.

The application of the GSTT depends upon the type of arrangement involved. In Example 80, the GSTT would be imposed upon the death of F (the life tenant).

CONCEPT SUMMARY 17–2
FEDERAL ESTATE TAX PROVISIONS

1. Both the Federal gift and estate taxes are excise taxes on the transfer of wealth.

2. The starting point for applying the Federal estate tax is to determine which assets are subject to tax. Such assets comprise a decedent's gross estate. The gross estate must be distinguished from the probate estate. The latter classification includes those assets subject to administration by the executor of the estate.

3. The gross estate generally will not include any gifts made by the decedent within three years of death. It does include any gift tax paid on these transfers.

4. Based on the premise that one should not continue to enjoy or control property and not have it subject to the estate tax, certain incomplete transfers are subject to inclusion in the gross estate.

5. Upon the death of a joint tenant, the full value of the property is included in the gross estate unless the survivor(s) made a contribution toward the cost of the property. Spouses are subject to a special rule that calls for automatic inclusion of one-half of the value of the property in the gross estate of the first tenant to die. As to joint tenancies (or tenancies by the entirety) between husband and wife, it makes no difference who furnished the original consideration. The creation of joint ownership is subject to the gift tax when a tenant receives a lesser interest in the property than is warranted by the consideration furnished.

6. A power of appointment is the right to determine who shall own or enjoy, presently or in the future, the property subject to the power. The exercise, lapse, or release of a general power of appointment during the life of the holder is subject to the gift tax. If the exercise, lapse, or release occurs at death, the property subject to the power is included in the holder's gross estate. If, however, a special power of appointment is involved, no gift or estate tax consequences result. Barring certain exceptions, a special power cannot be used to benefit the holder or his or her estate.

7. If the decedent is the insured, life insurance proceeds are included in the gross estate if either of two conditions is satisfied. First, the proceeds are paid to the estate or for the benefit of the estate. Second, the decedent possessed incidents of ownership (e.g., the right to change beneficiaries) over the policy. A transfer of an unmatured life insurance policy is subject to the gift tax. A gift also occurs when a policy matures and the owner of the policy is not the insured or the beneficiary.

8. In moving from the gross estate to the taxable estate, certain deductions are allowed. Under § 2053, deductions are permitted for various administration expenses (e.g., executor's commissions, funeral costs), debts of the decedent, and certain unpaid taxes. Casualty and theft losses incurred during the administration of an estate can be deducted in arriving at the taxable estate.

9. Charitable transfers are deductible if the designated organization holds qualified status with the IRS at the time of the gift or upon death.

10. Transfers to a spouse qualify for the gift or estate tax marital deduction. Except as noted in (11), such transfers are subject to the terminable interest limitation.

11. The terminable interest limitation will not apply if the transferee-spouse is given a general power of appointment over the property or the QTIP election is made. In the case of a lifetime transfer, the donor-spouse makes the QTIP election. In the case of a testamentary transfer, the executor of the estate of the deceased spouse has the election responsibility.

12. The tax base for determining the estate tax is the taxable estate plus all post-1976 taxable gifts. All available credits are subtracted from the tax.

13. Of prime importance in the tax credit area is the unified tax credit. Except for large taxable transfers, the unified tax credit is $192,800 (exemption equivalent of $600,000).

14. Other Federal estate tax credits include credits for state death taxes, gift taxes, tax on prior transfers, and foreign death taxes.

15. If due, a Federal estate tax return (Form 706) must be filed within nine months of the date of the decedent's death. The IRS grants extensions for estates that encounter difficulty in complying with the deadline.

The tax, however, is levied against the trust. In effect, it reduces the amount that is distributed to GD (the remainderperson).

In Example 81, the GSTT is imposed upon GM when the gift is made to GS. In this situation, not only will GM be subject to the GSTT but the amount of the tax represents an additional gift to GS.[69] Thus, if a gift is a direct skip (such as Example 81), the total transfer tax (the GSTT plus the gift tax) may exceed what the donee receives.

Though the GSTT seemingly yields a confiscatory result, every grantor is entitled to a $1 million exemption. The exemption can be applied to whichever transfers the grantor (or personal representative of the grantor) chooses. Any appreciation attributable to the exempted portion of the transfer is not subject to the GSTT.

─────────────── EXAMPLE 82 ───────────────

Assume the same facts as in Example 80 except that the trust created by GF contained assets valued at $1,000,000. Ten years later when F dies, the trust is now worth $3,000,000. If the exemption of $1,000,000 is used upon the creation of the trust, no GSTT results upon F's death. ◆

Tax planning for the Federal gift and estate tax is discussed in Chapter 18 in connection with family tax planning.

 TAX PLANNING
CONSIDERATIONS

PROBLEM MATERIALS

DISCUSSION QUESTIONS

1. The unified transfer tax adopts a different approach to the taxation of life and death transfers after 1976. Explain.

2. Why can the unified transfer tax be categorized as an excise tax? In this regard, how does it differ from an income tax?

3. Upon whom is the Federal gift tax imposed? What happens if that party is unable to pay the tax?

4. What are the major differences between the Federal estate tax and the typical inheritance tax levied by many states?

5. T, a resident and citizen of Canada, owns real estate located in Rochester, New York.

   a. Would T be subject to the U.S. gift tax if she transferred this property as a gift to her Canadian son?

   b. Would T be subject to the U.S. estate tax if she died and left the property to her Canadian son?

6. Explain what is meant by the statement that the Federal gift tax is cumulative in nature.

7. What effect, if any, do prior gifts made by a decedent have on the determination of the decedent's estate tax liability?

8. What effect, if any, does prior utilization of the $30,000 specific exemption have on the unified tax credit currently available?

9. What is meant by the exemption equivalent of the unified tax credit?

─────────────

69. § 2515.

10. Reg. § 25.2512–8 states: "A consideration not reducible to a value in money or money's worth, as love and affection, promise of marriage, etc., is to be wholly disregarded, and the entire value of the property transferred constitutes the amount of the gift."

    a. What does this Regulation mean?
    b. When might it apply?

11. X sells property to Y for $50,000. If the property is really worth $100,000, has X made a gift to Y? What additional facts would you want to know before answering this question?

12. In connection with gift loans, comment on the following points:

    a. Since any interest element recognized by the lender as income can be deducted by the borrower, the income tax effect is neutralized for the family unit.
    b. The borrower's net investment income for the year is less than $1,000.
    c. The gift loan involved only $95,000.
    d. The lender charged the borrower interest of 2 percent.

13. In the absence of § 2516, why would certain property settlements incident to a divorce be subject to the Federal gift tax?

14. In connection with § 2518 dealing with disclaimers, comment on the following:

    a. The role of state law.
    b. The avoidance of a Federal gift tax or the Federal estate tax.
    c. The disclaimer of only a partial interest.

15. What is the justification for the annual exclusion? In what manner does it resemble the gift tax treatment of the following?

    a. Tuition payments to an educational organization on behalf of another.
    b. Medical care payments on behalf of another.

16. What purpose is served by the § 2503(c) trust for minors?

17. In connection with the gift-splitting provision of § 2513, comment on the following:

    a. What it was designed to accomplish.
    b. How the election is made.
    c. Its utility in a community property jurisdiction.

18. D makes the following taxable gifts: $200,000 in 1975 and $450,000 in 1992. On the 1975 gift, D incurred and paid a Federal gift tax of $40,000. How should the gift tax be determined on the 1992 gift?

19. In connection with the filing of a Federal gift tax return, comment on the following:

    a. No Federal gift tax is due.
    b. The § 2513 election to split gifts is to be used.
    c. A gift of a future interest is involved.
    d. The donor uses a fiscal year for Federal income tax purposes.
    e. The donor obtained from the IRS an extension of time for filing his or her Federal income tax return.

20. Distinguish between the following:

    a. The gross estate and the taxable estate.
    b. The gross estate and the probate estate.

21. No taxable gifts made within three years of death are included in the gross estate of the donor. Evaluate the soundness of this statement.

22. Using community property, H creates a trust, life estate to W (H's wife), remainder to their children upon W's death.

    a. Is there any estate tax effect upon H's death four years later?
    b. Is there any estate tax effect upon W's death five years later?

23. It has been said that community property is much like a tenancy in common. Do you agree? Why or why not?

24. At the time of X's death, X was a joint tenant with Y in a parcel of real estate. With regard to the inclusion in X's gross estate under § 2040, comment on the following independent assumptions:

    a. The property was received by X and Y as a gift from D.
    b. Y provided all of the purchase price of the property.
    c. Y's contribution was received as a gift from X.
    d. X's contribution was derived from income generated by property received by X as a gift from Y.

25. Under what circumstances will the creation of a joint tenancy not constitute a gift when one of the tenants furnishes more of the consideration than the other (others)?

26. If the holder can use the power to appoint some of the property for his or her benefit, it is a general power of appointment. Do you agree? Why or why not?

27. T owns a policy on the life of S, with D as the designated beneficiary. Upon S's death, the insurance proceeds are paid to D.

    a. Are any of the proceeds included in S's gross estate?
    b. Does S's death generate any tax consequences to T?

28. For tax purposes, what difference does it make whether a casualty loss occurs before or after the death of the owner of the property?

29. In terms of the QTIP (qualified terminable interest property) election, comment on the following:

    a. Who makes the election.
    b. What the election accomplishes.
    c. The tax effect of the election upon the death of the surviving spouse.

30. Property passing to a surviving spouse who is not a U.S. citizen is not eligible for the estate tax marital deduction. Is this statement always true? Explain.

31. On a gift that is a "direct skip," it is possible that the total transfer taxes might exceed what the donee receives. Explain.

PROBLEMS

32. At the time of death, D held the following assets:

	Value on Date of Death	Value Six Months Later
Land	$ 900,000	$ 920,000
Stock in R Corporation	800,000	700,000
Stock in T Corporation	600,000	650,000
Total	$2,300,000	$2,270,000

The stock in R Corporation is sold by the estate for $730,000 eight months after D's death. The stock in T Corporation is sold by the estate for $660,000 four months after D's death.

    a. Is the alternate valuation date election available to the estate?
    b. If the election is available and is made, what value should be used?
    c. What value should be used if the election is not available or, if available, is not made?

33. In each of the following independent situations, indicate whether the transfer by D is, or could be, subject to the Federal gift tax:

    a. D makes a contribution to an influential political figure.
    b. D makes a contribution to B Corporation, of which he is not a shareholder.
    c. In consideration of his upcoming marriage to B, D establishes a savings account in B's name.

d. Same as (c). After their marriage, D establishes a joint checking account in the names of "D and B."

e. Same as (d). One year after the checking account is established, B withdraws all of the funds.

f. D exercises a special power of appointment in favor of B.

g. D enters into an agreement with B where he will transfer property to her in full satisfaction of her marital rights. One month after the agreement, the transfer occurs. Later D and B are divorced.

h. D purchases U.S. savings bonds, listing ownership as "D and B." Several years later, and after D's death, B redeems the bonds.

34. In each of the following independent situations, indicate whether the transfer by D is, or could be, subject to the Federal gift tax:

a. D purchases real estate and lists title as "D and B as joint tenants." D and B are brothers.

b. Same as (a), except that D and B are husband and wife.

c. D creates a revocable trust with B as the designated beneficiary.

d. Same as (c). One year after creating the trust, D releases all power to revoke the trust.

e. D takes out an insurance policy on his life, designating B as the beneficiary.

f. Same as (e). Two years later, D dies and the policy proceeds are paid to B.

g. D takes out an insurance policy on the life of W and designates B as the beneficiary. Shortly thereafter, W dies and the policy proceeds are paid to B.

h. D pays for B's college tuition.

35. In 1975, F purchased real estate for $300,000, listing ownership as follows: "F and D, equal tenants in common." F predeceases D in 1992 when the property is worth $800,000. Before 1975, F had not made any taxable gifts or utilized the $30,000 specific exemption. Assume F and D are father and daughter.

a. Determine F's gift tax consequences, if any, in 1975.

b. How much, if any, of the property should be included in F's gross estate?

36. In 1984, B purchased real estate for $500,000, listing title to the property as follows: "B and C, joint tenants with the right of survivorship." C predeceases B in 1992 when the real estate is worth $900,000. Assume B and C are sisters and that neither has made any other taxable gifts or utilized her $30,000 specific exemption.

a. Determine B's gift tax consequences, if any, in 1984.

b. How much, if any, of the property should be included in C's gross estate?

37. Assume the same facts as in Problem 36, except that B and C are husband and wife (rather than sisters).

a. Determine B's gift tax consequences, if any, in 1984.

b. How much, if any, of the property should be included in C's gross estate? Will any such inclusion generate an estate tax liability? Explain.

38. In January 1992, H and W enter into a property settlement under which H agrees to pay $500,000 to W in return for the release of her marital rights. At the time the agreement is signed, H pays W $100,000 as a first installment. Although the parties intended to obtain a divorce, H dies in July 1992 before legal proceedings have been instituted. After H's death, the executor of H's estate pays to W the $400,000 remaining balance due under the property settlement.

a. What are the gift tax consequences of the $100,000 payment made upon the signing of the agreement? Why?

b. What are the estate tax consequences of the $400,000 paid to W from estate assets after H's death? Why?

39. In 1992, M makes a gift to her daughter of securities worth $700,000. M has never made any prior taxable gifts or utilized her $30,000 specific exemption. F (M's husband), however, made a taxable gift of $500,000 in early 1976 upon which he paid a gift tax of $109,275. At the time of F's gift, F was not married to M.

    a. Determine M's gift tax liability on the 1992 transfer, assuming the parties chose not to make the election to split gifts under § 2513.

    b. What would the liability be if the election to split the gift were made?

40. D dies on July 7, 1992, at a time when he owns stock in Z Corporation and W Corporation. On June 3 of the same year both corporations authorized cash dividends payable on August 4. For Z Corporation, the dividend was payable to shareholders of record as of July 3, and W Corporation's date of record was July 10. After D's death, the executor of the estate received dividends in the following amounts: $6,000 from Z Corporation and $8,000 from W Corporation. D also owned some City of Minneapolis tax-exempt bonds. As of July 7, the accrued interest on the bonds was $7,500. On December 1, the executor of the estate received $10,000 in interest ($2,500 accrued since D's death) from the bonds. Concerning the dividends and interest, how much should be included in D's gross estate?

41. Before his death in 1992, F (a widower) made the following transfers:

    ▪ A gift of real estate (basis of $90,000 and fair market value of $400,000) to S (F's son). The gift was made in 1990 and resulted in a Federal gift tax of $20,000, which F paid. On the date of F's death, the property is worth $450,000.

    ▪ A gift of an insurance policy on F's life to D (the designated beneficiary). The policy was worth $10,000 but had a maturity value of $70,000. The gift was made in 1990 and resulted in no Federal gift tax liability.

    ▪ A gift of stock (basis of $40,000 and fair market value of $80,000) to T. The gift was made in 1981 and resulted in no Federal gift tax liability. On the date of F's death, the stock was worth $200,000.

    Presuming the alternate valuation date is not elected, how much should be included in F's gross estate as to these transfers?

42. In 1975, Q created a revocable trust with securities worth $200,000. T Trust Company was designated as the trustee. Under the terms of the trust, Q retained a life estate with remainder to her children. In 1990, Q releases her right to revoke the trust. Q dies in 1992 when the trust assets have a fair market value of $1,000,000.

    a. What, if any, are Q's gift tax consequences in 1975?

    b. What, if any, is included in Q's gross estate in 1992?

    c. Would your answer to (b) change if Q *also* released her life estate in 1990? Explain.

43. G would like to make a lifetime transfer in trust of $300,000 to his son, S, and accomplish the following objectives:

    ▪ Avoid any death tax on the deaths of G, S, and W (S's wife).

    ▪ Give S the right to determine what portion of the remainder should be allocated between W and their children, A and B.

    ▪ Give S some additional security by allowing him to reach the principal should the need materialize.

    ▪ Prevent S from squandering all of the principal to the detriment of W, A, or B.

    In light of § 2041, what do you suggest?

44. In each of the following independent situations, determine how much should be included in D's gross estate under § 2042 as to the various life insurance policies involved. Assume that none of the policies are community property.

    a. At the time of his death, D owned a paid-up policy on the life of B, with S as the designated beneficiary. The policy had a replacement cost of $80,000 and a maturity value of $300,000.

    b. W owns a policy on the life of D ($300,000 maturity value) with D's estate as the designated beneficiary. Upon D's death, the insurance company pays $300,000 to D's estate.

    c. Four years before his death, D transferred a policy on his life ($300,000 maturity value) to S as a gift. D retained the power to change beneficiaries. At the time of the transfer, the designated beneficiary was S. Because D had never exercised his right to change beneficiaries, the insurance company pays S $300,000 upon D's death.

d. Same as (c), except that D releases the power to change beneficiaries one year before his death.

45. In each of the following independent situations, determine the amount of the decedent's *gross estate.* All deaths occur in 1992.

	Decedents			
	A	B	C	D
Real estate	$400,000	$300,000	$600,000	$500,000
Dower interest claimed by C's surviving spouse (outright ownership of 50% of the real estate)	—	—	300,000	—
Pre-1976 taxable gifts	100,000	—	—	—
Post-1976 taxable gifts	—	—	—	200,000
Marketable securities	300,000	400,000	200,000	900,000
Fair market value of a note due from B's son that is forgiven in B's will	—	100,000	—	—

46. Comment on how each of the following independent situations should be handled for estate tax purposes:

a. Before her death, D issued a note payable to her daughter in the amount of $100,000. D never received any consideration for the note. After D's death, the daughter files a claim against the estate and collects $100,000 on the note.

b. At the time of her death, D (a widow) owned 10 cemetery lots (each worth $5,000), which she had purchased many years before for herself and her family.

c. At the time of his death, D was delinquent in the payment of back Federal income taxes. D's executor pays the taxes from assets of the estate.

47. In 1992, H places in trust $500,000 worth of securities. Under the terms of the trust instrument, W (H's wife) is granted a life estate, and on W's death, the remainder interest passes to H and W's children (as W determines in her will). Upon W's death 18 years later, the trust assets are valued at $2,000,000.

a. How much, if any, marital deduction will be allowed on the gift made in 1992?

b. How much, if any, of the trust will be included in W's gross estate upon W's death?

48. Assume the same facts as in Problem 47, except that H made the qualified terminable interest property election when the trust was created. Further assume that W has no choice as to which of her children will receive the remainder interest upon her death.

a. How much, if any, marital deduction will be allowed on the gift made in 1992?

b. How much, if any, of the trust will be subject to the Federal estate tax upon W's later death?

49. In each of the following independent situations, determine the decedent's final estate tax liability (net of any unified tax credit):

	Decedent			
	A	B	C	D
Year of death	1984	1985	1986	1992
Taxable estate	$600,000	$800,000	$700,000	$1,000,000
Pre-1977 taxable gift	—	250,000*	100,000*	—
Post-1976 taxable gift	200,000	—	—	250,000
Gift tax on pre-1977 taxable gift	—	49,725	15,525	—
Gift tax on post-1976 taxable gift	38,000	—	—	70,800

*The $30,000 specific exemption was used in full for each of these gifts. B's gift occurred on October 1, 1976, while C's took place in June 1976.

50. In each of the following independent situations, determine the decedent's final estate tax liability (net of any unified tax credit):

	Decedent			
	E	**F**	**G**	**H**
Year of death	1985	1986	1987	1992
Taxable estate	$800,000	$900,000	$1,100,000	$1,200,000
Pre-1977 taxable gift	250,000*	250,000*	—	—
Post-1976 taxable gift	—	—	500,000	80,000
Gift tax paid on post-1976 taxable gift	—	—	155,800	18,200
Gift tax paid on pre-1977 taxable gift	49,275	49,275	—	—

*The $30,000 specific exemption was used in full for each of these gifts. E's gift occurred in December 1976, while F's took place in December 1975.

51. In each of the following independent situations, determine the decedent's final estate tax liability for 1992 (net of any unified tax credit and credit for gift taxes paid). (Note: In some cases, you will have to compute the gift tax that was paid.)

	Decedent			
	I	**J**	**K**	**L**
Taxable estate	$600,000	$800,000	$900,000	$700,000
Taxable gift made in:				
1981	200,000	—	—	—
1979	—	200,000	—	—
1982	—	—	300,000	—
1983	—	—	—	200,000

52. In each of the following independent situations, determine the decedent's final estate tax liability for 1992 (net of any unified tax credit and credit for gift taxes paid), the year of death. (Note: In some cases, you will have to compute the gift tax that was paid.)

	Decedent			
	M	**N**	**O**	**P**
Taxable estate	$900,000	$700,000	$800,000	$1,100,000
Taxable gift made in:				
1980	200,000	—	—	—
1981	—	300,000	—	—
1982	—	—	150,000	—
1983	—	—	—	300,000

53. Assume the filing requirement for 1992 is a gross estate in excess of $600,000. What effect would each of the following transactions before the decedent's death in 1992 have on the filing requirement?

- Utilized $10,000 of the $30,000 specific gift tax exemption on a gift made in June 1976.
- Used the balance of the $30,000 specific gift tax exemption on a gift made in October 1976.
- Made a taxable gift of $100,000 in November 1976.
- Made a taxable gift of $100,000 in 1978.

COMPREHENSIVE TAX RETURN PROBLEM

During 1991, James and Mildred Smith (Social Security numbers 463-04-7964 and 466-36-4596) resided at 130 Elmwood Circle, Herndon, MI 48864. In their 25 years of marriage, the Smiths have always lived in common law states. James Smith is a trial lawyer, and Mildred Smith is a partner in a well-known internal medicine clinic. Both practices have been highly successful. Over the years, the Smiths have received gifts and inheritances from various relatives and have invested the funds wisely.

In 1991, the Smiths made the following transfers (without adjustment for the annual exclusion or the marital deduction):

	James Smith	Mildred Smith
Cash donation to the building fund of the Lutheran Church of Herndon, MI	$ 17,000	$ 19,000
Anniversary gift (diamond necklace) to Mildred	75,000	
Payment to Georgetown University for Larry Smith's (19-year-old son) tuition	15,000	4,000
Cash gift to Ann Smith (18-year-old daughter)	20,000	20,000
Gift of real estate (basis of $50,000 and fair market value of $250,000) to Gilbert Smith (23-year-old son)		200,000
Purchase of marketable securities in the name of Mark Smith (15-year-old son) under the Michigan Uniform Gifts to Minors Act. James Smith is named as the custodian of these securities.	100,000	140,000
Cash contribution to the campaign fund of Mark Walker who was running for Congress		12,000
Cash Christmas gift to Edith Jones, the Smith's maid for 15 years	11,000	

In past years, the Smiths have made the following *taxable* gifts:

Year	James Smith	Mildred Smith
1979	$200,000	$280,000
1985	101,000	200,000
1986	400,000	160,000
1987	110,000	110,000

For all past gifts, the Smiths have elected to use the gift-splitting provisions of § 2513.
Required:

a. Determine how much, if any, Federal gift tax will have been paid on the pre-1991 taxable gifts James and Mildred Smith have made.

b. Complete Form 709 (U.S. Federal Gift Tax Return) for the gifts made in 1991. As in the past, the § 2513 election is to be made.

RESEARCH PROBLEMS

RESEARCH PROBLEM   On October 1, 1976, H makes a gift of $66,000 to his son. In reporting the gift, W (H's wife) made the election under § 2513. As a result, no gift tax was due. W dies in 1992, and in completing Form 706, her executor claims a unified tax credit of $192,800.

a. Why was no gift tax due on the 1976 gift?

b. Did the executor of W's estate act correctly in claiming a unified tax credit of $192,800 on Form 706? Why or why not?

RESEARCH PROBLEM 2   Before her death in 1992, D entered into the following transactions:

a. In 1987, she borrowed $35,000 from a bank and promptly loaned that sum to her controlled corporation. The executor of D's estate repaid the bank loan but never attempted to collect the amount due D from the corporation.

b. In 1979, D promised her sister, S, a bequest of $200,000 if S would move in with her and care for her during an illness (which eventually proved to be terminal). D never kept her promise, and her will was silent on any bequest to S. After D's death, S sued the estate and eventually recovered $120,000 for breach of contract.

c. One of the assets in D's estate was a palatial residence that passed to R under a specific provision of the will. R did not want the residence, preferring cash instead. Per R's instructions, the residence was sold. Expenses incurred in connection with the sale were claimed as § 2053 expenses on Form 706 filed by D's estate.

d. Before her death, D incurred and paid certain medical expenses but did not have the opportunity to file a claim for partial reimbursement from her insurance company. After her death, the claim was filed by D's executor, and the reimbursement was paid to the estate.

Discuss the estate and income tax ramifications of each of these transactions.

Partial list of research aids:

Code §§ 61(a)(1) and (12), 111, 213, 691, 2033, and 2053.
Estate of Allie W. Pittard, 69 T.C. 391 (1977).
Estate of Myron M. Miller, 37 TCM 1547, T.C.Memo. 1978–374.
Joseph F. Kenefic, 36 TCM 1226, T.C.Memo. 1977–310.
Hibernia Bank v. U.S., 78–2 USTC ¶13,261, 42 AFTR2d 78–6510, 581 F.2d 741 (CA–9, 1978).
Rev.Rul. 78–292, 1978–2 C.B. 233.

RESEARCH PROBLEM 3 On August 1, 1987, H transfers securities in X Corporation to his son, S, under the Florida Uniform Gifts to Minors Act. Under the transfer, W (H's wife and mother of S) is designated as the custodian of the stock. On September 3, 1987, W transfers securities in X Corporation to her son, S, under the Florida Uniform Gifts to Minors Act. Under the transfer, H is designated as the custodian of the stock. H dies in 1992 as a result of an accident. Will any of the securities in X Corporation be included in H's gross estate?

Partial list of research aids:

Exchange Bank and Trust Co. v. U.S., 82–2 USTC ¶13,505, 51 AFTR2d 83–1317, 694 F.2d 1261 (CA–Fed.Cir., 1982).
Estate of Herbert Levy, 46 TCM 910, T.C.Memo. 1983–453.

RESEARCH PROBLEM 4 H dies on April 24, 1988, and under his will a major portion of the estate passes to a trust. The provisions of the trust grant a life estate to W (H's surviving spouse), remainder to their adult children. The income is payable to W quarter-annually or at more frequent intervals. Income accrued or held undistributed by the trust at the time of W's death shall pass to the remainder interest.

On January 24, 1989, H's estate filed a Federal estate tax return and made the QTIP election. On July 3, 1989, H's estate filed an amended return based on the premise that the QTIP election was improper. As a result of the loss of the marital deduction, the amended return was accompanied by a payment of additional estate taxes.

On February 11, 1989, W dies. All of her assets, including those in H's trust, pass to the children.

a. Why did H's estate file an amended return revoking the QTIP election?

b. Is the revocation of the election proper procedure?

c. Did H's estate ever qualify for the election?

Partial list of research aids:

Code §§ 2056(b)(7) and 2013.
Estate of Rose D. Howard, 91 T.C. 329 (1988), *rev'd* in 90–2 USTC ¶60,033, 66 AFTR2d 90–5994, 910 F. 2d 633 (CA–9, 1990).

CHAPTER

FAMILY TAX PLANNING

OBJECTIVES

Define and illustrate family tax planning objectives and techniques.

Review the rules governing the valuation of assets and business interests.

Explain the purpose and utility of special use valuation.

Discuss problems involved in valuing a closely held corporation.

Summarize income tax basis considerations of property acquired by gift or by inheritance.

Emphasize means by which the gift tax can be controlled.

Highlight various estate tax planning procedures.

Recognize and resolve problems of estate liquidity.

OUTLINE

VALUATION CONCEPTS

◆

Family tax planning involves procedures used by a family group to minimize the overall effect of taxation. To be fully effective, the planner must have a working knowledge of the gift, estate, and income tax ramifications of transfers within the family unit. The valuation process also affects both the amount of transfer tax liability and the basis of property for income tax purposes.

─────────────── EXAMPLE 1 ───────────────

In 1991, F dies with a disposable estate[1] of $1,640,000. Because the estate includes a large amount of marketable securities and the stock market declines, the value of the disposable estate is reduced to $1,500,000 in the six months after F's death. Under F's will, $1,000,000 passes to W (F's surviving spouse) with the remainder going to their adult children. F had never made any post-1976 taxable gifts, nor had he used any of his specific exemption (available before 1977). ◆

The first decision F's executor must make is whether to use the date of death value or elect the alternate valuation date (see Chapter 17). The estate tax consequence of each approach is summarized below:

	Date of Death Value	Alternate Valuation Date
Disposable estate	$1,640,000	$1,500,000
Less: Marital deduction	1,000,000	1,000,000
Taxable estate	$ 640,000	$ 500,000
Tentative tax (see Appendix A, page A–8)	$ 207,600	$ 155,800
Less: Unified tax credit	192,800	192,800
Estate tax due	$ 14,800	$ –0–

Since the election of the alternate valuation date saves $14,800 in estate taxes, is there any need to proceed further? Yes, because the estate tax valuation determines the income tax basis of the property to the estate and heirs. By electing the alternate valuation date, the parties sacrifice income tax basis of $140,000 [$1,640,000 (date of death value) − $1,500,000 (alternate valuation date)]. The key planning question becomes: Is the $14,800 estate tax saving worth the $140,000 lower income tax basis? This chapter identifies factors that must be taken into account in answering this question.

Example 1 demonstrates that meaningful family tax planning goes beyond the evaluation of isolated parts of the family unit and looks to the big picture. Family tax planning requires awareness of valuation concepts and knowledge of income, gift, and estate tax results. Consequently, it is one of the most sophisticated products a tax specialist can offer.

The satisfactory resolution of the valuation problem is an essential element of working with the tax law. Recall that the gift tax is predicated on the fair market value of the property on the date of the transfer. For the Federal estate tax, it is the fair market value on the date of the owner's death or the alternate valuation date (if available and elected) that controls. Even more subtle are the income tax considerations inherent in this problem.

─────────────────

1. For this purpose, the disposable estate includes the gross estate less all deductions (e.g., debts, administration and funeral expenses) except for the marital deduction. The term is not in the Code but is useful in evaluating tax planning options.

─────────────── EXAMPLE 2 ───────────────

D would like to give S an unimproved tract of land that he inherited from his grandmother 20 years ago. The importance of the value of the property on the date of the gift is clear, as this is the starting point in determining the gift tax implications of the transfer. A less apparent but equally important consideration is the determination of S's income tax basis in the property. To determine S's basis, D's adjusted basis in the property must be known. Since D inherited the property, basis is the land's fair market value as of 20 years ago. ◆

The fair market value of the land transferred in Example 2 is important in at least two respects: D's gift tax consequences and S's income tax basis upon the later disposition of the property in a taxable sale or exchange. Not mentioned, but consequential, is the effect the fair market value of the land had on the death taxes paid by the grandmother's estate.

Valuation in General

The Internal Revenue Code refers to "value" and "fair market value," but does not discuss these terms at length.[2] Code § 2031(b) comes closest to a definition when it treats the problem of stocks and securities for which no sales price information (the usual case with closely held corporations) is available. In such situations, "the value thereof shall be determined by taking into consideration, in addition to all other factors, the value of stock or securities of corporations engaged in the same or similar line of business which are listed on an exchange."

Regulation § 20.2031–1(b) is more specific in defining fair market value as "the price at which property would change hands between a willing buyer and a willing seller, neither being under any compulsion to buy or to sell and both having reasonable knowledge of relevant facts." The same Regulation makes clear that the fair market value of an item of property is not determined by a forced sale price. Nor is the fair market value determined by the sale price of the item in a market other than that in which the item is most commonly sold to the public. The item's location must also be considered. Thus, the fair market value of property that generally is obtained by the public in a retail market is the price at which the property (or comparable items) would be sold at retail.

─────────────── EXAMPLE 3 ───────────────

At the time of his death, D owned three automobiles. The automobiles are included in D's gross estate at their fair market value on the date of D's death or on the alternate valuation date (if elected). The fair market value of the automobiles is determined by looking to the price a member of the general public would pay for automobiles of approximately the same description, make, model, age, condition, etc. The price a dealer in used cars would pay for these automobiles is inappropriate, because an automobile is an item obtainable by the public in a retail market. ◆

If tangible personalty is sold as a result of an advertisement in the classified section of a newspaper and the property is of a type often sold in this manner, or if the property is sold at a public auction, the price for which it is sold is presumed to be the retail sales price of the item at the time of the sale. The retail sales price also is used if the sale is made within a reasonable period following the valuation date and there is no substantial change in market conditions

───────────────

2. See, for example, §§ 1001(b), 2031(a), and 2512(a). Sections 2032A(e)(7) and (8) set forth certain procedures for valuing farms and interests in closely held businesses.

affecting the value of similar items.[3] Tangible personalty includes all property except real estate and intangible property.

Valuation of Specific Assets

Stocks and Bonds. If there is a market for stocks and bonds on a stock exchange, in an over-the-counter market, or otherwise, the mean between the highest and lowest quoted selling prices on the valuation date is the fair market value per unit. A special rule applies if no sales occurred on the valuation date but did occur on dates within a reasonable period before and after the valuation date. The fair market value is the weighted average of the means between the highest and the lowest sales prices on the nearest date before and the nearest date after the valuation date. The average is weighted *inversely* by the respective number of trading days between the selling dates and the valuation date.[4]

--- EXAMPLE 4 ---

D makes a gift to S of shares of stock in X Corporation. The transactions closest to the date of the gift that involve this stock took place two trading days before the date of the gift at a mean selling price of $10 and three trading days after the gift at a mean selling price of $15. The $12 fair market value of each share of X stock is determined as follows.

$$\frac{(3 \times \$10) + (2 \times \$15)}{5} = \$12$$

◆

If no transactions occurred within a reasonable period before and after the valuation date, the fair market value is determined by taking a weighted average of the means between the bona fide bid and asked prices on the nearest trading dates before and after the valuation date. However, both dates must be within a reasonable period of time.

If no actual sales prices or bona fide bid and asked prices are available for dates within a reasonable period relative to the valuation date, the mean between the highest and lowest available sales prices or bid and asked prices on that date may be taken as the value.

If selling prices or bid and asked prices are not available, as is typically the case with securities of a closely held corporation, fair market value is determined by considering the following:

1. For bonds, the soundness of the security, the interest yield, the date of maturity, and other relevant factors.
2. For shares of stock, the corporation's net worth, prospective earning power, dividend-paying capacity, and other relevant factors.

Some of the "other relevant factors" are the goodwill of the business, the economic outlook in the particular industry, the company's position in the industry, and the value of securities of other corporations engaged in the same or similar lines of business.[5]

Shares in an open-end investment company (mutual fund) are valued at the redemption, or bid, price of the security.

---

3. Rev.Proc. 65–19, 1965–2 C.B. 1002.
4. Reg. §§ 20.2031–2(b) and 25.2512–2(b).
5. Reg. §§ 20.2031–2(f) and 25.2512–2(f). See also Rev.Rul.

59–60, 1959–1 C.B. 237, which discusses the subject at greater length than do the Regulations.

Interest in Businesses.   The fair market value of any interest in a business, such as a sole proprietorship or partnership, is the net amount that a willing purchaser would pay for the interest of a willing seller. Neither party must be under any compulsion to buy or sell, and both must have reasonable knowledge of the relevant facts.

The relevant facts to be considered in valuing the business are (1) a fair appraisal of the assets of the business, (2) the demonstrated earning capacity of the business, and (3) certain other factors used in arriving at the valuation of corporate stock to the extent applicable to the particular situation. Special attention should be given to determining an adequate value for the goodwill of the business if no bona fide purchase agreement exists.[6]

Notes Receivable.   The fair market value of notes, secured or unsecured, is the amount of unpaid principal plus interest accrued to the valuation date, unless the parties (e.g., executor, donor) establish a lower value or prove the notes are worthless. Factors such as a low interest rate and a distant maturity date are relevant in showing that a note is worth less than its face amount. Crucial elements in proving that a note is entirely or partially worthless are the financial condition of the borrower and the absence of any value for the property pledged or mortgaged as security for the obligation.[7]

─────────────────────── EXAMPLE 5 ───────────────────────

At the time of his death, D held a note (face amount of $50,000) issued by his son, S. Although S is solvent, he is relieved of the obligation because D forgives the note in his will. Presuming the note is payable on demand, it is included in D's gross estate at $50,000 plus accrued interest. If the note is not due immediately and/or the interest provided for is under the current rate, a discount may be in order, and the fair market value of the note would be less than $50,000. The burden of proof in supporting a discount for the note is on the executor. ◆

Insurance Policies and Annuity Contracts.   The value of a life insurance policy on the life of a person other than the decedent, or the value of an annuity contract issued by a company regularly engaged in selling annuities, is the cost of a comparable contract.[8]

─────────────────────── EXAMPLE 6 ───────────────────────

D purchased a joint and survivor annuity contract from an insurance company. Under the contract's terms, D is to receive payments of $60,000 per year for his life. Upon D's death, D's wife (W) is to receive $45,000 annually for her life. Ten years after the purchase of the annuity, when W is 40 years of age, D dies. The value of the annuity contract on the date of D's death [and the amount includible in D's gross estate under § 2039(a)] is the amount the insurance company would charge for an annuity providing for the payment of $45,000 annually for the life of a female 40 years of age. ◆

─────────────────────── EXAMPLE 7 ───────────────────────

At the time of her death, D owns an insurance policy (face amount of $200,000) on the life of her son, S. The policy is one on which no further payments need be made (e.g., a single premium policy or a paid-up policy). The value of the policy on the date of D's death (and the amount includible in D's gross estate under § 2033 as property owned by the decedent) is the amount the insurance company would charge for a single premium contract (face amount of $200,000) on the life of someone the same age as S. ◆

---

6. Reg. §§ 20.2031–3 and 25.2512–3. But see the special use valuation procedures of § 2032A(e)(8) discussed later.

7. Reg. §§ 20.2031–4 and 25.2512–4.

8. Reg. §§ 20.2031–8(a)(1) and 25.2512–6(a).

Determining the value of an insurance policy by using the amount charged for a comparable policy is more difficult when, on the date of valuation, the contract has been in force for some time and further premium payments are to be made. In such a case, the value may be approximated by adding to the interpolated terminal reserve the proportionate part of the gross premium last paid before the valuation date that covers the period extending beyond that date.[9]

The valuation of annuities issued by parties *not regularly engaged in the sale of annuities* (i.e., noncommercial contracts) requires the use of special tables issued by the IRS. Which table must be used depends on whether the valuation date occurs before 1971, after 1970 and before December 1, 1983, after November 30, 1983 and before May 1, 1989, or after April 30, 1989. The tables covering transfers after November 30, 1983, and before May 1, 1989, are reproduced in Appendix A.

--------------------- EXAMPLE 8 ---------------------

Under the terms of F's will, D (F's daughter) is entitled to receive an annuity of $20,000 payable annually for life. When D is 50 in March 1989, she assigns the annuity to S as a gift. From column 2 of Table A [Reg. § 25.2512–5(f)], the annuity factor for a person age 50 is 8.4743. Multiplying 8.4743 by the annual payment of $20,000 yields a fair market value of $169,486. Thus, when D assigns the annuity to S, she has made a gift of $169,486.[10] ◆

Life Estates, Terms for Years, Reversions, and Remainders.   As was true with noncommercial annuities, the valuation of life estates, income interests for a term of years, reversions, and remainders involves the use of tables. Again, it is important to ascertain when the transfer occurred.

--------------------- EXAMPLE 9 ---------------------

D transfers $100,000 in trust, specifying a life estate to W, remainder to S on W's death. The gift took place on May 3, 1988, when W was age 35.[11] Referring to Table A [Reg. § 25.2512–5(f)], a life estate for a person age 35 shows a factor of 0.93868 [column (3)]; the factor for a remainder interest is 0.06132 [column (4)]. Consequently, D has made a gift to W of $93,868 (0.93868 × $100,000) and a gift to S of $6,132 (0.06132 × $100,000). Thus, the value of the life estate ($93,868) plus the value of the remainder ($6,132) equals the total amount of the gift ($100,000). ◆

Due to constant fluctuations in interest rates, Congress enacted legislation requiring the IRS to issue new tables to reflect the current rate.[12] Effective for transfers after May 1989, these tables contain 20 different possibilities ranging from 8.2 percent to 12 percent.[13] *Only a portion of the tables is reproduced* in Appendix A.

The tables provide only the remainder factor. If the income interest (life estate) also has been transferred, the factor to be used is one minus the remainder factor.[14]

--------------------- EXAMPLE 10 ---------------------

Assume the same facts as in Example 9, except that the trust was created after April 1989. Further assume that the appropriate rate is 10.8%. Using the table extract in Appendix A

---

9. The terminal reserve value of a life insurance policy generally approximates the policy's cash surrender value. For an illustration on how to arrive at the interpolated terminal reserve value, see Reg. § 20.2031–8(a)(3) (Ex. 3).

10. The Regulations contain identical tables for transfers at death. See Reg. § 20.2031.

11. The pre-1971 and the current tables are unisex (no distinction is made between male and female). The tables applicable to transfers after 1970 and before December 1, 1983, do make a distinction between the sexes.

12. § 7520.

13. Notice 89–60, 1989–1 C.B. 700. The valuation factors in the tables represent 120 percent of whatever the Federal mid-term rate is for the month in which the valuation date falls.

14. Notice 89–24, 1989–1 C.B. 660.

[Table R(1)] for a person age 35 under the 10.8% column, the value of the remainder interest is $5,260 (.05260 × $100,000). The life estate factor is .9474 (1.00000 − .05260). Thus, D has made a gift to W of $94,740 and a gift to S of $5,260. ◆

In computing the value of an income interest for a term of years, a different table is used. Again, the table furnishes the remainder factor. The income interest factor is the difference between one and the remainder factor. *Only a portion of the tables is reproduced* in Appendix A.

─────────────── EXAMPLE 11 ───────────────

On April 30, 1992, T transfers $200,000 by gift to a trust. Under the terms of the trust, income is payable to R for eight years. After the eight-year period, the trust terminates, and the trust principal passes to U. For the month in which the trust was created, the appropriate rate was 10.8%. The present worth of $1 due at the end of eight years is $0.440232. Thus, T has made a gift to U of $88,046.40 (.440232 × $200,000) and a gift to R of $111,953.60 (.559768 × $200,000). ◆

What is the significance of dividing a gift into several distinct parts? The division becomes important in determining the applicability of the annual exclusion and the marital deduction. Under the facts of Example 9, an annual exclusion probably would be allowed for the gift to W but not for the interest passing to S (because of the future interest limitation). If W is D's spouse, no marital deduction is allowed because the life estate is a terminable interest. As noted in Chapter 17, however, this problem could be cured with a qualified terminable interest property (QTIP) election.

Special Use Valuation Method

Section 2032A permits an executor to elect to value certain classes of real estate used in farming or in connection with a closely held business at its "current" use, rather than the usual "highest," "best," or "most suitable" use. The major objective of the provision is to provide a form of limited relief to protect the heirs against the possibility of having to sell a portion of the family farm to pay estate taxes.

─────────────── EXAMPLE 12 ───────────────

At the time of his death, D owned a dairy farm on the outskirts of a large city. For farming purposes, the property's value is $300,000 (the current use value).[15] As a potential site for a shopping center, however, the property is worth $800,000 (the most suitable use value). The executor of D's estate can elect to include only $300,000 in the gross estate. ◆

The special use valuation procedure permits a reduction of no more than $750,000 in estate tax valuation.

─────────────── EXAMPLE 13 ───────────────

At the time of his death, D owned a farm with a most suitable use value of $2,000,000 but a current use value of $1,000,000. Assuming the property qualifies under § 2032A and the special use valuation election is made, D's gross estate must include $1,250,000. Only $750,000 can be excluded under § 2032A. ◆

The election of § 2032A affects the qualifying heir's income tax basis in the property. In Example 13, the use of § 2032A means the heir takes an income tax

─────────────────────

15. Sections 2032A(e)(7) and (8) set forth various methods of valuation to be applied in arriving at current use value.

basis of $1,250,000 in the farm. Had § 2032A not been elected and had the most suitable use value been included in D's gross estate, the income tax basis would have been $2,000,000.

The special use valuation election is available if *all* of the following conditions are satisfied:

1. At least 50 percent of the adjusted value of the gross estate consists of *real* or *personal* property devoted to a qualifying use (used for farming or in a closely held business) at the time of the owner's death.[16]
2. The *real* property devoted to a qualifying use comprises at least 25 percent of the adjusted value of the gross estate.
    For purposes of satisfying both the 50 percent test (condition 1) and the 25 percent test (condition 2), the qualifying property is considered at its most suitable use value. Thus, in Example 12, the property would be treated as if it had a value of $800,000 (not $300,000). The adjusted value of the gross estate is the gross estate less certain unpaid mortgages and other indebtedness.
3. The qualifying property passes to a qualifying heir of the decedent. A qualifying heir includes certain family members as set forth in § 2032A(e)(2).
4. The *real* property has been owned by the decedent or the decedent's family for five out of the eight years ending on the date of the decedent's death and was devoted to a qualifying use during that period.
5. The decedent or a member of the decedent's family has participated materially in the operation of the farm or business during the period specified under condition 4.[17]

Section 2032A(c) provides that the estate tax savings derived from the special use valuation method are recaptured from the heir, if he or she disposes of the property or ceases to use it as qualifying use property within a period of 10 years from the date of the decedent's death.

EXAMPLE 14

Assume the same facts as in Example 13. Further assume that by electing § 2032A, D's estate tax liability was reduced by $245,000. Three years after D's death, H (the qualifying heir) sells the farm for $3,000,000. At this point, H must pay the $245,000 additional estate tax liability that would have been imposed had § 2032A not been utilized. ◆

In this regard, the Code gives the IRS security for compliance with the terms of § 2032A by placing a special lien on the qualifying property.[18] In addition, the heir can elect to adjust the income tax basis upward.[19] The adjustment equals the reduction in the value of the gross estate due to § 2032A.

EXAMPLE 15

Assume the same facts as in Example 14. H can elect to add $750,000 to the farm basis in determining the gain or loss to be recognized on its sale. ◆

When a qualified heir elects to increase basis, he or she must pay interest on the amount of the estate tax that is recaptured. The interest is computed (at rates

---

16. §§ 2032A(b)(1)(A) and (b)(2). For a definition of "farm" and "farming," see §§ 2032A(e)(4) and (5).

17. § 2032A(b)(1)(C)(ii). "Material participation" is defined in § 2032A(e)(6).

18. § 6324B.

19. §§ 1016(c)(1) and (5).

in effect during the period involved) from nine months after the date of death to the due date of the recaptured estate tax.

Valuation Problems with a Closely Held Corporation

Goodwill Aspects.   If a closely held corporation's record of past earnings is higher than usual for the industry, the IRS is apt to claim the presence of goodwill as a corporate asset.

─────────────────── EXAMPLE 16 ───────────────────

D owned 70% of the stock of D Corporation, with the remaining 30% held by various family members. Over the past five years, D Corporation has generated average net profits of $100,000, and on the date of D's death, the book value of the corporation's stock was $250,000. If the IRS identifies 8% as an appropriate rate of return, one approach to the valuation of D Corporation stock would yield the following result:

Average net profit for the past five years	$100,000
8% of the $250,000 book value	20,000
Excess earnings over 8%	$ 80,000
Value of goodwill (5 × $80,000)	$400,000
Book value	250,000
Total value of the D stock	$650,000

◆

Thus, the IRS might contend that the stock should be included in D's gross estate at 70 percent of $650,000, or $455,000. If the estate wishes to argue for a lower valuation, relevant factors might include any of the following:

1. The average net profit figure for the past five years ($100,000) may not be representative. Perhaps it includes some extraordinary gains that normally do not occur or are extraneous to the business conducted by the corporation. An example might be a windfall profit for a specific year because of an unusual market situation. The corporation may have recognized a large gain from an appreciated investment held for many years. The figure may fail to take into account certain expenses that normally would be incurred but for some justifiable reason have been deferred. In a family business during periods of expansion and development, it is not uncommon to find an unusually low salary structure. Profits might be considerably less if the owner-employees of the business were being paid the true worth of their services.
2. The appropriate rate of return for this type of business may not be 8 percent. If it is higher, there would be less goodwill because the business is not as profitable as it seems.
3. If D was a key person in the operation of D Corporation, could some or all of any goodwill developed by the business be attributed to his or her efforts? If so, is it not reasonable to assume that the goodwill might be seriously impaired by D's death?

Other Factors.   Aside from the issue of goodwill, the valuation of closely held stock must take other factors into account.[20] For example, consider the percentage of ownership involved. If the percentage represents a *minority interest* and the

─────────────

20. These criteria are set forth in Reg. § 20.2031–2(f) and Rev.Rul. 59–60, 1959–1 C.B. 237.

corporation has a poor dividend-paying record, a substantial discount is in order.[21] The justification for the discount is the general inability of the holder of the minority interest to affect corporate policy, particularly with respect to the distribution of dividends. At the other extreme is an interest large enough to represent control, either actual or effective. Considered alone, a controlling interest calls for valuation at a premium.[22]

A controlling interest may be so large, however, that the disposition of the stock within a reasonable period of time after the valuation date could have a negative effect on the market for such shares. The *blockage rule* recognizes what may happen in terms of per unit value when a large block of shares is marketed at one time.[23] Most often, it is applied to stock that has a recognized market. The rule permits a discount from the amount at which smaller lots are selling on or about the valuation date.[24] The blockage rule could have a bearing on the valuation of other assets, but its application appears better suited to stocks and securities.[25]

Because most stock in closely held corporations does not trade in a recognized market, a discount for *lack of marketability* may be in order. The discount recognizes the costs that would have to be incurred in creating a market for such shares to effect their orderly disposition.[26] The discount could be significant considering typical underwriting expenses and other costs involved in going public.

Resolving the Valuation Problem for Stock in Closely Held Corporations. Since the valuation of closely held stock is subject to so many variables, planning should be directed toward bringing about some measure of certainty.

--------- EXAMPLE 17 ---------

D wants to transfer some of her stock in Z Corporation to a trust formed for her children. She also would like to make a substantial contribution to her alma mater, State University (S.U.). At present, the Z stock is owned entirely by D and has never been traded on any market or otherwise sold or exchanged. Z's past operations have proved profitable, and Z has established a respectable record of dividend distributions. Based on the best available information and taking into account various adjustments (e.g., discount for lack of marketability), D feels each share of Z stock possesses a fair market value of $120. ◆

If D makes a gift of some of the stock to the trust set up for the children and uses the $120 per share valuation, what assurance is there that the IRS will accept this figure? If the IRS is successful in increasing the fair market value per share, D could end up with additional gift tax liability.

D could hedge against any further gift tax liability. Concurrently with the gift of stock to the trust formed for the children, D could make an outright transfer of some of the shares to S.U., thereby generating an income tax deduction. D

---

21. See, for example, *Jack D. Carr*, 49 TCM 507, T.C.Memo. 1985–19.

22. See, for example, *Helvering v. Safe Deposit and Trust Co. of Baltimore, Exr. (Estate of H. Walters)*, 38–1 USTC ¶9240, 21 AFTR 12, 95 F.2d 806 (CA–4, 1938), *aff'g*. 35 B.T.A. 259 (1937), in which the court stated ". . . the influence of the ownership of a large number of shares upon corporate control might give them a value in excess of prevailing market quotations. . . ."

23. Reg. § 20.2031–2(e).

24. See, for example, *Estate of Robert Damon*, 49 T.C. 108 (1967).

25. In *Estate of David Smith*, 57 T.C. 650 (1972), the estate of a now-famous sculptor argued for the application of the blockage rule to 425 sculptures included in the gross estate.

26. See, for example, *Estate of Mark S. Gallo*, 50 TCM 470, T.C.Memo. 1985–363. In this case, the taxpayer also argued that a bad product image (i.e., the Thunderbird, Ripple, and Boone's Farm brands) would depress the value of the stock. Since the trend was toward better wines, association with cheaper products had a negative consumer impact.

would base the income tax deduction on the value used for gift tax purposes.[27] If the IRS later raises the value and assesses more gift tax, D can file an amended income tax return, claim a larger charitable contribution deduction, and obtain an offsetting income tax refund. To carry out this hedge, D's gift of Z stock would be derived by comparing her prevailing gift tax and income tax brackets for the year of the transfers. Note that no gift tax liability is incurred for the stock transferred to S.U. by virtue of the charitable deduction allowed for gift tax purposes by § 2522 (discussed in Chapter 17).

The Buy and Sell Agreement and Valuation. The main objective of a buy and sell agreement is to effect the orderly disposition of a business interest without the risk of the interest falling into the hands of outsiders. Moreover, a buy and sell agreement can ease the problems of estate liquidity and valuation.

Two types of buy and sell agreements exist: entity and cross-purchase arrangements. Under the entity type, the business itself (partnership or corporation) agrees to buy out the interest of the withdrawing owner (partner or shareholder). For a corporation, this normally takes the form of a stock redemption plan set up to qualify for income tax purposes under either § 302(b) or § 303. By making use of these provisions, corporate distributions can qualify for sale or exchange treatment rather than dividends (see Chapter 5). Under the cross-purchase agreement, the surviving owners (partners or shareholders) agree to buy out the withdrawing owner. The structures of the most typical buy and sell agreements are illustrated in Figure 18–1.

EXAMPLE 18

R, S, and D are equal and unrelated shareholders in T Corporation, and all three share in T's management. All agree to turn in their stock to the corporation for redemption at $100 per share if any one of them withdraws (by death or otherwise) from the business. Shortly thereafter, D dies, and the estate redeems the T stock at the agreed-upon price of $100 per share. ◆

EXAMPLE 19

Assume the same facts as in Example 18, except the agreement is the cross-purchase type under which each shareholder promises to buy a share of the withdrawing shareholder's interest. When D dies, the estate sells the T stock to R and S for $100 per share. ◆

Will the $100 per share paid to D's estate determine the amount to be included in D's gross estate? The answer is *yes*, subject to the following conditions:

1. The price is the result of a bona fide business agreement.
2. The agreement is not a device to transfer property to family members.
3. The agreement is comparable to other arrangements entered into by persons dealing at arm's length.[28]

Estate Freezes. Over the years, owners of closely held businesses have searched for ways to transfer the major value of the business to their heirs while retaining some security interest. The typical approach with corporations has

---

27. The use of fair market value as the measure of the charitable contribution deduction presumes the Z stock would yield long-term capital gain if sold by D. See § 170(e). However, the appreciation on the stock is a tax preference item and might create alternative minimum tax.

28. § 2703.

been for the owner to retain preferred stock and make gifts of common stock to the family. The approach *freezes* the amount that will be included in the owner's gross estate to the value of the preferred stock. Any post-gift appreciation in the business will be attributable to the common stock and *will not* be part of the owner's gross estate.

Under recent legislation, some degree of the estate tax freeze is permitted.[29] Unfortunately, current law is designed to maximize the amount of the gift made by the donor upon the creation of the freeze. Generally, the retained interest is valued at zero, thereby resulting in the transfer of the *full* value of the business.

EXAMPLE 20

F owns all of the stock in X Corporation valued as follows: $2,000,000 common stock and $500,000 preferred stock. The preferred stock is noncumulative, does not have a

---

FIGURE 18–1   **Structure of a Typical Buy and Sell Agreement**

Cross Purchase Type

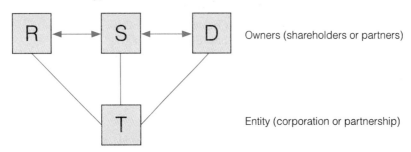

Structure: The owners (R, S, D) contract individually to purchase the deceased owner's interest in the entity (T).

Estate tax effect: The purchase price is included in the deceased owner's estate and generally *controls for valuation purposes.*

Entity Purchase Type

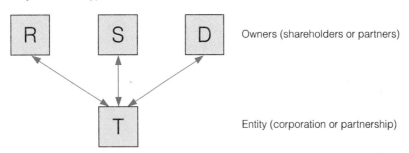

Structure: The entity (T) contracts to purchase the owner's (R, S, D) interest at death.

Estate tax effect: The purchase price is included in the deceased owner's estate and generally *controls for valuation purposes.*

---

29. § 2701.

redemption date, and possesses no liquidation preference. F gives the common stock to his adult children and retains the preferred stock. F has made a gift to the children of $2,500,000. The $500,000 worth of preferred stock F retained is treated as having no value. ◆

Special rules apply if the preferred stock is cumulative, has a redemption date, or carries certain other preferential rights. These rules allow some value to be assigned to the preferred stock, thereby reducing the amount of the gift. The adjustments can become complex and are not discussed further in the text.

The estate freeze rules *do not apply* to transfers of the following assets:

- Retained interests for which market quotations are readily available.
- Retained interests that are the same as those transferred (e.g., common stock, a partnership interest in which all partners share equally).

The response of the business community to the current estate freeze rules has not been positive. Consider some of the inherent disadvantages:

- Although the retained interest is deemed to be a gift, it will be included in the donor's gross estate upon death. In Example 20, therefore, the preferred stock is included in F's gross estate upon his subsequent death.
- The donor loses the use of any gift tax paid on the retained interest.

The estate freeze does, however, escape later estate taxation on any post-transfer appreciation that develops.

———————————— EXAMPLE 21 ————————————

Assume the same facts as in Example 20. F dies 10 years after the gift when the X Corporation common and preferred stock are worth $5,000,000 and $500,000, respectively. F's estate includes only $500,000 for the preferred stock. The $3,000,000 appreciation on the common stock ($5,000,000 − $2,000,000) has escaped a transfer tax. ◆

Valuation concepts are reviewed in Concept Summary 18–1.

INCOME TAX CONCEPTS
◆

F‌amily tax planning also involves an assessment of the income tax positions of the transferor (the donor or decedent) and the transferee (the donee or heir).

Basis of Property Acquired by Gift

The income tax basis of property acquired by gift depends on whether the donee sells the property for a gain or for a loss and, in certain cases, on when the gift occurred.

- If the gift took place before 1921, the donee's basis for gain or loss is the fair market value of the property on the date of the gift.[30]
- If the gift took place after 1920 and before 1977, the donee's basis for gain is the donor's adjusted basis plus any gift tax paid on the transfer (but not to exceed the fair market value on the date of the gift). The basis for loss is the lower of the basis for gain or the fair market value of the property on the date of the gift.

———————————

30. § 1015(c).

■ If the gift took place after 1976, the donee's basis for gain is the donor's adjusted basis plus only the gift tax attributable to the appreciation of the property to the point of the gift. The basis for loss is the lesser of the basis for gain or the fair market value of the property on the date of the gift.[31]

─────────────── EXAMPLE 22 ───────────────

In 1920, D received real estate as a gift from her grandfather. The property cost the grandfather $10,000 and was worth $25,000 on the date of the gift. D's income tax basis for gain or loss is $25,000. ◆

─────────────── EXAMPLE 23 ───────────────

In 1975, D receives stock as a gift from M. The stock cost M $10,000 and was worth $50,000 on the date of the gift. As a result of the transfer, M paid a gift tax of $5,000. D's income tax basis for gain or loss is $15,000 [$10,000 (M's basis) + $5,000 (gift tax paid by M)]. D does not have a different basis for loss; the fair market value of the property on the date of the gift ($50,000) is not less than the basis for gain ($15,000). ◆

─────────────── EXAMPLE 24 ───────────────

Assume the same facts as in Example 23, except that the gift took place in 1992.

M's adjusted basis on the date of the gift	$10,000
Gift tax attributable to the $40,000 appreciation [($40,000/$50,000) × $5,000]	4,000
D's income tax basis for gain	$14,000

D's basis for loss also is $14,000, based on the same reasoning as in Example 23. ◆

CONCEPT SUMMARY 18–1
VALUATION CONCEPTS

1. Fair market value is "the price at which property would change hands between a willing buyer and a willing seller, neither being under any compulsion to buy or to sell and both having reasonable knowledge of relevant facts."

2. Special rules govern the valuation of life insurance policies and annuity contracts. In the case of unmatured life insurance policies, value depends on whether the policies are paid-up or not. Resort to the IRS valuation tables is necessary when the annuities are issued by parties not regularly engaged in selling annuities.

3. The IRS valuation tables must be used to value multiple interests in property. Such interests include income for a term of years, life estates, and remainders.

4. Section 2032A provides valuation relief for the estates of persons who hold real estate used in farming or in connection with a closely held business. If the requirements of the provision are met and if the executor elects, the property can be valued at its *current use* rather than its *most suitable use*.

5. Determining the value of the stock in a closely held corporation presents unique problems. The presence or absence of *goodwill* at the corporate level has a direct bearing on the stock being valued. A discount may be in order for any of the following: a minority interest, lack of marketability, and the application of the blockage rule. The IRS will contend that a premium attaches to an interest that represents control of the corporation.

6. A properly structured buy and sell agreement will control the value to be assigned a deceased owner's interest in a partnership or a corporation.

7. An estate tax freeze is useful in avoiding post-transfer appreciation that develops on the partnership or corporate interest involved. However, the donor must consider the gift tax consequences that result when the freeze is created.

---

31. §§ 1015(a) and (d).

The effect of the rule illustrated in Example 24 is to deny a donee any increase in basis for the gift tax attributable to the donor's adjusted basis. In making the allocation, assume that $1,000 of the gift tax paid related to M's $10,000 basis and $4,000 to the $40,000 appreciation in the property.

Because the donee usually assumes the donor's basis in the property, transfers by gifts are considered carryover situations. Consistent with this approach, the donee's holding period includes that of the donor.[32]

Basis of Property Acquired by Death

General Rule.   Except as otherwise noted in the following sections, the income tax basis of property acquired from a decedent is the fair market value on the date of death or, if elected, on the alternate valuation date. When property has appreciated in value between acquisition and date of death, a step-up in income tax basis occurs for the estate or heir of the deceased owner. A step-up in basis means that appreciation existing at death escapes the application of the Federal income tax.

EXAMPLE 25

Upon her death in 1992, D owned real estate (adjusted basis of $100,000) worth $400,000 that she leaves to S. Presuming that the alternate valuation date is not elected, S's income tax basis in the property becomes $400,000. Thus, a subsequent sale of the real estate by S for $400,000 results in no gain or loss to S. ◆

EXAMPLE 26

Assume the same facts as in Example 25, except that, shortly before death, D sells the real estate for $400,000. Based on this assumption, D has a gain of $300,000 taxable under the income tax. ◆

By contrasting Examples 25 and 26, one can see that the rules place a premium on holding appreciated property until death, to take advantage of the step-up in basis rule. The same cannot be said for property that has declined in value. Here, death causes a step-down in basis. This result should be avoided if selling the property would generate a deductible income tax loss.

EXAMPLE 27

Upon his death in 1992, D held stock as an investment with an adjusted basis of $50,000 and a fair market value of $30,000. Because only $30,000 is included in the gross estate, the basis of the stock to the estate or heir is this amount. Had D sold the stock before his death, a deduction for some or all of the $20,000 loss might have been available. ◆

The holding period to the estate or heir of property acquired from a decedent is automatically treated as long term.[33]

Community Property.   Although there is usually no change in basis for property not part of a decedent's gross estate, a special exception applies to community property. In such situations, the surviving spouse's half of the community takes the same basis as the half included in the deceased spouse's gross estate.[34] The reason for and the effect of this special rule are illustrated in the following example.

---

32. § 1223(2).
33. § 1223(11).

34. § 1014(b)(6).

---------------------------------- EXAMPLE 28 ----------------------------------

D and W were husband and wife and lived in a common law state. At the time of D's death, he owned assets (worth $800,000 with a basis to him of $100,000), which he bequeathed to W. Presuming the transfer qualifies under § 2056, D's estate is allowed a marital deduction of approximately $800,000. As the property passes through D's estate, W receives a step-up in basis to $800,000. ◆

---------------------------------- EXAMPLE 29 ----------------------------------

Assume the same facts as in Example 28, except that D and W had always lived in California (a community property state). If the $800,000 of assets are community property, only one-half of this value is included in D's gross estate. Because the other half does not pass through D's estate (it already belongs to W), is it fair to deny W a new basis in it? Therefore, allowing the surviving spouse's share of the community to take on a basis equal to the half included in the deceased spouse's gross estate equalizes the income tax result generally achieved in common law states through the use of the marital deduction. By giving W an income tax basis of $800,000 ($400,000 for H's half passing to her plus $400,000 for her half) and including only $400,000 in D's gross estate, the tax outcome is the same as in Example 28. ◆

Step-Up in Basis and the One-Year Rule. To understand the need for § 1014(e), consider the following situation:

---------------------------------- EXAMPLE 30 ----------------------------------

H and W are husband and wife and reside in a common law state. When the parties learn that W has a terminal illness, H transfers property (basis of $50,000 and fair market value of $200,000) to W as a gift. W dies shortly thereafter, and under the provisions of W's will, the property returns to H. ◆

If it were not for § 1014(e), what have the parties accomplished? No gift tax occurs on the transfer from H to W because of the application of the marital deduction. Upon W's death, the bequest from W to H does not generate any estate tax because the inclusion of the property in W's gross estate is offset by the marital deduction. Through the application of the general rule of § 1014, H ends up with the same property, with its basis stepped up to $200,000. Thus, the procedure enables H to get a "free" increase in income tax basis of $150,000.

When applicable, § 1014(e) forces H (the original donor) to assume the property with the same basis it had to W immediately before W's death. W's basis would have been determined under § 1015 (basis of property acquired by gift). The basis would have been $50,000 (donor's adjusted basis) plus any gift tax adjustment (none in this case) and any capital additions made by the donee (none in this case), or $50,000. If § 1014(e) applies to Example 30, H ends up where he started (with $50,000) in terms of income tax basis.

For § 1014(e) to be operative, the following conditions must be satisfied:

- The decedent must have received appreciated property as a gift during the one-year period ending with his or her death.
- The property is acquired from the decedent by the donor (or the donor's spouse).

Example 30 concerns a transfer between spouses, but the application of § 1014(e) is not so limited. The provision applies with equal effect if, for example, the donor-heir were a daughter of the donee-decedent. In such cases, moreover, the technique used in Example 30 might be susceptible to the imposition of transfer taxes (viz., gift and estate taxes) because of the unavailability of the marital deduction.

Income in Respect of a Decedent.   Income in respect of a decedent (IRD) is income earned by a decedent to the point of his or her death but not reportable on the final income tax return under the method of accounting used. IRD is most frequently applicable to decedents using the cash basis of accounting. IRD also occurs, for example, when a taxpayer at the time of death held installment notes receivable on which the gain has been deferred.

IRD is included in the gross estate at its fair market value on the appropriate valuation date. However, the income tax basis of the decedent transfers to the estate or heirs. Neither a step-up nor a step-down is possible as is true of property received by death.[35] Furthermore, the recipient of IRD must classify it in the same manner (e.g., ordinary income, capital gain) as the decedent would have.[36]

How Conclusive Is the Value Used for Estate Tax Purposes?   Suppose a value is used for estate tax purposes and reflected on the estate tax return. At some future date, an heir to the property included in the gross estate believes the value used for estate tax purposes was incorrect. An heir might desire a change in value for countless reasons, including the following:

■ The property is sold. Higher value leads to higher basis and less income tax gain.
■ The property is depreciable. More basis means larger depreciation deductions.
■ A home equity loan is obtained. With a higher value, a larger loan is allowed.
■ If the heir is a charitable organization, higher value could improve its fund-raising potential.

Is there any chance of success in arguing for a different value and thereby changing the income tax basis? The answer is yes, but with definite reservations.

If the statute of limitations has not lapsed for the estate tax return, the heir may try for a higher income tax basis by having the estate tax valuation raised. Any new valuation, however, requires both cooperation from the decedent's executor and acceptance by the IRS.

If the statute of limitations has lapsed for the estate tax return, the success of the heir's challenge depends on the following factors:

1. The value reflected on the estate tax return and accepted by the IRS is presumed to be correct.[37] The heir must rebut the presumption.
2. To rebut the presumption of correctness, it is important to determine by what means the property was originally valued. Did the valuation result from a unilateral determination by the IRS, or was it the result of carefully considered compromise between the estate and the IRS? The presumption is more difficult for the heir to overcome in the latter instance.
3. Did the heir have a hand in setting the original value? If so, the doctrine of estoppel might prevent the heir from disputing the value. Under this doctrine, the courts might hold that the heir is now trying to obtain unfair advantage. The heir used or influenced the use of a lower value for

---

35. § 1014(c).
36. § 691(a)(3). See Chapter 19 for a further discussion of IRD.

37. Rev.Rul. 54–97, 1954–1 C.B. 113; *H. B. Levy*, 17 T.C. 728 (1951); and *Malcolm C. Davenport*, 6 T.C. 62 (1946).

estate tax purposes (thereby eliminating estate taxes) and now wants a higher value for income tax purposes (thereby reducing a recognized gain).[38]

4. Even if the heir can avoid the application of the doctrine of estoppel, justification for a new value must be produced. Perhaps the heir can present evidence unknown or not available to the executor of the estate when the property was originally valued. But was this evidence known to the parties involved in the original valuation and thereby taken into account? Remember that the valuation process does not involve hindsight but should consider only the factors reasonably available on the appropriate valuation date.

GIFT PLANNING
◆

One of the ways to carry out family tax planning is to start a program of lifetime giving. The objectives of such a program are to minimize transfer taxes while keeping income tax consequences in mind.

Minimizing Gift Taxes

The Federal gift tax can be avoided through proper use of the annual exclusion. Because a new annual exclusion is available each year, spacing gifts over multiple years increases the amount that can be transferred free of gift tax.

EXAMPLE 31

Starting in 1987, G makes annual gifts of $10,000 to each of her five grandchildren. Through 1992, G will have transferred $300,000 [$10,000 (annual exclusion) × 5 (number of donees) × 6 (number of years)] with no gift tax consequences. ◆

For married donors, the § 2513 election to split gifts provides the opportunity to double the amount that can be transferred.

EXAMPLE 32

Assume the same facts as in Example 31, except that G is married to M. If M consents to the § 2513 elections, G can transfer $600,000 [$20,000 (annual exclusion for two donors) × 5 (number of donees) × 6 (number of years)] with no gift tax consequences. ◆

From a practical standpoint, many donors who want to take advantage of the annual exclusion do not wish to give cash or near-cash assets (e.g., marketable securities). Where the value of the gift property substantially exceeds the amount of the annual exclusion, as is often the case with real estate, gifts of a partial interest are an attractive option.

EXAMPLE 33

F and M want to give a parcel of unimproved land to their three adult children and five grandchildren as equal owners. The land has an adjusted basis of $100,000, is held by

---

38. In *William A. Beltzer*, 74–1 USTC ¶9373, 33 AFTR2d 74–1173, 495 F.2d 211 (CA–8, 1974), *aff'g.* 73–2 USTC ¶9512, 32 AFTR2d 73–5250 (D.Ct.Neb., 1973), the doctrine of estoppel was *invoked against the taxpayer* since, as the executor of the estate, he had been instrumental in setting the original value reported on the death tax return.

F and M as community property, and has an appraised value of $320,000 as of December 21, 1991. On December 22, 1991, F and M convey a one-half undivided interest in the land to their children and grandchildren as tenants in common. This is followed by a transfer of the remaining one-half interest on January 2, 1992. Both transfers cause no gift tax consequences because each is fully covered by annual exclusions of $160,000 [$20,000 (annual exclusion for two donors) × 8 (number of donees)]. Thus, in a period of less than two weeks, F and M transfer $320,000 in value free of any Federal tax consequences. ◆

Further examination of Example 33 leads to the following observations:

- No income tax consequences ensue from the gift. However, had F and M first sold the land and made a gift of the cash proceeds, recognized gain of $220,000 [$320,000 (selling price) − $100,000 (adjusted basis)] would have resulted.
- The § 2513 election to split gifts is not necessary since the land was community property. If the land had been held by one of the spouses as separate property, the election would have been necessary to generate the same $320,000 of exclusions.
- Good tax planning generally dictates that sizable gifts of property be supported by reliable appraisals. In the case of successive gifts of partial interests in the same property, multiple appraisals should be obtained to cover each gift. This advice was not followed in Example 33 due to the short interval between gifts. Barring exceptional circumstances, the value of real estate will not change within a period of less than two weeks.

Minimizing Estate Taxes

Aside from the annual exclusion, do lifetime gifts offer any tax advantages over transfers at death? Someone familiar with the tax law applicable to post-1976 transfers would answer "no" to this question. Under the current unified transfer tax scheme, the tax rates and credit are the same. Consequently, there seems to be no transfer tax difference between transfer by gift and at death. However, as the following discussion shows, lifetime transfers may be preferable to those at death.

Avoiding a Transfer Tax on Future Appreciation. If property is expected to appreciate in value, a gift removes the appreciation from the donor's gross estate.

 EXAMPLE 34

In 1986, D transfers an insurance policy on her life to S, the designated beneficiary. At the time of the transfer, the policy had a fair market value of $50,000 and a face amount of $250,000. D dies in 1992, and the insurance company pays the $250,000 proceeds to S. By making the gift, D has kept $200,000 in value from being subject to a transfer tax. ◆

Besides life insurance, other assets that often appreciate in value include real estate, art objects, and special collections (e.g., rare books, coins, and stamps).

Preparing for the Special Use Valuation Method. The § 2032A election is not available for valuing transfers by gift. Yet, if its use is planned in estate tax situations, gifts of nonqualifying property may aid in meeting the requirements of § 2032A. Recall that one of the requirements of § 2032A is that qualified use property must constitute at least 50 percent of the adjusted value of the gross estate.

─────────────────────── EXAMPLE 35 ───────────────────────

In 1988, D's estate includes the following:

	Fair Market Value
Farm operated by D with current use value of $250,000	$1,000,000
Stock in a local bank	700,000
Marketable securities and cash	400,000

At this point, D's estate does not qualify for the § 2032A election. The qualifying property [$1,000,000 (farm)] does not equal or exceed 50% of the adjusted gross estate [$1,000,000 (farm) + $700,000 (bank stock) + $400,000 (marketable securities and cash)]. ◆

─────────────────────── EXAMPLE 36 ───────────────────────

Continuing with the facts of Example 35, D makes a gift of one-half of the bank stock in 1988. D dies in 1992 with no change in asset values. D's estate now qualifies for § 2032A treatment since $1,000,000 (farm) is 50% or more of $1,750,000 [$1,000,000 (farm) + $350,000 (bank stock) + $400,000 (marketable securities and cash)]. The election enables the estate to value the farm at $250,000 (current use). As a result, the estate tax on $500,000 in value is saved. ◆

Care must be taken to avoid gifts of property within three years of death. Though such gifts usually are not included in the gross estate of the donor for estate tax purposes, they are counted when testing for the percentage requirements of § 303 (stock redemptions to pay death taxes and administration expenses—refer to Chapter 5), § 2032A, and § 6166 (extension of time to pay estate taxes in installments—discussed below).[39]

─────────────────────── EXAMPLE 37 ───────────────────────

Assume the same facts as in Example 36, except that the gift occurs in 1990 (not 1988). Although only $350,000 of the bank stock is included in D's gross estate for estate tax purposes, $700,000 is used for the percentage requirements of § 2032A. As a result, the estate fails to qualify for the § 2032A election. ◆

Avoiding State Transfer Taxes.   Another element that may favor lifetime over death transfers is the state's transfer tax system. All states impose some type of death tax, but only a few impose a gift tax. Thus, a gift may completely avoid a state transfer tax.

The states currently imposing a state gift tax include Delaware, Louisiana, New York, North Carolina, Tennessee, and Wisconsin. Unfortunately, this could lead to multiple taxation of the same transfer. Unlike the *state death* tax credit (see the discussion of § 2011 in Chapter 17), the Code does not allow a credit for state gift taxes paid.

Effect of Gift Taxes Paid.   As to taxable gifts that generate a tax, consider the time value of the gift taxes paid. Since the donor loses the use of these funds, the predicted interval between the gift (and the imposition of the gift tax) and death (the imposition of the estate tax) may make the gift less attractive.

───────────────

39. §§ 2035(d)(3) and (4).

―――――――――――――――――――― EXAMPLE 38 ――――――――――――――――――――

In 1986, D makes a gift that results in a gift tax of $50,000. D dies five years later. Presuming a 10% rate of return, the gift tax paid would have been worth $80,550 at D's death. Therefore, D has lost $30,550 by making the gift. ♦

The analysis used in Example 38 requires refinement to yield a meaningful result. Variables that need to be questioned or interjected include the following:

- The life expectancy of the donor at the time of the gift. Actuarial tables can provide a start, but this kind of information must be adjusted for the general health and lifestyle of the donor. In any event, accurately predicting when a specific person will die is more chance than science.
- The interest factor used. Anticipating even short-rate changes, erratic at best, becomes mere guesswork as the time interval increases.
- Any change in the value of the property from the point of gift to the date of death. Appreciation in value during this interval makes the gift look like a wise choice. The opposite is true if value declines.
- The income tax ramifications of the gift. A donor escapes any post-transfer income yielded by the property. Thus, the income tax burden is shifted away from the donor to the donee.

A present value analysis finally must consider the estate tax effect of any gift tax paid. Except for gifts within three years of death (see Chapter 17), the gift tax paid itself is not subject to estate tax. Referring to Example 38, the $50,000 in gift taxes paid escapes inclusion in D's gross estate.

Income Tax Considerations

Income Shifting.   One way to lower the overall tax burden on the family unit is to shift income from high-bracket taxpayers to lower-bracket family members. To accomplish this shifting, however, income-producing property must be transferred.

If a gift of property is to shift income to the donee, the transfer must be *complete*. Continued dominion over the property by the donor may lead the IRS to question the finality of the gift.

―――――――――――――――――――― EXAMPLE 39 ――――――――――――――――――――

F, subject to a 31% marginal income tax rate, owns all of the stock in X, an S corporation. F transfers by gift 60% of the X stock to her four children. The children range in age from 14 to 19 years and are all in the 15% income tax bracket. After the transfer, F continues to operate the business. No shareholder meetings are held. Except for reporting 60% of the pass-through of X's profits, F's children have no contact with the business. Aside from the salary paid to F, X makes no cash distributions to its shareholders. ♦

The situation posed in Example 39 occurs frequently and is fraught with danger. If the purported gift by F lacks economic reality and F is the true economic owner of all of X's stock, the pass-through to the children is disregarded.[40] The profits are taxed to F at her 31 percent rate rather than to the children at their 15 percent rates. Consequently, the transfer has not accomplished the intended shifting of income.

―――――――――――――――――

40. *Michael F. Beirne*, 52 T.C. 210 (1969) and 61 T.C. 268 (1973).

What can be done to make the transfer in Example 39 tax-effective? First, a distribution of dividends would provide some economic benefit to the children. As the transfer is presently constituted, all that the children have received as a result of the gift is an economic detriment, because they must pay income taxes on their share of X's pass-through of profits. Second, some steps should be taken to recognize and protect the interests of the children as donees. One way to do this is to make use of the state's Uniform Gifts to Minors Act.[41] F could designate a family member as the custodian of the stock. The custodian would have a fiduciary responsibility to safeguard the interests of the children. Once the children reach age 21 and the custodianship relationship is terminated, shareholder meetings should be encouraged. That the children do not assume active participation in the business of X is of no consequence as long as they are given the opportunity to do so.

As was true in Example 39, income shifting techniques assume that the donee is in a lower tax bracket than the donor. When the donee is under the age of 14, however, kiddie tax treatment can neutralize the income tax effect of a gift. Under this provision, certain unearned income (e.g., interest, dividends) of a child is taxed at the marginal rate applicable to the parent.[42] In Example 39, suppose one of F's children was under 14 years of age. Giving X stock to the child would not serve any purpose. Even if the transfer was complete and the child recognized the profit pass-through, the applicable rate would be 31 percent, not 15 percent. Once the child reaches age 14, however, kiddie tax treatment no longer applies.

Income Tax Consequences to the Donor. Generally, a gift of property results in no income tax consequences to the donor. Two important exceptions exist, however, covering installment notes receivable and U.S. savings bonds.

A gift of an installment note receivable is a taxable disposition, and the donor is treated as if the note had been sold for its fair market value.[43] As a result, the donor must recognize the deferred profit.

EXAMPLE 40

In 1990, D sells real estate (basis of $100,000) to P (an unrelated party) for $400,000. P (the obligor) issues two notes of $200,000 each, one due in 1991 and one due in 1992. D (the obligee) does not elect out of the installment method. In 1991 and before the first note becomes due, D gives both notes to his son, S. On this date, the notes have a fair market value of $380,000. As a result of the gift to S, D recognizes a gain of $280,000 [$380,000 (fair market value of the notes) − $100,000 (D's unrecovered basis)]. ◆

A disposition also occurs if the notes become unenforceable.[44] Examples of unenforceability include a failure on the part of the obligee to pursue collection of the notes, a gift of the notes to the obligor, and cancellation or forgiveness of the notes. If the obligor and obligee are related, the face amount of the notes is treated as their fair market value.[45]

EXAMPLE 41

In 1990, D sells real estate (basis of $100,000) to S (D's son) for $400,000. S (the obligor) issues two notes for $200,000 each, one due in 1991 and one due in 1992. D (the

---

41. *Donald O. Kirkpatrick*, 36 TCM 1122, T.C.Memo. 1977–281.

42. § 1(i).

43. § 453B(a).

44. § 453B(f).

45. "Related person" is defined in § 453(f) indirectly by reference to other Code provisions.

obligee) does not elect out of the installment method. In 1991 and before the first note becomes due, D cancels both notes. At this point, the notes have a fair market value of $380,000. D's cancellation makes the notes unenforceable, and a disposition results. Since the obligor and obligee are related parties (mother and son), the fair market value of the notes is deemed to be $400,000 (the face amount), not $380,000. Thus, D has a recognized gain of $300,000. ◆

A gift of U.S. savings bonds is not effective unless the bonds are re-registered in the donee's name. This forces the donor to recognize any deferred income accrued on the bonds. The result may surprise donors who expect to postpone the recognition of interest income until the bonds are redeemed. Thus, the donor who desires to avoid income tax consequences should avoid gifts of installment notes receivable and U.S. savings bonds.

For purposes of contrasting tax results, what happens if these properties are passed by death? The results are summarized below:

- Installment notes receivable are taxed to whoever collects the notes (the estate or heirs).[46] If the notes are forgiven or canceled by the decedent's will, the income is taxed to the estate.
- Deferred interest income on U.S. savings bonds is taxed to whoever redeems the bonds (the estate or heirs).
- Recapture potential disappears at death.[47] The estate or heirs take the property free of any recapture potential existing at the time of the owner's death.

Carryover Basis Situations. When considering the income tax effect of a transfer on the donee or heir, the basis rules of §§ 1014 and 1015 warrant close examination. When appreciated property is involved, receiving the property from a decedent is preferred to a lifetime transfer.

EXAMPLE 42

F plans to transfer unimproved real estate (basis of $100,000 and fair market value of $400,000) to his daughter, D. If the property passes by death, D's basis is $400,000. If the property passes by gift, D's income tax basis (presuming no gift tax adjustment) is $100,000. The step-up effect of § 1014 provides D with an additional basis of $300,000. ◆

EXAMPLE 43

F plans to transfer unimproved real estate (basis of $150,000 and fair market value of $100,000) to his daughter, D. If the property passes by death, D's basis is $100,000. If the property passes by gift, D's income tax basis is $100,000 for losses and $150,000 for gains. Receiving the property as a gift, therefore, might be more advantageous to D than the complete step-down in basis under § 1014. ◆

For F, the options posed by Example 43 are not attractive. By making a gift or passing the property by death, F sacrifices the potential loss deduction of $50,000. Presuming the land is held as an investment, capital losses can be used to offset capital gains or can be applied against ordinary income to the extent of $3,000 per year. Unused capital losses can be carried over indefinitely but will not survive F's death.

---

46. § 453B(c).   47. §§ 1245(b)(1) and 1250(d)(1).

Estate planning considers the nontax and tax aspects of death. In the nontax area are the various steps that can be taken to reduce the costs of probating an estate. In the tax area, the focus is on controlling the amount of the gross estate and maximizing estate tax deductions.

Probate Costs

The probate estate consists of all properties subject to administration by an executor. The administration is conducted under the supervision of a local court, usually called a probate court. In certain states, probate functions are performed by county courts, surrogate courts, or orphan's courts.

Probate costs include: attorney fees, accountant fees, appraisal and inventory fees, court costs, expenses incident to the disposition of assets and satisfaction of liabilities, litigation costs needed to resolve will contests, and charges for the preparation of tax returns. The total amount of probate costs cannot be accurately predicted because so many variables are involved. A conservative range might be from 5 to 15 percent of the amount of the probate estate.

Many procedures can be used to reduce the probate estate and thereby save probate costs, including the following:

■ Owning property as joint tenants (or tenants by the entirety) with right of survivorship. Upon death, the property passes to the surviving tenant and generally is not subject to probate.
■ Making life insurance payable to a beneficiary other than the estate.
■ Utilizing a revocable trust. Upon the death of the creator, the trust becomes irrevocable and is not subject to probate. The revocable trust is often popularly referred to as a *living trust.*

Another advantage of bypassing the probate estate is that the beneficiary can obtain immediate possession and enjoyment of the property. The probate process can become prolonged, and the heir may have to await the final settlement of the estate before getting the property.

In terms of probate costs, the ownership of out-of-state real estate can cause horrendous problems. Out-of-state ownership is not uncommon with decedents who have relocated after retirement or who maintain vacation homes.

EXAMPLE 44

After retirement and five years before his death, D moved from Nebraska to Arizona. At death, D still owns a rental house in Nebraska and a vacation home in Idaho. To clear title to these properties, D's executor must institute ancillary probate proceedings in Nebraska and Idaho. This will result in additional attorney fees and court costs. ◆

The solution to the dilemma posed in Example 44 is to dispose of these properties before death. Although this may generate some legal fees, they will be far less than the cost of ancillary probate proceedings.

Controlling the Amount of the Gross Estate

Unlike the probate estate, the gross estate determines what property is subject to the Federal estate tax. In fact, many of the steps taken to reduce the probate estate will not have a similar effect on the gross estate—see the discussion of §§ 2036 and 2038 in Chapter 17.

Valuation procedures sometimes can be applied to control the amount of the gross estate. The special use valuation method of § 2032A can be elected when the estate consists of real estate used in farming or in connection with a closely held business. When the estate comprises assets that have declined in value shortly after death, the use of the alternate valuation date of § 2032 (see Chapter 17) is advised.

Proper Handling of Estate Tax Deductions

Estate taxes can be reduced either by decreasing the size of the gross estate or by increasing the total allowable deductions. The lower the taxable estate, the less estate tax is generated. Planning with deductions involves the following considerations:

- Making proper use of the marital deduction.
- Working effectively with the charitable deduction.
- Optimizing other deductions and losses allowed under §§ 2053 and 2054.

Approaches to the Marital Deduction. When planning for the estate tax marital deduction, both tax and nontax factors are taken into account. Two major tax goals guide the planning. They are the *equalization* and *deferral* approaches:

- Attempt to equalize the estates of both spouses. Clearly, for example, the estate tax on $2,000,000 is more than double the estate tax on $1,000,000 [compare $780,800 with $691,600 ($345,800 × 2)].
- Try to postpone estate taxation as long as possible. On a $1,000,000 amount, for example, what is the time value of $345,800 in estate taxes deferred for a period of, say, 10 years?

Barring certain circumstances, the deferral approach generally is preferable. By maximizing the marital deduction on the death of the first spouse to die, taxes are saved, and the surviving spouse can trim his or her future estate by entering into a program of lifetime giving. By making optimum use of the annual exclusion, considerable amounts can be shifted without incurring *any* transfer tax.

Tax planning must remain flexible and be tailored to the individual circumstances of the parties involved. The equalization approach may be most attractive in the following situations:

- Both spouses are of advanced age and/or in poor health, and neither is expected to survive the other for a prolonged period of time.
- The spouse who is expected to survive has considerable assets of his or her own. To illustrate, a spouse who passes a $250,000 estate to the survivor who already has assets of $1,000,000 is trading a 32 percent bracket for a later 43 percent bracket.
- Because of appreciation, property worth $250,000 today when it passes to the surviving spouse may be worth $1,000,000 five years later when the survivor dies.

The Marital Deduction—Sophistication of the Deferral Approach. When saving estate taxes for the family unit is the sole consideration, the equalization and deferral approaches can be combined with maximum effect.

―――――――――――――――――――― EXAMPLE 45 ――――――――――――――――――――

At the time of his death in 1992, H had never made any taxable gifts. Under H's will, H's disposable estate of $1,100,000 passes to W, H's surviving spouse. ◆

─────────────────── EXAMPLE 46 ───────────────────

Assume the same facts as in Example 45, except that H's will provides as follows: $600,000 to the children and the remainder ($500,000) to W. ◆

From a tax standpoint, which is the better plan? Although no estate tax results from either arrangement, Example 45 represents overkill in terms of the marital deduction. Why place an additional $600,000 in W's potential estate when it can pass free of tax to the children through the application of the $192,800 unified tax credit available for 1992? (The exemption equivalent of $192,800 is $600,000.) The exemption equivalent is known as the *by-pass amount*. The arrangement in Example 46 is to be preferred because it avoids unnecessary concentration of wealth in W's estate.

On occasion, disclaimers can be used to effect the deferral approach.

─────────────────── EXAMPLE 47 ───────────────────

Upon his death in 1992, H had never made any taxable gifts. Under H's will, the disposable estate of $1,500,000 passes as follows: $700,000 to S (H's adult son) and the remainder ($800,000) to W (H's surviving spouse). Shortly after H's death, S issues a disclaimer as to $100,000 of his $700,000 bequest. Such amount, therefore, passes to W as the remainderperson under H's will. ◆

S's disclaimer avoids an estate tax on $100,000. The result is to increase the marital deduction by $100,000 and eliminate *any* estate tax upon H's death.

Effectively Working with the Charitable Deduction. As a general guide to obtaining overall tax savings, lifetime charitable transfers are preferred over testamentary dispositions. For example, an individual who gives $10,000 to a qualified charity during his or her life secures an income tax deduction, avoids any gift tax, and reduces the gross estate by the amount of the gift. By way of contrast, if the $10,000 is willed to charity, no income tax deduction is available, and the amount of the gift is includible in the decedent's gross estate (though later deducted for estate tax purposes). In short, the lifetime transfer provides a double tax benefit (income tax deduction plus reduced estate taxes) at no gift tax cost. The testamentary transfer merely neutralizes the effect of the inclusion of the property in the gross estate (inclusion under § 2033 and then deduction under § 2055).

To ensure that an estate tax deduction is allowed for a charitable contribution, the designated recipient must fall within the classifications set forth in § 2055. The status of the organization on the date the transfer becomes effective controls and not the date the will authorizing the transfer was executed.

─────────────────── EXAMPLE 48 ───────────────────

In 1982, D drew up and executed a will in which he provided for $100,000 to pass to the XYZ Academy, a nonprofit educational organization described in § 2055(a)(2) and, at that time, approved by the IRS as a qualified recipient. In 1984, the qualified status of the academy was revoked for practicing racial discrimination in the enrollment of its student body.[48] D dies in 1992, and the executor of his estate, being compelled to satisfy the provisions of the will, transfers $100,000 to the academy. ◆

Even though D may have been unaware of the action taken by the IRS in 1984, no charitable deduction will be allowed his estate. The recipient was no longer qualified on the date of D's death. It may be that D, even if he had known about the

─────────────────────────────

48. Most of the organizations that are qualified recipients (which will permit the donor a charitable deduction) are listed in IRS Publication 78. This compilation, revised and supplemented from time to time, addresses § 170 (income tax deduction) transfers. Publication 78, with the exceptions noted in Chapter 17, also applies to § 2055 (estate tax deduction) and § 2522 (gift tax deduction) transfers.

probable loss of the charitable deduction, would still have wished the bequest carried out as originally conceived. If not, it is easy to see that the error was of D's own making because of his failure to review his estate planning situation.

One way to circumvent the quandary posed by Example 48 (other than changing D's will before D's death) is to express the charitable bequest in more flexible terms. The transfer to the XYZ Academy could have been conditioned on the organization's continued status as a qualified recipient at the time of D's death. Alternatively, D's will may grant D's executor the authority to substitute a different, but comparable, charitable organization *that is qualified* in the event of the disqualification of the named group.

On occasion, a charitable bequest depends on the issuance of a disclaimer by a noncharitable heir. Such a situation frequently arises with special types of property or collections, which the decedent may feel a noncharitable heir should have a choice of receiving.

EXAMPLE 49

D specified in her will that her valuable art collection is to pass to her son or, if the son refuses, to a designated and qualified art museum. At the time the will was drawn, D knew that her son was not interested in owning the collection. If, after D's death, the son issues a timely disclaimer, the collection passes to the museum, and D's estate takes a charitable deduction for its death tax value. ◆

EXAMPLE 50

D's will specifies that one-half of his disposable estate is to pass to his wife and the remainder of his property to a specified qualified charitable organization. If the wife issues a timely disclaimer after D's death, all of the property passes to the charity and qualifies for the § 2055 charitable deduction. ◆

Has the son in Example 49 acted wisely if he issues the disclaimer in favor of the museum? Although such a disclaimer will provide D's estate with a deduction for the value of the art collection, consider the income tax deduction alternative. If the son accepts the bequest, he can still dispose of the collection (and fulfill his mother's philanthropic objectives) through lifetime donation to the museum. At the same time, he obtains an income tax deduction under § 170. Whether this saves taxes for the family depends on a comparison of the mother's estate tax bracket with the estimated income tax bracket of the son. If the value of the collection runs afoul of the percentage limitations of § 170(b)(1), the donations could be spread over more than one year. If this is done, and to protect against the contingency of the son's dying before the entire collection is donated, the son can neutralize any potential death tax consequences by providing in his will for the undonated balance to pass to the museum.

The use of a disclaimer in Example 50 would be sheer folly. It would not reduce D's estate tax; it would merely substitute a charitable deduction for the marital deduction. Whether the wife issues a disclaimer or not, no estate taxes will be due. The wife should accept her bequest and, if she is so inclined, make lifetime gifts of it to a qualified charity. In so doing, she generates an income tax deduction for herself.

Proper Handling of Other Deductions and Losses under §§ 2053 and 2054. Many § 2053 and § 2054 deductions and losses may be claimed either as estate tax deductions or as income tax deductions by the estate on the fiduciary return (Form 1041), but not both.[49] The income tax deduction is not allowed unless the

---

49. § 642(g) and Reg. § 20.2053–1(d).

estate tax deduction is waived. It is possible for these deductions to be apportioned between the two returns.

Providing Estate Liquidity

Recognizing the Problem.   Even with effective predeath family tax planning directed toward a minimization of transfer taxes, the smooth administration of an estate necessitates a certain degree of liquidity. After all, probate costs will be incurred, and most important of all, death taxes must be satisfied. In the meantime, the surviving spouse and dependent beneficiaries may need financial support. Without funds to satisfy these claims, estate assets may have to be sold at sacrifice prices, and most likely, the decedent's scheme of testamentary disposition will be defeated.

EXAMPLE 51

At the time of D's death, D's estate was made up almost entirely of a large ranch currently being operated by S, one of D's two sons. Because the ranch had been in the family for several generations and was a successful economic unit, D hoped that S would continue its operation and share the profits with R, D's other son. Unfortunately, R, on learning that his mother had died without a will, demanded and obtained a partition and sale of his share of the property. Additional land was sold to pay for administration expenses and death taxes. After all of the sales had taken place, the portion remaining for S could not be operated profitably, and S was forced to give up the family ranch activity. ◆

What type of predeath planning might have avoided the result reached in Example 51? Certainly, D should have recognized and provided for the cash needs of the estate. Life insurance payable to her estate, although it adds to the estate tax liability, could have eased or solved the problem. This presumes that D was insurable or that the cost of the insurance would not be prohibitive. Furthermore, D made a serious error in dying without a will. A carefully drawn will could have precluded R's later course of action and perhaps kept much more of the ranch property intact. The ranch could have been placed in trust, life estate to S and R, remainder to their children. With such an arrangement, R would have been unable to sell the principal (the ranch).

Being able to defer the payment of death taxes may be an invaluable option for an estate that lacks cash or near-cash assets (e.g., marketable securities). In this connection, two major possibilities exist:

- The discretionary extension of time (§ 6161).
- The extension of time when the estate consists largely of an interest in a closely held business (§ 6166).

Discretionary Extension of Time to Pay Estate Taxes—§ 6161.   Currently, an executor or administrator may request an extension of time for paying the death tax for a period not to exceed 10 years from the date fixed for the payment. Such a request is granted by the IRS whenever there is "reasonable cause." Reasonable cause is not limited to a showing of undue hardship. It includes cases in which the executor or administrator is unable to marshal liquid assets readily because they are located in several jurisdictions. It also includes situations where the estate is largely made up of assets in the form of payments to be received in the future (e.g., annuities, copyright royalties, contingent fees, or accounts receivable), or the assets that must be liquidated to pay the estate tax must be sold at a sacrifice or in a depressed market.

Extension of Time When the Estate Consists Largely of an Interest in a Closely Held Business—§ 6166. Congress always has been sympathetic to the plight of an estate that consists of an interest in a closely held business. The immediate imposition of the estate tax in such a situation may force the liquidation of the business at distress prices or cause the interest to be sold to outside parties.

A possible resolution of the problem is § 6166, which, if applicable, requires the IRS to accept a 15-payment procedure (5 interest-only payments, followed by 10 installment payments of the estate tax). This delay will enable the business to generate enough income to buy out the deceased owner's interest without disruption of operations or other financial sacrifice.

To meet the requirements of § 6166, the decedent's interest in a farm or other closely held business must exceed 35 percent of the decedent's adjusted gross estate.[50] The adjusted gross estate is the gross estate less the sum allowable as deductions under § 2053 (expenses, indebtedness, and taxes) and § 2054 (casualty and theft losses during the administration of an estate).

An interest in a closely held business includes the following:[51]

- Any sole proprietorship.
- An interest in a partnership carrying on a trade or business, if 20 percent of the capital interest in the partnership is included in the gross estate *or* the partnership has 15 or fewer partners.
- Stock in a corporation carrying on a trade or business, if 20 percent or more of the value of the voting stock of the corporation is included in the gross estate *or* the corporation has 15 or fewer shareholders.

In meeting the preceding requirements, a decedent and his or her surviving spouse are treated as one owner (shareholder or partner) if the interest is held as community property, tenants in common, joint tenants, or tenants by the entirety. Attribution from family members is allowed, as described in § 267(c)(4).

―――――――――――――――――――――― EXAMPLE 52 ――――――――――――――――――――――

Decedent D held a 15% capital interest in the XYZ Partnership. D's son holds another 10%. XYZ had 16 partners including D and her son. Since the son's interest is attributed to D, the estate is deemed to hold a 25% interest, and XYZ (for purposes of § 6166) has only 15 partners. ◆

In satisfying the more-than-35 percent test for qualification under § 6166, interests in more than one closely held business are aggregated when the decedent's gross estate includes 20 percent or more of the value of each such business.[52]

―――――――――――――――――――――― EXAMPLE 53 ――――――――――――――――――――――

D's estate includes stock in X Corporation and Y Corporation, each of which qualifies as a closely held business. If the stock held in each entity represents 20% or more of the total value outstanding, the stocks can be combined for purposes of the more-than-35% test. ◆

If the conditions of § 6166 are satisfied and the provision is elected, the following results transpire:

- No payments on the estate tax attributable to the inclusion of the interest in a closely held business in the gross estate need be made with the first 5 payments. Then, annual installments are made over a period not longer than 10 years.

―――――――――――――――――

50. § 6166(a)(1).
51. § 6166(b)(1).

52. § 6166(c).

- From the outset, interest at the rate of 4 percent must be paid.[53] The rate is limited to the first $1,000,000 of estate tax value for the business.
- Acceleration of deferred payments may be triggered upon the disposition of the interest or failure to make scheduled principal or interest payments.[54]

In qualifying for § 6166, prune the potential estate of assets that may cause the 35 percent test to be failed. In this regard, lifetime gifts of such assets as marketable securities and life insurance should be considered.[55]

CONCEPT SUMMARY 18–2
ESTATE AND GIFT PLANNING

1. In reducing (or eliminating) gift taxes, take advantage of the annual exclusion and the election to split gifts. In the case of a single asset with high value (e.g., land), annual gifts of partial interests should be considered.

2. Gifts can reduce later estate taxes. This is accomplished by giving assets that will appreciate in value (e.g., life insurance policies, art works, rare collections). Unless the gifts are made within three years of death, any gift taxes paid will not be subject to the estate tax.

3. Timely gifts can help an estate qualify for § 2032A (special use valuation method), § 6166 (15-year payout of estate taxes), and § 303 (stock redemptions to pay death taxes). To be effective, the gift must avoid the three-year rule of § 2035.

4. Gifts can relieve the income tax burden on the family unit. This objective is accomplished by shifting the income from the gift property to family members who are in a lower income tax bracket. In this regard, make sure the gift is *complete* and circumvent kiddie tax treatment.

5. Avoid gifts of property that result in income tax consequences to the donor. Here, the major culprits are installment notes receivable and U.S. savings bonds upon which the interest has been deferred.

6. Potential *probate costs* can be an important consideration in meaningful estate planning. Some procedures that reduce these costs include joint tenancies with the right of survivorship, living trusts, and predeath dispositions of out-of-state real estate. Keep in mind that most of these procedures *do not reduce estate taxes*.

7. A program of lifetime giving and proper use of valuation techniques will reduce a decedent's *gross estate*. Further planning can reduce the *taxable estate* by proper handling of estate tax deductions.

8. For a married decedent, the most important deduction is the *marital deduction*. The two major approaches to the marital deduction are the *equalization* and *deferral* approaches. The objective of the equalization approach is to avoid concentrating wealth in the estate of the surviving spouse. This approach is beneficial when the surviving spouse has considerable assets or is not expected to survive for long. The objective of the deferral approach is to postpone estate tax consequences for as long as possible. The benefit can be considerable when the present value of estate taxes saved is projected over the life of a long-lived survivor.

9. Whether the equalization approach or the deferral approach is emphasized, make use of the *by-pass amount*. This is the amount of the exemption equivalent of the unified tax credit that can pass free of any transfer tax.

10. Lifetime charitable contributions are preferable to transfers by death. The lifetime contributions provide the donor with an income tax deduction, and the amount donated is not included in the gross estate. If transfers are to be made at death, however, make sure the charity is still a qualified organization. The status of the organization at death controls, not the status when the will was drawn up.

11. The *disclaimer* procedure can be used to control (either lower or raise) the amount of the marital deduction. It also can be used to increase the amount of the charitable deduction.

12. Predeath estate planning in an income tax context can be summarized as follows: avoid a *step-down* in income tax basis and seek a *step-up* in basis. Sell property for a loss to avoid a step-down in basis. Retain appreciated property to obtain a step-up in basis at death.

13. Gift planning can help ease potential *estate liquidity* problems (see item 3 above). After death, § 6166 can be useful if the estate qualifies. The provision allows installment payments of deferred estate taxes over an extended period of time. Except for interest at a set rate of 4%, payments begin in the sixth year after death. The deferral allows a closely held business to generate enough funds to meet the deceased owner's estate tax liability.

---

53. § 6601(j)(1).
54. § 6166(g).

55. A gift within three years of death is not effective for this purpose. § 2035(d)(4).

Some of the estate planning procedures covered in the last part of this chapter appear in Concept Summary 18–2.

PROBLEM MATERIALS

DISCUSSION QUESTIONS

1. D's gross estate is valued as follows: $1,100,000 on date of death and $1,010,000 on the alternate valuation date. Presuming D's estate qualifies, what factors should be considered before the alternate valuation date is elected?

2. Discuss the relevance of the following in defining "fair market value" for Federal gift and estate tax purposes:

   a. § 2031(b).
   b. The definition contained in Reg. § 20.2031–1(b).
   c. A forced sale price.
   d. The location of the property being valued.
   e. The sentimental value of the property being valued.
   f. The wholesale price of the property.
   g. Tangible personalty sold as a result of an advertisement in the classified section of a newspaper.

3. What factors should be considered in the valuation of bonds of a closely held corporation when selling prices and bid and asked prices are not available? In the valuation of stock in a closely held corporation under similar circumstances?

4. Two years before her death, M loaned her daughter (D) $100,000. The loan was intended to provide D funds to expand her business, which has proved profitable. D issued a note for the loan, made it payable on demand, and provided for a 10% rate of interest. No payments have been made on the note up to M's death. M's will forgives the note and any accrued interest. How should D's note be handled by M's estate?

5. At the time of his death, D held an annuity issued by Mutual of Omaha Insurance Company. Under the terms of the contract, the company is to pay S (D's surviving 65-year-old sister) $30,000 a year for life. For estate tax purposes, how is this survivorship annuity to be valued?

6. D creates a trust, specifying a life estate to W, remainder to S upon W's death.

   a. Why is it necessary to value the life estate and the remainder interest separately?
   b. In this regard, would it matter if the transfer occurred in 1970? In 1982? In 1991? Explain.

7. Contrast current use value with most suitable use value. Why might there be a difference between the two values?

8. Comment on the special use valuation method in connection with the following:

   a. The 50% test and the 25% test.
   b. Qualifying property.
   c. The five-out-of-eight-years requirement.
   d. The qualifying heir.
   e. The $750,000 limitation.
   f. The recapture possibility.

9. Assume the special use valuation method was elected and a premature disposition of the property occurs. Under the recapture rules, is an income tax basis adjustment appropriate? Explain.

10. Can a program of lifetime giving aid in planning for the election of the special use valuation method? Explain.

11. In valuing the stock of a closely held corporation, the IRS attributes a large amount to the goodwill of the business. What arguments can the taxpayers make to dispute this finding?

12. What effect, if any, will each of the following factors have on the valuation of stock in a closely held corporation?

   a. The "blockage rule."
   b. A minority interest is involved.
   c. A majority interest is involved.
   d. The cost the corporation would incur in going public.

13. During the same year in which the donor gives stock in a closely held corporation to family members, donations of some of the stock are made to a qualified charitable organization. In terms of tax planning, what might be accomplished by such a procedure?

14. Regarding buy and sell agreements, comment on the following:

   a. The difference between the entity and cross-purchase varieties.
   b. The purpose served.
   c. When the related transfer tax is recognized.

15. "The response of the business community to the current estate freeze rules has not been positive." Explain.

16. Review the income tax basis rules applicable when a donee sells property received as a gift after 1976.

17. What is meant by a step-up in basis for property acquired from a decedent? A step-down in basis?

18. What effect, if any, does the death of a spouse have on the income tax basis of the surviving spouse's share of the community property? Explain.

19. S gives property to his widowed mother. Nine months after the gift, S's mother dies. Under her will, the same property returns to S. Comment on the tax ramifications of these transfers.

20. H gives property to his wife, W. Thirteen months after the gift, W dies. Under her will, the same property returns to H. What are the gift, estate, and income tax consequences?

21. Assume the same facts as in Question 20, except that W dies 10 months after the gift. Again, comment on the gift, estate, and income tax consequences.

22. "The value assigned to property upon the death of the owner establishes a presumption of correctness as to income tax basis to an heir." Explain.

23. Same as Question 22. Give several reasons why an heir may want to rebut the presumption.

24. F and M (husband and wife) want to transfer real estate (estimated value of $400,000) to their four adult children and not exceed the annual exclusion. Any suggestions on how this result can be accomplished?

25. In terms of saving future estate taxes, give some examples of assets that should be transferred by gift.

26. "Any gift taxes previously paid by a decedent are not subject to estate taxation." Comment on this statement.

27. In considering the income tax ramifications of lifetime giving, discuss each of the following factors:

   a. The donee is under 14 years of age.
   b. The transferred property is an installment note receivable.
   c. The transferred property is a U.S. savings bond.
   d. The carryover basis result.

28. What are the advantages of bypassing the probate estate? How can this be accomplished?

29. D sold his business in New Jersey and moved to Florida to retire. D still owns rent property in New Jersey and a vacation cottage in Wisconsin. Comment on D's potential probate cost problems.

30. Explain the difference between the equalization and deferral approaches to the estate tax marital deduction.

31. For married persons, the real danger of an estate tax burden materializes upon the death of the surviving spouse. Do you agree? Why or why not?

31. In what fashion can disclaimers by heirs increase an estate's marital deduction? Increase the charitable deduction?

33. In connection with § 6166, comment on the following:

   a. The more-than-35% test.
   b. The definition of a closely held business.
   c. The family attribution rules.
   d. The business-aggregation rules.

34. The estate of T, currently still alive, almost qualifies for an election under § 6166. T is not concerned, however, because she plans on giving away her life insurance policy before her death. This, she believes, will allow her estate to meet the requirements of § 6166. Any comment?

PROBLEMS

35. When D died, she owned 3,000 shares of Y Corporation. The stock was traded in an over-the-counter market. The nearest trades before and after D's death were as follows:

	Mean Selling Price
Three days before D's death	$48 (per share)
Five days after D's death	50 (per share)

   Presuming the alternate valuation date is not elected, at what value should the Y stock be included in D's gross estate?

36. Under the terms of M's will, S (M's son) is entitled to receive an annuity of $40,000 payable annually for life. The annuity is to be paid from M's estate and is freely transferable. When S reaches age 58, he gives the annuity to D, his daughter, who is age 36. Using the appropriate table from Appendix A, determine the value of the transfer from S to D if the gift occurred in 1988.

37. F creates a trust with property valued at $800,000. Under the terms of the trust, G (age 44) receives a life estate, and H (age 15) receives the remainder interest. Determine the value of the gifts under each of the following assumptions:

   a. The trust was created in 1988.
   b. The trust was created after April 30, 1989. In the month the trust was created, the appropriate rate was 9.6%.

38. R transfers $500,000 in trust. Under the terms of the trust instrument, income is payable to S (age 16) for 12 years, remainder to D (age 40). Determine the taxable gifts under the following assumptions:

   a. The trust was created in 1988.
   b. The trust was created after April 30, 1989. In the month the trust was created, the appropriate rate was 9.4%.

39. M (age 65) creates a trust with property worth $800,000. Under the terms of the trust, M retains a life estate with the remainder interest passing to D (M's daughter) upon M's death. M dies in 1995 when the value of the trust is $1,100,000 and D is age 44.

   a. Determine the taxable gift, if any, if the trust was created in 1988.
   b. Determine the taxable gift, if any, if the trust was created in 1992. In the month the trust was created, the appropriate rate was 9.8%.

40. Assume the same facts as in Problem 39. How much, if any, of the trust is included in M's gross estate? Refer to Chapter 17 if necessary.

41. Comment on the following statements relating to § 2032A:

    a. Section 2032A applies even if the qualifying property is willed by the decedent to a nonfamily member.

    b. If § 2032A applies, current use value (as opposed to most suitable use value) can be used for the qualifying property, but not to exceed a limit on the adjustment of $1,000,000.

    c. The special use valuation method cannot be used in setting the valuation of a lifetime gift.

    d. Full recapture of the benefit of the special use valuation method would not occur if the qualifying heir were to sell the property 10 years after the decedent's death.

    e. Recapture occurs only if the qualifying property is sold.

    f. In any recapture situation, an income tax basis adjustment is required.

    g. Lifetime gifts of nonqualifying assets may help in satisfying the 50% and 25% requirements of § 2032A.

    h. In satisfying the 50% and 25% requirements, the qualifying property is valued at most suitable use value.

42. At the time of death, D owns 60% of the stock in X Corporation, with the remaining 40% held by family members. Over the past five years, X has generated average net profits of $200,000. On the date of D's death, the book value (corporate net worth) of the corporation's stock is $500,000. Assume that an appropriate rate of return for the type of business X conducts is 7%.

    a. Presuming that some goodwill exists, what value should be included in D's gross estate for the X stock?

    b. What arguments could D's executor make in maintaining that the value arrived at under (a) is too high?

43. F gives stock to D when the stock has a fair market value of $100,000. F acquired the stock 10 years before the gift at a cost of $20,000. Determine D's income tax basis for gain or loss under each of the following assumptions:

    a. The gift occurred in 1960. F paid a gift tax of $5,000 on the transfer.

    b. The gift occurred in 1992. F paid a gift tax of $5,000 on the transfer.

44. In the current year, M gives stock to S when the shares have a fair market value of $90,000. M acquired the stock four years ago at a cost of $100,000. As a result of the transfer, M incurred and paid a gift tax of $5,000. Determine S's gain or loss if the stock is sold later for:

    a. $75,000.

    b. $95,000.

    c. $105,000.

45. In 1980, M gives publicly traded stock to S when the shares have a fair market value of $300,000. M acquired the stock 10 years ago at a cost of $100,000. As a result of the transfer, M incurred and paid a gift tax of $18,000. Determine S's gain or loss if S sells the stock in 1992 for:

    a. $200,000.

    b. $110,000.

    c. $330,000.

46. In April 1991, T gives D a house (basis of $50,000 and fair market value of $150,000) to be used as D's personal residence. As a result of the transfer, T incurs and pays a gift tax of $9,000. Before her death in March 1992, D installs a swimming pool in the backyard at a cost of $10,000. The residence is worth $170,000 on the date of D's death, and D's estate does not elect the alternate valuation date. Determine the income tax basis of the property to the heir, based on the following independent assumptions:

    a. Under D's will, the residence passes to T.

    b. Under D's will, the residence passes to S (D's son).

47. F owns real estate (basis of $100,000 and fair market of $400,000). F and M (F's wife) would like to transfer this property equally to their four adult children without incurring any *taxable* gift. What do you suggest?

48. Comment on the problems that might arise in each of the following independent situations:

   a. In planning for the special use valuation election of § 2032A, W makes a gift of marketable securities two years before her death.
   b. D, a cash basis taxpayer, re-registers U.S. savings bonds in the name of his son.
   c. D gives his son installment notes received recently from the purchaser of real estate D sold.
   d. E gives stock in an S corporation to his 10-year-old daughter.
   e. F gives unimproved real estate to D. The real estate has an adjusted basis of $80,000 and a fair market value of $70,000.

49. At the time of her death in the current year, D held the following assets:

	Fair Market Value
Checking account at X National Bank (D listed as owner)	$ 40,000
Certificate of deposit at Z Savings Association (listed as "D and S as joint tenants with right of survivorship")	200,000
Insurance policy on D's life, issued by Y Company (D's estate is the designated beneficiary)	100,000
Insurance policy on D's life, issued by Z Company (Q is the designated beneficiary)	300,000
Living trust created by D four years ago (life estate to S, remainder to S's children)	800,000
Personal residence (title listed as "D and H, tenants by the entirety with right of survivorship")	400,000

   Presuming S, Q, and H survive D, how much is included in D's *probate* estate?

50. Among the assets included in D's gross estate are the following:

	Fair Market Value	
	Date of Death	Alternate Valuation Date
Stock in X Corporation	$200,000	$210,000
Stock in Y Corporation	300,000	250,000
Stock in Z Corporation	400,000	370,000
Real estate	500,000	500,000

   D's will provides that the above properties are to pass as follows: X Corporation stock to S (D's son), Y Corporation stock and real estate to H (D's husband), and Z Corporation stock to R Foundation (a qualified charity). Presume the estate qualifies under § 2032, and D's executor makes the election. How does the alternate valuation date affect

   a. S's inheritance?
   b. The marital deduction?
   c. The charitable deduction?

51. In the following independent situations, describe the effect of a disclaimer on the estate tax position of the parties.

   a. D's will passes $700,000 to S (her son) and the remainder of her assets to H (D's husband). S disclaims $200,000.
   b. D's will passes $900,000 to H (D's husband) and the $400,000 remainder to S (her son). H disclaims $200,000.
   c. D (a widow) provides in her will that $800,000 passes to S (her son, a priest) and the remainder to S's church. S disclaims $200,000.

52. Comment on the following statements relating to the § 6166 extension of time to pay tax, when the estate consists largely of an interest in a closely held business:

   a. No interest need be paid for the first five years.
   b. The value of the farm or other closely held business must be more than 35% of the gross estate.

c. Four percent is the rate charged on delayed payments up to the first $1,000,000 of gross estate value in the business.

d. If the interest consists of stock in a corporation, the corporation cannot have more than 15 shareholders.

e. The estate of a partner cannot qualify unless at least 20% of the capital interest in the partnership is included in the gross estate.

f. Annual installment payments of the deferred estate tax liability are made over a period of 15 years.

g. Acceleration of deferred payments occurs if the interest is disposed of prematurely.

h. In satisfying the more-than-35% test, interests in more than one business cannot be aggregated.

RESEARCH PROBLEMS

RESEARCH PROBLEM 1   At the time of his death, D held 100% of X Corporation, the stock of which has never been traded. Under D's will, the stock is to pass as follows: 51% to W (D's surviving spouse) and 49% to D's adult children. On audit by the IRS of the Form 706 filed by the estate, the parties agree that the correct value of the total X stock is $2,000,000. They disagree, however, on the value that should be assigned to the 51% passing to W. The IRS contends that the value of this interest is $1,020,000, while the estate argues that this amount is too low.

a. What is the source of the controversy?
b. Support the position of the IRS.
c. Support the position of the estate.

Partial list of research aids:

Reg. § 20.2031–2(f).
Estate of Dean A. Chenoweth, 88 T.C. 1577 (1987).

RESEARCH PROBLEM 2   For many years, the shares of X Corporation were held as follows:

Owner	Number of Shares
Mrs. T	60
Q	20
R	20

Neither Q nor R is related to the other or to Mrs. T.

In late 1991, Mrs. T is contacted by a group of investors who want to acquire control of X. While preliminary negotiations are in progress for the sale of the stock, Mrs. T creates four irrevocable trusts and transfers 15 shares of the stock to each. Mrs. T's son is designated as the trustee of all the trusts, with a different grandchild named as the beneficiary of each trust.

In early 1992, the trusts created by Mrs. T sell the shares to the group of investors for $400 each. Shortly thereafter, the investors acquire the remaining shares held by Q and R for $250 each.

On a timely filed gift tax return, Mrs. T reports the transfers to the four trusts. The gift tax paid by Mrs. T is based on a value of $250 per share.

a. Justify Mrs. T's position on the valuation of the stock for gift tax purposes.
b. How could the IRS dispute this determination?
c. Could Mrs. T suffer any income tax consequences from these transactions? Explain.

RESEARCH PROBLEM 3   In 1985, T created an irrevocable trust by transferring stock in Y Corporation (fair market value of $1,000,000) to X Trust Company. Under the terms of the trust, T retained the income for four years, remainder to T's children. X is exonerated from any requirement under applicable state law that compels a trustee to change investments in order to increase the income yield of trust corpus.

During the four-year life of the trust, the Y stock is retained as corpus. This was done even though the stock investment only yielded an annual return of 2/10 of 1%. X did not wish to sell the stock because of the income tax consequences and because Y was closely held.

In reporting the 1985 transfer, T filed a Form 709. The amount of the gift was computed by using Table B of Reg. § 25.2512–5(f). Under Table B, the factor for a remainder interest with an intervening four-year income interest is .683013. Thus, the gift was $683,013 [$1,000,000 (fair market value of the Y Corporation stock) × .683013 (Table B factor)].

Upon audit of T's Form 709, the IRS contends that the use of Table B is inappropriate. Table B is based on a 10% rate of return, which is not consistent with the income yield anticipated from the Y stock. Under the circumstances, T's gift of a remainder interest should be valued at $1,000,000 (the fair market value of the stock).

Which position is correct?

Partial list of research aids:

Reg. §§ 25.2511–1(e) and 25.2512–5(a).

RESEARCH PROBLEM 4   On June 1, D entered into a contract to sell real estate for $100,000 (adjusted basis of $20,000). The sale was conditioned on a rezoning of the property for commercial use. A $5,000 deposit placed in escrow by the purchaser was refundable if the rezoning were not accomplished. After considerable controversy, the application is approved on November 10, and two days later, the sum of $95,000 is paid to D's estate in full satisfaction of the purchase price. D died unexpectedly on November 1.

    a. Discuss the estate and income tax consequences of this set of facts, assuming that the sale of the real estate occurred after D's death.

    b. Before D's death.

    c. When do you think the sale occurred? Why?

Partial list of research aids:

§§ 691 and 1014.
George W. Keck, 49 T.C. 313 (1968), *rev'd.* 69–2 USTC ¶9626, 24 AFTR2d 69–5554, 415 F.2d 531 (CA–6, 1969).
Trust Company of Georgia v. Ross, 68–1 USTC ¶9133, 21 AFTR2d 311, 392 F.2d 694 (CA–5, 1967).

RESEARCH PROBLEM 5   Decedent D left an estate that consisted of, among other assets, a farm and a hardware business. The farm had a special use valuation of $400,000 but a best use value of $60,000. By itself, the farm comprised 42% of the adjusted gross estate. Combined with the hardware business, the value of both businesses totaled 53% of the adjusted gross estate. Although the farm included real estate, the hardware business did not, since it had been operated on leased premises. Thus, the value of the hardware business was entirely made up of personalty (e.g., inventory). Assuming that the conditions of § 2032A were satisfied, the executor of D's estate valued the farm at $60,000 for estate tax purposes. Upon audit by the IRS, § 2032A was deemed inapplicable, and the value of the farm was raised to $400,000. Which party is right, and why?

CHAPTER

INCOME TAXATION OF TRUSTS AND ESTATES

OBJECTIVES

Develop working definitions with respect to trusts, estates, beneficiaries, and other parties.

Identify steps by which to determine the accounting and taxable income of the trust or estate and the related taxable income of the beneficiaries.

Illustrate the uses and implications of distributable net income.

Examine effects of statutory restrictions on accounting periods and methods available to trusts and estates and on the taxation of distributions from accumulation trusts.

Present the special rules that apply to trusts that sell appreciated property received as a gift, that accumulate income, and over which the creator (grantor) of the trust retains certain rights.

OUTLINE

Taxpayers create trusts for a variety of reasons. Some trusts are established primarily for tax purposes while others are designed to accomplish a specific financial goal or to provide for the orderly management of assets in case of emergency. Figure 19–1 lists some of the more common reasons for creating a trust.

Because a trust is a separate tax entity, its gross income and deductions must be measured and an annual tax return must be filed. Similarly, when an individual dies, a legal entity is created in the form of his or her estate. This chapter examines the rules related to the income taxation of trusts and estates.

The income taxation of trusts and estates is governed by Subchapter J of the Internal Revenue Code, §§ 641 through 692. Certain similarities are apparent between Subchapter J and the income taxation of individuals (e.g., the definitions of gross income and deductible expenditures), partnerships (e.g., the conduit principle), and S corporations (e.g., the conduit principle and the trust as a separate taxable entity). Trusts also involve several important new concepts, however, including the determination of distributable net income and the tier system of distributions to beneficiaries.

The primary concern of this chapter is the income taxation of estates and ordinary trusts. Grantor trusts are discussed to a limited extent in a later section of the chapter. Special trusts, such as alimony trusts, trusts to administer the requirements of a court in the context of a bankruptcy proceeding, and qualified retirement trusts, are beyond the scope of this text.

Figure 19–2 illustrates the structure of a typical trust and estate.

What Is a Trust?

The Code does not contain a definition of a trust. However, the Regulations explain that the term "trust," as used in the Code, refers to an arrangement created by a will or by an *inter vivos* (lifetime) declaration, through which trustees take title to property for the purpose of protecting or conserving it for the beneficiaries.[1]

FIGURE 19–1	Type of Trust	Financial and Other Goals
Motivations For Creating A Trust	Life insurance trust	Holds life insurance policies on the insured, removes the proceeds of the policies from the gross estate (if an irrevocable trust), and safeguards against receipt of the proceeds by a young or inexperienced beneficiary.
	"Living" (revocable) trust	Manages assets, reduces probate costs, provides privacy for asset disposition, protects against medical or other emergencies, and provides relief from the necessity of day-to-day management of the underlying assets.
	Trust for minors	Provides funds for a college education, shifts income to lower-bracket taxpayers, and accumulates income without permanently parting with the underlying assets.
	"Blind" trust	Holds and manages the assets of the grantor without his/her input or influence (e.g., while the grantor holds political office or some other sensitive position).
	Retirement trust	A special tax-exempt trust that manages asset contributions under a qualified retirement plan.
	Alimony trust	Manages the assets of an ex-spouse and assures they will be distributed in a timely fashion to specified beneficiaries.
	Liquidation trust	Collects and distributes the last assets of a corporation that is undergoing a complete liquidation.

1. Reg. § 301.7701–4(a).

Typically, the creation of a trust involves at least three parties: (1) The *grantor* (sometimes referred to as the settler or donor) transfers selected assets to the trust entity. (2) The *trustee*, who may be either an individual or a corporation, is charged with the fiduciary duties associated with the trust. (3) The *beneficiary* is designated to receive income or property from the trust; the beneficiary's rights are defined by state law and by the trust document.

In some situations, fewer than three persons may be involved, as specified by the trust agreement. For instance, an elderly individual who no longer can manage his or her own property (e.g., because of ill health) may create a trust under which he or she is both the grantor and the beneficiary. In this case, a corporate trustee is charged with the management of the grantor's assets.

FIGURE 19–2   **Structure of a Typical Trust and Estate**

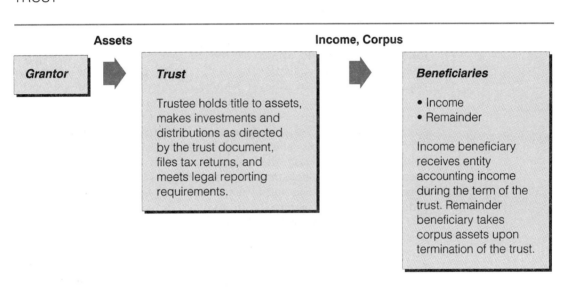

TRUST

Assets → **Income, Corpus**

Grantor → **Trust**
Trustee holds title to assets, makes investments and distributions as directed by the trust document, files tax returns, and meets legal reporting requirements.

→ **Beneficiaries**
- Income
- Remainder

Income beneficiary receives entity accounting income during the term of the trust. Remainder beneficiary takes corpus assets upon termination of the trust.

ESTATE

Assets, Liabilities → **Distributions**

Decedent → **Executor**
Executor manages assets of the decedent during administration period, satisfies liabilities, including estate taxes, and distributes net probate assets as directed by the controlling will. Terminates estate when required activities are completed.

→ **Beneficiaries**
Income and remainder beneficiaries exist during the life of the estate (i.e., the estate is a separate income tax entity) but these beneficiaries are chiefly corpus recipients.

In another situation, the grantor might designate him- or herself as the trustee of the trust assets. For example, a parent who wants to transfer selected assets to a minor child could use a trust entity to assure that the minor does not waste the property. By identifying him- or herself as the trustee, the parent retains virtual control over the property that is transferred.

Under the general rules of Subchapter J, the trusts just described are not recognized for income tax purposes. When only one party is involved (when the same individual is grantor, trustee, and sole beneficiary of the trust), Subchapter J rules do not apply, and the entity is ignored for income tax purposes.

Other Definitions

When the grantor transfers title of selected assets to a trust, those assets become the *corpus* (body), or principal, of the trust. Trust corpus, in most situations, earns *income*, which may be distributed to the beneficiaries or accumulated for the future by the trustee, as the trust instrument directs.

In the typical trust, the grantor creates two types of beneficiaries: one who receives the accounting income of the trust and one who receives the trust corpus that remains at the termination of the trust entity. Beneficiaries in the former category hold an *income interest* in the trust, and those in the latter category hold a *remainder interest* in the trust's assets. If the grantor retains the remainder interest, the interest is known as a *reversionary interest* (corpus reverts to the grantor when the trust entity terminates).

The trust document establishes the term of the trust. The term may be for a specific number of years (a *term certain*) or until the occurrence of a specified event. For instance, a trust might exist (1) for the life of the income beneficiary—in this case, the income beneficiary is known as a *life tenant* in trust corpus; (2) for the life of some other individual; (3) until the income or remainder beneficiary reaches the age of majority; or (4) until the beneficiary, or another individual, marries, receives a promotion, or reaches some specified age.

The trustee may be required to distribute the accounting income of the entity according to a distribution schedule specified in the agreement. Sometimes, however, the trustee is given more discretion with respect to the timing and nature of the distributions. If the trustee can determine, within guidelines that may be included in the trust document, either the timing of the income or corpus distributions or the specific beneficiaries who will receive them (from among those identified in the agreement), the trust is called a *sprinkling trust*. Here, the trustee can "sprinkle" the distributions among the various beneficiaries. As discussed in Chapters 17 and 18, family-wide income taxes can be reduced by directing income to those who are subject to lower marginal tax rates. Thus, by giving the trustee a sprinkling power, the income tax liability of the family unit can be manipulated via the trust agreement.

For purposes of certain provisions of Subchapter J, a trust must be classified as either a *simple trust* or a *complex trust*. A simple trust (1) is required to distribute its entire accounting income to designated beneficiaries every year, (2) has no beneficiaries that are qualifying charitable organizations, and (3) makes no distributions of trust corpus during the year. A complex trust is any trust that is not a simple trust.[2] These criteria are applied to the trust every year. Thus, every trust will be classified as a complex trust in the year in which it terminates (because it will be distributing all of its corpus during that year).

---

2. Reg. § 1.651(a)–1.

What Is an Estate?

An estate is created upon the death of every individual. The entity is charged with collecting and conserving all of the individual's assets, satisfying all liabilities, and distributing the remaining assets to the heirs identified by state law or the will.

Typically, the creation of an estate involves at least three parties: the *decedent*, all of whose probate assets are transferred to the estate for disposition; the *executor* or *executrix* (the latter is a female), who is appointed under the decedent's valid will (or the *administrator* or *administratrix*, if no valid will exists); and the *beneficiaries* of the estate, who are to receive assets or income from the entity, as the decedent has indicated in the will. The executor or administrator holds the fiduciary responsibility to operate the estate as directed by the will, applicable state law, and the probate court.

Recall that the assets that make up the probate estate are not identical to those that constitute the gross estate for transfer tax purposes (refer to Chapter 18). Many of the gross estate assets are not a part of the *probate estate* and thus are not subject to disposition by the executor or administrator. For instance, property held by the decedent as a joint tenant passes to the survivor(s) by operation of the applicable state's property law rather than through the probate estate. Proceeds of insurance policies on the life of the decedent, over which the decedent held the incidents of ownership, are not under the control of the executor or administrator. The designated beneficiaries of the policy receive the proceeds outright under the insurance contract.

An estate is a separate taxable entity. Under certain circumstances, taxpayers may find it profitable to prolong an estate's existence. This situation is likely to arise when the heirs are already in a high income tax bracket. Therefore, they would prefer to have the income generated by the estate assets taxed at the estate's lower marginal income tax rates. However, the tax authorities have recognized the possibility of shifting income to lower-bracket taxpayers. The Regulations state that if an estate's existence is unduly prolonged, it is terminated for Federal income tax purposes after the expiration of a reasonable period for completing the duties of administration.[3]

NATURE OF TRUST AND ESTATE TAXATION
◆

In general, the taxable income of a trust or an estate is taxed to the entity or to its beneficiaries to the extent that each has received the accounting income of the entity. Thus, Subchapter J creates a modified conduit principle relative to the income taxation of trusts, estates, and their beneficiaries. Whoever receives the accounting income of the entity, or some portion of it, is liable for the income tax that results.

──────── EXAMPLE 1 ────────

Beneficiary A receives 80% of the accounting income of Trust Z. The trustee accumulated the other 20% of the income at her discretion under the trust agreement and added it to trust corpus. A is liable for income tax only on the amount of the distribution, while Trust Z is liable for the income tax on the accumulated portion of the income. ◆

Filing Requirements

The fiduciary is required to file a Form 1041 (U.S. Fiduciary Income Tax Return) in the following situations:[4]

─────────────

3. Reg. § 1.641(b)–3(a).   4. § 6012(a).

- For an estate that has gross income for the year of $600 or more.
- For a trust that either has any taxable income or, if there is no taxable income, has gross income of $600 or more.

The fiduciary is responsible for filing Form 1041 and paying any income tax due, but has no personal liability for the tax. In general, the IRS must look to the assets of the estate or the trust for the tax due. The fiduciary may become personally liable for the tax if he or she makes excessive distributions of assets (e.g., payment of debts, satisfaction of bequests), thereby rendering the entity unable to pay the tax due. An executor or administrator may obtain from the IRS a discharge from such personal liability.[5] Taking advantage of this procedure is advisable before making any substantial distributions of estate assets.

The fiduciary return (and any related tax liability) is due no later than the fifteenth day of the fourth month following the close of the entity's taxable year. The return should be filed with the Internal Revenue Service Center for the region in which the fiduciary resides or has his or her principal place of business.

Tax Accounting Periods, Methods, and Payments

An estate or trust may use many of the tax accounting methods available to individuals. The method of accounting used by the grantor of a trust or the decedent of an estate does not carry over to the entity.

An estate has the same election available to any new taxpayer regarding the choice of a tax year. Thus, the estate of a calendar year decedent dying on March 3 can select any fiscal year or report on a calendar year basis.[6] If the latter is selected, the estate's first taxable year will include the period from March 3 to December 31. If the first or last tax years are short years (less than one calendar year), income for those years need not be annualized.

To eliminate the possibility of deferring the taxation of fiduciary-source income simply by using a fiscal tax year, § 645 requires that all trusts (other than charitable and tax-exempt trusts) use a calendar tax year.

Trusts and certain estates are required to make estimated Federal income tax payments using the same quarterly schedule that applies to individual taxpayers. This requirement applies to estates only for tax years that end two or more years after the date of the decedent's death.

In addition, if the trustee so designates on the fiduciary income tax return that is filed on or before the sixty-fifth day following the close of the trust tax year, an estimated income tax payment made by a trust can be assigned to a specified beneficiary. Under this rule, the payment is treated under § 643(g) as though it had been a timely filed fourth-quarter estimated tax payment of the beneficiary. This election is not available for an estate.

The two-year estimated tax exception for estates recognizes the liquidity problems that an executor often faces during the early months of the administration of the estate. The exception does not assure, however, that an estate whose existence measures less than 24 months will never be required to make an estimated tax payment.

EXAMPLE 2

X died on March 15, 1992. Her executor elected a fiscal year ending on July 31 for the estate. Estimated tax payments will be required from the estate starting with the tax year that begins on August 1, 1993. ◆

---

5. § 6905 and the Regulations thereunder.   6. § 441.

Tax Rates and Personal Exemption

A compressed tax rate schedule applies to estates and trusts. The 15 percent tax bracket is only $3,600 wide, so the ability to shift income in a tax-effective manner is restricted. Net long-term capital gains can be taxed at a nominal rate of no more than 28 percent. In addition to the regular income tax, an estate or trust may be subject to the alternative minimum tax imposed on tax preferences and adjustments.[7] Trusts may also be subject to a special tax imposed by § 644 on built-in gains from the sale or exchange of certain appreciated property.

Both trusts and estates are allowed a personal exemption in computing the fiduciary tax liability. All estates are allowed a personal exemption of $600. The exemption available to a trust depends upon the type of trust involved. A trust that is required to distribute all of its income currently is allowed an exemption of $300. All other trusts are allowed an exemption of only $100 per year.[8]

The classification of trusts as to the appropriate personal exemption is similar but not identical to the distinction between simple and complex trusts. The classification as a simple trust is more stringent.

EXAMPLE 3

Three trusts appear to operate in a similar fashion, but they are subject to different Subchapter J classifications and exemptions.

Trust X is required to distribute all of its current accounting income to Ms. A. Thus, it is allowed a $300 personal exemption. No corpus distributions or charitable contributions are made during the year. Accordingly, X is a simple trust.

Trust Y is required to distribute all of its current accounting income; it is allowed a $300 personal exemption. The beneficiaries of these distributions are specified in the trust instrument: one-half of accounting income is to be distributed to Mr. B, and one-half is to be distributed to State University, a qualifying charitable organization. Since Y has made a charitable distribution for the tax year, it is a complex trust.

The trustee of Trust Z can, at her discretion, distribute the current-year accounting income or corpus of the trust to Dr. C. As the trustee is not required to distribute current accounting income, only a $100 personal exemption is allowed. During the current year, the trustee distributed all of the accounting income of the entity to Dr. C, but made no corpus or charitable distributions. Nonetheless, because it lacks the current-year income distribution requirement, Z is a complex trust. ◆

Alternative Minimum Tax

The alternative minimum tax (AMT) may apply to a trust or estate in any tax year. Given the nature and magnitude of the tax preferences, adjustments, and exemptions that determine alternative minimum taxable income (AMTI), however, most trusts and estates are unlikely to incur the tax. Nevertheless, they could be vulnerable if they are actively engaged in a business that uses accelerated cost recovery or long-term construction contract tax accounting provisions. Similarly, an estate may be liable for the AMT if it receives a sizable portfolio of stock options shortly after the decedent's death under a deferred compensation plan. Charitable contributions of appreciated property may also cause an entity to incur AMT liability.

In general, derivation of AMTI for the entity follows the rules that apply to individual taxpayers. Thus, the corporate ACE adjustment does not apply to fiduciary entities, but AMTI may be created through the application of most of the other AMT preference and adjustment items discussed in Chapter 6.

---

7. § 55.

8. § 642(b).

The entity has a $20,000 annual exemption, similar to that available to a married individual who files a separate return. The exemption phases out at a rate of one-fourth of the amount by which AMTI exceeds $75,000.

The 24 percent alternative minimum tax rate is applied to AMTI. In addition, estimated tax payments for the entity must include any applicable AMT liability.

TAXABLE INCOME OF TRUSTS AND ESTATES
◆

Generally, the taxable income of an estate or trust is computed in a manner similar to that used for an individual. Subchapter J does, however, include several important exceptions and provisions that make it necessary to use a systematic approach to calculating the taxable income of these entities. Figure 19–3 illustrates the computation method followed in this chapter.

Entity Accounting Income

The first step in determining the taxable income of a trust or estate is to compute the entity's accounting income for the period. Although this prerequisite is not apparent from a cursory reading of Subchapter J, a closer look at the Code reveals a number of references to the income of the entity.[9] Wherever the term "income" is used in Subchapter J without some modifier (e.g., *gross* income or *taxable* income), the statute is referring to the accounting income of the trust or estate for the tax year.

FIGURE 19–3

Accounting Income, Distributable Net Income, and Taxable Income of the Entity and Its Beneficiaries (5 Steps)

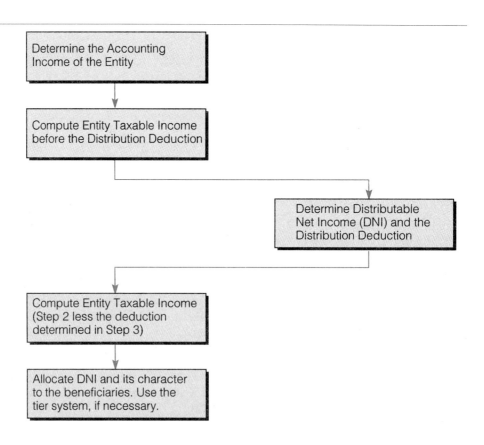

---

9. For example, see §§ 651(a)(1), 652(a), and 661(a)(1).

A definition of entity accounting income is critical to understanding the Subchapter J computation of fiduciary taxable income. Under state law, entity accounting income is the amount that the income beneficiary of the simple trust or estate is eligible to receive from the entity. More importantly, the calculation of accounting income is virtually under the control of the grantor or decedent (through a properly drafted trust agreement or will). If the document has been drafted at arm's length, a court will enforce a fiduciary's good faith efforts to carry out the specified computation of accounting income.

Entity (sometimes known as fiduciary) accounting income generally is defined by state laws that are derived from the Uniform Principal and Income Act. Most states have adopted some form of the Uniform Act, which constitutes Generally Accepted Accounting Principles in the fiduciary setting.

By allocating specific items of income and expenditure either to the income beneficiaries or to corpus, the desires of the grantor or decedent are put into effect. Figure 19-4 shows typical assignments of revenue and expenditure items to fiduciary income or corpus.

Where the controlling document is silent as to whether an item should be assigned to income or corpus, state law prevails. These allocations are an important determinant of the benefits received from the entity by its beneficiaries and the timing of those benefits.

------------------------------------ EXAMPLE 4 ------------------------------------

The A Trust is a simple trust. Mrs. B is its sole beneficiary. In the current year, the trust earns $20,000 in taxable interest and $15,000 in tax-exempt interest. In addition, the trust recognizes an $8,000 long-term capital gain. The trustee assesses a fee of $11,000 for the year. If the trust agreement allocates fees and capital gains to corpus, trust accounting income is $35,000, and Mrs. B receives that amount. Thus, the income beneficiary receives no immediate benefit from the trust's capital gain, and she bears none of the financial burden of the fiduciary's fees.

Interest income	$35,000
Long-term capital gain	±-0-*
Fiduciary's fees	±-0-*
Trust accounting income	$35,000

*Allocable to corpus.   ◆

------------------------------------ EXAMPLE 5 ------------------------------------

Assume the same facts as in Example 4, except that the trust agreement allocates the fiduciary's fees to income. The trust accounting income is $24,000, and Mrs. B receives that amount.

Allocable to Income	Allocable to Corpus	FIGURE 19-4
■ Ordinary and operating net income from trust assets.	■ Depreciation on business assets.	**Common Allocations of Items to Income or Corpus**
■ Interest, dividend, rent, and royalty income.	■ Casualty gain/loss on income-producing assets.	
■ Stock dividends.	■ Insurance recoveries on income-producing assets.	
■ One-half of fiduciary fees/commissions.	■ Capital gain/loss on investment assets.	
	■ Stock splits.	
	■ One-half of fiduciary fees/commissions.	

Interest income	$35,000
Long-term capital gain	± –0–*
Fiduciary's fees	–11,000
Trust accounting income	$24,000

*Allocable to corpus. ◆

─────────────────── Example 6 ───────────────────

Assume the same facts as in Example 4, except that the trust agreement allocates to income all capital gains and losses and one-half of the trustee's commissions. The trust accounting income is $37,500, and Mrs. B receives that amount.

Interest income	$35,000
Long-term capital gain	+8,000
Fiduciary's fees	–5,500*
Trust accounting income	$37,500

*One-half allocable to corpus. ◆

Gross Income

The gross income of an estate or trust is similar to that of an individual. In determining the gain or loss to be recognized by an estate or trust upon the sale or other taxable disposition of assets, the rules for basis determination are similar to those applicable to other taxpayers. Thus, the basis to an estate of property received from a decedent is stepped up or stepped down to gross estate value under § 1014 (refer to Chapter 18 for a more detailed discussion). Property received as a gift (the usual case in trust arrangements) is controlled by § 1015. Property purchased by the trust from a third party is assigned a basis equal to purchase price.

Property Distributions. In general, the entity does not recognize gain or loss upon its distribution of property to a beneficiary under the provisions of the will or trust document. The beneficiary of the distribution assigns to the distributed property a basis equal to that of the estate or trust. Moreover, the distribution absorbs distributable net income (DNI) and qualifies for a distribution deduction (both of which are explained later in this chapter) to the extent of the lesser of the distributed asset's basis to the beneficiary or the asset's fair market value as of the distribution date.[10]

─────────────────── Example 7 ───────────────────

The H Trust distributes a painting, basis of $40,000 and fair market value of $90,000, to beneficiary K. K's basis in the painting is $40,000. The distribution absorbs $40,000 of H's DNI, and H claims a $40,000 distribution deduction relative to the transaction. ◆

─────────────────── Example 8 ───────────────────

Assume the same facts as in Example 7, except that H's basis in the painting is $100,000. K's basis in the painting is $100,000. The distribution absorbs $90,000 of H's DNI, and H claims a $90,000 distribution deduction. ◆

A trustee or executor can elect to recognize gain or loss with respect to all of its in-kind property distributions for the year. If the election is made, the

─────────────────────────

10. § 643(e).

beneficiary's basis in the asset is equal to the asset's fair market value as of the distribution date. The distribution absorbs DNI and qualifies for a distribution deduction to the extent of the asset's fair market value. However, § 267 can restrict a trust's deduction for such losses.

────────────────── EXAMPLE 9 ──────────────────

The G Estate distributes an antique piano, basis to G of $10,000 and fair market value of $15,000, to beneficiary K. The executor elects that G recognize the related $5,000 gain on the distribution. Accordingly, K's basis in the piano is $15,000 ($10,000 basis to G + $5,000 gain recognized). Without the election, G would not recognize any gain, and K's basis in the piano would be $10,000. ◆

────────────────── EXAMPLE 10 ──────────────────

Assume the same facts as in Example 9, except that G's basis in the piano is $18,000. The executor elects that G recognize the related $3,000 loss on the distribution. Accordingly, K's basis in the piano is $15,000 ($18,000 – $3,000). Without the election, G would not recognize any loss, and K's basis in the piano would be $18,000. ◆

Income in Respect of a Decedent. The gross income of a trust or estate includes income in respect of a decedent (IRD).[11] For a cash basis decedent, IRD includes accrued salary, interest, rent, and other income items that were not constructively received before death. For both cash and accrual basis decedents, IRD includes, for instance, death benefits from qualified retirement plans and deferred compensation contracts. It also includes income from a partnership whose tax year does not end with the death of the deceased partner and collections of installment notes receivable.

The tax consequences of IRD are as follows:

- The fair market value of the right to IRD on the appropriate valuation date is included in the decedent's gross estate.[12] Thus, it is subject to the Federal estate tax.[13]
- The decedent's basis in the property carries over to the recipient (the estate or heirs). There is no step-up or step-down in the basis of IRD items.
- Gain or loss is recognized to the recipient of the income, measured by the difference between the amount realized and the adjusted basis of the IRD in the hands of the decedent. The character of the gain or loss depends upon the treatment that it would have received had it been realized by the decedent before death. Thus, if the decedent would have realized capital gain, the recipient must do likewise.
- Expenses related to the IRD (such as interest, taxes, and depletion) that properly were not reported on the final income tax return of the decedent may be claimed by the recipient if the obligation is associated with the IRD. These items are known as *expenses in respect of a decedent*. They are deductible for both Federal estate and income tax purposes.
- If the IRD item would have created an AMT preference or adjustment for the decedent (e.g., with respect to the collection of certain tax-exempt interest by the entity), an identical AMT item is created for the recipient.

───────────────────────

11. § 691 and the Regulations thereunder. The concept of IRD was introduced in Chapter 18.

12. § 2033.

13. To mitigate the effect of double taxation (imposition of both the estate tax and the income tax), § 691(c) allows the recipient an income tax deduction for the estate tax attributable to the income.

———————————————————— EXAMPLE 11 ————————————————————

K died on July 13 of the current year. On August 2, the estate received a check (before deductions) for $1,200 from K's former employer; this was K's compensation for the last pay period of his life. On November 23, the estate received a $45,000 distribution from the qualified profit sharing plan of K's employer, the full amount to which K was entitled under the plan. Both K and the estate are calendar year cash basis taxpayers.

The last salary payment and the profit sharing plan distribution constitute IRD to the estate. K had earned these items during his lifetime, and the estate had an enforceable right to receive each of them after K's death. Consequently, the gross estate includes $46,200 with respect to these two items. However, the income tax basis to the estate for these items is not stepped up (from zero to $1,200 and $45,000, respectively) upon distribution to the estate.

The estate must report gross income of $46,200 for the current tax year with respect to the IRD items. The gain recognized upon the receipt of the IRD is $46,200 [$1,200 + $45,000 (amounts realized) − $0 (adjusted basis)]. ♦

Including the IRD in both K's gross estate and the gross income of the estate may seem harsh. Nevertheless, it is similar to the treatment that applies to all of a taxpayer's earned income. The amount is subject to income tax upon receipt, and to the extent that it is not consumed by the taxpayer before death, it is included in the gross estate.

———————————————————— EXAMPLE 12 ————————————————————

Assume the same facts as in Example 11, except that K is an accrual basis taxpayer. IRD now includes only the $45,000 distribution from the qualified retirement plan. K's last paycheck is included in the gross income of his own last return (January 1 through date of death). The $1,200 salary is already properly recognized under K's usual method of tax accounting. It does not constitute IRD and is not gross income when received by the executor. ♦

———————————————————— EXAMPLE 13 ————————————————————

Assume the same facts as in Example 11. K's last paycheck was reduced by $165 for state income taxes that were withheld by the employer. The $165 tax payment is an expense in respect of a decedent and is allowed as a deduction *both* on K's estate tax return *and* on the estate's income tax return. ♦

Ordinary Deductions

As a general rule, the taxable income of an estate or trust is similar to that of an individual. Deductions are allowed for ordinary and necessary expenses paid or incurred in carrying on a trade or business; for the production or collection of income; for the management, conservation, or maintenance of property; and in connection with the determination, collection, or refund of any tax.[14] Reasonable administration expenses, including fiduciary fees and litigation costs in connection with the duties of administration, also are deductible.

The trust or estate must apply the 2 percent-of-AGI floor to any § 212 expenses that it incurs.[15] For this purpose, AGI appears to be the greater of (1) the pertinent-year AGI of the grantor of the trust or (2) the AGI of the trust or estate, computed as though the entity were an individual.

Expenses attributable to the production or collection of tax-exempt income are not deductible.[16] The amount of the disallowed deduction is found by using an apportionment formula, based upon the composition of the income elements of

—————————————————————

14. §§ 162 and 212.

15. § 67(c).

16. § 265.

entity accounting income for the year of the deduction. The apportionment of the § 212 deduction is made without regard to the accounting income allocation of such expenses to income or to corpus. The deductibility of the fees is determined strictly by the Code (under §§ 212 and 265), and the allocation of expenditures to income and to corpus is controlled by the trust agreement or will or by state law.

———————————————— EXAMPLE 14 ————————————————

The S Trust operates a business and invests idle cash in marketable securities. Its sales proceeds for the current year are $180,000. Expenses for wages, cost of sales, and office administration are $80,000. Interest income recognized is $20,000 from taxable bonds and $50,000 from tax-exempt bonds. The trustee claims a $35,000 fee for its activities. According to the trust agreement, $30,000 of this amount is allocated to the income beneficiaries and $5,000 is allocated to corpus.

Sales income	$180,000
Cost of sales	−80,000
Interest income ($50,000 is exempt)	+70,000
Fiduciary's fees, as allocated	−30,000
Trust accounting income	$140,000

◆

The sales proceeds are included in the gross income of the trust under § 61. The costs associated with the business are deductible in full under § 162. The taxable income is included in S's gross income under § 61, but the tax-exempt income is excluded under § 103. The fiduciary's fees are deductible by S under § 212, but a portion of the deduction is lost because of the § 265 prohibition against deductions for expenses incurred in the generation of tax-exempt income.

Specifically, 50/250 of the fees of $35,000 can be traced to tax-exempt income, and $7,000 of the fees is nondeductible. For purposes of the computation, only the income elements of the year's trust accounting income are included in the denominator. Moreover, the allocation of portions of the fees to income and to corpus is irrelevant in the calculation. The disallowed deduction for fiduciary's fees is computed as follows:

$$\$35,000^* \text{ (total fees paid)} \times \frac{\$50,000^{**} \quad (\textit{exempt} \text{ income elements of trust accounting income})}{\$250,000^{**} \quad (\textit{all} \text{ income elements of trust accounting income})}$$

= $7,000 (amount disallowed)

*All of the fees, and not just those that are allocated to income, are deductible by the trust under § 212.
**The numerator and denominator of this fraction are *not* reduced by expense items allocable to income (e.g., cost of sales).

Under § 642(g), amounts deductible as administration expenses or losses for death tax purposes (under §§ 2053 and 2054) cannot be claimed by the estate for income tax purposes unless the estate files a waiver of the death tax deduction. Although these expenses cannot be deducted twice, they may be allocated as the fiduciary sees fit between Forms 706 and 1041; they need not be claimed in their entirety on either return.[17] As discussed earlier, the prohibition against double

---

17. Reg. § 1.642(g)–2.

deductions does not extend to expenses in respect of a decedent. These are deductible both for estate tax purposes and on the income tax return of the recipient of the IRD.

Trusts and estates are allowed cost recovery deductions. However, such deductions are assigned proportionately among the recipients of the entity accounting income.[18]

EXAMPLE 15

L and M are the equal income beneficiaries of the N Trust. Under the terms of the trust agreement, the trustee has complete discretion as to the timing of the distributions from N's current accounting income. The trust agreement allocates all depreciation expense to income. In the current year, the trustee distributes 40% of the current trust accounting income to L and 40% to M; thus, 20% of the income is accumulated. The depreciation deduction allowable to N is $100,000. This deduction is allocated among the trust and its beneficiaries on the basis of the distribution of current accounting income: L and M can each claim a $40,000 deduction, and the trust can deduct $20,000. ◆

EXAMPLE 16

Assume the same facts as in Example 15, except that the trust agreement allocates all depreciation expense to corpus. L and M can each still claim a $40,000 depreciation deduction, and N retains its $20,000 deduction. The Code assigns the depreciation deduction proportionately to the recipients of entity accounting income. Allocation of depreciation to income or to corpus is irrelevant in determining which party can properly claim the deduction. ◆

When a trust sells property received by transfer from the grantor, the amount of depreciation subject to recapture includes the depreciation claimed by the grantor before the transfer of the property to the trust. However, depreciation recapture potential disappears at death. Thus, when an entity receives depreciable property from a decedent, the recapture potential is reduced to zero.

EXAMPLE 17

J transferred an asset to the S Trust via a lifetime gift. The asset's total depreciation recapture potential was $40,000. If S sells the asset at a gain, ordinary income not to exceed $40,000 is recognized by the trust. Had J transferred the asset after his death to his estate through a bequest, the $40,000 recapture potential would have disappeared. ◆

Deductions for Losses

An estate or trust is allowed a deduction for casualty or theft losses that are not covered by insurance or other arrangement. Such losses may also be deductible by an estate for Federal death tax purposes under § 2054. As a result, an estate is not allowed an income tax deduction unless the death tax deduction is waived.[19]

The net operating loss deduction is available for estates and trusts. The carryback of a net operating loss may reduce the distributable net income of the trust or estate for the carryback year and therefore affect the amount taxed to the beneficiaries for that year.

Certain losses realized by an estate or trust also may be disallowed, as they are for all taxpayers. Thus, the wash sales provisions of § 1091 disallow losses on

---

18. §§ 167(h) and 611(b)(3) and (4).
19. See Reg. § 1.642(g)–1 for the required statement waiving the estate tax deduction. In addition, see Reg. §§ 1.165–7(c) and 1.165–8(b), requiring that a statement be filed to allow an income tax deduction for such losses.

the sale or other disposition of stock or securities when substantially identical stock or securities are acquired by the estate or trust within the prescribed 30-day period. Likewise, § 267 disallows certain losses, expenses, and interest with respect to transactions between related taxpayers. Under § 267(b), the term "related taxpayers" includes the following:

- A grantor and a fiduciary of any trust.
- A fiduciary of a trust and a fiduciary of another trust, if the same person is a grantor of both trusts.
- A fiduciary and a beneficiary of the same trust.
- A fiduciary of a trust and a beneficiary of another trust, if the same person is a grantor of both trusts.
- A fiduciary of a trust and a corporation, more than 50 percent in value of the outstanding stock of which is owned by or for the trust or the grantor of the trust.

Except for the possibility of unused losses in the year of termination, the net capital losses of an estate or trust cannot be deducted by a beneficiary.[20] They are to be used only on the fiduciary income tax return. The tax treatment of these losses is the same as for individual taxpayers.

Charitable Contributions

An estate or complex trust is allowed a deduction for contributions to charitable organizations under the following conditions:

1. The contribution must be made pursuant to the will or trust instrument.
2. The recipient must be a qualified organization. For this purpose, qualified organizations include the same charities that qualify individual and corporate donors for the deduction, except that estates and trusts are permitted a deduction for contributions to certain foreign charitable organizations.
3. Generally, the contribution must be paid in the tax year claimed, but a fiduciary can treat amounts paid in the year immediately following as a deduction for the preceding year.[21] Under this rule, estates and complex trusts receive more liberal treatment than individuals or corporations.

Unlike individuals and corporations, estates and complex trusts are not limited in the extent of their deductible charitable contributions for the year (e.g., to a percentage of taxable or adjusted gross income). Nonetheless, an entity's contribution may not fully qualify for a deduction.[22] Specifically, the deduction is limited to amounts included in the gross income of the entity in the year of the contribution. A contribution is deemed to have been made proportionately from each of the income elements of entity accounting income. Thus, if the entity has tax-exempt income, the contribution is deductible only to the extent that the income elements of entity accounting income for the year of the deduction are included in the entity's gross income.

This rule is similar to that used to limit the § 212 deduction for fiduciary fees and other expenses incurred to generate tax-exempt income. However, if the will or trust agreement requires that the contribution be made from a specific type of income or from the current income from a specified asset, the document

20. § 642(h).
21. § 642(c)(1) and Reg. § 1.642(c)–1(b).
22. Reg. §§ 1.642(c)–3(b) and (c).

will control (the allocation of the contribution to taxable and tax-exempt income will not be required).

———————————————— EXAMPLE 18 ————————————————

The K Trust has gross rental income of $80,000, expenses attributable to the rents of $60,000, and tax-exempt interest from state bonds of $20,000. Under the trust agreement, the trustee is directed to pay 30% of the annual trust accounting income to the United Way, a qualifying organization. Accordingly, the trustee pays $12,000 to the charity in 1993 (i.e., 30% × $40,000). The charitable contribution deduction allowed for 1992 is $9,600 [($80,000/$100,000) × $12,000]. ◆

———————————————— EXAMPLE 19 ————————————————

Assume the same facts as in Example 18, except that the trust instrument also requires that the contribution be paid from the net rent income. The agreement controls, and the allocation formula need not be applied. The entire $12,000 is allowed as a charitable deduction. ◆

Deduction for Distributions to Beneficiaries

The modified conduit approach of Subchapter J is embodied in the deduction allowed to trusts and estates for the distributions made to beneficiaries during the year. When the beneficiary receives a distribution from the trust, some portion of that distribution may be subject to income tax on the beneficiary's own return. At the same time, the distributing entity is allowed a deduction for some or all of the distribution. Consequently, the modified conduit principle of Subchapter J is implemented. A good analogy to this operation is the taxability of corporate profits distributed to employees as taxable wages. The corporation is allowed a deduction for the payment, but the employee receives gross income in the form of compensation.

A critical value that is used in computing the amount of the entity's distribution deduction is *distributable net income* (*DNI*). DNI serves several functions as it is defined in Subchapter J:

- DNI is the maximum amount of the distribution on which the beneficiaries can be taxed.[23]
- DNI is the maximum amount that can be used by the entity as a distribution deduction for the year.[24]
- The makeup of DNI carries over to the beneficiaries (the items of income and expenses will retain their DNI character in the hands of the distributees).[25]

Subchapter J defines DNI in a circular manner, however. The DNI value is necessary to determine the entity's distribution deduction and therefore its taxable income for the year. Nonetheless, the Code defines DNI as a modification of the entity's taxable income itself. Using the systematic approach to determining the taxable income of the entity and its beneficiaries, as shown earlier in Figure 19–3, first compute *taxable income before the distribution deduction*, modify that amount to determine DNI and the distribution deduction, return to the calculation of *taxable income*, and apply the deduction that has resulted.

Taxable income before the distribution deduction includes all of the entity's items of gross income, deductions, gains, losses, and exemptions for the year. Therefore,

---

23. §§ 652(a) and 662(a).
24. §§ 651(b) and 661(c).

25. §§ 652(b) and 662(b).

to compute this amount, (1) determine the appropriate personal exemption for the year and (2) account for all of the other gross income and deductions of the entity.

The next step in Figure 19–3, is the determination of *distributable net income*, computed by making the following adjustments to the entity's *taxable income before the distribution deduction:*[26]

- Add back the personal exemption.
- Add back *net* tax-exempt interest. To arrive at this amount, reduce the total tax-exempt interest by charitable contributions and by related expenses not deductible under § 265.
- Add back the entity's *net* capital losses.
- Subtract any net capital gains taxable to the entity (those that are allocable to corpus). In other words, the only net capital gains included in DNI are those attributable to income beneficiaries or to charitable contributions.

Since taxable income before the distribution deduction is computed by deducting all of the expenses of the entity (whether they were allocated to income or to corpus), DNI is reduced by expenses that are allocated to corpus. The effect is to reduce the taxable income of the income beneficiaries. The actual distributions to the beneficiaries exceed DNI because the distributions are not reduced by expenses allocated to corpus. Aside from this shortcoming of Subchapter J, DNI offers a good approximation of the current-year economic income available for distribution to the entity's income beneficiaries.

DNI includes the net tax-exempt interest income of the entity, so that amount must be removed from DNI in computing the distribution deduction. Moreover, with respect to estates and complex trusts, the amount actually distributed during the year may include discretionary distributions of income and distributions of corpus permissible under the will or trust instrument. Thus, the distribution deduction for estates and complex trusts is computed as the lesser of (1) the deductible portion of DNI or (2) the amount actually distributed to the beneficiaries during the year. For a simple trust, however, full distribution is always assumed, relative to both the entity and its beneficiaries, in a manner similar to the partnership and S corporation conduit entities.

EXAMPLE 20

The Z Trust is a simple trust. Because of severe liquidity problems, its 1992 accounting income is not distributed to its sole beneficiary, M, until early in 1993. Z still is allowed a full distribution deduction for, and M still is taxable upon, the entity's 1992 income in 1992. ◆

EXAMPLE 21

The P Trust is required to distribute its current accounting income annually to its sole income beneficiary, Mr. B. Capital gains and losses and all other expenses are allocable to corpus. In the current year, P incurs the following items:

Dividend income	$25,000
Taxable interest income	15,000
Tax-exempt interest income	20,000
Net long-term capital gains	10,000
Fiduciary's fees	6,000

---

26. These and other (less common) adjustments are detailed in § 643.

1. Trust accounting income is $60,000; this includes the tax-exempt interest income, but not the fees or the capital gains, pursuant to the trust document. B receives $60,000 from the trust for the current year.

2. Taxable income before the distribution deduction is computed as follows:

Dividend	$25,000
Interest income	15,000
Net long-term capital gains	10,000
Fiduciary's fees (40/60)	(4,000)
Personal exemption	(300)
Total	$45,700

The tax-exempt interest is excluded under § 103. Only a portion of the fees is deductible because some of the fees are traceable to the tax-exempt income. The trust claims a $300 personal exemption as it is required to distribute its annual trust accounting income.

3. DNI and the distribution deduction are computed in the following manner:

Taxable income before the distribution deduction (from above)		$ 45,700
Add back: Personal exemption		300
Subtract: Net long-term capital gains of the trust		(10,000)
Add back: Net tax-exempt income—		
Tax-exempt interest	$20,000	
Less disallowed fees	(2,000)	18,000
Distributable net income		$ 54,000
Distribution deduction		
(DNI $54,000 − net tax-exempt income $18,000)		$ 36,000

4. Finally, return to the computation of the taxable income of the P Trust.

Taxable income before the distribution deduction	$45,700
Minus: Distribution deduction	36,000
Taxable income, P Trust	$ 9,700

A simple test should be applied at this point to assure that the proper figure for the trust's taxable income has been determined. On what is P to be taxed? P has distributed to Mr. B all of its gross income except the $10,000 net long-term capital gains. The $300 personal exemption reduces taxable income to $9,700. ◆

──────────────── EXAMPLE 22 ────────────────

The Q Trust is required to distribute all of its current accounting income equally to its two beneficiaries, Ms. F and the Universal Church, a qualifying charitable organization. Capital gains and losses and depreciation expenses are allocable to the income beneficiaries. Fiduciary fees are allocable to corpus. In the current year, Q incurs fiduciary fees of $18,000 and the following:

(1)	Rent income	$ 100,000
	Depreciation expense (rent income property)	−15,000
	Other expenses related to rent income	−30,000
	Net long-term capital gains	+20,000
	Accounting income, Q Trust	$ 75,000

(2)	Taxable rent income	$100,000
	Depreciation deduction	–0–
	Rental expense deductions	(30,000)
	Net long-term capital gains	20,000
	Fiduciary's fees	(18,000)
	Personal exemption	(300)
	Charitable contribution deduction	(37,500)
	Taxable income before the distribution deduction	$ 34,200

In the absence of tax-exempt income, a deduction is allowed for the full amount of the fiduciary's fees. Q is a complex trust, but since it is required to distribute its full accounting income annually, a $300 exemption is allowed. The trust properly does not deduct any depreciation for the rental property. The depreciation deduction is available only to the recipients of the entity's accounting income for the period. Thus, the deduction is split equally between Ms. F and the church. The deduction probably is of no direct value to the church since the church is not subject to the income tax. The trust's charitable contribution deduction is based upon the $37,500 that the charity actually received (one-half of trust accounting income).

(3)	Taxable income before the distribution deduction	$34,200
	Add back: Personal exemption	300
	Distributable net income	$34,500
	Distribution deduction	$34,500

The only adjustment necessary to compute DNI is to add back the trust's personal exemption, as there is no tax-exempt income. Subchapter J requires no adjustment relative to the charitable contribution. DNI is computed only from the perspective of Ms. F, who also received $37,500 from the trust.

(4)	Taxable income before the distribution deduction	$34,200
	Minus: Distribution deduction	34,500
	Taxable income, Q Trust	$ (300)

Perform the simple test (referred to above) to assure that the proper taxable income for the Q Trust has been computed. All of the trust's gross income has been distributed to Ms. F and the charity. As is the case with most trusts that distribute all of their annual income, the personal exemption is "wasted" by the Q Trust. ◆

In a year in which the AMT applies to the estate or trust, the distribution deduction is also applied against alternative minimum taxable income in deriving the amount that is subject to the § 55 tax.

Tax Credits

An estate or trust may claim the foreign tax credit allowed under § 901 to the extent that it is not allocable to the beneficiaries.[27] Similarly, other credits are apportioned between the estate or trust and the beneficiaries on the basis of the entity accounting income allocable to each.

---

27. § 642(a)(1).

The beneficiaries of an estate or trust receive taxable income from the entity under the modified conduit principle of Subchapter J. Distributable net income determines the maximum amount that can be taxed to the beneficiaries for any tax year. The constitution of the elements of DNI also carries over to the beneficiaries (e.g., net long-term capital gains retain their character when they are distributed from the entity to the beneficiary).

The timing of any tax consequences to the beneficiary of a trust or estate presents little problem except when the parties involved use different tax years. A beneficiary includes in gross income an amount based upon the DNI of the trust for any taxable year or years of the entity ending with or within his or her taxable year.[28]

--------------------------------- EXAMPLE 23 ---------------------------------

An estate uses a fiscal year ending on March 31 for tax purposes. Its sole income beneficiary is a calendar year taxpayer. For the calendar year 1993, the beneficiary reports the income assignable to her for the entity's fiscal year April 1, 1992, to March 31, 1993. If the estate is terminated by December 31, 1993, the beneficiary also includes any trust income assignable to her for the short year. This could result in a bunching of income in 1993. ◆

Distributions by Simple Trusts

The amount taxable to the beneficiaries of a simple trust is limited by the trust's DNI. However, since DNI includes net tax-exempt income, the amount included in the gross income of the beneficiaries could be less than DNI. When there is more than one income beneficiary, the elements of DNI are apportioned ratably according to the amount required to be distributed currently to each.

--------------------------------- EXAMPLE 24 ---------------------------------

A simple trust has ordinary income of $40,000, a long-term capital gain of $15,000 (allocable to corpus), and a trustee commission expense of $4,000 (payable from corpus). The two income beneficiaries, A and B, are entitled to the trust's annual accounting income, based on shares of 75% and 25%, respectively. Although A receives $30,000 as his share (75% × trust accounting income of $40,000), he is allocated DNI of only $27,000 (75% × $36,000). Likewise, B is entitled to receive $10,000 (25% × $40,000), but she is allocated DNI of only $9,000 (25% × $36,000). The $15,000 capital gain is taxed to the trust. ◆

Distributions by Estates and Complex Trusts

A problem arises with estates and complex trusts when more than one beneficiary receives a distribution from the entity and the controlling document does not require a distribution of the entire accounting income of the entity.

--------------------------------- EXAMPLE 25 ---------------------------------

The trustee of the W Trust has the discretion to distribute the income or corpus of the trust in any proportion between the two beneficiaries of the trust, Ms. K and Dr. L. Under the trust instrument, Ms. K must receive $15,000 from the trust every year. In the current year, the trust's accounting income is $50,000, and its DNI is $40,000. The trustee pays $15,000 to Ms. K and $25,000 to Dr. L. ◆

How is W's DNI to be divided between Ms. K and Dr. L? Several arbitrary methods of allocating DNI between the beneficiaries could be devised. Subchapter J resolves the problem by creating a two-tier system to govern the taxation of

---

28. §§ 652(c) and 662(c).

beneficiaries in such situations.[29] The tier system determines which distributions will be included in the gross income of the beneficiaries in full, which will be included in part, and which will not be included at all.

Income that is required to be distributed currently, whether or not it is distributed, is categorized as a *first-tier distribution*. All other amounts properly paid, credited, or required to be distributed are *second-tier distributions*.[30] First-tier distributions are taxed in full to the beneficiaries to the extent that DNI is sufficient to cover the distributions. If the first-tier distributions exceed DNI, however, each beneficiary is taxed only on a proportionate part of the DNI. Second-tier distributions are not taxed if the first-tier distributions exceed DNI. However, if both first-tier and second-tier distributions are made and the first-tier distributions do not exceed DNI, the second-tier distributions are taxed to the beneficiaries proportionately to the extent of the "remaining" DNI.

The following formula is used to allocate DNI among the appropriate beneficiaries when only first-tier distributions are made and those amounts exceed DNI:

| First-tier distributions to the beneficiary / First-tier distributions to all noncharitable beneficiaries | X | Distributable net income (without deductions for charitable contributions) | = | Beneficiary's share of distributable net income |

Amounts that pass to charitable organizations are disregarded in this formula.

When both first-tier and second-tier distributions are made and the first-tier distributions exceed DNI, the above formula is applied to the first-tier distributions. In this case, none of the second-tier distributions are taxed because all of the DNI has been allocated to the first-tier beneficiaries.

If both first-tier and second-tier distributions are made and the first-tier distributions do not exceed DNI, but the total of both first-tier and second-tier distributions does exceed DNI, the second-tier beneficiaries recognize income as follows:

| Second-tier distributions to the beneficiary / Second-tier distributions to all beneficiaries | X | Remaining distributable net income (after first-tier distributions and charitable contributions) | = | Beneficiary's share of distributable net income |

Charitable contributions are taken into account at this point.

──────────────── EXAMPLE 26 ────────────────

The trustee of the G Trust is required to distribute $10,000 per year to both Mrs. H and Mr. U, the two beneficiaries of the entity. In addition, she is empowered to distribute other amounts of trust income or corpus at her sole discretion. In the current year, the trust has accounting income of $60,000 and DNI of $50,000. However, the trustee distributes only the required $10,000 each to Mrs. H and to Mr. U. The balance of the income is accumulated and added to trust corpus.

29. §§ 662(a)(1) and (2).   **30.** Reg. §§ 1.662(a)–2 and –3.

In this case, only first-tier distributions have been made, but the total amount of the distributions does not exceed DNI for the year. Although DNI is the maximum amount that is included by the beneficiaries for the year, they can include no more in gross income than is distributed by the entity. Thus, both Mrs. H and Mr. U may be subject to tax on $10,000 as their proportionate shares of G's DNI. ◆

────────────────── EXAMPLE 27 ──────────────────

Assume the same facts in Example 26, except that DNI is $12,000. Mrs. H and Mr. U each receive $10,000, but they cannot be taxed in total on more than DNI. Each is taxed on $6,000 [DNI of $12,000 × ($10,000/$20,000 of the first-tier distributions)]. ◆

────────────────── EXAMPLE 28 ──────────────────

Return to the facts in Example 25. Ms. K receives a first-tier distribution of $15,000. Second-tier distributions include $20,000 to Ms. K and $25,000 to Dr. L. W's DNI is $40,000. The DNI is allocated between Ms. K and Dr. L as follows:

(1) First-tier distributions
    To Ms. K $15,000 DNI
    To Dr. L   –0–
    Remaining DNI = $25,000
(2) Second-tier distributions
    To Ms. K $11,111 DNI (20/45 × $25,000)
    To Dr. L $13,889 DNI (25/45 × $25,000)   ◆

────────────────── EXAMPLE 29 ──────────────────

Assume the same facts as in Example 28, except that accounting income is $80,000 and DNI is $70,000. The DNI is allocated between Ms. K and Dr. L as follows:

(1) First-tier distributions
    To Ms. K $15,000 DNI
    To Dr. L   –0–
    Remaining DNI = $55,000
(2) Second-tier distributions
    To Ms. K $20,000 DNI
    To Dr. L $25,000 DNI   ◆

────────────────── EXAMPLE 30 ──────────────────

Assume the same facts as in Example 28, except that accounting income is $18,000 and DNI is $12,000. The DNI is allocated between Ms. K and Dr. L as follows:

(1) First-tier distributions
    To Ms. K $12,000 DNI
    (limited to the DNI ceiling)
    To Dr. L   –0–
    Remaining DNI = $0
(2) Second-tier distributions
    To Ms. K $0 DNI
    To Dr. L $0 DNI   ◆

────────────────── EXAMPLE 31 ──────────────────

The Y Estate is required to distribute its income as follows: 50% to A, 25% to B, and 25% to C (a qualifying charitable organization). During the current year, it has accounting income of $40,000 and DNI (before any charitable contributions) of $27,000. Pursuant to the governing instrument, the following amounts are paid out: $20,000 to A (50% × $40,000), $10,000 to B, and $10,000 to C. A includes $18,000 in gross income

[($20,000/$30,000) × $27,000], and B includes $9,000 [($10,000/$30,000) × $27,000]. Note that the distribution to the charitable organization is not considered in allocating DNI to the first-tier beneficiaries (the denominator of the fraction is only $30,000).[31] ◆

─────────────── EXAMPLE 32 ───────────────

The will that created the V Estate requires that $20,000 be distributed annually to Mrs. V. If any accounting income remains, it may be either accumulated or distributed to Miss V or to W College, a qualifying charitable organization. In addition, the executor of the estate may invade corpus for the benefit of Mrs. V, Miss V, or the college. In the current year, the accounting income of the estate is $35,000 and DNI (before any charitable contributions) is $25,000. The executor pays $30,000 to Mrs. V and $10,000 each to Miss V and to the college. The DNI is to be allocated among the beneficiaries as follows:

(1) First-tier distributions

To Mrs. V	$20,000 DNI
To Miss V	–0–
To charity	–0–

Remaining DNI = $0

($25,000 DNI – first-tier distributions $20,000
      – charitable contributions $10,000)

The charitable contribution does not reduce the exposure to DNI for the first-tier distribution, but it is applied in computing the DNI that remains for the second-tier distributions.

(2) Second-tier distributions

To Mrs. V	$0 DNI
To Miss V	$0 DNI

◆

Separate Share Rule. For the sole purpose of determining the amount of DNI for a complex trust with more than one beneficiary, the substantially separate and independent shares of different beneficiaries in the trust are treated as *separate trusts*.[32] The following example illustrates the need for this special rule.

─────────────── EXAMPLE 33 ───────────────

Under the terms of the trust instrument, the trustee has the discretion to distribute or accumulate income on behalf of G and H (in equal shares). The trustee also has the power to invade corpus for the benefit of either beneficiary to the extent of that beneficiary's one-half interest in the trust. For the current year, the DNI of the trust is $10,000. Of this amount, $5,000 is distributed to G, and $5,000 is accumulated on behalf of H. In addition, the trustee pays $20,000 from corpus to G. Without the separate share rule, G would be taxed on $10,000 (the full amount of the DNI). With the separate share rule, G is taxed on only $5,000 (his share of the DNI) and receives the $20,000 corpus distribution tax-free. The trust is taxed on H's $5,000 share of the DNI that is accumulated. ◆

The separate share rule is designed to prevent the inequity that results if the corpus payments are treated under the regular rules applicable to second-tier beneficiaries. In Example 33, the effect of the separate share rule is to produce a two-trust result: one trust for G and one for H, each with DNI of $5,000.

Character of Income

Consistent with the modified conduit principle of Subchapter J, various classes of income (e.g., dividends, passive or portfolio gain and loss, AMT references,

───────────────

31. Reg. § 1.662(a)–2(e) (Ex.2).   **32.** Reg. § 1.663(c)–1(a).

and tax-exempt interest) retain the same character for the beneficiaries that they had when they were received by the entity. If there are multiple beneficiaries *and* if all of the DNI is distributed, a problem arises with respect to the allocation of the various classes of income among the beneficiaries.

Distributions are treated as consisting of the same proportion of each class of the items that enter into the computation of DNI as the total of each class bears to the total DNI of the entity. This allocation does not apply, however, if local law or the governing instrument specifically allocates different classes of income to different beneficiaries.[33]

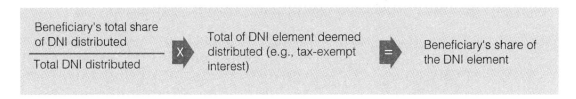

If the entity distributes only a part of its DNI, the amount of a specific class of DNI that is deemed distributed must first be determined.

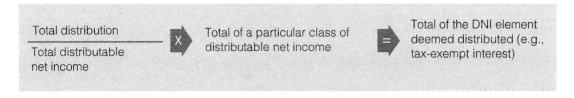

─────────────── EXAMPLE 34 ───────────────

The B Trust has DNI of $40,000, including the following: $10,000 of taxable interest, $10,000 of tax-exempt interest, and $20,000 of passive activity income. The trustee distributes, at her discretion, $8,000 to M and $12,000 to N, both noncharitable beneficiaries. The amount of each element of DNI that is deemed distributed is determined as follows:

Beneficiary	Amount Received	Income Type	
M	$ 8,000	Taxable interest [($8,000 distribution/$40,000 total DNI) × $10,000 taxable interest in DNI]	$2,000
		Exempt interest (8/40 × $10,000)	$2,000
		Passsive income (8/40 × $20,000)	$4,000
N	$12,000	Taxable interest [($12,000 distribution/$40,000 total DNI) × $10,000 taxable interest in DNI]	$3,000
		Exempt interest (12/40 × $10,000)	$3,000
		Passive income (12/40 × $20,000)	$6,000

─────────────── EXAMPLE 35 ───────────────

Continue with the facts of Example 34. The character of the income that flows through to beneficiaries M and N is effective for all other Federal income tax purposes. For

33. Reg. § 1.662(b)–1.

instance, the $2,000 exempt interest allocated to M is used in computing the taxable portion of any Social Security benefits M receives. If this exempt interest relates to nonessential activities of the issuing agency, M includes a $2,000 alternative minimum tax preference on the current-year return.

The $4,000 passive activity income that is allocated to M is available for offset against passive losses that M has incurred from limited partnerships and rental activities for the year. Similarly, the $3,000 taxable interest income allocated to N can be used to increase the amount of investment interest expense deductible by N in the year of the flow-through. The interest is treated as portfolio income to the same extent as that received directly by the taxpayer. ◆

Special Allocations.   Under certain circumstances, the parties may modify the character-of-income allocation method set forth above. A modification is permitted only to the extent that the allocation is required in the trust instrument and only to the extent that it has an economic effect independent of the income tax consequences of the allocation.[34]

EXAMPLE 36

Return to the facts in Example 34. Assume that the beneficiaries are elderly individuals who have pooled their investment portfolios to avail themselves of the trustee's professional asset management skills. Suppose the trustee has the discretion to allocate different classes of income to different beneficiaries and that she designates all of N's $12,000 distribution as being from the tax-exempt income. Such a designation *would not be recognized* for tax purposes, and the allocation method of Example 34 must be used.

Suppose, however, that the trust instrument stipulated that N was to receive all of the income from tax-exempt securities because only N contributed the exempt securities to trust corpus. Under this provision, the $10,000 of the nontaxable interest is paid to N. This allocation *is recognized*, and $10,000 of N's distribution is tax-exempt. ◆

Losses in the Termination Year

The ordinary net operating and capital losses of a trust or estate do not flow through to the entity's beneficiaries, as would such losses from a partnership or an S corporation. However, in the year in which an entity terminates its existence, the beneficiaries do receive a direct benefit from the loss carryovers of the trust or estate.[35]

Net operating losses and net capital losses are subject to the same carryover rules that otherwise apply to an individual. Consequently, net operating losses can be carried back 3 years and then carried forward 15 years while net capital losses can be carried forward only, and for an indefinite period of time. However, if the entity incurs a net operating loss in the last year of its existence, the excess of deductions over the entity's gross income is allowed to the beneficiaries (it will flow through to them directly). The net loss is available as a deduction *from* adjusted gross income in the beneficiary's tax year with or within which the entity's tax year ends. The amount allowed is in proportion to the relative amount of corpus assets that each beneficiary receives upon the termination of the entity and is subject to the 2-percent-of-AGI floor.

Any carryovers of the entity's other losses flow through to the beneficiaries in the year of termination in proportion to the relative amount of corpus assets that each beneficiary receives. The character of the loss carryover is retained by the

---

34. Reg. § 1.652(b)–2(b). This is similar to the § 704(b) requirement for partnerships.

35. Reg. §§ 1.642(h)–1 and –2.

beneficiary, except that a carryover of a net capital loss to a corporate beneficiary is always treated as short term. Beneficiaries who are individuals use these carryovers as deductions *for* adjusted gross income.

––––––––––––––––––––––––––––––– EXAMPLE 37 –––––––––––––––––––––––––––––––

The E Estate terminates on December 31, 1992. It had used a fiscal year ending July 31. For the termination year, the estate incurred a $15,000 net operating loss. In addition, the estate had an unused net operating loss carryover of $23,000 from the year ending July 31, 1989, and an unused net long-term capital loss carryover of $10,000 from the year ending July 31, 1991. D receives $60,000 of corpus upon termination, and Z Corporation receives the remaining $40,000. D and Z are calendar year taxpayers.

D can claim an itemized deduction of $9,000 [($60,000/$100,000) × $15,000] for the entity's net operating loss in the year of termination. This deduction is subject to the 2%-of-AGI floor on miscellaneous itemized deductions. In addition, D can claim a $13,800 deduction *for* adjusted gross income in 1992 (60% × $23,000) for the other net operating loss carryover of E, and she can use $6,000 of E's net long-term capital loss carryover with her other 1992 capital transactions.

Z receives ordinary business deductions in 1992 for E's net operating losses: $6,000 for the loss in the year of termination and $9,200 for the carryover from fiscal 1989. Moreover, Z can use the $4,000 carryover of E's net capital losses to offset against its other 1992 capital transactions, although the loss must be treated as short term.

With respect to both D and Z, the losses flow through in addition to the other tax consequences of E that they received on July 31, 1992 (at the close of the usual tax year of the entity), under Subchapter J. Moreover, if the beneficiaries do not use the operating loss carryforward in calendar year 1992, the short year of termination will exhaust one of the years of the usual carryover period (e.g., D can use E's net operating loss carryover for 15 tax years). ◆

BUILT-IN GAINS TAX COMPUTATION FOR TRUSTS
◆

Congress enacted § 644 to discourage taxpayers from transferring appreciated property to a trust, which would then sell the property. The purpose of the transfer was to shift the gain on the appreciation of the asset to the trust's lower tax rates. This provision, which can be described as the original "built-in gains tax," imposes a special liability on trusts that sell or exchange property at a gain within two years after it is transferred to the trust. The special tax applies only if the fair market value of the property at the time of the initial transfer exceeded the adjusted basis of the property immediately after the transfer (after any applicable adjustment for gift taxes paid).

The tax imposed by § 644 is equal to the amount of additional income tax that the transferor would have been required to pay (including any alternative minimum tax) had the gain been included in his or her gross income for the tax year of the sale. The tax applies only to an amount known as *includible gain*, which is the lesser of the following:

- The gain recognized by the trust on the sale or exchange of any property.
- The unrealized gain on the property at the time of the initial transfer to the trust. [36]

In several situations, the tax will not be imposed. For instance, the tax does not apply to the sale or exchange of property (1) acquired by the trust from a decedent or (2) that occurs after the death of the transferor.

––––––––––––––––––––––––––

36. §§ 644(b) and (d)(2).

————————————— EXAMPLE 38 —————————————

On July 1, 1992, G created an irrevocable trust with a transfer of 200 shares of Z Corporation stock. At the time of the transfer, the stock was a capital asset to G. It had a fair market value of $30,000; its basis to the trust was $20,000. On October 1, 1992, the trust sold the stock for $35,000. Section 644 applies because the stock was sold at a gain within two years after its transfer to the trust *and* its fair market value at the time of the initial transfer exceeded its adjusted basis to the trust immediately after the transfer. The trust must report a § 644 gain of $10,000 [the lesser of its gain recognized on the sale ($15,000) or the appreciation in the hands of G]. The $10,000 is taxed to the trust at G's 1992 income tax rates on a net capital gain. The remaining $5,000 of the gain is taxed to the trust under the usual Subchapter J rules. ◆

————————————— EXAMPLE 39 —————————————

Assume the same facts as in Example 38, except that the fair market value of the stock at the time of the transfer was $18,000. Section 644 will not apply to the subsequent sale by the trust since the fair market value of the stock on that date was less than the stock's basis to the trust. ◆

THE THROWBACK RULE
◆

To understand the purpose and rationale of the throwback provision, consider the general nature of taxation of trusts and their beneficiaries. The usual rule is that the income from trust assets is taxed to the trust itself or to the beneficiary, but not to both. Generally, a beneficiary is not taxed on any distributions in excess of the trust's distributable net income. Thus, trustees of complex trusts might be tempted to arrange distributions in a way that results in minimal income tax consequences to all of the parties involved. For instance, if the trust is subject to a lower marginal income tax rate than its beneficiaries, income could be accumulated at the trust level for several years before being distributed to the beneficiaries. Thus, the income that would be taxed to the beneficiaries in the year of distribution would be limited by the trust's DNI for that year. Further tax savings could be achieved by using multiple trusts. This device spreads the income during the accumulation period over more than one taxpaying entity and avoids the graduated tax rates.

To discourage the use of these tax minimization schemes, a *throwback rule* was added to the Code. Under the rule, a beneficiary's tax on a distribution of income accumulated by a trust in a prior year will approximate the increased tax that the beneficiary would have owed for that prior year if the income had been distributed in the year that it was earned by the trust. The tax as computed, however, is levied for the actual year of the distribution. The purpose of the throwback rule is to place the beneficiaries of complex trusts in the same nominal tax position they would have been in if they had received the distributions during the years in which the trust was accumulating the income.

A detailed description of the application of the throwback rule is beyond the scope of this text. However, some basic terms and concepts are presented in the following sections to familiarize the reader with the applicable statutory provisions and their purpose.

Basic Terms

The definitions of two terms are important in understanding the throwback rule: (1) *undistributed net income* and (2) *accumulation distribution*. Undistributed net income is defined in § 665(a) as the distributable net income of the trust reduced by first-tier and second-tier distributions and the income tax paid by the trust on any remaining undistributed DNI. Accumulation distribution is defined in

§ 665(b) as any distribution from a trust for a tax year in excess of the trust's DNI for the year.

The throwback rule applies only to complex trusts that do not distribute all current accounting income. The rule does not apply to estates or simple trusts. Moreover, the rule applies only in years when the complex trust makes an accumulation distribution. When this occurs, the distribution is "thrown back" to the earliest year in which the trust had any undistributed net income. The accumulation is thrown back to succeeding years sequentially until it is used up. Accumulation distributions may not be thrown back to years before 1969. Distributions of accounting income, capital gains that are allocable to corpus, and income accumulated before the beneficiary attained age 21 are not subject to the throwback procedure.[37]

Under the throwback rule, the beneficiary may be required to pay an additional income tax in the year of the accumulation distribution. The tax due for this year will be the sum of the tax on the beneficiary's taxable income (without the accumulation distribution) and the tax on the accumulation distribution.[38] The trust may not claim a refund (i.e., if the tax that it paid exceeded that which would have been paid by the beneficiary).[39]

EXAMPLE 40

In 1983, the T Trust was subject to a marginal Federal income tax rate of 19%, while its sole income beneficiary, O, was subject to a 33% marginal rate. O encouraged the trustee to accumulate $7,500 of the trust's DNI, which totaled $10,000. The balance of the DNI was distributed to O. If T's tax on this accumulation, after credits, is $1,200, T's undistributed net income for 1983 is $6,300 [$10,000 (DNI) − $2,500 (distribution of income) − $1,200 (taxes paid)].

By 1992, O's marginal rate had fallen to 15%, and O encouraged the trustee to distribute to him, in that year, an amount equal to the 1992 DNI of $12,000 plus the $6,300 that had been accumulated, after taxes, in 1983. When the trustee complied with O's wish, she made an accumulation distribution of $6,300.

The tax on the accumulation distribution is levied upon O in 1992. O's additional tax will approximate what O would have paid in 1983 had the trust distributed its full DNI in that year (the $6,300 accumulation distribution will be subject to approximately a 33% tax rate and not to O's prevailing 15% rate). ◆

Although no interest or penalty is due with the tax on the accumulation distribution, the additional tax discourages the manipulation of trust distributions for tax avoidance purposes.

Tax on Accumulation Distribution

The tax imposed on the accumulation distribution is determined by adding a fraction of the distribution to the beneficiary's taxable income for three of the five immediately preceding tax years (excluding both the year of the highest taxable income and the year of the lowest taxable income).[40] The fraction is calculated by dividing the accumulation distribution by the number of years in which it was earned by the trust. Once the additional tax on the adjusted taxable income for the three years is determined, the beneficiary must calculate an average additional tax for each of the three years. The tax is multiplied by the number of years over which the trust earned the income. The result is the tax on the accumulation distribution.

---

37. §§ 665(b) and (e).
38. § 668(a).
39. § 666(e).

40. § 667(b). For further details on calculating the tax, see the instructions to Schedule J (Form 1041).

The Sixty-Five-Day Rule

Amounts paid or credited to the beneficiaries in the first 65 days of the trust's tax year may be treated as paid on the last day of the preceding taxable year.[41] This provision offers the trustee some flexibility in timing distributions so that trust accumulations, and the resulting throwback procedures, can be avoided.

GRANTOR TRUSTS
◆

A series of special statutory provisions contained in §§ 671 through 679 of the Code applies when the grantor of the trust retains beneficial enjoyment or substantial control over the trust property or income. In that event, the grantor is taxed on the trust income, and the trust is disregarded for income tax purposes. The person who is taxed on the income is allowed to claim, on his or her own return, any deductions or credits attributable to the income.

These special rules concern only the Federal income tax treatment of the trust. Another part of the Code deals with the Federal estate and gift tax consequences of such incomplete transfers (refer to Chapters 17 and 18). The operation of these different Federal taxes is not completely correlated. Clearly, however, such taxes restrict the grantor's ability to redirect the income recognized from trust corpus to the trust or its beneficiaries.

Reversionary Trusts

For many years, taxpayers have used the so-called Clifford trust vehicle as a way to assign gross income to other taxpayers who presumably are subject to lower income tax rates. Although the surest way to assign income to other parties is to make a permanent transfer of the underlying assets to the transferee, few potential donors are willing to part with a sizable portion of the income-producing assets that they often have spent a lifetime accumulating.

The Code had allowed the use of the Clifford trust, under which the donor can part with the income-producing asset for only a temporary time period (defined in § 673 as greater than 10 years). During this period, any gross income earned is taxed to the income beneficiary of the trust (at the donee's lower rates). Upon the termination of the trust or upon the death of the income beneficiary, the trust assets revert to the grantor. Accordingly, the Clifford trust has offered a means by which income can be temporarily assigned to those in more favorable tax brackets without permanently transferring the income-producing property.

The Tax Reform Act (TRA) of 1986 severely limited the future use of a Clifford trust as an effective income-shifting device. The change repealed the § 673 exception from grantor trust status for trusts whose donor holds a reversionary interest that satisfies the time period.

Creation of a reversionary trust is subject to the Federal gift tax. If the grantor dies before the income interest expires, the present value of the reversionary interest is included in his or her gross estate under § 2033; thus, a Federal estate tax could also result.

Powers Retained by the Grantor

Sections 674 through 677 contain other restrictions on the extent of the powers over the trust that the grantor can retain without incurring grantor trust status.

---

41. See Reg. § 1.663(b)–2 for the manner and timing of the election.

If any of these provisions is violated, the income of the trust is taxed to the grantor, and the usual Subchapter J rules do not apply to the trust.

Section 674 provides that the grantor is taxed on the income if he or she retains (1) the beneficial enjoyment of corpus or (2) the power to dispose of the trust income without the approval or consent of any adverse party. An adverse party is any person having a substantial beneficial interest in the trust who would be affected adversely by the exercise or nonexercise of the power the grantor possesses over the trust assets.[42]

Section 674(b) contains several exceptions to this rule and lists a number of important powers that will *not* cause income to be taxed to the grantor:

- To apply the income toward the support of the grantor's dependents (except to the extent that it actually is applied for this purpose).[43]
- To allocate trust income or corpus among charitable beneficiaries.
- To invade corpus on behalf of a designated beneficiary.
- To postpone temporarily the payment of income to a beneficiary.
- To withhold income from a beneficiary during his or her minority or disability.
- To allocate receipts and disbursements between income and corpus.

The retention by the grantor or a nonadverse party of certain administrative powers over the trust will cause the income to be taxed to the grantor. Such powers include those to deal with trust income or corpus for less than full and

CONCEPT SUMMARY 19–1
PRINCIPLES OF FIDUCIARY TAXATION

1. Estates and trusts are temporary entities created to locate, maintain, and distribute assets and to satisfy liabilities according to the wishes of the decedent or grantor as expressed in the will or trust document.

2. Generally, the estate or trust acts as a conduit of the taxable income that it receives. To the extent that the income is distributed by the entity, it is taxed to the beneficiary. Taxable income retained by the entity is taxed to the entity itself.

3. The entity's accounting income must first be determined. Accounting conventions that are stated in the controlling document or, lacking such provisions, in state law allocate specific items of receipt and expenditure either to income or to corpus. Income beneficiaries typically receive payments from the entity that are equal to the accounting income.

4. The taxable income of the entity is computed using the scheme in Figure 19–3. The entity usually recognizes income in respect of a decedent. Deductions for fiduciary's fees and for charitable contributions may be reduced if the entity received any tax-exempt income during the year. Cost recovery deductions are assigned proportionately to the recipients of accounting income. Upon election, realized gain or loss on assets that properly are distributed in kind can be recognized by the entity.

5. A distribution deduction, computationally derived from distributable net income (DNI), is allowed to the entity. DNI is the maximum amount on which entity beneficiaries can be taxed. Moreover, the constitution of DNI is preserved for the recipients of the distributions.

6. Additional taxes are levied under Subchapter J to discourage (1) the transfer of appreciated assets to a lower-bracket estate or trust that quickly disposes of the assets in a taxable exchange, (2) the accumulation of trust income at the lower marginal tax rates of the entity followed by a subsequent distribution of the accumulation to beneficiaries, and (3) the retention of excessive administrative powers by the grantor of a trust when the gross income is taxed to a lower-bracket beneficiary.

---

42. §§ 672(a) and (b). See Reg. § 1.672(a)–1 for examples of adverse party situations.

43. § 677(b).

adequate consideration and to borrow from the trust without providing adequate interest or security.[44]

The grantor of a trust is taxed on the trust's income if he or she (or a nonadverse party) possesses the power to revoke the trust.[45] In addition, a grantor is taxed on all or part of the income of a trust when, without the consent of any adverse party, the income is or, at the discretion of the grantor or a nonadverse party (or both), may be

- Distributed to the grantor or the grantor's spouse.
- Held or accumulated for future distribution to the grantor or the grantor's spouse.
- Applied to the payment of premiums on insurance policies on the life of the grantor or the grantor's spouse.[46]

Moreover, trust income accumulated for the benefit of someone whom the grantor is *legally obligated* to support is taxed to the grantor but only to the extent that it is actually applied for that purpose.[47]

─────────────── EXAMPLE 41 ───────────────

F creates an irrevocable trust for his children with a transfer of income-producing property and an insurance policy on the life of M, F's wife. During the year, the trustee uses $3,000 of the trust income to pay the premiums on the policy covering M's life. F is taxed on $3,000 of the trust's income. ◆

─────────────── EXAMPLE 42 ───────────────

M creates an irrevocable accumulation trust. Her son, S, is the life beneficiary, and the remainder goes to any grandchildren. During the year, the trust income of $8,000 is applied as follows: $5,000 toward S's college tuition and other related educational expenses and $3,000 accumulated on S's behalf. If, under state law, M has an obligation to support S and this obligation includes providing a college education, M is taxed on the $5,000 that is so applied. ◆

Many of the tax planning possibilities for estates and trusts have been discussed in Chapter 18. However, several specific tax planning possibilities are available to help minimize the income tax effects on estates and trusts and their beneficiaries. These possibilities are discussed in the following sections in connection with postmortem tax planning and the use of trusts as income tax savings devices. Several examples illustrating the interrelationship among income, gift, and estate taxes are included.

**TAX PLANNING
CONSIDERATIONS**

Income Tax Planning for Estates

As a separate taxable entity, an estate can select its own tax year and accounting methods. The executor of an estate should consider selecting a fiscal year because this will determine when beneficiaries must include income distributions from the estate in their own tax returns. Beneficiaries must include the income for their tax year with or within which the estate's tax year ends. Proper selection of the estate's tax year can result in a smoothing out of income and a reduction of the income taxes for all parties involved.

44. See Reg. § 1.675–1(b) for a further discussion of this matter.
45. § 676.
46. § 677(a).
47. § 677(b).

Caution should be taken in determining when the estate is to be terminated. If a fiscal year has been selected for the estate, a bunching of income to the beneficiaries can occur in the year in which the estate is closed. Prolonging the termination of an estate can be effective income tax planning, but the IRS carefully examines the purpose of keeping the estate open. Since the unused losses of an estate will pass through to the beneficiaries, the estate should be closed when the beneficiaries can enjoy the maximum tax benefit of the losses.

The timing and amounts of income distributions to the beneficiaries also present important tax planning opportunities. If the executor can make discretionary income distributions, he or she should evaluate the relative marginal income tax rates of the estate and its beneficiaries. By timing the distributions properly, the overall income tax liability can be minimized. Care should be taken, however, to time the distributions in light of the estate's distributable net income.

EXAMPLE 43

For several years before his death on March 7, D had entered into annual deferred compensation agreements with his employer. These agreements collectively called for the payment of $200,000 six months after D's retirement or death. To provide a maximum 12-month period within which to generate deductions to offset this large item of income in respect of a decedent, the executor or administrator of the estate should elect a fiscal year ending August 31. The election is made simply by filing the estate's first tax return for the short period of March 7 to August 31. ◆

EXAMPLE 44

B, the sole beneficiary of an estate, is a calendar year cash basis taxpayer. If the estate elects a fiscal year ending January 31, all distributions during the period of February 1 to December 31, 1991, will be reported on B's tax return for calendar year 1992 (due April 15, 1993). Thus, any income taxes that result from a $50,000 distribution made by the estate on February 20, 1991, are deferred until April 15, 1993. ◆

EXAMPLE 45

Assume the same facts as in Example 44. If the estate is closed on December 15, 1992, the distributable net income for both the fiscal year ending January 31, 1992, and the final tax year ending December 15, 1992, is included in B's tax return for the calendar year 1992. To avoid the effect of this bunching of income, the estate should not be closed until calendar year 1993. ◆

EXAMPLE 46

Assume the same facts as in Example 45, except that the estate has a substantial net operating loss for the period February 1 to December 15, 1992. If B is subject to a high income tax rate for calendar year 1992, the estate should be closed in that year so that the excess deductions are passed through to its beneficiary. However, if B anticipates being in a higher tax bracket in 1993, the termination of the estate should be postponed. ◆

EXAMPLE 47

Review Examples 28 through 30 carefully. Note, for instance, the flexibility that is available to the executor or administrator in timing the second-tier distributions of income and corpus of the estate. To illustrate, if Dr. L is subject to a high tax rate, distributions to this beneficiary should be minimized except in years when DNI is low. In this manner, Dr. L's exposure to gross income from the distributions can be controlled so that most of the distributions that Dr. L receives will be free of income tax. ◆

In general, those beneficiaries who are subject to high income tax rates should be made beneficiaries of second-tier (but not IRD) distributions of the estate.

Most likely, these individuals will have less need for an additional steady stream of (taxable) income while their income tax savings can be relatively large. Moreover, a special allocation of tax-favored types of income and expenses should be considered. For example, tax-exempt income can be directed more easily to beneficiaries in higher income tax brackets.

Income Tax Planning with Trusts

The great variety of trusts provides the grantor, trustee, and beneficiaries with excellent opportunities for tax planning. Many of the same tax planning opportunities available to the executor of an estate are available to the trustee. For instance, the distributions from a trust are taxable to the trust's beneficiaries to the extent of the trust's distributable net income. If income distributions are discretionary, the trustee can time the distributions to minimize the income tax consequences to all parties.

Remember that the throwback rule applies to complex trusts. Consequently, the benefit from the timing of distributions may be more limited than it is for estates. Indeed, improper timing could result in a greater nominal tax than if the distributions had been made annually. The trustee of a complex trust should thus consider the *65-day rule.* The rule permits the trust to treat distributions made within 65 days of the end of its tax year as if they were made on the last day of that year. Proper use of this provision can help the trustee in both minimizing the overall income tax consequences and avoiding the throwback rule for the beneficiaries.

Tax Year and Payment Planning. TRA of 1986 reduced the benefits that arise from the traditional, tax-motivated use of trusts and estates by revising the rate schedules applicable to these entities. Specifically, accumulation within the entity of the otherwise taxable income of the trust or estate may no longer produce the same magnitude of tax benefits that were available under a more progressive tax rate schedule. The lower marginal rates of the trust are exhausted more quickly. They are also very similar to those that apply to the potential beneficiaries and may be higher for a trust. As a result, the absolute and relative values of income shifting are reduced.

Two other observations are pertinent with respect to the compressed marginal tax rate schedule that applies to fiduciaries:

1. The effective value of the entity's 15 percent bracket is only about $600 for 1992. Thus, the costs alone of planning to utilize this rate may exceed the eventual tax savings of using the entity. For example, establishing a number of different trusts to take advantage of the graduated rates may no longer produce a significant benefit. The costs associated with establishing and administering the trusts may exceed the per trust tax savings.
2. The timing of trust distributions themselves continue to be important to the planner. The rate differences between the entity and its beneficiaries might be as much as 16 percentage points at any one time (31% for the beneficiary − 15% for the entity). Consequently, it still may be a good idea to provide for a sprinkling power in the trust instrument.

Distributions of In-Kind Property

The ability of the trustee or executor to elect to recognize the realized gain or loss relative to a distributed noncash asset allows the gain or loss to be allocated to the optimal taxpayer.

─────────────── EXAMPLE 48 ───────────────

The Y Estate distributed some stock, basis of $40,000 and fair market value of $50,000, to beneficiary L. Y is subject to a 15% marginal income tax rate, and L is subject to a 31% marginal rate. The executor of Y should elect that the entity recognize the related $10,000 realized gain, thereby subjecting the gain to Y's lower marginal tax rate and reducing L's future capital gain income. ◆

─────────────── EXAMPLE 49 ───────────────

Assume the same facts as in Example 48, except that Y's basis in the stock is $56,000. The executor of Y should *not* elect that the entity recognize the related $6,000 loss, thereby shifting the $56,000 basis and the potential loss to L's higher marginal tax rates. ◆

Deductibility of Fiduciary Expenses

Many § 2053 and § 2054 estate tax deductions and losses may be claimed either as estate tax deductions or as income tax deductions of the estate on the fiduciary return (Form 1041), but the taxpayer must make an informed choice.[48] In such a case, the deduction for income tax purposes is not allowed unless the estate tax deduction is waived. These deductions can be apportioned between the two returns.

An expense deductible for estate tax purposes may not qualify as an income tax deduction. Interest expense incurred to carry tax-exempt bonds is disallowed for income tax purposes. If this expense is not claimed under § 2053 for estate tax purposes, it is completely lost.

Medical expenses incurred by the decedent but unpaid at the time of the decedent's death are covered by a special rule. If paid out of the estate during a one-year period beginning with the day after death, the expenses may be claimed as an income tax deduction in the year incurred or as an estate tax deduction, but not both.[49] The choice is between the decedent's appropriate Form 1040 and the estate's estate tax return. The expenses may be divided in any way between Form 1040 and the estate tax return.

Brokerage commissions and other expenses relating to the sale of estate property can be offset against the sale price of the property in computing taxable income of the estate or can be deducted on the estate tax return. The taxpayer chooses whether to claim these expenses as income tax or estate tax deductions.

─────────────── EXAMPLE 50 ───────────────

The executor of D's estate is paid a proper commission (authorized under local law and approved by the probate court) of $10,000 from estate assets. The commission expense can be claimed on the estate tax return (Form 706) or on the income tax return of the estate (Form 1041) or split in any way between the two returns. However, no more than $10,000 can be claimed. ◆

─────────────── EXAMPLE 51 ───────────────

The executor of D's estate pays $5,000 in burial expenses (authorized under local law and approved by the probate court) from estate assets. The $5,000 expense should be claimed on the estate tax return as it is not deductible for income tax purposes. ◆

─────────────── EXAMPLE 52 ───────────────

At the time of his death, D (a cash basis taxpayer) owed a local bank $10,000 on a business loan due in several months. On the due date of the loan, the executor of D's estate pays the bank $10,800, which represents the principal amount of the loan ($10,000), interest accrued before D's death ($700), and interest accrued after D's death ($100). The amount deductible on the estate tax return (Form 706) is $10,700. Because

─────────────────────────────

48. § 642(g) and Reg. § 20.2053–1(d).   **49.** § 213(c).

the interest accrued before D's death is an expense in respect of a decedent, it can also be claimed as an income tax deduction by whoever pays it. Since the interest was paid by the estate, it should be claimed on the estate's income tax return (Form 1041) along with the $100 of interest expense accrued after D's death. ◆

PROBLEM MATERIALS

DISCUSSION QUESTIONS

1. What is the importance of the accounting income of a trust or estate in determining its taxable income?

2. When must an income tax return be filed for an estate? A trust? When could the fiduciary be held liable for the income tax due from an estate or trust?

3. What is the general scheme of the income taxation of trusts and estates? How does the modified conduit principle relate to this general approach?

4. Under what circumstances can an estate or trust be taxed on a distribution of property to a beneficiary?

5. What is income in respect of a decedent? What are the tax consequences to a recipient of income in respect of a decedent?

6. How must an estate or trust treat its deductions for cost recovery? How does this treatment differ from the deductibility of administrative expenses or losses for estate tax purposes?

7. What happens to the net operating loss carryovers of an estate or trust if the entity is terminated before the deductions can be taken? How can this provision be used as a tax planning opportunity?

8. Discuss the income tax treatment of charitable contributions made by an estate or trust. How does this treatment differ from the requirements for charitable contribution deductions of individual taxpayers?

9. What is distributable net income? Why is this amount significant in the income taxation of estates and trusts and their beneficiaries?

10. Distinguish between first-tier and second-tier distributions from estates and complex trusts. Discuss the tax consequences to the beneficiaries receiving such distributions.

11. How must the various classes of income be allocated among multiple beneficiaries of an estate or trust?

12. What is the purpose of the built-in gains tax imposed on trusts by § 644? When is the tax applicable? How can it be avoided?

13. What is the throwback rule? When is it applicable? Why was such a rule adopted?

14. What is the 65-day rule, and under what circumstances can it be useful as a tax planning opportunity?

15. Under what circumstances may the grantor be taxed on all or part of the income of a trust? How might state law help to avoid taxation to the grantor?

16. Discuss the tax planning opportunities presented by the ability of an estate to select a noncalendar tax year.

PROBLEMS

17. The O Trust has generated $40,000 in depreciation deductions for the year. Its accounting income is $21,000. In computing this amount, pursuant to the trust document, depreciation was allocated to corpus. Accounting income was distributed at the trustee's discretion: $15,000 to Mr. H and $6,000 to Ms. J.

   a. Compute the depreciation deductions that H, J, and O may claim.
   b. Same as (a), except that depreciation was allocated to income.

    c. Same as (a), except that the trustee distributed $6,000 each to H and to J and retained the remaining accounting income.

    d. Same as (a), except that O is an estate (and not a trust).

18. The P Trust operates a welding business. Its current-year cost recovery deductions properly amounted to $35,000. P's accounting income was $150,000, of which $80,000 was distributed to first-tier beneficiary Q, $60,000 was distributed to second-tier beneficiary R, and $10,000 was accumulated by the trustee. R also received a $15,000 corpus distribution. P's distributable net income was $52,000. Identify the treatment of P's cost recovery deductions.

19. The J Trust incurred the following items in 1992 using the cash basis of tax accounting:

Taxable interest income	$40,000
Tax-exempt interest income	35,000
Long-term capital gains	25,000
Fiduciary's fees	10,000

The trustee distributed $12,000 to a qualified charitable organization in 1993, designating the payment as from 1992 accounting income. The trust instrument allocates capital gains and fiduciary fees to income.

    a. Compute J's 1992 charitable contribution deduction.

    b. Assume the same facts as in (a), except that capital gains are allocated to corpus.

    c. Assume the same facts as in (b), except that the trust instrument directs that all charitable contributions be paid from J's taxable interest income.

20. The W Estate collected a $10,000 bonus from W's employer after W's death under a qualified deferred compensation plan. State income taxes due on the payment were $1,000, and the executrix paid this amount during the first tax year of the estate. During this year, she also paid $1,200 for investment management fees relative to W's portfolio, which represented the bulk of the estate's assets. How is the estate's taxable income for the year affected by these transactions?

21. Determine the tax effects of the indicated losses for the Y Estate for both tax years. Y holds a variety of investment assets, which it received from the decedent, Mrs. Y. The estate's sole income and remainder beneficiary is Y, Jr.

Tax Year	Loss Generated
1993 (first tax year)	Taxable income ($300)
	Capital loss ($15,000)
1994 (final tax year)	Taxable income ($1,000)

22. The W Trust distributes $40,000 cash and a plot of land, basis of $15,000 and fair market value of $22,000, to its sole beneficiary, X. W's current-year distributable net income is $95,000. For each of the following independent cases, indicate (1) the amount of W's DNI deemed to be distributed to X, (2) W's distribution deduction for the land, and (3) X's basis in the land:

    a. No § 643(e) election is made.

    b. The trustee makes a § 643(e) election.

    c. Same as (a), except that W's basis in the land is $26,000.

    d. Same as (b), except that W's basis in the land is $26,000.

23. Assume the same facts as in Problem 22, except that W is an estate.

24. The X Trust had the following income for the year:

Dividends from a domestic corporation	$150,000
Taxable interest	75,000
Long-term capital gains	15,000
Tax-exempt interest	60,000
Total	$300,000

The trustee's fee for the year amounted to $20,000.

    a. How much of the trustee's fee is allocable to tax-exempt income?

    b. Can that amount be deducted by the trust?

25. Complete the following chart, indicating the comparative attributes of the typical trust and estate by answering yes/no or explaining the differences between the entities where appropriate.

Attribute	Estate	Trust
Separate income tax entity		
Controlling document		
Termination date is determinable from controlling document		
Legal owner of assets under fiduciary's control		
Document identifies both income and remainder beneficiaries		
Throwback rules apply		
Separate share rules apply		
Generally must use calendar tax year		

26. The LMN Trust is a simple trust that correctly uses the calendar year for tax purposes. Its three income beneficiaries (L, M, and N) are entitled to the trust's annual accounting income in shares of one-third each. For the current calendar year, the trust has ordinary income of $60,000, a long-term capital gain of $18,000 (allocable to corpus), and a trustee commission expense of $6,000 (allocable to corpus).

    a. How much income is each beneficiary entitled to receive?

    b. What is the trust's distributable net income?

    c. What is the trust's taxable income?

    d. How much will be taxed to each of the beneficiaries?

27. Assume the same facts as in Problem 26, except that the trust instrument allocates the capital gain to income.

    a. How much income is each beneficiary entitled to receive?

    b. What is the trust's distributable net income?

    c. What is the trust's taxable income?

    d. How much will be taxed to each of the beneficiaries?

28. Complete the chart below, indicating trust accounting income for each of the alternatives. For this purpose, use the following information:

Interest income, taxable	$60,000
Interest income, tax-exempt	10,000
Interest income, tax-exempt but AMT preference	20,000
Long-term capital gain	15,000
Trustee fee	8,000

Trust Agreement Provisions	Trust Accounting Income
Fees and capital gains allocable to corpus	
Capital gains allocable to corpus, one-half of fees allocable to income	
Capital gains allocable to income, silent concerning allocation of fees	
Fees and exempt income allocable to corpus, silent concerning allocation of capital gain/loss	

29. A trust is required to distribute $20,000 annually to its two income beneficiaries, A and B, in shares of 75% and 25%, respectively. If trust income is not sufficient to pay these amounts, the trustee is empowered to invade corpus to the extent necessary. During the current year, the trust has distributable net income of $12,000, and the trustee distributes $15,000 to A and $5,000 to B.

    a. How much of the $15,000 distributed to A is included in her gross income?
    b. How much of the $5,000 distributed to B is included in his gross income?
    c. Are these distributions first-tier or second-tier distributions?

30. Under the terms of the trust instrument, the trustee has discretion to distribute or accumulate income on behalf of W, S, and D in equal shares. The trustee also is empowered to invade corpus for the benefit of any of the beneficiaries to the extent of their respective one-third interest in the trust. In the current year, the trust has distributable net income of $48,000. Of this amount, $16,000 is distributed to W and $10,000 is distributed to S. The remaining $6,000 of S's share of DNI and D's entire $16,000 share are accumulated by the trust. Additionally, the trustee distributes $20,000 from corpus to W.

    a. How much income is taxed to W?
    b. To S?
    c. To D?
    d. To the trust?

31. During the current year, an estate has $60,000 of distributable net income composed of $30,000 in dividends, $20,000 in taxable interest, and $10,000 in tax-exempt interest. The trust's two noncharitable income beneficiaries, S and T, receive $20,000 each.

    a. How much of each class of income will be deemed to have been distributed?
    b. How much of each class of income is deemed to have been distributed to S? To T?

32. The trustee of the M Trust is empowered to distribute accounting income and corpus to the trust's equal beneficiaries, Mr. P and Dr. G. In the current year, the trust incurs the following:

Taxable interest income	$40,000
Tax-exempt interest income	60,000
Long-term capital gains—allocable to corpus	35,000
Fiduciary's fees—allocable to corpus	12,000

The trustee distributed $25,000 to P and $28,000 to G.

    a. What is M's trust accounting income?
    b. What is M's distributable net income?
    c. What is the amount of taxable income recognized by P from these activities? By G? By M?

33. Ms. D contributes 100 shares of Y Corporation stock to an irrevocable trust on July 1, 1991, income to her son, remainder to her grandson in 12 years. D's basis in the stock is $40,000; the fair market value of the stock at the date of the transfer is $300,000. On June 20, 1993, the trust sells the stock on the open market for $175,000. What is the amount of gain or loss recognized by the trust on the sale? How is the tax computed, and who is liable for it? How would the recognized gain have been treated had the stock been sold for $415,000?

34. Describe a tax planning situation where a tax adviser would properly make each of the following independent suggestions:

    a. A grantor trust be created.
    b. Trust accumulations be made, even though the tax on accumulation distributions will be levied on the eventual payments.
    c. A transfer of an appreciated asset to a trust be made, even though the § 644 tax will be levied on the entity.

35. In each of the following independent cases, determine whether the grantor of the trust is taxed on the entity's income:

    a. G transfers property in trust, income payable to W (his wife) for life, remainder to his grandson. G's son is designated as the trustee.

    b. G transfers income-producing assets and a life insurance policy to a trust, life estate to his children, remainder to his grandchildren. The policy is on the life of G's wife, and the trustee (an independent trust company) is instructed to pay the premiums with income from the income-producing assets. The trust is designated as the beneficiary of the policy.

    c. G transfers property in trust. The trust income is payable to G's grandchildren, as W (G's wife) sees fit. W and an independent trust company are designated as trustees.

    d. G transfers property in trust, income payable to W (G's ex-wife), remainder to G or his estate upon W's death. The transfer was made in satisfaction of G's alimony obligation to W. An independent trust company is designated as the trustee.

36. B is one of the income beneficiaries of the L Estate, which is subject to a 40% marginal Federal estate tax rate, a 30% marginal Federal income tax rate, and a 5% marginal state income tax rate. This year, B received $20,000 of sales commissions that were earned and payable to L (cash basis) at her death. Compute B's § 691(c) deduction for the current year, given the following financial data:

Sales commissions receivable	$40,000
Deferred gain on installment sale, three payments remaining	70,000

37. S is the sole income beneficiary of a well-endowed trust. She believes that the trustee should be accumulating the trust accounting income that is being earned so that S can receive it after she retires and, presumably, when she will be subject to a lower income tax rate. S currently is subject to a 40% combined state and Federal rate. Describe how the throwback rule inhibits the trustee from manipulating the timing of income distributions in this manner for each of the following independent cases:

    a. S is age 45.
    b. S is age 15.
    c. The trust allocates capital gains to income
    d. The entity is the estate of S's father.

38. W wishes to transfer some of the income from his investment portfolio to his daughter, age 6. W wants the trust to be able to accumulate income on his daughter's behalf and to meet any excessive expenses associated with the daughter's prep school and private college education. Furthermore, W wants the trust to protect his daughter against his own premature death without increasing his Federal gross estate. Thus, W provides the trustee with the powers to purchase insurance on his life and to meet tuition, fee, and book expenses of his daughter's education. The trust is created in 1987. A whole life insurance policy with five annual premium payments is purchased during that year. The trustee spends $10,000 for the daughter's college expenses in 1999 (but in no other year). W dies in 2005. Has the trust been tax-effective?

39. Complete the following chart, indicating the comparative attributes of the typical simple and complex trust by answering yes/no or explaining the differences between the entities where appropriate.

Attribute	Simple Trust	Complex Trust
Separate share rules apply	_____	_____
Throwback rules apply	_____	_____
Trust could incur its own tax liability for the year	_____	_____
Trust generally distributes all of DNI	_____	_____
Trust can deduct its charitable contributions in the year of, or the year after, payment	_____	_____
Trust could claim a foreign tax credit	_____	_____
Maximum 1991 tax rate on net long-term capital gains = 28%	_____	_____

Attribute	Simple Trust	Complex Trust
AMT preferences and adjustments flow through to beneficiaries ratably		
Amount of personal exemption		

COMPREHENSIVE TAX RETURN PROBLEM

Prepare the 1991 Fiduciary Income Tax Return (Form 1041) for the Kane Trust. In addition, determine the amount and character of the income and expense items that each beneficiary must report for 1991 and prepare a Schedule K–1 for Harold Kane.

The 1991 activities of the trust include the following:

Passive loss, activity acquired 1988 (rental of inherited farmland held for speculation; trust owned nondepreciable land only)	$400,000
Dividend income, all domestic stocks	550,000
Taxable interest income	100,000
Tax-exempt interest income	50,000
Net long-term capital gain	265,000
Fiduciary's fees	120,000

Under the terms of the trust instrument, depreciation, net capital gains and losses, and one-half of the fiduciary's fees are allocable to corpus. The trustee is required to distribute $150,000 to Harold every year. In 1991, the trustee distributed $200,000 to Harold and $85,000 to Patricia Kane. No other distributions were made.

The trust was created on December 14, 1953. It is not subject to any recapture taxes, nor does it have any tax credits. None of its income was derived under a personal services contract. The trust has no economic interest in any foreign trust.

The trustee, Wisconsin State National Bank, is located at 3100 East Wisconsin Avenue, Milwaukee, WI 53201. Its employer identification number is 84–7602487.

Harold lives at 9880 East North Avenue, Shorewood, WI 53211. His identification number is 498–01–8058.

Patricia lives at 6772 East Oklahoma Avenue, St. Francis, WI 53204. Her identification number is 499–02–6531.

RESEARCH PROBLEMS

RESEARCH PROBLEM 1   Thanks to a recent speech that you gave to the Kiwanis Club, Y has been convinced of the tax-saving opportunities that are presented by the creation of trusts. He recognizes that a great deal of income can be shifted to the marginal income tax rates that apply to his three children, and he is willing to give up as much control over the trust corpus assets as is necessary to avoid a grantor trust classification.

Y is very enthusiastic about trusts—so much so that he instructs you to place $30,000 into each of 12 trusts for each of his children. These 36 trusts would be administered separately by you, as trustee, but they would differ only in the assets that are used to fund them and in the termination date specified in the trust instrument. Specifically, one of each child's 12 trusts is scheduled to terminate annually, beginning in 15 years. Can the proliferation of multiple trusts, given the same grantor, the same trustee, the same beneficiaries, but different corpus assets and termination dates, be accepted under prevailing tax law?

RESEARCH PROBLEM 2   Your client has come to you for some advice regarding gifts of property. She has just learned that she must undergo major surgery, and she would like to make certain gifts before entering the hospital. On your earlier advice, she had established a plan of lifetime giving for four prior years. Consider each of the following assets that she is considering to use as gifts to family and friends. In doing so, evaluate the income tax consequences of having such property pass through her estate to the designated legatee.

    a. She plans to give a cottage to her son to fulfill a promise made many years ago. She has owned the cottage for the past 15 years and has a basis in it of $30,000 (fair market value of $20,000).

b. Since she has $100,000 of long-term capital losses that she has been carrying forward for the past few years, she is considering making a gift of $200,000 in installment notes to her daughter. Her basis in the notes is $100,000, and the notes' current fair market value is $190,000.

c. She has promised to make a special cash bequest of $25,000 to her grandson in her will. However, she does not anticipate having that much cash immediately available after her death. She requests your advice concerning the income tax consequences to the estate if the cash bequest is settled with some other property.

APPENDIX

TAX RATES AND TABLES

1991
Tax Rate
Schedules

Schedule X—Use if your filing status is **Single**

If taxable income is: Over—	But not over—	The tax is:	of the amount over—
$0	$20,350	.... 15%	$0
20,350	49,300	$3,052.50 + 28%	20,350
49,300	....	11,158.50 + 31%	49,300

Schedule Y-1—Use if your filing status is **Married filing jointly or Qualifying widow(er)**

If taxable income is: Over—	But not over—	The tax is:	of the amount over—
$0	$34,000	.... 15%	$0
34,000	82,150	$5,100.00 + 28%	34,000
82,150	....	18,582.00 + 31%	82,150

Schedule Y-2—Use if your filing status is **Married filing separately**

If taxable income is: Over—	But not over—	The tax is:	of the amount over—
$0	$17,000	.... 15%	$0
17,000	41,075	$2,550.00 + 28%	17,000
41,075	....	9,291.00 + 31%	41,075

Schedule Z—Use if your filing status is **Head of household**

If taxable income is: Over—	But not over—	The tax is:	of the amount over—
$0	$27,300	.... 15%	$0
27,300	70,450	$4,095.00 + 28%	27,300
70,450	....	16,177.00 + 31%	70,450

1992 Tax Rate Schedules

Single—Schedule X

If taxable income is: Over—	But not over—	The tax is:	of the amount over—
$0	$21,450	..........15%	$0
21,450	51,900	$3,217.50 + 28%	21,450
51,900	....	11,743.50 + 31%	51,900

Head of household—Schedule Z

If taxable income is: Over—	But not over—	The tax is:	of the amount over—
$0	$28,750	..........15%	$0
28,750	74,150	$4,312.50 + 28%	28,750
74,150	....	17,024.50 + 31%	74,150

Married filing jointly or Qualifying widow(er)—Schedule Y-1

If taxable income is: Over—	But not over—	The tax is:	of the amount over—
$0	$35,800	..........15%	$0
35,800	86,500	$5,370.00 + 28%	35,800
86,500	....	19,566.00 + 31%	86,500

Married filing separately—Schedule Y-2

If taxable income is: Over—	But not over—	The tax is:	of the amount over—
$0	$17,900	..........15%	$0
17,900	43,250	$2,685.00 + 28%	17,900
43,250	....	9,783.00 + 31%	43,250

INCOME TAX RATES — ESTATES AND TRUSTS

Tax Year 1991

Taxable Income		The tax is:	
Over—	But not over—		Of the amount over—
$ 0	$ 3,450	15%	$ 0
3,450	10,350	$ 517.50 + 28%	3,450
10,350	———	2,449.50 + 31%	10,350

Tax Year 1992

Taxable Income		The tax is:	
Over—	But not over—		Of the amount over—
$ 0	$ 3,600	15%	$ 0
3,600	10,900	$ 540 + 28%	3,600
10,900		2,584 + 31%	10,900

INCOME TAX RATES — CORPORATIONS

Taxable Income	Rate
$ 1–$ 50,000	15%
50,001 — 75,000	25
over $ 75,000	34
$100,000 —$335,000	5*

*Additional tax, "phases out" the lower marginal brackets.

Unified Transfer Tax Rates

For Gifts Made and For Deaths After 1976 and Before 1982

If the amount with respect to which the tentative tax to be computed is:	The tentative tax is:
Not over $10,000	18 percent of such amount.
Over $10,000 but not over $20,000	$1,800, plus 20 percent of the excess of such amount over $10,000.
Over $20,000 but not over $40,000	$3,800, plus 22 percent of the excess of such amount over $20,000.
Over $40,000 but not over $60,000	$8,200, plus 24 percent of the excess of such amount over $40,000.
Over $60,000 but not over $80,000	$13,000, plus 26 percent of the excess of such amount over $60,000.
Over $80,000 but not over $100,000	$18,200, plus 28 percent of the excess of such amount over $80,000.
Over $100,000 but not over $150,000	$23,800, plus 30 percent of the excess of such amount over $100,000.
Over $150,000 but not over $250,000	$38,800, plus 32 percent of the excess of such amount over $150,000.
Over $250,000 but not over $500,000	$70,800, plus 34 percent of the excess of such amount over $250,000.
Over $500,000 but not over $750,000	$155,800, plus 37 percent of the excess of such amount over $500,000.
Over $750,000 but not over $1,000,000	$248,300, plus 39 percent of the excess of such amount over $750,000.
Over $1,000,000 but not over $1,250,000	$345,800, plus 41 percent of the excess of such amount over $1,000,000.
Over $1,250,000 but not over $1,500,000	$448,300, plus 43 percent of the excess of such amount over $1,250,000.
Over $1,500,000 but not over $2,000,000	$555,800, plus 45 percent of the excess of such amount over $1,500,000.
Over $2,000,000 but not over $2,500,000	$780,800, plus 49 percent of the excess of such amount over $2,000,000.
Over $2,500,000 but not over $3,000,000	$1,025,800, plus 53 percent of the excess of such amount over $2,500,000.
Over $3,000,000 but not over $3,500,000	$1,290,800, plus 57 percent of the excess of such amount over $3,000,000.
Over $3,500,000 but not over $4,000,000	$1,575,800, plus 61 percent of the excess of such amount over $3,500,000.
Over $4,000,000 but not over $4,500,000	$1,880,800, plus 65 percent of the excess of such amount over $4,000,000.
Over $4,500,000 but not over $5,000,000	$2,205,800, plus 69 percent of the excess of such amount over $4,500,000.
Over $5,000,000	$2,550,800, plus 70 percent of the excess of such amount over $5,000,000.

UNIFIED TRANSFER TAX RATES

For Gifts Made and For Deaths in 1982

If the amount with respect to which the tentative tax to be computed is:	The tentative tax is:
Not over $10,000	18 percent of such amount.
Over $10,000 but not over $20,000	$1,800, plus 20 percent of the excess of such amount over $10,000.
Over $20,000 but not over $40,000	$3,800, plus 22 percent of the excess of such amount over $20,000.
Over $40,000 but not over $60,000	$8,200, plus 24 percent of the excess of such amount over $40,000.
Over $60,000 but not over $80,000	$13,000, plus 26 percent of the excess of such amount over $60,000.
Over $80,000 but not over $100,000	$18,200, plus 28 percent of the excess of such amount over $80,000.
Over $100,000 but not over $150,000	$23,800, plus 30 percent of the excess of such amount over $100,000.
Over $150,000 but not over $250,000	$38,800, plus 32 percent of the excess of such amount over $150,000.
Over $250,000 but not over $500,000	$70,800, plus 34 percent of the excess of such amount over $250,000.
Over $500,000 but not over $750,000	$155,800, plus 37 percent of the excess of such amount over $500,000.
Over $750,000 but not over $1,000,000	$248,300, plus 39 percent of the excess of such amount over $750,000.
Over $1,000,000 but not over $1,250,000	$345,800, plus 41 percent of the excess of such amount over $1,000,000.
Over $1,250,000 but not over $1,500,000	$448,300, plus 43 percent of the excess of such amount over $1,250,000.
Over $1,500,000 but not over $2,000,000	$555,800, plus 45 percent of the excess of such amount over $1,500,000.
Over $2,000,000 but not over $2,500,000	$780,800, plus 49 percent of the excess of such amount over $2,000,000.
Over $2,500,000 but not over $3,000,000	$1,025,800, plus 53 percent of the excess of such amount over $2,500,000.
Over $3,000,000 but not over $3,500,000	$1,290,800, plus 57 percent of the excess of such amount over $3,000,000.
Over $3,500,000 but not over $4,000,000	$1,575,800, plus 61 percent of the excess of such amount over $3,500,000.
Over $4,000,000	$1,880,800, plus 65 percent of the excess of such amount over $4,000,000.

UNIFIED TRANSFER TAX RATES

For Gifts Made and For Deaths in 1983

If the amount with respect to which the tentative tax to be computed is:	The tentative tax is:
Not over $10,000	18 percent of such amount.
Over $10,000 but not over $20,000	$1,800, plus 20 percent of the excess of such amount over $10,000.
Over $20,000 but not over $40,000	$3,800, plus 22 percent of the excess of such amount over $20,000.
Over $40,000 but not over $60,000	$8,200, plus 24 percent of the excess of such amount over $40,000.
Over $60,000 but not over $80,000	$13,000, plus 26 percent of the excess of such amount over $60,000.
Over $80,000 but not over $100,000	$18,200, plus 28 percent of the excess of such amount over $80,000.
Over $100,000 but not over $150,000	$23,800, plus 30 percent of the excess of such amount over $100,000.
Over $150,000 but not over $250,000	$38,800, plus 32 percent of the excess of such amount over $150,000.
Over $250,000 but not over $500,000	$70,800, plus 34 percent of the excess of such amount over $250,000.
Over $500,000 but not over $750,000	$155,800, plus 37 percent of the excess of such amount over $500,000.
Over $750,000 but not over $1,000,000	$248,300, plus 39 percent of the excess of such amount over $750,000.
Over $1,000,000 but not over $1,250,000	$345,800, plus 41 percent of the excess of such amount over $1,000,000.
Over $1,250,000 but not over $1,500,000	$448,300, plus 43 percent of the excess of such amount over $1,250,000.
Over $1,500,000 but not over $2,000,000	$555,800, plus 45 percent of the excess of such amount over $1,500,000.
Over $2,000,000 but not over $2,500,000	$780,800, plus 49 percent of the excess of such amount over $2,000,000.
Over $2,500,000 but not over $3,000,000	$1,025,800, plus 53 percent of the excess of such amount over $2,500,000.
Over $3,000,000 but not over $3,500,000	$1,290,800, plus 57 percent of the excess of such amount over $3,000,000.
Over $3,500,000	$1,575,800, plus 60 percent of the excess of such amount over $3,500,000.

UNIFIED TRANSFER TAX RATES

For Gifts Made and For Deaths after 1983 and before 1993

If the amount with respect to which the tentative tax to be computed is:	The tentative tax is:
Not over $10,000	18 percent of such amount.
Over $10,000 but not over $20,000	$1,800, plus 20 percent of the excess of such amount over $10,000.
Over $20,000 but not over $40,000	$3,800, plus 22 percent of the excess of such amount over $20,000.
Over $40,000 but not over $60,000	$8,200, plus 24 percent of the excess of such amount over $40,000.
Over $60,000 but not over $80,000	$13,000, plus 26 percent of the excess of such amount over $60,000.
Over $80,000 but not over $100,000	$18,200, plus 28 percent of the excess of such amount over $80,000.
Over $100,000 but not over $150,000	$23,800, plus 30 percent of the excess of such amount over $100,000.
Over $150,000 but not over $250,000	$38,800, plus 32 percent of the excess of such amount over $150,000.
Over $250,000 but not over $500,000	$70,800, plus 34 percent of the excess of such amount over $250,000.
Over $500,000 but not over $750,000	$155,800, plus 37 percent of the excess of such amount over $500,000.
Over $750,000 but not over $1,000,000	$248,300, plus 39 percent of the excess of such amount over $750,000.
Over $1,000,000 but not over $1,250,000	$345,800, plus 41 percent of the excess of such amount over $1,000,000.
Over $1,250,000 but not over $1,500,000	$448,300, plus 43 percent of the excess of such amount over $1,250,000.
Over $1,500,000 but not over $2,000,000	$555,800, plus 45 percent of the excess of such amount over $1,500,000.
Over $2,000,000 but not over $2,500,000	$780,800, plus 49 percent of the excess of such amount over $2,000,000.
Over $2,500,000 but not over $3,000,000	$1,025,800, plus 53 percent of the excess of such amount over $2,500,000.
Over $3,000,000*	$1,290,800, plus 55 percent of the excess of such amount over $3,000,000.

* For large taxable transfers (generally in excess of $10 million) there is a phase-out of the graduated rates and the unified tax credit.

UNIFIED TRANSFER TAX RATES

For Gifts Made and For Deaths After 1992

If the amount with respect to which the tentative tax to be computed is: | **The tentative tax is:**

Not over $10,000 .... 18 percent of such amount.

Over $10,000 but not over $20,000......... $1,800, plus 20 percent of the excess of such amount over $10,000.

Over $20,000 but not over $40,000......... $3,800, plus 22 percent of the excess of such amount over $20,000.

Over $40,000 but not over $60,000......... $8,200, plus 24 percent of the excess of such amount over $40,000.

Over $60,000 but not over $80,000......... $13,000, plus 26 percent of the excess of such amount over $60,000.

Over $80,000 but not over $100,000 .... $18,200, plus 28 percent of the excess of such amount over $80,000.

Over $100,000 but not over $150,000 .... $23,800, plus 30 percent of the excess of such amount over $100,000.

Over $150,000 but not over $250,000 .... $38,800, plus 32 percent of the excess of such amount over $150,000.

Over $250,000 but not over $500,000 .... $70,800, plus 34 percent of the excess of such amount over $250,000.

Over $500,000 but not over $750,000 .... $155,800, plus 37 percent of the excess of such amount over $500,000.

Over $750,000 but not over $1,000,000 ..... $248,300, plus 39 percent of the excess of such amount over $750,000.

Over $1,000,000 but not over $1,250,000 ... $345,800, plus 41 percent of the excess of such amount over $1,000,000.

Over $1,250,000 but not over $1,500,000 ... $448,300, plus 43 percent of the excess of such amount over $1,250,000.

Over $1,500,000 but not over $2,000,000 ... $555,800, plus 45 percent of the excess of such amount over $1,500,000.

Over $2,000,000 but not over $2,500,000 ... $780,800, plus 49 percent of the excess of such amount over $2,000,000.

Over $2,500,000 .... $1,025,800, plus 50 percent of the excess of such amount over $2,500,000.

Estate Tax Rates (before 1977)

(A) Taxable estate equal to or more than	(B) Taxable estate less than	(C) Tax on amount in column (A)	(D) Rate of tax on excess over amount in column (A) (Percentage)
0	$ 5,000	0	3
$ 5,000	10,000	$ 150	7
10,000	20,000	500	11
20,000	30,000	1,600	14
30,000	40,000	3,000	18
40,000	50,000	4,800	22
50,000	60,000	7,000	25
60,000	100,000	9,500	28
100,000	250,000	20,700	30
250,000	500,000	65,700	32
500,000	750,000	145,700	35
750,000	1,000,000	233,200	37
1,000,000	1,250,000	325,700	39
1,250,000	1,500,000	423,200	42
1,500,000	2,000,000	528,200	45
2,000,000	2,500,000	753,200	49
2,500,000	3,000,000	998,200	53
3,000,000	3,500,000	1,263,200	56
3,500,000	4,000,000	1,543,200	59
4,000,000	5,000,000	1,838,200	63
5,000,000	6,000,000	2,468,200	67
6,000,000	7,000,000	3,138,200	70
7,000,000	8,000,000	3,838,200	73
8,000,000	10,000,000	4,568,200	76
10,000,000		6,088,200	77

GIFT TAX RATES (BEFORE 1977)

(A) Amount of taxable gifts equal to or more than	(B) Amount of taxable gifts less than	(C) Tax on amount in column (A)	(D) Rate of tax on excess over amount in column (A) (Percentage)
0	$ 5,000	0	2¼
$ 5,000	10,000	$ 112.50	5¼
10,000	20,000	375.00	8¼
20,000	30,000	1,200.00	10½
30,000	40,000	2,250.00	13½
40,000	50,000	3,600.00	16½
50,000	60,000	5,250.00	18¾
60,000	100,000	7,125.00	21
100,000	250,000	15,525.00	22½
250,000	500,000	49,275.00	24
500,000	750,000	109,275.00	26¼
750,000	1,000,000	174,900.00	27¾
1,000,000	1,250,000	244,275.00	29¼
1,250,000	1,500,000	317,400.00	31½
1,500,000	2,000,000	396,150.00	33¾
2,000,000	2,500,000	564,900.00	36¾
2,500,000	3,000,000	748,650.00	39¾
3,000,000	3,500,000	947,400.00	42
3,500,000	4,000,000	1,157,400.00	44¼
4,000,000	5,000,000	1,378,650.00	47¼
5,000,000	6,000,000	1,851,150.00	50¼
6,000,000	7,000,000	2,353,650.00	52½
7,000,000	8,000,000	2,878,650.00	54¾
8,000,000	10,000,000	3,426,150.00	57
10,000,000		4,566,150.00	57¾

TABLE FOR COMPUTATION OF MAXIMUM CREDIT FOR STATE DEATH TAXES

(A) Adjusted Taxable Estate* equal to or more than	(B) Adjusted Taxable Estate* less than	(C) Credit on amount in column (A)	(D) Rate of credit on excess over amount in column (A) (Percentage)
0	$ 40,000	0	None
$ 40,000	90,000	0	0.8
90,000	140,000	$ 400	1.6
140,000	240,000	1,200	2.4
240,000	440,000	3,600	3.2
440,000	640,000	10,000	4.0
640,000	840,000	18,000	4.8
840,000	1,040,000	27,600	5.6
1,040,000	1,540,000	38,800	6.4
1,540,000	2,040,000	70,800	7.2
2,040,000	2,540,000	106,800	8.0
2,540,000	3,040,000	146,800	8.8
3,040,000	3,540,000	190,800	9.6
3,540,000	4,040,000	238,800	10.4
4,040,000	5,040,000	290,800	11.2
5,040,000	6,040,000	402,800	12.0
6,040,000	7,040,000	522,800	12.8
7,040,000	8,040,000	650,800	13.6
8,040,000	9,040,000	786,800	14.4
9,040,000	10,040,000	930,800	15.2
10,040,000		1,082,800	16.0

* Adjusted Taxable Estate = Taxable Estate − $60,000

VALUATION TABLES (After November 30, 1983, and before May 1, 1989)

Table A–10% Single Life, Unisex, Showing the Present Worth of an Annuity, of a Life Estate, and of a Remainder Interest [Reg. §§ 20.2031–7(f) and 25.2512–5(f)]

1 Age	2 Annuity	3 Life Estate	4 Remainder	1 Age	2 Annuity	3 Life Estate	4 Remainder
0	9.7188	0.97188	0.02812	55	8.0046	.80046	.19954
1	9.8988	.98988	.01012	56	7.9006	.79006	.20994
2	9.9017	.99017	.00983	57	7.7931	.77931	.22069
3	9.9008	.99008	.00992	58	7.6822	.76822	.23178
4	9.8981	.98981	.01019	59	7.5675	.75675	.24325
5	9.8938	.98938	.01062	60	7.4491	.74491	.25509
6	9.8884	.98884	.01116	61	7.3267	.73267	.26733
7	9.8822	.98822	.01178	62	7.2002	.72002	.27998
8	9.8748	.98748	.01252	63	7.0696	.70696	.29304
9	9.8663	.98663	.01337	64	6.9352	.69352	.30648
10	9.8565	.98565	.01435	65	6.7970	.67970	.32030
11	9.8453	.98453	.01547	66	6.6551	.66551	.33449
12	9.8329	.98329	.01671	67	6.5098	.65098	.34902
13	9.8198	.98198	.01802	68	6.3610	.63610	.36390
14	9.8066	.98066	.01934	69	6.2086	.62086	.37914
15	9.7937	.97937	.02063	70	6.0522	.60522	.39478
16	9.7815	.97815	.02185	71	5.8914	.58914	.41086
17	9.7700	.97700	.02300	72	5.7261	.57261	.42739
18	9.7590	.97590	.02410	73	5.5571	.55571	.44429
19	9.7480	.97480	.02520	74	5.3862	.53862	.46138
20	9.7365	.97365	.02635	75	5.2149	.52149	.47851
21	9.7245	.97245	.02755	76	5.0441	.50441	.49559
22	9.7120	.97120	.02880	77	4.8742	.48742	.51258
23	9.6986	.96986	.03014	78	4.7049	.47049	.52951
24	9.6841	.96841	.03159	79	4.5357	.45357	.54643
25	9.6678	.96678	.03322	80	4.3659	.43659	.56341
26	9.6495	.96495	.03505	81	4.1967	.41967	.58033
27	9.6290	.96290	.03710	82	4.0295	.40295	.59705
28	9.6062	.96062	.03938	83	3.8642	.38642	.61358
29	9.5813	.95813	.04187	84	3.6998	.36998	.63002
30	9.5543	.95543	.04457	85	3.5359	.35359	.64641
31	9.5254	.95254	.04746	86	3.3764	.33764	.66236
32	9.4942	.94942	.05058	87	3.2262	.32262	.67738
33	9.4608	.94608	.05392	88	3.0859	.30859	.69141
34	9.4250	.94250	.05750	89	2.9526	.29526	.70474
35	9.3868	.93868	.06132	90	2.8221	.28221	.71779
36	9.3460	.93460	.06540	91	2.6955	.26955	.73045
37	9.3026	.93026	.06974	92	2.5771	.25771	.74229
38	9.2567	.92567	.07433	93	2.4692	.24692	.75308
39	9.2083	.92083	.07917	94	2.3728	.23728	.76272
40	9.1571	.91571	.08429	95	2.2887	.22887	.77113
41	9.1030	.91030	.08970	96	2.2181	.22181	.77819
42	9.0457	.90457	.09543	97	2.1550	.21550	.78450
43	8.9855	.89855	.10145	98	2.1000	.21000	.79000
44	8.9221	.89221	.10779	99	2.0486	.20486	.79514
45	8.8558	.88558	.11442	100	1.9975	.19975	.80025
46	8.7863	.87863	.12137	101	1.9532	.19532	.80468
47	8.7137	.87137	.12863	102	1.9054	.19054	.80946
48	8.6374	.86374	.13626	103	1.8437	.18437	.81563
49	8.5578	.85578	.14422	104	1.7856	.17856	.82144
50	8.4743	.84743	.15257	105	1.6962	.16962	.83038
51	8.3874	.83874	.16126	106	1.5488	.15488	.84512
52	8.2969	.82969	.17031	107	1.3409	.13409	.86591
53	8.2028	.82028	.17972	108	1.0068	.10068	.89932
54	8.1054	.81054	.18946	109	.4545	.04545	.95455

VALUATION TABLES (After November 30, 1983, and before May 1, 1989, *continued*)

Table B–10% Table Showing the Present Worth of an Annuity for a Fixed Term of Years, of an Income Interest for a Fixed Term of Years, and of a Remainder Interest, Postponed for a Fixed Term of Years [Reg. §§ 20.2031–7(f) and 25.2512–5(f)]

1 Number of Years	2 Annuity	3 Term Certain	4 Remainder	1 Number of Years	2 Annuity	3 Term Certain	4 Remainder
1	.9091	.090909	.909091	31	9.4790	.947901	.052099
2	1.7355	.173554	.826446	32	9.5264	.952638	.047362
3	2.4869	.248685	.751315	33	9.5694	.956943	.043057
4	3.1699	.316987	.683013	34	9.6086	.960857	.039143
5	3.7908	.379079	.620921	35	9.6442	.964416	.035584
6	4.3553	.435526	.564474	36	9.6765	.967651	.032349
7	4.8684	.486842	.513158	37	9.7059	.970592	.029408
8	5.3349	.533493	.466507	38	9.7327	.973265	.026735
9	5.7590	.575902	.424098	39	9.7570	.975696	.024304
10	6.1446	.614457	.385543	40	9.7791	.977905	.022095
11	6.4951	.649506	.350494	41	9.7991	.979914	.020086
12	6.8137	.681369	.318631	42	9.8174	.981740	.018260
13	7.1034	.710336	.289664	43	9.8340	.983400	.016600
14	7.3667	.736669	.263331	44	9.8491	.984909	.015091
15	7.6061	.760608	.239392	45	9.8628	.986281	.013719
16	7.8237	.782371	.217629	46	9.8753	.987528	.012472
17	8.0216	.802155	.197845	47	9.8866	.988662	.011338
18	8.2014	.820141	.179859	48	9.8969	.989693	.010307
19	8.3649	.836492	.163508	49	9.9063	.990630	.009370
20	8.5136	.851356	.148644	50	9.9148	.991481	.008519
21	8.6487	.864869	.135131	51	9.9226	.992256	.007744
22	8.7715	.877154	.122846	52	9.9296	.992960	.007040
23	8.8832	.888322	.111678	53	9.9360	.993600	.006400
24	8.9847	.898474	.101526	54	9.9418	.994182	.005818
25	9.0770	.907704	.092296	55	9.9471	.994711	.005289
26	9.1609	.916095	.083905	56	9.9519	.995191	.004809
27	9.2372	.923722	.076278	57	9.9563	.995629	.004371
28	9.3066	.930657	.069343	58	9.9603	.996026	.003974
29	9.3696	.936961	.063039	59	9.9639	.996387	.003613
30	9.4269	.942691	.057309	60	9.9672	.996716	.003284

VALUATION TABLES (After April 30, 1989)

Table R(1) Single Life Remainder Factors Interest Rate

Age	9.4%	9.6%	9.8%	10.0%	10.2%	10.4%	10.6%	10.8%
0	.02027	.01989	.01954	.01922	.01891	.01864	.01838	.01814
1	.00910	.00871	.00834	.00801	.00770	.00741	.00715	.00690
2	.00899	.00857	.00819	.00784	.00751	.00721	.00693	.00667
3	.00916	.00872	.00832	.00795	.00760	.00728	.00699	.00671
4	.00951	.00904	.00862	.00822	.00786	.00752	.00721	.00692
5	.00998	.00949	.00904	.00862	.00824	.00788	.00755	.00724
6	.01054	.01002	.00954	.00910	.00869	.00832	.00796	.00764
7	.01118	.01064	.01013	.00966	.00923	.00883	.00846	.00811
8	.01192	.01134	.01081	.01031	.00986	.00943	.00904	.00867
9	.01276	.01216	.01159	.01107	.01059	.01014	.00972	.00933
10	.01372	.01308	.01249	.01194	.01142	.01095	.01051	.01009
11	.01481	.01414	.01351	.01293	.01239	.01189	.01142	.01098
12	.01601	.01529	.01463	.01402	.01345	.01292	.01243	.01197
13	.01726	.01651	.01582	.01517	.01457	.01401	.01349	.01300
14	.01850	.01771	.01698	.01630	.01567	.01508	.01453	.01402
15	.01969	.01886	.01810	.01738	.01672	.01610	.01552	.01498
16	.02084	.01997	.01917	.01842	.01772	.01707	.01646	.01589
17	.02194	.02103	.02018	.01940	.01866	.01798	.01734	.01674
18	.02302	.02207	.02118	.02035	.01958	.01886	.01818	.01755
19	.02412	.02312	.02218	.02131	.02050	.01974	.01903	.01837
20	.02524	.02419	.02320	.02229	.02143	.02064	.01989	.01919
21	.02638	.02527	.02424	.02328	.02238	.02154	.02075	.02002
22	.02757	.02640	.02532	.02430	.02336	.02247	.02164	.02087
23	.02881	.02759	.02644	.02538	.02438	.02345	.02257	.02176
24	.03016	.02888	.02767	.02655	.02550	.02451	.02359	.02273
25	.03164	.03029	.02902	.02784	.02673	.02569	.02472	.02381
26	.03328	.03186	.03052	.02928	.02811	.02701	.02598	.02502
27	.03509	.03360	.03219	.03088	.02965	.02849	.02741	.02639
28	.03708	.03550	.03403	.03264	.03134	.03013	.02898	.02790
29	.03925	.03760	.03604	.03458	.03322	.03193	.03072	.02958
30	.04162	.03988	.03825	.03671	.03527	.03391	.03264	.03143
31	.04421	.04238	.04067	.03905	.03753	.03610	.03475	.03348
32	.04702	.04510	.04329	.04160	.04000	.03849	.03707	.03573
33	.05007	.04806	.04616	.04438	.04269	.04111	.03961	.03819
34	.05336	.05125	.04926	.04738	.04561	.04394	.04236	.04087
35	.05690	.05469	.05260	.05063	.04877	.04702	.04535	.04378
36	.06068	.05836	.05617	.05411	.05215	.05031	.04856	.04690
37	.06470	.06228	.05999	.05783	.05578	.05384	.05200	.05025
38	.06899	.06646	.06407	.06180	.05965	.05761	.05568	.05385
39	.07356	.07092	.06841	.06604	.06379	.06165	.05962	.05770
40	.07841	.07565	.07303	.07055	.06820	.06596	.06383	.06181
41	.08355	.08067	.07794	.07535	.07288	.07054	.06832	.06620
42	.08896	.08596	.08312	.08041	.07784	.07539	.07306	.07085
43	.09466	.09154	.08858	.08576	.08308	.08052	.07808	.07576
44	.10067	.09743	.09434	.09141	.08861	.08594	.08340	.08097
45	.10699	.10362	.10042	.09736	.09445	.09167	.08901	.08648
46	.11362	.11013	.10680	.10363	.10060	.09770	.09494	.09230
47	.12059	.11697	.11352	.11022	.10707	.10406	.10119	.09843
48	.12787	.12412	.12055	.11713	.11386	.11073	.10774	.10487
49	.13544	.13157	.12787	.12433	.12094	.11769	.11458	.11160
50	.14331	.13931	.13548	.13182	.12831	.12494	.12172	.11862
51	.15150	.14737	.14342	.13963	.13600	.13251	.12917	.12596
52	.16004	.15579	.15172	.14780	.14405	.14044	.13698	.13366
53	.16896	.16458	.16038	.15635	.15247	.14875	.14517	.14172
54	.17822	.17372	.16940	.16524	.16124	.15740	.15370	.15014

VALUATION TABLES (After April 30, 1989, *continued*)

Table R(1) Single Life Remainder Factors Interest Rate

Age	9.4%	9.6%	9.8%	10.0%	10.2%	10.4%	10.6%	10.8%
55	.18785	.18322	.17878	.17450	.17039	.16642	.16261	.15893
56	.19785	.19310	.18854	.18414	.17991	.17583	.17190	.16811
57	.20824	.20338	.19870	.19419	.18984	.18564	.18160	.17769
58	.21904	.21407	.20927	.20464	.20018	.19587	.19172	.18770
59	.23023	.22515	.22024	.21551	.21093	.20652	.20225	.19812
60	.24178	.23659	.23158	.22674	.22206	.21753	.21316	.20893
61	.25366	.24837	.24325	.23831	.23353	.22890	.22442	.22009
62	.26584	.26045	.25524	.25020	.24532	.24059	.23601	.23158
63	.27832	.27284	.26754	.26240	.25742	.25260	.24793	.24339
64	.29111	.28555	.28016	.27493	.26987	.26495	.26019	.25556
65	.30429	.29865	.29317	.28787	.28271	.27771	.27286	.26815
66	.31788	.31217	.30663	.30124	.29601	.29093	.28600	.28120
67	.33191	.32614	.32053	.31508	.30978	.30462	.29961	.29474
68	.34638	.34055	.33488	.32937	.32401	.31879	.31371	.30877
69	.36120	.35533	.34961	.34405	.33863	.33336	.32822	.32322
70	.37634	.37043	.36468	.35907	.35361	.34829	.34310	.33804
71	.39171	.38578	.38000	.37436	.36886	.36349	.35826	.35316
72	.40733	.40138	.39558	.38991	.38439	.37899	.37373	.36858
73	.42321	.41725	.41143	.40575	.40021	.39479	.38950	.38432
74	.43940	.43345	.42763	.42195	.41639	.41096	.40565	.40046
75	.45598	.45004	.44424	.43856	.43301	.42758	.42226	.41706
76	.47297	.46706	.46129	.45563	.45009	.44467	.43937	.43417
77	.49033	.48447	.47873	.47311	.46761	.46221	.45693	.45175
78	.50800	.50220	.49652	.49094	.48548	.48013	.47488	.46973
79	.52582	.52009	.51448	.50897	.50356	.49826	.49306	.48795
80	.54366	.53802	.53248	.52705	.52171	.51647	.51133	.50628
81	.56134	.55579	.55035	.54499	.53974	.53457	.52950	.52451
82	.57875	.57331	.56796	.56270	.55753	.55245	.54745	.54254
83	.59581	.59047	.58523	.58007	.57500	.57001	.56510	.56026
84	.61253	.60731	.60218	.59713	.59216	.58726	.58245	.57770
85	.62896	.62387	.61886	.61392	.60906	.60428	.59956	.59492
86	.64496	.64000	.63511	.63030	.62555	.62088	.61627	.61173
87	.66031	.65548	.65071	.64602	.64139	.63683	.63233	.62790
88	.67507	.67037	.66574	.66117	.65666	.65221	.64783	.64350
89	.68952	.68495	.68045	.67601	.67163	.66730	.66304	.65882
90	.70379	.69938	.69502	.69071	.68646	.68226	.67812	.67402
91	.71770	.71343	.70921	.70504	.70093	.69686	.69285	.68888
92	.73087	.72674	.72267	.71864	.71466	.71073	.70684	.70300
93	.74317	.73918	.73524	.73135	.72750	.72370	.71994	.71622
94	.75446	.75061	.74680	.74303	.73931	.73562	.73198	.72838
95	.76468	.76096	.75727	.75362	.75001	.74644	.74291	.73941
96	.77377	.77015	.76657	.76303	.75953	.75606	.75262	.74923
97	.78203	.77852	.77504	.77160	.76819	.76481	.76147	.75816
98	.78948	.78606	.78267	.77931	.77599	.77270	.76944	.76621
99	.79635	.79302	.78971	.78644	.78319	.77998	.77680	.77365
100	.80273	.79947	.79624	.79304	.78987	.78673	.78362	.78054
101	.80880	.80561	.80245	.79932	.79622	.79315	.79010	.78708
102	.81512	.81200	.80892	.80586	.80283	.79983	.79685	.79390
103	.82181	.81878	.81577	.81279	.80983	.80690	.80399	.80111
104	.82924	.82630	.82338	.82048	.81760	.81475	.81192	.80912
105	.83846	.83563	.83282	.83003	.82726	.82451	.82178	.81907
106	.85187	.84922	.84659	.84397	.84137	.83879	.83623	.83368
107	.87147	.86911	.86676	.86443	.86211	.85981	.85751	.85523
108	.90383	.90201	.90020	.89840	.89660	.89481	.89304	.89127
109	.95704	.95620	.95537	.95455	.95372	.95290	.95208	.95126

VALUATION TABLES (After April 30, 1989 *continued*)

Table B Term Certain Remainder Factors Interest Rate

Years	9.4%	9.6%	9.8%	10.0%	10.2%	10.4%	10.6%	10.8%
1	.914077	.912409	.910747	.909091	.907441	.905797	.904159	.902527
2	.835536	.832490	.829460	.826446	.823449	.820468	.817504	.814555
3	.763744	.759571	.755428	.751315	.747232	.743178	.739153	.735158
4	.698121	.693039	.688003	.683013	.678069	.673168	.668312	.663500
5	.638136	.632335	.626597	.620921	.615307	.609754	.604261	.598827
6	.583305	.576948	.570671	.564474	.558355	.552313	.546348	.540457
7	.533186	.526412	.519737	.513158	.506674	.500284	.493985	.487777
8	.487373	.480303	.473349	.466507	.459777	.453156	.446641	.440232
9	.445496	.438233	.431101	.424098	.417221	.410467	.403835	.397322
10	.407218	.399848	.392624	.385543	.378603	.371800	.365131	.358593
11	.372228	.364824	.357581	.350494	.343560	.336775	.330137	.323640
12	.340245	.332869	.325666	.318631	.311760	.305050	.298496	.292094
13	.311010	.303713	.296599	.289664	.282904	.276313	.269888	.263623
14	.284287	.277110	.270127	.263331	.256719	.250284	.244022	.237927
15	.259860	.252838	.246017	.239392	.232957	.226706	.220634	.214735
16	.237532	.230691	.224059	.217629	.211395	.205350	.199489	.193804
17	.217123	.210485	.204061	.197845	.191828	.186005	.180369	.174914
18	.198467	.192048	.185848	.179859	.174073	.168483	.163083	.157864
19	.181414	.175226	.169260	.163508	.157961	.152612	.147453	.142477
20	.165826	.159878	.154153	.148644	.143340	.138235	.133321	.128589
21	.151578	.145874	.140395	.135131	.130073	.125213	.120543	.116055
22	.138554	.133097	.127864	.122846	.118033	.113418	.108990	.104743
23	.126649	.121439	.116452	.111678	.107108	.102733	.098544	.094533
24	.115767	.110802	.106058	.101526	.097195	.093056	.089100	.085319
25	.105820	.101097	.096592	.092296	.088198	.084289	.080560	.077003
26	.096727	.092241	.087971	.083905	.080035	.076349	.072839	.069497
27	.088416	.084162	.080119	.076278	.072627	.069157	.065858	.062723
28	.080819	.076790	.072968	.069343	.065905	.062642	.059547	.056609
29	.073875	.070064	.066456	.063039	.059804	.056741	.053840	.051091
30	.067527	.063927	.060524	.057309	.054269	.051396	.048680	.046111
31	.061725	.058327	.055122	.052099	.049246	.046554	.044014	.041617
32	.056422	.053218	.050202	.047362	.044688	.042169	.039796	.037560
33	.051574	.048557	.045722	.043057	.040552	.038196	.035982	.033899
34	.047142	.044304	.041641	.039143	.036798	.034598	.032533	.030595
35	.043092	.040423	.037924	.035584	.033392	.031339	.029415	.027613
36	.039389	.036882	.034539	.032349	.030301	.028387	.026596	.024921
37	.036005	.033652	.031457	.029408	.027497	.025712	.024047	.022492
38	.032911	.030704	.028649	.026735	.024952	.023290	.021742	.020300
39	.030083	.028015	.026092	.024304	.022642	.021096	.019658	.018321
40	.027498	.025561	.023763	.022095	.020546	.019109	.017774	.016535
41	.025136	.023322	.021642	.020086	.018645	.017309	.016071	.014923
42	.022976	.021279	.019711	.018260	.016919	.015678	.014531	.013469
43	.021002	.019415	.017951	.016600	.015353	.014201	.013138	.012156
44	.019197	.017715	.016349	.015091	.013932	.012864	.011879	.010971
45	.017548	.016163	.014890	.013719	.012642	.011652	.010740	.009902
46	.016040	.014747	.013561	.012472	.011472	.010554	.009711	.008937
47	.014662	.013456	.012351	.011338	.010410	.009560	.008780	.008065
48	.013402	.012277	.011248	.010307	.009447	.008659	.007939	.007279
49	.012250	.011202	.010244	.009370	.008572	.007844	.007178	.006570
50	.011198	.010221	.009330	.008519	.007779	.007105	.006490	.005929
51	.010236	.009325	.008497	.007744	.007059	.006435	.005868	.005351
52	.009356	.008508	.007739	.007040	.006406	.005829	.005306	.004830
53	.008552	.007763	.007048	.006400	.005813	.005280	.004797	.004359
54	.007817	.007083	.006419	.005818	.005275	.004783	.004337	.003934
55	.007146	.006463	.005846	.005289	.004786	.004332	.003922	.003551
56	.006532	.005897	.005324	.004809	.004343	.003924	.003546	.003205
57	.005971	.005380	.004849	.004371	.003941	.003554	.003206	.002892
58	.005458	.004909	.004416	.003974	.003577	.003220	.002899	.002610
59	.004989	.004479	.004022	.003613	.003246	.002916	.002621	.002356
60	.004560	.004087	.003663	.003284	.002945	.002642	.002370	.002126

APPENDIX

TAX FORMS

Form **709**	**United States Gift (and Generation-Skipping Transfer) Tax Return**		
(Rev. November 1991)	(Section 6019 of the Internal Revenue Code) (For gifts made after October 8, 1990, and before January 1, 1993)	OMB No. 1545-0020	
Department of the Treasury Internal Revenue Service	**Calendar year 19** .... ▶ **See separate instructions. For Privacy Act Notice, see the Instructions for Form 1040.**	Expires 8-31-93	

Part 1.—General Information

1 Donor's first name and middle initial	**2** Donor's last name **3** Social security number
4 Address (number, street, and apartment number)	**5** Legal residence (Domicile)
6 City, state, and ZIP code	**7** Citizenship

		Yes	No
8	If the donor died during the year, check here ▶ ☐ and enter date of death........................, 19		
9	If you received an extension of time to file this Form 709, check here ▶ ☐ and attach the Form 4868, 2688, 2350, or extension letter		
10	Enter the total number of separate donees listed on Schedule A—count each person only once . . . . ☐		
11a	Have you (the donor) previously filed a Form 709 (or 709-A) for any other year? If the answer is "No," do not complete line 11b .		
11b	If the answer to line 11a is "Yes," has your address changed since you last filed Form 709 (or 709-A)?		
12	Gifts by husband or wife to third parties.—Do you consent to have the gifts (including generation-skipping transfers) made by you and by your spouse to third parties during the calendar year considered as made one-half by each of you? (See instructions.) (If the answer is "Yes," the following information must be furnished and your spouse must sign the consent shown below. If the answer is "No," skip lines 13–18 and go to Schedule A.)		
13	Name of consenting spouse		
14	SSN		
15	Were you married to one another during the entire calendar year? (See instructions.)		
16	If the answer to 15 is "No," check whether ☐ married ☐ divorced or ☐ widowed, and give date (see instructions) ▶		
17	Will a gift tax return for this calendar year be filed by your spouse?		
18	Consent of Spouse—I consent to have the gifts (and generation-skipping transfers) made by me and by my spouse to third parties during the calendar year considered as made one-half by each of us. We are both aware of the joint and several liability for tax created by the execution of this consent.		

Consenting spouse's signature ▶   Date ▶

Part 2.—Tax Computation

1	Enter the amount from Schedule A, Part 3, line 15	**1**	
2	Enter the amount from Schedule B, line 3	**2**	
3	Total taxable gifts (add lines 1 and 2)	**3**	
4	Tax computed on amount on line 3 (see Table for Computing Tax in separate instructions). . .	**4**	
5	Tax computed on amount on line 2 (see Table for Computing Tax in separate instructions). . .	**5**	
6	Balance (subtract line 5 from line 4)	**6**	
7	Maximum unified credit (nonresident aliens, see instructions)	**7**	192,800 | 00
8	Enter the unified credit against tax allowable for all prior periods (from Sch. B, line 1, col. C) . .	**8**	
9	Balance (subtract line 8 from line 7)	**9**	
10	Enter 20% (.20) of the amount allowed as a specific exemption for gifts made after September 8, 1976, and before January 1, 1977 (see instructions)	**10**	
11	Balance (subtract line 10 from line 9)	**11**	
12	Unified credit (enter the smaller of line 6 or line 11)	**12**	
13	Credit for foreign gift taxes (see instructions)	**13**	
14	Total credits (add lines 12 and 13)	**14**	
15	Balance (subtract line 14 from line 6) (do not enter less than zero)	**15**	
16	Generation-skipping transfer taxes (from Schedule C, Part 3, col. H, total)	**16**	
17	Total tax (add lines 15 and 16)	**17**	
18	Gift and generation-skipping transfer taxes prepaid with extension of time to file	**18**	
19	If line 18 is less than line 17, enter BALANCE DUE (see instructions)	**19**	
20	If line 18 is greater than line 17, enter AMOUNT TO BE REFUNDED	**20**	

Under penalties of perjury, I declare that I have examined this return, including any accompanying schedules and statements, and to the best of my knowledge and belief it is true, correct, and complete. Declaration of preparer (other than donor) is based on all information of which preparer has any knowledge.

Donor's signature ▶   Date ▶

Preparer's signature (other than donor) ▶   Date ▶

Preparer's address (other than donor) ▶

(Left margin: Please attach check or money order here.)

For Paperwork Reduction Act Notice, see page 1 of the separate instructions for this form.   Cat. No. 16783M   Form **709** (Rev. 11-91)

Form 709 (Rev. 11-91)   Page **2**

SCHEDULE A	Computation of Taxable Gifts

Part 1.—Gifts Subject Only to Gift Tax. *Gifts less political organization, medical, and educational exclusions—see instructions*

A Item number	B Donee's name, relationship to donor (if any), and address and description of gift. If the gift was made by means of a trust, enter trust's identifying number below and attach a copy of the trust instrument. If the gift was securities, enter the CUSIP number(s), if available.	C Donor's adjusted basis of gift	D Date of gift	E Value at date of gift
1				

Part 2.—Gifts Which are Direct Skips and are Subject to Both Gift Tax and Generation-Skipping Transfer Tax. You must list the gifts in chronological order. *Gifts less political organization, medical, and educational exclusions—see instructions. (Also list here direct skips that are subject only to the GST tax at this time as the result of the termination of an "estate tax inclusion period." See instructions.)*

A Item number	B Donee's name, relationship to donor (if any), and address and description of gift. If the gift was made by means of a trust, enter trust's identifying number below and attach a copy of the trust instrument. If the gift was securities, enter the CUSIP number(s), if available.	C Donor's adjusted basis of gift	D Date of gift	E Value at date of gift
1				

Part 3.—Gift Tax Reconciliation

1	Total value of gifts of donor (add column E of Parts 1 and 2)	1	
2	One-half of items .... attributable to spouse (see instructions)	2	
3	Balance (subtract line 2 from line 1)	3	
4	Gifts of spouse to be included (from Schedule A, Part 3, line 2 of spouse's return—see instructions) . .	4	
	If any of the gifts included on this line are also subject to the generation-skipping transfer tax, check here ► ☐ and enter those gifts also on Schedule C, Part 1.		
5	Total gifts (add lines 3 and 4)	5	
6	Total annual exclusions for gifts listed on Schedule A (including line 4, above) (see instructions) . . .	6	
7	Total included amount of gifts (subtract line 6 from line 5)	7	

Deductions (see instructions)

8	Gifts of interests to spouse for which a marital deduction will be claimed, based on items ....of Schedule A	8		
9	Exclusions attributable to gifts on line 8	9		
10	Marital deduction—subtract line 9 from line 8	10		
11	Charitable deduction, based on items .... to .... less exclusions .	11		
12	Total deductions—add lines 10 and 11		12	
13	Subtract line 12 from line 7		13	
14	Generation-skipping transfer taxes payable with this Form 709 (from Schedule C, Part 3, col. H, Total) .		14	
15	Taxable gifts (add lines 13 and 14). Enter here and on line 1 of the Tax Computation on page 1 . . .		15	

(If more space is needed, attach additional sheets of same size.)

Form 709 (Rev. 11-91) — Page **3**

SCHEDULE A Computation of Taxable Gifts *(continued)*

16 Terminable Interest (QTIP) Marital Deduction. (See instructions.)

If a trust (or other property) meets the requirements of qualified terminable interest property under section 2523(f), and

    a. the trust (or other property) is listed on Schedule A, and

    b. the value of the trust (or other property) is entered in whole or in part as a deduction on line 8, Part 3 of Schedule A,

then the donor shall be deemed to have made an election to have such trust (or other property) treated as qualified terminable interest property under section 2523(f).

If less than the entire value of the trust (or other property) that the donor has included in Part 1 of Schedule A is entered as a deduction on line 8, the donor shall be considered to have made an election only as to a fraction of the trust (or other property). The numerator of this fraction is equal to the amount of the trust (or other property) deducted on line 10 of Part 3. The denominator is equal to the total value of the trust (or other property) listed in Part 1 of Schedule A.

If you make the QTIP election (see instructions for line 8 of Schedule A), the terminable interest property involved will be included in your spouse's gross estate upon his or her death (section 2044). If your spouse disposes (by gift or otherwise) of all or part of the qualifying life income interest, he or she will be considered to have made a transfer of the entire property that is subject to the gift tax (see Transfer of Certain Life Estates on page 3 of the instructions).

17 Election out of QTIP Treatment of Annuities

☐ ◄ Check here if you elect under section 2523(f)(6) **NOT** to treat as qualified terminable interest property any joint and survivor annuities that are reported on Schedule A and would otherwise be treated as qualified terminable interest property under section 2523(f). (See instructions.) Enter the item numbers (from Schedule A) for the annuities for which you are making this election ►

SCHEDULE B Gifts From Prior Periods

If you answered "Yes" on line 11a of Page 1, Part 1, see the instructions for completing Schedule B. If your answer is "No," skip to the Tax Computation on Page 1 (or Schedule C, if applicable).

A Calendar year or calendar quarter (see instructions)	B Internal Revenue office where prior return was filed	C Amount of unified credit against gift tax for periods after December 31, 1976	D Amount of specific exemption for prior periods ending before January 1, 1977	E Amount of taxable gifts

1 Totals for prior periods (without adjustment for reduced specific exemption) **1**

2 Amount, if any, by which total specific exemption, line 1, column D, is more than $30,000 . . . . . **2**

3 Total amount of taxable gifts for prior periods (add amount, column E, line 1, and amount, if any, on line 2) (Enter here and on line 2 of the Tax Computation on page 1.) **3**

(If more space is needed, attach additional sheets of same size.)

Form 709 (Rev. 11-91)   Page **4**

SCHEDULE C	Computation of Generation-Skipping Transfer Tax

Note: *Inter vivos direct skips which are completely excluded by the GST exemption must still be fully reported (including value and exemptions claimed) on Schedule C.*

Part 1.—Generation-Skipping Transfers

A Item No. (from Schedule A, Part 2, col. A)	B Value (from Schedule A, Part 2, col. E)	C Split Gifts (enter ½ of col. B) (see instructions)	D Subtract col. C from col. B	E Nontaxable portion of transfer	F Net Transfer (subtract col. E from col. D)
1					
2					
3					
4					
5					
6					

	Split gifts from spouse's Form 709 (enter item number)	Value included from spouse's Form 709	Nontaxable portion of transfer	Net transfer (subtract col. E from col. D)
If you elected gift splitting and your spouse was required to file a separate Form 709 (see the instructions for "Split Gifts"), you must enter all of the gifts shown on Schedule A, Part 2, of your spouse's Form 709 here. In column C, enter the item number of each gift in the order it appears in column A of your spouse's Schedule A, Part 2. We have preprinted the prefix "S-" to distinguish your spouse's item numbers from your own when you complete column A of Schedule C, Part 3. In column D, for each gift, enter the amount reported in column C, Schedule C, Part 1, of your spouse's Form 709.	S- S- S- S- S- S- S- S-			

Part 2.—GST Exemption Reconciliation (Code section 2631) and Section 2652(a)(3) Election

Check box ▶ ☐ if you are making a section 2652(a)(3) (special QTIP) election (see instructions)

Enter the item numbers (from Schedule A) of the gifts for which you are making this election ▶ ....

1	Maximum allowable exemption	1	$1,000,000
2	Total exemption used for periods before filing this return	2	
3	Exemption available for this return (subtract line 2 from line 1)	3	
4	Exemption claimed on this return (from Part 3, col. C total, below)	4	
5	Exemption allocated to transfers not shown on Part 3, below. You must attach a Notice of Allocation. (See instructions.)	5	
6	Add lines 4 and 5	6	
7	Exemption available for future transfers (subtract line 6 from line 3)	7	

Part 3.—Tax Computation

A Item No. (from Schedule C, Part 1)	B Net transfer (from Schedule C, Part 1, col. F)	C GST Exemption Allocated	D Divide col. C by col. B	E Inclusion Ratio (subtract col. D from 1.000)	F Maximum Estate Tax Rate	G Applicable Rate (multiply col. E by col. F)	H Generation-Skipping Transfer Tax (multiply col. B by col. G)
1					55% (.55)		
2					55% (.55)		
3					55% (.55)		
4					55% (.55)		
5					55% (.55)		
6					55% (.55)		
					55% (.55)		
					55% (.55)		
					55% (.55)		
					55% (.55)		

Total exemption claimed. Enter here and on line 4, Part 2, above. May not exceed line 3, Part 2, above		**Total generation-skipping transfer tax.** Enter here, on line 14 of Schedule A, Part 3, and on line 16 of the Tax Computation on page 1	

(If more space is needed, attach additional sheets of same size.)

Form **1120-A**
Department of the Treasury
Internal Revenue Service

U.S. Corporation Short-Form Income Tax Return
Instructions are separate. See them to make sure you qualify to file Form 1120-A.
For calendar year 1991 or tax year beginning ...., 1991, ending ...., 19 .....

OMB No. 1545-0890

1991

A Check this box if corp. is a personal service corp. (as defined in Temp. Regs. sec. 1.441-4T—see instructions) ▶ ☐

Use IRS label. Otherwise, please print or type.

Name

Number, street, and room or suite no. (If a P.O. box, see page 6 of instructions.)

City or town, state, and ZIP code

B Employer identification number

C Date incorporated

D Total assets (see Specific Instructions)
$

E Check applicable boxes: **(1)** ☐ Initial return **(2)** ☐ Change in address
F Check method of accounting: **(1)** ☐ Cash **(2)** ☐ Accrual **(3)** ☐ Other (specify) . . ▶

Income

1a Gross receipts or sales	**b** Less returns and allowances	**c** Balance ▶	**1c**
2 Cost of goods sold (see instructions)		**2**
3 Gross profit. Subtract line 2 from line 1c		**3**
4 Domestic corporation dividends subject to the 70% deduction		**4**
5 Interest		**5**
6 Gross rents		**6**
7 Gross royalties		**7**
8 Capital gain net income (attach Schedule D (Form 1120)) . . .		**8**
9 Net gain or (loss) from Form 4797, Part II, line 18 (attach Form 4797)		**9**
10 Other income (see instructions)		**10**
11 **Total income.** Add lines 3 through 10 . . . . ▶		**11**

(See instructions for limitations on deductions.)

Deductions

12 Compensation of officers (see instructions)	**12**
13a Salaries and wages **b** Less jobs credit **c** Balance ▶	**13c**
14 Repairs	**14**
15 Bad debts	**15**
16 Rents	**16**
17 Taxes	**17**
18 Interest	**18**
19 Contributions **(see instructions for 10% limitation)** . .	**19**
20 Depreciation (attach Form 4562) **20**	
21 Less depreciation claimed elsewhere on return **21a**	**21b**
22 Other deductions (attach schedule)	**22**
23 **Total deductions.** Add lines 12 through 22 . . . . . . ▶	**23**
24 Taxable income before net operating loss deduction and special deductions. Subtract line 23 from line 11 . .	**24**
25 **Less: a** Net operating loss deduction (see instructions) **25a**	
b Special deductions (see instructions) **25b**	**25c**

Tax and Payments

26 **Taxable income.** Subtract line 25c from line 24	**26**
27 **Total tax** (from page 2, Part I, line 7)	**27**
28 **Payments:**	
a 1990 overpayment credited to 1991 **28a**	
b 1991 estimated tax payments **28b**	
c Less 1991 refund applied for on Form 4466 **28c** ( ) Bal ▶ **28d**	
e Tax deposited with Form 7004 **28e**	
f Credit from regulated investment companies (attach Form 2439) . **28f**	
g Credit for Federal tax on fuels (attach Form 4136). See instructions . **28g**	
h Total payments. Add lines 28d through 28g	**28h**
29 Estimated tax penalty (see page 4 of instructions). Check if Form 2220 is attached . . . ▶ ☐	**29**
30 **Tax due.** If the total of lines 27 and 29 is larger than line 28h, enter amount owed	**30**
31 **Overpayment.** If line 28h is larger than the total of lines 27 and 29, enter amount overpaid . . .	**31**
32 Enter amount of line 31 you want: **Credited to 1992 estimated tax** ▶	**Refunded** ▶ **32**

Please Sign Here

Under penalties of perjury, I declare that I have examined this return, including accompanying schedules and statements, and to the best of my knowledge and belief, it is true, correct, and complete. Declaration of preparer (other than taxpayer) is based on all information of which preparer has any knowledge.

▶ _____   _____   _____
Signature of officer   Date   Title

Paid Preparer's Use Only

Preparer's signature ▶	Date	Check if self-employed ▶ ☐	Preparer's social security number
Firm's name (or yours if self-employed) and address ▶		E.I. No. ▶	
		ZIP code ▶	

For Paperwork Reduction Act Notice, see page 1 of the instructions.   Cat. No. 11456E   Form **1120-A** (1991)

Form 1120-A (1991)   Page **2**

Part I   Tax Computation

1 Income tax (see instructions to figure the tax). Check this box if the corp. is a qualified personal service corp. (see instructions) . . . . ▶ ☐   **1**

2a General business credit. Check if from: ☐ Form 3800 ☐ Form 3468 ☐ Form 5884 ☐ Form 6478 ☐ Form 6765 ☐ Form 8586 ☐ Form 8830 ☐ Form 8826   **2a**

b Credit for prior year minimum tax (attach Form 8827) **2b**

3 **Total credits.** Add lines 2a and 2b **3**

4 Subtract line 3 from line 1 . . . .   **4**

5 Recapture taxes. Check if from: ☐ Form 4255 ☐ Form 8611 . . . . . .   **5**

6 Alternative minimum tax (attach Form 4626). See instructions **6**

7 **Total tax.** Add lines 4 through 6. Enter here and on line 27, page 1 . . . .   **7**

Part II   Other Information (See page 15 of the instructions.)

1 Refer to the list in the instructions and state the principal:

   a Business activity code no. ▶ ....

   b Business activity ▶ ....

   c Product or service ▶ ....

2 Did any individual, partnership, estate, or trust at the end of the tax year own, directly or indirectly, 50% or more of the corporation's voting stock? (For rules of attribution, see section 267(c).) . . . . ☐ Yes ☐ No

If "Yes," attach schedule showing name, address, and identifying number.

3 Enter the amount of tax-exempt interest received or accrued during the tax year . . . . ▶ | $ |

4 Enter amount of cash distributions and the book value of property (other than cash) distributions made in this tax year . . . . ▶ | $ |

5a If an amount is entered on line 2, page 1, see the worksheet on page 11 for amounts to enter below:

   (1) Purchases (see instructions) . .

   (2) Additional sec. 263A costs (see instructions—attach schedule) .

   (3) Other costs (attach schedule) .

b Do the rules of section 263A (for property produced or acquired for resale) apply to the corporation? . . . . . . ☐ Yes ☐ No

6 At any time during the tax year, did the corporation have an interest in or a signature or other authority over a financial account in a foreign country (such as a bank account, securities account, or other financial account)? (See page 15 of the instructions for filing requirements for Form TD F 90-22.1.). . . . . ☐ Yes ☐ No

If "Yes," enter the name of the foreign country ▶ ....

Part III   Balance Sheets

		(a) Beginning of tax year		(b) End of tax year	
Assets	**1** Cash				
	2a Trade notes and accounts receivable				
	b Less allowance for bad debts	(	)	(	)
	3 Inventories				
	4 U.S. government obligations				
	5 Tax-exempt securities (see instructions)				
	6 Other current assets (attach schedule)				
	7 Loans to stockholders				
	8 Mortgage and real estate loans				
	9a Depreciable, depletable, and intangible assets				
	b Less accumulated depreciation, depletion, and amortization	(	)	(	)
	10 Land (net of any amortization)				
	11 Other assets (attach schedule)				
	12 Total assets				
Liabilities and Stockholders' Equity	**13** Accounts payable				
	14 Other current liabilities (attach schedule)				
	15 Loans from stockholders				
	16 Mortgages, notes, bonds payable				
	17 Other liabilities (attach schedule)				
	18 Capital stock (preferred and common stock)				
	19 Paid-in or capital surplus				
	20 Retained earnings				
	21 Less cost of treasury stock	(	)	(	)
	22 Total liabilities and stockholders' equity				

Part IV   Reconciliation of Income per Books With Income per Return (Must be completed by all filers.)

1 Net income per books . . . .

2 Federal income tax . . . .

3 Excess of capital losses over capital gains .

4 Income subject to tax not recorded on books this year (itemize) ....

5 Expenses recorded on books this year not deducted on this return (itemize)

6 Income recorded on books this year not included on this return (itemize) ....

7 Deductions on this return not charged against book income this year (itemize) ....

8 Income (line 24, page 1). Enter the sum of lines 1 through 5 less the sum of lines 6 and 7 . . .

Form **1120**

Department of the Treasury
Internal Revenue Service

U.S. Corporation Income Tax Return

For calendar year 1991 or tax year beginning .... , 1991, ending .... , 19 ...

▶ **Instructions are separate. See page 1 for Paperwork Reduction Act Notice.**

OMB No. 1545-0123

19**91**

A Check if a—		
(1) Consolidated return (attach Form 851)	☐	**Use IRS label. Other-wise, please print or type.**
(2) Personal holding co. (attach Sch. PH)	☐	
(3) Personal service corp. (as defined in Temp. Regs. sec. 1.441-4T— see instructions)	☐	

Name

Number, street, and room or suite no. (If a P.O. box, see page 6 of instructions.)

City or town, state, and ZIP code

B Employer identification number

C Date incorporated

D Total assets (see Specific Instructions)

$

E Check applicable boxes: (1) ☐ Initial return (2) ☐ Final return (3) ☐ Change in address

Income

1a	Gross receipts or sales	**b** Less returns and allowances	**c** Bal ▶	**1c**	
2	Cost of goods sold (Schedule A, line 7)	**2**	
3	Gross profit. Subtract line 2 from line 1c	**3**	
4	Dividends (Schedule C, line 19)	**4**	
5	Interest	**5**	
6	Gross rents	**6**	
7	Gross royalties	**7**	
8	Capital gain net income (attach Schedule D (Form 1120))	**8**	
9	Net gain or (loss) from Form 4797, Part II, line 18 (attach Form 4797) . .	**9**	
10	Other income (see instructions—attach schedule)	**10**	
11	**Total income.** Add lines 3 through 10 . . . . ▶	**11**	

Deductions (See instructions for limitations on deductions.)

12	Compensation of officers (Schedule E, line 4)	**12**	
13a	Salaries and wages	**b** Less jobs credit	**c** Balance ▶	**13c**	
14	Repairs	**14**	
15	Bad debts	**15**	
16	Rents	**16**	
17	Taxes	**17**	
18	Interest	**18**	
19	Contributions (**see instructions for 10% limitation**)	**19**	
20	Depreciation (attach Form 4562) **20**		
21	Less depreciation claimed on Schedule A and elsewhere on return . . **21a**	**21b**	
22	Depletion	**22**	
23	Advertising	**23**	
24	Pension, profit-sharing, etc., plans	**24**	
25	Employee benefit programs	**25**	
26	Other deductions (attach schedule)	**26**	
27	**Total deductions.** Add lines 12 through 26 . . . . ▶	**27**	
28	Taxable income before net operating loss deduction and special deductions. Subtract line 27 from line 11	**28**	
29	**Less:** **a** Net operating loss deduction (see instructions) **29a**		
	b Special deductions (Schedule C, line 20) **29b**	**29c**	

Tax and Payments

30	**Taxable income.** Subtract line 29c from line 28	**30**	
31	**Total tax** (Schedule J, line 10)	**31**	
32	**Payments: a** 1990 overpayment credited to 1991	**32a**		
b	1991 estimated tax payments . . .	**32b**		
c	Less 1991 refund applied for on Form 4466 **32c** ( ) **d** Bal ▶	**32d**	
e	Tax deposited with Form 7004	**32e**	
f	Credit from regulated investment companies (attach Form 2439) . . .	**32f**	
g	Credit for Federal tax on fuels (attach Form 4136). See instructions . .	**32g**	**32h**	
33	Estimated tax penalty (see page 4 of instructions). Check if Form 2220 is attached . . . ▶ ☐	**33**	
34	**Tax due.** If the total of lines 31 and 33 is larger than line 32h, enter amount owed	**34**	
35	**Overpayment.** If line 32h is larger than the total of lines 31 and 33, enter amount overpaid . .	**35**	
36	Enter amount of line 35 you want: **Credited to 1992 estimated tax** ▶	Refunded ▶	**36**	

Please Sign Here

Under penalties of perjury, I declare that I have examined this return, including accompanying schedules and statements, and to the best of my knowledge and belief, it is true, correct, and complete. Declaration of preparer (other than taxpayer) is based on all information of which preparer has any knowledge.

▶ Signature of officer   Date   ▶ Title

Paid Preparer's Use Only

Preparer's signature ▶	Date	Check if self-employed ☐	Preparer's social security number
Firm's name (or yours if self-employed) and address ▶		E.I. No. ▶	
		ZIP code ▶	

Cat. No. 11450Q

Form 1120 (1991)   Page **2**

Schedule A	**Cost of Goods Sold** (See instructions.)		

1	Inventory at beginning of year	**1**	
2	Purchases	**2**	
3	Cost of labor	**3**	
4a	Additional section 263A costs (see instructions—attach schedule)	**4a**	
b	Other costs (attach schedule)	**4b**	
5	**Total.** Add lines 1 through 4b	**5**	
6	Inventory at end of year	**6**	
7	**Cost of goods sold.** Subtract line 6 from line 5. Enter here and on line 2, page 1	**7**	

8a Check all methods used for valuing closing inventory:

   (i) ☐ Cost   **(ii)** ☐ Lower of cost or market as described in Regulations section 1.471-4 (see instructions)

   (iii) ☐ Writedown of "subnormal" goods as described in Regulations section 1.471-2(c) (see instructions)

   (iv) ☐ Other (Specify method used and attach explanation.) ▶ ....

  b Check if the LIFO inventory method was adopted this tax year for any goods (if checked, attach Form 970) . . . . . ▶ ☐

  c If the LIFO inventory method was used for this tax year, enter percentage (or amounts) of closing inventory computed under LIFO **8c**

  d Do the rules of section 263A (for property produced or acquired for resale) apply to the corporation? . . . . . ☐ Yes ☐ No

  e Was there any change in determining quantities, cost, or valuations between opening and closing inventory? If "Yes," attach explanation . . . . ☐ Yes ☐ No

Schedule C	**Dividends and Special Deductions** (See instructions.)	**(a)** Dividends received	**(b)** %	**(c)** Special deductions: (a) × (b)
1	Dividends from less-than-20%-owned domestic corporations that are subject to the 70% deduction (other than debt-financed stock)		70	
2	Dividends from 20%-or-more-owned domestic corporations that are subject to the 80% deduction (other than debt-financed stock)		80 see instructions	
3	Dividends on debt-financed stock of domestic and foreign corporations (section 246A)			
4	Dividends on certain preferred stock of less-than-20%-owned public utilities . . .		41.176	
5	Dividends on certain preferred stock of 20%-or-more-owned public utilities . . .		47.059	
6	Dividends from less-than-20%-owned foreign corporations and certain FSCs that are subject to the 70% deduction		70	
7	Dividends from 20%-or-more-owned foreign corporations and certain FSCs that are subject to the 80% deduction		80	
8	Dividends from wholly owned foreign subsidiaries subject to the 100% deduction (section 245(b))		100	
9	**Total.** Add lines 1 through 8. See instructions for limitation	/////	/////	
10	Dividends from domestic corporations received by a small business investment company operating under the Small Business Investment Act of 1958		100	
11	Dividends from certain FSCs that are subject to the 100% deduction (section 245(c)(1))		100	
12	Dividends from affiliated group members subject to the 100% deduction (section 243(a)(3))		100	
13	Other dividends from foreign corporations not included on lines 3, 6, 7, 8, or 11 .		/////	/////
14	Income from controlled foreign corporations under subpart F (attach Forms 5471) .		/////	/////
15	Foreign dividend gross-up (section 78)		/////	/////
16	IC-DISC and former DISC dividends not included on lines 1, 2, or 3 (section 246(d)) .		/////	/////
17	Other dividends	/////	/////	/////
18	Deduction for dividends paid on certain preferred stock of public utilities (see instructions)	/////	/////	
19	**Total dividends.** Add lines 1 through 17. Enter here and on line 4, page 1 . . ▶		/////	/////
20	**Total deductions.** Add lines 9, 10, 11, 12, and 18. Enter here and on line 29b, page 1 . . . . ▶			

Schedule E	**Compensation of Officers** (See instructions for line 12, page 1.)					

Complete Schedule E only if total receipts (line 1a plus lines 4 through 10 of page 1, Form 1120) are $500,000 or more.

	(a) Name of officer	(b) Social security number	(c) Percent of time devoted to business	Percent of corporation stock owned		(f) Amount of compensation
				(d) Common	(e) Preferred	
1			%	%	%	
			%	%	%	
			%	%	%	
			%	%	%	
			%	%	%	
2	Total compensation of officers					
3	**Less:** Compensation of officers claimed on Schedule A and elsewhere on return				( )	
4	Compensation of officers deducted on line 12, page 1					

Schedule J   Tax Computation

1   Check if you are a member of a controlled group (see sections 1561 and 1563) . . . . ▶ ☐

2   If the box on line 1 is checked:

   a   Enter your share of the $50,000 and $25,000 taxable income bracket amounts (in that order):

     (i) ☐ $ |_____| (ii) ☐ $ |_____|

   b   Enter your share of the additional 5% tax (not to exceed $11,750) . . . . ▶ $ |_____|

3   Income tax (see instructions to figure the tax). Check this box if the corporation is a qualified personal service corporation (see instructions on page 13) . . . . ▶ ☐   **3**

4a   Foreign tax credit (attach Form 1118) **4a**

   b   Possessions tax credit (attach Form 5735) **4b**

   c   Orphan drug credit (attach Form 6765) **4c**

   d   Credit for fuel produced from a nonconventional source (see instructions) . . .   **4d**

   e   General business credit. Enter here and check which forms are attached:

     ☐ Form 3800   ☐ Form 3468   ☐ Form 5884   ☐ Form 6478

     ☐ Form 6765   ☐ Form 8586   ☐ Form 8830   ☐ Form 8826 . . .   **4e**

   f   Credit for prior year minimum tax (attach Form 8827) **4f**

5   **Total.** Add lines 4a through 4f **5**

6   Subtract line 5 from line 3 . . . .   **6**

7   Personal holding company tax (attach Schedule PH (Form 1120)) **7**

8   Recapture taxes. Check if from: ☐ Form 4255   ☐ Form 8611 . . . . . .   **8**

9a   Alternative minimum tax (attach Form 4626). See instructions **9a**

   b   Environmental tax (attach Form 4626) **9b**

10   **Total tax.** Add lines 6 through 9b. Enter here and on line 31, page 1 . . . .   **10**

Schedule K   Other Information (See page 15 of the instructions.)

		Yes	No

1   Check method of accounting:

   a   ☐ Cash

   b   ☐ Accrual

   c   ☐ Other (specify) ▶ ....

2   Refer to the list in the instructions and state the principal:

   a   Business activity code no. ▶ ....

   b   Business activity ▶ ....

   c   Product or service ▶ ....

3   Did the corporation at the end of the tax year own, directly or indirectly, 50% or more of the voting stock of a domestic corporation? (For rules of attribution, see section 267(c).) . . . .

   If "Yes," attach a schedule showing: (a) name, address, and identifying number; (b) percentage owned; and (c) taxable income or (loss) before NOL and special deductions of such corporation for the tax year ending with or within your tax year.

4   Did any individual, partnership, corporation, estate, or trust at the end of the tax year own, directly or indirectly, 50% or more of the corporation's voting stock? (For rules of attribution, see section 267(c).) If "Yes," complete **a** and **b** . . . .

   a   Attach a schedule showing name, address, and identifying number.

   b   Enter percentage owned ▶ ....

5   Did one foreign person (see instructions for definition) at any time during the tax year own at least 25% of:

   a   The total voting power of all classes of stock of the corporation entitled to vote, or

   b   The total value of all classes of stock of the corporation?

   If "Yes," the corporation may have to file Form 5472.

   If "Yes," enter owner's country(ies) ▶ ....

   Enter number of Forms 5472 attached ▶

6   Was the corporation a U.S. shareholder of any controlled foreign corporation? (See sections 951 and 957.) . .

   If "Yes," attach Form 5471 for each such corporation. Enter number of Forms 5471 attached ▶ ....

7   At any time during the tax year, did the corporation have an interest in or a signature or other authority over a financial account in a foreign country (such as a bank account, securities account, or other financial account)? (See page 15 of the instructions for more information, including filing requirements for Form TD F 90-22.1.)

   If "Yes," enter name of foreign country ▶ ....

8   Was the corporation the grantor of, or transferor to, a foreign trust that existed during the current tax year, whether or not the corporation has any beneficial interest in it? . . . .

   If "Yes," the corporation may have to file Forms 3520, 3520-A, or 926.

9   During this tax year, did the corporation pay dividends (other than stock dividends and distributions in exchange for stock) in excess of the corporation's current and accumulated earnings and profits? (See sections 301 and 316.) . . . .

   If "Yes," file Form 5452. If this is a consolidated return, answer here for parent corporation and on **Form 851,** Affiliations Schedule, for each subsidiary.

10   Check this box if the corporation issued publicly offered debt instruments with original issue discount . . ▶ ☐

   If so, the corporation may have to file Form 8281.

11   Enter the amount of tax-exempt interest received or accrued during the tax year ▶ $ |_____|

12   If there were 35 or fewer shareholders at the end of the tax year, enter the number ▶

Form 1120 (1991)

Page **4**

Schedule L — Balance Sheets

Assets	Beginning of tax year (a)	(b)	End of tax year (c)	(d)
1 Cash				
2a Trade notes and accounts receivable				
b Less allowance for bad debts	( )		( )	
3 Inventories				
4 U.S. government obligations				
5 Tax-exempt securities (see instructions)				
6 Other current assets (attach schedule)				
7 Loans to stockholders				
8 Mortgage and real estate loans				
9 Other investments (attach schedule)				
10a Buildings and other depreciable assets				
b Less accumulated depreciation	( )		( )	
11a Depletable assets				
b Less accumulated depletion	( )		( )	
12 Land (net of any amortization)				
13a Intangible assets (amortizable only)				
b Less accumulated amortization	( )		( )	
14 Other assets (attach schedule)				
15 Total assets				
Liabilities and Stockholders' Equity				
16 Accounts payable				
17 Mortgages, notes, bonds payable in less than 1 year				
18 Other current liabilities (attach schedule)				
19 Loans from stockholders				
20 Mortgages, notes, bonds payable in 1 year or more				
21 Other liabilities (attach schedule)				
22 Capital stock: a Preferred stock				
b Common stock				
23 Paid-in or capital surplus				
24 Retained earnings—Appropriated (attach schedule)				
25 Retained earnings—Unappropriated				
26 Less cost of treasury stock		( )		( )
27 Total liabilities and stockholders' equity				

Schedule M-1 — Reconciliation of Income per Books With Income per Return *(This schedule does not have to be completed if the total assets on line 15, column (d), of Schedule L are less than $25,000.)*

1 Net income per books		7 Income recorded on books this year not included on this return (itemize):	
2 Federal income tax			
3 Excess of capital losses over capital gains		a Tax-exempt interest $	
4 Income subject to tax not recorded on books this year (itemize):			
....		8 Deductions on this return not charged against book income this year (itemize):	
5 Expenses recorded on books this year not deducted on this return (itemize):			
a Depreciation . . . . $		a Depreciation . . . . $	
b Contributions carryover $		b Contributions carryover $	
c Travel and entertainment $		....	
....		....	
....		9 Add lines 7 and 8	
6 Add lines 1 through 5		10 Income (line 28, page 1)—line 6 less line 9	

Schedule M-2 — Analysis of Unappropriated Retained Earnings per Books (Line 25, Schedule L) *(This schedule does not have to be completed if the total assets on line 15, column (d), of Schedule L are less than $25,000.)*

1 Balance at beginning of year		5 Distributions: a Cash	
2 Net income per books		b Stock	
3 Other increases (itemize):		c Property	
....		6 Other decreases (itemize):	
....		....	
....		7 Add lines 5 and 6	
4 Add lines 1, 2, and 3		8 Balance at end of year (line 4 less line 7)	

SCHEDULE PH
(Form 1120)

Department of the Treasury
Internal Revenue Service

U.S. Personal Holding Company Tax

▶ See separate instructions. Attach to tax return.

For Paperwork Reduction Act Notice, see page 1 of the Instructions for Forms 1120 and 1120-A.

OMB No. 1545-0123

1991

Name

Employer identification number

Part I—Undistributed Personal Holding Company Income

Additions

1	Taxable income before net operating loss deduction and special deductions. Enter amount from Form 1120, line 28. See instructions	1	
2	Contributions deducted in figuring line 1. Enter amount from Form 1120, line 19 . .	2	
3	Excess expenses and depreciation under section 545(b)(6). Enter amount from Schedule A, line 2. See instructions	3	
4	Total. Add lines 1 through 3	4	

Deductions

5	Federal and foreign income, war profits, and excess profits taxes not deducted in figuring line 1. See instructions (attach schedule)		5	
6	Contributions deductible under section 545(b)(2). See instructions for limitation		6	
7	Net operating loss for the preceding tax year deductible under section 545(b)(4). See instructions		7	
8a	Net capital gain. Enter amount from Schedule D (Form 1120), line 10. Foreign corporations, see instructions	8a		
b	**Less:** Income tax on this net capital gain (see section 545(b)(5)). Attach computation	8b		8c
9	Deduction for dividends paid (other than dividends paid after the end of the tax year). Enter amount from Schedule B, line 5		9	
10	Total. Add lines 5 through 9		10	
11	Subtract line 10 from line 4		11	
12	Dividends paid after the end of the tax year (other than deficiency dividends defined in section 547(d)), but not more than the smaller of line 11 or 20% of line 1, Schedule B. See instructions		12	
13	**Undistributed personal holding company income.** Subtract line 12 from line 11. Foreign corporations, see instructions		13	

Part II—Information Required Under Section 6501(f)—If the information on personal holding company income and stock ownership is not submitted with the corporation's return, the limitation period for assessment and collection of personal holding company tax is 6 years.

Personal Holding Company Income (See instructions.)

14	Dividends		14	
15a	Interest	15a		
b	**Less:** Amounts excluded under section 543(a)(1)(A), 543(a)(1)(B), 543(a)(1)(D), or 543(b)(2)(C). Attach schedule	15b	15c	
16	Royalties (other than mineral, oil, gas, or copyright royalties)		16	
17	Annuities		17	
18a	Rents	18a		
b	**Less:** Adjustments described in section 543(b)(2)(A) (attach schedule)	18b	18c	
19a	Mineral, oil, and gas royalties	19a		
b	**Less:** Adjustments described in section 543(b)(2)(B) (attach schedule)	19b	19c	
20	Copyright royalties		20	
21	Produced film rents		21	
22	Compensation received for use of corporation property by 25% shareholder		22	
23	Amounts received under personal service contracts and from their sale		23	
24	Amounts includible in taxable income from estates and trusts		24	
25	**Personal holding company income.** Add amounts in right column for lines 14 through 24 .		25	

Part III—Tax on Undistributed Personal Holding Company Income

26	**Personal holding company tax.** Enter 28% of line 13 here and on Schedule J (Form 1120), line 7, or on the proper line of the appropriate tax return	26	

Cat. No. 11465P

Schedule PH (Form 1120) 1991

Stock Ownership   Enter the names and addresses of the individuals who together owned directly or indirectly at any time during the last half of the tax year more than 50% in value of the outstanding stock of the corporation.

(a) Name	(b) Address	Highest percentage of shares owned during last half of tax year	
		(c) Preferred	(d) Common
		%	%
		%	%
		%	%
		%	%
		%	%

Schedule A   **Excess of Expenses and Depreciation Over Income From Property Not Allowable Under Section 545(b)(6)** (See instructions for Part I, line 3.)

(a) Kind of property	(b) Date acquired	(c) Cost or other basis	(d) Depreciation	(e) Repairs, insurance, and other expenses (section 162) (attach schedule)	(f) Total of columns (d) and (e)	(g) Income from rent or other compensation	(h) Excess (col. (f) less col. (g))
1							

2 Total excess of expenses and depreciation over rent or other compensation. Enter here and on line 3, Part I.
Note: *Attach a statement showing the names and addresses of persons from whom rent or other compensation was received for the use of, or the right to use, each property.*

Schedule B   **Deduction for Dividends Paid (Determined Under Section 562)**

1	Taxable dividends paid. Do not include dividends considered as paid in the preceding tax year under section 563 or deficiency dividends as defined in section 547	1	
2	Consent dividends. Attach Forms 972 and 973	2	
3	Taxable distributions. Add lines 1 and 2	3	
4	Dividend carryover from first and second preceding tax years. Attach computation	4	
5	Deduction for dividends paid. Add lines 3 and 4 and enter the result here and on Part I, line 9	5	

Form **4626**	**Alternative Minimum Tax—Corporations** (including environmental tax)	OMB No. 1545-0175
Department of the Treasury Internal Revenue Service	▶ See separate instructions. ▶ Attach to your tax return.	19**91**

Name	Employer identification number

1 Taxable income or (loss) before net operating loss deduction. (**Important:** See instructions if you are subject to the environmental tax.) **1**

2 Adjustments:

a Depreciation of tangible property placed in service after 1986 . . . . . . **2a**

b Amortization of certified pollution control facilities placed in service after 1986 . **2b**

c Amortization of mining exploration and development costs paid or incurred after 1986 . **2c**

d Amortization of circulation expenditures paid or incurred after 1986 (personal holding companies only) **2d**

e Basis adjustments in determining gain or loss from sale or exchange of property . **2e**

f Long-term contracts entered into after February 28, 1986 . . . . **2f**

g Installment sales of certain property **2g**

h Merchant marine capital construction funds **2h**

i Section 833(b) deduction (Blue Cross, Blue Shield, and similar type organizations only) . **2i**

j Tax shelter farm activities (personal service corporations only) **2j**

k Passive activities (closely held corporations and personal service corporations only) **2k**

l Certain loss limitations **2l**

m Other adjustments **2m**

n Combine lines 2a through 2m **2n**

3 Tax preference items:

a Depletion **3a**

b Tax-exempt interest from private activity bonds issued after August 7, 1986 . . **3b**

c Appreciated property charitable deduction **3c**

d Intangible drilling costs **3d**

e Reserves for losses on bad debts of financial institutions **3e**

f Accelerated depreciation of real property placed in service before 1987 . . . **3f**

g Accelerated depreciation of leased personal property placed in service before 1987 (personal holding companies only) **3g**

h Amortization of certified pollution control facilities placed in service before 1987 . **3h**

i Add lines 3a through 3h **3i**

4 Pre-adjustment alternative minimum taxable income. Combine lines 1, 2n, and 3i . **4**

5 Adjusted current earnings adjustment. Enter the amount from line 12 of the worksheet on page 7 of the instructions **5**

6 Combine lines 4 and 5. If zero or less, stop here (you are not subject to the alternative minimum tax) . . **6**

7 Adjustment based on energy preferences. (Do not enter more than 40% of line 6.) **7**

8 Alternative tax net operating loss deduction. (Do not enter more than the excess, if any, of: **(a)** 90% of line 6, over **(b)** line 7.) **8**

9 Alternative minimum taxable income. Subtract the sum of lines 7 and 8 from line 6 . . . . . . **9**

10 Exemption phase-out computation (if line 9 is $310,000 or more, skip lines 10a and 10b and enter -0- on line 10c):

a Subtract $150,000 from line 9 (if you are a member of a controlled group, see instructions). If the result is zero or less, enter -0- **10a**

b Multiply line 10a by 25% **10b**

c Exemption. Subtract line 10b from $40,000 (if you are a member of a controlled group, see instructions). If the result is zero or less, enter -0- **10c**

11 Subtract line 10c from line 9. If the result is zero or less, enter -0- **11**

12 Multiply line 11 by 20% **12**

13 Alternative minimum tax foreign tax credit. (See instructions for limitations.) **13**

14 Tentative minimum tax. Subtract line 13 from line 12 . . . . **14**

15 Regular tax liability before all credits except the foreign tax credit and possessions tax credit. . . **15**

16 Alternative minimum tax—Subtract line 15 from line 14. If the result is zero or less, enter -0-. Also enter the result on line 9a, Schedule J, Form 1120, or on the comparable line of other income tax returns . . **16**

17 Environmental tax—Subtract $2,000,000 from line 6 (computed without regard to your environmental tax deduction) and multiply the excess, if any, by 0.12% (.0012). Enter on line 9b, Schedule J, Form 1120, or on the comparable line of other income tax returns (members of a controlled group, see instructions) . . **17**

For Paperwork Reduction Act Notice, see separate instructions.   Cat. No. 12955I   Form **4626** (1991)

Form **1120S**	**U.S. Income Tax Return for an S Corporation**	OMB No. 1545-0130
Department of the Treasury Internal Revenue Service	For calendar year 1991, or tax year beginning .... , 1991, and ending .... , 19 ..... ▶ **See separate instructions.**	**1991**

A Date of election as an S corporation	Use IRS label. Otherwise, please print or type.	Name	**C** Employer identification number
		Number, street, and room or suite no. (If a P.O. box, see page 8 of the instructions.)	**D** Date incorporated
B Business code no. (see Specific Instructions)		City or town, state, and ZIP code	**E** Total assets (see Specific Instructions) $

F Check applicable boxes: (1) ☐ Initial return   (2) ☐ Final return   (3) ☐ Change in address   (4) ☐ Amended return
G Check this box if this S corporation is subject to the consolidated audit procedures of sections 6241 through 6245 (see instructions before checking this box) . ▶ ☐
H Enter number of shareholders in the corporation at end of the tax year . . . . ▶

Caution: Include only trade or business income and expenses on lines 1a through 21. See the instructions for more information.

Income

1a Gross receipts or sales |_____| **b** Less returns and allowances |_____| **c** Bal ▶	**1c**	
2 Cost of goods sold (Schedule A, line 8)	**2**	
3 Gross profit. Subtract line 2 from line 1c	**3**	
4 Net gain (loss) from Form 4797, Part II, line 18 *(attach Form 4797)*	**4**	
5 Other income (see instructions) *(attach schedule)*	**5**	
6 **Total income (loss).** Combine lines 3 through 5 . . . . ▶	**6**	

Deductions (See instructions for limitations.)

7 Compensation of officers	**7**	
8a Salaries and wages |_____| **b** Less jobs credit |_____| **c** Bal ▶	**8c**	
9 Repairs	**9**	
10 Bad debts	**10**	
11 Rents	**11**	
12 Taxes	**12**	
13 Interest	**13**	
14a Depreciation (see instructions)	14a			
b Depreciation claimed on Schedule A and elsewhere on return . .	14b			
c Subtract line 14b from line 14a	**14c**	
15 Depletion **(Do not deduct oil and gas depletion.)**	**15**	
16 Advertising	**16**	
17 Pension, profit-sharing, etc., plans	**17**	
18 Employee benefit programs	**18**	
19 Other deductions *(attach schedule)*	**19**	
20 **Total deductions.** Add lines 7 through 19 . . . . ▶	**20**	
21 Ordinary income (loss) from trade or business activities. Subtract line 20 from line 6	**21**	

Tax and Payments

22 **Tax:**		
a Excess net passive income tax *(attach schedule)*	22a		
b Tax from Schedule D (Form 1120S)	22b		
c Add lines 22a and 22b (see instructions for additional taxes)	**22c**	
23 **Payments:**		
a 1991 estimated tax payments	23a		
b Tax deposited with Form 7004	23b		
c Credit for Federal tax on fuels *(attach Form 4136)* . . .	23c		
d Add lines 23a through 23c . . . . ▶	**23d**	
24 Estimated tax penalty (see page 3 of instructions). Check if Form 2220 is attached . . ▶ ☐	**24**	
25 **Tax due.** If the total of lines 22c and 24 is larger than line 23d, enter amount owed. See instructions for depositary method of payment . . . . ▶	**25**	
26 **Overpayment.** If line 23d is larger than the total of lines 22c and 24, enter amount overpaid ▶	**26**	
27 Enter amount of line 26 you want: **Credited to 1992 estimated tax** ▶ |_____| **Refunded** ▶	**27**	

Please Sign Here

Under penalties of perjury, I declare that I have examined this return, including accompanying schedules and statements, and to the best of my knowledge and belief, it is true, correct, and complete. Declaration of preparer (other than taxpayer) is based on all information of which preparer has any knowledge.

▶ _____ _____ ▶ _____
Signature of officer   Date   Title

Paid Preparer's Use Only

Preparer's signature ▶	Date	Check if self-employed ▶ ☐	Preparer's social security number
Firm's name (or yours if self-employed) and address ▶		E.I. No. ▶	
		ZIP code ▶	

For Paperwork Reduction Act Notice, see page 1 of separate instructions. | Cat. No. 11510H | Form **1120S** (1991)

Schedule A **Cost of Goods Sold** (See instructions.)

1	Inventory at beginning of year	**1**
2	Purchases	**2**
3	Cost of labor	**3**
4	Additional section 263A costs (see instructions) *(attach schedule)*	**4**
5	Other costs *(attach schedule)*	**5**
6	**Total.** Add lines 1 through 5	**6**
7	Inventory at end of year	**7**
8	**Cost of goods sold.** Subtract line 7 from line 6. Enter here and on line 2, page 1	**8**

9a Check all methods used for valuing closing inventory:
    (i) ☐ Cost
    (ii) ☐ Lower of cost or market as described in Regulations section 1.471-4
    (iii) ☐ Writedown of "subnormal" goods as described in Regulations section 1.471-2(c)
    (iv) ☐ Other (specify method used and attach explanation) ▶ --
  b Check if the LIFO inventory method was adopted this tax year for any goods *(if checked, attach Form 970)*. . . . . . ▶ ☐
  c If the LIFO inventory method was used for this tax year, enter percentage (or amounts) of closing
    inventory computed under LIFO . . . . **9c** |
  d Do the rules of section 263A (for property produced or acquired for resale) apply to the corporation? . . . ☐ Yes ☐ No
  e Was there any change in determining quantities, cost, or valuations between opening and closing inventory? . . ☐ Yes ☐ No
    If "Yes," attach explanation.

Schedule B **Other Information**

                                                                                                Yes **No**

1 Check method of accounting: **(a)** ☐ Cash   **(b)** ☐ Accrual   **(c)** ☐ Other (specify) ▶ -----------------------------

2 Refer to the list in the instructions and state your principal:
  (a) Business activity ▶ ---------------------------------   **(b)** Product or service ▶ ---------------------------------

3 Did you at the end of the tax year own, directly or indirectly, 50% or more of the voting stock of a domestic corporation? (For rules of attribution, see section 267(c).) If "Yes," attach a schedule showing: **(a)** name, address, and employer identification number and **(b)** percentage owned.

4 Were you a member of a controlled group subject to the provisions of section 1561? . . . .

5 At any time during the tax year, did you have an interest in or a signature or other authority over a financial account in a foreign country (such as a bank account, securities account, or other financial account)? (See instructions for exceptions and filing requirements for form TD F 90-22.1.) . . . .
  If "Yes," enter the name of the foreign country ▶ --

6 Were you the grantor of, or transferor to, a foreign trust that existed during the current tax year, whether or not you have any beneficial interest in it? If "Yes," you may have to file Forms 3520, 3520-A, or 926 . . . .

7 Check this box if the corporation has filed or is required to file **Form 8264,** Application for Registration of a Tax Shelter . . . . ▶ ☐

8 Check this box if the corporation issued publicly offered debt instruments with original issue discount . . . ▶ ☐
  If so, the corporation may have to file **Form 8281,** Information Return for Publicly Offered Original Issue Discount Instruments.

9 If the corporation: **(a)** filed its election to be an S corporation after 1986, **(b)** was a C corporation before it elected to be an S corporation **or** the corporation acquired an asset with a basis determined by reference to its basis (or the basis of any other property) in the hands of a C corporation, and **(c)** has net unrealized built-in gain (defined in section 1374(d)(1)) in excess of the net recognized built-in gain from prior years, enter the net unrealized built-in gain reduced by net recognized built-in gain from prior years (see instructions) . . . . ▶ $------------------------

10 Check this box if the corporation had subchapter C earnings and profits at the close of the tax year (see instructions) . . . . ▶ ☐

Designation of Tax Matters Person (See instructions.)

Enter below the shareholder designated as the tax matters person (TMP) for the tax year of this return:

Name of designated TMP ▶	Identifying number of TMP ▶

Address of designated TMP ▶

Schedule K	Shareholders' Shares of Income, Credits, Deductions, etc.		
	(a) Pro rata share items		(b) Total amount

Income (Loss)

1	Ordinary income (loss) from trade or business activities (page 1, line 21)	1	
2	Net income (loss) from rental real estate activities (attach Form 8825)	2	
3a	Gross income from other rental activities **3a**		
b	Less expenses (attach schedule). **3b**		
c	Net income (loss) from other rental activities	3c	
4	Portfolio income (loss):		
a	Interest income	4a	
b	Dividend income	4b	
c	Royalty income	4c	
d	Net short-term capital gain (loss) (attach Schedule D (Form 1120S))	4d	
e	Net long-term capital gain (loss) (attach Schedule D (Form 1120S)).	4e	
f	Other portfolio income (loss) (attach schedule)	4f	
5	Net gain (loss) under section 1231 (other than due to casualty or theft) (attach Form 4797)	5	
6	Other income (loss) (attach schedule)	6	

Deductions

7	Charitable contributions (see instructions) (attach list)	7	
8	Section 179 expense deduction (attach Form 4562).	8	
9	Deductions related to portfolio income (loss) (see instructions) (itemize)	9	
10	Other deductions (attach schedule)	10	

Investment Interest

11a	Interest expense on investment debts	11a	
b (1)	Investment income included on lines 4a through 4f above	11b(1)	
(2)	Investment expenses included on line 9 above	11b(2)	

Credits

12a	Credit for alcohol used as a fuel (attach Form 6478)	12a	
b	Low-income housing credit (see instructions):		
(1)	From partnerships to which section 42(j)(5) applies for property placed in service before 1990	12b(1)	
(2)	Other than on line 12b(1) for property placed in service before 1990.	12b(2)	
(3)	From partnerships to which section 42(j)(5) applies for property placed in service after 1989	12b(3)	
(4)	Other than on line 12b(3) for property placed in service after 1989	12b(4)	
c	Qualified rehabilitation expenditures related to rental real estate activities (attach Form 3468) .	12c	
d	Credits (other than credits shown on lines 12b and 12c) related to rental real estate activities (see instructions).	12d	
e	Credits related to other rental activities (see instructions)	12e	
13	Other credits (see instructions)	13	

Adjustments and Tax Preference Items

14a	Accelerated depreciation of real property placed in service before 1987	14a	
b	Accelerated depreciation of leased personal property placed in service before 1987 . .	14b	
c	Depreciation adjustment on property placed in service after 1986	14c	
d	Depletion (other than oil and gas)	14d	
e (1)	Gross income from oil, gas, or geothermal properties	14e(1)	
(2)	Deductions allocable to oil, gas, or geothermal properties	14e(2)	
f	Other adjustments and tax preference items (attach schedule)	14f	

Foreign Taxes

15a	Type of income ▶		
b	Name of foreign country or U.S. possession ▶		
c	Total gross income from sources outside the United States (attach schedule)	15c	
d	Total applicable deductions and losses (attach schedule)	15d	
e	Total foreign taxes (check one): ▶ ☐ Paid ☐ Accrued	15e	
f	Reduction in taxes available for credit (attach schedule)	15f	
g	Other foreign tax information (attach schedule)	15g	

Other

16a	Total expenditures to which a section 59(e) election may apply	16a	
b	Type of expenditures ▶		
17	Total property distributions (including cash) other than dividends reported on line 19 below	17	
18	Other items and amounts required to be reported separately to shareholders (see instructions) (attach schedule)		
19	Total dividend distributions paid from accumulated earnings and profits	19	
20	**Income (loss)** (Required only if Schedule M-1 must be completed.). Combine lines 1 through 6 in column (b). From the result, subtract the sum of lines 7 through 11a, 15e, and 16a	20	

Form 1120S (1991) Page **4**

Schedule L	Balance Sheets	Beginning of tax year		End of tax year	
	Assets	**(a)**	**(b)**	**(c)**	**(d)**
1	Cash				
2a	Trade notes and accounts receivable . .				
b	Less allowance for bad debts				
3	Inventories				
4	U.S. Government obligations.				
5	Tax-exempt securities				
6	Other current assets (attach schedule). .				
7	Loans to shareholders				
8	Mortgage and real estate loans				
9	Other investments (attach schedule) . .				
10a	Buildings and other depreciable assets .				
b	Less accumulated depreciation				
11a	Depletable assets				
b	Less accumulated depletion				
12	Land (net of any amortization)				
13a	Intangible assets (amortizable only). . .				
b	Less accumulated amortization				
14	Other assets (attach schedule)				
15	Total assets				
	Liabilities and Shareholders' Equity				
16	Accounts payable				
17	Mortgages, notes, bonds payable in less than 1 year				
18	Other current liabilities (attach schedule)				
19	Loans from shareholders				
20	Mortgages, notes, bonds payable in 1 year or more				
21	Other liabilities (attach schedule) . . .				
22	Capital stock				
23	Paid-in or capital surplus				
24	Retained earnings				
25	Less cost of treasury stock		( )		( )
26	Total liabilities and shareholders' equity . .				

Schedule M-1 **Reconciliation of Income per Books With Income per Return** (You are not required to complete this schedule if the total assets on line 15, column (d), of Schedule L are less than $25,000.)

1	Net income per books		5 Income recorded on books this year not included on Schedule K, lines 1 through 6 (itemize):	
2	Income included on Schedule K, lines 1 through 6, not recorded on books this year (itemize):			
	....		**a** Tax-exempt interest $	
			....	
3	Expenses recorded on books this year not included on Schedule K, lines 1 through 11a, 15e, and 16a (itemize):		6 Deductions included on Schedule K, lines 1 through 11a, 15e, and 16a, not charged against book income this year (itemize):	
a	Depreciation $		**a** Depreciation $	
b	Travel and entertainment $		....	
	....		....	
	....		7 Add lines 5 and 6	
4	Add lines 1 through 3		8 Income (loss) (Schedule K, line 20). Line 4 less line 7	

Schedule M-2 **Analysis of Accumulated Adjustments Account, Other Adjustments Account, and Shareholders' Undistributed Taxable Income Previously Taxed** (See instructions.)

		(a) Accumulated adjustments account	(b) Other adjustments account	(c) Shareholders' undistributed taxable income previously taxed
1	Balance at beginning of tax year . . .			
2	Ordinary income from page 1, line 21 . .			
3	Other additions			
4	Loss from page 1, line 21.	( )		
5	Other reductions	( )	( )	
6	Combine lines 1 through 5			
7	Distributions other than dividend distributions .			
8	Balance at end of tax year. Subtract line 7 from line 6			

SCHEDULE K-1 (Form 1120S)	Shareholder's Share of Income, Credits, Deductions, etc.	OMB No. 1545-0130

Shareholder's Share of Income, Credits, Deductions, etc.
▶ See separate instructions.
For calendar year 1991 or tax year
beginning , 1991, and ending , 19

Department of the Treasury
Internal Revenue Service

1991

Shareholder's identifying number ▶	Corporation's identifying number ▶
Shareholder's name, address, and ZIP code	Corporation's name, address, and ZIP code

A Shareholder's percentage of stock ownership for tax year (see Instructions for Schedule K-1) . . . . . ▶ .... %
B Internal Revenue service center where corporation filed its return ▶ ....
C (1) Tax shelter registration number (see Instructions for Schedule K-1) . . . . . ▶ ....
(2) Type of tax shelter ▶ ....
D Check applicable boxes: **(1)** ☐ Final K-1 **(2)** ☐ Amended K-1

(a) Pro rata share items		(b) Amount	(c) Form 1040 filers enter the amount in column (b) on:
Income (Loss)			
1 Ordinary income (loss) from trade or business activities	1		See Shareholder's Instructions for Schedule K-1 (Form 1120S).
2 Net income (loss) from rental real estate activities	2		
3 Net income (loss) from other rental activities	3		
4 Portfolio income (loss):			
a Interest	4a		Sch. B, Part I, line 1
b Dividends	4b		Sch. B, Part II, line 5
c Royalties	4c		Sch. E, Part I, line 4
d Net short-term capital gain (loss)	4d		Sch. D, line 4, col. (f) or (g)
e Net long-term capital gain (loss)	4e		Sch. D, line 11, col. (f) or (g)
f Other portfolio income (loss) (attach schedule)	4f		(Enter on applicable line of your return.)
5 Net gain (loss) under section 1231 (other than due to casualty or theft)	5		See Shareholder's Instructions for Schedule K-1 (Form 1120S)
6 Other income (loss) (attach schedule)	6		(Enter on applicable line of your return.)
Deductions			
7 Charitable contributions (see instructions) (attach schedule)	7		Sch. A, line 13 or 14
8 Section 179 expense deduction	8		See Shareholder's Instructions for Schedule K-1 (Form 1120S)
9 Deductions related to portfolio income (loss) (attach schedule)	9		
10 Other deductions (attach schedule)	10		
Investment Interest			
11a Interest expense on investment debts	11a		Form 4952, line 1
b (1) Investment income included on lines 4a through 4f above	b(1)		See Shareholder's Instructions for Schedule K-1 (Form 1120S).
(2) Investment expenses included on line 9 above	b(2)		
Credits			
12a Credit for alcohol used as fuel	12a		Form 6478, line 10
b Low-income housing credit:			
(1) From section 42(j)(5) partnerships for property placed in service before 1990	b(1)		Form 8586, line 5
(2) Other than on line 12b(1) for property placed in service before 1990	b(2)		
(3) From section 42(j)(5) partnerships for property placed in service after 1989	b(3)		
(4) Other than on line 12b(3) for property placed in service after 1989	b(4)		
c Qualified rehabilitation expenditures related to rental real estate activities (see instructions)	12c		See Shareholder's Instructions for Schedule K-1 (Form 1120S).
d Credits (other than credits shown on lines 12b and 12c) related to rental real estate activities (see instructions)	12d		
e Credits related to other rental activities (see instructions)	12e		
13 Other credits (see instructions)	13		
Adjustments and Tax Preference Items			
14a Accelerated depreciation of real property placed in service before 1987	14a		See Shareholder's Instructions for Schedule K-1 (Form 1120S) and Instructions for Form 6251
b Accelerated depreciation of leased personal property placed in service before 1987	14b		
c Depreciation adjustment on property placed in service after 1986	14c		
d Depletion (other than oil and gas)	14d		
e (1) Gross income from oil, gas, or geothermal properties	e(1)		
(2) Deductions allocable to oil, gas, or geothermal properties	e(2)		
f Other adjustments and tax preference items (attach schedule)	14f		

For Paperwork Reduction Act Notice, see page 1 of Instructions for Form 1120S.   Cat. No. 11520D   **Schedule K-1 (Form 1120S) 1991**

Schedule K-1 (Form 1120S) (1991)   Page **2**

		(a) Pro rata share items	(b) Amount	(c) Form 1040 filers enter the amount in column (b) on:
Foreign Taxes	**15a**	Type of income ▶		Form 1116, Check boxes
	b	Name of foreign country or U.S. possession ▶		
	c	Total gross income from sources outside the U.S. *(attach schedule)* .	**15c**	} Form 1116, Part I
	d	Total applicable deductions and losses *(attach schedule)* .	**15d**	
	e	Total foreign taxes (check one): ▶ ☐ Paid ☐ Accrued . .	**15e**	Form 1116, Part II
	f	Reduction in taxes available for credit *(attach schedule)* . .	**15f**	Form 1116, Part III
	g	Other foreign tax information *(attach schedule)*	**15g**	See Instructions for Form 1116
Other	**16a**	Total expenditures to which a section 59(e) election may apply	**16a**	} See Shareholder's Instructions for Schedule K-1 (Form 1120S).
	b	Type of expenditures ▶		
	17	Property distributions (including cash) other than dividend distributions reported to you on Form 1099-DIV	**17**	
	18	Amount of loan repayments for "Loans From Shareholders" .	**18**	
	19	Recapture of low-income housing credit:		
	a	From section 42(j)(5) partnerships	**19a**	} Form 8611, line 8
	b	Other than on line 19a	**19b**	

20 Supplemental information required to be reported separately to each shareholder *(attach additional schedules if more space is needed)*:

Supplemental Information

Form **1065**
Department of the Treasury
Internal Revenue Service

U.S. Partnership Return of Income

For calendar year 1991, or tax year beginning ...., 1991, and ending............., 19....
▶ See separate instructions.

OMB No. 1545-0099

1991

A Principal business activity	Use the IRS label. Otherwise, please print or type.	Name of partnership	D Employer identification number
B Principal product or service		Number, street, and room or suite no. (If a P.O. box, see page 9 of the instructions.)	E Date business started
C Business code number		City or town, state, and ZIP code	F Total assets (see Specific Instructions) $

G Check applicable boxes: **(1)** ☐ Initial return **(2)** ☐ Final return **(3)** ☐ Change in address **(4)** ☐ Amended return

H Check accounting method: **(1)** ☐ Cash **(2)** ☐ Accrual **(3)** ☐ Other (specify) ▶ ....

I Number of partners in this partnership . . . .

Caution: *Include **only** trade or business income and expenses on lines 1a through 22 below. See the instructions for more information.*

Income

1a Gross receipts or sales	1a		
b Less returns and allowances.	1b	1c	
2 Cost of goods sold (Schedule A, line 8)		2	
3 Gross profit. Subtract line 2 from line 1c.		3	
4 Ordinary income (loss) from other partnerships and fiduciaries *(attach schedule)* . . .		4	
5 Net farm profit (loss) *(attach Schedule F (Form 1040))*		5	
6 Net gain (loss) from Form 4797, Part II, line 18.		6	
7 Other income (loss) (see instructions) *(attach schedule)*		7	
8 **Total income (loss).** Combine lines 3 through 7		8	

Deductions (see instructions for limitations)

9a Salaries and wages (other than to partners).	9a		
b Less jobs credit	9b	9c	
10 Guaranteed payments to partners		10	
11 Rent		11	
12 Interest		12	
13 Taxes		13	
14 Bad debts		14	
15 Repairs		15	
16a Depreciation (see instructions)	16a		
b Less depreciation reported on Schedule A and elsewhere on return	16b	16c	
17 Depletion **(Do not deduct oil and gas depletion.)**		17	
18 Retirement plans, etc.		18	
19 Employee benefit programs		19	
20 Other deductions *(attach schedule)*		20	
21 **Total deductions.** Add the amounts shown in the far right column for lines 9c through 20 .		21	
22 **Ordinary income (loss)** from trade or business activities. Subtract line 21 from line 8 . .		22	

Line 1 on Sch. K

Please Sign Here

Under penalties of perjury, I declare that I have examined this return, including accompanying schedules and statements, and to the best of my knowledge and belief, it is true, correct, and complete. Declaration of preparer (other than general partner) is based on all information of which preparer has any knowledge.

▶ _____
Signature of general partner

▶ _____
Date

Paid Preparer's Use Only

Preparer's signature ▶		Date	Check if self-employed ▶ ☐	Preparer's social security no.
Firm's name (or yours if self-employed) and address ▶			E.I. No. ▶	
			ZIP code ▶	

For Paperwork Reduction Act Notice, see page 1 of separate instructions. Cat. No. 11390Z Form **1065** (1991)

Schedule A Cost of Goods Sold

1	Inventory at beginning of year	**1**	
2	Purchases less cost of items withdrawn for personal use	**2**	
3	Cost of labor	**3**	
4	Additional section 263A costs (see instructions) *(attach schedule)*	**4**	
5	Other costs *(attach schedule)*	**5**	
6	**Total.** Add lines 1 through 5	**6**	
7	Inventory at end of year	**7**	
8	**Cost of goods sold.** Subtract line 7 from line 6. Enter here and on page 1, line 2	**8**	

9a Check all methods used for valuing closing inventory:

    (i) ☐ Cost

    (ii) ☐ Lower of cost or market as described in Regulations section 1.471-4

    (iii) ☐ Writedown of "subnormal" goods as described in Regulations section 1:471-2(c)

    (iv) ☐ Other (specify method used and attach explanation) ▶ ....

  b Check this box if the LIFO inventory method was adopted this tax year for any goods *(if checked, attach Form 970)* . . ▶ ☐

  c Do the rules of section 263A (for property produced or acquired for resale) apply to the partnership? . . ☐ **Yes** ☐ **No**

  d Was there any change in determining quantities, cost, or valuations between opening and closing inventory? ☐ **Yes** ☐ **No**
    If "Yes," attach explanation.

Schedule B Other Information

		Yes	No
1	Is this partnership a limited partnership?		
2	Are any partners in this partnership also partnerships?		
3	Is this partnership a partner in another partnership?		
4	Is this partnership subject to the consolidated audit procedures of sections 6221 through 6233? If "Yes," see **Designation of Tax Matters Partner** below		
5	Does this partnership meet **all** the requirements shown in the instructions for **Question 5?**		
6	Does this partnership have any foreign partners?		
7	Is this partnership a publicly traded partnership as defined in section 469(k)(2)?		
8	Has this partnership filed, or is it required to file, **Form 8264,** Application for Registration of a Tax Shelter? . .		
9	At any time during the tax year, did the partnership have an interest in or a signature or other authority over a financial account in a foreign country (such as a bank account, securities account, or other financial account)? (See the instructions for exceptions and filing requirements for form TD F 90-22.1.) If "Yes," enter the name of the foreign country. ▶		
10	Was the partnership the grantor of, or transferor to, a foreign trust which existed during the current tax year, whether or not the partnership or any partner has any beneficial interest in it? If "Yes," you may have to file Forms 3520, 3520-A, or 926		
11	Was there a distribution of property or a transfer (for example, by sale or death) of a partnership interest during the tax year? If "Yes," you may elect to adjust the basis of the partnership's assets under section 754 by attaching the statement described under **Elections** on page 5 of the instructions		

Designation of Tax Matters Partner (See instructions.)

Enter below the general partner designated as the tax matters partner (TMP) for the tax year of this return:

Name of
designated TMP ▶   Identifying
number of TMP ▶

Address of
designated TMP ▶ _____

Form 1065 (1991)

Page **3**

Schedule K Partners' Shares of Income, Credits, Deductions, Etc.

	(a) Distributive share items	(b) Total amount	

Income (Loss)

1	Ordinary income (loss) from trade or business activities (page 1, line 22)	**1**	
2	Net income (loss) from rental real estate activities *(attach Form 8825)*	**2**	
3a	Gross income from other rental activities **3a**		
b	Less expenses *(attach schedule)* **3b**		
c	Net income (loss) from other rental activities	**3c**	
4	Portfolio income (loss) (see instructions):		
a	Interest income	**4a**	
b	Dividend income	**4b**	
c	Royalty income	**4c**	
d	Net short-term capital gain (loss) *(attach Schedule D (Form 1065))*	**4d**	
e	Net long-term capital gain (loss) *(attach Schedule D (Form 1065))*	**4e**	
f	Other portfolio income (loss) *(attach schedule)*.	**4f**	
5	Guaranteed payments to partners	**5**	
6	Net gain (loss) under section 1231 (other than due to casualty or theft) *(attach Form 4797)*	**6**	
7	Other income (loss) *(attach schedule)*	**7**	

Deductions

8	Charitable contributions (see instructions) *(attach list)*	**8**	
9	Section 179 expense deduction *(attach Form 4562)*	**9**	
10	Deductions related to portfolio income (see instructions) (itemize)	**10**	
11	Other deductions *(attach schedule)*	**11**	

Investment Interest

12a	Interest expense on investment debts	**12a**	
b (1)	Investment income included on lines 4a through 4f above.	**12b(1)**	
(2)	Investment expenses included on line 10 above	**12b(2)**	

Credits

13a	Credit for income tax withheld.	**13a**	
b	Low-income housing credit (see instructions):		
(1)	From partnerships to which section 42(j)(5) applies for property placed in service before 1990	**13b(1)**	
(2)	Other than on line 13b(1) for property placed in service before 1990	**13b(2)**	
(3)	From partnerships to which section 42(j)(5) applies for property placed in service after 1989	**13b(3)**	
(4)	Other than on line 13b(3) for property placed in service after 1989	**13b(4)**	
c	Qualified rehabilitation expenditures related to rental real estate activities *(attach Form 3468)* . .	**13c**	
d	Credits (other than credits shown on lines 13b and 13c) related to rental real estate activities (see instructions)	**13d**	
e	Credits related to other rental activities (see instructions)	**13e**	
14	Other credits (see instructions)	**14**	

Self-Employment

15a	Net earnings (loss) from self-employment	**15a**	
b	Gross farming or fishing income	**15b**	
c	Gross nonfarm income	**15c**	

Adjustments and Tax Preference Items

16a	Accelerated depreciation of real property placed in service before 1987	**16a**	
b	Accelerated depreciation of leased personal property placed in service before 1987. .	**16b**	
c	Depreciation adjustment on property placed in service after 1986	**16c**	
d	Depletion (other than oil and gas).	**16d**	
e (1)	Gross income from oil, gas, and geothermal properties	**16e(1)**	
(2)	Deductions allocable to oil, gas, and geothermal properties	**16e(2)**	
f	Other adjustments and tax preference items *(attach schedule)*	**16f**	

Foreign Taxes

17a	Type of income ▶.................... **b** Foreign country or U.S. possession ▶..................		
c	Total gross income from sources outside the U.S. *(attach schedule)*.	**17c**	
d	Total applicable deductions and losses *(attach schedule)*	**17d**	
e	Total foreign taxes (check one): ▶ ☐ Paid ☐ Accrued	**17e**	
f	Reduction in taxes available for credit *(attach schedule)*	**17f**	
g	Other foreign tax information *(attach schedule)*	**17g**	

Other

18a	Total expenditures to which a section 59(e) election may apply	**18a**	
b	Type of expenditures ▶		
19	Other items and amounts required to be reported separately to partners (see instructions) *(attach schedule)*		

Analysis

20a	Income (loss). Combine lines 1 through 7 in column (b). From the result, subtract the sum of lines 8 through 12a, 17e, and 18a	**20a**	

b Analysis by type of partner:	(a) Corporate	(b) Individual		(c) Partnership	(d) Exempt organization	(e) Nominee/Other
		i. Active	ii. Passive			
(1) General partners						
(2) Limited partners						

Form 1065 (1991)   Page **4**

Caution: *Read the instructions for **Question 5** of Schedule B on page 14 of the instructions before completing Schedules L, M-1, and M-2.*

Schedule L — Balance Sheets

Assets	Beginning of tax year		End of tax year	
	(a)	(b)	(c)	(d)
1 Cash				
2a Trade notes and accounts receivable				
b Less allowance for bad debts				
3 Inventories				
4 U.S. government obligations				
5 Tax-exempt securities				
6 Other current assets (attach schedule) . . .				
7 Mortgage and real estate loans				
8 Other investments (attach schedule)				
9a Buildings and other depreciable assets . . .				
b Less accumulated depreciation				
10a Depletable assets				
b Less accumulated depletion				
11 Land (net of any amortization)				
12a Intangible assets (amortizable only).				
b Less accumulated amortization				
13 Other assets (attach schedule)				
14 **Total** assets				
Liabilities and Capital				
15 Accounts payable				
16 Mortgages, notes, bonds payable in less than 1 year .				
17 Other current liabilities (attach schedule) . . .				
18 All nonrecourse loans				
19 Mortgages, notes, bonds payable in 1 year or more .				
20 Other liabilities (attach schedule)				
21 Partners' capital accounts.				
22 **Total** liabilities and capital.				

Schedule M-1 — Reconciliation of Income per Books With Income per Return

1 Net income per books		5 Income recorded on books this year not included on Schedule K, lines 1 through 7 (itemize):	
2 Income included on Schedule K, lines 1 through 7, not recorded on books this year (itemize):		a Tax-exempt interest $	
....		6 Deductions included on Schedule K, lines 1 through 12a, 17e, and 18a, not charged against book income this year (itemize):	
3 Expenses recorded on books this year not included on Schedule K, lines 1 through 12a, 17e, and 18a (itemize):		a Depreciation $	
a Depreciation $		....	
b Travel and entertainment $		7 Total of lines 5 and 6	
....		8 Income (loss) (Schedule K, line 20a). Line 4 less line 7	
4 Total of lines 1 through 3			

Schedule M-2 — Analysis of Partners' Capital Accounts

1 Balance at beginning of year		6 Distributions: a Cash	
2 Capital contributed during year		b Property	
3 Net income per books		7 Other decreases (itemize):	
4 Other increases (itemize):		....	
....		8 Total of lines 6 and 7	
5 Total of lines 1 through 4		9 Balance at end of year. Line 5 less line 8 .	

SCHEDULE K-1 (Form 1065) Department of the Treasury Internal Revenue Service	**Partner's Share of Income, Credits, Deductions, Etc.** ▶ See separate instructions. For calendar year 1991 or tax year beginning ____, 1991, and ending ____, 19	OMB No. 1545-0099 **1991**

Partner's identifying number ▶ | **Partnership's identifying number** ▶

Partner's name, address, and ZIP code | Partnership's name, address, and ZIP code

A Is this partner a general partner? . . . ☐ Yes ☐ No
B Partner's share of liabilities (see instructions):
Nonrecourse . . . . $ ....
Qualified nonrecourse financing . . $ ....
Other . . . . $ ....
C What type of entity is this partner? . ▶ ....
D Is this partner a ☐ domestic or a ☐ foreign partner?
E IRS Center where partnership filed return:

F Enter partner's percentage of:

	(i) Before change or termination	**(ii)** End of year
Profit sharing	.... %	.... %
Loss sharing	.... %	.... %
Ownership of capital	.... %	.... %

G(1) Tax shelter registration number . ▶ ....
(2) Type of tax shelter ▶
H Check here if this partnership is a publicly traded partnership as defined in section 469(k)(2) . . . . ☐
I Check applicable boxes: **(1)** ☐ Final K-1 **(2)** ☐ Amended K-1

J Analysis of partner's capital account:

(a) Capital account at beginning of year	**(b)** Capital contributed during year	**(c)** Partner's share of lines 3, 4, and 7, Form 1065, Schedule M-2	**(d)** Withdrawals and distributions	**(e)** Capital account at end of year (combine columns (a) through (d))
			( )	

	(a) Distributive share item		**(b)** Amount	**(c)** 1040 filers enter the amount in column (b) on:
Income (Loss)	**1** Ordinary income (loss) from trade or business activities . . .	**1**		⎫ See Partner's Instructions for Schedule K-1 (Form 1065). ⎬
	2 Net income (loss) from rental real estate activities	**2**		
	3 Net income (loss) from other rental activities	**3**		⎭
	4 Portfolio income (loss):			
	a Interest	**4a**		Sch. B, Part I, line 1
	b Dividends	**4b**		Sch. B, Part II, line 5
	c Royalties	**4c**		Sch. E, Part I, line 4
	d Net short-term capital gain (loss)	**4d**		Sch. D, line 4, col. (f) or (g)
	e Net long-term capital gain (loss)	**4e**		Sch. D, line 11, col. (f) or (g)
	f Other portfolio income (loss) (attach schedule)	**4f**		(Enter on applicable line of your return.)
	5 Guaranteed payments to partner	**5**		⎫ See Partner's Instructions for Schedule K-1 (Form 1065). ⎬
	6 Net gain (loss) under section 1231 (other than due to casualty or theft)	**6**		⎭
	7 Other income (loss) (attach schedule)	**7**		(Enter on applicable line of your return.)
Deductions	**8** Charitable contributions (see instructions) (attach schedule) . .	**8**		Sch. A, line 13 or 14
	9 Section 179 expense deduction	**9**		⎫ See Partner's Instructions for Schedule K-1 (Form 1065). ⎬
	10 Deductions related to portfolio income (attach schedule) . . .	**10**		
	11 Other deductions (attach schedule)	**11**		⎭
Investment Interest	**12a** Interest expense on investment debts	**12a**		Form 4952, line 1
	b (1) Investment income included on lines 4a through 4f above .	**b(1)**		⎫ See Partner's Instructions for Schedule K-1 (Form 1065). ⎬
	(2) Investment expenses included on line 10 above	**b(2)**		⎭
Credits	**13a** Credit for income tax withheld	**13a**		⎫ See Partner's Instructions for Schedule K-1 (Form 1065). ⎬
	b Low-income housing credit:			
	(1) From section 42(j)(5) partnerships for property placed in service before 1990	**b(1)**		⎫
	(2) Other than on line 13b(1) for property placed in service before 1990	**b(2)**		
	(3) From section 42(j)(5) partnerships for property placed in service after 1989	**b(3)**		⎬ Form 8586, line 5
	(4) Other than on line 13b(3) for property placed in service after 1989	**b(4)**		
	c Qualified rehabilitation expenditures related to rental real estate activities (see instructions)	**13c**		⎭
	d Credits (other than credits shown on lines 13b and 13c) related to rental real estate activities (see instructions)	**13d**		⎫ See Partner's Instructions for Schedule K-1 (Form 1065). ⎬
	e Credits related to other rental activities (see instructions) . . .	**13e**		
	14 Other credits (see instructions)	**14**		⎭

from Sock

For Paperwork Reduction Act Notice, see Instructions for Form 1065. | Cat. No. 11394R | **Schedule K-1 (Form 1065) 1991**

	(a) Distributive share item		(b) Amount	(c) 1040 filers enter the amount in column (b) on:
Self-employment	**15a** Net earnings (loss) from self-employment	**15a**		Sch. SE, Section A or B
	b Gross farming or fishing income.	**15b**		(See Partner's Instructions for Schedule K-1 (Form 1065).)
	c Gross nonfarm income.	**15c**		
Adjustments and Tax Preference Items	**16a** Accelerated depreciation of real property placed in service before 1987	**16a**		(See Partner's Instructions for Schedule K-1 (Form 1065) and Instructions for Form 6251.)
	b Accelerated depreciation of leased personal property placed in service before 1987.	**16b**		
	c Depreciation adjustment on property placed in service after 1986	**16c**		
	d Depletion (other than oil and gas)	**16d**		
	e **(1)** Gross income from oil, gas, and geothermal properties . .	**e(1)**		
	(2) Deductions allocable to oil, gas, and geothermal properties	**e(2)**		
	f Other adjustments and tax preference items *(attach schedule)*	**16f**		
Foreign Taxes	**17a** Type of income ▶			Form 1116, Check boxes
	b Name of foreign country or U.S. possession ▶			
	c Total gross income from sources outside the U.S. *(attach schedule)*	**17c**		Form 1116, Part I
	d Total applicable deductions and losses *(attach schedule)*. . .	**17d**		
	e Total foreign taxes (check one): ▶ ☐ Paid ☐ Accrued . .	**17e**		Form 1116, Part II
	f Reduction in taxes available for credit *(attach schedule)* . . .	**17f**		Form 1116, Part III
	g Other foreign tax information *(attach schedule)*	**17g**		See Instructions for Form 1116.
Other	**18a** Total expenditures to which a section 59(e) election may apply	**18a**		See Partner's Instructions for Schedule K-1 (Form 1065).
	b Type of expenditures ▶			
	....			
	19 Recapture of low-income housing credit:			
	a From section 42(j)(5) partnerships	**19a**		Form 8611, line 8
	b Other than on line 19a.	**19b**		

20 Supplemental information required to be reported separately to each partner *(attach additional schedules if more space is needed):*

(Supplemental Information)

Form 1041 U.S. Fiduciary Income Tax Return 1991

Department of the Treasury—Internal Revenue Service

For the calendar year 1991 or fiscal year beginning _____ , 1991, and ending _____ , 19___ | OMB No. 1545-0092

A Type of Entity

- ☐ Decedent's estate
- ☐ Simple trust
- ☐ Complex trust
- ☐ Grantor type trust
- ☐ Bankruptcy estate
- ☐ Family estate trust
- ☐ Pooled income fund

Name of estate or trust (grantor type trust, see instructions)

Name and title of fiduciary

Number, street, and room or suite no. (If a P.O. box, see page 4 of instructions.)

City, state, and ZIP code

C Employer identification number

D Date entity created

E Nonexempt charitable and split-interest trusts, check applicable boxes (see instructions):

- ☐ Described in section 4947(a)(1)
- ☐ Not a private foundation
- ☐ Described in section 4947(a)(2)

B Number of Schedules K-1 attached (see instructions) . ▶

Check applicable boxes: ☐ Initial return   ☐ Final return   ☐ Amended return
Change in Fiduciary's ▶   ☐ Name or   ☐ Address

Income

1	Interest income	1
2	Dividends	2
3	Business income or (loss) (attach Schedule C (Form 1040))	3
4	Capital gain or (loss) (attach Schedule D (Form 1041))	4
5	Rents, royalties, partnerships, other estates and trusts, etc. (attach Schedule E (Form 1040))	5
6	Farm income or (loss) (attach Schedule F (Form 1040))	6
7	Ordinary gain or (loss) (attach Form 4797)	7
8	Other income (state nature of income)	8
9	**Total** income (combine lines 1 through 8) ▶	9

Deductions

10	Interest	10	
11	Taxes	11	
12	Fiduciary fees	12	
13	Charitable deduction (from Schedule A, line 6)	13	
14	Attorney, accountant, and return preparer fees	14	
15a	Other deductions NOT subject to the 2% floor (attach schedule)	15a	
b	Allowable miscellaneous itemized deductions subject to the 2% floor	15b	
c	Add lines 15a and 15b	15c	
16	**Total** (add lines 10 through 14, and 15c)		16
17	Adjusted total income or (loss) (subtract line 16 from line 9). Enter here and on Schedule B, line 1 ▶		17
18	Income distribution deduction (from Schedule B, line 17) (see instructions) (attach Schedules K-1 (Form 1041))		18
19	Estate tax deduction (including certain generation-skipping transfer taxes) (attach computation)		19
20	Exemption		20
21	**Total** deductions (add lines 18 through 20) ▶		21

Tax and Payments

22	Taxable income of fiduciary (subtract line 21 from line 17)	22
23	**Total** tax (from Schedule G, line 7)	23
24	Payments: **a** 1991 estimated tax payments and amount applied from 1990 return	24a
b	Treated as credited to beneficiaries (from Form 1041-T)	24b
c	Subtract line 24b from line 24a	24c
d	Tax paid with extension of time to file: ☐ Form 2758 ☐ Form 8736 ☐ Form 8800	24d
e	Federal income tax withheld	24e
	Credits: **f** Form 2439 _____ ; **g** Form 4136 _____ ; **h** Other _____ ; Total ▶	24i
25	**Total** payments (add lines 24c through 24e, and 24i) ▶	25
26	**Penalty** for underpayment of estimated tax (see instructions)	26
27	If the total of lines 23 and 26 is larger than line 25, enter **TAX DUE**	27
28	If line 25 is larger than the total of lines 23 and 26, enter **OVERPAYMENT**	28
29	Amount of line 28 to be: **a** Credited to 1992 estimated tax ▶ _____ ; **b** Refunded ▶	29

Please Sign Here

Under penalties of perjury, I declare that I have examined this return, including accompanying schedules and statements, and to the best of my knowledge and belief, it is true, correct, and complete. Declaration of preparer (other than fiduciary) is based on all information of which preparer has any knowledge.

▶ _____ Signature of fiduciary or officer representing fiduciary   Date

▶ _____ EIN of fiduciary (see instructions)

Paid Preparer's Use Only

Preparer's signature ▶	Date	Check if self-employed ▶ ☐	Preparer's social security no.

Firm's name (or yours if self-employed) and address ▶ _____
E.I. No. ▶ _____
ZIP code ▶ _____

Please attach check or money order here

For Paperwork Reduction Act Notice, see page 1 of the separate instructions.   Cat. No. 11370H   Form **1041** (1991)

Form 1041 (1991)   Page **2**

Schedule A   **Charitable Deduction—Do not complete for a simple trust or a pooled income fund.**

1	Amounts paid or permanently set aside for charitable purposes from current year's gross income	1
2	Tax-exempt interest allocable to charitable distribution (see instructions)	2
3	Subtract line 2 from line 1	3
4	Enter the net short-term capital gain and the net long-term capital gain of the current tax year allocable to corpus paid or permanently set aside for charitable purposes (see instructions) . .	4
5	Amounts paid or permanently set aside for charitable purposes from gross income of a prior year (see instructions)	5
6	**Total** (add lines 3 through 5). Enter here and on page 1, line 13	6

Schedule B   **Income Distribution Deduction (see instructions)**

1	Adjusted total income (from page 1, line 17) (see instructions)	1
2	Adjusted tax-exempt interest (see instructions)	2
3	Net gain shown on Schedule D (Form 1041), line 17, column (a). (If net loss, enter zero.) . . .	3
4	Enter amount from Schedule A, line 4	4
5	Long-term capital gain included on Schedule A, line 1	5
6	Short-term capital gain included on Schedule A, line 1	6
7	If the amount on page 1, line 4, is a capital loss, enter here as a positive figure	7
8	If the amount on page 1, line 4, is a capital gain, enter here as a negative figure	8
9	Distributable net income (combine lines 1 through 8)	9
10	Amount of income for the tax year determined under the governing instrument (accounting income) **10**	
11	Amount of income required to be distributed currently (see instructions)	11
12	Other amounts paid, credited, or otherwise required to be distributed (see instructions)	12
13	Total distributions (add lines 11 and 12). (If greater than line 10, see instructions.)	13
14	Enter the amount of tax-exempt income included on line 13	14
15	Tentative income distribution deduction (subtract line 14 from line 13).	15
16	Tentative income distribution deduction (subtract line 2 from line 9)	16
17	Income distribution deduction. Enter the smaller of line 15 or line 16 here and on page 1, line 18	17

Schedule G   **Tax Computation (see instructions)**

1	Tax: **a** ☐ Tax rate schedule or ☐ Schedule D_____; **b** Other taxes_____; Total ▶		1c
2a	Foreign tax credit (attach Form 1116).	**2a**	
b	Credit for fuel produced from a nonconventional source	**2b**	
c	General business credit. Check if from:		
	☐ Form 3800 or ☐ Form (specify) ▶_____	**2c**	
d	Credit for prior year minimum tax (attach Form 8801)	**2d**	
3	**Total** credits (add lines 2a through 2d) . . . . ▶		3
4	Subtract line 3 from line 1c		4
5	Recapture taxes. Check if from: ☐ Form 4255 ☐ Form 8611.		5
6	Alternative minimum tax (attach Form 8656)		6
7	**Total** tax (add lines 4 through 6). Enter here and on page 1, line 23 . . . . . ▶		7

Other Information (see instructions)   **Yes** | **No**

1	Did the estate or trust receive tax-exempt income? (If "Yes," attach a computation of the allocation of expenses.) Enter the amount of tax-exempt interest income and exempt-interest dividends ▶ $ _____	
2	Did the estate or trust have any passive activity losses? (If "Yes," enter these losses on **Form 8582,** Passive Activity Loss Limitations, to figure the allowable loss.)	
3	Did the estate or trust receive all or any part of the earnings (salary, wages, and other compensation) of any individual by reason of a contract assignment or similar arrangement?	
4	At any time during the tax year, did the estate or trust have an interest in or a signature or other authority over a financial account in a foreign country (such as a bank account, securities account, or other financial account)? (See the instructions for exceptions and filing requirements for Form TD F 90-22.1.) . . . . If "Yes," enter the name of the foreign country ▶ _____	
5	Was the estate or trust the grantor of, or transferor to, a foreign trust which existed during the current tax year, whether or not the estate or trust has any beneficial interest in it? (If "Yes," you may have to file Form 3520, 3520-A, or 926.).	
6	Check this box if this entity has filed or is required to file **Form 8264,** Application for Registration of a Tax Shelter . . ▶ ☐	
7	Check this box if this entity is a complex trust making the section 663(b) election . . . . ▶ ☐	
8	Check this box to make a section 643(e)(3) election (attach Schedule D (Form 1041)) . . . . . . ▶ ☐	
9	Check this box if the decedent's estate has been open for more than 2 years . . . . ▶ ☐	
10	Check this box if the trust is a participant in a Common Trust Fund that was required to adopt a calendar year ▶ ☐	

SCHEDULE J
(Form 1041)

Department of the Treasury
Internal Revenue Service

Trust Allocation of an Accumulation Distribution
(Under Code Section 665)

▶ File with Form 1041.
▶ See the separate Form 1041 instructions.

OMB No. 1545-0092

1991

Name of trust	Employer identification number

Part I Accumulation Distribution in 1991

See the regulations under sections 665-668 of the Internal Revenue Code for definitions and special rules.
See the Form 4970 instructions for certain income that minors may exclude and special rules for multiple trusts.

1 Other amounts paid, credited, or otherwise required to be distributed for 1991 (from Schedule B (Form 1041), line 12) **1**

2 Distributable net income for 1991 (from Schedule B of Form 1041, line 9) . . . **2**

3 Income required to be distributed currently for 1991 (from Schedule B of Form 1041, line 11). **3**

4 Subtract line 3 from line 2. If line 3 is more than line 2, enter zero **4**

5 Accumulation distribution for 1991. (Subtract line 4 from line 1.). **5**

Part II Ordinary Income Accumulation Distribution (Enter the applicable throwback years below.)

		Throwback year ending 19	Throwback year ending 19	Throwback year ending 19	Throwback year ending 19	Throwback year ending 19 ....
If the distribution is thrown back to more than five years (starting with the earliest applicable tax year beginning after December 31, 1968), attach additional schedules. (If the trust was a simple trust, see Regulations section 1.665(e)-1A(b).)						
6 Distributable net income (see instructions)	**6**					
7 Distributions (see instructions) .	**7**					
8 Subtract line 7 from line 6 .	**8**					
9 Enter amount from page 2, line 25 or line 31, as applicable	**9**					
10 Undistributed net income (Subtract line 9 from line 8) .	**10**					
11 Enter amount of prior accumulation distributions thrown back to any of these years	**11**					
12 Subtract line 11 from line 10	**12**					
13 Allocate the amount on line 5 to the earliest applicable year first. Do not allocate an amount greater than line 12 for the same year (see instructions) .	**13**					
14 Divide line 13 by line 10 and multiply result by amount on line 9	**14**					
15 Add lines 13 and 14 . . .	**15**					
16 Tax-exempt interest included on line 13 (see instructions) .	**16**					
17 Subtract line 16 from line 15	**17**					

For Paperwork Reduction Act Notice, see page 1 of the Instructions for Form 1041.   Cat. No. 11382Z   **Schedule J (Form 1041) 1991**

Schedule J (Form 1041) 1991 Page **2**

Part III Taxes Imposed on Undistributed Net Income (Enter the applicable throwback years below.)

If more than five throwback years are involved, attach additional schedules. If the trust received an accumulation distribution from another trust, see Regulations section 1.665 (d)-1A.

		Throwback year ending 19	Throwback year ending 19	Throwback year ending 19	Throwback year ending 19	Throwback year ending 19 ....
If the trust elected the alternative tax on capital gains, **OMIT** lines 18 through 25 **AND** complete lines 26 through 31. *(The alternative tax on capital gains was repealed for tax years beginning after December 31, 1978.)*						
18 Tax (see instructions) . . .	18					
19 Net short-term gain (see instructions).	19					
20 Net long-term gain (see instructions).	20					
21 Total net capital gain (Add lines 19 and 20.)	21					
22 Taxable income (see instructions)	22					
23 Enter percent (divide line 21 by line 22, but not more than 100%)	23	%	%	%	%	%
24 Multiply amount on line 18 by the percentage on line 23 .	24					
25 Tax on undistributed net income. (Subtract line 24 from line 18. Enter here and on page 1, line 9.)	25					
Complete lines 26 through 31 only if the trust elected the alternative tax on long-term capital gain.						
26 Tax on income other than long-term capital gain (see instructions)	26					
27 Net short-term gain (see instructions).	27					
28 Taxable income less section 1202 deduction (see instructions)	28					
29 Enter percent (divide line 27 by line 28, but not more than 100%)	29	%	%	%	%	%
30 Multiply amount on line 26 by the percentage on line 29 .	30					
31 Tax on undistributed net income. (Subtract line 30 from line 26. Enter here and on page 1, line 9.)	31					

Part IV Allocation to Beneficiary

Complete Part IV for each beneficiary. If the accumulation distribution is allocated to more than one beneficiary, attach an additional Schedule J with Part IV completed for each additional beneficiary. If more than five throwback years are involved, attach additional schedules.

Beneficiary's name | Identifying number

Beneficiary's address (number and street including apartment number or P.O. box)

City, state, and ZIP code

		Enter amount from line 13 allocated to this beneficiary **(a)**	Enter amount from line 14 allocated to this beneficiary **(b)**	Enter amount from line 16 allocated to this beneficiary **(c)**
32 Throwback year 19	32			
33 Throwback year 19	33			
34 Throwback year 19	34			
35 Throwback year 19	35			
36 Throwback year 19	36			
37 Total (Add lines 32 through 36.)	37			

SCHEDULE K-1 (Form 1041)	**Beneficiary's Share of Income, Deductions, Credits, Etc.**	OMB No. 1545-0092

SCHEDULE K-1 (Form 1041)

Department of the Treasury
Internal Revenue Service

Beneficiary's Share of Income, Deductions, Credits, Etc.

for the calendar year 1991, or fiscal year
beginning .... , 1991, ending .... , 19 ....
▶ Complete a separate Schedule K-1 for each beneficiary.

OMB No. 1545-0092

1991

☐ Amended K-1
☐ Final K-1

Name of estate or trust

Beneficiary's identifying number ▶	Estate's or trust's employer identification number ▶
Beneficiary's name, address, and ZIP code	Fiduciary's name, address, and ZIP code

	(a) Allocable share item	**(b)** Amount	**(c)** Calendar year 1991 Form 1040 filers enter the amounts in column (b) on:
1	Interest		Schedule B, Part I, line 1
2	Dividends		Schedule B, Part II, line 5
3a	Net short-term capital gain		Schedule D, line 4, column (g)
b	Net long-term capital gain		Schedule D, line 11, column (g)
4a	Business income and other non-passive income before directly allocable deductions. (see instructions)		Schedule E, Part III
b	Depreciation		
c	Depletion		
d	Amortization		
5a	Rental, rental real estate, and other passive income before directly allocable deductions. (see instructions)		
b	Depreciation		
c	Depletion		
d	Amortization		
6	Income for minimum tax purposes		
7	Income for regular tax purposes (add lines 1 through 5)		
8	Adjustment for minimum tax purposes (subtract line 7 from line 6)		Form 6251, line 5r
9	Estate tax deduction (including certain generation-skipping transfer taxes) (attach computation)		Schedule A, line 25
10	Foreign taxes (list on a separate sheet)		Form 1116 or Schedule A (Form 1040), line 7
11	Tax preference items (itemize):		
a	Accelerated depreciation		⎰ Include on the applicable ⎱
b	Depletion		⎱ line of Form 6251 ⎰
c	Amortization		
d	Exclusion items		1992 Form 8801
12	Distributions in the final year of estate or trust:		
a	Excess deductions on termination (attach computation)		Schedule A, line 20
b	Short-term capital loss carryover		Schedule D, line 5, column (f)
c	Long-term capital loss carryover		Schedule D, line 14, column (f)
d	Net operating loss (NOL) carryover		Form 1040, line 22
e			⎰ Include on the applicable line ⎱
f			⎱ of appropriate tax form ⎰
13	Other (itemize):		
a	Trust payments of estimated taxes credited to you		Form 1040, line 55
b	Tax-exempt interest		Form 1040, line 8b
c			
d			
e			⎰ Include on the applicable line ⎱
f			⎱ of appropriate tax form ⎰
g			
h			

For Paperwork Reduction Act Notice, see page 1 of the Instructions for Form 1041.   Cat. No. 11380D   **Schedule K-1 (Form 1041) 1991**

Form **8656**

Department of the Treasury
Internal Revenue Service

Alternative Minimum Tax—Fiduciaries

▶ See separate instructions.

▶ Attach to Forms 1041 or 990-T.

OMB No. 1545-1024

19**91**

Name of estate or trust | Employer Identification number

Part I Fiduciary's Share of Alternative Minimum Taxable Income

1	Adjusted total income or (loss) (from Form 1041, line 17)	**1**	
2	Net operating loss deduction (Do not enter as a negative amount.)	**2**	
3	Add lines 1 and 2	**3**	
4a	Interest	**4a**	
b	Taxes	**4b**	
c	Miscellaneous itemized deductions (from Form 1041, line 15b) . .	**4c**	
d	Refund of taxes	**4d** ( )	
e	Combine lines 4a through 4d	**4e**	
5	Adjustments:		
a	Depreciation of property placed in service after 1986	**5a**	
b	Circulation and research and experimental expenditures paid or incurred after 1986	**5b**	
c	Mining exploration and development costs paid or incurred after 1986	**5c**	
d	Long-term contracts entered into after February 28, 1986	**5d**	
e	Pollution control facilities placed in service after 1986	**5e**	
f	Installment sales of certain property	**5f**	
g	Adjusted gain or loss	**5g**	
h	Certain loss limitations	**5h**	
i	Tax shelter farm activities	**5i**	
j	Passive activities	**5j**	
k	Beneficiaries of other estates or trusts	**5k**	
l	Combine lines 5a through 5k	**5l**	
6	Tax preference items:		
a	Appreciated property charitable deduction	**6a**	
b	Tax-exempt interest from private activity bonds issued after August 7, 1986	**6b**	
c	Depletion	**6c**	
d	Combine lines 6a through 6c	**6d**	
7	Other items of tax preference:		
a	Accelerated depreciation of real property placed in service before 1987	**7a**	
b	Accelerated depreciation of leased personal property placed in service before 1987	**7b**	
c	Amortization of certified pollution control facilities placed in service before 1987	**7c**	
d	Intangible drilling costs	**7d**	
e	Combine lines 7a through 7d	**7e**	
8	Add lines 3, 4e, 5l, 6d, and 7e	**8**	
9a	Adjustment based on energy preferences	**9a**	
b	Alternative tax net operating loss deduction (see instructions for limitations)	**9b**	
c	Add lines 9a and 9b	**9c**	
10	Adjusted alternative minimum taxable income (line 8 less line 9c). Enter here and on line 13 .	**10**	
	Note: *Complete Part II before proceeding with line 11.*		
11a	Income distribution deduction from line 27	**11a**	
b	Estate tax deduction (from Form 1041, line 19)	**11b**	
c	Add lines 11a and 11b	**11c**	
12	Fiduciary's share of alternative minimum taxable income (line 10 less line 11c)	**12**	

For Paperwork Reduction Act Notice, see page 1 of the separate instructions. Cat. No. 64376F Form **8656** (1991)

Form 8656 (1991)   Page **2**

Part II   **Income Distribution Deduction on a Minimum Tax Basis**

13	Adjusted alternative minimum taxable income (from line 10).	13	
14	Adjusted tax-exempt interest (other than amounts included in line 6b)	14	
15	Net capital gain from Schedule D (Form 1041), line 17, column (a) (If a loss, enter -0-.)	15	
16	Capital gains allocable to corpus paid or set aside for charitable purposes (from Schedule A, Form 1041, line 4)	16	
17	Capital gains paid or permanently set aside for charitable purposes from current year's income (from Schedule A, Form 1041, line 1)	17	
18	Capital gains computed on a minimum tax basis included in line 10	18	( )
19	Capital losses computed on a minimum tax basis included in line 10 (Do not enter as a negative amount.)	19	
20	Distributable net alternative minimum taxable income (DNAMTI) (combine lines 13 through 19)	20	
21	Income required to be distributed currently	21	
22	Other amounts paid, credited, or required to be distributed	22	
23	Total distributions (add lines 21 and 22)	23	
24	Tax-exempt income included on line 23 (other than amounts included in line 6b)	24	
25	Tentative income distribution deduction on a minimum tax basis (line 23 less line 24)	25	
26	Tentative income distribution deduction on a minimum tax basis (line 20 less line 14)	26	
27	Income distribution deduction on a minimum tax basis (Enter the smaller of line 25 or line 26.) Enter here and on line 11a	27	

Part III   **Computation of Alternative Minimum Tax**

	Note: *If line 12 is $20,000 or less, you are not liable for the alternative minimum tax.*			
28	Enter amount from line 12		28	
29	Exemption amount	29 $20,000		
30	Phase-out of exemption amount	30 $75,000		
31	Line 28 less line 30 (If zero or less, enter -0-.)		31	
32	Multiply line 31 by 25% (.25)		32	
33	Line 29 less line 32 (If zero or less, enter -0-.)		33	
34	Line 28 less line 33		34	
35	Multiply line 34 by 24% (.24)		35	
36	Alternative minimum foreign tax credit (see instructions)		36	
37	Tentative minimum tax (line 35 less line 36)		37	
38a	Regular tax before credits (see instructions)	38a		
b	Section 644 tax (from line 1b, Schedule G, Form 1041)	38b		
c	Add lines 38a and 38b		38c	
39	Alternative minimum tax (line 37 less line 38c). Enter here and on line 6, Schedule G, Form 1041		39	

Form **851**
(Rev. January 1992)
Department of the Treasury
Internal Revenue Service

Affiliations Schedule

▶ **File with each consolidated income tax return**

Tax year ending .... , 19 ....

OMB No. 1545-0025

Expires 11-30-94

Common parent corporation	Employer identification number

Number, street, and room or suite no. (If a P.O. box, see instructions.)

City or town, state, and ZIP code

Part I Prepayment Credits

No.	Name and address of corporation	Employer identification number	Portion of Form 7004 tax deposits	Portion of estimated tax credits and deposits
			Prepayment Credits	
1	Common parent corporation	/////////		
	Subsidiary corporations:			
2				
3				
4				
5				
6				
7				
8				
9				
10				
	Totals (Must equal amounts shown on the consolidated tax return) . . . ▶			

Part II Voting Stock Information, Principal Business Activity, Etc. (See instructions.)

No.	Principal business activity (PBA)	PBA Code No.	Did the subsidiary make any nondividend distributions? (See instructions.) Yes	No	Number of shares	Percent of voting power	Percent of value	Owned by corporation no.
					Stock holdings at beginning of year			
1	Common parent corporation		/////////	/////////	/////////	/////////	/////////	/////////
	Subsidiary corporations:							
2						%	%	
3						%	%	
4						%	%	
5						%	%	
6						%	%	
7						%	%	
8						%	%	
9						%	%	
10						%	%	

For Paperwork Reduction Act Notice, see instructions.

Cat. No. 16880G

Form **851** (Rev. 1-92)

Part III **Changes in Stock Holdings During the Year** (See instructions.)

No.	Corporation Name	Stock-holder (Corpora-tion No.)	Date	(a) Changes		(b) Shares held after changes described in column (a)	
				Shares acquired	Shares disposed of	Percent of voting power	Percent of value
						%	%
						%	%
						%	%
						%	%
						%	%
						%	%
						%	%
						%	%

Note: *If additional stock was issued, or if any stock was retired during the year, show the dates and amounts for these transactions.*

If the equitable owners of any capital stock shown above were other than the holders of record, give full details.

Form 851 (Rev. 1-92)   Page **3**

Part IV	Additional Information (See instructions.)

1 During the tax year, did the corporation have more than one class of stock outstanding?

No.	Name	Answer to Question 1		If yes, list and describe each class of stock.
		Yes	**No**	

2 During the tax year, was there any member of the consolidated group that reaffiliated within 60 months of disaffiliation, or was there any member of the affiliated group that was deconsolidated under Rev. Proc. 91-11, 1991-1 C.B. 470 (as modified by Rev. Proc. 91-39, 1991-27 IRB 11)?

No.	Name	Answer to Question 2		If yes for any part of question 2, list and explain the circumstances.
		Yes	**No**	

3a During the tax year, was there any arrangement in existence by which one or more persons that were not members of the affiliated group could acquire any stock, or acquire any voting power without acquiring stock, in the corporation, other than a de minimis amount, from the corporation or another member of the affiliated group?

No.	Name	Answer to Question 3a		Item 3b (see instructions)	Item 3c (see instructions)	Item 3d (see instructions)
		Yes	**No**			
				%	%	%
				%	%	%
				%	%	%
				%	%	%

No.	Item 3e—Description of arrangements.

Please Sign Here

Under penalties of perjury, I declare that I have examined this form, including accompanying statements, and to the best of my knowledge and belief, it is true, correct, and complete for the tax year as stated.

▶ _____ |_____   ▶ _____
   Signature of officer   Date   Title

Instructions

(Section references are to the Internal Revenue Code.)

Paperwork Reduction Act Notice

We ask for the information on this form to carry out the Internal Revenue laws of the United States. You are required to give us the information. We need it to ensure that you are complying with these laws and to allow us to figure and collect the right amount of tax.

The time needed to complete and file this form will vary depending on individual circumstances. The estimated average time is:

Recordkeeping . . . . 8 hr., 51 min.
Learning about the law or the form . . . . . . 35 min.
Preparing and sending the form to the IRS . . . . 46 min.

If you have comments concerning the accuracy of these time estimates or suggestions for making this form more simple, we would be happy to hear from you. You can write to both the IRS and the Office of Management and Budget at the addresses listed in the instructions for the tax return with which this form is filed.

Purpose of Form

Form 851 is filed by the parent corporation for itself and for affiliated corporations in the affiliated group. File Form 851 by attaching it to the consolidated tax return for the group.

Affiliated Group

The term "affiliated group" means one or more chains of includible corporations (section 1504(a)) connected through stock ownership with a common parent corporation. The common parent must be an includible corporation and the following requirements must be met:

1. The common parent must own directly stock that represents at least 80% of the total voting power and at least 80% of the total value of the stock of at least one of the other includible corporations.

2. Stock that represents at least 80% of the total voting power, and at least 80% of the total value of the stock of each of the other corporations (except for the common parent) must be owned directly by at least one of the other includible corporations.

For this purpose, the term "stock" generally does not include any stock that (1) is nonvoting, (2) is nonconvertible, (3) is limited and preferred as to dividends and does not participate significantly in corporate growth, and (4) has redemption and liquidation rights that do not exceed the issue price of the stock (except for a reasonable redemption or liquidation premium).

Address

Include the suite, room, or other unit number after the street address. If the Post Office does not deliver mail to the street address and the corporation has a P.O. box, show the box number instead of the street address.

Corporation Numbers

When listing information in Parts II, III, and IV, be sure to use the same number for each corporation as you used in Part I, page 1.

Part II

PBA (Principal Business Activity) code number.—Enter in Part II the PBA code number for the parent corporation and each subsidiary. A list of the PBA code numbers can be found in the Instructions for Forms 1120 and 1120-A. Use the code number for the specific industry group from which the largest percentage of each corporation's total receipts is derived.

Also list for each subsidiary the corresponding principal business activity on which the code is based.

Nondividend distributions.—For purposes of Part II, nondividend distributions are any distributions (other than stock dividends and distributions in exchange for stock) paid during the tax year for which the consolidated tax return is filed that were in excess of the corporation's current and accumulated earnings and profits. See sections 301 and 316.

Part IV

Question 1.—For purposes of Question 1 only, disregard section 1504(a)(4).

Question 3a.—The term "arrangement" includes, but is not limited to, phantom stock, stock appreciation rights, an option, warrant, conversion feature, or similar arrangement. If you answer "Yes" to question 3a, complete items 3b through 3e.

Item 3b.—If you answer "Yes" to question 3a, show the percentage of the value of the outstanding stock that the person(s) could acquire.

Item 3c.—If you answer "Yes" to question 3a, and the arrangement was associated with voting stock, show the percentage of outstanding voting stock that the person(s) could acquire.

Item 3d.—If you answer "Yes" to question 3a, and the arrangement was associated with the acquisition of voting power without the acquisition of the related stock, show the percentage of voting power that the person(s) could acquire.

Item 3e.—If you answer "Yes" to question 3a, give a brief description of any arrangement (defined above) by which a person that is not a member of the affiliated group could acquire any stock, or acquire any voting power without acquiring stock, in the corporation.

Form **1122**
(Rev. December 1983)
Department of the Treasury
Internal Revenue Service

Authorization and Consent of Subsidiary Corporation to be Included in a Consolidated Income Tax Return

(Please type or print)

▶ For the first year a consolidated return is filed, this form must be attached for each subsidiary.

For the calendar year 19 ____ , or other tax year beginning _____ , 19 ____ and ending _____ , 19 ____

Name | **Employer identification number**

Number and street

City or town, State, and ZIP code

Name of common parent corporation | **Employer identification number**

The subsidiary corporation named above authorizes its common parent corporation to include it in a consolidated return for the tax year indicated and for each later year the group must make a consolidated return under the regulations. If the parent corporation does not make a consolidated return on behalf of the subsidiary, the subsidiary authorizes the Commissioner or District Director of Internal Revenue to do so.

The subsidiary consents to be bound by the provisions of the consolidated return regulations.

Signature

Under penalties of perjury, I declare that the subsidiary named above has authorized me to sign this form on its behalf, that I have examined this form, and the information contained herein, and to the best of my knowledge and belief, it is true, correct, and complete.

▶ _____ ▶ _____
Signature of officer   Date   Title

Form **1122** (Rev. 12-83)

APPENDIX

GLOSSARY OF TAX TERMS

The words and phrases appearing below have been defined to reflect their conventional use in the field of taxation. Such definitions may therefore be incomplete for other purposes.

A

Accounting method. The method under which income and expenses are determined for tax purposes. Important accounting methods include the cash basis and the accrual basis. Special methods are available for the reporting of gain on installment sales, recognition of income on construction projects (the completed contract and percentage of completion methods), and the valuation of inventories (last-in, first-out and first-in, first-out). §§ 446–474. See also *accrual basis, cash basis, completed contract method, percentage of completion method,* etc.

Accounting period. The period of time, usually a year, used by a taxpayer for the determination of tax liability. Unless a fiscal year is chosen, taxpayers must determine and pay their income tax liability by using the calendar year (January 1 through December 31) as the period of measurement. An example of a fiscal year is July 1 through June 30. A change in accounting periods (e.g., from a calendar year to a fiscal year) generally requires the consent of the IRS. Some new taxpayers, such as a newly formed corporation, are free to select either an initial calendar or fiscal year without the consent of the IRS. §§ 441–443. See also *annual accounting period concept.*

Accrual basis. A method of accounting that reflects expenses incurred and income earned for any one tax year. In contrast to the cash basis of accounting, expenses need not be paid to be deductible, nor need income be received to be taxable. Unearned income (e.g., prepaid interest and rent) generally is taxed in the year of receipt regardless of the method of accounting used by the taxpayer. § 446(c)(2). See also *accounting method, cash basis,* and *unearned income.*

Accumulated adjustments account. An account that comprises an S corporation's post-1982 income, loss, and deductions for the tax year (including nontaxable income and nondeductible losses and expenses). After the year-end income and expense adjustments are made, the account is reduced by distributions made during the tax year.

Accumulated earnings credit. A reduction allowed in arriving at accumulated taxable income in determining the accumulated earnings tax. See also *accumulated earnings tax* and *accumulated taxable income.*

Accumulated earnings tax. A special tax imposed on corporations that accumulate (rather than distribute) their earnings beyond the reasonable needs of the business. The accumulated earnings tax and related interest are imposed on accumulated taxable income in addition to the corporate income tax. §§ 531–537.

Accumulated taxable income. The base upon which the accumulated earnings tax is imposed. Generally, it is the taxable income of the corporation as adjusted for certain items (e.g., the Federal income tax, excess charitable contributions, the dividends received deduction) less the dividends paid deduction and the accumulated earnings credit. § 535.

Acquiescence. Agreement by the IRS on the results reached in most of the regular decisions of the U.S. Tax Court; sometimes abbreviated *acq.* or *A.* See also *nonacquiescence.*

Acquisition. See *corporate acquisition.*

Ad valorem tax. A tax imposed on the value of property. The most common ad valorem tax is that imposed by states, counties and cities on real estate. Ad valorem taxes can, however, be imposed on personal property as well. See also *personalty.*

Adjusted basis. The cost or other basis of property reduced by depreciation allowed or allowable and increased by capital improvements. Other special adjustments are provided in § 1016 and the Regulations thereunder. See also *basis.*

Adjusted current earnings (ACE). An adjustment in computing corporate alternative minimum taxable income (AMTI), computed at 75 percent of the excess of adjusted current earnings and profits computations over AMTI. ACE computations reflect longer and slower cost recovery deductions and other restrictions on the timing of certain recognition events. Exempt interest, life insurance proceeds, and other receipts that are included in earnings and profits but not in taxable income also increase the ACE adjustment. See also *alternative minimum tax* and *earnings and profits.*

Adjusted gross estate. The gross estate of a decedent reduced by § 2053 expenses (e.g., administration, funeral) and § 2054 losses (e.g., casualty). The determination of the adjusted gross estate is necessary in testing for the extension of time for installment payment of estate taxes under § 6166. See also *gross estate.*

Adjusted gross income. A tax determination peculiar to individual taxpayers. Generally, it represents the gross income of an individual, less business expenses and less any appropriate capital gain or loss adjustment. See also *gross income.*

Adjusted ordinary gross income. A determination peculiar to the personal holding company tax imposed by § 541. In ascertaining whether a corporation is a personal holding company, personal holding company income divided by adjusted ordinary gross income must equal 60 percent or more. Adjusted ordinary gross income is the corporation's gross income less capital gains, § 1231 gains, and certain expenses. § 543(b)(2). See also *personal holding company income.*

Adjusted taxable estate. The taxable estate reduced by $60,000. The adjusted taxable estate is utilized in applying § 2011 for determining the limit on the credit for state death taxes paid that will be allowed against the Federal estate tax. See also *taxable estate.*

Administration. The supervision and winding up of an estate. The administration of an estate runs from the date of an individual's death until all assets have been distributed and liabilities paid.

Administrator. A person appointed by the court to administer (manage or take charge of) the assets and liabilities of a decedent (the deceased). Such person may be a male (administrator) or a female (administratrix). See also *executor.*

Affiliated group. An affiliated group of corporations can elect to file federal income tax returns on a consolidated basis, thereby offsetting the income of some of the group members against the losses of others. Alternatively, affiliated group members qualify for a 100% dividends-received deduction. Affiliated groups exist when at least 80 percent of the equity of the members is held within the group, and an obvious parent corporation can be identified.

AFTR. Published by Prentice-Hall, *American Federal Tax Reports* contain all of the Federal tax decisions issued by the U.S. District Courts, U.S. Claims Court, U.S. Court of Appeals, and the U.S. Supreme Court.

AFTR2d. The second series of the *American Federal Tax Reports,* dealing with 1954 and 1986 Code case law.

Alimony. Alimony deductions result from the payment of a legal obligation arising from the termination of a marital relationship. Designated alimony payments generally are included in the gross income of the recipient and are deductible *for* AGI by the payer.

Allocable share of income. Certain entities receive conduit treatment under the Federal income tax law. This means the earned income or loss is not taxed to the entity, but such amounts are allocated to the owners or beneficiaries thereof, regardless of the magnitude or timing of corresponding distributions. The portion of the entity's income that is taxed to the owner or beneficiary is the allocable share of the entity's income or loss for the period. Such allocations are determined by (1) the partnership agreement relative to the partners, (2) a weighted-average stock ownership computation relative to shareholders of an S corporation, and (3) the controlling will or trust instrument relative to the beneficiaries of an estate or trust.

Allocation. The assignment of income for various tax purposes. A multistate corporation's nonbusiness income usually is allocated to the state where the nonbusiness assets are located; it is not apportioned with the rest of the entity's income. The income and expense items of an estate or trust are allocated between income and corpus components. Specific items of income, expense, gain, loss, and credit can be allocated to specific partners or shareholders in an S corporation, if a substantial economic nontax purpose for the allocation is established. See also *apportionment* and *substantial economic effect.*

Alternate valuation date. Property passing from a person by death may be valued for death tax purposes as of the date of death or the alternate valuation date. The alternate valuation date is six months from the date of death or the date the property is disposed of by the estate, whichever comes first. The use of the alternate valuation date requires an affirmative election on the part of the executor or administrator of the estate. The election of the alternate valuation date is not available unless it decreases the amount of the gross estate *and* reduces the estate tax liability.

Alternative minimum tax (AMT). Simply stated, the AMT is a fixed percentage of alternative minimum taxable income (AMTI). AMTI generally starts with the taxpayer's adjusted gross income (for individuals) or taxable income (for other taxpayers). To this amount, the taxpayer (1) adds designated preference items (e.g., the appreciation on charitable contribution property), (2) makes other specified adjustments (e.g., to reflect a longer, straight-line cost recovery deduction), (3) subtracts certain AMT itemized deductions for individuals (e.g., interest incurred on housing but not taxes paid), and (4) subtracts an exemption amount (e.g., $40,000 on an individual joint return). The taxpayer must pay the greater of the resulting AMT (reduced by only the foreign tax credit) or the regular income tax (reduced by all allowable tax credits).

Amortization. The tax deduction for the cost or other basis of an intangible asset over the asset's estimated useful life. Examples of amortizable intangibles include patents, copyrights, and leasehold interests. The intangible goodwill cannot be amortized for income tax purposes because it possesses no estimated useful life. As to tangible assets, see *depreciation.* As to natural resources, see *depletion.* See also *estimated useful life* and *goodwill.*

Amount realized. The amount received by a taxpayer upon the sale or exchange of property. The measure of the amount realized is the sum of the cash and the fair market value of any property or services received by the taxpayer, plus any related debt assumed by the buyer. Determining the amount realized is the starting point for arriving at realized gain or loss. § 1001(b). See also *realized gain or loss* and *recognized gain or loss.*

Annual accounting period concept. In determining a taxpayer's income tax liability, only those transactions taking place during a specified tax year are taken into consideration. For reporting and payment purposes, therefore, the tax life of taxpayers is divided into equal annual accounting periods. See also *accounting period* and *mitigation of the annual accounting period concept.*

Annual exclusion. In computing the taxable gifts for any one year, each donor may exclude the first $10,000 of a gift to each donee. Usually, the annual exclusion is not available for gifts of future interests. § 2503(b). See also *gift splitting* and *future interest.*

Annuity.   A fixed sum of money payable to a person at specified times for a specified period of time or for life. If the party making the payment (i.e., the obligor) is regularly engaged in this type of business (e.g., an insurance company), the arrangement is classified as a commercial annuity. A private annuity involves an obligor that is not regularly engaged in selling annuities (e.g., a charity or family member).

Anticipatory assignment of income.   See *assignment of income.*

Appellate court.   For Federal tax purposes, appellate courts include the Courts of Appeals and the Supreme Court. If the party losing in the trial (or lower) court is dissatisfied with the result, the dispute may be carried to the appropriate appellate court. See also *Court of Appeals* and *trial court.*

Apportionment.   The assignment of the business income of a multistate corporation to specific states for income taxation. Usually, the apportionment procedure accounts for the property, payroll, and sales activity levels of the various states, and a proportionate assignment of the entity's total income is made thereby, using a three-factor apportionment formula. These activities indicate the commercial domicile of the corporation, relative to that income. Some states exclude nonbusiness income from the apportionment procedure; they *allocate* nonbusiness income to the states where the nonbusiness assets are located. See also *domicile, nonbusiness income, payroll factor, property factor,* and *sales factor.*

Arm's length.   The standard under which unrelated parties would carry out a particular transaction. Suppose, for example, X Corporation sells property to its sole shareholder for $10,000. In determining whether $10,000 is an arm's length price, one would ascertain the amount for which the corporation could have sold the property to a disinterested third party.

Articles of incorporation.   The legal document specifying a corporation's name, period of existence, purpose and powers, authorized number of shares, classes of stock, and other conditions for operation. These articles are filed by the organizers of the corporation with the state of incorporation. If the articles are satisfactory and other conditions of the law are satisfied, the state will issue a charter recognizing the organization's status as a corporation.

Assessment.   The process whereby the IRS imposes an additional tax liability. If, for example, the IRS audits a taxpayer's income tax return and finds gross income understated or deductions overstated, it will assess a deficiency in the amount of the tax that should have been paid in light of the adjustments made. See also *deficiency.*

Assignment of income.   A procedure whereby a taxpayer attempts to avoid the recognition of income by assigning to another the property that generates the income. Such a procedure will not avoid the recognition of income by the taxpayer making the assignment if it can be said that the income was earned at the point of the transfer. In this case, usually referred to as an anticipatory assignment of income, the income will be taxed to the person who earns it.

Association.   An organization treated as a corporation for Federal tax purposes even though it may not qualify as such under applicable state law. What is designated as a trust or a partnership, for example, may be classified as an association if it clearly possesses corporate attributes. Corporate attributes include centralized management, continuity of existence, free transferability of interests, and limited liability. § 7701(a)(3).

At-risk amount.   The taxpayer has an amount at risk in a business or investment venture to the extent that it has subjected personal assets to the risks of the business. Typically, the taxpayer's at-risk amount includes (1) the amount of money or other property that the investor contributed to the venture for the investment, (2) the amount of any of the entity's liabilities for which the taxpayer personally is liable and that relate to the investment, and (3) an allocable share of nonrecourse debts incurred by the venture from third parties in arm's length transactions, with respect to real estate investments.

At-risk limitation.   Generally, a taxpayer can deduct losses relative to a trade or business, S corporation, partnership, or investment asset only to the extent of the at-risk amount.

Attribution.   Under certain circumstances, the tax law applies attribution rules to assign to one taxpayer the ownership interest of another taxpayer. If, for example, the stock of X Corporation is held 60 percent by M and 40 percent by S, M may be deemed to own 100 percent of X Corporation if M and S are mother and son. In such a case, the stock owned by S is attributed to M. Stated differently, M has a 60 percent direct and a 40 percent indirect interest in X Corporation. It can also be said that M is the constructive owner of S's interest.

Audit.   Inspection and verification of a taxpayer's return or other transactions possessing tax consequences. See also *correspondence audit, field audit,* and *office audit.*

B

Bailout.   Various procedures whereby the owners of an entity can obtain the entity's profits with favorable tax consequences. With corporations, for example, the bailout of corporate profits without dividend consequences might be the desired objective. The alternative of distributing the profits to the shareholders as dividends generally is less attractive since dividend payments are not deductible. See also *preferred stock bailout.*

Bargain sale or purchase.   A sale of property for less than fair market value. The difference between the sale or purchase price and the fair market value of the property may have tax consequences. If, for example, a corporation sells property worth $1,000 to one of its shareholders for $700, the $300 difference probably represents a constructive dividend to the shareholder. Suppose, instead, the shareholder sells the property (worth $1,000) to his or her corporation for $700. The $300 difference probably represents a contribution by the shareholder to the corporation's capital. Bargain sales and purchases among members of the same family may lead to gift tax consequences. See also *constructive dividends.*

Basis.   The acquisition cost assigned to an asset for income tax purposes. For assets acquired by purchase, basis would be cost (§ 1012). Special rules govern the basis of property received by virtue of another's death (§ 1014) or by gift (§ 1015), the basis of stock received on a transfer of property to a controlled corporation (§ 358), the basis of the property transferred to the corporation (§ 362), and the basis of property received upon the liquidation of a corporation (§ 334). See also *adjusted basis.*

Beneficiary.   A party who will benefit from a transfer of property or other arrangement. Examples include the beneficiary of a trust, the beneficiary of a life insurance policy, and the beneficiary of an estate.

Bequest.   A transfer by will of personal property. To bequeath is to leave such property by will. See also *devise* and *personal property.*

Blockage rule.   A factor to be considered in valuing a large block of stock. Application of this rule generally justifies a discount in the fair market value since the disposition of a large amount of stock at any one time may depress the value of such shares in the market place.

Bona fide. In good faith, or real. In tax law, this term is often used in connection with a business purpose for carrying out a transaction. Thus, was there a bona fide business purpose for a shareholder's transfer of a liability to a controlled corporation? § 357(b)(1)(B). See also *business purpose*.

Book value. The net amount of an asset after reduction by a related reserve. The book value of machinery, for example, is the amount of the machinery less the reserve for depreciation.

Boot. Cash or property of a type not included in the definition of a nontaxable exchange. The receipt of boot will cause an otherwise tax-free transfer to become taxable to the extent of the lesser of the fair market value of such boot or the realized gain on the transfer. For example, see transfers to controlled corporations under § 351(b) and like-kind exchanges under § 1031(b). See also *like-kind exchange* and *realized gain or loss*.

Brother-sister corporations. More than one corporation owned by the same shareholders. If, for example, C and D each own one-half of the stock in X Corporation and Y Corporation, X and Y are brother-sister corporations.

B.T.A. The Board of Tax Appeals was a trial court that considered Federal tax matters. This Court is now designated as the U.S. Tax Court.

Built-in gains tax. A penalty tax designed to discourage a shift of the incidence of taxation on unrealized gains from a C corporation to its shareholders, via an S election. Under this provision, any recognized gain during the first 10 years of S status generates a corporate-level tax on a base not to exceed the aggregate untaxed built-in gains brought into the S corporation upon its election from C corporation taxable years.

Burden of proof. The requirement in a lawsuit to show the weight of evidence and thereby gain a favorable decision. Except in cases of tax fraud, the burden of proof in a tax case generally is on the taxpayer. See also *fraud*.

Business bad debts. A tax deduction allowed for obligations obtained in connection with a trade or business that have become either partially or completely worthless. In contrast with nonbusiness bad debts, business bad debts are deductible as business expenses. § 166. See also *nonbusiness bad debts*.

Business purpose. A justifiable business reason for carrying out a transaction. It has long been established that mere tax avoidance is not an acceptable business purpose. The presence of a business purpose is crucial in the area of corporate reorganizations and certain liquidations. See also *bona fide*.

Buy and sell agreement. An arrangement, particularly appropriate in the case of a closely held corporation or a partnership, whereby the surviving owners (shareholders or partners) or the entity agrees to purchase the interest of a withdrawing owner. The buy and sell agreement provides for an orderly disposition of an interest in a business and may aid in setting the value of such interest for death tax purposes. See also *cross-purchase buy and sell agreement* and *entity buy and sell agreement*.

C

C corporation. A regular corporation governed by Subchapter C of the Code. Distinguished from S corporations, which fall under Subchapter S of the Code.

Calendar year. See *accounting period*.

Capital asset. Broadly speaking, all assets are capital except those specifically excluded by the Code. Major categories of noncapital assets include property held for resale in the normal course of business (inventory), trade accounts and notes receivable, and depreciable property and real estate used in a trade or business (§ 1231 assets). § 1221. See also *capital gain* and *capital loss*.

Capital contribution. Various means by which a shareholder makes additional funds available to the corporation (placed at the risk of the business) without the receipt of additional stock. Such contributions are added to the basis of the shareholder's existing stock investment and do not generate income to the corporation. § 118.

Capital expenditure. An expenditure that should be added to the basis of the property improved. For income tax purposes, this generally precludes a full deduction for the expenditure in the year paid or incurred. Any cost recovery in the form of a tax deduction would come in the form of depreciation, depletion, or amortization. § 263.

Capital gain. The gain from the sale or exchange of a capital asset. See also *capital asset*.

Capital loss. The loss from the sale or exchange of a capital asset. See also *capital asset*.

Capital stock tax. A state-level tax, usually imposed on out-of-state corporations for the privilege of doing business in the state. The tax may be based on the entity's apportionable income or payroll, or on its apportioned net worth as of a specified date.

Cash basis. A method of accounting that reflects deductions as paid and income as received in any one tax year. However, deductions for prepaid expenses that benefit more than one tax year (e.g., prepaid rent and prepaid interest) usually must be spread over the period benefited rather than deducted in the year paid. § 446(c)(1). See also *constructive receipt of income*.

Cash surrender value. The amount of money that an insurance policy would yield if cashed in with the insurance company that issued the policy.

CCH. Commerce Clearing House (CCH) is the publisher of a tax service and of Federal tax decisions (USTC series).

Centralized management. A concentration of authority among certain persons who may make independent business decisions on behalf of the entity without the need for continuing approval by the owners of the entity. It is a characteristic of a corporation since day-to-day business operations are handled by appointed officers and not by the shareholders. Reg. § 301.7701–2(c). See also *association*.

Cert. den. By denying the Writ of Certiorari, the U.S. Supreme Court refuses to accept an appeal from a U.S. Court of Appeals. The denial of certiorari does not, however, mean that the U.S. Supreme Court agrees with the result reached by the lower court. See also *certiorari*.

Certiorari. Appeal from a U.S. Court of Appeals to the U.S. Supreme Court is by Writ of Certiorari. The Supreme Court need not accept the appeal and usually does not (*cert. den.*), unless a conflict exists among the lower courts that must be resolved or a constitutional issue is involved. See also *cert. den.*.

Claims Court. A trial court (court of original jurisdiction) that decides litigation involving Federal tax matters. Previously known as the U.S. Court of Claims, appeal from the U.S. Claims Court is to the Court of Appeals for the Federal Circuit.

Closely held corporation. A corporation, the stock ownership of which is not widely dispersed. Rather, a few shareholders are in control of corporate policy and are in a position to benefit personally from such policy.

Collapsing. To disregard a transaction or one of a series of steps leading to a result. See also *step-transaction approach, substance vs. form concept,* and *telescoping.*

Common law state. See *community property.*

Community property. The states with community property systems are Louisiana, Texas, New Mexico, Arizona, California, Washington, Idaho, Nevada, and Wisconsin. The rest of the states are common law property jurisdictions. The difference between common law and community property systems centers around the property rights possessed by married persons. In a common law system, each spouse owns whatever he or she earns. Under a community property system, one-half of the earnings of each spouse is considered owned by the other spouse. Assume, for example, H and W are husband and wife and their only income is the $50,000 annual salary H receives. If they live in New York (a common law state), the $50,000 salary belongs to H. If, however, they live in Texas (a community property state), the $50,000 salary is owned one-half each by H and W. See also *separate property.*

Completed contract method. A method of reporting gain or loss on certain long-term contracts. Under this method of accounting, gross income and expenses are recognized in the tax year in which the contract is completed. Reg. § 1.451–3. See also *percentage of completion method.*

Complex trusts. Complex trusts are those that are not simple trusts. Such trusts may have charitable beneficiaries, accumulate income, and distribute corpus. §§ 661–663. See also *simple trusts.*

Concur. To agree with the result reached by another, but not necessarily with the reasoning or the logic used in reaching such a result. For example, Judge R agrees with Judges S and T (all being members of the same court) that the income is taxable but for a different reason. Judge R would issue a concurring opinion to the majority opinion issued by Judges S and T.

Condemnation. The taking of property by a public authority. The taking is by legal action, and the owner of the property is compensated by the public authority.

Conduit concept. An approach the tax law assumes in the tax treatment of certain entities and their owners. The approach permits specified tax characteristics to pass through the entity without losing their identity. Under the conduit concept, for example, long-term capital losses realized by a partnership are passed through as such to the individual partners. Varying forms of the conduit concept are applicable for partnerships, trusts, estates, and S corporations.

Consent dividends. For purposes of avoiding or reducing the penalty tax on the unreasonable accumulation of earnings or the personal holding company tax, a corporation may declare a consent dividend. In a consent dividend, no cash or property is distributed to the shareholders, although the corporation obtains a dividends paid deduction. The consent dividend is taxed to the shareholders and increases the basis in their stock investment. § 565.

Consolidated return. A procedure whereby certain affiliated corporations may file a single return, combine the tax transactions of each corporation, and arrive at a single income tax liability for the group. The election to file a consolidated return is usually binding on future years. See §§ 1501–1505 and the Regulations thereunder.

Consolidated taxable income. The taxable income construct of an affiliated group that has elected to file on a consolidated basis. Consolidated taxable income reflects (a) the elimination of a few intercompany transactions, (b) computation of certain transactions on a consolidated basis, and (c) deferral of certain gains and losses realized relative to intercompany transfers.

Consolidation. The combination of two or more corporations into a newly created corporation. Thus, A Corporation and B Corporation combine to form C Corporation. A consolidation may qualify as a nontaxable reorganization if certain conditions are satisfied. §§ 354 and 368(a)(1)(A).

Constructive dividends. A taxable benefit derived by a shareholder from the shareholder's corporation, although such benefit was not designated as a dividend. Examples include unreasonable compensation, excessive rent payments, bargain purchases of corporate property, and shareholder use of corporate property. Constructive dividends generally are a problem limited to closely held corporations. See also *bargain sale or purchase, closely held corporation,* and *unreasonable compensation.*

Constructive ownership. See *attribution.*

Constructive receipt of income. If income is unqualifiedly available although not physically in the taxpayer's possession, it is subject to the income tax. An example would be accrued interest on a savings account. Under the constructive receipt of income concept, such interest is taxed to a depositor in the year available, rather than the year actually withdrawn. The fact that the depositor uses the cash basis of accounting for tax purposes is irrelevant. See Reg. § 1.451–2. See also *cash basis.*

Continuity of life or existence. The death or other withdrawal of an owner of an entity does not terminate the existence of such entity. This is a characteristic of a corporation since the death or withdrawal of a shareholder does not affect the corporation's existence. Reg. § 301.7701–2(b). See also *association.*

Contributions to the capital of a corporation. See *capital contribution.*

Contributory qualified pension or profit sharing plan. A plan funded with both employer and employee contributions. Since the employee's contributions to the plan are subject to income tax, a later distribution of such contributions to the employee generally are tax-free. See also *qualified pension or profit sharing plan.*

Controlled foreign corporation. Any foreign corporation in which more than 50 percent of the total combined voting power of all classes of stock entitled to vote or the total value of the stock of the corporation is owned by "U.S. shareholders" on any day during the taxable year of the foreign corporation. For purposes of this definition, a U.S. shareholder is any U.S. person who owns, or is considered as owning, 10 percent or more of the total combined voting power of all classes of voting stock of the foreign corporation. Stock owned directly, indirectly, and constructively is used in this measure.

Controlled group. A controlled group of corporations is required to share the lower corporate tax rates and various other tax benefits among its members. A controlled group may be either a brother-sister or a parent-subsidiary group. A controlled group exists with respect to those corporations for which at least 80 percent ownership is held within the group. In addition, aggregate common ownership in excess of 50 percent is required of the members of a brother-sister controlled group.

Corporate acquisition. The takeover of one corporation by another if both parties retain their legal existence after the transaction. An acquisition can be effected via a stock purchase or through a tax-free exchange of stock. See also *corporate reorganization* and *merger*.

Corporate liquidation. Occurs when a corporation distributes its net assets to its shareholders and ceases its legal existence. Generally, a shareholder recognizes capital gain or loss upon such liquidation of the entity regardless of the corporation's balance in its earnings and profits account. However, the distributing corporation recognizes gain and loss on assets that it distributes to shareholders in kind.

Corporate reorganization. Occurs, among other instances, when one corporation acquires another in a merger or acquisition, a single corporation divides into two or more entities, a corporation makes a substantial change in its capital structure, or a corporation undertakes a change in its legal name or domicile. The exchange of stock and other securities in a corporate reorganization can be effected favorably for tax purposes if certain statutory requirements are followed strictly. Such tax consequences include the nonrecognition of any gain that is realized by the shareholders except to the extent of boot received. See also *corporate acquisition* and *merger*.

Corpus. The body or principal of a trust. Suppose, for example, G transfers an apartment building into a trust, income payable to W for life, remainder to S upon W's death. Corpus of the trust is the apartment building.

Correspondence audit. An audit conducted by the IRS by mail. Typically, the IRS writes to the taxpayer requesting the verification of a particular deduction or exemption. The completion of a special form or the remittance of copies of records or other support is all that is requested of the taxpayer. See also *audit, field audit*, and *office audit*.

Court of Appeals. Any of 13 Federal courts that consider tax matters appealed from the U.S. Tax Court, a U.S. District Court, or the U.S. Claims Court. Appeal from a U.S. Court of Appeals is to the U.S. Supreme Court by Writ of Certiorari. See also *appellate court* and *trial court*.

Credit for prior transfers. The death tax credit for prior transfers applies when property is taxed in the estates of different decedents within a 10-year period. The credit is determined using a decreasing statutory percentage, with the magnitude of the credit decreasing as the length of time between the multiple deaths increases.

Criminal fraud. See *fraud*.

Cross-purchase buy and sell agreement. Under this type of arrangement, the surviving owners of the business agree to buy out the withdrawing owner. Assume, for example, R and S are equal shareholders in T Corporation. Under a cross-purchase buy and sell agreement, R and S would contract to purchase the other's interest should that person decide to withdraw from the business. See also *buy and sell agreement* and *entity buy and sell agreement*.

Current earnings and profits. A corporate distribution is deemed to be first from the entity's current earnings and profits and then from accumulated earnings and profits. Shareholders recognize dividend income to the extent of the earnings and profits of the corporation. A dividend results to the extent of current earnings and profits even if there is a larger negative balance in accumulated earnings and profits.

Current use valuation. See *special use value*.

Curtesy. A husband's right under state law to all or part of his wife's property upon her death. See also *dower*.

D

Death benefit. A payment made by an employer to the beneficiary or beneficiaries of a deceased employee on account of the death of the employee. Under certain conditions, the first $5,000 of such payment is exempt from the income tax. § 101(b)(1).

Death tax. A tax imposed on property transferred by the death of the owner. See also *credit for prior transfers, estate tax*, and *inheritance tax*.

Decedent. An individual who has died.

Deduction. The Federal income tax is not imposed upon gross income. Rather, it is imposed upon net income. Congressionally identified deductions are subtracted from gross income to arrive at the tax base taxable income.

Deductions in respect of a decedent. Deductions accrued to the point of death but not recognizable on the final income tax return of a decedent because of the method of accounting used. Such items are allowed as deductions on the estate tax return and on the income tax return of the estate (Form 1041) or the heir (Form 1040). An example of a deduction in respect of a decedent is interest expense accrued up to the date of death by a cash basis debtor.

Deferred compensation. Compensation that will be taxed when received and not when earned. An example is contributions by an employer to a qualified pension or profit sharing plan on behalf of an employee. Such contributions will not be taxed to the employee until they are distributed (e.g., upon retirement). See also *qualified pension or profit sharing plan*.

Deficiency. Additional tax liability owed by a taxpayer and assessed by the IRS. See also *assessment* and *statutory notice of deficiency*.

Deficiency dividends. Once the IRS has established a corporation's liability for the personal holding company tax in a prior year, the tax may be reduced or avoided by the issuance of a deficiency dividend under § 547. The deficiency dividend procedure is not available in cases where the deficiency was due to fraud with intent to evade tax or to a willful failure to file the appropriate tax return [§ 547(g)]. Nor does the deficiency dividend procedure avoid the usual penalties and interest applicable for failure to file a return or pay a tax.

Deficit. A negative balance in the earnings and profits account.

Delaware subsidiary holding company. An entity established to optimize the state income tax liabilities of a multistate corporation. A subsidiary is formed and domiciled with nexus in Delaware or some other state that exempts portfolio income from the state tax base. The subsidiary then holds and manages all of the corporation's nonbusiness assets.

Demand loan. A loan payable upon request by the creditor, rather than on a specific date.

Depletion. The process by which the cost or other basis of a natural resource (e.g., an oil or gas interest) is recovered upon extraction and sale of the resource. The two ways to determine the depletion allowance are the cost and percentage (or statutory) methods. Under the cost method, each unit of production sold is assigned a portion of the cost or other basis of the interest. This is determined by dividing the cost or other basis by the total units expected to be recovered. Under the percentage (or statutory) method, the tax law provides a special percentage factor for different types of minerals and other natural resources. This percentage is multiplied by the gross income from the interest to arrive at the depletion allowance. §§ 613 and 613A.

Depreciation. The deduction for the cost or other basis of a tangible asset over the asset's estimated useful life. As to intangible assets, see *amortization*. As to natural resources, see *depletion*. See also *estimated useful life*.

Depreciation recapture. Upon the disposition of depreciable property used in a trade or business, gain or loss is measured by the difference between the consideration received (the amount realized) and the adjusted basis of the property. Such gain recognized could be § 1231 gain and qualify for long-term capital gain treatment. The recapture provisions of the Code (e.g., §§ 219, 1245, and 1250) may operate to convert some or all of the previous § 1231 gain into ordinary income. The justification for depreciation recapture is that it prevents a taxpayer from converting a dollar of ordinary deduction (in the form of depreciation) into deferred tax-favored income (§ 1231 or long-term capital gain). The depreciation recapture rules do not apply when the property is disposed of at a loss or via a gift. See also *Section 1231 gains and losses*.

Determination letter. Upon the request of a taxpayer, an IRS District Director will comment on the tax status of a completed transaction. Determination letters are frequently used to clarify employee status, determine whether a retirement or profit sharing plan qualifies under the Code, and determine the tax-exempt status of certain nonprofit organizations.

Devise. A transfer by will of real estate. See also *bequest*.

Disclaimer. The rejection, refusal, or renunciation of a claim, power, or property. Section 2518 sets forth the conditions required to avoid gift tax consequences as the result of a disclaimer.

Discretionary trusts. Trusts under which the trustee or another party has the right to accumulate (rather than distribute) the income for each year. Depending on the terms of the trust instrument, such income may be accumulated for future distributions to the income beneficiaries or added to corpus for the benefit of the remainderperson. See also *corpus* and *income beneficiary*.

Disproportionate. Not pro rata or ratable. Suppose, for example, X Corporation has two shareholders, C and D, each of whom owns 50 percent of its stock. If X Corporation distributes a cash dividend of $2,000 to C and only $1,000 to D, the distribution is disproportionate. The distribution would have been proportionate if C and D had received $1,500 each.

Disregard of corporate entity. To treat a corporation as if it did not exist for tax purposes. In such event, each shareholder would account for an allocable share of all corporate transactions possessing tax consequences. See also *entity*.

Dissent. To disagree with the majority. If, for example, Judge B disagrees with the result reached by Judges C and D (all of whom are members of the same court), Judge B could issue a dissenting opinion.

Distributable net income (DNI). The measure that determines the nature and amount of the distributions from estates and trusts that the beneficiaries thereof must include in income. DNI also limits the amount that estates and trusts can claim as a deduction for such distributions. § 643(a).

Distributions in kind. A transfer of property "as is." If, for example, a corporation distributes land to its shareholders, a distribution in kind has taken place. A sale of land followed by a distribution of the cash proceeds would not be a distribution in kind of the land.

District Court. A Federal District Court is a trial court for purposes of litigating Federal tax matters. It is the only trial court for which a jury trial can be obtained. See also *trial court*.

Dividend. A nondeductible distribution to the shareholders of a corporation. A dividend constitutes gross income to the recipient if it is from the current or accumulated earnings and profits of the corporation.

Dividends received deduction. A deduction allowed a corporate shareholder for dividends received from a domestic corporation. The deduction usually is 70 percent of the dividends received, but it could be 80 or 100 percent depending upon the ownership percentage held by the payee corporation. §§ 243–246.

Dock sale. A purchaser uses its owned or rented vehicles to take possession of the product at the seller's shipping dock. In most states, the sale is apportioned to the operating state of the purchaser, rather than the seller. See also *apportionment* and *sales factor*.

Domestic corporation. A corporation created or organized in the United States or under the law of the United States or any state or territory. § 7701(a)(4). Only dividends received from domestic corporations qualify for the dividends received deduction (§ 243). See also *foreign corporation*.

Domicile. A person's legal home.

Donee. The recipient of a gift.

Donor. The maker of a gift.

Double-weighted apportionment formula. A means by which the total taxable income of a multistate corporation is assigned to a specific state. Usually, the payroll, property, and sales factors are equally treated, and the weighted average of these factors is used in the apportionment procedure. In some states, however, the sales factor may receive a double weight, or it may be the only factor considered. These latter formulas place a greater tax burden on the income of out-of-state corporations. See also *apportionment, payroll factor, property factor, sales factor,* and *UDITPA*.

Dower. A wife's right to all or part of her deceased husband's property, unique to common law states as opposed to community property jurisdictions. See also *curtesy*.

E

Earned income. Income from personal services. Distinguished from passive, portfolio, and other unearned income. Sometimes referred to as "active" income. See §§ 469, 911, and the Regulations thereunder.

Earnings and profits. Measures the economic capacity of a corporation to make a distribution to shareholders that is not a return of capital. Such a distribution will result in dividend income to the shareholders to the extent of the corporation's current and accumulated earnings and profits.

Employee stock ownership plan (ESOP). A type of qualified profit sharing plan that invests in securities of the employer. In a noncontributory ESOP, the employer usually contributes its shares to a trust and receives a deduction for the fair market value of such stock. Generally, the employee recognizes no income until the stock is sold after its distribution to him or her upon retirement or other separation from service. See also *qualified pension or profit sharing plan.*

En banc. The case was considered by the whole court. Typically, for example, only one of the judges of the U.S. Tax Court will hear and decide on a tax controversy. However, when the issues involved are unusually novel or of wide impact, the case will be heard and decided by the full Court sitting *en banc.*

Entity. An organization or being that possesses separate existence for tax purposes. Examples are corporations, partnerships, estates, and trusts. See also *disregard of corporate entity.*

Entity accounting income. Entity accounting income is not identical to the taxable income of a trust or estate, nor is it determined in the same manner as the entity's financial accounting income would be. The trust document or will determines whether certain income, expenses, gains, or losses are allocated to the corpus of the entity or to the entity's income beneficiaries. Only those items that are allocated to the income beneficiaries are included in entity accounting income.

Entity buy and sell agreement. A buy and sell agreement whereby the entity is to purchase the withdrawing owner's interest. When the entity is a corporation, the agreement generally involves a stock redemption on the part of the withdrawing shareholder. See also *buy and sell agreement* and *cross-purchase buy and sell agreement.*

Escrow. Money or other property placed with a third party as security for an existing or proposed obligation. C, for example, agrees to purchase D's stock in X Corporation but needs time to raise the necessary funds. The stock is placed by D with E (the escrow agent), with instructions to deliver it to C when the purchase price is paid.

Estate. An entity that locates, collects, distributes, and discharges the assets and liabilities of a decedent.

Estate tax. A tax imposed on the right to transfer property by death. Thus, an estate tax is levied on the decedent's estate and not on the heir receiving the property. See also *death tax* and *inheritance tax.*

Estimated useful life. The period over which an asset will be used by the taxpayer. Assets such as goodwill do not have an estimated useful life. The estimated useful life of an asset is essential to measuring the annual tax deduction for depreciation and amortization.

Estoppel. The process of being stopped from proving something (even if true) in court due to prior inconsistent action. It is usually invoked as a matter of fairness to prevent one party (either the taxpayer or the IRS) from taking advantage of a prior error.

Excess lobbying expenditures. An excise tax is applied on otherwise tax-exempt organizations with respect to the excess of total lobbying expenditures over *grass roots lobbying expenditures* for the year.

Excess loss account. When aggregate operating losses of a subsidiary exceed the acquisition price thereof, an excess loss account is created. Essentially, this construct represents a negative basis in the subsidiary's stock. Thus, if the stock is sold while an excess loss account exists, gain is recognized equal to the balance in the excess loss account.

Excise tax. A tax on the manufacture, sale, or use of goods or on the carrying on of an occupation or activity, or a tax on the transfer of property. Thus, the Federal estate and gift taxes are, theoretically, excise taxes.

Executor. A person designated by a will to administer (manage or take charge of) the assets and liabilities of a decedent. Such party may be a male (executor), female (executrix), or a trust company (executor). See also *administrator.*

Exemption. An amount by which the tax base is reduced for all qualifying taxpayers. Individuals can receive personal and dependency exemptions, and taxpayers apply an exemption in computing their alternative minimum taxable income. Often, the exemption amount is phased out as the tax base becomes sizable.

Exemption equivalent. The maximum value of assets that could be transferred to another party without incurring any Federal gift or death tax because of the application of the unified tax credit.

Exempt organization. An organization that is either partially or completely exempt from Federal income taxation. § 501.

F

Fair market value. The amount at which property would change hands between a willing buyer and a willing seller, neither being under any compulsion to buy or to sell and both having reasonable knowledge of the relevant facts. Reg. § 20.2031–1(b).

Federal Register. The first place that the rules and regulations of U.S. administrative agencies (e.g., the U.S. Treasury Department) are published.

F.2d. An abbreviation for the Second Series of the *Federal Reporter,* the official series in which decisions of the U.S. Claims Court and of the U.S. Court of Appeals are published.

F.Supp. The abbreviation for *Federal Supplement,* the official series in which the reported decisions of the U.S. Federal District Courts are published.

Feeder organization. An entity that carries on a trade or business for the benefit of an exempt organization. However, such a relationship does not result in the feeder organization itself being tax-exempt. § 502.

Fiduciary. A person who manages money or property for another and who must exercise a standard of care in such management activity imposed by law or contract. A trustee, for example, possesses a fiduciary responsibility to the beneficiaries of the trust to follow the terms of the trust and the requirements of applicable state law. A breach of fiduciary responsibility would make the trustee liable to the beneficiaries for any damage caused by such breach.

Field audit. An audit conducted by the IRS on the business premises of the taxpayer or in the office of the tax practitioner representing the taxpayer. See also *audit, correspondence audit,* and *office audit.*

FIRPTA. Under the Foreign Investment in Real Property Tax Act, gains or losses realized by nonresident aliens and non-U.S. corporations on the disposition of U.S. real estate create U.S.-source income and are subject to U.S. income tax.

First-in, first-out (FIFO). An accounting method for determining the cost of inventories. Under this method, the inventory on hand is deemed to be the sum of the cost of the most recently acquired units. See also *last-in, first-out (LIFO).*

Fiscal year. See *accounting period*.

Foreign corporation. A corporation that is not organized under the laws of one of the states or territories of the United States. § 7701(a)(5). See also *domestic corporation*.

Foreign currency transaction. An exchange that could generate a foreign currency gain or loss for a U.S. taxpayer. For instance, if A contracts to purchase foreign goods, payable in a currency other than U.S. dollars, at a specified date in the future, any change in the exchange rate between the dollar and that currency will generate a foreign currency gain or loss upon completion of the contract. This gain or loss is treated as separate from the underlying transaction; it may create ordinary or capital gain or loss.

Foreign earned income exclusion. The Code allows exclusions for earned income generated outside the United States to alleviate any tax base and rate disparities among countries. In addition, the exclusion is allowed for housing expenditures incurred by the taxpayer's employer with respect to the non-U.S. assignment, and self-employed individuals can deduct foreign housing expenses incurred in a trade or business.

Foreign personal holding company (FPHC). A foreign corporation in which (1) 60 percent or more of the gross income for the taxable year is FPHC income and (2) more than 50 percent of the total combined voting power or the total value of the stock is owned, directly or indirectly, by five or fewer individuals who are U.S. persons (the U.S. group) at any time during the taxable year. The 60 percent of gross income test drops to 50 percent or more after the 60 percent requirement has been met for one tax year, until the foreign corporation does not meet the 50 percent test for three consecutive years or the stock ownership requirement is not met for an entire tax year.

Foreign sales corporation. An entity qualifying for a partial exemption of its gross export receipts from U.S. tax. Most FSCs must maintain a presence in a foreign country. In addition, an FSC cannot issue preferred stock, nor can it have more than 25 shareholders.

Foreign tax credit or deduction. A U.S. citizen or resident who incurs or pays income taxes to a foreign country on income subject to U.S. tax may be able to claim some of these taxes as a deduction or a credit against the U.S. income tax. §§ 27 and 901–905.

Form 706. The U.S. Estate Tax Return. In certain cases, this form must be filed for a decedent who was a resident or citizen of the United States.

Form 709. The U.S. Gift Tax Return.

Form 709–A. The U.S. Short Form Gift Tax Return.

Form 870. The signing of Form 870 (Waiver of Restriction on Assessment and Collection of Deficiency in Tax and Acceptance of Overassessments) by a taxpayer permits the IRS to assess a proposed deficiency without issuing a statutory notice of deficiency (90-day letter). This means the taxpayer must pay the deficiency and cannot file a petition to the U.S. Tax Court. § 6213(d).

Form 872. The signing of this form by a taxpayer extends the period during which the IRS can make an assessment or collection of a tax. In other words, Form 872 extends the applicable statute of limitations. § 6501(c)(4).

Form 1041. The U.S. Fiduciary Income Tax Return, required to be filed by estates and trusts. See Appendix B for a specimen form.

Form 1065. The U.S. Partnership Return of Income. See Appendix B for a specimen form.

Form 1120. The U.S. Corporation Income Tax Return. See Appendix B for a specimen form.

Form 1120–A. The U.S. Short-Form Corporation Income Tax Return. See Appendix B for a specimen form.

Form 1120S. The U.S. Small Business Corporation Income Tax Return, required to be filed by S corporations. See Appendix B for a specimen form.

Fraud. Tax fraud falls into two categories: civil and criminal. Under civil fraud, the IRS may impose as a penalty an amount equal to as much as 75 percent of the underpayment [§ 6653(b)]. Fines and/or imprisonment are prescribed for conviction of various types of criminal tax fraud (§§ 7201–7207). Both civil and criminal fraud require a specific intent on the part of the taxpayer to evade the tax; mere negligence is not enough. Criminal fraud requires the additional element of willfulness (i.e., done deliberately and with evil purpose). In practice, it becomes difficult to distinguish between the degree of intent necessary to support criminal, rather than civil, fraud. In either situation, the IRS has the burden of proving fraud. See also *burden of proof*.

Free transferability of interests. The capability of the owner of an entity to transfer his or her ownership interest to another without the consent of the other owners. It is a characteristic of a corporation since a shareholder usually can freely transfer the stock to others without the approval of the existing shareholders. Reg. § 301.7701–2(e). See also *association*.

Fringe benefits. Compensation or other benefits received by an employee that are not in the form of cash. Some fringe benefits (e.g., accident and health plans, group term life insurance) may be excluded from the employee's gross income and thus are not subject to the Federal income tax.

Future interest. An interest that will come into being at some future point in time. It is distinguished from a present interest, which is already in existence. Assume, for example, that D transfers securities to a newly created trust. Under the terms of the trust instrument, income from the securities is to be paid each year to W for her life, with the securities passing to S upon W's death. W has a present interest in the trust since she is currently entitled to receive the income from the securities. S has a future interest since he must wait for W's death to benefit from the trust. The annual exclusion of $10,000 is not allowed for a gift of a future interest. § 2503(b). See also *annual exclusion* and *gift splitting*.

G

General partner. A partner who is fully liable in an individual capacity for the debts of the partnership to third parties. A general partner's liability is not limited to the investment in the partnership. See also *limited partner*.

General power of appointment. See *power of appointment*.

Gift. A transfer of property for less than adequate consideration. Gifts usually occur in a personal setting (such as between members of the same family). They are excluded from the income tax base but may be subject to a transfer tax.

Gift splitting. A special election for Federal gift tax purposes is available, whereunder a husband and wife can treat a gift by one of them to a third party as being made one-half by each. If, for example, H (the husband) makes a gift of $20,000 to S, W (the wife) may elect to treat $10,000 of the gift as coming from her. The major advantage of the election is that it enables the parties to take advantage of the nonowner spouse's (W in this case) annual exclusion and unified credit. § 2513. See also *annual exclusion*.

Gift tax.   A tax imposed on the transfer of property by gift. Such tax is imposed upon the donor of a gift and is based on the fair market value of the property on the date of the gift.

Gifts within three years of death.   Some taxable gifts automatically are included in the gross estate of the donor if death occurs within three years of the gift. § 2035.

Goodwill.   The reputation and built-up business of a company. For accounting purposes, goodwill has no basis unless it is purchased. In the purchase of a business, goodwill generally is the difference between the purchase price and the value of the assets acquired. The intangible asset goodwill cannot be amortized for tax purposes. Reg. § 1.167(a)–3. See also *amortization*.

Grantor.   A transferor of property. The creator of a trust is usually designated as the grantor of the trust.

Grantor trust.   A trust under which the grantor retains control over the income or corpus (or both) to such an extent that such grantor will be treated as the owner of the property and its income for income tax purposes. The result is to make the income from a grantor trust taxable to the grantor and not to the beneficiary who receives it. §§ 671–678. See also *reversionary interest*.

Grass roots lobbying expenditures.   Exempt organizations are prohibited from engaging in political activities, but expenses incurred to influence the opinions of the general public relative to specific legislation are permitted by the law. See also *excess lobbying expenditures*.

Gross estate.   The property owned or previously transferred by a decedent that is subject to the Federal death tax. Distinguished from the probate estate, which is property actually subject to administration by the administrator or executor of an estate. §§ 2031–2046. See also *adjusted gross estate* and *taxable estate*.

Gross income.   Income subject to the Federal income tax. Gross income does not include all economic income. That is, certain exclusions are allowed (e.g., interest on municipal bonds). For a manufacturing or merchandising business, gross income usually means gross profit (gross sales or gross receipts less cost of goods sold). § 61 and Reg. § 1.61–3(a). See also *adjusted gross income* and *taxable income*.

Gross up.   To add back to the value of the property or income received the amount of the tax that has been paid. For gifts made within three years of death, any gift tax paid on the transfer is added to the gross estate. § 2035.

Group term life insurance.   Life insurance coverage permitted by an employer for a group of employees. Such insurance is renewable on a year-to-year basis, and typically no cash surrender value is built up. The premiums paid by the employer on such insurance are not taxed to the employees on coverage of up to $50,000 per person. § 79 and Reg. § 1.79–1(b).

Guaranteed payments.   Payments made by a partnership to a partner for services rendered or for the use of capital to the extent that such payments are determined without regard to the income of the partnership. Such payments are treated as though they were made to a nonpartner and thus are usually deductible by the entity.

Guardianship.   A legal arrangement under which one person (a guardian) has the legal right and duty to care for another (the ward) and his or her property. A guardianship is established because of the ward's inability to legally act on his or her own behalf (e.g., because of minority [he or she is not of age] or mental or physical incapacity).

H

Head of household.   An unmarried individual who maintains a household for another and satisfies certain conditions set forth in § 2(b). Such status enables the taxpayer to use a set of income tax rates that are lower than those applicable to other unmarried individuals but higher than those applicable to surviving spouses and married persons filing a joint return.

Heir.   A person who inherits property from a decedent.

Hobby.   An activity not engaged in for profit. The Code restricts the amount of losses that an individual can deduct with respect to hobby activities so that such transactions cannot be used to offset income from other sources. § 183.

Holding period.   The period of time during which property has been held for income tax purposes. The holding period is significant in determining whether gain or loss from the sale or exchange of a capital asset is long term or short term. § 1223.

H.R. 10 plans.   See *Keogh plans*.

Hot assets.   Unrealized receivables and substantially appreciated inventory under § 751. When hot assets are present, the sale of a partnership interest or the disproportionate distribution of such assets can cause ordinary income to be recognized.

I

Imputed interest.   For certain long-term sales of property, the IRS can convert some of the gain from the sale into interest income if the contract does not provide for a minimum rate of interest to be paid by the purchaser. The application of this procedure has the effect of forcing the seller to recognize less long-term capital gain and more ordinary income (interest income). § 483 and the Regulations thereunder.

Incident of ownership.   An element of ownership or degree of control over a life insurance policy. The retention by an insured of an incident of ownership in a life insurance policy will cause the policy proceeds to be included in the insured's gross estate upon death. § 2042(2) and Reg. § 20.2042–1(c). See also *gross estate* and *insured*.

Includible gain.   Section 644 inposes a built-in gains tax on trusts that sell or exchange property at a gain within two years after the date of its transfer in trust by the transferor. The provision applies only if the fair market value of the property at the time of the initial transfer exceeds the adjusted basis of the property immediately after the transfer. The tax imposed by § 644 is the amount of additional tax the transferor would pay (including any minimum tax) had the gain been included in the transferor's gross income for the tax year of the sale. However, the tax applies only to an amount known as *includible gain*. This is the lesser of the following: the gain recognized by the trust on the sale or exchange of any property, or the excess of the fair market value of such property at the time of the initial transfer in trust by the transferor over the adjusted basis of such property immediately after the transfer.

Income beneficiary. The party entitled to income from property. In a typical trust situation, A is to receive the income for life with corpus or principal passing to B upon A's death. In this case, A is the income beneficiary of the trust.

Income in respect of a decedent. Income earned by a decedent at the time of death but not reportable on the final income tax return because of the method of accounting that appropriately is utilized. Such income is included in the gross estate and will be taxed to the eventual recipient (either the estate or heirs). The recipient will, however, be allowed an income tax deduction for the estate tax attributable to the income. § 691.

Income shifting. Occurs when an individual tranfers some of his or her gross income to a taxpayer who is subject to a lower tax rate, thereby reducing the total income tax liability of the group. Income shifting produces a successful assignment of income. It can be accomplished by transferring income-producing property to the lower-bracket taxpayer or to an effective trust for his or her benefit, or by transferring ownership interests in a family partnership or in a closely held corporation.

Incomplete transfer. A transfer made by a decedent during lifetime that, because of certain control or enjoyment retained by the transferor, is not considered complete for Federal estate tax purposes. Thus, some or all of the fair market value of the property transferred is included in the transferor's gross estate. §§ 2036–2038. See also *gross estate* and *revocable transfer*.

Individual retirement account (IRA). Individuals with earned income are permitted to set aside up to 100 percent of such income per year (not to exceed $2,000) for a retirement account. The amount so set aside can be deducted by the taxpayer and is subject to income tax only upon withdrawal. The Code limits the amount of this contribution that can be deducted *for* AGI depending upon (1) whether the taxpayer or spouse is an active participant in an employer-provided qualified retirement plan and (2) the magnitude of the taxpayer's AGI before the IRA contribution is considered. § 219. See also *simplified employee pensions.*

Inheritance tax. A tax imposed on the right to receive property from a decedent. Thus, theoretically, an inheritance tax is imposed on the heir. The Federal estate tax is imposed on the estate. See also *death tax* and *estate tax*.

In kind. See *distributions in kind.*

Installment method. A method of accounting enabling certain taxpayers to spread the recognition of gain on the sale of property over the collection period. Under this procedure, the seller computes the gross profit percentage from the sale (the gain divided by the selling price) and applies it to each payment received, to arrive at the gain to be recognized. § 453.

Insured. A person whose life is the subject of an insurance policy. Upon the death of the insured, the life insurance policy matures, and the proceeds become payable to the designated beneficiary. See also *life insurance.*

Intangible asset. Property that is a "right" rather than a physical object. Examples are patents, stocks and bonds, goodwill, trademarks, franchises, and copyrights. See also *amortization* and *tangible property.*

Inter vivos transfer. A transfer of property during the life of the owner. Distinguished from testamentary transfers, wherein the property passes at death.

Interest-free loans. Bona fide loans that carry no interest (or a below-market rate). If made in a nonbusiness setting, the imputed interest element is treated as a gift from the lender to the borrower. If made by a corporation to a shareholder, a constructive dividend could result. In either event, the lender may have interest income to recognize. § 7872.

Internal Revenue Code. The collected statutes that govern the taxation of income, property transfers, and other transactions in the United States and the enforcement of such provisions. Enacted by Congress, the Code is amended frequently, but it has not been reorganized since 1954. Because of the extensive revisions to the statutes that occurred with respect to the Tax Reform Act of 1986, Title 26 of the U.S. Code is now known as the Internal Revenue Code of 1986.

Interpolated terminal reserve. The measure used in valuing insurance policies for gift and estate tax purposes when the policies are not paid up at the time of their transfer. Reg. § 20.2031–8(a)(3), Ex. (3).

Intestate. No will exists at the time of death. Under such circumstances, state law prescribes who will receive the decedent's property. The laws of intestate succession generally favor the surviving spouse, children, and grandchildren, and then parents and grandparents and brothers and sisters.

Investment income. Consisting of virtually the same elements as portfolio income, a measure by which to justify a deduction for interest on investment indebtedness. See also *investment indebtedness* and *portfolio income.*

Investment indebtedness. Debt incurred to carry or incur investments by the taxpayer in assets that will produce portfolio income. Limitations are placed upon interest deductions that are incurred with respect to such debt (generally to the corresponding amount of investment income).

Investment tax credit. A special tax credit equal to 6 or 10 percent of the qualified investment in tangible personal property used in a trade or business. Expired as of the end of 1985.

Involuntary conversion. The loss or destruction of property through theft, casualty, or condemnation. Any gain realized on an involuntary conversion can, at the taxpayer's election, be deferred for Federal income tax purposes if the owner reinvests the proceeds within a prescribed period of time in property that is similar or related in service or use. § 1033.

IRA. See *individual retirement account.*

Itemized deductions. Personal and employee expenditures allowed by the Code as deductions from adjusted gross income. Examples include certain medical expenses, interest on home mortgages, and charitable contributions. Itemized deductions are reported on Schedule A of Form 1040.

J

Jeopardy assessment. If the collection of a tax appears in question, the IRS may assess and collect the tax immediately without the usual formalities. The IRS can terminate a taxpayer's taxable year before the usual date if it feels that the collection of the tax may be in peril because the taxpayer plans to leave the country. §§ 6851 and 6861–6864.

Joint and several liability. Permits the IRS to collect a tax from one or all of several taxpayers. A husband and wife who file a joint income tax return usually are collectively or individually liable for the full amount of the tax liability. § 6013(d)(3).

Joint tenancy.   The undivided ownership of property by two or more persons with the right of survivorship. Right of survivorship gives the surviving owner full ownership of the property. Suppose, for example, B and C are joint owners of a tract of land. Upon B's death, C becomes the sole owner of the property. As to the death tax consequences upon the death of a joint tenant, see § 2040. See also *tenancy by the entirety* and *tenancy in common.*

Joint venture.   A one-time grouping of two or more persons in a business undertaking. Unlike a partnership, a joint venture does not entail a continuing relationship among the parties. A joint venture is treated like a partnership for Federal income tax purposes. § 7701(a)(2).

K

Keogh plans.   A designation for retirement plans available to self-employed taxpayers. They are also referred to as H.R. 10 plans. Under such plans a taxpayer may deduct each year up to either 20 percent of net earnings from self-employment or $30,000, whichever is less.

Kiddie tax.   Synonym for *tax on unearned income of a child under age 14.*

L

Lapse.   The expiration of a right either by the death of the holder or upon the expiration of a period of time. Thus, a power of appointment lapses upon the death of the holder if such holder has not exercised the power during life or at death (through a will).

Last-in, first-out (LIFO).   An accounting method for valuing inventories for tax purposes. Under this method, it is assumed that the inventory on hand is valued at the cost of the earliest acquired units. § 472. See also *first-in, first-out (FIFO).*

Legacy.   A transfer of cash or other property by will.

Legal age.   The age at which a person may enter into binding contracts or commit other legal acts. In most states, a minor reaches legal age or majority (comes of age) at age 18.

Legal representative.   A person who oversees the legal affairs of another; for example, the executor or administrator of an estate or a court appointed guardian of a minor or incompetent person.

Legatee.   The recipient of property under a will and transferred by the death of the owner.

Lessee.   One who rents property from another. In the case of real estate, the lessee is also known as the tenant.

Lessor.   One who rents property to another. In the case of real estate, the lessor is also known as the landlord.

LEXIS.   An on-line database system, produced by Mead Data Services, by which the tax researcher can obtain access to the Internal Revenue Code, Regulations, administrative rulings, and court case opinions.

Life estate.   A legal arrangement under which the beneficiary (the life tenant) is entitled to the income from the property for his or her life. Upon the death of the life tenant, the property is transferred to the holder of the remainder interest. See also *income beneficiary* and *remainder interest.*

Life insurance.   A contract between the holder of a policy and an insurance company (the carrier) under which the company agrees, in return for premium payments, to pay a specified sum (the face value or maturity value of the policy) to the designated beneficiary upon the death of the insured. See also *insured.*

Like-kind exchange.   An exchange of property held for productive use in a trade or business or for investment (except inventory and stocks and bonds) for other investment or trade or business property. Unless non-like-kind property (boot) is received, the exchange is nontaxable. § 1031. See also *boot.*

Limited liability.   The liability of an entity and its owners to third parties is limited to the investment in the entity. This is a characteristic of a corporation since shareholders generally are not responsible for the debts of the corporation and, at most, may lose the amount paid in for the stock issued. Reg. § 301.7701–2(d). See also *association.*

Limited partner.   A partner whose liability to third-party creditors of the partnership is limited to the amount invested by such partner in the partnership. See also *general partner* and *limited partnership.*

Limited partnership.   A partnership in which some of the partners are limited partners. At least one of the partners in a limited partnership must be a general partner. See also *general partner* and *limited partner.*

Liquidating distribution.   A distribution by a partnership or corporation that is in complete liquidation of the entity's trade or business activities. Typically, such distributions generate capital gain or loss to the investors without regard, for instance, to the earnings and profits of the corporation or to the partnership's basis in the distributed property. They can, however, lead to recognized gain or loss at the corporate level.

Liquidation.   See *corporate liquidation.*

Lobbying expenditure.   An expenditure made for the purpose of influencing legislation. Such payments can result in the loss of the exempt status of, and the imposition of Federal income tax on, an exempt organization.

Long-term capital gain or loss.   Results from the sale or other taxable exchange of a capital asset that had been held by the seller for more than one year or from other transactions involving statutorily designated assets, including § 1231 property and patents.

Lump-sum distribution.   Payment of the entire amount due at one time rather than in installments. Such distributions often occur from qualified pension or profit sharing plans upon the retirement or death of a covered employee.

M

Majority.   See *legal age.*

Malpractice.   Professional misconduct; an unreasonable lack of skill.

Marital deduction.   A deduction allowed against the taxable estate or taxable gifts upon the transfer of property from one spouse to another.

Market value.   See *fair market value.*

Merger.   The absorption of one corporation by another under which the corporation being absorbed loses its legal identity. X Corporation is merged into B Corporation, and the shareholders of

X Corporation receive stock in B Corporation in exchange for their stock in X Corporation. After the merger, X Corporation ceases to exist as a separate legal entity. If a merger meets certain conditions, it is nontaxable to the parties involved. § 368(a)(1)(A). See also *corporate acquisition* and *corporate reorganization.*

Minimum tax.   See *alternative minimum tax.*

Minority.   See *legal age.*

Mitigation.   To make less severe. See also *mitigation of the annual accounting period concept* and *mitigation of the statute of limitations.*

Mitigation of the annual accounting period concept. Various tax provisions that provide relief from the effect of the finality of the annual accounting period concept. For example, the net operating loss carryover provisions allow the taxpayer to apply the negative taxable income of one year against a corresponding positive amount in another tax accounting period. See also *annual accounting period concept.*

Mitigation of the statute of limitations.   A series of tax provisions that prevents either the IRS or a taxpayer from obtaining a double benefit from the application of the statute of limitations. It would be unfair, for example, to permit a taxpayer to depreciate an asset previously expensed, but which should have been capitalized, if the statute of limitations prevents the IRS from adjusting the tax liability for the year the asset was purchased. §§ 1311–1315. See also *statute of limitations.*

Mortgagee.   The party who holds the mortgage; the creditor.

Mortgagor.   The party who mortgages the property; the debtor.

Most suitable use value.   For gift and estate tax purposes, property that is transferred normally is valued in accordance with its most suitable or optimal use. Thus, if a farm is worth more as a potential shopping center, the value as a shopping center will control, even though the transferee (the donee or heir) continues to use the property as a farm. For an exception to this rule concerning the valuation of certain kinds of real estate transferred by death, see *special use value.*

Multistate corporation.   A corporation that has operations in more than one of the states of the United States. Issues arise relative to the assignment of appropriate amounts of the entity's taxable income to the states in which it has a presence. See also *allocation, apportionment, nexus,* and *UDITPA.*

Multistate Tax Commission.   A regulatory body of the states that develops operating rules and regulations for the implementation of UDITPA and other provisions that assign the total taxable income of a multistate corporation to specific states. See also *allocation, apportionment,* and *UDITPA.*

Multi-tiered partnerships.   See *tiered partnerships.*

N

Necessary.   Appropriate and helpful in furthering the taxpayer's business or income-producing activity. §§ 162(a) and 212. See also *ordinary.*

Negligence.   Failure to exercise the reasonable or ordinary degree of care of a prudent person in a situation that results in harm or damage to another. Code § 6653(a) imposes a penalty on taxpayers who show negligence or intentional disregard of rules and Regulations with respect to the underpayment of certain taxes.

Net operating loss.   To mitigate the effect of the annual accounting period concept, § 172 allows taxpayers to use an excess loss of one year as a deduction for certain past or future years. In this regard, a carryback period of 3 years and a carryforward period of 15 years currently is allowed. See also *mitigation of the annual accounting period concept.*

Net worth method.   An approach used by the IRS to reconstruct the income of a taxpayer who fails to maintain adequate records. Under this method, the gross income for the year is estimated as the increase in net worth of the taxpayer (assets in excess of liabilities) with appropriate adjustment for nontaxable receipts and nondeductible expenditures. The net worth method often is used when tax fraud is suspected.

Nexus.   A multistate corporation's taxable income can be apportioned to a specific state only if the entity has established a sufficient presence, or nexus, with that state. State law, which often follows UDITPA, specifies various activities that lead to such nexus in various states. See also *apportionment* and *UDITPA.*

Ninety-day letter.   See *statutory notice of deficiency.*

Nonacquiescence.   Disagreement by the IRS on the result reached by the U.S. Tax Court in a Regular Decision. Sometimes abbreviated *non-acq.* or *NA.* See also *acquiescence.*

Nonbusiness bad debts.   A bad debt loss incurred not in connection with a creditor's trade or business. Such loss is classified as a short-term capital loss and will be allowed only in the year the debt becomes entirely worthless. In addition to family loans, many investor losses fall into the classification of nonbusiness bad debts. § 166(d). See also *business bad debts.*

Nonbusiness income.   Income generated from investment assets or from the taxable disposition thereof. In some states, the nonbusiness income of a multistate corporation is held out of the apportionment procedure and allocated to the state in which the nonbusiness asset is located. See also *allocation* and *apportionment.*

Noncontributory qualified pension or profit sharing plan. A plan funded entirely by the employer with no contributions being made by the covered employees. See also *qualified pension or profit sharing plans.*

Nonliquidating distribution.   A payment made by a partnership or corporation to the entity's owner is a nonliquidating distribution when the entity's legal existence does not cease thereafter. If the payor is a corporation, such a distribution can result in dividend income to the shareholders. If the payor is a partnership, the partner usually assigns a basis in the distributed property that is equal to the lesser of the partner's basis in the partnership interest or the basis of the distributed asset to the partnership. In this regard, the partner first assigns basis to any cash that he or she receives in the distribution. The partner's remaining basis, if any, is assigned to the noncash assets according to their relative bases to the partnership.

Nonrecourse debt.   Debt secured by the property that it is used to purchase. The purchaser of the property is not personally liable for the debt upon default. Rather, the creditor's recourse is to repossess the related property. Nonrecourse debt generally does not increase the purchaser's at-risk amount.

Nonresident alien.   An individual who is not a citizen or resident of the United States. Citizenship is determined under the immigration and naturalization laws of the United States. Residency is determined under § 7701(b) of the Internal Revenue Code.

Nonseparately stated income. The net income of an S corporation that is combined and allocated to the shareholders. Other items, such as capital gains and charitable contributions, that could be treated differently on the individual tax returns of the shareholders are not included in this amount but are allocated to the shareholders separately.

O

Obligee. The party to whom someone else is obligated under a contract. Thus, if C loans money to D, C is the obligee and D is the obligor under the loan.

Obligor. See *obligee.*

Office audit. An audit conducted by the IRS in the agent's office. See also *audit, correspondence audit,* and *field audit.*

On all fours. A judicial decision exactly in point with another as to result, facts, or both.

Optimal use value. Synonym for most suitable use value.

Ordinary. Common and accepted in the general industry or type of activity in which the taxpayer is engaged. It comprises one of the tests for the deductibility of expenses incurred or paid in connection with a trade or business; for the production or collection of income; for the management, conservation, or maintenance of property held for the production of income; or in connection with the determination, collection, or refund of any tax. §§ 162(a) and 212. See also *necessary.*

Ordinary and necessary. See *necessary* and *ordinary.*

Ordinary gross income. A concept peculiar to personal holding companies and defined in § 543(b)(1). See also *adjusted ordinary gross income.*

P

Partner. See *general partner* and *limited partner.*

Partnership. For income tax purposes, a partnership includes a syndicate, group, pool, or joint venture, as well as ordinary partnerships. In an ordinary partnership, two or more parties combine capital and/or services to carry on a business for profit as co-owners. § 7701(a)(2). See also *limited partnership* and *tiered partnerships.*

Passive investment income. Passive investment income means gross receipts from royalties, certain rents, dividends, interest, annuities, and gains from the sale or exchange of stock and securities. With certain exceptions, if the passive investment income of an S corporation exceeds 25 percent of the corporation's gross receipts for three consecutive years, S status is lost.

Passive foreign investment company (PFIC). A non-U.S. corporation that generates a substantial magnitude of personal holding company income. Upon receipt of an excess distribution from the entity or the sale of its shares, its U.S. shareholders are taxable on their pro rata shares of the tax that has been deferred with respect to the corporation's taxable income, plus an applicable interest charge.

Passive loss. Any loss from (1) activities in which the taxpayer does not materially participate, (2) rental activities, or (3) tax shelter activities. Net passive losses cannot be used to offset income from nonpassive sources. Rather, they are suspended until the taxpayer either generates net passive income (and a deduction of such losses is allowed) or disposes of the underlying property (at which time the loss deductions are allowed in full). Landlords who actively participate in the rental activities can deduct up to $25,000 of passive losses annually. However, this amount is phased out when the landlord's AGI exceeds $100,000. See also *portfolio income.*

Payroll factor. The proportion of a multistate corporation's total payroll that is traceable to a specific state. Used in determining the taxable income that is to be apportioned to that state. See also *apportionment.*

Pecuniary bequest. A bequest of money to an heir by a decedent. See also *bequest.*

Percentage depletion. See *depletion.*

Percentage of completion method. A method of reporting gain or loss on certain long-term contracts. Under this method of accounting, the gross contract price is included in income as the contract is completed. Reg. § 1.451–3. See also *completed contract method.*

Personal and household effects. Items owned by a decedent at the time of death. Examples include clothing, furniture, sporting goods, jewelry, stamp and coin collections, silverware, china, crystal, cooking utensils, books, cars, televisions, radios, stereo equipment, etc.

Personal holding company. A corporation that satisfies the requirements of § 542. Qualification as a personal holding company means a penalty tax will be imposed on the corporation's undistributed personal holding company income for the year.

Personal holding company income. Income as defined by § 543. Such income includes interest, dividends, certain rents and royalties, income from the use of corporate property by certain shareholders, income from certain personal service contracts, and distributions from estates and trusts. Such income is relevant in determining whether a corporation is a personal holding company and is therefore subject to the penalty tax on personal holding companies. See also *adjusted ordinary gross income.*

Personal property. Generally, all property other than real estate. It is sometimes designated as personalty when real estate is termed realty. Personal property can also refer to property not used in a taxpayer's trade or business or held for the production or collection of income. When used in this sense, personal property could include both realty (e.g., a personal residence) and personalty (e.g., personal effects such as clothing and furniture). See also *bequest.*

Personalty. Personalty is all property that is not attached to real estate (realty) and is movable. Examples of personalty are machinery, automobiles, clothing, household furnishings, inventory, and personal effects. See also *ad valorem tax* and *realty.*

P-H. Prentice-Hall is the publisher of a tax service and of Federal tax decisions (AFTR and AFTR2d series).

PHINet. An on-line database system, produced by Prentice-Hall Information Services, by which the tax researcher can obtain access to the Internal Revenue Code, Regulations, administrative rulings, and court case opinions.

Portfolio income. Income from interest, dividends, rentals, royalties, capital gains, or other investment sources. Net passive losses cannot be used to offset net portfolio income. See also *passive loss* and *investment income.*

Power of appointment. A legal right granted to someone by will or other document that gives the holder the power to dispose of property or the income from property. When the holder may appoint the property to his or her own benefit, the power usually is designated as a general power of appointment. If the holder cannot benefit himself or herself but may only appoint to certain other persons, the power is a special power of appointment. For example, assume G places $500,000 worth of securities in trust granting D the right to determine each year how the trustee is to divide the income between A and B. Under these circumstances, D has a special power of appointment. If D had the further right to appoint the income to himself, he or she probably possesses a general power of appointment. For the estate tax and gift tax effects of powers of appointment, see §§ 2041 and 2514. See also *testamentary power of appointment.*

Preferred stock bailout.   A process wherein the issuance, sale, and later redemption of a preferred stock dividend was used by a shareholder to obtain long-term capital gains without any loss of voting control over the corporation. In effect, therefore, the shareholder was able to bail out corporate profits without suffering the consequences of dividend income treatment. This procedure led to the enactment by Congress of § 306, which, if applicable, converts the prior long-term capital gain on the sale of the stock to ordinary income. Under these circumstances, the amount of ordinary income is limited to the shareholder's portion of the corporation's earnings and profits existing when the preferred stock was issued as a stock dividend. See also *bailout.*

Present interest.   See *future interest.*

Presumption.   An inference in favor of a particular fact. If, for example, the IRS issues a notice of deficiency against a taxpayer, a presumption of correctness attaches to the assessment. Thus, the taxpayer has the burden of proof of showing that he or she does not owe the tax listed in the deficiency notice. See also *rebuttable presumption.*

Previously taxed income (PTI).   Before the Subchapter S Revision Act of 1982, the undistributed taxable income of an S corporation was taxed to the shareholders as of the last day of the corporation's tax year and usually could be withdrawn by the shareholders without tax consequences at some later point in time. The role of PTI has been taken over by the accumulated adjustments account. See also *accumulated adjustments account.*

Principal.   Property as opposed to income. The term is often used as a synonym for the corpus of a trust. If, for example, G places real estate in trust with income payable to A for life and the remainder to B upon A's death, the real estate is the principal, or corpus, of the trust.

Private foundation.   An exempt organization that is subject to additional statutory restrictions on its activities and on contributions thereto. Excise taxes may be levied on certain prohibited transactions, and the Code places more stringent restrictions on the deductibility of contributions to private foundations. § 509.

Probate.   The legal process wherein the estate of a decedent is administered. Generally, the probate process involves collecting a decedent's assets, liquidating liabilities, paying necessary taxes, and distributing property to heirs.

Probate court.   The usual designation for the state or local court that supervises the administration (probate) of a decedent's estate.

Probate estate.   The property of a decedent that is subject to administration by the executor or administrator of an estate. See also *administration.*

Property factor.   The proportion of a multistate corporation's total property that is traceable to a specific state. Used in determining the taxable income that is to be apportioned to that state. See also *apportionment.*

Property tax.   An *ad valorem* tax, usually levied by a city or county government, on the value of real or personal property that the taxpayer owns on a specified date. Most states exclude intangible property and assets owned by exempt organizations from the tax base, and some exclude inventory, pollution control or manufacturing equipment, and other items to provide relocation or retention incentives to the taxpayer.

Prop.Reg.   An abbreviation for Proposed Regulation. A Regulation may first be issued in proposed form to give interested parties the opportunity for comment. When and if a Proposed Regulation is finalized, it is designated as a Regulation (abbreviated Reg.).

Pro rata.   Proportionately. Assume, for example, a corporation has 10 shareholders, each of whom owns 10 percent of the stock. A pro rata dividend distribution of $1,000 would mean that each shareholder would receive $100.

Public Law 86–272.   A congressional limit on the ability of the state to force a multistate corporation to assign income to that state. Under P.L. 86–272, where orders for tangible personal property are both filled and delivered outside of the state, the entity must establish more than the mere solicitation of such orders before any income can be apportioned to the state. See also *apportionment.*

Public policy limitation.   A concept developed by the courts precluding an income tax deduction for certain expenses related to activities deemed to be contrary to the public welfare. In this connection, Congress has incorporated into the Code specific disallowance provisions covering such items as illegal bribes, kickbacks, and fines and penalties. §§ 162(c) and (f).

Q

Qualified pension or profit sharing plan.   An employer-sponsored plan that meets the requirements of § 401. If these requirements are met, none of the employer's contributions to the plan will be taxed to the employee until distributed to him or her (§ 402). The employer will be allowed a deduction in the year the contributions are made (§ 404). See also *contributory qualified pension or profit sharing plan, deferred compensation,* and *noncontributory pension or profit sharing plan.*

Qualified terminable interest property (QTIP).   Generally, the marital deduction (for gift and estate tax purposes) is not available if the interest transferred will terminate upon the death of the transferee spouse and pass to someone else. Thus, if H places property in trust, life estate to W, and remainder to their children upon W's death, this is a terminable interest that will not provide H (or H's estate) with a marital deduction. If, however, the transfer in trust is treated as qualified terminable interest property (the QTIP election is made), the terminable interest restriction is waived and the marital deduction becomes available. In exchange for this deduction, the surviving spouse's gross estate must include the value of the QTIP election assets, even though he or she has no control over the ultimate disposition of the asset. Terminable interest property qualifies for this election if the donee (or heir) is the only beneficiary of the asset during his or her lifetime and receives income distributions relative to the property at least annually. As to gifts, the donor spouse is the one who makes the QTIP election. As to property transferred by death, the executor of the estate of the deceased spouse has the right to make the election. §§ 2056(b)(7) and 2523(f).

R

RAR. A Revenue agent's report, which reflects any adjustments made by the agent as a result of an audit of the taxpayer. The RAR is mailed to the taxpayer along with the 30-day letter, which outlines the appellate procedures available to the taxpayer.

Realized gain or loss. The difference between the amount realized upon the sale or other disposition of property and the adjusted basis of such property. § 1001. See also *adjusted basis, amount realized, basis,* and *recognized gain or loss.*

Realty. Real estate. See also *personalty.*

Reasonable needs of the business. The usual justification for avoiding the penalty tax on unreasonable accumulation of earnings. In determining the amount of taxable income subject to this tax (accumulated taxable income), § 535 allows a deduction for "such part of earnings and profits for the taxable year as are retained for the reasonable needs of the business." § 537.

Rebuttable presumption. A presumption that can be overturned upon the showing of sufficient proof. See also *presumption.*

Recapture. To recover the tax benefit of a deduction or a credit previously taken. See also *depreciation recapture.*

Recapture potential. A measure with respect to property that, if disposed of in a taxable transaction, would result in the recapture of depreciation (§§ 1245 or 1250), deferred LIFO gain, or deferred installment method gain.

Recognized gain or loss. The portion of realized gain or loss subject to income taxation. See also *realized gain or loss.*

Regulations. The U.S. Treasury Department Regulations (abbreviated Reg.) represent the position of the IRS as to how the Internal Revenue Code is to be interpreted. Their purpose is to provide taxpayers and IRS personnel with rules of general and specific application to the various provisions of the tax law. Regulations are published in the *Federal Register* and in all tax services.

Related parties. Various Code Sections define related parties and often include a variety of persons within this (usually detrimental) category. Generally, related parties are accorded different tax treatment from that which applies to other taxpayers who would enter into similar transactions. For instance, realized losses that are generated between related parties are not recognized in the year of the loss. However, these deferred losses can be used to offset recognized gains that occur upon the subsequent sale of the asset to a nonrelated party. Other uses of a related-party definition include the conversion of gain upon the sale of a depreciable asset into all ordinary income (§ 1239) and the identification of constructive ownership of stock relative to corporate distributions, redemptions, liquidations, reorganizations, and compensation.

Remainder interest. The property that passes to a beneficiary after the expiration of an intervening income interest. If, for example, G places real estate in trust with income to A for life and remainder to B upon A's death, B has a remainder interest. See also *life estate* and *reversionary interest.*

Remand. To send back. An appellate court may remand a case to a lower court, usually for additional fact finding. In other words, the

appellate court is not in a position to decide the appeal based on the facts determined by the lower court. Remanding is abbreviated "rem'g."

Reorganization. See *corporate reorganization.*

Restoration event. The transaction that triggers recognition of a gain or loss that previously was realized between members of a consolidated group.

Return of capital. When a taxpayer reacquires financial resources that he or she previously had invested in an entity or venture, the return of his or her capital investment itself does not increase gross income for the recovery year. A return of capital may occur with respect to an annuity or insurance contract, the sale or exchange of any asset, or a distribution from a partnership or corporation.

Revenue neutral. A change in the tax system that results in the same amount of revenue. Revenue neutral, however, does not mean that any one taxpayer will pay the same amount of tax as was previously the case. Thus, as a result of a tax law change, corporations could pay more taxes, but the excess revenue will be offset by lesser taxes on individuals.

Revenue Procedure. A matter of procedural importance to both taxpayers and the IRS concerning the administration of the tax laws is issued as a Revenue Procedure (abbreviated Rev.Proc.). A Revenue Procedure is first published in an *Internal Revenue Bulletin* (I.R.B.) and later transferred to the appropriate *Cumulative Bulletin* (C.B.). Both the *Internal Revenue Bulletins* and the *Cumulative Bulletins* are published by the U.S. Government Printing Office.

Revenue Ruling. A Revenue Ruling (abbreviated Rev.Rul.) is issued by the National Office of the IRS to express an official interpretation of the tax law as applied to specific transactions. It is more limited in application than a Regulation. A Revenue Ruling is first published in an *Internal Revenue Bulletin* (I.R.B.) and later transferred to the appropriate *Cumulative Bulletin* (C.B.). Both the *Internal Revenue Bulletins* and the *Cumulative Bulletins* are published by the U.S. Government Printing Office.

Reversed (Rev'd.). An indication that a decision of one court has been reversed by a higher court in the same case.

Reversing (Rev'g.). An indication that the decision of a higher court is reversing the result reached by a lower court in the same case.

Reversionary interest. The property that reverts to the grantor after the expiration of an intervening income interest. Assume, for example, G places real estate in trust with income to A for 11 years, and upon the expiration of this term, the property returns to G. Under these circumstances, G holds a reversionary interest in the property. A reversionary interest is the same as a remainder interest, except that, in the latter case, the property passes to someone other than the original owner (e.g., the grantor of a trust) upon the expiration of the intervening interest. See also *grantor trust* and *remainder interest.*

Revocable transfer. A transfer of property whereby the transferor retains the right to recover the property. The creation of a revocable trust is an example of a revocable transfer. § 2038. See also *incomplete transfer.*

Rev.Proc. Abbreviation for an IRS Revenue Procedure. See *Revenue Procedure.*

Rev.Rul. Abbreviation for an IRS Revenue Ruling. See *Revenue Ruling.*

Right of survivorship. See *joint tenancy.*

S

S corporation. The designation for a small business corporation. See also *Subchapter S*.

Sales factor. The proportion of a multistate corporation's total sales that is traceable to a specific state. Used in determining the taxable income that is to be apportioned to that state. See also *apportionment*.

Sales tax. A state- or local-level tax on the retail sale of specified property. Generally, the purchaser pays the tax, but the seller collects it, as an agent for the government. Various taxing jurisdictions allow exemptions for purchases of specific items, including certain food, services, and manufacturing equipment. If the purchaser and seller are in different states, a *use tax* usually applies.

Schedule PH. A tax form required to be filed by corporations that are personal holding companies. The form must be filed in addition to Form 1120 (U.S. Corporation Income Tax Return).

Section 306 stock. Preferred stock issued as a nontaxable stock dividend that, if sold or redeemed, would result in ordinary income recognition. § 306(c). See also *preferred stock bailout*.

Section 306 taint. The ordinary income that would result upon the sale or other taxable disposition of § 306 stock.

Section 1231 assets. Depreciable assets and real estate used in a trade or business and held for the appropriate holding period. Under certain circumstances, the classification also includes timber, coal, domestic iron ore, livestock (held for draft, breeding, dairy, or sporting purposes), and unharvested crops. § 1231(b). See also *Section 1231 gains and losses*.

Section 1231 gains and losses. If the combined gains and losses from the taxable dispositions of § 1231 assets plus the net gain from business involuntary conversions (of both § 1231 assets and long-term capital assets) is a gain, such gains and losses are treated as long-term capital gains and losses. In arriving at § 1231 gains, however, the depreciation recapture provisions (e.g., §§ 1245 and 1250) are first applied to produce ordinary income. If the net result of the combination is a loss, such gains and losses from § 1231 assets are treated as ordinary gains and losses. § 1231(a). See also *depreciation recapture* and *Section 1231 assets*.

Section 1244 stock. Stock issued under § 1244 by qualifying small business corporations. If § 1244 stock becomes worthless, the shareholders may claim an ordinary loss rather than the usual capital loss, within statutory limitations.

Section 1245 recapture. Upon a taxable disposition of § 1245 property, all depreciation claimed on such property is recaptured as ordinary income (but not to exceed recognized gain from the disposition).

Section 1250 recapture. Upon a taxable disposition of § 1250 property, some of the depreciation or cost recovery claimed on the property may be recaptured as ordinary income.

Separate property. In a community property jurisdiction, separate property is that property that belongs entirely to one of the spouses. Generally, it is property acquired before marriage or acquired after marriage by gift or inheritance. See also *community property*.

Sham. A transaction without substance that will be disregarded for tax purposes.

Short-term capital gain or loss. Results from the sale or other taxable exchange of a capital asset that had been held by the seller for one year or less or from other transactions involving statutorily designated assets, including nonbusiness bad debts.

Simple trusts. Simple trusts are those that are not complex trusts. Such trusts may not have a charitable beneficiary, accumulate income, or distribute corpus. See also *complex trusts*.

Simplified employee pensions. An employer may make contributions to an employee's individual retirement account (IRA) in amounts not exceeding the lesser of 15 percent of compensation or $30,000 per individual. § 219(b)(2). See also *individual retirement account*.

Small business corporation. A corporation that satisfies the definition of § 1361(b), § 1244(c)(2), or both. Satisfaction of § 1361(b) permits an S election, and satisfaction of § 1244 enables the shareholders of the corporation to claim an ordinary loss on the worthlessness of stock.

Special power of appointment. See *power of appointment*.

Special use value. An option that permits the executor of an estate to value, for death tax purposes, real estate used in a farming activity or in connection with a closely held business at its current use value rather than at its most suitable or optimal use value. Under this option, a farm is valued for farming purposes even though, for example, the property might have a higher potential value as a shopping center. For the executor of an estate to elect special use valuation, the conditions of § 2032A must be satisfied. See also *most suitable use value*.

Spin-off. A type of reorganization wherein, for example, A Corporation transfers some assets to B Corporation in exchange for enough B stock to represent control. A Corporation then distributes the B stock to its shareholders.

Split-off. A type of reorganization wherein, for example, A Corporation transfers some assets to B Corporation in exchange for enough B stock to represent control. A Corporation then distributes the B stock to its shareholders in exchange for some of their A stock.

Split-up. A type of reorganization wherein, for example, A Corporation transfers some assets to B Corporation and the remainder to Z Corporation in return for which it receives enough B and Z stock to represent control of each corporation. The B and Z stock is then distributed by A Corporation to its shareholders in return for all of their A stock. The result of the split-up is that A Corporation is liquidated, and its shareholders now have control of B and Z Corporations.

Sprinkling trust. When a trustee has the discretion to either distribute or accumulate the entity accounting income of the trust and to distribute it among the trust's income beneficiaries in varying magnitudes, a sprinkling trust exists. The trustee can "sprinkle" the income of the trust.

Standard deduction. A minimum amount allowed to individual taxpayers as a deduction *from* AGI to minimize recordkeeping responsibilities. An additional standard deduction amount is allowed to taxpayers who are either blind or age 65 or older. A limited standard deduction is allowed to a taxpayer who is claimed as a dependent on another's tax return.

Statute of limitations. Provisions of the law that specify the maximum period of time in which action may be taken on a past event. Code §§ 6501–6504 contain the limitation periods applicable to the IRS for additional assessments, and §§ 6511–6515 relate to refund claims by taxpayers.

Statutory notice of deficiency. Commonly referred to as the 90-day letter, this notice is sent to a taxpayer upon request, upon the expiration of the 30-day letter, or upon exhaustion by the taxpayer of his or her administrative remedies before the IRS. The notice gives the taxpayer 90 days in which to file a petition with the U.S. Tax Court. If such a petition is not filed, the IRS will issue a demand for payment of the assessed deficiency. §§ 6211–6216. See also *deficiency* and *thirty-day letter*.

Step-transaction approach. Disregarding one or more transactions to arrive at the final result. Assume, for example, that the shareholders of A Corporation liquidate the corporation and thereby receive cash and operating assets. Immediately after the liquidation, the shareholders transfer the operating assets to newly formed B Corporation. Under these circumstances, the IRS may contend that the liquidation of A Corporation be disregarded (thereby depriving the shareholders of capital gain treatment). What may really have happened is a reorganization of A Corporation with a distribution of boot (ordinary income) to A's shareholders. If this is so, there will be a carryover of basis in the assets transferred from A Corporation to B Corporation.

Step-up in basis. An increase in the income tax basis of property. The classic step-up in basis occurs when a decedent dies owning appreciated property. Since the estate or heir acquires a basis in the property equal to the property's fair market value on the date of death (or alternate valuation date if available and elected), any appreciation is not subject to the income tax. Thus, a step-up in basis is the result, with no income tax consequences.

Stock attribution. See *attribution*.

Stock redemption. Occurs when a corporation buys back its own stock from a specified shareholder. Typically, the corporation recognizes any realized gain or loss on the noncash assets that it uses to effect a redemption, and the shareholder obtains a capital gain or loss upon receipt of the purchase price.

Subchapter S. Sections 1361–1379 of the Internal Revenue Code. An elective provision permitting certain small business corporations (§ 1361) and their shareholders (§ 1362) to elect to be treated for income tax purposes in accordance with the operating rules of §§ 1363–1379. Of major significance is the fact that S corporations usually avoid the corporate income tax and corporate losses can be claimed by the shareholders.

Substance vs. form concept. A standard used when one must ascertain the true reality of what has occurred. Suppose, for example, a father sells stock to his daughter for $1,000. If the stock is really worth $50,000 at the time of the transfer, the substance of the transaction is probably a gift to her of $49,000.

Substantial economic effect. Partnerships are allowed to allocate items of income, expense, gain, loss, and credit in any manner that is authorized in the partnership agreement, provided that such allocation has an economic effect aside from the corresponding tax results. The necessary substantial economic effect is present, for instance, if the post-contribution appreciation in the value of an asset that was contributed to the partnership by a partner were allocated to that partner for cost recovery purposes.

Surviving spouse. When a husband or wife predeceases the other spouse, the survivor is known as a surviving spouse. Under certain conditions, a surviving spouse may be entitled to use the income tax rates in § 1(a) (those applicable to married persons filing a joint return) for the two years after the year of death of his or her spouse.

Survivorship. See *joint tenancy*.

T

Tangible property. All property that has form or substance and is not intangible. See also *intangible asset*.

Tax benefit rule. A rule that limits the recognition of income from the recovery of an expense or loss properly deducted in a prior tax year to the amount of the deduction that generated a tax saving. Assume, for example, that last year T (an individual) had medical expenses of $3,000 and adjusted gross income of $30,000. Because of the 7.5 percent limitation, T was able to deduct only $750 of these expenses [$3,000 − (7.5% × $30,000)]. If, in this year, T is reimbursed by his insurance company for $900 of these expenses, the tax benefit rule limits the amount of income from the reimbursement to $750 (the amount previously deducted with a tax saving).

Tax Court. The U.S. Tax Court is one of three trial courts of original jurisdiction that decide litigation involving Federal income, death, or gift taxes. It is the only trial court where the taxpayer must not first pay the deficiency assessed by the IRS. The Tax Court will not have jurisdiction over a case unless the statutory notice of deficiency (90-day letter) has been issued by the IRS and the taxpayer files the petition for hearing within the time prescribed.

Tax on unearned income of a child under age 14. Passive income, such as interest and dividends, that is recognized by such a child is taxed *to him or her* at the rates that would have applied had the income been incurred by the child's parents, generally to the extent that such income exceeds $1,000. The additional tax is assessed regardless of the source of the income or the income's underlying property. If the child's parents are divorced, the custodial parent's rates are used. The parents' rates reflect any applicable alternative minimum tax and the phase-outs of lower tax brackets and other deductions.

Tax preference items. Those items that may result in the imposition of the alternative minimum tax. §§ 55–58. See also *alternative minimum tax*.

Tax year. See *accounting period*.

Taxable estate. Defined in § 2051, the taxable estate is the gross estate of a decedent reduced by the deductions allowed by §§ 2053–2057 (e.g., administration expenses, marital, charitable, and ESOP deductions). The taxable estate is the amount that is subject to the unified transfer tax at death. See also *adjusted taxable estate* and *gross estate*.

Taxable gift. Defined in § 2503, a taxable gift is the amount of the gift that is subject to the unified transfer tax. Thus, a taxable gift has been adjusted by the annual exclusion and other appropriate deductions (e.g., marital and charitable).

Taxable income. The tax base with respect to the prevailing Federal income tax. Taxable income is defined by the Internal Revenue Code, Treasury Regulations, and pertinent court cases. Currently, taxable income includes gross income from all sources except those specifically excluded by the statute. In addition, taxable income is reduced for certain allowable deductions. Deductions for business taxpayers must be related to a trade or business. Individuals also can deduct certain personal expenses in determining their taxable incomes. See also *gross income*.

Tax-free exchange. Transfers of property specifically exempted from income tax consequences by the tax law. Examples are a transfer of property to a controlled corporation under § 351(a) and a like-kind exchange under § 1031(a).

T.C. An abbreviation for the U.S. Tax Court used to cite a Regular Decision of the U.S. Tax Court.

T.C. Memo. An abbreviation used to refer to a Memorandum Decision of the U.S. Tax Court.

Telescoping. To look through one or more transactions to arrive at the final result. It is also designated as the *step-transaction approach* or the *substance vs. form concept* (see these terms).

Tenancy by the entirety. Essentially, a joint tenancy between husband and wife. See also *joint tenancy* and *tenancy in common.*

Tenancy in common. A form of ownership whereby each tenant (owner) holds an undivided interest in property. Unlike a joint tenancy or a tenancy by the entirety, the interest of a tenant in common does not terminate upon that individual's death (there is no right of survivorship). Assume, for example, B and C acquire real estate as equal tenants in common, each having furnished one-half of the purchase price. Upon B's death, his one-half interest in the property passes to his estate or heirs, not to C. For a comparison of results, see also *joint tenancy* and *tenancy by the entirety.*

Terminable interest. An interest in property that terminates upon the death of the holder or upon the occurrence of some other specified event. The transfer of a terminable interest by one spouse to the other may not qualify for the marital deduction. §§ 2056(b) and 2523(b). See also *marital deduction.*

Testamentary disposition. The passing of property to another upon the death of the owner.

Testamentary power of appointment. A power of appointment that can be exercised only through the will (upon the death) of the holder. See also *power of appointment.*

Thin capitalization. When debt owed by a corporation to the shareholders becomes too large in relation to the corporation's capital structure (i.e., stock and shareholder equity), the IRS may contend that the corporation is thinly capitalized. In effect, this means that some or all of the debt will be reclassified as equity. The immediate result is to disallow any interest deduction to the corporation on the reclassified debt. To the extent of the corporation's earnings and profits, interest payments and loan repayments are treated as dividends to the shareholders.

Thirty-day letter. A letter that accompanies a revenue agent's report issued as a result of an IRS audit of a taxpayer (or the rejection of a taxpayer's claim for refund). The letter outlines the taxpayer's appeal procedure before the IRS. If the taxpayer does not request any such procedures within the 30-day period, the IRS will issue a statutory notice of deficiency (the 90-day letter). See also *statutory notice of deficiency.*

Three-factor apportionment formula. A means by which the total taxable income of a multistate corporation is assigned to a specific state. Usually, the payroll, property, and sales factors are treated equally, and the weighted average of these factors is used in the apportionment procedure. In some states, however, the sales factor may receive a double weight, or it may be the only factor considered. These latter formulas place greater tax burden on the income of out-of-state corporations. See also *apportionment, payroll factor, property factor, sales factor,* and *UDITPA.*

Throwback rule. If there is no income tax in the state to which a sale would otherwise be assigned for apportionment purposes, the sale essentially is exempt from state income tax, even though the seller is domiciled in a state that levies an income tax. Nonetheless, if the seller's state has adopted a throwback rule, the sale is attributed to the *seller's* state, and the transaction is subjected to a state-level tax. See also *apportionment* and *sales factor.*

Tiered partnerships. An ownership arrangement wherein one partnership (the parent or first tier) is a partner in one or more partnerships (the subsidiary/subsidiaries or second tier). Frequently, the first tier is a holding partnership, and the second tier is an operating partnership.

Trade or business. Any business or professional activity conducted by a taxpayer. The mere ownership of rental or other investment assets does not constitute a trade or business. Generally, a trade or business generates relatively little passive investment income.

Transfer tax. A tax imposed upon the transfer of property. See also *unified transfer tax.*

Transferee liability. Under certain conditions, if the IRS is unable to collect taxes owed by a transferor of property, it may pursue its claim against the transferee of such property. The transferee's liability for taxes is limited to the extent of the value of the assets transferred. For example, the IRS can force a donee to pay the gift tax when such tax cannot be paid by the donor making the transfer. §§ 6901–6905.

Treasury Regulations. See *Regulations.*

Trial court. The court of original jurisdiction; the first court to consider litigation. In Federal tax controversies, trial courts include U.S. District Courts, the U.S. Tax Court, and the U.S. Claims Court. See also *appellate court, Claims Court, District Court,* and *Tax Court.*

Trust. A legal entity created by a grantor for the benefit of designated beneficiaries under the laws of the state and the valid trust instrument. The trustee holds a fiduciary responsibility to manage the trust's corpus assets and income for the economic benefit of all of the beneficiaries.

Trustee. An individual or corporation that takes the fiduciary responsibilities under a trust agreement.

U

UDITPA. The Uniform Division of Income for Tax Purposes Act has been adopted in some form by many of the states. The Act develops criteria by which the total taxable income of a multistate corporation can be assigned to specific states. See also *allocation, apportionment, Multistate Tax Commission,* and *nexus.*

Undistributed personal holding company income. The penalty tax on personal holding companies is imposed on the corporation's undistributed personal holding company income for the year. The adjustments necessary to convert taxable income to undistributed personal holding company income are set forth in § 545.

Unearned income. Income received but not yet earned. Normally, such income is taxed when received, even for accrual basis taxpayers.

Unified tax credit. A credit allowed against any unified transfer tax. §§ 2010 and 2505.

Unified transfer tax. A set of tax rates applicable to transfers by gift and death made after 1976. § 2001(c).

Uniform Gift to Minors Act. A means of transferring property (usually stocks and bonds) to a minor. The designated custodian of the property has the legal right to act on behalf of the minor without requiring a guardianship. Generally, the custodian possesses the right to change investments (e.g., sell one type of stock and buy another), apply the income from the custodial property to the minor's support, and even terminate the custodianship. In this regard, however, the custodian is acting in a fiduciary capacity on behalf of the minor. The custodian could not, for example, appropriate the property for his or her own use, because it belongs to the minor. During the period of the custodianship, the income from the property is taxed to the minor. The custodianship terminates when the minor reaches legal age. See also *guardianship* and *legal age.*

Unitary state.   A state that has adopted the unitary theory in its apportionment of the total taxable income of a multistate corporation to the state.

Unitary theory.   Under the unitary theory, the sales, property, and payroll of related corporations are combined for *nexus* and *apportionment* purposes, and the worldwide income of the unitary entity is apportioned to the state. Subsidiaries and other affiliated corporations that are found to be part of the corporation's unitary business (because they are subject to overlapping ownership, operation, or management) are included in the apportionment procedure. This approach can be limited if a *water's edge election* is in effect.

Unrealized receivables.   Amounts earned by a cash basis taxpayer but not yet received. Because of the method of accounting used by the taxpayer, such amounts have no income tax basis. When unrealized receivables are distributed to a partner, they generally convert a transaction from nontaxable to taxable, or they convert otherwise capital gain to ordinary income.

Unreasonable compensation.   A deduction is allowed for ''reasonable'' salaries or other compensation for personal services actually rendered. To the extent compensation is ''excessive'' (''unreasonable''), no deduction is allowed. The problem of unreasonable compensation usually is limited to closely held corporations, where the motivation is to pay out profits in some form that is deductible to the corporation. Deductible compensation therefore becomes an attractive substitute for nondeductible dividends when the shareholders also are employed by the corporation.

Unrelated business income.   Income recognized by an exempt organization that is generated from activities not related to the exempt purpose of the entity. For instance, the pharmacy located in a hospital often generates unrelated business income. § 511.

Unrelated business income tax.   Levied on the unrelated business taxable income of an exempt organization.

Use tax.   A sales tax that is collectible by the seller where the purchaser is domiciled in a different state.

U.S.-owned foreign corporation.   A foreign corporation in which 50 percent or more of the total combined voting power or total value of the stock of the corporation is held directly or indirectly by U.S. persons. A U.S. corporation is treated as a U.S.-owned foreign corporation if dividend or interest income paid by such corporation is classified as foreign source under § 861.

U.S. real property interest.   Any direct interest in real property situated in the United States and any interest in a domestic corporation (other than solely as a creditor) unless the taxpayer can establish that a domestic corporation was not a U.S. real property holding corporation during the shorter of the period after June 18, 1980, during which the taxpayer held an interest in such corporation, or for the five-year period ending on the date of disposition of such interest (the base period).

USSC.   An abbreviation for the U.S. Supreme Court.

U.S. Tax Court.   See *Tax Court.*

USTC.   Published by Commerce Clearing House, *U.S. Tax Cases* contain all of the Federal tax decisions issued by the U.S. District Courts, U.S. Claims Court, U.S. Courts of Appeals, and the U.S. Supreme Court.

V

Value.   See *fair market value.*

Vested.   Absolute and complete. If, for example, a person holds a vested interest in property, such interest cannot be taken away or otherwise defeated.

Voting trust.   A trust that holds the voting rights to stock in a corporation. It is a useful device when a majority of the shareholders in a corporation cannot agree on corporate policy.

W

Wash sale.   A loss from the sale of stock or securities that is disallowed because the taxpayer has, within 30 days before or after the sale, acquired stock or securities substantially identical to those sold. § 1091.

Water's edge election.   A limitation on the worldwide scope of the unitary theory. If a corporate water's edge election is in effect, the state can consider only the activities that occur within the boundaries of the United States in the apportionment procedure. See also *apportionment* and *unitary theory.*

WESTLAW.   An on-line database system, produced by West Publishing Company, by which the tax researcher can obtain access to the Internal Revenue Code, Regulations, administrative rulings, and court case opinions.

Writ of Certiorari.   See *certiorari.*

APPENDIX

TABLE OF CODE SECTIONS CITED

[See Title 26 U.S.C.A.]

APPENDIX

TABLE OF REGULATIONS CITED

APPENDIX

TABLE OF REVENUE PROCEDURES AND REVENUE RULINGS CITED

Appendix

Table of Cases Cited

SUBJECT INDEX

G

Q

R

S

T

U

UNIFIED TRANSFER TAX RATES
For Gifts Made and For Deaths after 1983 and before 1993

If the amount with respect to which the tentative tax to be computed is:	The tentative tax is:
Not over $10,000	18 percent of such amount.
Over $10,000 but not over $20,000..............	$1,800, plus 20 percent of the excess of such amount over $10,000.
Over $20,000 but not over $40,000..............	$3,800, plus 22 percent of the excess of such amount over $20,000.
Over $40,000 but not over $60,000..............	$8,200, plus 24 percent of the excess of such amount over $40,000.
Over $60,000 but not over $80,000..............	$13,000, plus 26 percent of the excess of such amount over $60,000.
Over $80,000 but not over $100,000	$18,200, plus 28 percent of the excess of such amount over $80,000.
Over $100,000 but not over $150,000	$23,800, plus 30 percent of the excess of such amount over $100,000.
Over $150,000 but not over $250,000	$38,800, plus 32 percent of the excess of such amount over $150,000.
Over $250,000 but not over $500,000	$70,800, plus 34 percent of the excess of such amount over $250,000.
Over $500,000 but not over $750,000	$155,800, plus 37 percent of the excess of such amount over $500,000.
Over $750,000 but not over $1,000,000	$248,300, plus 39 percent of the excess of such amount over $750,000.
Over $1,000,000 but not over $1,250,000	$345,800, plus 41 percent of the excess of such amount over $1,000,000.
Over $1,250,000 but not over $1,500,000	$448,300, plus 43 percent of the excess of such amount over $1,250,000.
Over $1,500,000 but not over $2,000,000	$555,800, plus 45 percent of the excess of such amount over $1,500,000.
Over $2,000,000 but not over $2,500,000	$780,800, plus 49 percent of the excess of such amount over $2,000,000.
Over $2,500,000 but not over $3,000,000	$1,025,800, plus 53 percent of the excess of such amount over $2,500,000.
Over $3,000,000[*]................................	$1,290,800, plus 55 percent of the excess of such amount over $3,000,000.

*For large taxable transfers (generally in excess of $10 million) there is a phase-out of the graduated rates and the unified tax credit.

For gifts made and for deaths after 1992, see the rates in Appendix A, p. A–9.